THE NATIONAL ROLL OF THE GREAT WAR.

The National Roll of the Great War

One of the most sought-after sets of reference books of the First World War is the *National Roll of the Great War*. The National Publishing Company attempted, shortly after hostilities ceased, to compile a brief biography of as many participants in the War as possible. The vast majority of entries refer to combatants who survived the Great War and the *National Roll* is often the only source of information available. Fourteen volumes were completed on a regional basis; **the Naval & Military Press has compiled a fifteenth volume which contains an alphabetic index to the fourteen now republished volumes**.

The National Roll - complete 15 vol. set	ISBN: 1 847340 33 4	£285.00
Section I - London	ISBN: 1 847340 34 2	£22.00
Section II - London	ISBN: 1 847340 35 0	£22.00
Section III - London	ISBN: 1 847340 36 9	£22.00
Section IV - Southampton	ISBN: 1 847340 37 7	£22.00
Section V - Luton	ISBN: 1 847340 38 5	£22.00
Section VI - Birmingham	ISBN: 1 847340 39 3	£22.00
Section VII - London	ISBN: 1 847340 40 7	£22.00
Section VIII - Leeds	ISBN: 1 847340 41 5	£22.00
Section IX - Bradford	ISBN: 1 847340 42 3	£22.00
Section X - Portsmouth	ISBN: 1 847340 43 1	£22.00
Section XI - Manchester	ISBN: 1 847340 44 X	£22.00
Section XII - Bedford & Northampton	ISBN: 1 847340 45 8	£22.00
Section XIII - London	ISBN: 1 847340 46 6	£22.00
Section XIV - Salford	ISBN: 1 847340 47 4	£22.00
Section XV - Index to all 14 volumes	ISBN: 1 847340 48 2	£22.00

The Naval & Military Press Ltd
Unit 10, Ridgewood Industrial Park, Uckfield,
East Sussex, TN22 5QE, England
Tel: 01825 749494   Fax: 01825 765701
www.naval-military-press.com
www.military-genealogy.com

THE NATIONAL ROLL
OF THE GREAT WAR
1914-1918

CONTAINED WITHIN
THE PAGES OF THIS
VOLUME WILL BE
FOUND THE NAMES
AND RECORDS OF
SERVICE OF THOSE
WHO HELPED TO
SECURE VICTORY FOR
THE EMPIRE DURING
THE GREAT WAR OF
1914-1918.

THE
NAVAL &
MILITARY
PRESS LTD
2006

Published by

The Naval & Military Press Ltd

Unit 10, Ridgewood Industrial Park,

Uckfield, East Sussex,

TN22 5QE England

Tel: +44 (0) 1825 749494

Fax: +44 (0) 1825 765701

www.naval-military-press.com

www.military-genealogy.com

FOREWORD

WHEN we quietly consider what the Great War, with its gains and losses, its cares and anxieties, has taught us, we are at once struck by the splendid heroism of all who took part in it. Many by reason of special qualities of mind or soul stand out more prominently than the rest ; but the names and deeds of others, who toiled no less meritoriously are officially left unsung.

Yet it is well, if only for purely personal and family reasons, that there should be some abiding record of the self-sacrificing services of all men and women who answered their Country's call in her hour of need, and who, whether on land or sea, or in the air, in hospital, or camp, or workshop, were ready to lay down life itself, if need be, that Britain might live and Right prevail over Might.

It is for this reason primarily that the present " National Roll of the Great War " was projected. In the pages of this and of succeeding volumes will be found records of devotion and patriotism of which the individual, the family, and the nation have every reason to be proud.

The National Roll makes no claim to being a complete book of reference—in fact no such record could be compiled—but it may safely claim to supply a wonderful memorial of splendid services, truly worthy of the thankful remembrance of a grateful Empire.

To all who by their Faith and Courage helped to bring Victory to our arms, we dedicate this book.

THE EDITOR.

1, York Place,
Baker Street,
London, W.1

The utmost care is taken to verify particulars contained herein, but the Editors accept no responsibility for their accuracy.

THE NATIONAL ROLL OF THE
1914　　GREAT WAR　　1918

SECTION V.

A

ABBISS, A. D., A/Corporal, 43rd Queen's Own Cameron Highlanders.
He volunteered in July 1915, and in the following February was drafted to the Western Front. He took part in various engagements, including those of Arras and the Somme, and was killed in action at Ypres on October 8th, 1916. He was entitled to the General Service and Victory Medals.
27, Bedford Street, Hitchin. 1621/B.

ABBISS, B., Pte., R.M.L.I. (H.M.S. "Sapphire.")
He volunteered in January 1915, and in the same year proceeded to the Dardanelles and served at Suvla Bay and Mudros. In 1916 he was transferred to France, where he was engaged on the Somme and at Beaumont-Hamel, Grandcourt, Givenchy and Arras. He was afterwards drafted to Malta, Egypt and India. He was discharged as medically unfit for further duty in June 1919, and holds the 1914-15 Star, and the General Service and Victory Medals.
55, Pondswick Road, Luton. 1/A.

ABBISS, F., Corporal (Signals), anti-Aircraft Section, attached Royal Garrison Artillery.
He joined in May 1916, and in the same year was drafted to Salonika, where he was in action on the Vardar and Struma Fronts, and was wounded. In 1918 he was sent to Italy, and was engaged on the Piave. He also served for a time in Constantinople, and suffered badly from malaria. After returning home, he was demobilised in November 1919, holding the General Service and Victory Medals, and the Médaille Militaire d'Honneur Bronze avec Glaives.
55, Pondswick Road, Luton. 1/B.

ABBISS, F. E., Sapper, Royal Engineers.
He joined in August 1916, and on the completion of his training was sent to the Western Front in April of the following year. He did excellent work in the mining company at Arras, Messines and Ypres, but owing to illness contracted on service, was invalided home in July 1917. After his discharge from hospital in the following year he performed light duties until he was finally demobilised in February 1919. He holds the General Service and Victory Medals.
83, Sun Street, Biggleswade. Z1257.

ABBISS, R., A.B., Royal Navy.
He volunteered in November 1915, and served in H.M.S. "Repulse" in the Battle of Heligoland Bight, and in the North Sea laying mines. He was engaged with the first battle-cruiser squadron on important duties at Zeebrugge, and did valuable work there. He was still serving in 1920, and holds the 1914-15 Star, and the General Service and Victory Medals. 27, Bedford Street, Hitchin. 1621/A.

ABBOTT, A. E., Cadet, Royal Air Force.
He joined in August 1918, and was going through his course of training up to the time of the Armistice. He was not successful, therefore, in being drafted overseas while hostilities continued, but he rendered valuable service with his Squadron until demobilised in 1919. 16, Bedford Road, Hitchin. 1625.

ABBOTT, E., Stoker, R.N., and Gunner, R.G.A.
He joined in October 1917, and was engaged on patrol boats in the North Sea and the Mediterranean in escorting troop-ships through submarine areas. He was afterwards transferred to the Royal Garrison Artillery and sent to India, where he was still serving in the Punjab in 1920. He holds the General Service and Victory Medals.
62, Cambridge Street, Luton. 3.

ABBOTT, E. A., Sapper, Royal Engineers.
He volunteered in March 1915, and in November of the same year was drafted to Egypt, and in the same year he did much valuable work. In 1916 he was transferred to Egypt, and afterwards to France, where he took part in many important engagements, including those of Cambrai and the Retreat and Advance of 1918. He was demobilised in March 1919, after returning home, and holds the 1914-15 Star, and the General Service and Victory Medals.
89, Feamley Street, Watford. X5.

ABBOTT, F., A/Corporal, Royal Air Force.
He volunteered in 1915, and after being engaged on important duties in Ireland, was drafted to the Western Front. He served in various sectors, and was employed as an aeroplane engine-fitter on duties which demanded a high degree of technical skill and accuracy. He was demobilised in December 1919, and holds the General Service and Victory Medals.
Ganders Ash, Leavisden Green, Watford. X6/B.

ABBOTT, G. J., Steward, R.N., H.M.S. "Mars" and "Legion."
He was serving at the outbreak of hostilities, and during the war was on duty with the Grand Fleet in the North Sea. He took part in various engagements of importance, including the Battle of Heligoland Bight. He was demobilised in February 1919, and holds the 1914-15 Star, and the General Service and Victory Medals.
96, Oak Road, Luton. 2/B.

ABBOTT, H., Private, 1st Bedfordshire Regt.
He was serving at the outbreak of war, and in September 1914 was drafted to the Western Front, where he took part in the Battles of Ypres and Arras, and was killed in action at Hill 60 on April 17th, 1915. He was entitled to the 1914 Star, and the General Service and Victory Medals.
96, Oak Road, Luton. 2/A.

ABBOTT, H., Private, Machine Gun Corps.
He volunteered in January 1915, and after his training was drafted to the Western Front. He took an active part in many great engagements, including those of Ypres, the Somme and Arras, and was twice wounded. He was discharged in January 1918, in consequence of his service, and holds the 1914-15 Star, and the General Service and Victory Medals.
Ganders Ash, Leavisden Green, Watford. X6/A.

ABBOTT, H., Private, R.A.S.C.
Volunteering in November 1914, he was drafted in July 1915 to the Western Front, where he took part in many important engagements, including those of Ypres, Loos, Vimy Ridge, the Somme and Arras, and in January 1918 was invalided home. He was demobilised in February 1919, and holds the 1914-15 Star, and the General Service and Victory Medals.
66, Sotheron Road, Watford. X7.

ABBOTT, H., Sergeant, 5th Yorkshire Regt.
He volunteered in August 1914, and was afterwards drafted to Egypt, and later to Palestine. He rendered valuable services on this fighting front, and took part in the important engagements at Gaza and Haifa, and those near Jerusalem and the River Jordan. He was killed in action on July 1st, 1918, and was entitled to the 1914-15 Star, and the General Service and Victory Medals.
11, Moreton Road, Luton. 8/A.

ABBOTT, W. C., Private, Duke of Wellington's (West Riding Regiment).
He volunteered in August 1914, and in the following year was drafted to the Western Front, where he took part in the Battles of Ypres, Festubert, the Somme, Passchendaele and Cambrai, and was twice wounded. He was discharged as medically unfit for further service in July 1918, and holds the 1914-15 Star, and the General Service and Victory Medals. 11, Moreton Road, Luton. 8/B.

ABRAHAMS H., Private, Machine Gun Corps.
He volunteered in August 1914, and after performing valuable service with his unit for some time, was drafted to Egypt in July 1917, where he served with General Allenby's Forces in the Palestine Campaign at Gaza. In May 1918 he was sent to the Western Front, where he was in action at Cambrai and Ypres, and was wounded at Valenciennes in October. He was invalided home in consequence, and was eventually demobilised in March 1919, holding the General Service and Victory Medals.
19, East Street, Leighton Buzzard. 1261.

ABRAHAMS, W. E., Sapper, Royal Engineers.
He volunteered in September 1914, and in July of the following year was drafted to Gallipoli, where he took part in the engagements at Suvla Bay and Anzac. He was killed in action at Chocolate Hill on September 2nd, 1915, and was entitled to the 1914-15 Star, and the General Service and Victory Medals.
6, Selbourne Road, Luton.   9.

ABRAMS, A. E., Private, Royal Sussex Regiment.
He joined in May 1918, and after his training served on important duties at various stations with his unit. After the conclusion of hostilities he proceeded to Germany in December 1918, and was stationed at Cologne until February in the following year, when he returned to England and was demobilised.
21, York Street, Luton.   10.

ADAMS, B. J., Private, Bedfordshire Regiment.
He joined in 1917, and in the same year was drafted to the Western Front, where he took part in many important engagements, including those of Cambrai and the Somme, and was demobilised in January 1919 after his return to England, and holds the General Service and Victory Medals.
12, Cannon Street, St. Albans.   11/C.

ADAMS, D., Private, Bedfordshire Regiment.
He volunteered in August 1914, and in September of the same year was drafted to the Western Front, where he took part in numerous engagements, including those at Ypres, Hill 60, Verdun and the Somme, and was severely wounded. He was invalided home, and died on July 29th, 1916, and was entitled to the 1914 Star, and the General Service and Victory Medals.
13, Blacksmith Lane, St. Albans.   12/A.

ADAMS, E. W., Private, 1st Hertfordshire Regt.
He volunteered in April 1915, and in the following year proceeded to the Western Front, where he took part in numerous important engagements in the Ypres salient, and was killed in action there on September 23rd, 1917. He was entitled to the General Service and Victory Medals.
3, Rightofway, New Town, Hatfield.   X13/B.

ADAMS, F., Sergeant, Grenadier Guards.
He volunteered in March 1915, and having completed his training, proceeded to France in the following June. While in this theatre of war he took a prominent part in many engagements, including those of the Somme (where he was gassed), Ypres, Arras and Cambrai. He was demobilised in March 1919, and holds the 1914-15 Star, and the General Service and Victory Medals.
2, West Alley, Hitchin.   1809.

ADAMS, F. E., Sergeant, Loyal North Lancashire Regiment.
He volunteered in October 1915, and in December of the following year was drafted to the Western Front. He was killed in action in the attack on Greenland Hill, near Plouvain, on April 28th, 1917, and was entitled to the General Service and Victory Medals.
Ferndale, Cumberland Street, Houghton Regis, Dunstable.
                                                           14/B.

ADAMS, F. G., Sapper, Royal Engineers.
He volunteered in April 1915, and in the same year proceeded to France. He was engaged in several important battles, including those at Ypres, the Somme, Arras and Cambrai, and was wounded. After returning to England he was demobilised in February 1919, and holds the 1914-15 Star, and the General Service and Victory Medals.
5, Weymouth Street, Apsley, Herts.   X15.

ADAMS, G. W., Corporal, R.A.F. (late R.N.A.S.)
He volunteered in November 1914, and proceeded to the Western Front, where he took part in many important engagements, including those at Ypres and the Somme, and was wounded. He was killed in an air-raid whilst guarding German prisoners at Dunkirk, on September 24th, 1918, and was entitled to the 1914-15 Star, and the General Service and Victory Medals.
12, Cannon Street, St. Albans.   11/B.

ADAMS, H. R., 2nd Lieut., Bedfordshire Regt.
He volunteered in August 1914, and in the following year proceeded to the Dardanelles, and took part in many important engagements, including those at Suvla Bay and Anzac, and was wounded. He returned home in the same year, and was afterwards engaged on the East Coast on various defence duties. He was demobilised in March 1919, and holds the 1914-15 Star, and the General Service and Victory Medals.
12, Cannon Street, St. Albans.   11/A.

ADAMS, J., Private, Queen's (Royal West Surrey Regiment) and Labour Corps.
Volunteering at the outbreak of war, he was sent to the Dardanelles in 1915, and took part in all the chief engagements there, up to the date of the Evacuation. In January 1917 he was drafted to France, where he saw much service until December of the same year. He was wounded three times, and after being invalided home, was discharged in December 1917 as medically unfit for further military duty. He holds the 1914-15 Star, and the General Service and Victory Medals.
64, Church Street, Leighton Buzzard.   1260.

ADAMS, J., Private, 5th Bedfordshire Regt.
He volunteered in August 1914, and in January 1915 was drafted to France, where he took part in numerous engagements, including those at Ypres, Loos and St Quentin, and was wounded. On his recovery he was sent to Egypt, and served in the Battle of Gaza and the Capture of Jerusalem. After his return home he was demobilised in February 1919, and holds the 1914-15 Star, and the General Service and Victory Medals.
183, Heath Road, Leighton Buzzard.   1287.

ADAMS, P., Private, Yorkshire and Essex Regts.
He volunteered in 1915, and during his training served with the Cyclist Battalion of the Yorkshire Regiment. After being transferred to the Essex Regiment, he was drafted to the Eastern Front in 1917, and saw much active service in Palestine, taking part in many engagements, including those of Jaffa, Haifa, and the Capture of Jerusalem. After returning home he was demobilised in March 1920, and holds the General Service and Victory Medals.
6, Chapel Street, Woburn Sands, Beds.   Z16.

ADAMS, S. W., Corporal, Bedfordshire and Northamptonshire Regiments.
Volunteering in September 1914, he was sent immediately to France, where he played an important part in numerous engagements, including those at Ypres, Arras, Cambrai and St. Quentin. During his service he was wounded twice. He was demobilised in March 1919 after returning home, and holds the 1914 Star, and the General Service and Victory Medals.
Mill Lane, Welwyn.   17.

ADAMS, W. H., Private, 16th Cheshire Regiment.
He joined in February 1916, and in December of that year was drafted to the Western Front, where he took part in the Battles of Arras, Ypres and the Somme, and was severely wounded. He was consequently discharged in February 1918 as unfit for further duty, and holds the General Service and Victory Medals.
Ferndale, Cumberland Street, Houghton Regis, Dunstable.
                                                           14/A.

ADAMSON, F., Gunner, R.G.A.
He joined in June 1916, and in the following September was drafted to France, where he served in several important engagements up to the close of the fighting, including those at Arras, Cambrai, the Somme and Amiens. He was demobilised in January 1919 on returning to England, and holds the General Service and Victory Medals.
39, Harcourt Street, Luton.   18/A.

ADAMSON, W., Private, Bedfordshire Regt.
He joined in June 1916, and in the following October proceeded to France. He took part in much severe fighting in the Somme, Arras, Ypres, Cambrai, St. Quentin and numerous other sectors of the front, and during his service was wounded. He was demobilised in September 1919, and holds the General Service and Victory Medals.
39, Harcourt Street, Luton.   18/B.

ADDINGTON, E. R., Private, 3rd Bedfordshire Regiment.
He volunteered in September 1914, and on the completion of his training was sent to France, where he served in numerous engagements on various sectors of the front, including those of the Somme and Ypres. He was severely gassed at Cambrai in April 1918, and invalided home. He was demobilised in March 1919, and holds the 1914-15 Star, and the General Service and Victory Medals.
40, Lattimore Road, St. Albans.   X19.

ADKINS, R., Private, 9th Duke of Wellington's (West Riding Regiment).
He was serving at the outbreak of war, and was immediately drafted to France. He took part in the fierce fighting at Mons, La Bassée, Ypres, the Somme, Arras and Cambrai, and was wounded three times. He was killed in action near Cambrai in September 1918, during the Advance of that year, and was entitled to the Mons Star, and the General Service and Victory Medals.
11, Hartwell Grove, Leighton Buzzard.   1581.

ADOLPH, C., Corporal, 30th Middlesex Regiment.
He volunteered in August 1914, and on the completion of his training 'was retained at various stations on important duties with his unit, but was not drafted overseas while hostilities continued. He was transferred to France in December 1918, and served at Lille and Armentières until April 1919, when he was sent home for demobilisation.
7, Lower Paxton Road, St. Albans. X21.

AFFORD, A., L/Corporal, Sherwood Foresters.
Volunteering in April 1915, he was drafted to the Dardanelles on the completion of his training, and took part in the Gallipoli campaign. On the Evacuation of the Peninsula he was sent to Egypt, and served in the Palestine operations, being present at the engagement at Gaza. Later he was transferred to France, where he remained until after the conclusion of hostilities, when he returned to England and was demobilised in April 1919, holding the 1914-15 Star, and the General Service and Victory Medals.
Ling's Cottages, Temple Normanton, Derbyshire. 22/A.

AFFORD, D. (Miss), Special War Worker.
During the war this lady held an important position at Messrs. Chesterfield Tube Works, Ltd. Her services proved of the utmost value, and the manner in which she carried out her arduous duties was worthy of the highest commendation.
" Sunnymead," Luton Road, Harpenden, Herts. 22/B.

AITCHISON, F., Gunner, Tank Corps.
He joined in January 1917, and on completion of his training served at various stations on important duties with his unit. He was not successful in obtaining his transfer overseas before the cessation of hostilities, and was demobilised in November 1919.
Station Road, Flitwick, Beds. 23.

ALBON, H., Queen's (Royal West Surrey Regt.)
Joining in June 1918, on completion of his training he served at various stations on important duties with his unit. He was unsuccessful in obtaining his transfer overseas before the cessation of hostilities, and was demobilised in April 1919.
14, Shakespeare Street, North Watford, Herts. X24.

ALBONE, C., Private, 4th Northamptonshire Regiment.
He volunteered in April 1915, and in the following July was drafted to the Dardanelles and took part in the landing at Suvla Bay. He contracted dysentery and enteric fever and was invalided to Egypt, and thence home. On his recovery he was sent, in September 1916, to France, and served on the Somme and at Ypres, Arras, and Albert. In November 1917 he proceeded to Italy, and was in action on the Piave and Trentino Fronts. He returned home and was demobilised in March 1919, and holds the General Service and Victory Medals.
2, Britains Yard, Biggleswade, Beds. Z1522.

ALBONE, H. G., Private, Machine Gun Corps.
He joined in 1916, and on the completion of a brief training was sent overseas in the same year. He took part in the Battles of the Somme and Arras, and was killed in action on October 12th, 1917. He was entitled to the General Service and Victory Medals.
18, Cowfairlands, Biggleswade, Bedfordshire. Z1255/A.

ALBURY, A. W., Sergeant, 11th Bedfordshire Regiment.
He volunteered in June 1915, and after his training served at various stations on important duties with his unit. He rendered valuable service, but was unable to obtain his transfer overseas owing to being medically unfit. He was demobilised in February 1919.
Southill, Beds. Z25.

ALCOCK, E. G., L/Corporal, R.A.S.C. (M.T.)
He joined in February 1917, and on completion of his training served at various stations on important transport duties. He was unable to obtain his transfer overseas owing to being medically unfit, and was demobilised in April 1920.
70, Waterlow Road, Dunstable. 179/B.

ALDERMAN, C., Private, 1st Hertfordshire Regt.
Volunteering in March 1915, he was shortly afterwards drafted to France, where he took part in severe fighting on various sectors of the front. He was killed in action on September 14th, 1917, and was entitled to the 1914-15 Star, and the General Service and Victory Medals.
13, Hampstead Road, Watford. X26.

ALDERMAN, H. T., Private, R.A.S.C.
He joined in October 1916, and after completing his training was engaged on important duties at various stations until drafted to Salonica in November 1918. After serving there for some time he was sent to the Dardanelles, where he remained until February 1920, when he returned to England and was demobilised. He holds the General Service and Victory Medals.
444, Hitchin Road, Luton, Beds. 27.

ALDOUS, A. F., Private, Middlesex Regiment.
Volunteering in 1914, he was immediately sent to France, where he served in the Retreat from Mons. He was reported missing in 1914, and is presumed to have been killed. He was entitled to the Mons Star, and the General Service and Victory Medals.
22, Watford Fields, Watford. X31/C.

ALDOUS, E. F., Private, Machine Gun Corps.
He joined in January 1916, and on completion of his training proceeded to France, where he served in numerous engagements, including those at Arras, Ypres and Cambrai. He was demobilised in November 1919, and holds the General Service and Victory Medals.
22, Watford Fields, Watford. X31/B.

ALDOUS, S., Gunner, Royal Garrison Artillery.
He was serving at the outbreak of war, and was immediately drafted to France, where he took part in the Retreat from Mons, and the engagements at Ypres and Arras and other places. During his service he was wounded three times, and after the cessation of hostilities, returned to England and was demobilised in May 1920. He holds the Mons Star, and the General Service and Victory Medals.
22, Watford Fields, Watford. X31/A.

ALDRED, H. W., Private, 1st Bedfordshire Regt.
He joined in April 1918, and on the completion of his training served at various stations on important duties with his unit. He was not successful in obtaining his transfer abroad owing to being medically unfit for service overseas, and was demobilised in November 1919.
Leighton Road, Toddington, Beds. 28.

ALDRIDGE, B., Gunner, Royal Field Artillery.
He volunteered in 1915, and in the following year was sent to France, where he served in numerous engagements, including those at Ypres, Arras and Cambrai. He was demobilised in June 1919, and holds the General Service and Victory Medals.
15, Wellclose Street, St. Albans, Herts. 29.

ALDRIDGE, F. W., Gunner, Royal Marine Artillery.
He volunteered in March 1915, and was posted for duty with H.M.S. " Malaya " off the coast of German East Africa. Later he was stationed in Irish waters, and in 1920 was still serving with his ship, cruising off Scotland. He holds the General Service and Victory Medals.
68, Holywell Road, Watford, Herts. X30/B.

ALDRIDGE, G. H., Gunner, Royal Marine Artillery.
He volunteered in 1915, and served on H.M.S. " Shannon " and " Barham," engaged on patrol duties in the North Sea and Mediterranean. He holds the General Service and Victory Medals, and was still serving on H.M.S. " Barham " in 1920.
68, Holywell Road, Watford, Herts. X30/C.

ALLAM, J., Private, Royal Air Force.
He volunteered in February 1915, and at the conclusion of his training was sent to the Orkneys. He was engaged on highly important duties, patrolling the North Sea, and was attached to the seaplane section of the Royal Navy. He continued to serve in this valuable capacity until the cessation of hostilities, and was demobilised in June 1919, holding the General Service and Victory Medals.
11, Ratcliffe Road, Hitchin. 1811.

ALLEN, A., Private, Queen's (Royal West Surrey Regiment).
Volunteering in 1914, on completion of his training he served at various stations engaged on important duties with his unit. He was not able to obtain his transfer overseas owing to being medically unfit, and was discharged in 1917, having rendered valuable service.
471, Whippendell Road, Watford, Herts. 32.

ALLEN, A., Private, Bedfordshire Lancers.
He volunteered in October 1914, and in March of the following year was drafted to the Western Front, where he took part in the Battles of Ypres (II.), Loos, the Somme and Arras. He was killed in action near Cambrai in August 1918, and was entitled to the 1914-15 Star, and the General Service and Victory Medals.
Primrose Cottage, West Street, Dunstable. 2441/A.

ALLEN, A., Sergeant, 2nd Border Regiment.

Volunteering in September 1914, on completion of his training he was drafted to France, where he served at Neuve Chapelle, Festubert, and the Somme, and on various other sectors of the Front. He was severely wounded on July 1st, 1916, and died on the following day. He was entitled to the 1914 Star, and the General Service and Victory Medals.

22, Cavendish Road, St. Albans, Herts.   X33.

ALLEN, A. C., Private, South Wales Borderers.

He volunteered in November 1915, and in the following year was drafted to Mesopotamia, where he took part in numerous engagements, including those at Basra and Kut-el-Amara. He returned home and was demobilised in February 1919, holding the General Service and Victory Medals.

27, Buxton Road, Luton.   35/B.

ALLEN, A. J., Leading Aircraftsman, R.A.F.

He volunteered in November 1915, and after having completed his training served as a wireless operator in France and Italy. On April 18th, 1918, he was mentioned in Despatches for bravery and devotion to duty. During his service overseas he was gassed, and after the conclusion of hostilities returned to England and was demobilised in February 1919, holding the General Service and Victory Medals.

30, Oswald Road, St. Albans.   X36/B.

ALLEN, C., Gunner, Royal Field Artillery.

He joined in 1916, and on completion of his training was drafted to France, where he served in numerous engagements, including those at Arras and on the Somme. During his service he was badly gassed. He was demobilised in 1919, and holds the General Service and Victory Medals.

132, High Street, Markyate, Beds.   37.

ALLEN, E., Air Mechanic, Royal Air Force.

He joined in February 1918, and proceeded to the Western Front, where he was engaged as an aeroplane fitter. His work demanded a high degree of technical skill, and he rendered valuable services. He was demobilised in May 1920, and holds the General Service and Victory Medals.

30, Oswald Road, St. Albans, Herts.   X36/A.

ALLEN, E., Cpl., 4th East Anglian Ammunition Column, Royal Field Artillery.

He volunteered in August 1914, and in January of the following year was drafted to the Western Front, where he served at Ypres. In March of the same year he was transferred to Egypt, and later to Palestine, and served in various engagements, including those at Gaza. He returned home and was demobilised in August 1919, and holds the General Service and Victory Medals.

27, Church Road, Watford.   X4583/C.

ALLEN, E. G., Rflmn., King's Royal Rifle Corps.

He was serving in the Merchant Service at the outbreak of war, but in 1918 joined the Army. After having completed his training he was drafted to Germany with the Army of Occupation. He was still serving in 1920.

16, Havelock Road, Biggleswade, Beds.   Z1251.

ALLEN, F. A., Private, 5th Bedfordshire Regiment and Royal Army Medical Corps.

He volunteered in September 1914, and in December of the same year was discharged as medically unfit. He re-enlisted in July 1916, and on completion of his training was drafted to France, where he served on the Somme and at Cambrai. He was demobilised in June 1919, and holds the General Service and Victory Medals.

27, Buxton Road, Luton, Beds.   35/A.

ALLEN, F. J., Leading Seaman, R.N., H.M.S. "Warspite."

He volunteered in August 1914, and after his training was posted to H.M.S. "Warspite." Whilst in this vessel he took part in the Battle of Jutland, and subsequently served on important and dangerous duties off the coast of Spain and in the North Sea. He holds the 1914-15 Star, and the General Service and Victory Medals, and in 1920 was still serving with the Fleet off the Algerian coast.

73, Warwick Road, Luton.   38/B.

ALLEN, G., Sergeant, 3rd Bedfordshire Regt.

He volunteered in August 1914, and after his training served at various stations as an instructor of musketry. He was discharged in 1916 as medically unfit for further service.

91, Church Street, Dunstable, Beds.   177.

ALLEN, H., Private, 13th Essex Regiment.

He joined in August 1916, and in November of the same year was drafted to the Western Front, where he took part in important engagements, including those at Arras and Ypres. He was demobilised in March 1919, and holds the General Service and Victory Medals.

16, Russell Rise, Luton, Beds.   39.

ALLEN, H., Private, 2nd Norfolk Regiment.

He volunteered in April 1915, and having completed his training was sent to Mesopotamia. He served at Kut, Magdhaba and Baghdad, and suffered seriously from fever, on account of which he was invalided to India. He returned home after the cessation of hostilities, and was demobilised in February 1919, holding the General Service and Victory Medals.

Town Yard, Barton, Ampthill.   1807.

ALLEN, H. O., Private, 2nd Royal Welch Fusiliers.

He volunteered in 1914, and was drafted to the Western Front, where he took part in many engagements, including those of the Somme, Arras and Ypres, and was wounded. He was invalided home and discharged in 1917, and holds the General Service and Victory Medals.

471, Whippendale Road, Watford, Herts.   X40.

ALLEN, J., Private, East Lancashire Regiment.

He joined in March 1916, and in the same year was drafted to the Western Front, where he took part in numerous engagements, including those at Arras, Ypres and Cambrai. He was demobilised in August 1919, and holds the General Service and Victory Medals.

50, Ridgway Road, Luton, Beds.   41.

ALLEN, J., Private, Machine Gun Corps.

He joined in October 1916, and in February of the following year was sent to the Western Front, where he served at Cambrai and on the Somme, and was twice wounded. On his recovery he was sent to Italy and later to Salonica, and after the signing of the Armistice served on special duties at Constantinople, and Tiflis, in Russia. He was finally demobilised in December 1919, and holds the General Service and Victory Medals.

17, Back Street, Biggleswade, Bedfordshire.   Z1256.

ALLEN, J. T., Private, 2nd Bedfordshire Regt.

He joined in December 1916, and in February of the following year was drafted to India. He was engaged on various important garrison duties and rendered valuable services. He returned home and was demobilised in December 1919, and holds the General Service and Victory Medals.

2, Lyndhurst Road, Luton.   42.

ALLEN, J. W., Sergeant, 7th Bedfordshire Regt.

He volunteered in September 1914, and in December of the following year was drafted to the Western Front, where he took part in many engagements, including those on the Somme and at Arras, Ypres, Cambrai and Petit Miraumont, and was three times wounded. He was demobilised in April 1919, and holds the 1914-15 Star, and the General Service and Victory Medals.

109, High Street, Houghton Regis.   43.

ALLEN, L., L/Corporal, Royal Engineers.

He volunteered in September 1914, and having completed his training proceeded to France in the following year. He took part in numerous engagements, including those at Ypres, the Somme, Arras and the Aisne, and was wounded. In March 1919 he returned to England and was demobilised, holding the 1914-15 Star, and the General Service and Victory Medals.

Wheathampstead Road, Harpenden, Herts.   44.

ALLEN, M., Gunner, R.H.A. and R.F.A.

He enlisted in August 1908, and in November 1914 was drafted to Mesopotamia, where he served throughout the campaign against the Turks and was wounded. After the cessation of hostilities he returned to England, and in August 1919 was demobilised, holding the 1914-15 Star, and the General Service and Victory Medals.

11, Welldon Crescent, Harrow, Middlesex.   X45.

ALLEN, R., Private, 6th Bedfordshire Regiment.

He joined in January 1917, and after a brief training was drafted to France. Shortly after his arrival on this front he was killed in action at Vimy Ridge on April 20th, 1917, and was entitled to the General Service and Victory Medals.

63, Havelock Road, Luton, Bedfordshire.   46/B.

ALLEN, R., Private, 2nd Suffolk Regiment.

He volunteered in June 1915, and in the following September was drafted to the Western Front. Whilst serving in this theatre of war he took part in the Battles of the Somme, Arras, Ypres and Cambrai, and in the Retreat of 1918. After the Armistice he proceeded to Germany with the Army of Occupation, and served at Cologne until April 1919, when he returned to England and was demobilised.

119, High Street, Markyate, Beds.   47.

ALLEN, R. S., Sergeant, R.E. (Signals).
He volunteered in November 1914, and owing to his ability as an Instructor, was retained for the training of recruits in signalling and other military duties. In 1918 he was eventually drafted overseas, and served in Russia with the Relief Force. He was invalided home and discharged as medically unfit for further duty in January 1919, and holds the Victory Medal.
165, Dallow Road, Luton. 48.

ALLEN, R. W., O.S., R.N., H.M.S. " Royal Arthur."
He joined the Navy in July 1918, and after his training was posted to H.M.S. " Royal Arthur," and served with the Grand Fleet in the North Sea. He was engaged with his vessel on important and hazardous duties at Scapa Flow and in the Mediterranean Sea. In 1920 he was still serving, and holds the General Service and Victory Medals.
73, Warwick Road, Luton. 38/C.

ALLEN, S. R., Private, Royal Dublin Fusiliers.
He joined in October 1916, and after his training was drafted to the Western Front in April 1917. He took part in the engagements at Messines and Armentières, and was wounded and invalided home. On his recovery he returned to France, and on March 21st, 1918, was taken prisoner during the Retreat. He was held in captivity until after the Armistice, when he was released and returned to England. He holds the General Service and Victory Medals, and was demobilised in March 1919.
215, High Town Road, Luton, Beds. 49.

ALLEN, T., L/Corporal, Royal Engineers.
He volunteered in 1915, and after his training proceeded to the Western Front, where he was in action on the Somme and at Ypres and Cambrai. During his service overseas he was wounded, and on the conclusion of hostilities returned to England and was demobilised, holding the General Service and Victory Medals.
43, Judge Street, North Watford, Herts. X50.

ALLEN, T. H., Private, 1st Hertfordshire Regt.
He volunteered in 1915, and proceeded to the Western Front, where he took part in numerous important engagements, including those of Loos and Arras. He also served in the Retreat of 1918. Later, on June 16th, 1918, he died of wounds received in action, and was entitled to the 1914-15 Star, and the General Service and Victory Medals.
16, Weymouth Street, Apsley End, Herts. X51.

ALLEN, V. Z., Private, Staffordshire Regiment.
He volunteered in January 1915, and in the same year was sent to the Western Front. Whilst in this theatre of war he took part in the fighting on the Somme, and at Arras and Cambrai. After four years' service in France he was demobilised in January 1919, and holds the 1914-15 Star, and the General Service and Victory Medals.
73, Warwick Road, Luton. 38/A.

ALLEN, W. Private, 6th Bedfordshire Regiment and Royal Army Medical Corps.
He joined in 1916, and after his training served at various stations on important duties with his unit. He rendered valuable services, but was not successful in obtaining his transfer overseas before the cessation of hostilities. He was demobilised in January 1920.
63, Havelock Road, Luton, Beds. 46/A.

ALLEN, W. G., Private, R.A.S.C.
He joined in December 1916, and immediately proceeded to the Western Front, where he was engaged on transport duties at Dunkirk. Later, owing to ill-health, he was invalided home and discharged in May 1917. He holds the General Service and Victory Medals.
3, Church Street, Wheathampstead, Herts. 52.

ALLISON, E., Private, Norfolkshire Regiment.
He volunteered in March 1915, and having completed his training proceeded to France later in the year. He took part in several important engagements, including those of Loos, the Somme, Arras, Cambrai and Ypres, where he was wounded in 1918. He came home and was demobilised in February 1919, holding the 1914-15 Star, and the General Service and Victory Medals.
Southill, Beds. Z53/B.

ALLISON, H., C.S.M., Bedfordshire Regiment.
He was serving at the outbreak of hostilities, having enlisted in 1902, and was immediately drafted to France, where he took a prominent part in the fierce fighting at Mons and in later engagements at La Bassée, Ypres, Loos, the Somme, Arras and Cambrai. He was twice wounded during his service. He holds the Mons Star, and the General Service and Victory Medals, and in 1920 was still serving, chiefly on recruiting duties.
Southill, Beds. Z53/A.

ALLISON, H. (M.M.), C.S.M., 1st Bedfordshire and Hertfordshire Regiments.
He was serving at the outbreak of war, and in August 1914 was drafted to the Western Front. Whilst in this theatre of war he took a prominent part in the fighting at the Marne, the Aisne, La Bassée, Ypres, Hill 60, the Somme and Arras. He was afterwards sent to Italy, where he did excellent service until his return to the Western Front for the final stages of the war. He was twice wounded during his service, and in August 1918 was awarded the Military Medal for assuming command of his company at Achiet-le-Petit when all the officers were casualties, and capturing enemy gun-emplacements and many prisoners. After the Armistice he went to Germany, and in 1920 he was still serving. He holds, in addition to the Military Medal, the 1914 Star, and the General Service and Victory Medals.
19, Estcourt Road, Watford. X54.

ALLOM, J., Private, 13th Bedfordshire Regt.
He joined in 1917, and after his training was retained on important dock duties with his unit. He rendered valuable services, but was not successful in obtaining his transfer overseas before the cessation of hostilities. He was demobilised in February 1919.
135, Lower Marlowes, Hemel Hempstead. X55.

ALMOND, J. W., Private, King's (Liverpool Regt.)
He volunteered in 1915, and having completed his training proceeded to France in the following year. He took part in several important engagements up to the cessation of hostilities, including those of Vimy Ridge, the Somme, Arras and Cambrai, and was both wounded and gassed. After his return home he was demobilised in January 1919, and holds the General Service and Victory Medals.
Lower Luton Road, Harpenden. 56/B.

ALMOND, P., Private, 9th King's (Liverpool Regiment).
He volunteered in November 1915, and after rendering valuable services with his unit, was drafted in 1917 to France, where he fought at Bullecourt, Messines and Ypres in that year. He was severely wounded on the Somme in March 1918, but on his recovery after treatment in England returned to the lines in October 1918. He was demobilised in July 1919, and holds the General Service and Victory Medals.
24, Surrey Street, Luton. 57.

ALMOND, S., Rifleman, King's Royal Rifle Corps.
He joined in September 1918, and after his training was engaged with his unit on important duties. He rendered valuable services, chiefly as a guard of prisoners of war, but was not successful in obtaining his transfer overseas before the cessation of hostilities. He was demobilised in October 1919.
Lower Luton Road, Harpenden, Herts. 56/A.

AMBLER, G. H. (Mrs.), Special War Worker.
On the outbreak of war this lady immediately volunteered for work of national importance and accepted a responsible position in a large munition factory. She continued her work in this connection until after the conclusion of hostilities, when she relinquished her appointment.
Sycamore House, Limburg Road, Leagrave. 59.

AMBRIDGE, A. J., Private, Machine Gun Corps.
He joined in March 1916, and after his training was drafted to France, where he took part in various engagements, and was invalided home through causes due to his service. On his recovery he was drafted in 1917 to Mesopotamia, where he rendered valuable service until 1919. He returned to England for his demobilisation in April 1919, and holds the General Service and Victory Medals.
Sharpenhoe Road, Barton, Beds. 60/A.

AMBRIDGE, A. W., Private, 5th Bedfordshire Regiment.
He volunteered in August 1914, and after being retained for a time on important duties was later sent to the Western Front, where he took part in many important engagements in the later years of the war, including those of Arras and the Somme. He was discharged in May 1918 in consequence of his service, and holds the General Service and Victory Medals.
Waller Cottage, Letchworth Road, Leagrave, near Luton. 61.

AMBRIDGE, C. T., 5th Bedfordshire Regiment.
He volunteered in August 1914, and was engaged on important duties with his unit until July of the following year, when he was sent to the Dardanelles. He took part in the severe fighting at Suvla Bay and Anzac, and was reported missing after the engagements on Chocolate Hill, where he is believed to have been killed in action on August 15th, 1915. He was entitled to the 1914-15 Star, and the General Service and Victory Medals.
74, Dane Road, Luton. 62/A.

AMBRIDGE, E., Corporal, Labour Corps.
He volunteered in August 1914, and was quickly drafted to the Western Front. He took part in the heavy fighting during the Retreat from Mons and in the engagements at Lille, Loos and Arras. He was killed in action near Cambrai on September 13th, 1918, and was entitled to the General Service and Victory Medals.
103, High Street, Silsoe, Ampthill.   63—64/C.

AMBRIDGE, W. J., Private, Northamptonshire Regiment.
He volunteered in August 1914, and in the same year proceeded to the Western Front. He took part in much heavy figh ing in the early part of the war, including the engagements of the Somme and Arras, and was wounded and gassed. He was invalided home and discharged owing to his wound in 1917, holding the 1914 Star, and the General Service and Victory Medals.
30, Gardenia Avenue, Leagrave, near Luton.   65.

AMBROSE, F., Private, Bedfordshire Regiment.
He joined in 1916, and in the same year, after finishing his training, was sent to France, where he took part in the severe fighting at Ypres and Arras. He was taken prisoner in 1917, and remained in German hands until the Armistice. On his release he returned home and was demobilised in 1919, holding the General Service and Victory Medals.
54, Piccotto End, Hemel Hempstead.   X66.

AMBROSE, F., Sapper, Royal Engineers.
He volunteered in August 1914, and was sent in the same year to France, where he took a prominent part in the Battle of Ypres, Hill 60, Arras and Cambrai, and in much other heavy fighting during the war. He was blown up on Hill 60, and was six times wounded. He returned home and was demobilised in February 1919, and holds the 1914 Star, and the General Service and Victory Medals.
8, White Lion Street, Apsley End, Herts.   X67/B.

AMES, J., Private, R.A.O.C.
He volunteered in December 1915, and after valuable service at various stations was, in 1916, drafted to Mesopotamia. There he did excellent service in a travelling workshop, engaged chiefly in repairing 18-pounder guns. He suffered severely from dysentery in the East, and in August 1919 was discharged as medically unfit for further service. He holds the General Service and Victory Medals.
63, Leighton Street, Woburn, Beds.   Z68.

AMES, W. J., Corporal, 7th East Surrey Regt.
Volunteering in August 1914, he was shortly afterwards drafted to India and later to Mesopotamia. In this fighting area he took part in many engagements of importance, including those around Kut-el-Amara, and along the Tigris, and was wounded. After his return home he was discharged in November 1919 as medically unfit for further service, and holds the 1914-15 Star, and the General Service and Victory Medals.
6, Back Street, Biggleswade.   1253—1254/A.

ANDERSEN, S. A., Sapper, Royal Engineers.
He joined in March 1917, and in the following July, at the close of his training, was sent to France. He rendered valuable service and saw much fighting at Passchendaele, Cambrai, the Somme and the Marne, and other later engagements up to the cessation of hostilities. He returned to England and was demobilised in October 1919, holding the General Service and Victory Medals.
34, Gardenia Avenue, Leagrave, near Luton.   69.

ANDERSON, A., Sapper, Royal Engineers.
He volunteered in August 1914, and in the following year was sent to France. While there he did valuable work, and took part in several important engagements, including those of Ypres, the Somme and Cambrai. In November 1918 he was drafted to Russia, where he was employed on important duties until July 1919, when he came home and was demobilised. He holds the 1914-15 Star, and the General Service and Victory Medals.
48, Butlin Road, Luton.   71/A.

ANDERSON, A., 1st Air Mechanic, R.A.F.
He joined in December 1917, and after his training served with his unit as an engine fitter on important duties, which demanded high technical skill. He rendered valuable services but was not successful in obtaining his transfer overseas before the cessation of hostilities. He was demobilised in November 1919.
10, Ashton Road, Luton.   72.

ANDERSON, B., Private, R.A.M.C.
He volunteered in September 1914, and was afterwards sent to the Western Front, where he rendered valuable services in various sectors until the close of hostilities, especially at Ypres, Arras and Cambrai. After the Armistice he went with the Army of Occupation to Germany, and in June 1919 returned to England and was demobilised. He holds the 1914-15 Star, and the General Service and Victory Medals.
3, Spring Place, Luton.   73/A.

ANDERSON, C., Driver, R.A.S.C.
He volunteered in September 1914, and in the following year was sent to Egypt and Palestine, where he did much valuable transport work in the Canal Zone and at Suez, Port Said, Gaza, Haifa and Damascus. Having contracted malaria he died at Damascus on October 15th, 1918, and was buried there. He was entitled to the 1914-15 Star, and the General Service and Victory Medals.
3, Spring Place, Luton.   73/B.

ANDERSON, E., Private, 5th Bedfordshire Regt.
He volunteered in October 1914, and on the conclusion of his training was drafted to the Dardanelles, where he fought in several important engagements, and was killed in action at Chocolate Hill on August 15th, 1915. He was entitled to the 1914-15 Star, and the General Service and Victory Medals.
27, Brache Street, Luton.   74.

ANDERSON, E., Sapper, Royal Engineers.
He joined in January 1917, and after his training was drafted to France. While there he rendered valuable services at Cambrai, and was also employed in bridge building and in guarding German prisoners of war at various camps. During his service he was gassed. He came home and was demobilised in March 1919, holding the General Service and Victory Medals.
1, Lowbell Lane, London Colney, near St. Albans.   75/B.

ANDERSON, F., Private, Middlesex Regiment.
He joined in May 1916, and was soon afterwards sent to France, where he took an active part in the Somme Offensive and the Battles of Ypres and Arras, where he was severely wounded in 1917. In December 1918 he was demobilised, and holds the General Service and Victory Medals.
73, Saxon Road, Luton.   76/A.

ANDERSON, G., Sapper, R.E. (R.O.D.)
He joined in June 1917, and was in the following September sent to Egypt, where he took part in the Advance in Palestine. While there he rendered valuable services in the Railway Operating Department of the Royal Engineers at Gaza, Acre and Damascus. He came home and was demobilised in November 1919, holding the General Service and Victory Medals. 51, Oak Road, Luton.   77.

ANDERSON, H., Gunner, Royal Field Artillery.
He volunteered in April 1915, and on the conclusion of his training was drafted to the Western Front. There he took a prominent part in many important engagements, including those of Arras, Passchendaele and Cambrai. After the Armistice he went with the Army of Occupation to Germany, but later proceeded to India, where he was still serving in 1920. He holds the General Service and Victory Medals.
3, Lowbell Lane, London Colney, near St. Albans.   75/A.

ANDERSON, H., Private, 5th Bedfordshire Regt.
He volunteered in 1915, and after his training was drafted to the Eastern Front, where he rendered valuable service at the Dardanelles and in Egypt and Palestine. He took part in several important engagements, including the three Battles of Gaza, Haifa and Acre, and was wounded. He also did excellent work for a time at Suez Docks. After his return home he was demobilised in July 1919, holding the 1914-15 Star, and the General Service and Victory Medals.
73, Laxon Road, Luton.   76/C.

ANDERSON, H., Private, Sherwood Foresters.
He joined in February 1916, and having completed his training was retained on important duties with his unit. He was afterwards sent to France, where, after but a short period of service, he was taken prisoner on the Somme in April 1918. After his release he was drafted to Germany in the Army of Occupation, and on his return was demobilised in January 1920, holding the General Service and Victory Medals. 73, Laxon Road, Luton.   76/B.

ANDERSON, H. H., Corporal, 24th Canadian Regiment (Victoria Rifles).
He volunteered in August 1914, and having completed his training proceeded to France in the following year. While there he fought in several important engagements, including those of Ypres, the Somme, Arras, Cambrai, the Marne and the Aisne. He afterwards served with the Army of Occupation in Cologne, until he was sent home for demobilisation in July 1919. He holds the 1914-15 Star, and the General Service and Victory Medals.
106, Norfolk Road, Rickmansworth, Herts.   X73.

ANDERSON, H. W. (D.C.M.), Staff-Sergeant, Royal Army Service Corps.

He volunteered in September 1914, and was drafted to Egypt in the following year. He rendered valuable services at Cairo and Alexandria and took a prominent part in the fighting in the Palestine Campaign at Gaza, Haifa, Aleppo and Damascus. He was awarded the Distinguished Conduct Medal for great gallantry in the Field, and in addition holds the 1914–15 Star, and the General Service and Victory Medals. He was demobilised in 1919.
54, Regent Street, North Watford.   X79.

ANDERSON, J., Private, Labour Corps.

He joined in September 1916, and was sent to France in the following March, where he did much valuable work with his corps in various parts of the Front, particularly at Ypres, Dickebusch and Arras, right up to the cessation of hostilities. He returned to England and was demobilised in January 1919, holding the General Service and Victory Medals.
" Fitzroy," Symington Street, Harpenden.   80.

ANDERSON, J. W. (M.M.), L/Corporal, M.G.C.

He volunteered in February 1915, and in July of the same year was drafted to the Western Front. He took part in heavy fighting on the Somme and at Arras, Ypres and Cambrai, and was awarded the Military Medal for bravery in the Field. After the Armistice he proceeded with the Army of Occupation to Germany, where he remained until he returned home and was demobilised in February 1919. He holds, in addition to the Military Medal, the 1914–15 Star, and the General Service and Victory Medals.
77, Church Street, Dunstable.   178.

ANDERSON, P., Gunner, Royal Field Artillery.

He volunteered in November 1915, and having completed his training was drafted to the Western Front in August 1916. While overseas he rendered valuable services in several important engagements, including those of the Somme, Arras, Ypres, Passchendaele and Cambrai until the cessation of hostilities. He returned home, and was demobilised in May 1919, holding the General Service and Victory Medals.
25, Orchard Road, Walsworth, Hitchin.   1628.

ANDERSON, W., Private, East Surrey Regt.

He joined in February 1917, and in April of the same year was drafted to the Western Front, where he took part in the Battles of Arras, Cambrai and the Somme. He was also engaged in guarding German prisoners, and in important sanitary duties. He was demobilised in April 1919 after returning home, and holds the General Service and Victory Medals.
6, Austins Lane, Ampthill.   1523.

ANDREW, H. G., Private, Royal Engineers.

He volunteered in November 1915, and after a period of training proceeded to Egypt in the following year. While in this theatre of war he took part in various important engagements, and on March 27th, 1917, was killed in action at the Battle of Gaza. He was entitled to the General Service and Victory Medals.
34, Ashburnham Road, Luton.   89.

ANDREWS, A., Private, Grenadier Guards.

He was serving at the outbreak of war, and being over age for service abroad was engaged on important duties at various stations. He rendered valuable service until March 1919, when he was demobilised.
90, Burr Street, Luton, Beds.   83/A.

ANDREWS, A. G., Sapper, Royal Engineers.

He joined in June 1917, and in September of the same year was drafted to Egypt. He took part in the Palestine Campaign, being in action at Haifa and Gaza, and was present at the Capture of Jerusalem. He returned home and was demobilised in March 1920, and holds the General Service and Victory Medals.
Rose Bank, Marsh End, Leagrave, Beds.   84—85.

ANDREWS, C., Private, 11th Queen's (Royal West Surrey Regiment).

He joined in 1917, and in the same year proceeded to France, where he took part in several engagements on various sectors of the Front, including those at Arras, Passchendaele, Cambrai and the Somme. He was reported missing on October 1st, 1918, and is believed to have been killed in action. He was entitled to the General Service and Victory Medals.
40, Regent Street, Leighton Buzzard.   1288—1289/E.

ANDREWS, F., Private, 2nd Bedfordshire Regt.

Joining in May 1915, in the following October he proceeded to France and took part in numerous engagements, including those of Vimy Ridge, the Somme, Passchendaele, Cambrai and Ypres. He also fought in the Retreat and Advance of 1918, and was wounded at Ypres. He was demobilised in March 1920, and holds the 1914–15 Star, and the General Service and Victory Medals.
40, Regent Street, Leighton Buzzard.   1288—1289/A.

ANDREWS, F. G., Sergeant, Royal Engineers.

He volunteered in May 1915, and in January of the following year was sent to Egypt. He took part in the Palestine Campaign, being present at numerous important engagements, including that at Gaza and the Capture of Jerusalem. He returned home and was demobilised in May 1919, and holds the General Service and Victory Medals.
4, Buxton Road, Luton, Beds.   86.

ANDREWS, F. G., Private, 1st Bedfordshire Regiment.

He volunteered in January 1915, and in the following July proceeded to the Western Front, where he took part in many important engagements, including those on the Somme, and at Arras and Ypres. On August 23rd, 1918, he was killed in action at Albert, and was entitled to the General Service and Victory Medals.
50, St. Mary's Street, Dunstable,   87.

ANDREWS, H. W., Driver, R.E. ; and Air Mechanic, Royal Air Force.

He volunteered in March 1915, but after a short period was discharged as medically unfit. Later he rejoined in the Royal Air Force, and was stationed at various depôts on responsible duties connected with aeroplane engine fitting. He rendered valuable services until July 1919, when he was demobilised.
72, Cambridge Street, Luton.   88.

ANDREWS, J., Private, R.A.S.C.

He joined in January 1916, and in the following July was drafted to France and served on the Somme and at Arras, Ypres and Cambrai, being engaged on transporting supplies and ammunition to the Front Lines. He rendered valuable services, and was demobilised in February 1919. He holds the General Service and Victory Medals.
40, Regent Street, Leighton Buzzard.   1288—1289/D.

ANDREWS, L., Pte., Canadian Overseas Forces.

He volunteered in August 1914, and came to England with the first contingent. He was sent to France in 1915, and took part in the Battles of Festubert, the Somme, Arras and Cambrai. He was demobilised in 1919, and holds the 1914–15 Star, and the General Service and Victory Medals.
Church Street, Westoning, Beds.   1521.

ANDREWS, L., Gunner, Royal Field Artillery.

He was mobilised with the Territorial Force on the declaration of war, and after a course of training was drafted to Mesopotamia in 1915. In this theatre of war he took part in heavy fighting, and was in many of the engagements that led to the Capture of Baghdad and the Occupation of Mosul. On the conclusion of hostilities he returned to England, and was demobilised in March 1919. He holds the 1914–15 Star, and the General Service and Victory Medals.
100, Harwood Road, Watford, Herts.   X90.

ANDREWS, W. H., L/Corporal, M.G.C.

He joined in 1916, and in the same year was sent overseas. He served in several sectors of the Western Front, and among the battles in which he took part were those at Ypres, and on the Somme (II.), Aisne (III.), and Marne (II.). In the course of these actions he was gassed, but served till the end of the war, when he returned to England. He holds the General Service and Victory Medals, and was demobilised in 1919.
105, Lower Paddock Road, Oxhey, Watford.   X91.

ANGELL, G. E., Private, Labour Corps.

He joined in December 1916, and on completion of his training was engaged on agricultural duties, being medically unfit for service overseas. He rendered valuable services until October 26th, 1918, when he died of influenza in the Aylesbury hospital.
Breachwood Green, near Welwyn.   92/C.

ANGELL, H., Private, Labour Corps.

He joined in September 1916, and served at various stations on important duties with his unit. He was not successful in obtaining his transfer overseas before the cessation of hostilities, but afterwards was attached to the Army of Occupation and served on the Rhine until February 1920, when he was demobilised.
Breachwood Green, near Welwyn.   92/B.

ANGELL, W., Private, R.A.S.C. (M.T.)
He joined in January 1917, and shortly afterwards was drafted to the Western Front, and was engaged on important duties in the workshops at various places. He was demobilised in January 1917, and holds the General Service and Victory Medals.
Breachwood Green, near Welwyn.   92/A.

ANNING, A. G., Private, Queen's Own (Royal West Kent Regiment).
He joined in April 1916, and after a period of training proceeded to France, where he took part in various engagements, including those on the Somme, and at Arras and Cambrai, and was wounded four times. In March 1918 he was taken prisoner and was held in captivity until after the Armistice, when he was released and returned to England. He was demobilised in February 1919, and holds the General Service and Victory Medals.
24, Benskin Road, Watford, Herts.   X93.

ANNING, E., Private, Loyal North Lancashire Regiment.
He volunteered in 1915, and after a period of training proceeded to France. While in this theatre of war he took part in various engagements, including those of Arras and Cambrai, and was wounded twice in action. In 1918 he was demobilised, and holds the General Service and Victory Medals.
110, Harwood Road, Watford, Herts.   X94/B.

ANNING, W., Rifleman, King's Royal Rifle Corps.
He volunteered in 1915, and in the same year proceeded to France, where he took part in various important engagements. On August 24th, 1916, he was killed in action at Ypres, and was entitled to the General Service and Victory Medals.
110, Harwood Road, Watford, Herts.   X94/A.

ANSELL, B. G., Gunner, Royal Field Artillery.
Having volunteered in October 1915, he was later drafted to Mesopotamia, and took part in numerous engagements during his service in that theatre of war. He returned home and was demobilised in May 1919, and holds the General Service and Victory Medals.
17, Upper Culver Road, St Albans, Herts.   X95.

ANSELL, C., Sapper, Royal Engineers.
He volunteered in September 1914, and after his training was, in August of the following year, drafted to the Western Front, and took a prominent part in the heavy fighting at Loos, Vimy Ridge, Beaumont-Hamel and Cambrai. He returned home and was demobilised in April 1919, and holds the 1914-15 Star, and the General Service and Victory Medals.
11, Camp View Road, St. Albans, Herts.   X97.

ANSELL, C. G., C.S.M., 26th Royal Fusiliers.
He volunteered in 1914, and was engaged at various stations as Drill Instructor until September 1918, when he was drafted to the Western Front. Later in the same year he proceeded with the Army of Occupation to Germany. He returned home and was demobilised in April 1919, and holds the General Service and Victory Medals
14, Breakspear Road, Abbots Langley, Herts.   X96.

ANSELL, G., Private, 2nd East Surrey Regiment.
He volunteered in September 1914, and in February of the following year was drafted to the Western Front and took part in severe fighting at Hill 60, Ypres, where he was wounded, and Arras. In 1916 he was transferred to Salonica, and was again wounded. After the Armistice he proceeded to Turkey, and in January 1919 returned home and was demobilised, holding the 1914-15 Star, and the General Service and Victory Medals
1, Breakspear Road, Abbots Langley, Herts.   X98.

ANSELL, G., Corporal, 190th Light Trench Mortar Battery.
He joined in January 1917, and after a short period of training was drafted overseas in April of the same year. He saw much active service on the Western Front, and was engaged in severe fighting at various places, including Ypres, Passchendaele and the Somme. He was killed in action at Bapaume on August 24th, 1918, and was entitled to the General Service and Victory Medals.
Princess Street, Toddington, Beds.   99/B.

ANSELL, H., Private, Bedfordshire Regiment.
He volunteered in August 1914, and was immediately drafted to the Western Front, where he was killed in action during the Retreat from Mons. He was entitled to the Mons Star, and the General Service and Victory Medals.
5, Bell's Lane, Shillington, Beds.   1626.

ANSELL, H., Sergeant, Rifle Brigade.
He joined in 1916, and in the same year was drafted to France, where he took part in many important engagements, including those at Ypres, Cambrai, St. Quentin and the Somme, and was twice wounded. After the signing of the Armistice he went with the Army of Occupation into Germany, and returned home to be demobilised in September 1919. He holds the General Service and Victory Medals.
49, Norfolk Road, Rickmansworth, Herts.   X100.

ANSELL, H. V., Air Mechanic, Royal Air Force.
He joined in May 1918, and was engaged at various stations on important duties, which required a high degree of technical skill, in connection with the repair and upkeep of aeroplanes used on air-patrol and other work. He rendered valuable services till his demobilisation in January 1919.
Old Marford, Wheathampstead, Herts.   101/B.

ANSELL, J., Private, R.A.S.C.
He joined in 1916, and after his training served on important duties with his unit at various stations. He rendered valuable service, but was not successful in obtaining his transfer to a theatre of war prior to the termination of hostilities. He was demobilised in 1919.
Church Street, Shillington, Beds.   1624.

ANSELL, S., Private, Northumberland Fusiliers.
He volunteered in 1915, and in January of the following year was drafted to the Western Front, where he took part in action at Albert and on the Somme. In 1917 he was transferred to Italy and served on the Piave Front. He returned to France in 1918, and was engaged in the Retreat and Advance of that year. He was three times wounded and invalided home, and was demobilised in January 1919, holding the General Service and Victory Medals.
Parsonage Lane, Shillington.   2438.

ANSELL, S. W., Private, 4th Bedfordshire Regt.
He volunteered in September 1914, and on completion of his training was drafted to France, and served at Hill 60, Givenchy, the Somme, Passchendaele and Cambrai. During his service he was wounded three times. He was demobilised in February 1919, and holds the 1914-15 Star, and the General Service and Victory Medals.
56, Dudley Street, Luton.   103.

ANSELL, V. A., Private, 28th Canadian Infantry.
He volunteered in December 1914, and in January 1916 was drafted to the Western Front, where he saw much active service. He was engaged in heavy fighting in the Ypres sector and on the Somme, and was wounded and taken prisoner. Released on the signing of the Armistice he was repatriated in December 1918, and demobilised in May of the following year. He holds the General Service and Victory Medals.
New Marford, Wheathampstead, Herts.   101/C.

ANSELL, W., Private, 5th Bedfordshire Regt.
He volunteered in August 1914, and in the following year was sent to the Dardanelles, where he took part in the landing at Suvla Bay, and was wounded and invalided home. He was discharged as medically unfit for further service in July 1916, and holds the 1914-15 Star, and the General Service and Victory Medals.
Austins Lane, Ampthill, Beds.   1524.

ANSTEE, A. E., Private, R.A.M.C.
Joining in August 1916, on completion of his training he was drafted to Salonika, and served on the Doiran and other Fronts. On the cessation of hostilities he was attached to the Army of Occupation in Constantinople until September 1919, when he was sent home and demobilised. He holds the General Service and Victory Medals.
100, Ashton Road, Luton, Beds.   105.

ANSTEE, E., Private, 7th Bedfordshire Regt.
He joined in July 1916, and in the following November was drafted to France, where he took part in several engagements. He was killed in action at Arras in May 1917, and was entitled to the General Service and Victory Medals.
17, Cowper Street, Luton.   106.

ANSTEE, F. C., A.B., Royal Navy.
He was serving in the Navy when war was declared, and being posted to H.M.S. "Canada" was engaged on patrol duties with the Grand Fleet in the North Sea. During his service he took part in the Battle of Jutland and several minor engagements. He holds the 1914 Star, and the General Service and Victory Medals, and in 1920 was serving in H.M.S. "Aquarius."
7, Longmire Road, St. Albans.   X104.

ANTHONY, H. J., A.B., Royal Navy.
He joined in May 1917, and was posted for duty with H.M. Motor Lighter "K.55," with which he served on patrol duties in the Mediterranean Sea until May 1919, when he returned to England. He was demobilised in July 1919, and holds the General Service and Victory Medals.
17, Shaftesbury Road, Watford.   107/B.

ANTHONY, J. H., Private, 1st Bedfordshire Regt.
Volunteering in May 1915, on the completion of his training he was drafted to France. He served on the Somme, and was taken prisoner at Beaucourt in February 1917. On the cessation of hostilities he was released, and returning to England was demobilised in March 1919. He holds the General Service and Victory Medals.
17, Shaftesbury Road, Watford. 107/A.

APPLEBY, H., Private, Bedfordshire Regiment.
Joining in May 1916, he was shortly afterwards sent to France, where he took part in the severe fighting on the Somme and at Vimy Ridge, and was wounded. He was invalided home and discharged in August 1917, and holds the General Service and Victory Medals.
56, Albert Road, Luton. 108/B.

APPLEBY, P., (M.M.), Corporal, Bedfordshire Regiment.
Volunteering in June 1915, he was shortly afterwards drafted to France, where he took part in numerous engagements, including those at Loos, Albert, and many other places. Later he was transferred to Italy and served on the Piave. Returning to the Western Front in 1918, he was wounded and suffered the loss of an eye whilst in action at Ypres. He was awarded the Military Medal for bravery in the Field, and in addition holds the 1914–15 Star, and the General Service and Victory Medals, and was demobilised in December 1918.
56, Albert Road, Luton. 108/A.

ARCHER, A., Private, 3rd Bedfordshire Regt.
He volunteered in November 1914, and in the following year was sent overseas. He saw much active service in many sectors of the Western Front, and was engaged at several important battles, including those of Hill 60, Ypres, Arras, Givenchy and the Somme. He holds the 1914–15 Star, and the General Service and Victory Medals, and was demobilised in March 1919
Grove Road, Harpenden, Herts. 109/B.

ARCHER, A. J. (D.C.M.), Sergeant, M.G.C.
Serving at the outbreak of the war, he was immediately drafted to France, where he took part in the Retreat from Mons and the engagements at Messines, Passchendaele, the Somme and Ypres. He was wounded whilst in action at Amiens, and again at Guillemont Farm. During his service he was awarded the Distinguished Conduct Medal and the Medaille Militaire for conspicuous bravery and gallantry in the Field, and also holds the Mons Star, and the General Service and Victory Medals. In 1920 he was still serving.
Marsh Road, Leagrave, near Luton. 110—111/A.

ARCHER, C., Private, R.A.M.C.
He joined in April 1917, and was engaged on H.M. Hospital Ship " Western Australia " on important duties conveying the wounded to Dover from Boulogne and to Southampton from Rouen. After the cessation of hostilities he continued to serve, travelling between Southampton and Germany repatriating prisoners of war. He was demobilised in March 1920, and holds the General Service and Victory Medals.
19, Upper Heath Road, St. Albans. 112.

ARCHER, E., Private, Royal Air Force.
Joining in February 1918, he served with his unit at various stations on important duties which demanded a high degree of technical skill. He rendered valuable service but was not successful in obtaining his transfer overseas before the cessation of hostilities. He was demobilised in February 1919. Lower Luton Road, Harpenden. 113.

ARCHER, F. W. A., Private, Essex Regiment.
He joined in October 1916, and in the following December, was drafted to France, where he served on the Somme and at Arras. In January 1918 he proceeded to Italy, where he took part in the campaign against the Austrians and was in action on the Piave. He returned to England and was demobilised in January 1919, holding the General Service and Victory Medals.
Park Road, Toddington, Beds. 114.

ARCHER, T., Special Constable, Bedford Constabulary.
He joined in April 1915, and served in the Leagrave Division until the end of the war, during which time he rendered valuable service and was on duty during numerous air-raids. He has been awarded the Long Service Medal.
Marsh Road, Leagrave, near Luton. 110—111/B.

ARGENT, C. E., Sergeant, Hertfordshire Regt.
He volunteered in January 1915, and later in the same year was drafted to France, where he took part in the Battle of the Somme and numerous other engagements. After the Armistice he proceeded to Germany with the Army of Occupation with which he served until February 1920, when he returned to England and was demobilised, holding the 1914–15 Star, and the General Service and Victory Medals.
5, Temperance Street, St Albans, Herts. 115.

ARGENT, H. F., Private, Machine Gun Corps.
He joined in February 1917, and shortly afterwards was drafted to Egypt, where he was in action in several engagements. He was killed on December 27th, 1917, and was entitled to the General Service and Victory Medals.
32, Liverpool Road, St. Albans. 116.

ARGER, H., Private, 1/1st Hertfordshire Regt.
He volunteered in November 1915, and was attached to the transport section of his regiment and sent overseas in 1917. He was engaged in numerous sectors of the Western Front in transporting supplies and ammunition, and served on the Somme and at Arras, Messines, Ypres, Cambrai and Amiens. In April 1919 he was demobilised, and holds the General Service and Victory Medals.
69, Sun Street, Biggleswade, Bedfordshire. Z1258.

ARGER, T. L., Private, Queen's (Royal West Surrey Regiment.)
He joined in August 1917, and in March of the following year was drafted to France, where he served in various engagements during the Retreat and Advance of 1918, notably at Albert and St. Quentin. He was severely wounded at Amiens in August 1918, and invalided home to hospital, and after treatment was finally demobilised in May 1919. He holds the General Service and Victory Medals.
69, Sun Street, Biggleswade, Bedfordshire. Z1259.

ARIS, W., Private, Suffolk Regiment.
He joined in January 1917, and in the following July was drafted to the Western Front, where he took part in the Battles of Ypres (III.), Cambrai and the Somme (II.). He was severely wounded in the Retreat, and died in hospital on August 21st, 1918. He was entitled to the General Service and Victory Medals.
77, South Street, Leighton Buzzard, Beds. 471.

ARMIGER, C., Corporal, Royal Sussex Regiment.
He volunteered in August 1914, and in the following January was drafted to France, where he served on the Somme, and was wounded. On his recovery he took part in further engagements, including those at Ypres and Cambrai. He was still serving in 1920, and holds the General Service and Victory Medals.
17, Capson Road, Dunstable. 117/B.

ARMIGER, H., Sapper, Royal Engineers.
Volunteering in August 1914, he was drafted to Egypt in the following month. Later he was transferred to France, where he served on various sectors of the Front, including those of Ypres, the Somme, Arras, Cambrai and Menin Road. He was demobilised in April 1919, and holds the 1914–15 Star, and the General Service and Victory Medals.
17, Capson Road, Dunstable. 117/A.

ARMITAGE, A., Artificer, Royal Navy.
Joining in February 1918, he served on T.B. " No 8." and was engaged on patrol duties in the North Sea. He also was present when the German Fleet was escorted to Scapa Flow. He was demobilised in October 1919, and holds the General Service and Victory Medals.
14, Park Road West, Luton, Beds. 119.

ARMITAGE, H., Private, Hertfordshire Regt.
He volunteered in August 1914, and was immediately drafted to the Western Front, where he took part in the Retreat from Mons and the Battles of Ypres and the Somme, and was three times wounded. He was taken prisoner at St. Julien in 1916, and held in captivity until after the Armistice, when he was released. He returned to England and was demobilised in December 1918, holding the Mons Star, and the General Service and Victory Medals.
5, Thorpe's Yard, Queen Street, Hitchin, Herts. 1627.

ARMITAGE, H. G., Private, Royal Inniskilling Fusiliers.
He was serving at the outbreak of hostilities, and was drafted to France in August 1914. He took part in the Retreat from Mons, during which he was wounded on two occasions, and also served in numerous other engagements. He was wounded for the third time at Givenchy in July 1915, and was invalided home and discharged in the following June. He holds the Mons Star, and the General Service and Victory Medals.
" Rosebank," Kershaw's Hill, Hitchin, Herts. 1623.

ARMITAGE, W. G., Private, 1st Bedfordshire Regiment.
He was serving at the outbreak of war, and was immediately sent to France. He served in the Retreat from Mons and other engagements until April 20th, 1915, when he was wounded at Hill 60. He was invalided home, and in December 1915 was discharged as medically unfit for further service, holding the Mons Star, and the General Service and Victory Medals.
Lilley, near Luton, Beds. 121.

ARMOND, F., Private, East Surrey Regiment.
Volunteering in September 1914, he was drafted to the Western Front in the succeeding year, and whilst in this theatre of war, took part in the Battles of Ypres and Messines Ridge, and was wounded in both engagements. On recovery he was sent to Mesopotamia, where he served until he was invalided home in 1919. He was demobilised in October of that year, and holds the 1914–15 Star, and the General Service and Victory Medals.
Royston Street, Potton, Bedfordshire.   Z1252.

ARMSDEN, C., Private, 1st Norfolk Regiment.
He joined in December 1916, and on completion of his training was drafted to France, where he served on the Somme, and at Cambrai. He was taken prisoner on April 15th, 1918, during the Retreat, and was held in captivity until after the cessation of hostilities, when he was released and returned to England. He was demobilised in November 1919, and holds the General Service and Victory Medals.
23, Cobden Street, Luton, Beds.   122/A.

ARMSTRONG, A., Rifleman, King's Royal Rifle Corps.
He joined in June 1918, and after having completed his training served with his unit on important duties at various stations. He was not successful in obtaining his transfer overseas prior to the cessation of hostilities, but in October 1919 was sent to India, where he was still serving in 1920.
Chaul End, Near Luton, Beds.   118.

ARMSTRONG, A. C., Private, 7th Bedfordshire Regiment.
Volunteering in September 1914, he was shortly afterwards drafted to France, where he served at Ypres, the Somme, Arras, Cambrai and St. Quentin, and was wounded twice. He was demobilised in February 1919, and holds the 1914–15 Star, and the General Service and Victory Medals.
9, Stuart Street, Luton.   120/C.

ARMSTRONG, F. W., Private, 7th Bedfordshire Regiment.
He volunteered in September 1914, and on completion of his training proceeded to France, where he took part in numerous engagements. He was killed in action on the Somme on July 1st, 1916, and was entitled to the 1914–15 Star, and the General Service and Victory Medals.
9, Stuart Street, Luton.   120/B.

ARMSTRONG, H. J., Private, 4th Bedfordshire Regiment.
He joined in June 1916, and in the following year was drafted to the Western Front, and took part in the Battles of the Somme, Arras, Ypres and Cambrai, and was twice wounded. He returned home and was demobilised in October 1919, and holds the General Service and Victory Medals.
Chequers Lane, Preston, Herts.   2440.

ARMSTRONG, J., Sapper, Royal Engineers.
Joining in 1916, he was drafted to France in the same year. He was engaged on important duties in the workshops at Rouen until September 1919, when he was demobilised. He holds the General Service and Victory Medals.
43, St. Albans Road, Watford, Herts.   123.

ARNOLD, O., Sapper, Royal Engineers.
He volunteered in May 1915, and having completed his training was en route for Gallipoli on board H.M.S. " Hythe," when the vessel was torpedoed and sunk on October 28th, 1915, and he was drowned. He was entitled to the 1914–15 Star, and the General Service and Victory Medals.
Mill Road, Greenfield, Beds.   1520.

ARNOLD, S., Private, 2nd Bedfordshire Regt.
Volunteering in 1914, on completion of his training he was drafted to France, where he served in many engagements, including those at Hill 60, Ypres, Festubert, Arras, and the Somme, and was wounded twice. He was demobilised in 1919, and holds the 1914–15 Star, and the General Service and Victory Medals.
The Folly, Wheathampstead, Herts.   124/B.

ARNOLD, S. W., Private, East Surrey Regiment.
He joined in May 1916, and on completion of his training proceeded to India and served at Poona and Rawal Pindi. Later he was drafted to Mesopotamia, and was in action at Kut, Baghdad, Mosul and other places. He was sent home and demobilised in January 1919, and holds the General Service and Victory Medals.
101, Albert Road, Luton.   125.

ARNOLD, W., Corporal, 1/5th Bedfordshire Regt.
He volunteered in September 1914, and on completion of his training was drafted to Gallipoli, where he took part in the landing at Suvla Bay and numerous other engagements on that Front. Later he was sent to Egypt, and served in the Battle of Gaza, and was wounded. He was demobilised in March 1919, and holds the General Service and Victory Medals.
54, Warwick Road, Luton.   127.

ARNOLD, W., R.Q.M.S., R.F.A.
He volunteered in August 1914, and immediately proceeded to France, where he served in the Retreat from Mons and at Ypres, and the Somme 1916. He was discharged as medically unfit in July 1917, and holds the Mons Star, and the General Service and Victory Medals.
Flamstead, near Dunstable, Beds.   126.

ARTHURS, J., Private, R.A.S.C
He joined in 1916, and after completing his training and rendering valuable service with his unit was sent to France in the following year. While overseas he did excellent work as a baker at Le Havre and performed his duties with efficiency until after the cessation of hostilities. On returning home he was demobilised in August 1919, holding the General Service and Victory Medals.
149, Sandringham Road, Watford.   X667/B.

ASBURY, A. J , Gunner, R.G.A.
He volunteered in September 1914, and after his training was drafted in July 1915 to Salonika, where he saw much service as a gunner on the Vardar, Struma and Monastir Fronts until hostilities ceased. He returned home and was demobilised in September 1919, holding the General Service and Victory Medals.
High Street, Whitwell, Herts.   129.

ASBURY, C., Bombardier, R.F.A.
He volunteered in August 1914, and in the following month was sent to France. He served in numerous engagements of importance, including those at Ypres, Loos, Hill 60, Vimy Ridge, and was killed in action on the Somme in September 1916. He was entitled to the 1914 Star, and the General Service and Victory Medals.
Pretoria Cottages, Harlington, Beds.   128/C.

ASBURY, W., Private, East Surrey Regiment.
He joined in June 1916, and shortly afterwards was drafted to France, where he took part in numerous engagements, including those of the Somme, Arras, Ypres and Cambrai. He was killed in action near Cambrai in the victorious Advance of October 1918, and was entitled to the General Service and Victory Medals.
Midland Cottages, Harlington, Beds.   130.

ASHBY, A., Private, Bedfordshire Regiment.
He was mobilised at the outbreak of hostilities, and immediately proceeded to France, where he fought gallantly at Mons and Le Cateau, and was killed in action on September 15th, 1914. He was entitled to the Mons Star, and the General Service and Victory Medals.
High Street, Barton, Ampthill.   1808/A.

ASHBY, A., Corporal, Bedfordshire Regiment.
He volunteered in August 1914, and in the same year proceeded to Egypt and Palestine, where he took part in many important operations, including those at Gaza, Haifa and Jaffa, and was wounded three times. He was also engaged for a time at the Dardanelles, where he was again in action. He returned home and was demobilised in April 1919, and holds the 1914–15 Star, and the General Service and Victory Medals.
Clifton Road, Shefford, Beds.   Z132.

ASHBY, A. A., Private, R.A.M.C.
He was mobilised in August 1914, and in the following year was drafted overseas. He saw much active service in Gallipoli, and did valuable work with the Field Ambulance at Anzac and other places. He was afterwards sent to Palestine and served in many engagements, including those near Gaza and Jerusalem, after the fall of which he was sent to France. On this Front he served at Arras and was gassed. He holds the 1914–15 Star, and the General Service and Victory Medals, and was demobilised in August 1919.
29, Frederic Street, Luton.   133.

ASHBY, C. E., Private, Lancashire Fusiliers.
He joined in July 1916, and in the same year was drafted to the Western Front, where he took part in several important engagements, including those at Arras, Ypres and Lens. He was killed in action at Dickebusch on May 9th, 1918. He was entitled to the General Service and Victory Medals.
444, Hitchin Road, Luton.   134/A.

ASHBY, E. O., Sapper, R.E. (R.O.D.)

He was mobilised on the outbreak of hostilities in August 1914, and in the following year was drafted to the Western Front, where he remained until after the cessation of hostilities. He was engaged on important railway operating duties in various sectors, and took part in many great battles, including those at Ypres and the Somme. In February 1919 he returned to England for demobilisation, and holds the 1914-15 Star, and the General Service and Victory Medals.
81, Fearnley Street, Watford.   X135/A.

ASHBY, H., Corporal, 5th Bedfordshire Regt.

He volunteered in 1914, and in the following year was drafted overseas. He first saw action in Gallipoli, where he took part in the landing at Suvla Bay, and the heavy fighting at Anzac, and was wounded. He was afterwards sent to Egypt, and took part in several engagements, including those in the Canal Zone, after which he went through the Advance on Jerusalem. Under General Allenby he fought at Gaza and Haifa, and also served with the Mounted Police. He was demobilised in 1919, and holds the 1914-15 Star, and the General Service and Victory Medals.
444, Hitchin Road, Luton.   134/B.

ASHBY, H., Sergeant-Major, Bedfordshire Regt.

He was mobilised in August 1914, and soon proceeded to France, where he took a distinguished part in the Battle of Ypres and was severely wounded. After his recovery he rendered valuable services as an Instructor at various stations until his demobilisation in March 1919. He holds the 1914 Star, and the General Service and Victory Medals.
High Street, Burton, Ampthill.   1808/B.

ASHBY, J., Private, Bedfordshire Regiment.

He volunteered in August 1914, and was immmediately drafted to the Western Front, where he took part in the Battles of Mons, Loos, Vimy Ridge, the Somme, Arras, Ypres (III.) and Cambrai. He also served in the Retreat and Advance of 1918. He was demobilised in February 1919, and holds the Mons Star, and the General Service and Victory Medals.
Near Church, Harlington.   2435.

ASHBY, L., Private, 6th Northamptonshire Regt.

He volunteered in 1915, and having undergone a course of training was sent to the Western Front in the following year. He took part in many important engagements, including the Battles of the Somme, and was killed in action at Grandcourt on February 17th, 1917. He was entitled to the General Service and Victory Medals.
86, Breakspeare Road, Abbots Langley, Herts.   X136/A.

ASHBY, W., Private, R.A.S.C. (M.T.)

He volunteered in May 1915, and was soon drafted to France, where he saw service in many sectors. He rendered valuable transport services in connection with supplies for the firing line, and was present at the Battles of the Somme, Arras, Ypres and Cambrai. He also served through the closing stages of the war, and after the close of hostilities was sent back to England for his demobilisation in March 1919. He holds the 1914-15 Star, and the General Service and Victory Medals.
86, Liverpool Road, Watford.   X137.

ASHBY, W. J., Private, Bedfordshire Regiment.

He volunteered in July 1915, and being physically unfit for active service overseas, was detailed for agricultural work. His special qualifications enabled him to render valuable service in the production of food supplies until 1919, when he was demobilised.
3, Grover Road, Oxhey, Herts.   X138.

ASHBY, W. J. J., Private, Hertfordshire and Royal Buckinghamshire Regiments and Trench Mortar Battery.

He volunteered in April 1915, and after his training was retained on various important duties with his unit. In July 1917 he was drafted to the Western Front, and took part in the severe fighting at the Battles of Arras, Ypres and St. Julien, and was twice wounded He died of wounds on September 1st, 1918, and was entitled to the General Service and Victory Medals.
8, King's Road, St. Albans.   139.

ASHER, C. G. R., L/Corporal, R.A.S.C. (M.T.)

He joined in March 1916, and after the completion of his training was engaged on important duties with his unit at various stations. Owing to medical unfitness he was not successful in securing his transfer overseas before the cessation of hostilities, but he rendered valuable services with the anti-aircraft section at Dover and at Head-quarters at Canterbury, until his demobilisation in November 1919.
90, Bury Park Road, Luton.   140.

ASHMAN, W. A. (M.M.), Sergeant, Royal Army Veterinary Corps and Royal Field Artillery.

He volunteered in October 1915, and in the following year was drafted to the Western Front. He took part in the Battles of Arras, Ypres, Passchendaele and Cambrai, and was mentioned in Despatches and awarded the Military Medal for great bravery at Armentières in 1918. He was demobilised in April 1919, and holds besides the Military Medal, the General Service and Victory Medals.
15, Grove Road, Harpenden.   141.

ASHMORE, A., Private, R.A.S.C.

He volunteered in November 1914, and having completed his training was retained on important duties and then sent to Salonika in 1916. While overseas he saw much fighting for nearly three years, and rendered valuable services on the Struma, Monastir and Vardar Fronts. After his return to England he was demobilised in March 1919, holding the General Service and Victory Medals.
" Fowey," Grange Road, Leagrave, Beds.   663/B.

ASHPOOL, F., Private, R.A.M.C.

He joined in October 1916, and after a course of training was drafted to the Western Front. He was engaged in hospitals on highly important duties as operator's attendant, and rendered valuable services until his demobilisation in October 1919. He holds the General Service and Victory Medals.
39, Old Bedford Road, Luton.   142/B.

ASHTON, C. S., Sergeant, Herts Dragoons.

He volunteered in September 1914, and in August of the following year was sent to Palestine, where he took part in various engagements, including that at Gaza and the taking of Jerusalem. In 1917 he was transferred to Mesopotamia, where he was again in action. He returned home and was demobilised in November 1919, and holds the 1914-15 Star, and the General Service and Victory Medals.
Bake-house, Preston, Herts.   2439.

ASHWELL, W. J., Private, Surrey Regiment.

He joined in 1917, and at the conclusion of his training served on highly important duties. He did much good work on the land in connection with food productions, but was not able to secure his transfer overseas before the cessation of hostilities. He was demobilised in 1919.
8, Moggerhanger, Sandy, Beds.   1806.

ASKER, F., Private, Northamptonshire Regt.

He joined in January 1916, but was not successful in obtaining his transfer overseas before the cessation of hostilities on account of physical unfitness for active service. He was engaged on important defence duties on the East Coast, and rendered valuable services. He was demobilised in February 1919, but in the following April he re-enlisted and was sent to India, where he was still serving in 1920.
45, Summer Street, Slip End.   143.

ASTLEY, F., Staff-Sergeant, R.A.S.C.

He joined in 1916, and after valuable services with his unit was drafted to Salonica, where he served with distinction on the Doiran and Vardar Fronts. In 1918 he proceeded with the Army of Occupation to Constantinople, where he was still serving in 1920. He holds the General Service and Victory Medals.
Pine House, Grange Road, Leagrave, Beds.   144.

ASTLING, F. S., Private, Royal Fusiliers.

He joined in January 1917, and in the following July proceeded to France, where he served in the fierce engagements at Ypres, Passchendaele, the Somme and the Retreat and Advance of 1918. He was demobilised in December 1919 on returning home, and holds the General Service and Victory Medals.
32, St. Mary's Road, Dunstable.   176/B.

ASTLING, H. J., Private, Northumberland Regiment and Labour Corps.

He joined in July 1916, and on completing his training proceeded to France, where he served in numerous engagements, including those at Arras, Cambrai, the Somme, and the Retreat and Advance of 1918. During his service he was twice wounded on the Arras Front. He was demobilised in February 1919, and holds the General Service and Victory Medals.
32, St Mary's Street, Dunstable.   176/A.

ASHTON, H., Private, Bedfordshire Regiment.

He was mobilised in August 1914, and in the following month was drafted to the Western Front, where he took part in many important engagements. He was wounded at Ypres in April 1917, and being invalided home,was discharged in August 1918 on account of his injuries. He holds the 1914 Star, and the General Service and Victory Meda
4, Francis Place, High Street, Watford.   145.

ASTON, W. T., Private, R.A.S.C.
He volunteered in November 1915, and in January 1917, after having rendered valuable service with his unit, was drafted to the Western Front, where he was engaged on important transport and supply duties at Arras, Ypres and Dunkirk. He returned home and was discharged in June 1918 in consequence of his service, and holds the General Service and Victory Medals.
3, Chaters Yard, High Street, Watford.   X146.

ATKINS, E. A., Stoker (R.N.), H.M.S. " Wessex."
He volunteered in August 1914, and throughout the war rendered valuable service in his ship in many waters, including the North and the Baltic Seas, taking part in numerous important engagements. He was still serving in 1920, and holds the 1914-15 Star, and the General Service and Victory Medals.
116, Judge Street, North Watford.   X148/A.

ATKINS, A. G., Private, Machine Gun Corps.
He joined in June 1916, and in the same year was sent to France, where he took an important part in several engagements. He rendered valuable services on the Somme and Ypres Fronts, and was afterwards drafted to Italy, where he did excellent work on the Piave as a machine gunner. He was wounded during his service. He came home and was demobilised in February 1919, holding the General Service and Victory Medals.
29a, Plantation Road, Leighton Buzzard.   472.

ATKINS, C., Private, R.A.S.C.
Joining in January 1916, in the following July he proceeded to France, where he was engaged until hostilities ceased on important transport duties, conveying food and ammunition to the front line. He was wounded once during his service, and was demobilised in September 1919, holding the General Service and Victory Medals.
2, Clarence Road, Leighton Buzzard.   1286.

ATKINS, E., Private, 13th Royal Fusiliers.
He joined in January 1917, and after a short period of training was drafted to the Western Front in the following March. He was in action in only one engagement, at Arras, where on April 28th, 1917, he was killed. He was entitled to the General Service and Victory Medals.
47, Branch Road, Park Street, near St. Albans.   X149.

ATKINS, E. Pte., 16th Northumberland Fusiliers.
He volunteered in October 1915, and after a period of training proceeded to the Western Front, where he took part in various important engagements, including those of the Somme and Ypres. On December 1st, 1917, he was killed in action at Bourlon Wood, and was entitled to the General Service and Victory Medals.
23, Breakspeare Road, Abbots Langley.   X150.

ATKINS, E. W., L/Corporal, 7th Bedfordshire Regiment.
He volunteered in May 1915, and in the same year proceeded to France. While in this theatre of war he took part in various important engagements, including that of Vimy Ridge, and was killed in action on the Somme on July 1st, 1916. He was entitled to the General Service and Victory Medals.
13, The Camp, St. Albans.   X151.

ATKINS, G., Bandsmen, R.M.L.I.
He volunteered in August 1914, and being posted to H.M.S " Commonwealth," took part in the Battles of Heligoland Bight, Dogger Bank and Jutland. He also fought in several engagements on the Western Front until hostilities ended. He was demobilised in May 1920 and holds the 1914-15 Star, and the General Service and Victory Medals.
52, Holywell Road, Watford.   X152/A.

ATKINS, H., Private, 4th Norfolk Regiment.
He joined in January 1917, and after undergoing a course of training was drafted to Egypt in July of the same year. He saw much active service in this Eastern theatre of war and was engaged in several Battles, including that of Gaza, in the Advance under General Allenby through Syria and Palestine. He was demobilised in April 1920, after returning to England, and holds the General Service and Victory Medals.
10, Castle Road, St. Albans.   X153/A.

ATKINS, H. B., Leading Stoker, R.N., H.M.S. " Burslem."
He volunteered in 1915, and while serving with the Grand Fleet in the North Sea, took part in many important engagements. He also rendered valuable service in the Baltic and other waters. He was demobilised in April 1920, and holds the 1914-15 Star, and the General Service and Victory Medals.
116, Judge Street, North Watford.   X148/B.

ATKINS, J., Private, Royal Air Force.
He joined in May 1918, and after his training did good work with his unit in connection with air patrols and anti-aircraft defences until the end of the war. He was not successful in obtaining his transfer overseas before the cessation of hostilities, but rendered valuable services until his demobilisation in March 1919.
99, Regent Street, North Watford.   X154/A.

ATKINS, J., Trooper, Herts Dragoons.
He joined in 1916, and was soon drafted overseas. He saw much active service on the Western Front, where he took part in the Battles of Arras, and was afterwards sent to Palestine. In this theatre of war he was in action in many of the Battles of the Advance under General Allenby, including those around Gaza, Jaffa, Haifa, Aleppo and Damascus. He holds the General Service and Victory Medals, and was demobilised in June 1919, after his return to England.
112, Norfolk Road, Rickmansworth.   X155/B.

ATKINS, L., Private, 3rd Northamptonshire Regt.
He joined in March 1916, and shortly afterwards was drafted to France, where he took part in the severe fighting at Vimy Ridge and Albert. On September 26th, 1916, he was killed in action on the Somme. He was entitled to the General Service and Victory Medals.
76, Breakspeare Road, Abbots Langley.   X156.

ATKINS, T., Bombardier, 1st Hertford Battery, Royal Field Artillery.
Having enlisted in the Territorials before the war, he was mobilised on the outbreak of hostilities and was, in November 1915, drafted overseas. He was in much heavy fighting around Loos before he was sent to Egypt in February 1916. In that theatre of war he took part in General Allenby's Advance on Jerusalem and fought at Gaza and in other Battles in Syria and Palestine. He was demobilised in May 1919, and holds the 1914-15 Star, and the General Service and Victory Medals.
10, Castle Road, St. Albans.   X153/B.

ATKINS, T., Private, 9th Royal Fusiliers.
He volunteered in June 1915, and after a period of training proceeded to the Western Front in the following November. While overseas he took part in the fighting on the Somme, at Arras and Cambrai, and many other important battles until hostilities ceased, and was wounded. In February 1919 he was demobilised after returning home, and holds the 1914-15 Star, and the General Service and Victory Medals.
25, Bernard Street, St. Albans.   X157.

ATKINS, W. A., Driver, R.A.S.C. (M.T.)
He volunteered in May 1915, and after a period of training was drafted to the Western Front in June of the following year. He was engaged on important duties in connection with the transport of ammunition and supplies to the forward areas, and was present at the Battles of Ypres, Arras and the Somme. He holds the General Service and Victory Medals, and was demobilised in March 1919.
112, Norfolk Road, Rickmansworth.   X155/A.

ATKINSON, J. W., C.S.M., 6th Sherwood Foresters.
He volunteered in November 1914, and after being retained on important duties with his unit for a time, went to Ireland, where he helped to suppress the Sinn Fein troubles in 1916. During his service in France he took a conspicuous part in the Battles of Bullecourt and Ypres and many other engagements, and was killed in action near Cambrai on March 21st, 1918. He was entitled to the General Service and Victory Medals.
100, Sutton Street, Watford.   X158/B.

ATTWELL, R. S., Staff-Sergeant, Military Provost Staff Corps.
He was serving at the outbreak of war, and proceeded to France in August 1915. While in this theatre of war he took a prominent part in several important engagements, and in November 1916 was wounded in action on the Somme. He also served with the Grenadier Guards and did excellent work at General Headquarters. In 1920 he was still in the Army, and holds the 1914-15 Star, and the General Service and Victory Medals.
61, Cardiff Road, Watford.   X159.

ATTWOOD, A. C., 1st Class Gun Layer, R.M.A.
He was called up from the Reserve in August 1914, and served in H.M.S. " Good Hope." He was drowned when this vessel was sunk in the battle against superior forces at Coronel on November 1st, 1914. He was entitled to the 1914-15 Star, and the General Service and Victory Medals.
38, Waterside, King's Langley.   X160.

ATWOOD, F. W., A.B., R.N., H.M.S. " Vigour."

He joined in 1917, and after a period of training was posted to H.M.S. " Vigour." While with this ship he was engaged on highly dangerous duties in connection with the blowing up of mines in the North Sea and the Baltic, and also served off the coast of Spain. In 1920 he was still serving, and holds the General Service and Victory Medals.
81, Sopwell Lane, St. Albans. X161.

AUBEN, F., Gunner, Royal Garrison Artillery.

He volunteered in 1915, and having completed his training was sent to Singapore, where he did much good work. After serving there until 1916 he returned to England, and in 1917 was drafted to the Western Front, where he fought at Arras and the Somme, and in many engagements during the Retreat and Advance of 1918. After the cessation of hostilities he returned home and was demobilised in 1919, holding the 1914–15 Star, and the General Service and Victory Medals.
42, Bancroft Street, Hitchin. 1810/A.

AUBURN, E., Private, 3rd Northamptonshire Regiment.

He joined in May 1918, and after his training was engaged on important duties with his unit at various stations. He was not successful in securing a transfer overseas before hostilities ceased, but rendered valuable services until his demobilisation in 1919.
8, High Street, Redbourne, Herts. 162.

AUBURN, W. C. (M.M.), Private, 4th Bedfordshire Regiment.

He volunteered in February 1915, and in the same year was drafted to the Western Front, where he took part in numerous engagements, including those at Loos, the Somme, Arras, Ypres and Cambrai. He also served in the Retreat and Advance of 1918, and was wounded and gassed. He was awarded the Military Medal for gallantry and devotion to duty, and also holds the 1914–15 Star, and the General Service and Victory Medals, and was demobilised in December 1919.
Upper Green, Eckleford, Hitchin. 2437.

AUSTIN, F. A., Corporal, R.A.S.C.

He volunteered in May 1915, and in the following August proceeded to France. While in this theatre of war he was engaged on various important transport and supply duties during the engagements of the Somme, Arras, Ypres and Cambrai. In May 1919 he was demobilised after returning to England, and holds the 1914–15 Star, and the General Service and Victory Medals.
208, Beech Hill, Luton. 164.

AUSTIN, C. J., A/Sergeant, Northumberland Fusiliers.

He volunteered in October 1914, and in the following year was drafted to Mesopotamia. He did valuable work in this field of war, and was engaged in many of the important battles that led to the capture of Baghdad. Whilst on active service there he contracted fever, and died on July 19th, 1917. He was entitled to the 1914–15 Star, and the General Service and Victory Medals.
2, Lea Mead, Hatfield. X163.

AUSTIN, F. A. A., Private, 1st Border Regiment.

He joined in April 1916, and was drafted to the Western Front on completing his training. He saw much active service whilst overseas, and took part in many important battles, including those at Arras and Cambrai. He was killed in action on September 3rd, 1918, and was entitled to the General Service and Victory Medals.
27, Leavensden Road, Watford. X165/B.

AUSTIN, G. R., Sapper, Royal Engineers.

He volunteered in December 1915, and after concluding his training was drafted in February 1916 to the Western Front. Whilst in this theatre of war he rendered valuable service with his unit at the Somme, Arras and Cambrai, and in many other important engagements up to the cessation of hostilities. He was demobilised in March 1919, and holds the General Service and Victory Medals.
8, Upper Culver Road, St. Albans. X166.

AUSTIN, H. M., Sergeant, Royal Field Artillery.

He volunteered in December 1914, and after six months' training proceeded to the Western Front. He took a prominent part in the heavy fighting at Ypres, the Somme, Guillemont, Arras, Passchendaele and Cambrai, and in many later engagements until fighting ceased. He was demobilised in July 1919, and holds the 1914–15 Star, and the General Service and Victory Medals.
2, Devonshire View, Hitchin. 1622.

AUSTIN, W. J., Drummer, 5th Bedfordshire Regt.

He volunteered in July 1917, and after a period of training was engaged at several stations on important duties with his unit. He did good work in the band and on various guard duties until his demobilisation in September 1919, but was not transferred to a fighting front.
108, Cotterell's Road, Hemel Hempstead. X167.

AUTON, G., Private, Black Watch.

He volunteered in October 1915, and at the end of his training in the following March was drafted to the Western Front. Here he took part in many important engagements, notably those of the Somme, Arras, and Passchendaele. He was wounded three times, and after being invalided home for treatment was discharged in April 1917 as medically unfit for further military service. He holds the General Service and Victory Medals.
48, Dagnall Street, St. Albans. X168.

AUTON, W., Private, 53rd Royal Sussex Regt.

He joined in October 1917, and in the following March was drafted to the Western Front, where he took part in the heavy fighting in many engagements during the Retreat and Advance of 1918 in the closing stages of the war. He was afterwards sent with the Army of Occupation into Germany, and was engaged on garrison duty on the Rhine until he returned to England for his demobilisation in March 1919. He holds the General Service and Victory Medals.
48, Dagnall Street, St. Albans. X169.

AVERY, W., Private, 23rd Middlesex Regiment.

He joined in June 1918 on attaining military age, and after completing a course of training was sent into Germany with the Army of Occupation. He was stationed at Cologne, and was chiefly engaged as a driver on important transport duties. He returned to England and was demobilised in March 1920.
Adelaide Cottages, Harlington, near Dunstable. 170.

AXTELL, F. H., Private, Royal Sussex Regt.

He joined in April 1917, and in the same year, after finishing his training, was drafted to Egypt. He was in action in several important engagements in the Palestine Campaign under General Allenby until the end of the war. He holds the General Service and Victory Medals, and was demobilised in December 1919 after his return to England.
84, Regent Street, North Watford. X171.

AXTELL, H., Air Mechanic, Royal Air Force.

He joined in 1917, but owing to physical unfitness for active service was not drafted overseas. He did very valuable work with his unit in connection with the rigging and fitting of aeroplanes, until he was demobilised in February 1919.
120, High Street, Redbourne, Herts. 172.

AYLOTT, C. G., Private, Royal Air Force.

He joined in December 1917, and after his training served on important duties with his unit. His work as an engine-fitter demanded a high degree of technical knowledge, and was carried out with efficiency. He was not successful in obtaining his transfer overseas before the termination of the war, and was demobilised in September 1919.
89, Cowper Street, Luton. 174.

AYLOTT, C. H., Bombardier, R.F.A.

He was mobilised on the outbreak of hostilities, and was immediately drafted to France, where he was in action in several important battles, including those of Ypres, Festubert, the Somme, Arras and Armentières, and was once wounded. After returning home he was sent to India, where in 1920 he was still serving. He holds the 1914–15 Star, and the General Service and Victory Medals.
51, Ashton Road, Luton. 173.

AYRE, H. B., Private, 606th H.S. Emp. Coy.

He joined in November 1917, and was engaged afterwards at various stations on important duties with his unit until June 1918, when he was discharged as medically unfit for further service. 111, St. James' Road, Watford. 175/B.

AYRE, J. M., Sapper, Royal Engineers.

Joining in February 1917, he was immediately drafted to the Western Front, where he rendered valuable service at Arras and Vimy Ridge. He died on May 27th of the same year from the effects of an illness contracted while overseas. He was entitled to the General Service and Victory Medals.
111, St. James' Road, Watford. 175/A.

B

BACHCINI, C., Private, R.A.M.C.

He volunteered in August 1914, and in the following year was drafted to the Western Front, where he served in numerous engagements up to the close of hostilities, including those at Hill 60, Ypres, Vimy Ridge, the Somme, Messines and Cambrai. He returned home and was demobilised in March 1919, holding the 1914–15 Star, and the General Service and Victory Medals. 25, Alma Street, Luton. 579/B.

**BACKLER, R., Trooper, 3rd (Prince of Wales')
Dragoon Guards.**
He volunteered in November 1915, and in the same year was
drafted to the Western Front. He was subsequently in
action on the Somme, at Ypres and Cambrai, and also did
excellent work with his unit during the Retreat and Advance
of 1918. He was demobilised in February 1919, and holds the
1914-15 Star, and the General Service and Victory Medals.
105, St. Jame's Road, Watford.   X189.

BACON, A., Private, 1st Bedfordshire Regiment.
He volunteered in September 1914, and in the following May
was drafted to the Western Front,where he took part in many
important engagements,including those at Ypres, the Somme,
Arras and Cambrai. In November 1917 he was sent to
Italy, and was in action on the Piave and at Trentino. He
returned to France in April 1918, and served in the final
stages of the war, remaining overseas until after the signing
of the Armistice. He was demobilised in April 1919, and
holds the 1914-15 Star, and the General Service and Victory
Medals.
44, King's Road, St. Albans.   190/A.

BACON, H., Private, Durham Light Infantry.
Joining in June 1916, he was drafted to France at the conclusion of his training. During his service in this theatre of
war he fought in many battles, and was subsequently
killed in action at Beaumont-Hamel on November 5th, 1916.
He was entitled to the General Service and Victory Medals.
31, New England Street, St. Albans.   191.

BACON, R., Private, 2nd Bedfordshire Regt.
Volunteering in September 1914, he was drafted to France
in the following May. Subsequently he took part in several
engagements, notably those at Givenchy and Loos, where
he was severely wounded in October 1915. He was invalided
home, and after protracted treatment in hospital was discharged as medically unfit in July 1916. He holds the
1914-15 Star, and the General Service and Victory Medals.
44, King's Road, St. Albans.   190/B.

**BADRICK, C., Trooper, County of London
Yeomanry.**
He volunteered in October 1914, and in the following March
was drafted to Egypt. He afterwards proceeded to Palestine, where he served in the General Offensive under General
Allenby. During his service in this theatre of war he took
part in the Battles of Gaza and the Entry into Jerusalem,
and subsequently fought at Aleppo. He returned to England
and was demobilised in January 1919, and holds the 1914-15
Star, and the General Service and Victory Medals.
High Street, Wing, Leighton Buzzard, Bucks.   1605/B.

BADRICK, H. G., Private, Labour Corps.
He joined in January 1917, and in the following July was
drafted to France. During his service on the Western Front
he was engaged with his unit on important road construction
and trenching duties in the forward areas, especially at Cambrai and the Somme (II.), and in various engagements in the
Retreat and Advance of 1918. After the cessation of hostilities he was sent to Germany with the Army of Occupation,
and was stationed at Cologne until his return home in
November 1919 for demobilisation. He holds the General
Service and Victory Medals.
High Street, Wing, Leighton Buzzard, Bucks.   1605/A.

BADRICK, W. Driver, Royal Field Artillery.
He was mobilised from the Reserve in August 1914, and early
in the following month was sent to the Western Front, where
he took part in the final stages of the Retreat from Mons.
Subsequently he served at Ypres, Loos, Arras and Cambrai,
and on one occasion was gassed and wounded. He was
demobilised after his return to England in January 1919, and
holds the Mons Star, and the General Service and Victory
Medals.
35, Sotheron Road, Watford.   192.

**BADSWORTH, W. P., Private, 7th Bedfordshire
Regiment.**
He volunteered in December 1915, and in the following
September was drafted to the Western Front. Whilst in
this theatre of war he fought on the Somme and at Arras,
and on two occasions was severely wounded. He was
invalided home, and after protracted treatment in hospital
was discharged as medically unfit for further service in July
1918. He holds the General Service and Victory Medals.
32, Jubilee Street, Luton, Bedfordshire.   193.

BADWELL, F. J., Pioneer, Royal Engineers.
He volunteered in September 1914, and on completion of his
training was sent to the Western Front, where he did excellent
work with his unit in many sectors, including those of the
Somme and Arras. Returning to England he was demobilised in May 1919, and holds the 1914-15 Star, and the
General Service and Victory Medals.
6, Park Gate Road, Callowland, Watford, Herts.   X194.

BAILEY, E. A., A.B , R.N., H.M.S. " Excellent."
He joined in July 1918, and for the remaining period of war
was engaged on duties of a special nature at the Portsmouth
School of Gunnery. He rendered excellent services until
February 1919, when he was demobilised.
40, Grove Road, Luton.   196.

BAILEY, H., Private, R.A.S.C.
He joined in 1916, and in the same year was sent to Salonika,
where he was engaged on important transport duties in
various sectors. He was afterwards drafted to the Western
Front and in a similar capacity served at the Battles of
Ypres, the Somme and Cambrai. Returing to England after
the cessation of hostilities he was demobilised in December
1919, and holds the General Service and Victory Medals.
4, Brightwell Road, Watford.   197/A.

BAILEY, H. C., Private, R.A.S.C.
Volunteering in January 1915, he was drafted to Salonika
at the conclusion of his training. He was engaged on
important transport work in the forward areas, and in this
capacity saw service during engagements on the Vardar
Front and at Monastir. He was demobilised after his
return to England in February 1919, and holds the General
Service and Victory Medals.
2, Boundary Road, St. Albans, Herts.   X198.

BAILEY, H. P., Aircraftsman, R.A.F.
He joined in July 1918, and after his training served at
various stations with his squadron. He was engaged on
important duties, which demanded a high degree of technical
knowledge and skill, and rendered valuable services, but
was unable to obtain a transfer overseas before the termination of the war. He was demobilised in April 1919.
152, Hitchin Road, Luton.   199.

BAILEY, J., Private, Bedfordshire Regiment.
He volunteered in January 1915, and after his training was
sent overseas in the following September. He subsequently
fought at Ypres,on the Somme and at Loos,and was wounded
and invalided home on three occasions during his service.
He was demobilised in January 1919, and holds the 1914-15
Star, and the General Service and Victory Medals.
37, Ashton Road, Luton.   T200.

BAILEY, J. H., Corporal, R.G.A.
He volunteered in April 1915, and in July of the following
year was drafted to the Western Front, where he took part
in the heavy fighting at Arras, Ypres, Passchendaele,
Cambrai, the Somme, and Albert. He returned home and
was demobilised in January 1919, holding the General
Service and Victory Medals.
12, Barker's Cottages, Hitchin Hill, Hitchin.   2451.

BAILEY, L. T., Private, Tank Corps.
He volunteered in June 1915, and in the following January
was drafted to the Western Front, where he was in action on
the Somme and at Bullecourt, Passchendaele and Cambrai.
He also served in the Retreat of 1918,and after the conclusion
of hostilities returned to England and was demobilised,
holding the General Service and Victory Medals.
108, High Street, South Dunstable.   3850—3851/B.

BAINES, J., Rifleman, Rifle Brigade.
He joined in July 1917, and in the same year was drafted to
the Western Front, where he took part in numerous engagements, including those of Lens, Cambrai, the Retreat and
Advance of 1918, and was wounded. He returned home and
was demobilised in November 1919, and holds the General
Service and Victory Medals.
6, Chambers Lane, Ickleford, Hitchin.   2444.

BAINES, W., Sapper, Royal Engineers.
Joining in June 1916, he was quickly drafted to the Western
Front, where he was engaged on road construction, making
and wiring trenches and other important work. Whilst
carrying out these duties near Ypres, in 1917, he was severely
wounded, but on his recovery he rejoined his unit and served
until the termination of war. He was demobilised in
November 1919, and holds the General Service and Victory
Medals.
50, Baker Street, Leighton Buzzard.   1292.

BAINES, W. J., Private, Cheshire Regiment.
Volunteering in June 1915 he was drafted to Egypt in the
same year and subsequently served with General Allenby's
Forces in the Palestine Campaign. He took part in the
Battles of Gaza and the Capture of Jerusalem, and at the end
of 1917 was sent to India, where he was engaged on special
duties at various garrison outposts. He returned home and
was discharged as medically unfit for further service in
August 1918, and holds the 1914-15 Star, and the General
Service and Victory Medals.
Ley Green, King's Walden, Herts.   201/B.

BAKER, A. G., Corporal, R.A.O.C.

Joining in October 1916, he was sent to France two months' later. During his service overseas he was engaged on important duties in the forward areas and was present at many engagements, including those of Arras and the Somme. In the latter part of 1917 he was gassed, and early in the following year was severely wounded. He was demobilised on his return to England in February 1919, and holds the General Service and Victory Medals.
" Wyken," Houghton Regis, Beds. 202.

BAKER, E., Sapper, Royal Engineers.

He volunteered in 1915, and until the early part of 1918, when he was sent to France, was engaged on duties of an important nature. Subsequently he served in the Retreat and Advance of that year, during which he did excellent work with his unit, notably at Cambrai and Béthune.. Returning to England he was demobilised in March 1919, and holds the General Service and Victory Medals.
45, Upper Heath Road, St. Albans. X203.

BAKER, E., Private, Royal Sussex Regiment.

He joined in 1916, and was quickly drafted to the Western Front. Here he served in many important engagements, notably those on the Somme, at Arras and Ypres, where he was severely wounded. He was demobilised in May 1919, and holds the General Service and Victory Medals.
8, Hockliffe Road, Leighton Buzzard. 1294/B.

BAKER, G., Private, Gloucestershire Regiment.

He joined in May 1917, and in November of the same year was drafted to the Western Front, where he took part in heavy fighting at Ypres and on the Somme. He also served in the Retreat and Advance of 1918, and was killed in action on August 23rd, 1918, and was entitled to the General Service and Victory Medals.
86, Fishpool Street, St. Albans. 205/A.

BAKER, G., Private, Hertfordshire Regiment, and Rifleman, Rifle Brigade.

He volunteered in November 1914, and on the completion of his training was drafted to India. He served at Rawal Pindi, in the Punjab and at other stations, and was engaged on duties of an important nature. He returned home and was demobilised in July 1919, and holds the General Service and Victory Medals.
26, Willow Lane, Watford. X204.

BAKER, G. W., Private, 22nd London Regiment (The Queen's).

He volunteered in August 1914, and after his training was sent overseas. During his service in France, which lasted for nearly four years, he served in many notable engagements, and was wounded in action at Loos. He was demobilised in February 1919, and holds the 1914-15 Star, and the General Service and Victory Medals.
10, College Place, St. Albans. 206.

BAKER, H., Driver, Royal Field Artillery.

He volunteered in July 1915, and after his training was engaged on special duties until drafted to the Western Front in March 1917. Subsequently he took part in engagements at Arras, Ypres, Passchendaele and the Somme, and did good work with his battery throughout his service overseas, which lasted two years. He was demobilised in May 1919, and holds the General Service and Victory Medals.
7, Jubilee Street, Luton. 207/B.

BAKER, H., Private, R.A.M.C.

He volunteered in August 1915, and in the same year was drafted to the Western Front. Here he served as a stretcher-bearer in several important battles, including those of Ypres, the Somme and Arras, and was severely gassed. He was invalided home and discharged in October 1916, and holds the 1914-15 Star, and the General Service and Victory Medals.
10, Croak Log, London Road, Bushey, Herts. X208.

BAKER, H. G., Private, 4th Bedfordshire Regt.

He volunteered at the outbreak of hostilities and was drafted to the Western Front shortly afterwards. During his service in this theatre of war he served in several engagements, notably that at Ypres, and was severely wounded. Returning to England he was invalided out of the Service in January 1916, and holds the 1914-15 Star, and the General Service and Victory Medals.
30, Willow Lane, Watford. X209.

BAKER, J., Bombardier, R.F.A.

He volunteered in November 1915, and after his training was retained for special duties as an Instructor at the School of Gunnery, until the early part of 1918. He was then drafted to France, and subsequently served in the Retreat and Advance of that year, during which he participated in some heavy fighting. Returning to England in December 1918, he was demobilised in the following February, and holds the General Service and Victory Medals.
11, Smith Street, Watford. 210.

BAKER, J., Gunner, Royal Field Artillery.

He volunteered in 1915, and was quickly drafted to France. Here he took part in engagements in many important sectors of the Front, including those of Ypres, Cambrai, the Somme and Arras. He was demobilised after his return to England in January 1919, and holds the General Service and Victory Medals. 55, Piccotts End, Hemel Hempstead, Herts. 211.

BAKER, L., Private, 1st Hertfordshire Regiment, and Driver, Royal Field Artillery.

Volunteering in September 1914, he was sent to the Western Front in the following year and subsequently took part in several engagements. In February 1916 he was drafted to Egypt and thence to Palestine, where, with General Allenby's Forces, he served in the Battles of Gaza, Jaffa, and in other operations during that campaign. Returning to England he was demobilised in June 1919, and holds the 1914-15 Star, and the General Service and Victory Medals.
9, Carey Place. Watford. 212/B.

BAKER, L. A., Private, Middlesex Regiment.

He volunteered in June 1915, and in the following December was drafted to France, where he served in many engagements, notably those at Ypres, the Somme, Loos, Arras and Cambrai. He was demobilised on his return to England in February 1919, and holds the 1914-15 Star, and the General Service and Victory Medals.
2, Bury Dell Lane, Park Street, near St. Albans, Herts.
213/A.

BAKER, T., Pioneer, Royal Engineers.

He volunteered in April 1915, and on completing his training in the following January was sent overseas. He subsequently served on the Somme, at Arras, Ypres and Cambrai, and in many other sectors, and did excellent work with his unit until the conclusion of hostilities. He was demobilised on his return to England in March 1919, and holds the General Service and Victory Medals.
67, Sutton Road, Watford, Herts. X214.

BAKER, W., Pioneer, Royal Engineers.

He volunteered in August 1915, and in the same month was sent to the Western Front. Whilst in this theatre of war he served at Loos, the Somme, Arras, and in many other sectors, and did good work with his unit. In May 1917, owing to ill-health, he was invalided home, and in November was discharged as medically unfit for further service. He holds the 1914-15 Star, and the General Service and Victory Medals.
7, Jubilee Street, Luton. 207/A.

BAKER, W., L/Corporal, Royal Army Service Corps and Bedfordshire Regiment.

Volunteering at the commencement of hostilities he was sent to the Western Front in the following year. Subsequently he served in many engagements, notably those at Ypres, the Somme, Cambrai, Arras and St. Quentin, and did excellent work with his unit. Returning to England in 1919 he was demobilised, and holds the 1914-15 Star, and the General Service and Victory Medals.
55, Regent Street, North Watford, Herts. X215.

BAKER, W. A., Private, R.A.S.C.

He volunteered in January 1915, and in the same month was drafted to Egypt, where he served until the end of that year, when he was sent to the Western Front. Here he was engaged in conveying supplies of food and ammunition to the various forward areas, including the Somme, and during 1918 carried out similar duties on the Piave in Italy. After the cessation of hostilities he returned to England, and in April 1919 was demobilised. He holds the 1914-15 Star, and the General Service and Victory Medals.
" Woodcote," Ferndale Road, Luton. 216.

BALDOCK, A. G., Private, 6th Bedfordshire Regt.

He volunteered in August 1914, and was shortly afterwards drafted to France. During his service in this theatre of war he fought in numerous engagements, including those at Arras and Cambrai, and was taken prisoner. Held in captivity for three years he was released after the Armistice, and returning to England was demobilised in February 1919. He holds the 1914-15 Star, and the General Service and Victory Medals.
Bowman's Cottages, London Colney, near St. Albans.
217/A.

BALDWIN, A., Private, 1/10th Royal Scots.

He joined in August 1916, and after completing his training served with his battalion at various stations on garrison duties until January 1918, when he proceeded overseas. He was in action on the Western Front, and took part in the fighting on the Somme, at St. Quentin and Cambrai during the German Offensive and subsequent Allied Advance. He was demobilised in October 1919, and holds the General Service and Victory Medals.
42, Warwick Road, Luton. 218/B.

BALDWIN, A. E., Rifleman, Rifle Brigade.
He joined in 1916, and in the same year was drafted overseas
He served on the Western Front, and was in action in the
first Battle of the Somme and the subsequent engagements
at Arras and Ypres. He was wounded at Arras, and after
recovery returned to the firing line, where he was engaged
until the end of the war. He was demobilised in March 1919,
and holds the General Service and Victory Medals.
60, Park Road West, Luton.   219/A.

BALDWIN, C., Private, 1/5th Bedfordshire Regt.
He volunteered at the outbreak of war and was engaged
with his unit on various duties until 1916, when he was sent
to France. In this theatre of war he took part in the Battles
of Ypres, the Somme, Arras, Passchendaele, St. Julien and
Cambrai, and returned to England after the Armistice. He
holds the General Service and Victory Medals, and was
demobilised in February 1919.
42, Warwick Road, Luton.   218/A.

BALDWIN, F. G., Private, Royal Fusiliers.
He joined in June 1916, and in December of the same year
was drafted to the Western Front, where he took part in
engagements and was wounded. He was invalided home,
and after a period in hospital was discharged as medically
unfit for further service in February 1918, holding the General
Service and Victory Medals.
69, Liverpool Road, Watford.   X220/B.

BALDWIN, H., Private, 4th Bedfordshire Regt.
He volunteered in September 1914, and was drafted to the
Western Front in the following March. He was in action at
Neuve Chapelle and Festubert, and owing to ill-health was
invalided to hospital in England in August 1915. He was
subsequently discharged as medically unfit for further service
in September 1916, and holds the 1914–15 Star, and the
General Service and Victory Medals.
2b, Liverpool Road, Watford.   X221.

BALDWIN, H., Sapper, Royal Engineers.
He volunteered in August 1914, and was drafted to Gallipoli
in the following year. He took part in the landing at Suvla
Bay, and was present during the subsequent fighting until
the Evacuation of the Peninsula. He was then sent to
Egypt, and serving under General Allenby in the British
Advance through Palestine, was engaged in the forward
areas whilst operations were in progress. He holds the
1914–15 Star, and the General Service and Victory Medals.
60, Park Road West, Luton.   219/B.

BALDWIN, J. E., Driver, Royal Field Artillery.
He volunteered in July 1915, and was drafted to the Western
Front in February 1916. Whilst in this theatre of war he
was in action at Arras, Ypres and on the Somme, where,
during heavy fighting his horses were killed from under him.
He suffered from shell-shock and was sent home, and after
receiving hospital treatment was invalided out of the Service
in October 1918. He holds the General Service and Victory
Medals.
110, Norfolk Road, Rickmansworth, Herts.   X222.

BALDWIN, J. W., Pte., 19th Canadian Infantry.
He volunteered in October 1914, and in September of the
following year was drafted to the Western Front, where he
served in various sectors and took part in fighting at St. Eloi,
Festubert, Loos and Lens. He was demobilised in April
1919, and holds the 1914–15 Star, and the General Service
and Victory Medals.
61, Cardiff Road, Watford.   X223.

BALDWIN, J. W., Leading Signalman, R.N.
He was in the Navy at the outbreak of hostilities, and during
the war served in H.M.S. " Tarantella," which vessel was
engaged on important patrol and other duties in the Persian
Gulf, North Sea, and in various other waters. His ship was
also in action in the Battle of Jutland and had many
encounters with the German Fleet. He was demobilised in
March 1919, and holds the 1914–15 Star, and the General
Service and Victory Medals.
31, Church Road, Watford.   X224/C.

BALDWIN, W. (M.M.), Bombardier, R.F.A.
He volunteered in September 1914, and after his training
was drafted to France, where he took part in the fighting in
various sectors and was in action in many battles, including
those of Arras, Ypres, the Somme, Cambrai and St. Quentin.
He was awarded the Military Medal for conspicuous bravery
and devotion to duty in the Field. On the cessation of
hostilities he was sent with the Army of Occupation to
Germany, and was stationed at Cologne. He was still serving
in 1920, and holds the 1914–15 Star, and the General Service
and Victory Medals.
85, Breakspeare Road, Abbots Langley, Herts.   225/A.

BALDWIN, W. G., Air Mechanic, R.A.F.
He joined in June 1916, and in the same year proceeded with
his squadron overseas. During his service in France he was
employed as an aero engine-fitter, work which demanded a
high degree of technical skill. Early in 1918 he was invalided
home on account of ill-health, and was discharged from the
Service in consequence in May of that year. He has since
died, and was entitled to the General Service and Victory
Medals.
85, Breakspeare Road, Abbots Langley, Herts.   225/B.

BALDWIN, W. H., Private, Bedfordshire Regt.
He joined in July 1917, and in the same year was drafted to
the Western Front, where he took part in severe fighting at
Arras, Cambrai and the Somme, and was twice wounded.
He was killed in action on the Somme on August 30th, 1918,
and was entitled to the General Service and Victory Medals.
69, Liverpool Road, Watford.   X220/A.

BALFOUR, H. E., Private, R.A.S.C. (M.T.)
He volunteered in February 1915, and in the following May
was sent to the Western Front. He was engaged on important transport duties to the forward areas, and was present
at the Battles of Ypres, the Somme, Arras and many others
until the close of the war. He was demobilised in April
1919, and holds the 1914–15 Star, and the General Service
and Victory Medals.
8, Breadcroft Lane, Harpenden, Herts.   226.

**BALL, F. C., Trooper, Bedfordshire Lancers, and
Private, Machine Gun Corps.**
He volunteered in September 1914, and in the following
April was drafted to France, where he took part in severe
fighting at Hill 60, Ypres, and Loos, and was wounded.
He was invalided home in 1916. On recovery he was sent to
Egypt in 1917, and was in action in several engagements
during the British Advance through Palestine. In the
following year he returned to France and fought on the
Somme, at Cambrai, and in the Retreat and Advance of 1918.
He was demobilised in February 1919, and holds the
1914–15 Star, and the General Service and Victory Medals.
Campton Villa, Shefford, Beds.   228/A.

BALL, H., L/Corporal, Royal Engineers.
He volunteered in September and served with his unit at
various stations until 1916, when he was sent to Egypt.
Whilst in this theatre of war he served under General
Allenby in Palestine, and was engaged on special duties in
connection with operations at Jaffa and Gaza. He returned
to England and was demobilised in March 1919, and holds
the General Service and Victory Medals.
Campton Villa, Shefford, Beds.   228/C.

BALL, H. H., Driver, Royal Engineers.
Volunteering in September 1914, he was employed at home
for a time on important work. In 1916 he proceeded to
Egypt, where he was engaged on duties in the forward areas,
and was present during the fighting at Gaza, Jaffa, Jerusalem
and Damascus, and was wounded. He holds the General
Service and Victory Medals, and after returning to England
was demobilised in February 1919.
Campton Villa, Shefford, Beds.   228/B.

BALL, W. H., 1st Class Stoker, Royal Navy.
He joined the Royal Navy in 1912, and during the war
served in H.M.S. " Rattlesnake," " Platypus," " Jupiter,"
" Euryalus " and T.B.D. " No. 19." These vessels were
engaged on important duties in the North Sea, and other
waters, and H.M.S " Rattlesnake " took part in the naval
operations at the Dardanelles. In 1920 he was still serving,
and holds the 1914–15 Star, and the General Service and
Victory Medals.
9, Cardigan Street, Luton.   230.

BALLAM, A. E., Ordinary Seaman, Royal Navy.
He joined in 1918, and after his training was posted to H.M.S.
" Royal Oak," in which ship he served with the Mediterranean Sea Fleet on patrol and other duties. After the Armistice his ship was stationed in Turkish waters, guarding British
interests at Constantinople. He holds the General Service
and Victory Medals, and in 1920 was still serving.
43, Windsor Road, Callowland, Watford.   X231/A.

BALLAM, A. J., Private, R.A.S.C.
He volunteered in December 1914, and in the following year
proceeded overseas. During his service on the Western
Front, he was engaged on various duties with his unit and
was frequently in the forward areas whilst operations were
in progress, and was present at the Battles of Ypres, Arras
and the Somme. He was demobilised in February 1919, and
holds the 1914–15 Star, and the General Service and Victory
Medals.
42, Windsor Road, Callowland, Watford.   X231/B.

BALLANTINE, A., Private, Royal Marine Engineers.
He joined in April 1918, and at the conclusion of his training served with his unit at various stations on important duties. He did much good work, but was not able to secure his transfer overseas owing to medical unfitness. He was demobilised in February 1919.
Lower Luton Road, Harpenden, Herts. 232.

BALLARD, A. C., Private, Queen's Own (Royal West Kent Regiment); and Rifleman, King's Royal Rifle Corps.
He enlisted in May 1914, and at the outbreak of war served with his regiment on important garrison and other duties at various stations until April 1918, when he was drafted to the Western Front. He was engaged in the fighting at Arras and Cambrai, during the German Offensive and subsequent Allied Advance of that year, and after the Armistice returned to England and was demobilised in February 1919. He holds the General Service and Victory Medals.
108, Estcourt Road, Watford. X233/A.

BALLARD, E. J., C.Q.M.S., Queen's Own (Royal West Kent Regiment).
He enlisted in February 1911, and early in 1915 was drafted to Mesopotamia, where he served with his unit and took part in many important engagements until the cessation of hostilities. He returned to England in January 1919, and was sent to Germany to the Army of Occupation, and in 1920 he was still serving there. He holds the 1914-15 Star, and the General Service and Victory Medals.
108, Estcourt Road, Watford. X233/B.

BALLARD, G., Private, 7th Royal Fusiliers.
He volunteered in 1915 and in the same year was drafted to the Western Front. He was engaged in the heavy fighting in many battles, including those of the Somme (1916), Ypres (1917), and Cambrai (1918), and was three times wounded. He was demobilised in March 1919, and holds the 1914-15 Star, and the General Service and Victory Medals.
126, Sandringham Road, Watford. 234/B.

BALLARD, H., Private, Middlesex Regiment.
He joined in May 1916, and in the following September was drafted to the Western Front, where he took part in the Somme Offensive, during which he was killed in action on September 29th, 1916. He was entitled to the General Service and Victory Medals.
17, Alfred Road, Houghton Road. Dunstable. 235/A.

BALLARD, L., L/Corporal, 8th Leicestershire Regiment.
He volunteered in November 1914, and at the conclusion of his training served with his unit at various stations on important duties until November 1916, when he proceeded overseas. Whilst on the Western Front he fought in many engagements, and was reported missing on May 3rd, 1917, but was later presumed to have been killed in action on that date. He was entitled to the General Service and Victory Medals.
42, High Street, Houghton Regis, Dunstable. 235/B.

BAMBROOK, A., Corporal, R.G.A.
He volunteered in November 1915, and in the following year was drafted to France. He served in many engagements, including those on the Somme and at Ypres, and was severely wounded during the Retreat of March 1918. He was invalided home and discharged as unfit for further service in December 1918, and holds the General Service and Victory Medals.
52, New Road, Linslade, Bucks. 1582.

BANDY, A., Gunner, Royal Field Artillery.
He volunteered in August 1914, and in the following January was drafted overseas. During his service on the Western Front he did excellent work as a gunner in the Battles of Loos, the Somme, Passchendaele, Bullecourt and the Retreat of 1918, in which he was severely wounded and gassed. He was demobilised in February 1919, and holds the 1914-15 Star, and the General Service and Victory Medals.
Church Street, Wing, Bucks. 1607/B.

BANDY, A. E., Sapper, Royal Engineers.
He joined in December 1916, and after his training served at various stations on important coastal defence duties. He rendered valuable services, but owing to being medically unfit was unable to obtain his transfer overseas. He was demobilised in January 1919.
Beaulah, Alfred Street, Dunstable, Bedfordshire. 183.

BANDY, A. F. W., Driver, R.F.A.
He volunteered in December 1915, and after his training was, in 1917, drafted to the Western Front, where he took part in important engagements and was wounded at Messines. He was invalided home, and discharged as medically unfit for further service in March 1918, and holds the General Service and Victory Medals.
Myrtle Cottage, Queen's Road, Harpenden, Herts. 236.

BANDY, E. L., Private, Machine Gun Corps.
He joined in March 1917, but was not successful in obtaining his transfer overseas before the cessation of hostilities owing to being medically unfit for active service. He was engaged on important duties at various stations, and rendered valuable services until he was demobilised in March 1920.
8, West Parade, Dunstable, Beds. 237/C.

BANDY, E. W., Private, Bedfordshire Regiment.
He volunteered in August 1914, and in the following April was drafted to Egypt, where he remained until January 1917, when he was transferred to the Western Front. He took part in the engagements at Arras, Ypres, the Somme and Cambrai, and in the Retreat of 1918, and after the conclusion of hostilities returned to England and was demobilised in February 1919, holding the General Service and Victory Medals.
Chequer's Hill, Flamstead, near Dunstable, Beds. X476.

BANDY, J. A., Private, East Surrey Regiment.
He volunteered in January 1915, and on the completion of his training, after serving on important duties at various stations, was drafted to France in July 1916. He took part in the heavy fighting in the Battle of the Somme, and in January 1917 was severely wounded and suffered from shell-shock. After being for some months under treatment in hospital he was discharged in July 1917 as medically unfit for further military duty. He holds the General Service and Victory Medals.
Church Street, Wing, Bucks. 1607/A.

BANDY, R., Private, Bedfordshire Lancers.
He volunteered in September 1914, and in January of the following year was drafted to the Western Front, and took part in severe fighting at the Battle of Loos and on the Somme. In 1917 he was transferred to Egypt and served at the Battle of Gaza, and later in important engagements in Palestine. Afterwards he served in Ireland for a time, prior to his demobilisation in April 1919. He holds the 1914-15 Star, and the General Service and Victory Medals.
8, West Parade, Dunstable, Beds. 237/A.

BANDY, W. G., Private, 5th Norfolk Regiment.
He joined in April 1916, and after his training was, in August of the same year, drafted to the Western Front. He took part in the Battle of the Somme (I.), and was killed in action at Arras on April 27th, 1917. He was entitled to the General Service and Victory Medals.
Cliftonville, Alfred Street, Dunstable, Beds. 238.

BANDY, W. J., Private, Bedfordshire Lancers.
He volunteered in September 1914, and in January of the following year was sent to the Western Front, where he took part in severe fighting at the Battle of Ypres and on the Somme. In 1917 he was transferred to Egypt, and served at the Battle of Gaza and in various important engagements in Palestine. He returned home and was demobilised in February 1919, and holds the 1914-15 Star, and the General Service and Victory Medals.
8, West Parade, Dunstable, Beds. 237/B.

BANFIELD, B., Private, R.A.S.C.
He joined in November 1916, but was not successful in obtaining his transfer overseas owing to being medically unfit for service abroad. He was engaged on important duties at various stations, and rendered valuable services until he was demobilised in November 1919.
40, Cotterels Road, Hemel Hemstead, Herts. X239.

BANGLE, A., Private, 6th Royal Sussex Regt.
He joined in August 1916, and after his training was, in February of the following year, drafted to India. He was engaged on various important duties at Rawal Pindi and on the Frontier; and rendered valuable services. He returned home and was demobilised in April 1919, and holds the General Service and Victory Medals.
Wynn Stanley, Symington Street, Harpenden, Herts. 240/B.

BANGS, G., Private, 4th Bedfordshire Regiment.
He volunteered in December 1914, and was drafted to Egypt and Palestine, where he took part in important engagements. He was later transferred to France, where he was in action at Ypres, the Somme and Cambrai, and was wounded. He was demobilised in February 1919, and holds the 1914-15 Star, and the General Service and Victory Medals.
Lodge Cottages, Lower Luton Road, Harpenden, Herts. 241/A.

BANGS, H., A.B. (R.N.), H.M.S. "Braemar Castle."
He volunteered in 1914, and served in the North Sea and the Mediterranean. He was engaged in the transport of troops between England and the Dardanelles and Egypt, and rendered valuable services. He was discharged in November 1918 as medically unfit, and holds the 1914-15 Star, and the General Service and Victory Medals.
Lodge Cottages, Lower Luton Road, Harpenden, Herts. 241/B.

BANKS, A., Private, Royal Defence Corps.
He volunteered in May 1915, and was engaged at various stations on important duties. He rendered valuable services protecting bridges and guarding prisoners of war until March 1919, when he was demobilised.
Castle Hill, Ridgmont, Beds. Z242/A.

BANKS, C., Private, The Buffs (East Kent Regt.)
He joined in May 1916, and in December of the same year, was drafted to the Western Front, where he took part in the Battles of Arras (I.), Ypres (III.), and Cambrai He also served in the Retreat and Advance of 1918, and was wounded on the Somme. He was demobilised in September 1919, and holds the General Service and Victory Medals.
St. Asaph, Alfred Street, Dunstable, Beds. 243.

BANKS, G., Private, Bedfordshire Lancers.
He volunteered in August 1914, and in the same year was sent to the Western Front, where he took part in the Retreat from Mons, and the Battles of Loos, Arras and Cambrai. After the Armistice he proceeded with the Army of Occupation to Germany, where he remained until March 1919, when he returned to England and was demobilised, holding the Mons Star, and the General Service and Victory Medals.
51, St. Mary's Street, Dunstable, Beds. 244.

BANKS, J., Private, 2nd Bedfordshire Regiment.
He was mobilised in August 1914, and in September of the same year was drafted to the Western Front, and took part in severe fighting at the Battles of La Bassée, Ypres (I.), Loos, the Somme and Cambrai. He also fought in the Retreat and Advance of 1918. He was still serving in 1920, and holds the 1914 Star, and the General Service and Victory Medals.
24, Winfield Street, Dunstable, Beds. 245.

BANKS, P., Gunner, Royal Field Artillery.
He joined in May 1917, and after his training proceeded to France in the following year. While in this theatre of war he took part in various engagements, including the Advance of 1918. Later he was attached to the Army of Occupation and drafted to Germany. He returned to England for his demobilisation in November 1919, and holds the General Service and Victory Medals.
37, Prosperous Row, Dunstable, Beds. 246.

BARBER, F. C., Private, 3rd Royal Sussex Regt.
He enlisted in February 1914, and in the same year proceeded to France. While in this theatre of war he took part in various engagements, including those on the Marne and at La Bassée, Hill 60, Ypres, Albert, the Somme and Cambrai, and was twice wounded. In November 1919 he was demobilised, and holds the 1914 Star, and the General Service and Victory Medals.
Monkdale, Blandell Road, Leagrave, Luton. 247.

BARBER, W. B., Private, R.A.M.C.
He volunteered in March 1915, and after a period of training, proceeded to the Western Front in the following year. While in this theatre of war he was engaged on important duties at Ypres, the Somme and Cambrai. In December 1919 he was demobilised, and holds the General Service and Victory Medals.
15, Adelaide Street, Luton. 248.

BARBER, W. G., Private, 8th Durham Light Infantry.
He joined in June 1917, and in April of the following year, was drafted to the Western Front. Shortly afterwards he was reported missing, and is presumed to have been killed at Cambrai. He was entitled to the General Service and Victory Medals.
Grace Lynn, St. Peter's Road, Dunstable, Beds. 249.

BARBOUR, J. R., Gunner, 1st Herts. R.F.A.
He volunteered in September 1914, and after completing a course of training in the following year was drafted to India, where he was engaged on garrison duties at various stations. He was demobilised in November 1919, and holds the General Service and Victory Medals.
18, Upper Culver Road, St. Albans, Herts. X250/A.

BARBOUR, W., Private, R.A.V.C.
He volunteered in October 1914, and after a course of training was drafted overseas in the following year. He served in many sectors of the Western Front until 1916 when he was sent to Salonika. In this theatre of war he was engaged in attending to sick and wounded horses and mules. He holds the 1914-15 Star, and the General Service and Victory Medals, and was demobilised in March 1919.
18, Upper Culver Road, St. Albans, Herts. X250/B.

BARFE, L., Private, 20th Hussars.
He was mobilised in 1914, and was sent to the Western Front, where he took part in the severe fighting during the Retreat from Mons, and was in action at Ypres, Arras, Passchendaele and Cambrai, and was five times wounded. He was invalided home and was discharged as medically unfit in September 1918, holding the Mons Star, and the General Service and Victory Medals.
Ganders Ash, Leavesden, Watford. X254.

BARFOOT, F., Private, 2nd Royal Sussex Regt.
He volunteered in September 1914, and after training was drafted to France in August 1916. He was severely wounded at the Battle of the Somme in the following month, and on recovery served at Ypres and Passchendaele Ridge. In February 1919 he was demobilised, and holds the General Service and Victory Medals.
4, Baker Street, Ampthill, Bedfordshire. 251/A.

BARFOOT, I. (Miss), Special War Worker.
During the war this lady offered her services for work of National importance, and was engaged at a munition factory in the painting of fuses. Her duties were carried out in an efficient manner and to the entire satisfaction of the firm.
4, Baker Street, Ampthill, Bedfordshire. 251/B.

BARFORD, E., L/Corporal, Royal Engineers.
He volunteered in March 1917, and in the following month was drafted to the Western Front, and took part in important engagements, including those at Arras, Ypres and the Somme. He returned home and was demobilised in November 1919, and holds the General Service and Victory Medals.
72, Hartley Road, Luton, Beds. 255.

BARFORD, P. R., Private, East Surrey Regt.
He joined in July 1916, and on the completion of his training was drafted to the Western Front in September 1917. He was in action at Messines and numerous other engagements, and owing to ill-health was invalided home, and discharged as medically unfit in May of the succeeding year. He holds the General Service and Victory Medals.
7, Bigtham Road, Dunstable. 256.

BARHAM, C. L., Private, 6th Queen's (Royal West Surrey Regiment).
He joined in May 1916, and in the following November was sent to the Western Front, where he was engaged for three years on special duties. He served at Ypres (III.), Albert and Cambrai, and was wounded. After the signing of the Armistice he proceeded to Germany with the Army of Occupation and was stationed at Cologne until November 1919, when he returned home and was demobilised. He holds the General Service and Victory Medals.
41, Potton Road, New Town, Biggleswade. Z1266.

BARKER, A., Private, 1/5th Bedfordshire Regt. and Machine Gun Corps.
Volunteering in September 1914, in the following July he proceeded to the Dardanelles, where he served in several engagements. Later he was drafted to Egypt and took part in the Palestine Campaign, being in action at Gaza. During his service he was wounded, and after the conclusion of hostilities returned to England and was demobilised in June 1919, holding the 1914-15 Star, and the General Service and Victory Medals.
5, Buxton Road, Luton. 257.

BARKER, A., Private, 1st Bedfordshire Regt.
He joined in November 1916, and in April of the following year was drafted to the Western Front. He took part in numerous engagements, and was wounded at Passchendaele Ridge in October 1917, and again at Bapaume in August 1918. In September he was invalided home, and after his recovery was demobilised in July 1919. He holds the General Service and Victory Medals.
140, Hartley Road, Luton. 260.

BARKER, A. E., Sapper, Royal Engineers.
He volunteered in November 1915, and in April of the following year, was sent to the Western Front. In this theatre of war he served at Arras, Ypres and Cambrai and in numerous other engagements until the conclusion of hostilities. He was demobilised in May 1919, and holds the General Service and Victory Medals.
84, Hartley Road, Luton. 261.

BARKER, C., Private, 13th Royal Sussex Regt.
He joined in March 1916, and having completed his training was drafted to the Western Front in June of the same year. While overseas he saw much fighting at Arras, Ypres and Passchendaele, and was taken prisoner at Cambrai in 1918. He was held in captivity until after the Armistice, when he returned home, and was demobilised in November 1919, holding the General Service and Victory Medals.
43, Sunnyside, Hitchin. 1611/A.

BARKER, C., Rifleman, King's Royal Rifle Corps.
He joined in March 1916, and in the same year, proceeding to France, took part in the Battles of the Somme, Arras, Lens and Cambrai, and in many important engagements, in the Retreat and Advance of 1918 up to the date of the Armistice. After returning home he was demobilised in November 1919, holding the General Service and Victory Medals. 4, Telegraph Place, Hitchin. 1817.

BARKER, C., Private, 11th Essex Regiment.
On attaining military age he joined in February 1918, and in the following month was drafted to France, where he took part in severe fighting, and was killed in action near Cambrai on May 28th, 1918. He was entitled to the General Service and Victory Medals.
26, Back Street, Luton. 259/A.

BARKER, E., Private, 2nd Bedfordshire Regt.
He was called up from the Reserve in August 1914, and after his training proceeded to France, where he took part in engagements at Vimy Ridge and numerous other places. He was reported missing in July 1916, and is believed to have been killed in action. He was entitled to the 1914-15 Star, and the General Service and Victory Medals.
26, Back Street, Luton. 259/B.

BARKER, G., Private, 3rd Essex Regiment.
He joined in January 1916, and in the following August was drafted to France. While in this theatre of war he took part in the severe fighting in the Somme and Ypres sectors, and was killed in action at Arras on April 24th, 1917. He was entitled to the General Service and Victory Medals.
15, Sunny Side, Hitchin. 1818.

BARKER, G., Private, Royal Engineers.
Volunteering in August 1915, in the following December he was sent to France, where he took part in numerous engagements, including those at Hill 60, Ypres, Vimy Ridge, the Somme, Arras and Cambrai. He was demobilised in March 1919, and holds the 1914-15 Star, and the General Service and Victory Medals.
124, Baker Street, Luton. 258.

BARKER, G. H., Air Mechanic, R.A.F.
Joining in June 1918, he was shortly afterwards drafted to France and served on important duties at Dunkirk, Ypres, Arras and on the Somme. He was demobilised in November 1919, and holds the General Service and Victory Medals.
124, Baker Street, Luton. 258/A.

BARKER, R. H., Sergeant, Sherwood Foresters.
He volunteered at the outbreak of war, and in July 1915 was sent to Egypt. From there he was transferred to Gallipoli, where he served in the campaign against the Turks. On January 25th, 1918, he died of pneumonia, and was entitled to the 1914-15 Star, and the General Service and Victory Medals.
102, Iddesleigh Road, Queen's Park. 262/A.

BARKER, W., Private, R.A.S.C.
He volunteered in May 1915, and after his training rendered valuable services in the transport section at various depôts. He was not successful in obtaining his transfer overseas, owing to being medically unfit, and was discharged in September 1916.
34, Lammas Road, Watford. X263/A.

BARKER, W., Air Mechanic, Royal Air Force.
He joined in September 1918, being still under military age, and served at various stations on important work in connection with the repair of aeroplanes until January 1919, when he was demobilised.
5, Buxton Road, Luton. 257/B.

BARLOW, H., Bombardier, R.F.A.
He volunteered in August 1915, and in the following January was drafted to France. He took part in the heavy fighting on the Somme, and was wounded and invalided home. In May 1917 he was discharged as medically unfit for further service, and holds the General Service and Victory Medals.
29, Friday Street, Leighton Buzzard. 1584.

BARNELL, P. H., Private, R.A.M.C.
He volunteered in September 1915, and after a course of training was drafted to the Western Front, where he served in important engagements, including those at Arras, Cambrai, Albert and Delville Wood. He returned home and was demobilised in February 1919, and holds the General Service and Victory Medals.
70, Salisbury Road, Luton, Beds. 265/A.

BARNELL, R. G., Private, R.A.M.C.
He volunteered in September 1914, and after his training was, in 1916, sent to Egypt. He served in the Palestine Campaign, and was present at various engagements, including those at Gaza and Haifa. Later he was drafted to Russia, where he remained until July 1919, when he returned home and was demobilised, holding the General Service and Victory Medals. 70, Salisbury Road, Luton, Beds. 265/B.

BARNES, A., Private, 4th Bedfordshire Regt.
He joined in 1916, and having completed his training proceeded to France. While there he took part in several important engagements, including those of Verdun, Vimy Ridge, Givenchy and Arras. During his service he suffered from shell-shock, and on the conclusion of hostilities returned to England and was demobilised, holding the General Service and Victory Medals.
High Street, London Colney. X273.

BARNES, A. W., Private, 1st Bedfordshire Regt.
He volunteered in August 1914, and served with his unit at various stations until he was sent to France in 1916. Whilst overseas he took part in the engagements at Arras, Cambrai and Ypres, where he was gassed. He returned home in June 1919 and was demobilised, holding the General Service and Victory Medals.
Lilly Ville, London Colney. X274/A.

BARNES, B., Private, 2nd Devonshire Regt.
He volunteered in September 1914, and was sent to the Western Front, where he took part in various engagements, including that at Messines. He was later transferred to Salonika, where he was again in action, and after the conclusion of hostilities returned home and was demobilised in January 1919, holding the 1914-15 Star, and the General Service and Victory Medals.
Belmont Cottages, Lower Luton Road, Barford, Harpenden. 267.

BARNES, F. W., Gunner, R.F.A.
He volunteered in May 1915, and in the following year was drafted to France, where he served in numerous important engagements, including those of the Somme, Arras, Ypres, Passchendaele and Cambrai. During his service overseas he was wounded, and on the conclusion of hostilities he returned to England and was demobilised in 1919, holding the General Service and Victory Medals.
63, Breakspeare Road, Abbots Langley, Herts. X272/A.

BARNES, G., Private, R.A.S.C. (M.T.)
He joined in August 1916, but was not successful in obtaining his transfer overseas before the cessation of hostilities, owing to being medically unfit. He was engaged at various stations on important duties, and rendered valuable services until he was demobilised in February 1919.
Sunnymede, St. Julian's Road, St. Albans. X266.

BARNES, G. R., Sergeant, 3rd Suffolk Regt.
He joined in January 1918, and in the following October was drafted to the Western Front, where he took part in engagements at Ypres and elsewhere during the Advance. After the Armistice he proceeded to Germany with the Army of Occupation, and in 1920 was still serving at Cologne. He holds the General Service and Victory Medals.
"Inglewood," Marsh Road, Luton. 264.

BARNES, J., Private, R.A.S.C.
He volunteered in August 1915, and in the same year proceeded to the Western Front, where he was engaged on important duties at Etaples in the Commissariat until 1917, when he was invalided to England and discharged as medically unfit for further service. He holds the 1914-15 Star, and the General Service and Victory Medals.
Lilly Ville, London Colney. X274/B.

BARNES, J. E., Private, 3rd Bedfordshire Regt.
He volunteered in July 1915, and was immediately sent to France, where he fought in several important engagements. Whilst overseas he was in action at Hill 60, St. Julian, the Somme and Arras, and was severely wounded. He was invalided home, and in December 1919 was discharged as medically unfit for further service. He holds the 1914-15 Star, and the General Service and Victory Medals.
63, Breakspeare Road, Abbots Langley. X272/C.

BARNES, J. G. M., Private, 1st Hertfordshire Regiment.
He volunteered in December 1914, and having completed his training was drafted to France in the following year. While in this theatre of war he fought in several important engagements, including those of Ypres, the Somme, Arras and Cambrai, and was wounded. After the conclusion of hostilities he returned to England and was demobilised in 1919, holding the 1914-15 Star, and the General Service and Victory Medals.
63, Breakspeare Road, Abbots Langley, Herts. X272/B.

BARNES, S. I., Sapper, Royal Engineers.
He joined in January 1916, and in the following June was drafted to France, where he was engaged on important duties until after the conclusion of hostilities, when he returned to England. He was demobilised in September 1919, and holds the General Service and Victory Medals.
27, Brighton Road, Watford. X270.

BARNES, W., Private, The Buffs (East Kent Regiment.

He volunteered in August 1914, and after completing his training was drafted to France, where he took part in the Battles of Arras and Cambrai. Later he was transferred to Mesopotamia and served in the campaign against the Turks. During his service overseas he was twice wounded, and after the conclusion of hostilities returned to England and was demobilised in March 1919. He holds the General Service and Victory Medals.

Bowman's Green Cottages, London Colney.

                             X268/A—X269/B.

BARNES, W., Corporal, Royal Engineers.

He joined in September 1916, and in the same year was drafted to the Western Front, where he was engaged on important duties on the railways. He served at Albert, the Somme, Vimy Ridge, Ypres, Passchendaele and Cambrai, and after the conclusion of hostilities returned to England and was demobilised in February 1919, holding the General Service and Victory Medals.

East End, Flitwick.   1544.

BARNETT, H., L/Corporal, Bedfordshire Regt.

He volunteered in August 1914, and was immediately afterwards sent to the Western Front and took part in the severe fighting at Mons, Ypres, Hill 60, the Somme and elsewhere. During his service he was three times wounded, and on the conclusion of hostilities returned home and was demobilised in 1919, holding the Mons Star, and the General Service and Victory Medals.

40, Brightwell Road, Watford, Herts.   X275/B.

BARNWELL, C. J., A.B., R.N., H.M.S. " Terror."

He volunteered in August 1916, and was posted for duty with the Fleet in the Mediterranean. Later he served with the monitors off the coast of Belgium and took part in engagements at Zeebrugge and Ostend. He holds the General Service and Victory Medals, and was demobilised in February 1919.

Mount Pleasant, Aspley Guise.   Z271.

BARR, H., Corporal, Royal Field Artillery.

He volunteered in August 1914, and on completion of his training was drafted to France, where he served for a while. Later he was sent to Egypt and took part in the Palestine Offensive, being present at the Battle of Gaza. He returned home and was demobilised in March 1919, holding the General Service and Victory Medals.

10, Grosvenor Road, E., St. Albans.   279.

BARRALET, Corporal, Oxfordshire and Buckinghamshire Light Infantry.

He volunteered in July 1915, and after his training was sent to Mesopotamia. During his service in this theatre of war he took part in heavy fighting in many engagements. He returned home and was demobilised in October 1919, and holds the General Service and Victory Medals.

36, Longmine Road, St. Albans.   X280.

BARRALET, J. J., Rifleman, Rifle Brigade.

He joined in March 1917, and after his training served at various stations on important duties with his unit. He rendered valuable services, but was not successful in obtaining his transfer overseas before the cessation of hostilities. He was demobilised in October 1919.

36, Longmine Road, St. Albans.   X278.

BARRETT, E., Driver, Royal Engineers.

He volunteered in September 1914, and in the following year was drafted to the Dardanelles and was engaged at Suvla Bay and Anzac. Later he was transferred to Egypt, where he served in the Canal Zone and at Gaza, Haifa, Damascus and Beyrout. He returned home and was demobilised in March 1919, and holds the 1914-15 Star, and the General Service and Victory Medals.

5, Windmill Street, Luton.   282/C.

BARRETT, E. H., Sapper, Royal Engineers.

He joined in February 1916, and after his training served at various stations on important duties until September 1918 when he was drafted to Russia. He served in the campaign against the Bolshevists until 1919, when he returned to England and was demobilised. He holds the Victory Medal.

55, Souldem Street, Watford.   281.

BARRETT, F. T., Gunner, Royal Field Artillery.

Volunteering in May 1915, on completion of his training he served at various stations on important duties with his unit. He was not successful in obtaining his transfer overseas, being medically unfit for foreign service. He was demobilised in January 1919.

23, Lyndhurst Road, Luton.   277.

BARRETT, S. D., Corporal, Royal Engineers.

He volunteered in August 1915, and in the following January was drafted to the Western Front, where he took part in numerous engagements. On December 1st, 1918, he was drowned near Cambrai, and was entitled to the General Service and Victory Medals.

73, Dallow Road, Luton.   276.

BARSBY, G., Sapper, Royal Engineers.

He joined in 1916, and in the following year was drafted to the Western Front, where he took an important part in many engagements, including those at Passchendaele, Bullecourt, Cambrai and Béthune. He was demobilised in 1919, and holds the General Service and Victory Medals.

The Folly, Wheathampstead, Herts.   283/A.

BARSLEY, R., Private, 13th Royal Fusiliers.

Volunteering in 1915, in the same year he was sent to the Western Front, where he was in action in several sectors. Among the important battles in which he took part were those of Ypres, Arras, Bullecourt, Cambrai and the Somme. He served until the end of the war, and was demobilised in January 1919. He holds the 1914-15 Star, and the General Service and Victory Medals.

Lower Luton Road, Harpenden, Herts.   284.

BARTLE, J. S., Corporal, 4th Bedfordshire Regt.

Volunteering in September 1914, on completion of his training he was drafted to France, and was in action at Vimy Ridge, and on the Somme. Later he was transferred to Egypt, and served at Gaza and Aleppo, and was present at the Capture of Jerusalem. He returned home and was demobilised in July 1919, holding the 1914-15 Star, and the General Service and Victory Medals.

69, Victoria Road, Dunstable, Beds.   289/A.

BARTLE, W. R., Private, 4th Bedfordshire Regt.

He volunteered in September 1914, and in the following January was drafted to France, where he took part in numerous engagements, on various sectors of the Front. He was killed while fighting near Arras in April 1917, and was entitled to the 1914-15 Star, and the General Service and Victory Medals.

69, Victoria Street, Dunstable.   289/B.

BARTON, A., Private, Loyal North Lancashire Regiment.

Volunteering in July 1915, he was shortly afterwards drafted to France, where he served at Ypres and the Somme, and in numerous other engagements. On the cessation of hostilities he was sent to Germany, and served on the Rhine until May 1919, when he was demobilised. He holds the General Service and Victory Medals.

33, Dorset Street, Luton.   292.

BARTON, A. E. (sen.), Private, Royal Army Medical Corps and Machine Gun Corps.

He volunteered in September 1914, and was sent to Mesopotamia in 1916. He was in action at Kut and Baghdad, and later was transferred to Egypt. In 1918 he went to Palestine and took part in the capture of Haifa, Damascus and Beyrout. He returned home and was demobilised in April 1919, and holds the 1914-15 Star, and the General Service and Victory Medals.

26, Henry Street, Luton.   288/C.

BARTON, A. E., Private, 5th Bedfordshire Regt.

He volunteered in August 1914, and in the following year was sent to the Western Front, and took part in many engagements, including those on the Somme and at Arras, Béthune and Cambrai. He returned home and was demobilised in February 1919, and holds the 1914-15 Star, and the General Service and Victory Medals.

26, Henry Street, Luton.   288/B.

BARTON, A. J., Private, Queen's Own (Royal West Kent Regiment).

Joining in February 1916, he was soon afterwards sent to France, where he served on the Somme and at Arras, Cambrai and Ypres, where he was wounded and gassed in 1917. He was wounded again in October 1918, and returning home was demobilised in February 1919, and holds the General Service and Victory Medals.

17, Brighton Road, Watford.   291.

BARTON, C. B., Private, 5th Bedfordshire Regt.

He volunteered in August 1914, and after having completed his training was drafted to the Dardanelles in the following July. He took part in the engagement at Suvla Bay, and on August 15th, 1915, died of wounds received in action at Chocolate Hill. He was entitled to the 1914-15 Star, and the General Service and Victory Medals.

18, Brache Street, Luton.   285/A.

BARTON, C. W., Private, 6th Royal Fusiliers.
He joined in April 1917, and in December of the same year was drafted to the Western Front. He took part in many important engagements, and was taken prisoner at Messines in 1918. On his release he returned home and was demobilised in September 1919, and holds the General Service and Victory Medals.
70, Park Road West, Luton, Beds.   287/B.

BARTON, F., Gunner, Royal Garrison Artillery.
Joining in July 1916, he was shortly afterwards drafted to France, where he took part in numerous engagements in various sectors of the Front. He was killed in action on September 26th, 1917, while fighting near Ypres, and was entitled to the General Service and Victory Medals.
142, Cranelles Road, Harpenden.   290.

BARTON, F. A., Private, 29th Middlesex Regt.
He joined in 1916, but was not successful in obtaining his transfer overseas before the cessation of hostilities. He was engaged on important duties at various stations with his unit, and rendered valuable services. He was demobilised in 1918.
23, Chabham Street, Luton.   286/A.

BARTON, J., Private, Middlesex Regiment.
He joined in June 1917, but was not successful in obtaining his transfer overseas before the cessation of hostilities. He was engaged on important duties with his unit, and rendered valuable services until he was demobilised in 1918.
26, Henry Street, Luton.   288/A.

BARTON, J. W., Private, 5th Bedfordshire Regt. and Army Cyclist Corps.
He volunteered in September 1914, and in the following year was drafted to the Dardanelles and took part in the landing at Suvla Bay. He was later transferred to Egypt and Palestine, where he served in many important engagements, including that at Gaza. He returned home and was demobilised in March 1919, and holds the 1914-15 Star, and the General Service and Victory Medals.
80, Cambridge Street, Luton, Beds.   293.

BARTON, R., Private, 2nd Suffolk Regiment.
He volunteered in September 1914, and having completed his training was drafted to the Western Front in 1916. He took part in numerous important engagements, including the Battle of Ypres, and was killed in action on October 28th, 1918, during the Advance. He was entitled to the General Service and Victory Medals.
18, Brache Street, Luton, Beds.   285/B.

BARTRAM, E. E., Sapper, Royal Engineers.
He volunteered in December 1914, and in July of the following year was drafted to the Western Front, where he rendered valuable service in the Battles of Ypres, Loos, Vimy Ridge, the Somme, Arras, Cambrai and many other engagements until hostilities ceased, and was four times wounded. He was chiefly engaged in the maintenance of the lines of communication. He was demobilised in February 1919, and holds the 1914-15 Star, and the General Service and Victory Medals.
Saunder's Piece, Ampthill.   1545/A.

BARTRAM, W. E., Private, 11th Bedfordshire Regiment.
He joined in May 1917, and after his training served at various stations on important duties with his unit. He rendered valuable services, but was not successful in obtaining his transfer overseas while hostilities continued. He was discharged in June 1918 as medically unfit for further Service.
Saunder's Piece, Ampthill.   1545/B.

BASEY, A. C., Sergeant, Rifle Brigade.
He volunteered in November 1915, and on the completion of his training rendered valuable service with his unit until he was drafted to British East Africa, where he served at Nairobi on garrison duty. He returned home and was demobilised in August 1919, and holds the General Service and Victory Medals.
45, Oak Road, Luton.   294.

BASS, A. H., A.B., Royal Navy.
He joined in September 1916 and was posted to H.M.S. "Orion," on which vessel he was engaged in patrol duties in the North Sea and at Scapa Flow. He was afterwards transferred to H.M.S. "Thanet" for service to the Baltic and other Russian waters, and in 1920 was still serving. He holds the General Service and Victory Medals.
89, Albert Road, Luton.   295/C.

BASS, A. H., Private, Northamptonshire Regt.
He joined in 1916, and after completing his training was drafted to France, where he rendered much valuable service. He took a prominent part in various engagements, and was killed in action on February 17th, 1917. He was entitled to the General Service and Victory Medals.
112, Cotterell's Road, Hemel Hempstead.   296/B.

BASS, C., Private, 10th Hampshire Regt.
He volunteered in April 1915, and in the following November was drafted to Egypt, where for a short time he was stationed at Alexandria, and was attached to the Royal Army Medical Corps as a hospital orderly. In January 1916 he was sent to Salonika, and whilst in this theatre of war took part in various important engagements on the Balkan Front. He contracted pneumonia on service, and died on October 2nd, 1918. He was entitled to the 1914-15 Star, and the General Service and Victory Medals.
97, Bury Park Road, Luton.   297.

BASS, C. W., Driver, Royal Army Service Corps, attached to Royal Marine Engineers.
He joined in 1916, and after the conclusion of his training served on important duties at various stations. He was also engaged on the repair of ships in the Channel. He did excellent work, but was not successful in obtaining his transfer overseas before the termination of the war. In February 1919 he was demobilised.
Cotton End, Beds.   Z298.

BASS, M. E., Private, 4th Northamptonshire Regiment.
He joined in March 1917, and in April was sent to the Western Front, where he took an active part in the Battles of Arras, Cambrai and the Somme, and also served in the Retreat and Advance of 1918. In March 1919 was demobilised after his return home, and holds the General Service and Victory Medals.
67, Cowper Street, Luton.   299.

BASS, T., Private, 2nd Suffolk Regiment.
He joined in 1916, and after his training was drafted to the Western Front. He was in action at the Somme, Arras, and in many other engagements, and was killed in an engagement in January 1918. He was entitled to the General Service and Victory Medals.
19, York Street, Luton.   300/B.

BASS, T., Driver, R.A.S.C., and R.F.A.
He joined in April 1918, and on the conclusion of his training served with his unit at various stations on important duties. He did much good transport work, but was not able to secure his transfer overseas before the cessation of hostilities. He was demobilised in May 1919.
8, Ickleford Road, Hitchin.   1819.

BASS, W., Sergeant, Hertfordshire Regiment.
He volunteered in August 1914, and at once proceeded to the Western Front. While overseas he took a prominent part in many severe engagements, including those of Mons, the Marne, the Aisne, Ypres, Loos, the Somme, Arras, Lens and Cambrai, and was severely wounded. He came home and was demobilised in 1919, holding the Mons Star, and the General Service and Victory Medals.
5, Winifred Road, Apsley End.   X302.

BASS, W., A.B., Royal Navy.
He was in the Navy at the outbreak of hostilities, and served in H.M.S. "Hawkins." Throughout the war he was engaged with his ship on the important work of patrolling different seas, and also took an active part in the Battles of Heligoland Bight and Jutland. He was still serving in 1920, and holds the 1914-15 Star, and the General Service and Victory Medals.
21, Greatham Road, Bushey, Watford.   X301.

BASS, W. C., Corporal, 11th Queen's (Royal West Surrey Regiment).
Joining in March 1917, he was put through a course of training and was soon drafted to the Western Front. He took an active part in several important engagements, including those of Arras, Bullecourt, Messines, Cambrai and the Somme. He was demobilised in November 1919 after returning home, and holds the General Service and Victory Medals.
89, Albert Road, Luton.   295/B.

BASS, W. J., Private, 2nd Bedfordshire Regt.
He joined in June 1916, and after completing his training was drafted to France in the following October. While there he took an active part in many engagements, including those of Cambrai and the Somme, and was killed in action on March 28th, 1918. He was entitled to the General Service and Victory Medals.
26, Limbury Road, Leagrave.   303.

BASS, W. J., Gunner, R.G.A.

He joined in July 1916, and in October of the same year was sent to the Western Front. Here he served in many important engagements, including those of the Somme and Ypres. He was killed in action at Dickebusch on September 27th, 1917, and was buried at Bailleul. He was entitled to the General Service and Victory Medals.
89, Albert Road, Luton.   295/A.

BASSAM, A., Driver, R.A.S.C.

He volunteered in September 1914, and was at once sent to France, where he rendered valuable transport services in the early stages of the struggle, and in many later engagements. He suffered severely from shell-shock, and after more than two years' treatment in home hospitals was finally discharged in May 1918 as unfit for military duty. He holds the 1914 Star, and the General Service and Victory Medals.
Salford Road, Apsley Guise.   Z304.

BASSELL, G., Private, 1st West Yorkshire Regt.

He was serving at the outbreak of war and was immediately sent to the Western Front, where he served in many important battles until hostilities ceased, including those at Mons, Ypres, Arras and Cambrai, and was three times wounded. He was demobilised in March 1919, after returning home, and holds the Mons Star, and the General Service and Victory Medals.
7, Midland Terrace, St. Albans.   X305.

BASSETT, C., Private, R.A.V.C.

He volunteered in August 1914, and after concluding his training and performing important duties for a time with his unit, was sent in 1917 to the Western Front, where he rendered valuable veterinary services at Abbeville and other depôts. In consequence of an injury through being thrown from a horse he was invalided home, and discharged as medically unfit for further service in October 1918. He holds the General Service and Victory Medals.
7a, Hastings Street, Luton.   306.

BASSETT, D., Private, 1st Welch Regiment.

He volunteered in August 1914, and immediately afterwards was drafted to the Western Front, where he took part in the Battles of Marne and Festubert. He was severely wounded at Ypres and suffered the loss of both legs. He was invalided home, and discharged as medically unfit in October 1915, and holds the 1914 Star, and the General Service and Victory Medals.
92, Rushbymead, Letchworth.   2442.

BASSETT, G. S., Private, Royal Defence Corps.

He volunteered in August 1914, and rendered valuable services with his unit until the cessation of hostilities. He was chiefly engaged at Woolwich and Bedford in guarding ammunition and factories and in training duties. He was demobilised in December 1919.
4, Caroline Cottages, Capel Road, Oxhey.   X307/A.

BASSILL, A. W. G., Corporal, 53rd Bedfordshire Regiment.

He joined in August 1917, and after his training was engaged on important duties with his unit. He was not successful in securing his transfer overseas before hostilities ceased, but in 1919 was sent to Germany with the Army of Occupation. He rendered valuable services there until his return home for demobilisation in March 1920.
37, Arthur Road, St. Albans.   X308.

BASSILL, J. W., Private, 1st Queen's Own (Royal West Kent Regiment).

Serving at the outbreak of war, he was immediately drafted to the Western Front, where he took part in the Retreat from Mons. He was also in action at Neuve Chapelle, Hill 60, and Trônes Wood, and was killed in the fierce fighting on the Somme on September 9th, 1916. He was entitled to the Mons Star, and the General Service and Victory Medals.
12, Parker Street, Watford.   X310.

BASTIN, J., Private, Labour Corps.

He joined in March 1917, but was not successful in obtaining his transfer overseas before the cessation of hostilities owing to medical unfitness. He was engaged on various important agricultural duties, and rendered valuable services until demobilised in March 1919.
41, Shaftesbury Road, Watford.   X309.

BATCHELOR, A. H., L/Corporal, Military Foot Police.

He joined in July 1916, and having completed his training proceeded to Salonika in the following year. While in this theatre of war he rendered valuable services on the Vardar Front, and later went to Constantinople. He returned home and was demobilised in November 1919, holding the General Service and Victory Medals.
Trowley Bottom, Flamstead.   X475.

BATCHELOR, A. T., Private, 7th Border Regt.

He volunteered in April 1915, and on the completion of his training was sent to the Western Front, where he was frequently in action. He served at Bullecourt, Ypres, Cambrai, and Amiens, and was twice wounded. He was demobilised in January 1919 after returning home, and holds the General Service and Victory Medals.
41, Liverpool Road, Watford.   X311.

BATCHELOR, E., Sergeant, Hertfordshire Regt.

He volunteered in 1914, and in the following year was drafted to France, where he took a leading part in various important battles until hostilities ceased, including those of Somme, Arras and Cambrai, and was wounded. He was demobilised in March 1919 after coming back to England, and holds the 1914–15 Star, and the General Service and Victory Medals.
Trowley Bottom, near Flamstead.   X312.

BATCHELOR, E. C., Sapper, R.E. (Signals).

He volunteered in November 1914, and after a period of training was drafted to the Western Front, where he took part in many important engagements, including those at Hill 60, Ypres, the Somme, where he was wounded, Cambrai and St. Quentin. He returned to England and was demobilised in April 1919, holding the 1914–15 Star, and the General Service and Victory Medals.
26, Baker Street, Luton.   313/B.

BATCHELOR, E. G., Private, Buffs (East Kent Regiment).

He volunteered in June 1915, and in November of the following year, after performing important duties with his unit, was sent to France. After serving in various engagements, including those of the Somme and Ypres, he was taken prisoner at St. Quentin in March 1918. After the Armistice he was sent home, and in January of the next year was demobilised. He holds the General Service and Victory Medals.
46, York Road, Watford.   X314.

BATCHELOR, E. T., Sapper, Royal Engineers.

He volunteered in January 1915, and in the same year, after concluding his training, was sent to the Western Front, where he was engaged on important sapping and mining operations, chiefly at Arras, Ypres and Cambrai, and was twice wounded. In January 1919 he was demobilised after his return to England, and holds the 1914–15 Star, and the General Service and Victory Medals.
3, Meeting Alley, Watford.   X315.

BATCHELOR, F., Private, Bedfordshire Regt.

Volunteering in September 1914, after his training he was drafted to France, and took part in numerous engagements, including those on the Somme, at Arras and Ypres, in each of which he was wounded. He was killed in action on September 20th, 1918, near Cambrai. He was entitled to the 1914–15 Star, and the General Service and Victory Medals.
River Hill, Flamstead.   477/B.

BATCHELOR, F. F., Rifleman, 5th King's Royal Rifle Corps.

He joined in March 1918, but was not successful in obtaining his transfer overseas before the cessation of hostilities on account of his youth. He was engaged with his unit on important duties at various stations, and rendered valuable services until demobilised in January 1919.
126, Sandringham Road, Watford.   234/A.

BATCHELOR, F. F. (sen.), Driver, R.A.S.C.

He joined in April 1918, and after his training was engaged on important duties. He was not successful on account of his age in securing his transfer overseas before hostilities ended, but rendered valuable services in connection with Agricultural work until his demobilisation in April 1919.
126, Sandringham Road, Watford.   234/C.

BATCHELOR, G. H., Private, Bedfordshire Regt.

He joined in June 1916, and after a short training was sent to the Western Front in the following September. From that time onwards he took part in many engagements, and was killed in action on March 13th, 1917, near Béthune. He was entitled to the General Service and Victory Medals.
131, Judge Street, Callowland, Watford.   X316.

BATCHELOR, H., Private, Labour Corps.

He joined in July 1917, and in October of the same year was sent out to Palestine, where he saw considerable service and did valuable work in road repairs at Gaza, Haifa and Damascus. He returned home and was demobilised in June 1919, and holds the General Service and Victory Medals.
2, Oak Road, Luton.   317.

BATCHELOR, H., Private, 8th Bedfordshire Regiment.
He volunteered in May 1915, and on the completion of his training was sent to the Western Front early in 1916. He served in various engagements for eight months, and was killed in the heavy fighting on the Somme on September 15th, 1916. He was entitled to the General Service and Victory Medals.
Trowley Bottom, Flamstead. X318.

BATCHELOR, H. L., Private, M.G.C.
He joined in December 1917, and after his training served on important duties with his unit. He was not successful in securing his transfer overseas while hostilities lasted, but did excellent work until January 1919 when he was demobilised.
41, Liverpool Road, Watford. X311/B.

BATCHELOR, J., A.B., Royal Navy, H.M.S. "Marlborough."
He volunteered in January 1915, and after a period of training was posted to H.M.S. "Marlborough." Whilst in this vessel he was engaged on important and dangerous duties in the North Sea, and took a prominent part in the Battle of Jutland. Later he did valuable work off the coasts of Egypt and Russia and in the Baltic. He holds the 1914–15 Star, and the General Service and Victory Medals, and in 1920 was still serving.
75, Fearnley Street, Watford. TX319.

BATCHELOR, J. P., Private, Middlesex Regt.
He joined in June 1916, and having completed his training was sent to Malta in October of the same year. While there he rendered valuable services, and in 1917 proceeded to France, where he fought at Arras, Ypres, Cambrai, and in the Offensive of 1918. He came home, and was demobilised in April 1919, holding the General Service and Victory Medals.
Trowley Bottom, near Flamstead. X474.

BATCHELOR, P., L/Corporal, Bedfordshire Regt.
He volunteered in September 1914, and in the following June proceeded to France. He took part in much severe fighting in various sectors of the Front, and was badly wounded on the Somme in 1916. On his recovery he returned to the line and served at Arras, Cambrai, and in numerous engagements in the Retreat and Advance of 1918. He was demobilised in February 1919, and holds the 1914–15 Star, and the General Service and Victory Medals.
River Hill, Flamstead. X77/A.

BATCHELOR, P. S., L/Corporal, 17th Queen's (Royal West Surrey Regiment).
He joined in October 1916, and after his training was drafted to the Western Front, where he took part in many important engagements up to the close of fighting, including those at Arras and Ypres, and was gassed. He was demobilised in October 1919 after returning home, and holds the General Service and Victory Medals.
26, Baker Street, Luton. 313/A.

BATE, O., Private, 11th Suffolk Regiment.
He joined in June 1916, and in the same year, after his training, proceeded to the Western Front, where he saw considerable service. He took part in the important engagements of the Somme, Arras, Ypres, Cambrai and St. Quentin, and was killed in action on March 21st, 1918. He was entitled to the General Service and Victory Medals.
3, Cassiobridge Road, Watford. X320/A.

BATEMAN, A., Private, 7th East Surrey Regt.
He volunteered in September 1914, and in January of the following year he was drafted to France, where he fought at Neuve Chapelle, Ypres, and was wounded at Festubert. Having recovered he went back to the lines, and on March 16th, 1916, in the Battle of Loos, he was killed in action. He was entitled to the 1914–15 Star, and the General Service and Victory Medals.
3, Cross Street West, Dunstable. 321/A.

BATEMAN, A., Private, Bedfordshire Regiment.
He volunteered in September 1914, and after his training served on important duties with his unit. He rendered valuable services as an army cook, but was not successful in obtaining his transfer overseas before the cessation of hostilities. He was demobilised in March 1919.
3, Cross Street West, Dunstable. 321/B.

BATEMAN, J. (Mrs.), Special War Worker.
From June 1917 to December 1918, this lady was engaged on munition work of National importance, being employed on important duties in the fuse department at Messrs. Kent's Factory, Luton. Her steady and consistent services gave great satisfaction.
3, Cross Street West, Dunstable. 321/C.

BATEMAN, W., Gunner, Royal Field Artillery.
He joined in May 1916, and after his training was completed proceeded to France in the same year. He served at Arras, Passchendaele and Cambrai, and in many later engagements up to the cessation of hostilities. During his service he was wounded. He returned home and was demobilised in February 1919, holding the General Service and Victory Medals.
16, King Street, Dunstable. 322.

BATES, A., Gunner, Royal Garrison Artillery.
He was mobilised at the outbreak of war, and in July 1915 was sent to the Dardanelles, where he saw much heavy fighting. He was wounded at the landing at Suvla Bay, and was in action at Anzac Bay and at Chocolate Hill. After the Evacuation of the Peninsula he was drafted to the Western Front, and served at Arras, Ypres, Passchendaele, Cambrai and on the Somme, and was twice gassed during this period. He was demobilised in June 1919, and holds the 1914–15 Star, and the General Service and Victory Medals.
100, Hartley Road, Luton. 323.

BATES, A., Air Mechanic, Royal Air Force.
He joined in October 1918, and served at various stations on important duties which demanded a high degree of technical skill. He did excellent work as an aero-engine fitter, but was not successful in securing a transfer abroad before the termination of the war. He was demobilised in February 1919. Prior to his service in the Royal Air Force he had been engaged on work of National importance at the Vauxhall Motor Co.'s Factory, Luton.
Downsview, Borough Road, Dunstable. 187.

BATES, A. B., Private, 1st Bedfordshire Regt.
He volunteered in November 1914, and having completed his training was sent to Gallipoli in the following July. While in this theatre of war he fought in several important engagements, and afterwards took part in the Palestine Campaign. During his service he was wounded in Gallipoli and at Gaza. He returned home and was demobilised in July 1919, holding the 1914–15 Star, and the General Service and Victory Medals.
Mount View, Borough Road, Dunstable. 324/B.

BATES, A. H., Private, 6th Leicestershire Regt.
He volunteered in November 1914, and in the following year proceeded to the Western Front, where he took part in many notable engagements, including those of Ypres, the Somme, Arras and Cambrai. He was severely wounded, and after hospital treatment was discharged in March 1918 as medically unfit for further service. He holds the 1914–15 Star, and the General Service and Victory Medals.
46, Union Street, Leighton Buzzard. 1269.

BATES, C. (D.C.M.), Sergeant, Royal Berkshire Regiment.
He was serving in the Army at the outbreak of war and immediately proceeded to France. While in this theatre of war he took a distinguished part in many great engagements, including the Retreat from Mons and the Battles of Ypres, Arras, Passchendaele and St. Quentin, and was twice wounded. He was awarded the Distinguished Conduct Medal for conspicuous bravery on the Field at Passchendaele, and also holds the Mons Star, and the General Service and Victory Medals. He was demobilised in March 1919.
47, Church Road, Watford. X325.

BATES, C. G., Rflmn., Rifle Brigade (Cyclist Bn.)
He joined in October 1918 immediately on attaining the age for service, and after going through a course of training was drafted to the Army of Occupation in Germany, where he was engaged on important duties, and was still serving in 1920.
Kenmore, Beechwood Road, Leagrave, Beds. 326.

BATES, E., Gunner, Royal Field Artillery.
He joined in January 1917, and after a period of training was drafted to the Western Front, where he took part in the severe fighting at the Battles of Ypres and Arras, and was wounded. He returned home and was discharged owing to his injuries in July 1918, and holds the General Service and Victory Medals.
3, Whitby Road, Luton. 327.

BATES, F., Private, 17th Middlesex Regiment.
He joined in April 1916, and in July of the same year was drafted to the Western Front. He took part in many important engagements, including those of Ypres, Arras and Vimy Ridge, and was wounded and taken prisoner in April 1917. On his release in November 1918 he returned home, and was demobilised in April 1919, holding the General Service and Victory Medals.
Earl's Court, Toddington, Beds. 328.

BATES, F., L/Corporal, Norfolk Regiment.

He volunteered in March 1915, and in the following year proceeded to the Western Front, where he took part in the Battles on the Somme and Passchendaele. In September 1917 he was wounded on the Lens Front and invalided home. He was discharged in September 1918 owing to his injuries, and holds the General Service and Victory Medals.
Dagnall Road, Eddlesborough, near Dunstable.   Z1530.

BATES, F., Corporal, Bedfordshire Regiment.

He volunteered in September 1914, and in the following December was sent to France, where he saw much fighting and was severely wounded at Neuve Chapelle in March 1915. On his recovery he was drafted to the Balkan Front in November 1915, where he took part in many engagements and was wounded the second time. After treatment in hospital at Cairo he returned home in 1916, and was subsequently stationed in Ireland until February 1919, when he was demobilised. He holds the 1914-15 Star, and the General Service and Victory Medals.
2, Ship Yard, Queen Street, Hitchin.   1820.

BATES, G. (Mrs.), Special War Worker.

From July 1915 until May 1917 this lady was engaged on munition duties of great importance at Luton, and subsequently was employed for six months as a canteen worker at Stockwood Park, Luton. In both posts she rendered services which were much appreciated.
Downsview, Borough Road, Dunstable.   324/C.

BATES, H., Corporal, R.A.S.C.

He joined in April 1916, and after a period of training was drafted to the Western Front. He was engaged on important duties with the Military Police at Le Havre and rendered valuable services. He was demobilised in April 1919, and holds the General Service and Victory Medals.
23, Vernon Road, Luton.   329.

BATES, H. E., Rifleman, 9th London Regiment (Queen Victoria's Rifles).

He volunteered in November 1915, and after being retained on important duties with his unit he was drafted to the Western Front in December 1916. After taking part in important engagements he died of wounds received at Vimy Ridge in April 1917. He was entitled to the General Service and Victory Medals.
57, Buxton Road, Luton.   330.

BATES, L., Private, 10th Queen's (Royal West Surrey Regiment).

He joined in October 1918 immediately on attaining military age, and on the conclusion of his training was drafted in April 1919 to the Army of Occupation on the Rhine, where he did valuable work as a signaller until his demobilisation in March 1920.
Mount View, Borough Road, Dunstable.   324/A.

BATES, L. F., Sergeant, Oxfordshire and Buckinghamshire Light Infantry.

He joined in May 1916, and in November of the same year was drafted to the Western Front. He took part in the severe engagements of the Somme, Ypres, Cambrai, and St. Julien, and was wounded and invalided home. On his recovery he returned to France in March 1918, and took part in the Retreat and Advance of that year. After subsequent service in Palestine he returned home and was demobilised in November 1919, holding the General Service and Victory Medals.
54, Lyndhurst Road, Luton.   332.

BATES, W., Private, 7th Bedfordshire Regiment.

He joined in June 1916, and in November of the same year was drafted to the Western Front, where he took part in many important engagements, including those of the Somme, Ypres and Cambrai, when he was wounded and taken prisoner. He died of his injuries on May 14th, 1918, and was entitled to the General Service and Victory Medals.
55, Vale Road, Bushey.   333.

BATH, H., Private, 2nd Bedfordshire Regiment.

He volunteered in November 1915, and after the conclusion of his training was drafted overseas in the following year. He took part in many important engagements, including those of the Somme, Arras, Ypres and Cambrai. On his return home he was demobilised in October 1919, holding the General Service and Victory Medals.
60, Grove Road, Hitchin.   1812/B.

BATH, W., Rifleman, 2nd Rifle Brigade.

He was mobilised in August 1914, and immediately proceeded to the Western Front. While in this theatre of war he fought in the Retreat of Mons and the Battle of La Bassée, and was killed in action on May 3rd, 1915, in the second Battle of Ypres. He was entitled to the Mons Star, and the General Service and Victory Medals.
60, Grove Road, Hitchin.   1812/A.

BATTAMS, A. T., Driver, Royal Engineers.

He enlisted previously to the outbreak of hostilities in April 1914, and served at various stations on important duties with his unit. He was eventually drafted to France in January 1919, and served at Boulogne until February 1920, when he returned home and was demobilised.
51, Hartley Road, Luton.   334/A.

BATTAMS, C. E., Private, Bedfordshire Regiment.

He joined in June 1917, and in June of the following year was drafted to the Western Front, where he took part in the severe fighting in the last Battles of Ypres and Cambrai, and other engagements, and was wounded. He was still serving in 1920, and holds the General Service and Victory Medals.
22, Collingdon Street, Luton.   336/A.

BATTAMS, H. V., Gunner, R.F.A.

He volunteered in October 1914, and in the following February was drafted to the Western Front. Whilst in this theatre of war he took part in the fighting at Hill 60, Ypres, the Somme and Arras, and in various subsequent engagements until the conclusion of the war. He was sent home and demobilised in April 1919, and holds the 1914-15 Star, and the General Service and Victory Medals.
51, Hartley Road, Luton.   334/B.

BATTAMS, J. H., Driver, Royal Field Artillery.

He volunteered in August 1914, and having completed his training was drafted to the Western Front. Employed as driver in an ammunition column he saw much service in several sectors and did very valuable work in many engagements until fighting ceased. On the conclusion of hostilities he was sent with the Army of Occupation into Germany, where he was employed on garrison and other duties until his return to England for demobilisation in April 1919. He holds the General Service and Victory Medals.
75, Copsewood Road, Watford.   X335/A.

BATTAMS, T., A/Corporal, Bedfordshire and Hertfordshire Regiments.

He joined in July 1916, and in the same year was drafted to India, where he was engaged on important training and garrison duties at various stations. He returned home and was demobilised in January 1920, holding the General Service and Victory Medals.
24, Vandyke Road, Leighton Buzzard.   1291.

BATTAMS, W., Air Mechanic, Royal Air Force.

He joined in July 1917, and after his training served at various stations on important duties which demanded a high degree of technical skill. In the following year he was sent to France, and was stationed at Dunkirk and Boulogne, in both of which places he rendered valuable services in the aeroplane repair shops. He was demobilised after returning to England in 1919, and holds the General Service and Victory Medals.
51, Hartley Road, Luton.   334/C.

BATTEN, A. H., Private, 1st Bedfordshire Regt.

He volunteered in August 1914, and proceeded in July 1915 to the Western Front, where he took part in many important engagements until the close of hostilities, including those of the Somme, Arras, Messines, Ypres and Cambrai. Later he was transferred to Italy, where he was again in action. He returned home and was demobilised in March 1919, holding the 1914-15 Star, and the General Service and Victory Medals.
228, Chester Road, Watford.   X337.

BATTRICK, A. V., Private, Machine Gun Corps.

He joined in November 1916, and after a course of training was drafted to the Western Front in December 1917. He took part in the severe fighting in various engagements until the end of the war, including those of Arras, the Somme and Ypres. He was demobilised in April 1919, and holds the General Service and Victory Medals.
22, Oak Road, Luton.   338.

BATTRICK, B., A.B., Royal Navy.

He volunteered in October 1915, and during the remainder of the war period was engaged in H.M.S. " Coventry " in the North Sea and other waters on important patrolling and anti-submarine duties. He also took part in the engagement off Zeebrugge. He was still serving in the Navy in 1920, and holds the 1914-15 Star, and the General Service and Victory Medals.
" Raleigh," St. Peter's Road, Dunstable.   339/B.

BATTRICK, G., Cpl., 2nd Lancashire Fusiliers.

He volunteered in September 1914, and in March of the following year was drafted to the Western Front, where he took part in numerous engagements until the cessation of hostilities, including those of Ypres, the Somme, Arras and Armentières. He was demobilised in April 1919, and holds the 1914-15 Star, and the General Service and Victory Medals.
" Raleigh," St. Peter's Road, Dunstable.   339/A.

BAULK, G. W., Gunner, Royal Field Artillery.
He joined in 1916, and having completed his training was sent to France in the following year. While on this Front he played a prominent part as a gunner and signaller in the Battles of Ypres, the Somme, Passchendaele and Cambrai. Suffering severely from shell-shock he was invalided to England, and was finally discharged in March 1919 as medically unfit for further duties. He holds the General Service and Victory Medals.
Ampthill Road, Shefford, near Bedford.   Z340.

BAVISTER, H. E., Sapper, Royal Engineers.
He volunteered in August 1915, and after the completion of his training was drafted to France in February 1917. He took part in the fighting at Ypres, Arras and on the Somme, and was twice severely wounded and gassed in action at Cambrai in 1918. He was invalided home, and after treatment in hospital was subsequently demobilised in February 1919. He holds the General Service and Victory Medals.
112, Hartley Road, Luton.   341/A.

BAVISTER, W., Private, Bedfordshire Regiment.
He volunteered in December 1914, and was drafted to the Western Front in the following year. While in this theatre of war he fought at Hill 60, Ypres, Festubert and the Somme, where he was severely wounded. He died from his injuries on August 10th, 1916, and was entitled to the 1914-15 Star, and the General Service and Victory Medals.
Asby's Cottages, Westoning, Ampthill.   1540.

BAXTER, A. L., Private, 19th Hussars.
He was mobilised at the outbreak of war, and immediately proceeded to France, where he was engaged in several important battles, including those of Mons, Ypres, the Somme, Arras and the Aisne, until August 1918 when he was sent to Egypt. After valuable service there he returned home and was demobilised in June 1919, holding the Mons Star, and the General Service and Victory Medals.
5, Lower Paddock Road, Oxhey, Watford.   X342/A.

BAXTER, T. R., Driver, R.A.S.C. (M.T.)
He joined in June 1918, and in the following September was sent to the Western Front, where he did valuable work on motor transport duties at Havrincourt, Cambrai and the Somme. He remained in France until July 1919 when he was demobilised, and holds the General Service and Victory Medals.
31, Ash Road, Luton.   343.

BAXTER, W. A., Sapper, Royal Engineers.
Volunteering in September 1914, he was sent to Gallipoli in July of the following year, and took part in the landing at Suvla Bay, and in other operations on the Peninsula, up to the Evacuation in December. He then served in Egypt in the defence of the Suez Canal against the attacks of the Turks, and after was drafted to Salonika, where he was in action on the Vardar Front until the conclusion of hostilities. He returned home and was demobilised in May 1919, holding the 1914-15 Star, and the General Service and Victory Medals.
68, Ridgway Road, Luton.   344.

BAYES, J. W., L/Corporal, Hertfordshire and Leicestershire Regiments.
He volunteered in November 1915 at the age of 16, and in 1917 was drafted to the Western Front, where he was in action at Ypres, Cambrai, the Somme and St. Quentin, and was wounded. After being a prisoner of war for some time he returned home and was demobilised in January 1919, holding the General Service and Victory Medals.
Wheathamstead Road, Harpenden.   345.

BAYLEY, V., Sergeant, 22nd London Regiment (Queen's).
He volunteered in June 1915, and after his training was drafted in 1916 to Egypt, whence he proceeded to take part in the Palestine Campaign. He was in action in the Battles of Gaza and Haïfa, and was present at the Entry into Jerusalem and the attacks on Damascus and Aleppo. He was wounded during his service. While at Cairo he assisted in quelling the riots. In 1920 he returned home but remained in the Army. He holds the General Service and Victory Medals.
12, Merton Road, Watford.   TX346.

BAYLISS, F., Sergeant, Royal Garrison Artillery.
He was mobilised at the outbreak of war and was immediately drafted to the Western Front, where he took part in the Retreat from Mons. He also served in many later engagements, including those of the Marne, Ypres, the Somme and Arras, and was wounded. He was demobilised in 1919 after returning home, and holds the Mons Star, and the General Service and Victory Medals.
32a, Hagden Lane, Watford.   X347/A.

BAYNES, G., Gunner, Royal Garrison Artillery.
He joined in October 1917, and after his training was drafted to the Western Front in February 1918. While in this theatre of war he fought on the Somme and Cambrai Fronts, and rendered valuable services in the Retreat and Advance of 1918. He came home and was demobilised in November 1919, holding the General Service and Victory Medals.
71, South Street, Leighton Buzzard.   473.

BEACH, C., Gunner, Royal Garrison Artillery.
He volunteered in June 1915, and after his training served on important aircraft defence duties at various stations. He did excellent work but was not successful in obtaining a transfer overseas before the conclusion of hostilities. He was demobilised in February 1919.
3, Right of Way, New Town, Hatfield.   X348.

BEACHER, J., Corporal, R.A.M.C.
He volunteered in August 1915, and in October of the same year was drafted to Egypt and served at Alexandria, Kubri, El Arish, Gaza and other places. He returned home and was demobilised in August 1919, and holds the 1914-15 Star, and the General Service and Victory Medals.
29, Old Bedford Road, Luton.   349.

BEADLE, W. H., Driver, R.A.S.C. (M.T.) and Private, East Surrey Regiment.
He joined in May 1916, and in the following year proceeded to the Western Front, where he served at the Battle of Ypres. Later he was transferred to Mesopotamia and took part in the campaign against the Turks. During his service overseas he was wounded, and after the conclusion of hostilities returned to England and was demobilised in December 1919, holding the General Service and Victory Medals.
Grove Mill Farm, Walsworth, Hitchin.   1620.

BEAL, A., Private, The Queen's (Royal West Surrey Regiment).
He volunteered in 1915, and having completed his training was drafted to France in the following year. He fought in the Somme Offensive in July, and was killed in action in September 1916. He was entitled to the General Service and Victory Medals.
Maulden Road, Flitwick, East End.   1543.

BEAL, D., Private, Royal Air Force.
He joined in June 1918, and on the completion of his training was engaged with his unit at various stations until he went to Germany with the Army of Occupation. He was employed on garrison and other duties, and in 1920 was still serving.
Upper Sundon, near Dunstable.   350/C.

BEAL, H., Sapper, Royal Engineers.
He joined in December 1916, and immediately proceeded to France, where he saw much fighting in several important engagements. While overseas he served at Arras, Ypres, Cambrai and the Somme, and after the Armistice with the Army of Occupation on the Rhine. He returned to England and was demobilised in February 1919, holding the General Service and Victory Medals.
Ridgeway, Flitwick.   1542.

BEAL, H. W., Private, Labour Corps.
He joined in March 1916, and after a course of training was sent to the Western Front in the same year. He was engaged on important duties in connection with the construction of roads and trenches in several sectors, and was present at many important actions, including those on the Somme and at Arras, Ypres and Cambrai. On the conclusion of hostilities he returned to England for demobilisation in January 1919, and holds the General Service and Victory Medals.
Upper Sundon, near Dunstable.   350/B.

BEAL, J., Private, R.A.S.C.
He volunteered in November 1915, and in the following March was sent to the Western Front. Engaged on important duties in connection with the transport of supplies and ammunition to the forward areas, he saw much active service in many sectors, and was present at the Battles of the Somme, Ypres, Arras and Cambrai. He holds the General Service and Victory Medals, and was demobilised in February 1919.
Upper Sundon, near Dunstable.   350/A.

BEALE, A., Sergeant, 6th Bedfordshire Regiment.
He volunteered in September 1914, and in July of the following year was drafted to the Western Front, and was in action on the Somme, where he was wounded. On his recovery he rejoined his unit and took an important part in numerous engagements until the closing stages of the war. He holds the 1914-15 Star, and the General Service and Victory Medals, and was demobilised in February 1919.
6, Railway Terrace, Bedford Street, Watford.   X351.

BEALE, F. J., Driver, Royal Field Artillery.

He was called up from the Reserve at the outbreak of war, and was immediately drafted to the Western Front, where he took part in the Retreat from Mons. He also served on the Marne, and at La Bassée, Ypres (I.) and Hill 60, where he was severely wounded. He was invalided home, and in October 1917 was discharged as medically unfit for further duty. He holds the Mons Star, and the General Service and Victory Medals.

Ampthill Road, Shefford, near Bedford.   Z352.

BEALE, H., Private, R.A.S.C.

He joined in May 1917, and served at various stations on important duties with his unit. He rendered valuable services, but owing to being medically unfit was unable to obtain his transfer abroad. He was demobilised in July 1919.

5, Charles Street, Watford.   X353/A.

BEALE, P. D., Driver, Royal Field Artillery.

Volunteering in September 1915, he proceeded to France in the same year and was in action at numerous engagements, including those of Vimy Ridge, Ypres and Passchendaele, and was wounded. He was demobilised in April 1919, and holds the 1914–15 Star, and the General Service and Victory Medals.

5, Charles Street, Watford.   X353/C.

BEALE, S. H. (M.M.), Sergeant, 2nd Wiltshire Regiment.

He volunteered in January 1915, and in the same year was sent to the Western Front and took a prominent part in the fighting at Ypres, Vimy Ridge and Arras. He was awarded the Military Medal for conspicuous bravery in the Field, and holds in addition the 1914–15 Star, and the General Service and Victory Medals. He was demobilised in April 1919.

5, Charles Street, Watford.   X353/B.

BEAN, W. J., Private, Suffolk Regiment.

He joined in April 1917, and in the following year was drafted to the Western Front, where he took part in the second Battle of the Marne and in the last engagement at Ypres. He was also present at the entry into Lille and in many other engagements in the Advance of 1918. He holds the General Service and Victory Medals, and was demobilised in October 1919.

23a, Upper Paddock Road, Oxhey, Watford.   X355.

BEANEY, F. E., Private, Labour Corps.

He joined in June 1916, and after his training served at various stations on important duties with his unit. He rendered valuable services, but was not successful in obtaining his transfer overseas before the cessation of hostilities owing to his medical unfitness. He was demobilised in November 1919.

71, Victoria Street, Dunstable.   2647/A.

BEARD, A., Private, 2/5th Bedfordshire Regt.

He joined in July 1916, and on the completion of his training was drafted to the Western Front in January of the following year. He saw much heavy fighting at Arras, Bullecourt and Cambrai, and in other engagements, and was killed in action near Ypres on July 2nd, 1918. He was entitled to the General Service and Victory Medals.

65, Edward Street, Dunstable.   356.

BEASLEY, H. C., Private, 6th Bedfordshire Regt.

He volunteered in September 1914, and in the following year was sent overseas. He served at Ypres and in various other engagements, and was killed in action on August 3rd, 1916. He was entitled to the 1914–15 Star, and the General Service and Victory Medals.

44, Victoria Road, North Watford.   X357.

BEAUMONT, C., Private, Duke of Cornwall's Light Infantry.

He volunteered in January 1915, and in the same year was drafted to France, where he took part in much heavy fighting on the Somme, Arras and Cambrai Fronts, and in numerous other engagements, and was wounded and gassed. He was afterwards transferred to India where he was still serving in 1920 on important garrison duties. He holds the 1914–15 Star, and the General Service and Victory Medals.

177, Heath Road, Leighton Buzzard.   2455/B.

BEAUMONT, C., Private, Duke of Cornwall's Light Infantry.

He volunteered in August 1914, and after a course of training served at various stations with his unit until he was drafted overseas. He saw active service in several sectors of the Western Front, and among the important battles in which he took part were those at Arras, Ypres and Cambrai. He was later sent to India, where he was still serving in 1920. He holds the General Service and Victory Medals.

103a, North Street, Luton.   358/A.

BEAUMONT, F., Rifleman, 18th London Regt. (London Irish Rifles.)

Having enlisted in the Territorials before the war he was mobilised on the outbreak of hostilities, and in 1915 was drafted to the Western Front. Here he was engaged in severe fighting, and was wounded in the Battle of Loos and sent to hospital. On recovery he served in other sectors, and was gassed near Ypres in July 1917. In March of the following year he was taken prisoner in the second Battle of the Somme, but effected his escape in September and served through the last stages of the war. He holds the Territorial Efficiency Medal, the 1914–15 Star, and the General Service and Victory Medals.

Mill Lane, Welwyn.   359.

BEAUMONT, G., Rifleman, 9th London Regt. (Queen Victoria's Rifles).

He volunteered in November 1914, and in the following May was drafted to the Western Front. Whilst in this theatre of war he was in several important engagements, including the Battle of the Somme, in which he was killed on July 1st, 1916. He was entitled to the 1914–15 Star, and the General Service and Victory Medals.

40, Capel Road, Oxhey, Herts.   X360/A.

BEAUMONT, H., Private, R.A.S.C. (M.T.)

He joined in June 1916, and in the following year was sent overseas. He was in the Advance on Jerusalem through Egypt and Palestine, and was engaged on important transport duties during several battles, including those at Gaza, Aleppo and Damascus. He was demobilised in November 1919, and holds the General Service and Victory Medals.

103, Norfolk Road, Rickmansworth.   X361.

BEAUMONT, H., Leading Seaman, Royal Navy.

He volunteered in August 1914, and was posted to H.M.S. " Osea Malden." Serving on board this vessel he was engaged in patrol and convoy duties in the North Sea. He took part in the Battle of Jutland and in several minor engagements, and also served in the Baltic. He holds the 1914–15 Star, and the General Service and Victory Medals, and in 1920 was still serving.

40, Capel Road, Oxhey.   X360/B.

BEAUMONT, R., Sergeant, Bedfordshire Regt.

He volunteered in August 1914, and was drafted to Salonica in January of the following year. After rendering valuable service on the Vardar Front, he returned home and was discharged as time-expired. He rejoined in March 1916 and was sent to France, where he took part in the Battles of the Somme and Arras, and was killed in action near the latter place in June 1917. He was entitled to the 1914–15 Star, and the General Service and Victory Medals.

177, Heath Road, Leighton Buzzard.   2455/C.

BEAUMONT, W. F., Private, Bedfordshire Regt.

Volunteering in September 1914 he was drafted in January 1915 to the Western Front, where he took part in various engagements, including those of Loos, the Somme, Arras and Cambrai, and was gassed. He was demobilised in January 1919 after his return home, and holds the 1914–15 Star, and the General Service and Victory Medals.

177, Heath Road, Leighton Buzzard.   2455/A.

BEAZLEY, T. C., Private, 1st Essex Regiment.

He joined in June 1916, and in the same year saw active service on the Western Front, where he took part in several important battles. After being engaged at Combles he was in action at Arras, Ypres and Cambrai, and continued serving in the Western theatre of war until the end of hostilities. He holds the General Service and Victory Medals, and was demobilised in August 1919.

Parkville, London Colney.   X362.

BECK, H. W., Rifleman, Rifle Brigade.

He was serving at the outbreak of war and was immediately drafted to the Western Front, where he took part in the continuous fighting during the Retreat from Mons. He was engaged in many subsequent battles, including those at Ypres, Neuve Chapelle and the Somme, and was gassed and twice wounded. He served until the cessation of hostilities, and returning home was demobilised in October 1919. He holds the Mons Star, and the General Service and Victory Medals.

50, Ebury Road, Watford.   X363/4A.

BECKETT, F., Pte., R.A.S.C. and Labour Corps.

He volunteered in July 1915, and early in the following year was drafted to the Western Front. Engaged on important duties in connection with the transport of supplies to the forward areas, he served at many engagements, including the Battle of Cambrai. He was later transferred to the Labour Corps and did good work with that unit in constructing bridges and roads until he was demobilised in February 1919. He holds the General Service and Victory Medals.

The Bridge, Kings Langley   X365/A.

BECKETT, F. L., Private, Oxfordshire and Buckinghamshire Light Infantry.
He volunteered in April 1915, and in the following year was sent to the Western Front. He was in fierce fighting in several sectors, including those of Arras, Ypres and the Somme, and was killed in action on August 22nd, 1917, at St. Julien, where he was buried. He was entitled to the General Service and Victory Medals.
Station Road, Woburn Sands. Z366/B.

BECKINSALE, G., Sergeant, R.A.V.C.
Volunteering in an infantry regiment in November 1914, he was immediately sent to the Western Front. He saw much active service in various sectors, and among other important actions took part in the Battle of Ypres. On his being transferred to the Royal Army Veterinary Corps in 1916 his special knowledge was utilised at various base hospitals, where he did valuable work in attending to sick and wounded horses. He was demobilised in March 1919, and holds the 1914 Star, and the General Service and Victory Medals.
79, Liverpool Road, Watford. X367.

BECKWITH, S. C., Private, R.A.M.C.
He volunteered in September 1914, and after a course of training was engaged at various hospitals attending to sick and wounded soldiers. He was drafted to the Western Front in 1917, and during the engagements at Polygon Wood, Kemmel Hill and Ypres, did valuable work with the Field Ambulance. He was gassed in the course of his duties on the Somme in April 1918, and after returning to England was demobilised in April 1919, holding the General Service and Victory Medals.
15, Albert Road, Houghton Regis, Dunstable. 368.

BEDFORD, G., Private, Bedfordshire Regiment.
Volunteering in June 1915, he was drafted to France in the following year on the conclusion of his course of training. He was in action in the third Battle of Ypres, in which he was wounded, and subsequently took part in the Battles of the Marne and Cambrai. He holds the General Service and Victory Medals, and was demobilised in September 1919.
54, Cambridge Road, St. Albans. X369/A.

BEDFORD, P., Air Mechanic, Royal Air Force.
He joined in December 1917, and was shortly afterwards drafted to the Western Front. He was engaged on important duties at the Calais aircraft base, where his qualifications and technical skill were of great value. He was demobilised in January 1919 after his return home, and holds the General Service and Victory Medals.
54, Cambridge Road, St. Albans. X369/B.

BEEBY, J. W., Sergeant, 1st Hertfordshire and 7th Bedfordshire Regiments.
He was serving when war broke out, and after discharging important duties at various stations was drafted to the Western Front in 1918. After being in action in the Ypres sector he was invalided home on account of gas-poisoning and shell-shock. He holds the General Service and Victory Medals, and was demobilised in February 1919.
33, Buxton Road, Luton. 370.

BEES, W. G., Corporal (Saddler), R.A.S.C.
Volunteering in October 1914, after a course of training he was sent to the Western Front in the following year. He served in various sectors in this theatre of war and was present at many important engagements, notably those at Loos, Ypres, and the Somme. He took part in the closing stages of the war and saw further fighting at Cambrai. He was demobilised in May 1919, and holds the 1914–15 Star, and the General Service and Victory Medals.
116, Harwood Road, Watford. X371/A.

BEESON, E. W., Private, Machine Gun Corps.
He joined in May 1916, and in September of the same year was drafted to the Western Front. He fought at the Somme, Arras and Ypres, and in Autumn of 1917 was transferred to Italy, where he took part in the British Offensive on the Piave front until 1918. After returning home he was demobilised in September 1919, holding the General Service and Victory Medals.
39, Shaftesbury Road, Watford. X372.

BEESON, S., Corporal, Royal Engineers.
He volunteered in August 1914, and later was drafted to the Western Front. After taking part in much heavy fighting in this theatre of war he was drafted to Egypt and Palestine, where he rendered valuable services at Gaza and Jerusalem, and was severely wounded. He returned home and was demobilised in February 1919, holding the General Service and Victory Medals.
33, Meeting Alley, Watford. X373/B.

BEETON, R., Private, Kent Cyclist Battalion and Queen's Own (Royal West Kent Regt.)
He joined in July 1917, and was immediately drafted to Africa, where he rendered valuable services for some months. He was then sent to India, and while there was engaged on important duties in the Punjab at Rawal Pindi, Lahore and Firozpur, and on the Frontier. He returned home and was demobilised in January 1920, holding the General Service and Victory Medals.
8, Merton Road, Watford. X374.

BEETON, W. J., Private, Bedfordshire Regt.
He volunteered in February 1915, and in the following year was drafted to France, where he took part in the Battles of the Somme and Cambrai. He was killed in action on June 21st, 1918, and was entitled to the General Service and Victory Medals.
18, Trevour Road, Hitchin. 1821.

BELCHER, E., L/Cpl., Somerset Light Infantry.
He volunteered in 1914, and on the conclusion of his training was drafted in 1915 to the Western Front. He was in this fighting area for only three weeks, during which he fought at the Battle of Ypres and was killed in action. He was entitled to the 1914–15 Star, and the General Service and Victory Medals.
64, Brightwell Road, Watford. X375/A.

BELCHER, H., Private, Bedfordshire Regiment, 7th and 11th Queen's (Royal West Surrey Regiment), and Labour Corps.
He joined in June 1916, and in the following August was drafted to the Western Front, where he took part in numerous engagements, including those at Ypres, Albert, the Somme and St. Quentin, and was three times wounded. He returned home and was demobilised in April 1919, and holds the General Service and Victory Medals.
19, Mill Street, Apsley End. X376.

BELCHER, S. J., Farrier-Sergeant, R.F.A.
He volunteered in 1914, and in the following year proceeded to France. While overseas he rendered valuable services in many sectors of the line as farrier-sergeant to his unit until the cessation of hostilities. He returned home and was demobilised in May 1919, holding the 1914–15 Star, and the General Service and Victory Medals.
38, Holywell Road, Watford. X377/B.

BELL, E. (M.M.), Private, R.A.M.C.
He volunteered in September 1914, and in the following year was drafted to the Dardanelles, where he did excellent service at Suvla Bay and Anzac. After serving there for some time he was transferred to the Western Front, and after serving on the Somme was awarded the Military Medal for conspicuous gallantry in the Field. He was demobilised in March 1919, and holds, in addition to the Military Medal, the 1914–15 Star, and the General Service and Victory Medals.
62, Cobden Street, Luton. 378.

BELL, E. A., Private, 17th (Duke of Cambridge's Own) Lancers.
He joined in May 1918, and up to the date of the Armistice was engaged on important duties with his unit. He was then sent to Germany in the Army of Occupation, and rendered valuable services at Cologne until he returned to England for demobilisation in November 1919.
2, Marquis Lane, Harpenden. 379/A.

BELL, F. A., Private, Duke of Cornwall's Light Infantry.
He volunteered in August 1914, and was quickly sent to France, where he fought at Mons, Ypres and several other engagements until 1916. He was then drafted to Salonika and took part in various important battles until hostilities ceased. He returned home and was demobilised in December 1918, holding the Mons Star, and the General Service and Victory Medals. He has since then been killed by accident on October 29th, 1919.
31, Fearnley Street, Watford. X380.

BELL, H. E., Private, Bedfordshire Regiment.
He was mobilised in August 1914, and was at once sent to the Western Front, where he fought in many great battles, including those of Mons, Arras and Cambrai, and was twice wounded. He was afterwards drafted to India and rendered valuable services at various stations. He was still serving in 1920, and holds the Mons Star, and the General Service and Victory Medals.
10, Dolphin Yard, St. Albans. X381/B.

BELL, L. J., Private, Middlesex Regiment.

He was called up from the Reserve in August 1914, and after being retained on important duties with his unit was drafted to France in November 1916. There he took part in many important engagements up to the close of hostilities, including those of Ypres, Passchendaele and the Somme, and was twice wounded. After returning home he was demobilised in July 1919, holding the General Service and Victory Medals.
14, Camp View, St. Albans.   X382.

BELL, P. G., Gunner, Royal Field Artillery.

He joined in June 1916, and in the following November proceeded to the Western Front, where he took an active part in many important engagements up to the close of hostilities, including those of Cambrai, Albert, Bapaume and other operations in the Retreat and Advance of 1918. After the Armistice he went to Germany with the Army of Occupation, and on his return was demobilised in September 1919. He holds the General Service and Victory Medals.
2, Marquis Lane, Harpenden.   379/B.

BELL, W., Bombardier, Royal Field Artillery.

He volunteered in August 1914, and in the following year was drafted to the Western Front, where he took part in much severe fighting at Ypres and the Somme. In 1916 he was sent to Salonika, and after much valuable service then proceeded to Russia. In March 1919, after his return to the West, he joined the Army of Occupation in Germany, where he remained until his demobilisation in September 1920. He holds the 1914–15 Star, and the General Service and Victory Medals.
Maiden Croft Lane, Gosmore, near Hitchin.   2448/A.

BELL, W., Private, Labour Corps.

He volunteered in July 1915, and after his training was drafted to France, where he rendered valuable services in various sectors on trench-digging and guarding duties. He was afterwards engaged with the Royal Army Ordnance Corps in the Relief Force in North Russia. He was demobilised in January 1919 after his return home, and holds the General Service and Victory Medals.
2, Grove Circus, Watford.   X383.

BELL, W. R. W., Private, 9th (Queen's Royal) Lancers.

He volunteered in August 1914, and having completed his training proceeded to the Western Front. He took part in much severe fighting at Ypres and in other engagements, and was killed in action on July 30th, 1916. He was entitled to the General Service and Victory Medals.
10, Dolphin Yard, St. Albans.   X381/A.

BELLINGHAM, J., Private, R.A.M.C.

He volunteered in April 1915, and after his training was drafted to the Western Front. While in this theatre of war he rendered valuable medical services at Arras, Cambrai, and other important engagements, attending to the wounded on the field, and was himself wounded. He holds the General Service and Victory Medals, and was demobilised in June 1919.
Myrtle Villa, Seaton Road, London Colney.   X384.

BELLIS, F. T., Driver, Royal Field Artillery.

He volunteered in May 1915, and after his training was in November of the same year drafted to Egypt. He took part in the campaign in Palestine and was present in the engagements preceding the capture of Jericho. He returned home and was demobilised in May 1919, holding the 1914–15 Star, and the General Service and Victory Medals.
366, Whippendell Road, Watford.   X386/C.

BELLIS, H. H., Private, Queen's (Royal West Surrey Regiment).

He joined in May 1916, and after his training was in the same year drafted to the Western Front. He took part in the severe fighting at the Somme, Cambrai and in the Retreat and Advance of 1918, and was killed in action on September 21st, 1918. He was entitled to the General Service and Victory Medals.
366, Whippendell Road, Watford.   X386/B.

BELLIS, J. W., Gunner, Royal Field Artillery.

He volunteered in July 1915, and in the same year he was drafted to Egypt. He took part in the Palestine campaign and fought in numerous engagements, including those in the vicinity of Beersheba, Jerusalem and Jericho. He returned home and was demobilised in July 1919, holding the 1914–15 Star, and the General Service and Victory Medals.
366, Whippendell Road, Watford.   X386/A.

BENNELL, J. A., Staff-Sergeant, R.A.S.C.

He volunteered in November 1914, and in April of the following year was sent to the Western Front, where he was stationed at Le Havre. He was engaged on important duties in connection with the food supplies for his unit, and rendered valuable services until 1919. He was demobilised in February of that year, and holds the 1914–15 Star, and the General Service and Victory Medals.
113, Villiers Road, Oxhey, Watford.   X387.

BENNETT, A., Corporal, Mounted Military Police, 15th Division.

Volunteering in April 1915, he was shortly afterwards drafted to the Western Front, where he was on Police duties in various sectors. He did valuable work during several important battles, including those on the Somme and at Arras and Cambrai, and returned to England on the conclusion of hostilities and was demobilised in July 1919. He holds the 1914–15 Star, and the General Service and Victory Medals.
53, Breakspeare Road, Abbots Langley.   X389/A.

BENNETT, A., Private, R.A.V.C.

He joined in January 1916, and after his training served at various stations on important duties with his unit. He rendered valuable services, but was not successful in obtaining his transfer overseas before the cessation of hostilities. He was demobilised in March 1919.
Upper Sundon, near Dunstable, Beds.   388.

BENNETT, A. E., Private, 17th Royal Fusiliers.

Joining in February 1918, on completion of his training he was drafted to France, where he was engaged on salvage duties. He was accidentally killed by the explosion of a bomb on October 18th, 1918, and was entitled to the General Service and Victory Medals.
60, Silver Lane, Haynes, near Bedford.   Z390/A.

BENNETT, A. E., Private, Bedfordshire Regt.

He volunteered in 1915, and in the same year was drafted to the Western Front. He took part in heavy fighting at Hill 60, Arras, Cambrai, St. Julien, St. Quentin and the Somme, and was three times wounded. He was demobilised in January 1919, and holds the 1914–15 Star, and the General Service and Victory Medals.
8, Garden Road, Abbots Langley.   X391/B.

BENNETT, C., Gunner, Royal Field Artillery.

He joined in September 1917, and after his training was drafted to the Western Front, and took part in many important engagements, including the Battle of Cambrai. He returned home and was demobilised in November 1919, and holds the General Service and Victory Medals.
32, Tavistock Street, Luton.   392/A.

BENNETT, C. D., Private, 7th Bedfordshire Regt.

He volunteered in September 1914, and after his training was sent to the Western Front. He took part in the fighting at Cambrai, Albert and Fricourt, and was wounded, and after the conclusion of hostilities returned to England and was demobilised in February 1919, holding the General Service and Victory Medals.
69, Beech Road, Luton.   393/A.

BENNETT, E. W., Private, Hertfordshire Regt.

He volunteered in May 1915, and after a period of training was drafted to the Western Front. He took part in the fighting at the Battles of Ypres and the Somme, and was killed in action at the latter place on September 4th, 1916. He was entitled to the General Service and Victory Medals.
The Old Rectory, Welwyn.   394/B.

BENNETT, F., 2nd Corporal, Royal Engineers and Bedfordshire Regiment.

He enlisted in 1907, and in 1914 was drafted to the Western Front, where he took part in the Retreat from Mons and the Battle of Ypres, and was wounded at Kemmel. In 1915 he was transferred to Salonika, until 1919, when he returned home and was demobilised, holding the Mons Star, and the General Service and Victory Medals.
8, Garden Road, Abbots Langley, Herts.   X391/A.

BENNETT, H. J., Private, 1/5th Bedfordshire and 1/5th Suffolk Regiments.

He joined in 1916, and in the following year was drafted to Egypt, where he served in numerous engagements in Palestine under General Allenby, including those at Gaza and Jerusalem. He returned home and was demobilised in January 1919, and holds the General Service and Victory Medals.
60, Silver Lane, Haynes, near Bedford.   390/B.

BENNETT, J., Gunner, Royal Horse Artillery.

He joined in December 1917, and after his training was in the following April sent to the Western Front, where he was in action at Bapaume, Cambrai and Ypres. After the Armistice he proceeded with the Army of Occupation to Germany, where he served until he returned home and was demobilised in November 1919. He holds the General Service and Victory Medals.

Wilshamstead, Beds. Z395/B.

BENNETT, J. J. G., Gunner, R.F.A.

He was serving at the outbreak of war, and was immediately afterwards sent to the Western Front, and took part in the Battles of Mons and Ypres. He was severely wounded and invalided home, and was discharged as medically unfit for further service in August 1915, holding the Mons Star, and the General Service and Victory Medals.

Back Street, Hatfield. X396.

BENNETT, P., Sergeant, King's Royal Rifle Corps.

He volunteered in August 1914, and in the following year was drafted to the Western Front, and took part in the fighting at Ypres, Arras, the Somme, Passchendaele and St. Quentin. He returned home and was demobilised in February 1919, and holds the 1914-15 Star, and the General Service and Victory Medals.

30, Boyle Street, Luton. 397/A.

BENNETT, R. E., Sapper, Royal Engineers.

He joined in June 1918, and after his training served at various stations on important duties as search-light operator and engine driver, work which demanded a high degree of technical skill. He rendered valuable services, but was not successful in obtaining his transfer overseas before the cessation of hostilities. He was demobilised in November 1919.

38, Watson's Walk, St. Albans. X398.

BENNETT, R. F., Private, 2nd Bedfordshire Regt.

He joined in January 1916, and in May of the same year was drafted to France, and took part in the Battles of Vimy Ridge and the Somme. He was wounded near Trones Wood in July 1916 and invalided home. On his recovery he returned to the Western Front, and was in action at Messines and Passchendaele, and was again wounded. He returned home and was demobilised in March 1919, and holds the General Service and Victory Medals.

Wilshamstead, Beds. Z395/A.

BENNETT, W., Private, R.A.S.C.

He joined in 1916, and after his training was sent to the Western Front, where he was engaged on important duties with his unit. He was present at numerous engagements, including those at Ypres and Cambrai, and after the cessation of hostilities returned home and was demobilised in December 1919, holding the General Service and Victory Medals.

32, Tavistock Street, Luton. 392/B.

BENNETT, W. C., Private, R.A.S.C.

He volunteered in August 1914, and in the following October was drafted to the Western Front, and served in the Retreat from Antwerp and at La Bassée, Ypres, Armentières and the Somme. He was demobilised in March 1919, and holds the 1914 Star, and the General Service and Victory Medals.

The Old Rectory, Welwyn. 394/A.

BENNETT, W. G., Private, R.A.M.C.

He volunteered in September 1914, and in June of the following year was sent to the Western Front. He was attached to the 45th Field Ambulance, and served in the Battles of Ypres, the Somme and Arras, and in many other engagements. He was demobilised in February 1919, and holds the 1914-15 Star, and the General Service and Victory Medals.

Primrose Hill, King's Langley. 399/A.

BENNIFER, C. H., Gunner, Royal Field Artillery.

He volunteered in May 1915, and after his training served at various stations on important duties with his unit until June 1917, when he was sent to the Western Front and took part in the heavy fighting at Arras and Ypres. On July 23rd, 1917, he died of wounds received in action, and was entitled to the General Service and Victory Medals.

13, Southern Road, Watford. X400/B.

BENNIFER, T. W., Private, Queen's (Royal West Surrey Regiment).

He joined in February 1916, and in the following July was drafted to the Western Front, and took part in the Battles of the Somme and Ypres. He was wounded and invalided home, and on his recovery returned to France and was again in action. Later he was taken prisoner, and died whilst in captivity on May 19th, 1917. He was entitled to the General Service and Victory Medals.

13, Southern Road, Watford. X400/C.

BENT, A., Private, 6th Northamptonshire Regt.

He joined in March 1916, and in July of the same year was drafted to the Western Front, and took part in the Battles of Arras, Vimy Ridge, the Somme and Passchendaele. He was killed in action on March 14th, 1917, and was entitled to the General Service and Victory Medals.

18, Bolton Road, Luton. 401.

BENT, H., Private, 7th Northamptonshire Regt.

He volunteered in June 1915, and in the following December was drafted to the Western Front, and took part in many important engagements, including those at Arras and Vimy Ridge, and was twice wounded. He returned home and was discharged in consequence of his wounds in February 1918, and holds the 1914-15 Star, and the General Service and Victory Medals.

Locklong, Marsh Road, Leagrave, near Luton. 402.

BENT, H. W., 2nd Air Mechanic, R.A.F.

He volunteered in March 1915, and after his training was drafted in October 1916 to the Western Front. He took part in the Battles of the Somme and Bapaume, and was wounded and invalided home. He was demobilised in January 1919, and holds the General Service and Victory Medals.

Royal Oak, Leagrave, near Luton. 403.

BENT, S. C., Sergeant, Royal Army Pay Corps.

He joined in October 1916, and on the completion of his training was engaged on highly important clerical duties with his unit. He was not successful in securing his transfer to a fighting front before the cessation of hostilities, but he rendered valuable clerical services until his demobilisation in January 1919.

26, Kingston Road, Luton. 4051/A.

BENTLEY, C., Private, Suffolk Regiment and Machine Gun Corps.

He volunteered in August 1914, and in the following year proceeded to the Western Front, where he took part in the Battles of Ypres, the Somme, Givenchy and Arras, and was wounded and invalided home. On his recovery he returned to France, and after serving in numerous engagements was again wounded. Owing to his wounds he was discharged in September 1918, and holds the 1914-15 Star, and the General Service and Victory Medals.

36, Shott Lane, Letchworth. 2445/B.

BENTLEY, E. M., Private, Women's Legion and Member, Women's Army Auxiliary Corps.

She volunteered in July 1917, and during her service in the Women's Legion and the W.A.A.C., discharged the varied duties assigned to her with commendable skill and efficiency. She was demobilised in October 1918.

36, Shott Lane, Letchworth. 2445/A.

BENTLEY, F., Sapper, Royal Engineers.

He volunteered in 1915, and after a course of training was drafted to the Western Front, where he took part in the Battles of Ypres and Cambrai and many other engagements, and was gassed. He returned home and was demobilised in March 1919, and holds the General Service and Victory Medals.

Thatch Cottage, High Street, Harpenden. 404.

BENTLEY, H. J., Rifleman, 8th London Regt. (Post Office Rifles).

He volunteered in 1915, and after his training was drafted to the Eastern Front and served in Egypt and Salonika. He took part in many engagements, including the taking of Jerusalem, and after the conclusion of hostilities he returned home and was demobilised in March 1919, holding the General Service and Victory Medals.

High Street, Harpenden. 405.

BERRIDGE, A., Private, Labour Corps.

He joined in March 1916, and in the same year was drafted to the Western Front. He served on the Somme and at Arras, Ypres and Givenchy, engaged in the repair of roads and railways, and rendered valuable services. He was demobilised in 1919, and holds the General Service and Victory Medals.

Clifton Road, Shefford, Bedford. Z406.

BERRINGTON, H., Private, Duke of Cornwall's Light Infantry.

He joined in March 1917, and after his training was engaged on important duties at various stations with his unit until April 1918, when he was sent to the Western Front and took part in the fighting at Cambrai and Ypres. He was demobilised in February 1919, and holds the General Service and Victory Medals.

Cotton End, near Bedford. Z407/B.

BERRINGTON, H. J., Private, Essex Regiment.
He volunteered in December 1915, and in the following year
proceeded to the Western Front and took part in severe
fighting at Albert and on the Somme. He was taken prisoner
near Ypres in July 1917 and sent to Germany. On his
release he returned home and was demobilised in January
1919, and holds the General Service and Victory Medals.
Cotton End, near Bedford.   Z407/A.

BERRY, A. L., Private, 11th Essex Regiment.
He volunteered in December 1915, and in the following year
was drafted to the Western Front, where he took part in important engagements, including those on the Somme and at
Arras, Ypres and Cambrai. Later he proceeded with the
Army of Occupation to Germany,. He returned home and
was demobilised in April 1919, and holds the General Service
and Victory Medals.
1, Mission Cottages, New Town, Hatfield.   X408/B.

BERRY, G. H., Private, Grenadier Guards.
He joined in January 1918, and after his training served at
various stations on important duties with his unit. He
rendered valuable services, but was not successful in obtaining his transfer overseas before the cessation of hostilities.
He was demobilised in February 1919.
The Hill, Welwyn.   409/B.

BERRY, G. W., Gunner, Royal Field Artillery.
He volunteered in September 1915, and in the following year
was sent to Mesopotamia, where he took part in the campaign
against the Turks and was in action in numerous engagements,
including those at Baghdad and Kut. He returned home and
was demobilised in May 1919, and holds the General Service
and Victory Medals.
The Hill, Welwyn, Herts.   409/A.

BERRY, G. W., Sapper, Royal Engineers.
He joined in 1916, and on the completion of his training was
sent in the same year to France. He was engaged on important duties on the Somme and at Arras and Cambrai until
after the Armistice, when he was drafted to Germany with
the Army of Occupation. He returned home and was demobilised in March 1919, and holds the General Service and
Victory Medals.
16, The Leys, Woburn Sands.   Z410/A.

BERRY, V. W., L/Corporal, R.A.S.C. (M.T.)
He joined in June 1916, and after his training served at
various stations on important duties with his unit, being
employed as an engine-fitter. He rendered valuable services,
but was not successful in obtaining his transfer overseas
before the cessation of hostilities. He was demobilised in
September 1919.
1, Mission Cottages, New Town, Hatfield.   X408/A.

BERRY, W. H., Private, Bedfordshire Regiment.
He joined in June 1916, and in the same year was drafted to
France, where he took part in numerous engagements. On
March 21st, 1918, he was killed in action at St. Quentin
during the Retreat, and was entitled to the General Service
and Victory Medals.
2nd Right of Way, New Town, Hatfield.   X411.

BESSANT, A., Private, 44th Canadian Infantry.
He joined in 1916, and in January of the following year was
drafted overseas. He served at Arras, Passchendaele,
Cambrai and the Somme, and was wounded near Ypres and
invalided home. On his recovery he served in England until
he was demobilised in September 1919. He holds the General
Service and Victory Medals.
17, Summer Street, Leighton Buzzard.   1586/B.

BEST, A. E., L/Corporal, Royal Fusiliers.
He was serving at the outbreak of war, and in 1914 was
drafted to the Western Front, where he took part in the
Retreat from Mons and the Battles of the Marne, the Aisne,
La Bassée, Ypres and the Somme, and was four times wounded.
In May 1919 he was sent to Russia with the Relief Force, and
served at Archangel until the withdrawal of the expedition.
He holds the Mons Star, and the General Service and Victory
Medals, and was demobilised in December 1919.
High Street, Toddington, Dunstable.   412.

BEST, W., Sapper, Royal Engineers.
He volunteered in August 1914, and in the following July was
drafted to Egypt. He took part in the Palestine Campaign,
and was present at the Battle of Gaza and also served at the
capture of Jerusalem. During his service overseas he was
chiefly engaged on important duties in connection with the
wiring of the lines of communication, and after the conclusion
of hostilities returned to England and was demobilised in June
1919, holding the 1914-15 Star, and the General Service and
Victory Medals.
2, Bower Lane, Eaton Bray, Dunstable.   413.

BEST, W., Sapper, Royal Engineers.
He volunteered in May 1915, and in the same year was drafted
to the Western Front, where he was engaged on important
wiring duties at Ypres, Arras, Cambrai and the Somme. He
holds the 1914-15 Star, and the General Service and Victory
Medals, and was demobilised in July 1919.
56, Norfolk Road, Rickmansworth.   X414.

BETHELL, H. J., Leading Seaman, R.N., H.M.S. "Scott."
He was serving at the outbreak of war, and was posted for
duty with the Grand Fleet in the North Sea. He took part
with his ship in the repulse of the German raiders off Hartle-
pool and also served in the Battle of Jutland and the engagement at Zeebrugge. He holds the 1914-15 Star, and the
General Service and Victory Medals, and was discharged in
consequence of his service in May 1918.
26, Neal Street, Watford.   415/A.

BETHELL, W. P., Sergeant, R.A.M.C.
He volunteered in December 1914, and after the completion of
his training was drafted to the Dardanelles, where he served in
the Gallipoli Campaign. Later he was transferred to Egypt,
and was engaged on important duties at the Military Hospital,
Cairo, where he continued to serve until after the conclusion of
hostilities, when he returned to England and was demobilised
in May 1919. He holds the General Service and Victory
Medals.
26, Neal Street, Watford.   415/B.

BETTLE, A. S., Corporal, Royal Flying Corps.
He joined in January 1916, and after having completed his
training was drafted to Mesopotamia, where he served on
important duties as a photographer until February 1918, when
he was invalided to England and discharged in consequence
of his service. He holds the General Service and Victory
Medals.
94, Sutton Road, Watford.   X416/A.

BETTLE, G., Private, 1st Bedfordshire Regiment.
He was serving at the outbreak of war, and was immediately
sent to France, where he took part in the Retreat from Mons
and the Battles of La Bassée, Hill 60, Festubert, the Somme,
Passchendaele and Cambrai. In 1918 he was transferred to
Italy, and served on the Piave and the Asiago Plateaux. During
his service he was wounded, and after the conclusion of
hostilities returned home and was demobilised in July 1920,
holding the Mons Star, and the General Service and Victory
Medals.
Station Grove, Woburn Sands, Beds.   417.

BETTLE, J. S., Private, R.A.O.C.
He volunteered in May 1915, and after his training was drafted
to the Dardanelles, where he served in the Gallipoli operations.
Later he was transferred to Egypt, where he was engaged on
important duties. He also served in the Palestine Campaign
under General Allenby, and was afterwards sent to the Western
Front, and was present at the Battles of Ypres and Arras. He
holds the General Service and Victory Medals, and was demobilised in June 1919.
94, Sutton Road, Watford.   416/B.

BETTS, W. T., Aircraftsman, Royal Air Force.
He joined in July 1918, and after his training served as a fitter
at various depôts on important duties which required a high
degree of technical knowledge and skill. He rendered valuable
service, but owing to physical unfitness was unable to obtain
his transfer overseas. He was demobilised in February 1919.
47, London Terrace, High Street, Dunstable, Bedfordshire.
                                                    186.

BEXLEY, F. A., Private, R.A.F.
He volunteered in 1915, and on completion of his training was
drafted to France, where he served in various sectors of the
Front engaged on important duties. He was demobilised
in February 1919, and holds the General Service and Victory
Medals.
27, Harley Street, St. Albans.   418—419/A.

BICKERTON, T. A., Private, Essex Regiment.
Volunteering in August 1915, in the following December he
was sent to France, and was in action at Arras, Ypres and
Cambrai. He was taken prisoner in March 1918, and was
held in captivity until after the Armistice, when he was repatriated. He was demobilised in January 1919, and holds
the 1914-15 Star, and the General Service and Victory Medals.
90, Holywell Hill, St. Albans.   420.

BIDEWELL, H., Colour-Sergeant-Major, Norfolk Regiment.
Volunteering at the outbreak of the war, in the following year
he was drafted to the Dardanelles, where he served in
numerous engagements in various sectors of the Front.
He was sent home and demobilised in 1919, and holds the
1914-15 Star, and the General Service and Victory Medals.
123, Regent Street, North Watford.   421/B.

BIERTON, A. R., Gunner, Royal Field Artillery.
He joined in 1916, and on completion of his training was drafted to Salonika, where he served in various sectors of the Front with the anti-aircraft section. He returned home and was demobilised in January 1919, and holds the General Service and Victory Medals.
36, Merton Road, Watford. 422.

BIERTON, D., Private, East Yorkshire Regiment.
He volunteered in November 1915, but after five months' service the strain of military duties proved too severe for his health, and he was discharged in March 1916 as medically unfit for further duty.
32, Regent Street, Leighton Buzzard. 2462.

BIERTON, J., L/Corporal, 4th Middlesex Regt.
He joined in January 1916, and having completed his training was drafted to the Western Front in the following October. He took part in the Battle of the Somme, and later was killed in action near Arras on February 17th, 1917. He was entitled to the General Service and Victory Medals.
9, George Street, Leighton Buzzard. 480.

BIGGADIKE, B. J., 5th Northamptonshire Regt.
Volunteering in August 1914, on completion of his training he was drafted to France, where he served in various sectors of the Front. He was wounded at Ypres and invalided home, and was discharged as medically unfit for further service in June 1916. He holds the 1914–15 Star, and the General Service and Victory Medals.
1, Ivy Road, Luton. 424.

BIGGERSTAFF, L., Corporal, R.A.S.C.
Joining in March 1916, he was shortly afterwards sent to Egypt. He served on important transport duties during the Palestine Campaign, and was present at the engagements at Gaza and Jerusalem, rendering valuable services. He was sent home and demobilised in March 1920, and holds the General Service and Victory Medals.
1, Local Board Road, Luton. 426.

BIGGS, C., Private, Gloucestershire Regiment.
He volunteered in July 1915, and in the same year was drafted to France, where he served in numerous engagements in various sectors of the Front. Later he was transferred to Mesopotamia, and was in action at Kut and Baghdad. He was demobilised in October 1919, and holds the 1914–15 Star, and the General Service and Victory Medals.
29, Grover Road, Oxhey, Herts. 427/A.

BIGGS, F. A., Private, West Riding Regiment.
Volunteering in March 1915, on completion of his training he was sent to France, where he took part in several engagements and was severely wounded on August 21st, 1918. He was invalided home, and was still in hospital in 1920. He holds the General Service and Victory Medals.
80, Ashton Road, Luton. 428.

BIGGS, G., Gunner, Royal Field Artillery.
He volunteered in April 1915, and after his training was drafted to the Dardanelles, where he took part in the Gallipoli operations. On the Evacuation of the Peninsula he was transferred to Mesopotamia, and served in the campaign against the Turks, being present at the engagements at Kut and Baghdad. After the conclusion of hostilities he returned to England, and in April 1919 was demobilised, holding the 1914–15 Star, and the General Service and Victory Medals.
29, Grover Road, Oxhey. 427/B.

BIGMORE, H. J., Private, 2/5th Sherwood Foresters.
Joining in September 1916, shortly afterwards he was drafted to France, where he took part in several engagements, including those at Passchendaele, Arras and Cambrai. He was killed in action on September 27th, 1917, and was entitled to the General Service and Victory Medals.
Ramridge End, Stopsley. 429.

BIGNELL, F. G., Private, Royal Sussex Regiment.
Joining in June 1918, on completion of his training he served at various stations on important duties with his unit. He rendered valuable service, but was not successful in obtaining his transfer overseas before the cessation of hostilities. He was demobilised in February 1919.
5, Bury Dell Lane, Park Street, near St. Albans. 430.

BIGNELL, H. A., Private, 3rd Buffs (East Kent Regiment).
He joined in January 1916, and after his training served at various stations on important transport duties, and for a time in Ireland. He rendered valuable services, but was not successful in obtaining his transfer overseas before the cessation of hostilities. He was demobilised in September 1919.
71, Liverpool Road, Watford. 432.

BILCOCK, E., Private, Machine Gun Corps.
He joined in May 1916, and in the following December was drafted to the Western Front, where he took part in the engagements at Arras, Vimy Ridge, Messines, Ypres and the Somme. On October 18th, 1918, he died of wounds received in action at Kemmel Hill, and was entitled to the General Service and Victory Medals.
Grange Lane, Lower Caldecote, Biggleswade. Z1539.

BILEY, W. H., Bombardier, Royal Field Artillery.
He volunteered in December 1915, and in the following March was drafted to Mesopotamia, where he served in the campaign against the Turks. During his service in this theatre of war he took part in the fighting on the Kut-el-Amara front, and was wounded. He finally returned to England and was demobilised in January 1920, and holds the General Service and Victory Medals.
Church Street, Wing, Bucks. 1606.

BILLING, A. F., Pioneer, Royal Engineers.
He volunteered in November 1915, and on completion of his training was drafted to France, and was present at several engagements. He was severely wounded on the Somme and invalided home, and was discharged as medically unfit for further service in January 1918.
29, Park Street, near St. Albans, Herts. 433.

BILLING, F. H., (D.C.M.) (M.M.), Private, Grenadier Guards.
He enlisted in December 1906, and in October 1914 was drafted to the Western Front, where he served at Ghent, Antwerp, Ypres, Neuve Chapelle, Festubert, Cambrai and the Somme. He was awarded the Distinguished Conduct Medal for attacking a German patrol single-handed and capturing prisoners. Later he was granted the Military Medal for conspicuous gallantry in conveying rations to a company which had been cut off by the enemy. In addition he holds the 1914 Star, and the General Service and Victory Medals, and was demobilised in March 1920.
75, Estcourt Road, Watford. X434.

BILLINGHAM, T., Rifleman, 16th King's Royal Rifle Corps.
He joined in May 1916, and having completed his training was sent to the Western Front in the following year. He took an active part in the Battles of Cambrai and on the Somme and other important engagements until the cessation of hostilities. Returning home he was demobilised in November 1919, and holds the General Service and Victory Medals.
34, Orchard Road, Wakworth, Hitchin. 1815.

BILLINGTON, A. (Miss), Special War Worker.
From June 1916 to November 1917 this lady was engaged on work of National importance at Messrs. Kent's Munition Factory, Luton. She was chiefly employed on fuse-filling, and carried out her dangerous duties with care and skill.
Upper Sundon, Dunstable. 435/B.

BILLINGTON, C., Private, East Surrey Regt.
He joined in February 1916, and in the following July was drafted to France, where he fought in the Battles of the Somme, Arras and Ypres, and was killed in action on August 10th, 1917. He was entitled to the General Service and Victory Medals.
Upper Sundon, near Dunstable. 436.

BILLINGTON, F., Private, Bedfordshire Regt.
Joining in April 1916, he was drafted in the following November to France, where he served in several engagements, including those of Bullecourt, Ypres, Cambrai and the second Battle of the Somme, where he was wounded in 1918. He was demobilised in September 1919, and holds the General Service and Victory Medals.
Upper Sundon, near Dunstable. 437.

BILLINGTON, F. R., Stoker, Royal Navy.
He was serving at the outbreak of hostilities, and in H.M.S. " Talisman " was engaged on important patrol duties in the North Sea and the Channel. He took part in several minor operations, including those off Dunkirk and Zeebrugge, and also rendered valuable services in Chinese waters. He was discharged in June 1918 in consequence of his service, and holds the 1914–15 Star, and the General Service and Victory Medals.
High Street, Flitwick. 438.

BILLINGTON, H., Gunner, R.G.A.
He joined in April 1916, and after his training was, in March of the following year, drafted to Mesopotamia. During his service in this theatre of war he took part in many engagements, including those around Kut-el-Amara and Baghdad, and suffered much from fever. He returned home and was demobilised in April 1919, and holds the General Service and Victory Medals.
Brewery Lane, Ampthill. 1526.

BILLINGTON, H., Private, Cheshire Regiment.
Joining in September 1916, he was in the same year sent to France, where he took part in many important engagements, including those of Arras, Passchendaele, Cambrai and the last Battle of Ypres. He was demobilised in January 1919, and holds the General Service and Victory Medals.
34, Camp View Road, St. Albans.　　　　439.

BILLINGTON, H. F., Gunner, R.H.A. & R.F.A.
He volunteered in December 1914, and in the following June, on the completion of his training, was drafted to France, where he served in numerous engagements, including those of Givenchy, the Somme, Arras, Ypres and Cambrai, and was gassed at Arras. He was demobilised in February 1919, and holds the 1914-15 Star, and the General Service and Victory Medals.
11, Duke Street, Luton.　　　　440—441.

BILLINGTON, J., Private, 5th Bedfordshire Regt.
He volunteered in June 1915, and in the following month was drafted to the Dardanelles, where he took part in the engagements at Suvla Bay, Anzac and in other operations. Upon the Evacuation of the Peninsula he was transferred to Egypt and did valuable work in the Canal Zone defences, and afterwards in the Palestine Campaign at Gaza, Haifa, Acre and other important engagements until the cessation of hostilities. After returning home he was demobilised in February 1919, and holds the 1914-15 Star, and the General Service and Victory Medals.
21, Windmill Street, Luton.　　　　442.

BILLINGTON, L., L/Cpl., Bedfordshire Regt.
He volunteered in August 1915, and having completed his training was drafted to France in March of the following year. While in this theatre of war he fought at the Somme, Arras, Ypres, Cambrai and in the Retreat and Advance of 1918, and often took charge in bombing raids. He came home and was demobilised in February 1919. He holds the General Service and Victory Medals.
Upper Sundon, near Dunstable.　　　　443/B.

BILLINGTON, O. (Miss), Special War Worker.
From March 1915 to November 1918 this lady was engaged on important capstan work at Messrs. Kent's Munition Factory, Luton. Throughout her period of service she discharged her responsible duties with great efficiency.
Upper Sundon, near Dunstable.　　　　435/C.

BILLINGTON, V. (Miss), Special War Worker.
For more than three years during the war this lady rendered services of a valuable nature at Messrs. Kent's Munition Works, Luton. Her duties of lacquering fuses were carried out in an efficient manner, and she received high commendation for her work.
Upper Sundon, near Dunstable.　　　　435/A.

BILLINGTON, W., Sapper, Royal Engineers.
He joined in January 1917, and immediately proceeded to France, where he was engaged on important duties with his unit, particularly in connection with road-making at Vimy Ridge, Ypres, Cambrai and on the Somme. He remained overseas until after the cessation of hostilities, and returned home to be demobilised in March 1919. He holds the General Service and Victory Medals.
Barton Cottages, Clophill, near Ampthill.　　　　1822.

BILLINGTON, W., Air Mechanic, Royal Air Force (late Royal Naval Air Service).
He volunteered in July 1915, and on completing his training was engaged for a time on important duties with his squadron. In 1917 he was drafted to France, where he rendered valuable services in the fitting of aeroplanes until after the close of hostilities, at Dunkirk and other important air-stations. Returning to England in August 1919 he did good work as a carpenter for the Royal Air Force up to his demobilisation in July 1920. He holds the General Service and Victory Medals.
Mount Pleasant, Aspley Guise.　　　　Z444/A.

BILLINGTON, W. C., Private, 7th Bedfordshire Regiment.
He was mobilised in September 1914, and immediately proceeded to France, where he took part in several engagements of importance, including that of Festubert, and was killed in action on September 28th, 1916. He was entitled to the 1914 Star, and the General Service and Victory Medals.
Mount Pleasant, Aspley Guise.　　　　Z444/B.

BINGHAM, A., Private, 1st Bedfordshire Regt.
He was mobilised in August 1914, and proceeding at once to France took part in the Retreat from Mons and in several engagements of importance, including those of the Marne, Ypres, the Somme, Arras and Cambrai. He was wounded at Hill 60 and Trones Wood. After returning home he was demobilised in February 1919, and holds the Mons Star, and the General Service and Victory Medals.
99, Boyle Street, Luton.　　　　445/A.

BIRCH, A., Private, 2nd Lincolnshire Regiment.
He was serving at the outbreak of war, and in November 1914 was drafted to France, After taking part in several early engagements he was killed in the fierce fighting at Neuve Chapelle on March 10th, 1915. He was entitled to the 1914 Star, and the General Service and Victory Medals.
61, Cardiff Road, Watford.　　　　X181.

BIRCH, G. W. (M.M.), L/Cpl., Royal Fusiliers.
He was mobilised on the outbreak of hostilities, and in the first month was in action in the Battle and Retreat from Mons. He also served in many other sectors of the Western Front, taking part in several important battles, including those of Ypres and the Somme, and was frequently wounded. He was awarded the Military Medal for conspicuous bravery and devotion to duty in the Field, and also holds the Mons Star, and the General Service and Victory Medals. He was demobilised in 1919.
52, Holywell Road, Watford.　　　　X152/C.

BIRCH, L., Corporal, Duke of Cornwall's Light Infantry.
He was mobilised at the outbreak of war, and immediately proceeded to the Western Front, where he took part in the Retreat from Mons and the Battles of Ypres and Neuve Chapelle. He was subsequently sent to Mesopotamia, and while fighting near Kut was killed in action on March 6th, 1916. He was entitled to the Mons Star, and the General Service and Victory Medals.
14, Neal Street, Watford.　　　　447/B.

BIRCH, L., Private, Duke of Cornwall's Light Infantry and Dorsetshire Regiment.
He volunteered in August 1914, and later was drafted to France, where he took part in several engagements of importance. In 1915 he was drafted to the Dardanelles, and afterwards to India, where he was killed in action on the Frontier on March 15th, 1916. He was entitled to the 1914 Star, and the General Service and Victory Medals.
38, Hagden Lane, Watford.　　　　X446.

BIRCH, W., Private, Labour Corps.
He joined in March 1915, and later in the year was drafted to France, where he rendered valuable services with his unit and took part in several engagements, including the Battle of Ypres and the Retreat and Advance of 1918. He was demobilised in December 1918, and holds the 1914-15 Star, and the General Service and Victory Medals.
8, Fearnley Street, Watford.　　　　X449.

BIRCH, W., Petty Officer, R.N.A.S.
He joined in October 1917, and on the completion of his training was engaged with his squadron on important duties. He rendered valuable services in testing seaplanes along the East Coast, but was not successful in obtaining his transfer overseas before the cessation of hostilities. He was demobilised in June 1919.
106, Villiers Road, Oxhey.　　　　448.

BIRCH, W. A., Leading Signalman, Royal Navy.
He was serving in the Navy when war was declared, and on board H.M.S. "Triad" was engaged on important duties in the North Sea, and took part in the Battle of Jutland. He was afterwards sent to Turkey, and thence to Baku, where he was taken prisoner by the Bolshevists. Released from captivity, he returned home and was demobilised in December 1919. He holds the 1914-15 Star, and the General Service and Victory Medals.
31, Church Road, Watford.　　　　X224/A.

BIRCH, W. G., (M.M.), Private, Royal Fusiliers.
He was mobilised at the outbreak of hostilities, and was immediately drafted to France, where he took part in the Retreat from Mons and was wounded. He was afterwards sent to the Dardanelles and took part in the landing and other operations there. Returning to the Western Front, he again fought in many important engagements, including those of Arras, Bullecourt and Cambrai. During his service he was awarded the Military Medal for great gallantry and devotion to duty in the Field, and also holds the Mons Star, and the General Service and Victory Medals. He was demobilised in March 1919.
14, Neal Street, Watford.　　　　447/C.

BIRD, A., Private, Buffs (East Kent Regiment).
He joined in October 1917, and after his training was engaged at various stations on important duties with his unit. He rendered valuable services in the East coastal defences, but was not successful in obtaining his transfer overseas before the cessation of hostilities. He was demobilised in September 1919.
Grange Road, Leagrave.　　　　450.

BIRD, A., Private, Royal Army Ordnance Corps and Queen's (Royal West Surrey Regiment).

He joined in October 1916, and in June of the following year was drafted to France, where he fought at Ypres and other engagements until October. He was then sent to Italy, and remained there until February 1918, when he returned to the Western Front in time for take part in many engagements in the Retreat and Advance. He was demobilised in March 1919, and holds the General Service and Victory Medals.

106, Althorpe Road, Luton. 459/A.

BIRD, A. G., Private, R.A.M.C.

He volunteered in November 1915, and in June of the following year was sent to France, where he rendered valuable services in important operations until 1919, including those of the Somme and Ypres. After the Armistice he returned home, and was demobilised in March 1919. He holds the General Service and Victory Medals.

240, North Street, Luton. 451.

BIRD, B., Private, 4th Essex Regiment.

He volunteered in September 1914, and after the completion of his training was drafted in March 1915 to Egypt. After valuable service there he was engaged in the campaign in Mesopotamia and Palestine, and took part in the engagements round Kut-el-Amara and Gaza, where he was wounded. After his return home he was demobilised in March 1919, and holds the 1914–15 Star, and the General Service and Victory Medals.

18, Winfield Street, Dunstable. 184.

BIRD, C., Private, 17th Royal Fusiliers.

He joined in January 1917, and on the conclusion of his training was drafted overseas, where he was actively engaged in many sectors of the Western Front. He fought at the Battles of Ypres and Cambrai, and during his service was severely gassed. After his return home he was demobilised in October 1919, and holds the General Service and Victory Medals.

17, Upper Heath Road, St. Albans. X452/B.

BIRD, G., Private, Royal Army Veterinary Corps.

He joined in August 1916, and on the completion of his training was drafted to Salonika, and subsequently to Italy and the Western Front. In all these fighting areas he rendered valuable services with his unit, attending to sick and wounded animals. After the Armistice he passed into Germany with the Army of Occupation. During his service he suffered much from malaria and other maladies. He returned home and was demobilised in December 1919, holding the General Service and Victory Medals.

93, Cambridge Street, Luton. 453.

BIRD, G. W., Private, R.M.L.I.

He was mobilised at the outbreak of hostilities, and was chiefly engaged in mine-sweeping in the North Sea and the Baltic. He also took part in the Battles of the Falkland Islands and Jutland, and for a time was engaged on hospital trains to and from Scotland. He was still serving in 1920, and holds the 1914–15 Star, and the General Service and Victory Medals.

64, Grantham Road, Bushey. X454.

BIRD, H., Private, 29th Middlesex Regiment.

He joined in July 1916, but during the course of his training the strain of military duties proved too severe for his health, and he was in consequence discharged in December of the same year as medically unfit for further service.

57, High Street, Houghton Regis, Dunstable. 455/B.

BIRD, H. G., Private, King's Shropshire Light Infantry.

He volunteered in October 1915, and having completed his training proceeded to the Western Front. He took part in many engagements of importance and was killed on April 20th, 1917, by shell fire while asleep in his dug-out. He was buried near Ypres. He was entitled to the General Service and Victory Medals.

20, Gloucester Road, Luton. 456.

BIRD, H. W., Private, 10th Middlesex Regiment.

He joined in 1916, and in the same year was drafted to India, where he took part in various engagements on the Frontier. He also rendered valuable services at Rawal Pindi and in various stations on the Ganges until 1919, when he came home and was demobilised in November. He holds the General Service and Victory Medals.

17, Upper Heath Road, St. Albans. X452/A.

BIRD, J., Private, York and Lancaster Regiment.

He joined in February 1917, and after his training was sent in the following September to the Western Front. He fought in several important engagements in the Retreat and Advance of 1918, and was wounded. After his return home he was demobilised in November 1919, holding the General Service and Victory Medals.

71, Lancaster Road, Hitchin. 1823/A

BIRD, J. S., Private, Norfolk Regiment.

He joined in 1916, and in the same year was drafted to the Western Front, where he took part in the Battles of the Somme, the Ancre, Arras, Ypres, Passchendaele, Cambrai, the second battle of the Somme, and other engagements until fighting ceased. In December of that year, after the Armistice was signed, he proceeded to Germany with the Army of Occupation, remaining until March 1920, when he returned home and was demobilised. He holds the General Service and Victory Medals.

Oak Road, Leagrave. 457.

BIRD, L., Private, 4th Bedfordshire Regiment.

He volunteered in May 1915, and in February of the succeeding year was drafted to the Western Front. He was wounded in action on the Somme on July 1st, 1916, and was invalided home and in hospital for three months. On his recovery he returned to France and took part in the engagement at Beaumont-Hamel, where he was severely wounded, and in consequence lost his right leg. After being again invalided home he was discharged as unfit for further service in September 1918. He holds the General Service and Victory Medals.

28, High Street, Houghton Regis, Dunstable. 458.

BIRD, L., Private, 51st Bedfordshire Regiment.

He joined in April 1918, and after the completion of his training was engaged on important duties with his unit. He was not successful in securing his transfer overseas before the cessation of hostilities, but after the Armistice went into Germany with the Army of Occupation. He returned to England in November 1919, and was demobilised in March 1920.

57, High Sreet, Houghton Regis, Dunstable. 455/A.

BIRD, P., Private, Northamptonshire Regiment.

He joined in August 1916, and in the December following was drafted to France. He took part in important engagements at the Somme, Ypres and Vimy Ridge, and was taken prisoner. He remained in captivity until the Armistice, when he was repatriated. He was finally demobilised in September 1919, and holds the General Service and Victory Medals.

106, Althorpe Road, Luton. 459/B.

BIRD, P. A., Trooper, 1st Bedfordshire Lancers.

He volunteered in June 1915, and was sent to France in the following September. He saw much fighting on the Somme Front in 1915-16, but owing to a breakdown in health was invalided home and discharged in July 1916 as medically unfit for further service. He holds the 1914–15 Star, and the General Service and Victory Medals.

3, Wright's Yard, Houghton Regis, Dunstable. 460/A.

BIRD, S. (M.M.), Private, East Surrey Regiment.

He joined in June 1917, and in December of the same year was drafted to the Western Front, where he served in many important engagements until May 1918, when he was sent to Italy. He returned to France in July after three months' service on the Italian Front, and took part in the Allied Advance and was wounded in October. He was awarded the Military Medal for distinguished gallantry on the Field, and in addition holds the General Service and Victory Medals. He was demobilised in June 1919.

Victoria Road, Leagrave. 461.

BIRD, S., Driver, Royal Field Artillery.

He joined in May 1916, and in October was drafted to Salonika, where he saw much service. He took part in many engagements on the Vardar and in the recapture of Monastir, and was in action in several operations on the Bulgarian and Rumanian fronts. In May 1919 he was sent to Egypt, and was stationed at Cairo and Alexandria until September, when he proceeded home and was demobilised. He holds the General Service and Victory Medals.

38, Henry Street, Luton. 462

BIRDSEY, H. F. Corporal, 7th Royal Warwickshire Regiment.

He volunteered in August 1915, and after a period of training proceeded to France. While in this theatre of war he took part in various engagements round Ypres, and in July 1916 was killed in action in the Battle of the Somme. He was entitled to the 1914–15 Star, and the General Service and Victory Medals.

100, Sutton Road, Watford. X158/A.

BIRDSEY, J. C., Corporal, Lincolnshire Regt.

He volunteered in November 1914, and owing to his success as an Instructor was retained to drill recruits. Later he was drafted to France, and was in action at Arras and Cambrai. In March 1918 he was wounded and taken prisoner during the German Offensive, and was held in captivity until the Armistice. He was subsequently demobilised in April 1919, and holds the General Service and Victory Medals.

8, Summer Street, Leighton Buzzard. 1270.

BIRDSEY, W. T., Sergeant-Major, 51st Bedfordshire Regiment.
He volunteered in August 1914, and in the following February was drafted to France. He took a distinguished part in the Battles of Hill 60, Ypres, the Somme, Arras and Cambrai, and was three times wounded and invalided home. He was demobilised in February 1920 after his return to England, and holds the 1914-15 Star, and the General Service and Victory Medals.
23, Beaudesert, Leighton Buzzard.   1589.

BIRKATT, G. W., Driver, Royal Engineers.
Volunteering in November 1914, he was retained on important duties until 1917, when he was sent to the Western Front. Whilst in this theatre of war he did excellent work as a Royal Engineer driver and was in action at Arras, Ypres, Cambrai, the Somme, and in many other engagements in the Retreat and Advance of 1918. He holds the General Service and Victory Medals, and was demobilised in May 1919.
" Chestnut Row," Lilley, near Luton.   463.

BISHOP, A. H., Steward, R.N., H.M.S. " Vera."
He was mobilised in August 1914, and during the whole course of the war was engaged in the North Sea on important patrol duties, and was twice blown up. He was demobilised in March 1919, and holds the 1914-15 Star, and the General Service and Victory Medals.
45, Cowper Street, Luton.   465.

BISHOP, A. J., 1st Air Mechanic, Royal Air Force (late Royal Flying Corps).
He joined in January 1916, and after his training was engaged with his squadron on highly important duties which demanded great technical skill. He rendered valuable services, but was not successful in obtaining his transfer overseas owing to physical unfitness. He was demobilised in August 1919. 44, Catherine Street, St. Albans. X464/A.

BISHOP, C., Private, Oxfordshire and Buckinghamshire Light Infantry.
He volunteered in January 1915, and the same year was sent to Mesopotamia, where he took part in many engagements, and was severely wounded at Kut in May 1916. On recovery he was sent to the Indian Frontier, where he rendered valuable service at various stations until 1920, when he returned home and was demobilised in January, holding the 1914-15 Star, and the General Service and Victory Medals.
44, Catherine Street, St. Albans.   X464/B.

BISHOP, F., A.B., Royal Navy.
He volunteered in 1915, and being unfit for active service, was engaged at Harwich on important electrical work in connection with the construction of torpedoes, which demanded a high degree of skill and accuracy. He rendered valuable services until discharged as medically unfit for further service in 1916.
21, Essex Street, Luton.   T466/B.

BISHOP, F., Private, Bedfordshire Regiment.
He volunteered in July 1915, and after completing his training was in January of the following year drafted to Egypt and Palestine. He took part in much severe fighting at Gaza and Jaffa and in Syria, and was wounded. He returned home and was demobilised in August 1919, and holds the General Service and Victory Medals.
33, Waterside, King's Langley.   X468.

BISHOP, J. W., Sapper, Royal Engineers.
He volunteered in May 1915, and on the completion of his training proceeded to the Western Front, where he took part in various engagements, including that at Cambrai. He was also engaged as an Engineer on special duties at Headquarters, and rendered valuable services. He was demobilised in May 1919, and holds the General Service and Victory Medals.
Waterside, London Colney, St. Albans.   X467.

BISNEY, E., Private, Norfolk Regiment.
He joined in May 1916, and in the same year was sent to the Western Front, where he took part in many important engagements, including those at Albert, Vimy Ridge, Messines and Ypres. In 1918 he proceeded with the Army of Occupation to Germany, and after over a year's service there returned home to be demobilised in February 1920. He holds the General Service and Victory Medals.
5, Fishery Cottages, Boxmoor.   X469/B.

BISNEY, H., Corporal, Hertfordshire Regiment.
Volunteering in December 1914, he was drafted in the following year to the Western Front, and took part in many engagements from Ypres and Festubert in 1915 down to Cambrai and the Somme in 1918. He was twice wounded and was taken prisoner in March 1918. On his release he returned home and was demobilised in February 1919. He holds the 1914-15 Star, and the General Service and Victory Medals.
5, Fishery Cottages, Boxmoor.   X469/C.

BISNEY, P., Private, Queen's (Royal West Surrey Regiment).
He joined in January 1917, and after a course of training was drafted to the Western Front. He took part in severe fighting at Bullecourt, Messines Ridge, Ypres, the Somme and Cambrai. He returned home and was demobilised in January 1919, holding the General Service and Victory Medals.
5, Fishery Cottages, Boxmoor.   X469/A.

BISNEY, W. J., Private, Queen's (Royal West Surrey Regiment).
Joining in February 1917, after his training he was drafted to Egypt. On the voyage out his vessel, the " Transylvania," was sunk, and he was drowned on May 4th, 1917. He was entitled to the General Service and Victory Medals.
6, Fishery Cottages, Boxmoor.   X470.

BLACKBURN, J. V., Private, 1st Bedfordshire Regiment.
He volunteered in May 1915, and after his training served in France and Italy. He took part in the Battles of Arras and Ypres, and was twice wounded. On August 23rd, 1918, he was killed in action at Achiet-le-Petit, and was entitled to the General Service and Victory Medals.
30, Albert Road, Luton.   481.

BLACKWELL, A., Bombardier, R.F.A.
He volunteered in January 1915, and in the following May was drafted to France, where he took part in the Battles of Ypres and Loos. Later he was transferred to Mesopotamia, and was present at the Capture of Kut and Baghdad. In February 1918 he returned to the Western Front, and served at Cambrai and Le Cateau during the Advance. After the conclusion of hostilities he returned to England and in May 1919 was demobilised, holding the 1914-15 Star, and the General Service and Victory Medals.
13, The Rookery, Watford.   X482.

BLACKWELL, A., Special War Worker.
In January 1917 this lady accepted an important position with the Navy and Army Canteen Board at the Isle of Sheppey, where she rendered valuable services until June 1919, when she relinquished her appointment. The manner in which she carried out the arduous duties allotted to her was worthy of the highest commendation.
24, Brighton Road, Watford.   483—484/E.

BLACKWELL, A. F., Private, Essex Regiment.
He joined in April 1917, and after his training was drafted to the Western Front, where he took part in numerous engagements, including the Battle of Ypres, and was wounded. He returned home and was demobilised in December 1918, and holds the General Service and Victory Medals.
24, Brighton Road, Watford.   483—484/A.

BLACKWELL, E., Member, Q.M.A.A.C.
She joined in December 1917, and was sent to France, where she served at Abbeville. Her duties, which were of a highly important nature, were carried out in a most efficient manner, and she rendered valuable services. Meeting with an accident she was sent home and discharged as medically unfit for further service in January 1920, and holds the General Service and Victory Medals.
24, Brighton Road, Watford.   483—484/D.

BLACKWELL, G. T., Private, Royal Fusiliers and Labour Corps.
He volunteered in October 1915, and after his training was drafted to France, where he was engaged on important duties. Later he returned to England, and in August 1917 was discharged in consequence of his service. He holds the General Service and Victory Medals.
60, Burr Street, Luton.   485.

BLACKWELL, H. C., Sergeant, The Cameronians (Scottish Rifles).
He volunteered in December 1914, and in the following year was drafted to the Western Front, where he took part in the Battles of Ypres, the Somme and Arras, and numerous other engagements, and was wounded. He was invalided to England and in February 1918 was discharged as medically unfit for further service, holding the 1914-15 Star, and the General Service and Victory Medals.
59, Benskin Road, Watford.   X486.

BLACKWELL, J. W., Pte., 3rd Middlesex Regt.
He volunteered in March 1915, and during his period of service overseas took part in many important engagements on the Western Front and in Salonika, including the Battles of Loos, and was wounded. He returned home and was demobilised in May 1919, and holds the General Service and Victory Medals.
24, Brighton Road, Watford.   483—484/B.

BLACKWELL, R., Special War Worker.

From January 1917, until June 1919 this lady held an important position with the Navy and Army Canteen Board at the Isle of Sheppey. During this time the manner in which she carried out her arduous duties gave entire satisfaction.
24, Brighton Road, Watford.   483—484/C.

BLADON, E. J., Private, 2nd Bedfordshire Regt.

He volunteered in August 1914, and in the following February was drafted to France, where he was killed in action at Hill 60 in May 1915. He was entitled to the 1914-15 Star and the General Service and Victory Medals.
93, St. John's Road, Boxmoor.   487/A.

BLADON, F. C., Private, 8th Devonshire Regt.

He volunteered in September 1914, and in the following year was drafted to the Western Front, where he was in action at Ypres and in numerous other engagements. On October 7th, 1916 he was killed at the Battle of the Somme, and was entitled to the 1914-15 Star, and the General Service and Victory Medals.
15, Sopwell Lane, St. Albans.   X488.

BLAKE, A., L/Corporal, Royal Sussex Regt.

He joined in February 1918, and having completed his training was sent to France in August of the same year. Whilst overseas he took part in numerous engagements, including those of Kemmel Hill and Le Cateau, and after the Armistice served with the Army of Occupation on the Rhine. He holds the General Service and Victory Medals, and was demobilised in October 1919.
14, Parker Street, Watford.   X490/B.

BLAKE, C., Sergeant, 3rd Bedfordshire Regt.

He volunteered at the outbreak of war, and in the same year was sent to the Western Front, where he served in many notable engagements. He was wounded in action at Hill 60, and on recovery fought at Ypres, the Somme, Arras and Cambrai. He was finally demobilised in June 1919, and holds the 1914 Star, and the General Service and Victory Medals.
5, Chobham Street, Luton, Bedfordshire.   491.

BLAKE, E., Corporal, R.A.S.C. (M.T.)

He joined in August 1916, and after his training served on important transport and supply duties with his unit. He rendered valuable services, but was not successful in obtaining his transfer overseas before the cessation of hostilities on account of his medical unfitness. He was demobilised in December 1919.
Tilsworth Road, Stanbridge, near Leighton Buzzard.
                    2456.

BLAKE, E., Bugler, 2nd Bedfordshire Volunteers.

Being under age for service in the Regular Army he joined the Luton Volunteers in March 1918, and rendered valuable services with his unit until after the cessation of hostilities, when he was discharged.
21, Holly Walk, Luton.   492/B.

BLAKE, F., Private, Machine Gun Corps.

He volunteered in September 1914, and in July of the following year was sent to the Dardanelles, where he took part in the landing at Suvla Bay, and in other operations in Gallipoli until the Evacuation of the Peninsula. In February 1916 he was drafted to Mesopotamia, and was wounded at Sanna-i-Yab. Later he proceeded to Palestine, where he fought in the Battles of Gaza, and was wounded at Samarra. He returned home in April 1919 and was demobilised in May, holding the 1914-15 Star, and the General Service and Victory Medals.
21, Holly Walk, Luton.   493.

BLAKE, H., Rifleman, King's Royal Rifle Corps.

He joined in July 1918, and after his training served at various stations on important duties with his unit. He gave valuable services, but was not successful in obtaining his transfer overseas before the cessation of hostilities. He was demobilised in November 1919.
21, Holly Walk, Luton.   492/A.

BLAKE, L., Private, 19th London Regiment.

He volunteered in August 1914, and in the following March was drafted to the Western Front. In May 1915 he was severely wounded near Ypres and was invalided home. On his recovery he served at various stations on important duties with his unit until March 1919, when he was demobilised. He holds the 1914-15 Star, and the General Service and Victory Medals.
14, Parker Street, Watford.   490/A.

BLAKE, W. J., Trooper, Bedfordshire Lancers.

He volunteered in November 1914, and in February of the following year was drafted to the Western Front. In 1916 he was sent to Egypt and took part in the Palestine Offensive, being present at the Battle of Gaza. The next year he proceeded to Salonika, where he served on the Vardar and in various other engagements. He returned home and was demobilised in May 1919, and holds the General Service and Victory Medals.
71, Church Street, Dunstable.   185.

BLAKIE, A., Gunner, Royal Field Artillery.

He joined in 1916, and after his training was drafted to the Western Front, He took part in the fighting in many engagements, and was gassed. He died at Poperinghe from the effects of gas-poisoning on January 2nd, 1918, and was entitled to the General Service and Victory Medals.
86, St. John's Road, Boxmoor, Herts.   X489/A.

BLANCHARD, F. W., Lieutenant, R.F.A.

He was called up from the Reserve at the outbreak of the war, and in August 1914 was drafted to France, and took part in numerous engagements, including those at Mons, Ypres and the Somme. He also served in Mesopotamia for a time. He was still serving in 1920, and holds the Mons Star, and the General Service and Victory Medals.
23, Hockliffe Road, Leighton Buzzard.   1293/B.

BLAND, B. W., Private, Machine Gun Corps.

He volunteered in July 1915, and in January of the following year was sent overseas, and fought in the Battle of the Somme and at Arras, Messines and Ypres. He was severely wounded and gassed at Passchendaele on October 18th, 1917, and taken to hospital at Etaples, where he died three days later on October 21st. He was entitled to the General Service and Victory Medals.
Meppershall Road, Shefford.   Z494/C.

BLAND, E. H., Corporal, Machine Gun Corps.

He joined in July 1916, and in the same year was sent to the Western Front, where he saw much service. He took part in the Battles of the Somme, Arras, Ypres, Albert and in various engagements in the Retreat and Advance of 1918. After the Armistice was signed he proceeded to Germany with the Army of Occupation, and was stationed on the Rhine until his return to England in August 1919, when he was demobilised. He holds the General Service and Victory Medals.
North Bridge Street, Shefford.   Z495.

BLAND, F. J., Private, 8th Leicestershire Regt.

He volunteered in November 1914, and in July of the following year was drafted to the Western Front, where he served at Festubert and Loos. He also fought in the Battle of the Somme, and was severely wounded on July 15th, 1916. After this engagement he was reported missing, and is presumed to have been killed. He was entitled to the 1914-15 Star, and the General Service and Victory Medals.
Meppershall Road, Shefford.   Z494/B.

BLAND, L. V., Trooper, Norfolk Dragoons (King's Own Royal Regiment).

He joined in January 1918, and after his training was drafted to France in the following June. During his service overseas he took part in the second Battle of Cambrai, and later volunteered to give 1½ pints of his blood for transfusion in order to save the life of a comrade. He was invalided home in September 1918, and after treatment in hospital was demobilised in the following December, holding the General Service and Victory Medals.
North Bridge Street, Shefford.   496/B.

BLAND, S., Sapper, Royal Engineers.

He volunteered in January 1915, and in February of the following year was drafted to German East Africa, where he served in many operations during that campaign. He was invalided home with malaria in June 1917, and on recovery in November was sent to Mesopotamia. He took part in several engagements, but died after some months' service from small pox at Basra on April 18th, 1918. He was entitled to the General Service and Victory Medals.
North Bridge Street, Shefford.   Z496/A.

BLAND, W. H., Private, Bedfordshire Regiment.

He joined in February 1916, and in July was drafted to the Western Front, where he took part in various engagements. He was invalided home in January 1917, owing to ill-health brought on during his service, and on recovery was transferred to the Labour Corps. He rendered valuable services on agricultural work until his demobilisation in March 1919, and holds the General Service and Victory Medals.
Meppershall Road, Shefford.   Z494.

BLEANEY, B., Private, Bedfordshire Lancers.
He volunteered in November 1914, and in the same year
was drafted to the Western Front, where he took part in
various notable engagements. He served on the Somme,
and at Arras and Ypres, and in many other battles. After
the Armistice was signed he proceeded to Germany with the
Army of Occupation, and was stationed on the Rhine until
July 1919, when he returned home and was demobilised.
He holds the 1914-15 Star, and the General Service and
Victory Medals.
73, High Street, Houghton Regis, Dunstable,   497.

BLEANEY, C., Sapper, Royal Engineers.
He joined in December 1916, and on the completion of his
training was sent to the Western Front in January of the
following year. He took part in the Battles of Arras, Ypres
(III.), Messines, Passchendaele, and numerous other engagements. After the conclusion of hostilities he returned to
England and was demobilised in March 1919, holding the
General Service and Victory Medals.
132, High Street, Houghton Regis, Dunstable.   498.

BLEANEY, W., Pte., 1/5th Bedfordshire Regt.
He volunteered in November 1914, and after his training
was drafted to Egypt in February 1916. He served in the
Offensive on Palestine with General Allenby's Forces, and
took part in the Battles of Gaza and Jaffa, and was present
at the entry into Jerusalem. He returned home and was
demobilised in March 1919, and holds the General Service
and Victory Medals.
22, King Street, Houghton Regis, Dunstable.   499.

**BLEW, H., Private, Oxfordshire and Buckingham-
shire Light Infantry.**
He volunteered in 1914, and was engaged at various stations
on important defence duties guarding the coast, railways
and munition works. He rendered valuable services, but was
not successful in obtaining his transfer overseas on account
of being over age for active service. He was discharged in
August 1918.
School Lane, Wing.   2458/B.

BLEW, W. J., Corporal, R.A.S.C.
He volunteered in October 1915, and after his training served
at various stations on important duties, including the
guarding of German prisoners. He rendered valuable services,
but was not successful in obtaining his transfer overseas
before the cessation of hostilities. Owing to the strain of
military service his health broke down, and he died on
February 19th, 1919.
School Lane, Wing.   2458/A.

BLIGH, A., Driver, Royal Engineers.
He volunteered in August 1914, and in 1917 was drafted to
Egypt. He took part in the Palestine campaign, and was
present at the engagements at Gaza, Haifa, Acre and Beyrout.
After the conclusion of hostilities he returned to England, and
in November 1919 was demobilised, holding the General
Service and Victory Medals.
99, Boyle Street, Luton.   445/B.

BLINCO, E., Sapper, Royal Engineers.
He volunteered in August 1915, and having completed his
training was drafted to Egypt in January of the following
year. While in this theatre of war he was in action at Gaza
and Jerusalem, and was engaged on making roads, wiring
trenches and building bridges. During his service overseas
he was wounded, and on the conclusion of hostilities returned
to England and was demobilised in May 1919, holding the
General Service and Victory Medals.
10, Plantation Road, Leighton Buzzard.   479.

BLINDELL, W., Corporal, Royal Engineers.
He volunteered in December 1915, and in June of the following year was drafted to the Western Front. During his service
he was engaged on important duties in the forward areas
whilst operations were in progress, and was in action on the
Somme and at Ypres, Arras, Passchendaele Ridge and
Albert. He was demobilised after his return to England
in November 1919, and holds the General Service and
Victory Medals.
6, Duke's Lane, Hitchin, Herts.   1824.

BLISS, F., Private, 6th Bedfordshire Regiment.
He volunteered in December 1915, and in May of the following year was sent overseas. He served on the Somme and
at Beaumont-Hamel and Ypres, and was taken prisoner
at Zillebeke on October 9th, 1917. He was held in captivity
in Germany until December 1918, when he was released,
and in February of the following year was demobilised. He
holds the General Service and Victory Medals.
19, High Street, Houghton Regis, Dunstable.   500.

BLISS, T. W., Private, Worcester Regiment.
He joined in March 1917, and after his training was sent to
France in April of the following year. He took part in the
heavy fighting during the Retreat and Advance, and was
killed in action near Cambrai on September 25th, 1918.
He was entitled to the General Service and Victory Medals.
8, High Street, Houghton Regis, Dunstable.   501.

**BLISS, W. S. (M.M), Trumpeter, 1st King
Edward's Horse Regiment.**
He volunteered in November 1914, and was sent to the
Western Front in the following year. Whilst in this theatre
of war he took part in many notable engagements, including
the Battles of Ypres, the Somme and Cambrai. Later he
was drafted to Italy, where he served until the termination
of hostilities. During his service overseas he was awarded
the Military Medal for distinguished gallantry in the Field,
and holds in addition the 1914-15 Star, and the General
Service and Victory Medals. He was demobilised in 1919.
45, Sotheron Road, Watford.   X502/B.

BLOOMFIELD, W. J., Corporal, R.G.A.
He joined in October 1916, and in the following April was
sent overseas. During his service in France he took part
in the Battles of Ypres, Arras, Cambrai and Albert, and in
the Advance from Amiens. After the Armistice he proceeded
to Germany with the Army of Occupation, with which he
remained until demobilised in November 1919. He holds the
General Service and Victory Medals.
1, Brickfield, Hitchin Hill, Hitchin.   1825.

BLOOR, J. A., Private, Bedfordshire Regiment.
He volunteered in November 1914, and in the following year
was drafted to France, where he served at Ypres, Festubert,
Loos, Givenchy and on the Somme, where he was wounded.
He was invalided home, and after treatment in hospital was
discharged in February 1918 as medically unfit for further
service. He holds the 1914-15 Star, and the General Service
and Victory Medals.
17, Weymouth Street, Apsley.   X503.

BLOXAM, H., Private, 1st Hertfordshire Regt.
He was mobilised at the outbreak of war, and in November
1914 was drafted to the Western Front, where he took part
in the Battle of Ypres and numerous other engagements.
Later, his health having broken down through the strain of
active service, he was invalided home in 1915, and died
four years later on May 22nd, 1919. He was entitled to the
1914 Star, and the General Service and Victory Medals.
6, Radlett Road, Watford.   X504.

BLOXHAM, J., Sergeant, Bedfordshire Regt.
He was mobilised at the outbreak of war, and was sent to
France, where he took a prominent part in several important
engagements, including those of Mons, Ypres, the Somme
and Arras. During his service overseas he was wounded and
gassed, and also contracted fever, but continued to serve on
the Western Front until August 1919, when he returned to
England and was demobilised, holding the Mons Star, and
the General Service and Victory Medals.
8, Saint Michael's Mount, Hitchin.   1608.

BLUNDEN, A. G., Gunner, Royal Field Artillery.
He volunteered in January 1915, and in the same year was
sent to the Western Front. During his service overseas he
took part in the Battles of Arras, Ypres, Passchendaele, and
Cambrai, and was wounded three times. He was demobilised in February 1919, and holds the General Service and
Victory Medals.
28, Lammas Road, Watford.   X505/A.

**BOARD, H., Pte., 1/5th Bedfordshire Regiment
and M.G.C.; and Rifleman, Rifle Brigade.**
He was serving at the outbreak of war, having joined the
Army in May 1914, and was drafted to the Western Front
in April 1916. He took part in the Battles of the Somme,
Ypres (III.), and St. Quentin, and also served at Nieuport,
and was wounded. He was invalided home in October
1918, and was demobilised in January 1919, holding the
General Service and Victory Medals.
35, Winston Road, Luton.   506.

**BOATMAN, F. C., Corporal, Bedfordshire Regt.
(transferred Royal Army Pay Corps.)**
He joined in March 1916, and after his training served at
various stations on important clerical duties. He did excellent work, but owing to being medically unfit was unable
to obtain a transfer abroad before the termination of the war.
He was demobilised in August 1919.
Glencoe, Shakespeare Road, Harpenden.   507.

BODDY, C., Private, Queen's Own (Royal West Kent Regiment).
He volunteered in November 1915, and after his training was drafted to Salonika, where he took part in many important engagements on the Balkan fronts. He was wounded during his service and invalided to hospital, and in April 1918 was sent home and discharged as medically unfit for further military duty. He holds the General Service and Victory Medals.
62, Acme Road, North Watford. X508.

BODSWORTH, E., Pte., 8th Bedfordshire Regt.
He joined in May 1916, and after a brief training was sent to France, where he took part in the heavy fighting on the Somme. He was killed in action on September 15th, 1916, and was entitled to the General Service and Victory Medals.
Leighton Street, Woburn. Z509/B.

BODSWORTH, F. C., Private, 4/7th East Surrey Regiment.
He volunteered in September 1914, and in the same year was sent overseas. He served in various engagements in France and was wounded three times and gassed. Later he was taken prisoner and held in captivity in Germany for 2½ years. After the Armistice he was released and returned home and was demobilised in February 1919. He holds the 1914 Star, and the General Service and Victory Medals.
Leighton Street, Woburn, Bedfordshire. Z509/C.

BODSWORTH, F. P., Sapper, Royal Engineers.
He volunteered in September 1914, and on the completion of his training was drafted to Gallipoli, where he took part in the landing at Suvla Bay and in other operations, until the Evacuation of the Peninsula. He was sent home and discharged in consequence of his service in March 1916. He holds the 1914-15 Star, and the General Service and Victory Medals.
24, Dane Road, Luton. 510.

BODSWORTH, J. W., Private, 1/5th Bedfordshire Regiment.
He volunteered in September 1914, and in January of the following year was drafted to the Western Front. Whilst in this theatre of war he took part in various engagements. In the latter part of 1915 he was sent to Egypt, and served in the Palestine Offensive, being in action at Gaza and Haïfa. During his service overseas he was wounded, and after the conclusion of hostilities returned to England and was demobilised in June 1919. He holds the 1914-15 Star, and the General Service and Victory Medals.
Leighton Street, Woburn. Z509/A.

BOLT, D. V., Private, 19th Welch Regiment.
He joined in June 1916, and in February of the following year was sent to the Western Front, where he saw much service, and took part in the Battles of Ypres, Armentières, Passchendaele Ridge, and the Somme. He was demobilised in February 1919, and holds the General Service and Victory Medals.
High Street, Flitwich, Ampthill. 511.

BOLTON, A., Private, 11th Norfolk Regiment.
He joined in 1916, and after his training served at various stations on important duties with his unit. He rendered valuable services on agricultural work for two years, and was discharged in consequence of his service in October 1918.
34, Ridgway Road, Luton. 512.

BOLTON, A. W., Company Sergeant-Major, Duke of Cornwall's Light Infantry.
He was mobilised in August 1914, and served at various stations on important duties with his unit until May 1918, when he was drafted to the Western Front, and took part in heavy fighting at Cambrai and Arras. He returned home and was demobilised in January 1919, and holds the General Service and Victory Medals.
28, St. Mary's Road, Watford. X513.

BOLTON, A. W., Gunner, R.F.A.
He volunteered in May 1915, and in the same year was sent to France. He took an important part in numerous engagements, including those of Ypres, the Somme and Cambrai, and was gassed. He holds the 1914-15 Star, and the General Service and Victory Medals, and was demobilised in February 1919. Littleworth Wing, near Leighton Buzzard. 514.

BOLTON, B., Corporal, Australian Imperial Forces.
He volunteered in September 1914, and after having completed his training was drafted to the Dardanelles, where he took part in the Gallipoli campaign. On the Evacuation of the Peninsula he was transferred to the Western Front, and was in action on the Somme and at Arras and Ypres, and was twice wounded. He holds the 1914-15 Star, and the General Service and Victory Medals, and was demobilised in 1918.
Vicarage Lane, Wing, near Leighton Buzzard. 515.

BOLTON, J., Gunner, Royal Garrison Artillery.
He joined in June 1916, and in the following September was sent to the Western Front, where he served in numerous important engagements. After the cessation of hostilities he returned home and was demobilised in March 1919. He holds the General Service and Victory Medals.
Rothschild Road, Wing. 1604.

BOLTON, J., Private, Oxfordshire and Buckinghamshire Light Infantry.
Volunteering in December 1914, he was drafted to France in the following March, and whilst in this theatre of war took part in the fighting at Ypres and Loos. In January 1916 he was sent to Salonika, and during his service on the Balkan front was in action in the Vardar and the Struma sectors. After the cessation of hostilities he returned home and was eventually demobilised in March 1919. He holds the 1914-15 Star, and the General Service and Victory Medals.
7, Lily Crescent, Leighton Road, Wing. 1602.

BONAR, W. Y., Sapper, Royal Engineers.
He joined in 1916, and in the same year proceeded to the Western Front. During his service overseas he took part in many important engagements, including those at Arras, Ypres and the Somme, and was wounded. He returned home and was demobilised in 1919, and holds the General Service and Victory Medals.
8, Lower Paxton Road, St. Albans. X517.

BONE, C. G, Private, 15th West Yorkshire Regt.
He joined in May 1917, and after his training was drafted in the same year to the Western Front, where he took part in severe fighting at Arras, Ypres, Passchendaele, Cambrai, the Somme and the Aisne. He was demobilised in February 1919, and holds the General Service and Victory Medals.
29, Liverpool Road, Watford. X518.

BONE, E. J., Sergeant, Bedfordshire Regiment.
He volunteered in August 1914, and was immediately afterwards sent to the Western Front, where he took part in numerous engagements, including those at Mons, Ypres, Hill 60 and the Somme, and was three times wounded. He was still serving in 1920, and holds the Mons Star, and the General Service and Victory Medals.
222, Chester Road, Watford. X519.

BONE, F., Private, Bedfordshire Regiment.
He volunteered in August 1914, and in the following year was drafted to the Western Front, where he took part in many engagements, including those at Arras, Vimy Ridge and Messines. He was killed in action at Ypres on July 26th, 1917, and was entitled to the 1914-15 Star, and the General Service and Victory Medals.
1, Queen's Place, Hemel Hempstead. X420/B.

BONE, H. J., Gunner, Royal Marine Artillery.
Joining in October 1916, on completion of his training he was drafted to France, where he took part in the fighting on the Somme. Later he was wounded at Ostend on October 17th, 1918. He was demobilised in August 1919, and holds the General Service and Victory Medals.
29, Brighton Road, Watford. X521.

BONE, N., Private, R.A.V.C.; and Gunner, R.F.A.
He volunteered in April 1915, and was the same year drafted to France, where he served on important duties at various stations attending to wounded horses. He was demobilised in January 1919, and holds the 1914-15 Star, and the General Service and Victory Medals.
59, Lower Paddock Road, Oxhey. X522.

BONESS, G. H., Private, 1st Bedfordshire Regt.
Volunteering in December 1914, he proceeded to the Western Front in the following year, and took a prominent part in various engagements, including those at Ypres, Festubert, Loos and Dickebusch. He was killed in action in the heavy fighting on the Somme on July 27th, 1916, and was entitled to the 1914-15 Star, and the General Service and Victory Medals.
Anchor Yard, Sun Street, Biggleswade. Z1265.

BONEFIELD, J., Sapper, Royal Engineers.
He volunteered in January 1915, and was drafted to France in the following year. While in this theatre of war he rendered valuable services in several important engagements. Later he was sent to Salonica, where he saw much fighting, and after the Armistice returned home and was demobilised in March 1919, holding the General Service and Victory Medals.
76, Rushby Walk, Letchworth. 9101.

BONHAM, A., Sergeant, York and Lancaster Regiment.
He volunteered in September 1914, and in January of the following year was drafted to the Western Front, where he took part in the Battles of Loos and the Somme, and was wounded and invalided home. On his recovery he was sent to Italy, where he was again in action on the Piave Front. He returned home and was demobilised in March 1919, holding the 1914–15 Star, and the General Service and Victory Medals.
80, Old Road, Linslade, near Leighton Buzzard. 2459/B.

BONHAM, H., Rifleman, King's Royal Rifle Corps.
He volunteered in December 1915, and in July of the following year proceeded to Salonica, where he was engaged on the Vardar Front. Having contracted malaria he was invalided home, but on his recovery six months later he was sent to France, where he took part in various engagements up to the close of hostilities. After serving with the Army of Occupation in Germany, he returned home and was demobilised in September 1919. He holds the General Service and Victory Medals.
80, Old Road, Linslade, near Leighton Buzzard. 2459/A.

BONNER, E., Private, Labour Corps.
He joined in March 1916, and after training served at various stations on important duties with his unit. He did excellent work, but was not successful in obtaining his transfer overseas before the cessation of hostilities. He was demobilised in September 1918.
50, Edward Street, Dunstable. 188.

BONNER, H. J., Private, Bedfordshire Regt.
He volunteered in May 1915, and in the same year was drafted to Egypt and thence to Palestine, where he took part in the engagements at Gaza and Jaffa, and was wounded. After the cessation of hostilities he returned to England, and was demobilised in February 1919, holding the 1914–15 Star, and the General Service and Victory Medals.
Sandon Road, Harlington, near Dunstable. 523.

BONNER, J., Private, Norfolk Regiment.
He joined in August 1917, and was the following December drafted to France, where he took part in much heavy fighting on the Somme and at Cambrai, and was severely wounded. He was invalided home and discharged as medically unfit for further service in June 1918. He holds the General Service and Victory Medals.
88, Ash Road, Luton. 524/B.

BONNER, J. E., Private, Bedfordshire Regiment and Machine Gun Corps.
He was mobilised at the outbreak of war and in the following July was drafted to Gallipoli, where he took part in the engagements at Suvla Bay. He was later sent to Egypt and thence to Palestine, and served at Gaza, afterwards proceeding to Mesopotamia and India, being once wounded. He returned to England and was demobilised in April 1919, holding the 1914–15 Star, and the General Service and Victory Medals.
Sandon Road, Harlington, near Dunstable. 525.

BONNER, S. M., Private, 6th Bedfordshire Regt.
He joined in October 1916, and in the same year was drafted to the Western Front, where he took part in numerous engagements, including those on the Somme and at Arras. He was killed in action at the latter place on April 12th, 1917, and was entitled to the General Service and Victory Medals.
2, Coventry Cottages, Westoning, Ampthill. 1541/A.

BONNER, T. H., Private, 17th (Duke of Cambridge's Own) Lancers.
He volunteered in April 1915, and in the same year was drafted to the Western Front, where he took part in numerous engagements, including those at Festubert, Albert, Loos, Vimy Ridge and the Somme. He was demobilised in March 1919, and holds the 1914–15 Star, and the General Service and Victory Medals.
2, Coventry Cottages, Westoning, Ampthill. 1541/B.

BONNER, W., L/Corporal, 5th Royal Fusiliers.
He joined in August 1917, and on the completion of his training was drafted to France, where he took part in the fighting on the Somme and at Bapaume, Cambrai and St. Quentin, and was twice wounded. He was demobilised in February 1919, and holds the General Service and Victory Medals.
88, Ash Road, Luton. 524/A.

BOON, F., Private, Bedfordshire Regiment.
He was serving at the outbreak of war, and was drafted to Egypt, where he took part in numerous engagements. On October 17th, 1918, he died of wounds received in action, and was entitled to the 1914–15 Star, and the General Service and Victory Medals.
28, St. Anne's Road, Luton. 526/B.

BOON, T. F., Pte., Loyal North Lancashire Regt.
He joined in January 1916, and on the completion of his training was drafted to the Western Front, where he took part in much heavy fighting at Arras and Cambrai, and was wounded. He was demobilised in February 1919, and holds the General Service and Victory Medals.
2, St. Peter's Cottages, New Town, Hatfield. 527.

BOON, W. E., Private, Bedfordshire Regiment.
He volunteered in March 1915, and was in the same year drafted to the Western Front, where he took part in the heavy fighting at Loos (where he was wounded), on the Somme and at Arras, Ypres and Cambrai. In April 1918 he was taken prisoner and sent to Germany, where he suffered many privations during his captivity. After the Armistice he was repatriated, and in February 1919 was demobilised, holding the 1914–15 Star, and the General Service and Victory Medals.
High Street, Woburn Sands, Beds. 528.

BOON, W. J., Private, Bedfordshire Regiment.
He was serving at the outbreak of war, and was speedily drafted to the Western Front, where he took part in much heavy fighting, and was killed in action at Festubert on May 17th, 1915. He was entitled to the 1914 Star, and the General Service and Victory Medals.
28, St. Anne's Road, Luton. 526/A.

BOONE, J., Private, Royal Defence Corps.
He joined in March 1916, and was stationed at various places on important duties with his unit on the East Coast. He was also for a time employed on guarding German prisoners. He rendered valuable services until he was discharged in September 1918.
121, West Street, Dunstable. 529/B.

BOONE, W. J., Private, Queen's (Royal West Surrey Regiment).
He joined in August 1918, on attaining military age, and on the completion of his training was drafted overseas in December 1918. He served with the Army of Occupation at Cologne until October 1919, when he returned home and was demobilised.
121, West Street, Dunstable. 529/A.

BORLEY, C., Private, Suffolk Regiment.
He was mobilised at the outbreak of war, and was drafted overseas in July 1915. He served at the Dardanelles, and was wounded at Suvla Bay and invalided home. Later he was discharged as medically unfit for further service in March 1916. He holds the 1914–15 Star, and the General Service and Victory Medals.
32, Frogmore, near St. Albans. X530.

BOSLEY, E., Sapper, Royal Engineers.
He volunteered in 1915, and was in the same year drafted to France, where he took part in much heavy fighting at Loos, Arras and Cambrai. He was afterwards transferred to Egypt, and took part in the Palestine campaign, and later to Mesopotamia, where he served in the operations against the Turks. During his service overseas he was once wounded, and after the cessation of hostilities returned home and was demobilised in February 1919. He holds the 1914–15 Star, and the General Service and Victory Medals.
1, Park Street, Hatfield, Herts. X531B—X532/B.

BOSLEY, H., C.Q.M.S., Norfolk Regiment.
He joined in April 1916, and on the completion of his training served in Ireland on important duties as Machine Gun Instructor with his unit. He rendered valuable services, but was unsuccessful in obtaining his transfer overseas prior to the cessation of hostilities. He was demobilised in November 1919.
91, Norfolk Road, Rickmansworth. X533/A.

BOSLEY, S., Private, Manchester Regiment.
He volunteered in September 1914, and on the completion of his training was drafted to the Western Front, where he took part in heavy fighting at Ypres, Arras, the Somme, Bullecourt and Passchendaele. Later he proceeded to Italy, and fought in the engagements on the Piave. He was demobilised in March 1919, and holds the General Service and Victory Medals.
91, Norfolk Road, Rickmansworth. X533/B.

BOSTON, C. H., Corporal, 9th East Surrey Regt.
Volunteering in 1914, on the completion of his training he was drafted to the Western Front in 1915, and was in action at Givenchy and Loos in the same year. In 1916 he served in the heavy fighting on the Somme, and was killed in action at Delville Wood on September 3rd. He was entitled to the 1914–15 Star, and the General Service and Victory Medals.
Railway Cottages, Potton. Z1285/A.

BOTSFORD, A. A., Private, 4th Yorkshire Regt.
Joining in September 1916, in the following January he proceeded to France, where he took part in many engagements, including those at Arras, Bullecourt, Ypres and on the Somme. He was wounded in 1918 and invalided home, and in April 1919 was demobilised, holding the General Service and Victory Medals.
25, Clarence Road, Leighton Buzzard.   1290.

BOTSFORD, H., Private, Royal Sussex Regt.
Volunteering in 1914, he was drafted in the following year to the Western Front and saw much service. He took part in the engagements at Hill 60, the Somme, Arras, Ypres, Cambrai and Givenchy, and during this period suffered from shell-shock. He was eventually demobilised in 1919, and holds the 1914–15 Star, and the General Service and Victory Medals.
6, Union Street, Leighton Buzzard.   1268.

BOTTOMS, B. J., Private, Norfolk Regiment.
He joined in June 1918, and on the completion of his training served in Ireland on important duties with his unit. He rendered valuable services, but was not successful in obtaining his transfer to a fighting Front prior to the cessation of hostilities. He was still serving in 1920.
Church Court, Lidlington, Beds.   Z534A—535/A.

BOTTOMS, F. G., Private, R.A.S.C. (M.T.)
He joined in May 1916, and in the following year was drafted to India. He was shortly afterwards sent to Mesopotamia, where he was in action at Kut and Baghdad. He also served in Russia, and returned to England and was demobilised in March 1919. He holds the General Service and Victory Medals.
77, Cowper Street, Luton.   536.

BOTTOMS, H., Sergeant, Bedfordshire Regiment.
He volunteered in January 1915, and in the same year was sent to the Dardanelles and took part in the landing at Suvla Bay, and in other operations in Gallipoli. After the Evacuation of the Peninsula he was drafted to Egypt and served in the Palestine Campaign, being present at the Battles of Gaza and the entry into Jerusalem. After the conclusion of hostilities he returned to England, and was subsequently demobilised in April 1919. He holds the 1914–15 Star, and the General Service and Victory Medals.
10, Road Houses, Silsoe, Beds.   1826.

BOTTOMS, W. C., Private, Norfolk Regiment.
He joined in May 1918, and on the completion of his training was drafted to Germany in February 1919. He served with the Army of Occupation at Coblentz and Cologne until May 1920, when he returned to England and was demobilised.
Church Court, Lidlington.   Z535B—Z534/B.

BOUGHTON, F., Sapper, Royal Engineers.
He joined in 1916, and on the completion of his training served at Richborough on important duties in connection with the Train Ferry to France. He rendered valuable services, but was unsuccessful in obtaining his transfer overseas, and was demobilised in 1919.
19, Pinner Road, Oxhey.   X537.

BOULTWOOD, G., Corporal, R.A.S.C.
He joined in 1917, and was in the same year drafted to the Western Front, where he served at Ypres, the Somme and the Aisne during much heavy fighting. He was demobilised in 1919, and holds the General Service and Victory Medals.
51, Lower Paddock Road, Oxhey.   X538.

BOURNE, C. T., L/Corporal, Bedfordshire Regt.
He joined in February 1916, and was in the same year drafted to the Western Front, where he took part in the heavy fighting at Ypres, Cambrai and the Somme, and was killed in action at Arras on September 1st, 1918. He was entitled to the General Service and Victory Medals.
124, Estcourt Road, Watford.   X539/A.

BOURNE, G., Pioneer, Royal Engineers.
He volunteered in August 1915, and was in the same year drafted to the Western Front, where he took part in much heavy fighting at Arras and on the Aisne. For a time he was engaged on special duties in connection with road construction. He was demobilised in January 1919, and holds the 1914–15 Star, and the General Service and Victory Medals.
39, Fishpool Street, St. Albans.   X540/B.

BOURNE, G. W., Rifleman, King's Royal Rifle Corps.
He joined in July 1917, and on the completion of his training was drafted to the Western Front, where he took part in much fierce fighting at Ypres, Cambrai, and on the Marne and the Aisne. He was demobilised in December 1919, and holds the General Service and Victory Medals.
39, Fishpool Street, St. Albans.   X540/A.

BOURNE, L. W., Wireless Operator, Royal Navy.
He joined in February 1918, and on the completion of his training served at various stations on special and important duties with his unit. He rendered valuable services, but was unsuccessful in obtaining his transfer overseas before the cessation of hostilities. He was demobilised in January 1919.
124, Estcourt Road, Watford.   X539/B.

BOURNE, T., Private, Bedfordshire Regiment.
He volunteered in January 1915, and was in the same year drafted to France, where he took part in the heavy fighting at Hill 60 and Verdun, and was killed in action on February 22nd, 1916. He was entitled to the 1914–15 Star, and the General Service and Victory Medals.
53, Sopwell Lane, St. Albans.   X541/B.

BOWDEN, A. H., Private, Hertfordshire Regt.
He volunteered in November 1914, and on the completion of his training was drafted to France, where he took part in numerous engagements of importance, and was severely wounded at Arras. He was invalided home, and in June 1917 was discharged as medically unfit for further service. He holds the General Service and Victory Medals.
3, Coltswood Road, Harpenden.   542/B.

BOWDEN, H. E., Private, R.A.S.C.
He joined in November 1917, and was speedily drafted to France. He rendered valuable transport service at Ypres, Arras and the Somme, where he was gassed in 1918. He was demobilised in November 1919 after returning home, and holds the General Service and Victory Medals.
3, Coltswood Road, Harpenden.   542/A.

BOWDEN, S. A., Private, Queen's Own (Royal West Kent Regiment).
He volunteered in November 1915, and in the following July was sent to France, where he took part in the Battles of the Somme and Arras, and was killed in action at the third Battle of Ypres, on August 9th, 1917. He was entitled to the General Service and Victory Medals.
10, St. Peter's Road, Dunstable.   543.

BOWER, A., Private, Oxfordshire and Buckinghshire Light Infantry.
Volunteering in October 1914, he served on the Western Front for nearly three years' During this time he took part in many important engagements, including those of the Somme, Arras and Cambrai, and was wounded. He also fought in the Retreat and Advance of 1918, and after the Armistice proceeded to Germany, where in 1920 he was still serving with the Army of Occupation. He holds the General Service and Victory Medals.
35, Vale Road, Bushey.   X544/B.

BOWER, H. J., Private, Royal Defence Corps.
An ex-soldier, who had previously seen service in India and in the South African Campaign, he volunteered in December 1914. Throughout the war he was engaged on defence and guard duties of an important nature, which he carried out at various stations in England. He was demobilised in February 1919.
35, Vale Road, Bushey.   X544/A.

BOWERS, B. W., Sergeant, 5th Bedfordshire Regt.
He volunteered at the outbreak of war, and in September was sent to the Western Front, where he served at La Bassée, Festubert, Loos, the Somme, Arras and Ypres. He also took part in the Retreat and Advance of 1918. In February of the following year he was demobilised, and holds the 1914 Star, and the General Service and Victory Medals.
10, Manchester Place, Dunstable.   182.

BOWLER, F. S., Private, Labour Corps.
He volunteered in May 1915, and after being engaged on important duties was drafted to France, where he rendered valuable service in the fighting in the Somme area and was severely wounded at Albert. He was invalided home, and on recovery was sent to Ireland on special duties until demobilised in April 1919. He holds the General Service and Victory Medals.
Mount Pleasant, Aspley Guise.   Z545.

BOWLES, A. C., Private, Bedfordshire Lancers.
He was serving at the outbreak of hostilities, and after the completion of his training was engaged at various stations on important duties with his unit. Owing to ill-health he was unable to secure his transfer to a fighting front, and was discharged in August 1916 as time-expired. He died six months later.
41, Alexandra Terrace, Biggleswade.   Z1262/A.

BOWLES, H., Private, 10th Hampshire Regiment.
He volunteered in December 1914, and having completed his training was sent to Egypt in the following September. While in this theatre of war he saw much service, and also on the Vardar front at Salonica. In 1918 he served in Russia, and afterwards returned home to be demobilised in April 1919. He holds the 1914-15 Star, and the General Service and Victory Medals.
56, Tavistock Street, Luton.   546/A.

BOWLES, S., Private, 5th Bedfordshire Regt.
He volunteered in August 1914, and after being engaged for some time on important duties with his unit, proceeded in 1916 to Egypt, where he rendered valuable services in the defence of the Canal Zone and in several other engagements. He afterwards joined the expedition through Palestine, and fought at Gaza, Haifa and Acre until the close of hostilities. Returning home he was demobilised in March 1919, and holds the General Service and Victory Medals.
56, Tavistock Street, Luton.   546/B.

BOWLEY, J. A., Private, 8th Lincolnshire Regt.
He volunteered soon after the outbreak of war and was speedily drafted to France. He took part in the Battles of La Bassée, Ypres and Loos, where he was taken prisoner in September 1915. He suffered many privations during his long captivity, and after being repatriated in November 1918, was demobilised in the following March. He holds the 1914 Star, and the General Service and Victory Medals.
2, Saulbury Road, Linslade.   1583.

BOWLEY, R., Private, R.A.S.C. (M.T.)
He joined in March 1917, and in the following May was drafted to France, where he rendered valuable service for two years. He was stationed at Rouen, and was chiefly engaged on important transport duties and in repairing motor vehicles. He was demobilised in May 1919, and holds the General Service and Victory Medals.
13, Pinner Road, Oxhey.   X547.

BOWTELL, E., Rifleman, 2nd Rifle Brigade.
He volunteered in September 1914, and in February of the following year was drafted to the Western Front. He took part in the heavy fighting at Ypres and the Somme and numerous later engagements, and was twice severely wounded and invalided home to hospital. After over four years' service in France he returned to England and was demobilised in March 1919, holding the 1914-15 Star, and the General Service and Victory Medals.
5, Sotheron Road, Watford.   X548/A.

BOWYER, A. F., Private, Lancashire Fusiliers.
He joined in 1916, and in the same year, after completing his training, was drafted to the Western Front. In the course of his service overseas he was in action at Loos, Albert, Vimy Ridge, and other important engagements until fighting ceased. He was demobilised in February 1919, and holds the General Service and Victory Medals.
70, Villiers Road, Oxhey.   X549.

BOXFORD, W. S., A/Bombardier, R.F.A.
He joined in September 1916, and after his training was drafted to the Western Front, where he took part in various engagements, including those at Bapaume and St. Quentin. He also served in the Retreat and Advance of 1918. He was demobilised in October 1919, and holds the General Service and Victory Medals.
Potters Bar, Middlesex.   550.

BOYCE, W. J., Corporal, Bedfordshire Regiment.
He volunteered in August 1914, and in the following month was drafted to the Western Front, where he took part in the severe fighting at the Battle of La Bassée, Loos, the Somme, Ypres, Cambrai and during the Retreat and Advance of 1918, and was wounded. He was demobilised in March 1919, and holds the 1914 Star, and the General Service and Victory Medals.
25, Mill Road, Leighton Buzzard.   2461/A.

BOZIER, A. G. W., Private, Bedfordshire Regt.
Volunteering in September 1914, he was drafted to the Western Front on the completion of his training. He fought with distinction in the Battle of Ypres and was severely wounded. After protracted hospital treatment he was discharged in January 1916 as totally unfit for further service. He holds the 1914-15 Star, and the General Service and Victory Medals.
59, May Street, Luton.   553.

BOZIER, P. C., Private, 3rd King's Shropshire Light Infantry and Welch Regiment.
He volunteered in 1914, and in the following year was drafted to France. He subsequently took part in numerous important engagements, including those at Ypres, the Somme and Cambrai, and was gassed during his service in France. In March 1919 he was demobilised, and holds the 1914-15 Star, and the General Service and Victory Medals.
Bury Green, near Wheathampstead.   551/A.

BOZIER, V., Private, Middlesex Regiment.
He joined in March 1917, and after his training did valuable work at various places, where he was principally engaged in important agricultural duties. He was unsuccessful, owing to medical reasons, in obtaining a transfer overseas while hostilities lasted, and was demobilised in March 1919 after exactly two years' service.
157, High Street, Houghton Regis, Dunstable.   552.

BRACEY, A. W., Private, Bedfordshire Regt.
He volunteered in August 1914, and at the conclusion of his training was drafted overseas in July 1915. He fought in many engagements on the Arras and Somme Fronts, and was twice wounded in 1916. On his recovery he took part in the Battle of Vimy Ridge, and was there captured in April 1917. Being repatriated after the cessation of hostilities he was demobilised in March 1919, holding the 1914-15 Star, and the General Service and Victory Medals.
6, St. Michael's Mount, Walsworth Road, Hitchin.   1609/A.

BRACEY, F. (D.C.M.), Corporal, 24th Royal Fusiliers.
He was mobilised at the outbreak of hostilities, and immediately proceeded to the Western Front. While overseas he rendered valuable services in various engagements until hostilities ceased, including those of Mons, Ypres, Armentières, Arras and the Somme, where he was wounded. He came home and was demobilised in June 1919, holding the Mons Star, and the General Service and Victory Medals.
6, St. Michael's Mount, Walsworth Road, Hitchin.   1609/B.

BRACEY, R., Private, Bedfordshire Regiment.
He joined in May 1916, and after he had finished his training served at various depôts on important guard and coastal defence duties with his unit. He was medically unfit for foreign service, but did excellent work until he was finally demobilised in April 1919.
26, Longmire Road, St. Albans.   X554.

BRACKLEY, H., Private, Royal Air Force.
He joined in May 1918, and after his training served at various stations on important duties, which demanded a high degree of technical skill. He was chiefly engaged as an aeroplane rigger and rendered valuable services, but was not successful in obtaining his transfer overseas before the termination of the war. He was demobilised in February 1919. 31, Weymouth Street, Apsley.   X555.

BRADBURY, J. E., Bugler, R.M.L.I.
He joined the Royal Marines in November 1917, and after a period of training was posted to H.M.S. "Galatea." Whilst in this vessel he was engaged on important and dangerous duties with the Grand Fleet in the North Sea until hostilities ceased. In 1920 he was still serving, and holds the General Service and Victory Medals.
42, Chatsworth Road, Luton.   556.

BRADBURY, T. H., Cpl., 9th Middlesex Regt.
He volunteered in August 1914, and in the same year was sent to India and served on the Frontier. In 1917 he was transferred to Mesopotamia and thence to Palestine, and was engaged at Gaza. He contracted malaria, and later returned to India in 1918. He came home and was demobilised in 1919, and holds the 1914-15 Star, and the General Service and Victory Medals.
70, Holywell Road, Watford.   X557.

BRADER, P., 1st Air Mechanic, R.A.F.
He joined in July 1916, and after a period of training served with his unit at various stations on important duties which demanded a high degree of technical knowledge and skill. He rendered valuable services, but was not successful in obtaining a transfer overseas before the termination of the war. He was demobilised in February 1919.
15, Portland Street, St. Albans.   558.

BRADFORD, F. W., Private, 9th North Staffordshire Regiment.
Volunteering in October 1914, he was retained for a time on important duties, and proceeded to the Western Front in February 1916. He served at Loos and Gommecourt, and was wounded at Lens. After his recovery he took part in other important engagements, until the termination of the war. He was demobilised in January 1919 after returning home, and holds the General Service and Victory Medals.
51, Cavendish Road, St. Albans.   X559.

BRADFORD, P. J., Private, Bedfordshire Regt.
He volunteered in August 1914, and in July of the following year was sent to the Western Front, where he was in action at Loos and on the Somme. He was invalided home in March 1916, owing to illness contracted in the trenches, and did not return to France until July of the succeeding year. He then took part in the Battles of Ypres, Cambrai, Albert and other important engagements until the cessation of hostilities. He was demobilised in February 1919, and holds the 1914-15 Star, and the General Service and Victory Medals.
Mount Pleasant, Aspley Guise.   Z560/A.

BRADSHAW, A. E., Private, 12th East Surrey Regiment.

Joining in May 1918, he was sent to the Western Front two months later and took part in many engagements in the Advance of that year, including those of Cambrai and Ypres. He returned to England in February 1919, when he was demobilised, and holds the General Service and Victory Medals.

15, Jubilee Street, Luton.   561/B.

BRADSHAW, F., Gunner, Royal Marine Artillery, H.M.S. "Ajax."

He joined in September 1917, and was posted to H.M.S. "Ajax," which vessel was engaged on important duties in the North Sea and off the coast of Russia. In October 1918 he was injured in an accident whilst at Scapa Flow, but after his recovery was sent to the Black Sea, where he was still serving in 1920. He holds the General Service and Victory Medals.

15, Jubilee Street, Luton.   561/A.

BRAMBLEBY, F. J., Cpl., Duke of Cornwall's Light Infantry.

He joined in 1917, and after his training was drafted in November of the following year to India, where he was engaged on various important duties. He was later transferred to Russia and afterwards to Salonika. He returned home and was demobilised in November 1919, and holds the General Service and Victory Medals.

5, Wharf Lane, Rickmansworth.   X5446/B.

BRAMFORD, W., Cpl., 18th Canadian Infantry.

He volunteered in September 1914, and in the following January was drafted to France. He served at Neuve Chapelle and Ypres, and was wounded and taken prisoner near Loos in August 1915. He suffered many privations during his long captivity, and was repatriated after the Armistice. He was demobilised in October 1919, and holds the 1914–15 Star, and the General Service and Victory Medals.

11, Summer Street, Leighton Buzzard.   1587.

BRAMPTON, W. A., Private, R.A.O.C.

He volunteered in October 1915, and in the following year was drafted to German East Africa. Whilst in this sphere of war he was engaged on important clerical duties in connection with the rationing of the troops. He rendered valuable services for three years, and returned home in January 1919 when he was demobilised. He holds the General Service and Victory Medals.

130, London Road, St. Albans.   X562.

BRANDOM, C., Private, Queen's (Royal West Surrey Regiment).

He joined in March 1918 on attaining military age, and after completing his training was sent overseas. He served with the Army of Occupation on the Rhine for over twelve months, and returned to England to be demobilised in January 1920.

28, Regent Street, Leighton Buzzard.   1588/A.

BRANDOM, E., Private, Worcestershire Regt.

He joined in February 1916, and in the following July was drafted to the Western Front, where he took part in the heavy fighting at the Somme, Arras, Bullecourt and Cambrai. He also served in the Retreat and Advance of 1918, and was wounded. He was demobilised in February 1919 after returning home, and holds the General Service and Victory Medals.

26, Regent Street, Leighton Buzzard.   1590/B.

BRANDOM, G. A., Sapper, Royal Engineers.

He volunteered in August 1914, and on the completion of his training was sent to France, where he served for the remainder of the war on important field company duties, chiefly in connection with laying wires and trenching. After the Armistice he proceeded to Germany with the Army of Occupation, and was engaged on guard duty on the Rhine. After his return to England he was demobilised in May 1919, and holds the General Service and Victory Medals.

49, Copsewood Road, Watford.   563/A.

BRANDOM, S. C., Sergeant, R.A.V.C.

Vounteering in 1915 he was drafted to the Western Front in March of the following year. Whilst in this theatre of war he rendered valuable services with his unit in all important engagements until the conclusion of hostilities, especially at Béthune. He was demobilised in May 1919 after returning to England, and holds the General Service and Victory Medals.

12, Cecil Street, North Watford.   X564.

BRANDOM, W., Aircraftsman, Royal Air Force.

He joined in November 1917, and after a period of training was engaged on important duties which demanded a high degree of technical ability. He did excellent work but was not successful in obtaining a transfer overseas before the conclusion of the war. He was demobilised in February 1919.

49, Copsewood Road, Watford.   563/B.

BRANDOM, W., Sergeant, 2nd Bedfordshire Regt.

He volunteered at the outbreak of war and was almost immediately drafted to France. He took part in the fighting at La Bassée, Ypres, where he was wounded, and Hill 60, and was killed in action at Loos in September 1915. He was entitled to the 1914 Star, and the General Service and Victory Medals.

114, Long Row, Vandyke Road, Leighton, Buzzard. 1585/B.

BRANDOM, W. J., Private, 5th Bedfordshire Regiment.

He volunteered in August 1914, and in the following March was drafted to the East. He was present at the landing at Gallipoli, and the engagement at Krithia. After the Evacuation he proceeded to Egypt and took part in the Capture of Gaza, Jerusalem and Aleppo. He was demobilised in June 1919, and holds the 1914–15 Star, and the General Service and Victory Medals.

28, Regent Street, Leighton Buzzard.   1588/B.

BRANDON, A. (D.C.M.), Private, Welch Regt.

He joined in June 1916, and in December of the following year was drafted to the Western Front, where he took part in important engagements, including those at Ypres, Armentières and Cambrai, and was wounded. He was awarded the Distinguished Conduct Medal for conspicuous bravery whilst acting as despatch-bearer between his company and battalion headquarters during a critical period at Delville Wood, and in addition holds the General Service and Victory Medals. He was demobilised in January 1919.

57, Cromwell Road, Luton.   566—565.

BRANDON, A. E., Private, Machine Gun Corps.

He joined in December 1917, and in March of the following year, on the conclusion of his training, was sent to the Western Front, where he served with distinction in the second Battle of the Somme, Cambrai and the last Battle of Ypres. He was demobilised in April 1919 after returning home, and holds the General Service and Victory Medals.

15, Moor Street, Luton.   567.

BRANDON, B., Gunner, Royal Garrison Artillery.

He was mobilised in August 1914, and was immediately drafted to the Western Front, where he took part in the Retreat from Mons, and was killed in action in the fierce fighting at the Battle of the Aisne on September 25th, 1914. He was entitled to the Mons Star, and the General Service and Victory Medals.

64, Holywell Road, Watford.   X568/B.

BRANDON, C., Private, Middlesex Regiment.

Volunteering in 1915, he was engaged on the completion of his training at various stations on important duties with his unit. He rendered valuable services, but was not successful in obtaining his transfer overseas before the conclusion of the war. He was demobilised in 1918.

64, Holywell Road, Watford.   X568/A.

BRANDON, W., Sapper, Royal Engineers.

He volunteered in December 1914, and in the following July was drafted to Gallipoli, where he did valuable service at Suvla Bay for six months. He then proceeded to Egypt and took an active part in the Campaign through Palestine, especially at Gaza and Jerusalem. He returned home and was demobilised in July 1919, holding the 1914–15 Star, and the General Service and Victory Medals.

75, Cowper Street, Luton.   570.

BRANDON, W., Sapper, Royal Engineers.

Volunteering in September 1914, he was retained after the completion of his training on important duties with his unit until August 1917, when he was drafted to Salonika. During the remainder of the war he did valuable service in the Vardar and Doiran sectors of this Front, and returning home was demobilised in March 1919, holding the General Service and Victory Medals.

3, Brache Street, Luton.   569.

BRANSON, C. J., Sapper, Royal Engineers.

Volunteering in August 1914, he was drafted on completing his training, first to Gallipoli and then to Egypt and Palestine. In both theatres of war he was engaged on important duties in connection with the operations and was frequently in the forward areas. He was wounded during his service overseas, and for a time was in hospital. After his return to England he was demobilised in June 1919, and holds the General Service and Victory Medals.

29, Grove Road, Luton.   571/B.

BRANSON, E. D., Air Mechanic, Royal Air Force.

He joined in June 1917, and after his training was completed served at various stations on important engineering duties which demanded a high degree of technical skill. He did excellent work, but was not able to secure his transfer overseas before the termination of the war. He was demobilised in July 1919.

29, Grove Road, Luton.   571/A.

BRASIER, S., A.B., Royal Navy.
He joined in December 1916, and on the completion of his training was engaged with the Grand Fleet on important duties in the North Sea. He took part in several minor engagements, including that outside Scapa Flow. He was demobilised in January 1919, and holds the General Service and Victory Medals.
Sharpenhoe Road, Barton.   T1549.

BRASIER, W., Air Mechanic, Royal Air Force.
He joined in June 1916, and after his training served at various air depôts on important duties which demanded a high degree of proficiency. He did excellent work but was not successful in obtaining his transfer overseas before the cessation of hostilities. He was demobilised in March 1919.
Sharpenhoe Road, Barton.   T1547.

BRAUNTON, W. J. H., Gunner, R.F.A.
Volunteering in 1914, he proceeded to the Western Front later in the year, and took part in many important engagements, including that at Ypres. He was subsequently killed in action on April 4th, 1916, and was entitled to the 1914-15 Star, and the General Service and Victory Medals.
89, Norfolk Road, Rickmansworth.   572/B.

BRAWN, W. E., Corporal, Bedfordshire, East Surrey and Northamptonshire Regiments.
He volunteered in August 1914, and after being retained for some time on important duties with his unit was, in 1917, drafted to France. He took part in the severe fighting at Cambrai, where he was wounded. On recovery he served in many important engagements in the Retreat and Advance of 1918. He was demobilised in January of the following year, and holds the General Service and Victory Medals.
23a, Bailey Street, Luton.   573.

BRAY, H. W., Pte., 11th Royal Berkshire Regt.
He joined in June 1916, and in the following October was drafted to the Western Front, where he saw much service. During his time in France he took part in the fighting on the Somme, Arras and Cambrai Fronts, and was severely gassed in an engagement near Cambrai in 1918. He was invalided home to hospital, and after prolonged treatment died from the effects of the poisoning on October 16th, 1919. He was entitled to the General Service and Victory Medals.
Holly Hill, Wing.   1603.

BRAY, P., Gunner, Royal Field Artillery.
He was mobilised in August 1914, and owing to his ability as an Instructor in riding was retained to train recruits until 1918. He was sent in February of that year to France, where he took part in the second Battle of Cambrai and other important engagements. He was demobilised in July 1919 after returning home, and holds the General Service and Victory Medals.
11, Shaftesbury Road, Watford.   X574/B.

BRAY, R. A., Gunner, Royal Garrison Artillery.
He volunteered in June 1915, and in November 1917 was drafted to France, where he took part in the fighting at Arras, Ypres, Cambrai, and in the second Battle of Le Cateau in 1918. After the signing of the Armistice he was sent to Germany, where he was engaged with the Army of Occupation on garrison duty until May 1919 when he was demobilised. He holds the General Service and Victory Medals.
11, Shaftesbury Road, Watford.   X574/A.

BRAYBROOK, F., Private, 3rd Bedfordshire Regiment.
He volunteered in March 1915, and on the completion of his training was drafted to India, where he was engaged on special duties at various garrison outposts and did valuable work. He was sent home and discharged for causes due to his service in July 1918. He holds the General Service and Victory Medals.
3, Park Road West, Luton.   576/A.

BRAYBROOK, F. L., Driver, Royal Engineers.
Volunteering in January 1915, he was at first drafted to the Dardanelles and later to Egypt. After valuable service there he joined the Palestine Campaign, and took part in the Battles of Gaza, and in other engagements in General Allenby's great Offensive. He died in Egypt on October 14th, 1918, and was entitled to the General Service and Victory Medals.
3, Park Road West, Luton.   576/B.

BRAYBROOKS, F. J., Private, 7th Bedfordshire Regiment.
He volunteered in September 1914, and after his training was drafted to France. During his service overseas he took part in severe fighting at Festubert, Loos, Vimy Ridge and the Somme, and was killed in action at Cambrai on December 8th, 1917. He was entitled to the 1914-15 Star, and the General Service and Victory Medals.
Moggerhanger, Sandy.   Z1816/A.

BRAZIER, E., Private, 5th Bedfordshire Regt.
He volunteered in September 1914, and in the following year was sent to France, where he took part in various important engagements, and was wounded. In December 1919 he was drafted to the Eastern theatre of war, and while serving in the Palestine Campaign was again wounded. He was killed in action on September 21st, 1918, in the great Advance under General Allenby, and was entitled to the 1914-15 Star, and the General Service and Victory Medals.
Princess Street, Toddington.   577/A.

BRAZIER, H., Sapper, Royal Engineers.
He joined in August 1916, and in the same year, after completing his training, was sent to France, where he was engaged on wiring, pontooning and trench work on the Somme and Arras Fronts, and was wounded. In July 1917 he was drafted to Egypt, and served on similar duties in the Offensive in Palestine, at Gaza, and other places. He returned home in November 1919, and was demobilised in December, holding the General Service and Victory Medals.
Princess Street, Toddington.   577/B.

BRAZIER, J., Private, 1st Bedfordshire Regiment.
He was mobilised at the outbreak of war, and was immediately drafted to the Western Front, where he took part in the Retreat from Mons. He also served with distinction in the Battle of Ypres, and was killed fighting on October 2nd, 1914. He was entitled to the Mons Star, and the General Service and Victory Medals.
Bull Yard, Wheathampstead.   578.

BRAZIER, W., C.S.M., A/R.S.M., Bedfordshire Regiment.
He was mobilised in August 1914, and in the following year was sent to the Dardanelles, where he was engaged at Suvla Bay, Anzac and Chocolate Hill. After the Evacuation he was transferred to Egypt, where he rendered distinguished service in the Canal Zone in many important engagements. He also acted for some time at Kantara as Regimental Sergeant-major. After returning home he was demobilised in January 1920, and holds the 1914-15 Star, and the General Service and Victory Medals.
25, Alma Street, Luton.   579/A.

BRAZIER, W., Private, Northamptonshire Regt.
He joined in February 1917, and after a short period of training was drafted to the Western Front. He was killed in action at Ypres in his first engagement on July 31st, 1917. He was entitled to the General Service and Victory Medals.
Bury Road, Stopsley, near Luton.   580.

BREED, A., Corporal, 1st Bedfordshire Regiment.
He volunteered in August 1914, and was sent immediately afterwards to the Western Front, where he took part in the heavy fighting in the Retreat from Mons and at La Bassée, Festubert, Arras, Cambrai, the Somme and many other engagements, and was wounded. He was demobilised in May 1919 after his return home, and holds the Mons Star, and the General Service and Victory Medals.
Clifton Road, Shefford.   Z581.

BREED, A. C., Private, Machine Gun Corps.
He volunteered in May 1915, and after a course of training was, in the same year, sent overseas. He was in action on the Western Front at Festubert, Loos, and the first Battle of the Somme, and after taking part in the Battles of Ypres, Vimy Ridge and Cambrai, did valuable service until the end of the war. He holds the 1914-15 Star, and the General Service and Victory Medals, and was demobilised in March 1919.
Brook End, Potton.   Z1267/B.

BREED, B., Corporal, 5th Bedfordshire Regt.
He was mobilised in August 1914, and in December of the same year was drafted to the Western Front, where he took part in the Battles of St. Eloi, Hill 60, Ypres, the Somme, Beaumont-Hamel, Arras, Cambrai and many other engagements. He later proceeded with the Army of Occupation to Germany. He returned home and was demobilised in March 1919, and holds the 1914-15 Star, and the General Service and Victory Medals.
Meppershall Road, Shefford.   Z582.

BREED, F., Sergeant, 13th London Regiment (Kensington's).
He volunteered in August 1914, and in October of the same year was drafted to the Western Front, where he took part in the Battles of La Bassée, Neuve Chapelle, Ypres, Lens and Cambrai, and was twice wounded. After returning home he was engaged as an Instructor at the Cadet Schools at Crowborough and the Isle of Wight, and at the Guards' training depôt at Shorncliffe. In January 1919 he was demobilised, and holds the 1914 Star, and the General Service and Victory Medals.
Church Cottage, Campton, Shefford.   Z583.

BREED, F., Private, Bedfordshire Regiment.
He volunteered in August 1915, and in the following February was sent to the Western Front. He took part in the severe fighting in the first Battle of the Somme, and was invalided home on account of wounds received there. On his recovery he returned to France, and was engaged at Ypres, Arras, Messines and Cambrai, and was again sent home. He rejoined his unit in the Field in August 1918, and died of wounds received in action on October 10th of the same year. He was entitled to the General Service and Victory Medals.
Brook End, Potton. Z1267/A.

BREED, W., Private, 4th Suffolk Regiment.
He volunteered in December 1915, and after his training was engaged on various important duties with his unit until November of the following year, when he was drafted to the Western Front. He took part in many important engagements, and was killed in action on the Ypres Front on April 23rd, 1917. He was entitled to the General Service and Victory Medals.
109, St. James Road, Watford. X584/A.

BRENT, T., Private, 1st Northamptonshire Regt.
He volunteered at the outbreak of war, and was immediately drafted to the Western Front, where he took part in the Retreat from Mons, and in the Battles of Arras, Ypres and Cambrai. He was also engaged for a time in Egypt and Palestine, where he did much valuable work. During his whole service abroad he was wounded three times. He holds the Mons Star, and the General Service and Victory Medals, and was demobilised in March 1919.
101, Highbury Road, Luton. 695/A.

BRETT, B., Gunner, Royal Field Artillery.
He joined in January 1916, and in June of the same year was drafted to the Western Front. During his three years' service overseas he took part in the severe fighting on the Somme and at Arras, Ypres, Cambrai and many other engagements until hostilities ceased. He was demobilised in July 1919, and holds the General Service and Victory Medals.
Grove Road, Harpenden. 585.

BRETT, J. H., Pte., 11th West Yorkshire Regt.
He joined in September 1916, and on the conclusion of his training was drafted to the Western Front, where he saw much fighting, and was killed in action near Ypres on September 29th, 1917. He was entitled to the General Service and Victory Medals.
Hope Villa, Kershaw's Hill, Hitchin. 1617.

BREWER, C. A., 1st Class Stoker, R.N., T.B.D. "Sylvia."
He volunteered in October 1915, and served until the close of hostilities in the North Sea and Baltic, where he was engaged in chasing submarines and on other important duties. He was demobilised in January 1919, and holds the General Service and Victory Medals.
10, Pretoria Road, Watford. X586/B.

BREWER, E. E., Private, Hertfordshire Regt.
He joined in 1916, and after his training served at various stations on important coastal defence duties with his unit. He rendered valuable services, but was not successful in obtaining his transfer overseas before the cessation of hostilities. He was demobilised in 1919.
79, London Road, St. Albans. X587.

BREWER, J. E., Corporal, R.A.P.C.
He joined in October 1916, and after his training was engaged on important clerical duties with his unit. He did not succeed in securing his transfer to a fighting Front while fighting continued, but rendered much valuable service, and was still serving in 1920.
98, Talbot Road, Luton. 588.

BREWER, J. T. G., Private, Bedfordshire Regt. and Royal Welsh Fusiliers.
He volunteered in 1915, and in the same year was drafted to the Western Front, where he took part in numerous engagements, including those at Ypres, Arras and Cambrai. He also served in the Retreat and Advance of 1918 up to the Entry into Mons, and was three times wounded during his service. He was demobilised in January 1919, and holds the 1914-15 Star, and the General Service and Victory Medals.
10, Pretoria Road, Watford. X586/A.

BREWER, J. W., Sapper, Royal Engineers.
Volunteering in September 1914, he was attached to the Inland Water Transport section, and on the completion of his training was drafted to Mesopotamia, where he served on the Kut-el-Amara front, rendering valuable services until hostilities ceased. He was sent home and demobilised in May 1919, and holds the General Service and Victory Medals.
40, Watson's Walk, St. Albans. 478.

BREWSTER, F. W., Sergeant, 1st Brigade, Royal Field Artillery (A.I.F.)
He volunteered in August 1914, and in the same year was sent to France, where he took a prominent part in the operations at La Bassée and Ypres. Later he was sent to Gallipoli, and saw much fighting at Suvla Bay, and Anzac. After further service he was demobilised in August 1919, holding the 1914 Star, and the General Service and Victory Medals.
1, Charles Street, Hemel Hempstead. X589.

BRIARS, C. (Miss), Special War Worker.
During the war this lady was engaged on important work at large military equipment factories at Letchworth and Luton. She was chiefly occupied in the manufacture of fuses, bandoliers and ammunition boxes, and carried out her duties with care and efficiency.
Bury Road, Stopsley, Luton. 590.

BRICE, A. J., Private, 15th Royal Sussex Regt.
Joining in November 1916, he was sent to the Western Front at the conclusion of his training a year later. During his service overseas he was engaged on special duties in connection with the water supply, and rendered valuable service in many battles in the last year of fighting, notably those of the Somme, the Aisne, the Marne, Ypres and Cambrai. Returning to England in December 1918 he was demobilised in the following March, and holds the General Service and Victory Medals.
23, Thorpe Road, St. Albans. X591.

BRICE, H., Corporal, 1st Bedfordshire Regiment.
He volunteered in October 1914, and on the completion of his training was drafted to France, when he took part in the Battle of the Somme and was wounded. After his recovery, while serving in an engagement near Cambrai, he was again wounded in October 1917, and was subsequently killed in action in the heavy fighting on the Somme Front on August 23rd, 1918. He was entitled to the General Service and Victory Medals.
Meppershall Road, Shefford. Z592.

BRICE, H. A., Private, Essex Regiment, attached Machine Gun Corps.
Volunteering in November 1915, he was drafted to France in January 1917. He took part in the Battle of Ypres, Cambrai and the Somme, and was severely gassed in action. After his return to England he was demobilised in January 1919, and holds the General Service and Victory Medals.
10, Queen's Street, Luton. 593/B.

BRICE, V. A., Private, Royal Army Service Corps and 1/5th Yorkshire Regiment.
He volunteered in November 1915, and in the following year was drafted to France, where he served at Arras, Ypres and Passchendaele. He was reported missing on March 30th, 1918, after the second Battle of the Somme, and has not been heard of since then. He was entitled to the General Service and Victory Medals.
33, Merton Road, Watford. X594.

BRIDCUTT, C. A., Private, East Surrey Regt.
He joined in June 1916, and after his training was sent to the Western Front in the following October. He served with distinction at Beaumont-Hamel, Arras and Vimy Ridge, where he was killed in action on May 3rd, 1917. He was entitled to the General Service and Victory Medals.
8, Cape Road, Fleetville, St. Albans. X595.

BRIDGE, W. A., A.B., Royal Navy.
He was serving in the Navy when hostilities were begun, and was posted to H.M. Submarine "E.47," in which vessel he did very valuable work in the Dardanelles and subsequently in the Bight of Heligoland, where he was drowned in August 1917. He was entitled to the 1914-15 Star, and the General Service and Victory Medals.
31, Church Road, Watford. X224/B.

BRIDGES, A., Driver, R.A.S.C.
He volunteered in September 1914, and in January of the following year was sent out to France. During his service he was present at the Battles of Ypres and the Somme, and did valuable work as a transport driver until the close of the war. He was demobilised in April 1919, and holds the 1914-15 Star, and the General Service and Victory Medals.
23, Pinner Road, Oxhey. X596.

BRIDGES, F. W. J., Private, 7th Norfolkshire Regiment.
He volunteered in June 1915, and in the following December was drafted overseas. During his service in France he took part in much heavy fighting, and was in action at the Somme, Arras and Cambrai, and throughout the Retreat and Advance of 1918. After his return to England he was demobilised in February 1919, and holds the 1914-15 Star, and the General Service and Victory Medals.
10, Black Horse Lane, Sunnyside, Hitchin. 1827.

BRIDGES, G. J., Private, R.A.S.C. (M.T.)
Volunteering in May 1915, he was soon drafted to the Western
Front, where he served on important transport duties at
Rouen, Ypres and other important sectors of the line, and
was chiefly engaged in conveying rations to the troops. In
November 1917 he was sent to German East Africa, and
rendered valuable services until his return home for demobi-
lisation in April 1919. He holds the 1914–15 Star, and the
General Service and Victory Medals.
90, Norfolk Road, Rickmansworth.   X597.

BRIGHT, A., Private, Royal Air Force.
He joined in September 1918, and after his training served in
the aeroplane shops at various stations on important duties
which demanded a high degree of technical skill. He rendered
valuable services, but was unable, on medical grounds, to
obtain a transfer overseas before the termination of the war.
He was demobilised in April 1919.
84, Waterlow Road, Dunstable.   598.

BRIGHT, L. C., Private, 17th Middlesex Regiment.
He joined in April 1916, and on September of the same year,
after completing his training, was sent to the Western Front.
He fought at Albert and in the Somme sector, and was taken
prisoner on February 28th, 1917. He was held in captivity
in Germany until December 1918, when he was released and
sent home. He was demobilised in the following August,
and holds the General Service and Victory Medals.
31, High Street, Houghton Regis, near Dunstable.   599.

BRIGHT, S., Private, 7th Lincolnshire Regt.
He joined in March 1917, and 11 months later, on the completion of his training, was drafted to France. After only a
few weeks' service on the Western Front he was killed in
action at Sailly-Sailly on March 23rd, 1918. He was entitled
to the General Service and Victory Medals.
87, High Street, Houghton Regis, Dunstable.   600.

BRIGHTMAN, A., Corporal, Hertfordshire Regt.
He joined in April 1918, and after his training was engaged
on important duties with his unit. He rendered valuable
services, but was not successful in obtaining his transfer
overseas before the cessation of hostilities. He was demobilised in 1919.
Manor Road, Barton, near Ampthill.   601/B.

BRIGHTMAN, K. (Miss), Special War Worker.
From 1916 until 1918 this lady was engaged on work of
National importance as a Woolwich Inspector in Messrs.
Kent's Munition Factory, Luton. She carried out her
responsible duties with great efficiency, and rendered valuable
services throughout.
Manor Road, Barton, near Ampthill.   601/A.

**BRIGINSHAW, W., Drummer, 5th Bedfordshire
Regiment.**
He volunteered in August 1914, and after his training was
engaged on important guard duties at various stations with
his unit. He rendered valuable services, but was not successful in obtaining his transfer overseas before the cessation of
hostilities. He was demobilised in February 1919.
58, Warwick Road, Luton.   602.

BRIM, E. E., Private, 7th Norfolk Regiment.
He joined in 1916, and in the same year was drafted to the
Western Front. During his service he was in action at the
Somme, Arras and Ypres, and was taken prisoner by the
enemy in an engagement on November 30th, 1917. After
being held in captivity in Germany until 1918 he was
repatriated and demobilised. He holds the General Service
and Victory Medals.
34, Grange Street, St. Albans.   X603.

BRIMLEY, F., 1st Air Mechanic, R.A.F.
He joined in March 1917, and proceeded to Mesopotamia in
the same year. He took part in many engagements, and also
did valuable work in the repair of aeroplanes at Baghdad
Aerodrome until hostilities ceased. He returned home and
was demobilised in May 1919, and holds the General Service
and Victory Medals.
3, Belgrave Avenue, Watford.   X604.

BRINKLOW, A., Private, Norfolk Regiment.
He was mobilised at the outbreak of war, and in the following
July was drafted to Egypt. He joined the Advance into
Palestine, where he took part in the Battles of Gaza, and was
badly wounded. On returning to the lines after three months'
hospital treatment he took part in many subsequent engage-
ments. He returned to England and was demobilised in
May 1919, and holds the 1914–15 Star, and the General
Service and Victory Medals.
Watling Street, Hockliffe, near Leighton Buzzard.   1608/B.

BRINKLOW, D., Private, 5th Bedfordshire Regt.
He volunteered in March 1915, and in April of the following
year was drafted to Egypt. He afterwards proceeded to
Palestine, where he took part in the fighting at Gaza, and
was severely wounded. On his recovery he served at Alleppo
until the conclusion of hostilities. He returned to England in
December 1918, and was demobilised in January, holding
the General Service and Victory Medals.
Watling Street, Hockliffe, near Leighton Buzzard.   1608/A.

BRINKLOW, F., Stoker, Royal Navy.
He was serving at the outbreak of hostilities, and in 1914
and 1915 on board H.M.S. "Inflexible" gave much valuable
service in the North Sea and the Atlantic and Pacific
Oceans. He also took part in the Battle of the Falkland
Islands. From 1915 onwards he was in hospital owing to
severe illness, and in March 1919 was demobilised, holding
the 1914–15 Star, and the General Service and Victory Medals.
105, Apsley End, Herts.   X605.

BRINKLOW, H., Private, 6th Cheshire Regiment.
He volunteered in November 1914, and after concluding his
training was engaged on important guard duties with his
unit. He was not successful, on medical grounds, in obtaining
his transfer to a fighting Front, but rendered valuable service
until discharged in October 1915 as unfit for further military
duty.
27, Bury Hill, Hemel Hempstead.   X606.

**BRINKLOW, J. C., Private, King's Own (York-
shire Light Infantry).**
He joined in June 1917, and having completed his training
with his unit was drafted to France in August the same year.
He fought at Ypres, Lens and Cambrai, but owing to heart
trouble was invalided home. After a long stay in hospital at
Hull he was discharged in February 1919 as medically unfit
for further service. He holds the General Service and
Victory Medals.
Home Farm, Houghton Conquest, near Ampthill.   Z607/A.

BRINKLOW, L., Private, Essex Regiment.
He joined in 1916, and on completing his training was sent
to France in the same year, where he took part in several
important engagements, including those of the Somme,
Arras, Ypres, Cambrai, and the Retreat and Advance of 1918.
He returned home and was demobilised in September 1919,
holding the General Service and Victory Medals.
114, Harwood Road, Watford.   X608/B.

BRINKLOW, S C., Private, Royal Fusiliers.
He volunteered in April 1915, and in the same year was
drafted to the Western Front, where he took part in many
important engagements, and was killed in action on October
13th, 1916. He was entitled to the 1914–15 Star, and the
General Service and Victory Medals.
128, Cotterell's Road, Hemel Hempstead.   X609/B.

**BRITCHFORD, C. C., Private, 1st Buffs (East
Kent Regiment).**
He volunteered in September 1914, and in the following
year, after finishing his course of training, was drafted to the
Western Front, where he took part in several important
engagements, including those of Loos, Ypres, Cambrai and
Havrincourt, and was wounded. He was killed in action on
the Ypres Front on September 19th, 1918, and was entitled
to the 1914–15 Star, and the General Service and Victory
Medals.
5, Watson's Row, St. Albans.   X610.

**BRITNELL, P. W., L/Corporal, 1st Gloucester-
shire Regiment.**
He joined in 1916, and in the same year was drafted to the
Western Front. He took part in the heavy fighting at Arras,
Ypres, Cambrai and the Somme, and was gassed and severely
wounded. He died of his injuries on November 1st, 1918, and
was entitled to the General Service and Victory Medals.
Aspley Guise, Beds.   Z611.

BRITTANY, G., Private, Royal Defence Corps.
He volunteered in November 1914, and after his training was
engaged on important duties with his unit. He rendered
valuable services as a guard of government property at
Woolwich Arsenal until he was discharged in January 1918.
37, Chapel Street, Hemel Hempstead.   X612/A.

BRITTANY, T., Pte., 9th Seaforth Highlanders.
He volunteered in August 1914, and immediately proceeded
to the Western Front. While overseas he took part in much
severe fighting at Ypres, the Somme, Arras and in other
engagements until hostilities ceased, and was four times
wounded and gassed. On returning home he was demobilised
in February 1919, holding the 1914 Star, and the General
Service and Victory Medals.
37, Chapel Street, Hemel Hempstead.   X612/B.

BROCK, A., Private, R.M.L.I.
He joined in 1916, and was posted for duty in H.M.S. " Furious." He served in many waters, including the North Sea, the Baltic and Mediterranean, and was also at Scapa Flow. He rendered valuable services until demobilised in November 1919, and holds the General Service and Victory Medals.
62, Norfolk Road, Rickmansworth. X613.

BROCK, L., Corporal, Royal Field Artillery.
He volunteered in August 1914, and served at various stations on important duties with his unit until June 1917, when he was sent to Mesopotamia, and took part in heavy fighting at Baghdad and Kut-el-Amara. In April 1919 he proceeded to India, where he remained until November 1919, when he returned home and was demobilised, holding the General Service and Victory Medals.
33, York Road, Watford. X614.

BRONSELL, A. H., Private, Machine Gun Corps.
He volunteered in January 1916, and in the following June proceeded to France, where he was engaged in the heavy fighting. In November of the same year he was sent to Egypt, in which theatre of war he was in action in the British Advance through Palestine, and took part in the Battles of Gaza and the capture of Jerusalem. He returned to England in November 1919, and in the following month was demobilised, and holds the General Service and Victory Medals.
123, Herkomer Road, Bushey, Herts. X615/C.

BROOK, J. J., Sapper, Royal Engineers.
He volunteered in October 1914, and after his training served on important duties with his unit until July 1915, when he was sent to France, where he served till 1919. During his service overseas he took part in many engagements, including those at Arras, the Somme and Béthune. He was demobilised in April 1919, and holds the 1914-15 Star, and the General Service and Victory Medals.
12, Cassiobridge Road, Watford. X616.

BROOKER, J. G., Saddler, R.A.S.C.
He was serving at the outbreak of war, and was immediately afterwards sent to France. During his service overseas he was present at many engagements, including those at La Bassée, Hill 60 and Ypres, and was wounded and gassed. After the Armistice he was drafted to Constantinople with the Army of Occupation. He returned home and was demobilised in January 1920, and holds the 1914 Star, and the General Service and Victory Medals.
Heath Road, Harpenden. 617.

BROOKES, B., Private, Royal Fusiliers.
He volunteered in June 1915, and in the following year was drafted to the Western Front, where he took part in numerous engagements, including those on the Somme and at Ypres, and was twice wounded. He was invalided home, and was discharged in June 1918 as medically unfit for further service, and holds the General Service and Victory Medals.
Hillford End, Shillington. 2446.

BROOKES, H., Private, 6th Essex Regiment.
He joined in February 1916, and after his training was drafted to Egypt. During his service in this theatre of war he took part in the Palestine Campaign, being present at many engagements, including those at Gaza and Haifa. He returned to England in June 1919, and later was sent to Ireland, where he remained until he was demobilised in August 1919. He holds the General Service and Victory Medals.
3, Ivel Terrace, Biggleswade. Z1532.

BROOKES, J., Corporal, Royal Air Force.
He joined in September 1916, and at the conclusion of his training was sent overseas in 1917. He took part in many important engagements on the Western Front, including the Battle of the Somme, and after the Armistice proceeded to Germany with the Army of Occupation, with which he was still serving in 1920, holding the General Service and Victory Medals.
25, Bedford Road, St. Albans. X618/A.

BROOKS, A. C., L/Corporal, 10th South Wales Borderers.
He joined in June 1918, and in the following August was drafted to France, where he took part in the Battles of the Somme and Cambrai. Later he was drafted to Italy, where he served until December 1919, when he returned to England and was demobilised. He holds the General Service and Victory Medals.
108, Ridgway Road, Luton. 619/B.

BROOKS, A. E., Rifleman, Rifle Brigade.
He joined in April 1916, and in May of the following year was drafted to France, where he took part in several engagements and was wounded. He was invalided home, and on his recovery served on important duties with his unit at various stations until April 1919, when he was demobilised, holding the General Service and Victory Medals.
108, Ridgway Road, Luton. 619/A.

BROOKS, C., Gunner, Royal Garrison Artillery.
He joined in 1916, and in the same year was drafted to France, where he fought in numerous engagements, including the Battles of Ypres, and was wounded. After the cessation of hostilities he returned to England and in 1919 was demobilised, holding the General Service and Victory Medals.
94, Judge Street, North Watford. X620/A.

BROOKS, E. W., Sergeant, 4th London Regiment (Royal Fusiliers).
He volunteered in October 1914, and in the following year was drafted to the Dardanelles, where he took part in the engagement at Suvla Bay, and was wounded. Later he was transferred to the Western Front, where he was killed in action at Menin Road on September 30th, 1917. He was entitled to the 1914-15 Star, and the General Service and Victory Medals.
108, Ridgway Road, Luton. 619/C.

BROOKS, F., Private, R.A.M.C.
He volunteered in October 1914, and was drafted to the Western Front. During his service in this theatre of war he was present at engagements at Ypres, Arras and Kemmel Hill. He was taken prisoner in April 1917 and held in captivity in Germany for ten months. He was then released and sent home and demobilised in February 1919. He holds the 1914-15 Star, and the General Service and Victory Medals.
69, Bury Park Road, Luton. 621.

BROOKS, G., Sapper, Royal Engineers.
He volunteered in 1915, and during his four years' service on the Western Front took part in numerous important engagements, including those of the Somme, Arras and Cambrai. On his return to England he was demobilised in 1919, holding the 1914-15 Star, and the General Service and Victory Medals.
94, Judge Street, North Watford. X620/B.

BROOKS, H., Gunner, Royal Field Artillery.
He joined in October 1916, and on the completion of his training was drafted to the Western Front in October of the following year. He took part in the engagements at Ypres, Passchendaele Ridge, Cambrai and Bapaume, and did excellent work as a gunner. He was demobilised in November 1919, and holds the General Service and Victory Medals.
59, Union Street, Dunstable. 622.

BROOKS, W., Sergeant, Sherwood Foresters.
He was serving at the outbreak of war, and proceeded immediately afterwards to the Western Front, where he took part in many important engagements, including the Retreat from Mons and the Battles of Ypres and Loos, and was twice wounded. He was invalided home and was discharged as medically unfit in November 1916, holding the 1914 Star, and the General Service and Victory Medals.
9, Newcombe Road, Luton. 624.

BROOM, H., Private, 7th Royal Fusiliers.
He joined in June 1916, and was drafted to the Western Front, where he served in various important engagements, including that at Passchendaele. He was taken prisoner on April 5th in the German Offensive of 1918, and was held in captivity until the conclusion of hostilities, when he was released and returned to England and was demobilised in April 1919, holding the General Service and Victory Medals.
Chapel Cottage, Leavesden Green, near Watford. X625.

BROOME, H. J., Private,, 16th Middlesex Regt.
He joined in May 1916, and a year later was drafted to the Western Front. Whilst in this theatre of war he served in the heavy fighting at Ypres and was taken prisoner at Cambrai in November 1917. He was held in captivity in Germany until November 1918, when he was released, and returning to England, was demobilised in April 1919, holding the General Service and Victory Medals.
9, Bailey Street, Luton. 626.

BROUGHALL, W., Pte., 1st Hertfordshire Regt.
He volunteered in October 1914, and in July of the following year was drafted to the Western Front, where he served in various engagements, including those at La Bassée and Ypres, and was wounded and taken prisoner in September 1917. On his release he returned home and was demobilised in February 1919, and holds the 1914-15 Star, and the General Service and Victory Medals.
115, Oak Road, Luton. 653.

BROWN, A., Gunner, Royal Field Artillery.
He volunteered in December 1915, and in September of the following year was drafted to Mesopotamia, where he took part in the engagements on the Tigris and in the Offensive on Kut-el-Amara. He was present also at the capture of Baghdad and the occupation of Mosul by the British Forces. He returned home and was demobilised in May 1919, and holds the General Service and Victory Medals.
46, Arthur Street, Luton. 627.

BROWN, A., Private, Bedfordshire Regiment.

He was serving at the outbreak of hostilities, and was almost immediately drafted to the Western Front and took part in the Retreat from Mons. He also served on the Marne and at Festubert, the Somme, Ypres and Cambrai. During this period he was three times wounded, and was severely gassed in action and invalided home. Later he was discharged as unfit for further duty in March 1918. He re-enlisted, however, as a transport driver in 1919, and was still serving in the following year. He holds the Mons Star, and the General Service and Victory Medals.
3, Back Street, Biggleswade. Z1535—Z1536/B.

BROWN, A. J., Private, Bedfordshire Regiment.

He was called up from the Reserve at the outbreak of hostilities, and in October was sent to the Western Front, where he took part in the engagements at La Bassée and Ypres. He was killed in action at Festubert on May 14th, 1915, and was entitled to the 1914 Star, and the General Service and Victory Medals.
27, Cobden Street, Luton. 628/B.

BROWN, A. P., Sapper, Royal Engineers.

He volunteered in September 1914, and saw much varied service. He was sent first to Gallipoli, where he did valuable work throughout the campaign until the Evacuation of the Peninsula. He then proceeded to Egypt and the Soudan, and served in Palestine with General Allenby's Forces until the termination of the war. He returned home and was demobilised in June 1919, and holds the General Service and Victory Medals.
27, Vernon Road, Luton. 629.

BROWN, A. W., L/Corporal, Royal Engineers.

He volunteered in August 1914, and was sent out to the Western Front on the completion of his training. He took part in the Battles of the Somme, Arras, Ypres and Cambrai, and in many subsequent engagements until the conclusion of the war. He was demobilised in March 1919, and holds the General Service and Victory Medals.
49, Brunswick Street, Luton. 630.

BROWN, C., Sapper, Royal Engineers.

He joined in May 1916, and in the following year was drafted to the Western Front. During his service overseas he was engaged on important duties in the forward areas whilst operations were in progress, and was present at the engagements at Arras, Cambrai and Albert. He was gassed in the Advance of 1918, but on recovery proceeded to Germany with the Army of Occupation and was stationed on the Rhine until his return to England, when he was demobilised in September 1919. He holds the General Service and Victory Medals.
11, Telegraph Terrace, Hitchin. 1828.

BROWN, C., Private, Hertfordshire Regiment.

He volunteered in October 1914, and was drafted to the Western Front in the following year. Whilst in this theatre of war he took part in many important engagements, including those on the Somme and at Arras and Cambrai, and was wounded. After the conclusion of hostilities he returned to England and was demobilised in February 1919. He holds the 1914-15 Star, and the General Service and Victory Medals.
4, Cross Street West, Dunstable. 631.

BROWN, C. H., Private, 6th Essex Regiment.

He was serving at the outbreak of war, and in October of the same year was sent to the Western Front, and took part in the Battles of Ypres and Neuve Chapelle, and was wounded. In August 1915 he was transferred to the Dardanelles, and was in action at Suvla Bay and Anzac. Later he proceeded to Egypt, where he was in many engagements, including those of Gaza and Jaffa and the Capture of Jerusalem. He returned home and was demobilised in March 1919, and holds the 1914 Star, and the General Service and Victory Medals.
3, Brittain's Yard, Hitchin Street, Biggleswade. Z1529.

BROWN, C. J., Trooper, Bedfordshire Lancers.

He volunteered in 1915, and in the following year was drafted to Salonika, where he took part in various important operations in the Balkan Campaign. He suffered severely from malaria, and was also wounded in action, and was eventually discharged as medically unfit for further military duty in May 1919. He holds the General Service and Victory Medals.
62, Leighton Street, Woburn. Z632/B.

BROWN, C. L., Trooper, Herts. Dragoons; and Private, Royal Defence Corps.

He volunteered in November 1915, and was engaged on important guard duties, and later conducting horses to France. Whilst thus employed he met with an accident which rendered him unfit for service overseas. He was transferred to the Royal Defence Corps, and was engaged on important duties at various stations until he was demobilised in January 1919. He holds the General Service and Victory Medals.
57, Diamond Street, Watford. X633/B.

BROWN, C. T., Trooper, Herts. Dragoons.

He volunteered in November 1915, and after his training was drafted to the Western Front, where he took part in heavy fighting at Ypres and on the Somme. Later he was transferred to Egypt and served in the Palestine Campaign. After the Armistice he was sent to Turkey, where he served until June 1919, when he returned home and was demobilised, holding the General Service and Victory Medals.
57, Diamond Road, Watford. X633/A.

BROWN, D., Private, 12th Hampshire Regiment.

He joined in June 1916, and in September of the following year was drafted to Salonika, where he was engaged on the Vardar, Struma and Doiran fronts, and was severely wounded and invalided home. He was demobilised in August 1919, and holds the General Service and Victory Medals.
4, Barker's Cottages, Hitchin Hill. 2450/A.

BROWN, D. T., Gunner, Royal Garrison Artillery.

He joined in June 1916, and after his training in the same year was drafted to Italy, where he took part in the campaign against the Austrians, and was in action on the Piave and the Asiago Plateau. After the termination of hostilities he returned to England, and in March 1919 was demobilised, holding the General Service and Victory Medals.
14, Neal Street, Watford. 447/A.

BROWN, E., Private, 5th Bedfordshire Regiment.

He volunteered in June 1915, and in January of the following year was drafted to Egypt. He served in the Palestine Campaign and took part in many engagements, including those at Gaza, Jaffa, Jericho and the Capture of Jerusalem. He returned home and was demobilised in April 1919, and holds the General Service and Victory Medals.
4, Barker's Cottages, Hitchin Hill. 2450/B.

BROWN, E., (M.M.), Private, Bedfordshire Regt.

He volunteered in 1914, and in the following year was sent to the East and served in the Palestine Offensive with General Allenby's Forces. Whilst in this theatre of war he took part in the fighting at Gaza and Haifa and in other engagements throughout the campaign. He was awarded the Military Medal for distinguished bravery and devotion to duty on the Field, and holds in addition the 1914-15 Star, and the General Service and Victory Medals. He was demobilised after his return to England in 1919.
3, Back Street, Biggleswade. Z1535C—Z1536/C.

BROWN, E. J., Sergeant, King's Royal Rifle Corps.

He volunteered in May 1915, and after a period of training was drafted to the Western Front. During his service overseas he took part in the Battles of the Somme, Ypres and Cambrai, and was wounded. He holds the 1914-15 Star, and the General Service and Victory Medals, and was demobilised in 1919.
34, Shakespeare Street North, Watford. X635.

BROWN, E. J., Private, 5th Bedfordshire Regt.

He volunteered in June 1915, and at the conclusion of his training was drafted to the Dardanelles in August of the same year. He took part in the landing at Suvla Bay, and after serving at several other engagements, proceeded to Egypt, where he saw much fighting during the Palestine Campaign at Jaffa, Gaza and Jerusalem, and was twice wounded. He was awarded the Military Medal for devotion to duty during a bombing raid, and holds in addition the 1914-15 Star, and the General Service and Victory Medals. He was demobilised in March 1919.
29, Alexandra Terrace, Biggleswade. Z1537.

BROWN, F., 1st Hertfordshire Regiment.

He volunteered in September 1914, and in the following month was drafted to the Western Front, where he took part in heavy fighting at La Bassée, Ypres, St. Eloi, Hill 60, Givenchy and the Somme. He was wounded and invalided home on two occasions, but returning to France, he served in the Retreat and Advance of 1918. He was demobilised in January 1919, and holds the 1914 Star, and the General Service and Victory Medals.
3, West Alley, Hitchin. 2449/A.

BROWN, F., Cpl., 7th Buffs (East Kent Regt.)

He joined in May 1916, and in the same year was drafted to France, where he saw much fighting. Whilst overseas he took part in the Somme Offensive, and was twice wounded, and later fought at Arras, where he was taken prisoner in May 1917. After nineteen months in captivity he was released, and returning to England was demobilised in September 1919, holding the General Service and Victory Medals.
Biggrave's Cottages, Ickle Yard, Hitchin. 1619.

BROWN, F. C., Private, 2nd Bedfordshire Regt.
He volunteered in February 1915, and in September of the same year was drafted to the Western Front, where he took part in many important engagements, including those on the Somme and at Arras and Ypres, and was wounded. He was invalided home, and in September 1917 was discharged as medically unfit, holding the 1914-15 Star, and the General Service and Victory Medals.
118, Old Bedford Road, Luton. 637.

BROWN, F. C., Private, 11th Royal Sussex Regt.
He joined in March 1916, and after his training served on important duties with his unit until September of the following year, when he was drafted to the Western Front. He took part in the engagements at Beaumont-Hamel and Thiepval, and was wounded, and after the cessation of hostilities returned to England and was demobilised in September 1920, holding the General Service and Victory Medals.
56, Stanley Street, Luton. 638.

BROWN, F. C., Sapper, Royal Engineers.
He volunteered in August 1914, and was drafted to the Western Front. During his service overseas he took part in numerous important engagements, including those on the Somme and at Arras and Ypres. He was demobilised in January 1919, and holds the 1914 Star, and the General Service and Victory Medals.
15, York Street, Luton. 639.

BROWN, F. F., Private, 8th Bedfordshire Regt.
He volunteered in September 1914, and in August of the following year was sent to the Western Front, where he took part in the Battle of the Somme and many other engagements, and was killed in action on April 11th, 1916. He was entitled to the 1914-15 Star, and the General Service and Victory Medals.
7, Parcels Place, Hitchin. 2449/B.

BROWN, F. J., Private, 26th Royal Fusiliers.
He joined in September 1918, and after completing his training served with his unit at various stations until the following January, when he was drafted overseas and served with the Army of Occupation in Germany for a year. He was demobilised in February 1920.
138, Liverpool Road, Watford. X640/B.

BROWN, G., Corporal, 2nd Bedfordshire Regt.
He was serving at the outbreak of war, and immediately proceeded to France, where he was in action in the Retreat from Mons and the subsequent Battles of La Bassée, Ypres and Hill 60. He was killed during the engagement at Loos on October 6th, 1915. He was entitled to the Mons Star, and the General Service and Victory Medals.
25, Chase Street, Luton. 641/B.

BROWN, G. E., Private, Bedfordshire Lancers.
Volunteering in August 1914, he was sent overseas in the following year, and during his service in France took part in the fighting at Festubert, Loos and the Somme. He was also in action at Messines Ridge, Ypres and Cambrai in 1917, and was wounded and in hospital for a time. After the conclusion of the war he was invalided home, and subsequently discharged as medically unfit for further duty. He holds the 1914-15 Star, and the General Service and Victory Medals.
45, Nightingale Road, Hitchin. 1829.

BROWN, H., Private, 1st Bedfordshire Regiment.
He volunteered in August 1914, and in the following year was drafted overseas. During his service in France he fought at the Battles of Ypres, Loos, the Somme and Arras. He also took part in engagements during the Retreat and Advance of 1918. After the conclusion of hostilities he returned home and was demobilised in January 1919, holding the 1914-15 Star, and the General Service and Victory Medals.
3, Brown's Yard, St. Andrew's Street, Hitchin. 1830.

BROWN, H., Private, 1st Royal Inniskilling Fusiliers.
A serving soldier, he was drafted to France on the declaration of war, and fought in the Retreat from Mons and the Battles which followed, including those of Ypres. He was severely wounded in action, and died from the effects of his wounds on March 22nd, 1916. He was entitled to the Mons Star, and the General Service and Victory Medals.
36, Sutton Road, Watford. X648/C.

BROWN, H., Private, 9th Essex Regiment.
He joined in April 1917, and in August of the same year was sent to France and took part in various engagements, including that at Cambrai. He was wounded at Albert in April 1918, and taken prisoner at Epéhy in September of the same year. On his release he returned home and was demobilised in March 1919, and holds the General Service and Victory Medals.
Princess Street, Toddington. 642.

BROWN, H. S., Private, 1st Hertfordshire Regt.
He volunteered in September 1914, and after his training served on important duties with his unit until August 1916, when he was sent to the Western Front. He took part in many important engagements, including those at Ypres, Arras, Armentières and Cambrai, and was wounded on the Somme in March 1918. He was demobilised in February 1919, and holds the General Service and Victory Medals.
Luton Road, Toddington. 643.

BROWN, H. W., Sapper, Royal Engineers.
He volunteered in February 1915, and in December of the same year was drafted to the Western Front, and took part in the Battles of Ypres, Loos, Vimy Ridge, the Somme, Cambrai and many other important engagements. In December 1918 he proceeded with the Army of Occupation to Germany. He returned home and was demobilised in April 1919, and holds the 1914-15 Star, and the General Service and Victory Medals.
27, South Road, Luton. 644.

BROWN, H. W., Sapper, Royal Engineers.
He joined in June 1917, and in September of the same year was drafted to Egypt. In this theatre of war he did valuable work with the railway company in the Advance on Jerusalem under General Allenby, and was present at the Battles of Gaza, Jaffa and Jerusalem. He was demobilised in February 1920, and holds the General Service and Victory Medals.
10, Havelock Road, Biggleswade. Z1273.

BROWN, J., Private, 4th Bedfordshire Regiment and Queen's Own (Royal West Kent Regt.)
He was called up from the Reserve in August 1914, and in the same month was drafted to France, where he took part in the Retreat from Mons and the engagements on the Marne and at Ypres and Givenchy. He was wounded and buried by the explosion of a shell, and was invalided home. On his recovery he was drafted to Mesopotamia in 1916, and served at the capture of Kut-el-Amara and Baghdad. In 1917 he was invalided home through ill-health, and later served on important agricultural duties until his demobilisation in March 1919. He holds the Mons Star, and the General Service and Victory Medals.
6, West Alley, Hitchin. 1831.

BROWN, J., Private, 1st Bedfordshire Regiment.
He was serving in the Territorials at the outbreak of hostilities, and was mobilised and drafted to France in September 1914. In this theatre of war he took part in the Retreat from Mons and the Battle of La Bassée, in which he was killed in action on November 5th, 1914. He was entitled to the Mons Star, and the General Service and Victory Medals.
25, Chase Street, Luton. 641/C.

BROWN, J., Private, 1st Cambridgeshire Regt.
He joined in June 1917, and after his training was drafted to the Western Front, where he took part in important engagements, including those of Ypres, Passchendaele and Cambrai, and was wounded. He was discharged in August 1918 owing to his wound, and holds the General Service and Victory Medals.
35, Red Lion Yard, Watford. X645.

BROWN, J. D., Sergeant, Machine Gun Corps.
He joined in January 1917, and in the following May was drafted to the Western Front. Whilst overseas he took part in the fighting at Arras, Passchendaele and in many other engagements, and was severely wounded in action on the Somme in March 1918. On his recovery he was sent to Palestine in August 1919, and served there until February 1920, when he returned to England and was demobilised in the following month. He holds the General Service and Victory Medals.
138, Liverpool Road, Watford. X640/A.

BROWN, J. E., Private, 4th Middlesex Regiment.
He was serving with the Colours when war was declared, and was drafted to France with the First Expeditionary Force. He was engaged in the fighting during the Retreat from Mons, and was reported missing on August 28th, 1914, but was afterwards believed to have been killed in action on that date. He was entitled to the Mons Star, and the General Service and Victory Medals.
17, High Street, Lilley, Luton. 646/A.

BROWN, L., Private, Lincolnshire Regiment.
He joined in February 1917, and in January of the following year was drafted to the Western Front, where he took part in various engagements, including those at Cambrai and Albert, and was killed in action near Amiens on May 19th, 1918. He was entitled to the General Service and Victory Medals.
4, Barker's Cottages, Hitchin Hill. 2450/C.

BROWN, L. C. (Miss), Special War Worker.
This lady was engaged at Messrs. Kent's Factory, Luton, in the capstan, lathe and tool-setting departments. Her duties, which were of a responsible nature, were carried out with great care and efficiency, and she rendered valuable services during the war.
17, Elizabeth Street, Luton. 647.

BROWN, L. W., Air Mechanic, Royal Air Force.
He volunteered in August 1914, and after his training served with his squadron at various stations on important duties which demanded a high degree of technical skill. He rendered valuable services, but was not successful in obtaining his transfer overseas before the cessation of hostilities. He was demobilised in March 1919.
34, Alexandra Road, Hitchin. 2452.

BROWN, R. W. (M.M.), Private, Bedfordshire Regiment.
He volunteered at the outbreak of war, and was almost immediately drafted to France, and took part in the Retreat from Mons. He also served on the Marne and at Festubert, the Somme and Arras, where he was killed in action on April 23rd, 1917. He won the Military Medal for conspicuous gallantry and devotion to duty on the Field, and was entitled in addition to the Mons Star, and the General Service and Victory Medals.
3, Back Street, Biggleswade. Z1535/A—Z1536/A.

BROWN, S., Corporal, 1st Bedfordshire Regt.
He was mobilised in August 1914, and was almost immediately sent to France, where he fought in the Retreat from Mons and the operations which followed, until killed in action on September 22nd, 1914. He was entitled to the Mons Star, and the General Service and Victory Medals.
36, Sutton Road, Watford. X648/B.

BROWN, S. J., Riflmn, King's Royal Rifle Corps.
He volunteered in November 1914, and in May of the following year was drafted to the Western Front, where he took part in the Battle of Ypres (I.), and was wounded and invalided home. On his recovery he returned to France and served at Ypres, Arras and the Somme, and was again wounded and sent home, but returned to France shortly afterwards. During the fighting at Cambrai he was again wounded, and afterwards transferred to the Labour Corps. He was demobilised in February 1919, and holds the 1914-15 Star, and the General Service and Victory Medals.
72, Hitchin Street, Biggleswade. Z1538.

BROWN, T. W., Trumpeter, Royal Engineers.
He volunteered in 1915, and in the following year proceeded overseas. During his service in France he served with his unit in various sectors, and was present at many engagements, including those of Albert, Vimy Ridge, the Somme, Ypres and Cambrai, and was twice wounded. He was demobilised in April 1919, and holds the General Service and Victory Medals. 61, Ramridge Road, Luton, Beds. 649/A.

BROWN, W., Gunner, Royal Garrison Artillery.
He joined in April 1916, and in July of the same year was drafted to the Western Front, where he took part in the Battles of the Somme, Arras, Ypres and Cambrai, and many other engagements. He was demobilised in February 1919, and holds the General Service and Victory Medals.
2, Francis Place, High Street, Watford. X650.

BROWN, W. G., Gunner (Signaller), R.G.A.
He volunteered in April 1915, and after his training served at various stations on important duties with his unit. He rendered valuable services, but was not successful in obtaining his transfer overseas before the cessation of hostilities. He was demobilised in January 1919.
46, Kirby Road, Dunstable. 651.

BROWN, W. R., Sergeant, 2nd Bedfordshire Regiment and Royal Engineers.
He was mobilised when war was declared, and later proceeded to France, where he served in many engagements, and was wounded in action on the Somme in July 1916. On recovery he returned to the firing-line, and was again wounded at Arras in 1917. He was later engaged at Ypres in 1918, and through the final stages of the war. He was demobilised in February 1919, and holds the 1914-15 Star, and the General Service and Victory Medals. He had previously served through the South African War.
36, Sutton Road, Watford. X648/A.

BROWNE, C. H., Sapper, Royal Engineers.
He volunteered in September 1914, and in the following year was drafted to the Western Front, where he took part in many important engagements, including those at Ypres, the Somme and Cambrai. He was afterwards transferred to Salonika, where he was again in action. He returned home and was demobilised in March 1919, and holds the 1914-15 Star, and the General Service and Victory Medals.
River Hill, Flamstead, near Dunstable. X652.

BRUDENELL, W. P., Private, R.A.S.C.
He joined in August 1916, and in the following month was drafted to the Western Front. He was engaged on important transport duties in various sectors, including the Somme, Ypres, Arras, Albert and Cambrai, and rendered valuable services until after hostilities ceased. He was demobilised in June 1919, and holds the General Service and Victory Medals.
111, Sun Street, Biggleswade. Z1528.

BRUNT, C., Sergeant, Royal Field Artillery.
He was mobilised on the declaration of war, and was drafted to France shortly afterwards. He was engaged in the Battle of and Retreat from Mons, and took part in the subsequent Battles of La Bassée, Neuve Chapelle and Festubert. Suffering from gas-poisoning, he was sent to England for treatment, and on recovery, having returned to the line, was in action at Cambrai, the Somme and Amiens. He was demobilised in February 1919, and holds the Mons Star, and the General Service and Victory Medals.
Northill, near Biggleswade. Z1272/B.

BRUNT, J. R., Sergeant, 7th Bedfordshire Regt.
He volunteered in September 1914, and after his training served for a time on important duties with his unit until he was drafted to the Western Front in 1915. In this theatre of war he took part in the heavy fighting at Ypres, Loos, the Somme, Bapaume and Cambrai, and in other sectors until the close of hostilities. He was demobilised in February 1919, and holds the 1914-15 Star, and the General Service and Victory Medals.
Northill, near Biggleswade. Z1272/A.

BRUNTON, J. G., Corporal, Royal Engineers.
He volunteered in September 1914, and served as a Drill Instructor until May 1916, when he was drafted to the Western Front. He took part in many important engagements, including those at Messines and St. Julien, and was wounded. He was discharged in September 1917 in consequence of his service, and holds the General Service and Victory Medals.
Mimram Road, Welwyn. 656.

BRUTON, A. C., Private, 1st Hertfordshire Regt.
He volunteered in September 1914, and was sent overseas in the following January. Whilst on the Western Front he was engaged in the heavy fighting at Neuve Chapelle, Béthune, Givenchy, Festubert, and was seriously wounded in action at Vermelles. He subsequently died from the effects of his wounds on October 3rd, 1915, and was entitled to the 1914-15 Star, and the General Service and Victory Medals.
New Marford, Wheathampstead. 654/A.

BRUTON, E. W., Private, 9th Essex Regiment.
He joined in February 1916, and after his training was engaged on important duties with his unit until January of the following year, when he was drafted to the Western Front. He took part in several important engagements, and was wounded. He died from the effects of his injuries on May 8th, 1918, and was entitled to the General Service and Victory Medals.
55, Ash Road, Luton. 655.

BRUTON, R. B., Private, Northamptonshire Regt.
He joined in April 1918, and after completing his training was sent to Ireland, where he was employed on guard and other important duties. He did good work, but was not successful in securing his transfer to a theatre of war before hostilities ceased. He was demobilised in December 1919.
New Marford, Wheathampstead. 654/B.

BRUTY, C., Private, R.A.S.C.
Volunteering in August 1914, he went through a course of training and was employed on important duties at various depôts until drafted to the Western Front. He did very valuable work in several sectors in transporting supplies to the lines, and was present at many engagements until fighting ceased. On the termination of hostilities he was sent home and demobilised in March 1919. He holds the General Service and Victory Medals.
103, North Street, Luton. 358/C.

BRYANT, D., Private, Bedfordshire Regiment.
He volunteered in February 1915, and on the completion of his training was sent to the Western Front, where he was in action at the Somme. In April 1917 he was severely wounded in an engagement near Vimy Ridge, and was invalided home. After being for many months in hospital he was transferred to the Labour Corps and was stationed at Ampthill, where he did valuable work until demobilised in April 1919. He holds the General Service and Victory Medals.
42, Cemetery Street, Biggleswade Z1271.

BRYANT, G. W., Private, Bedfordshire Regiment.
He volunteered in August 1914, and was immediately sent to the Western Front, where he took part in the Battles of Mons, the Marne, the Aisne, Ypres, the Somme and numerous other engagements. He was wounded five times, and on three occasions was invalided home. He was demobilised in 1919, and holds the Mons Star, and the General Service and Victory Medals.
35, Diamond Road, Watford.   X657.

BRYANT, H. L., Staff-Sergeant, R.F.A.
He volunteered in August 1914, and in November of the following year was sent to France, where he took a prominent part in engagements on the Arras and Ypres Fronts. Afterwards he was transferred to Egypt and Palestine, where he again rendered valuable service. He returned home and was demobilised in April 1919, holding the 1914–15 Star, and the General Service and Victory Medals.
1, Alexandra Road, St. Albans.   X658.

BUCK, E. J., Sergt.-Major, 1st (Royal) Dragoons.
He was serving in South Africa at the outbreak of war, and proceeding to the Western Front, took part in the Battles of the Marne, La Bassée and Ypres, where he was wounded. On his recovery after hospital treatment at Liverpool he was engaged at York as an Instructor until 1917, when he returned to France, and was in action at Messines and Lens. He was demobilised in January 1920, and holds the 1914 Star, and the General Service and Victory Medals.
7, Benson's Row, Shortmead Street, Biggleswade.   Z1531.

BUCK, E. V. (Miss), Nurse, Territorial Force Nursing Service.
From March 1917 until March 1919 this lady rendered valuable service on the nursing staff at the 3rd London General Hospital, Wandsworth, and won high praise by her zeal and efficiency.
20, Banbury Street, Watford.   X659/A.

BUCKINGHAM, A., Sergeant, 5th Bedfordshire Regiment and Army Cyclist Corps.
He volunteered in August 1914, and was retained for a time on important duties as sergeant over escorts and at General Headquarters. In 1915 he was drafted to Gallipoli, and landing at Suvla Bay in August, rendered much valuable service on the coast of the Sea of Marmora at Lala, Barbara Beach and the Australian Gulf. After his return to England he was discharged in September 1917 in consequence of his service, and holds the 1914–15 Star, and the General Service and Victory Medals.
Ireland, Shefford, Beds.   Z660.

BUCKINGHAM, A., Private, 5th Bedfordshire Regiment.
He was mobilised at the outbreak of war, and on the conclusion of his training was sent to the Dardanelles in the following year. While in that fighting area he took part in many engagements, including that of Suvla Bay, and afterwards proceeded to Egypt and Palestine, where he fought at Gaza and in other important operations. He returned home and was demobilised in April 1919, holding the 1914–15 Star, and the General Service and Victory Medals.
29, Buxton Road, Luton.   661/C.

BUCKINGHAM, A. F., Private, 1st Hertfordshire Regiment.
He volunteered in February 1915, and shortly afterwards was drafted to France, where he fought at Ypres and the Somme, and was twice wounded. On his recovery he was sent to Egypt, where he saw much fighting in the Palestine Campaign until the cessation of hostilities. He was still serving in 1920, and holds the General Service and Victory Medals.
7, St. John's Road, Watford.   X662/C.

BUCKINGHAM, B. W., Private, 7th Lincolnshire Regiment.
He joined in December 1916, and was drafted to France in the following year. While in this theatre of war he fought in several important engagements, including those of Arras, Vimy Ridge, Passchendaele, Cambrai and the Somme, and was twice wounded. After the cessation of hostilities he came home, and was demobilised in September 1919, holding the General Service and Victory Medals.
Fowley, Grange Road, Leagrave.   663/A.

BUCKINGHAM, E., Gunner (Signaller), R.F.A.
He joined in March 1916, and in the same year was drafted to the Western Front, where he took part in various important engagements. He was killed near Givenchy on April 23rd, 1917, and was entitled to the General Service and Victory Medals.
Ireland, Shefford, Beds.   Z604.

BUCKINGHAM, E., Private, Northumberland Fusiliers.
He volunteered in September 1914, and after a period of training was engaged at various stations on important duties with his unit. He was unable to obtain his transfer overseas, being over military age, but did valuable work until demobilised in March 1919.
9, Cross Street, Luton.   665/A.

BUCKINGHAM, G., Shoeing Smith, Bedfordshire Lancers.
He volunteered in February 1915, and after a period of training was sent to Ireland, where he was engaged on important guard duties, and served during the Dublin riots. He was discharged in November 1917 as medically unfit for further service, and died shortly afterwards.
Luton Road, Toddington, near Dunstable.   666/A.

BUCKINGHAM, G., Driver, R.A.S.C.
He joined in June 1918, and after his training was engaged at various stations on important duties with his unit. He rendered valuable horse-transport service, but was not successful in obtaining his transfer overseas before the cessation of hostilities. He was demobilised in February 1919.
149, Sandringham Road, Watford.   X667/A.

BUCKINGHAM, G., Sergeant, R.A.S.C.
He volunteered in August 1915, and while he was proceeding soon after to Salonika his ship was torpedoed by a German submarine. He was picked up and interned by the Spanish authorities. He escaped to England 12 months later, and after doing much valuable work with his unit was demobilised in June 1919, holding the 1914–15 Star, the General Service and Victory Medals.
5, Florence Street, Hitchin.   1618.

BUCKINGHAM, G. E. W., Private, M.G.C.
He joined in 1918, and after his training was engaged with his unit on important duties at various stations until the cessation of hostilities. He was then drafted with the Army of Occupation to Cologne on the Rhine, where he rendered valuable service until he was demobilised in April 1920.
113, St. James' Road, Watford.   X668.

BUCKINGHAM, H., Private, 1st Bedfordshire Regiment.
He volunteered in November 1914, and a year later was drafted to the Western Front, where he took an active part in the Battles of the Somme, Arras, Ypres and Cambrai in 1918. During the last engagement he was badly gassed, and was under treatment at Boulogne Hospital. After his return home he was demobilised in October 1919, and holds the 1914–15 Star, and the General Service and Victory Medals.
Luton Road, Toddington.   666/B.

BUCKINGHAM, H. C., Private, 5th Bedfordshire Regiment
He volunteered in May 1915, and in the following year was drafted to Egypt. He afterwards proceeded to Palestine, where he served with General Allenby's Forces in many important battles. He was wounded at Gaza in 1917, and was present at the entry into Jerusalem and the fighting before Aleppo. After his return to England he was demobilised in April 1919, and holds the General Service and Victory Medals.
5, Spencer Road, Luton.   1201/B.

BUCKINGHAM, H. G., Private, Sherwood Foresters.
He joined in August 1916, and on the conclusion of his training was drafted in the following year to Egypt, where he rendered valuable service at Cairo and other stations. He afterwards took an active part in the campaign through Palestine, and fought in the Battles of Gaza, the Jordan, Haifa and Aleppo. He was also present at the entry into Jerusalem. After his return to England he was demobilised in February 1919, and holds the General Service and Victory Medals.
40, Duke Street, Luton.   669.

BUCKINGHAM, J., Gunner, R.F.A.
Volunteering at the outbreak of hostilities, he was immediately drafted overseas, and took part in the Retreat from Mons. He also fought at the Marne, Ypres and the Somme, where he was severely wounded in 1916. He was invalided home to hospital, and after prolonged treatment was finally discharged as medically unfit for further service in February 1919. He holds the Mons Star, and the General Service and Victory Medals.
15, Walsworth, Hitchin.   1814.

BUCKINGHAM, J. E., Sergeant, 5th Bedfordshire Regiment.
He volunteered at the outbreak of war, and was drafted to
the Dardanelles in July 1915. He was wounded during the
operations at Suvla Bay, and invalided home. After his
recovery he served for a time with the Labour Corps in
England, but was finally discharged as unfit for further duty
in March 1918. He holds the 1914–15 Star, and the General
Service and Victory Medals.
11, Cross Street, Luton. 665/B.

BUCKINGHAM, L. M. (Miss), Special War
Worker.
This lady was engaged on work of National importance at
Messrs. Kent's Factory, Luton, for a period of over 3½ years.
Her duties, which were in connection with fuse-making, were
carried out with great efficiency, and were much appreciated.
Princess Street, Toddington. 670.

BUCKINGHAM, P., Private, 2nd Bedfordshire
Regiment.
He volunteered at the outbreak of war, and was immediately
drafted to France, where he took part in the Retreat from
Mons and the Battle of Ypres. He was mortally wounded
in a later engagement, and subsequently died on November
4th, 1916, being buried at Warlencourt British Cemetery.
He was entitled to the Mons Star, and the General Service
and Victory Medals. 136, North Street, Luton. 671.

BUCKINGHAM, R., Private, 1st Hertfordshire
Regiment.
He was mobilised soon after the outbreak of hostilities, and
in November 1914 proceeded to the Western Front, where he
fought in several important engagements until the close of
hostilities, including those of Ypres, the Somme, and the
Retreat and Advance of 1918. He returned home in January
1919, and was demobilised in the following month, holding
the 1914 Star, and the General Service and Victory Medals.
7, St. John's Road, Watford. X662/B.

BUCKINGHAM, R. S., Corporal, Oxfordshire and
Buckinghamshire Light Infantry.
He volunteered in April 1915, and in the following December
was drafted to Mesopotamia, where he rendered valuable
service in the operations in the Persian Gulf, and was killed
in action on April 6th, 1916. He was entitled to the 1914–15
Star, and the General Service and Victory Medals.
Dorset Villa, Marsh Road, Leagrave. 672.

BUCKINGHAM, S., Private, 5th Bedfordshire
Regiment.
He volunteered in July 1915, and after a period of training
was drafted overseas. After doing valuable work at the
Dardanelles and proceeding to Egypt, he took part in the
chief engagements in the campaign through Palestine, and
was wounded. He was demobilised in January 1919, and
holds the 1914–15 Star, and the General Service and Victory
Medals.
7, Dordans Road, Leagrave. 673.

BUCKINGHAM, S. G., Private, Labour Corps.
He joined in March 1918, and having completed his training was sent to France. While in this theatre of war he
rendered valuable services with his unit until November 1919,
when he returned home and was demobilised, holding the
General Service and Victory Medals.
29, Buxton Road, Luton. 661/B.

BUCKINGHAM, W. (Mrs.), Special War Worker.
During the war this lady was engaged on work of an important nature at the Filling Station, Watford, where she held a
very responsible position as head forewoman. She rendered
valuable service, and performed her duties in a highly satisfactory manner until compelled to resign owing to illness.
7, St. John's Road, Watford. X662/A.

BUCKINGHAM, W., Sergeant, 5th and 7th
Bedfordshire Regiment.
He was mobilised with the Territorials at the outbreak of
war, and having completed his training was drafted to the
Dardanelles in July of the following year. He was severely
wounded at Suvla Bay. On his recovery he was sent to
France, where he took an important part in engagements at
Ypres and the Somme. He was killed in action on March
23rd, 1918, and was entitled to the 1914–15 Star, and the
General Service and Victory Medals.
29, Buxton Road, Luton. 661/A.

BUCKINGHAM, W. C., Private, Bedfordshire
Regiment.
He joined in April 1916, and in the following September, at
the close of his training, was drafted to France. He fought
at the Somme, Arras and Ypres, and was killed in action on
the Somme Front on September 15th, 1917. He was
entitled to the General Service and Victory Medals.
Luton Road, Toddington. 674.

BUCKLEY, J., Driver, Royal Field Artillery.
He volunteered in April 1915, and after a period of training
was drafted overseas. He rendered valuable service in
Egypt and India, and while taking part in the Campaign in
Mesopotamia died of enteric fever at Kut on July 15th, 1916.
He was entitled to the General Service and Victory Medals.
1, Dordans Road, Leagrave. 675.

BUCKOKE, W., Private, Hertfordshire, Bedfordshire and Manchester Regiments.
He volunteered in January 1915, and in the same year was
drafted overseas. He took part in much severe fighting on
the Western Front at Ypres, the Somme, St. Julien and
Armentières, and was wounded. He was demobilised in
January 1919, and holds the 1914–15 Star, and the General
Service and Victory Medals.
20, Breakspeare Road, Abbots Langley. X677.

BUDD, F., Corporal, Machine Gun Corps.
He volunteered at the outbreak of war, and after a period of
training was drafted overseas. He served on the Western
Front during the heavy fighting at Arras, and Ypres, and was
killed in action near Cambrai on March 29th, 1918. He was
entitled to the General Service and Victory Medals.
2, Brighton Road, Watford. X678.

BUDDEN, W. H., Sergeant, Royal Engineers.
He volunteered in January 1915, and in the following September was drafted to France. After two months' service
there he proceeded to Salonika, and was engaged on special
duties until hostilities ceased, building pontoon bridges on
the Vardar, Doiran and Struma fronts. For his distinguished
gallantry in the Field he was awarded the Greek Military
Medal. He also holds the 1914–15 Star, and the General
Service and Victory Medals, and was demobilised in February
1919.
Hillside, Lidlington, Beds. Z679.

BUGG, E. E., Private, 2nd Leicestershire Regt.
He joined in June 1916, and at the close of his training was
drafted to India in the following November. After a few
months' service there he was transferred to Mesopotamia,
and took part in the engagements near Kut and Baghdad.
In December 1917 he proceeded to Egypt, where he served
for a time at Alexandria and Cairo, and afterwards joined the
expedition into Palestine. In this theatre of war he took
part in many engagements, including those at Acre, Haifa and
Aleppo until hostilities ceased. He returned home and was
demobilised in April 1919, holding the General Service and
Victory Medals.
34, Park Road West, Luton. 680.

BULL, S., Stoker, R.N., H.M.S. "Barham."
He volunteered in August 1914, and was posted to H.M.S.
"Barham," in which battleship he was engaged on important
duties in the North, Mediterranean and Baltic Seas and other
waters until the cessation of hostilities. He returned home
and was demobilised in 1919, holding the 1914–15 Star, and
the General Service and Victory Medals.
84, Benskin Road, Watford. X682/B.

BULL, V. S., Private, Devonshire Regiment and
Royal Air Force.
He volunteered in November 1915, and in the following May
was drafted to Egypt, whence he took part in the Offensive
in Palestine, and was in action at Gaza and Jaffa. Later he
was sent to India, where he did valuable work at Secunderabad and Rawal Pindi until August 1919, when he returned
home and was demobilised. He re-enlisted in September
in the Royal Air Force, but owing to medical unfitness was
discharged in June 1920. He holds the General Service and
Victory Medals.
Clifton Fields, Shefford, Beds. Z681.

BULLEN, W. A., L/Corporal, 13th Bedfordshire
Regiment.
He was mobilised at the outbreak of war, and was immediately drafted to the Western Front, where he took part in
the Retreat from Mons. He was also in action at Festubert
and Ypres, and was there severely wounded. After his
recovery he was retained on important duties with his unit
until March 1919, when he was demobilised. He holds the
Mons Star, and the General Service and Victory Medals.
19, Garfield Street, Watford. X684.

BULWER, F. W., Private, 10th Essex Regiment.
He volunteered in August 1914, and on the conclusion of his
training was drafted to the Western Front. During his
service in France he took part in several engagements, and
was wounded in action. He was reported missing after the
fierce encounter near Albert on July 20th, 1916, and is
presumed to have been killed on that date. He was entitled
to the 1914–15 Star, and the General Service and Victory
Medals.
3, Parker Street, Watford. X685/B—X686/B.

BULWER, M. H., Sapper, Royal Engineers.
He volunteered in August 1914, and after his training was drafted overseas. During his service on the Western Front he was engaged on important duties as a telephone operator and telegraphist, and was frequently in the fighting areas. He was invalided home suffering from the effects of severe shell-shock, and after being in hospital for some time was discharged as medically unfit for further service in 1916. He holds the 1914-15 Star, and the General Service and Victory Medals.
3, Parker Street, Watford. X685/A—X686/A.

BUNCE, C. E., Private, Machine Gun Corps.
He was serving in the Regular Army in India at the outbreak of hostilities, and remained there on important garrison duties throughout the war. He did excellent work at various frontier stations and at Rawal Pindi. He returned home and was demobilised in March 1919, holding the 1914-15 Star, and the General Service and Victory Medals.
2, Francis Place, High Street, Watford. X687.

BUNCE, F., Pioneer, Royal Engineers.
He volunteered at the outbreak of war, and after a period of training was sent to the Western Front. He rendered valuable service in various sectors of the line, particularly on the Somme and Cambrai, and was wounded. After the conclusion of hostilities he returned home and was demobilised in March 1919, holding the General Service and Victory Medals.
39, Meeting Alley, Watford. X689.

BUNCE, F., Sergeant, 7th Bedfordshire Regt.
He volunteered in September 1914, and was soon drafted to France, where he took a prominent part in the Battle of Ypres and various other engagements. He was killed by a shell explosion in a dug-out in the Somme sector on June 27th, 1916. He was entitled to the 1914 Star, and the General Service and Victory Medals.
54, Ebury Road, Watford. X688.

BUNCE, F. W., Sergeant, Royal Field Artillery (Anti-Aircraft Section).
Volunteering in May 1915, he was retained for special duties as a gymnastic instructor at Hythe. He rendered most valuable services there, but was unable to secure his transfer overseas before hostilities ceased. He was demobilised in February 1919.
63, Sutton Road, Watford. X690.

BUNKER, A., Private, Royal Marine Labour Corps.
He joined in July 1917, and in August was sent out to France, where he did valuable work with his unit at Ypres, Cambrai, Amiens and other important sectors of the line until hostilities ceased. After returning home he was demobilised in April 1919, and holds the General Service and Victory Medals.
2, Field Terrace, Watford. X692.

BUNKER, A., Private, East Lancashire Regt.
He joined in 1916, and on the completion of his training was drafted to the Western Front, where he saw much service in many important engagements up to the close of the fighting, including those of Arras, Ypres, Lens, Cambrai, the Somme and Albert. He was demobilised in February 1919, after returning to England, and holds the General Service and Victory Medals.
Station Road, Ridgmont, Beds. Z691.

BUNKER, A. E., Private, 1st Royal Fusiliers.
He joined in January 1917, and proceeding to France on the conclusion of his training, took part in several engagements on the Somme and Arras Fronts. He was killed in action on July 31st, 1917, and was entitled to the General Service and Victory Medals.
12, Millbrook, near Ampthill. 3181/A.

BUNKER, F. G., Pioneer, R.E. (Signals).
After volunteering in April 1915, and going through a course of training, he was sent to Egypt and Palestine, and did valuable work in connection with the engagements near Gaza, Beersheba, Jerusalem, Jericho, Es Salt and Aleppo. He returned home and was demobilised in June 1919, and holds the General Service and Victory Medals.
Church Cottage, West End, Silsoe. 63/A—64/A.

BUNKER, F. J., Private, Grenadier Guards.
He joined in April 1918, but after his training, owing to the state of his health, was not successful in obtaining his transfer overseas before the cessation of hostilities. He was engaged on various important duties with his unit, and rendered valuable services until demobilised in November 1919.
103, High Street, Silsoe. 63/F—64/F.

BUNKER H., Driver, Royal Engineers.
He volunteered in April 1915, and in January of the following year was drafted to Egypt. He rendered valuable service at Cairo, and afterwards in the Palestine Campaign at Gaza and other places until fighting ceased. He returned home and was demobilised in July 1919, and holds the General Service and Victory Medals.
103, High Street, Silsoe. 63B—64/B.

BUNKER, H. C. E., Private, 2nd Bedfordshire Regiment.
He volunteered in September 1914, and in November of the same year was drafted to the Western Front, where he took part in heavy fighting at the Battles of Hill 60, Ypres, Loos and the Somme, and was wounded. He was killed in action at Trones Wood on August 11th, 1916, and was entitled to the 1914 Star, and the General Service and Victory Medals.
The Old Vicarage, Tilsworth. 2457.

BUNKER, H. S., Private, R.A.S.C.
He volunteered in August 1914, and in February of the succeeding year was sent to the Western Front. He was chiefly engaged on important transport duties conveying supplies for the troops in various sectors, particularly the Somme, Arras, Ypres and Cambrai, and suffered severely from shell-shock. He was demobilised in 1919, and holds the 1914-15 Star, and the General Service and Victory Medals.
110, West Street, Dunstable. 694.

BUNKER, R. H., Electrical Artificer, R.N., H.M.S. " Galatea."
He joined the Navy in April 1918, and was posted to H.M.S. " Galatea." Whilst in this vessel he was engaged in the blockade of Russia, and also served on important patrol duties in the Sea of Marmora, the North Sea and the Baltic. In 1920 he was still serving, and holds the Victory Medal.
50, Hampton Road, Luton. 693/B.

BUNTING, J. S., Sergeant-Major, 1/6th Sherwood Foresters.
He was mobilised at the outbreak of war, and in the following February was drafted to the Western Front, where he served with distinction at Neuve Chapelle, Loos, Vimy Ridge, Gommecourt, Ypres, Kemmel and St. Quentin. After four years' active service in France he returned home and was demobilised in March 1919. He holds the 1914-15 Star, and the General Service and Victory Medals.
Derwent House, Alfred Street, Dunstable. 696.

BUNYAN, A., Private, Machine Gun Corps.
He joined in July 1916, and on finishing his training in the following July was sent overseas. He rendered valuable service in the Arras, Somme and Ypres sectors, and was wounded. He returned to England on the cessation of hostilities and was demobilised in January 1919, holding the General Service and Victory Medals.
56, King's Road, Luton. 697.

BUNYAN, A., Private, 11th Suffolk Regiment.
He joined in June 1916, and later in the same year was drafted to the Western Front. He took part in many great engagements, including those of Arras, Cambrai and Amiens, and was twice wounded and gassed. He was demobilised in September 1919, after his return to England, and holds the General Service and Victory Medals.
Red Lion Cottages, Upper Woodside, near Luton. 701/B.

BUNYAN, A. E., Private, 12th Royal Sussex Regiment.
He joined in February 1917, and in August of the same year, after concluding his training, was drafted to France. He took part in various engagements, including those at Ypres and Menin Road, where he was severely wounded in November 1917. After a long stay in hospital he was discharged in May 1918 as medically unfit for further duty. He holds the General Service and Victory Medals.
14, Elizabeth Street, Luton. 698.

BUNYAN, E., Private, Labour Corps.
He joined in July 1916, and was engaged on important Agricultural duties. He rendered valuable services, but for medical reasons was unable to obtain a transfer abroad before the termination of the war. He was demobilised in August 1919.
Ivy Cottage, Aley Green, near Luton. 699.

BUNYAN, F., Sergeant, Bedfordshire Yeomanry (Lancers).
He volunteered in September 1914, and after being retained on important duties for a time was, in 1916, drafted to Egypt. He afterwards served through the Palestine Campaign, and fought with distinction at Gaza, and before the Entry into Jerusalem. After his return home he was on duty in Ireland until March 1919, when he was demobilised. He holds the General Service and Victory Medals.
83, Princes Street, Dunstable. 700.

BUNYAN, F., Private, 7th Bedfordshire Regt.
He joined in September 1916, and after the conclusion of his training was drafted to the Western Front in the same year. He took part in various important engagements, including those at Ypres, where he was wounded, Arras, Cambrai and Amiens. He was invalided home, and discharged in 1918 as medically unfit for further military duty. He holds the General Service and Victory Medals.
Red Lion Cottages, Upper Woodside, near Luton.   701/C.

BUNYAN, F. J., Gunner, Royal Field Artillery.
Volunteering in April 1915, he was afterwards drafted to France, where he served in numerous engagements up to the cessation of hostilities, including those of the Somme, Arras, Cambrai and Ypres. He was demobilised in April 1919 after his return home, and holds the General Service and Victory Medals. 27, Harley St., St. Albans. 418/B—419/B.

BUNYAN, H., Sergeant, Sherwood Foresters.
He joined the Army in 1910, and was sent overseas immediately after the declaration of war. He took a distinguished part in various early engagements, including the Battle of Ypres, and was killed in action on August 9th, 1915. He was entitled to the 1914 Star, and the General Service and Victory Medals.
84, Langley Road, Luton.   702.

BUNYAN, H. (M.M.), Private, 6th Leicestershire Regiment.
He was mobilised at the outbreak of hostilities, and was drafted to France in the following year. While overseas he fought in several important engagements, including those of Ypres, Arras, Messines and the Somme, and was killed in action at Lys on April 16th, 1918. He was awarded the Military Medal for bravery on the Field in October 1917, and was also entitled to the 1914-15 Star, and the General Service and Victory Medals.
6, St. Anne's Road, Luton.   703/B.

BUNYAN, H. R., Private, 4th Durham Light Infantry.
Joining in September 1917, he was engaged on the conclusion of his training at various stations on important duties with his unit, chiefly in connection with observation work. He was not successful in obtaining his transfer overseas before the cessation of hostilities, but rendered valuable services until demobilised in March 1919.
23, Cobden Street, Luton.   122/B.

BUNYAN, S., Corporal, Machine Gun Corps.
He volunteered at the outbreak of war, and was soon drafted to France. Whilst in this theatre of war he took part in many notable battles, including those of Ypres and the Somme and was three times wounded. In 1919 he proceeded to India, where he was still serving in 1920. He holds the 1914 Star, and the General Service and Victory Medals.
Red Lion Cottages, Upper Woodside, near Luton.   701/A.

BUNYAN, T., Sapper, Royal Engineers.
He joined in June 1916, and having completed his training was drafted to the Western Front in November of the same year. While there he saw much severe fighting in several battles, including those of the Somme, Vimy Ridge, Ypres, Cambrai and the Retreat and Advance in 1918. After his return home he was demobilised in March 1919, holding the General Service and Victory Medals.
126, High Street, Markyate.   704.

BUNYAN, W. C., Private, Suffolk Regiment.
Joining in 1917, in the same year he proceeded to France, where he was in action at Cambrai, Albert, Le Cateau, and numerous other operations in the Retreat and Advance of 1918. On the cessation of hostilities he was attached to the Army of Occupation, and served on the Rhine until October 1919, when he returned home and was demobilised. He holds the General Service and Victory Medals.
27, Harley Street, St. Albans.   418/C—419/C.

BUNYAN, W. G., 1st Air Mechanic, R.A.F.
He joined in June 1917, and after his training served at various stations on important aircraft duties, which demanded a high degree of technical knowledge and skill. He rendered valuable services, but owing to heart trouble was unable to take part in the fighting overseas before hostilities ceased. He was demobilised in January 1919.
21, Portland Street, St. Albans.   705.

BURCH, F. G., L/Corporal, 1st Hertfordshire Regiment.
He volunteered in January 1915, and in August was drafted to France, where he took part in various important engagements, including those of Ypres and St. Julien, where he was captured on July 31st, 1917. He was held prisoner in Germany until after the Armistice, and after his return home was demobilised in February 1919. He holds the 1914-15 Star, and the General Service and Victory Medals.
25, Vale Road, Bushey.   707/A.

BURCH, W., Private, 1st Hertfordshire Regt.
He joined in 1916, and after a period of training was drafted to France in August of the same year. He took a prominent part in the severe fighting on the Somme, where he was killed in action on November 14th, 1916. He was entitled to the General Service and Victory Medals.
25, Vale Road, Bushey.   707/B.

BURCHELL, W., Gunner, R.G.A.
He joined in December 1916, and after his training served at various stations on important duties with his unit. He rendered valuable services, but was not successful in obtaining his transfer overseas owing to his medical unfitness. He was discharged in March 1918 owing to his physical disabilities.
2, Mentmor Road, Linslade, near Leighton Buzzard.   2460.

BURGE, E. P., Private, 5th Bedfordshire Regt.
He was mobilised in August 1914, and in July of the following year was drafted to Gallipoli, where he took part in the Landing at Suvla Bay, and other operations until the Evacuation of the Peninsula. In January 1916 he was drafted to France, where he served in the Battles of the Somme, Arras and Cambrai, and was wounded. He returned home and was demobilised in 1920, and holds the 1914-15 Star, and the General Service and Victory Medals.
Arthur Street, Ampthill.   723.

BURGESS, A., Special War Worker.
From June 1917 until November 1918 this lady was engaged on work of great importance as a Woolwich Examiner in the fuse department of Messrs. Kent's Munition Factory, Luton, and carried out her reponsible duties with the utmost care and efficiency.
65, Selbourne Road, Luton.   710/B.

BURGESS, A., Air Mechanic, Royal Air Force (late Royal Naval Air Service).
He volunteered in November 1915, and in June of the following year was drafted to France, where he was engaged on special duties in connection with aeroplane engine repairs. He rendered excellent service until he was demobilised in February 1919, holding the General Service and Victory Medals.
21, Stanmore Road, Watford.   X708.

BURGESS, A., Gunner, Royal Field Artillery.
He joined in June 1916, and was afterwards drafted to Salonika, where he took part in various engagements on the Balkan Front. Later he returned to France and served at Arras and St. Quentin, and in other battles until the Armistice was signed. He then proceeded to Germany with the Army of Occupation and was stationed on the Rhine until his return home, to be demobilised in September 1919. He holds the General Service and Victory Medals.
Harris's Lane, Stopsley, Luton.   709.

BURGESS, A. G., Private, Machine Gun Corps.
He volunteered in December 1915, and after his training was drafted to the Western Front, where he took part in many important engagements, including those at Arras, Cambrai, Ypres and St. Quentin, and was wounded. He was discharged in November 1918 in consequence of his wounds, and holds the General Service and Victory Medals.
Melton House, Summer Street, Slip End.   711.

BURGESS, A. H., Private, 2nd Queen's (Royal West Surrey Regiment).
He joined in 1918, and on completing his training was engaged on important duties with his unit. He was not successful in securing his transfer to a fighting front before the cessation of hostilities, but after the Armistice proceeded to Germany in the Army of Occupation. After valuable service at Cologne he returned home and was demobilised in 1919.
167, Whippendell Road, Watford.   706/B.

BURGESS, C., Gunner, Royal Field Artillery.
He joined in April 1917, and in August of the same year was sent to France. After only one month's service overseas he was badly gassed in action at Poperinghe, and died from the effects on September 28th, 1917. He was entitled to the General Service and Victory Medals.
1, Etna Road, St. Albans.   714.

BURGESS, E., Gunner, Royal Garrison Artillery.
He joined in March 1916, and in the following year was drafted to the Western Front, where he took part in important engagements, including those of Arras, Ypres, Cambrai, St. Quentin and many others. He returned home, and was demobilised in November 1919, and holds the General Service and Victory Medals.
Angel Cottages, Offley.   2447.

BURGESS, E., Sergeant, Royal Engineers.
He joined in July 1916, and in the following September was drafted to India, where as artificer sergeant he did excellent work at Poona until November 1919. After his return home he was demobilised in the following month, holding the General Service and Victory Medals.
65, Selbourne Road, Luton. 710/C.

BURGESS, E. A., Driver, R.F.A.
He volunteered in October 1915, and after a period of training was drafted to France in September 1916. He took part in the Offensive on the Somme, and in the engagements at Arras, Bullecourt, Cambrai and other places until the cessation of hostilities. He was demobilised in January 1919, and holds the General Service and Victory Medals.
24, Hedley Road, St. Albans. X713/A.

BURGESS, F. G., Private, Grenadier Guards.
He joined in June 1918, and was engaged at various stations on important duties with his unit. He was unsuccessful in obtaining his transfer overseas while hostilities continued, and was demobilised in December 1919, after rendering valuable services.
134, Ridgway Road, Luton. 715/B.

BURGESS, H., Private, R.A.F. (late R.F.C.)
He joined in January 1917, and in the same year was drafted to France. He did much valuable work at Dunkirk, Rouen, and Ypres, and after the cessation of hostilities proceeded with the Army of Occupation to Cologne. He remained there until 1919, when he returned home and was demobilised, holding the General Service and Victory Medals.
134, Ridgway Road, Luton. 715/A.

BURGESS, H. H., Private, 8th Bedfordshire Regt.
He volunteered in 1914, and after his training was drafted to the Western Front in the following year. He took part in various important battles, including those of Festubert, Loos, Ypres (where he was twice wounded), and the Somme, where he was again severely wounded in three places. After being invalided home he was discharged as medically unfit for further duty in November 1918. He holds the 1914-15 Star, and the General Service and Victory Medals.
167, Whippendell Road, Watford. X706/A.

BURGESS, J. J., Chief Motor Mechanic, R.N., Motor Boat 2506.
He joined in March 1918, and during his service was engaged on important patrol duties along the coast and as a skilled fitter in the workshops. He rendered much valuable service until his demobilisation in March 1919.
Batterdale, Hatfield. X716/B.

BURGESS, L. (Mrs.), Special War Worker.
This lady was engaged at Messrs. Kent's Munition Factory, Luton, for three years, and was employed as an inspector of the fuses for anti-aircraft shells. Her duties, which were of a dangerous and responsible nature, were carried out with great care and efficiency, and she rendered valuable services.
86, Saxon Road, Luton. 717.

BURGESS, P. J., Private, Northamptonshire Regiment.
He joined in August 1916, and in the same year, on concluding his training, was drafted to France. He took part in the Battle of Ypres, and also fought at Passchendaele, Cambrai, the Somme and in several engagements in the Retreat and Advance of 1918. In September 1919 he was demobilised after returning home, and holds the General Service and Victory Medals.
167, Whippendell Road, Watford. 706/C.

BURGESS, S., Private, 2nd Bedfordshire Regt.
He was mobilised from the Reserve in August 1914, and was immediately afterwards sent to France. He took part in the Battles of Mons, the Marne and Ypres, and being wounded was invalided home. On his recovery he returned to France, and was killed in action on October 12th, 1916. He was entitled to the Mons Star, and the General Service and Victory Medals.
23, Buxton Road, Luton. 720.

BURGESS, S., Private, 8th Bedfordshire Regt.
He volunteered in May 1915, and in February of the following year was drafted to the Western Front, where he took part in the Battles of the Somme and Cambrai, and many other important later engagements. He was gassed near Ypres in August 1918. He was demobilised in April 1919, and holds the General Service and Victory Medals.
Caddington, near Luton. 719.

BURGESS, S. (M.S.M), Sergt.-Major, R.A.S.C.
He was serving at the outbreak of war and proceeded immediately to the Western Front. He rendered distinguished service in the Retreat from Mons and at Ypres, Arras, Cambrai and other engagements until hostilities ceased. He was awarded the Meritorious Service Medal for his excellent work and the Croix-de-Guerre for great bravery. He also holds the Mons Star, and the General Service and Victory Medals, and in 1920 was still serving.
208, North Street, Luton. 718.

BURGESS, W. E., Private, R.A.S.C.
He joined in August 1918, and immediately proceeded to North Russia. While in this theatre of war he rendered valuable transport services in several important operations, and died at Archangel on November 5th, 1918. He was entitled to the Victory Medal.
448, Hitchin Road, Luton. 721/A.

BURGESS, W. E., Private, 14th London Regt. (London Scottish).
He volunteered in October 1915, and after his training was engaged on important duties with his unit. He rendered valuable services, but was not successful in obtaining his transfer overseas owing to medical unfitness. He was discharged in July 1916. 22, Bury Park Road, Luton. 722.

BURGIN, A., Private, Norfolk Regiment.
He joined in June 1916, and in the same year was drafted to the Western Front, where he took part in many engagements, including those on the Somme and at Ypres. He was taken prisoner at Cambrai in November 1917 and sent to Germany. On his release he returned home and was demobilised in May 1919, and holds the General Service and Victory Medals.
192, Chester Road, Watford. 724.

BURGIN, W., Private, R.A.S.C.
He volunteered in June 1915, and after his training served at various stations on important duties with his unit. He rendered valuable services, but was not successful in obtaining his transfer overseas before the cessation of hostilities. He was demobilised in January 1919.
12, Chapman Yard, Watford. X725/B.

BURGOINE, H. J., Private, M.G.C.
He joined in October 1918, and after his training served at various stations on important agricultural duties. Owing to being medically unfit for service overseas he was not able to secure his transfer to the Front, and in March 1919 he was demobilised.
"Magpie Row," George St., Maulden, near Ampthill. 1832.

BURGOYNE, C., Driver, Royal Engineers.
He was mobilised at the outbreak of hostilities, and having completed his training, was drafted to France in 1918. Whilst in this theatre of war he fought on the Somme and at Ypres and Cambrai, and after the cessation of hostilities returned home and was demobilised in June 1919, holding the General Service and Victory Medals.
15, Brache Street, Luton. 727/A.

BURGOYNE, H., Private, 5th Bedfordshire Regt
He volunteered in October 1915, and after his training was retained on important duties with his unit until 1917, when he was drafted to France. He remained there until 1919, and during that period took part in engagements at Ypres (where he was severely wounded), Arras, the Somme, and Cambrai, where he was wounded again. Returning home he was demobilised in May 1919, holding the General Service and Victory Medals.
15, Brache Street, Luton, Beds. 727/B.

BURGOYNE, J., Private, R.A.M.C.
He volunteered in August 1914, and after a course of training was drafted overseas. During his period of service abroad he served in Egypt and France, and was engaged on important duties in connection with the Field Ambulance, and rendered valuable services. He was demobilised in April 1919, and holds the General Service and Victory Medals.
1, Park Road West, Luton. 726.

BURGOYNE, O. P., Driver, R.F.A.
He joined in May 1917, and in the following June was drafted to the Western Front, where he took part in many engagements, including those at Ypres, the Somme, Armentières and Cambrai. He returned home and was demobilised in February 1919, and holds the General Service and Victory Medals. 138, New Town Street, Luton. 728.

BURKETT, C. E. (M.M.), Corporal, R.F.A.
He was serving at the outbreak of war, and was immediately afterwards sent to France, where he took part in the Retreat from Mons and the Battles of Ypres, Arras, Cambrai and St. Quentin, and was twice wounded. He was awarded the Military Medal for gallantry on the Field, and in addition holds the Mons Star, and the General Service and Victory Medals, and was demobilised in February 1919.
Ramridge End, Stopsley 729.

BURLEY, F., Gunner, Royal Garrison Artillery.
. Volunteering in 1915, he was drafted overseas at the conclusion of his training. During his service on the Western Front, which lasted nearly four years, he took part in many battles, notably those at Arras, Ypres, Passchendaele, the Somme and Cambrai, and was severely wounded. Returning to England he was demobilised in February 1919, and holds the 1914–15 Star, and the General Service and Victory Medals.
71, Warwick Road, Luton.   730/B.

BURLEY, F. P., Private, Labour Corps.
He joined in June 1917, and after his training was engaged on special duties at various stations. He was unable to secure his transfer overseas before the cessation of hostilities, but afterwards was sent with the Army of Occupation to Cologne, where he remained until the latter part of 1919. Returning to England he was demobilised in November of that year.
36, Bury Park Road, Luton.   731/A.

BURLEY, F. R., Private, 3rd Royal Fusiliers.
Joining in July 1918, he had not completed his training when hostilities ceased. Afterwards, however, he was sent with the Army of Occupation to Germany, where in 1920 he was still serving.
36, Bury Park Road, Luton.   731/B.

BURLEY, J., Private, Bedfordshire Regiment.
He volunteered in August 1914, and was sent to France in in the following year. Whilst in this theatre of war he fought in several battles, including those of Ypres, Hill 60, Givenchy, the Somme, Loos, and Cambrai, where he was severely wounded, losing a leg. Returning to England he was invalided out of the Service in 1918, and holds the 1914–15 Star, and the General Service and Victory Medals.
71, Warwick Road, Luton.   730/C.

BURLEY, J. H., Private, 2nd Bedfordshire Regt.
He volunteered in August 1914, and immediately afterwards was sent to the Western Front, where he took part in the Retreat from Mons, and the Battles of Hill 60 and Loos, and numerous other engagements, and was twice wounded. He was demobilised in October 1919, and holds the Mons Star, and the General Service and Victory Medals.
20, Kimpton Road, Luton.   732.

BURLEY, R., Private, Royal Field Artillery.
Volunteering in September 1914, he was drafted to France on the completion of his training, subsequently taking part in engagements at Ypres and Hill 60. In 1916 he was sent to Egypt, and in the following year served in the Palestine Campaign with General Allenby's Forces, and participated in much heavy fighting. From 1918 until after the cessation of hostilities he saw service in Salonika, and was demobilised after his return to England in January 1919. He holds the the 1914–15 Star, and the General Service and Victory Medals.
71, Warwick Road, Luton.   730/A.

BURLS, J. A. E., Lieutenant, R.A.V.C.
He joined in February 1917, and in the following October was drafted to France, where he was in charge of the hospital for horses at Rouen. Later, in February 1918, he was sent to Mesopotamia, where he was stationed at Baghdad and Mosul. He holds the General Service and Victory Medals, and was still serving in 1920.
Roseneath, Avondale Road, Luton.   733.

BURNAGE, A. G., Private, 1st Hertfordshire Regiment.
He was mobilised in August 1914, and was immediately afterwards drafted to the Western Front, where he took part in the Battles of Mons, La Bassée, Ypres, Neuve Chapelle, St. Eloi, the Somme, Arras and Passchendaele, and was wounded. He was invalided home and discharged as medically unfit in October 1918, and holds the Mons Star, and the General Service and Victory Medals.
32, Alexandra Road, Hitchin.   2453.

BURNAGE, A. J., Private, South Irish Horse.
He joined in January 1916, and after his training served at various stations on important duties with his unit. He rendered valuable services, but was not successful in obtaining his transfer overseas before the cessation of hostilities. He was demobilised in September 1919.
North Bridge Street, Shefford, near Bedford.   Z735/B.

BURNAGE, F., Sergeant, 5th Bedfordshire Regt.
He volunteered in June 1915, and in the same year was sent to the Dardanelles. Later he was transferred to Egypt, and served in the Palestine Offensive, taking part in numerous engagements, including that at Gaza and Jerusalem. He returned home and was demobilised in March 1919, and holds the 1914–15 Star, and the General Service and Victory Medals.
Campton, Shefford.   Z737.

BURNAGE, F. E., Pte., R.A.M.C., & Gnr., R.F.A.
He volunteered in October 1915, and in the following January was drafted to Egypt. He served at various stations and took part in the Palestine Campaign, being present at the engagements at Gaza, Haifa and Beyrout. He was demobilised in August 1919, and holds the General Service and Victory Medals.
24, Wenlock Street, Luton.   738.

BURNHAM, A. E., Private, R.A.S.C.
He volunteered in June 1915, and in the same year proceeded to the Western Front, where he was engaged on important duties with his unit. He was present at engagements on the Somme and at Arras and Cambrai, and after the termination of hostilities returned to England and was demobilised, holding the 1914–15 Star, and the General Service and Victory Medals. 54, Holywell Road, Watford.   X734/C.

BURNHAM, C., L/Corporal, Royal Engineers.
He volunteered in November 1914, and in the following July was drafted to the Dardanelles and was in action at Suvla Bay. Later he was transferred to Egypt, and served in the Palestine Campaign, taking part in the Battle of Gaza. Finally he was sent to France, where he was present at the Battle of Cambrai, and was twice wounded. He holds the 1914–15 Star, and the General Service and Victory Medals, and was demobilised in May 1919.
110, Cobden Street, Luton.   739.

BURNHAM, E., Private, R.A.S.C.
He volunteered in July 1915, and in the same year was drafted to France, where he served on important duties in various sectors of the Front. He was present at engagements at Arras, Ypres, Cambrai and the Somme, and after the conclusion of hostilities returned to England and was demobilised in January 1919, holding the 1914–15 Star, and the General Service and Victory Medals.
54, Holywell Road, Watford.   X734/A

BURNHAM, E., Private, R.A.V.C.
He joined in June 1917, and after his training served at various stations on important duties with his unit. He rendered valuable services, but was not succesful in obtaining his transfer overseas before the cessation of hostilities. He was demobilised in February 1919.   X736.
25, York Road, Watford.

BURNHAM, H. T., Private, Bedfordshire and Norfolk Regiments.
He joined in 1916, and in the following year was drafted to France, where he was in action on the Somme and at Arras and Cambrai, and was gassed. He holds the General Service and Victory Medals, and was demobilised in September 1919.
54, Holywell Road, Watford.   X734/B.

BURNIDGE, J., Private, King's Liverpool Regt.
He joined in October 1916, and after a period of training was drafted to North Russia. He served on the Vaga and Dvina Fronts until September 1919, when he returned to England and was demobilised. He holds the Victory Medal.
28, Leighton Street, Woburn.   Z740.

BURR, E. G., Rifleman, K.R.R.C.
He joined in May 1917, and a year later was drafted overseas. He served on the Western Front on the Marne and at Amiens, and was later invalided home through ill-health. He was demobilised in March 1919, and holds the General Service and Victory Medals.
29, Bolton Road, Luton.   741.

BURR, S. R., Private, 2nd Bedfordshire Regiment.
He joined in June 1916, and in the same year was drafted to the Western Front, where he was in action on the Ancre and at Passchendaele, where he was wounded and gassed. On recovery he took part in the fierce fighting at Bapaume and Cambrai. He was demobilised in October 1919, and holds the General Service and Victory Medals.
Manor Road, Barton, near Ampthill.   T1546.

BURRAGE, D., Private, 4th London Regiment (Royal Fusiliers).
He joined in June 1916, and after a period of training was drafted to France, where he took part in many engagements, including those on the Somme, and at Arras and Ypres, where he was killed in action on October 26th, 1917. He was entitled to the General Service and Victory Medals.
206, Harwood Road, Watford.   X742.

BURRELL, P., Sapper, Royal Engineers.
He volunteered in August 1914, and in the following July was drafted to the Dardanelles, where he was in action at Suvla Bay, and other engagements. Later he was transferred to Egypt, and took part in the Palestine Campaign, being present at the Battle of Gaza. He holds the 1914–15 Star, and the General Service and Victory Medals, and was demobilised in March 1919.
" Ingleside," Beechwood Road, Leagrave, near Luton.   743.

BURRIDGE, C. E., Private, 8th Royal Sussex Regiment.

He volunteered in September 1914, and in July of the following year was sent to the Western Front, where he took part in the heavy fighting at Festubert, Loos, the Somme, Arras, Ypres and Cambrai. He was killed in action near Albert on May 9th, 1918, and was entitled to the 1914–15 Star, and the General Service and Victory Medals.
6, Lower Dagnall Street, St. Albans. X744.

BURROWS, E. W., Private, Norfolk Regiment.

He joined in 1916, and after his training was drafted to the Western Front in the same year. He served in the engagements at Arras, Ypres, Cambrai, the Somme and St. Quentin, and after the signing of the Armistice went to Germany with the Army of Occupation and was stationed on the Rhine. He holds the General Service and Victory Medals, and was demobilised in 1919.
Flitton, near Ampthill. T1550.

BURROWS, J., Private, Royal Fusiliers.

He volunteered in 1915, and in the same year was drafted to the Western Front, where he took part in many important engagements, including those at Neuve Chapelle, Arras, Ypres, Cambrai, the Somme and Armentières, and was wounded. He was invalided home and discharged as medically unfit in October 1918, and holds the General Service and Victory Medals.
Clifton Road, Shefford, Bedford. Z745.

BURROWS, J. V., Gunner, R.F.A.

He volunteered in May 1915, and in 1917 was drafted to the Western Front, where during his service he took part in the Battles of Arras, Ypres and Cambrai. He was also in action on the Marne in 1918, and in other engagements in the Advance of that year. He was demobilised in July 1919, and holds the General Service and Victory Medals.
Sharpenhoe Road, Barton. T1548.

B URROWS, L., Driver, Royal Field Artillery.

He volunteered in September 1914, and in the following year was sent to France, where he took part in severe fighting at Hill 60, the Somme, Ypres, Cambrai and St. Quentin, and was wounded. He was demobilised in January 1919, and holds the 1914–15 Star, and the General Service and Victory Medals.
22, Cobden Street, Luton. 746.

BURROWS, P. C., Private, Middlesex Regiment.

He volunteered in May 1915, and in September of the same year was drafted to the Western Front, where he took part in heavy fighting at Loos, and on the Somme, and was wounded. He was invalided home suffering from frost-bite and dysentery, and was discharged as medically unfit for further service in November 1916. He holds the 1914–15 Star, and the General Service and Victory Medals.
35, Union Street, Dunstable. 747.

BURROWS, P. J., Sapper, Royal Engineers.

He joined in May 1916, and in the following May was drafted overseas. During his service in France, he was engaged on important duties with his unit in various sectors of the Front, and was wounded at St. Julien in October 1917. Later he was invalided home through ill-health, and was finally demobilised in April 1919, holding the General Service and Victory Medals.
11, Bearton Road, Hitchin. 1833.

BURTON, J. L., Gunner, Royal Field Artillery.

He joined in December 1916, and after his training was drafted to the Western Front, and took part in heavy fighting at Ypres, the Somme and many other important engagements. He was discharged in May 1918, and holds the General Service and Victory Medals.
73, Beech Road, Luton. 748.

BURTON, T., Private, East Surrey Regiment.

He volunteered in August 1914, and in October of the same year was drafted to the Western Front, where he took part in the Battles of Ypres, the Somme, and many other engagements. He was killed in action at Arras on May 1st, 1917, and was entitled to the 1914 Star, and the General Service and Victory Medals.
Clifton Road, Shefford, Bedford. Z749.

BURTON, W., L/Corporal (Signaller), R.G.A.

He joined in November 1915, and after his training was drafted to the Western Front, where he took part in many engagements, including those at Ypres, Cambrai and Bullecourt. Later he proceeded with the Army of Occupation to Germany. He returned home and was demobilised in October 1919, and holds the General Service and Victory Medals.
99, Highbury Road, Luton. 750.

BUSBY, G. C., Private, Australian Imperial Forces.

He volunteered in January 1915, and in the following July was drafted to the Dardanelles, where he was killed in action in September of the same year. He was entitled to the 1914–15 Star, and the General Service and Victory Medals.
28, Brixton Road, Watford. X751/A.

BUSE, C., Private, 8th Bedfordshire Regiment.

He volunteered in November 1914, and having completed his training was drafted to France in 1916. Whilst serving on this Front he saw much fighting at numerous engagements, including those of the Somme, Arras, Ypres and Cambrai. Returning home after the cessation of hostilities, he was demobilised in March 1919, holding the General Service and Victory Medals.
Dunstable Street, Ampthill. 752.

BUSHBY, E. J., Private, Grenadier Guards.

Joining in January 1918, after completing his training he was engaged at various stations on important duties with his unit. As he was medically unfit for service overseas he was unable to secure his transfer to a theatre of war, and was demobilised in January 1919.
Jack's Lane, Clophill, Ampthill. 1834/B.

BUSHBY, G. F., Private, 2nd London Regiment (Royal Fusiliers).

He joined in June 1916, and in the following year was drafted to France. Soon after his arrival on this Front he was wounded and taken prisoner. He was held in captivity in Germany until after the Armistice, when he was released and subsequently sent home and demobilised in March 1919. He holds the General Service and Victory Medals.
Jack's Lane, Clophill, Ampthill. 1834/A.

BUSHBY, W., Rifleman, King's Royal Rifles.

He volunteered in October 1915, and in April of the following year was drafted to Egypt, and later proceeded to Palestine. Whilst in this theatre of war he took part in the fighting at Gaza, Jaffa and Haifa and in other operations throughout the Campaign. He returned home and was subsequently demobilised in April 1919, and holds the General Service and Victory Medals.
Jack's Lane, Clophill, Ampthill. 1834/C.

BUSHBY, W. G., Private, 5th Bedfordshire and Essex Regiments.

He volunteered in September 1914, and was drafted to Gallipoli in July of the following year. While in this theatre of war he saw much fighting, being in action at Suvla Bay and Chocolate Hill. Later he returned to England, but was afterwards sent to France, where he fought on the Somme and at Vimy Ridge, St. Quentin, and Cambrai. After the cessation of hostilities he returned to England, and was demobilised in February 1919, holding the General Service and Victory Medals.
15, Essex Street, Luton. 753.

BUTCHER, A., Private, R.A.S.C.

He joined in December 1916, and after his training proceeded to France. While overseas he was present at several engagements, including those of Ypres, Arras, Cambrai and the Somme. He rendered valuable services until the cessation of hostilities, when returning home he was finally demobilised in May 1919, holding the General Service and Victory Medals.
63, Edward Street, Dunstable. 754.

BUTCHER, A. B., Pte., 2nd Hertfordshire Regt.

He volunteered in August 1914, and in the following January was drafted to the Western Front. Later he was transferred to Egypt and took part in the Palestine Campaign, being in action in numerous engagements. After the cessation of hostilities he returned to England, and was demobilised in August 1919, holding the 1914–15 Star, and the General Service and Victory Medals.
89, Cardiff Road, Watford. X755/B.

BUTCHER, A. L., Private, Northamptonshire Regiment.

He volunteered in 1914, and in the same year was drafted to Egypt and took part in the Battle of Gaza. He was later transferred to Salonika, and thence to France, where he served in the Battles of the Somme and Arras. He was also engaged in the Retreat and Advance of 1918, and was twice wounded. He was demobilised in April 1919, and holds the 1914–15 Star, and the General Service and Victory Medals.
11, Victoria Place, Biggleswade. Z1534.

BUTCHER, A. P., Sergeant, 2nd Hertfordshire Regiment.
He was mobilised at the outbreak of war, and after his training served at various stations on important duties with his unit. He rendered valuable services, but was not successful in obtaining his transfer overseas before the cessation of hostilities. He was discharged in June 1917.
89, Cardiff Road, Watford. X755/A.

BUTCHER, C., Private, 1st Bedfordshire Regt.
Serving in the Army before war broke out, in 1914 he was sent to France with the original Expeditionary Force and was in heavy fighting in the Retreat from Mons and on the Aisne, the Marne and at Ypres. He was wounded in this last engagement, and on recovery rejoined his unit to take part in the Battles of Neuve Chapelle, Hill 60, Givenchy and Festubert, and was killed in action at Loos on October 28th, 1915. He was entitled to the Mons Star, and the General Service and Victory Medals.
1, Foundry Lane, Biggleswade. Z1527/A.

BUTCHER, E. C., Private, Bedfordshire and Hertfordshire Regiments.
Volunteering in August 1914, he was sent to the Western Front in the following year, and whilst in this theatre of war served at Ypres, Festubert, the Somme, Arras and Cambrai, and was wounded four times. Later he was drafted to India, where in 1920 he was still serving in the Deccan. He holds the 1914-15 Star, and the General Service and Victory Medals.
17, Victoria Place, Biggleswade. Z1263.

BUTCHER, F. T., Rifleman, The Cameronians (Scottish Rifles).
He volunteered in September 1914, and in the following year was drafted to France, where he took part in the Battle of Arras and numerous other engagements. In March 1918 he was taken prisoner near Ypres and was kept in captivity in Germany until after the Armistice, when he was released and returned to England and was demobilised, holding the 1914-15 Star, and the General Service and Victory Medals.
240, Wellington Street, Luton. 756.

BUTCHER, G., Sapper, R.E. (Signals).
He joined in October 1916, and in January of the following year proceeded to German East Africa. He was engaged in various parts on the maintenance of telegraph lines, and on postal duties, and rendered valuable services. He returned home and was demobilised in March 1919, and holds the General Service and Victory Medals.
51, Upper Culver Road, St. Albans. X758/B.

BUTCHER, J. H., Corporal, 6th Leicester Regt.
He volunteered in November 1915, and after his training was drafted to the Western Front, where he took part in heavy fighting at Ypres, Arras and Cambrai, and was wounded. Later he proceeded with the Army of Occupation to Germany. He returned home and was demobilised in January 1919, and holds the General Service and Victory Medals.
51, Upper Culver Road, St. Albans. X758/A.

BUTCHER, J. H., Gunner, R.F.A.
He volunteered in October 1915, and having completed his training was drafted to Mesopotamia in 1917. Whilst in this theatre of war he took part in several engagements, and was present at the Capture of Baghdad. He also served in India for a time. After his return home on the cessation of hostilities, he was demobilised in April 1919, holding the General Service and Victory Medals.
32, Upper Culver Road, St. Albans. X757.

BUTCHER, W., Sapper, Royal Engineers.
He volunteered in 1915, and in the same year was drafted to the Western Front, where he did valuable work in the Battles of Neuve Chapelle, Ypres, the Somme, Messines and Cambrai, and was wounded. He was demobilised in February 1919 after his return home, and holds the 1914-15 Star, and the General Service and Victory Medals.
Park Street, Ampthill. 1525.

BUTLER, R. G., Private, R.A.S.C. (M.T.)
He joined in August 1916, and after his training was drafted in the following March to the Western Front, where he rendered valuable service at many engagements, including those of Arras, Cambrai, and the Retreat and Advance of 1918. He afterwards proceeded with the Army of Occupation to Germany, and on his return home was demobilised in February 1919, holding the General Service and Victory Medals.
79, Frederic Street, Luton. 769.

BUTLER, W. P., Private, 2nd Cheshire Regiment.
He joined in June 1916, and in November of the same year was sent to Salonika. He served in various engagements, and was taken prisoner by the Bulgarians in July 1918, and died in captivity on September 17th of the same year. He was entitled to the General Service and Victory Medals.
47, Diamond Road, Watford. X770.

BUTT, H. F., Private, R.A.S.C. and R.A.M.C.
He volunteered in August 1914, and in October of the following year was drafted overseas, and served at the Dardanelles, being present at numerous engagements. Later he was transferred to Palestine, where he remained until he returned home and was demobilised in June 1919. He holds the General Service and Victory Medals.
11, Althorp Road, Luton. 771.

BUTTELL, E. B., Private, Royal Air Force.
He joined in January 1916, and after his training served at various stations on important duties with his unit. He rendered valuable services, but was not successful in obtaining his transfer overseas before the cessation of hostilities. He was demobilised in February 1919.
169, Sandringham Road, Callowland, Watford. X773/A.

BUTTELL, E. O. (Mrs.), Special War Worker.
This lady was engaged as forewoman at the Watford Munition Factory in the danger zone of the shell-filling department. Her duties, which were of a dangerous and responsible nature, were carried out with great care and efficiency, and she rendered valuable services during the war.
169, Sandringham Road, Callowland, Watford. X773/B.

BUTTERFIELD, A., Private, 1st Bedfordshire Regiment.
He volunteered at the outbreak of war, and immediately proceeded to France, where he took part in numerous important engagements, including those of Mons, Neuve Chapelle, Arras, Ypres and Oppy Wood, and was wounded six times. He also saw service in Italy for a short period, and returning home was demobilised in March 1919, holding the Mons Star, and the General Service and Victory Medals
45, Hitchin Hill, Hitchin. 1612.

BUTTERFIELD, A., Sergeant, 3rd Bedfordshire Regiment.
He volunteered in September 1914, and having completed his training was drafted to France in August of the following year. Whilst overseas he took part in several important engagements, including the Battles of the Somme, Arras and Ypres. Later he served in Russia for a time. He returned home and was demobilised in August 1919, holding the 1914-15 Star, and the General Service and Victory Medals.
45, Hitchin Hill, Hitchin. 1613.

BUTTERFIELD, A., L/Corporal, R.G.A.
He volunteered at the outbreak of war, and was immediately drafted to France. He fought in the Battles of the Marne, the Aisne, Ypres, Loos and the Somme, and later proceeded to Mesopotamia, where he suffered from malaria. Afterwards he was transferred to India, remaining there until August 1919, when he returned home and was demobilised. He holds the 1914 Star, and the General Service and Victory Medals.
" Aspinall," Alfred Street, Dunstable. 774.

BUTTERFIELD, A. G., Sapper, Royal Engineers.
He volunteered in September 1914, and in the following July was drafted to the Dardanelles, and later transferred to the Western Front, where he took part in the fighting at Arras, on the Somme and at Ypres. He was demobilised in February 1919, and holds the 1914-15 Star, and the General Service and Victory Medals.
32, Cowper Street, Luton. 775.

BUTTERFIELD, E., Driver, Royal Engineers.
On attaining military age he joined in July 1918, and was drafted overseas after the cessation of hostilities. He served with the Army of Occupation at Cologne on the Rhine for 12 months and was demobilised in February 1920.
8, Luton Road, Markyate. 776/B.

BUTTERFIELD, G. (D.C.M.), Bombardier, Royal Garrison Artillery.
He volunteered at the outbreak of war, and was shortly afterwards drafted overseas. He served in India and Mesopotamia, and was awarded the Distinguished Conduct Medal for his conspicuous gallantry in the Field. During the operations at Kut he was wounded and taken prisoner and sent to Turkey. His injuries proved fatal and he subsequently died in captivity on September 13th, 1917. He was entitled to the 1914-15 Star, and the General Service and Victory Medals.
8, Luton Road, Markyate. 776/C.

BUTTERFIELD, G., Private, M.G.C.
He volunteered in July 1915, and in the same year was drafted overseas. He served on the Western Front during the fighting on the Somme, and at Arras, Ypres, and Cambrai, and was twice wounded. In March 1918 he was taken prisoner and sent to Germany, remaining in captivity for nine months. He was repatriated and demobilised in January 1919, and holds the 1914-15 Star, and the General Service and Victory Medals.
24, Upper Heath Road, St. Albans. X779/A.

BUTTERFIELD, G., Gunner, R.G.A.
He joined in October 1916, and was in the same year drafted overseas. He served on the Western Front, and took part in many engagements, including those at Ypres, Messines Ridge and Delville Wood, where he was killed in action on April 15th, 1918. He was entitled to the General Service and Victory Medals.
43, Church Street, St. Albans. X777.

BUTTERFIELD, H., Gunner, R.G.A.
He joined in July 1916, and in the following November was drafted to France, where he took part in various engagements, including those on the Somme and at Vimy Ridge and Arras, where he was killed in action on June 5th, 1917. He was entitled to the General Service and Victory Medals.
51, Arthur Street, Luton. 778/A.

BUTTERFIELD, H., Driver, R.F.A.
He joined in March 1917, and after a short period of training was drafted to India. He served at Secunderabad and on the North West Frontier until 1919, when he returned to England and was demobilised in January 1920, holding the General Service and Victory Medals.
8, Luton Road, Markyate. 776/A.

BUTTERFIELD, J., Sergeant, Royal Engineers.
He joined in April 1918, and in the following June was drafted overseas. He remained a few months in France, and was then transferred to Egypt, where he served at Alexandria and Cairo. He holds the General Service and Victory Medals, and was still serving in 1920.
105, Park Street, Luton. 780/A.

BUTTERFIELD, J., Private, M.G.C.
He volunteered in November 1915, and was drafted to France, where he saw much fighting. While overseas he took part in several battles, including Arras, Cambrai, Albert and Ypres, and was wounded. After the Armistice he returned home, and was demobilised in April 1919, holding the General Service and Victory Medals.
25, Dacre Road, Hitchin. 1615.

BUTTERFIELD, J. H., Rifleman, Royal Irish Rifles.
He volunteered in November 1915, and after completing his training was drafted overseas. He served on the Somme and at Ypres, Vimy Ridge and Passchendaele, and was wounded at Cambrai. He was demobilised in March 1919, and holds the General Service and Victory Medals.
51, Arthur Street, Luton. 778/B.

BUTTERFIELD, O., Shoeing Smith, R.F.A.
He was serving at the outbreak of war, and was drafted overseas in 1915. He fought in many sectors of the Western Front, and took part in the engagements at Ypres, on the Somme, Arras and Cambrai. He was demobilised in September 1919, and holds the 1914-15 Star, and the General Service and Victory Medals.
5, Cleveland Road, Markyate. 1655.

BUTTERFIELD, P., Sapper, Royal Engineers.
He volunteered at the outbreak of hostilities, and a year later was drafted overseas. He served at Gallipoli, being present at engagements at Suvla Bay, Anzac, and was later transferred to Egypt, and took part in the Palestine campaign, being in action at Gaza and Jerusalem. He was demobilised in March 1919, and holds the 1914-15 Star, and the General Service and Victory Medals
105, Park Street, Luton. 780/B.

BUTTERTON, G., Private, R.A.S.C.
He joined in April 1917, and after a period of training served at various stations on important transport duties with his unit. He was unsuccessful in obtaining his transfer overseas before fighting ceased, but did valuable work until demobilised in March 1919.
26, Pondswick Road, Luton. 781.

BUTTON, H. J., Private, Border Regiment.
He joined in April 1916, and was shortly afterwards drafted to France. He took part in the fierce fighting on the Somme and at Arras, and was killed in action near Ypres on April 23rd, 1917. He was entitled to the General Service and Victory Medals.
41, Yarmouth Road, Callowland, Watford. 782/C.

BUTTON, S. G., Private, 4th Middlesex Regiment.
He joined in May 1916, and in the following August was drafted to France. He took part in the severe fighting on the Somme, at Beaumont-Hamel, Arras, Bullecourt and Vimy Ridge, where he was killed in action on April 23rd, 1917. He was entitled to the General Service and Victory Medals.
41, Yarmouth Road, Callowland, Watford. X782/A.

BUTTON, W. A., Private, Labour Corps.
He joined in March 1917, and was the same year drafted to France. He was engaged until October 1919 on the Western Front in making roads and doing other important work at Ypres, Arras, the Somme and Cambrai, often during much heavy firing. He was demobilised in November 1919 after his return home, and holds the General Service and Victory Medals.
41, Yarmouth Road, Callowland, Watford. 782/B.

BUTTS, F., Private, 2nd Lincolnshire Regiment
He had previously served 12 years in the Regular Army, and was in India at the outbreak of hostilities. After his arrival on the Western Front in November 1914, he took part in the fighting at Hill 60, Ypres, Festubert, Loos, the Somme, Arras, Albert and Cambrai, and in other engagements until the cessation of hostilities. After the Armistice he proceeded to Germany with the Army of Occupation, and was stationed at Cologne until his return to England for demobilisation in April 1919. He holds the 1914 Star, and the General Service and Victory Medals.
6, Verulam Road, Hitchin. 1835/A.

BUTTS, W., Private, 1st Hertfordshire Regiment.
He volunteered in August 1914, and in the following November was drafted to France. A fortnight later he was killed in action in his first engagement, at Ypres, on November 19th, 1914 He was entitled to the 1914 Star, and the General Service and Victory Medals.
6, Verulam Road, Hitchin. 1835/B.

BUTTS, W., Private, Labour Corps and R.A.S.C.
He volunteered in October 1915, and was drafted to Gallipoli in November. After a few weeks' service on that Front at Anzac and Cape Helles, he was transferred to France, where he did excellent work in many sectors until the cessation of hostilities. He returned home and was demobilised in February 1919, holding the 1914-15 Star, and the General Service and Victory Medals.
12, Water Lane, Hitchin. 1607.

BYE, R. H., Private, Bedfordshire Regiment.
He volunteered at the outbreak of war, and was immediately drafted to France, where he took part in the fierce fighting during the Retreat from Mons, and also served in the engagements of Hill 60, the Somme, Arras, Ypres and Verdun. He was afterwards transferred to Italy and did valuable work on the Piave Front. He was discharged in January 1918 in consequence of his service, and holds the Mons Star, and the General Service and Victory Medals.
41, Albert Street, St. Albans. X783/A.

BYFIELD, F. T., Private, R.A.S.C.
He volunteered in January 1915, and in the following March was drafted to France, where he was engaged for nearly four years on highly important transport duties in many sectors of the Front. He was demobilised in January 1919, and holds the 1914-15 Star, and the General Service and Victory Medals.
28, Yarmouth Road, Callowland, Watford. X785.

BYGRAVE, L. J., Corporal, Royal Irish Fusiliers.
He was serving at the outbreak of war, and was immediately drafted to France, where he was engaged in the fierce fighting during the Retreat from Mons and in the Battle of Ypres. He then proceeded to Egypt and Palestine, and took part in the campaign up to Jerusalem. He also served for a period in Salonika and Serbia. After his return home he was demobilised in June 1919, and holds the Mons Star, and the General Service and Victory Medals.
Station Road, Puzzle Gardens, Toddington. 784.

BYGRAVE, P., Private, Labour Corps.
He volunteered in July 1915, and was engaged on important duties at various stations on the completion of his training. Owing to ill-health he was not successful in obtaining his transfer overseas before the cessation of hostilities, but he rendered valuable service until demobilised in January 1919.
Church Path, Ickleford, Hitchin. 1616.

BYGRAVES, F., Bombardier, R.F.A.
He joined in April 1916, and in the following year was drafted to the Western Front, where he took part in important engagements, including those at Ypres, the Somme, Arras and Cambrai. In consequence of illness, which rendered him unfit for active service, he was transferred to the Military Police. He was demobilised in January 1919, and holds the General Service and Victory Medals.
13, Alexander Terrace, Biggleswade. Z1533.

BYGRAVES, S., Private, 11th Queen's (Royal West Surrey Regiment).
He joined in April 1916, and after a short training was drafted to the Western Front in July. He fought with distinction in several engagements, including that at Arras, and was killed in action on June 7th, 1917, near Ypres. He was mentioned in Despatches and recommended for the Military Medal on the very day on which he died. He was entitled to the General Service and Victory Medals.
New Town, Biggleswade.   Z1264.

BYRAM, R. A., L/Corporal, 7th Lincolnshire Regt.
He was mobilised at the outbreak of war, and was at once drafted to France. He took part in the Retreat from Mons, and in the Battles of Loos, Vimy Ridge, the Somme, Albert and Cambrai. During the Retreat in April 1918 he was taken prisoner and was held in captivity in Germany until February 1919. After his return to England he was demobilised in the following month, and holds the Mons Star, and the General Service and Victory Medals.
54, Sunnyside, Hitchin.   1813/A.

BYSOUTH, S., Private, R.A.S.C.
He joined in September 1916, and in the following month was drafted to France. He rendered much valuable transport service and took part in many engagements, including those of the Somme, Arras and Achiet-le-Grand. He was demobilised in October 1919, after his return home, and holds the General Service and Victory Medals.
162, Dallow Road, Luton.   786.

C

CADDEY, J., Private, R.A.S.C. (M.T.)
Volunteering in April 1915, he was sent overseas in the following month, and subsequently served on important motor transport duties at Loos, the Somme, Arras, Armentières and Albert, until after the cessation of hostilities. After returning to England he was demobilised in June 1919, and holds the 1914-15 Star, and the General Service and Victory Medals.   31, Brixton Road, Watford.   X802.

CADMAN, A. T., Corporal, Machine Gun Corps.
He was serving in India at the outbreak of hostilities, and after being retained on important duties there for a time was drafted to France in 1916. From that date until the close of the war he took part in many important engagements, including those of the Somme, Arras and Cambrai. After his return to England he was demobilised in January 1919, and holds the General Service and Victory Medals.
94, St. James' Road, Watford.   X803/B.

CADMAN, G., Corporal, Royal Engineers.
He volunteered in January 1915, and was drafted to France later in the same year. While in this theatre of war he saw much severe fighting in several engagements, including those of Arras, Ypres, Cambrai and the Somme. After over four years' service he returned home, and was demobilised in March 1919, holding the 1914-15 Star, and the General Service and Victory Medals.
94, St. James' Road, Watford.   X803/A.

CAIN, A. A., Sergeant, 2nd Bedfordshire Regt.
After service in India prior to the outbreak of hostilities, he was transferred to the Western Front early in the war. He took a prominent part in many important engagements, and was killed in action in the neighbourhood of Lille in 1915. He was entitled to the 1914 Star, and the General Service and Victory Medals. 61, Hastings Street, Luton.   814/B.

CAIN, A. C., Private, Bedfordshire Regiment.
He volunteered in 1915, and later in that year was drafted to France. During his service on the Western Front he was in action at Festubert, Vimy Ridge, the Somme, Arras, Cambrai and the Retreat and Advance of 1918. He was demobilised in 1919, holding the 1914-15 Star, and the General Service and Victory Medals. 20, Portmill Lane, Hitchin.   1836.

CAIN, F., Gunner, Royal Field Artillery.
He volunteered in 1915, and in the same year was drafted to the Western Front. He took part in many important engagements until October 3rd, 1917, when he died in hospital from wounds received in action. He was buried at Zuydschoote. He was entitled to the 1914-15 Star, and the General Service and Victory Medals.
Lower Luton Road, Batford, Harpenden.   800.

CAIN, G., Private, Royal Army Service Corps.
He volunteered in December 1914, and in the following year, on the conclusion of his training, was drafted to France. He was engaged until the close of hostilities on important duties with the supply column, transporting rations and munitions of all kinds to and from the lines, particularly in the engagements at Ypres, Arras, the Marne and St. Quentin. After his return home he was demobilised in March 1919, holding the 1914-15 Star, and the General Service and Victory Medals   204, Chester Road, Watford.   X805.

CAIN, H., Gunner, Royal Field Artillery.
He joined in February 1918, and in the following May was sent to Salonika, where he was engaged in several important battles. Later he rendered valuable service with the Relief Force in North Russia until January 1920, when he returned home and was demobilised. He holds the General Service and Victory Medals.
57, Ash Road, Luton.   806.

CAIN, H. E., Private, R.A.M.C.
Being unfit for service with the Colours, he joined the 2nd Bedfordshire Volunteers in October 1914, and served as honorary quartermaster until April 1917, when he joined the Royal Army Medical Corps. He was not successful in securing his transfer overseas, but rendered valuable services until demobilised in January 1919.
61, Clarendon Road, Luton.   807.

CAIN, H. W., Private, 1st Hertfordshire Regiment.
He volunteered in September 1914, and after completing his training was sent to the Western Front in the following year. While overseas he fought in several engagements, and was killed in action at Ypres in 1917. He was buried in the British Cemetery south of that town, and was entitled to the 1914-15 Star, and the General Service and Victory Medals.
Angel Cottage, Offley.   1605.

CAIN, J., Private, Royal Defence Corps.
Though too old for overseas service, he volunteered in 1915, and at the conclusion of his training served at various stations on important duties. He did much valuable work guarding railways and munition factories until the close of his service. He was discharged in December 1917.
3, Cross Street, Luton.   809/C.

CAIN, P. H., L/Corporal, 5th Bedfordshire Regt.
He volunteered in September 1914, and having completed his training was sent in the following July to the Dardanelles, where he fought in several engagements, including that at Suvla Bay, and was wounded. On his recovery he was transferred to Egypt, and afterwards took part in the Palestine campaign, in which he fought at Gaza, Jaffa and in other engagements. He was demobilised in January 1919, and holds the 1914-15 Star, and the General Service and Victory Medals.
33, Gloucester Road, Luton.   804.

CAIN, S., Sapper, Royal Engineers.
He volunteered in November 1915, and in the following March was drafted to Egypt, where he was engaged on important duties at forward areas. In the Palestine Expedition he rendered valuable service at Gaza and Jerusalem building pontoon bridges and making trenches. On his return home he was demobilised in February 1919, holding the General Service and Victory Medals.
3, Cross Street, Luton.   809/B.

CAIN, T., Private, Duke of Wellington's (West Riding Regiment).
He volunteered in April 1915, and, having completed his training, was drafted to France. He saw much fighting in several severe engagements, and was killed in action near Albert on September 24th, 1916. He was entitled to the General Service and Victory Medals.
4, Newcombe Street, Harpenden.   808/A.

CAIN, W., Private, R.M.L.I.
He joined in October 1916, and was posted for duty with H.M.S. " Vincent " in the North Sea, and took part in the engagement near Scapa Flow. Later he was transferred to H.M.S. " Renown," and served in that vessel during the Prince of Wales' voyages to Canada and Australia. He holds the General Service and Victory Medals, and was still serving in 1920.
3, Cross Street, Luton.   809/A.

CAIN, W., Private, Norfolk Regiment.
He joined in March 1916, and on the conclusion of his training was drafted to the Western Front. Whilst in this theatre of war he took part in several engagements until the close of hostilities, including those of St. Quentin and Albert. After returning home he was demobilised in February 1919, holding the General Service and Victory Medals.
4, Newcombe Street, Harpenden.   808/B.

CALCOTT, B. F., Sapper, Royal Engineers.
He joined in April 1917, and on the conclusion of his training served with his unit at various stations on important duties. He did much good work in the construction of huts and drains, but was not able to secure his transfer overseas before the cessation of hostilities owing to medical unfitness. He was demobilised in February 1919.
8, Queen Street, Houghton Regis, Dunstable.   810.

CALCRAFT, W. E., Pte., Sherwood Foresters.
He joined in September 1917, and after having completed his training was drafted to France in the following April. He was killed in action on August 31st, 1918, and was entitled to the General Service and Victory Medals.
66, Ridge Avenue, Letchworth. 2769.

CALLAGHAN, H., Private, R.A.S.C.
He joined in April 1917, and having completed his training was sent to German East Africa. Whilst in this theatre of war he was engaged on important transport and supply duties until the Armistice. Returning home, he was demobilised in March 1919, and holds the General Service and Victory Medals.
58, St. Mary's Street, Dunstable. 811.

CALLAN, B. A., Gunner, R.F.A.
He joined in January 1917, and in the same year was drafted to the Western Front, where he took an active part in several important engagements for a period of nearly twelve months. In January 1918 he was sent to the Italian Front, and did excellent work until hostilities ceased. Returning home, he was demobilised in February 1919, and holds the General Service and Victory Medals.
11, Newcombe Road, Luton. 812.

CALVER, H., Private, 13th Middlesex Regiment.
He volunteered in January 1915, and at the conclusion of his training was sent to the Western Front in the following September. He took an active part in several engagements, and was killed in action near Loos on January 27th, 1916. He was entitled to the 1914–15 Star, and the General Service and Victory Medals.
Meppershall Road, Shefford. 813.

CAMP, E., Private, Machine Gun Corps.
He joined in 1916, and having completed his training was sent to Turkey. After much valuable service there he proceeded to France, where he took part in many important battles until fighting ceased, including those of Arras and Cambrai. After his return home he was demobilised in December 1919, and holds the General Service and Victory Medals.
61, Hastings Street, Luton. 814/A.

CAMP, H. H. (M.S.M.), Quartermaster-Sergeant, Bedfordshire and Hertfordshire Regiments.
He joined the Army in 1898, and was drafted to France in October 1914. After taking part in several battles, including that of Ypres, he was sent home in the following February and was retained on important duties with his unit until January 1920, when he was demobilised. He holds the Queen's and King's South African Medals, the Long Service Medal, the Meritorious Service Medal, the 1914 Star, and the General Service and Victory Medals.
71, Boyle Street, Luton. 815.

CANDERTON, J. T., Private, 3rd Queen's (Royal West Surrey Regiment).
He joined in May 1916, and having completed his training was drafted to the Western Front in the following August. He took part in the Somme Offensive and was killed in action there on October 26th, 1916. He was entitled to the General Service and Victory Medals.
24, Maple Road, Luton. 816/A.

CANDERTON, W. E. E., Private, Bedfordshire and Royal Sussex Regiments.
He volunteered in November 1914, and after being retained on important duties for some time was drafted to France in August 1916. He took an active part in several important engagements, including those of the Somme, Vimy Ridge, Ypres and Cambrai, and was twice wounded. On returning home he was demobilised in May 1919, and holds the General Service and Victory Medals.
24, Maple Road, Luton. 816/B.

CANHAM, A. C., L/Corporal, M.G.C.
He was serving at the outbreak of war, and in the following year was drafted to the Western Front, where he took part in the heavy fighting at Loos, the Somme, Arras, Cambrai and the Retreat and Advance in 1918. He was demobilised in March 1919 after returning home, and holds the 1914–15 Star, and the General Service and Victory Medals.
Millbrook, near Ampthill. T1555.

CANNON, A. E., Sapper, Royal Engineers.
He volunteered in August 1914, and in the following year was drafted to Ireland, where he was retained on important duties until 1917. He was then drafted to Egypt, and proceeding afterwards to Palestine, rendered valuable services with his unit at Gaza, Haifa, Damascus and Beyrout, until the cessation of hostilities. He holds the General Service and Victory Medals, and in 1920 was still serving.
17, Warwick Road, Luton. 817/B.

CANNON, E., Corporal, 24th London Regiment (Queen's).
He volunteered in September 1914, and at the conclusion of his training was drafted to France in the following year. Whilst in this theatre of war he saw much severe fighting at Hill 60, Loos, Vimy Ridge, the Somme, Arras, Ypres and Cambrai, and was wounded. After returning home he was demobilised in March 1919, and holds the 1914–15 Star, and the General Service and Victory Medals.
62, Chapel Street, Luton. 818/B.

CANNON, E. C., Air Mechanic, R.A.F.
He joined in July 1918, and was speedily sent to Egypt, where he was engaged with his squadron for several months on important aeroplane repair duties at Aboukir aerodrome. After returning home he was demobilised in March 1919, and holds the General Service and Victory Medals.
62, Chapel Street, Luton. 818/A.

CANNON, E. G., Gunner, Royal Marine Artillery.
He joined in July 1916, and was posted for duty with H.M.S. "Collingwood," and served in the Mediterranean, Black Sea and North Sea. Later he was transferred to H.M.S. "Iron Duke," and was still serving in that vessel in 1920. He holds the General Service and Victory Medals.
62, Albert Street, St. Albans. X819.

CANNON, F. J., Private, Royal Fusiliers.
He joined in March 1918, and having completed his training was drafted to the Western Front in the same year. Whilst overseas he took part in many of the last engagements of the war, including those of Cambrai and St. Quentin, and after the Armistice proceeded with the Army of Occupation to Germany. Returning home, he was demobilised in December 1919, and holds the General Service and Victory Medals.
17, Warwick Road Luton. 817/A.

CANNON, G., Private, 9th Essex Regiment.
He joined in July 1916, and in the following November was drafted to the Western Front. He took part in an engagement near Albert in February 1917, and was severely wounded. On his recovery he served at Arras, Ypres, Cambrai and in other engagements until hostilities ceased. In February 1919 he was demobilised after his return to England, and holds the General Service and Victory Medals.
43, Highbury Road, Hitchin. 1594.

CANNON, H. J., Private, Bedfordshire Regiment.
He volunteered in August 1914, and at the conclusion of his training served with his unit at various stations on important duties. He did much good work, but was not able to secure his transfer overseas before the cessation of hostilities. He was discharged in April 1918.
17, Warwick Road, Luton. 817/C.

CANNON, M. T., Private, 5th Bedfordshire Regt.
He volunteered in September 1915, and after completing his training was drafted in 1917 to Palestine, where he took part in many important engagements, including the second and third Battles of Gaza, and was wounded in November 1917. He returned home and was demobilised in May 1919, and holds the General Service and Victory Medals.
54, Cobden Street, Luton. 820/B.

CANNON, R., Private, 2nd London Regiment (Royal Fusiliers).
He volunteered in September 1914, and after his training served on important duties with his unit until August 1916, when he was drafted to the Western Front. He took part in many engagements until hostilities ceased, including those of the Somme, Arras and Cambrai, and was twice wounded. He was demobilised in April 1919, and holds the General Service and Victory Medals.
54, Cobden Street, Luton. 820/A.

CANYIN, A. W. G., Driver, R.F.A.
He was mobilised in August 1914, and was immediately drafted to France, where he took part in the Retreat from Mons. Later he served at Hill 60, Ypres, Loos and Arras, and in various subsequent engagements until the termination of the war. He was demobilised after his return home in February 1919, and holds the Mons Star, and the General Service and Victory Medals.
41, Clifford Street, Watford. X821/A.

CANWELL, J., Private, Bedfordshire Regiment.
He joined in March 1916, and during a short period of service did good work with his unit at Kempston Barracks. The strain of military duties proved too severe for his health, and he was discharged in June 1916 as unfit for further service.
Cemetery Lane, Flitton, near Ampthill. T1552.

CAPELL, G., Private, 1st Bedfordshire Regiment.
He volunteered in August 1914, and immediately afterwards
was sent to the Western Front, where he took part in the
Battles of Mons, Ypres, the Somme, Arras and the Retreat
of 1918, in which he was wounded. He was then invalided
home to a Glasgow hospital, and holds the Mons Star, and the
General Service and Victory Medals.
73, South Street, Leighton Buzzard. 2786.

CAPELL, T., Private, Queen's (Royal West Surrey Regiment).
He volunteered in August 1914, and immediately afterwards
proceeded to the Western Front, where he took part in the
Battles of Mons, Ypres, Hill 60, Loos and numerous other
engagements until the close of the war, and was twice
wounded. He was demobilised in April 1919, and holds the
Mons Star, and the General Service and Victory Medals.
20, Fearnley Street, Watford. X822/B.

CAPP, F., Private, Oxfordshire and Buckinghamshire Light Infantry.
He volunteered in November 1915, and in the following year
was drafted to Mesopotamia, where he rendered valuable
services in various parts of the Front until hostilities ceased.
He returned home and was demobilised in March 1919, and
holds the General Service and Victory Medals.
32, Leys Terrace, Woburn Sands. Z823/B.

CAPP, W., Private, Royal Warwickshire Regt.
He volunteered in November 1915, and in the following year
was drafted to the Western Front, where he took part in
numerous engagements, including those of the Somme, Arras,
Vimy Ridge, Ypres and Cambrai. He was afterwards transferred to Italy, and did good service on the Piave before
returning to France in 1919. He was demobilised in February of that year, and holds the General Service and Victory
Medals.
32, Leys Terrace, Woburn Sands. Z823/A.

CAPPER, C. S., Air Mechanic, R.A.F.
He volunteered in February 1915, and after his training was
drafted to the Western Front, where he served with his unit
at the Battles of the Somme, Arras, Cambrai and many other
engagements, and was three times wounded. He was demobilised in June 1919, holding the General Service and
Victory Medals.
83, Lea Road, Luton. 824.

CARD, F. L., Private, 4th Bedfordshire Regt.
Being mobilised in 1914, he was shortly afterwards drafted
to the Western Front, where he took part in the Battle of
Neuve Chapelle, and was badly wounded. He was invalided
home in consequence, and was discharged in December 1915
as unfit for further military duties. He holds the 1914-15
Star, and the General Service and Victory Medals.
23, Cannon Road, Watford. X825.

CARELESS, A. F. W., Private, 3rd Bedfordshire Regiment.
He volunteered in November 1915, and in the following year
was drafted to the Western Front, where he took part in the
Battles of the Somme, Ypres and Cambrai. and many other
engagements until fighting ceased, and was twice wounded.
He was demobilised in April 1919, and holds the General
Service and Victory Medals.
31, Langley Street, Luton. 826.

CARPENTER, A. F., Private, 2nd Suffolk Regt.
He joined in March 1917, and in November of the same year
was drafted to the Western Front. After taking part in
numerous engagements, including those of the Somme, Cambrai and Bapaume, he was killed in action on August 30th,
1918. He was entitled to the General Service and Victory
Medals.
24, Brixton Road, Watford. X828/B.

CARPENTER, B., Gunner, Royal Field Artillery.
He volunteered in December 1914, and in July of the
following year was sent to Egypt. He took part in many
important engagements in the Palestine Campaign, including
those at Gaza and preceding the taking of Jerusalem, and was
wounded. After returning home he was demobilised in May
1919, and holds the 1914-15 Star, and the General Service
and Victory Medals.
28, Sandringham Road, Watford. X829.

CARPENTER, C., Private, R.M.L.I.
He volunteered in 1915, and after his training proceeded to
the Western Front, where he took part in many important
engagements, including those of the Somme and Arras. He
was killed in action on July 14th, 1917, and was entitled to
the General Service and Victory Medals.
3, Terrace Gardens, St. Albans. X830.

CARPENTER, E., Private, R.A.S.C. (M.T.)
He joined in 1916, and in the same year was drafted to
India. He was chiefly engaged in transporting the sick and
wounded by motor ambulance from the North-West Frontier
to hospital, and rendered valuable services. He returned
home and was demobilised in March 1919, and holds the
General Service and Victory Medals.
6, Chalk Hill, Oxhey. X833/B.

CARPENTER, H. G., Corporal, R.H.A.
He joined in September 1916, and in September of the following year was drafted to the Western Front, where he took
part in the Battles of Cambrai and the Somme. In June
1918 he was transferred to Egypt, and rendered valuable
service in many operations until hostilities ceased. He
returned home and was demobilised in December 1919,
holding the General Service and Victory Medals.
24, Brixton Road, Watford. X828/A.

CARPENTER, J., Driver, R.A.S.C.
Volunteering in December 1914, he was drafted overseas in
the following year, and rendered valuable services as a driver
in the Battles of Ypres, Loos, Lens and other important engagements until the close of the war. After the conclusion
of hostilities he was demobilised in 1919, and holds the
General Service and Victory Medals.
1, Fearnley Street, Watford. X798.

CARPENTER, J., Corporal, R.A.O.C.
He joined in 1916, and in the same year was drafted to the
Western Front. He was engaged at Boulogne on important
duties with his unit, and rendered valuable services until
after the cessation of hostilities. He was demobilised in
August 1919, and holds the General Service and Victory
Medals.
24, Chapel Street, Hemel Hempstead. X832.

CARPENTER, JAMES, Private, 4th Bedfordshire Regiment.
He joined in June 1916, and in August of the same year was
drafted to the Western Front, where he took part in the
heavy fighting in the Somme Offensive. He was killed in
action near Ypres on April 10th, 1917, and was entitled to the
General Service and Victory Medals.
12, Elfrida Road, Watford. X831/A.

CARPENTER, JOHN, Shoeing Smith, R.F.A.
Volunteering in August 1914, he was drafted to the Western
Front in November of the following year. In February 1916
he was transferred to Egypt and Palestine, and was engaged
at his station at the Base. After rendering valuable service he
was demobilised in July 1919, and holds the 1914-15 Star,
and the General Service and Victory Medals.
12, Elfrida Road, Watford. X831/B.

CARPENTER, W., Pte., 1st Bedfordshire Regt.
Volunteering in September 1914, he was in the following year
drafted to France, where he took part in the severe fighting
on the Somme and in many other engagements. He was
killed in action at Vimy Ridge on April 23rd, 1917, and was
entitled to the 1914-15 Star, and the General Service and
Victory Medals.
6, Chalk Hill, Oxhey. X833/A.

CARR, M. (Miss), Special War Worker.
This lady was engaged at Messrs. Kent's Munition Factory,
Biscot Road, Luton, for one year. Her duties, which were
of an important nature, were carried out in an efficient
manner, and she rendered valuable services.
36, Summer Street, Luton. 834.

CARRICK, W., Private, Machine Gun Corps.
He volunteered in October 1915, and in the following year
was drafted to the Western Front, where he took part in
numerous engagements until fighting ceased, including those
of the Somme, Arras, Ypres and Cambrai, and was wounded
and gassed. He was demobilised in March 1919, and holds
the General Service and Victory Medals.
38, Cowper Street, Luton. 835/A.

CARRINGTON, A., Pte., 2nd Coldstream Guards.
Volunteering in July 1915, he was in the following year
drafted to the Western Front, where he took part in the heavy
fighting on the Somme, and at Arras and Ypres. He was
killed in action on August 10th, 1917, and was entitled to the
General Service and Victory Medals.
39, Queen's Street, Hemel Hempstead. X836.

CARRINGTON, A., Private, Cheshire Regiment.
Volunteering in August 1915, he was retained for a time on
important duties, and was later drafted to the Western
Front, where he took part in many engagements, including
those at Arras, Bullecourt, Ypres, the Somme and Cambrai.
He was demobilised in December 1919, after his return home,
and holds the General Service and Victory Medals.
2, South Road, Luton. 837/B.

CARRINGTON, ALBERT, Private, 24th London Regiment (Queen's).
He volunteered in September 1914, and in the following year was drafted to the Western Front, where he took part in numerous engagements during the remainder of the war, including those of Ypres, Loos, Albert, Arras, Messines, the Somme and Cambrai. He was demobilised in March 1919, and holds the 1914-15 Star, and the General Service and Victory Medals.
2, South Road, Luton. 837/A.

CARRINGTON, E., Private, M.G.C.
Joining in April 1918, he proceeded in the following month to the Western Front, after a short course of training at Woolwich. He did not take part in any engagements, but rendered valuable services with his unit until his return home to be demobilised in November 1919. He holds the General Service and Victory Medals.
2, South Road, Luton. 837/C.

CARRINGTON, H., Driver, R.F.A.
He volunteered in 1915, and in the same year was sent to the Dardanelles, where he was engaged at Suvla Bay and Anzac. After the Evacuation he was transferred to Egypt, and in 1916 to Salonica, where he was again in action on the Monastir front. He returned home and was demobilised in 1919. holding the 1914-15 Star, and the General Service and Victory Medals.
28, Cherry Bounce, Hemel Hempstead. X838/B.

CARRINGTON, J., Private, R.A.S.C.
He volunteered in June 1915, and after his training was drafted in the same year to the Western Front. At Le Havre Rouen and other depôts he carried out important duties with his unit, and rendered valuable services. He was also engaged for some time in Paris and Verdun. He returned home and was demobilised in April 1918, holding the 1914-15 Star, and the General Service and Victory Medals.
28, Cherry Bounce, Hemel Hempstead. X838/A.

CARRINGTON, W. E., Private, Middlesex Regt.
He joined in June 1916, and after his training was sent to Salonika, where he did two years' valuable service on the Vardar, Monastir and Struma fronts. In June 1918 he was transferred to France, where he took part in many of the last engagements, including those of Albert, the Somme, Cambrai, Ypres and St. Quentin. He was demobilised in October 1919, and holds the General Service and Victory Medals.
39, Baker Street, Luton. 839.

CARRITT, H. N., R.Q.M.S., R.A.O.C.
He was serving at the outbreak of war, and proceeded to France in the same year. After two years' valuable service there he proceeded to Salonika. On both fronts he was engaged in issuing supplies to troops and many other important duties in connection with his corps, and carried out his responsible duties with great efficiency. He was demobilised in March 1919, and holds the 1914 Star, and the General Service and Victory Medals.
119, Queen's Road, Watford. X840.

CARTER, A., Private, 4th York and Lancaster Regiment.
He volunteered in 1915, and in the same year was drafted to the Western Front, where he took part in the heavy fighting at the Battles of Hill 60, Ypres, Loos and the Somme. He was killed in action at Messines on June 11th, 1917, and was entitled to the 1914-15 Star, and the General Service and Victory Medals.
37, Tavistock Street, Luton. 841.

CARTER, A., Private, 1st Bedfordshire Regt.
He joined in November 1916, and after his training was, in October of the following year, drafted to the Western Front, where he took part in many great engagements. In December 1917 he was transferred to Italy, and saw much service on the Piave front for four months. Subsequently he returned to France for the last stages of the fighting. He returned home and was demobilised in January 1919, holding the General Service and Victory Medals.
70, Boyle Street, Luton. 842.

CARTER, A., Sergeant, Bedfordshire Regiment.
He volunteered in 1914, and in the same year was sent to the Western Front. He took part in the heavy fighting during the Retreat from Mons and at Hill 60, Givenchy, Passchendaele and many other battles, and was twice wounded. He was demobilised in 1919, and holds the Mons Star, and the General Service and Victory Medals.
The Folly, Wheathampstead. 283/C.

CARTER, A., 2nd Class Warrant Officer, Royal Marine Light Infantry.
A Reservist, he had originally enlisted in March 1888, and was called up on the outbreak of war. In August 1914 he was drafted to Ostend, and later served at Antwerp during the siege. In 1915 he was sent to the Dardanelles, and after taking part in the Gallipoli Campaign, served in Egypt for a time. Afterwards he was in Greece, and finally in France, where he took part in numerous engagements. He holds the 1914 Star, and the General Service and Victory Medals, and was demobilised in February 1919.
The Chequers, Preston, Hitchin. 1602*

CARTER, A. J., Bombardier, R.F.A.
Volunteering in August 1914, he was immediately afterwards sent to the Western Front, where he took part in many great battles, including those of the Aisne, Ypres, Festubert and the Somme. He was killed in action at Arras on April 23rd, 1917, and was entitled to the 1914 Star, and the General Service and Victory Medals.
5, Cross Street South, St. Albans. X843.

CARTER, A. J., Private, Bedfordshire Regiment.
He joined in 1916, and after a period of training was drafted to the Western Front, where he fought in many battles, including those at Arras, Ypres, the Somme and Cambrai. He was severely wounded and lost the sight of his right eye, and was discharged in 1919, holding the General Service and Victory Medals.
7, Biggleswade Road, Potton. Z1275.

CARTER, A. R., Private, R.A.S.C.
He joined in February 1917, and after completing his training was, in the same year, sent to the Western Front. He was engaged on the transport of supplies to the various sectors of the front, and rendered valuable services until the conclusion of hostilities. He was demobilised in March 1919, and holds the General Service and Victory Medals.
7, Albion Road, St. Albans. X844.

CARTER, B. H., Private, Royal Sussex Regt.; and Rifleman, King's Royal Rifle Corps.
He joined in March 1916, and in June of the same year was drafted to the Western Front, where he fought in numerous engagements, including those round Ypres, the Somme, Beaumont-Hamel and Ploegsteert, and was wounded. Owing to illness he was absent from the Front during part of 1917 and 1918, but returned to France in September 1918, in time for the concluding phases of the war. He was mentioned in Despatches for his valuable work, and holding the General Service and Victory Medals, was demobilised in February 1919.
34, Clarendon Road, Luton. 845.

CARTER, C., Private, Army Cyclist Corps.
He volunteered in September 1914, and in the following July was drafted to the Dardanelles and took part in the landing at Suvla Bay and in subsequent operations in Gallipoli. He contracted dysentery in the course of his service, and died on the homeward voyage on October 14th, 1915. He was entitled to the 1914-15 Star, and the General Service and Victory Medals.
112, Hartley Road, Luton. 341/B.

CARTER, C. W., Gunner (Signaller), R.H.A.
Joining in September 1916, he was in April of the following year drafted to the Western Front. He took an active part in the heavy fighting at Cambrai, the Somme and many other important engagements until hostilities ceased. He was demobilised in February 1919, and holds the General Service and Victory Medals.
34, Clarendon Road, Luton. 846/A.

CARTER, E., Private, Middlesex Regiment.
He joined in 1915, and in the same year he was drafted to the Western Front. During his service overseas he took part in numerous engagements, including those at Hill 60, Ypres, Loos, Vimy Ridge and Cambrai, and was twice wounded. He was demobilised in 1919, and holds the 1914-15 Star, and the General Service and Victory Medals.
The Folly, Wheathampstead. 283/B.

CARTER, F., Private, 1st Hertfordshire Regiment.
He volunteered in August 1914, and in the following year was drafted to the Western Front, where he took part in numerous engagements, including those at Hill 60, Ypres, Arras, Passchendaele, the Aisne, the Marne, Cambrai and St. Quentin, and was four times wounded. He returned home and was discharged as medically unfit in February 1919, holding the 1914-15 Star, and the General Service and Victory Medals.
25, Breakspeare Road, Abbot's Langley. X847

CARTER, F., Private, 8th East Surrey Regiment.
He volunteered in September 1914, and on the completion of
his training was drafted to France in August of the succeeding year. During his service on the Western Front he took
part in the fighting at Loos and Delville Wood, and was subsequently killed in action in the severe fighting on the Somme
on July 1st, 1916. He was entitled to the 1914–15 Star,
and the General Service and Victory Medals.
King Street, Potton.   Z1281/C–1282/C.

CARTER, F. C., Corporal, 5th Bedfordshire Regt.
He volunteered in August 1914, and was in training at various
camps, but his health could not stand the strain of military
duties, and he was discharged in November 1914 as medically
unfit for further service. 14, Brunswick Street, Luton.   848.

CARTER, F. J., Private, 6th Lancashire Fusiliers.
He joined in January 1917, and later in that year was drafted
to France, where he took part in many important engagements, including those of Ypres, Cambrai, the Somme and
the Retreat and Advance of 1918. He returned home and
was demobilised in February 1919, holding the General
Service and Victory Medals.
96, Talbot Road, Luton.   849.

CARTER, G., L/Corporal, Military Foot Police.
He volunteered in October 1915, and in the following year
was drafted to France. During his service on the Western
Front he was engaged on important military police duty
behind the lines in the Somme, Arras, Ypres and Cambrai
sectors. He returned home and was demobilised in August
1919, holding the General Service and Victory Medals.
36, Liverpool Road, Luton.   850.

CARTER, G., Private, Bedfordshire Regiment.
He volunteered in August 1914, and in the same year was
drafted to France, where he took part in much of the early
fighting, and was wounded at Neuve Chapelle in March 1915.
After recovering he was sent to Mesopotamia in 1916, and
served in the engagements at Kut and in the Offensive on
Kut-el-Amara. After the cessation of hostilities he returned
home, and in December 1919 was demobilised, holding the
1914 Star, and the General Service and Victory Medals.
Clifton Road, Shefford.   Z851.

CARTER, G. H., L/Corporal, R.F.A. and M.F.P.
He joined in December 1917, and in March 1918 was drafted
to the Western Front, where he took part in many engagements, including those on the Somme and at Cambrai and
Ypres. In January 1919 he joined the Army of Occupation
in Germany, and did good service at Cologne. He returned
home and was demobilised in November 1919, holding the
General Service and Victory Medals.
34, Clarendon Road, Luton.   846/B.

CARTER, H., L/Corporal, 16th Middlesex Regt.
Volunteering in August 1915, he was drafted to the Western
Front in the following year. During his service in France
he took part in the severe fighting at Arras, Ypres, Cambrai,
Albert and Amiens, and was wounded. After the cessation
of hostilities he returned home and was demobilised in
January 1919. He holds the General Service and Victory
Medals.
1, Vicarage Lane, Wing, near Leighton Buzzard.   852.

CARTER, H., Private, 17th Middlesex Regiment.
He joined in April 1916, and in the following November was
sent to France, where he fought in the Battle of the Somme
and in various subsequent engagements. During his service
he contracted cerebro-spinal meningitis, and after his death
in hospital at Rouen in March 1917 was buried in Rouen
Cemetery. He was entitled to the General Service and
Victory Medals. 6, Alfred Street, Luton.   853.

CARTER, H., Pte., 1st Bedfordshire Regiment.
He volunteered in 1915, and after his training was drafted to
France in the following July. Whilst in this theatre of war
he served in the Battle of the Somme, and in November
1916 was invalided home suffering from trench feet. After
his recovery he returned to France in March 1917, and took
part in the fighting at Arras and Ypres. Later he was sent to
Italy and was engaged in the Offensive on the Piave, but
in March 1918 he returned to France. After serving at
Albert he was severely wounded near Cambrai on June 14th,
1918, and as a result died on the same day. He was entitled
to the General Service and Victory Medals.
King Street, Potton.   Z1281/D–1282/D.

CARTER, H. G., Private, R.A.S.C. (M.T.)
He volunteered in September 1914, and in the same year
was drafted to the Western Front. During his service in
France he did good work with the Field Ambulance Section,
notably at Ypres, Arras and Cambrai. In 1917 he was sent
to Italy, and was present for similar duties in many engagements until the termination of the war. He returned home
and was demobilised in April 1919, holding the 1914 Star,
and the General Service and Victory Medals.
9, Church Road, Watford.   X854.

CARTER, H. J., Sapper, Royal Engineers.
He volunteered in September 1915, and on the completion of
his training, being drafted to Egypt in January of the following year, served in the Offensive in Palestine. Here he was
engaged on important duties, such as wiring, trenching and
pontooning, in connection with the operations, and was
frequently in the forward areas. He returned home and was
demobilised in August 1919, and holds the General Service
and Victory Medals.
8, Chiltern Road, Dunstable.   855.

**CARTER, J., Private, Bedfordshire and Hertford-
shire Regiments.**
He was mobilised at the outbreak of war, and in the following
year was drafted to France, where he took part in numerous
important engagements, including those at Ypres, the Somme,
Arras, Cambrai and Albert, and was twice wounded. In
1920 he was still serving with the Colours, and holds the
1914–15 Star, and the General Service and Victory Medals.
8, Lammas Road, Watford.   X856/B.

CARTER, O., Private, 1st Middlesex Regiment.
He volunteered in March 1915, and in the following December
was drafted to France. During his service on the Western
Front he took part in the fighting at Vimy Ridge, Albert,
Arras and Cambrai, and was killed in action in the Ypres
sector on December 7th, 1917. He was buried at Ypres
Cemetery, and was entitled to the 1914–15 Star, and the
General Service and Victory Medals.
Clifton Road, Shefford.   Z857.

CARTER, T. H., Pte., 4th Middlesex Regiment.
Joining in June 1916, he proceeded in the same year to the
Western Front, where he served in numerous important
engagements up to the close of hostilities, including those of
the Somme, Arras, Ypres, Cambrai and St. Quentin. During
his service he was gassed. He was demobilised in August
1919, after his return home, and holds the General Service
and Victory Medals
94, Ridgway Road, Luton.   858.

CARTER, T. W., Sergeant-Farrier, R.F.A.
He volunteered in August 1915, and on the completion of his
training was drafted overseas in November of the following
year. During his service in France he did good work with
his battery in the Somme, Arras and Cambrai sectors, and in
various subsequent engagements until the cessation of hostilities. He returned home and was demobilised in May
1919, and holds the General Service and Victory Medals.
16, Upper Culver Road, St. Albans.   X859.

CARTER, V. R., Private, Sherwood Foresters.
He volunteered in May 1915, and in January 1917 was drafted
to the Western Front, where he took part in the Battles of
Arras, Bullecourt and Ypres. He was killed in action in
November 1917, and was entitled to the General Service and
Victory Medals.
1, Garden Road, Dunstable.   930/B.

**CARTER, W. C., Drummer, 1st Hertfordshire
Regiment.**
He was mobilised at the outbreak of war, and was immediately drafted to the Western Front, where he served in the
Retreat from Mons and at La Bassée, Neuve Chapelle and
other engagements, and was gassed. In consequence he was
invalided home and discharged in August 1915 as medically
unfit for further military duty. He holds the Mons Star,
and the General Service and Victory Medals
13, Lattimore Road, St. Albans.   X861.

CARTER, W. H., Private, Royal Welch Fusiliers.
He joined in May 1916, and in the following month was
drafted to France, where he took part in the heavy fighting
on the Somme, and was gassed in action. On his recovering
he served at Ypres and Cambrai and in many subsequent
engagements until the termination of the war. He was
demobilised in February 1919, after his return home, and
holds the General Service and Victory Medals.
64, Waterlow Road, Dunstable.   860.

CARVELL, J., Sapper, Royal Engineers.
He joined in 1916, and after his training was completed was
drafted to Italy, and whilst in this theatre of war served on
the Piave. He was engaged on important duties in the
forward areas whilst operations were in progress, and was
frequently under fire. He was sent home and subsequently
demobilised in May 1919, and holds the General Service and
Victory Medals.
3, Inkerman Street, St. Albans.   X862.

CASEY, T., R.S.M., 3rd Northumberland Fusiliers.
Volunteering in 1915, he was engaged on special duties training recruits until the following year, when he was drafted to France. During his service on the Western Front he took part in the fighting on the Somme and at Arras, Ypres and Cambrai, and was in action in the Retreat and Advance of 1918. After the Armistice was signed he proceeded to Germany with the Army of Occupation, and was stationed on the Rhine until his return home in September 1919, when he was demobilised. He holds the General Service and Victory Medals.
14, San Remo Road, Aspley Guise, Beds.   Z863/A.

CASTLE, A., Sergeant, Middlesex Regiment.
Volunteering in January 1915, he was drafted to France in the following year. During his service on the Western Front he took part in the fighting on the Somme and at Arras, Cambrai, St. Quentin and St. Julien, and was twice wounded. and in hospital. After the cessation of hostilities he returned home and was demobilised in January 1919, and holds the 1914-15 Star, and the General Service and Victory Medals.
59, Old Park Road, Hitchin.   1601/B.

CASTLE, F., Private, R.A.S.C.
He volunteered in 1914, and on the completion of his training was drafted to France in the following year. During his service on the Western Front he took part in the fighting at Ypres and in various subsequent engagements, including that of Amiens, in 1918. He returned home and was demobilised in March 1919, and holds the 1914-15 Star, and the General Service and Victory Medals.
58, Victoria Road, North Watford.   X864.

CASTLE, F. G. (D.S.M.), Leading Stoker, R.N., H.M.S. " Valentine."
He was serving at the outbreak of hostilities, and was posted for duty with H.M.S. " Valentine " in the North Sea. He took part in the Battle of Heligoland Bight, the raid on Cuxhaven on Christmas Day, 1914, and the Battle of Jutland, and was also for a time in the submarine service. He was awarded the Distinguished Service Medal for gallantry in action, and in addition holds the 1914-15 Star, and the General Service and Victory Medals. He was still serving in 1920.
Hall Yard, Hatfield.   X865.

CASTLE, W., Private, 1st Bedfordshire Regiment.
He volunteered in 1915, and in the same year was sent to the Western Front, where he took part in the Battles of the Somme, Arras and Ypres. He was killed in action in the Advance of 1918 on October 23rd of that year, and was entitled to the 1914-15 Star, and the General Service and Victory Medals.
15, St. Andrew's Place, Hitchin.   1604.

CATLIN, A., Private, Tank Corps.
He joined in May 1917, and in the following December was drafted to France. During his service on the Western Front he fought in the second Battle of the Somme, at Amiens and other engagements. He returned home and was demobilised in October 1919, and holds the General Service and Victory Medals.
26, Cowper Street, Luton.   866.

CATLIN, F., Private, Royal Fusiliers.
He joined in May 1918, and after his training served at various stations on important duties with his unit. In January 1919 he proceeded to Germany with the Army of Occupation, and served there until the following August, when he returned home and was demobilised.
47, Kimberley Road, Fleetville, St. Albans.   X870/B.

CATLIN, F. J., Private, R.A.S.C. (M.T.)
He joined in October 1916, and in the same month was drafted overseas. During his service in France de did excellent work in the Motor Transport Section on the Somme and at Ypres, and in numerous other engagements. After the Armistice he proceeded to Germany with the Army of Occupation, and remained there until his return to England in March 1920. He was demobilised in the following month, and holds the General Service and Victory Medals.
16, North Common, Redbourn, Herts.   867.

CATLIN, G., Private, 1st Suffolk Regiment.
He volunteered in 1915, and after his training served at various coastal stations on important defence duties with his unit. He rendered valuable services, but owing to being medically unfit for duty abroad was not able to secure his transfer overseas before the termination of the war. He was demobilised in February 1919.
42, Guildford Street, Luton.   868.

CATLIN, W., Pioneer, Royal Engineers.
He volunteered in August 1915, and in the following year was drafted to France. During his service on the Western Front he was engaged on important duties in the forward areas. He was severely wounded in the Battle of the Somme on November 15th, 1916, and was invalided home to hospital and discharged in the following January. He died from the effects of his wounds on December 29th, 1919, and was entitled to the General Service and Victory Medals.
47, Kimberley Road, Fleetville, St. Albans.   X870/A.

CATLING, C. R., Driver, Royal Field Artillery.
He volunteered in April 1915, and after serving at various stations on important duties was drafted to the Western Front in 1916. During his service in France he fought at Vimy Ridge, the Somme, Cambrai and Armentières, and in later engagements until the conclusion of hostilities. He returned home and was demobilised in August 1919, and holds the General Service and Victory Medals.
24a, Queen's Street, Luton.   869/B.

CATLING, E. J., Corporal, R.A.M.C.
He was mobilised at the outbreak of war, and was almost immediately drafted to France, where he was wounded in the Retreat from Mons, and later served at Ypres. In August 1915 he was sent to Gallipoli, and was present at the landing at Suvla Bay and in the subsequent engagements until the Evacuation of the Peninsula. He then proceeded to Mesopotamia, and served at the fall of Kut, the capture of Baghdad and the occupation of Mosul. He returned home and was demobilised in November 1919, and holds the Mons Star, and the General Service and Victory Medals.
24a, Queen's Street, Luton.   869/A.

CATO, B. (M.M.), Private, 8th Leicestershire Regt.
He joined in February 1916, and in the following November was drafted to France, where he took part with distinction in numerous important engagements. He was taken prisoner in May 1918 near Ypres, and was held in captivity in Germany until the following December, when he was repatriated and demobilised. He was awarded the Military Medal for conspicuous bravery and devotion to duty in the Field, and also holds the General Service and Victory Medals.
16, Hitchin Road, Luton.   871.

CATTON, W. J., Sergeant, 18th London Regiment (London Irish Rifles).
He volunteered in August 1914, and served on important duties with his unit until June 1916, when he was drafted to the Western Front. He took part in important engagements, including that at Festubert, and was wounded near Vimy Ridge in October 1916, and invalided home. He was demobilised in March 1919, and holds the General Service and Victory Medals.
15, Sutton Road, Watford.   X872.

CAVANAGH, J., Private, 5th Bedfordshire Regt.
He was mobilised in August 1914, and in July of the following year was drafted to the Dardanelles and took part in the landing at Suvla Bay. In 1916 he was transferred to Egypt and served in the Palestine Campaign, being present at the Battle of Gaza. He returned home and was demobilised in January 1920, and holds the 1914-15 Star, and the General Service and Victory Medals.
Silverdale, Icknield Street, Dunstable.   873/B.

CAVE, T. W., Private, Queen's Own (Royal West Kent Regiment).
He joined in 1917, and was drafted to the Western Front in the same year, where he took part in heavy fighting on the Somme and at Cambrai, and was wounded. He was demobilised in 1919, and holds the General Service and Victory Medals.
153, Lower Marlowes, Hemel Hempstead.   X874/B.

CAVES, H. C., Driver, Royal Field Artillery.
He volunteered in August 1914, and was immedialtely afterwards sent to the Western Front, where he took part in many engagements, including the Retreat from Mons and the Battles of the Marne, the Aisne, Albert, the Somme, Loos and Cambrai. He also served in the Retreat and Advance of 1918. He was demobilised in 1920, and holds the Mons Star, and the General Service and Victory Medals.
Hillside, Lidlington, near Ampthill.   Z875.

CAWDELL, H., Sapper, Royal Engineers.
He volunteered in January 1915, and in the following August was drafted to the Dardanelles, and was engaged at Suvla Bay and Anzac. In December of the same year he was transferred to Egypt and served in the Canal zone. In 1917 he took part in various engagements, including those at Gaza, Jaffa, Haifa, Acre and Beyrout. He was demobilised in July 1919, and holds the General Service and Victory Medals.
13, Wood Street, Luton.   876.

CAWDELL, S., Rifleman, 15th London Regt. (Civil Service Rifles).

He volunteered in December 1915, and in May of the following year was drafted to the Western Front, where he took part in various engagements. He was killed in action at Ypres in January 1917, and was entitled to the General Service and Victory Medals.
244, High Town Road, Luton.   877/A.

CHALK, F., Private, R.M.L.I.

He enlisted in October 1911, and on the outbreak of war was posted for duty with the Grand Fleet in the North Sea. He took part in the Battle of Heligoland Bight, and was also on active service in the Baltic and Mediterranean. After the conclusion of hostilities he was for a time with the Army of Occupation at Cologne, and in 1920 was still serving in Scotland. He holds the 1914–15 Star, and the General Service and Victory Medals.
142, New Town Street, Luton.   796/C.

CHALKLEY, A., Trooper, King Edward's Horse.

He volunteered in August 1914, and was immediately afterwards drafted to the Western Front, where he was engaged on important duties with his unit, and was present at the Battle of Albert. He died in hospital at Rouen on June 14th, 1918, and was entitled to the 1914 Star, and the General Service and Victory Medals.
2, Gosmore Road, Gosmore, Hitchin.   2776.

CHALKLEY, H., Sapper, Royal Engineers.

He volunteered in April 1915, and after his training served on important duties with his unit until 1917, when he was drafted to the Western Front. He took part in numerous important engagements, including those on the Somme and at Arras, Passchendaele, Cambrai and the Marne, and was wounded. He was demobilised in February 1919, and holds the General Service and Victory Medals.
40, Ivy Road, Luton.   878.

CHALKLEY, H., Private, 1st Bedfordshire Regt.

He joined in October 1916, and was drafted to the Western Front, where he took part in various engagements, including those at Vimy Ridge, Passchendaele, Lens, the Marne and Bapaume. He was killed in action at Beaumont-Hamel on September 25th, 1918, and was entitled to the General Service and Victory Medals.
112, North Street, Luton.   879/A.

CHALKLEY, H., Private, The Buffs (East Kent Regiment).

He joined in May 1916, and six months later was sent to France. He took part in much heavy fighting at Loos, and was wounded at Hulluch. He was invalided home, and after a long period in hospital was discharged in March 1918, holding the General Service and Victory Medals.
67, Buxton Road, Luton.   880.

CHALKLEY, P., Private, Bedfordshire Regiment.

He was serving at the outbreak of war, and was immediately drafted to the Western Front. He took part in the fierce fighting during the Retreat from Mons and in the Battles of Arras and Ypres, being twice wounded. He was invalided home and discharged in January 1918, and holds the Mons Star, and the General Service and Victory Medals.
14, Front Street, Slip End.   881.

CHALKLEY, S., Sapper, Royal Engineers.

He joined in May 1918, and after his training was drafted in August of the same year to Italy, where he served on the Piave and at Taranto on important duties with his unit, and rendered valuable services. He afterwards went to Constantinople, and was still serving in 1920. He holds the General Service and Victory Medals.
112, North Street, Luton.   879/B.

CHALKLEY, S., Private, 8th Bedfordshire Regt.

He volunteered in May 1915, and at the conclusion of his training proceeded to the Western Front in February of the following year. After taking part in several engagements he was killed in action at Ypres on April 19th, 1916, and was entitled to the General Service and Victory Medals.
42, Hitchin Hill, Hitchin.   1837/A.

CHALKLEY, W., Private, 4th Bedfordshire Regt.

He volunteered in October 1915, and after having completed his training was drafted to the Western Front in December of the following year. He took part in the Battle of the Somme, and on April 25th, 1917, was killed in action at Arras. He was entitled to the General Service and Victory Medals.
42, Hitchin Hill, Hitchin.   1837/B.

CHALLIS, E., Private, 1/4th Norfolk Regiment.

He volunteered in August 1914, and on the conclusion of his training was drafted in the following year to the Dardanelles. Here he took part in various engagements in Gallipoli until the Evacuation of the Peninsula, and in 1917 was sent to Mesopotamia, where he remained until the conclusion of the war. He returned home and was demobilised in January 1919, and holds the 1914–15 Star, and the General Service and Victory Medals.
20, Flamley Street, Watford.   X822/A.

CHAMBERLAIN, H., 2nd Lieutenant, R.G.A.

He joined as a gunner in April 1916, and was gazetted to a commission in March 1918. He proceeded to the Western Front in July 1918, and took part in important engagements during the Advance of that year, including those of the Marne, Cambrai and Ypres. He was demobilised in November 1919, and holds the General Service and Victory Medals.
2a, Stockwood Crescent, Luton.   883/A.

CHAMBERLAIN, H., Captain, R.A.O.C.

He joined in August 1892, and during the Great War was engaged on important duties at various stations. He rendered valuable service, but was not successful in obtaining his transfer overseas prior to the cessation of hostilities. He was still serving in 1920.
2a, Stockwood Crescent, Luton.   83/B.

CHAMBERLAIN, H. (M.M.), L/Corporal, Bedfordshire Regiment.

He volunteered in May 1915, and in January of the following year was drafted to Egypt and Palestine, where he took part in various engagements, including those at Umbrella Hill, Gaza, Haïfa, Aleppo and Jerusalem, and was awarded the Military Medal for gallantry in the Field. He returned home and was demobilised in February 1919, and holds in addition to the Military Medal the General Service and Victory Medals.
59, Queen's Street, Luton.   882/B.

CHAMBERLAIN, H. J. (M.M.), Private, Bedfordshire Regiment.

He volunteered in September 1914, and after a period of training was sent to the Dardanelles, and served at Suvla Bay. He was later transferred to Egypt and took part in the Palestine Campaign, being present at the engagements at Gaza and Jaffa, and was awarded the Military Medal for conspicuous bravery in holding a trench single-handed. He also holds the 1914–15 Star, and the General Service and Victory Medals, and was demobilised in January 1919.
80, Cambridge Street, Luton.   884.

CHAMBERLAIN, J., Private, Bedfordshire Regt.

He volunteered in January 1915, and after a period of training was engaged on important duties at various stations with his unit. He rendered valuable service, but was unsuccessful in obtaining his transfer overseas, and was demobilised in March 1919.
5, Mice Road, Leighton Buzzard.   1593.

CHAMBERLAIN, W. F., Corporal, Labour Corps.

He volunteered in 1915, and in the same year was drafted overseas. He served in many sectors of the Western Front, and took part in the heavy fighting at Ypres, Arras, the Somme and Cambrai, and was wounded and gassed. He was demobilised in 1919, and holds the 1914–15 Star, and the General Service and Victory Medals.
39, Cassio Bridge Road, Watford.   X885.

CHAMBERS, G. H., Private, York and Lancaster Regiment.

He volunteered in September 1914, and in the following year was drafted to France. He served at Neuve Chapelle, Hill 60 and Ypres, and was wounded. On recovery he took part in the fighting on the Somme and at Arras, Ypres and Cambrai. He was demobilised in February 1919, and holds the 1914–15 Star, and the General Service and Victory Medals.
51, Old Road, Linslade.   1594.

CHAMBERS, H., Corporal, Royal Engineers.

He volunteered in August 1915, and at the conclusion of his training served with his unit at various stations on important duties. He rendered valuable service, but was not able to secure his transfer overseas before the cessation of hostilities. He was demobilised in February 1919.
33, Bedford Street, Hitchin.   1838.

CHAMBERS, H., Gunner, R.G.A.

He joined in June 1916, and in the following November was drafted to France. He took part in various engagements, including those at Ypres, the Somme and Cambrai, and after the Armistice proceeded to Germany with the Army of Occupation, with which he remained until he returned home and was demobilised in September 1919. He holds the General Service and Victory Medals.
29, Alfred Street, Luton.   836.

CHAMBERS, H., Private, Worcestershire Regt.
He joined in February 1916, and in the following April was drafted overseas. He served on the Western Front, and during the Battle of the Somme was severely wounded. He was invalided home, and after a period in hospital was discharged in June 1917 as medically unfit for further service. He holds the General Service and Victory Medals.
5, Shaftesbury Road, Watford. X888.

CHAMBERS, H., Private, 5th Bedfordshire Regiment.
He enlisted in the Territorial Force in May 1914, and was mobilised on the outbreak of hostilities. He was engaged on important duties with his unit at various stations until March 1918, when he was drafted to the Western Front. He served at Cambrai, and on April 13th, 1918, died of wounds received in action. He was entitled to the General Service and Victory Medals.
75, Wimbourne Road, Luton. 887.

CHAMBERS, H. N., Private, Bedfordshire Regt.
He was mobilised in August 1914, and in the following year was drafted overseas. He served at the Dardanelles, and was in action at Suvla Bay and was later transferred to Egypt. Afterwards he was sent to the Western Front, and took part in several engagements. He was demobilised in January 1919, and holds the 1914-15 Star, and the General Service and Victory Medals.
41, Wellington Street, Luton. 889.

CHAMBERS, J., Gunner, R.G.A.
He volunteered in August 1914, having previously served in the Boer War, and on the completion of his training was sent to France, where he was engaged on important duties. He served on the Somme and at Arras, Ypres and Cambrai, and during his service abroad suffered from shell-shock. He was demobilised in December 1918, and holds the 1914-15 Star, and the General Service and Victory Medals.
73, Hastings Street, Luton. 890.

CHAMBERS, W. J., Private, 1st Essex Regt.
He volunteered in September 1914, and after his training was sent to the Western Front in the following year. He served at Hill 60, Ypres, Arras and Cambrai, and in many other engagements, and was gassed and wounded three times. He was eventually demobilised in February 1919, and holds the 1914-15 Star, and the General Service and Victory Medals.
28, Lammas Road, Watford. X505/B.

CHAMPKIN, F., Private, East Surrey Regiment.
Joining in June 1916, he was sent to the Western Front at the conclusion of his training in the following September. Subsequently he took part in several engagements, including that on the Somme, where he was wounded, and on October 11th, 1917, was killed in action near Ypres. He was entitled to the General Service and Victory Medals.
13, King Street, Dunstable. 1022.

CHAMPKINS, A., 2nd Corporal, R.E.
He volunteered in January 1915, and in October of the same year was drafted to France. Whilst in this theatre of war he saw much fighting at several battles, including those of Loos, Arras, Ypres, Cambrai and the Somme. He remained overseas until after the cessation of hostilities, when he returned home and was demobilised in July 1919, holding the 1914-15 Star, and the General Service and Victory Medals.
138, Ridgway Road, Luton. 891.

CHANCE, A., Private, 1st Suffolk Regiment.
He volunteered in June 1915, and after having completed his training was drafted to the Western Front, where he took part in the Battles of Loos, the Somme, Arras, Ypres, Passchendaele and Cambrai. He was killed in action near Albert on September 23rd, 1918, and was entitled to the 1914-15 Star, and the General Service and Victory Medals.
90, Burr Street, Luton. 83/B.

CHANCE, E., L/Corporal, 21st (Empress of India's) Lancers.
He enlisted in July 1912, and in 1915 was drafted to India, where he was stationed at Rawal Pindi and Poona. In 1919 he served on the North West Frontier and took part in the fighting against the Afghans. He holds the India General Service Medal (with clasp, Afghanistan, North West Frontier, 1919), the General Service and Victory Medals, and returned to England and was demobilised in November 1919.
49, Langley Street, Luton. 892.

CHANCE, P., Corporal, 6th Bedfordshire Regt.
He volunteered in December 1915, and was sent to France, where he saw considerable service. While in this theatre of war he fought on the Somme and at Arras, Lens and Cambrai, and in April 1918 was killed in action at Ypres. He was entitled to the General Service and Victory Medals.
90, Burr Street, Luton. 83/C.

CHANCE, F. G., 8th Bedfordshire Regiment.
He volunteered in November 1915, and on the conclusion of his training was drafted to the Western Front in the following May. He was killed in action on the Somme on September 25th, 1916, and was entitled to the General Service and Victory Medals.
Randall's Cottages, Luton Road, Toddington. 893.

CHANCE, G., Private, East Surrey Regiment and Royal Army Service Corps.
He joined in February 1917, and in the following May was drafted to the Western Front, where he served at Arras and Ypres. He returned to England in September 1918, and in the following April was demobilised, holding the General Service and Victory Medals.
53, Sotheron Road, Watford. 894/B.

CHANCE, G. H., Seaman (Gunner), R.N.
He volunteered in August 1915, and was posted for duty with H.M.S. "Whitshed." He was engaged on submarine patrol work in the North Sea and Russian waters, and was still serving in 1920. He holds the 1914-15 Star, and the General Service and Victory Medals.
53, Sotheron Road, Watford. 894/A.

CHANCE, H., Private, Durham Light Infantry.
He joined in September 1916, and after training served on important duties at various stations. He did excellent work with his unit, but was not able to secure his transfer overseas before the cessation of hostilities. He was demobilised in January 1920.
31, Meeting Alley, Watford. 895.

CHANCE, H., Private, 2nd Bedfordshire and Hertfordshire Regiments.
He joined in January 1918, and after his training was drafted to the Western Front, and took part in the fighting in various engagements until the conclusion of hostilities. In 1919 he went to India, where in the following year he was still serving. He holds the General Service and Victory Medals.
21, Greatham Road, Bushey. 896.

CHANDLER, A. E., Stoker, R.N., H.M.S. "Royal Oak."
He joined in 1916, and after training was posted to H.M.S. "Royal Oak," and whilst in this vessel took part in the Battles of Jutland and Heligoland Bight. He was engaged on important and dangerous duties in the North Sea and the Baltic until the conclusion of the war, and in 1920 was still serving with the Channel Fleet. He holds the General Service and Victory Medals.
76, Holywell Road, Watford. 897/B.

CHANDLER, E., Private, 9th Cheshire Regt.
He volunteered in August 1915, and on the completion of his training was drafted to France in the following year. He served at Ypres and on the Somme, and was wounded, and for a time in hospital. After the conclusion of hostilities he returned to England, and in April 1919 was demobilised, holding the General Service and Victory Medals.
76, Holywell Road, Watford. 897/C.

CHANDLER, F., Private, 7th Bedfordshire Regt.
Volunteering in September 1914, he was sent overseas in the following August, and during his service in France was in action on the Ypres Front and in the Battle of the Somme, where he was wounded. On recovery he took part in the fighting in various engagements, including Arras, and was twice severely gassed. After the cessation of hostilities he was demobilised in January 1919, and holds the 1914-15 Star, and the General Service and Victory Medals.
5, Cumberland Street, Houghton Regis. 898/C.

CHANDLER, J. C., Private, East Surrey Regt.
He joined in March 1917, and on the completion of his training was drafted to France, where he took part in much heavy fighting on the Somme, and at Arras and Cambrai. He was killed in action on August 23rd, 1918, at the Battle of Amiens, and was entitled to the General Service and Victory Medals.
The Baulk, Biggleswade. Z1558.

CHANDLER, P. H., Private, Duke of Wellington's (West Riding Regiment).
Volunteering in February 1915, on completion of his training he was sent to France, and took part in severe fighting in various sectors of the Front, including Ypres, Cambrai and Rheims. On the cessation of hostilities he was attached to the Army of Occupation, and proceeded to Germany, where he served until demobilised in July 1919. He holds the General Service and Victory Medals.
82, Bassett Road, Leighton Buzzard. 1296.

CHANDLER, S., Private, 1/5th Bedfordshire Regiment.
He was mobilised in August 1914, and after training was drafted to Egypt in the following year and proceeded to Palestine, where he took part in the fighting at Gaza and other engagements in the campaign. During his service in the East he was wounded, and after the conclusion of hostilities returned to England and was demobilised in March 1919. He holds the 1914–15 Star, and the General Service and Victory Medals.
5, Cumberland Street, Houghton Regis. 898/B.

CHANDLER, S. H., Private, 10th Essex Regt.
Joining in October 1916, in the following February he was drafted to France, where he took part in the numerous engagements, including those at Arras, Ypres, Cambrai and the Somme, and was wounded three times. He was demobilised in January 1919, and holds the General Service and Victory Medals.
90, Bassett Road, Leighton Buzzard. 1295.

CHANDLER, W., Corporal, 7th Bedfordshire Regiment.
He volunteered in August 1914, and on the completion of his training was drafted overseas in the following August. During his service on the Western Front he took part in the fighting at Ypres and in numerous other engagements, and was killed at the Battle of the Somme on July 1st, 1916. He was entitled to the 1914–15 Star, and the General Service and Victory Medals.
5, Cumberland Street, Houghton Regis. 898/A.

CHANDLER, W. H., Bombardier, R.G.A.
He joined in June 1916, and in the following November was drafted overseas. During his service on the Western Front he took part in the battles at Vimy Ridge, Messines, Ypres, Passchendaele, Cambrai and the Somme. After the conclusion of the war he finally returned home and was demobilised in May 1919, and holds the General Service and Victory Medals.
22, Adrian Road, Abbots Langley. 899.

CHANDLER, W. T., Corporal, Bedfordshire Regiment.
He volunteered at the outbreak of war, and in the following year was drafted to France. Whilst in this theatre of war he took part in the fighting at Hill 60, Ypres, the Somme and Cambrai, and was wounded. After the cessation of hostilities he returned home and was demobilised in 1919, holding the 1914–15 Star, and the General Service and Victory Medals.
76, Holywell Road, Watford. 897/A.

CHANDLER, W. T., Private, 8th Leicestershire Regiment.
He joined in March 1916, and having completed his training was drafted to France in August of the same year. While in this theatre of war he fought on the Somme, and at Arras, Vimy Ridge and Bullecourt, where he was wounded and taken prisoner. After the cessation of hostilities he was released, and returning to England was demobilised in August 1919. He holds the General Service and Victory Medals.
74, Bassett Road, Leighton Buzzard. 1301/A.

CHANNING, H. C., Private, Duke of Wellington's (West Riding Regiment).
He joined in December 1916, and was sent to the Western Front, where he saw much heavy fighting. He served at Arras, Messines, Ypres, Cambrai, the Somme and Béthune, and was wounded three times. He returned home and was demobilised in April 1919, and holds the General Service and Victory Medals.
30, Pondswick Road, Luton. 900/B.

CHAPMAN, A., Private, R.A.M.C.
He volunteered in March 1915, and after his training served at various stations on important duties with his unit. He rendered valuable services, but was not successful in obtaining his transfer overseas before the cessation of hostilities, owing to being medically unfit. He was demobilised in August 1919.
45, Old Road, Linslade, near Leighton Buzzard. 2784/B.

CHAPMAN, A. W., Private, 4th Bedfordshire Regiment.
He joined in January 1917, and on completion of his training was drafted overseas. During his service he took part in the fighting at Arras, Ypres (where he was wounded and gassed), Cambrai and numerous other engagements. He was demobilised after his return home in February 1919, and holds the General Service and Victory Medals.
3, Dordans Road, Leagrave. 901.

CHAPMAN, B., Pte., Northumberland Fusiliers.
He volunteered in March 1915, and in the same year was sent to France. Whilst in this theatre of war he took part in many important engagements, and served at Ypres, the Somme and Arras, where he was severely wounded. He was invalided home, and in December 1917 was discharged as medically unfit for further duty. He holds the 1914–15 Star, and the General Service and Victory Medals.
New Marford, Wheathampstead. 902/C.

CHAPMAN, C., Private, Labour Corps.
He joined in February 1917, and after his training served on important guard duties with his unit. He rendered valuable services, but owing to being medically unfit for duty abroad, was unable to obtain his transfer overseas. He was discharged in October 1917.
7, Cross Street South, St. Albans. 903.

CHAPMAN, C., Private, 4th Northumberland Fusiliers.
He joined in April 1916, and on the completion of his training was drafted to the Western Front. After a brief service overseas he was killed in action in an engagement on August 16th, 1916. He was entitled to the General Service and Victory Medals.
4, Newcombe Street, Harpenden. 904.

CHAPMAN, C., Private, 1st Hertfordshire Regt.
He volunteered in March 1915, and in the same year was drafted to France. During his service overseas he took part in the fighting at Ypres, the Somme and at Arras, and was severely wounded and taken prisoner at Ypres on July 31st, 1917. He was held in captivity in Germany until after the Armistice, when he was released, and returning to England was demobilised in March 1919. He holds the 1914–15 Star, and the General Service and Victory Medals.
New Marford, Wheathampstead. 902/A.

CHAPMAN, F., Private, 4th (Queen's Own) Hussars.
He volunteered at the outbreak of war, and was almost immediately drafted to the Western Front and took part in the Retreat from Mons, and was wounded. On recovery he served in the Battle of Ypres, where he was again wounded, and also fought on the Somme and at Arras and Cambrai, and was wounded for the third time. He was finally demobilised after his return home in March 1919, and holds the Mons Star, and the General Service and Victory Medals.
32, Chapel Street, Hemel Hempstead. 905.

CHAPMAN, G., Private, Labour Corps.
He volunteered in August 1915, and in the following January was drafted to France, where he served on the Somme and at Vimy Ridge and Cambrai on road making and repairing duties. He holds the General Service and Victory Medals, and was demobilised in February 1919.
24, Bolton Road, Luton. 906.

CHAPMAN, J., Private, 3rd Bedfordshire Regt.
He volunteered in March 1915, and in August of the same year was drafted to the Western Front. While in this theatre of war he saw much fighting, and was severely wounded in the first Battle of the Somme in August 1916. He was invalided home, and discharged as medically unfit in June 1917. He holds the General Service and Victory Medals.
4, St. Michael's Mount, Hitchin. 1606/B.

CHAPMAN, S. J., Pte., 1/5th Bedfordshire Regt.
He volunteered in August 1914, and in the same year was drafted to the Western Front, and was wounded in action at Neuve Chapelle. In July 1915 he was sent to Gallipoli, where he took part in the landing at Suvla Bay and in subsequent engagements, and was again severely wounded. In the following September he went to Malta and afterwards proceeded to Salonika, where he served at Monastir and Vardar Ridge, and finally was in action in Mesopotamia, at Kut (II.), and was present at the capture of Baghdad and the occupation of Mosul. After the cessation of hostilities he returned home and was demobilised in February 1919. He holds the 1914–15 Star, and the General Service and Victory Medals.
31, Ashton Street, Luton. 907.

CHAPMAN, V., Sergeant, R.H.A.
He volunteered in September 1915, and in the same year was drafted to Mesopotamia, where he took part in numerous engagements, including that at Kut-el-Amara. He returned home and was demobilised in May 1919, and holds the 1914–15 Star, and the General Service and Victory Medals.
45, Ridge Avenue, Letchworth. 2766.

CHAPMAN, W., Private, 10th Hampshire Regt.
He volunteered in September 1914, and after his training served on important duties with his unit. In October 1915 he was drafted to Salonika, but on the outward voyage contracted dysentery and died at sea on October 28th. He was entitled to the 1914–15 Star, and the General Service and Victory Medals.
New Marford, Wheathampstead, Herts. 902/B.

CHAPPEL, H., Private, Machine Gun Corps.
He was serving at the outbreak of war, and was immediately sent to the Western Front, where he took part in the Retreat from Mons and the Battles of Albert, Ypres, Festubert, Loos, the Somme, Arras and Cambrai. He also served in the Retreat and Advance of 1918. In 1920 he was still serving, in Russia, and holds the 1914 Star, and the General Service and Victory Medals.
Castle Hill, Ridgmont, Beds. Z242 /B.

CHAPPELL, A. E., Sapper, Royal Engineers.
He volunteered in September 1914, and served at various stations on important duties with his unit. He rendered valuable services but, owing to being over age for duty abroad, was unable to obtain a transfer overseas, and was demobilised in March 1919.
9, Bedford Road, Houghton Regis, Dunstable.
908—909—910 /D.

CHAPPELL, A. S. S. (Miss), Special War Worker.
For three years during the war, from September 1915 until the cessation of hostilities, this lady held a responsible post at the T.N.T. Explosive Works, Chaul End, Luton. Her duties, which were of a highly dangerous character, consisted in the inspection of 106 Fuse detonator holders, and she carried out her work in a consistently commendable manner, and to the complete satisfaction of those in authority.
9, Bedford Road, Houghton Regis, near Dunstable.
908—909—910 /C.

CHAPPELL, C., Private, 11th Suffolk Regiment.
He volunteered in September 1914, and in the following April was sent to the Western Front. During his service in France he took part in the fighting on the Somme, and at Arras and Ypres, and also was engaged in important duties at Rouen, Boulogne and Calais. He returned home and was subsequently demobilised in March 1919, and holds the 1914–15 Star, and the General Service and Victory Medals.
37, Branch Road, Park Street, St. Albans. X788.

CHAPPELL, E. G., Private, The Buffs (6th East Kent Regiment).
He joined in June 1916, and in the following September was drafted to France, where he fought in the Battle of the Somme. He was killed in action in an engagement near Rheims on October 28th, 1916, and was entitled to the General Service and Victory Medals.
Rectory Lane, Houghton Conquest, near Ampthill. 911.

CHAPPELL, G. L. (Miss), Special War Worker.
This lady offered her services for work of National importance during the war, and from September 1916 until the cessation of hostilities was engaged at the T.N.T. Explosive Works at Chaul End, Luton. Her duties, which consisted in the inspection of 106 fuses were of a responsible and highly dangerous nature, and she carried them out with great care and efficiency, and in an entirely satisfactory manner.
9, Bedford Road, Houghton Regis, near Dunstable.
908—909—910 /A.

CHARGE, J., Corporal, Bedfordshire Regiment.
Volunteering at the outbreak of war he was immediately drafted overseas, and took part in the Retreat from Mons. Subsequently he fought in the Battles of Arras, Ypres, Cambrai and other engagements until the cessation of hostilities, and during his service was severely wounded. After returning to England, he was demobilised in April 1919, and holds the Mons Star, and the General Service and Victory Medals.
37, Meeting Alley, Watford. 912.

CHARGE, R., Private, 6th Bedfordshire Regt.
He joined in June 1916, and in the same year was drafted to the Western Front, where he took part in the fighting at Arras and Cambrai and the final operations of the war. After the conclusion of hostilities he was demobilised on his return home in February 1919, and holds the General Service and Victory Medals.
13, Butcher's Yard, High Street, Watford. 913 /A.

CHARLES, A. G. C., Private, R.A.M.C.
He volunteered in August 1914, and on the conclusion of his training was drafted to Gallipoli, and served at the landing at Suvla Bay, Anzac and in various other operations until the Evacuation of the Peninsula. Later he was sent to Egypt, and subsequently proceeded to Palestine, where he was present at the Battles of Gaza, Haïfa and Damacus. During his service he was wounded. He returned to England and was demobilised in April 1919, holding the 1914–15 Star, and the General Service and Victory Medals.
54, Langley Road, Luton. 914 /B.

CHARLES, H., Private, 1st Lincolnshire Regt.
He joined in April 1917, and after his training was completed he was sent to France. During his service overseas he took part in the fighting at Cambrai, and was subsequently killed in action on April 16th, 1918. He was entitled to the General Service and Victory Medals.
54, Langley Road, Luton. 914 /A.

CHARNOCK, G., Private, 2nd York and Lancaster Regiment.
He volunteered in September 1914, and in the following year was drafted to France, where he saw much heavy fighting. He took part in the engagements at Hill 60, Ypres, Vimy Ridge, the Somme, Arras, Cambrai and St. Quentin, and was severely wounded in a subsequent engagement on September 18th, 1918, when he lost a leg in action. He was sent home to hospital, and after treatment was eventually demobilised in May 1919. He holds the 1914–15 Star, and the General Service and Victory Medals.
Littleworth, Wing, near Leighton Buzzard. 915.

CHARTER, A. R., Private, East Surrey Regt.
He volunteered in September 1914, and in the following year was drafted to France, where he fought at Arras, Ypres and the Somme. He was severely wounded, and after being invalided home was subsequently discharged as unfit for further service in August 1916. He holds the 1914–15 Star, and the General Service and Victory Medals.
King Street, Potton. Z1277.

CHARTER, T. J., Private, 8th East Surrey Regt.
He volunteered in September 1914, and in the following year was drafted to the Western Front, where he took part in many severe engagements, including those of the Somme, Cambrai and Ypres, and was wounded at Albert, Dickebusch and again at Albert. He was demobilised in February 1919, and holds the 1914–15 Star, and the General Service and Victory Medals.
48, Sun Street, Biggleswade. Z1565.

CHASE, F., Private, 6th Bedfordshire Regiment.
He volunteered in August 1915, and in May of the succeeding year, after finishing his training, was drafted to France. After three months' active service on the Western Front he was killed in the severe fighting on the Somme on July 10th, 1916. He was entitled to the General Service and Victory Medals.
Watling Street, Hockliffe, near Leighton Buzzard. 1610.

CHASE, W. A., Gunner, No. 3 Light Car Patrol, 21st Indian Infantry Brigade.
He joined in January 1915, and later in the same year was drafted to Egypt, and took part in the Palestine Campaign and was wounded. Afterwards he was sent to Italy, and served in the operation against the Austrians, and in January 1918 to the Western Front, where he remained until after the cessation of hostilities, when he returned home, and was demobilised in November 1919. He holds the General Service and Victory Medals.
49, Church Road, Watford. 916.

CHASE, W. T., Private, Middlesex Regiment.
He was serving at the outbreak of war, and was drafted to France in January 1915. During his service there he took part in many engagements, and was wounded at Neuve Chapelle on March 10th. Later he was sent to Egypt, and afterwards proceeded to Palestine, where he took part in numerous engagements, including those at Gaza. After his return to England, he was demobilised in March 1919, and holds the 1914–15 Star, and the General Service and Victory Medals.
63, Vale Road, Bushey. 917.

CHATTEN, E. M., Steward, R.N.R.
He volunteered in August 1914, and was posted for duty with H.M.S. "Moresby" in the North Sea. Later he was engaged on special transport duties from Mexico to France. During his service he was wounded, and in July 1918 was discharged in consequence. He holds the Naval General Service, the General Service, Victory and Life Saving Medals.
19, Church Street, Leighton Buzzard. 2783.

CHEESMAN, W., Private, R.A.V.C.
He joined in 1917, and in the same year was drafted to the Western Front. He was engaged with his unit in many sectors, including those of Cambrai, the Somme and Amiens attending to sick and wounded horses and rendered valuable services. He was demobilised in November 1919, and holds the General Service and Victory Medals.
29, Weymouth Street, Apsley. X1202 /A.

CHENERY, T., Corporal, R.A.S.C.
He joined in July 1916, and after his training served at various depôts on important duties with his unit. He did excellent work as a shoeing-smith, but was not successful in obtaining his transfer overseas before the cessation of hostilities. He was demobilised in May 1919.
2, Norfolk Place, Church Street, Biggleswade. Z1280.

CHERRY, A., Private, Machine Gun Corps.
He volunteered in June 1915, and in January of the following year was drafted to the Western Front, where he took part in numerous important engagements, including those of the Somme, Bullecourt, Arras, Messines, Ypres and Delville Wood. Afterwards he was transferred to Italy and rendered valuable services on the Piave and Asiago fronts. In 1918 he returned to France, and was engaged in the Advance of that year. He was demobilised in 1919, and holds the General Service and Victory Medals.
8, Biggin Lane, Hitchin. 2777.

CHERRY, J. H., Private, 20th Hussars.
He volunteered in November 1914, and after his training was completed was drafted to France in the following year. He took part in various engagements while hostilities continued, including those of the Somme, Arras and Cambrai, and the Retreat and Advance of 1918. After the cessation of hostilities he returned home and was demobilised in February 1919, holding the 1914-15 Star, and the General Service and Victory Medals.
Mill Lane, Greenfield, near Ampthill. 918.

CHERRY, R. H., Farrier, Bedfordshire Lancers.
He volunteered in August 1914, and having completed his training at various stations was sent to France. While overseas he was engaged on important work at Loos and the Somme, but after contracting fever died at Boulogne on November 20th, 1916. He was entitled to the 1914-15 Star, and the General Service and Victory Medals.
Home Farm, Houghton Conquest, near Ampthill. Z607/B.

CHERRY, W. H., Private, Norfolk Regiment.
He joined in April 1916, and after the conclusion of his training saw much varied service in Mesopotamia, Persia and India. After taking part in several engagements, and doing good work throughout, he was demobilised on his return home in December 1919. He holds the General Service and Victory Medals.
25, Ramridge Road, Luton. 919.

CHERRY, W. L., Private, 37th Northumberland Fusiliers.
He joined in September 1916, and in the following February was drafted overseas. During his service on the Western Front he took part in the severe fighting at Arras, Cambrai and the Somme, and served in the Advance at Amiens and in all subsequent engagements. After the cessation of hostilities he was sent home and demobilised in January 1919, holding the General Service and Victory Medals.
18, Regent Street, Luton. 920.

CHESHER, S., Private, R.E. and R.D.C.
He joined in April 1917, and at the conclusion of his training served with his unit at various stations on important duties. He did much good work in connection with railway construction and in guarding German prisoners, but was not able to secure his transfer overseas before the cessation of hostilities. He was demobilised in 1919.
21, Chobham Street, Luton. 921.

CHESHIRE, A., Private, Queen's (Royal West Surrey Regiment).
He joined in June 1916, and in October of the same year, after finishing his training, was drafted to France. During his service he was severely wounded in the Battle of the Somme, but on his recovery went back to the Lines and took part in the fighting at Bullecourt, Cambrai, and the Retreat and Advance of 1918. After the conclusion of hostilities he returned home and was demobilised in March 1919, holding the General Service and Victory Medals.
Rose Cottages, Stuart Street, Dunstable. 922/A.

CHESHIRE, A. A., Corporal, Bedfordshire Regt. and Royal Army Medical Corps.
He volunteered in June 1915, and on the conclusion of his training was drafted to the Western Front in November of the following year. Whilst in this theatre of war he took an active part in the engagements on the Somme, and in July 1917 was severely gassed at Ypres. On his recovery after hospital treatment at home he was transferred to the Royal Army Medical Corps, in which he was engaged on important duties as hospital orderly until his demobilisation in May 1919. He holds the General Service and Victory Medals.
6, Gove Road, Dunstable. 923.

CHESHIRE, C., Private, R.A.M.C.
He volunteered in April 1915, and after his training did valuable work with his unit as a hospital nursing orderly. He rendered skilled service, but was not successful in obtaining his transfer overseas while hostilities continued. He was demobilised in August 1919.
4, The Cottages, Napsbury. X925.

CHESHIRE, E., Sergeant, R.A.V.C.
He joined in January 1916, and having completed his training was drafted to France in the same year. He was chiefly engaged in attending to wounded horses in the forward areas in various sectors, and conveying them to the veterinary hospital. After three years' valuable service he returned home and was demobilised in April 1919, holding the General Service and Victory Medals.
17, Park Road West, Luton. 924.

CHESHIRE, F., Driver, Royal Field Artillery.
He volunteered at the outbreak of hostilities, and on the conclusion of his training was sent to France. He was present in several important engagements, and later was sent to Egypt. He took part in the Palestine Campaign, and fought at Gaza, Haïfa, Damascus and Alleppo. He came home and was demobilised in June 1919, holding the General Service and Victory Medals.
64, Fearnley Street, Watford. X926/A.

CHESHIRE, F. W., Private, Bedfordshire Regt.
He joined in March 1916, and after his training was drafted in the same year to the Western Front. He afterwards took part in much heavy fighting at Arras, Cambrai, Givenchy, St. Quentin and in many other engagements, and was wounded in March 1917. He was demobilised in February 1919, and holds the General Service and Victory Medals.
75, Edward Street, Dunstable. 927.

CHESHIRE, H. J., Sapper, Royal Engineers.
He was mobilised in August 1914, and was drafted to the Dardanelles, when he served at Suvla Bay and Anzac. He was later transferred to Egypt and Palestine, and took part in numerous engagements, including those of Gaza, Jaffa and others up to the taking of Jerusalem and the close of hostilities. He returned home and was demobilised in June 1919, and holds the 1914-15 Star, and the General Service and Victory Medals.
37, Dumfries Street, Luton. 928/A.

CHESHIRE, L. W., Private, Royal Munster Fusiliers.
He volunteered in June 1915, and after his training was drafted to the Western Front, where he took part in the heavy fighting at Arras, Passchendaele and Cambrai. He was later transferred to Italy, where he was again in action. He returned home and was demobilised in March 1919, and holds the General Service and Victory Medals.
28, Oswald Road, St. Albans. X929.

CHESHIRE, R., Gunner, Royal Field Artillery.
He volunteered in 1915, and in the same year proceeded to Mesopotamia, where he saw much fighting in several engagements, including those of Kut and Baghdad. He remained overseas until the cessation of hostilities, and after returning home was demobilised in April 1919, holding the 1914-15 Star, and the General Service and Victory Medals.
64, Fearnley Street, Watford. X926/B.

CHESHIRE, R. G., Private, 4th Royal Welch Fusiliers.
He joined in January 1916, and in July of the same year was drafted to the Western Front, where he took part in many severe engagements, including those of the Somme, Arras, Ypres, Cambrai, and the Retreat and Advance of 1918. He was demobilised in May 1919 after his return to England, and holds the General Service and Victory Medals.
1, Garden Road, Dunstable. 930/A.

CHESHIRE, W. W. W., Corporal, R.M.L.I.
He enlisted in April 1894, and at the outbreak of war was posted to H.M.S. "Carmania." Whilst serving in this vessel he took part in the engagement with the German armed merchantman, "Cap Trafalgar," and was severely wounded. Later he died in hospital in December 1914, and was entitled to the 1914-15 Star, and the General Service and Victory Medals.
"Red House," Toddington, Dunstable. 931.

CHESSUM, E., Private, R.A.S.C. and Essex Regt.
He joined in March 1917, and in the same year was sent to France. While in this theatre of war he saw much service at Ypres, where he was twice wounded. On his recovery he fought at the Somme and Cambrai, and in other engagements until hostilities ceased. Later he went to Germany with the Army of Occupation. He returned to England and was demobilised in October 1919, holding the General Service and Victory Medals.
102, Nightingale Road, Hitchin. 1839.

CHESTER, F., Sergeant, 21st London Regiment (1st Surrey Rifles).
He joined in 1917, and was drafted to the Western Front in the following year. Whilst there he took part in many important engagements, including those of the Somme, Ypres and Cambrai, and did excellent work. He was demobilised in September 1919 after his return to England, and holds the General Service and Victory Medals.
73, Grover Road, Oxhey. X933/A.

CHESTER, F., L/Corporal, Northamptonshire Regiment.
He volunteered in December 1915, and in December of the following year was drafted to the Western Front, where he took part in the severe fighting at the Somme and Passchendaele, and was wounded near Arras in October 1917. He was invalided home and discharged owing to his wounds in March 1918. He holds the General Service and Victory Meda s. 13, Park Road, Bushey. X932.

CHICK, W., Shoeing Smith, R.A.S.C.
Volunteering in October 1915, he was shortly afterwards drafted to France. He rendered valuable service in many great battles until hostilities ceased, including those of the Somme, Arras and Ypres. He was demobilised in 1919, and holds the 1914–15 Star, and the General Service and Victory Medals.
7, Grosvenor Terrace, Boxmoor. X934.

CHIEZA, A., Private, 4th Bedfordshire Regiment.
Volunteering in August 1914, he was immediately drafted to France. He served at Mons, Armentières and Ypres, and in December 1915 was discharged as unfit for further service. He subsequently died on February 14th, 1920, and was entitled to the Mons Star, and the General Service and Victory Medals.
15, Temperance Street, St. Albans. 935.

CHILD, C., Private, Royal Army Service Corps.
He volunteered in 1915, and in the same year was drafted overseas. He was engaged with the Field Ambulance Section in many sectors of the Western Front, and was present at the Battles of the Somme, Ypres, Arras and Cambrai. He was demobilised in 1919, and holds the 1914–15 Star, and the General Service and Victory Medals.
224, Chester Road, Watford. X936.

CHILD, H. W. (M.M.), Private, R.A.S.C.
He volunteered in November 1914, and in the same month proceeded to the Western Front, where he rendered valuable service in various engagements until hostilities ceased, including those of Ypres, the Somme and Arras. He was awarded the Military Medal for conspicuous bravery in the Field, and in addition holds the 1914 Star, and the General Service and Victory Medals. He was demobilised in March 1919. Somersham, Harpenden Rise. 937/B.

CHILDS, D. A., Private, 1st Hertfordshire Regt.
He volunteered in January 1915, and served on important duties with his unit. He rendered valuable services, but was not successful in obtaining his transfer overseas owing to his medical unfitness. He was discharged in the same year.
Lowbell Lane, London Colney, near St. Albans. X938/A

CHILDS, E., Private, 14th London Regiment (London Scottish).
After volunteering in November 1915, he was drafted in May of the following year to the Western Front, where he took part in many important engagements until fighting ceased, including those of the Somme, Arras and Ypres. He was demobilised in September 1919 on his return home, and holds the General Service and Victory Medals.
Somersham, Harpenden Rise. 937/A.

CHILDS, F. H., Private, R.A.S.C.
He volunteered in May 1915, and in the following month was drafted to the Western Front, where he was engaged at Calais and Le Havre in the Base Supply Depôts, and rendered valuable services. He was demobilised in July 1919, and holds the 1914–15 Star, and the General Service and Victory Medals.
19, Ebury Road, Watford. X939/A.

CHILDS, W., Gunner, Royal Garrison Artillery.
He was serving at the outbreak of war, having enlisted in 1908, and was drafted to India, where he was engaged at Nowgong, Peshawar and Multan on important duties with his battery. In 1916 he was transferred to the Persian Gulf, and afterwards proceeded north to Mesopotamia, where he took part in much heavy fighting. He was taken prisoner at Kut with General Townshend in April 1916, and died in captivity at Angora on January 19th, 1917. He was entitled to the 1914–15 Star, and the General Service and Victory Medals.
32, Dorset Street, Luton. 941/A.

CHILDS, W., Sapper, Royal Engineers.
He joined in September 1916, and after being retained for important duties with his unit was drafted to the Western Front in 1918. He rendered valuable services during the Advance on the Cambrai Front, and after the cessation of hostilities did important salvage work until he returned to England and was demobilised in December 1919. He holds the General Service and Victory Medals.
Gas Street, Toddington. 940.

CHIPPETT, C. S., Private, Queen's (Royal West Surrey Regiment).
He joined in February 1916, and in the following month was drafted to Salonika, where he took part in many important engagements until the close of the war, especially in the Vardar sector. He returned home and was demobilised in February 1919, holding the General Service and Victory Medals.
10, Cavendish Road, St. Albans. X942/B.

CHIPPETT, S. C., Rifleman, Royal Irish Rifles.
He joined in February 1916, and in January of the following year was drafted to the Western Front, where he took part in the heavy fighting at Messines, Ypres, St. Quentin and Cambrai. He was demobilised in November 1919 after returning to England, and holds the General Service and Victory Medals.
10, Cavendish Road, St. Albans. X942/A.

CHIVERS, H., Private, 23rd Royal Fusiliers (Sportsman Battalion).
He volunteered in October 1914, and in the following year was drafted to the Western Front, where he took part in important engagements, including those at Givenchy and Loos, and was wounded on the Somme in 1916. He was invalided home, and after a period in hospital was discharged as medically unfit for further service, owing to his wounds, in March 1917, and holds the 1914–15 Star, and the General Service and Victory Medals.
Lower Green, Ickleford, Hitchin. 2771.

CHRISTMAS, A., Corporal, R.H.A.
He volunteered in August 1914, and in the same year was drafted to the Western Front, where he took part in numerous important engagements until the last year of the war, and was killed in action on March 22nd, 1918. He was entitled to the 1914 Star, and the General Service and Victory Medals.
7, Heath Road, St. Albans. X943/B.

CHRISTMAS, ALBERT, Corporal, R.F.A.
After volunteering in 1914, he was drafted in the following year to the Western Front. During his period of service overseas he took part in the heavy fighting in many engagements down to the Advance of 1918. He was demobilised in June 1919 after his return to England, and holds the 1914–15 Star, and the General Service and Victory Medals.
7, Heath Road, St. Albans. X943/A.

CHUBB, H. E., Private, 14th Suffolk Regiment and Labour Corps.
He joined in October 1916, and after his training served at various stations on important coastal defence duties with his unit. He rendered valuable services, but was not successful in obtaining his transfer overseas before the cessation of hostilities owing to his medical unfitness. He was demobilised in February 1919.
London Road, Woburn. Z944.

CHURCH, C., Private, York and Lancaster Regt.
He joined in July 1917, and after completing his course of training was drafted in the following year to Italy, where he took part in many important engagements on the Piave Front, and was twice wounded. He returned home and was demobilised in March 1919, and holds the General Service and Victory Medals.
46, Acme Road, North Watford. X945.

CHURCH, F., A.B., Royal Navy.
He was serving at the outbreak of hostilities, and during the whole period of the war was engaged on cruising and patrol duties in the North Sea and various other waters. He rendered valuable services until he was demobilised in June 1919, holding the 1914–15 Star and the General Service and Victory Medals.
Ramridge End, Stopsley. 946/C.

CHURCH, H., Private, Lincolnshire Regiment.
He volunteered in August 1914, and in the following year was drafted to the Western Front, where he took part in the Battles of Arras, Cambrai, St. Quentin and many other engagements, and was three times wounded. He was demobilised in March 1919, and holds the 1914–15 Star, and the General Service and Victory Medals.
Ramridge End, Stopsley. 946/A.

CHURCH, W., Gunner, Royal Field Artillery.
After joining in April 1916, he was in the same year drafted to the Western Front, where he took part in many important engagements, including those of Ypres, the Somme and Cambrai. In November 1918 he was severely wounded in action, and lost a leg in consequence. He was invalided home, and after a period in hospital was discharged as medically unfit for further service. He holds the General Service and Victory Medals.
58, Talbot Road, Luton. 949.

CHURCH, J., Private, Royal Fusiliers.
He joined in June 1916, and in the following September was drafted to the Western Front. In 1917 he was transferred to Italy, and saw much service on the Piave front. In 1918 he returned to France and took part in various engagements during the Retreat and Advance of that year, including that of the Somme, where he was wounded. He was demobilised in June 1919, and holds the General Service and Victory Medals.
Ramridge End, Stopsley. 947.

CHURCH, T., Private, 3rd Bedfordshire Regt.
Volunteering in December 1914, he shortly afterwards proceeded to the Western Front, where he took part in numerous engagements, including those of Ypres, Arras, Albert and Cambrai. He returned home and was discharged in September 1918 in consequence of his service, and holds the 1914-15 Star, and the General Service and Victory Medals.
12, St. Anne's Road, Luton. 948.

CHURCH, T., Private, 6th Bedfordshire Regt.
He volunteered in August 1914, and after completing his training was drafted to the Western Front, where he took part in many important engagements, including those of Arras, Ypres and Passchendaele, and was wounded. He was discharged in September 1918 in consequence of his injuries, and holds the General Service and Victory Medals.
Ramridge End, Stopsley. 946/B.

CHURCHHOUSE, C. E., Private, York and Lancaster Regiment.
He joined in 1916, and in the same year proceeded to the Western Front, where he fought in numerous engagements, including those of the Somme and the Marne, and was wounded. He also served in the Retreat of 1918, and was killed in action on the Cambrai front on July 21st, 1918. He was entitled to the General Service and Victory Medals.
15, Bernard Street, St. Albans. X950.

CIRCUIT, F. (jun.), Corporal, Northamptonshire Regiment.
He joined in April 1918, but was not successful in obtaining his transfer overseas before the cessation of hostilities. He was engaged on various important duties with his unit, and rendered valuable services until his demobilisation in November 1919.
73, Lancaster Road, Hitchin. 2779/B.

CIRCUIT, F., Sapper, Royal Engineers.
He volunteered in June 1915, and after his training served at various stations with his unit. He rendered valuable services, but was not successful in obtaining his transfer overseas, and was discharged in December 1917 in consequence of his service.
73, Lancaster Road, Hitchin. 2779/A.

CIRCUIT, S. J., Driver, R.A.S.C.; and Private, Sussex Regiment.
He joined in March 1918, and after his training served at various stations on important duties in connection with the maintenance of supplies for the troops. He rendered highly efficient services, but was not able to secure his transfer overseas before the fighting ended. He was demobilised in December 1919.
13, Souldon Street, Watford. X951.

CLAMP, H., C.Q.M.S., 5th Leicestershire Regt.
He volunteered in November 1914, and after being retained on important duties with his unit was sent in 1916 to the Western Front, where he took a distinguished part in much severe fighting in various sectors, including those of Arras, Ypres and Cambrai, and the Retreat and Advance of 1918. He returned home and was demobilised in July 1919, and holds the General Service and Victory Medals.
13, Holly Walk, Luton. 952.

CLAPHAM, F., Rifleman, 8th London Regiment (Post Office Rifles).
He joined in March 1917, and in the same year was drafted to the Western Front. During his service there he took part in the fighting at Vimy Ridge, Messines, Cambrai and the Somme, and was severely wounded and invalided home to hospital. He was demobilised in 1919, and holds the General Service and Victory Medals.
Leighton Street, Woburn. Z953/A.

CLARE, C., L/Corporal, 4th Worcestershire Regt.
He was mobilised from the Reserve at the outbreak of war, and was immediately drafted to the Western Front, where he took part in the Retreat from Mons. He served also at La Bassée, Ypres (I.), Hill 60, the Somme, Arras, Bullecourt, Passchendaele, Cambrai, and in other engagements until fighting ceased. After the conclusion of hostilities he demobilised in January 1919, and holds the Mons Star, and the General Service and Victory Medals.
Sandfield Cottages, Woburn Sands. Z954.

CLARIDGE, N. F. (Miss), Special War Worker.
During the war this lady was engaged on work of National importance at Messrs. Kent's Munition Factory, Luton. She was employed on drilling work, and carried out her duties with much skill.
98, Man Grove, near Luton. 955.

CLARIDGE, S. C., Private, Royal Fusiliers.
He volunteered in January 1915, and was drafted to the Western Front in the same year. While overseas he fought in several engagements, including that of Monchy, where he was wounded in 1916. On his recovery he was again in action, and was wounded for the second time at Cambrai in 1918. After being invalided home he was demobilised in February 1919, holding the 1914-15 Star, and the General Service and Victory Medals.
22, Back Street, Luton. 956.

CLARK, A., Private, 13th Bedfordshire Regt.
He joined in December 1916, and after his training served at various stations on important guard duties with his unit. He rendered valuable services, but was not successful in obtaining his transfer overseas before the termination of the war. He was demobilised in March 1919.
Mill House, Barton. T1551.

CLARK, A. G., Private, R.A.M.C.
He joined in 1916, and having completed his training was drafted to France in the following year. Whilst in this theatre of war he saw much fighting, and did good work in the Battles of the Somme, Arras, Ypres and Cambrai. After the Armistice he served with the Army of Occupation on the Rhine until his demobilisation in May 1919. He holds the General Service and Victory Medals.
33, Beech Road, Luton. 994.

CLARK, A. J., Gunner, Royal Field Artillery.
He volunteered in 1914, and was afterwards drafted to the Western Front. During his service in France he took part in numerous engagements in various sectors until August 1918, when he was killed in action in the Advance. He was entitled to the 1914-15 Star, and the General Service and Victory Medals.
14, Alma Road, Hemel Hempstead. X981/B—982/B.

CLARK, B., A.B., Royal Naval Division.
He volunteered in November 1915, and in July of the following year proceeded to the Western Front, where he took part in many important engagements, including that at Arras, and was wounded. He was invalided home, and on his recovery was employed on various important duties until he was demobilised in September 1919. He holds the General Service and Victory Medals.
Upper Woodside, near Luton. 1003.

CLARK, B. A., Driver, R.A.V.C.
He joined in August 1916, and after his training served at various stations on important duties with his unit. He rendered valuable services attending to the needs of sick horses, but was not successful in obtaining his transfer overseas before the cessation of hostilities. He was demobilised in February 1919.
16, Buxton Road, Luton. 1001.

CLARK, B. E., Gunner, R.G.A.
He volunteered in May 1915, and in the same year was drafted to the Western Front. Whilst in this theatre of war he took an active part in several important battles until hostilities ceased, including those of the Somme, Arras, Ypres and Cambrai, and was gassed. Upon returning home he was demobilised in March 1919, and holds the General Service and Victory Medals.
12, Piccotts End, Hemel Hempstead. X2193/B.

CLARK, C. G., Sergeant, Royal Fusiliers.
Joining in July 1918, he went through his course of training, and in the following November was drafted to France in time for the last days of the fighting. After the Armistice he proceeded with the Army of Occupation into Germany, and was engaged on important guard duties on the Rhine for several months. He returned home and was demobilised in November 1919, holding the General Service and Victory Medals.
1, Swan Cottages, High Street, Watford. X980/B.

CLARK, E., Private, Royal Army Service Corps.
He was serving at the outbreak of war, and in the same month was drafted to the Western Front, where he was present at the Battles of Mons, the Marne, the Aisne and Ypres. He was invalided home and discharged as medically unfit for further service in April 1916, and holds the Mons Star, and the General Service and Victory Medals.
4, Shott Lane, Letchworth 2768

CLARK, E., Private, Tank Corps.
He joined in July 1917, and after his training was engaged on important duties as a fitter at various stations with his unit. His duties, which demanded a high degree of technical skill, were carried out with great efficiency, and he rendered valuable services, but was not successful in obtaining his transfer overseas before the cessation of hostilities. He was demobilised in December 1918.
29, Henry Street, Luton. 1010.

CLARK, F., Private, Lancashire Fusiliers
Joining in April 1917, he went through his training and was afterwards engaged on special duties until February 1918. He was then drafted to France, where he took part in many engagements during the Retreat and Advance of that year, notably those at Ypres and Armentières. He was demobilised on his return to England in November 1919, and holds the General Service and Victory Medals.
14, Collingdon Street, Luton. 1021/A.

CLARK, F., Private, 5th Bedfordshire Regiment.
He volunteered in April 1915, and after his training was engaged on important duties until March 1916, when he was drafted to Egypt, and subsequently to Palestine. He took part in much heavy fighting, particularly near Gaza (where he was wounded), and Aleppo, and was also present at the capture of Jerusalem. Returning to England in 1919, he was demobilised in April of that year, and holds the General Service and Victory Medals.
17, Manchester Place, Dunstable. 1023.

CLARK, F. A., Driver, R.A.S.C. (M.T.)
He joined in May 1916, and having completed his training was drafted to Egypt and Palestine in the following year. He was present at El-Arish, Rafa, Gaza and Haifa, and subsequently saw the final stages of the fighting at Salonika. After returning home, he was demobilised in October 1919, and holds the General Service and Victory Medals.
9, Gardenia Avenue, Leagrave. 996.

CLARK, F. G., Corporal, Machine Gun Corps.
He volunteered at the outbreak of war, and in the same year was drafted to Mesopotamia, where he served under General Townshend. During his service overseas he was severely wounded near Kut, and after leaving hospital took part in the capture of Baghdad, and in the occupation of Mosul. He returned home and was demobilised in May 1919, and holds the 1914–15 Star, and the General Service and Victory Medals.
14, Alma Road, Hemel Hempstead. X981—982/C.

CLARK, F. S., L/Corporal, R.A.M.C.
He volunteered in September 1915, and in the following year was drafted to France, where he did good work attending to the wounded at various hospitals. He remained there until after the cessation of hostilities, and after returning home was demobilised in May 1919. He holds the General Service and Victory Medals.
54, Dudley Street, Luton. 989.

CLARK, F. W., Private, Queen's (Royal West Surrey Regiment) and Labour Corps.
Joining in March 1917, he was shortly afterwards drafted to France, where he did much valuable salvage and road work at Messines, Passchendaele Ridge, Lens and in the Retreat and Advance of Cambrai in 1918. During his service he was gassed. He was demobilised in February 1919, after returning home, and holds the General Service and Victory Medals.
84, Shortmead Street, Biggleswade. Z1556.

CLARK, H., Sapper, Royal Engineers.
He volunteered in February 1915, and in September of the same year was sent to the Western Front. He was engaged with his unit on important duties in many sectors until hostilities ceased, and was present at the Battles of Loos, Armentières and the Somme. He was wounded on the Somme Front in July 1916. He was demobilised in January 1920, and holds the 1914–15 Star, and the General Service and Victory Medals.
3, Benskin Road, Watford. 1163/B.

CLARK, H., Sapper, Royal Engineers.
After joining in May 1916, he was, in the following year, drafted to the Western Front. During his service in France he was engaged on important duties in many sectors of the line, and was present in the Battles of Arras, Cambrai and the Somme, where he was wounded. After the conclusion of hostilities he returned home and was demobilised in May 1919, holding the General Service and Victory Medals.
23, New Street, Luton. 983.

CLARK, H., Private, 7th Bedfordshire Regiment.
He volunteered in December 1914, and on the conclusion of his training was drafted to the Western Front in 1915. Whilst in this theatre of war he fought in several battles until hostilities ceased, including those of Hill 60, Ypres, Festubert, the Somme and Cambrai. On returning home after a period of over three years' service overseas he was demobilised in February 1919, holding the 1914–15 Star, and the General Service and Victory Medals.
River Hill, Flamstead. X995.

CLARK, H. (M.M.), Corporal, 9th Seaforth Highlanders.
He volunteered in August 1914, and after his training was drafted overseas in March of the following year. He took a prominent part in several engagements, including those of the Somme, Arras, Albert and Cambrai, and was twice wounded. He was mentioned in Despatches and awarded the Military Medal for conspicuous bravery in the Field. On his return home he was demobilised in April 1919, holding the Military Medal, the 1914–15 Star, and the General Service and Victory Medals.
17, Francis Street, Luton. 993.

CLARK, H., Private, Royal Welch Fusiliers.
He joined in February 1916, and after a period of training, was drafted overseas. He took part in the severe fighting at Ypres, Cambrai and the Somme, where he was severely wounded. In spite of considerable hospital treatment he lost the use of his right arm, and was in consequence discharged in 1919. He holds the General Service and Victory Medals.
Wagstaff Terrace, Potton. X1279.

CLARK, H., Sergeant, 2nd Bedfordshire Regt.
He was mobilised in August 1914, and was at once sent to France, where he took a prominent part in many important battles, including those of Mons, Ypres, Hill 60, Arras, and was three times wounded. On his recovery he proceeded to India, where he rendered valuable service, and was still serving in 1920. He holds the Mons Star, and the General Service and Victory Medals.
11, Bell Terrace, Redbourn. 1207/B.

CLARK, J., L/Corporal, 13th Essex Regiment.
He joined in July 1916, and having completed his training, was drafted to France in the following October. After taking part in the several important engagements, including those of the Somme, Bullecourt, Oppy Wood and Ypres, he was taken prisoner near Cambrai in December 1917. He returned home after the Armistice, and was demobilised in February 1919. He holds the General Service and Victory Medals.
4, Elfrida Road, Watford. X1000.

CLARK, J., Private, 1st Lincolnshire Regiment.
He was mobilised at the outbreak of war, and immediately proceeded to France, where he saw much severe fighting in several early engagements, and was killed in the Battle of the Aisne on September 19th, 1914. He was entitled to the 1914 Star, and the General Service and Victory Medals.
11, St. Mitchael's Mount, Walsworth, Hitchin. 1840/B.

CLARK, J., Sapper, Royal Engineers.
He joined in June 1918, and after his training served at various stations on important duties with his unit. He did much valuable work but was not successful in obtaining his transfer overseas before the conclusion of the war. He was demobilised in January 1919.
123, Judge Street, Callowland, Watford. X1012.

CLARK, J., Rifleman, King's Royal Rifle Corps.
He joined in January 1916, and was in the same year drafted to France, where he did good service at Arras, Cambrai, Ypres and the Somme, and in other engagements until fighting ceased. He was demobilised in August 1919, after his return home, and holds the General Service and Victory Medals.
Baulk Road, Biggleswade. Z1557.

CLARK, J. W., Private, Royal Fusiliers and Air Mechanic, Royal Air Force.
He joined in March 1917, and on the conclusion of his training served with his unit at various stations on important duties. He did much good work as a draughtsman, but was not able to secure his transfer overseas before the cessation of hostilities. He was demobilised in February 1919.
48, Reginald Street, Luton. 988.

CLARK, L., Special War Worker.
This lady was engaged for two years during the war at the Chaulend Filling Factory, where she did most important work. Afterwards she went to Messrs. Kent's Munition Factory, Luton, and for a further period of nearly a year was engaged on shell-work, which she carried out in a highly satisfactory manner.
14, Collingdon Street, Luton. 1021/B

CLARK, P. E. V., Corporal, R.A.P.C.
He joined in January 1916, and after his training served on important duties with his unit. He rendered valuable services but was not successful in obtaining his transfer overseas before the cessation of hostilities. He was demobilised in February 1919.
253, Dunstable Road, Luton.   1005.

CLARK, R. L., Drummer, Bedfordshire Regiment.
He joined in July 1917, and was for a time engaged on important guard duties. Later he was drafted to France and was present at the Battle of Cambrai. He returned to England after the conclusion of hostilities, and in September 1919 was demobilised, holding the General Service and Victory Medals.
1, Swan Cottages, High Street, Watford.   980/A.

CLARK, W., Sapper, Royal Engineers.
He was mobilised at the outbreak of war, and in December 1915 was sent to Egypt, and served on the banks of the Suez Canal, where he was in action against the Turks in various attacks, notably at Ismalia. Later he was invalided home and was discharged in November 1916 as medically unfit for further military duty. He holds the 1914–15 Star, and the General Service and Victory Medals.
104, Hartley Road, Luton.   1016.

CLARK, W. C., Sapper, Royal Engineers.
He joined in March 1916, and after his training served on important duties at various stations. In June 1917 he was drafted to Egypt, and was engaged on important duties during the Palestine Offensive, being present at the entry into Jerusalem in December 1917. After the cessation of hostilities he returned home and was finally demobilised in September 1919, holding the General Service and Victory Medals.
76, Frederic Street, Luton.   985.

CLARK, W. J., Private, Suffolk Regiment.
He joined in April 1916, and was later drafted overseas. He served on the Western Front on the Somme, and at Arras, and in September 1917, was reported missing and is presumed to have been killed in action near Cambrai. He was entitled to the General Service and Victory Medals.
76, Wing Road, Leighton Buzzard.   1595.

CLARKE, A. C., Private, 4th Bedfordshire Regt.
He volunteered in August 1914, and after having completed his training was drafted to the Western Front, where he took part in the Battles of Arras, Passchendaele and Cambrai. On October 30th, 1917, he was killed in action, and was entitled to the General Service and Victory Medals.
41, New England Street, St. Albans.   1019.

CLARKE, A. G., Private, 5th Bedfordshire Regt.
He joined in October 1917, and in the following year was drafted to Egypt, where he took part in various important engagements, and was wounded. He returned home and was demobilised in January 1920, and holds the General Service and Victory Medals.
28, Park Road West, Luton.   1006.

CLARKE, C., Private, Bedfordshire Regiment.
He volunteered in November 1915, and after training served on important duties with his unit. In February 1917, he was drafted overseas, and took part in the Battles of Arras, Cambrai and the Somme. He was killed in action in an engagement at Savy, near St. Quentin, on March 21st, 1918, and was entitled to the General Service and Victory Medals.
Duke Street, Aspley Guise.   Z984.

CLARKE, C., Private, Bedfordshire Regiment.
He volunteered in August 1914, and at the conclusion of his training was drafted to France in the following year. He saw much fighting at Ypres, Loos, Arras and the Somme, and remained overseas until the cessation of hostilities, after which he returned home, and was demobilised in February 1919. He holds the 1914–15 Star, and the General Service and Victory Medals.
11, Belgrave Avenue, Watford.   X998/B.

CLARKE, C., Private, Machine Gun Corps.
He joined in 1916, and having completed his training was drafted to Egypt in the following year. He saw much fighting at El Arish, Gaza, Medjel, Haifa and Beyrout, and in 1918 was sent to Cairo, where he remained on special duties until the cessation of hostilities, when he returned home, and was demobilised in February 1919. He holds the General Service and Victory Medals.
4, Stanley Cottages, Batford Road, Harpenden.   992.

CLARKE, C., Private, Labour Corps.
He joined in June 1916, and at the conclusion of his training in the following November, was drafted to France. During his overseas service he was attached to the Royal Engineers, and was engaged in constructing roads and light railways in various sectors of the Front, notably those of the Somme, Arras, Ypres and Cambrai. He was demobilised after his return to England in April 1919, and holds the General Service and Victory Medals.
18, St. Mary's Street, Dunstable.   1024/B.

CLARKE, E., Sergeant, Royal Defence Corps.
He was mobilised in August 1914, and was engaged at various stations on important coastal defence duties with his unit, and rendered valuable services. He was demobilised in March 1919.
3, Chequer Street, Luton.   1007/A.

CLARKE, E. (Mrs.), Special War Worker.
In November 1916 this lady accepted an important position at the Greenford Munition Factory, and was engaged on responsible work in the shell-filling department until November 1918, when she relinquished her appointment. During her service the manner in which she carried out the arduous duties assigned to her was worthy of the highest praise, and the services which she rendered to her Country were of the utmost value.
69, Waterside, King's Langley.   997/B.

CLARKE, E., Private, Bedfordshire Lancers.
He volunteered in January 1915, and in the following July was sent to the Western Front, where he took part in many important engagements, including those at Loos, the Somme and Vimy Ridge. In February 1917 he was transferred to Egypt, and served at Gaza and Jerusalem. He returned home and was demobilised in March 1919, and holds the 1914–15 Star, and the General Service and Victory Medals.
8, Bower Lane, Eaton Bray, Dunstable.   976/B.

CLARKE, E. D., Private, 1st Hertfordshire Regt.
He joined in July 1916, and was later drafted to the Western Front, where he took part in various engagements, including that at Ypres. He was invalided home with trench feet in the following year, and was afterwards transferred to the Labour Corps, with which he served on important duties until he was demobilised in January 1919. He holds the General Service and Victory Medals.
31, John Street, Luton.   1004.

CLARKE, E. H. R., Private, Northumberland Fusiliers.
He joined in April 1918, and was almost immediately drafted to France, where he took part in the fighting at St. Quentin and in other engagements. He suffered from severe shell-shock, and after a period of treatment was eventually discharged in February 1919. He holds the General Service and Victory Medals.
9, Summer Street, Slip End.   1015.

CLARKE, E. R., Stoker, Royal Navy, H.M.S. "Galatea."
He joined in June 1916, and was posted for duty with H.M.S. "Galatea." He also served for a time in H.M.S. "Glatton," and was on board that vessel when she was blown up in the Channel, but fortunately was amongst the survivors. He took part in the engagement at Zeebrugge, and during his service was wounded on two occasions. He holds the General Service and Victory Medals, and in 1920 was still serving.
3, Chequer Street, Luton.   1007/B.

CLARKE, F. (M.M.), Bombardier, R.G.A.
He joined in 1916, and after having completed his training was drafted to the Western Front, where he took part in the Battles of Arras and Cambrai. He was awarded the Military Medal for conspicuous gallantry, and in addition holds the General Service and Victory Medals, and was demobilised in February 1919.
11, Belgrave Avenue, Watford.   998/A.

CLARKE, F., Private, 4th Bedfordshire Regiment.
He was mobilised at the outbreak of war, and in the following November was drafted to France, where he took part in the fighting at Neuve Chapelle and was wounded in March 1915. Later he was sent to Egypt, and served in the Palestine campaign, being present at the Battles of Gaza and other engagements. After the conclusion of hostilities he returned to England and was demobilised in June 1919, holding the 1914 Star, and the General Service and Victory Medals.
3, Old Park Road, Hitchin.   1599.

CLARKE, F., 5th Bedfordshire Regiment.
He joined in 1916, and having completed his training was drafted to France. Whilst in this theatre of war he saw much fighting at several engagements, including those of Ypres, the Somme and Arras. He was severely gassed, and on August 20th, 1918, was killed in action. He was entitled to the General Service and Victory Medals.
94, Baker Street, Luton. 990/B.

CLARKE, F., Private, Bedfordshire Regiment.
He joined in July 1916, and after the completion of his training served in France on the Somme, and at Ypres and Arras, and was wounded. On recovery he returned to the fighting line and took part in many subsequent engagements until hostilities ceased. He holds the General Service and Victory Medals, and was demobilised in February 1919.
32, Hampton Road, Luton. 1014.

CLARKE, F. C., Gunner, R.G.A.
He volunteered in October 1915, and in May of the following year was sent to France. In this theatre of war he did good work as a gunner on the Somme, and at Arras and Ypres, and was twice severely gassed. After the conclusion of hostilities he proceeded to Germany with the Army of Occupation and served until March 1920, when he was demobilised. He holds the General Service and Victory Medals.
76, New Town Street, Luton. 986.

CLARKE, F. W., Leading Aircraftsman, R.A.F.
He joined in August 1917, and in the following year, after the completion of his training, was drafted to France, where he was engaged on important duties at Boulogne. Later, owing to ill-health, he was invalided home. He holds the General Service and Victory Medals, and in 1920 was still serving.
30, Saxon Road, Luton. 1002.

CLARKE, G., Sapper, Royal Engineers.
He volunteered in June 1915, and in the following year was drafted to the Western Front, where he was engaged on important duties in connection with engineering on various fronts, and rendered valuable services. He was demobilised in March 1919, and holds the General Service and Victory Medals.
Hoo Lane Cottages, Offley. 2773.

CLARKE, H. F., Private, R.A.V.C.
He volunteered in January 1915, and having completed his training was drafted to Salonika in the following year. While overseas he rendered valuable services, tending sick and wounded horses, and after the Armistice returned home and was demobilised in 1919. He holds the General Service and Victory Medals.
11, Queen Street, St. Albans. 1013/B.

CLARKE, J., Private, 6th Lincolnshire Regiment.
He joined in March 1916, and in the following June was drafted to the Western Front, where he took part in various engagements, including those at Ypres, Arras and the Somme, and was wounded. He was invalided home, and after a period in hospital was engaged on various important duties until he was demobilised in February 1919. He holds the General Service and Victory Medals.
147, High Street, Houghton Regis, Dunstable. 977.

CLARKE, J., Private, R.A.M.C.
He joined in August 1916, and after his training served at various stations on important duties with his unit. He rendered valuable services, but was not successful in obtaining his transfer overseas, owing to medical unfitness, before the cessation of hostilities. He was demobilised in February 1919.
69, Waterside, King's Langley. X997/A.

CLARKE, J., Corporal, Royal Defence Corps.
He volunteered in August 1914, and after his training served at various stations on important duties with his unit. He rendered valuable services, but was not successful in obtaining his transfer overseas before the cessation of hostilities. He was demobilised in March 1919.
11, Queen Street, St. Albans, Herts. 1013/C

CLARKE, J. (M.S.M.), 1st Class W.O., R.A.F.
He volunteered in November 1914, and served at various stations on important duties with his unit. He met with a serious flying accident in a Twin Curtis machine, and on his recovery was engaged in building and repairing aeroplanes and other responsible work, which demanded a high degree of technical skill. He rendered valuable services, but was not successful in obtaining his transfer overseas before the cessation of hostilities. He was awarded the Meritorious Service Medal for his consistent good work, and was demobilised in May 1920.
Minnis Farm, Ewell Minnis, near Dover. Z1276.

CLARKE, J., Sapper, Royal Engineers.
Volunteering in June 1915, he joined the Staffordshire Regiment, later being transferred to the Royal Engineers. During his training he was stationed in Ireland and did valuable work during the Sinn Fein riots in 1916. He was afterwards drafted to France, where he took part in many engagements, notably those at Arras, Albert and Cambrai, and was taken prisoner at St. Quentin during the German Offensive in March 1918. Released after the signing of the Armistice, he returned to England, and in March 1919 was demobilised, holding the General Service and Victory Medals. 132, Wenlock Street, Luton. 1020

CLARKE, J. A., Flight-Sergeant, R.A.F.
He joined in June 1916, and after his training served at various stations on important duties, which required a high degree of technical skill. In May 1918 he was drafted to France, and rendered valuable services as an observer on the Cambrai Front and in other sectors. He was finally demobilised in June 1919, and holds the General Service and Victory Medals. 18, Arthur Road, St. Albans. X787.

CLARKE, J. W., Private, Royal Welch Fusiliers.
He volunteered in January 1915, and in the same year was drafted to the Western Front, where he took an active part in several important engagements. He fought at Festubert, Loos and the Somme, and was severely wounded and gassed. He was invalided home, and was discharged as medically unfit in June 1917, holding the 1914-15 Star, and the General Service and Victory Medals.
2, Whimbush Grove, Hitchin. 1841.

CLARKE, P. J., Corporal, Rifle Brigade.
He joined in 1916, and on the completion of his training was drafted to France, where he took part in the Battles of the Somme, Arras, Ypres and Cambrai. In February 1917 he was mentioned in Despatches for gallantry at Bullecourt, and was awarded the Military Medal for conspicuous bravery. In addition he holds the General Service and Victory Medals. During his service he was three times wounded, and after the conclusion of hostilities returned to England and was demobilised in 1919.
11, Queen Street, St. Albans, Herts. 1013/A.

CLARKE, R. W., Trumpeter, 1st Bedfordshire Lancers.
He volunteered in September 1914, and at the conclusion of his training was sent to France in June of the following year. He saw much fighting at several engagements, including those of Loos and the Somme, and returning home was discharged in February 1917, in consequence of his service. He holds the 1914-15 Star, and the General Service and Victory Medals. 65, Leagrave Road, Luton. 987.

CLARKE, T., Pte., 2nd Bedfordshire Regiment.
He volunteered in January 1915, and in October of the same year was drafted to the Western Front, where he took part in heavy fighting at the Battles of Loos, Vimy Ridge, the Somme, Arras, Ypres (III.) and Armentières, and was wounded. He was demobilised in March 1919, and holds the 1914-15 Star, and the General Service and Victory Medals.
Luton Road, Toddington, near Dunstable. 978.

CLARKE, T., Sapper, Royal Engineers.
He volunteered in February 1915, and at the conclusion of his training served with his unit at various stations on important duties. He rendered valuable service, but was not able to secure his transfer overseas before the cessation of hostilities. He was demobilised in February 1919.
1, Brampton Park Road, Hitchin. 1842.

CLARKE, T. H., Private, 10th Queen's (Royal West Surrey Regiment).
He joined in May 1917, and in the same year was drafted to the Western Front, where he took part in various engagements, including those at Kemmel, Ypres, Passchendaele and Menin. He was demobilised in March 1920, and holds the General Service and Victory Medals.
Mill Road, Greenfield, near Ampthill. 1011.

CLARKE, T. J., Rifleman, Rifle Brigade.
He joined on attaining military age in June 1918, but had not completed his training when hostilities ceased. Afterwards, however, he was sent with the Army of Occupation to Germany, where he was engaged on special duties. He was demobilised on his return to England in April 1920.
18, St. Mary's Street, Dunstable. 1024/A.

CLARKE, T. W., Private, R.A.S.C.
Having previously been engaged on work of National importance at No. 2. Filling Station, Watford, where he did valuable work, he joined the Army in April 1916. After his training he was drafted to Egypt, and subsequently served as a caterpillar tractor driver during the Palestine campaign, being present at the Battle of Gaza and the capture of Jerusalem. In September 1918 he returned to England in consequence of ill-health, and a month later was invalided out of the Service. He holds the General Service and Victory Medals.
20, Neal Street, Watford. X999.

CLARKE, V. G., Private, Labour Corps and the Queen's (Royal West Surrey Regiment).
He joined in 1916, and after having completed his training was drafted to the Western Front in the same year. Whilst serving overseas he was present at the Battles of Arras and Ypres and numerous other engagements. He holds the General Service and Victory Medals, and was demobilised in 1918.
High Street, Barton, Ampthill. 1018.

CLARKE, W., L/Corporal, The Buffs (East Kent Regiment).
He volunteered in June 1915, and in the same year was drafted to Mesopotamia and was engaged at Kut. He rendered valuable services until March 1919, when he returned home and was demobilised, holding the 1914-15 Star, and the General Service and Victory Medals.
8, Bower Lane, Eaton Bray, Dunstable. 976/A.

CLARKE, W., Wireless Operator, R.N., H.M.S. " Resolution."
He joined in August 1917, and during his service was engaged as a wireless operator off the coasts of Malta and Spain, and in the North Sea and at Scapa Flow, and rendered valuable services. He was still serving in 1920, and holds the General Service and Victory Medals.
104, Biscot Road, Luton. 4279/A.

CLARKE, W., Sergeant, R.A.S.C.
He joined in February 1917, and at the conclusion of his training served with his unit at various stations on important duties. He rendered valuable service, but was not able to secure his transfer overseas before the cessation of hostilities. He was demobilised in December 1919.
94, Baker Street, Luton. 990/A.

CLARKE, W. C., Driver, R.H.A. and R.F.A.
He joined in October 1916, and in the following January was drafted to France. During his service on the Western Front he was engaged on important duties as a driver attached to the ammunition column, and was present at the engagements at Ypres, Cambrai and the Somme. After the termination of hostilities he returned home and was demobilised in November 1919, holding the General Service and Victory Medals.
Luton Road, Toddington. 979.

CLARKE, W. D., Private, 2nd Bedfordshire Regt.
He volunteered in January 1915, and after having completed his training was drafted to France, and took part in numerous engagements, and was twice wounded. On July 26th, 1917, he was killed in action, and was entitled to the General Service and Victory Medals.
Summer Field House, Summer Street, Slip End. 1017.

CLARKE, W. H., Private, 1st Bedfordshire Regt.
He volunteered in August 1914, and at the conclusion of his training was drafted to the Western Front in February of the following year. He fought at Neuve Chapelle, and later, on April 20th, 1915, was killed in action at Hill 60. He was entitled to the 1914-15 Star, and the General Service and Victory Medals.
39, Castle Road, St. Albans. X991.

CLATWORTHY, G., Private, R.A.S.C.
He volunteered in August 1914, and in the following January was drafted to the Western Front. Whilst in this theatre of war he was present at the engagements at Ypres and on the Somme, and was subsequently severely wounded. He was invalided home in December 1917, and after protracted treatment in hospital was finally demobilised in February 1919. He holds the 1914-15 Star, and the General Service and Victory Medals.
14, Collingdon Street, Luton. 962.

CLAY, J., Private, 2nd Leicestershire Regiment.
He was serving at the outbreak of war, and in 1915 was sent overseas. During his service on the Western Front he took part in the fighting at Ypres, Arras, Cambrai and Albert. Later he was drafted to Mesopotamia, and finally to India. He was still serving in 1920, and holds the 1914-15 Star, and the General Service and Victory Medals.
27, Peache Street, Luton. 957/A.

CLAY, W., Pioneer-Sergeant, 1/5th Leicestershire Regiment.
He volunteered in August 1914, and was drafted to France, where he took part in the heavy fighting at Ypres and was severely wounded. He was invalided home, and after treatment in hospital was discharged as physically unfit for further military service in December 1915. He holds the 1914-15 Star, and the General Service and Victory Medals.
27, Peache Street, Luton. 957/B.

CLAYDEN, F. R., Corporal, R.A.S.C.
He joined in February 1917, and in the following July was drafted to the Western Front, where he was attached to the head-quarters on important duties. He was later transferred to Egypt, and served in the Palestine campaign, and was present at the Battle of Gaza. He returned home and was demobilised in March 1920, and holds the General Service and Victory Medals.
5, Church Road, Linslade, Bucks. 1596/A.

CLAYDEN, W. R., Private, Devonshire Regiment.
He joined in July 1918, and after his training served at various stations on important duties with his unit. He rendered valuable services, but was not successful in obtaining his transfer overseas before the cessation of hostilities. In December 1918 he was drafted to Germany with the Army of Occupation, with which he served until March 1920, when he returned home and was demobilised.
5, Church Road, Linslade. 1596/B.

CLAYDON, W., Gunner, Royal Field Artillery.
Volunteering in 1915, he was drafted to the Western Front in the same year, and took part in the Battles of the Somme, Ypres, Arras and Cambrai. After the cessation of hostilities he returned to England, and in May 1919 was demobilised, holding the 1914-15 Star, and the General Service and Victory Medals.
6, Oxhey Street, Oxhey. X958.

CLAYTON, C., Gunner, Royal Field Artillery.
He volunteered in November 1915, and in the following January was drafted to the Western Front. Whilst in this theatre of war he took part in the Battles of the Somme, Arras, Ypres (III.) and Cambrai, and after hostilities had ceased was finally demobilised in April 1919. He holds the General Service and Victory Medals.
58, Clarendon Road, Luton. 959/A.

CLAYTON, G., Sergeant, Bedfordshire Lancers and 8th Hussars.
He was mobilised in August 1914, and in the following year was drafted to France, where he served at Givenchy, Loos, the Somme, Arras, Ypres and Cambrai, and was wounded at Passchendaele. He was demobilised in February 1919, and holds the 1914-15 Star, and the General Service and Victory Medals.
59, The Baulk, Biggleswade. Z1564/A.

CLAYTON, H. G., Corporal, R.A.S.C.
He joined in February 1917, and in the same year was drafted to Salonika, and during his service on the Balkan Front did good work in the Advance on Vardar and in the engagements at Monastir. In December 1918 he was sent to Constantinople, where he served with the Army of Occupation until the following March, when he returned home and was demobilised, holding the General Service and Victory Medals.
132, Biscot Road, Luton. 960.

CLAYTON, H. M., Driver, R.F.A.
He volunteered in 1915, and in the following April was sent overseas. During his service on the Western Front he did excellent work as a driver in various important engagements, including those at Vimy Ridge, Ypres and Armentières. He was severely wounded in action in July 1918 and invalided home to hospital, and finally demobilised in February 1919. He holds the General Service and Victory Medals.
96, Althorp Road, Luton. 961.

CLAYTON, L., Private, Suffolk Regiment.
He volunteered in 1915, and in the same year was drafted to Egypt, where he served in the Palestine campaign, taking part in the engagements at Gaza and Jerusalem. Later he returned to England and was afterwards sent to the Western Front, and took part in the Advance. He was killed in action on October 14th, 1918, and was entitled to the 1914-15 Star, and the General Service and Victory Medals.
59, The Baulk, Biggleswade. Z1564/B.

CLAYTON, S., Sapper, Royal Engineers.
He volunteered in November 1915, and in the following March was sent overseas. During his service on the Western Front he carried out important duties as a despatch rider, and was in action on the Somme and at Ypres. He was severely wounded and invalided home in June 1917, and after his recovery was drafted to Egypt, where in 1920 he was still serving. He holds the General Service and Victory Medals.
58, Clarendon Road, Luton. 959/B.

CLEAVER, A. F. C., Trooper, Bedfordshire Lancers.
Volunteering in September 1914, he was sent to the Western Front early in the following year, and subsequently served on the Somme, and at Arras and Ypres. He also took part in the Retreat of 1918, and in March of that year was reported missing, and is believed to have been killed in action. He was entitled to the General Service and Victory Medals.
81, Church Street, Dunstable, Beds. 1025.

CLEAVER, A. J., Seaman (Gunner), Royal Navy.
He joined in October 1916, and served for a time in the North Sea, being engaged on patrol and submarine chasing duties. Later he was stationed in the Mediterranean and was serving in H.M.S. "Agamemnon," when the Armistice with Turkey was signed on board. Afterwards he proceeded with the Fleet to Constantinople, and in March 1919, having returned to England, was demobilised, holding the General Service and Victory Medals.
56, Stanbridge Road, Leighton Buzzard. 2787.

CLEAVER, B. G., Corporal, M.G.C.
He volunteered in November 1914, and on the completion of his training was drafted to the Western Front in December 1916. During his service in France he took part in the fighting at Arras, Bourlon Wood, Cambrai and Gouzeaucourt. After the cessation of hostilities he returned home and was subsequently demobilised in February 1919, and holds the General Service and Victory Medals.
Downs Villa, Toddington. 964.

CLEAVER, J. S., Private, 17th Middlesex Regt.
He joined in March 1916, and in the following month was sent to France. In this theatre of war he was engaged in heavy fighting at Vimy Ridge, and was subsequently killed in action at the Battle of the Somme in November 1916. He was entitled to the General Service and Victory Medals.
"The Rising Sun," Harlington, Beds. 965/A.

CLEAVER, S. C., Sapper, Royal Engineers.
He volunteered in December 1914, and in the following April was drafted to Egypt and proceeded into Palestine with General Allenby's Forces. During his service he was engaged on important duties in the forward areas whilst operations were in progress. He was wounded at Gaza in November 1917, and subsequently killed in action near Jerusalem on April 8th, 1918. He was entitled to the 1914-15 Star, and the General Service and Victory Medals.
"The Rising Sun," Harlington, Beds. 965/C.

CLEAVER, W. J., Private, 2nd Bedfordshire Regt.
Volunteering in September 1914, he was drafted to France in the following January. During his service overseas he took part in the fighting at Loos, the Somme, Arras, Ypres and Cambrai, and was twice wounded. He was killed in action during the Retreat on April 25th, 1918, and was entitled to the 1914-15 Star, and the General Service and Victory Medals.
"The Rising Sun," Harlington, Beds. 965/B.

CLEMENTS, A., Private, 1/5th Bedfordshire Regiment.
Volunteering in September 1914, he was shortly afterwards drafted to Egypt, where he served on the banks of the Suez Canal, and at Katia, Gaza and Jerusalem. He was demobilised in July 1919, and holds the General Service and Victory Medals.
8, Baker Street, Leighton Buzzard. 1299/B.

CLEMENTS, C., Private, Gordon Highlanders.
He joined in November 1916, and in the following February was drafted to France, where he took part in numerous engagements, including those at Vimy Ridge, Ypres and the Retreat and Advance of 1918. On the cessation of hostilities he was attached to the Army of Occupation and served on the Rhine until demobilised in November 1919. He holds the General Service and Victory Medals.
8, Baker Street, Leighton Buzzard. 1299/A.

CLEMENTS, E. W. F., Air Mechanic, R.A.F.
He joined in November 1917, and after his training was completed served at various stations on important duties which demanded a high degree of technical knowledge and skill. He rendered valuable service but was not able to secure his transfer overseas before the conclusion of the war, and was demobilised in January 1919.
1, Claremont Road, Luton. 966/A.

CLEMENTS, H., Pte., Northumberland Fusiliers.
He was called up from the Reserve in August 1914, and in the following January proceeded to France, where he served in numerous engagements in various sectors of the front, including the Retreat and Advance of 1918. He was demobilised in May 1919, and holds the 1914-15 Star, and the General Service and Victory Medals.
8, Baker Street, Leighton Buzzard. 1300.

CLEMENTS, H. G., C.S.M., 1st Hertfordshire Regiment.
He was serving at the outbreak of war, and in November 1915 was sent to France. Whilst in this theatre of war he was engaged on important special duties in connection with the guarding of German prisoners of war at a large camp at Rouen. He was finally demobilised in October 1919, and holds the 1914-15 Star, and the General Service and Victory Medals.
1, Station Road, Harpenden. 967.

CLEMENTS, J. R., Sergeant, Bedfordshire Regt.
He volunteered at the outbreak of war, and was later drafted to Egypt. He served in the Palestine campaign, being present at the engagements at Gaza and Jerusalem and was wounded. He returned to England and was demobilised in April 1919, and holds the 1914-15 Star, and the General Service and Victory Medals.
30, Mill Road, Leighton Buzzard. 1591.

CLEMENTS, P. W., Flight-Sergeant, R.A.F.
He volunteered in January 1915, and in the following July was drafted to France, where he was engaged as an observer and also took part in numerous bombing raids on the enemy positions. He holds the 1914-15 Star, and the General Service and Victory Medals, and was demobilised in February 1920.
"Park View," Stanbridge Road, Leighton Buzzard. 2788.

CLEMENTS, W., Private, R.A.M.C.
He joined in June 1917, and in November of the same year was drafted to Salonika, and served on the Vardar front. He contracted malaria and was invalided home in August 1918, and after a period in hospital was engaged on important duties with his unit until April 1920, when he was demobilised, and holds the General Service and Victory Medals.
3, St. Katherine Cottages, Ickleford, Hitchin. 2770.

CLEMENTS, W. A., Private, 2nd Luton Vols.
He joined the Volunteer Training Corps in 1915, and rendered valuable services on important guard duties until 1917, when he was discharged.
1, Claremont Road, Luton. 966/B.

CLEWS, A., Private, 2nd Bedfordshire Regiment.
He volunteered in September 1914, and in the following year was sent to the Western Front, where he took part in the Battles of the Somme, Ypres, Armentières and many other engagements, and was three times wounded. He was demobilised in February 1919, and holds the 1914-15 Star, and the General Service and Victory Medals.
5, Alfred Street, Dunstable. 969—970/B.

CLEWS, F., Private, 7th Bedfordshire Regiment.
He volunteered in September 1914, and in April of the following year was drafted to the Western Front, where he took part in numerous important engagements. He was killed in action on December 4th, 1915, and was entitled to the 1914-15 Star, and the General Service and Victory Medals.
5, Alfred Street, Dunstable. 969—970/C.

CLEWS, J. W., Gunner, Royal Garrison Artillery.
He joined in October 1917, and in March of the following year was drafted to the Western Front, where he took part in important engagements, including those on the Somme and at Cambrai. After the Armistice he proceeded with the Army of Occupation to Germany, where he served until December 1919, when he returned home and was demobilised, holding the General Service and Victory Medals.
Hazeldene, St. Peter's Road, Dunstable. 969—970/A.

CLIBBON, W., Pioneer, R.E. (Signals).
He joined in August 1918, and in May of the following year was drafted to Egypt and stationed at Beyrout, where he served on important duties until 1920. After his return to England he was demobilised in April of that year.
27, Cavendish Road, St. Albans. X792/B.

CLIBBON, W., Private, Queen's Own (Royal West Kent Regiment).
He volunteered in May 1915, and in the following August was drafted overseas. During his service on the Western Front he took part in the Battle of the Somme, and was afterwards reported missing and is presumed to have been killed in action on July 22nd, 1916. He was entitled to the 1914-15 Star, and the General Service and Victory Medals.
27, Cavendish Road, St. Albans. X792/A.

CLIFTON, S. E. W., Engineer (W.O.), R.N., H.M.S. " Albion " and " Daphne."
He volunteered in August 1914, and served on coastal patrol duties off German South-West Africa and at the Dardanelles, where he was present at the landing at Suvla Bay. He was also stationed in the North Sea, Scapa Flow and the Baltic. He was demobilised in January 1920, and holds the 1914-15 Star, and the General Service and Victory Medals.
27, Selbourne Road, Luton. 971.

CLODE, F. A., Leading Stoker, R.N., H.M.S. " Blake."
He was serving at the outbreak of hostilities, and throughout the war was engaged on important duties off the coasts of German African territory. He rendered valuable services, and was still serving in 1920. He holds the 1914-15 Star, and the General Service and Victory Medals.
2, Dumfries Street, Luton. 5012/F—5013/F.

CLODE, S. I. (Mrs.), Special War Worker.
For 3½ years during the war this lady held an important position in a large Explosives factory, where she was engaged on responsible work in connection with the manufacture of pellets and in filling bombs. The manner in which she carried out the arduous duties assigned to her was worthy of the highest commendation.
2, Dumfries Street, Luton. 5012/G—5013/G.

CLOUT, D. T., Private, R.A.S.C. (M.T.)
He volunteered in March 1915, and in the same month was drafted to the Western Front, where he was engaged in the transport of ammunition and supplies, and rendered valuable services. He was demobilised in June 1919, and holds the 1914-15 Star, and the General Service and Victory Medals.
14, Shaftesbury Road, Watford. 972/C—973/C.

CLOUT, E. D., Corporal, R.F.A.
He joined in February 1917, and in the same year was drafted to the Western Front. He was attached to the anti-aircraft section and served in various engagements, including that at Cambrai, and was gassed. He was demobilised in February 1919, and holds the General Service and Victory Medals.
14, Shaftesbury Road, Watford. 972/A—973/A.

CLOUT, W. T., Gunner, Royal Field Artillery.
He volunteered in May 1915, and in November of the same year was drafted to the Western Front, where he served in the Ypres and Arras sectors. In January 1916 he was sent to Egypt and served in the Palestine Campaign, taking part in various engagements, including those at Gaza and Jaffa, and being wounded. He returned home and was demobilised in June 1919, and holds the 1914-15 Star, and the General Service and Victory Medals.
14, Shaftesbury Road, Watford. 972/D—973/D.

CLOUT, W. R., Private, Royal Air Force.
He joined in August 1918, and after his training served in Ireland on important duties with his unit. He rendered valuable services, but was not successful in obtaining his transfer overseas before the cessation of hostilities. He was demobilised in April 1919.
14, Shaftesbury Road, Watford. 972/B—973/B.

CLUBB, R. E., Private, 4th Middlesex Regiment.
He volunteered in August 1914, and in the following year was drafted to the Western Front, where he took part in many important engagements, including those at Hill 60, Ypres and Festubert. He was killed in action at Loos on March 4th, 1916, and was entitled to the 1914-15 Star, and the General Service and Victory Medals.
66, Pondswick Road, Luton. 974.

CLUTTEN, A. V., Sapper, Royal Engineers.
He was mobilised in August 1914, and served on important duties with his unit until September 1917, when he was drafted to the Western Front, where he took part in various important engagements, including those at Ypres, Cambrai and the Somme, and was gassed. He was demobilised in February 1919, and holds the General Service and Victory Medals.
7, Norman Road, Leagrave Road, Luton. 975/A.

CLUTTEN, H. W., Private, Royal Fusiliers.
He volunteered in September 1914, and in the following year proceeded to the Western Front, where he took part in heavy fighting at Hooge and Ypres, and was severely wounded. He was invalided home, and after two years in hospital was discharged as medically unfit for further service in June 1917. Later he died of influenza on October 15th, 1918, and was entitled to the 1914-15 Star, and the General Service and Victory Medals.
7, Norman Road, Leagrave Road, Luton. 975/B.

COATES, A., Private, 8th Royal Sussex Regt.
He volunteered in October 1915, and in December 1917 was drafted to France. He took part in the Battles of Ypres, St. Quentin, Villers-Bretonneux and Aveluy Wood, and was wounded. He was demobilised in December 1918, and holds the General Service and Victory Medals.
117, Maple Road, Luton. 1059.

COBB, F., Private, R.A.F. (Police).
He was mobilised in August 1914, and in the same month was drafted to the Western Front, where he was engaged on police duties, and also acted as stretcher-bearer for a time. He was present at various engagements, including that at Cambrai, and also served in the Retreat and Advance of 1918, and was wounded. He was invalided home, and after a period in hospital was demobilised in February 1919, and holds the 1914 Star, and the General Service and Victory Medals.
14, St. Andrew's Street, Leighton Buzzard. 2785.

COBLES, W., Private, Cheshire Regiment.
He was serving at the outbreak of war, and in the following year was drafted to France, where he took part in much heavy fighting at Loos, Festubert, Albert, Cambrai and on the Somme, being twice wounded and gassed. He was demobilised in 1919, and holds the 1914-15 Star, and the General Service and Victory Medals.
Lower Caldecote, Biggleswade. Z1561.

COCHRANE, A., Private, R.D.C. and R.A.S.C.
He volunteered in 1915, and was placed in the Royal Defence Corps, but later was transferred to the Royal Army Service Corps. He was engaged on important duties with his unit, and rendered valuable services, but was not successful in obtaining his transfer overseas before the cessation of hostilities. He was demobilised in June 1919.
46, Saint Mary Street, Dunstable. 1120/B.

COGGLES, A. G., Private, Royal Fusiliers.
He joined in June 1916, and after training was sent to the Western Front, where he saw considerable service. He took part in the Battles of Ypres (III.) and Cambrai, and was wounded in action. After the conclusion of hostilities he returned home and was demobilised in February 1919, and holds the General Service and Victory Medals.
92, Hampton Road, Luton. 1147.

COKER, A. E., Sapper, Royal Engineers.
He joined in November 1916, and in March of the following year proceeded overseas. He did excellent work with his unit on the Western Front until invalided home, owing to severe illness. On recovery, he returned to France in March 1918, and was present at several battles, including those of Ypres and the Somme. He was demobilised in November 1919, and holds the General Service and Victory Medals.
7, Diamond Road, Watford. X1170.

COLE, A. J., Private, Bedfordshire Regiment.
He volunteered in January 1915, and on the completion of his training was drafted to France, where he served on the Somme and at Arras and Cambrai, and was three times wounded. He was invalided home and was demobilised in March 1919, holding the General Service and Victory Medals.
56, The Baulk, Biggleswade. Z1559.

COLE, F., Private, 1st Bedfordshire Regiment.
He volunteered in November 1914, and in the following January was drafted overseas. He first saw service in France, where he was wounded in the Battle of Hill 60, and in 1916 was sent to Italy. After taking part in heavy fighting on the Piave and in the Trentino Advance, he returned to the Western Front, was in action on the Somme, at Arras, Ypres and Cambrai, and was wounded for the second time. Demobilised in February 1919, he holds the 1914-15 Star, and the General Service and Victory Medals.
George Street, Maulden, near Ampthill, Beds. 1171

COLE, F. H., Private, Bedfordshire Regiment; and Sapper, Royal Engineers.
Joining in October 1916, he was drafted overseas in the following year. He saw much active service in several sectors of the Western Front, and, employed on important duties in forward areas, was present at many battles, including those at Cambrai, Arras and Ypres. He was gassed whilst in France, and at the end of the war he returned to England. He was demobilised in September 1919, and holds the General Service and Victory Medals.
37, New England Street, St. Albans. 1168.

COLE, G., Gunner, Royal Field Artillery.
He volunteered in 1915, and was drafted to the Western Front in the same year. He took part in heavy fighting at the Battles of Loos, St. Eloi and the Somme, and was killed in action at Cambrai on November 1st, 1917. He was entitled to the 1914-15 Star, and the General Service and Victory Medals.
Church Street, Shillington. 2772.

COLE, G., Private, Machine Gun Corps.

He joined in October 1918, and at the conclusion of his training was engaged on important agricultural duties. He rendered valuable service, but was not able to secure his transfer overseas owing to being medically unfit for duty abroad. He was demobilised in January 1919.
Magpie Row, George Street, Maulden, near Ampthill. 1843.

COLE, R. H., Private, 2nd Coldstream Guards.

He volunteered in December 1915, and in the following year was drafted to the Western Front, where he took part in numerous engagements, including those at Arras, Ypres, Cambrai and the Somme. He was demobilised in March 1919, and holds the General Service and Victory Medals.
Gosmore, Hitchin. 2775.

COLEMAN, A., Private, 2nd South Wales Borderers and Labour Corps.

He volunteered at the outbreak of hostilities, and immediately proceeded to France, where he took part in the Retreat from Mons, and was severely wounded. On his recovery he was drafted to Gallipoli in July 1915, and was in action at Suvla Bay and Anzac. Later he returned to France, where he saw much fighting at several engagements, including the Somme, Arras, Ypres, Passchendaele and Cambrai. He was wounded again at Béthune, and remained overseas until after the Armistice had been signed, when he returned to England and was demobilised in March 1919, holding the Mons Star, and the General Service and Victory Medals.
3, Essex Street, Luton. 1126/A.

COLEMAN, F., Driver, Royal Field Artillery.

He volunteered in August 1914, and throughout the war was engaged on important duties in connection with the transport of horses to the Western Front. During his service he met with a serious accident, being thrown from a horse, and was under treatment for some time. He holds the 1914-15 Star, and the General Service and Victory Medals, and was demobilised in March 1919.
3, Essex Street, Luton. 1126/B.

COLEMAN, P. W., Private, Highland L.I.

He volunteered in February 1915, and in the same year was drafted overseas, and served at Ypres and on the Somme, and was wounded. In 1917 he was sent to Palestine, where he took part in the Battle of Gaza and other engagements of that campaign, and was wounded on two further occasions. He returned home after the cessation of hostilities, and was demobilised in March 1919, and holds the General Service and Victory Medals.
2, Hillside Road, Luton. 1145/A.

COLEMAN, T. B., L/Corporal, M.G.C.

He joined in February 1916, and in the following May was drafted overseas. During his service on the Western Front he took part in the Battles of the Somme, Ypres and Cambrai. He was severely wounded in action at Armentières in April 1918, and was invalided to hospital, and after some months' treatment was discharged as medically unfit for further service in October of the same year. He holds the General Service and Victory Medals.
14, Alexandra Road, Hitchin. 1596.

COLEMAN, W. G., Private, 3rd Somerset L.I.

He joined in 1917, and on the completion of his training was drafted to France, where he saw considerable service in the Retreat and Advance of 1918. After the termination of the war he was sent home and subsequently demobilised in January 1919. He holds the General Service and Victory Medals.
Station Grove, Woburn Sands, Beds. Z1054.

COLEMAN, W. J., Corporal, R.A.S.C.

He volunteered in May 1915, and was almost immediately drafted to the Western Front. During his service in France he was wounded in the Battle of the Somme, and on recovering was present at the engagements at Arras, Ypres and Cambrai. He was demobilised in May 1919, after exactly four years' service with the Colours, and holds the 1914-15 Star, and the General Service and Victory Medals.
28, Hagden Lane, Watford. X1095.

COLEMAN, W. L., Private, 3rd Bedfordshire Lancers and Royal Army Service Corps.

He volunteered in April 1915, and in the following April was sent to the Western Front. During his service overseas he took part in the Battle of Ypres (III.), and was severely wounded and invalided to hospital. He was discharged as medically unfit for further duty in May 1918, and died in August 1919 from the effects of wounds. He was entitled to the General Service and Victory Medals.
2, Hillside Road, Luton. 1145/B.

COLES, A., Driver, Royal Engineers.

He volunteered in September 1914, and after his training was drafted, in March 1916, to Egypt. He was engaged on the transport of supplies to various parts, including Gaza and Jerusalem, and rendered valuable services. He was demobilised in July 1919, and holds the General Service and Victory Medals.
55, Spencer Road, Luton. 4234/B.

COLES, F. R., Sapper, Royal Engineers.

He joined in April 1917, and having undergone a course of training was engaged on important duties with his unit. He was unable to secure his transfer overseas before hostilities ceased, but did valuable work until demobilised in March 1919.
34, Victoria Road, North Watford. X1158.

COLES, G. D., Private, Queen's (Royal West Surrey Regiment).

He joined in February 1918, and in the following August was drafted to the Western Front, where he took part in the fighting in the Somme area, and was severely wounded near Lens. After the cessation of hostilities he was sent home and demobilised in February 1919, and holds the General Service and Victory Medals.
32, Union Road, Hitchin. 1600.

COLES, G. H., Private, Machine Gun Corps.

Volunteering in January 1915 he went through his training, and in July 1917 was drafted to Palestine, where he served at Gaza and in other engagements. In June 1918 he was sent to France and took part in the Battle of Cambrai and in other important battles in the Advance of that year. He was demobilised in May 1919, and holds the General Service and Victory Medals.
Chalgrave, Toddington. 1066.

COLES, G. W., Sapper, Royal Engineers.

He joined in February 1917, and was almost immediately drafted to the Western Front. Throughout his service overseas he was engaged on important duties in the Somme, Arras and Cambrai areas, constructing railways and roads as the infantry advanced. He returned home in December 1918, and in the following March was demobilised, holding the General Service and Victory Medals.
41, George Street, Leighton Buzzard. 791.

COLES, H. C., Private, Bedfordshire Regiment.

He volunteered in August 1914, and after being retained for some time on important duties with his unit, was drafted to the Western Front, where he took part in the severe fighting at the Battles of Arras, Vimy Ridge, Ypres and Cambrai, and was gassed. He was demobilised in February 1919, after returning home, and holds the General Service and Victory Medals.
7, Ship Road, Leighton Buzzard. 1072.

COLES, H. J., Sapper, Royal Engineers.

Volunteering in November 1915, he was speedily drafted overseas, and until the conclusion of hostilities rendered valuable service in Egypt, Palestine and Syria, being present at the entry into Jerusalem and the battles near Haïfa, Acre and Aleppo. After his return to England he was demobilised in March 1919, and holds the General Service and Victory Medals.
36, Smart Street, Luton. 1062.

COLES, J., Staff-Sergeant, Royal Engineers.

He volunteered in June 1915, and after being engaged on important duties for some time at various stations, was in 1917 drafted to the Egyptian front. He took part in the Palestine campaign and rendered valuable service at Gaza, Haïfa, Acre, Damascus and Beyrout. After the close of hostilities he returned to England and was demobilised in April 1919, holding the General Service and Victory Medals.
60, Baker Street, Luton. 1116.

COLES, P. R., Gunner, Royal Field Artillery.

He volunteered in December 1915, and in February 1917 was drafted to the Western Front, where he saw much service. He took part in the engagements at Vimy Ridge, Messines, Ypres, Passchendaele, the second Battle of the Somme and other operations until September 1918, when he returned home. He was demobilised in the December following, and holds the General Service and Victory Medals.
84, Russell Rise, Luton. 1065.

COLES, R. T., Private, R.M.L.I.

Volunteering in August 1914, he was, during his service, engaged on important patrol duties in the North Sea and at Scapa Flow, and rendered valuable services. He died on June 12th, 1915, from illness contracted during the war, and was entitled to the 1914-15 Star, and the General Service and Victory Medals.
The Grange, High Street, Toddington. 1042/B.

COLES, S., Private, 4th Bedfordshire Regiment.
He volunteered in September 1914, and was going through his course of training at Dover, when his health gave way under the strain of military duties. He was therefore discharged in November 1914 as unfit for further service owing to heart trouble.
High Street, Toddington.   1041.

COLES, S. G., Pte., King's Liverpool Regiment.
He volunteered in August 1915, and after his training served on important duties with his unit until January 1917, when he was drafted to the Western Front. He took part in the severe engagements at Arras, Bullecourt and Ypres, and was killed in action near Arras on August 29th, 1917. He was entitled to the General Service and Victory Medals.
Park Road, Toddington.   1039.

COLEWELL, P. J. (M.M.), L/Corporal, M.G.C.
He volunteered in August 1914, and in the following January was drafted to Egypt. In charge of a machine gun squad he took a prominent part in the operations on this front and in the Advance through Palestine, where he fought in the Battles of Gaza and before the entry into Jerusalem. He was awarded the Military Medal for conspicuous bravery in action and devotion to duty, and in addition holds the 1914-15 Star, and the General Service and Victory Medals. He was demobilised in March 1919.
Carpenter's Arms, Harlington.   1134.

COLLARBONE, A. E., Gunner, R.G.A.
He joined in December 1916, and in January of the following year was drafted to the Western Front, where he took part in the severe fighting at Ypres, Lens, Cambrai, the Somme, Amiens and many other later engagements. He was demobilised in February 1919, and holds the General Service and Victory Medals.
Arm & Sword Yard, Hatfield.   X1154/C.

COLLARBONE, H. H., Private, 1st Hertfordshire Regiment.
He volunteered in September 1914, and in January of the following year was drafted to the Western Front. He took part in many important engagements until the close of hostilities, including those of Festubert in 1915, and the Somme, the Marne and Amiens in 1918, and was wounded and twice gassed. He was demobilised in April 1919, after returning home, and holds the 1914-15 Star, and the General Service and Victory Medals.
Arm & Sword Yard, Hatfield.   X1154/A.

COLLARBONE, W., Sergeant, East Surrey Regt.
After having previously served he volunteered in August 1914, and in November of the following year was drafted to the Western Front, where he took part in various engagements, including that of Ypres, and was wounded. In 1916 he was transferred to Salonika and rendered valuable service there until fighting ended. He was demobilised in April 1919, and holds the 1914-15 Star, and the General Service and Victory Medals.
Arm & Sword Yard, Hatfield.   X1154/B.

COLLER, W., Private, Royal Welch Fusiliers.
He volunteered in 1915, and in the same year was drafted to the Western Front, where he fought in many important engagements, including those at Ypres, the Somme, Cambrai, Arras and the Aisne, and was gassed. He was demobilised in 1919, and holds the 1914-15 Star, and the General Service and Victory Medals.
12, Grover Road, Oxhey.   1096/B.

COLLETT, A. G., L/Corporal, R.A.M.C.
He volunteered in November 1914, and in the following January was sent to France, where he served as a stretcher-bearer in the engagements at Ypres, the Somme, Arras and Cambrai. He also did valuable skilled work in the hospitals. He was demobilised in April 1919, and holds the 1914-15 Star, and the General Service and Victory Medals.
50, Stanbridge Road, Leighton Buzzard.   1298.

COLLETT, R., Private, R.A.S.C.
He volunteered in 1915, and in the same year was drafted to Egypt, where he was present at various engagements, including those at Gaza and Haifa. In 1918 he was transferred to France, and served in the Retreat and Advance of 1918, during which he was employed in the transport of ammunition and supplies to the front lines. He was demobilised in March 1919, and holds the 1914-15 Star, and the General Service and Victory Medals.
14, Rushby Mead, Letchworth.   2767.

COLLEY, A., Sapper, Royal Engineers.
He joined in 1916, and after his training was drafted to France, where he was engaged at Cambrai and other battles. He was chiefly employed on important duties in connection with wiring and general telephonic work, and rendered valuable services. In November 1919 he was demobilised, after his return to England, and holds the General Service and Victory Medals.
23, Lowestoft Road, Watford.   X1152.

COLLEY, A. J., Sergeant, Queen's Own (Royal West Kent Regiment).
Joining in June 1916, he was drafted in the next month to India, where he served in various minor engagements on the Frontier. In 1917 he was transferred to Mesopotamia, and served with distinction at Baghdad and Mosul. He returned home and was demobilised in March 1919, holding the General Service and Victory Medals.
110a, Liverpool Road, Watford.   X1079.

COLLIER, G., L/Corporal, 11th South Lancashire Regiment.
Volunteering in November 1914, he was retained for important duties in England until September 1918, when he was drafted to France. He then served at Cambrai and Ypres and in other engagements up to the date of the Armistice. He was demobilised after his return to England in June 1919, and holds the General Service and Victory Medals.
65, Queen Street, Hemel Hempstead.   X1043.

COLLIER, H. J., Stoker, Royal Navy.
He was mobilised at the outbreak of war, and did valuable and highly dangerous duty in the North Sea on board the mine-sweeper "Poppy." He also rendered good service on H.M.S. "Lord Clive" in many important operations. He was demobilised in February 1919, and holds the 1914-15 Star, and the General Service and Victory Medals.
118, Liverpool Road, Watford.   X1153.

COLLIER, H. W., Private, 5th Lincolnshire Regt.
He joined in February 1917, and in the same year, on concluding his training, was sent out to France, where he served at Cambrai, the Somme and other engagements until hostilities ceased, and was wounded. He holds the General Service and Victory Medals, and was demobilised in November 1919.
11, Piccotts End, Hemel Hempstead.   X1109/B.

COLLIER, T., Private, R.A.V.C.
He joined in December 1916, and after his training was drafted to Salonika, and served at Vardar and Monastir. He was principally engaged in attending to wounded and sick horses, and rendered valuable services. He contracted fever while on this front, and died in November 1918. He was entitled to the General Service and Victory Medals.
47, Bury Park Road, Luton.   1127.

COLLINS, A., Private, 22nd London Regiment (Queen's).
He volunteered in July 1915, and after his training was sent to France in October and served at Loos. In December of the same year he was drafted to Salonika, and rendered valuable service in many engagements on the Vardar, Struma and Doiran fronts. He finished his foreign service in Egypt, where he remained until his return home to be demobilised in July 1919. He holds the 1914-15 Star, and the General Service and Victory Medals.
21, St. Michael's Street, St. Albans.   1044.

COLLINS, C. C., Private, Bedfordshire Regiment.
He volunteered in August 1914, and in the following January was drafted to Egypt. He afterwards proceeded into Palestine, and was present in the fighting at Gaza, and at the Fall of Jerusalem. He returned home and was subsequently demobilised in March 1919, holding the 1914-15 Star, and the General Service and Victory Medals.
Church Lane, King's Langley.   X1094/C.

COLLINS, F., Corporal, Bedfordshire Regiment.
Volunteering in August 1914, he proceeded immediately afterwards to the Western Front, where he took part in the Retreat from Mons and the Battles of Ypres, Arras, St. Quentin and many other engagements, and was wounded. He also rendered valuable service in the Dardanelles expedition in 1915. He returned home after the conclusion of hostilities, and was demobilised in March 1919, holding the Mons Star, and the General Service and Victory Medals.
High Street, Toddington.   1128/A.

COLLINS, F., Petty Officer, R.N., H.M.S. "Virginian."
He was serving in the Navy at the outbreak of hostilities, and for over three years was engaged on patrol work off the coast of Iceland. He also rendered valuable services on transport ships passing through highly dangerous waters. He was demobilised in January 1919, and holds the 1914-15 Star, and the General Service and Victory Medals.
15, Cromer Road, Watford.   X1151.

COLLINS, G. F. H., Air Mechanic, R.A.F.

He joined in May 1918, and was drafted to the Western Front. As an armourer he was engaged on important work which demanded considerable technical skill and great care, and rendered valuable services. He afterwards proceeded with the Army of Occupation to Germany, and on his return home was demobilised in August 1919, holding the General Service and Victory Medals.

9, Oxhey Street, Oxhey. X1098.

COLLINS, H. A., Private, 8th Bedfordshire Regt.

He joined in March 1916, and in September of the same year was drafted to France, where he fought in the Battles of the Somme and Arras, and was severely wounded in April 1917. He was invalided home, and after treatment was discharged in November 1917 as medically unfit for further service. He holds the General Service and Victory Medals.

Cotton End, near Bedford. Z1105.

COLLINS, J. W., Private, 9th East Surrey Regt.

He joined in April 1917, and after a brief training was drafted to France. He was killed in action at St. Julien on August 5th, 1917, and in one of his first engagements, and was entitled to the General Service and Victory Medals.

17, Dacre Road, Hitchin. 1597.

COLLINS, T., Private, Lincolnshire Regiment.

He volunteered in 1916, and in the same year was drafted to the Western Front, where he took part in numerous engagements until hostilities ended, including those of the Somme, Arras, Ypres and the Aisne. He returned home and was demobilised in December 1919, holding the General Service and Victory Medals.

5, Oxhey Street, Oxhey. X1097.

COLLYER, L. W. (M.M.), Rifleman, 6th London Regiment (Rifles).

He volunteered in 1914, and was drafted to the Western Front in the following year. He served in several sectors, and amongst the important battles in which he was engaged were those of the Somme, Arras and Cambrai. He was awarded the Military Medal for conspicuous gallantry in the Field and devotion to duty, and was killed in action on March 23rd, 1918. In addition to the Military Medal he was entitled to the 1914-15 Star, and the General Service and Victory Medals.

23, Souldern Street, Watford. X1164.

COLMAN, E. C., Private, 5th Bedfordshire Regt.

Volunteering in August 1914, he was drafted to France, and whilst in this theatre of war was in action at Ypres and the Somme and Arras. Later he was drafted to Italy, where he took part in various engagements against the Austrians. During his service overseas he was wounded and gassed three times. He returned home and was demobilised in February 1919, and holds the 1914-15 Star, and the General Service and Victory Medals.

52, Dudley Street, Luton. 1146/B.

COMPTON, F. J., Corporal, Bedfordshire Regt.

He joined in February 1916, and during his service on the Western Front took part in the Battles of the Somme, where he was wounded. On his recovery he returned to the fighting line, and was in action at Arras, Ypres and Cambrai. In 1918 he was again severely wounded. After his return home he was demobilised in August 1919, and holds the General Service and Victory Medals.

1, New England Street, St. Albans. 1051.

CONGREVE, C., Private, Norfolk and North Staffordshire Regiments.

He joined in January 1917, and in September was sent to France, where he took part in the Battle of Cambrai and was wounded. On his recovery he served in the Somme sector, and was again wounded in April 1918. He was also gassed in action in an engagement in October, and after the termination of the war was sent home to be demobilised in January 1919. He holds the General Service and Victory Medals.

3, Bury Lane, Rickmansworth. X1049.

CONQUEST, A., Private, 1st Bedfordshire Regt.

He joined in June 1918, and after his training served at various stations on important duties with his unit. He rendered valuable services, but was not successful in obtaining his transfer overseas before the termination of the war. In 1920 he was still in the Army.

77, Salisbury Road, Luton. 1113.

CONQUEST, H. J., Corporal, Royal Engineers.

He was serving at the outbreak of war, and being sent to the Western Front was present at many important engagements, including those of Arras, Ypres, Cambrai, Amiens and Albert. During his service of 3½ years in France he was twice wounded. He holds the 1914 Star, and the General Service and Victory Medals, and in 1920 was still serving.

41, Albert Road, Luton. 1094/A.

CONSTABLE, E. A., Private, R.A.S.C. (M.T.)

He joined in 1916, and being drafted to the Western Front in the following year was engaged on important transport duties in several sectors, conveying supplies of all kinds to the lines at Ypres, Cambrai and the Somme. He was demobilised in July 1919, after returning home, and holds the General Service and Victory Medals.

2, Albion Terrace, Hatfield. X1155.

CONSTABLE, P., Private, 1st Bedfordshire Regt.

Volunteering in February 1915, he was drafted overseas in January of the following year. After serving on the Western Front, where he was wounded at Ypres, he was sent to Italy and took part in the Advance on the Piave. He returned to France in March 1918, and was engaged on the Somme and at Cambrai, and was again wounded. He was demobilised in March 1919, and holds the General Service and Victory Medals.

7, Union Lane, New Town, Hatfield. X1156/A.

CONWAY, S. E., Private, Machine Gun Corps.

Joining in October 1916, he proceeded overseas in the following January, and was on active service on the Western Front until hostilities ceased. He took part in much heavy fighting in several sectors, and fought in the Battles of Arras, Ypres and Cambrai. He was demobilised in November 1919, after returning to England, and holds the General Service and Victory Medals.

78, Holywell Hill, St. Albans. X1173.

COOK, A., Gunner, R.F.A.; and Private, Labour Corps.

He joined in 1916, and on the completion of his training served at various stations on important duties with his unit. He rendered valuable services, but was not successful in obtaining his transfer overseas before the cessation of hostilities. He was demobilised in March 1919.

35, Housbourne Crawley, Aspley Guise. Z1106.

COOK, A., Sapper, Royal Engineers.

He volunteered in July 1915, but, both on account of his age and on medical grounds, was unfit for service overseas. He did valuable work with his unit and was discharged on account of his service in March 1918.

27, Church Street, Ridgmont. Z1103.

COOK, A. E., E.R.A., R.N., H.M.S. "Dalhousie" and "Firefly."

He volunteered in May 1914, and did valuable service with the Grand Fleet in the North Sea, and at the Battle of Heligoland Bight. He was later drafted to Mesopotamia, and took part in the bombardment of Kut. He returned home and was discharged as medically unfit for further service in September 1919, and holds the 1914-15 Star, and the General Service and Victory Medals.

70, Queen's Street, Luton. 1118.

COOK, A. G., Private, Royal Army Service Corps.

He volunteered in October 1914, and after being retained on important duties was, in August 1916, drafted to Salonika, where he rendered valuable service as a farrier on the Struma and Vardar fronts. Afterwards he went to Russia, where he did excellent work until his return home in June 1919 to be demobilised. He holds the General Service and Victory Medals.

61, Shaftesbury Road, Watford. X1088.

COOK, A. H., Sapper, Royal Engineers.

He volunteered in September 1914, and was sent to the Western Front on the completion of his training. While in France he was engaged on important work in various sectors, including those of Armentières, Ypres and Cambrai. He remained overseas until after the Armistice, and returning home was demobilised in April 1919, holding the General Service and Victory Medals.

60, Arthur Street, Luton. 1063/A.

COOK, A. J., Private, R.A.S.C.

He joined in January 1916, and in the following August was drafted to Mesopotamia, where he remained for nearly two years. During this time he did valuable transport work in several places until hostilities ceased, and afterwards proceeded to India, where he was stationed at Bangalore. Returning home, he was demobilised in April 1920, holding the General Service and Victory Medals.

10, Clarendon Road, Luton. 1068.

COOK, A. J., Gunner, Royal Field Artillery.

He volunteered in 1915, and having completed his training was drafted to France in the same year. Whilst in this theatre of war he rendered valuable services in many sectors of the line, and was later sent to Palestine, where he fought in several important engagements. After returning home he was demobilised in 1919, and holds the 1914-15 Star, and the General Service and Victory Medals.

38, Holywell Road, Watford. X/377A.

COOK, A. R., Private, Royal Army Medical Corps.

He volunteered in September 1914, and, proceeding to France in January of the following year, did valuable work in the Battles of Ypres and the Somme (where he was gassed), Arras, Passchendaele, Cambrai, Kemmel Hill and in subsequent engagements until the cessation of hostilities. He was demobilised in February 1919, and holds the 1914-15 Star, and the General Service and Victory Medals.
81, Station Road, Ridgmont. Z1102/A.

COOK, A. W., Private, Bedfordshire Regiment and Sherwood Foresters.

He joined in June 1916, and after his training was drafted to the Western Front, where he took part in the severe fighting at the Somme, Arras, Ypres and in other important engagements until the close of hostilities, and was twice wounded. He was demobilised in 1919, and holds the General Service and Victory Medals.
13, Cross Street West, Dunstable. 1121.

COOK, B. W., Rifleman, Rifle Brigade.

He joined in October 1918, and was going through his course of training when hostilities ceased. He afterwards proceeded to Germany with the Army of Occupation and rendered valuable service at Cologne. In 1920 he was still serving in His Majesty's Forces.
114, Baker Street, Luton. 1115.

COOK, C., L/Corporal, 14th Army Cyclist Corps.

Volunteering in September 1914, he was drafted in the following year to the Western Front, where he took part in many important engagements, including those of Ypres and the Somme. In 1916 he was transferred to Italy and served in the final Advance of the Allies. He returned home and was demobilised in February 1919, and holds the 1914-15 Star, and the General Service and Victory Medals.
59, Hitchin Road, Luton. 1071/A.

COOK, C., L/Corporal, Oxfordshire and Buckinghamshire Light Infantry.

He volunteered in August 1914, and in the following month was drafted to France. He took part in many great engagements, including those of Ypres, Festubert, Loos and the Somme, where he was wounded. He was invalided home in consequence, and in August 1917 was discharged as unfit for further service. He holds the 1914 Star, and the General Service and Victory Medals.
24, Saulbury Road, Linslade. 1597.

COOK, C. J., Private, 1st Essex Regiment.

Joining in March 1917, he went through a course of training and was drafted overseas in July of the same year. He was engaged in much heavy fighting in several sectors of the Western Front, and was killed in action on August 23rd, 1918, in the Battle of Bapaume. He was entitled to the General Service and Victory Medals.
1, Copsewood Road, Watford. X1165/A.

COOK, D., Sapper, Royal Engineers.

He volunteered in September 1914, and in December of the same year was drafted to the Western Front, where he did valuable work in the Battles of the Somme, Arras, Ypres, Passchendaele and many other engagements. He was discharged in September 1917 in consequence of his service, and holds the 1914-15 Star, and the General Service and Victory Medals.
113, High Street, Houghton Regis, Dunstable. 1075.

COOK, E., Private, Norfolk Regiment.

He joined in October 1918, on attaining military age, and having completed his training was drafted to India, where he was engaged on important garrison duties at various stations. In 1920 he was still serving.
7, Chapel Yard, Eaton Bray, Dunstable. 797/A.

COOK, E., Pte., 9th South Lancashire Regiment.

He joined in January 1916, and in July of the same year, on the conclusion of his training, was drafted to India. While there he rendered valuable garrison duties at various stations until his return home to be demobilised in December 1919. He holds the General Service and Victory Medals.
61, West Street, Dunstable. 1110/C.

COOK, E., Private, Northumberland Fusiliers.

He joined in September 1916, and after the completion of his training was engaged on important guard duties at various stations. He rendered valuable services, but was not successful in obtaining his transfer overseas before the termination of the war. He was demobilised in March 1919.
25, New England Street, St. Albans. 1050.

COOK, E. E., Air Mechanic, Royal Air Force (late Royal Naval Air Service).

He joined in 1916, and was drafted to the Western Front on completing his training. During his service overseas he was engaged as an areo-engine fitter and carried out his duties, which demanded a high degree of technical skill, with great care and efficiency. He was demobilised in May 1919, and holds the General Service and Victory Medals.
11, Chapel Street, Hemel Hempstead. X1033/A.

COOK, E. H., Sapper, Royal Engineers.

He joined in March 1916, and in the same year was drafted to India, where he was engaged on important garrison duties. He was afterwards drafted to Mesopotamia, and he took part in heavy fighting at Baghdad, Kut-el-Amara and in many other engagements. On his return home he was demobilised in September 1919, and holds the General Service and Victory Medals.
52, Yarmouth Road, Callowland. X1036/B.

COOK, E. R., Special War Worker.

For 18 months of the war he was engaged on highly important aeroplane work at Messrs. Hewlett and Blondeau's Factory, Leagrave, and discharged his responsible and skilled duties throughout with thoroughness and skill.
60, Arthur Street, Luton. 1063/B.

COOK, F., Private, 27th Durham Light Infantry.

He volunteered in November 1914, and after his training served on important duties with his unit. He was not successful in securing his transfer while fighting continued, but rendered valuable service until his discharge in October 1918 as medically unfit for further service owing to heart trouble.
High Street, Liddington. Z1111.

COOK, F. J., Private, 6th Yorkshire Regiment.

He joined in June 1916, and after his training did good work at various stations with his unit. In January 1917 he was transferred to the Bedfordshire Regiment and later to the 24th Middlesex. He was not successful in obtaining his transfer abroad before the conclusion of the war, and was demobilised in January 1919.
79, Cambridge Street, Luton. 1114.

COOK, G. E., L/Corporal, R.A.O.C. and Oxfordshire and Buckinghamshire Light Infantry.

He joined in January 1918, and in the same year was drafted to the Western Front, where he was engaged on various important duties with his unit at Dieppe and other stores. Returning home he was demobilised in February 1920, and holds the General Service and Victory Medals.
High Street, Wheathampstead. 1056/B.

COOK, G. H., Air Mechanic, Royal Air Force.

He joined in July 1917, and on the conclusion of his training served with his unit at various stations on important duties which required considerable skill. He did much good work, but was not able to secure his transfer overseas before the cessation of hostilities. He was demobilised in 1919.
19, Balmoral Road, Hitchin. 1844.

COOK, G. S., Private, Royal Army Service Corps.

Volunteering in April 1915, he proceeded to France in the following month, when for a time he rendered valuable service on the ines of communication in various important sectors of the Front. Afterwards he was attached to the Royal Engineers and did good work on the railways until hostilities ended. He was demobilised in February 1919, and holds the General Service and Victory Medals.
41, Spencer Street, St. Albans. X1144.

COOK, H., Private, R.A.M.C.

He joined in 1916, and on the conclusion of his training did much valuable work as an orderly in Ripon Military Hospital. He was not able to secure his transfer overseas before the cessation of hostilities, and was demobilised in November 1919.
27, Hastings Street, Luton. 1132.

COOK, H., Gunner, Royal Field Artillery.

He joined in April 1918, and after completing his training was drafted to the Western Front, where he took part in several of the last engagements of the war, including those at Cambrai and St. Quentin. He afterwards proceeded with the Army of Occupation to Germany. Returning home he was demobilised in October 1919, and holds the General Service and Victory Medal.
59, Hitchin Road, Luton. 1071/B.

COOK, H., Corporal, Bedfordshire Regiment.

Volunteering in June 1915, he was engaged on important duties with his unit at various stations until sent to France in 1918. He was in action in many important engagements towards the close of hostilities, including those of Havrincourt and Cambrai, and was gassed and wounded. He returned home and was demobilised in February 1919, holding the General Service and Victory Medals.
31, Edward Street, Dunstable. 1137.

COOK, H. E., A/Sergeant, 5th Bedfordshire Regt.
He was mobilised in August 1914, and in the following year was drafted to the Dardanelles, where he took part in the landing at Suvla Bay and other operations. In December 1915, after the evacuation he was transferred to Egypt, and in the subsequent Palestine Campaign fought with distinction in the Battles of Gaza and many other important engagements. He returned home in May 1919, and was demobilised in June, holding the 1914-15, Star and the General Service and Victory Medals.
2, St. Peter's Road, Dunstable.   1074.

COOK, H. W., C.S.M., Norfolk Regiment and Lancashire Fusiliers.
He volunteered in September 1914, and after completing his training rapidly won promotion by reason of his efficiency, becoming Company Sergeant-Major in February 1917. He was retained for special duties as Drill Instructor and other purposes until February 1918, when he was drafted to the Western Front, and took a prominent part in many engagements in the Retreat and Advance of that year. He fought with distinction in the last Battles of the Somme and Ypres, and was wounded several times. He was mentioned in Despatches for his valuable work in June 1918, and holds the General Service and Victory Medals. He was demobilised in March 1919.
High Street, Wheathampstead.   1056/A.

COOK, H. W., L/Corporal, Bedfordshire Regt. (Machine Gun Company).
He joined in August 1916, and on the conclusion of his training saw much service on the Egyptian and Palestine Fronts and in France. In the East he took part in many important engagements, including those of Gaza and Haifa, and during his service he was wounded. He was still serving in 1920, and holds the General Service and Victory Medals.
8, Dumfries Street, Luton.   1117/A.

COOK, J. W., Private, Norfolk Regiment.
He joined in December 1916, and in February of the following year was drafted to the Western Front, where he took part in many important engagements, and was killed in action at the Battle of Ypres on August 4th, 1917. He was entitled to the General Service and Victory Medals.
35, Astley Hill, Hemel Hempstead.   X1034.

COOK, L., Sapper, R.E. (R.O.D.)
He joined in March 1917, and in May of the same year was drafted to Egypt, where he rendered valuable service in many important engagements, including those near Gaza, Jaffa, Jerusalem and Jericho. He returned home and was demobilised in April 1920, and holds the General Service and Victory Medals.
8, Elfrida Road, Watford   X1100.

COOK, M. E., Private, Labour Corps.
He joined in June 1916, and after a period of training was drafted to the Western Front, where he served for over two years. He was engaged on important duties, and rendered valuable service in trench digging and road repairs in many sectors. He was demobilised in December 1919, and holds the General Service and Victory Medals.
11, Ashton Street, Luton.   1060.

COOK, R., Private, Royal Army Medical Corps.
He volunteered in September 1914, and in February of the following year was drafted overseas. During his service in France he was present at the Battles of Ypres, Messines and Albert, and was engaged as a stretcher-bearer and hospital orderly. In November 1917 he was severely gassed in the Battle of Cambrai, and was invalided home to hospital. After protracted treatment he was eventually demobilised in February 1919, holding the 1914-15 Star, and the General Service and Victory Medals.
Mount Pleasant, Aspley Guise.   Z1052.

COOK, R. C., Sergeant, 9th Norfolk Regiment.
He volunteered in October 1915, and in the same year was drafted to France, where he took part in heavy fighting on the Somme, at Arras, Cambrai and St. Quentin, and was four times wounded. He died of his injuries on Armistice Day 1918, and was entitled to the 1914-15 Star, and the General Service and Victory Medals.
High Street, Wheathampstead.   1056/B.

COOK, R. J., Private, Royal Sussex Regiment.
He joined in May 1918, and on the completion of his training did good work with his unit. He was not successful in securing his transfer overseas before the Armistice, but in March 1919 joined the Army of Occupation in Germany. He rendered valuable service there until August 1919, when he returned home and was demobilised in the following October.
25, Periwinkle Lane, Hitchin.   1845.

COOK, S., Private, Labour Corps.
He joined in July 1910, and in the following November was drafted to the Western Front. Whilst in this theatre of war he was engaged on important duties in several sectors, including those of the Somme, Ypres, at Arras and Cambrai. He remained overseas until after the cessation of hostilities, and after returning home was demobilised in March 1919, holding the General Service and Victory Medals.
7, Chapel Yard, Eaton Yard, Dunstable.   797/C.

COOK, S. F., Sapper, Royal Engineers.
Volunteering in May 1915, he was drafted to Egypt in the following September. After being engaged for some time there he was sent to France, and later to Italy, and rendered valuable services in all three theatres of war. He was demobilised in March 1919, after his return home, and holds the 1914-15 Star, and the General Service and Victory Medals.
1, Copsewood Road, Watford.   1165/B.

COOK, S. T., Private, Bedfordshire Regiment.
He joined in August 1917, and after his training proceeded in the following year to North Russia, where he was engaged on various important duties with his unit, and rendered valuable services. He was still serving in 1920, and holds the Victory Medal.
8, Dumfries Street, Luton.   1117/B.

COOK, T., Driver, Royal Field Artillery,
Volunteering in March 1915, he proceeded to France in the following month. During his service there, which lasted four years, he took part in many important engagements, including those of Festubert, Loos, the Somme, Arras, Ypres and Cambrai. He was demobilised after his return home in April 1919, and holds the 1914-15 Star, and the General Service and Victory Medals.
41, Cardiff Road, Watford.   X794/B.

COOK, T., Gunner, R.F.A. and R.G.A.
He joined in May 1918, and on concluding his training was sent with the Army of Occupation to Germany in November 1918. He was stationed at Cologne, and rendered valuable services there until April 1920, when he was demobilised.
8, Station Road, Ridgmont.   Z1102/B.

COOK, T. A., Pte., Bedfordshire and Hertfordshire Regiments.
Joining in May 1917, he went through his course of training and later in that year proceeded to the Western Front. While there he took an active part in many operations in the later stages of the war, and being killed in action on August 20th, 1918, was buried at Bagneux. He was entitled to the General Service and Victory Medals.
422, Hitchin Lane, Luton.   1135.

COOK, T. G., Private, 1st Bedfordshire Regiment.
He volunteered in August 1914, and in February of the following year was drafted to the Western Front, where he took part in the heavy fighting at Neuve Chapelle, Hill 60 Ypres and other important engagements. He was killed in action near Lens on April 23rd, 1917, and was entitled to the 1914 15 Star, and the General Service and Victory Medals.
11, Chapel Street, Hemel Hempstead.   X1033/B.

COOK, W., Stoker, R.N., H.M.S. " Superb."
He was serving in the Navy at the outbreak of war, and was posted to H.M.S. " Superb." Throughout the war he was engaged on important duties of a dangerous nature in the North Sea and the Mediterranean, and was wounded in a severe air-raid over Chatham in September 1917. He was demobilised in May 1919, and holds the 1914-15 Star, and the General Service and Victory Medals.
Mount Pleasant, Aspley Guise.   Z1048.

COOK, W., Private, Middlesex Regiment.
He joined in May 1916, and on completing his training was drafted to France, where he saw much service in many sectors of the Front. He was killed in action at St. Julien on July 31st, 1917, and was entitled to the General Service and Victory Medals.
Bowman's Green Cottages, London Colney, near St. Albans.   X1077/B.

COOK, W. E., Private, Bedfordshire Regiment.
Volunteering in January 1915, he was in the same year drafted to the Egyptian Front. He rendered valuable service there and in the Palestine Campaign, in which he fought in the Battles of Gaza and those leading up to the taking of Jerusalem, and was wounded. He returned home and was demobilised in February 1919, and holds the 1914-15 Star, and the General Service and Victory Medals.
52, Yarmouth Road, Callowland.   X1036/A.

COOK, W. J., Corporal, R.A.M.C.
He volunteered in September 1914, and on the conclusion of his training proceeded to France in the following year. He acted as a stretcher-bearer in the Battles of Ypres and Arras and other engagements, but owing to ill-health was invalided to England, where he was discharged as medically unfit for further service in May 1918. He holds the 1914-15 Star, and the General Service and Victory Medals.
66, Dudley Street, Luton. 1078.

COOK, W. J., Private, 5th Bedfordshire Regiment.
He joined in November 1916, and in March of the following year was drafted to France, where he was in action at Arras, Vimy Ridge, and Messines. He was severely wounded in the Battle of Ypres, and being invalided home was subsequently discharged as medically unfit for further duty in May 1918. He holds the General Service and Victory Medals.
58, Leighton Street, Woburn. Z1053.

COOK, W. L., Private, Suffolk Regiment.
He joined in 1916, and in the same year was drafted to France, where he took part in numerous engagements until fighting ceased, including those of the Somme, Arras, Ypres and Cambrai. During his service he was gassed. After the cessation of hostilities he returned home and was demobilised in 1919, holding the General Service and Victory Medals.
50, Church Street, Leighton Buzzard. 1283.

COOK, W. T., Private, 1/5th Bedfordshire Regt.
He volunteered at the outbreak of war, and after his training was sent to the Dardanelles in March of the following year. Whilst in this theatre of war he took part in the landing at Gallipoli in April, and in other engagements until the Evacuation of the Peninsula. He then proceeded to Egypt and advanced into Palestine, where he fought at Gaza and in many subsequent battles. He returned home and was demobilised in June 1919, and holds the General Service and Victory Medals.
80, Victoria Terrace, Victoria Street, Dunstable. 1133/A.

COOKE, C., Private, Essex Regiment.
He volunteered in January 1915, and in the following July was sent overseas. During his service on the Western Front he took part in the Battles of Loos and the Somme. He was mortally wounded near Arras on May 3rd, 1917, and died from his injuries two days later on May 5th. He was entitled to the 1914-15 Star, and the General Service and Victory Medals.
Watling Street, Hockliffe, near Leighton Buzzard 1612/A.

COOKE, E. G., Private, 5th Wiltshire Regiment.
He volunteered in November 1915, and in the following year was drafted to Mesopotamia, where he took part in various important engagements, and was killed in action on March 29th, 1917. He was entitled to the General Service and Victory Medals.
28, Leys Terrace, Woburn Sands, Beds. Z1055.

COOKE, J., Private, 1st Hertfordshire Regiment.
Mobilised at the outbreak of war in August 1914, he was shortly afterwards drafted to the Western Front, in many sectors of which he was engaged in severe fighting. Amongst the important battles in which he took part were those of Ypres, Arras and the Somme. He holds the 1914 Star, and the General Service and Victory Medals, and was demobilised in 1919.
15, Queen Street, St. Albans. 1167.

COOKE, P. G., Artificer, R.N., H.M.S. "Bristol."
He joined in January 1916, and was posted to H.M.S. "Bristol," and whilst in this vessel served off the coasts of France, Italy and South America. He rendered valuable service, and was finally demobilised in July 1919. He holds the General Service and Victory Medals.
16, Bury Park Road, Luton. 1148.

COOKSEY, S. P., Private, Labour Corps.
He joined in April 1917, and after his training served at various stations on important duties with his unit. He rendered valuable services, but was not successful in obtaining his transfer overseas before the cessation of hostilities. He was demobilised in September 1919.
40, Hatfield Road, Watford. X1076.

COOLEY, W., Gunner, Royal Field Artillery.
Joining in 1916, he was trained and sent overseas in the same year. He served with his battery in most of the important engagements fought in the different sectors of the Western Front, including the third Battle of Ypres, until the end of the war. He was demobilised in 1918, and holds the General Service and Victory Medals.
3, Benskin Road, Watford. X1163/A.

COONEY, J. M. F., Sergeant, 1/6th Seaforth Highlanders.
He was mobilised at the outbreak of war, and in the following year was drafted to France, where he served at first on important duties at the Base. Later he voluntarily gave up this work in order to go up to the firing line, and was killed in action at Beaumont-Hamel on November 13th, 1916. He was entitled to the 1914-15 Star, and the General Service and Victory Medals.
24. Housbourne Crawley Aspley Guise, Beds. Z1107/A.

COOPER, A., Private, Lancashire Fusiliers.
He joined in 1916, and having completed a course of training, in the following year was drafted overseas. He served on the Western Front, and was in heavy fighting in several sectors until he was killed in action near Ypres on September 6th, 1917. He was entitled to the General Service and Victory Medals.
Ramridge End, Stopsley, Luton. 1161/A.

COOPER, A., Private, 1/5th Norfolk Regiment.
He joined in April 1916, and was drafted to France, where he was in action at Béthune and Cambrai, and was wounded. Later he was sent to Egypt, and from thence proceeded to Palestine, and took part in the fighting during the campaign against the Turks, and was again wounded. He returned home and was demobilised in November 1919, and holds the General Service and Victory Medals.
15, Pondswick Road, Luton. 1061.

COOPER, A., Private, Tank Corps.
He joined in February 1917, and was in the following year drafted to the Western Front, where he served at Arras, Ypres, Cambrai and the Somme. He was demobilised in January 1919, and holds the General Service and Victory Medals.
Beeston, Sandy, Beds. Z1563.

COOPER, A. G., Private, R.A.V.C.
He joined in 1916, but being unfit for active service was unable to obtain his transfer overseas. He rendered valuable service at various stations tending sick and wounded horses, until he was demobilised in 1919.
Ramridge End, Stopsley, Luton. 1161/B.

COOPER, B., Private, 2nd Bedfordshire Regt.
He volunteered in November 1915, and in March of the following year was drafted to the Western Front, where he took part in the Battles of the Somme and Ypres, and was wounded and invalided home. On his recovery he returned to France and was again in action, and was taken prisoner near Cambrai in March 1918. On his release he returned home and was demobilised in February 1919, and holds the General Service and Victory Medals.
25, High Street, Lilley, near Luton, Beds. 1131.

COOPER, B. S., Private, 1/5th Bedfordshire Regt.
He volunteered in August 1914, and in July of the succeeding year was sent to the Dardanelles, where he took part in many engagements in the Gallipoli Campaign. He was later drafted to Egypt, whence he served in the Offensive on Palestine, and fought at Jaffa and in the engagements at Gaza. He returned home in December 1918 and was demobilised in the following February, and holds the 1914-15 Star, and the General Service and Victory Medals.
26, Langley Street, Luton. 1143.

COOPER, C., Sergeant, Bedfordshire and Essex Regiments.
He was serving in India at the outbreak of war, and was engaged at various stations on important duties with his unit until 1916, when he was drafted to Mesopotamia, where he took part in many actions, including those at Kut, Baghdad and Mosul. He returned home and was demobilised in August 1919, and holds the 1914-15 Star, and the General Service and Victory Medals.
23, York Street, Luton. 1069.

COOPER, C., Private, 2nd Bedfordshire Regt.
He was serving in South Africa when war was declared, and in September 1914 arrived on the Western Front and took part in the Battles of the Marne, La Bassée and Ypres (I.), in which he was severely wounded. Later he died as a result of his injuries on November 28th, 1914, and was entitled to the 1914 Star, and the General Service and Victory Medals.
Lidshill, Ridgmont, Beds. Z1104/A.

COOPER, E., L/Corporal, Bedfordshire and Hertfordshire Regiments.
He volunteered in September 1914, and in the following year was drafted to the Western Front, where he took part in heavy fighting at Hill 60, Ypres, Vimy Ridge, the Somme and numerous other engagements, including those in the Retreat and Advance of 1918, and was wounded. He was demobilised in January 1919, and holds the 1914-15 Star, and the General Service and Victory Medals.
42, Upper Paddock Road, Oxhey, Watford X1086.

COOPER, F., Private, The Queen's (Royal West Surrey Regiment)

He joined in August 1917, and after his training was engaged on important duties with his unit at various stations. He rendered valuable service, but owing to being medically unfit for duty abroad was unable to obtain his transfer to the Front. He was demobilised in January 1919.
30, Harley Street, St. Albans. 1045/B.

COOPER, F., 2nd Air Mechanic, R.A.F.

He volunteered in November 1914, and having completed his training was sent to the Western Front. Whilst in this theatre of war he was serving with his squadron at St. Omer, Arras, Cambrai and the Somme, and was engaged on duties which called for a high degree of technical skill. Returning home he was demobilised in March 1919, holding the 1914–15 Star, and the General Service and Victory Medals.
Anchor Cottage, Walsworth, Hitchin. 1846/A.

COOPER, F., Private, R.A.M.C.

He volunteered in August 1914, and after his training was engaged on special duties attending to the wounded on hospital ships voyaging between England and Egypt and South Africa. He rendered valuable services for four years, and was finally demobilised in March 1919. He holds the 1914–15 Star, and the General Service and Victory Medals.
Lidshill, Ridgmont, Beds. Z1104/B.

COOPER, F. J., Corporal, 9th Lancers.

He volunteered in August 1914, and on the completion of his training was drafted to France, where he served in the fighting on the Somme and at Arras, Cambrai and Ypres, and was wounded at the Hohenzollern Redoubt. He was demobilised in 1919, and holds the 1914–15 Star, and the General Service and Victory Medals.
High Road, Beeston, Sandy, Beds. Z1560.

COOPER, G., Private, 1/5th Bedfordshire Regt.

A Reservist, he was mobilised in August 1914, and in the following year was in action at Gallipoli, taking part in the landing at Suvla Bay and other heavy fighting until, on the evacuation of the Peninsula, he was sent to Egypt. In this theatre of war he was in General Allenby's Advance into Palestine, and amongst other battles fought in that of Gaza. Demobilised in March 1919, he holds the Long Service and Good Conduct Medal, and the 1914–15 Star, and the General Service and Victory Medals.
Caddington, near Luton, Beds. 1159.

COOPER, H. J., Sergeant, M.G.C.

He volunteered in September 1914, and in the following year was transferred to Mesopotamia, where he took part in various engagements. He returned home and was demobilised in October 1919, and holds the 1914–15 Star, and the General Service and Victory Medals.
26, Trevor Road, Hitchin. 2780.

COOPER, J. H., Private, 5th and 2nd Bedfordshire Regiment.

He was serving at the outbreak of war, and in November of the same year was drafted to the Western Front, where he took part in the Battles of Ypres, Neuve Chapelle, St. Quentin and Hill 60, where he was wounded. He was invalided home, and after a period in hospital was discharged as medically unfit for further service in May 1916, and holds the 1914–15 Star, and the General Service and Victory Medals.
New Road, Clifton, Shefford. Z1008.

COOPER, J. W., Driver, R.A.S.C.

He volunteered in May 1915, and after his training saw much varied service in Salonika, France and Egypt. Throughout his time overseas he was engaged on important transport duties in conveying rations to the troops on all fronts. He holds the 1914–15 Star, and the General Service and Victory Medals, and was demobilised in 1919.
34, Acme Road, North Watford. X1092.

COOPER, R. C., Private, R.A.M.C. and M.G.C.

He volunteered in September 1914, and after training was drafted to the Western Front in September 1917. He served at Cambrai, and was severely wounded in action and invalided to hospital and thence home in January 1918. He was demobilised in December of the same year, and holds the General Service and Victory Medals.
26, Langley Street, Luton. 1142.

COOPER, S. T., Sapper, Royal Engineers.

He volunteered in January 1915, and in July was sent to the Dardanelles, where he took part in the memorable landing at Suvla Bay and in other engagements until the evacuation of Gallipoli. He then proceeded to Palestine, and in this theatre of war served at Gaza and was present at the fall of Jerusalem. He returned to England and was demobilised in July 1919, and holds the 1914–15 Star, and the General Service and Victory Medals.
36, King's Road, Luton. 1058.

COOPER, W., 2nd Corporal, R.E. and R.A.F.

He volunteered in March 1915, and after his training served at various stations on important duties with his unit. He rendered valuable services, but was not successful in obtaining his transfer overseas before the cessation of hostilities. He was afterwards transferred to the Royal Air Force, and was in training as a cadet when Armistice was signed. He was demobilised in February 1919. 1070.
154, Hitchin Road, Luton.

COOPER, W., Private, 5th Yorkshire Regiment.

He joined in March 1916, and after his training served at various stations on important duties with his unit. He rendered valuable services, but was not successful in obtaining his transfer overseas before the cessation of hostilities. He was demobilised in March 1919.
26, King's Road, Luton. 1125/B.

COOPER, W. H., Cpl., 5th Bedfordshire Regt.

He volunteered in August 1914, and was later drafted to the Western Front, where he took part in important engagements, including that at Ypres. He was killed whilst gallantly leading his section into action on the Somme on September 4th, 1916, and was entitled to the 1914–15 Star, and the General Service and Victory Medals.
New Road, Clifton, Shefford. Z1031.

COOTE, F., Private, 5th Bedfordshire Regt.

Volunteering in September 1914, he was sent to the Dardanelles after the conclusion of his training in the following year. There he saw much fighting at Suvla Bay, Anzac and in other engagements. After the Evacuation he was transferred to the Western Front and fought at the Somme, Arras and Ypres. In March 1918 he was captured near Cambrai, and returning home after the Armistice was demobilised in May 1919. He holds the 1914–15 Star, and the General Service and Victory Medals.
54, Ivy Road, Luton. 795/B.

COOTE, H., Gunner, Royal Field Artillery.

He volunteered in October 1914, and having completed his training was sent to the Western Front He took part in several great engagements during his service there, among which were those at Ypres, Loos, the Somme, Arras, Passchendaele and Cambrai. Returning home after the Armistice, he was demobilised in April 1919, and holds the 1914–15 Star, and the General Service and Victory Medals.
54, Ivy Road, Luton. 795/A.

COPELAND, A. E., Private, Middlesex Regt.

He joined in September 1918, and after his training served on various important duties with his unit. He rendered valuable services, but on medical grounds was not successful in obtaining his transfer overseas before the cessation of hostilities. He was demobilised in January 1919.
168, Queen's Road, Watford. X1099.

COPLEY, G. C., Rifleman, 21st London Regt. (1st Surrey Rifles).

He volunteered in May 1915, and in the following month was drafted to the Western Front, where he was in action in the Somme area. In September of the same year he was transferred to Salonika, and afterwards to Palestine, where he served in many battles, including those of Gaza and those leading up to the taking of Jerusalem. He returned home and was demobilised in June 1919, and holds the 1914–15 Star, and the General Service and Victory Medals.
77, Shaftesbury Road, Watford. X1087/A.

COPLEY, H., Rifleman, King's Royal Rifles.

He joined in March 1917, and was drafted to the Western Front in the same year He took part in numerous engagements, including that at Cambrai and the Retreat and Advance of 1918, and was wounded. He was demobilised in September 1919 after returning to England, and holds the General Service and Victory Medals.
77, Shaftesbury Road, Watford. X1087/C.

COPLEY, J., Private, 8th Middlesex Regiment.

He volunteered in September 1914, and in January of the following year was sent to Gibraltar. After four months' service there he was transferred to Egypt, and in August of the same year to the Western Front, where he took part in many important engagements, and was killed in action on the Somme on July 17th, 1916. He was entitled to the 1914–15 Star, and the General Service and Victory Medals.
77, Shaftesbury Road, Watford. X1087/B.

COPPERWAITE, A., Sergeant, South Wales Borderers.

He joined in January 1916, and later in that year proceeded to France. While in this theatre of war he saw much fighting on the Somme, and at Arras, Vimy Ridge and Ypres, and was twice wounded. After his return home he was demobilised in September 1919, and holds the General Service and Victory Medals.
Clifton, Shefford. Z1030/A.

COPPERWAITE, A. W., Private, 2nd Bedfordshire Regiment.
Volunteering in 1914, he was drafted overseas in the following year. He was engaged in much heavy fighting on the Western Front, at Festubert, Loos, Givenchy and Delville Wood, and being seriously wounded was invalided home to hospital. He was discharged in March 1918 as unfit for further service, but in 1920 was still under treatment for his injuries. He holds the 1914-15 Star, and the General Service and Victory Medals.
New Road, Clifton, Shefford. Z1138.

COPPERWAITE, W. G., Private, Royal Irish Fusiliers.
He joined in June 1916, and in the same year proceeded overseas. Whilst on the Western Front he fought in several engagements, including those of the Somme and Vimy Ridge, and was gassed and captured at St. Quentin. After the Armistice he was repatriated, and was demobilised in September 1919, holding the General Service and Victory Medals.
Clifton, Shefford. Z1030/B.

COPPIN, J. A., Private, 13th Royal Fusiliers.
He joined in July 1916, and in September of the same year was drafted to the Western Front, where he took part in much heavy fighting and was seriously wounded. He was invalided home, and died in London from the effect of his injuries on December 19th, 1916. He was entitled to the General Service and Victory Medals.
73, Sotheron Road, Watford. X1080/A.

COPSON, A., Corporal, Royal Engineers.
He volunteered in January 1915, and in May of the same year was sent to France, where he took part in the engagements at Loos, Beaumont-Hamel, Cambrai and Albert. After nearly four years' service he returned home and was demobilised in January 1919. He holds the 1914-15 Star, and the General Service and Victory Medals.
6, Camp View Road, St. Albans. X1067.

CORBETT, G., Private, R.A.S.C. (M.T.)
He joined in 1917, and after his training was in the same year drafted to Italy, where he was engaged on various parts of the Front in the transport of ammunition and supplies, and rendered valuable services. He returned home and was demobilised in 1919, and holds the General Service and Victory Medals.
25, Upper Paddock Road, Oxhey, Watford. X1085.

CORFIELD, J., Sergeant, R.A.V.C.
He joined in 1916, and in the same year was despatched to the Western Front. He was engaged on important duties in connection with sick and wounded horses and mules in many sectors, and was present at the Battles of Ypres, Arras and the Somme. At the end of the war he returned to England for demobilisation in January 1919, and holds the General Service and Victory Medals.
71, Benskin Road, Watford. X1172.

CORKETT, E., Private, Royal Fusiliers.
He joined in June 1916, and in the following October was drafted to France. He saw much fighting on the Somme and at Arras and Messines Ridge, and finally at Cambrai. After the cessation of hostilities he returned home and was demobilised in March 1919, holding the General Service and Victory Medals.
2, Black Horse Lane, Sunnyside, Hitchin. 1847.

CORKETT, F. A., Air Mechanic, R.A.F.
He joined in July 1918, and in September of the same year was drafted to the Western Front, where he was engaged as a fitter in the aeroplane shops at various stations, his duties demanding a high degree of technical skill. After the Armistice he proceeded with the Army of Occupation to Germany, where he served until August 1919, when he returned home and was demobilised. He holds the General Service and Victory Medals.
3, Rothschild Road, Wing, near Leighton Buzzard.
2790-2789.

CORLEY, H., Private, 1st Middlesex Regiment.
He volunteered in August 1914, and in the following year was drafted to the Western Front, where he took part in heavy fighting at Hill 60, Ypres and Loos. He was killed in action on the Somme on October 23rd, 1916, and was entitled to the 1914-15 Star, and the General Service and Victory Medals.
8, The Camp, St. Albans. X1082/B.

CORLEY, L. J., Seaman, R.N., H.M.S. "Marlborough."
He volunteered in 1915, and served with the Grand Fleet in the North Sea and the Baltic. He was engaged in chasing enemy submarines and other important duties, and rendered valuable services. He was still serving in 1920, and holds the General Service and Victory Medals.
8, The Camp, St. Albans. X1082/A.

COSBY, H., Sergeant, Royal Engineers.
He joined in June 1917, and in the following November was sent to the Western Front. During his service overseas he was engaged on important duties in connection with operations in the forward areas, and was also frequently in action in the Retreat and Advance of 1918. He returned home and was demobilised in November 1919, and holds the General Service and Victory Medals.
12, East Street, Leighton Buzzard. 789.

COSTER, H. G., Petty Officer, R.N., H.M.S. "Lowestoft."
He was serving in the Navy at the outbreak of hostilities, and was posted immediately to H.M.S. "Lowestoft." Whilst in this vessel he took part in the fighting at Heligoland Bight and Dogger Bank, and later served on important and dangerous duties in the North Sea, Black Sea, and off the coasts of Russia. He was finally demobilised in April 1919, and holds the 1914-15 Star, and the General Service and Victory Medals.
8, Albert Street, Watford. X1090/A-1091/A.

COTCHIN, J., Private, Bedfordshire Regiment.
He joined in 1916, and in the same year was drafted to the Western Front, where he took part in the Battles of the Somme, Arras and Cambrai. He holds the General Service and Victory Medals, and was demobilised in 1919, but has since joined the Territorials.
High Street, Ridgmont, Beds. Z1101.

COTCHIN, J., 2nd Lieutenant, Bedfordshire Regt.
He was serving as a Rifleman in the King's Royal Rifle Corps at the outbreak of war, and was almost immediately sent to the Western Front, where he took part in the Retreat from Mons and also served with distinction at the Marne and at Festubert. Later he returned to England to undergo training for a commission, and on being gazetted went back to France, and after taking part in several engagements was killed in action in the heavy fighting at Ypres on October 9th, 1917. During his service overseas he was wounded four times and gassed, and was recommended for the Military Cross for conspicuous bravery and devotion to duty on the Field. He was entitled to the Mons Star, and the General Service and Victory Medals.
79, Station Road, Ridgmont, Beds. Z1112.

COTTAM, J. J., Private, Sherwood Foresters.
He volunteered in September 1914, and on the completion of his training was drafted overseas. He took part in the Battle of Ypres and in the engagement at the Hooge Redoubt and at Loos, and was severely wounded. He was invalided home, and in October 1915 was discharged as medically unfit for further military duty. He holds the 1914-15 Star, and the General Service and Victory Medals.
52, Dudley Street, Luton. 1146/A.

COTTERELL, G. W., Private, 2/1st East Riding Yorkshire Lancers.
He joined in October 1916, and after his training served on important duties with his unit at various stations, and was for a time in Ireland. He rendered valuable services, but was not successful in obtaining his transfer overseas before the cessation of hostilities. He was demobilised in December 1919. 96, Regent Street, North Watford. X1150.

COTTERELL, W., L/Corporal, Bedfordshire Regt.
He volunteered in September 1914, and after a period of service with his unit at various stations was drafted overseas in 1916. Serving on the Western Front he was engaged in several important actions, including those at Ypres, Lens and Cambrai, and was taken prisoner in March 1918. He was repatriated at the conclusion of the war, and demobilised in March 1919. He holds the General Service and Victory Medals.
14, Keyfield West, St. Albans, Herts. 1169.

COTTINGHAM, G., Private, 1/5th Leicester Regiment.
He volunteered in November 1914, and was sent abroad in the following year. Serving in various sectors of the Western Front, he was in many important engagements, including those on the Somme and at Ypres, Béthune and Cambrai. On the conclusion of hostilities he returned to England for demobilisation in May 1919, and holds the 1914-15 Star, and the General Service and Victory Medals.
4, South Road, Luton. 1160.

COTTON, A., Private, Bedfordshire Regiment.
He volunteered in November 1915, and having completed his training was drafted to the Western Front in January of the following year. He fought in numerous engagements, including those of the Somme, Arras, Ypres, Bullecourt and Cambrai, and also took part in the Retreat and Advance in 1918, and was wounded. Returning home he was demobilised in March 1919, holding the General Service and Victory Medals.
51, Hitchin Hill, Hitchin. 1848.

COULDWELL, W. M. (Miss), Special War Worker.
This lady was engaged at the Admiralty Inspection Offices, Brent Road, and was employed as fuse inspector. Her duties, which were of a dangerous and responsible nature, were carried out with great care and efficiency, and she rendered valuable services during the war.
40, Lyndhurst Road, Luton.   1122.

COUSINS, B., Air Mechanic, R.A.F.
He joined in August 1916, and served at various stations on important duties which required a high degree of technical skill. He rendered valuable services, but was not successful in obtaining his transfer overseas before the cessation of hostilities. He was demobilised in July 1919.
3, Duke's Place, Hitchin.   2781.

COUSINS, F., Aircraftsman, Royal Air Force.
He joined in January 1918, and was engaged on patrol duties in the North Sea, being attached to the seaplane section on board H.M.S. " Furious." He holds the General Service and Victory Medals, and was demobilised in March 1919.
23, Bunyan Road, Hitchin.   1849/A.

COUSINS, H., Private, 1st Hertfordshire Regt.
He joined in October 1916, and at the conclusion of his training was drafted to France in the following year. He saw much fighting at Ypres, Arras, Messines, the Somme and Cambrai, and was killed in action in the Advance on August 23rd, 1918, at Achiet-le-Grand. He was entitled to the General Service and Victory Medals.
23, Bunyan Road, Hitchin.   1849/B.

COUSINS, J., Private, 1st Hertfordshire Regt.
He volunteered in 1915, and in the same year was drafted overseas and took part in the fighting on the Somme and at Ypres, Cambrai and St. Quentin, and was gassed. On recovery he served in various engagements until the conclusion of the war. He was demobilised in February 1919, and holds the 1914-15 Star, and the General Service and Victory Medals.
2, Hope Cottages, Old Park Road, Hitchin.   1603.

COUSINS, P., Sapper, Royal Engineers.
Volunteering in August 1915, he was drafted to France before the close of the year and did excellent work in several sectors. In the course of his overseas service he was present at several battles, including those of Ypres, St. Quentin, Armentières, Cambrai and the Somme, and on the termination of the war he returned to England. He was demobilised in March 1919, and holds the 1914-15 Star, and the General Service and Victory Medals.
Hillside Cottage, Woodside, Luton.   1162.

COVE, E. G., Private, Hertfordshire Regiment.
He volunteered in February 1915, and after having completed his training was drafted to the Western Front later in the same year. He took part in the engagements at Loos, Vimy Ridge and Cambrai, and was wounded and gassed, and after the Armistice proceeded to Germany with the Army of Occupation. He served on the Rhine until February 1919, when he returned to England and was demobilised, holding the General Service and Victory Medals.
63, Park Corner, St. Albans.   X1046.

COVE, J. F., Driver, Royal Field Artillery.
He volunteered at the outbreak of war and saw much varied service during his five years overseas. He was first drafted to the Western Front and took part in the Retreat from Mons and the Battles of Ypres (I.) and Loos. Towards the end of 1915 he was sent to Egypt, and whilst in this theatre of war was in action at Gaza and other engagements during the Palestine Campaign. He finally proceeded to Mesopotamia, where he remained until the completion of his service, being present at the capture of Baghdad in 1917. He subsequently returned home and was demobilised in August 1919, and holds the Mons Star, and the General Service and Victory Medals.
63, Park Corner, St. Albans.   X1047.

COVE, W. G., Private, 2nd Queen's (Royal West Surrey Regiment).
He joined in June 1916, and at the conclusion of his training served with his unit at various stations on important duties. He rendered valuable service, but was not able to secure his transfer overseas owing to being medically unfit. He was discharged in March 1918.
41, Union Street, Dunstable.   1026.

COWARD, M. E., Private, 7th Lincolnshire Regt.
He joined in February 1917, and on the completion of his training was drafted to France, where he took part in the fighting in various engagements. He was killed in action on the Somme in March 1918, and was entitled to the General Service and Victory Medals.
13, Broughton Hill, Letchworth.   1598.

COX, A., Sapper, Royal Engineers.
He volunteered in August 1914, and in the following year was drafted to the Western Front, where he took part in many engagements, including those at Ypres, Arras and Cambrai. He returned home and was sent to Longmore, where he was still serving in 1920, and holds the 1914-15 Star, and the General Service and Victory Medals.
9, Wright's Cottages, St. Albans Road, Watford.   X1037.

COX, A., Corporal, Canadian Overseas Forces.
He volunteered in January 1915, and was sent to the Western Front, where he took part in numerous engagements, including those at Arras, Ypres and Cambrai, and was three times wounded. He was demobilised in June 1919, and holds the General Service and Victory Medals.
43, Copsewood Road, Watford.   X1149/B.

COX, A., Private, East Surrey Regiment.
He volunteered in November 1915, and in the same year was sent to France, where he saw much service. He was wounded and gassed at Arras, and on recovery took part in the engagements at Ypres, Passchendaele, St. Julien and St. Quentin. He was demobilised in February 1919, and holds the 1914-15 Star, and the General Service and Victory Medals.
The Hill, Wheathampstead, Herts.   1057

COX, A. C., Gunner, Royal Garrison Artillery.
He joined in August 1916, and after his training served at various stations on important duties with his unit. He rendered valuable services, but was not successful in obtaining his transfer overseas before the cessation of hostilities. He was demobilised in January 1919.
The Hill, Wheathampstead, Herts.   1141.

COX, A. F., Flight-Sergeant, R.A.F.
He was serving at the outbreak of war, and in 1915 was posted to H.M.S. " Manxman," and later to H.M.S. " Yarmouth," and served at Malta, Italy and Mudros, also at Heligoland and the Dardanelles with submarines. He was serving as an engineer on H.M.S. " Yarmouth " when a Zeppelin was brought down in 1917. He was demobilised in May 1920, and holds the 1914-15 Star, and the General Service and Victory Medals.
Near Pond, Clifton, Shefford.   Z1009.

COX, A. G., Gunner, R.F.A.
He joined in April 1917, and in May of the following year was drafted to Palestine, where he served on important special duties at Damascus, Aleppo, Jaffa and Beyrout. He returned home and was demobilised in April 1920, and holds the General Service and Victory Medals.
72, Dane Road, Luton.   1119.

COX, A. W., Regimental Sergeant-Major, R.E.
He joined in June 1916, and in July of the same year was drafted to the Western Front, where he took part in various engagements and was gassed near Armentières. He was also for a time engaged on important clerical duties, and rendered valuable services. He was demobilised in May 1919, and holds the General Service and Victory Medals.
The Common, King's Langley.   X1035/B.

COX, A. W. T., Staff-Sergeant, R.A.S.C. (M.T.)
He volunteered in December 1914, and in the following year was drafted to the Western Front, where he served in many sectors, including Ypres and Armentières. He afterwards was transferred to Serbia and Macedonia, and was engaged on the transport of guns and supplies. He returned home and was demobilised in April 1919, and holds the 1914-15 Star, and the General Service and Victory Medals.
140, Cravells Road, Harpenden.   1083.

COX, B., Private, Bedfordshire Regiment.
He volunteered in December 1914, and after training was sent to the Western Front, where he took part in the Battles of Ypres (II.), the Somme and Arras, and was wounded. He was eventually demobilised in May 1919, and holds the 1914-15 Star, and the General Service and Victory Medals.
88, St. John's Road, Boxmoor, Herts.   X1108.

COX, B. S., Corporal, R.F.C., and 10th Lincolnshire Regiment.
He joined in July 1916, and in November of the same year was drafted to the Western Front, and was attached to the Kite Balloon Section on observation duties. He was later transferred to the 10th Lincolnshire Regiment, and took part in various engagements. He was killed in action at Kemmell Hill on April 17th, 1918, and was entitled to the General Service and Victory Medals.
The Common, King's Langley.   X1035/A.

COX, C., Corporal, 5th Bedfordshire Regiment.

He volunteered in August 1914, and in April of the following year was drafted to the Dardanelles. He was later transferred to Egypt and Palestine, and took part in many engagements, including that at Gaza and the capture of Jerusalem, and was wounded. He returned home and was demobilised in March 1919, and holds the 1914–15 Star, and the General Service and Victory Medals.

12 and 14, Mill Road, Leighton Buzzard.   1592 /C.

COX, C., Private, 6th Bedfordshire Regiment.

He volunteered in August 1914, and after having completed his training was drafted to the Western Front in July 1915. He took part in numerous engagements, and on July 26th, 1916, died of wounds received in action in the Battle of the Somme. He was entitled to the 1914–15 Star, and the General Service and Victory Medals.

Woodland Villa, Dunstable Street, Ampthill.   1566 /A.

COX, C. E., Sapper, Royal Engineers (Signals).

He joined in 1917, and after his training served at various stations as despatch-rider with his unit. He rendered valuable services, but was not successful in obtaining his transfer overseas before the cessation of hostilities. He was demobilised in April 1919.

60, Benskin Road, Watford.   X1130.

COX, C. G., L/Corporal, 7th Bedfordshire Regt.

He volunteered in December 1914, and proceeded in the following year to the Western Front, where he took part in numerous engagements, including those at Hill 60 and Ypres, and was wounded. He was killed in action at Carnoy, near Albert, on July 1st, 1916, and was entitled to the 1914–15 Star, and the General Service and Victory Medals.

166, North Street, Luton.   1073 /B.

COX, E., Sapper, Royal Engineers (R.O.D.)

He joined in February 1916, and in September was drafted to the Western Front, and took part in the engagements on the Somme, at Arras, Ypres and Cambrai. During his service in France he was also engaged in important transport duties on the railways. He was finally demobilised in June 1919, and holds the General Service and Victory Medals.

Woodland Villas, Ampthill.   1567 /A.

COX, E., Sapper, Royal Engineers (R.O.D.)

He volunteered in February 1915, and in April was sent to the Western Front, where he carried out important railway duties in various sectors. He served at Loos, the Somme, Ypres and Albert, and was engaged in transporting ammunition and food supplies to the lines. He was demobilised in July 1919, and holds the 1914–15 Star, and the General Service and Victory Medals.

Dunstable Street, Ampthill.   T1553.

COX, E. C., Sapper, Royal Engineers.

Mobilised on the outbreak of hostilities in August 1914, he was soon afterwards sent to France, where he served in the Retreat from Mons, and in several subsequent battles, including those of Arras, Ypres and Cambrai. At the end of the war he returned home, and in December 1919 was demobilised, holding the Mons Star, and the General Service and Victory Medals.

55, King's Road, St. Albans.   1139 /A.

COX, F., Bombardier, Royal Horse Artillery.

He volunteered in October 1915, and on the completion of his training was sent to France in the following January. Whilst in this theatre of war he took part in the fighting on the Somme, and at Ypres and Cambrai, and in various engagements in the Retreat and Advance of 1918. After the signing of the Armistice he proceeded to Germany with the Army of Occupation, remaining there until April 1919, when he was demobilised after his return to England. He holds the General Service and Victory Medals.

18, Stanmore Road, Watford.   X1093.

COX, F., Private, 7th (Queen's Own) Hussars.

He volunteered in August 1914, and in the following year proceeded to Mesopotamia, where he took part in numerous engagements, including those at Baghdad, Kut and Mosul. He returned home and was demobilised in 1919, and holds the 1914–15 Star, and the General Service and Victory Medals.

78, Judge Street, North Watford.   X1081.

COX, F. (D.C.M.), Corporal, 2nd Border Regt.

He volunteered in September 1914, and served on important duties with his unit until he was drafted to the Western Front. During his service in France he was attached to the Machine Gun Corps, and took part in numerous important engagements, including those at Ypres, Passchendaele and Cambrai, and was three times wounded. He was awarded the Distinguished Conduct Medal for gallantry in the Field, and in addition holds the General Service and Victory Medals, and was demobilised in May 1919.

43, Copsewood Road, Watford.   X1149 /C.

COX, F., Corporal, Bedfordshire Regiment.

He volunteered at the outbreak of war, and in the following year was drafted to the Western Front. He took part in many engagements, including those at Ypres, Albert, Passchendaele Ridge and the Somme, where he was killed in action on August 6th, 1916. He was entitled to the 1914–15 Star, and the General Service and Victory Medals.

Woodland Villas, Dunstable Street, Ampthill.   1566 /B.

COX, G., Private, 1st Hertfordshire Regiment.

He volunteered in 1915, and in the same year proceeded to the Western Front, where he took part in several engagements, including those of Hill 60 and Ypres. He was taken prisoner during an engagement at Festubert, and was held in captivity in Germany until the signing of the Armistice, when he was released and returned to England, and was demobilised in December 1918. He holds the 1914–15 Star, and the General Service and Victory Medals.

13, White Lion Street, Apsley End, Herts.   X1136.

COX, H., Trooper, Herts. Dragoons.

He volunteered in 1915, and in the same year was drafted to the Western Front, where he took part in the Battles of the Somme, Ypres and Cambrai, and also served in the Retreat and Advance of 1918. He returned home and was demobilised in March 1919, and holds the 1914–15 Star, and the General Service and Victory Medals.

12 & 14, Mill Road, Leighton Buzzard.   1592 /B.

COX, H., Leading Signaller, H.M.S. "Commonwealth."

He was in the Navy at the outbreak of war, and was posted for duty with H.M.S. "Commonwealth" in the North Sea. He also served in Russian waters for a time. He was demobilised in January 1920, and holds the General Service and Victory Medals.

43, Copeswood Road, Watford.   X1149 /A.

COX, H. J., Private, R.A.M.C.; and Air Mechanic, Royal Air Force.

He volunteered in September 1914, and in the following year was drafted to the Western Front. In the early part of his service overseas he was engaged in attending to the wounded, but later being transferred to the Royal Air Force, he was employed at Dunkirk and in the Ypres sector on repair work to aeroplanes. His duties, which demanded a high degree of technical skill, were carried out in a most efficient manner, and he rendered valuable services. He was demobilised in January 1919, and holds the 1914–15 Star, and the General Service and Victory Medals.

166, North Street, Luton.   1073 /A.

COX, J., Gunner, Royal Field Artillery.

He volunteered in June 1915, and after his training served at various stations on important duties with his unit. He rendered valuable services, but was not successful in obtaining his transfer overseas before the cessation of hostilities. He was discharged as medically unfit for further service in April 1919.

12 & 14, Mill Road, Leighton Buzzard.   1592 /A.

COX, J., Private, Cheshire Regiment.

Volunteering in March 1915, he was drafted in the following November to Salonika, where he served in the first Battle of the Vardar and in the General Offensive on the Doiran Front. Later he was invalided home suffering from malaria, and subsequently was discharged as medically unfit for further duty in August 1917. He holds the 1914–15 Star, and the General Service and Victory Medals.

Woodland Villas, Dunstable Street, Ampthill.   1567 /B.

COX, J. C., L/Corporal, 2nd Buffs (East Kent Regiment).

He joined in August 1917, and was drafted overseas in the following year. He first saw active service in France, where amongst other engagements he was in those at Cambrai and St. Quentin, being wounded and twice gassed. He was subsequently sent to India, where in 1920 he was still serving. He holds the General Service and Victory Medals.

Hobbs Hill, Welwyn, Herts.   1157.

COX, J. M., Sapper, Royal Engineers.

He volunteered in March 1915, and was sent to France in the following October. During his service overseas he was engaged on important duties in connection with operations in the forward areas, and in maintaining the lines of communication, and was present at engagements on the Somme and at Arras, Ypres and Cambrai. He was eventually demobilised in September 1919, and holds the 1914–15 Star, and the General Service and Victory Medals.

57, South Street, Leighton Buzzard.   790.

COX, J. S, Private, 1st Bedfordshire Regiment.

He volunteered in July 1915, and in January of the following year was drafted to India, where he served at various stations on important duties with his unit, and rendered valuable services. He returned home and was demobilised in March 1919, and holds the General Service and Victory Medals.

Kirkham Cottages, High St., Toddington, West Dunstable. 1040.

COX, J. W., Sergeant, Northamptonshire Regt.

He joined in May 1916, and after a period of training was drafted overseas. He served on the Western Front, taking part in the heavy fighting on the Somme and at Arras, Ypres and Cambrai, and was wounded during the Advance of 1918. He was demobilised in March 1919, and holds the General Service and Victory Medals.

29, St. John's Street, Biggleswade. Z1274.

COX, L., Special War Worker.

In January 1915 he accepted an important appointment at Messrs. Sankey & Sons, where he was engaged on responsible duties in connection with the output of munitions. The services which he rendered to the country whilst with the firm were of the utmost value, and all work which he undertook was carried out with a promptitude and excellence which was worthy of the highest praise.

65, Selbourne Road, Luton. 710/A.

COX, P. H., Leading Cook's Mate, Royal Navy.

He volunteered in November 1914, and being posted to H.M.S. " North Star," was engaged in patrol duties in the North Sea, the Mediterranean and other seas. He was later attached to the Dover Patrol, and was killed in action on April 23rd, 1918, at Zeebrugge. He was entitled to the 1914-15 Star, and the General Service and Victory Medals.

The Cottage, Popes Road, Abbots Langley, Herts.. 136/B.

COX, P. W., Private, King's Own (Royal Lancaster Regiment).

He joined in 1917, and after training was drafted to France in the same year. He served in various sectors taking part in heavy fighting in several engagements, including the first Battle of Cambrai, and the second Battle of the Somme. Reported missing on March 28th, 1918, in the latter battle, he was presumed to have been killed in action on that date. He was entitled to the General Service and Victory Medals.

55, King's Road, St. Albans. 1139/B.

COX, T., Private, 1st Connaught Rangers.

He volunteered in August 1914, and was immediately afterwards sent to the Western Front, where he took part in the Battles of Mons, Ypres and other engagements. He was killed in action on October 3rd, 1915, and was entitled to the Mons Star, and the General Service and Victory Medals.

Ireland, Shefford, Beds. Z1032.

COX, V. C., Sapper, Royal Engineers.

He volunteered in August 1914, and on the completion of his training served at various stations on important duties with his unit. In 1917 he was drafted to Egypt, but his ship was torpedoed outside Alexandria Harbour on December 30th, and he was drowned. He was entitled to the General Service and Victory Medals.

88, Hagden Lane, Watford. X1089.

COX, W. J., Private, 2nd Cavalry Reserve, 4th Queen's Own Hussars.

He was mobilised on the outbreak of war, having previously had 20 years' service in the Army and been through the South African War. He was immediately drafted to the Western Front, and took part in the Retreat from Mons. He was afterwards stationed in Ireland, where he rendered valuable service until discharged on medical grounds in March 1919. He holds the Queen's and King's South African Medal, the Mons Star, and the General Service and Victory Medals.

64, Newcombe Road, Luton. 793.

COX, W. W., Private, 8th Leicestershire Regt.

He joined in February 1917, and having taken his course of training was drafted to the Western Front in the following year. He was taken prisoner in action near Cambrai in May 1918, and died in Germany on December 28th, 1918. He was entitled to the General Service and Victory Medals.

14, Stanmore Road, Watford. 1166.

COY, W. H., Staff-Sergeant, Royal Fusiliers, attached M.P.S.C.

He volunteered in September 1914, and being unfit for active service was attached to the Military Police Staff Corps. He did much excellent work with it until his demobilisation in April 1920.

124, High Street, Redbourn. 1140.

CRABTREE, J. E., Sapper, Royal Engineers.

Volunteering in 1914, he was soon drafted to the Western Front, and, attached to the Sappers and Miners, did very valuable work in the forward areas during several important engagements. He was blown up in an explosion at Hill 60, and after being invalided home was discharged as medically unfit for further service in 1915. He holds the 1914 Star, and the General Service and Victory Medals.

66, Souldern Road, Watford. 1192/B.

CRAMPHORN, W., Corporal, M.G.C.

Having enlisted in the Army before the war, he was drafted to France soon after hostilities broke out, and was engaged in the fierce fighting in the Retreat from Mons, and in the first Battle of Ypres. He was afterwards sent to Palestine, and did valuable service in that theatre of war before he returned to France in 1916. During this second period of active service on the Western Front, he took part in many engagements in the Somme and Cambrai areas, and was twice wounded. He was invalided home and subsequently discharged unfit for further military service in September 1917. He holds the Mons Star, and the General Service and Victory Medals.

18, Blacksmith Lane, St. Albans. 1185.

CRAMPHORN, W. A., Corporal, M.G.C.

He volunteered in August 1914, and immediately proceeded to France. While overseas he took an active part in the Battles at Mons, Ypres, the Somme and Arras, and was twice wounded. He was discharged in consequence of his injuries in September 1917, holding the Mons Star, and the General Service and Victory Medals.

11, Bell Terrace, Lamb Lane, Redbourn. 1207/A.

CRANFIELD, G. W., Private, Bedfordshire Regt.

Volunteering in August 1914, he went through his course of training and was drafted to France in the following year. During his service on the Western Front he took part in the severe fighting at Festubert, Arras and Ypres, where he was killed in action on September 9th, 1917. He was entitled to the 1914-15 Star, and the General Service and Victory Medals. " Ivy Dene," Ampthill Road, Flitwick. 1554/A.

CRANFIELD, H., Private, Royal Fusiliers.

Volunteering in August 1914, he was drafted to France in the following year, and whilst in this theatre of war took part in the Battles of Festubert, the Somme, Arras and Cambrai. After the signing of the Armistice he proceeded into Germany with the Army of Occupation, and was stationed on the Rhine until his return home in 1919 to be demobilised. He holds the 1914-15 Star, and the General Service and Victory Medals.

" Ivy Dene " Ampthill Road, Flitwick. 1554/B.

CRAWFORD, C. A., Private, 1st King Edward's Horse.

He volunteered in December 1914, and was, in April 1916, drafted to the Western Front. He took part in the heavy fighting at the Somme and Cambrai, and was afterwards transferred to the Italian Front, where he remained until 1919. He then returned home and was demobilised in February of that year, holding the General Service and Victory Medals.

23, Estcourt Road, Watford. X1210.

CRAWLEY, A. F., L/Corporal, R.A.S.C. (M.T.)

Mobilised on the outbreak of war, he was shortly afterwards drafted to France. During his service overseas he was engaged on important duties in connection with the transport of ammunition and supplies to the forward areas, and was present in the Retreat from Mons, and the Battles of Ypres, Festubert, the Somme, Arras and Cambrai. On the cessation of hostilities, he was sent into Germany with the Army of Occupation, and was employed on garrison and other duties until he was demobilised in February 1919. He holds the Mons Star, and the General Service and Victory Medals.

42, Waterside, King's Langley. X1193.

CRAWLEY, A. R., Private, 2nd London Regt. (Royal Fusiliers).

He joined in 1917, and in the same year was drafted to the Western Front, where he took part in the heavy fighting in the Ypres, Cambrai and Somme areas, and was wounded. Afterwards he was transferred to Egypt and served in the Palestine Offensive at Jaffa and other places. He returned home and was demobilised in April 1920, holding the General Service and Victory Medals.

Back Lane, Preston, Hitchin. 2774.

CRAWLEY, B. J., Driver, R.F.A.

He volunteered in October 1915, and in June 1917, after being retained on important duties with his unit, was drafted to Mesopotamia. He served as a driver in the Battle of Kut-el-Amara and other engagements, taking guns into action. He returned to England after hostilities ceased, and was demobilised in May 1919, holding the General Service and Victory Medals.

24, Hedley Road, St. Albans. X713/C.

CRAWLEY, C. F., Private, 8th Lincolnshire Regt.
Volunteering in December 1915, he was drafted in the following year to the Western Front. Whilst in this theatre of war he took part in many important engagements, including the Battles of the Somme and Ypres. He was killed in action on October 4th, 1917, in the course of heavy fighting near Arras, and was entitled to the General Service and Victory Medals.
Monk's Island, King's Langley.   X1177.

CRAWLEY, C. W., Private, Manchester Regt.
He joined in January 1916, and in the following June, after the completion of his training, was drafted to the Western Front. He took part in numerous engagements until fighting ceased, including those of Ypres and the Somme. He was demobilised in November 1919 on his return to England, and holds the General Service and Victory Medals.
23, Inkerman Road, St. Albans.   X1217.

CRAWLEY, D., Private, Hertfordshire Regiment.
He joined in May 1917, and in the same year, after the completion of his training, was drafted to France. He took part in the severe fighting at Messines, Ypres, the Somme and Cambrai, and was wounded. He was demobilised in 1919 after his return home, and holds the General Service and Victory Medals.
10, Grosvenor Terrace, Boxmoor.   X1205/A.

CRAWLEY, D. T., Gunner, R.F.A.
He volunteered in October 1915, and after the completion of his training was drafted to Mesopotamia. He took part in several important engagements, including those at Kut-el-Amara, and other places on the Tigris. He was demobilised in May 1919, and holds the General Service and Victory Medals.
24, Hedley Road, St. Albans.   X713/B.

CRAWLEY, E. G., Private, Bedfordshire Regt.
He volunteered in August 1914, and was shortly afterwards drafted to France, where he took part in much heavy fighting and was severely wounded at Neuve Chapelle. He was also gassed during his service. He was, in consequence, invalided home, and was eventually discharged in June 1916. He holds the 1914 Star, and the General Service and Victory Medals.
2, Leyton Road, Harpenden.   1208.

CRAWLEY, F. W. P., Sergeant, R.A.S.C. (Canteens).
He joined in July 1917, and was shortly afterwards drafted overseas. He was engaged on responsible canteen duties in Mesopotamia, and did valuable work at Basra through the remainder of the campaign in that country. He was demobilised in December 1920, and holds the General Service and Victory Medals.
97, Oak Road, Luton.   1188.

CRAWLEY, G. W., Private, Labour Corps.
Joining in September 1916, he was drafted to Italy in the following year. Whilst there he was employed with his unit at various bases on important duties which he carried out with much success. He returned to England and was demobilised in January 1920, holding the General Service and Victory Medals.
65, Cromwell Road, Luton.   1187/A.

CRAWLEY, H., Corporal, 8th Leicestershire Regiment.
He joined in April 1916, and after his training was sent to France in September of the same year. During his service overseas he took an active part in many important engagements, and being taken prisoner at Ypres in May 1918 was kept in captivity until the signing of the Armistice. He was repatriated and demobilised in November 1918, holding the General Service and Victory Medals.
65, Cromwell Road, Luton.   1187/B.

CRAWLEY, H., Private, Royal Fusiliers.
He joined in January 1918, and in the following May was drafted to the Western Front. During his service overseas he was engaged in several important operations, and was wounded in the La Bassée sector during the Advance of 1918, and invalided home. He was demobilised in October 1919, and holds the General Service and Victory Medals.
65, Cromwell Road, Luton.   1187/C.

CRAWLEY, H., Private, Queen's (Royal West Surrey Regiment).
He joined in October 1917, and in the same year was drafted overseas. He took part in numerous engagements of importance on the Western Front until hostilities ceased, including those of the Somme, Arras and Cambrai. He was demobilised in 1919 after his return to England, holding the General Service and Victory Medals.
10, Grosvenor Terrace, Boxmoor.   X1205/B.

CRAWLEY, R., Q.M.S., Bedfordshire Regiment.
He volunteered in 1915, and in the following year was drafted to the Western Front, where he took a prominent part in many engagements in the Somme, Ypres and Cambrai sectors. In 1917 he was transferred to Italy, and served with distinction on the Asiago, Piave and Trentino fronts. In March 1918 he returned to France in time for the Retreat and Advance of that year. He was demobilised in 1919, and holds the General Service and Victory Medals.
127, Bearton Road, Hitchin.   2778.

CRAWLEY, S. P., Sergeant, Hertfordshire and Bedfordshire Regiments.
He was mobilised at the beginning of hostilities and proceeded with the First Expeditionary Force to France. He was in the Retreat from Mons, and fought in several other important battles, including those of Albert and Ypres, right down to the cessation of hostilities. He was wounded during his service overseas, and after his return home was demobilised in 1919. He holds the Mons Star, and the General Service and Victory Medals.
4, Felden Lane, Apsley End.   X1174.

CRAWLEY, W. (M.M.), Private, 7th Bedfordshire Regiment.
He volunteered in September 1914, and in July of the following year was sent to France. In this theatre of war he took a prominent part in the severe fighting near Arras, Thiepval and the Somme, and was awarded the Military Medal for conspicuous bravery in the Field and devotion to duty in September 1916. He was invalided home on account of wounds received in the battle of Ypres in August 1917, and discharged as unfit for further service in June 1918. In addition to the Military Medal he holds the 1914-15 Star, and the General Service and Victory Medals.
Primrose Vale, King's Langley.   X1179.

CRAWLEY, W. J., Staff-Sergeant, R.A.S.C.
He volunteered in 1914, and proceeded overseas in the following year. Whilst on the Western Front he was employed in the instruction and training of drivers, and was also engaged on responsible duties in superintending the transport of ammunition and supplies to the forward areas in various sectors until the cessation of hostilities. He was demobilised in March 1919, and holds the 1914-15 Star, and the General Service and Victory Medals.
22, Pretoria Road, Watford.   X1181.

CRAY, A. H., Private, 4th North Staffordshire Regiment.
He joined in February 1916, and in the same year proceeded overseas. He saw much active service in several sectors of the Western Front, and took part in the Battles of Vimy Ridge, the Somme, Ypres and Cambrai. Returning to England after the cessation of hostilities he was demobilised in April 1919, and holds the General Service and Victory Medals.
36, Yarmouth Road, Watford.   X1190/B.

CRAY, T. E., Private, 1st Hertfordshire Regiment.
He volunteered in September 1914, and after his training was engaged on important duties with his unit at various stations. Owing to physical disability he was not sent overseas, and in April 1915 was discharged as medically unfit for further military service.
36, Yarmouth Road, Watford.   X1190/A.

CREAMER, A., Private, East Surrey Regiment.
He joined in February 1917, and after completing his course of training was drafted overseas in the following August. During his service on the Western Front he was engaged in severe fighting in various sectors, and was wounded and taken prisoner near Cambrai in the Retreat of 1918. Repatriated after the signing of the Armistice he was demobilised in March 1919, and holds the General Service and Victory Medals.
8, Union Street, Dunstable.   1195.

CREAMER, R. W., Gunner, R.F.A.
He joined in August 1916, and after his training was drafted to Salonika in the following January. Whilst in this theatre of war he took part in the fighting on the Vardar front, and being sent later to Egypt proceeded into Palestine with General Allenby's Forces. During his service here he was in action at Gaza, but contracted malaria from which he died on October 19th, 1918. He was entitled to the General Service and Victory Medals.
Watling Street, Hockliffe, near Leighton Buzzard.   1611.

CREASY, S., Private, Welch Regiment.
He volunteered in September 1914, and in the following December was drafted to the Western Front. He took part in the fighting on the Somme, and was wounded near Cambrai in December 1917. After returning to England in March 1918 he was demobilised in February 1919, and holds the 1914-15 Star, and the General Service and Victory Medals.
36, Lowestoft Road, Watford.   X1216.

CREED, A. G., Private, 1st Hertfordshire Regt.
He volunteered in February 1915, and in the same year was drafted to the Western Front, where he was in action at Ypres, the Somme and Poperinghe, in which engagement he was killed on April 26th, 1918. He was entitled to the 1914-15 Star, and the General Service and Victory Medals.
40, Souldern Road, Watford, Herts.   X1209.

CREES, A. C., Cpl., Royal Engineers (Driver).
He joined in June 1916, and in the following year was drafted to Salonika. He did excellent work on the Doiran and Struma fronts and at Strumnitza, and was mentioned in Despatches for gallant conduct under fire at Salonika on November 1st, 1918. He returned home and was demobilised in December 1919, and holds the General Service and Victory Medals.
Princess Street, Toddington.   1200.

CREMER, W., Private, Queen's (Royal West Surrey Regiment).
Joining in February 1917, he went to France in the same month. He went through the heavy fighting at Arras, Vimy Ridge and Messines, and being severely wounded was invalided home. On recovering from the effects of his wounds he was sent to Lincolnshire, and employed on agricultural work until his demobilisation in March 1919. He holds the General Service and Victory Medals.
Mount Pleasant, Aspley Guise.   Z1175.

CREW, A. E., L/Corporal, 4th Bedfordshire Regt.
He volunteered in September 1915, and in the following July was drafted to the Western Front. He was engaged in several operations in the Somme Offensive, and was wounded in August 1916. On his recovery he rejoined his unit and took part in the Battles of Ypres, Albert, Cambrai and several other engagements until hostilities ceased. Demobilised in February 1919, he holds the General Service and Victory Medals.
55, High Street, Houghton Regis, Dunstable.   1189/A.

CREW, B. W., Private, Queen's (Royal West Surrey Regiment).
Volunteering in October 1914, he passed through a course of training, and after carrying out important duties with his unit at various depôts was drafted to France in May 1917. During his service overseas he took part in heavy fighting in several engagements, including those of Poperinghe and Ypres, and was invalided home suffering from shell-shock. After undergoing treatment in hospital he was discharged in November 1917 as medically unfit for further service, and subsequently died from the effects of the shock on July 1st, 1919. He was entitled to the General Service and Victory Medals.
55, High Street, Houghton Regis, Dunstable.   1189/A.

CREW, F., L/Corporal, R.A.O.C.
He joined in August 1916, and in the following November was drafted overseas. He did valuable work with his unit on the Western Front in many engagements until fighting ceased, including those at Arras, Vimy Ridge, Bullecourt, Bapaume, Albert and Péronne. He was demobilised in August 1919 after returning home, and holds the General Service and Victory Medals.
65, Ashton Road, Luton.   1213.

CRICK, B. F., Gunner, Royal Field Artillery.
Joining in August 1916, he was engaged with his unit on important duties at various stations until drafted overseas in October 1918. On the Western Front he took part in the last Battle of Cambrai, and in other important engagements in the closing stages of the war, and returned to England for demobilisation in March 1919. He holds the General Service and Victory Medals.
7, Frogmore Cottages, near St. Albans.   X1184.

CRIPPS, F. A. V., Private, Royal Fusiliers.
He joined in December 1916, and in the following February was sent to France. He took part in much heavy fighting, and was wounded at Ypres. He also served at Arras, Vimy Ridge, Passchendaele Ridge and Cambrai. He was demobilised in November 1919 after his return home, and holds the General Service and Victory Medals.
Caddington, Luton.   1214.

CRIPPS, G., Sapper, Royal Engineers.
He volunteered in 1915, and in the following year, after the completion of his training, was drafted to India, where he served at various stations, including Poona and Rawal Pindi, on important duties with his unit and rendered valuable services. He was accidentally killed on July 30th, 1919, and was entitled to the General Service and Victory Medals.
29, Weymouth Street, Apsley.   X1202/C.

CRIPPS, H., Private, Queen's Own (Royal West Kent Regiment).
He joined in 1916, and after his training was engaged on important duties with his unit at various stations until drafted to France in 1918. He saw much active service, and took part in many engagements in the final stages of the war, and on the conclusion of hostilities was sent into Germany with the Army of Occupation. He was demobilised in December 1919, and holds the General Service and Victory Medals.
53, Piccotts End, Hemel Hempstead.   X1196/A.

CRIPPS, T., A.B., R.N., H.M.S. " Malaya."
He volunteered in 1915 at the age of 16, and served with the Grand Fleet in the North Sea, where he took part in various engagements, and was wounded. He was killed in action at the Battle of Jutland on May 31st, 1916, and was entitled to the 1914-15 Star, and the General Service and Victory Medals.
29, Weymouth Street, Apsley.   X1202/B.

CRIPPS, W., Private, Bedfordshire Regiment.
He volunteered in 1915, and after serving at various stations with his unit was drafted in 1917 to the Western Front, where he took part in much heavy fighting in various sectors and was wounded on the Somme. On his recovery he went to Egypt and fought in several important engagements in General Allenby's victorious Advance in Palestine. He holds the General Service and Victory Medals, and was demobilised in June 1919.
53, Piccotts End, Hemel Hempstead.   X1196/B.

CRISP, C. J., Gunner, Royal Garrison Artillery.
After joining in July 1916 he went through a course of training and was sent overseas in the following year. He saw much active service on the Western Front, and amongst the important engagements in which he fought were the Battles of Arras and Cambrai. After the conclusion of hostilities he returned to England and was demobilised in February 1919, holding the General Service and Victory Medals.
4, Garfield Street, Watford.   X1176.

CRITCHER, E. C., Driver, R.A.S.C.
Joining in February 1916, he was dispatched overseas in the following April, and served on the Western Front. He was engaged on important duties transporting ammunitions and supplies to the forward areas, and was present at many important engagements, including those of the Somme, Arras, Ypres and Cambrai. From France he proceeded to Egypt, and in General Allenby's Advance through Palestine did excellent work at Gaza and in many notable actions. He was demobilised in September 1919 after returning home, and holds the General Service and Victory Medals.
16, Brixton Road, Watford.   X1178.

CROFT, A., Driver, R.A.S.C. (H.T.)
Volunteering in April 1915, he was shortly afterwards drafted to France. After being employed on important duties there he was transferred to Salonika and subsequently to Egypt and Palestine. Throughout his service on all these fronts he did excellent supply and transport work, and was present at many important engagements. After the cessation of hostilities he returned home, and in September 1919 was demobilised, holding the 1914-15 Star, and the General Service and Victory Medals.
22, College Place, St. Albans.   1218.

CROFT, F., Private, 10th Duke of Cornwall's Light Infantry.
He joined in November 1916, and having completed his training was drafted to France in December of the following year. While overseas he fought in several engagements, until hostilities ceased, including those of Ypres, Passchendaele, Cambrai and the Somme. After the Armistice had been signed he returned home and was demobilised in January 1919, holding the General Service and Victory Medals.
6, St. Anne's Road, Luton.   703/A.

CROFT, F. C., Sapper, Royal Engineers.
He volunteered in November 1914, and in the following year was drafted to Gallipoli. He was engaged in the heavy fighting in the landing at Cape Helles and in other operations, and on the Evacuation of the Peninsula went to Egypt. After a period of service on this Eastern front he was sent in June 1916 to France, where he did good work in several sectors, and was present at the Battles of Armentières. He was demobilised in March 1919, and holds the 1914-15 Star, and the General Service and Victory Medals.
45, Cambridge Street, Luton.   1199.

CROFT, J. W., Private, Bedfordshire Regiment.
He was serving at the outbreak of war, and was immediately drafted to France. He took part in much heavy fighting in the opening stages of hostilities, and was killed in action at Ypres on October 26th, 1914. He was entitled to the 1914 Star, and the General Service and Victory Medals.
118, Harwood Road, Watford.   X1212.

CROFT, W., Private, Royal Defence Corps.

He volunteered in November 1914, and did valuable work in the Royal Defence Corps as he was unfit for overseas service. After his training he was engaged on various important duties, including the guarding of German prisoners of war at detention camps in different parts of the country until the cessation of hostilities. He was demobilised in February 1919.
7, Warwick Road, Luton.　　　　　　　　　　1198/A.

CRONE, J. B., Sergt.-Major, M.G.C.

Volunteering in December 1914, he joined in the Bedfordshire Regiment, but in the course of his training was transferred to the Machine Gun Corps. In March 1916 he was drafted to the Western Front, and was severely wounded whilst in action at Ypres in the following October, and was invalided to England. After his recovery he was stationed at Grantham, where he was engaged on important duties as an Instructor until March 1918, when he returned to France and served in the concluding stages of the war. He was demobilised in April 1919, and holds the General Service and Victory Medals.
52, Bedford Street, Hitchin.　　　　　　　　3294.

CROOK, A. E., Private, 17th Royal Sussex Regt.

He joined in June 1917, and in the following October, on the completion of his training, was sent to Egypt. He took part in General Allenby's Offensive in Palestine and served at Gaza, Haïfa, Damascus and Aleppo. After returning to England he was demobilised in January 1920, and holds the General Service and Victory Medals.
40, May Street, Luton.　　　　　　　　　　1203.

CROOK, A. E., Gunner, Royal Horse Artillery.

He was mobilised at the outbreak of hostilities, and was drafted at once to France. He took part in the Retreat from Mons, the Battle of Ypres and many other engagements until the conclusion of hostilities. He was demobilised in February 1919 after his return to England, and holds the Mons Star, and the General Service and Victory Medals.
51, Benskin Road, Watford.　　　　　　　　X1211/B.

CROOK, H. R., Sergeant, R.A.S.C. (M.T.)

He volunteered in April 1915, and in the same month was sent to the Western Front, where he was engaged on important motor transport duties at Loos, Ypres, the Somme, Messines, Arras and Cambrai. After the Armistice he advanced into Germany with the Army of Occupation and was employed on the Rhine on special duties. He was mentioned in Despatches for devotion to duty on the Field in July 1916, and holds the 1914-15 Star, and the General Service and Victory Medals. On his return from Germany he served for a time at Abbeville, and was eventually demobilised in July 1919.
10, Nightingale Road, Hitchin.　　　　　　　1595.

CROOK, W., L/Corporal, Rifle Brigade.

He joined in April 1918, and having gone through his course of training was, in the following December, drafted to Germany, where he was engaged on guard duties with the Army of Occupation on the Rhine. He remained overseas until January 1920, when he returned home and was demobilised.
40, May Street, Luton.　　　　　　　　　　1204.

CROOK, W. J., Petty Officer, R.N., H.M.S. "Swift."

Volunteering in August 1914, he was posted to H.M.S. "Swift," and served in many waters. He took an active part in the Battle of the Falkland Islands in 1914, and in the engagements in the Dardanelles in 1915. He holds the 1914-15 Star, and the General Service and Victory Medals, and was still serving in 1920.
51, Benskin Road, Watford.　　　　　　　　X1211/A.

CROOT, H. J., Private, Royal Welch Fusiliers.

He joined in February 1916, and after his training was sent to Mesopotamia, where he served in the Tigris operations at Kut-el-Amara and Baghdad. He was invalided to India in 1917 with malaria, and on his recovery, being transferred to Egypt, took part in the Battles of Jaffa and Haïfa in the campaign through Palestine. He returned home later, and after service in Ireland was demobilised in September 1919, holding the General Service and Victory Medals.
Carter's Lane, Potton.　　　　　　　　　　Z1278.

CROPLEY, A. L., Private, Royal Fusiliers.

He joined in February 1918, and in the following July was drafted to France. During his service on the Western Front he took part in the severe fighting at Amiens and Bapaume, and was severely wounded in the second Battle of Cambrai in October 1918. He was invalided home to hospital, and after treatment was discharged in March 1919 as medically unfit for further military service. He holds the General Service and Victory Medals.
4, St. John's Street, Biggleswade.　　　　　Z1284/A.

CROPLEY, P., Air Mechanic, R.A.F.

He joined in March 1917, and after his training was engaged at various stations in England and Ireland on important aircaft duties which demanded a high degree of technical skill. He was unable, on medical grounds, to secure a transfer overseas before fighting ceased, and after doing good work with his squadron, was demobilised in 1919.
The Chequers, Whipsnade, Dunstable.　　　　Z1248/B.

CROSS, A., Farrier Q.M.S., R.A.S.C. (Remounts); and Leading Aircraftsman, R.A.F.

He was serving in the Army at the outbreak of war, and being immediately drafted to France was engaged in the heavy fighting in the Retreat from Mons, and in several subsequent actions. In 1916 he was sent to Egypt, where he was employed on important duties until the cessation of hostilities. He also did excellent work as leading aircraftsman in the R.A.F. He was demobilised in March 1919, and holds the Mons Star, and the General Service and Victory Medals.
6, Brighton Road, Watford.　　　　　　　　X1194.

CROSS, F. W., Private, Norfolk Regiment.

He joined in 1916, and on completing his training was sent to the Western Front in the following year. During his service overseas he was engaged in much heavy fighting in several important battles, including those of Ypres (where he was wounded), Cambrai and Amiens. Returning to England on the conclusion of hostilities he was demobilised in June 1919, and holds the General Service and Victory Medals.
41, Longmire Road, St. Albans.　　　　　　X1191/B.

CROSS, J. J., Private, 22nd Queen's (Royal West Surrey Regiment).

He volunteered in June 1915, and after completing his training was drafted overseas. During his service on the Western Front he was employed at Le Havre and other bases on important duties in connection with the loading and unloading of ammunition and other stores until the cessation of hostilities. He was demobilised in March 1919, and holds the General Service and Victory Medals.
41, Longmire Road, St. Albans.　　　　　　X1191/A.

CROSS, J. S., Private, 6th Queen's (Royal West Surrey Regiment).

He joined in June 1918, and in the following autumn was dispatched to France. Whilst overseas he took part in several important engagements in the final stages of the war, and fought in the second Battle of Cambrai. After returning to England he was demobilised in February 1920, and holds the General Service and Victory Medals.
136, New Town Street, Luton.　　　　　　　1182.

CROUCH, A., Private, Machine Gun Corps.

He volunteered in October 1915, and after a period of training was drafted to France. He did valuable service at Neuve Chapelle and the Somme, and was later transferred to Palestine, where he was present during the campaign to Jerusalem and beyond. He was demobilised in June 1919, and holds the General Service and Victory Medals.
39, Upper Heath Road, St. Albans.　　　　　X1215.

CROUCH, J., Private, Bedfordshire Regiment.

Volunteering in 1914, he was sent overseas in the same year. During his service on the Western Front, he was engaged in much heavy fighting in various sectors, and amongst the battles in which he took part were those at the Somme and Arras. He was twice wounded during his service. He returned to England on the termination of hostilities and was demobilised in January 1919, holding the 1914 Star, and the General Service and Victory Medals.
2, Cross Street North, Dunstable.　　　　　1186.

CROUCHER, W. R., Gunner, R.G.A.

He volunteered in October 1914, and in the following year, after completing his training, was drafted to the Dardanelles. He was present at the landing at Suvla Bay, and was killed in action on August 7th, 1915. He was entitled to the 1914-15 Star, and the General Service and Victory Medals.
2, Prospect Place, Chalk Hill, Oxhey.　　　　X1219.

CROWE, F. W., Sapper, Royal Engineers; and Private, Royal Defence Corps.

He volunteered in April 1915, and in January of the following year was drafted to the Western Front, where he took part in various engagements, including those near St. Quentin, Cléry and Ypres, and was wounded. He was invalided home, and being transferred to the Royal Defence Corps, after a period in hospital, was employed on important guard and training duties until he was demobilised in March 1919. He holds the General Service and Victory Medals.
5, Spencer Road, Luton.　　　　　　　　　1201/A.

CROW, G., Special Constable, Woburn Division.
He volunteered in June 1915, and from that date till January 1919, rendered valuable services as a special constable. He took regular patrol work and was also on duty during several air-raids. The remainder of his available time he devoted to responsible and arduous agricultural work. In January 1919 he was demobilised, and received high commendation for his efficient services throughout.
Church End, Hockliffe, near Leighton Buzzard.   1609/B.

CROW, P. G., Air Mechanic, Royal Air Force.
He joined in March 1918, and after the completion of his training served at various stations on important duties, which demanded considerable technical skill. He was medically unfit for duty overseas, but he rendered valuable service as an aeroplane fitter and tester until demobilised in November 1919.
Church End, Hockliffe, Leighton Buzzard.   1609/A.

CROWCHER, G., Corporal, 1st Royal Berkshire Regiment.
He volunteered in 1914, and was sent to the Western Front immediately. He fought at Mons, Ypres and the Somme, and other engagements, and was three times wounded. He died from his injuries in Netley Hospital on February 8th, 1919, and was entitled to the Mons Star, and the General Service and Victory Medals.
5, Lower Paddock Road, Oxley.   X342/B.

CROWSLEY, A., Sergeant, City of London Lancers (Rough Riders).
He volunteered in October 1914, and after a period of service with his unit at several stations, was sent overseas in July 1916. He did excellent work in Egypt, and in the Advance into Palestine under General Allenby, and was in action at Gaza, Jaffa, Jerusalem and Damascus. He was seriously wounded in the last action, taken prisoner, and died afterwards from the effects of his wounds. He was entitled to the General Service and Victory Medals.
5, North Bridge Street, Shefford.   Z1180.

CROXFORD, W. G., Corporal, Queen's (Royal West Surrey Regiment).
He joined in May 1917, and having completed his training was drafted to France in the January following. He saw much severe fighting in various battles, including those of Albert, St. Quentin, Cambrai and others in the Retreat and Advance in 1918. Returning home after the cessation of hostilities, he was demobilised in September 1919, and holds the General Service and Victory Medals.
Pretoria Cottages, Harlington.   1206/A.

CROXFORD, T., Sapper, Royal Engineers.
He volunteered in April 1915, and in October of the same year was drafted to France. While in this theatre of war he did excellent work in many important areas, including the Somme, Arras, Ypres and Cambrai, and was chiefly engaged in wiring and trenching. He remained overseas carrying out his duties until after the Armistice, and returning home, was demobilised in March 1919. He holds the 1914-15 Star, and the General Service and Victory Medals.
Pretoria Cottages, Harlington.   1206/B.

CRUMPLIN, C. H., Private, Bedfordshire Regt.
Joining in July 1916, he completed a course of training, and was drafted overseas. Whilst on the Western Front he saw much active service in various sectors, especially round Ypres, and took part in much heavy fighting. He was killed in action at Messines Ridge in June 1917, and was entitled to the General Service and Victory Medals.
Batford Mills, Harpenden.   1183/A.

CRUMPLIN, F., Rifleman, King's Royal Rifles.
He was serving in the Army at the outbreak of hostilities, and was immediately sent to France. There he fought in the Retreat from Mons and in the subsequent engagements at Ypres, the Somme, Arras and Cambrai, and was twice wounded. He was afterwards transferred for some time to Italy, where he did valuable work. After returning to England he was discharged in December 1918, and holds the Mons Star, and the General Service and Victory Medals.
Batford Mills, Harpenden.   1183/B.

CULLING, A., Private, R.A.M.C.
He volunteered in October 1914, and in the following year was drafted to the Western Front, where he was engaged on important medical duties with his unit in the Somme and Cambrai areas. During his time in France he suffered from severe shell-shock. He was demobilised in June 1919 after his return to England, and holds the 1914-15 Star, and the General Service and Victory Medals.
83, Saxon Road, Luton.   1230/B.

CULLING, H. H., L/Corporal, 20th Durham Light Infantry.
He joined in June 1917, and in April of the following year was drafted to France. Whilst in this theatre of war he took part in severe fighting at the Somme, Cambrai and Ypres, and after the cessation of hostilities proceeded into Germany with the Army of Occupation. He was stationed at Cologne until November 1919, when he returned home and was demobilised. He holds the General Service and Victory Medals.
83, Saxon Road, Luton.   1230/A.

CULLING, L., Sergeant, R.A.V.C.
He volunteered in October 1915, and in the following year was drafted to France. He was engaged at Rouen and in various sectors including Ypres and Arras, in attending to sick and wounded horses, and rendered valuable services. He was demobilised in April 1919, and holds the General Service and Victory Medals.
59, Beech Road, Luton.   1236.

CULLIS, G. J., A.B., Royal Navy.
He joined in April 1918, and was engaged in important mine-sweeping duties in the North Sea, the Mediterranean and the Baltic, where he rendered highly valuable services. He was still serving in 1920, and holds the General Service and Victory Medals.
13, Alfred Street, Luton.   1242/A.

CULLIS, J. R., Private, 5th Bedfordshire Regt.
He was mobilised in August 1914, and was sent to the Dardanelles, where he took part in the landings at Anzac and Suvla Bay. Afterwards he was transferred to Egypt and Palestine, where he rendered good service in various important engagements. He was demobilised in June 1919 after his return home, and holds the 1914-15 Star, and the General Service and Victory Medals.
84, Queen's Street, Luton.   1241.

CULLOCH, M., Sapper, Royal Engineers.
He joined in 1916, and after his training was engaged at various stations in Ireland on important engineering duties with his unit. He rendered valuable services, but was not successful in obtaining his transfer overseas, and was discharged in 1918 as medically unfit for further service.
High Street, Wheathampstead.   1247.

CULVERHOUSE, A. J., Private, Bedfordshire Regiment.
Joining in September 1916, he went through his training and afterwards served at various stations on important duties with his unit. He did much valuable guard work, but was not successful in obtaining his transfer overseas before all fighting ceased. He was demobilised in February 1920.
36, Souldern Street, Watford.   X1237/A.

CULVERHOUSE, B., Private, Hertfordshire Regiment.
Volunteering in 1915, he was shortly afterwards drafted to the Western Front. He took part in the heavy fighting in the Somme Offensive, and was killed in action at St. Julien on July 31st, 1917. He was entitled to the 1914-15 Star, and the General Service and Victory Medals.
30, Souldern Street, Watford.   X1222.

CULVERHOUSE, H. H., Private 7th Hertfordshire Regiment.
He volunteered in March 1915, and in March of the following year was drafted to the Western Front, where he took part in important engagements. He was killed in action on the Somme on October 14th, 1916, and was entitled to the General Service and Victory Medals.
14, St. Mary's Road, Watford.   X1248.

CULVERHOUSE, W. C., Private, 7th Middlesex Regiment.
He joined in June 1918, and after his training served at various stations on important duties with his unit. He rendered valuable services, but was not successful in obtaining his transfer overseas, before the cessation of hostilities. After the signing of the Armistice he was sent to Germany with the Army of Occupation, with which he served until April 1920, when he returned to England and was demobilised.
53, Souldern Street, Watford.   X1240.

CUMBERLAND, G., Private, 6th Northamptonshire Regiment.
He joined in April 1918, and in the following August was drafted to the Western Front, where he took part in various engagements and was wounded at Le Cateau on September 20th, 1918. He was demobilised in November 1919, and holds the General Service and Victory Medals.
144, Hartley Road, Luton.   1246.

CUMBERLAND, H., Private, R.A.S.C. (M.T.)
He joined in August 1916, and after his training served on important duties at various stations until May 1918, when he was drafted to Italy. He was engaged with the motor transport on the Piave and at Taranto, and other places, until after the conclusion of hostilities, when he returned home in October 1919, and was demobilised in the following December. He holds the General Service and Victory Medals.
Marsh Road, Leagrave, Beds.　　　1234/A.

CUMBERLAND, H., Private, 4th Bedfordshire Regiment.
He joined in May 1917, and in the following April was sent to the Western Front. During his service in France, he took part in the fighting at Armentières and was later killed in action near Cambrai on September 5th, 1918. He was entitled to the General Service and Victory Medals.
Marsh Road, Leagrave, Luton.　　　1234/B.

CUMBERLAND, J. E., Private, Bedfordshire Regiment.
He joined in April 1916, and in the following December was drafted to France. During his service on the Western Front he fought at the capture of Vimy Ridge and was severely wounded in April 1917. He was invalided home to hospital and discharged as medically unfit for further duty in the same month. He holds the General Service and Victory Medals.
School Lane, Leagrave.　　　1233.

CUMBERLAND, P. F., Private, Middlesex Regt.
He joined in May 1916, and in the following October was drafted overseas. He served on the Western Front during the Battles on the Somme and at Arras, where he was killed in action on March 1st, 1917. He was entitled to the General Service and Victory Medals.
11, Capron Road, Dunstable.　　　1228.

CUMBERLAND, S., Private, 5th Bedfordshire Regiment.
He volunteered in September 1914, and in the following year was drafted to the Dardanelles, where he took part in the landing at Suvla Bay. In 1916 he was transferred to Egypt and served in various engagements, including those on the Canal zone and at Gaza, Haifa, Acre and Beyrout. He was demobilised in February 1919, and holds the 1914-15 Star, and the General Service and Victory Medals.
6, Windmill Street, Luton.　　　1238.

CUMBERLAND, S., Private, Bedfordshire and Norfolk Regiments.
He volunteered in December 1915, and after a period of training was drafted overseas. He served in many sectors of the Western Front, taking part in the fighting at Arras, the Somme, Ypres and Albert, and suffered from trench fever. He was demobilised in April 1919, and holds the General Service and Victory Medals.
28, Edward Street, Luton.　　　1223.

CUMBERLAND, T. S., Special War Worker.
He was engaged on munition work at Luton, being too young to join the Service, and was employed on various important work. His duties, which were of a responsible nature, were carried out in an efficient manner, and he rendered valuable service during the war.
Kozi-Kot, Queen's Street, Houghton Regis.　　　1239.

CUMBERLAND, V., Gunner, R.F.A.
He volunteered in May 1915, and in March 1917, was drafted to the Western Front, where he took part in the Battles of the Somme, Ypres and Cambrai and many other engagements. He was demobilised in March 1919, and holds the General Service and Victory Medals.
Kozi-Kot, Queen's Street, Houghton Regis.　　　1235.

CUMNER, F. C., Battery Sergeant-Major, R.F.A. and R.H.A.
He enlisted in June 1893, and served in the Soudan Expedition of 1898 and in the South African War. In 1915 he was sent to the Western Front, where he took part in the heavy fighting at Festubert and Loos. He afterwards returned home and was engaged as an Instructor in the School of Gunnery, and rendered valuable services. He was demobilised in December 1919, and holds the Khedive's and Queen's Medals for the Soudan, the Queen's and King's South African Medals, the 1914-15 Star, and the General Service, Victory and Good Conduct Medals.
32, Richmond Hill, Luton.　　　1245.

CUNNINGHAM, C. A., Sergeant, R.E.
He joined in September 1916, and after completing his training, was drafted to Mesopotamia, taking part in various engagements, including those at Samara and Tekrit. He returned to England and was demobilised in February 1919 and holds the General Service and Victory Medals.
34, Chatsworth Road, Luton.　　　1227.

CURCHIN, E. A., Chief Stoker, Royal Navy.
He was serving at the outbreak of hostilities, and was posted for duty with H.M.S. "Superb." He was engaged on patrol duties in the North Sea, and also served for a time with the Fleet in the Dardanelles. He holds the 1914-15 Star, and the General Service and Victory Medals, and was finally demobilised in February 1919
2, Wootton Terrace, Walsworth, Hitchin.　　　1850.

CURL, A. T., Private, R.A.V.C.
He joined in September 1916, and after a period of training was drafted to Salonika and thence to France, where he was present at various engagements. He was demobilised in April 1919, holding the General Service and Victory Medals.
Lower Luton Road, Harpenden, Herts.　　　1226.

CURL, E. D., Private, 10th (Prince of Wales' Own Royal) Hussars.
He volunteered at the outbreak of war, and immediately afterwards was sent to France, where he was killed in action on August 16th, 1914. He was entitled to the 1914-15 Star, and the General Service and Victory Medals.
Slate Corner, Flamstead, Dunstable.　　　X1244.

CURL, W., Private, Bedfordshire Regiment.
He volunteered in August 1914, and served at various stations on important duties with his unit, but was unsuccessful in obtaining his transfer overseas, owing to being unfit for service abroad. He was discharged in 1917.
15, Chobham Street, Luton.　　　1231.

CURME, R., Air Mechanic, Royal Air Force.
He joined in June 1918, and after a period of training was stationed at various places with his squadron, on important duties, which called for a high degree of technical skill. He rendered valuable service but was unsuccessful in obtaining his transfer overseas before the cessation of hostilities. He was demobilised in January 1919.
46, Pinner Road, Oxhey, Herts.　　　X/1220.

CURRANT, D., Private, 2nd Bedfordshire Regt.
He volunteered in August 1914, and in the following year was drafted to the Western Front, where he took part in the Battles of Hill 60, Vimy Ridge the Somme, Arras and Cambrai. He was demobilised in November 1919, and holds the 1914-15 Star, and the General Service and Victory Medals.
12, Ridgway Road, Luton.　　　1243.

CURRANT, F., Corporal, Middlesex Regiment.
He volunteered at the outbreak of war and was almost immediately drafted overseas. He served in much heavy fighting in many sectors of the Western Front, including the Battles of Ypres and the Somme, and was gassed and wounded. He was demobilised in March 1919, and holds the 1914 Star, and the General Service and Victory Medals.
14, Upper Heath Road, St. Albans, Herts.　　　X1221.

CURRANT, G. H., Trooper, Hertfordshire Dragoons.
He volunteered at the outbreak of war and was almost immediately drafted to France and took part in the Retreat from Mons and the Battle of Ypres. During his service, he fought in engagements in the Dardanelles campaign, and in Egypt, and, after the Armistice was signed, proceeded to Germany with the Army of Occupation and was stationed on the Rhine. He was demobilised in March 1919, and holds the Mons Star, and the General Service and Victory Medals.
5, Temperance Street, St. Albans.　　　799.

CURRINGTON, A. E., Private, R.A.M.C.
He joined in May 1918, on the attainment of military age, and after the completion of his training was drafted to Germany with the Army of Occupation in December 1918. He served at Cologne on important garrison duties until April 1920, when he returned home and was demobilised.
88, Hitchin Road, Luton.　　　1229/B.

CURRINGTON, W. (D.C.M.), Pte., 2nd Bedfordshire Regiment.
He volunteered in September 1914, and after serving on important duties with his unit was drafted to France in 1916. He took part in the fighting on the Somme, and was wounded at Arras, and again at Ypres and was for a time in hospital at Boulogne. He was awarded the Distinguished Conduct Medal for conspicuous bravery on the Field, and holds, in addition, the General Service and Victory Medals, and was demobilised in March 1919.
88, Hitchin Road, Luton.　　　1229/A.

CURRY, W., Sapper, Royal Engineers.
He volunteered in December 1915, and in the following March was sent to Egypt and thence to Palestine, where he was engaged on important duties for a period of three years. He served at Jaffa, Jerusalem, Gaza, Jericho, and on the River Jordan, and after the conclusion of hostilities returned home and was demobilised in March 1919, holding the General Service and Victory Medals.
5, Devonshire View, Highbury, Hitchin. 1851/A.

CURRY, W. J., Private, 9th Welch Regiment.
He joined in February 1917, and having completed his training was drafted to France in April 1918. He saw much fighting in several battles, including those of the Somme and Amiens, and was severely wounded in the Advance of 1918. Returning home he was demobilised in November 1919, holding the General Service and Victory Medals.
5, Devonshire View, Highbury, Hitchin. 1851/B.

CURTIS, B. J., Private, Bedfordshire and Cheshire Regiments.
He volunteered in May 1915, and after his training was drafted to the Western Front, where he took part in numerous engagements, including those at Arras, Ypres, Cambrai and the Somme, and was wounded. He was killed in action near Péronne on March 21st, 1918, and was entitled to the General Service and Victory Medals.
Chapel House, Southill. Z1249.

CURTIS, S., Trooper, Royal Horse Guards.
He volunteered in August 1914, and was immediately afterwards sent to the Western Front, where he took part in important engagements, including the Retreat from Mons, and was wounded. He was invalided home and discharged in December 1914 as medically unfit for further service, and holds the Mons Star and the General Service and Victory Medals.
Holly Cottage, King's Waldon. 1250.

CURTIS, T. H., Private, King's Royal Irish Hussars.
He volunteered in April 1915, and in the following October was drafted to France, and served on the Somme in many engagements. Later he was sent to Egypt, and took part in the Battle of Gaza and the capture of Jerusalem. Whilst on this Front he contracted enteric, and was invalided home to hospital and was discharged in February 1919, holding the General Service and Victory Medals.
56, Clarence Road, Leighton Buzzard. 1297.

CUSTANCE, V., Private, Bedfordshire Regiment.
He volunteered in September 1914, and was immediately sent to France, where he took part in the fierce fighting during the Retreat from Mons, and was severely wounded. He subsequently died as a result of his injuries in January 1915. He was entitled to the Mons Star, and the General Service and Victory Medals.
138, Wenlock Street, Luton. 1224.

CUTLER, A. E., Private, Bedfordshire Regt.
He volunteered in September 1914, and after his training served at various stations on important duties with his unit. He rendered valuable services, but was not successful in obtaining his transfer overseas before the cessation of hostilities. He was demobilised in March 1919.
4, White Hill, Hitchin. 2782.

CUTLER, F., Private, Oxfordshire and Buckinghamshire Light Infantry and M.G.C.
He joined in 1916, and in the following year was drafted to the Western Front, where he served as a Lewis gunner in the Passchendaele and Lens sectors. He was taken prisoner during the fighting near Cambrai in November 1917, and suffered many privations during his captivity. After the Armistice he was repatriated and was demobilised in March 1919. He holds the General Service and Victory Medals.
7, Taskers Row, Eddlesborough, near Dunstable. Z1562.

CUTLER, H. W., Private, Norfolk and Bedfordshire Regiments.
He joined in February 1917, and was shortly afterwards drafted to France, where he took part in the Battles of Ypres and Cambrai. After the Armistice he proceeded to Germany, and remained with the Army of Occupation on the Rhine until October 1919, when he returned home, and was demobilised, holding the General Service and Victory Medals.
69, Leavesden Road, Watford. X1225.

CUTLER, H. W., Private, Queen's (Royal West Surrey Regiment) and Labour Corps.
He joined in March 1916, and after a period of training was drafted overseas. He served on the Western Front during many engagements, including those at Arras, the Somme and Ypres, and suffered from shell-shock. He was demobilised in 1919, and holds the General Service and Victory Medals.
1, Flowerdale, Markyate, Herts. 1232.

D

DALTON, H. H., A.B., R.N., H.M.S. " Warspite."
He joined in 1918, and after his training was engaged on hazardous duties in the North Sea, the Baltic, and off the coasts of Italy and Constantinople. He was demobilised after his return home in May 1919, and holds the General Service and Victory Medals.
6, Shakespeare Street, North Watford. X1327.

DANES, F. D., Corporal, 8th Bedfordshire Regt.
He volunteered in September 1914, and in the following year was drafted to the Western Front, and whilst in this theatre of war fought at the Somme, Ypres, Cambrai, St. Quentin and Albert, and was severely gassed. After the cessation of hostilities he returned home, and in January 1919 was demobilised, holding the 1914-15 Star, and the General Service and Victory Medals.
High Street, Toddington. 1322.

DANIELS, E., Corporal, R.A.S.C.
He volunteered in January 1915, and after his training was engaged at various stations on important duties with his unit. He rendered valuable services, but was not successful in obtaining his transfer overseas before the termination of hostilities. He was demobilised in November 1919.
15, Ivy Road, Luton. 1323/A.

DANIELS, F. S. C, Private, Bedfordshire Lancers.
He volunteered in 1915, and in the following year was drafted to Egypt. He took part in the campaign through Palestine to Jerusalem, and at one time while on patrol duty was reported missing, but subsequently was able to rejoin his unit. He was subsequently transferred to the Western Front, and took part in important engagements near Arras, Cambrai and the Somme. He was demobilised in February 1919, and holds the General Service and Victory Medals.
Woodland Villa, Dunstable Street, Ampthill. T1569.

DANIELS, O., Private, Grenadier Guards.
He volunteered in August 1914, and after his training was drafted overseas. During his long-continued service in France he took part in the fighting at Hill 60, Ypres, the Somme, Cambrai and in various subsequent engagements in the Retreat and Advance of 1918. He was twice wounded. After his return home he was demobilised in January 1919, and holds the 1914-15 Star, and the General Service and Victory Medals.
25, Warwick Road, Luton. 1324.

DANIELS, S., A.B., Royal Naval Division.
He joined in June 1917, and in the following October was drafted to France. During his service on the Western Front he fought in numerous engagements of importance, including those at Passchendaele, Cambrai and St. Quentin, and was severely gassed in March 1918. After his return to England he was demobilised in February 1919, and holds the General Service and Victory Medals.
George Street, Maulden, near Ampthill. 1326.

DANSEY, L. J., Private, London Regiment (Royal Fusiliers).
Volunteering in October 1915, he was drafted overseas in the following December. During his service in France he was in action at Loos and on the Somme Front, and was wounded and taken prisoner in 1916. He was held in captivity in Germany until the Armistice, when he was repatriated. In January 1919 he was demobilised, and holds the 1914-15 Star, and the General Service and Victory Medals.
32, Yarmouth Road, Callowland, Watford. X1325/B.

DANSEY, W. G., Private, 4th London Regiment (Royal Fusiliers).
He volunteered in October 1915, and in the same year proceeded to the Western Front, where he took an active part in the Battles of the Somme, Arras, Cambrai, and in many operations in the Retreat and Advance of 1918. During his service he was wounded. He was demobilised in February 1919, and holds the 1914-15 Star, and the General Service and Victory Medals.
32, Yarmouth Road, Callowland, Watford. X1325/A.

DARBY, H., Private, Labour Corps.
He joined in June 1917, and in the following October was drafted to the Western Front. During his service in France he was engaged on important duties in connection with road construction and the conveyance of ammunition up the line, and was frequently under fire whilst operations were in progress. He was demobilised in January 1919, after the cessation of hostilities, and holds the General Service and Victory Medals.
108, Victoria Street, Dunstable. 1328.

DARBY, W J., L/Corporal, 11th Royal Fusiliers.
He volunteered in July 1915, and in the following November
was drafted to the Western Front, where he served in numerous important engagements. He took part in the fighting
at Arras, Ypres, Passchendaele and St. Quentin, and was
severely wounded at Albert. After the Armistice he returned home in December 1918, and was demobilised in the
following February, holding the 1914-15 Star, and the General
Service and Victory Medals.
6, Cannon Cottages, Sunnyside, Hitchin.   1589.

DARDY, P. R., Driver, Royal Field Artillery.
He joined in March 1916, and in the following December
was drafted to France. Whilst in this theatre of war he did
excellent work with his battery at Messines, Ypres and
Bapaume, where he was wounded. After his recovery he
served in the last Battle of Ypres, and afterwards was sent to
Italy, where he took part in the operations on the Piave until
the conclusion of hostilities. He was demobilised after his
return to England in March 1919, and holds the General
Service and Victory Medals.
62, Pondswick Road, Luton.   1329.

DARLING, G. R., Private, 6th Northamptonshire
    Regiment.
Joining in September 1916, he went through his course of
training and in the same year was drafted to France. During
his service on the Western Front he fought in many important engagements, including those of Ypres and the second
Battle of the Somme, and was killed in action on April 5th,
1918. He was entitled to the General Service and Victory
Medals.
52, Ebury Road, Watford.   X1330.

DARLOW, A., Private, 1st Lincolnshire Regt.
He volunteered in August 1914, and was soon drafted to the
Western Front, where he served in the Battles of the Marne,
Festubert, Loos, the Somme, Ypres and Cambrai. In the
Retreat of April 1918 he was taken prisoner, and was sent to
Germany. During his captivity he fell ill and died at Charle-
ville War Hospital. He was entitled to the 1914 Star, and
the General Service and Victory Medals.
King Street, Potton.   Z1302.

DARNELL, C., Private, Bedfordshire Regt.
He was serving at the outbreak of war, having enlisted in
1899, and was shortly afterwards drafted to France. Whilst
on the Western Front he took part in the fierce fighting at
Mons, Ypres and Armentières. He was discharged in February 1916 as a time-expired man, and holds the Mons Star,
and the General Service and Victory Medals.
South View, Upper Caldecote, Biggleswade.   Z1571.

DARNELL, R., Private, East Yorkshire Regt.
He was mobilised at the outbreak of war, and in the following
month was drafted to the Western Front. He fought at the
Battles of the Marne, the Aisne and La Bassée, and was
killed in the fierce conflict at Dickebusch on October 28th,
1914. He was entitled to the Mons Star, and the General
Service and Victory Medals.
King Street, Potton.   Z2571/B.

DARNELL, S., Private, Bedfordshire Regt.
He joined in August 1916, and after a period of training was
sent to the Western Front, where he took part in the Battles
of Arras, Ypres, Cambrai and the Somme. He was invalided
to England with fever in March 1918, and was demobilised in
March 1919, holding the General Service and Victory
Medals.
Seddington, Biggleswade.   Z1572.

DARSLEY, W. R., Private, R.A.S.C. (M.T.)
He was mobilised from the Reserve at the outbreak of hostilities, and was immediately drafted to the Western Front,
where he took part in the Retreat from Mons. He also
rendered valuable service in the Battles of the Marne, the
Aisne, Ypres, the Somme and in subsequent engagements
until August 1918, when in consequence of severe wounds he
was invalided home. After treatment in hospital he was
demobilised in the following February, and holds the Mons
Star, and the General Service and Victory Medals.
39, Ashby Road, Watford.   X1331.

DARTON, J. W., Pioneer, Royal Engineers.
He volunteered in June 1915, and in November 1916 was
drafted to France, where he was engaged on important duties
in connection with the operations, and was frequently in the
forward areas. In 1918 he was invalided home, and after
his recovery served at various stations in England and Ireland
until his demobilisation in January 1919. He holds the
General Service and Victory Medals.
3, Bedford Street, Hitchin.   1852.

DARTON, W. J., Private, R.A.S.C. (Canteens).
Volunteering in August 1915, he was drafted to Egypt in the
following year and advanced into Palestine with General
Allenby's Forces. Whilst in this theatre of war he rendered
valuable service on important duties at Gaza, Haifa and
Aleppo. In 1920 he was still serving with the Colours, and
holds the General Service and Victory Medals.
3, Bedford Street, Hitchin.   1853.

DARVILL, J., Gunner, Royal Garrison Artillery.
Volunteering in August 1914, he was drafted to the Western
Front after the completion of his training in the following
year. During his service in France he did good work as a
gunner in numerous important engagements, and was killed
in action near Arras on April 27th, 1917. He was entitled
to the 1914-15 Star, and the General Service and Victory
Medals.
41, Regent Street, North Watford.   X1332/B.

DARVILL, W., Corporal, R.A.S.C.
He joined in September 1916, and in the following year was
drafted to Mesopotamia, where he was engaged on important
transport duties in connection with the operations until the
conclusion of hostilities, especially at Kut, Baghdad and
Mosul. After returning home he was demobilised in August
1919, and holds the General Service and Victory Medals.
41, Regent Street, North Watford.   X1332/A.

DAVENPORT, G., Private, 7th Royal Fusiliers.
He volunteered in February 1915, and after a period of training was drafted overseas. He served in several sectors of
the Western Front, and among the important battles in
which he took part were those at Arras and Ypres. He was
wounded and gassed during his service, and was taken
prisoner on April 5th, 1918, in the heavy fighting near Cambrai. Released from captivity after the Armistice, he was
demobilised in March 1919, and holds the General Service
and Victory Medals.
75, Copsewood Road, Watford.   X335/C.

DAVENPORT, P. W., A.B., Royal Navy.
He joined in 1918, and being posted to H.M.S. "Sparrow-
hawk," was engaged on patrol duties in the North Sea and
the Baltic. His ship was one of the force that convoyed the
German Fleet to Rosyth and Scapa Flow. He holds the
General Service and Victory Medals, and was still serving
in 1920. 75, Copsewood Road, Watford.   X335/B.

DAVEY, W., Corporal, Royal Engineers (E.A.)
He volunteered in August 1914, and on the conclusion of his
training was drafted to Egypt. He afterwards took a prominent part in many engagements in the Palestine Campaign
until fighting ceased, including those at Gaza. He returned
home and was demobilised in May 1919, holding the General
Service and Victory Medals.
69, Beech Road, Luton.   393/B.

DAVIES, B., Private, Sherwood Foresters.
He volunteered in May 1915, and on finishing his training
was drafted overseas in the following year. During his
service in France he took part in numerous important engagements, including the Battles of the Somme and Marne in 1918.
After the cessation of hostilities he proceeded to Ireland,
where he served until February 1920, when he was demobilised. He holds the General Service and Victory Medals.
4, Dorset Street, Luton.   1333.

DAVIES, C., Sapper, Royal Engineers.
He volunteered in November 1914, and in the following year
was drafted to the Western Front. During his service in
France he was frequently engaged in the forward areas whilst
operations were in progress, notably at Loos, Vimy Ridge
and Beaumont-Hamel, and was twice wounded. In 1920
he was still serving in France, and holds the 1914-15 Star,
and the General Service and Victory Medals.
5, Cape Road, Fleetville, St. Albans.   X1334.

DAVIES, E. L., Private, R.A.S.C. (M.T.)
He volunteered in September 1915, and in the following year
was drafted to Mesopotamia, where he was engaged on important transport duties at Kut, Baghdad and Mosul. In
1919 he proceeded to India, and did duty with his unit at
Bangalore until March of the same year, when he was drafted
for special work in Persia until August. After his return home
he was demobilised in 1919, and holds the General Service
and Victory Medals.
4, Charles Street, Luton.   1335.

DAVIES, F., Rifleman, King's Royal Rifle Corps.
He volunteered in August 1914, and after his training was
drafted to France in the following year. During his service
on the Western Front he fought at Festubert, Loos, Albert,
the Somme, Arras, Vimy Ridge, Messines and Cambrai, where
he was wounded. He was afterwards discharged as medically
unfit for further service, and holds the 1914-15 Star, and the
General Service and Victory Medals.
6, St. Andrew's Street, Queen Street, Hitchin.   1854.

DAVIES, H., Gunner, Royal Garrison Artillery.
He volunteered in June 1915, and in the following year was drafted to France. During his service on the Western Front he took part in the Battles of the Somme, Ypres, Cambrai, the Marne, and in many subsequent engagements until the cessation of hostilities. He returned home and was demobilised in January 1919, and holds the General Service and Victory Medals.
4, Dorset Street, Luton. 1336.

DAVIES, P. H., Sergeant, Royal Air Force.
He volunteered in October 1915, and after his training served at various stations, where he was engaged on important duties which demanded a high degree of skill. He did excellent work throughout, but was not successful in obtaining a transfer overseas before the cessation of hostilities. He was demobilised in 1920.
4, Armours Cottages, Shefford. Z1337.

DAVIES, W., Private, Durham Light Infantry.
He joined in November 1916, and after his training served at various stations on important coastal defence duties with his unit. He rendered valuable services, but on medical grounds was not able to secure his transfer overseas before fighting ceased. He was demobilised in February 1919.
68, Talbot Road, Luton. 1338.

DAVIES, W. W., L/Corporal, Middlesex Regt.
After joining in October 1916, he went through his course of training, and being attached to the Labour Corps, did valuable work, especially in connection with camp sanitation. He was not successful in obtaining his transfer to a fighting area before hostilities were over, but rendered excellent service until his demobilisation in June 1919.
40, Lower Dagnall Street, St. Albans. X1339.

DAVIS, E., L/Corporal, 2nd Bedfordshire Regt.
Volunteering at the commencement of hostilities, he was quickly drafted to the Western Front, and served in the Retreat from Mons. He also took an active part in many of the subsequent engagements, including those at the Somme and Arras, and was killed in action during the Advance on September 2nd, 1918. He was entitled to the Mons Star, and the General Service and Victory Medals.
21, Duke Street (The Rear), Luton. 1340.

DAVIS, E. G., Corporal, Guards' Machine Gun Regiment.
Called from the Reserve at the outbreak of war, he was immediately drafted to the Western Front, where he took part in the Retreat from Mons and the subsequent engagements at Hill 60, Ypres, the Somme, Arras and Cambrai. His service overseas lasted until May 1918, and after his return to England he was engaged on duties of an important nature until his demobilisation in January 1919. He holds the Mons Star, and the General Service and Victory Medals.
9, Bailey Street, Luton. 1341.

DAVIS, G., Driver, Royal Engineers.
He volunteered in 1915, and after his training saw service in Salonika and on the Western Front, where he was engaged on important duties in the forward areas until hostilities ceased. Whilst in the East he contracted malaria. He holds the 1914-15 Star, and the General Service and Victory Medals, and was still serving in 1920.
10, Park Street, Hitchin. 4567/B.

DAVIS, G., Private, 7th Norfolk Regiment.
He joined in January 1917, and on the conclusion of his training in the following February was sent to France. Subsequently he went into action, and on April 28th, 1917, after taking part in the fighting at Monchy, was reported missing. He is now presumed to have been killed on that date. He was entitled to the General Service and Victory Medals.
Stopsley Green, Luton. 1342/B.

DAVIS, G. F., Private, Labour Corps.
Joining in March 1917, he was drafted to France at the conclusion of his training, and was subsequently engaged on important duties in the fighting areas of Lens and Cambrai. He was demobilised after his return to England in November 1919, and holds the General Service and Victory Medals.
109, Cambridge Street, Luton. 1343.

DAVIS, H., Private, Labour Corps.
He volunteered in 1915, and having completed his training was drafted to France in the following year. He did valuable work with the Salvage Company in the Somme, Messines and Passchendaele areas, and was killed near Passchendaele on September 10th, 1917. He was entitled to the General Service and Victory Medals.
Falda Road, Barton. 1578/B.

DAVIS, H., Private, Royal Welch Fusiliers.
Joining in January 1916, he was drafted to the WesternFront in the following July. Whilst overseas he acted as a pioneer for his battalion, and in this capacity rendered valuable service in many sectors, notably those of the Somme, Arras and Cambrai. He was demobilised after his return to England in March 1919, and holds the General Service and Victory Medals.
Stopsley Green, Luton. 1342/A.

DAVIS, J., Corporal, 13th King's (Liverpool Regiment).
He volunteered in June 1915, and on the conclusion of his training in the following November was drafted to France. Subsequently he fought in the Battle of Loos and was wounded on the Somme, where he was afterwards killed in action on July 14th, 1916. He was entitled to the 1914-15 Star, and the General Service and Victory Medals.
69, High Street, Markyate. 1344/B.

DAWBORN, H., Corporal, Bedfordshire Regt.
He joined in March 1916, and after his training at Ampthill was sent to the Western Front. His overseas service lasted for three years, during which time he was engaged in the fighting at Vimy Ridge, the Somme, Beaumont-Hamel, Ypres and Cambrai, and in the Retreat and Advance of 1918. He was demobilised after his return to England in February 1919, and holds the General Service and Victory Medals.
Moulsoe Buildings, near Newport Pagnell, Bucks. Z1345/B.

DAWBORN, W., Sergeant, 7th BedfordshireRegt.
Volunteering in September 1914, he was drafted to the Western Front early in the following year. Whilst in this theatre of war he participated in the fighting at Hill 60, Albert, Ypres, the Somme and Cambrai, and was subsequently wounded in action at St. Quentin. He was invalided to hospital at Newport, and after treatment was discharged as physically unfit in August 1919. He holds the 1914-15 Star, and the General Service and Victory Medals.
Great Brickhill, near Bletchley, Bucks. Z1345/A.

DAWES, C., Pte., Bedfordshire and Dorsetshire Regiments.
Volunteering in June 1915, he was drafted to Mesopotamia in the following November, and subsequently fought at Kut-el-Amara and Baghdad. Throughout his service overseas he did excellent work, and holds the 1914-15 Star, and the General Service and Victory Medals. He was demobilised in March 1919.
6, Englands Lane, Dunstable. 1318.

DAWES, S. H., L/Corporal, Machine Gun Corps.
He volunteered in May 1915, and at the conclusion of his training in the following December was drafted to the Western Front. Whilst in this theatre of war he was engaged in the fighting at Loos, Albert,Arras, Vimy Ridge, the Somme, Passchendaele and Cambrai, and after the Retreat and subsequent Advance of 1918 was sent to Germany with the Army of Occupation. He was demobilised after his return to England in July 1919, and holds the 1914-15 Star, and the General Service and Victory Medals.
27, Union Street, Luton. 1346.

DAWKS, H. N., Sergeant, 2nd Bedfordshire Regt.
A serving soldier, he was drafted to France in October 1914, and subsequently fought at Neuve Chapelle, Ypres, Festubert and Loos, where in the following September he was severely wounded and gassed. He was invalided home, and on his recovery was found to be unfit for further foreign service, and was engaged on special duties until he was demobilised in February 1919. He holds the 1914-Star, and the General Service and Victory Medals.
George Street, Maulden, near Ampthill. 1347.

DAWSON, A., Private, Royal Fusiliers.
Joining in June 1916, he was sent to the Western Front at the conclusion of his training, and was subsequently in almost continuous fighting until he was killed in action on May 28th, 1917. He was entitled to the General Service and Victory Medals.
Marsom Place, Stopsley, Beds. 1348.

DAWSON, R., Sapper, Royal Engineers.
Called from the Reserve at the outbreak of war, he was engaged on special duties until 1915, when he was drafted to the Dardanelles, and took part in the landing at Suvla Bay and in the subsequent engagements. After the evacuation of the Peninsula he was sent to Egypt, where he saw service in the Canal zone, and later took part in the Palestine campaign, during which he participated in heavy fighting at Gaza, Haifa and Aleppo, and in the capture of Damascus. He was demobilised after his return to England in July 1919, and holds the 1914-15 Star, and the General Service and Victory Medals.
85, Oak Road, Luton. 349.

DAWSON, S. C., Drummer, 7th Bedfordshire Regiment.
He volunteered in August 1914, and was drafted to France in the following July. In the capacity of brigade-runner he was present at many engagements, including those at Loos and Albert, and in July 1916 was wounded in the Somme sector. He was then invalided home, but on his recovery in the following January returned to the Western Front and served at Arras, Ypres and Messines. Returning to England after the cessation of hostilities, he was demobilised in March 1919, and holds the 1914-15 Star, and the General Service and Victory Medals.
Victoria Cottage, Ampthill Road, Shefford.　　　Z1350/A.

DAWSON, W., Special War Worker.
Early in 1915 he was appointed manager of the mechanical fuse department at Messrs. Kent's, Ltd., Luton. In this capacity his exceptional abilities proved of the utmost value, and he worked with untiring energy until the conclusion of hostilities, when he relinquished his position.
18, Chatsworth Road, Luton.　　　1351.

DAY, A., Rifleman, King's Royal Rifle Corps.
He joined in 1917, and early in the following year was drafted to France, where he served in the final stages of the war and subsequently advanced into Germany with the Army of Occupation. He holds the General Service and Victory Medals, and was demobilised after his return to England in December 1919.
5, St. John's Road, Watford.　　　X1356.

DAY, A., Private, Bedfordshire Regiment.
He joined in January 1916, and after his training was sent to the Western Front, where he served for three years. During this time he took part in several engagements, notably those at Arras and Cambrai, and did valuable work with his unit. He was demobilised after his return to England in February 1919, and holds the General Service and Victory Medals.
58, Cravells Road (Lower), Harpenden, Herts.　　　1355.

DAY, A., Private, Bedfordshire and Hampshire Regiments.
Volunteering in December 1914, he was drafted to Salonika in the following September, and subsequently took part in much of the fighting on that front until the cessation of hostilities. He was demobilised after his return to England in April 1919, and holds the 1914-15 Star, and the General Service and Victory Medals.
55, Vale Road, Bushey, Watford.　　　X1354.

DAY, A., Gunner, R.G.A. (Siege Battery).
Joining in November 1916, he was sent to the Western Front in the following March, and subsequently fought in several engagements, notably those at Ypres and Arras. In December 1917, in consequence of ill-health, he was invalided home, and after his recovery was engaged on duties of an important nature at various stations until his demobilisation, which took place in January 1919. He holds the General Service and Victory Medals.
27, Claremont Road, Luton.　　　1353.

DAY, A., Private, Middlesex Regiment.
He joined in November 1916, and on completion of his training in the following July was drafted to Egypt and thence to Palestine. During the campaign on this front he did excellent work with his unit, and took part in the capture of Jerusalem and Jericho. He was demobilised after his return to England in March 1919, and holds the General Service and Victory Medals.
37, Marsh Road, Leagrave, Luton.　　　1352.

DAY, A. E., Private, 3rd Suffolk Regiment.
He joined in 1918, and after his training was engaged at various stations on important agricultural work. He was unable to secure his transfer overseas before the cessation of hostilities, but nevertheless did valuable work until his demobilisation, which took place in January 1919.
32, North Common, Redbourn, Herts.　　　1357/A.

DAY, A. T., Private, Labour Corps.
He joined in February 1917, and after his training was engaged on duties of an important nature at various stations with his unit. He was unsuccessful in obtaining his transfer overseas before the cessation of hostilities, but rendered valuable services until his demobilisation, which took place in 1919.
111, Windmill Road, Luton.　　　1358.

DAY, A. V. G., Corporal, Middlesex Regiment.
He joined in May 1916, and saw varied service in South Africa, India, Salonika, Egypt, Italy and France, where he took part in the fighting in the Arras sector. After the cessation of hostilities he returned to England, and in June 1919 was demobilised, holding the General Service and Victory Medals.
" Frère," Alfred Street, Dunstable.　　　1028.

DAY, A. W., Private, R.A.S.C. (M.T.)
He joined in April 1918, but owing to physical unfitness was unable to secure his transfer overseas. He was engaged on important transport duties at various stations, and rendered valuable services until his demobilisation, which took place in March 1919.
Red Lion Cottage, Upper Woodside, near Luton.　　　1360.

DAY, A. W., Private, 8th Northamptonshire Regt.
Joining in June 1916, he was drafted to France in the following September, and on his arrival was sent to the Somme sector, where operations were then in progress. Subsequently he fought at Ypres and Arras, but after having been severely wounded in March 1917 was invalided home. He was discharged in December of that year, and holds the General Service and Victory Medals.
46, King's Road, St. Albans.　　　1359.

DAY, B., Private, R.A.S.C. (M.T.)
Volunteering in October 1914, he was quickly sent to France, where he served for nearly five years. During this time he was engaged on important duties in the forward areas, and was present at the Battles of Loos, Ypres, Arras and Cambrai. He was demobilised on his return to England in February 1919, and holds the 1914 Star, and the General Service and Victory Medals.
Clipstone Cottages, High Street, Barton.　　　1361.

DAY, B. D., Private, Bedfordshire Regiment.
He volunteered at the commencement of hostilities and early in 1915 was sent to France. Subsequently he was engaged in the fighting at Ypres, Hill 60, Festubert, Loos and the Somme, and was almost continuously in action until July 27th, 1916, when he was killed at Longueval Wood. He was entitled to the 1914-15 Star, and the General Service and Victory Medals.
74, Queen's Street, Hitchin.　　　1855/A.

DAY, C. R. G., Driver, Hertfordshire R.F.A.
Volunteering at the commencement of hostilities, he was sent to Egypt early in 1915, and subsequently took part in several minor engagements. Later he fought under General Allenby in the Palestine campaign, and on December 30th, 1917, was accidentally killed. He was entitled to the 1914-15 Star, and the General Service and Victory Medals
29, Temperance Street, St. Albans.　　　1362.

DAY, E., Air Mechanic, R.A.F. (late R.N.A.S.)
He joined in July 1917, and after his training was engaged on important duties which called for a high degree of technical knowledge and skill. He was unable to secure his transfer to a theatre of war before the cessation of hostilities, but nevertheless rendered valuable services until his demobilisation, which took place in April 1919.
" Verona," Luton Road, Harpenden.　　　1363.

DAY, E., Rifleman, Rifle Brigade.
He joined in September 1918 immediately on attaining military age, and after his training was drafted to France in the following November. On the cessation of hostilities he proceeded to Germany with the Army of Occupation, with which he served until March 1919, when he returned to England and was demobilised, holding the General Service and Victory Medals.
13, Lamb Lane, Redbourn.　　　1364/B.

DAY, F., Private, 1st Bedfordshire Regiment.
Volunteering at the commencement of hostilities he was drafted to France, and took part in the Retreat from Mons and the subsequent Battles of Ypres and Loos. In 1916 he was sent to Egypt and thence to Palestine, where he participated in heavy fighting at Gaza, Haïfa and Medjil. Later he did excellent work with his unit in helping to suppress the riots which broke out in Cairo. He was demobilised after his return to England in June 1919, and holds the Mons Star, and the General Service and Victory Medals.
7, Queen's Street, Hitchin.　　　1587.

DAY, F., Gunner, Royal Field Artillery.
He volunteered in August 1914, and was quickly sent to the Western Front, where he served in the final stages of the Retreat from Mons. Subsequently he was engaged on the fighting on the Marne, at Albert, La Bassée, Ypres, Festubert, Loos, Vimy Ridge and the Somme, and was wounded. He was discharged after his return to England in October 1918, and holds the Mons Star, and the General Service and Victory Medals.
4, Fountain Yard, Biggleswade.　　　Z1310.

DAY, F. A., Private, 2nd Bedfordshire Regt.
Volunteering in September 1914, he was sent to the Western Front on completion of his training, and was subsequently in action in many important sectors, notably those of Ypres and Festubert. He was reported missing after an engagement on June 16th, 1915, but was later presumed to have been killed in action on that date. He was entitled to the 1914-15 Star, and the General Service and Victory Medals.
17, Wellclose Street, St. Albans.　　　1365.

DAY, F. G., Rifleman, Rifle Brigade.

Volunteering in March 1915, he was sent to France at the conclusion of his training, and subsequently, in the capacity of signaller, was present at many engagements, including those at Ypres, Passchendaele and Cambrai. On one occasion he was wounded, but after being treated at the Base was able to rejoin his unit. He holds the General Service and Victory Medals, and was demobilised after his return to England in March 1919.

4, Shaw Cottages, Hatfield, Herts. X1366.

DAY, H., Private, 1st Hertfordshire Regiment.

He volunteered in November 1914, and after his training served in France for nearly two years, during which time he took part in many notable battles. Returning to England in 1916 he was discharged through causes due to his service, and holds the 1914–15 Star, and the General Service and Victory Medals.

11, Park Street, Hitchin. 2706.

DAY, H., Private, Royal Army Service Corps.

He volunteered in May 1915, and after his training served on important duties with his unit at various stations. Owing to being medically unfit for duty abroad he was unable to procure his transfer to a theatre of war, but nevertheless rendered valuable services until his demobilisation in March 1919. 13, Lamb Lane, Redbourn. 1364/C.

DAY, H., Private, Royal Army Medical Corps.

He volunteered in December 1914, and until 1916, when he was sent to France, was engaged on special duties at various hospitals in England. Subsequently he served in Italy, Egypt and Palestine, and did valuable work with his unit on each of these fronts, on one occasion being wounded. He holds the General Service and Victory Medals, and in 1920 was serving in Cairo.

6a, Brache Street, Luton. 4759/C.

DAY, J. (D.C.M.), C.S.M., 1/5th Bedfordshire Regiment.

Volunteering in September 1914 he was drafted to the Dardanelles in the following year, and subsequently took part in the landing at Suvla Bay and the engagements which followed. After the Evacuation of the Peninsula he was sent to Egypt, where he saw service in the Canal zone, and later fought with distinction in many sectors of the Palestine front, including those of El Arish, Gaza, Haïfa and Beyrout. Whilst overseas he was wounded on two occasions, but after receiving treatment at a Base hospital was able to rejoin his unit. He was twice mentioned in Despatches, and in July 1917 was awarded the Distinguished Conduct Medal for the conspicuous bravery and devotion to duty he displayed at a critical moment at Umbrella Hill. In addition he holds the Médaille Militaire, awarded for gallantry, the 1914–15 Star, and the General Service and Victory Medals. He was demobilised in May 1919.

6, Gaitskell Row, Luton. 1368.

DAY, J., Private, 4th Bedfordshire Regiment.

Volunteering in November 1915 he was sent to the Western Front in the following March, and subsequently went into action on the Somme. He also served at Arras, Ypres and Cambrai, and in the Retreat and Advance of 1918, and was wounded. Returning to England after the cessation of hostilities he was demobilised in March 1919, and holds the General Service and Victory Medals.

Upper Sundon, near Dunstable. 1367/B.

DAY, J. W., Private, 12th Middlesex Regiment.

He joined in May 1916, and having completed his training was drafted to France in August of the same year. Whilst overseas he fought on the Somme, and was killed in action at Albert on September 26th, 1916. He was entitled to the General Service and Victory Medals.

56, Park Hill, Ampthill. 1570/B.

DAY, P., Private, 4th Bedfordshire Regiment.

He volunteered in November 1915, and after his training was sent to France. His service in this theatre of war lasted for over three years, and during this time he took an active part in many important battles, notably those of Vimy Ridge, the Somme, Arras, Ypres and Cambrai. He holds the General Service and Victory Medals, and was demobilised in February 1919.

Upper Sundon, near Dunstable. 1367/A.

DAY, P., Private, 4th Bedfordshire Regiment.

He volunteered in November 1915, and after his training was sent to France in the following March. Subsequently he was engaged in the fighting on the Somme and at Arras and Ypres, but in January 1918 returned to England in consequence of ill-health. He was invalided out of the Service a month later, and holds the General Service and Victory Medals.

Upper Sundon, near Dunstable. 1317.

DAY, P. B., Sapper, Royal Engineers.

He volunteered in August 1915, and after his training served in Egypt and Palestine for three years. During this time he did valuable work with his unit in the Canal zone, and at El Arish, Gaza, Haïfa, Beyrout and Damascus. He holds the General Service and Victory Medals, and was demobilised after his return to England in March 1919.

174, North Street, Luton. 1370.

DAY, P. G., Private, 22nd London Regiment (The Queen's).

He joined in April 1918, and having completed his training was drafted to the Western Front in the following October and served in the Somme sector. In 1919 he was sent to Egypt, and thence to Palestine, where he was stationed at Jerusalem. Later he returned to England, and in April 1920 was demobilised, holding the General Service and Victory Medals.

56, Park Hill, Ampthill. 1570/A.

DAY, S., Private, 1/5th Bedfordshire Regiment.

Volunteering in September 1914, he was sent to the Dardanelles in the following year, and subsequently took part in the landing at Suvla Bay and in the engagements which followed. In November 1915 he returned to England in consequence of ill-health, and on his recovery in the following March was drafted to Egypt. He also served in the Palestine campaign, during which he participated in heavy fighting, including that at Gaza and Jaffa. He was demobilised on his return to England in June 1919, and holds the 1914–15 Star, and the General Service and Victory Medals.

"Maybank," Kingston Road, Luton. 1371.

DAY, W., Private, Coldstream Guards.

He volunteered in December 1914, and in the following year was drafted to France, where he took part in numerous engagements, including the Battles of the Somme, Arras and Cambrai, and was wounded. He holds the 1914–15 Star, and the General Service and Victory Medals, and was still serving in 1920.

13, Lamb Lane, Redbourn. 1364/A.

DAY, W., Private, 1st Bedfordshire Regiment.

He volunteered at the outbreak of hostilities, and at the conclusion of his training served with his unit at various stations on important duties. He rendered valuable service, but was not able to secure his transfer overseas owing to medical unfitness. He was discharged in December 1914.

80, High Street South, Dunstable. 1027.

DAYTON, S. G., Sapper, Royal Engineers.

Volunteering in January 1915, he was sent to the Western Front at the conclusion of his training. He was engaged on important work in the forward areas, and was subsequently killed in the discharge of his duties at Arras on September 21st, 1917. He was entitled to the General Service and Victory Medals.

86, Victoria Street, St. Albans. X1372/C.

DEACON, F., Private, Labour Corps.

He joined in 1916, and after his training served at various stations on important duties until he was sent overseas in the following year. He was present during his service in France at the Battles of Cambrai and Ypres and in subsequent engagements until the cessation of hostilities. In January 1919 he returned home and was demobilised, and holds the General Service and Victory Medals.

56, Husbourne Crawley, Beds. Z1373

DEACON, H., Private, 1st Hertfordshire Regt.

He volunteered in May 1915, and in the same year was drafted to the Western Front. Here he took part in various engagements, including those at Ypres, Arras and Cambrai. In March 1918 he was taken prisoner and held in captivity in Germany until his release after the Armistice. He was finally demobilised in February 1919, and holds the 1914–15 Star, and the General Service and Victory Medals.

20, Watford Fields, Watford. X1374

DEACON, J., Private, R.A.S.C.

He volunteered in September 1914, and in the following year was drafted overseas. During his service on the Western Front he was engaged on important duties in the forward areas transporting rations and ammunition to the front lines, and was present at the engagement at Vimy Ridge. He was finally demobilised in April 1919, and holds the 1914–15 Star, and the General Service and Victory Medals.

9, Cross Street, St. Albans. X1375.

DEACON, W., Private, Bedfordshire Regiment.

He volunteered in November 1914, and in the following June was drafted to the Western Front. During his service in France he fought at Festubert, Loos, the Somme, Messines, Passchendaele, Cambrai and Albert, and was wounded three times. He was finally demobilised in February 1919 after his return to England, and holds the 1914–15 Star, and the General Service and Victory Medals.

The Grove, Lidlington, Beds. Z1376.

DEALEY, A., Pioneer, Royal Engineers.

He volunteered in August 1915, and after a short training was sent to the Western Front, where he was engaged on important duties in connection with the operations, and was frequently in the forward areas, notably at Loos. In January 1916 he was invalided home through ill-health, brought on by active service, and after a period in hospital was discharged as medically unfit for further military duty in the following April. He holds the 1914-15 Star, and the General Service and Victory Medals.
33, Watford Fields, Watford. X1377/A—1378/A.

DEALEY, A. T., 1st Class Stoker, R.N., H.M.S. "Bacchante."

He joined in November 1917, and was posted for duty with H.M.S. "Bacchante," and was engaged on important patrol work in the North Sea. Later he was stationed with his ship off the West Coast of Africa, in the region of Sierra Leone. He holds the General Service and Victory Medals, and in March 1919 was demobilised.
33, Watford Fields, Watford. 1377/B—1378/B.

DEALEY, E., Private, Northamptonshire Regt.

He joined in 1916, and in the same year was drafted to France, where he took part in the fighting in various engagements, including those at Arras, Ypres and Béthune. He was severely gassed and was invalided home to hospital, and discharged as medically unfit for further duty in April 1918. He holds the General Service and Victory Medals.
38, St. John's Road, Boxmoor, Herts. X1379.

DEAMER, E., Trooper, Hertfordshire Dragoons.

He volunteered in 1915, and in the same year was drafted to Mesopotamia. Whilst in this theatre of war he took part in various important engagements, including those at Kut, Baghdad and Mosul. After the cessation of hostilities he returned home and was demobilised in April 1919, and holds the General Service and Victory Medals.
2, Grove Cottages, Grove Road, Harpenden. 1380.

DEAMER, G., Private, Royal Fusiliers and Labour Corps.

He joined in June 1916, and after his training was sent to the Western Front, where he served on important special duties at Dunkirk. He was mainly engaged in guarding German prisoners at the internment camps, but was also for a time employed at the docks. He was demobilised in January 1919 after his return home, and holds the General Service and Victory Medals.
Stopsley Green, Luton. 1381.

DEAMER, S., Gunner, Royal Field Artillery.

He joined in March 1916, and after his training was drafted to Salonika, where he served in the anti-aircraft section on important duties. He returned home and was demobilised in September 1919, and holds the General Service and Victory Medals.
81, Althorp Road, Luton. 1320.

DEAMER, W. L., Private, R.A.V.C.

He joined in July 1916, and after his training was drafted to Salonika in April of the following year. Whilst in this theatre of war he was engaged in tending sick and wounded horses. In May 1918 he was sent to France and was stationed at Rouen, where he was employed on important duties until April 1919, when he returned home and was demobilised, holding the General Service and Victory Medals.
9, Portland Street, St. Albans. 1382.

DEAN, A., Signal Instructor, R.F.A.

He volunteered in September 1914, and owing to his ability as an instructor was retained to drill and train recruits in signalling duties. He served at various stations and did excellent work, and after the conclusion of hostilities was finally demobilised in March 1919.
108, Judge Street, North Watford. X1383.

DEAN, A., Private, M.G.C. and Bedfordshire Regt.

He joined in May 1917, and in the same year was sent to the Western Front, where he took part in the fighting at Arras, Cambrai and the Somme, and in subsequent engagements until the cessation of hostilities. He was demobilised after his return home in January 1919, and holds the General Service and Victory Medals.
27, Greatham Road, Bushey, Herts. X1384/B.

DEAN, A. E., Corporal, Hertfordshire Regiment.

He volunteered in February 1915, and after a brief training was drafted to France. During his service on the Western Front he took part in the fighting at Hill 60, Ypres, Festubert, Vimy Ridge and Cambrai, and in March 1918 was taken prisoner. He was held in captivity in Germany until after the Armistice, when he was released and returned home and was discharged. He holds the 1914-15 Star, and the General Service and Victory Medals.
27, Greatham Road, Bushey, Herts. X1384/C.

DEAN, A. E., Private, 7th Norfolk Regiment.

He joined in January 1917, and in the following June was drafted to France. After taking part in several important engagements he was killed in action at Gonnelieu on November 20th, 1917, and was entitled to the General Service and Victory Medals.
45, Bailey Street, Luton. 1385.

DEAN, J. H., Private, 1st Hertfordshire Regt.

Mobilised with the Territorials at the outbreak of war, he was drafted to the Western Front in November 1914, and subsequently took part in the first Battle of Ypres in which he was severely wounded. He was invalided home and after protracted hospital treatment was discharged suffering from shell-shock in 1916. He holds the 1914 Star, and the General Service and Victory Medals.
86, Estcourt Road, Watford. X1386/B.

DEAN, J. M., Private, 6th Queen's Own (Royal West Kent Regiment).

He joined in May 1916, and was drafted to France immediately upon the completion of his training, subsequently taking part in fighting on the Somme. He was afterwards invalided home in consequence of ill-health, but on his recovery in May 1917 returned to the Western Front and took part in the Battle of Ypres. In the following July he was severely wounded in action at Arras, and died on the 15th of that month. He was entitled to the General Service and Victory Medals.
86, Estcourt Road, Watford. X1386/A.

DEAN, J. W., Private, Bedfordshire and Hampshire Regiments.

He volunteered in November 1914, and in the following September was sent to Salonika, where he took part in various important operations against the Bulgarians, notably at Vardar Ridge. He was reported missing after an engagement on December 7th, 1915, and was later presumed to have been killed in action on that date. He was entitled to the 1914-15 Star, and the General Service and Victory Medals.
27, Greatham Road, Bushey. X1384/A.

DEAR, A., Rifleman, King's Royal Rifle Corps.

He joined in September 1918, but had not completed his training when hostilities ceased. Afterwards, however, he was sent with the Army of Occupation to Germany, where he was engaged on special duties, and in 1920 was still serving.
89, Highbury Road, Luton. 1388/C.

DEAR, A. J., Rifleman, 8th London Regiment (Post Office Rifles).

He joined in August 1916, and in the following November was sent to the Western Front, where he subsequently took part in several engagements. In July 1917 he was severely wounded whilst in action at Ypres, and in August was invalided home. He was discharged in December of the same year as physically unfit for further service, and holds the General Service and Victory Medals.
The Old Rectory, Mill Lane, Welwyn. 1389.

DEAR, C., Sapper, Royal Engineers.

He volunteered in August 1915, and after his training was engaged on important duties until 1917, when he was sent to Egypt and thence to Palestine. Subsequently he saw service at Jaffa, Beersheba and in the Jordan Valley, and was present at the capture of Jerusalem. He holds the General Service and Victory Medals, and was demobilised after his return to England in August 1919.
89, Highbury Road, Luton. 1388/B.

DEAR, C. J., Private, Royal Army Service Corps.

He joined in September 1916, and after his training was engaged on duties of an important nature at various stations with his unit. He was unsuccessful in obtaining his transfer overseas before the cessation of hostilities, but nevertheless did valuable work until he was demobilised in April 1919.
140, Rushymead, Letchworth. 1591.

DEAR, F., Private, 4th Bedfordshire Regiment.

A serving soldier, he was drafted to the Western Front immediately upon the outbreak of war, and took part in the Retreat from Mons. He also served in the engagements which followed, and was subsequently killed in action at Hill 60 on June 16th, 1915. He was entitled to the Mons Star, and the General Service and Victory Medals.
"Oakdene," Kershaw's Hill, Hitchin. 1856/A.

DEAR, F., Sergeant, 8th London Regiment (Post Office Rifles).

He joined in January 1917, and after his training was engaged on important duties until March 1918, when he was sent to the Western Front. Subsequently he served in the final stages of the war, during which he participated in heavy fighting on the Somme and at St. Quentin and Cambrai. He was demobilised in October 1919, and holds the General Service and Victory Medals.
High Street, Welwyn, Herts. 1390

DEAR, G., Private, R.A.S.C.

Joining in 1916 he was sent to Salonika after his training, and subsequently served on the Struma and the Doiran fronts. Later he was invalided home in consequence of ill-health, and after his recovery was drafted to France, where he did excellent work with his unit during the Retreat and Advance of 1918. Returning to England after the cessation of hostilities he was demobilised in 1919, and holds the General Service and Victory Medals.

4, Pea Hen Yard, St. Andrew Street, Hitchin. 1857/B.

DEAR, H., Sapper, Royal Engineers.

Joining in March 1916, he was sent to France at the conclusion of his training in the following December, and served there for nearly three years. During this time he was engaged on important duties in various sectors, including those of Vimy Ridge, the Somme, Arras, Ypres and Cambrai, and on one occasion was wounded. He was demobilised after his return to England in January 1919, and holds the General Service and Victory Medals.

89, Highbury Road, Luton. 1388/A.

DEAR, P. W., Sapper, Royal Engineers.

He volunteered in September 1914, and in December of the following year was drafted to Egypt. He served in the Canal zone at Ismailia, and later with the Egyptian Expeditionary Force in the Palestine Campaign. He was present at numerous engagements, including those at Gaza, Haïfa, Jaffa, Medjil and Beyrout, and was twice wounded. After the cessation of hostilities he returned to England, and in April 1919 was demobilised, holding the General Service and Victory Medals.

61, Ramridge Road, Luton. 649/B.

DEAR, R., Private, Bedfordshire Regiment.

He joined in March 1917, but after his training was found to be physically unfit for further service, and on these grounds was discharged in the following August.

4, Pea Hen Yard, St. Andrew's Street, Hitchin. 1857/A.

DEAR, R. F., L/Corporal, 6th Queen's (Royal West Surrey Regiment).

He joined in November 1916, and at the conclusion of his training was sent to the Western Front, where he took part in several engagements, including those at Cambrai and Armentières, and was subsequently severely wounded. He returned to England, and after treatment was invalided out of the Service in October 1918. He holds the General Service and Victory Medals.

35, Norman Road, Luton. 1387.

DEARING, W. E., Private, Machine Gun Corps.

Joining in February 1916, he was engaged for nearly two years on important duties at various stations. In January 1918 he was sent to the Western Front, where he took part in heavy fighting during the Retreat and Advance of that year, and after the cessation of hostilities went with the Army of Occupation to Germany. He was demobilised after his return to England in November 1919, and holds the General Service and Victory Medals.

20, Bedford Street, Watford. X1391.

DEEBLE, H., Private, 29th Middlesex Regiment.

He joined in July 1916, and served on various important duties with his unit. He rendered valuable services, but was not successful in obtaining his transfer overseas owing to a physical disability which resulted in his being discharged as unfit for further service in January 1917.

King's Street, Potton. Z1312.

DEELEY, E. W., Driver, R.F.A.

He volunteered in August 1914, and in the following year was sent to Salonika and thence to Egypt and Palestine. He took part in many important engagements, including those at Gaza, Haïfa, Damascus and Aleppo. He returned home and was demobilised in June 1919, and holds the 1914-15 Star, and the General Service and Victory Medals.

71, Victoria Road, North Watford. X1392/A.

DEELEY, J. P., Private, Northumberland Fusiliers.

Joining in 1917 he was in the same year sent to the Western Front. During his service in this theatre of war he took part in much heavy fighting, including that at Cambrai, and was twice wounded. He returned home and was demobilised in December 1919, and holds the General Service and Victory Medals.

71, Victoria Road, North Watford. X1392/B.

DEFOE, W., Private, 3rd Bedfordshire Regt.

He joined in May 1916, and after his training served at various stations on important duties with his unit. He rendered valuable services, but was not successful in obtaining his transfer overseas before the cessation of hostilities. He was demobilised in September 1919.

226, High Street, Watford. X1393/A.

DELL, G. G., Private, R.A.M.C.

He volunteered in September 1915, and in March of the following year was drafted to the Western Front, where he served in important engagements, including those on the Somme and at Ypres and Poperinghe, also in the Retreat and Advance of 1918, and was wounded. He was demobilised in February 1919, and holds the General Service and Victory Medals. 57, Ashby Road, Watford. X1395.

DELL, P., Private, Hertfordshire Regiment.

Volunteering in 1914, he was drafted to the Western Front in the same year. He took part in heavy fighting at the Battles of Ypres, the Somme, Arras and many other important engagements, and was wounded and invalided home. Later he was discharged in April 1918 as medically unfit for further service, and holds the 1914-15 Star, and the General Service and Victory Medals.

1, Cotterall Hill, Hemel Hempstead. X1394/A.

DELLAR, T. C., Private, 2nd Essex Regiment.

He volunteered in September 1914, and in the following year was sent to Gallipoli, where he took part in various engagements, and was wounded. He was invalided home and was discharged in September 1916 as medically unfit, holding the 1914-15 Star, and the General Service and Victory Medals. 37, Essex Street, Luton. 1396.

DELLAR, S. F. (Miss), Special War Worker.

In August 1916 this lady accepted an important position on the staff of the Navy and Army Canteen Board. She rendered valuable services in this connection, and ultimately was appointed manageress of the canteen at the Royal Engineers' Camp, Sandy.

55, Cemetery Street, Biggleswade. Z1305/B.

DELLER, A. W., Private, 2nd Bedfordshire Regt.

He volunteered in December 1914, and having completed his training was sent to the Western Front in the following year. While in this theatre of war he fought in several engagements, including those at Festubert and Loos, and was killed in action on the Somme in July 1916. He was entitled to the General Service and Victory Medals.

Waterloo Terrace, Hitchin Street, Biggleswade. Z1574/A.

DELLER, G., Sergeant, R.M.L.I. and R.A.F.

He volunteered in August 1914, and in the following year was sent to Egypt and thence to the Dardanelles. He was afterwards transferred to France, where he took part in the Battle of Arras and other important engagements, and was wounded. He was demobilised in 1920, and holds the 1914-15 Star, and the General Service and Victory Medals.

14, Manchester Place, Dunstable. 1397.

DENHAM, W. J., Private, Queen's Own (Royal West Kent Regiment).

Volunteering in September 1914, he was sent to the Western Front in December of the same year. He took part in severe fighting at Loos, the Somme, Ypres, the Marne and other important engagements, and was twice wounded and gassed. He was demobilised in April 1919, and holds the 1914-15 Star, and the General Service and Victory Medals.

70, Estcourt Road, Watford. X1398.

DENNER, A. (Mrs.), Special War Worker.

In July 1917 this lady accepted an important position on the staff of the Navy and Army Canteen Board. She rendered valuable services, and the manner in which she carried out the responsible duties assigned to her was most praiseworthy.

21, Waterside, King's Langley. X1399/B.

DENNER, S., Private, Royal Army Service Corps.

He joined in October 1916, and after his training served at various stations on important duties with his unit. He rendered valuable services, but was not successful in obtaining his transfer overseas owing to being medically unfit for active service. He was discharged in October 1916 owing to his physical disabilities.

21, Waterside, King's Langley. X1399/A.

DENNER, S., Special War Worker.

During the war he held an important position on the entertainment staff of the Navy and Army Canteen Board. His untiring efforts to provide amusement for the troops in their hours of recreation were greatly appreciated by the men, and the services which he rendered in this connection were of the utmost value.

21, Waterside, King's Langley. X1399/C.

DENNETT, H., Private, 5th Northamptonshire Regiment.

He volunteered in 1915, and in December of the same year was drafted to the Western Front, where he took part in the Battles of the Somme, Arras, Cambrai and many other engagements, and was twice wounded. He returned home and was discharged in September 1918 owing to his wounds, and holds the 1914-15 Star, and the General Service and Victory Medals. 23, Smart Street, Luton. 1400.

DENNIS, H., Gunner, Royal Garrison Artillery.
He joined in August 1916, and after his training served at various stations on important duties with his battery. He rendered valuable services, but was not successful in obtaining his transfer overseas before the cessation of hostilities owing to his medical unfitness for active service. He was demobilised in February 1919.
4, Fox & Crown, Biggleswade Road, Potton.   Z1303.

DENNIS, J., Sergeant, Royal Field Artillery.
He was mobilised in August 1914, and was sent to France in the same month. He took part in the Retreat from Mons, and the Battles of the Aisne, La Bassée, Ypres, Hill 60, Loos, the Somme and Messines, and was killed whilst in charge of a party taking ammunition up to the line on the Ypres Front on August 15th, 1917. He was entitled to the Mons Star, and the General Service and Victory Medals.
8, New Town, Potton.   Z1308/B.

DENNIS, P. C., Stoker, R.N., H.M.S. " Dunedin."
He joined in May 1918 and during his period of service in the war was engaged on patrol duty off the Norwegian coast. He also took part in the bombardment of the south Russian coast, and served in the Baltic for a time. He was still serving in 1920, and holds the General Service and Victory Medals.
Brook End, Potton.   Z1307.

DENNIS, T., Private, The Buffs (East Kent Regiment).
Joining in June 1918 he was sent in October of the same year to France, where he took part in severe fighting at Cambrai and Amiens. He was wounded in November 1918 and invalided home, and in February 1919 was discharged as medically unfit, holding the General Service and Victory Medals.
8, New Town, Potton.   Z1308/A.

DENNIS, V. L., Rifleman, Rifle Brigade.
Volunteering in May 1915, he was sent to France in the same year. During his service overseas he took part in severe fighting on the Somme, and in various other engagements. He was killed in action near Albert on October 23rd, 1916, and was entitled to the 1914–15 Star, and the General Service and Victory Medals.
8, Muriel Avenue, Watford.   X1401.

DENNIS, W. A., Private, Tank Corps.
He volunteered in January 1915, and in June of the following year was drafted to the Western Front, where he took part in many important engagements, including the Battles of Arras and Ypres. He was demobilised in February 1919, and holds the General Service and Victory Medals.
29, Marsh Road, Leagrave.   1402.

DENNIS, W. W., Trooper, Bedfordshire Lancers.
He volunteered in August 1914, and after his training served at various stations on important duties with his unit. He rendered valuable service, but was not successful in obtaining his transfer overseas, and was finally discharged as medically unfit for further service in November 1914.
24, Back Street, Biggleswade.   Z1577/B.

DENNY, W. E., Sergeant, Royal Engineers.
He volunteered in February 1915, and in the following July was drafted overseas. He served on the Western Front and took part in various engagements, being in charge of trenching and mining parties. He was demobilised in January 1919, and holds the 1914–15 Star, and the General Service and Victory Medals.
26, Saulbury Road, Linslade, Bucks.   1598.

DENT, W., Private, Northamptonshire Regiment.
He volunteered at the outbreak of war, and after completing his training was drafted to the Western Front. He served at Neuve Chapelle, Festubert, Loos, Arras, Ypres and Cambrai, during much heavy fighting, and after the cessation of hostilities, proceeded to Germany with the Army of Occupation on the Rhine. He was demobilised in January 1919, and holds the 1914–15 Star, and the General Service and Victory Medals.
Beeston, Sandy, Beds.   Z1573.

DENTON, A., L/Corporal, Suffolk Regiment.
He joined in October 1916, and in the following year was drafted to Egypt and thence to Palestine, where he took part in various engagements, including that at Gaza and was present at the capture of Jerusalem. He returned home and was demobilised in January 1920, and holds the General Service and Victory Medals.
Goswell End, Harlington.   1408/B.

DENTON, A. P., Private, R.A.S.C. (M.T.)
Joining in January 1917 he was sent to the Western Front in May of the following year, and was engaged as a motor driver in the Cambrai sector, transporting ammunition and supplies. He was demobilised in November 1919, and holds the General Service and Victory Medals.
Luton Road, Toddington.   1404/A.

DENTON, C., Private, Bedfordshire Regiment.
He volunteered in May 1915, and after his training served at various stations on important duties with his unit. He rendered valuable services, but was not successful in obtaining his transfer overseas. He was discharged as medically unfit for further service in March 1916.
Near Post Office, Harlington.   1405.

DENTON, G. F., Shoeing Smith, R.E.
He volunteered in September 1914, and after his training served at various stations on important duties in connection with his trade. He rendered valuable services, but was not successful in obtaining his transfer overseas. He was discharged as medically unfit for further service in May 1918.
125, New Town Street, Luton.   1406.

DENTON, H. J., Sergeant, Royal Air Force.
He volunteered in January 1915, and in the following July was sent to France, where he served in numerous sectors of the front, including Loos, Vimy Ridge, the Somme, Arras and Ypres. He was demobilised in March 1919, and holds the General Service and Victory Medals.
Pretoria Cottages, Harlington, Beds.   128/A.

DENTON, J. H., Private, R.A.S.C. (M.T.)
He joined in September 1916, and in May of the following year was drafted to Salonika and served on the Vardar and Struma fronts. He was engaged as a motor driver, transporting guns, ammunition and supplies, and rendered valuable services. He was demobilised in October 1919, and holds the General Service and Victory Medals.
Luton Road, Toddington.   1404/B.

DENTON, W., Sergeant-Major, R.A.F.
Volunteering in January 1915 he proceeded to the Western Front in the following July, and was present during the severe fighting at Loos, Vimy Ridge, the Somme, Arras, Passchendaele and Cambrai. He was demobilised in March 1919, and holds the General Service and Victory Medals.
Pretoria Cottages, Harlington, Beds.   128/B.

DENTON, W., Gunner, Royal Garrison Artillery.
He volunteered in December 1915, and in the following year was drafted to the Western Front, where he took part in numerous engagements, including those on the Somme and at Arras, Ypres, Cambrai and St. Quentin. He was demobilised in January 1919, and holds the General Service and Victory Medals.
2, Nursing Cottages, Old Bedford Road, Luton.   1407/B.

DENTON, W., Private, Bedfordshire Regiment.
Volunteering in January 1915 he was sent to France in the following July and took part in the heavy fighting at Vimy Ridge, the Somme, Arras, Ypres and Cambrai, and was twice wounded. He returned home and was discharged in October 1918 owing to his wounds, and holds the 1914–15 Star, and the General Service and Victory Medals.
Goswell End, Harlington.   1408/A.

DENTON, W. (M.S.M.), Sergeant-Major, R.A.F.
Volunteering in January 1915 he was sent to France in the following year. He was present at various engagements, including those at Arras and Ypres, and was awarded the Meritorious Service Medal for devotion to duty. He was demobilised in March 1919, and holds the General Service, Victory and Meritorious Service Medals.
Hornbeam House, Grange Road, Leagrave.   1403/A.

DEPLEDGE, R. C., Corporal, Northumberland Fusiliers.
Volunteering in October 1914, he was later drafted to the Western Front, where he took part in the severe fighting in the Ypres, Arras, Albert and Cambrai sectors, and was wounded. He was invalided home and discharged owing to his wounds in July 1917, and holds the General Service and Victory Medals.
5, Edward Street, Luton.   1409.

DERBYSHIRE, E., Private, King's (Liverpool Regiment) and Machine Gun Corps.
He volunteered in August 1915, and after his training was engaged at various stations on important duties with his unit. He rendered valuable services as guard, but was not successful in obtaining his transfer overseas while hostilities continued. He was discharged in March 1918.
49, Bermack Row, Apsley End.   X1410/A.

DESBOROUGH, A. G., Private, Bedfordshire Regiment.
He volunteered in 1915, and after his training was drafted to the Western Front, where he took part in the Battles of Arras, Ypres and Passchendaele, and other important engagements. He returned home, and was discharged in June 1918 in consequence of his service, and holds the General Service and Victory Medals.
2, Lowbell Lane, London Colney, St. Albans.   X1411/C.

DESBOROUGH, G., Corporal, Royal Engineers.
Volunteering in January 1915, he was later sent to the Western Front. He was engaged on important duties on the line of communication at the Loos, Ypres and Vimy Ridge fronts, and was wounded. He was invalided home and discharged owing to his injuries in July 1916, and holds the 1914-15 Star, and the General Service and Victory Medals.
2, Lowbell Lane, London Colney, near St. Albans. X1411/B.

DESBOROUGH, G. W., Driver, R.F.A.
He was serving at the outbreak of war, and was afterwards sent to the Western Front. He took part in the severe fighting at Arras, Ypres, Cambrai and in many other engagements, and was wounded. He returned home and was demobilised in October 1919, and holds the General Service and Victory Medals.
2, Lowbell Lane, London Colney, near St. Albans. X1411/A

DESORMEAUX, V., Sergeant, R.A.S.C.
He was serving at the outbreak of war and in the following year was drafted to the Western Front. He was engaged in the transport of supplies to the various fronts, and in bringing down the wounded to the Clearing Stations. In these capacities he rendered valuable services until hostilities ceased. He was demobilised in November 1919, and holds the 1914-15 Star, and the General Service and Victory Medals.
30, Elfrida Road, Watford.   X1412.

DEVERELL, S. G., Private, R.A.S.C.
He volunteered in August 1915, and after his training was engaged on important duties with his unit until July 1917, when he was drafted to the Western Front. He was present at numerous important engagements until hostilities ceased, including those at Ypres and Armentières. He was demobilised in March 1919, and holds the General Service and Victory Medals.
Eaton Bray, Dunstable.   1413.

DEVEREUX, A. E., Sergeant, Royal Welch Fusiliers and Tank Corps.
He volunteered in December 1914 and was retained at various stations for training and gymnastic purposes, until he was sent to France in September 1916. After being transferred to the Tank Corps he saw much service on the Arras, Ypres, Messines and Cambrai fronts. He was severely wounded and gassed in 1918 whilst in action in a Whippet Tank on the Somme front, and after being invalided home was eventually discharged in February 1919, holding the General Service and Victory Medals.
Campton, Shefford.   Z1414/A.

DEVEREUX, E., Corporal, 8th Bedfordshire Regt.
He volunteered in October 1914, and in the following year was drafted to the Western Front, where he took part in much severe fighting at Loos and Albert. He was killed in action near Ypres on March 16th, 1916, and was buried near the Menin Road. He was entitled to the 1914-15 Star, and the General Service and Victory Medals.
Campton, Shefford.   Z1414/B.

DEVEREUX, H., Private, 5th Bedfordshire and 7th Essex Regiments.
He volunteered in June 1915, and after his training was retained at various stations on important duties with his unit. He rendered valuable services, but was not successful in obtaining his transfer overseas before the cessation of hostilities. He was demobilised in March 1919.
16, Swiss Cottage, Campton, Shefford.   Z1415.

DEW, S., Driver, Royal Engineers.
He volunteered in July 1915, and in September of the same year was drafted to the Western Front, where he took part in many important engagements, including those of the Somme, Lens, Loos and Béthune. He was demobilised in May 1919 after returning home, and holds the 1914-15 Star, and the General Service and Victory Medals.
8, Crown Terrace, Watford.   X1417.

DEWAR, C. D., Private, Queen's Own (Royal West Kent Regiment).
Joining in June 1918 he went through a course of training, after which he was sent to the Western Front, where he was engaged on motor transport duties with his unit. He had previously served voluntarily in France from January 1915 to June 1916 with the British Ambulance Committee, and was awarded the Croix-de-Guerre for rescuing French wounded under fire. He was demobilised in May 1919, and holds the General Service and Victory Medals.
23, High Street, Lilley, near Luton.   1416.

DIBSDALE, F., Trumpeter, R.F.A.
He volunteered in August 1914, and proceeded to France in November of the following year. In February 1916 he was transferred to Egypt, and afterwards served in the Palestine campaign at Gaza and Jerusalem. Whilst in this theatre of war he contracted an illness from which he died on November 23rd, 1918. He was entitled to the 1914-15 Star, and the General Service and Victory Medals.
11, Arthur Road, St. Albans.   X1418.

DICKENS, A., Sapper, Royal Engineers.
Volunteering in October 1914, he proceeded in July of the following year to France, where he took a prominent part in the Battles of the Somme, Arras, Ypres, Passchendaele and Cambrai and various other engagements. He was demobilised in March 1919 after returning home, and holds the 1914-15 Star, and the General Service and Victory Medals.
22, Bedford Road, Houghton Regis, near Dunstable. 1424.

DICKENS, A., Private, 7th Bedfordshire Regt.
Volunteering in August 1914, he was drafted to France in April of the following year, and took part in much heavy fighting at the Somme, Arras, Ypres and Passchendaele, and was twice wounded. He was demobilised in March 1919, and holds the 1914-15 Star, and the General Service and Victory Medals.
22, Bedford Road, Houghton Regis, near Dunstable. 1419.

DICKENS, F., Private, 5th Bedfordshire Regt.
He volunteered in September 1914, and was drafted to Egypt in December of the following year. After serving in the Canal zone until February 1917 he proceeded towards Palestine. He took part in many engagements during his service, including those at El Arish, Rafa, Jaffa and Gaza. He was killed in action in November 1917, and was entitled to the 1914-15 Star, and the General Service and Victory Medals.
3, Harcourt Street, Luton.   1420/A.

DICKENS, G., Private, Bedfordshire Regiment.
Volunteering in 1914, he was immediately afterwards sent to France, where he took part in the Retreat from Mons, and the Battles of the Marne, Festubert, Loos, the Somme, Arras, Cambrai and many other important engagements. He was killed in action in 1918, and was entitled to the Mons Star, and the General Service and Victory Medals.
8, Ivel Terrace, Biggleswade.   Z1315/A.

DICKENS, H., Private, Bedfordshire and Hertfordshire Regiments.
He joined in April 1916, and after his training served on various important duties with his unit until 1918, when he was drafted to India. He rendered valuable service there until he contracted fever, and in 1919 was invalided home. He was still serving in 1920.
22, Bedford Road, Houghton Regis, near Dunstable. 1421.

DICKENS, W. A., Sergeant-Instructor, Bedfordshire Regiment.
Having previously served, he was mobilised in August 1914 and was drafted to India. He was engaged while there on important instructional duties at various garrison stations, including Poona, Rawal Pindi and Bangalore, and rendered valuable services. He was still serving in 1920, and holds the General Service and Victory Medals.
Hornbeam House, Grange Road, Leagrave.   1403/B.

DICKERSON, F., Private, 2/6th South Staffordshire Regiment.
He volunteered in November 1914, and after having completed his training was engaged on important duties with his unit at various stations. He rendered valuable service, but owing to being medically unfit for duty abroad was unable to procure his transfer to a theatre of war. He was discharged in April 1915.
New Marford, Wheathampstead, Herts.   1422.

DICKERSON, H., Rifleman, Rifle Brigade.
He volunteered in March 1915, and after his training was retained at various stations on important guard duties with his unit. He rendered valuable services, but was not successful in obtaining his transfer overseas before fighting ceased. He was discharged in August 1917 in consequence of injuries received during the course of his duties.
New Marford, Wheathampstead.   1423

DICKERSON, W., Rifleman, Royal Irish Rifles.
He joined in August 1916, and in February of the following
year was drafted to the Western Front, where he saw much
service in the Ypres and Somme sectors. In consequence
of severe illness he was invalided home, and was discharged
in December 1917 as medically unfit for further service.
He holds the General Service and Victory Medals.
Rosellen Cottages, Potton.   Z1313.

DICKINSON, A., Trooper, 1st Herts. Dragoons.
Volunteering in May 1915, he was drafted in January of the
following year to Egypt and Palestine, where he took part
in many important engagements until the close of the campaign, including those at Gaza and Jaffa. He returned
home and was demobilised in May 1919, holding the General
Service and Victory Medals.
49, Waterside, King's Langley.   X1426/A.

DICKINSON, A. M., Sapper, Royal Engineers.
Volunteering in June 1916 he was sent to Mesopotamia in
the same year, and served on the Amara and Kut-el-Amara
fronts. He was engaged on important duties connected
with his branch of the service, particularly in connection
with bridge-building, and did valuable work until the
campaign was over. He returned home and was demobilised in February 1919, and holds the General Service and
Victory Medals.
27, Camp View Road, St. Albans.   X1425.

DICKINSON, S., Private, R.A.S.C. (M.T.)
He volunteered in June 1915, and in the same year was
drafted to the Western Front. He was engaged as a motor-
driver in the transport of supplies to the various fronts, and
rendered valuable services. He was severely wounded at
Ficheux during an air raid in August 1918, and lost his left
leg. He was subsequently discharged in January 1920,
and holds the 1914–15 Star, and the General Service and
Victory Medals.
49, Waterside, King's Langley.   X1426/B.

DICKSON, G. L., Private, R.A.S.C.
He joined in November 1916, and in the same month proceeded to France, where he rendered valuable service in the
Beaumont-Hamel, Somme, Bullecourt, Ypres and Cambrai
areas. He remained abroad until after hostilities ceased,
and on his return home in June 1919 was demobilised,
holding the General Service and Victory Medals.
28, Chatsworth Road, Luton.   1427.

DIGGINS, E. G., Private, 4th Bedfordshire Regt.
After volunteering in November 1915, and going through
a course of training, he proceeded in July of the following
year to the Western Front, and took part in much severe
fighting at Arras, Ypres, Cambrai and Neuve Chapelle.
He was killed in action at Achiet-le-Petit on August 23rd,
1918, and was entitled to the General Service and Victory
Medals.
Hall End, Maulden, Ampthill.   1858/A.

DIGGINS, H. T., Private, 4th Bedfordshire Regt.
He volunteered in November 1915, and in July of the
following year was drafted to the Western Front, where he
took part in numerous engagements in the Somme Offensive.
He was killed in action on the Somme on November 13th,
1916, after four months' service overseas, and was entitled
to the General Service and Victory Medals.
Hall End, Maulden, Ampthill.   1858/B.

DIGGINS, O. A., Corporal, 1st King's Shropshire
Light Infantry.
Volunteering in November 1914 he was retained on important
duties with his unit until March 1918, when he was drafted
to the Western Front. He took part in numerous engagements in the Retreat and Advance of 1918, including those
near Arras, Ypres, the Marne and the Aisne. He was
demobilised in February 1919 after returning home, and
holds the General Service and Victory Medals.
Hall End, Maulden, near Ampthill.   1858/C.

DILKS, J. A., Private, Royal Army Service Corps.
Volunteering in 1914, he was in the following year sent to
the Western Front, where he fought in numerous engagements, including those at Ypres, the Somme, Arras, Cambrai
and Amiens. He returned home and was demobilised in
March 1919, and holds the 1914–15 Star, and the General
Service and Victory Medals.
100, Villiers Road, Oxhey.   X1428.

DILLEY, A., Private, 5th Sherwood Foresters.
He joined in October 1916, and was drafted to France in
February of the following year. He took part in much severe
fighting in the Somme sector, and at Ypres and Cambrai, and
was wounded. He was taken prisoner near Bullecourt in
March 1918, but on his release returned home and was
demobilised in February 1919. He holds the General Service
and Victory Medals.
8, Milton Road, Luton.   1429/C.

DILLEY, A. J., Private, R.A.M.C. and Gordon
Highlanders.
Volunteering in October 1915 he proceeded to France in the
following year, where he was in action at Ypres, Arras and
Albert. He was severely wounded on the Somme in March
1918, and in consequence lost a hand. He was discharged
in December 1919, holding the General Service and Victory
Medals, but was still under hospital treatment in 1920.
Ampthill Road, Shefford.   Z1321/B.

DILLEY, C., Private, Grenadier Guards.
He was mobilised in August 1914, and was immediately
afterwards sent to France, where he took part in the Retreat
from Mons and the Battles of Albert, Festubert, Loos, the
Somme, Arras, Cambrai and many other engagements until
hostilities ceased. He was demobilised in March 1919 on
the completion of 12 years' valuable service, and holds the
Mons Star, and the General Service and Victory Medals.
Clifton Road, Shefford.   Z1430.

DILLEY, D., A/Corporal, 1st Bedfordshire Regt.
Volunteering in July 1915 he was retained after his training
on important duties with his unit until December 1916, when
he was drafted to France. While on this front he took part
in the fighting in various engagements, and was killed in
action near Lens on April 23rd, 1917. He was entitled to
the General Service and Victory Medals.
8, Milton Road, Luton.   1429/B.

DILLEY, E., Private, Bedfordshire Regiment;
and Machine Gun Corps.
He volunteered in May 1915, and in March of the following
year was drafted to the Western Front. He was in action at
St. Eloi, Albert and the Somme, and being wounded was
invalided home in September 1916. On his recovery he
returned to France in January of the following year, and was
in action on the Somme, when he was again wounded. After
his recovery he was transferred to the Machine Gun Corps
and sent to France for the third time, and served at Cambrai
and Ypres. He was eventually demobilised in May 1919,
and holds the General Service and Victory Medals.
Campton, Shefford.   Z1321/A.

DILLEY, E. G., Private, Northamptonshire Regt.
He joined in July 1918, and after his training was engaged
at various stations on important duties with his unit. He
rendered valuable services, but was not successful in obtaining
his transfer overseas before the cessation of hostilities. He
was demobilised in November 1919.
Clifton Road, Shefford.   Z1431.

DILLEY, W., Private, Royal Army Medical Corps.
He volunteered in October 1915, and in September of the
following year was drafted to the Western Front, where he
did valuable work in the Battles of Arras and Cambrai. In
November 1917 he was transferred to Italy, and was engaged
in the last Advance. He returned home and was demobilised
in April 1919, and holds the General Service and Victory
Medals.
14, Milton Road, Luton.   1429/A.

DILLINGHAM, G. W., Private, R.A.M.C.
He joined in August 1916, and was drafted to France in April
of the following year, where he was engaged on important
duties in the field and in hospital for a period of two years.
While in this theatre of war he saw much fighting in the
Ypres, Albert, Arras and Cambrai sectors. Returning home
he was demobilised in July 1919, and holds the General
Service and Victory Medals.
Arthur Street, Ampthill.   1568/A.

DILLINGHAM, J. T., Private, R.A.M.C.
He volunteered in October 1915, and having completed his
training was sent to Mesopotamia in May of the following
year. While on this front he did excellent medical work
in many engagements on the Tigris, including those at
Kut-el-Amara and Baghdad. He remained overseas until
after the cessation of hostilities, and on his return home was
demobilised in October 1919, holding the General Service
and Victory Medals.
Arthur Street, Ampthill.   1568/C.

DILLINGHAM, P., Private, 389th Home Service
Labour Corps.
He joined in October 1916, and after a course of training
was engaged at various stations on work of importance with
his unit. His duties, which were of a responsible nature,
were carried out with great care and efficiency, and he
rendered valuable services. He was demobilised in July
1919.
31, King's Road, Luton.   1432.

DILLINGHAM, S. A., Corporal, R.A.M.C.

Joining in 1916, he went through his course of training and afterwards was retained on important duties at various hospitals with his unit. He was not successful in obtaining his transfer overseas before the cessation of hostilities, but rendered most valuable services. He was still serving in 1920.   84, Hartley Road, Luton.   1433.

DILLINGHAM, W., Corporal, Northumberland Fusiliers.

He volunteered in September 1914, and after his training was retained on important duties with his unit until September 1918, when he was drafted to the Western Front. He took part in many engagements in the last stages of hostilities, including those in the Somme, Kemmel Hill and the Marne areas. He was demobilised in February 1919, and holds the General Service and Victory Medals.
79, Chase Street, Luton.   1434.

DILLINGHAM, W. D., Trooper, 1st Scottish Horse.

He joined in April 1916, and after his training served in Ireland with his unit on important duties. He rendered valuable services, but was not successful in obtaining his transfer to a theatre of war while hostilities continued. When he was returning home on leave on October 10th, 1918, his vessel, the "Leinster," was torpedoed by a German submarine and he was drowned.
High Street, Westoning, Ampthill.   1575/B—1568/B.

DIMMOCK, A. G., Private, Bedfordshire Regt.

He volunteered in May 1915, and in the same year was drafted to the Western Front, where he took part in the Battles of the Somme, Arras, Ypres, Passchendaele and Cambrai, and other engagements up to the cessation of hostilities, and was three times wounded. He was demobilised in February 1919, and holds the 1914-15 Star, and the General Service and Victory Medals.
51, Dordans Road, Leagrave.   1436B.

DIMMOCK, A. J., Sapper, Royal Engineers (E.A.)

He volunteered in July 1915, and after his training was drafted to the Western Front, where he was engaged on special railway work in various sectors. His duties, which demanded a high degree of skill, were carried out with great efficiency. During his period of service overseas he was wounded in October 1918. He was demobilised in January 1919 and holds the General Service and Victory Medals.
1, Park Road West, Luton.   1435.

DIMMOCK, A. W., Private, R.A.M.C.

He joined in 1916, and after completing his training was engaged on various important hospital duties with his unit. He rendered valuable services, but was not successful in obtaining his transfer overseas before the cessation of hostilities. He was demobilised in August 1919.
The Cottages, Napsbury.   X1437.

DIMMOCK, C., Private, 4th Bedfordshire Regt.

He was serving at the outbreak of war, having enlisted in 1909, and was immediately afterwards sent to France, where he took part in numerous engagements, including those at the Marne, the Aisne, Ypres, Hill 60, Arras, Cambrai and Welsh Ridge. He was demobilised in August 1919 after returning home, and holds the 1914 Star, and the General Service and Victory Medals.
85, Lea Road, Luton.   1438/A.

DIMMOCK, F., Private, Royal Fusiliers.

He joined in January 1916, and in April of the same year proceeded to the Western Front, where he took part in much severe fighting at Albert, the Somme, Arras, Ypres, Passchendaele and Cambrai. He was demobilised in October 1919, and holds the General Service and Victory Medals.
51, Dordans Road, Leagrave.   1436/A.

DIMMOCK, H., L/Corporal, R.E. (E.A.)

He volunteered at the outbreak of war, and in July 1915 was drafted overseas. He was engaged on the Western Front on important duties in mining, road-making, and trench-making, especially in the Somme area. He was demobilised in March 1919, and holds the 1914-15 Star, and the General Service and Victory Medals.
62, Church Street, Leighton Buzzard.   1600.

DIMMOCK, H., Private, 5th Bedfordshire Regt.

He volunteered in November 1914, and in the following year was drafted to the Dardanelles, where he took part in the landing at Anzac and Suvla Bay, and in many subsequent engagements until the Evacuation of the Peninsula. In January 1917 he was transferred to the Western Front, where he served in the Battles of Vimy Ridge, Passchendaele, Cambrai and the second Battle of the Somme. During his service overseas he was twice wounded. He returned to England and was demobilised in February 1919, and holds the 1914-15 Star, and the General Service and Victory Medals.
51, Dordans Road, Leagrave.   1436/C.

DIMMOCK, H., Sapper, Royal Engineers.

He joined in March 1917, and in the following August was drafted to the Western Front. During his service in France he was engaged on highly important duties, wiring, trenching, pontooning and maintaining communication in connection with the operations that were being carried on, especially at Arras, Ypres, Cambrai and the Somme. He was demobilised after his return to England in April 1919, and holds the General Service and Victory Medals.
Luton Road, Toddington.   1439.

DIMMOCK, J., Private, Royal Fusiliers and Royal Air Force.

He joined in March 1916, and in the following November was drafted to France. During his service on the Western Front he was severely wounded near Arras. After six months' treatment at home he returned to France in 1918, and was transferred to the Observation Balloon Section of the Royal Air Force. He served in the Cambrai sector until the conclusion of hostilities, and was demobilised in April 1919, holding the General Service and Victory Medals.
66, Bassett Road, Leighton Buzzard.   2707/A.

DIMMOCK, L., Private, 5th Bedfordshire Regt. and Machine Gun Corps.

Volunteering in September 1914, he was drafted to the Dardanelles and was engaged at Anzac and Suvla Bay. He was afterwards transferred to Egypt and Palestine and took part in various engagements, including those at Gaza, Haifa, Damascus and Beyrout. He returned home and was demobilised in February 1919, and holds the 1914-15 Star, and the General Service and Victory Medals.
85, Lea Road, Luton.   1438/B.

DIMMOCK, P., Private, 4th Bedfordshire Regt.

He joined in November 1916, and in the following February proceeded overseas. During his service in France he took part in the Battles of Vimy Ridge, Messines, Passchendaele, Lens, Cambrai, and the second Battle of the Somme, and suffered from fever, and was gassed during this period. He was demobilised after his return home in December 1919, and holds the General Service and Victory Medals.
37, John Street, Luton.   1440.

DIMMOCK, W., Sapper, Royal Engineers.

He joined in February 1917, and later in the same year was drafted to the Western Front. During his service in France he was engaged as an engine-driver and in other important duties in connection with the railways until the cessation of hostilities. He returned home and was demobilised in December 1919, holding the General Service and Victory Medals.
25, York Street, Luton,   1442.

DIMMOCK, W. A., Private, East Surrey Regt.

He joined in March 1916, and after a short training was drafted to France in the following May. He took part in several engagements until December, when he was transferred to Italy. Whilst in this theatre of war he served in numerous important operations against the Austrians until the cessation of hostilities. He then went into Germany with the Army of Occupation, and was stationed at Cologne until October 1919, when he returned to England and was demobilised. He holds the General Service and Victory Medals.
23, Longmire Road, St. Albans.   X1441.

DIMMOCK, W. M., Private, Essex Regiment.

He volunteered in October 1915, and in the following April was sent to France. After only about a month's service on the Western Front he was very severely wounded in an engagement near Ypres in May 1916, and was invalided home. A year later he died from the effects of his injuries on May 27th, 1917. He was entitled to the General Service and Victory Medals.
3, Black Horse Lane, Sunnyside, Hitchin.   1588.

DIMSFORD, R., L/Corporal, 3rd London Regt. (Royal Fusiliers).

He was mobilised at the outbreak of hostilities and was immediately drafted to France, where he took part in the Retreat from Mons. He fought also at Albert, Neuve Chapelle, Hill 60, Ypres, Festubert, Loos, the Somme, Arras, Lens and Cambrai, and other engagements until hostilities ceased. He was demobilised in June 1919 after returning home, and holds the Mons Star, and the General Service and Victory Medals.
Poultry Cottages, King's Langley.   X1443.

DINGLEY, G., Private, Bedfordshire and Northamptonshire Regiments.

He volunteered in December 1915, and in the following July, on completing his training, was drafted to the Western Front. During his service in France he took part in the severe fighting in the Somme Offensive, and was afterwards killed in action on February 17th, 1917. He was entitled to the General Service and Victory Medals.
7, Windmill Road, Luton.   1444/B.

DINGLEY, H., Private, 5th Bedfordshire Regt.
Volunteering at the commencement of hostilities he was drafted to Egypt in 1915, and afterwards advanced into Palestine with General Allenby's Forces. Whilst in this theatre of war he took part in the fighting at Gaza, Haïfa, Acre, Damascus and Aleppo. He returned to England and was demobilised after five years' service in August 1919, holding the 1914–15 Star, and the General Service and Victory Medals. 7, Windmill Road, Luton. 1444/A.

DINHAM, W. A., Gunner, Royal Field Artillery.
He volunteered in May 1915, and in the following year, after being retained for a time on important duties, was drafted overseas. He took part in much heavy fighting at the Somme, Ypres and Arras, and was wounded. He was later killed in action near Cambrai on April 3rd, 1918, and was entitled to the General Service and Victory Medals. 17, Summer Street, Leighton Buzzard. 1586/A.

DINSEY, W. J., Private, 3rd Lancashire Fusiliers.
He joined in 1917, and in the same year, on the conclusion of his training was drafted to France. In this theatre of war he took part in many important engagements, including those at Bullecourt, Messines, Cambrai and the Somme, and was gassed and wounded during the Offensive in March 1918. He was demobilised in January 1919, and holds the General Service and Victory Medals. Manor Road, Barton, near Ampthill. T1579.

DINTINGER, C., Private, 36th Regiment of Infantry.
He joined the French Army in 1915, and after his training was sent to the fighting front. During his service he took part in engagements at Ypres, Arras and Verdun, and was awarded the Croix de Guerre for conspicuous gallantry in the Field. He was killed in action on July 11th, 1918, and was entitled to the Victory Medal. 19, Belgrave Avenue, Watford. X1445/B.

DIX, E. F., Sergeant, Tank Corps.
He joined in February 1916, and after his training was retained with his unit on important duties as an Instructor of recruits. He rendered valuable services, but was not able to secure his transfer overseas before the cessation of hostilities. He was demobilised in December 1919. 6, Grover Road, Oxhey. X1446/B.

DIX, F., Private, Yorkshire Regiment.
He volunteered in 1915, and on the completion of his training was drafted to France in the same year. While overseas he saw much service at Ypres, Loos, Albert, Vimy Ridge and Le Cateau, where he was severely wounded. He afterwards died from his injuries on October 29th, 1918. He was entitled to the 1914–15 Star, and the General Service and Victory Medals. Church End, Westoning, Ampthill. 1576/B.

DIX, G. R., Private, 4th Bedfordshire Regiment.
He was mobilised in August 1914, and immediately proceeded to France. While in this theatre of war he took part in the Retreat from Mons and the Battles of Hill 60, Festubert, Loos the Somme, the Ancre, Arras and Cambrai. He was severely wounded during his service, and died of his injuries on February 8th, 1920. He was entitled to the Mons Star, and the General Service and Victory Medals. Church End, Westoning, Ampthill. 1576/A.

DIX, H. W., Private, Royal Army Service Corps.
He joined in July 1916, and on the completion of his training was engaged at various stations on important duties in connection with transport. He did excellent work, but on medical grounds was not successful in obtaining a transfer overseas while hostilities continued. He was demobilised in December 1919. 6, Grover Road, Oxhey. X1446/A.

DIXON, C., Pioneer, Royal Engineers.
He volunteered in May 1915, and after his training was drafted to the Western Front in the following January. During his service in France he was engaged on important duties in the forward areas whilst operations were in progress, notably on the Somme, and was killed there in February 26th, 1917, being buried at Armentières. He was entitled to the General Service and Victory Medals. 36, King's Road, Hitchin. 1859.

DIXON, J., Private, R.A.V.C.
Volunteering in October 1914, he was sent overseas a year later and served on important veterinary duties in the Ypres and Arras sectors until March 1916. He was then drafted to Salonika, and from there to Egypt in 1917. Whilst on the Palestine Front he did valuable work in attendance on the sick and wounded horses at Haïfa, Jaffa, Jericho, Jordan and in other sectors until the cessation of hostilities. He returned home and was demobilised in April 1919, and holds the 1914–15 Star, and the General Service and Victory Medals. 11, Bardwell Road, St. Albans. X1447.

DIXON, S. G., Trooper, Herts. Dragoons.
He volunteered at the commencement of hostilities, and in 1915 proceeded first to France and later to the Dardanelles, where he took part in the landing at Suvla Bay and in subsequent engagements until the evacuation of the Peninsula. He was then drafted to Egypt, and advancing into Palestine was severely wounded in the first Battle of Gaza. Subsequently he returned home and was demobilised in April 1919, holding the 1914–15 Star, and the General Service and Victory Medals. 94, St. Mary's Road, Watford. X1448/A.

DIXON, W. G., Private, Buffs (East Kent Regt.)
He joined in June 1918 on attaining military age, and in the following October was drafted to France. He took part in the last stages of the Advance, and after the Armistice proceeded into Germany with the Army of Occupation on the Rhine. He was demobilised in March 1919 after returning home, and holds the General Service and Victory Medals. 9, Hartwell Grove, Leighton Buzzard. 1599.

DOBBS, E. C., Private, 5th Bedfordshire Regt.
He was mobilised on the outbreak of hostilities, and in September 1914 was drafted to France, where he took part in numerous engagements. In August 1915 he returned to England and was discharged, and until July 1918 was engaged on important work at the Vauxhall Motor Co., Ltd., in connection with the output of munitions. He then joined the Royal Navy, and was posted for duty with H.M.S. " New Zealand " with which he served as a Petty Officer until June 1920, when he was demobilised, holding the 1914 Star, and the General Service and Victory Medals. 112, Clarendon Road, Luton. 1449.

DOBBS, G. L., Private, Somerset Light Infantry.
He joined in May 1916, and after his training was retained at various stations on important duties until 1918, when he was drafted to France. He then took part in the severe fighting in the second Battles of the Somme and Cambrai, and in other engagements until the cessation of hostilities. He returned home and was demobilised in 1919, holding the General Service and Victory Medals. 3, Union Road, Hitchin. 1592.

DOBBS, M. (Miss), Special War Worker.
Early in the war this lady volunteered for work of National importance and was engaged at the Vauxhall Motor Works, Luton. She was engaged on important duties in the manufacture of ammunition boxes and accessories for motor cars in use at the Front. She carried out her responsible work very efficiently for over four years. 4, Brunswick Street, Luton. 1319.

DOCKERILL, F. S., Private, R.A.V.C.
He joined in February 1916, and after his training served at various stations on important duties with his unit. He did very valuable work, but owing to ill-health was unable to secure a transfer overseas while hostilities continued, and was discharged in February 1918. 13, Anderson's Row, Florence Street, Hitchin. 1860.

DODD, H., Special War Worker.
He offered his services in July 1918, and being engaged at Messrs. Lowe & Sons' Factory, Burton-on-Trent, did excellent work in connection with the manufacture of guns. His duties were carried out in an efficient manner. 65, Piccotts End, Hemel Hempstead. X1450.

DODDS, E., A.B., R.N., H.M.S. " Benbow."
He volunteered at the commencement of hostilities, and after his training was posted to H.M.S. " Benbow." Whilst in this vessel he served on important and dangerous duties at Malta, Gibraltar, the North Sea, and the Baltic, and took part in the Battle of Jutland. After the cessation of hostilities he was demobilised in August 1919, and holds the 1914–15 Star, and the General Service and Victory Medals. 5, Chapman's Terrace, Hatfield. X1451/B.

DODDS, T. G., Private, R.A.S.C. (M.T.)
Volunteering in January 1915, he was sent to the Western Front, where he served on important motor transport duties in various sectors. On August 29th, 1918, he was killed by a shell whilst driving his motor near Arras, and was buried in Faubourg d'Amiens cemetery. He was entitled to the 1914–15 Star, and the General Service and Victory Medals. 5, Chapman's Terrace, Hatfield. X1451/A.

DODKIN, H. (M.M.), Private, 8th Middlesex Regiment.
He joined in June 1916, and in the same year was drafted overseas. During his service on the Western Front he fought with distinction at the Somme, Ypres and Cambrai, and in many subsequent engagements until the cessation of hostilities. He was awarded the Military Medal for distinguished gallantry on the Field, and holds in addition the General Service and Victory Medals. In May 1919 he was demobilised. 24, Rushley Mead, Letchworth. 2708.

DODSON, A. J., Private, Labour Corps.

He volunteered in April 1915, and after being retained for a period on important duties was drafted to the Western Front in 1917. During his service in France he did valuable work in the Somme sector, and was gassed near Arras in April 1918. In the following March he was demobilised, and holds the General Service and Victory Medals.
Station Road, Toddington. 1452.

DODSON R. J., Private, 5th Bedfordshire Regt.

He joined in October 1916, and after his training served at various stations on various important duties, including those of a Military Policeman. He rendered valuable services, but was not successful in obtaining his transfer to a fighting area before the conclusion of hostilities. He was demobilised in May 1919.
50, Warwick Road, Luton. 1453.

DOGGETT, E. C., Private, 3rd North Staffordshire Regiment.

Volunteering in September 1914, he proceeded to France in the following year. During his services on the Western Front he took part in the fighting at Hill 60, Ypres, and the Somme, where he was severely gassed. He was invalided home in consequence, and discharged as unfit for further military duty in August 1916. He holds the 1914–15 Star, and the General Service and Victory Medals.
12, Muriel Avenue, Watford. X1454.

DOGGETT, J., Private, Bedfordshire Regiment.

He volunteered in September 1914, and was speedily drafted to France, where he took part in the fighting at Ypres, Arras, Cambrai and numerous subsequent engagements until hostilities ceased, and was wounded. He returned home and was demobilised in 1919, holding the 1914–15 Star, and the General Service and Victory Medals.
42, Brightwell Road, Watford. X1455.

DOGGETT, J., Sapper, Royal Engineers (E.A.)

He volunteered in August 1915, and after the completion of his training was drafted to Egypt, where he served at Cairo, Alexandria and in the Suez Canal zone, at Kubri and Port Said. Later he proceeded to Palestine, and whilst in this theatre of war was engaged with the water supply column in laying water pipes through the desert. He was frequently in the forward areas whilst operations were in progress, and was present at Gaza, Jaffa, Haifa and Beyrout. He returned home and was demobilised in August 1919, and holds the General Service and Victory Medals.
9, Belmont Cottages, Hatfield. X1456/B.

DOGGETT, T., Private, R.A.S.C. (M.T.)

He volunteered in 1915, and after his training served at Aldershot on important transport duties with his unit. He rendered valuable services, but was not successful owing to medical unfitness, in obtaining his transfer overseas before the cessation of hostilities. He was demobilised in 1919.
40, Brightwell Road, Watford. X275/C.

DOGGETT, W. J., Driver, R.A.S.C. (M.T.)

He joined in 1916, and when his training was completed was drafted to Salonika. Whilst in this theatre of war he was engaged on important transport duties, conveying rations to the lines on the Vardar front. He returned home and was demobilised in August 1919, and holds the General Service and Victory Medals.
9, Belmont Cottages, Hatfield. X1456/A.

DOHERTY, E., Private, R.A.V.C.

Volunteering in 1915, he was drafted to the Western Front, where he was subsequently engaged on important duties in many sectors, including those of Ypres and Arras. He did valuable work throughout his service overseas, which lasted for three years, and was demobilised after his return to England in February 1919. He holds the 1914–15 Star, and the General Service and Victory Medals.
86, Fishpool Street, St. Albans. X1457.

DOLAMORE, G., Private, 2nd Middlesex Regt.

He joined in October 1918, but had not completed his training when hostilities ceased. Afterwards, however, he was drafted to Egypt, where he was engaged on duties of an important nature, and in 1920 was still serving.
3, St. John's Road, Watford. X1458/B.

DOLAMORE, W. F., Gunner (Fitter), R.F.A.

He volunteered in March 1915, and at the conclusion of his training in the following November was sent to France. In this theatre of war he took part in several engagements, and later was drafted to Egypt. He also served in the Palestine campaign, during which he participated in the fighting at Gaza and in the capture of Jerusalem and Jericho. He was demobilised on his return to England in June 1919, and holds the 1914–15 Star, and the General Service and Victory Medals.
3, St. John's Road, Watford. X1458/A.

DOLBY, P., Sergeant, 1/5th Bedfordshire Regt.

He volunteered in August 1914, and in the following year was drafted to the Dardanelles, subsequently taking part in the landing at Suvla Bay and in the engagements which followed. After the evacuation of the Peninsula he was sent to Egypt and thence to Palestine, where he fought in many battles, including that of Gaza. On one occasion he was wounded, but after receiving treatment at the Base rejoined his unit and remained overseas until 1919. He was demobilised after his return to England in September of that year, and holds the 1914–15 Star, and the General Service and Victory Medals.
80, New Town Street, Luton. 1459.

DOLEMORE, F. D., Sapper, Royal Engineers.

Volunteering in November 1915, he was drafted to France a year later and was subsequently engaged on duties of an important nature in the forward areas. He was twice wounded and after being blown up by an explosion in the Arras sector, suffered from a severe form of shell-shock. In January 1918 he returned to England, and in the following September was invalided out of the Service. He holds the General Service and Victory Medals.
"Wingfield House," Princess Street, Dunstable. 1460.

DOLLIMORE, C. T., Corporal, R.F.A.

He volunteered in July 1915, and in the following October was sent to the Western Front. In this theatre of war he served for over three years, during which time he fought in many important sectors, notably those of the Somme and Ypres, and in the Retreat and Advance of 1918. Returning to England in January 1919 he was demobilised a month later, and holds the 1914–15 Star, and the General Service and Victory Medals.
4, St. Mary's Road, Watford. X1461.

DOLLIMORE, E. G., Sergeant, R.A.F.

He volunteered in July 1915, and after his training was engaged on duties of an important nature which called for a high degree of technical knowledge and skill. In January 1918 he was drafted to the Western Front, where he did valuable work with scouting and bombing squadrons until the cessation of hostilities. He was demobilised after his return to England in March 1919, and holds the General Service and Victory Medals.
High Street, Wing, Leighton Buzzard. 2699.

DOLLIMORE, E. J., Private, Bedfordshire Regt.

He volunteered in May 1915, and after his training was engaged on special duties until January 1916, when in consequence of ill-health he was discharged. He then obtained work of National importance at a munition factory in Hitchin, where he did valuable work for the remaining period of hostilities.
10, Rushly Mead, Letchworth. 2698/B.

DOLLIMORE, E. J. (jun.), Sergt., R.A.S.C.

Volunteering in June 1915, he was sent to the Western Front at the conclusion of his training. Subsequently he was engaged on important transport work, and in this capacity saw service in many sectors, including those of the Somme, Arras, Ypres, Cambrai and Vimy Ridge. He did excellent work until the cessation of hostilities, and after his return to England in 1919 was placed on the Reserve. He holds the General Service and Victory Medals.
10, Rushly Mead, Letchworth. 2698/C.

DOLLIMORE, F. G., Private, 1st Bedfordshire Regiment.

Joining in October 1916, he was drafted to France in the following May, and after taking part in several engagements was killed in action at Menin Road on October 5th, 1917. He was entitled to the General Service and Victory Medals.
10, Rushly Mead, Letchworth. 2698/A.

DOLTON, G. H., 2nd Corporal, Royal Engineers.

Volunteering in 1915, he was sent to the Western Front at the conclusion of his training. He was subsequently engaged on important duties in many sectors, including those of Ypres, the Somme, Beaumont-Hamel and Cambrai, and on one occasion was severely gassed. After the cessation of hostilities he advanced with the Army of Occupation into Germany, where he served until 1919. Returning to England he was demobilised in April of that year, and holds the 1914–15 Star, and the General Service and Victory Medals.
Vicarage Street, Woburn Sands, Beds. Z1462.

DOLTON, W. G., Private, Labour Corps.

He volunteered in September 1914, and after his training, being physically unfit for foreign service, was engaged on duties of an important nature at various stations with his unit. Although he was unable to secure his transfer overseas, he did valuable work until his demobilisation, which took place in February 1919.
Woburn Road, Ampthill. 1463.

DORLING, A., Private, Royal Fusiliers.
Joining in February 1917, he was sent to France on completing his training in the following August, and a month later was killed in action. He was entitled to the General Service and Victory Medals.
Longwood, near Winchester, Hants.   1464.

DORLING, F., Private, Hertfordshire Regiment; and Royal Army Medical Corps.
He volunteered early in 1916, and after his training was engaged on important duties at various stations. He was unable to secure his transfer overseas, but nevertheless did valuable work until his death, which occurred on October 26th, 1918, from an illness contracted in the service.
38, Longmire Road, St. Albans.   1465/B.

DORNHORST, F. S., Private, Middlesex Regt.; and Labour Corps.
He joined in September 1916, and at the conclusion of his training was drafted to France. Subsequently he was engaged on important duties in the forward areas, and was present during engagements at Ypres, Lens, the Somme and Cambrai. Owing to ill-health he returned to England in 1918, and in November of that year was invalided out of the Service. He holds the General Service and Victory Medals.
"Campton Cottage," Shefford, near Bedford.   Z1466.

DORRINGTON, E. H., Corporal, R.E.
Called up from the Reserve at the outbreak of hostilities he was first sent to Egypt and later to the Dardanelles, subsequently rendering valuable service with his unit during the Gallipoli campaign. After the Evacuation of the Peninsula he was drafted to Salonika, where he was engaged on duties of an important nature in the forward areas. He holds the 1914-15 Star, and the General Service and Victory Medals, and was demobilised after his return to England in April 1919.
6, Albion Road, Luton.   1467.

DORRINGTON, H. G., A.B., Royal Naval Division.
Joining in June 1917, he was drafted to the Western Front at the conclusion of his training. He subsequently took part in many important engagements, notably those on the Somme and at Cambrai and Bullecourt, and was wounded and gassed. Returning to England after the cessation of hostilities he was demobilised in February 1919, and holds the General Service and Victory Medals.
34, Regent Street, Luton.   1468.

DOUGHTY, T. H., Sergeant, 5th Queen's (Royal West Surrey Regiment).
He volunteered in July 1915, having previously served with the East Lancashire Regiment in the Boer War. He served at various stations on important duties with his unit and rendered valuable services, but was not successful in obtaining his transfer overseas before the cessation of hostilities. He was demobilised in December 1919.
73, Sothern Road, Watford.   X1080/B.

DOUGLAS, M., L/Corporal, 10th Argyll and Sutherland Highlanders.
He volunteered in August 1914, but at the conclusion of his training was found to be physically unfit for foreign service. He did valuable work however, until March 1915, when in consequence of continued ill-health he was discharged.
Hillford End, Shillington, Beds.   1590.

DOUGLAS, W. D., Private, R.A.S.C.
He volunteered in March 1915, and in the same year was drafted to the Western Front, where he was engaged on important duties as an ambulance driver in numerous sectors. He was demobilised after the cessation of hostilities in May 1919, and holds the General Service and Victory Medals.
63, Leighton Street, Woburn, Beds.   Z1469.

DOUGLAS, W. E., Gnr., Royal Marine Artillery.
He volunteered in February 1915, and in the same year was drafted to France. Whilst in this theatre of war he was engaged on important duties, and served at Ypres, the Somme, Kemmel, Armentières and Cambrai. He was demobilised when hostilities ceased in November 1918, and holds the 1914-15 Star, and the General Service and Victory Medals.   4, Commerce Avenue, Letchworth.   1593.

DOVASTON, T., Sapper, Royal Engineers.
He volunteered in June 1915, and in the following December was drafted to Egypt, where he served on special work in the Canal zone, and at Ismailia. In 1917 he took part in the advance into Palestine, and was frequently engaged on important duties in the forward areas whilst operations were in progress, notably at Gaza, Haïfa and Beyrout. He returned home and was demobilised in August 1919, and holds the General Service and Victory Medals.
18, Selbourne Road, Luton.   1470/B.

DOVASTON, W., Private, 8th Middlesex Regt.
He was mobilised with the Territorials at the outbreak of war, and in June 1915 was sent to the Western Front. Here he fought in the Battles of Loos and Vimy Ridge, and in several subsequent engagements. He was killed in action on the Somme in September 1916, and was entitled to the 1914-15 Star, and the General Service and Victory Medals.
18, Selbourne Road, Luton.   1470/A.

DOVER, H. R., Sergeant, R.A.V.C.
Volunteering at the outbreak of hostilities he was sent overseas in September 1914. During his service in France he was engaged on special duties at Ypres, Neuve Chapelle, Vimy Ridge, Arras and Cambrai, and also served in the Retreat and Advance of 1918. He returned home and was demobilised in April 1919, and holds the 1914 Star, and the General Service and Victory Medals.
New Street, Shefford, Beds.   Z1471.

DOWMAN, A. H., Sapper, Royal Engineers.
He volunteered in July 1915, and served on important duties at various stations until 1917, when he was drafted to France. He was then engaged on special work in connection with the operations, and was frequently in the forward areas, notably at Arras, Cambrai and the Somme, and was twice wounded. In 1919 he returned home and was demobilised, and holds the General Service and Victory Medals.
65, High Street, Markyate, Herts.   1472/A.

DOWNING, H., Sapper, Royal Engineers.
He volunteered in February 1915, and in the same year was drafted to the Western Front, where he was engaged on important duties in connection with the operations and was frequently in the forward areas, and was wounded. He served at Arras, Ypres, Cambrai and St. Quentin, and in subsequent engagements until the cessation of hostilities. He returned home and was demobilised in August 1919, and holds the 1914-15 Star, and the General Service and Victory Medals.
Mill Road, Greenfield, near Ampthill.   1473/B.

DOWNING, W., Private, Labour Corps.
Volunteering in August 1914, he was drafted to the Western Front in the following year. During his service in France he was present at Arras, Cambrai and St. Quentin, and was severely gassed. In 1918 he was sent home and was demobilised in April of the following year, holding the 1914-15 Star, and the General Service and Victory Medals.
Mill Road, Greenfield, near Ampthill.   1473/A.

DOWSE, F. G., Private, Middlesex Regiment.
He joined in May 1918, and after his training was completed served at various stations on important Guard and Military Police duties. Later he was drafted to Germany, where he was stationed on the Rhine, and engaged in similar work until April 1920, when he returned to England and was demobilised.
Ganders Ash, Leavesden Green, Watford.   X1474.

DOWSE, G., Air Mechanic, R.A.F. (late Royal Naval Air Service).
He joined in 1917, and after his training served at various stations on important duties with his unit as an aero-engine fitter. His work, which demanded a high degree of technical skill, was carried out in a most efficient manner, and he rendered valuable services, but was not successful in obtaining his transfer overseas before the cessation of hostilities. He was demobilised in 1918.
90, Breakspeare Road, Abbots Langley.   X1475.

DRACKLEY, T. G., L/Corporal, R.E.
He was serving at the outbreak of war, and was immediately drafted to the Western Front, where he took part in the Retreat from Mons. He also rendered valuable service at Ypres, the Somme, Cambrai and in many other engagements until hostilities ceased, and was wounded 15 times during this period. He was demobilised in October 1919 after returning home, and holds the Mons Star, and the General Service and Victory Medals.
3, Cassio Bridge Road, Watford.   X320/B.

DRAKE, A., Private, 6th Bedfordshire Regiment.
He volunteered in 1914, and was drafted immediately afterwards to the Western Front, where he took part in numerous engagements, including those at Mons and Ypres. He was killed in action at Arras on April 23rd, 1917, and was entitled to the Mons Star, and the General Service and Victory Medals.
58, Holywell Road, Watford.   X1476/B.

DRAKE, D., L/Corporal, Machine Gun Corps.
Volunteering in 1915, he was drafted to France in the same year. He took part in severe fighting on the Somme and at Arras, Ypres, Cambrai and many other important engagements, and after the conclusion of hostilities returned home and was demobilised in April 1919. He holds the 1914-15 Star, and the General Service and Victory Medals.
58, Holywell Road, Watford.   X1476/A.

DRAKE, F. E., Private, 3rd Wiltshire Regiment.

He enlisted in July 1911, and immediately after the outbreak of war was sent to France, where he took part in the Battle of Mons and other engagements, and was gassed. In June 1915 he was transferred to the Dardanelles, and was in action at Anzac, and later went to Egypt and Palestine, and served at Gaza. He afterwards proceeded to Italy and was engaged on the Trentino Front. He returned home and was demobilised in April 1919, and holds the 1914 Star, and the General Service and Victory Medals.

12, Waddington Street, St. Albans. 1478 /B.

DRAKE, G. M. (M.M.), Sergeant, Manchester Regiment.

He volunteered in August 1914, and in the same year was drafted overseas. He served on both the Western and Gallipoli Fronts, and took part in engagements at Suvla Bay, the Somme, Arras and Cambrai. During his service he was wounded, and was awarded the Military Medal for conspicuous gallantry. In addition he holds the 1914 Star, and the General Service and Victory Medals, and was demobilised in April 1919.

7, Lower Paddock Road, Oxhey, Watford. X1477.

DRAKE, H., Private, Northumberland Fusiliers.

Volunteering in 1914, he was sent immediately afterwards to the Western Front, where he took part in heavy fighting at the Battles of Ypres, Arras, Cambrai and numerous other engagements. He was killed in action on October 22nd, 1917, and was entitled to the 1914 Star, and the General Service and Victory Medals.

12, Grover Road, Oxhey. X1096 /A.

DRAKE, H., Private, 1st Essex Regiment.

He volunteered in September 1915, and in December of the following year was drafted to the Western Front, where he took part in important engagements, including those at Ypres and Passchendaele, and was twice wounded. He was killed at Achiet-le-Grande on August 27th, 1918, and was entitled to the General Service and Victory Medals.

12, Waddington Road, St. Albans. 1478 /A.

DRANSFIELD, J. R., A/Bombardier, R.F.A.

Volunteering in January 1915, he was sent in the following July to the Dardanelles, where he did valuable service until December of the same year, when he was transferred to France and took part in the Battle of the Somme, and was wounded. In December 1916 he proceeded to Mesopotamia and served at Baghdad, Ramadich and Hit. He was demobilised in March 1919, and holds the 1914-15 Star, and the General Service and Victory Medals.

281, High Town Road, Luton. 1316.

DRAPER, A. C., L/Corporal, Welch Regiment.

He was mobilised with the Herts. Territorials in August, and later was transferred to the Welch Regiment. In June 1915 he was drafted to the Western Front, where he took part in the Battles of Ypres, Lens and the Somme, and was wounded. He was demobilised in March 1919, and holds the 1914-15 Star, and the General Service and Victory Medals.

New Marford, Wheathampstead. 1479 /A.

DRAPER, A. W., Gunner, Royal Field Artillery.

He volunteered in 1914, and on the completion of his training was drafted to the Western Front. During his service in France he took part in much heavy fighting in the Somme and Cambrai sectors, and was badly injured by accident, in consequence of which he was discharged in 1917. He holds the General Service and Victory Medals.

44, Elizabeth Street, Luton. 1480.

DRAPER, D., Private, 6th Northamptonshire Regiment.

Volunteering in May 1915, he was sent to France in the same year. While there he took part in numerous engagements, including those at Thiepval, Ypres, Zillebeke, and was three times wounded. He was invalided home and discharged in February 1918 in consequence of his injuries. He holds the 1914-15 Star, and the General Service and Victory Medals.

3, Luton Road, Toddington. 1481.

DRAPER, E. A., Private, R.A.M.C.

He volunteered in November 1915, and on completing his training was drafted to France in the following year. During his service overseas he did good work as a stretcher-bearer on the Somme and at Ypres, Arras and Cambrai. He was killed in action by a shell on March 21st, 1918, and was entitled to the General Service and Victory Medals.

13, Newcombe Road, Luton. 1428.

DRAPER, F. A., Corporal, 22nd London Regt. (Queen's).

He volunteered in 1914, and after his training served in France, Salonika and Palestine. On each of these Fronts he took an active part in many notable engagements, and was with General Allenby's Forces at the capture of Jerusalem. Throughout his service overseas, which lasted for over four years, he did excellent work with his unit, and was demobilised on his return to England in March 1919. He holds the 1914-15 Star, and the General Service and Victory Medals.

20, College Place, St. Albans. 1483.

DRAPER, F. C., Driver, Royal Field Artillery.

He volunteered in June 1915, and after his training was sent in the following year to France, where he was engaged during the remainder of the war in transporting guns to their selected positions on the various fronts, and was wounded. He returned home and was demobilised in May 1919, holding the General Service and Victory Medals.

15, Dacie Road, Hitchin. 1861.

DRAPER, F. T., Private, R.A.M.C.

Volunteering in September 1915, he was, in November of the same year, drafted to Egypt and Palestine. During his period of service in this theatre of war he was present at many important battles in the Palestine Offensive, including those at Gaza. He was demobilised in March 1919 after his return home, and holds the 1914-15 Star, and the General Service and Victory Medals.

14, Beech Road, Luton. 1484.

DRAPER, G. A., Stoker, R.N., H.M.S. " Yarmouth."

Joining in February 1918, he was posted to H.M.S. " Yarmouth," and while engaged on important cruising duties in the North Sea, rendered valuable services. He was demobilised in February 1919, and holds the General Service and Victory Medals.

37, Dallow Road, Luton. 1485.

DRAPER, G. W., Private, Machine Gun Corps.

He joined in October 1916, and was sent to France in February of the following year. He took part in heavy fighting at the Battles of Arras, Messines, Passchendaele, Cambrai and many other engagements, and was killed in action on the Somme on March 28th, 1918. He was entitled to the General Service and Victory Medals.

11, Norton Road, Leagrave, near Luton. 1486.

DRAPER, H., L/Corporal, Oxfordshire and Buckinghamshire Light Infantry.

Volunteering in October 1915, he was drafted in December of the following year to the Western Front, where he took part in numerous engagements, including those at the Somme, Ypres, St. Quentin, Armentières and Passchendaele, and was wounded near Cambrai. He was demobilised in May 1919, and holds the General Service and Victory Medals.

3, Portland Street, St. Albans. 1487.

DRAPER, J., Driver, Royal Field Artillery.

He volunteered in April 1915, and after a course of training was drafted to Mesopotamia, where he took part in numerous engagements, including that at Baghdad. He returned home and was demobilised in May 1919, and holds the General Service and Victory Medals.

Fernleigh, London Colney. X1488.

DRAPER, L. W., Private, 2nd Suffolk Regiment.

Volunteering in September 1914, he was sent to France in the following year and took part in severe fighting at Neuve Chapelle and Ypres. He was afterwards, in 1917, transferred to Egypt and thence to Palestine, and served in various engagements, including those at Gaza, Haïfa, Aleppo and Damascus. He was wounded at Gaza and on two other occasions, and after the conclusion of hostilities returned to England and was demobilised in February 1920. He holds the 1914-15 Star, and the General Service and Victory Medals.

New Marford, Wheathampstead. 1479 /B.

DRAPER, P., Private, Bedfordshire Regiment.

He volunteered in September 1914, and was sent to France in the following January. He was engaged on the Ypres, Somme and Cambrai fronts, and was wounded three times, being twice invalided home for treatment. He died of his injuries in October 1918, and was entitled to the 1914-15 Star, and the General Service and Victory Medals.

13, Blacksmith Lane, St. Albans. 12 /C.

DRAPER, S., Corporal, 3rd Bedfordshire Regt.

He volunteered in November 1914, and was sent to France in the following year and took part in severe fighting on the Somme and Arras. He was killed in action near Bullecourt on May 26th, 1917, and was entitled to the 1914-15 Star, and the General Service and Victory Medals.

51, Union Street, Dunstable. 1489.

DRAPER, W., Private, Machine Gun Corps.

Joining in May 1918, he went through a course of training, after completing which he was drafted to the Western Front in the following August. He was engaged on various important duties until after the signing of the Armistice, when he proceeded with the Army of Occupation to Germany. He was demobilised in October 1919, and holds the General Service and Victory Medals.

26, Bedford Road, Houghton Regis.   1490.

DRAPER, W., Corporal, R.A.S.C.

He was mobilised at the outbreak of hostilities and in the following September was drafted overseas. Whilst on the Western Front he was present at the Battles of Ypres, the Somme, Arras, and Cambrai, and at various engagements in the Retreat and Advance of 1918. In June 1919 he was demobilised after his return to England, and holds the 1914 Star, and the General Service and Victory Medals.

28, Union Street, Dunstable.   1491.

DRAPER, W. H., Private, Royal Fusiliers.

He joined in July 1916, and in the following December was drafted to France. Here he took part in the fighting on the Somme, and at Arras, Messines and Ypres, where he was severely wounded. He was invalided home to hospital, and after treatment was eventually discharged as medically unfit for further service in 1918. He holds the General Service and Victory Medals.

9, Norton Road, Leagrave, near Luton.   1492.

DRAYCOTT, M. (Miss), Special War Worker.

For three years during the war this lady held a responsible position at Chawl End Bomb Factory, Luton. She was engaged on highly dangerous work, including fuse-filling, and carried out her duties in a most efficient manner and to the entire satisfaction of the Firm.

92, Ashton Road, Luton.   1493/B.

DRAYCOTT, W. H., Private, R.A.V.C.

Volunteering in November 1914, he was drafted to Egypt in the following year, and served under General Allenby in the British Advance through Palestine. He was engaged on important duties tending sick and wounded horses at Gaza, Jaffa and Beyrout, and was present at the entry into Jerusalem, and during his service was wounded. He returned to England in March 1919 and was demobilised, and holds the 1914–15 Star, and the General Service and Victory Medals.

92, Ashton Road, Luton.   1493/A.

DREW, A. C., Private, Labour Corps.

He volunteered in March 1915, and in the following year was drafted to France, where he served on important duties in various sectors, notably the Somme, Arras and Cambrai. He was demobilised in March 1920 after his return to England, and holds the General Service and Victory Medals.

Brook End, Potton.   Z1314.

DREWITT, W., L/Corporal, R.H.A. and R.F.A.

A serving soldier, he was engaged for the first three years of the war on important duties at various stations and was for a time in Ireland. In 1917 he was drafted to France, and took part in the heavy fighting at Arras, Vimy Ridge, Ypres, Cambrai and the Somme, and in subsequent engagements until the cessation of hostilities. He returned home and was discharged in March 1920, having served over 12½ years with the Colours, and holds the General Service and Victory Medals.

40, Leighton Street, Woburn, Beds.   Z1494.

DRIVER, H. C., Corporal, 7th Middlesex Regt.

He joined in May 1916, and after his training served at various stations on important duties with his unit. He was engaged as a Drill Instructor to recruits and was also employed on responsible clerical and escort work. He rendered valuable services, but was not successful in obtaining his transfer overseas before the cessation of hostilities. He was demobilised in January 1919.

Greyhound Inn, Park Street West, Luton.   1495.

DRURY, G. H. (D.C.M.), C.S.M.,1st Hertfordshire and 3rd Bedfordshire Regiments.

He was mobilised with the Territorials in August 1914, and in the following January was drafted to France, where he took part in the fighting at Ypres, the Somme and Arras, and was awarded the Distinguished Conduct Medal for conspicuous gallantry in capturing a German gun. In February 1918 he was sent to Italy, and served in various operations against the Austrians, until the following September,when he proceeded to Russia, where after six months' active service he was reported missing in March 1919, and is presumed to have been killed in action. In addition to holding the Distinguished Conduct Medal, he was entitled to the 1914–15 Star, and the General Service and Victory Medals.

20, Shott Lane, Letchworth.   2700/A.

DRURY, R. G., Private, Hertfordshire Regt. and Labour Corps.

He volunteered in October 1914, and after his training served at various coastal stations on important guard and training duties. He rendered valuable services, but was unable to secure his transfer abroad before the cessation of hostilities. He was demobilised in February 1919.

20, Shott Lane, Letchworth.   2700/B.

DRYERRE, H. E., Gunner (Signaller), R.G.A.

He joined in August 1916, and after his training was drafted to France in the following August. He served on important signalling duties at Ypres, Amiens and Villers-Brettoneux, and in subsequent engagements until the cessation of hostilities. He returned home and was demobilised in January 1919, and holds the General Service and Victory Medals.

37, Buxton Road, Luton.   1496.

DUCK, T. H., Private, 7th Northamptonshire Regiment.

He joined in May 1916, and in the following September was drafted to France, where he was in action on the Somme and at Arras. He was severely wounded at Monchy in May 1917, and again at Cambrai in October 1918, when he was invalided home to hospital. After prolonged treatment he was finally discharged in February 1920, and holds the General Service and Victory Medals.

19, Cavendish Road, St. Albans.   X1497.

DUDDRIDGE, G. H., Private, R.A.S.C.

He volunteered in January 1915, and after his training was engaged on important duties at various places. Owing to being medically unfit for duty overseas he was unable to obtain his transfer to a theatre of war, but rendered valuable service until October 1919, when he was demobilised.

3, Stanbridge Road, Leighton Buzzard.   2701.

DUDEY, F., Pte., 2/6th South Staffordshire Regt.

He volunteered in July 1915, and after his training was engaged on important duties at various stations. He rendered valuable service, but owing to being medically unfit for duty abroad, was unable to obtain his transfer overseas. He was demobilised in February 1919.

176, Fishpool Street, St. Albans.   1498/A.

DUDLEY, E. D., Drummer, 2/3rd London Regt. (Royal Fusiliers).

Volunteering in November 1914, he served on important duties at various stations until 1916, when he was drafted to the Western Front. Whilst in this theatre of war he fought on the Somme and was gassed, and after his recovery served at Passchendaele, St. Quentin and Villers-Bretonneux, and in subsequent engagements until the cessation of hostilities. He was demobilised in February 1919 after his return to England, and holds the General Service and Victory Medals.

9, Arthur Street, Luton.   3042/B.

DUDLEY, G., Private, The Buffs (East Kent Regiment).

He joined in June 1916, and in the following January was sent overseas, and took part in the fighting at Arras, Ypres and Cambrai. In 1918 he was taken prisoner in an engagement during the Retreat, and was held in captivity in Germany until released in January 1919, when he was sent home and demobilised. He holds the General Service and Victory Medals.

Primrose Cottage, West Street, Dunstable.   2441/B.

DUDLEY, P., Private, Bedfordshire Regiment.

He volunteered in August 1914, and after serving on important duties at various stations was drafted to Egypt in 1916, and took part in the Advance through Palestine under General Allenby. He fought in many important engagements during the campaign, and after nearly 3¼ years' service in the East, returned home and was demobilised in June 1919. He holds the General Service and Victory Medals.

3, King Street, Dunstable.   1499.

DUDLEY, T., Gunner, Royal Garrison Artillery.

He joined in October 1916, and in the following February was sent to France. He did excellent work as a gunner in various engagements on the Somme, but owing to illness contracted whilst on active service he was invalided home in November 1917. He was finally demobilised in February 1919, and holds the General Service and Victory Medals.

The Green, Caddington, Beds.   1500.

DUDLEY, T., Gunner, Royal Garrison Artillery.

He joined in October 1917, and in February 1918 was drafted to France. Whilst in this theatre of war he took part in the Battle of the Somme, and in various subsequent engagements, until the cessation of hostilities. He returned home and was demobilised in February 1919, and holds the General Service and Victory Medals.

Caddington, near Luton.   1501.

DUDLEY, W., Private, 6th Bedfordshire Regt.
He volunteered in February 1915, and in the following
August was drafted overseas, where he saw much heavy
fighting. He was in action at Vimy Ridge, the Somme,
Ypres and various subsequent engagements, and was
wounded and gassed three times during his service. He
died from the effects of severe gas poisoning on May 8th,
1918, and was entitled to the 1914-15 Star, and the General
Service and Victory Medals.
15, North Common, Redbourn, Herts.   1502.

DUDLEY, W. A., Gunner (Signaller), R.F.A.
Volunteering in November 1915, he was drafted to the
Western Front in the following year. He served on important signalling duties with the field batteries, and was
in action at the Battles of the Somme, Arras, Ypres and
Passchendaele, and in many engagements during the Retreat
and Advance of 1918. He was demobilised in May 1919
after his return home, and holds the General Service and
Victory Medals.
18, Yarmouth Road, Callowland, Watford.   X1503.

DUFFIN, J., Private, 4th Bedfordshire Regiment.
He volunteered in 1915, and in the following year was sent
overseas. During his service on the Western Front he took
part in the fighting on the Somme, at Arras, Ypres and
Cambrai, and was gassed in action. He was demobilised
in 1918, and holds the General Service and Victory Medals.
Wagstaff Terrace, Potton.   Z1311/B.

DUKES, C. E., Private, 5th Bedfordshire Regt.
Volunteering in August 1914, he served on important duties
at various stations until 1915, when he was drafted to the
Dardanelles. Whilst serving in this theatre of war he was
wounded, and, contracting malaria, was invalided home to
hospital. After his recovery he was sent in 1917 to the
Western Front, where he was in action at Arras, Messines
and Cambrai, and was again wounded in an engagement
in March 1918. During his service in France he acted as
signaller, attached to the Royal Engineers, and was engaged
on important duties throughout. He returned home and was
demobilised in March 1919, and holds the 1914-15 Star, and
the General Service and Victory Medals.
North Bridge Street, Shefford.   Z1504.

**DUKES, H. H., Private, 4th Queen's Own
Cameron Highlanders.**
Volunteering in December 1914, he was sent to France in
the following April, and was subsequently killed in action
on May 11th, 1915. He was entitled to the 1914-15 Star,
and the General Service and Victory Medals.
23, Shaftesbury Road, Watford.   X1505.

**DUMBELTON, G. J., Rifleman, The Cameron-
ians (Scottish Rifles).**
He joined in April 1917, and after his training served at
various stations on important duties with his unit. He
rendered valuable services, but was not successful in obtaining his transfer overseas before the cessation of hostilities
owing to his medical unfitness for active service. He was
demobilised in December 1919.
30, Liverpool Road, Watford.   X1506/A.

**DUMBELTON, H. W., Trooper, 1st Herts.
Dragoons.**
Volunteering in November 1915, he was sent to Egypt in
September of the following year, where he took part in
numerous engagements, including those at Gaza, Haifa and
Beyrout. In 1919 he was transferred to Turkey, where he
served until he returned home and was demobilised in June
of the same year. He holds the General Service and Victory
Medals.
30, Liverpool Road, Watford.   X1506/B.

**DUMPLETON, P., Private, 5th Bedfordshire
Regiment.**
He volunteered in October 1914, and in January 1916 was
drafted to Egypt, and took part in important engagements
in the Sinai Peninsula. Contracting malaria, he was
invalided to hospital at Cairo, where he died in October 1916.
He was entitled to the General Service and Victory Medals.
37, Hartley Road, Luton.   1507.

**DUNFORD, H. E., Private, Queen's (Royal West
Surrey Regiment).**
After volunteering in December 1915, he went through a
course of training and was then drafted to the Western Front,
where he took part in severe fighting at Cambrai, Amiens,
and many other engagements, and was wounded. He was
demobilised in October 1919, and holds the General Service
and Victory Medals.
40, Brighton Road, Watford.   X1508/A.

DUNFORD, J., Private, Royal Defence Corps.
Volunteering in January 1915, he was engaged at various
stations on important guard duties with his unit until January
1917, when he was discharged in consequence of his service.
40, Brighton Road, Watford.   X1508/B.

DUNKLEY, A., Sergeant, R.A.S.C.
He joined in September 1916, and after his training was
drafted to the Western Front. During his service overseas
he was present at numerous engagements, and after the
conclusion of hostilities returned home and was demobilised
in October 1919. He holds the General Service and Victory
Medals.
25, Albert Street, St. Albans.   X1509.

DUNN, P. E., Private, Machine Gun Corps.
He joined in January 1918, and after his training served
at various stations on important duties with his unit. He
rendered valuable services, but was not successful in obtaining
his transfer overseas before the cessation of hostilities. He
was demobilised in February 1919.
31, Ridge Avenue, Letchworth.   2702/A.

**DUNN, L. A., Private, Herts. Regiment; and
1st Air Mechanic, Royal Air Force.**
Joining in September 1914, he was sent in the following year
to France, where he was present at various engagements,
including those at Albert, the Somme, and Cambrai. During
his service he was chiefly engaged in the repair of aeroplanes,
on work which required a high degree of technical skill.
He was demobilised in May 1919, and holds the 1914-15 Star,
and the General Service and Victory Medals.
31, Ridge Avenue, Letchworth.   2702/B.

DUNNETT, W. J., Private, R.M.L.I.
He was serving at the outbreak of war, and was immediately
afterwards sent to the Western Front, where he took part
in the Battles of Mons, Ypres, Hill 60, the Somme, Arras,
Passchendaele and Cambrai. He was demobilised in March
1919, and holds the Mons Star, and the General Service and
Victory Medals.
Victoria Terrace, Leedon, Leighton Buzzard.   1306.

DUNNING, S. C., Gunner, R.G.A.
He volunteered in August 1914, and in October of the same
year was sent to the Western Front, where he took part in
the Battles of Ypres, the Somme, Arras, Cambrai and
numerous other engagements. He was demobilised in
February 1919, and holds the 1914 Star, and the General
Service and Victory Medals.
Hockcliffe, near Leighton Buzzard.   1613.

**DUNTON, J. E., Ordinary Seaman, R.N.,
H.M.S. "Danae."**
He joined in August 1916, and was posted for duty with
H.M.S. "Danae." He served in the North Sea, at Scapa
Flow and in Russian waters, and took part in the Battle
of Zeebrugge. He was still serving in 1920, and holds the
General Service and Victory Medals.
48, Ebury Road, Watford.   X1511.

DURHAM, C. W., Private, Bedfordshire Regt.
He joined in February 1916, and in the following year was
drafted to the Western Front, where he took part in the
Battles of Ypres, Arras, Cambrai and the Somme, and was
wounded and invalided home. He was demobilised in
February 1919, and holds the General Service and Victory
Medals.
2, New Town, Potton.   Z1304/A.

**DURHAM, H. C., Private, The Buffs (East Kent
Regiment).**
He joined in May 1918, and in the following September was
drafted overseas and served on transport duties at Armentières, where he was injured in an accident. He then fought
at Epéhy, and was severely wounded on September 21st,
1918, and invalided to hospital in France. In February
1919 he was sent home and was under treatment in various
hospitals until February 1920, when he was demobilised,
holding the General Service and Victory Medals.
2, New Town, Potton.   Z1304/B.

DURHAM, J., Gunner, Royal Field Artillery.
He was mobilised in August 1914, and after his training served
on important duties with the Mounted Military Police at
various stations. In February 1918 he was drafted overseas,
and was severely gassed near Cambrai, and was in action also
at Albert and Amiens. After the signing of the Armistice
he proceeded to Germany with the Army of Occupation and
was stationed at Cologne until August 1919, when he was
sent home and demobilised. He holds the General Service
and Victory Medals.
40, Back Street, Biggleswade.   Z1309.

DURRANT, A., Private, 17th Manchester Regt.

He volunteered in May 1915, and in the following October proceeded to the Western Front. After taking part in several minor engagements he fought in the Battles of the Somme and was severely wounded in 1916, and suffered from shell-shock. He was invalided home to hospital, and was discharged as unfit for further military duty in the following July. He holds the 1914–15 Star, and the General Service and Victory Medals.
48, Lake Street, Leighton Buzzard.   2703.

DURRANT, M., Sapper, Royal Engineers.

He volunteered in October 1915, and in the following May was drafted to France. There he was engaged on important duties in connection with the operations, and was frequently in the forward areas, notably at Ypres and Cambrai, and was wounded. After the signing of the Armistice he proceeded to Germany with the Army of Occupation and served there until May 1919, when he was demobilised, holding the General Service and Victory Medals.
2, Dorset Street, Luton.   1512/A.

DURRANT, M. W., Private, Queen's (Royal West Surrey Regiment) and Labour Corps.

He joined in February 1917, and was drafted to the Western Front in the following month. During his service overseas he fought at Arras and Ypres, where he was wounded and gassed. He was invalided home to hospital, but on his recovery returned to France, where he continued to serve until February 1919, when he was demobilised, holding the General Service and Victory Medals.
26, Essex Street, Luton.   1513.

DURRANT, R., Gunner, R.G.A.

He volunteeerd in November 1915, and in the following July was drafted to France, where he did excellent work as a gunner at Ypres, Cambrai and Amiens. In November 1918, after the Armistice was signed, he proceeded to Germany and served on important guard duties on the Rhine until September 1919, when he was demobilised after his return to England. He holds the General Service and Victory Medals.
Church Lane, King's Langley.   1514/B.

DURRANT, S. E., Private, R.A.M.C.

He joined in November 1916, and in May of the succeeding year was drafted to the Western Front. Whilst in this theatre of war he served on important duties at Bullecourt, Cambrai, the Aisne and the Somme, and in subsequent engagements, until the cessation of hostilities. He returned home and was demobilised in January 1919, and holds the General Service and Victory Medals.
49, Buxton Road, Luton.   1515.

DURRANT, S. H., Private, Bedfordshire Lancers.

He volunteered in August 1914, and after his training served at various stations on important duties with his unit. In 1919 he proceeded to Ireland on special duties in connection with the suppression of the Sinn Fein risings. He rendered valuable services throughout, but was unable to secure his transfer to a fighting front owing to physical unfitness. He was demobilised in March 1919.
47, Wing Road, Leighton Buzzard   2704.

DUVALL, V., Private, 12th (Prince of Wales' Royal) Lancers.

He was serving at the outbreak of war, and in 1915 was sent to France, and took part in the second Battle of Ypres, and later served at Arras. Subsequently he was seriously injured in an accident, and was invalided home, and later discharged as physically unfit for further duty in September 1919. He holds the 1914–15 Star, and the General Service and Victory Medals.
King William's Inn, Waterside, King's Langley. X1516/B.

DUVALL, W. G., Private, Norfolk Regiment.

Volunteering in August 1914, he was drafted to Egypt in the following year, and took part in the British Advance through Palestine under General Allenby. He fought at Gaza and Jaffa, and was present at the entry into Jerusalem, and during his service suffered from shell-shock. He was demobilised after his return to England in June 1919, and holds the 1914–15 Star, and the General Service and Victory Medals.
King William's Inn, Waterside, King's Langley. X1516/C.

DUVALL, W. T., Q.M.S., Bedfordshire Regiment.

He was mobilised in 1914, and in the following year was drafted to Egypt, where he served on important clerical work at Headquarters. He rendered valuable services, but on account of being over age for further duty was sent home and discharged in May 1917. He holds the 1914–15 Star, and the General Service and Victory Medals.
King William's Inn, Waterside, King's Langley. X1516/A.

DYDE, J., Gunner, Royal Garrison Artillery.

He volunteered at the outbreak of war, and in the following year was drafted to Egypt, and served in the Palestine Offensive with General Allenby's Forces. He did excellent work as a gunner at Gaza, but later was severely wounded and invalided home to hospital. In February 1918 he was discharged as medically unfit for further military duty, and holds the 1914–15 Star, and the General Service and Victory Medals.   275, High Street, Watford.   X1517.

DYER, A., Private, 2nd Northamptonshire Regt.

He joined in November 1916, and in March of the following year was drafted overseas. Whilst on the Western Front he saw much fighting at several engagements, including those of Passchendaele and Cambrai, and served in the Retreat and Advance in 1918. He was with the Army of Occupation on the Rhine, and in 1920 was drafted to India. He holds the General Service and Victory Medals.
30, St. Mary's Street, Dunstable.   1029/B.

DYER, E. J., Sapper, Royal Engineers.

He volunteered in 1915, and in the same year was drafted to France, where he was engaged on important duties in connection with the operations, and was almost continually in the front lines, notably at Armentières and La Bassée. He sustained severe shell-shock, and died on December 23rd, 1917. He was entitled to the General Service and Victory Medals.
4, Grover Road, Oxhey, Herts.   X1518.

DYER, F., Corporal, Northamptonshire Regt.

He was serving at the outbreak of hostilities, and was almost immediately drafted to France and took part in the Retreat from Mons. Subsequently he served in other engagements, and was later killed in action on May 9th, 1915. He was entitled to the Mons Star, and the General Service and Victory Medals.
Garden Field, Offley, Herts.   2705/C.

DYER, S. J., Gunner (Signaller), R.G.A.

He joined in March 1917, and after his training served at various stations on important duties. He did excellent work, but owing to medical unfitness was unable to secure his transfer overseas before the cessation of hostilities. He was demobilised in April 1919.
23, Princess Street, Dunstable.   1519.

DYSON, E., Private, 6th Bedfordshire Regiment.

He volunteered in September 1914, and was drafted to the Western Front in the following year. Whilst in this theatre of war he served at Hill 60, Ypres, the Somme, Arras and St. Quentin, and was severely gassed in action. On his recovery he fought in several subsequent engagements, and was afterwards demobilised in 1919. He holds the 1914–15 Star, and the General Service and Victory Medals.
39, Regent Street, South Watford.   1520.

E

EADLE, J., Private, Oxfordshire and Buckinghamshire Light Infantry.

He volunteered in June 1915, and during his service on the Western Front took part in many engagements, notably those at Arras, Ypres and Cambrai, and was wounded. He holds the General Service and Victory Medals, and was still serving in 1920.
19, Loates Lane, Watford.   X2964/B.

EAGER, F. E., Private, Q.M.A.A.C.

She joined in February 1918, and during her service did valuable work as a cook at Dollington Camp, Northampton, where she was attached to the 53rd Rifle Brigade. She was discharged in October 1918.
40, Lyndhurst Road, Luton.   1568/A.

EAGER, W. F., Private, 10th London Regiment.

Volunteering in October 1914, he was sent to France in June 1916, and subsequently served on the Somme and in other sectors until the following January. He was then drafted to Salonika, and, after taking part in fighting on the Vardar front, was transferred to Egypt in August 1917. Later he fought in the Palestine campaign, during which he fought in the engagements at Gaza and Aleppo, and in the capture of Jerusalem and Jericho. He was demobilised after his return to England in April 1919, and holds the General Service and Victory Medals.
40, Lyndhurst Road, Luton.   1568/B.

EAGLES, L. (Mrs.), R.A.O.C.

She joined in February 1917, and during her service was engaged on important clerical duties. She served until August 1918, when she was discharged.
202, Dunstable Road, Luton.   1560/A.

EAGLES, S. A., 2nd Lieutenant, R.A.F.
He joined in April 1917, and was stationed at Farnborough, where he was engaged on important flying duties throughout his service. On one occasion his machine crashed, but fortunately he escaped serious injury. He was demobilised in February 1919.
202, Dunstable Road, Luton.   1560/B.

EALING, F. H., Corporal, Royal Engineers.
He was mobilised at the outbreak of war, and in 1915 was drafted to Gallipoli, where he was present at the landing at Suvla Bay and in the engagements which followed. After the evacuation of the Peninsula he was sent to Egypt, and thence to the Western Front, where he was engaged on duties of an important nature in the Somme and other sectors. On one occasion he was wounded at Ypres, but after treatment was able to rejoin his unit, and remained in France until February 1919. He was demobilised after his return to England, and holds the 1914–15 Star, and the General Service and Victory Medals.
45, Frederic Street, Luton.   1581/A.

EAMES, A. J., L/Corporal, R.M.L.I.
He joined in March 1916, and in the following July was drafted overseas. During his service in France he took part in the Battles of the Somme, Beaumont-Hamel and Arras, and was killed in action in the fierce fighting at the capture of Vimy Ridge on April 28th, 1917. He was entitled to the General Service and Victory Medals.
12, Cassio Bridge Road, Watford.   2709/A.

EAMES, G. W., Private, Bedfordshire Regiment.
Volunteering in August 1914, he was at once sent to France. He was engaged in the fighting at Mons, Ypres, the Somme, Arras and Cambrai, and in other important sectors, and did excellent work throughout his overseas service, which lasted for nearly five years. He was demobilised in March 1919, and holds the Mons Star, and the General Service and Victory Medals. 60, Alexandra Road, St. Albans.   X1529/C.

EAMES, J., Private, Tank Corps.
He joined in June 1916, and in the same year was drafted to France. He took part in numerous important engagements, including those of the Somme, Arras, Cambrai and the Retreat and Advance of 1918. He was demobilised in June 1919 after his return home, and holds the General Service and Victory Medals.
17, Summer Street, Leighton Buzzard.   1586/C.

EAMES, J. W., Private, 5th Bedfordshire and 4th Dorsetshire Regiments.
He joined in June 1916, and after serving in India was drafted to Mesopotamia. In this Eastern field of war he took part in the operations for the Relief of Kut and in many of the engagements in the Advance to Baghdad. He was demobilised in April 1919 after returning to England, and holds the General Service and Victory Medals.
116, Harwood Road, Watford.   X371/B.

EAMES, T., Private, Lincolnshire Regiment.
Joining in January 1917, he was sent to France a year later, and after taking part in engagements at the Somme and St. Quentin, was taken prisoner at Cambrai in April 1918. Released after the Armistice, he returned to England and in November 1919 was demobilised. He holds the General Service and Victory Medals.
21, Branch Road, Park Street, St. Albans.   X1571/B.

EAMES, W., Corporal, R.A.S.C.
He volunteered in September 1915, and was drafted to Salonika at the conclusion of his training early in the following year. During his service overseas he was engaged as a shoeing-smith, and in this capacity did valuable work on the Vardar front. He was accidentally injured in the course of his service, and lost his left thumb in consequence. He was demobilised after his return to England in June 1919, and holds the General Service and Victory Medals.
21, Branch Road, Park Street, St. Albans.   X1571/A.

EARL, G. L., A.B., Royal Navy
He joined in August 1918, and after finishing his training at Harwich, was posted to H.M.S. "Inconstant," in which he subsequently served in the Clyde and at Milford Haven. In 1920 he was still serving.
33, King's Road, Luton.   1566/A.

EARL, H. S., A.B., Royal Navy.
He was in the Navy when war broke out, and throughout the period of hostilities served on board H.M.S "Cleopatra." This vessel was engaged on important duties in the North Sea, the Baltic and off the coast of Scotland, and also took part in several naval engagements, including that off Heligoland Bight. He holds the 1914–15 Star, and the General Service and Victory Medals, and in 1920 was still serving.
33, King's Road, Luton.   1566/B.

EARL, R., Gunner, Royal Garrison Artillery.
He volunteered in July 1915, and on the conclusion of his training in the following April was drafted overseas. His service on the Western Front lasted for two years, during which time he did excellent work with his battery in the Battles of Ypres, Passchendaele Ridge, Arras, the Somme and Cambrai. He was severely wounded in the German Offensive of March 1918, and in consequence was invalided to England. He was demobilised in February 1919, and holds the General Service and Victory Medals.
24, High Street, Lilley, near Luton.   1535.

EARLEY, D. J., Trooper, 1st (Royal) Dragoons.
Joining in November 1917, he was sent to the Western Front on completing his training in the following April. He fought in many engagements during the Retreat and Advance of 1918, and after the cessation of hostilities served with the Army of Occupation in Germany until October 1919. He was demobilised on his return to England, and holds the General Service and Victory Medals.
6, Crispin Terrace, Hitchin.   T2710.

EARTHEY, H. R., Sergeant, R.F.A.
Volunteering at the commencement of hostilities, he was quickly sent to the Western Front, where he fought in many notable battles, including that of Ypres. He afterwards became seriously ill, and after his return to England was, in September 1916, invalided out of the Service. He holds the 1914–15 Star, and the General Service and Victory Medals.
12, Austin Place, Hemel Hempstead.   X1556.

EAST, A., A.B., Royal Navy.
He volunteered in January 1915, and after his training was posted to H.M.S. "Lion." On board this vessel, which during the period of hostilities was engaged in cruising in the North Sea, and off the coasts of Africa, he served for over four years, and did most valuable work. Returning to his base he was demobilised in February 1920, and holds the 1914–15 Star, and the General Service and Victory Medals.
15, Ivy Road, Luton.   1323/B.

EAST, A. F., Trumpeter, R.G.A.
Volunteering in March 1915, he was sent to the Western Front at the conclusion of his training in the following year, and served at the Somme, Passchendaele, Havrincourt Wood and Cambrai. Later he returned to England, and in June 1917 was discharged through causes arising out of his service. He holds the General Service and Victory Medals.
80, Norman Road, Luton.   1561/B.

EAST, C. W., Private, 1st Middlesex Regiment.
Volunteering in May 1915, he was drafted to the Western Front at the conclusion of his training. He was subsequently engaged in the severe fighting at Ypres and Arras, and was wounded and gassed. He was afterwards taken prisoner whilst in action at the Somme and was held in captivity until after the cessation of hostilities. After returning to England he was demobilised in November 1919, and holds the General Service and Victory Medals.
The Hill, Wheathampstead.   2711/B.

EAST, C. W., Private, 44th Canadian Infantry.
Volunteering in 1915, he was retained on important duties for some time after the completion of his training, and was sent to France in June 1917. Subsequently he served in several important engagements, and was in action almost continuously until his death on October 20th of that year. He was entitled to the General Service and Victory Medals.
18, Brightwell Road, Watford.   X1536.

EAST, D., Corporal, R.A.S.C.
He volunteered in August 1914, and until 1916, when he was sent to Salonika, was retained for special duties. Subsequently he served on the Vardar, Struma and Doiran fronts, and was engaged throughout in transporting food and ammunition to the forward areas. He was demobilised on his return to England in April 1919, and holds the General Service and Victory Medals.
12, Cassio Bridge Road, Watford.   X2712.

EAST, G., Driver, R.A.S.C. (M.T.)
Volunteering in October 1915, he was sent to Egypt in the following March, and was subsequently transferred to Palestine. Throughout his service overseas he was engaged in motor-driving, transporting food and ammunition to the troops in the forward areas, and in this capacity was present at several engagements, notably that at Gaza. He holds the General Service and Victory Medals, and was demobilised after his return to England in December 1919.
8, Oxford Terrace, West Street, Dunstable.   1550.

EAST, J., Private, 1st Hertfordshire Regiment.
He volunteered in October 1914, but during the course of his training was found to be medically unfit for service. He was therefore discharged in the following month.
10, Willow Lane, Watford.   2713/B.

EAST, P. A., Private, R.A.M.C.

He volunteered in November 1915, and in the following May, after completing his training, was drafted to France. During his service overseas he was engaged at Vimy Ridge, the Somme, where in September 1916 he was wounded, Arras, Messines and Cambrai, and did excellent work with his unit throughout. He was demobilised after his return to England in 1919, and holds the General Service and Victory Medals.

80, Norman Road, Luton.   1561/A.

EAST, W. G., 1st Air Mechanic, R.A.F.

He joined in August 1916, and on the completion of his training in the following March was sent to the Western Front. During his service in this theatre of war he was engaged on important aeronautical duties which called for a high degree of technical skill, and did valuable work at many air depôts, including those of St. Omer and Marquise. He was demobilised on his return to England in January 1919, and holds the General Service and Victory Medals.

6, Liverpool Road, Watford.   X2714.

EAST, W. J., Private, R.A.S.C.

He volunteered at the commencement of hostilities, and was soon afterwards drafted to the Western Front. His service in this theatre of war lasted for nearly five years, during which time he was engaged on important transport work in various sectors, including those of Ypres, the Somme and Amiens. On one occasion he was wounded. He holds the 1914 Star, and the General Service and Victory Medals, and was demobilised after his return to England in 1919.

2, Caroline Cottages, Capell Road, Oxhey.   2715/B.

EASTON, C. J., Corporal, Worcestershire Regt.

Called from the Reserve at the outbreak of war, he was sent to France early in 1915. While there he fought in many sectors, including that of the Somme, and was wounded in action at Cambrai in November 1917. He was also wounded a second time at Merville during the German Offensive in April 1918. He was demobilised after his return to England in March 1919, and holds the 1914-15 Star, and the General Service and Victory Medals.

8, Bunyan Road, Hitchin.   2716.

EASTON, C. W., Bombardier, R.F.A.

He volunteered in June 1915, and on the completion of his training was sent to Salonika in December 1916. He took part in the Advance across the Struma and in the engagements at Vardar, and was wounded. In December 1918 he returned home and was demobilised in February of the following year, holding the General Service and Victory Medals.

41, Sotheron Road, Watford.   X502/A.

EATON, A., L/Corporal, Royal Engineers.

He volunteered in November 1914, and during his service on the Western Front, which lasted for two years, was engaged on duties of an important nature in the Arras, Ypres and Cambrai sectors. Returning to England after the cessation of hostilities he was demobilised in March 1919, and holds the General Service and Victory Medals.

21, South Road, Luton.   2717.

EATON, F., Sergeant-Major, R.F.A.

He volunteered at the commencement of hostilities, and was retained for important duties with his Battery. His efficient work soon won for him promotion, and he became an instructor at the Hythe School of Gunnery. He was unable to secure his transfer to a theatre of war before the signing of the Armistice, but rendered valuable services until he was discharged in August 1918.

16, Ladysmith Road, St. Albans.   X1527/A.

EATON, F., Q.M.S., Royal Field Artillery.

He volunteered in August 1914, and was afterwards drafted to France and thence to Egypt. After taking part in several minor engagements on this front he was transferred to Palestine, and subsequently was engaged in the fighting at Gaza and Jaffa, and in the Occupation of Haïfa and Beyrout. On one occasion he was wounded. He was demobilised after his return to England in March 1919, and holds the General Service and Victory Medals.

16, Ladysmith Road, St. Albans.   X1527/B.

EATON, O. (Miss), Special War Worker.

This lady held an important post with the London General Omnibus Company for three years during the war. She thus released a man for active service, and performed her duties with much efficiency. On resigning in September 1919 she was presented with a certificate in recognition of her good work.

16, Ladysmith Road, St. Albans.   X1527/C.

EBBS, L., Private, Labour Corps.

He joined in February 1917, and after completing his training was drafted to the Western Front, where he was engaged on important duties in the Ypres and Béthune areas until after the cessation of hostilities. He holds the General Service and Victory Medals, and was demobilised on his return to England in October 1919.

17, New Street, Luton.   2718.

ECOTT, B., Corporal, 2nd Grenadier Guards.

Called from the Reserve at the outbreak of hostilities he was immediately sent to France, and was badly wounded during the Retreat from Mons. On his recovery in the following February he returned to the Western Front and fought at Ypres, Loos, the Somme, where in July 1916 he was wounded a second time, Arras and Lens. During his service he was commended by the G.O.C. of his division for the great courage and gallantry he displayed whilst in charge of a Lewis-gun section, and in recognition of this was awarded a certificate. After the cessation of hostilities he advanced into Germany with the Army of Occupation, and remained there for some time. He was demobilised in March 1919, and holds the Mons Star, and the General Service and Victory Medals.

New Street, Shefford, near Bedford.   Z2719/A.

ECOTT, F. G., Private, 5th Bedfordshire and Lincolnshire Regiments.

Joining in January 1916, he obtained his training at Colchester, and in February of the following year was sent to France. He was subsequently engaged in the fighting at Arras, Ypres, Lens and the Somme, and in May 1918 was severely wounded on the Aisne front and invalided to England. He was demobilised in May 1919, and holds the General Service and Victory Medals.

New Street, Shefford, near Bedford.   Z2719/B.

EDEN, H., Sergeant, Herts Dragoons and R.F.A.

He volunteered in September 1914, and on completing his training early in the following year was drafted to Egypt, where he took part in several minor engagements. Later he served in the Palestine Campaign, during which he was engaged in the fighting at Gaza and in the Occupation of Haïfa and the capture of Jerusalem. Throughout his service overseas, which lasted for nearly four years, he did excellent work, and was demobilised after his return to England in July 1919. He holds the 1914-15 Star, and the General Service and Victory Medals.

11, Pinner Road, Oxhey.   X1537.

EDENS, J., Gunner, Royal Marine Artillery.

Volunteering in May 1915, he was sent to France in July of the following year. He took an active part in the Battles of the Somme, Ypres, Arras and Cambrai, and did valuable work until May 1919, when he returned to England and was demobilised. He holds the General Service and Victory Medals.

1, Parker Street, Watford.   X1546.

EDMONDS, G., Private, Machine Gun Corps.

Called from the Reserve at the outbreak of hostilities, he was quickly drafted to France and took part in the Retreat from Mons. He also served in many of the subsequent engagements, notably those of Ypres, La Bassée, Loos, Festubert and Givenchy, and remained overseas until December 1918. He was demobilised in the following February, and holds the Mons Star, and the General Service and Victory Medals.

41, Prosperous Row, Dunstable.   1564.

EDWARDS, A. B., Private, 2nd Sherwood Foresters.

He volunteered in December 1915, and after finishing his training was drafted to the Western Front, where he took part in many notable battles until hostilities ceased, including those of the Somme, Ypres and Cambrai. On two occasions he was wounded, but after treatment was able to rejoin his unit. He holds the General Service and Victory Medals, and was demobilised after his return to England in September 1919.

12, Tucker Street, Watford.   X1533.

EDWARDS, C., Private, 4th Suffolk Regiment.

He joined on attaining military age in July 1918, but had not completed his training when hostilities ceased. During his service, however, he did much valuable work at various stations until his demobilisation, which took place in November 1919.

20, Vandyke Road, Leighton Buzzard.   2720.

EDWARDS, D., Private, Royal Air Force.

He joined in 1917, and after his training was engaged on important duties in connection with engine repairs, which demanded a high degree of technical knowledge and skill. He was not successful in obtaining his transfer overseas before the cessation of hostilities, but did valuable work until he was demobilised in 1919.

66, Brightwell Road, Watford.   X2721.

EDWARDS, H., Private, Gloucestershire Regt.
Volunteering in September 1914, he was sent to the Western Front in the following July, where he took an active part in several battles, including those of Loos and the Somme, in which he was severely wounded in July 1916. After his recovery in November he was drafted to Salonika, where he served for two years, during which time he did excellent work with his unit. He then returned to France and rendered valuable services in the final stages of the war. He holds the 1914-15 Star, and the General Service and Victory Medals, and in 1919 was discharged through causes arising out of his service.
139, St. James' Road, Watford.   2722.

EDWARDS, J., Private, 9th Warwickshire Regt.
He joined in April 1917, and two months later was drafted to Mesopotamia, where he took an active part in several engagements, including that at Deli Abbas. In August 1918 he was sent with the Military Mission to Russia, and served in the occupation and subsequent evacuation of Baku. He was demobilised after his return to England in January 1920, and holds the General Service and Victory Medals.
19, Oak Road, Luton.   2723.

EDWARDS, S. C., Private, 2nd Volunteer Battalion, Bedfordshire Regiment.
Joining in June 1917, he was engaged on important defence duties on the East Coast. He carried out these responsible duties in an efficient manner, and rendered valuable services, until demobilised in February 1919.
47, Chatsworth Road, Luton.   2726/A.

EDWARDS, S. W., A.B., Royal Naval Division.
Joining in August 1917, he was quickly drafted to France, and subsequently served at Ypres, the Somme and Cambrai, where in 1918 he was taken prisoner. Released after the cessation of hostilities he returned to England, and in May 1919 was demobilised. He holds the General Service and Victory Medals.
29, Merton Road, Watford.   X2724.

EDWARDS, T. H., L/Corporal, Royal Engineers (2nd Field Survey Company).
Joining in July 1916, he was sent to the Western Front on the completion of his training early in the ensuing year. He was subsequently engaged on important duties as observer in the forward areas, and during the course of his service was present at many battles, including those of Ypres, the Somme and Cambrai. Returning to England he was demobilised in April 1919, and holds the General Service and Victory Medals.
23, The Baulk, Biggleswade.   Z1522.

EDWARDS, W., Private, Queen's (Royal West Surrey Regiment).
He joined in June 1917, and in the following September was drafted to the Western Front, where he took part in the heavy fighting at Ypres, Cambrai and the Somme, and many subsequent engagements. He was demobilised in May 1919 after returning to England, and holds the General Service and Victory Medals.
47, Chatsworth Road, Luton.   2726/B.

EDWARDS, W., Private, Border Regiment.
He was mobilised at the outbreak of war, and being sent to France in September 1914, was a month later taken prisoner whilst in action at Ypres. During his captivity in Germany, which lasted for nearly four years, he worked in the salt mines, and suffered greatly from privation. On his release in November 1918 he returned to England, and in December of the following year was demobilised. He holds the 1914 Star, and the General Service and Victory Medals.
68, Saxon Road, Luton.   2725.

EDWARDS, W. S., Gunner, R.F.A.
Joining in October 1914, he was drafted to the Western Front on the completion of his training in the following year. During his service overseas he took part in many engagements, including those at Givenchy, the Somme, Albert, Arras and Cambrai, and was wounded and gassed. He was demobilised in July 1919, and holds the 1914-15 Star, and the General Service and Victory Medals.
29, Brighton Road, Watford.   X2727.

EFFORD, F. E., Private, 25th London Regiment (Cyclists.)
He volunteered in September 1914, and after his training served at various stations on important duties with his unit. He rendered valuable services, but owing to injuries received, was not successful in obtaining his transfer overseas before the cessation of hostilities. He was demobilised in February 1919.
Hill View, Ferndale Road, Luton.   1573.

EGAN, J., Corporal, East Surrey Regiment.
He enlisted in October 1909, and in August 1914 was sent to the Western Front. He took part in the Retreat from Mons, where he was four times wounded and taken prisoner on August 23rd. In November 1918, after over four years' captivity, he was released and returned home. He was demobilised in March 1919, and holds the Mons Star, and the General Service and Victory Medals.
8, Sapwell Lane, St. Albans.   X2728.

EKINS, L., Private, 2nd Northumberland Fusiliers:
Volunteering in November 1914, he was sent to Mesopotamia in June of the following year, and there took part in the operations at Basra, Kut, Baghdad and Mosul. In 1918 he was transferred to India, and rendered valuable service at Bangalore, Rawal Pindi and Delhi. He returned home and was demobilised in February 1920, and holds the 1914-15 Star, and the General Service and Victory Medals.
72, Hitchin Road, Luton.   1580.

ELBOURN, G., Private, R.A.S.C. (M.T.)
Volunteering in November 1915, he was sent to France in March of the following year, where he was engaged in the Somme, Arras, Ypres and Cambrai sectors in the transport of supplies of all kinds. He rendered valuable services until his return home to be demobilised in February 1919, and holds the General Service and Victory Medals.
39, Arthur Road, St. Albans.   X1539/A.

ELBOURN, H., Shoeing Smith, R.A.V.C.
He joined in January 1916, and in December of the same year proceeded to the Western Front, where he was engaged at various stations on important duties in attendance on sick and wounded horses. In 1917 he was transferred to Italy, and did valuable work on the Piave and other fronts. He was demobilised in March 1919 after his return home, and holds the General Service and Victory Medals.
32, Cavendish Road, St. Albans.   X2729.

ELBOURN, H., Private, Royal Fusiliers.
He joined in April 1918, and after his training was sent to France in the following August. He took part in the severe fighting at Cambrai in that month, and was taken prisoner. On his release he returned home and was subsequently demobilised in February 1920, holding the General Service and Victory Medals.
39, Arthur Road, St. Albans.   X1539/B.

ELBOURN, R. P., Ordinary Seaman, R.N.
He joined in January 1918, and was posted to the "Andrew Sack," a mine-sweeping vessel, with which he served in the North Sea until August 1919, when he was demobilised, holding the General Service and Victory Medals. Later he served in the 4th (Queen's Own) Hussars from January till March 1920, when he was discharged as unfit for further military duty.
67, Cavendish Road, St. Albans.   X2730.

ELCOME, R., Corporal, R.A.S.C.
Volunteering in August 1914, he was immediately afterwards sent to the Western Front, where he did valuable work in the Battles of Mons, the Aisne, Ypres, the Somme, Arras, Cambrai and other engagements until hostilities ceased. He returned home and was demobilised in 1919, and holds the Mons Star, and the General Service and Victory Medals.
53, Benskin Road, Watford.   X1570/C.

ELDRED, E., L/Corporal, Queen's (Royal West Surrey Regiment).
He joined in October 1916, and was drafted to France in January of the following year. Remaining there until hostilities ceased, he took part in severe fighting on the Somme and at Arras, Ypres and Cambrai, and after the Armistice proceeded with the Army of Occupation to Germany. He returned home and was demobilised in October 1919, and holds the General Service and Victory Medals.
14, Ivy Road, Luton.   1584.

ELEMENT, A., Private, 15th Essex Regiment.
Volunteering in 1915, he was drafted to France in the same year, and there took part in much severe fighting at the Somme, Arras and Cambrai, and in many other important engagements, and was wounded. He was demobilised in January 1919, and holds the 1914-15 Star, and the General Service and Victory Medals.
36, Queen Street, Hemel Hempstead.   X1553.

ELEMENT, G., Gunner, Royal Field Artillery.
He joined in 1917, and in the same year, after completing his training, was sent to the Western Front, where he took part in numerous engagements, including those at the Somme, Arras and Cambrai, and was severely gassed. He returned home and was demobilised in 1920, holding the General Service and Victory Medals.
11, Two Waters Road, Hemel Hempstead.   X1552/A.

ELEMENT, J., Private, Bedfordshire Regiment.
Volunteering in 1915, he was sent in the same year to France, where he took part in the severe fighting at Hill 60, Ypres, the Somme, Givenchy and many other engagements. He was killed in action in March 1918, and was entitled to the 1914–15 Star, and the General Service and Victory Medals.
11, Two Waters Road, Hemel Hempstead.   X1552/B.

ELEMENT, J. W., Private, 6th Buffs (East Kent Regiment).
He joined in February 1917, and was shortly afterwards drafted to France. Whilst serving in one of his first engagements he was killed in action at Monchy, near Arras, on August 17th, 1917. He was entitled to the General Service and Victory Medals.
9, Duke Street, Watford.   968/A.

ELEMENT, J. W., Private, 9th Middlesex Regt.
He volunteered in January 1915, and after his training was completed served at various stations on important duties with his unit. He was principally engaged in guarding ammunition factories and railways. He was discharged in September 1916 as medically unfit for further military duty.
9, Duke Street, Watford.   X968/B.

ELKERTON, J., Sapper, Royal Engineers.
He volunteered in April 1915, and in September of the same year was sent to the Western Front, where he did valuable wiring, trenching, and pontooning work in connection with many engagements, including the Battle of Loos. Being wounded he was invalided home, and on his recovery six months later was drafted to Salonika, where he served on the Vardar front. He returned home and was demobilised in April 1919, and holds the 1914–15 Star, and the General Service and Victory Medals.
126, Heath Road, Leighton Buzzard.   1523.

ELKINS, J. C., Driver, Royal Engineers.
He volunteered in April 1915, and in the following September was sent to the Western Front, where he was engaged in the Battles of the Somme, Messines, Ypres and other important engagements. He also did much valuable work in the transport of supplies. Owing to heart trouble he returned home in 1918, and was demobilised in January 1919, holding the 1914–15 Star, and the General Service and Victory Medals.
Southill, Beds.   Z2731.

ELKINS, R. J., Gunner, Royal Garrison Artillery.
Volunteering in October 1915, he was drafted to France in March of the following year. During his service overseas he took part in much heavy fighting at the Somme, Arras, Ypres, Passchendaele, Lens, Cambrai and St. Quentin. He was demobilised in June 1919, and holds the General Service and Victory Medals.
17, Cherry Bounce, Hemel Hempstead.   X1526.

ELLEMENT, W., Private, R.A.S.C.
He volunteered in September 1914, and in January of the following year was drafted to France. He rendered valuable transport services in many sectors, including those of Ypres, the Somme, Arras and Albert, until the war ended. He was demobilised in April 1919, and holds the 1914–15 Star, and the General Service and Victory Medals.
58, Cardiff Road, Watford.   X2732/A.

ELLINGHAM, E., Sapper, Royal Engineers.
Volunteering in September 1914, he was sent to France in June of the following year. He served on the Somme on important trenching and wiring duties in connection with his branch of the Service, and did much valuable work. He was severely wounded in 1916, and after hospital treatment was discharged as medically unfit for further service in February 1917. He holds the 1914–15 Star, and the General Service and Victory Medals.
110, Princess Street, Dunstable.   1549.

ELLINGHAM, E. H., Corporal, Royal Engineers.
He joined in April 1916, and after his training was sent to France in May of the following year. He did excellent work in connection with many important engagements until hostilities ceased, including those at Ypres, the Somme, Arras and Albert. He was demobilised in September 1919, and holds the General Service and Victory Medals.
62, Spencer Road, Luton.   2733.

ELLINGHAM, H. A., Private, Bedfordshire Regt.
Joining in 1916, he was shortly afterwards sent to France, where he took part in the severe fighting at the Somme, Arras, Ypres, Cambrai and other important engagements, and was wounded. He returned home and was discharged in consequence of his injuries in April 1918. He holds the General Service and Victory Medals.
3, Lower Paddock Road, Oxhey   X2734.

ELLINGHAM, S., Private, 2nd Cheshire Regt.
He joined in July 1916, and in December of the same year was sent to Salonika, where he was engaged on the Monastir, Doiran and Vardar fronts. During his service abroad he was wounded and contracted malaria. He returned home and was demobilised in December 1919, and holds the General Service and Victory Medals.
2, Letchworth Road, Leagrave, near Luton.   1563.

ELLIOT, A., Corporal, Royal Field Artillery.
Volunteering in October 1915, he was sent to Egypt in December of the same year, and from there to France in the following March. He took part in the severe fighting at Kemmel, the Somme, Beaumont-Hamel, Arras, Vimy Ridge, Lens, and Serre Wood and other engagements until the war ended. He was demobilised in May 1919, and holds the 1914–15 Star, and the General Service and Victory Medals.
47, Portland Street, St. Albans.   1544.

ELLIS, A. C., Air Mechanic, R.A.F. (late R.N.A.S.)
He joined in March 1917, and after his training was sent to Malta in the same year. He was engaged with the Headquarters Staff at Valetta on various important duties, and rendered valuable services. He returned home and was demobilised in December 1919, and holds the General Service and Victory Medals.
45, Buxton Road, Luton.   1557.

ELLIS, A. E., Corporal, R.A.S.C. (M.T.)
Volunteering in March 1915, he was drafted to France in the same year. After valuable transport service at the Base there, he proceeded to France, where he did similar work in the Vardar, Struma and Doiran areas, and later on the Bulgarian and Turkish fronts until hostilities ceased. He returned home and was demobilised in March 1919, and holds the 1914–15 Star, and the General Service and Victory Medals.
69, Sutton Road, Watford.   X2735/B.

ELLIS, C. W., Sergeant, 6th Northamptonshire Regiment.
He joined in May 1917, and on the completion of his training was sent to France in the following August, where he took part in the severe fighting at Arras, Albert, Le Cateau and other engagements up to the close of the war. He was demobilised in December 1919 after returning home, and holds the General Service and Victory Medals.
69, Sutton Road, Watford.   X2735/C.

ELLIS, F., Bombardier, Royal Field Artillery.
He volunteered in September 1914, and after his training served on the Western Front for nearly four years. During this time he participated in many important engagements, notably those on the Somme, at Ypres, Arras and Cambrai, and did excellent work with his battery throughout. He holds the 1914–15 Star, and the General Service and Victory Medals, and was demobilised in February 1919.
38, Spenser Road, Luton.   2736/A.

ELLIS, F., Special War Worker.
When war broke out he obtained work of National importance at Messrs. Kent's, Ltd., Luton, where throughout the period of hostilities he was engaged on important duties in connection with the manufacture of fuses. He carried out this work in a highly satisfactory manner, which was greatly appreciated by the firm.
38, Spenser Road, Luton.   2736/B.

ELLIS, F. H., Corporal, Royal Welch Fusiliers.
Volunteering in September 1914, he proceeded to the Western Front in July of the following year. He took part in the severe fighting at the Somme, Albert, Arras, Ypres, Passchendaele and many other important engagements, and was twice wounded. He returned to England in consequence in September 1918, and was demobilised in January 1920, holding the 1914–15 Star, and the General Service and Victory Medals.
2, Bigthan Road, Dunstable.   1582.

ELLIS, F. L., Private, Bedfordshire Regiment.
He volunteered in September 1914, and in the following year was drafted to the Western Front, where he took part in numerous engagements, including those at Loos, the Somme, Delville Wood, Arras, Ypres and Cambrai. He was three times wounded and gassed. After being invalided home he was demobilised in December 1918, and holds the 1914–15 Star, and the General Service and Victory Medals.
Lower Green, Ickleford, Hitchin.   2933/A.

ELLIS, R. P., Gunner, Royal Field Artillery.
Volunteering in August 1915, he was sent to France on the completion of his training in the same year. There he took part in the severe fighting at the Somme, Albert, Ypres, Arras, Cambrai and other engagements until hostilities ceased. He was demobilised in February 1919, and holds the 1914–15 Star, and the General Service and Victory Medals.
10, Anderson's Row, Florence Street, Hitchin.   2737.

ELLIS, S., Private, 17th Royal Sussex Regt.

He joined in March 1917, and after serving at various depôts on important duties was drafted in the following year to France, where he was in action at Cambrai and in subsequent engagements until the cessation of hostilities. In July 1919 he was sent to Egypt, and proceeding later to Palestine, remained there until April 1920, when he returned home and was demobilised. He holds the General Service and Victory Medals.

84, Bury Road, Hemel Hempstead. X1554.

ELLIS, W. A. (D.C.M.), Sergeant, 2nd Bedford-shire Regiment.

Volunteering in November 1914, he was drafted to France in the following year. Whilst in this theatre of war he took a distinguished part in the fighting at the Somme, Thiepval, Bray, Trônes Wood, Passchendaele and Le Cateau. He was awarded the Distinguished Conduct Medal and Bar for his conspicuous bravery and devotion to duty in the Field on many occasions, and also holds the 1914-15 Star, and the General Service and Victory Medals. He was demobilised in March 1919.

41, Pinner Road, Bushey. X2735/A.

ELLIS, W. G., Private, Bedfordshire Regiment.

He volunteered in December 1914, and in the following July was drafted to the Western Front. He took an active part in the Battles of the Somme, Givenchy, Arras, Ypres and other engagements until hostilities ceased, and was three times wounded. He was demobilised in March 1919, and holds the 1914-15 Star, and the General Service and Victory Medals.

Trowley Hill, Flamstead. X1585.

ELSDON, E. J., Private, 8th Bedfordshire Regt.

He volunteered in January 1915, and after being retained on important duties at various stations was drafted overseas in October of the succeeding year. He was wounded in an engagement near Ypres in April 1917, and after his recovery fought at Hulluch. He was reported missing after this engagement on July 12th, 1917, and was later presumed to have been killed there. He was entitled to the General Service and Victory Medals.

40, Collingdon Street, Luton. 1531/A.

ELSDON, P. H., Driver, Royal Field Artillery.

He volunteered in January 1915, and after his training was drafted to France in the following March. He took part in numerous engagements, including those at Neuve Chapelle, Ypres, Loos and the Somme, and later was in action at Gommecourt and in other engagements until the termination of hostilities. He was demobilised in June 1919, on his return to England, and holds the 1914-15 Star, and the General Service and Victory Medals.

40, Collingdon Street, Luton. 1531/B.

ELSE, B., Sapper, Royal Engineers.

He volunteered in September 1914, and was retained on important duties at various stations until 1917, when he was drafted to France. While there he was engaged in the forward areas whilst operations were in progress, notably at Ypres, Maubeuge and Cambrai, and was gassed. He was demobilised in March 1919, and holds the General Service and Victory Medals.

11, York Street, Luton. 2738.

ELSE, C. F., Private, 5th Middlesex Regiment.

He joined in August 1918, and after his training served at various stations on important duties with his unit. He did not proceed overseas while hostilities were in progress, but in March 1919 he was drafted to Germany to the Army of Occupation, and was stationed on the Rhine until the following March, when he returned home and was demobilised.

27, Periwinkle Lane, Hitchin. 2739.

ELSEY, M. W. F., Private, Bedfordshire Regt.

He joined in June 1916, and in the following month was sent overseas, and took part in the Battle of the Somme. In the following January he was invalided home through illness contracted while overseas, and on his recovery was engaged on various Home defence duties, as he was medically unfit for further trench warfare. He was demobilised in April 1919, and holds the General Service and Victory Medals.

20, George Street, Markyate. 1551.

ELSON, A., Gunner, Royal Garrison Artillery.

He joined in June 1916, and in the same year was drafted to the Western Front. He took part in the Battles of Menin Road, Cambrai and St. Quentin, and was gassed in action. After his recovery he did good work in various subsequent engagements until the cessation of hostilities, and in February 1919, after returning home, was demobilised. He holds the General Service and Victory Medals.

50, York Road, Watford X2741.

ELSTON, E., Private, 5th Bedfordshire Regt.

He volunteered in September 1914, and after his training was engaged at various stations on important duties with his unit. He rendered valuable services, but was not successful in obtaining his transfer overseas before the cessation of hostilities. He was discharged in August 1916 as medically unfit for further military duties.

13, Jubilee Street, Luton. 634/A.

ELSTON, T. G., Sergeant, 5th Bedfordshire Regt.

He was mobilised at the outbreak of hostilities, and after being retained on important duties with his unit was drafted to Egypt in 1916. While in this theatre of war he took a prominent part in several important engagements on the Canal zone and the Sinai Peninsula, and proceeding afterwards on the Palestine Expedition, fought at El Arish, Gaza, Haifa, Acre and Beyrout. After his return home he was demobilised in June 1919, and holds the General Service and Victory Medals.

13, Jubilee Road, Luton. 634/B.

ELSTON, W., Private, Royal Fusiliers.

He joined in March 1917, and in the following May was drafted to France. During his service on the Western Front he took part in the fighting at Ypres and in the Somme sector until September 1917. He then returned home and was discharged in consequence of his service in the following December. He holds the General Service and Victory Medals.

168, Wellington Street, Luton. 2740/A.

ELVEY, R. M., Special War Worker.

He volunteered for work of National importance, and was engaged abroad on the construction of aeroplane hangars at Dunkirk and on the Island of Lemnos. He did excellent work, but owing to illness contracted overseas had to return home and resigned his post.

Brentwood Villa, Blundell Road, Leagrave. 2742.

EMERTON, H., Private, R.A.M.C.

He joined in September 1917, and in the following January was drafted to Salonika, where he did valuable work with his unit on the Vardar and Monastir fronts. He returned home after the cessation of hostilities, and was demobilised in March 1919, holding the General Service and Victory Medals.

9, Lea Road, Luton. 1576.

EMERTON, H. J. (D.C.M.), Corporal, 5th Bedfordshire Regiment.

He had joined the Territorials in June 1914, and in July of the following year was sent to the Dardanelles, where he took part in the landing at Suvla Bay and in subsequent operations until the Evacuation of the Peninsula. He was next drafted to Egypt, and proceeding thence on the Palestine Expedition, fought in the Battle of Gaza, where he was awarded the Distinguished Conduct Medal for conspicuous gallantry and devotion to duty under fire. He also holds the 1914-15 Star, and the General Service and Victory Medals, and was demobilised after his return home in May 1919.

44, Inkerman Road, St. Albans. X1540.

EMERTON, M., Sapper, Royal Engineers.

He joined in December 1917, and after his training served at Chepstow on important duties with his unit. He rendered valuable services, but was unsuccessful in obtaining his transfer overseas before the cessation of hostilities. In January 1919 he was demobilised.

133, Lower Marlowes, Hemel Hempstead. X1575.

EMERTON, P., Private, Labour Corps.

He joined in July 1916, and in the following October was drafted to the Western Front, where he did valuable work in the Battles of the Somme, Arras, Messines, Ypres, Passchendaele and Cambrai. After the termination of hostilities he returned home and was demobilised in February 1919, holding the General Service and Victory Medals.

10, Cumberland Street, Luton. 1559.

EMERTON, W. P., Private, 10th Queen's (Royal West Surrey Regiment).

He joined in October 1918, and in the following month was drafted to Germany, where he served with the Army of Occupation at Cologne until April 1920. He then returned to England and was demobilised.

2, Blacksmith's Lane, St. Albans. 2743.

EMERY, A. J., 1st Air Mechanic, Royal Air Force.

He joined in October 1916, and after his training served at various stations on important duties which demanded a high degree of technical skill. He did excellent work with his squadron, but for medical reasons was not able to secure his transfer overseas. He was demobilised in February 1919.

18, Victoria Road, North Watford. X1543.

EMERY, A. J., Sergeant, Royal Engineers.

He volunteered in April 1915, and in the following month was drafted to France. During his service on the Western Front he was engaged on important duties in connection with the operations, and was frequently in the forward areas at Ypres, the Somme, Arras and Cambrai. He was demobilised in March 1919 after his return to England, and holds the 1914-15 Star, and the General Service and Victory Medals.

115, Estcourt Road, Watford.   X2744/B.

EMERY, D. H., 2nd Lieutenant, 11th Essex Regt.

He joined as a private in April 1917, and in September 1918, after having been retained on important duties with his unit, was drafted to the Western Front in time for the final stages of hostilities. He took part in several operations, and was gassed. During his two years' service he did much valuable work, and attained commissioned rank. He was demobilised in April 1919, and holds the General Service and Victory Medals.

115, Estcourt Road, Watford.   X2744/A.

EMERY, J., Private, 2nd Bedfordshire Regiment.

Volunteering in January 1915, he was drafted to France in the following October, and saw much heavy fighting in the Battles of Loos, the Somme, Beaumont-Hamel, Ypres, Passchendaele Ridge, Cambrai, and in the engagements which followed until the cessation of hostilities. During the Battle of the Somme in October 1916 he was buried by a shell explosion. He was demobilised in March 1919, and holds the 1914-15 Star, and the General Service and Victory Medals.

New Town, Potton.   Z1525.

EMERY, S., Private, 6th North Staffordshire Regiment.

Volunteering at the commencement of hostilities, he was drafted overseas on the conclusion of his training in 1915. During his service in France he took part in the fighting at Hill 60, Ypres and the Somme, where he was severely wounded. After being invalided home he was discharged in March 1917 as medically unfit for further duty. He holds the 1914-15 Star, and the General Service and Victory Medals.

11, Park Lane, Luton.   1534.

EMERY, W., Private, Bedfordshire Regiment.

He volunteered at the commencement of hostilities, and was soon drafted to the Western Front. Whilst in this theatre of war he took part in the fighting at Ypres and the Somme, and was severely wounded at Arras. In 1917 he was sent to Egypt, and after rendering valuable service at Kantara proceeded with General Allenby's Forces in the Advance through Palestine, and was in action at Gaza, Haïfa and Beyrout. He returned home and was demobilised in June 1919, and holds the 1914-15 Star, and the General Service and Victory Medals.

27, Weymouth Street, Apsley.   X1572.

EMERY, W. C., Private, 5th Bedfordshire Regt.

He volunteered in August 1914, and in the following January was drafted to the Western Front, where he took part in the fighting at Ypres and Hill 60 in April 1915, and was severely wounded. On his recovery he was sent to Egypt in the succeeding February, and served in the British Advance through Palestine under General Allenby. He fought in the Battles of Gaza, and was present at the entry into Jerusalem. He returned home and was demobilised in June 1919, and holds the 1914-15 Star, and the General Service and Victory Medals.

81, Waterside, King's Langley.   X1579.

EMES, W. G., Sergeant, 1st West Yorkshire Regt.

He volunteered in August 1914, and soon afterwards was drafted to France. There he took part in the fighting at Neuve Chapelle and other engagements, and was severely wounded and invalided home. After much hospital treatment he was discharged as medically unfit for further service in 1915, and holds the 1914 Star, and the General Service and Victory Medals.

115, Pinner Road, Oxhey.   X2745.

EMSDEN, L. H. (D.C.M.), Sergeant, Bedfordshire Regiment; and Pilot, R.A.F.

He volunteered in 1914, and in the following year was drafted to France, where he took a prominent part in the engagements at Hill 60, Ypres, the Somme, Cambrai and St. Quentin. During his service he was transferred to the Royal Air Force, and had a hand in bringing down 25 enemy aeroplanes. He was awarded the Distinguished Conduct Medal for his conspicuous bravery in action. He was twice severely injured, and was finally discharged as disabled in November 1918. He holds in addition to the Distinguished Conduct Medal the 1914-15 Star, and the General Service and Victory Medals.

107, Church Street, Dunstable.   1565.

ENDERSBY, F. W., Private, Bedfordshire and Dorsetshire Regiments.

He volunteered in October 1914, and after his training was retained at various stations on important duties with his unit. After his transfer to the Dorsetshire Regiment he was sent to India in 1916, and later to Mesopotamia, where he was in action at Kut and Baghdad. He returned home and was demobilised in April 1919, and holds the General Service and Victory Medals.

59, Cowfair Lands, Biggleswade.   Z1524.

ENDERSBY, W. C., Private, Royal Warwickshire Regiment.

He joined in April 1916, and in the following December was sent overseas. During his service on the Western Front he fought at Arras, Vimy Ridge and Lens, but owing to illness contracted abroad was invalided home, and after prolonged treatment was demobilised in September 1919. He holds the General Service and Victory Medals.

The Baulk, Beeston, Sandy.   Z1521.

ENGLAND, E., Private, 4th Bedfordshire Regt.

Volunteering in September 1914, he was drafted to the Western Front in the following year. During his service in France he fought at the Somme, Arras, Cambrai, and in subsequent engagements until October 1918, when he was discharged on account of his service. He holds the General Service and Victory Medals.

1, Charles Street, Hemel Hempstead.   X1555.

ENGLAND, F. E. E., Corporal, Royal Engineers.

He volunteered in August 1914, and after being retained for a time on important duties was sent to France in May 1916. He did valuable work in numerous engagements in various sectors of the Front, including those of the Somme, Vimy Ridge and Passchendaele. He was demobilised in February 1919 after returning home, and holds the General Service and Victory Medals.

4, Bury Dell Lane, near St. Albans.   431/B.

ENGLAND, G. W., Gunner, Royal Field Artillery.

Volunteering in August 1914, he was retained on important duties after the completion of his training until 1917, when he proceeded to France. While there he saw much service until hostilities ceased, and took part in many engagements, including those of Arras and Messines. After his return to England he was demobilised in May 1919, and holds the General Service and Victory Medals.

4, Bury Dell Lane, near St. Albans.   431/A.

ENGLAND, H. D., Private, Machine Gun Corps.

He volunteered in 1915, and after serving on important duties at various stations was drafted to France in February 1917. After taking part in the Battles of Arras and Ypres, he was sent later in the same year to Palestine, and served at the Battle of Gaza. In the ensuing year he proceeded to India, and assisted in the suppression of the Afghan risings. He returned home and was demobilised in December 1919, and holds the General Service and Victory Medals, and the India General Service Medal (with Clasp, Afghanistan, N.W. Frontier, 1919).

64, Adrian Road, Abbots Langley.   X2746.

ENGLAND, J. J., Gunner, Royal Field Artillery.

He volunteered in 1915, and in the same year was drafted to France, where he served at Ypres and was gassed in a subsequent engagement in July 1915. On his recovery he fought at the Somme, Arras, Cambrai, and in the battles that followed until the cessation of hostilities. After the Armistice he proceeded to Germany with the Army of Occupation, and remained until May 1919, when he was demobilised. He holds the 1914-15 Star, and the General Service and Victory Medals.

6, Adrian Road, Abbots Langley.   X2747.

ENGLAND, T., Private, R.A.O.C.

He joined in 1916, and in the same year was sent to France, where he was engaged on important duties in connection with the supply of ammunition at Rouen and other depôts. He did excellent work until the cessation of hostilities, and was demobilised in 1919, holding the General Service and Victory Medals.

53, London Road, Boxmoor.   X1574.

ENSTEN, A. J., Rifleman, 13th Rifle Brigade.

He joined in February 1917, and in the following January was drafted overseas. During his service in France he took part in the Retreat and Advance of 1918, including the Battle of Cambrai, and being severely wounded in action at Achiet-le-Grand on August 28th, 1918, died of his injuries on the same day. He was entitled to the General Service and Victory Medals.

39, Sotheron Road, Watford.   X2748.

ENSTONE, W. C., Private, R.A.O.C.

He volunteered in April 1915, and in the following November was drafted overseas. During his service in France he was employed on important duties with his unit in many engagements, including that of Ypres. He did excellent work until May 1919, when he returned home. He was demobilised in the succeeding month, and holds the 1914–15 Star, and the General Service and Victory Medals.

55, Diamond Road, Watford. X2749.

ENTWISTLE, J. W., Private, King's (Liverpool Regiment).

Volunteering in April 1915, he joined the Royal Fusiliers, and after his training was drafted to France. He took an active part in many important engagements, notably those at Ypres, Festubert and Loos, and on two occasions was severely wounded. He then returned to England, and in April 1917 was invalided out of the Service. In the following March, however, he rejoined in the Queen's Own Cameron Highlanders, but eight months later was discharged. Later he enlisted in the King's Liverpool Regiment, in which in 1920 he was still serving. He holds the 1914–15 Star, and the General Service and Victory Medals.

8, Hagden Lane, Watford. X2750.

ESSEX, H., Private, Worcestershire Regiment.

He joined in March 1918, and in the following May was drafted to the Western Front. He was in action at the Battles of the Somme and Cambrai, and was gassed. He was afterwards transferred to Egypt, where he did much valuable salvage work. After returning home he was demobilised in March 1920, and holds the General Service and Victory Medals.

Leighton Road, Wing, Leighton Buzzard. 1614/A.

ESSEX, W., Royal Garrison Artillery.

Volunteering in October 1915, he was sent to France in February of the following year. He was engaged in moving guns into position, and in the transport of ammunition and supplies on the Somme, Arras and Cambrai fronts, and rendered valuable services. He was demobilised in June 1919, and holds the General Service and Victory Medals.

Leighton Road, Wing, Leighton Buzzard. 1614/B.

ESTWICK, S., Sapper, Royal Engineers (Signals).

He volunteered in July 1915, and proceeded in the same year to the Western Front, where he took a prominent part in the Battles of Loos, the Somme, Arras, Albert and Ypres, and was wounded at the Somme. He was discharged as medically unfit for further service in December 1918, and holds the 1914–15 Star, and the General Service and Victory Medals.

52, York Street, Watford. X2751.

ETCHES, F., Sergeant, M.G.C. (Motor).

Volunteering in January 1915, he proceeded to France in the following March, and took part in the Battles of Neuve Chapelle and Loos. He was then drafted to Russia, and after being ice-bound in the White Sea from December 1915 to May 1916, was engaged on the Caucasian front in August. In the winter of 1917–18 he rendered valuable service on the Roumanian and Galician fronts, and afterwards in Mesopotamia. On the conclusion of his varied and eventful service overseas he returned home and was demobilised in April 1919. He holds the St. George's Cross, a Russian decoration, and in addition the 1914–15 Star, and the General Service and Victory Medals.

Aley Green, near Luton. 2752.

EUINTON, E. A., Corporal, R.A.P.C.

He joined in January 1917, and after his training served at his depôt on important duties with his unit. He rendered valuable clerical services, but on account of medical unfitness was not able to secure his transfer overseas before the cessation of hostilities. He was demobilised in May 1919.

84, Cambridge Street, Luton. 1558/B.

EUINTON, D. L. (Miss), Special War Worker.

For over a year during the war this lady was engaged on important and highly dangerous duties in the manufacture of fuses at the Vauxhall Motor Works, Luton. She carried out her work with great care and efficiency, and was commended for her services.

84, Cambridge Street, Luton. 1558/A.

EVANS, A., Driver, Royal Engineers (Signals).

He was mobilised in 1914, and was sent immediately afterwards to France, where he took part in the Retreat from Mons and the Battle of Ypres. In 1916 he was transferred to Italy, and rendered valuable service on the Piave and Asiago fronts until the war ceased. He was demobilised in February 1919 after returning home, and holds the 1914 Star, and the General Service and Victory Medals.

65, Vale Road, Bushey. X1538

EVANS, B. W. G., Private, R.A.M.C.

Volunteering in October 1915, he was sent to the Western Front in the following year, and there served on the Somme as a stretcher-bearer and did valuable work in hospital. In March 1917 he was transferred to Italy, and was engaged on the Piave front until the war ceased. He was demobilised in February 1919, and holds the General Service and Victory Medals.

High Street, Toddington. 1548/A.

EVANS, C., Private, Durham Light Infantry.

He volunteered at the outbreak of hostilities, and after being retained for important duties with his unit was sent to France in October of the following year. He took part in the heavy fighting at Loos, the Somme, Arras, Ypres, Lens and Cambrai, and was wounded three times. He was killed by accident on August 30th, 1918, and was entitled to the 1914–15 Star, and the General Service and Victory Medals.

38, Warwick Road, Luton. 1578.

EVANS, E. A., Pioneer, Royal Engineers.

He joined in May 1917, and in the same year was sent to France, where he was present at the Battles of Arras and Ypres, and was twice wounded. In September 1919 he was transferred to Egypt, and did good service with his unit at Kantara. He was still serving in 1920, and holds the General Service and Victory Medals.

44, Watson's Walk, St. Albans. X2753.

EVANS, E. J., Private, R.A.S.C. (M.T.)

Joining in December 1916, he was afterwards drafted to the Western Front. He was engaged until the close of the war in the transport of ammunition and supplies to the various fronts, and rendered valuable service. After the Armistice he proceeded with the Army of Occupation to Germany, and on his return home was demobilised in October 1919, holding the General Service and Victory Medals.

2, Jones' Yard, St. Albans. 2754.

EVANS, F., Private, 7th Bedfordshire Regiment.

Volunteering in August 1914, he was sent in the following year to France, where he took part as a Brigade-runner in many important engagements, including those at Loos, Albert, Vimy Ridge and the Somme. He was severely wounded at Lens in August 1917, and after being invalided home, was discharged owing to his injuries in the same month. He holds the 1914–15 Star, and the General Service and Victory Medals.

Victoria Cottage, Ampthill Road, Shefford. 1350/B.

EVANS, F., Bombardier, Royal Field Artillery.

He volunteered in August 1914, and in February of the following year was drafted to the Western Front, and a month later to Egypt. He afterwards took part in the Palestine Campaign, and fought in the Battle of Gaza. After returning to France in March 1918 he was in action at Cambrai and other engagements, and was wounded. He was demobilised in January 1919, and holds the 1914–15 Star, and the General Service and Victory Medals.

59, Old London Road, St. Albans. X1541.

EVANS, F. J., Private, Bedfordshire Regiment.

He volunteered in December 1914, and after a period of training was drafted overseas in 1915. During his service on the Western Front he took an active part in many engagements of great importance, and was killed in action on June 25th, 1916. He was entitled to the 1914–15 Star, and the General Service and Victory Medals.

24, Upper Heath Road, St. Albans. X779/B.

EVANS, G., Private, Labour Corps.

He joined in June 1917, and after his training was engaged on various farms in Scotland on general agricultural duties. He rendered valuable services, but was not successful, for medical reasons, in obtaining his transfer overseas before the cessation of hostilities. He was demobilised in August 1919.

The Laurels, Luton Road, Toddington. 1577.

EVANS, G., Private, 16th (The Queen's) Lancers.

He was serving at the outbreak of war, and was immediately drafted to France, where he took part in the Retreat from Mons, and the Battles of Ypres, Hill 60, Arras, the Somme and many other engagements. He was discharged in 1917 in consequence of his service, and holds the Mons Star, and the General Service and Victory Medals.

13, Upper Paddock Road, Oxhey. X2755.

EVANS, G. E., Private, R.M.L.I.

Joining in May 1918, he was engaged from that year onwards in covering British troops in their operations in Russia, and in other important duties. After rendering valuable services, he was demobilised in 1920, and holds the General Service and Victory Medals.

23, Bernard Street, St. Albans. X1532.

EVANS, G. H., Trooper, Sussex Dragoons.

He volunteered in December 1915, and was shortly afterwards sent to Ireland, where he was present during the
Dublin Riots. He was drafted in August 1916 to France,
and took part in the Battles of the Somme, Arras, Ypres,
Cambrai and the Retreat of 1918, and was wounded. He
was demobilised in January 1919, and holds the General
Service and Victory Medals.
23, Regent Street, Leighton Buzzard.   1601.

EVANS, H., Private, Machine Gun Corps.

He joined in July 1916, and in the following September was
sent to Salonika. Whilst in this theatre of war he served in
the General Offensive of the Allies on the Doiran front and
in the Advance on Vardar. After the cessation of hostilities
he remained overseas until November 1919, when he returned
home and was demobilised, holding the General Service and
Victory Medals.
7, Summer Street, Slip End.   1567.

EVANS, J., Gunner, Royal Garrison Artillery.

Joining in February 1917, he went through his course of
training and was afterwards sent to France, where he remained for nearly two years. During his service overseas
he took part in many important engagements, including those
at Cambrai and Ypres. He was demobilised in February
1919 after his return home, and holds the General Service
and Victory Medals.
59, Saxon Road, Luton.   2756.

EVANS, J. J., Private, Lancashire Fusiliers.

Joining in June 1917, he was sent overseas at the conclusion
of his training. His service in France lasted for two years,
during which time he was engaged in the fighting in many
sectors, notably those of the Somme and Cambrai, and was
wounded and gassed. He holds the General Service and
Victory Medals, and was demobilised after his return to
England in December 1919.
2, Caroline Cottages, Capel Road, Oxhey.   2715/A.

EVANS, L. F., Rifleman, Royal Irish Rifles.

Joining in November 1916, he was drafted to France in
January of the following year, and took part in numerous
engagements until hostilities ceased, including those at
Albert, St. Quentin, Arras and Cambrai. He was demobilised in February 1919, after his return to England, and
holds the General Service and Victory Medals.
High Street, Toddington.   1548/B.

EVANS, M. P., Private, 2nd Bedfordshire Regt.

He joined in November 1916, and in the same year was
drafted to the Western Front. There he saw much heavy
fighting at Vimy Ridge, and was wounded at Albert, and
again at Kemmel Hill. He was invalided home in consequence, and discharged as unfit for further military duty in
February 1918. He holds the General Service and Victory
Medals.
52, Selbourne Road, Luton.   1562.

EVANS, O., Private, R.A.S.C.

He volunteered in March 1915, and in the same year was
drafted to the Western Front. During his service in France
he was engaged on important transport duties, conveying
rations and ammunition up to the front lines in the Somme,
Arras, Ypres and Cambrai sectors. He was discharged as
medically unfit for further duty in November 1918, and holds
the 1914-15 Star, and the General Service and Victory Medals.
6, Caroline Cottages, Capell Road, Oxhey.   X2757/A.

EVANS, W., Boy, R.N., H.M.S. " Ganges."

He joined the Navy in June 1918, and whilst in training on
H.M.S. " Ganges " became seriously ill. He died on January
28th, 1919.
6, Caroline Cottages, Capell Road, Oxhey.   X2757/B.

EVANS, W., Private, 1st Hertfordshire Regt.

He volunteered in January 1915, and in the same year was
sent to France. Whilst in this theatre of war he took part
in the fighting at Loos and the Somme, where he was gassed.
After his recovery he served at Arras, Ypres and Albert,
and in the subsequent engagements until the cessation of
hostilities. He was demobilised after his return to England
in March 1919, and holds the 1914-15 Star, and the General
Service and Victory Medals.
6, Caroline Cottages, Capell Road, Oxhey.   X2757/C.

EVANS, W., Rifleman, 18th London Regiment (London Irish Rifles).

He volunteered in May 1915, and later in the same year,
after completing his training, was drafted to the Western
Front. After taking part in several minor engagements he
was killed in the heavy fighting in the Somme Offensive on
September 16th, 1916, and was buried in the British cemetery
there. He was entitled to the General Service and Victory
Medals.
New Street, Shefford.   Z2758.

EVANS, W. J., Sapper, Royal Engineers.

He volunteered in August 1914, and on the completion of
his training was sent to the Dardanelles, where he was engaged on important duties in connection with the operations
until the evacuation of the Peninsula. He was then drafted
to the Western Front, and rendered valuable services as a
carpenter with the Inland Water Transport until the war
ended. He fought in the Battle of Cambrai. After his
return home he was demobilised in January 1919, and holds
the 1914-15 Star, and the General Service and Victory
Medals.
5, Upper Culver Road, St. Albans.   X1547.

EVERETT (née SEWELL), A. E. (Mrs.), N.C.O., Women's Legion and Q.M.A.A.C.

She volunteered in February 1917, and during the following
two years did valuable work with these two bodies of women
workers at St. John's Wood and Regent's Park. She acted
as head waitress, and by her efficient services rose to the
responsible position of forewoman. She was discharged in
April 1919.
14, Bardwell Street, St. Albans.   X2759.

EVERETT, F., Driver, Royal Engineers.

He volunteered in September 1915, and after his training
served on important duties with his unit until July of the
following year, when he was drafted to the Western Front.
While there he rendered excellent service in numerous en-
gagements, including those of the Somme, Arras, Ypres and
Cambrai. He was demobilised in May 1919, and holds the
General Service and Victory Medals.
The Grange, High Street, Toddington.   1042/A.

EVERITT, A. T., Private, 8th Bedfordshire Regt.

Volunteering in September 1914, he was drafted in the
following year to the Western Front, where he fought at
Hill 60 and in several subsequent engagements. He was
killed in action near Ypres on March 1st, 1916, and was
entitled to the 1914-15 Star, and the General Service and
Victory Medals.
62, Apsley End, Herts.   X1583.

EVERITT, B., Private, 1st Hertfordshire Regt.

He volunteered in August 1915, and after his training was
completed served at various stations on important duties
with his unit. In January 1917 he was drafted to France,
and took part in the Battles of Ypres and Cambrai, and in
the engagements which followed during the Retreat and
Advance of 1918. He was demobilised in January 1919, and
holds the General Service and Victory Medals.
20, Ashton Road, Luton.   1530.

EVERITT, W. S., Pioneer, Royal Engineers.

He volunteered in December 1914, and after his training
was completed was drafted to Gallipoli in the following
July. Whilst in this theatre of war he took part in the
landing at Suvla Bay and in the subsequent operations until
the Evacuation of the Peninsula. He was then sent to Egypt,
and advanced with the British forces under General Allenby
into Palestine. Here he was engaged on important duties
in connection with the operations and was frequently under
fire. He returned home in April 1919, and was demobilised
in the following month, holding the 1914-15 Star, and the
General Service and Victory Medals.
25, Bailey Street, Luton.   2760.

EVETTS, J. H. (Mrs.), Nurse.

This lady was appointed Junior Staff Nurse at Graylingwell
War Hospital, Chichester, in May 1918. For nearly a year
she carried out her responsible duties with skill and efficiency,
and resigned her position in April 1919.
Morval, Kneller Road, Brockley, S.E.4   X2761/B.

EVETTS, W. A. (M.C.), Major, R.G.A.

He volunteered in October 1914, and in September of the
following year was drafted to France. Whilst in this theatre
of war he took a prominent part in the Battles of Loos,
the Somme, Arras, Ypres, Kemmel and the Aisne. In
May 1917 he was mentioned in Despatches by Sir Douglas
Haig, and was awarded the Military Cross for distinguished
gallantry in the Field in January 1918. In the following
October he gained the French Legion d'Honneur for conspicuous bravery in action. He holds in addition to these
medals the 1914-15 Star, and the General Service and
Victory Medals, and was demobilised in May 1919.
Morval, Kneller Road, Brockley, S.E.4   X2761/A.

EVINTON, A. E., Private, R.A.M.C.

He volunteered in August 1914, and being medically unfit
for overseas warfare was retained on important duties as
hospital orderly in a large military hospital at Blackpool.
He carried out his work with great care and efficiency, and
was discharged in October 1918 on medical grounds.
54, Ridgway Road, Luton.   1569.

EWER, C. W., L/Corporal Queen's (Royal West Surrey Regiment).
He volunteered in 1914, and during the war saw much varied service. He was drafted to France in 1915, and fought at Ypres and Festubert. In the following year he was sent to Salonika, where he was engaged at the recapture of Monastir, and later proceeded to Egypt and served in the Palestine campaign. Here he took part in the fighting at Gaza, Jaffa, Haifa, Damascus and Aleppo, and was present at the fall of Jerusalem. In August 1919 he returned home and was demobilised, holding the 1914-15 Star, and the General Service and Victory Medals.
18, College Place, St. Albans. 1528.

EWER, W., Private, 2nd Bedfordshire Regiment.
He volunteered in September 1914, and in the following July, after completing his training, was drafted to France. In October of that year he was wounded at Ypres, and again in July 1916 in the Battle of the Somme. He was invalided home and discharged as medically unfit for further military service in July 1917, and holds the 1914-15 Star, and the General Service and Victory Medals.
Watland Place, Frogmore, near St. Albans. X1542.

EWINGTON, H. J., Private, Cheshire Regiment.
He joined in October 1916, and after his training was completed was drafted to France. During his service on the Western Front he took part in the Battle of Cambrai and many other engagements, and was wounded. He was demobilised in November 1919 after returning to England, and holds the General Service and Victory Medals.
Holly Cottage, King's Walden. 2762/B.

EZRA, G., Gunner, Royal Field Artillery.
He volunteered in 1914, and in the same year was drafted to India, where he was engaged on important garrison duties at Rawal Pindi, Poona and other stations until 1916. He was then sent to Mesopotamia, and took part in the Battles of Kut and the capture of Baghdad, and was present at the occupation of Mosul. He was demobilised after his return to England in 1919, and holds the General Service and Victory Medals.
3, Grove Cottages, Grove Road, Harpenden. 2763/A.

F

FACER, C., Corporal, Royal Sussex Regiment.
He volunteered at the outbreak of hostilities, and in the following June was sent to the Western Front, where he took part in the heavy fighting on the Somme and at Ypres, and in the Retreat and Advance of 1918, and was wounded. He holds the 1914-15 Star, and the General Service and Victory Medals, and was still serving in 1920.
17, Capron Road, Dunstable. 117/B.

FACER, H., Private, 5th Bedfordshire Regiment.
He volunteered in August 1914, and in March of the following year was sent to the Dardanelles and served in the landing at Gallipoli. Later in the same year he proceeded to Egypt, and was transferred to the Royal Army Medical Corps, and was engaged on hospital duties. In 1917 he returned home, but afterwards was sent to Salonika, where he was killed in action on the Vardar front on July 13th, 1918, and was entitled to the 1914-15 Star, and the General Service and Victory Medals.
141, High Street, Dunstable. 2791.

FAIERS, J. W., Sergeant, Royal Irish Fusiliers.
He was serving in 1914, and in October of the same year was sent to the Western Front, where he took part in the Retreat from Mons and the Battle of Arras and other important engagements, and was twice wounded. He was afterwards transferred to Egypt and thence to Palestine, and finally to Salonika. He was demobilised in November 1919, and holds the 1914 Star, and the General Service and Victory Medals.
Luton Road, Harpenden. 2792.

FAIREY, A., Gunner, Royal Horse Artillery.
Joining in May 1916, he went through a course of training and afterwards served at various stations on important duties with his battery. He rendered valuable services, but was not successful in obtaining his transfer overseas before the cessation of hostilities, owing to being medically unfit. He was demobilised in September 1919.
3, Garden Cottages, Lyles Row, Hitchin. 2793.

FALLOWFIELD, G., Gunner, R.G.A.
He volunteered in November 1915, and after his training served at various stations on important duties with his battery. He rendered valuable services, but was not successful in obtaining his transfer overseas owing to being medically unfit, and was discharged in June 1916. In 1917 he re-enlisted, but was discharged later in the same year owing to his physical disabilities.
2, King's Road, Hitchin. 2794.

FAREY, E., L/Corporal, 5th, 8th and 4th Bedfordshire Regiment.
Volunteering in September 1914, he was sent to Gallipoli in August of the following year and took part in the landing at Suvla Bay. On the Evacuation of the Peninsula he returned home, and in 1917 was drafted to the Western Front, where he served in numerous engagements, including those on the Somme and at Cambrai, and was twice wounded. He was demobilised in January 1919, and holds the 1914-15 Star, and the General Service and Victory Medals.
5, Salisbury Road, Luton. 2795.

FAREY, M., Private, 7th Hertfordshire Regt.
He volunteered in August 1914, and in the same year was sent to the Western Front, where he took part in many important engagements, including those at Ypres, Béthune and Lens, and was wounded. He died of his injuries on December 5th, 1915, and was entitled to the 1914 Star, and the General Service and Victory Medals.
5, Penn's Yard, St. Andrew's Street, Hitchin. 2796.

FARNHAM, J., Sergeant, Labour Corps.
He was serving at the outbreak of war and was shortly afterwards sent to the Western Front, where he took part in many important engagements, including those on the Somme and at Cambrai, Ypres and Bapaume, and was twice wounded. He was demobilised in March 1919, and holds the 1914-15 Star, and the General Service and Victory Medals.
14, Holly Walk, Luton. 2797.

FARMER, A. E., Private, 3rd Bedfordshire Regt.
After volunteering in August 1914, he was drafted to the Western Front. He took part in heavy fighting during the Retreat from Mons and at the Battle of the Marne, and was killed in action on April 17th, 1915. He was entitled to the Mons Star, and the General Service and Victory Medals.
Ivy Cottage, The Leys, Woburn Sands. Z2800/B.—Z2801/B.

FARMER, H., Private East Surrey Regiment.
Volunteering in September 1914, he was drafted to France in the following year and took part in numerous engagements, including those at Ypres and on the Somme, and was severely gassed. He was invalided home and discharged in April 1916, and holds the 1914-15 Star, and the General Service and Victory Medals.
10, Duke Street, Luton. 2798/A.

FARMER, H. R., Sergeant, Middlesex Regiment.
He volunteered in August 1914, and was sent to France in the following year and took part in heavy fighting at the Battles of Ypres and Arras. He was discharged suffering from shell-shock in May 1917, but rejoined in September 1918, and was engaged on various important duties until January 1919, when he was demobilised. He holds the 1914-15 Star, and the General Service and Victory Medals.
48, Holywell Road, Watford. X2799/A.

FARMER, J., Private, Machine Gun Corps.
He volunteered in 1915, and in the same year was drafted to the Western Front, where he served in numerous engagements, including those at Loos, Lens, Arras and Cambrai, and was taken prisoner. On his release he returned home and was demobilised in August 1919, and holds the 1914-15 Star, and the General Service and Victory Medals.
Ivy Cottage, The Leys, Woburn Sands. Z2800/C—Z2801/C.

FARMER, J., Private, R.A.V.C.
Volunteering in August 1915, he was sent in the following December to France, where he was engaged in attending to sick and wounded horses, and rendered valuable services. He was afterwards transferred to Salonika and served on the Struma and Monastir fronts. He was demobilised in May 1919, and holds the General Service and Victory Medals.
3, Right-of-Way, New Town, Hatfield. X28002/B.

FARMER, L., Private, 22nd Manchester Regt.
He joined in January 1917, and was sent to the Western Front, where he took part in severe fighting at Ypres, Passchendaele and Cambrai. In 1918 he was transferred to Egypt, where he served at Cairo and Port Said, and later was drafted to Austria with the Army of Occupation. He was demobilised in February 1920, and holds the General Service and Victory Medals.
3, Right-of-Way, New Town, Hatfield. X2802/A.

FARMER, R., Sapper, Royal Engineers.
He joined in June 1918, and after his training served on important duties with his unit until December of the same year, when he was drafted to the Army of Occupation in Germany, where he remained until February 1920, when he returned home and was demobilised.
10, Duke Street, Luton. 2798/B.

FARMER, W., Private, Lancashire Fusiliers.
He joined in February 1917, and in July of the same year was drafted to the Western Front, where he took part in numerous engagements, including those at Ypres, Passchendaele, Cambrai, Amiens and the Somme, and was wounded and gassed. He was demobilised in November 1919, and holds the General Service and Victory Medals.
98, Baker Street, Luton.   2803/A.

FARMER, W. G., Private, Oxfordshire and Buckinghamshire Light Infantry.
Joining in 1914 he was sent to India, where he served at various stations on important duties. In 1916 he was transferred to Mesopotamia, and took part in engagements at Kut-el-Amara and on the Tigris. He was demobilised in 1919, and holds the 1914-15 Star, and the General Service and Victory Medals.
Ivy Cottage, The Leys, Woburn Sands. Z2800/A—Z2801/A.

FARNHAM, A., Sergeant, R.A.M.C.
Joining in October 1916, he went through a course of training, and in August of the following year was sent to France, where he served at the Battles of Ypres, the Somme and many other important engagements. He was demobilised in April 1920, and holds the General Service and Victory Medals.
16, Surrey Street, Luton.   2804/A.

FARNHAM, H., Private, Essex Regiment.
He joined in May 1916, and was sent to France in the same year. He served in numerous engagements, and was wounded and taken prisoner during the Retreat of March 1918. On his release he returned home and was demobilised in April 1919, and holds the General Service and Victory Medals.
Stopsley, near Luton.   2804/C.

FARNHAM, L. F., Pte., 5th Bedfordshire Regt.
He was mobilised with the Territorials in August 1914, and was drafted to France in May of the following year, but later was sent home owing to being under age. In June 1917 he again proceeded to France, where he served in various engagements, and was taken prisoner in March 1918. On his release he returned home and was demobilised in April 1919, and holds the 1914-15 Star, and the General Service and Victory Medals.
16, Surrey Street, Luton.   2804/B.

FARR, C. W., Private, Royal Fusiliers.
He joined in October 1916 and was drafted to France in the same year, and took part in many engagements, including those on the Somme. He was killed in action at Ypres on October 9th, 1917, and was entitled to the General Service and Victory Medals.
Ireland, Shefford.   Z2805.

FARR, F., Private, 5th Bedfordshire Regiment.
Volunteering in November 1914, he was sent to the Western Front in April of the following year, and took part in severe fighting in various engagements, including that at Ypres, where he was wounded. He was invalided home and discharged owing to his injuries in March 1917, and holds the 1914-15 Star, and the General Service and Victory Medals.
142, New Town Street, Luton.   796/B.

FARR, H., Private, Royal Berkshire Regiment and Labour Corps.
He joined in January 1917, and after his training was drafted to the Western Front, where he took part in severe fighting at Cambrai and Albert, and was wounded. He was afterwards transferred to the Labour Corps, with which he served until January 1919 when he was demobilised, holding the General Service and Victory Medals.
33, Grove Road, Luton.   2806/A—2807/A.

FARROW, C. G., Private, 3rd Bedfordshire Regt.
He joined in April 1917, and in the following July was drafted to Egypt, and thence to Palestine. In this theatre of war he took part in several important engagements, including those at Gaza and Jaffa, and did excellent work with his unit until October 1919, when he returned to England and was demobilised. He holds the General Service and Victory Medals.
29, Hitchin Hill, Hitchin.   2808.

FATHERS, E. G., Private, 1st Bedfordshire Regt.
Volunteering at the commencement of hostilities, he was sent to France in November 1914, and subsequently took an active part in the Battles of Neuve Chapelle, Ypres and the Somme. In September 1916 he was drafted to India, where, for the remaining period of his service he was engaged on special duties. He was demobilised on his return to England in May 1919, and holds the 1914 Star, and the General Service and Victory Medals.
21, Stoke Road, Linslade, Leighton Buzzard.   2809.

FAULDER, P. G., Corporal, 1st Hertfordshire Regiment.
He volunteered in April 1915, and was sent to the Western Front on completion of his training. During his service overseas, which lasted for nearly four years, he took an active part in numerous engagements, including those at Passchendaele Ridge and Cambrai, and did excellent work with his unit. He holds the 1914-15 Star, and the General Service and Victory Medals, and was demobilised in January 1919.
29, New England Street, St. Albans.   ·   2810.

FAULKNER, A., Private, Bedfordshire Regt.
He volunteered in September 1914, but whilst in training contracted pneumonia, of which he subsequently died in hospital on February 1st, 1915.
Southill, Beds.   Z2811.

FAULKNER, A. G., Private, Oxfordshire and Buckinghamshire Light Infantry.
He volunteered in August 1914, and in the following June was sent to France, where he served for three months. Later he was transferred to Salonika, and subsequently fought on the Vardar and Struma fronts. He was also engaged for a time in conveying food and ammunition to the forward areas, and in this capacity did excellent work. Returning to England, he was demobilised in May 1919, and holds the 1914-15 Star, and the General Service and Victory Medals.
38, Baker Street, Leighton Buzzard.   2812/B.

FAULKNER, C., Gunner, R.G.A.
He joined in 1918, and after his training was engaged on important duties on the anti-aircraft guns. He was not successful in obtaining his transfer overseas before the termination of hostilities, but nevertheless rendered valuable services until his demobilisation, which took place in 1919.
15, Church Street, St. Albans.   2813/B.

FAULKNER, C. A., Private, 2nd Bedfordshire Regiment.
He joined in 1918, but had not completed his training when hostilities ceased. Afterwards, however, he was sent with the Army of Occupation to Germany, where he was engaged on duties of a special nature until the latter part of 1919, when he returned to England and was demobilised.
15, Church Street, St. Albans.   2813/A.

FAULKNER, L. (M.S.M.), Sergeant, 1st Lincolnshire Regiment.
A serving soldier, he was drafted to the Western Front at the outbreak of hostilities, and took part in the Retreat from Mons. He subsequently fought in many other important engagements, including those at Ypres, Arras, Passchendaele, Cambrai, St. Quentin and Beaumont-Hamel, and was wounded five times. In May 1918 he was awarded the Meritorious Service Medal for his efficient work in the Field and in addition holds the Mons Star, and the General Service and Victory Medals. He was discharged in March 1919.
17, Cherry Bounce, Hemel Hempstead.   X2814.

FAULKNER, T. G., Private, 1/6th South Staffordshire Regiment.
Joining in March 1916, he was sent to the Western Front at the conclusion of his training. He was subsequently engaged in the fighting at Loos and Albert, and was killed in action during the operations at Vermelles on May 12th, 1917. He was entitled to the General Service and Victory Medals.
New Street, Shefford, Bedford.   Z2815/A.

FAULKNER, W., Private, Queen's Own (Royal West Surrey Regiment).
He volunteered in January 1915, and on the completion of his training was, in the following July, drafted to France, where he took part in numerous engagements, and was wounded at the Battle of the Somme in July 1916. He was invalided home, but on his recovery returned to France, and was killed in action at Cambrai on March 14th, 1918. He was entitled to the 1914-15 Star, and the General Service and Victory Medals.
13, Butcher's Yard, Watford.   913/B.

FAUNCH, J., Air Mechanic, Royal Air Force.
He had previously volunteered, but was rejected on medical grounds, and finally joined the Royal Air Force in July 1918. Two months later he was drafted to France, where, during the Advance of that year, he was engaged on important duties which called for a high degree of technical skill. He was demobilised on his return to England in January 1919, and holds the General Service and Victory Medals.
27, Stanbridge Road, Leighton Buzzard.   2816.

FAVELL, E., Private, 1/5th Bedfordshire Regt.
He volunteered at the commencement of hostilities and in March 1915 was drafted to Egypt and served with General Allenby's Forces in the Advance through Palestine. Whilst in this theatre of war he took part in the three Battles of Gaza and was severely wounded in 1917. After his recovery he was present at the capture of Jerusalem, and later fought at Aleppo and in subsequent engagements until the termination of the war. He returned home and was demobilised in March 1919, after exactly four years' overseas service, and holds the 1914-15 Star, and the General Service and Victory Medals.
12, Barrow Path, Leighton Buzzard   2817.

FAVELL, G., Sergeant-Major, Bedfordshire Regt.
He volunteered in August 1914, and was drafted to the Western Front and fought in the Battles of Ypres, Loos and the Somme, where he was wounded. After his recovery he was in action at Arras and Cambrai, and in various subsequent engagements. During his service in France he acted for a time as Instructor, and after hostilities were concluded he proceeded to India, where he was employed on special duties at various garrison outposts, and in 1920 was still serving there. He holds the 1914 Star, and the General Service and Victory Medals.
12, Barrow Path, Leighton Buzzard.   2818.

FEARN, A. E., Private, 1st Hertfordshire Regt.
He volunteered in April 1915, and in the following year was drafted to France, where he took part in the heavy fighting on the Somme and in the third Battle of Ypres. He was wounded in action and taken prisoner on July 31st, 1917, and held in captivity in Germany until his release early in 1919. He was then sent home and demobilised in March, and holds the General Service and Victory Medals.
28, College Place, St. Albans.   2819.

FEARN, C. E., Corporal, Royal Engineers.
He volunteered in October 1915, and after his training was drafted to Salonika in January 1917. Whilst in this theatre of war he was engaged on important duties in connection with the operations at various points of the Macedonian Front. He returned home, and was demobilised in July 1919, and holds the General Service and Victory Medals..
7, Grange Street, St. Albans.   X2820.

FEARN, W., Private, R.A.S.C.
Volunteering in September 1914, he was engaged at various stations on important duties with his unit until September 1917, when he was drafted overseas. Whilst in France he served on transport work conveying supplies up to the lines, and was present at many engagements in the Somme, Arras and Cambrai sectors. He was severely wounded near Ypres in January 1918, and was invalided to hospital and finally demobilised in March 1919. He holds the General Service and Victory Medals.
43, Edward Street, Dunstable, Luton.   2821—2822.

FEAZEY, W. E., Corporal, Machine Gun Corps.
He joined in January 1916, and in the following year was drafted to France, where he took part in the fighting at Arras, Ypres, Cambrai and St. Quentin, and was wounded and gassed. He was demobilised after the conclusion of hostilities in January 1919, and holds the General Service and Victory Medals.
High Street, Flitwick, Beds.   2823.

FELKS, A., Sapper, Royal Engineers.
He volunteered in October 1914, and in the following year was drafted to the Dardanelles, and took part in the landing at Suvla Bay and in subsequent engagements in Gallipoli, until the Evacuation of the Peninsula. Later he was sent to Salonika and from there to Egypt, where he was engaged on important duties at Ismalia and in the Canal zone. In 1917 he proceeded to Palestine, and served at Gaza, Haifa, Acre and Beyrout. He was finally demobilised after his return to England in June 1919, and holds the General Service and Victory Medals.
23, John Street, Luton.   2824/A.

FELKS, H., Rifleman, King's Royal Rifle Corps.
He joined in September 1918, and in the following December was drafted to Mesopotamia, where he was stationed at Baghdad, and was engaged on important garrison duties. In 1920 he was still serving, and holds the Victory Medal.
23, John Street, Luton.   2824/B.

FELKS, T., Private, Bedfordshire Regiment.
He volunteered in April 1915, and was drafted to the Dardanelles, and took part in the landing at Suvla Bay and in the engagements which followed until the Evacuation of Gallipoli. In 1917 he was sent to Egypt, and served with the British Forces under General Allenby in the Advance on Palestine, and fought in the Battle of Gaza. He was killed in action in a later engagement on July 21st, 1917, and holds the 1914-15 Star, and the General Service and Victory Medals.
23, John Street, Luton.   2824/C.

FELKS, T S., L/Corporal, Royal Fusiliers.
He joined in March 1916, and in the following September was drafted to the Western Front, where he served for 2½ years. He fought on the Somme and at Vimy Ridge, Ypres, Passchendaele and Cambrai, and in numerous subsequent engagements until the conclusion of hostilities. He was demobilised after his return home in February 1919, and holds the General Service and Victory Medals.
63, Dordans Road, Leagrave   2825.

FELL, N., Sergeant, Royal Welch Fusiliers.
Volunteering in January 1915, he was drafted to Mesopotamia later in the same year and served in the campaign against the Turks, being present at the capture of Baghdad. On August 10th, 1918, he was drowned whilst bathing in the River Tigris, and was entitled to the 1914-15 Star, and the General Service and Victory Medals.
3, Common View Square, Letchworth.   2826/B.

FELLOWS, S., Private, 1st East Surrey Regt.
He joined in August 1917, and in April of the following year was sent to the Western Front, where he fought at Lens and was severely gassed. On recovery he proceeded to North Russia in August 1918, and served with the Relief Forces until November 1919. He was then sent home, and in January 1920 drafted to Ireland, where he was engaged on important duties at various stations until May of the same year, when he was demobilised. He holds the General Service and Victory Medals, and the Russian Order of St. George.
38, Cecil Street, North Watford.   X2827.

FELLS, H., Private, Machine Gun Corps.
He volunteered in June 1915, and on the completion of his training was drafted overseas. During his service in France he fought at Arras and St. Quentin, and was wounded. On recovery he served in various engagements during the Advance until the conclusion of hostilities. He was demobilised in February 1919, and holds the General Service and Victory Medals.
Lichfield, Cowper Road, Harpenden.   2828.

FENEMORE, L. T., 1st Class Petty Officer, R.N., H.M.S. " Queen."
He was mobilised at the outbreak of war, and served in H.M.S. " Queen," and was engaged in the bombardment of the Dardanelles Forts during the naval operations against the Turks. After the Evacuation of the Gallipoli Peninsula he served in Grecian waters and off the coast of Italy until the conclusion of hostilities. He was finally demobilised in April 1919, and holds the 1914-15 Star, and the General Service and Victory Medals.
47, Souldern Street, Watford.   X2829.

FENLEY, J., Private, Labour Corps.
He volunteered at the commencement of hostilities, and was drafted to the Dardanelles and took part in the first landing at Gallipoli, and was wounded. On recovery he was sent to Mesopotamia, where he served at Kut-el-Amara and in the British success on the Tigris. Later he proceeded to Egypt, was with General Allenby's Forces in the Advance through Palestine, and was in action at Gaza and Haifa, and was wounded. Afterwards he was drafted to the Western Front, where he served until demobilised in March 1919. He holds the 1914-15 Star, and the General Service and Victory Medals.
Millbrook, near Ampthill.   2830.

FENSOM, L., Private, Machine Gun Corps.
He joined in October 1918 on the attainment of military age, and after his training served at various stations on important duties with his unit. He rendered valuable services, but not having completed his training before the termination of hostilities, was unable to procure his transfer overseas. He was demobilised in March 1919.
Bidwell Farm, Dunstable.   2831.

FENSOM, W. W., Private, 2nd Bedfordshire Regt.
He volunteered in December 1914, and in the following year was drafted to the Western Front. During his service in France he fought in the Battles of the Somme, Arras and Cambrai, and was wounded. In May 1918 he was killed in action in an engagement near Ypres, and was entitled to the 1914-15 Star, and the General Service and Victory Medals.
15, Merton Road, Watford.   2832.

FENSOME, A., Private, Bedfordshire Regiment and Labour Corps.
He joined in July 1916, and in the following December was drafted to the Western Front. There he was engaged on important duties in connection with the upkeep of roads in the Somme, Arras, Cambrai and the Marne areas, and in subsequent engagements, until the cessation of hostilities. He was demobilised after his return to England in March 1919, and holds the General Service and Victory Medals.
Upper Woodside, near Luton.   2833

FENSOME, A. H., Private, 7th Bedfordshire Regt.
He joined in May 1916, and in the following January was
sent to France. He soon went into action and was wounded
at Irles in the next month. After his recovery he took part
in the fighting at Arras, Ypres and the Somme, and in the engagements which followed until the conclusion of hostilities.
He was demobilised in October 1919 after returning home,
and holds the General Service and Victory Medals.
3, Stanley Street, Luton.   2835.

**FENSOME, A. J., Private, 5th Bedfordshire Regt.
and Driver, Royal Army Service Corps.**
He joined in November 1916, and in the following March
was sent to the Western Front, where he was severely
wounded at the capture of Vimy Ridge in May, and was
invalided home. After a year's treatment he returned to
France in May 1918, and fought in the second Battle of the
Somme and in subsequent engagements until the cessation of
hostilities. After the Armistice he advanced into Germany
with the Army of Occupation and remained there until
October 1919, when he was demobilised, after his return to
England. He holds the General Service and Victory Medals.
84, Ashton Road, Luton.   2836.

FENSOME, B., Private, Labour Corps.
He joined in February 1917, and in the same year was
drafted to the Western Front, where he was engaged on
important duties with his company at Vimy Ridge, Ypres,
Cambrai and on the Somme. He was demobilised in November 1919 after returning to England, and holds the General
Service and Victory Medals.
36, Henry Street, Luton.   2837.

**FENSOME, C. F., L/Corporal, North Staffordshire
Regiment.**
He volunteered in October 1914, and in the same year was
drafted to the Western Front, where he took part in numerous engagements, including the Battles of Hill 60, Ypres
(where he was wounded), Loos and the Somme, where he
was wounded for the second time. He was invalided home
and in October 1916 was discharged as medically unfit for
further service. He holds the 1914 Star, and the General
Service and Victory Medals.
1, Reginald Street, Luton.   2838.

FENSOME, C. H., Corporal, Royal Irish Fusiliers.
Volunteering at the outbreak of war he was drafted to
Salonika in the following July. Whilst in this theatre of
war he took part in the Serbian Retreat, and in the Advance
across the Struma River. In 1917 he was sent to Palestine,
and was in action at Gaza and Beersheba, and in the subsequent engagements of the campaign until May 1918, when
he proceeded to France, where he served up to the cessation
of hostilities. He was demobilised in May 1920, and holds
the 1914-15 Star, and the General Service and Victory
Medals. 30, Ashton Road, Luton.   2839.

FENSOME, C. R., Private, R.A.S.C. (M.T.)
Volunteering at the commencement of hostilities he was
drafted to the Western Front in the same year, and was
engaged on important transport duties at Ypres, the
Somme and Arras. In 1917 he was sent to Salonika, and
was present at various engagements on the Balkan front,
including the Advance on Vardar. Finally he proceeded
to Russia, where he rendered excellent service at Murmansk
until June 1919, when he returned home and was demobilised.
He holds the 1914 Star, and the General Service and Victory
Medals.
120, Cowper Street, Luton.   2840.

**FENSOME, E. A., Corporal, 11th Royal Sussex
Regiment.**
He joined in April 1916, and in the following December
was drafted to France, where he took part in the Battle of the
Somme. In July 1917 he was wounded in action at Ypres,
and after his recovery was again wounded at St. Julien in the
following November. He was demobilised in September
1919, and holds the General Service and Victory Medals.
1a, Sutton Road, Watford.   X2841.

FENSOME, E. W., Private, 5th Bedfordshire Regt.
He volunteered in June 1915, and after his training served
at various stations on important duties with his unit. He
rendered valuable services, but for medical reasons was unable
to secure his transfer overseas before the close of hostilities.
He was demobilised in February 1919.
6, Spring Place, Luton.   2842.

FENSOME, F., L/Corporal, Bedfordshire Regt.
He volunteered in 1914, and in the following year was drafted
to France, where he saw much service. He took part in
the fighting at Hill 60, and was wounded at Ypres. On his
recovery he was in action on the Somme, and was again
wounded at Passchendaele and also at Cambrai. He was
demobilised in February 1919, and holds the 1914-15 Star,
and the General Service and Victory Medals.
31, Windmill Street, Luton.   2843.

FENSOME, G., Corporal, Bedfordshire Regiment.
Volunteering at the outbreak of hostilities, he was drafted to
the Western Front in the following November. During his
service in France he fought at Neuve Chapelle, Ypres, Loos,
the Somme, Arras, Passchendaele and in the engagements
which followed in the Retreat and Advance of 1918. He
was demobilised after his return to England in February
1919, and holds the 1914 Star, and the General Service and
Victory Medals.
Bury Road, Stopsley, near Luton.   2844.

FENSOME, G., Private, Machine Gun Corps.
Volunteering at the outbreak of hostilities, he was drafted
in the following month to the Western Front, where he
served for upwards of 4½ years. He took part in the engagements at La Bassée, Festubert, Loos, the Somme (where he
was gassed), Arras, Ypres and the subsequent battles until
the cessation of hostilities. He was demobilised in February
1919, and holds the 1914 Star, and the General Service and
Victory Medals.
Slate Corner, Flamstead.   X2845.

FENSOME, G. A., Private, 6th Yorkshire Regt.
He joined in October 1916, and on the completion of his training served at various stations on important duties with his
unit. He afterwards proceeded to North Russia and did
much valuable work at Archangel. He was accidentally
killed at Bakaritza in August 1919. He was entitled to the
General Service and Victory Medals.
14, Brache Street, Luton.   2846.

FENSOME, H., Sapper, R.E. (Signals).
He joined in April 1918, and after his training was engaged
at various stations on important duties in the signal section
of the Royal Engineers. Early in 1919 he proceeded to Russia,
where he was engaged as wireless operator at Murmansk.
After eight months' valuable service he returned home, and
was demobilised in October 1919, holding the General Service
and Victory Medals.
42, Park Road West, Luton.   2847.

FENSOME, H. C., L/Corporal, Royal Engineers.
He volunteered in April 1915, and after being engaged on
important duties at various stations was drafted to France
in September 1917. Whilst in this theatre of war he was
engaged in the forward areas whilst operations were in progress, notably at Ypres, Cambrai and the Somme, and was
wounded. After his recovery he served until the termination
of hostilities, and was demobilised in June 1919. He holds
the General Service and Victory Medals.
9, Chatsworth Road, Luton.   2848.

**FENSOME, L., Private, 6th Buffs (East Kent
Regiment).**
He joined in June 1916, and after his training was drafted
to France in the following October. During his service on
the Western Front he fought at the Somme, Arras and Ypres,
and was killed in action on October 2nd, 1917, and buried at
Monchy. He was entitled to the General Service and
Victory Medals.
47a, May Street, Luton.   2849.

FENSOME, P., Private, Suffolk Regiment.
He joined in July 1916, and after his training was sent to the
Western Front, where he served for upwards of two years.
During this period he took part in the fighting at Armentières,
Arras and Albert, and was twice wounded in action. He
was demobilised in February 1919 after his return to England,
and holds the General Service and Victory Medals.
54, May Street, Luton.   2850.

FENSOME, P. E., Cpl., 5th Bedfordshire Regt.
He volunteered in September 1914, and a year later was
drafted to Gallipoli, where he served in various operations
until the Evacuation of the Peninsula in December 1915.
He was then sent to Egypt, and advancing with the British
Forces through Palestine, took part in numerous engagements until the conclusion of the campaign. He returned
home and was demobilised in April 1919, holding the 1914-15
Star, and the General Service and Victory Medals.
56, Lyndhurst Road, Luton.   2851.

FENSOME, S., Private, Labour Corps.
He volunteered in March 1915, and after being retained
for important duties at various stations was drafted to
France in March 1917. During his service on the Western
Front he was engaged in road construction and repairs, in
the Arras, Ypres, Cambrai and Somme sectors, and was on
many occasions under fire until the conclusion of hostilities.
He was demobilised in February 1919, after his return to
England, and holds the General Service and Victory Medals.
The Grove, Woodside.   2852/A.

FENSOME, S. C., Private, Lancashire Fusiliers.
He joined in March 1917, and after a short training was drafted to France in the following May. After taking part in various engagements he was killed in the fierce fighting at Passchendaele Ridge on October 9th, 1917. He was entitled to the General Service and Victory Medals.
21, Granville Road, Luton. 2853/A

FENSOME, T., Driver, Royal Engineers.
He volunteered in March 1915, and after being drafted to Egypt in February of the following year joined in the British Advance through Palestine. Here he was engaged on important duties in connection with the operations, and was frequently in the forward areas, notably at Gaza and Jaffa. He was also present at the fall of Jerusalem. He was demobilised after his return to England in July 1919, and holds the General Service and Victory Medals.
21, Granville Road, Luton. 2853/B.

FENSOME, W., Private, Bedfordshire Regiment.
Volunteering in August 1914, he was drafted to France a year later, and stationed for a time at Le Havre. Later he took part in the severe fighting at the Battle of the Somme, and was severely wounded and gassed in action. He was invalided home, and after hospital treatment was discharged as medically unfit for further service in December 1917. He subsequently died through the effects of gas-poisoning in November 26th, 1919. He was entitled to the 1914-15 Star, and the General Service and Victory Medals.
24, Duke Street, Luton. 2854.

FENSOME, W., Private, 12th Suffolk Regiment.
He volunteered in September 1915, and in the following May, on the completion of his training, was drafted to France, where he served for only four months before being shot by a sniper and taken prisoner. He died from his injuries on September 20th, 1916, and was entitled to the General Service and Victory Medals.
104, Chapel Street, Luton. 2855.

FICKLING, E., Gunner, Royal Field Artillery; and Private, 1st London Regt. (Royal Fusiliers)
He volunteered in March 1915, and in the same year was drafted to France, where he served in various important battles, including those at Arras, Ypres and Cambrai. He was also engaged in conveying rations and ammunition up to the front lines, and was wounded and gassed during this period. He was demobilised in February 1919, and holds the 1914-15 Star, and the General Service and Victory Medals.
25, Ashdon Road, Bushey. 2856.

FIDLER, L., Sergeant, Royal Garrison Artillery.
He volunteered at the outbreak of hostilities, and in the following year was drafted to France, where he served in various engagements, and was in action at Arras and Albert. Later he returned to England and was engaged at various stations as Gunnery instructor to the Officers' Training Corps, and rendered valuable services. He was demobilised in January 1919, and holds the 1914-15 Star, and the General Service and Victory Medals.
59, Old Park Road, Hitchin. 1601/A.

FIELD A., Private, Bedfordshire Regiment.
He volunteered in March 1915, and in the same year proceeded to France. During his service on the Western Front he was severely wounded in the heavy fighting at the Battle of the Somme in 1916, and was invalided home to hospital. Subsequently he was discharged as unfit for further military duty in June 1917, and holds the 1914-15 Star, and the General Service and Victory Medals.
17, Stanbridge Road, Leighton Buzzard. 2857/B.

FIELD, A. C., Private, Suffolk Regiment.
He joined in January 1917, and after his training served at various stations on important duties with his unit. In 1918 he proceeded to Germany with the Army of Occupation, and remained there until November 1919, when he returned home and was demobilised.
8, Heath Terrace, Landridge Road, St. Albans. X2858/B.

FIELD, C. F., Corporal, 1st Hertfordshire Regt.
He volunteered in August 1914, and was shortly afterwards sent to France. He took part in heavy fighting at the Battles of Mons, Albert, Ypres, the Somme, Arras and many other engagements, and was three times wounded. He was demobilised in 1919, and holds the Mons Star, and the General Service and Victory Medals.
1, Ratcliffe Road, Hitchin. 2872/B.

FIELD, E., Leading Stoker, R.N., H.M.S. " Birmingham."
He was serving in the Navy at the outbreak of war, and was posted to H.M.S. " Birmingham." Whilst in this vessel he was engaged on important patrol duties in the North Sea, and also took part in the Battle of Jutland. Later he was employed with his ship in conveying troops to France, and in bringing back German prisoners from the Western Front to England until the cessation of hostilities. In 1920 he was still serving, and holds the 1914-15 Star, and the General Service and Victory Medals.
17, Stanbridge Road, Leighton Buzzard. 2857/A.

FIELD, E. J., Sergeant, Queen's Own (Royal West Kent Regiment).
Volunteering in 1915, he was drafted in the same year to Egypt and served with the British Forces under General Allenby in the Advance through Palestine. He took part in the Battles of Gaza, and was present at the entry into Jerusalem, and afterwards was in action in subsequent engagements until the conclusion of the campaign. He returned home in March 1920, and was demobilised in the following month, and holds the 1914-15 Star, and the General Service and Victory Medals.
10, Yarmouth Road, Callowland, Herts. X2859/B.

FIELD, F., Sapper, Royal Engineers.
Volunteering in April 1915, he was sent to France in the following year, and was engaged on important duties in connection with the operations and was frequently in the forward areas. He served at Ypres, the Somme, Arras, Armentières and Cambrai, and in various later engagements until the conclusion of hostilities. He was demobilised in March 1919, and holds the General Service and Victory Medals.
21, Dunstable Place, Luton. 2862/A.

FIELD, F., Private, Royal Defence Corps.
He volunteered in October 1914 at 49 years of age, and served at various stations on important duties, protecting bridges and guarding prisoners of war. He was demobilised after over four years' service in January 1919.
8, Beech Road, Luton. 2860.

FIELD, F., A.B., R.N., H.M.S. " Lion."
He joined in April 1917, and after training was posted to H.M.S. " Lion." Whilst in this vessel he served on important and dangerous submarine patrol duties in the North Sea, and took part in the engagement in Heligoland Bight in April 1918. In 1920 he was still serving in South African Waters, and holds the General Service and Victory Medals.
21, Charles Street, Luton. 2861/A.

FIELD, F. F., Private, R.A.M.C.
He volunteered in March 1915, and in the following January was drafted overseas. During his service in France he was engaged on important duties, and was present at the Battle of the Somme, and was twice severely wounded. In July 1916 he was invalided home to hospital, and in September of the following year was discharged as medically unfit for further service. He holds the General Service and Victory Medals.
32, Ashton Road, Luton. 2864.

FIELD, G., L/Corporal, 9th Royal Fusiliers.
He volunteered in August 1914, and was almost immediately drafted to France, where he took part in the fighting at Ypres and Loos. On July 7th, 1916, he was mortally wounded in action on the Somme, and was invalided home to hospital, where he died 12 days later. He was entitled to the 1914 Star, and the General Service and Victory Medals.
121, Pinner Road, Oxhey, Herts. X2863/A.

FIELD, G. E., Private, Middlesex Regiment and Labour Corps.
He joined in February 1917, and in the following year was drafted overseas, and took part in the Battle of Cambrai, where he was severely wounded. After his recovery he was transferred to the Labour Corps, and was engaged on important duties at various stations in France until the conclusion of hostilities. He was demobilised in February 1919, and holds the General Service and Victory Medals.
50, Burmack Row, Apsley End, Herts. X2865.

FIELD, G. E., Sergeant, Royal Field Artillery.
He volunteered in October 1915, and in the same year was drafted to Mesopotamia. Whilst in this theatre of war he took part in the fighting at Kut, the capture of Baghdad and numerous other engagements. He was demobilised after his return to England in April 1919, and holds the 1914-15 Star, and the General Service and Victory Medals.
8, Heath Terrace, Landridge Road, St. Albans. X2858/A.

FIELD, H., Private, Royal Defence Corps.
He joined in April 1917, and served at various stations on
on important guard duties. He rendered valuable services,
until March 1919, when he was demobilised.
21, Charles Street, Luton.   2861/B.

FIELD, J., Corporal, 6th Bedfordshire Regiment.
Volunteering in August 1914, he was almost immediately
drafted to France and took part in the Retreat from Mons,
and was wounded. After his recovery he served at Ypres,
Loos, the Somme and Arras, and in numerous subsequent
engagements until the cessation of hostilities. He was
finally demobilised in July 1919, and holds the Mons Star,
and the General Service and Victory Medals.
43, Queen Street, Hemel Hempstead.   X2866.

FIELD, J., Private, 2nd Wiltshire Regiment.
He joined in January 1918, and in the following month was
drafted to France. After taking part in various engagements he was killed in action on October 21st, 1918, and
was entitled to the General Service and Victory Medals.
121, Pinner Road, Oxhey, Herts.   X2863/B.

FIELD, J. G., Q.M.S., R.A.O.C.
He volunteered in December 1914, and in the following
year was drafted to Salonika. Throughout the Balkan campaign he was engaged on important duties, and was present
at the Battles of the Vardar and Struma, and at the recapture
of Monastir. He was finally demobilised after his return to
England in May 1919, and holds the 1914-15 Star, and the
General Service and Victory Medals.
10, Yarmouth Road, Callowland, Herts.   X2859/A.

FIELD, L., Private, Bedfordshire Regiment.
Volunteering in August 1914, he was drafted to France in the
following November, and took part in the heavy fighting at
Ypres. In January 1915 he was invalided home to hospital
suffering from severe shell-shock, and on his recovery was sent
to India in November of the same year. Here he served on
various important duties until June 1917, when he was again
invalided home through ill-health. Later he was transferred
to the Royal Defence Corps with which he served until
January 1918, when he was discharged as medically unfit for
further military duty. He holds the 1914 Star, and the
General Service and Victory Medals.
44, Old Road, Linslade, near Leighton Buzzard.   2867.

**FIELD, P., Private, Queen's (Royal West Surrey
    Regiment).**
He joined in June 1918, and after a short training was drafted
to France in the following October. A month later he returned
to England, having been severely wounded in an engagement near Cambrai. After his recovery he was demobilised
in March 1919, and holds the General Service and Victory
Medals.
47, Spencer Road, Luton.   2868.

FIELD, R., Private, A/Sergeant, R.A.M.C.
He volunteered early in August 1914, and in the same year
was drafted to France, where he served on important duties
in various sectors of the Western Front. Whilst acting as a
stretcher-bearer at Hill 60 he was severely gassed, but on
recovery was present at the Battles of the Somme, Arras,
Ypres and subsequent engagements until the conclusion
of hostilities. He returned to England and was demobilised
in 1919, and holds the 1914 Star, and the General Service
and Victory Medals.
22, Temperance Street, St. Albans.   2869.

FIELD, S., Sergeant, Royal Field Artillery.
He volunteered in June 1915, and after his training was
drafted to the Western Front. During his service in France
he fought at Arras and Cambrai, and in the third Battle of
Ypres, and took part in various later engagements in the
Retreat and Advance of 1918. In September 1919 he was
demobilised after his return to England, and holds the
General Service and Victory Medals.
46, Garfield Street, Watford.   X2870.

**FIELD, T., Private, 14th London Regiment
    (London Scottish).**
He joined in September 1917, and in the same year was
drafted to France and fought in the third Battle of Ypres
and at Passchendaele and the Somme. He was wounded
and taken prisoner on the Cambrai Front in August 1918,
and held in captivity in Germany until after the Armistice,
when he was released and sent home and demobilised. He
holds the General Service and Victory Medals.
10, Yarmouth Road, Callowland, Watford.   X2871.

FIELD, W., Sergeant, Military Foot Police.
He volunteered in 1915, and after his training was sent to
Ireland, where he served on important military police duties
during the Sinn Fein risings in 1916. He returned to England
in 1919, and was demobilised in January of the following
year.
1, Ratcliffe Road, Hitchin.   2872/A.

FIELD, W. A., Gunner, R.N., H.M.S. " Barham."
Volunteering in August 1914, he served in H.M.S." Barham "
in the North Sea and the Baltic. He took part in numerous
engagements, including the Battle of Jutland, where he was
wounded. He was demobilised in December 1919, and
holds the 1914-15 Star, and the General Service and
Victory Medals.
1, Ratcliffe Road, Hitchin.   2872/C.

**FIELD, W. A., Private, Bedfordshire and Suffolk
    Regiments, and Royal Defence Corps.**
He joined in February 1916, and after his training served at
various stations on important duties with his unit. He
rendered valuable services, but was not successful in obtaining
his transfer overseas. He was discharged in December 1917.
78, Queen's Street, Hitchin.   2873.

FIELD, W. T., Bombardier, Royal Field Artillery.
He joined in March 1917, and in the same year was drafted
to the Western Front. During his service in France he was
in action at Ypres, the Somme and Cambrai, and was twice
severely wounded. In 1919 he proceeded to Germany, where
he remained until October in that year, when he returned
home and was demobilised. He holds the General Service
and Victory Medals.
7, St. Paul's Road, Luton.   2764/B.

FIGG, A., Gunner, Royal Field Artillery.
Volunteering in 1915, he was drafted in the same year
to the Western Front, where he took part in the Battles of
Hill 60, Loos, the Somme, Vimy Ridge and various other
engagements. He was invalided home and discharged as
medically unfit for further service in September 1918, and
holds the 1914-15 Star, and the General Service and Victory
Medals.
14, College Place, St. Albans.   2874/C.

FIGG, H., L/Corporal, Royal Fusiliers.
He joined in 1917, and was sent to France in the same year.
He took part in severe fighting at Ypres, Amiens, Cambrai
and numerous other engagements, and was gassed. He
returned home and was demobilised in 1919, and holds the
General Service and Victory Medals.
14, College Place, St. Albans.   2874/B.

FIGG, W. G., Private, R.A.S.C. (M.T.)
Joining in 1917, he was sent to the Western Front in the
same year and served in many important engagements,
including those on the Somme and at Ypres. He was killed
in action on October 1st, 1918, and was entitled to the
General Service and Victory Medals.
14, College Place, St. Albans.   2874/A.

**FILLER, C. D., Private, Queen's (Royal West
    Surrey Regiment).**
He joined in October 1916, and was sent to France in the same
year. He took part in severe fighting on the Somme and at
Arras, Ypres and Cambrai, and was wounded. In 1918 he
proceeded with the Army of Occupation to Germany. He
was demobilised in April 1920, and holds the General Service
and Victory Medals.
Church Street, Hatfield.   X2875.

FINAL, G., Private, Grenadier Guards.
He had previously served in the South African War, and
re-enlisted in August 1914, and was almost immediately sent
overseas. He took part in the memorable Retreat from
Mons, and was subsequently killed in action in December
1914. He was entitled to the Mons Star, and the General
Service and Victory Medals.
9, Duke Street, Watford.   X968/C.

FINAR, G. W., Private, 4th Bedfordshire Regt.
Volunteering in August 1914, he was immediately afterwards sent to France, where he took part in much severe
fighting at Mons, Ypres, Hill 60, Vimy Ridge, the Somme
and Passchendaele. He returned home and was discharged
in consequence of his service in December 1917, and holds
the Mons Star, and the General Service and Victory Medals.
69, Cotterell's Road, Hemel Hempstead.   X2876/C.

FINEL, L., Private, Hertfordshire Regiment.
He volunteered in August 1914, and in the following year
was drafted to the Western Front, where he took part in
numerous engagements, including those at Hill 60 and
Ypres. In 1916 he returned home, and was engaged on
important duties with his unit until he was demobilised in
1919. He holds the 1914-15 Star, and the General Service
and Victory Medals.
49, Astley Hill, Hemel Hempstead.   X28771/A.

FISHER, A., Sergeant, 15th (The King's) Hussars.
He volunteered in February 1915, and in the following year
was sent to France, where he took part in severe fighting at
Vimy Ridge, the Somme, Arras, Ypres and Cambrai. He
was demobilised in March 1919, and holds the 1914-15 Star,
and the General Service and Victory Medals.
Sleaford End, Maulden, near Ampthill.   1545.

FISHER, F., Sergeant, Royal Field Artillery.
He enlisted in July 1906, and was drafted to the Western Front in October 1914, and took part in many important engagements. In November 1915 he was transferred to Salonika, where he was seriously injured by being thrown from his horse, and was invalided home. On his recovery he returned to France, where he was again in action. He was demobilised in February 1919, and holds the 1914 Star, and the General Service and Victory Medals.
56, Queen's Street, Hitchin. 2878.

FISHER, G. F., 1st Class Petty Officer, R.N., H.M.S. " Carnarvon."
He volunteered in August 1914, and during his period of service was engaged with his ship in the North Sea and the Baltic, and took part in numerous actions. He was still serving in 1920, and holds the 1914-15 Star, and the General Service and Victory Medals.
49, Ratcliffe Road, Hitchin. 2879/A.

FISHER, G. W., C.Q.M.S., 1st Hertfordshire Regt.
He was mobilised in August 1914,and in the following November was sent to the Western Front, where he took part in heavy fighting at Ypres, the Somme and Arras, and was wounded. He was demobilised in December 1918, and holds the 1914 Star, and the General Service and Victory Medals.
61, Old London Road, St. Albans. X2880.

FISHER, H. J., Sapper, Royal Engineers.
He joined in June 1918, and after his training served at various stations on important duties with his unit. He rendered valuable services, but was not successful in obtaining his transfer overseas before the cessation of hostilities. He was demobilised in April 1919.
36, Brightwell Road, Watford. X2881.

FISHER, J., Gunner, Royal Field Artillery.
He volunteered in 1914, and was drafted to the Western Front in the following year, and took part in many important engagements, and was wounded. In 1918 he proceeded to Germany with the Army of Occupation, and later served at Malta for a time. He was demobilised in 1919, and holds the 1914-15 Star, and the General Service and Victory Medals.
30, Fearnley Street, Watford. X2882.

FISHER, S. W., Private, Suffolk Regiment.
He joined in April 1917, and in the same year was drafted to the Western Front, where he took part in heavy fighting at Arras, Cambrai and the Somme, and was wounded and invalided home. On his recovery he returned to France, where he was again in action. After the Armistice he proceeded with the Army of Occupation to Germany, where he served until he was demobilised in September 1919. He holds the General Service and Victory Medals.
Delma Cottage, 18, Banks Road, Biggleswade. Z2883.

FISHER, W., Gunner, Royal Field Artillery.
He volunteered in August 1914, and was immediately afterwards sent to the Western Front, where he took part in the Battles of Mons, Ypres and numerous other important engagements. He was later transferred to Italy, where he was again in action. He was demobilised in January 1919, and holds the Mons Star, and the General Service and Victory Medals. 69, Ridge Avenue, Letchworth. 2885.

FISHER, W. J., Private, 1st Wiltshire Regiment.
Volunteering in August 1914, he was shortly afterwards sent to the Western Front, where he took part in various important engagements. He was killed in action at Neuve Chapelle on October 28th, 1914, and was entitled to the 1914 Star, and the General Service and Victory Medals.
97, Fearnley Street, Watford. X2884/B.

FISHER, W. M. J., Private, Bedfordshire and Suffolk Regiments.
He joined in 1918, and after his training served at various stations on important duties with his unit. He rendered valuable services, but was not successful in obtaining his transfer overseas before the cessation of hostilities. He was demobilised in January 1919.
22, Weymouth Street, Apsley End. X2886.

FITZJOHN, A. V., Pte., 1st Hertfordshire Regt.
He volunteered in July 1915, but during the course of his training was found to be physically unfit for military service and was discharged in February 1916.
6, Inkerman Road, St. Albans. 2887.

FLACK, A. G., Private, R.A.S.C. (M.T.)
He joined in January 1917, and in the same year was drafted to the Western Front, where he was present at numerous engagements. He was afterwards transferred to Italy, where he served in the campaign against the Austrians. After the conclusion of hostilities he returned to England and was demobilised in April 1919, holding the General Service and Victory Medals.
4, School Walk, Letchworth. 2888.

FLECKNEY, C., Private, R.A.S.C. (M.T.)
Joining in February 1917, he was drafted to Egypt in the same year. He was present at the engagements at Gaza and at the capture of Jerusalem, and was employed on transporting ammunition and supplies, and rendered valuable services. He was demobilised in January 1920, and holds the General Service and Victory Medals.
Red House, The Square, Toddington. 2889.

FLECKNEY, C. W., 3rd Middlesex Regiment.
He joined in January 1917, and after his training was drafted to the Western Front, where he took part in severe fighting at Ypres, St. Quentin and many other engagements, and was wounded and gassed. He was still serving in 1920, and holds the General Service and Victory Medals.
Station Road, Toddington. 2890.

FLECKNEY, S., Private, Labour Corps.
He joined in October 1916, and after his training served at various stations on important duties with his unit. He rendered valuable services, but was not successful in obtaining his transfer overseas before the cessation of hostilities. He was demobilised in March 1919.
73, Marsh Road, Leagrave. 2891/B.

FLECKNEY, T., Private, York and Lancaster Regiment.
Joining in March 1916, he was drafted to the Western Front in October of the same year, and took part in severe fighting at Albert and other engagements. He was killed in action on the Somme on December 11th, 1916, and was entitled to the General Service and Victory Medals.
34, Cobden Street, Luton. 2892.

FLECKNOE, E. W., Corporal, King's Royal Rifle Corps.
He joined in June 1918, but was not successful in obtaining his transfer overseas before the cessation of hostilities. In November 1918 he proceeded to the Army of Occupation in Germany, and rendered valuable services until February 1919, when he was demobilised.
Marson Place, Stopsley. 2893/A.

FLECKNOE, W. T., Private, Machine Gun Corps.
He volunteered in November 1915, and in June of the following year was drafted to the Western Front, where he took part in numerous engagements, including those on the Somme and at Arras, Ypres and Cambrai. He was demobilised in March 1919, and holds the General Service and Victory Medals.
Marson Place, Stopsley. 2893/B.

FLEET, A., Private, Essex Regiment and Labour Corps.
He joined in March 1918, and after his training served at various stations on important duties with his unit. He rendered valuable services, but was not successful in obtaining his transfer overseas before the cessation of hostilities. In December 1918 he proceeded to the Army of Occupation in Germany, where he served until March 1920, when he was demobilised.
64, Boyle Street, Luton. 2894.

FLEMING, D. G., Observer, Royal Air Force.
He was serving at the outbreak of hostilities, and throughout the war was engaged on aerial patrol duties in the North Sea. For a time he was attached to H.M.S. " Collingwood," and was with that vessel at the Battle of Jutland. He holds the 1914-15 Star, and the General Service and Victory Medals, and was still serving in 1920.
Grove View, Leopold's Road, Linslade, Leighton Buzzard. 2895.

FLETCHER, A., Corporal, R.F.A.
He joined in June 1916, and in the following January was drafted to the Western Front, where he was engaged on important duties with the Ammunition Column conveying supplies to the front lines. He served in the Retreat and Advance of 1918 and was wounded, and after the cessation of hostilities returned to England and was demobilised, holding the General Service and Victory Medals.
Talbot House, Talbot Road, Luton. 2896/A.

FLETCHER, C. V., Private, 9th (Queen's Royal) Lancers.
Volunteering in August 1914, he was shortly afterwards drafted to the Western Front, where he took part in severe fighting at Arras, Ypres and Cambrai, and in other important engagements, and was twice wounded. He also served in Africa for a time, and on the conclusion of hostilities returned to England and was demobilised in February 1919, holding the 1914 Star, and the General Service and Victory Medals.
Talbot House, Talbot Road, Luton. 2896/B.

FLETCHER, F., Gunner, R.F.A.
Joining in July 1916, he was drafted in January of the following year to Mesopotamia, where he took part in various engagements, including those at Kut and Amara. He returned home and was demobilised in March 1919, and holds the General Service and Victory Medals.
Upper Sundon, near Dunstable.   2897.

FLETCHER, F. G., Private, King's Own (Royal Lancaster Regiment).
Joining in July 1916, he was drafted to Mesopotamia in January of the following year, and took part in numerous engagements, including those at Kut and Amara. He returned home and was demobilised in September 1919, and holds the General Service and Victory Medals.
Upper Sundon, near Dunstable.   2898.

FLETCHER, G., 1st Hertfordshire Regiment.
He joined in August 1916, and was sent to France in the same year and took part in heavy fighting at Vimy Ridge, the Somme, Arras and Ypres, and was severely wounded. He was demobilised in January 1919, and holds the General Service and Victory Medals.
10, Spring Place, Luton.   2899.

FLETCHER, H. F., Private, Bedfordshire Lancers.
He volunteered in August 1914, and was drafted to the Western Front in June of the following year, and took part in numerous engagements, including those at Hill 60, Loos, Vimy Ridge, the Somme and Cambrai, and was wounded. On his recovery he returned to the front line, and was again in action. He was demobilised in February 1919, and holds the 1914–15 Star, and the General Service and Victory Medals.
Park Road, Toddington.   2900.

FLETCHER, J., Private, Royal Fusiliers.
Joining in May 1916, he was drafted to France in the same year and took part in severe fighting at Ypres, the Somme, Cambrai and various other engagements, and was wounded. He was demobilised in October 1919, and holds the General Service and Victory Medals.
29, College Place, St. Albans.   2901.

FLETTON, A., C.Q.M.S., King's Royal Rifle Corps.
He volunteered in August 1914, and was sent to the Western Front in the following year. He took part in numerous important engagements, including those at La Bassée and the Marne, and was wounded. He was demobilised in February 1919, and holds the 1914–15 Star, and the General Service and Victory Medals.
Kimberley House, Beale Street, Dunstable.   2902/A.

FLETTON, W., Corporal, Norfolk Regiment.
Joining in May 1918, he proceeded to France in July of the same year and took part in various engagements, including that at Arras. After the Armistice he was sent to Germany, where he served with the Army of Occupation until March 1920, when he returned to England and was demobilised, holding the General Service and Victory Medals.
Kimberley House, Beale Street, Dunstable.   2902/B.

FLINT, F. J., Staff-Sergeant, R.H.A.
Volunteering in April 1915, he was drafted to the Dardanelles in the following July, and subsequently took part in many of the engagements which followed. After the Evacuation of the Peninsula he was sent to France, where he fought in important sectors, and from June 1918 until the ensuing year served in Egypt. After being on service in Belgium for a time, he was demobilised on his return to England in June 1919, and holds the 1914–15 Star, and the General Service and Victory Medals.
46, Cecil Street, North Watford.   X2903.

FLINT, H. A. C., Private, 4th Suffolk Regiment.
Joining in February 1916, he was sent to France at the conclusion of his training in the following July. He was subsequently engaged in the fighting on the Somme, at Thiepval and Beaumont-Hamel, where in November he was wounded, and in March 1918 was again wounded during the German Offensive. He remained on the Western Front, however, until August 1919, and was demobilised on his return to England a month later. He holds the General Service and Victory Medals.
1, Garfield Street, Watford.   2904.

FLINT, J. O., 1st Class Stoker, Royal Navy.
He joined in August 1916, and after his training was posted to H.M.S. "Ramillies." This vessel was engaged on important work in the North Sea and the Baltic, and also took part in several Naval engagements. Throughout his service he did excellent work, and on returning to his Base in February 1919 was demobilised. He holds the General Service and Victory Medals.
48, Victoria Road, North Watford.   X2905.

FLINT, M., Private, Labour Corps.
He joined in October 1916, and after his training was sent to the Western Front, where he was engaged on important duties in the forward areas. On one occasion he was severely gassed, but after being treated at the Base was able to rejoin his unit, and remained in France until 1919. He was demobilised on his return to England, and holds the General Service and Victory Medals.
41, Adrian Road, Abbots Langley, Herts.   X2906.

FLINT, R., Private, R.A.M.C.
Joining in October 1916, he was sent to France immediately upon the completion of his training. He was subsequently engaged on important duties at the various hospitals, and rendered valuable services with his unit until after the cessation of hostilities. He holds the General Service and Victory Medals, and was demobilised on his return to England in September 1919.
29, Parker Street, Watford   X2907.

FLINT, T. H., A.B., Royal Navy.
He was already in the Navy, and during the period of hostilities served on board H.M.S. "Parker." This vessel was engaged with the Grand Fleet in the North Sea and also took part in many Naval engagements, notably the Battle of Jutland. He did valuable work until October 1919, when he returned to his Base and was demobilised. He holds the 1914–15 Star, and the General Service and Victory Medals.
Mimram Road, Welwyn, Herts.   2908.

FLITTON, B., Private, Queen's (Royal West Surrey Regiment).
He joined in 1917, and during his service on the Western Front, which began later in that year, took part in many important engagements until hostilities ceased, including those of Arras and the Somme, and was wounded. He holds the General Service and Victory Medals, and was demobilised after his return to England in January 1919.
Trowley Bottom, Flamstead.   X2909.

FLITTON, C. G., Bugler, King's Royal Rifle Corps.
He joined in June 1918, and on the completion of his training was drafted to Germany in the following December. He served with the Army of Occupation for 18 months, at the end of which time he returned to England, where he was still serving in 1920.
Letchworth Road, Leagrave, near Luton.   2910/B.

FLITTON, H., L/Sergeant, King's Royal Rifle Corps.
He volunteered in August 1914, and in the same year was sent overseas. He took part in many of the early engagements, including the Battle of Ypres, and was killed in action on March 20th, 1915. He was entitled to the 1914 Star, and the General Service and Victory Medals.
11, Piccotts End, Hemel Hempstead.   X1109/A.

FLITTON, H., Sapper, Royal Engineers.
Volunteering in December 1915, he was drafted to France early in the following year. He was subsequently engaged with his unit on duties of an important nature in many sectors, notably those of Ypres, the Somme and Cambrai, and throughout his service overseas, which lasted for nearly three years, did excellent work. He holds the General Service and Victory Medals, and was demobilised after his return to England in March 1919.
River Hill, Flamstead.   X2911.

FLITTON, H., Private, Bedfordshire Regiment.
He volunteered in December 1914, and after completing his training was engaged on duties of an important nature at various stations. He was unable to secure his transfer overseas before the termination of hostilities, but rendered valuable services until his demobilisation, which took place in April 1919.
Trowley Bottom, Flamstead.   X2912.

FLITTON, W. G., Private, 5th Bedfordshire Regt.
He volunteered in August 1914, and in May 1916 was drafted to Egypt. He served in the Canal zone and the Sinai Peninsula, and took part in the engagements at El Arish, Gaza and Umbrella Hill. On July 22nd, 1918, he was killed in action at Medjl, and was entitled to the General Service and Victory Medals.
Letchworth Road, Leagrave, near Luton.   2910/A.

FLOYD, T., Private, 4th Bedfordshire Regt.
Volunteering in 1915, he was sent to the Western Front early in the following year. He was afterwards engaged in the fighting in many important sectors, notably in that of Ypres, until the cessation of hostilities, and throughout his service overseas, which lasted for three years, did excellent work with his unit. He was demobilised on his return to England in January 1919, and holds the General Service and Victory Medals.
54, Oxford Street, Watford.   X2913.

FLYNN, E. C., Leading Stoker, Royal Navy.
Volunteering in August 1914, he was first posted to H.M.S. "Sutlej," in which he was engaged for ten months with the North Sea Patrol. He subsequently served on board H.M.S. "General Craufurd" and "Anemone." For two years and seven months his vessel was on special patrol service off the Belgian Coast, and afterwards was engaged on mine-sweeping duties for a further period of ten months. He was demobilised in May 1919, and holds the 1914–15 Star, and the General Service and Victory Medals.
63, Lilley, Luton. 2914.

FOGG, W., Private, 10th Sherwood Foresters.
He volunteered in November 1915, and after his training was sent to the Western Front in January 1916. During his service in this theatre of war, which lasted for three years, he fought in many important battles until the close of the war, including those of the Somme and Cambrai, and was wounded at Arras in 1917. A year later he was twice wounded in action at Ypres. Returning to England in May 1919 he was demobilised in June, and holds the General Service and Victory Medals.
11, The Rookery, Watford. X2915.

FOLDS, E. C., L/Corporal, Queen's Own (Royal West Kent Regiment).
Joining in 1916, he was sent to France in the same year on the completion of his training. He took an active part in operations on the Somme, at Arras and Cambrai, but in 1917, in consequence of ill-health, returned to England, and was subsequently invalided out of the Service. He holds the General Service and Victory Medals.
32, Landridge Road, St. Albans. X2916/B.

FOLDS, W. C., Driver, Royal Horse Artillery.
He volunteered in February 1915, and at the conclusion of his training was sent to the Western Front. His service in this theatre of war lasted for over three years, during which time he did excellent work in the operations at Loos, the Somme, St. Quentin, Arras and Cambrai. He also served in the Retreat and Advance of 1918, and was wounded. He holds the 1914–15 Star, and the General Service and Victory Medals, and on his return to England in February 1919 was demobilised.
32, Landridge Road, St. Albans. X2916/A.

FOLKS, J. O., L/Corporal, 13th Middlesex Regt.
He joined in May 1916, and after his training was drafted in April 1917 to the Western Front, where he subsequently took part in several engagements. In November 1917 he was invalided home, but on his recovery a year later returned to France and served for a further period of eight months. He was demobilised in September 1919, and holds the General Service and Victory Medals.
14, Cambridge Street, Luton. 2917.

FORD, G. W., Driver, Royal Field Artillery; and Private, Bedfordshire Regiment.
He volunteered in September 1914, and after his training was retained on important duties until sent to Egypt in 1916. He subsequently served in the Palestine campaign, during which he took part in the fighting at Gaza and in the occupation of Haifa, Beyrout and Damascus. Returning to England in 1919, he was demobilised in March of that year, and holds the General Service and Victory Medals.
81, Benskin Road, Watford. X2918.

FORD, H. R., Pte., R.A.M.C.; and Driver, R.A.S.C.
Volunteering in September 1914, he was retained for special duties for some time after his training. In February 1916 he was drafted to Salonika, where he did valuable work during the operations on the Doiran, Vardar and Struma fronts, and at Monastir. His service overseas lasted for three years, and on his return to England in March 1919 he was demobilised. He holds the General Service and Victory Medals.
31, Buxton Road, Luton. 2919.

FORD, J., Private, Royal Army Service Corps.
Volunteering in August 1914, he was sent to the Western Front at the conclusion of his training early in the following year. He was engaged on important transport work in the forward areas, and on two occasions was wounded in the discharge of his duties. He returned to England in 1918, and in July of that year was invalided out of the Service in consequence of his wounds. He holds the 1914–15 Star, and the General Service and Victory Medals.
13, Lower Paddock Road, Oxhey, Herts. X2920/B.

FORD, R. H., Private, R.M.L.I.
He joined in February 1917, and during his service in France, which lasted for nearly two years, took an active part in many engagements, notably those at Arras, the Somme and Cambrai. On one occasion he was wounded, but was afterwards able to rejoin his unit. He was demobilised in December 1919 after his return to England, and holds the General Service and Victory Medals.
13, Lower Paddock Road, Oxhey. X2920/C.

FORD, W., Sapper, Royal Engineers.
He joined in 1917, and on the conclusion of his training was engaged on important duties with his unit at various stations. Although unsuccessful in obtaining his transfer to a theatre of war before fighting ceased, he rendered valuable service until his demobilisation in 1919.
13, Lower Paddock Road, Oxhey. X2920/A.

FORDHAM, H., Private, R.M.L.I.
He was mobilised at the commencement of hostilities, and was afterwards engaged on duties of an important nature at various stations. He was not successful in obtaining his transfer to a theatre of war, but rendered valuable services until his demobilisation in May 1919.
96, Hartley Road, Luton. 2921.

FORDHAM, R., Private, 2nd Norfolk Regiment.
Joining in August 1916, he served on the Western Front from the following April until March 1919. During this period he took an active part in operations at Arras, Ypres, Messines, Passchendaele, the Somme and Cambrai, and also did excellent work with his unit during the Retreat and Advance of 1918. He holds the General Service and Victory Medals, and in 1920 was still serving.
100, Collingdon Street, Luton. 2922.

FORSDICK, J. F., Private, R.A.S.C.
He volunteered in May 1915, and on the conclusion of his training three months later was sent to the Western Front. His service in this theatre of war lasted for nearly four years, during which period he did valuable work with his unit in connection with the transport of supplies to the forward areas and was present at the Battles of the Somme and Arras. He was demobilised on his return to England in March 1919, and holds the 1914–15 Star, and the General Service and Victory Medals.
12, Francis Place, High Street, Watford. X2923.

FOSKETT, F. G., Private, Bedfordshire Regt.
Volunteering at the commencement of hostilities, he was sent to France early in 1915, and subsequently fought at St. Eloi, Givenchy, Festubert, Ypres, Loos, the Somme, Arras and Cambrai. On two occasions he was wounded, but after his recovery rejoined his unit and continued his service until hostilities ceased. He was demobilised in March 1919, and holds the 1914–15 Star, and the General Service and Victory Medals.
Back of Church, Ickleford, Hitchin. 2925.

FOSKETT, G., L/Corporal, Machine Gun Corps.
Joining in June 1916, he was soon afterwards sent to the Western Front and fought in many engagements, including those of the Somme, Ypres, Arras and Cambrai. After the cessation of hostilities he advanced into Germany with the Army of Occupation, and on his return to England in February 1919 was demobilised. He holds the General Service and Victory Medals.
Rose Cottage, Puller Road, Boxmoor. X2924/A.

FOSS, A. W., Sergeant, 2nd Welch Regiment.
He volunteered in November 1915, and after his training was engaged at various stations on important duties with his unit. He rendered valuable services, but was not successful in obtaining his transfer overseas before the cessation of hostilities owing to his medical unfitness. He was demobilised in January 1920.
40, Cannon Street, St. Albans. 2926/B.

FOSSEY, A. G., Private, R.A.V.C.
Joining in August 1916, he was drafted to France in May of the following year. He was engaged on the Ypres, Arras, Albert and Somme fronts in attending to sick and wounded horses and mules, and rendered valuable services. He was demobilised in May 1919 after his return home, and holds the General Service and Victory Medals.
21, Saunder's Piece, Ampthill. 2927.

FOSSEY, E., Private, Machine Gun Corps.
He joined in June 1916, and after his training served at various stations on important duties with his unit. He did much valuable work, but on medical grounds was not successful in obtaining his transfer overseas before the close of the war. He was demobilised in March 1919.
High Street, Clophill, near Ampthill. 2928.

FOSSEY, H., Private, R.A.M.C.
Joining in May 1917, he went through his course of training and was afterwards drafted to Egypt. During the Palestine Campaign he rendered valuable service in many important engagements, including those at Gaza and Aleppo. He was demobilised in October 1919, after his return to England, and holds the General Service and Victory Medals.
25, Ash Road, Luton. 2929

FOSSEY, H. F. J., Private, 4th Royal Fusiliers.
He joined in February 1917, and in July of the same year was drafted to German East Africa, where he served in various engagements. In June 1918 he was transferred to France, and took part in the severe fighting in the Cambrai area. He was demobilised in February 1919, and holds the General Service and Victory Medals.
20, Saunder's Piece, Ampthill. 2930.

FOSSEY, H. G., Private, Royal Sussex Regiment.
He volunteered in November 1914, and after the completion of his training served on important duties with his unit until 1916, when he was drafted to the Western Front. He took part in many severe engagements, including those at Loos and Le Cateau, where he was killed in action while serving with a machine-gun unit in October 1919. He was entitled to the General Service and Victory Medals.
Mount Pleasant, Aspley Guise. Z2931.

FOSSEY, W. C., Rifleman, 5th London Regiment (London Rifle Brigade).
Volunteering in January 1915, he was soon drafted to France, and took part in numerous engagements, including those at Neuve Chapelle, Festubert, Ypres, the Somme, Arras and Cambrai. He was demobilised in March 1919 after returning home, and holds the 1914-15 Star, and the General Service and Victory Medals.
Finnings, Flitwick. 2932.

FOSTER, A., Private, 1st Hertfordshire Regt.
He volunteered in 1914, and in the following year was drafted to the Western Front, where he took part in the heavy fighting at Hill 6c, Festubert, the Somme, Messines, Albert and Ypres, and was twice wounded. He was taken prisoner at Cambrai in March 1918, and after his return home was demobilised in December 1919, holding the 1914-15 Star, and the General Service and Victory Medals.
Lower Green, Ickleford, Hitchin. 2933/B.

FOSTER, A., L/Corporal, Machine Gun Corps.
Joining in April 1917, he was drafted to France in April 1918, and took part in the heavy fighting in the Retreat and Advance of that year. In consequence of being severely wounded in August 1918 he was invalided home, and after long hospital treatment was discharged in November 1919, holding the General Service and Victory Medals.
12, St. Michael's Mount, Hitchin. 1840/A.

FOSTER, A. H., Gunner, Royal Field Artillery.
He volunteered in August 1914, and in the following year was drafted to France, where he took part in the severe fighting at Ypres, Loos, the Somme and in other important engagements, and was killed in action on May 3rd, 1917. He was entitled to the 1914-15 Star, and the General Service and Victory Medals.
Brook End, Potton. Z2934/A.

FOSTER, A. H., Private, 6th Northamptonshire Regiment.
Joining in June 1916, he was quickly sent to France in the same year. He took part in various important engagements in the Somme Offensive and was killed in action near Pozières, on October 27th, 1916. He was entitled to the General Service and Victory Medals.
2, Heber Cottages, London Colney. 2935/A.

FOSTER, C. W. E., Pte., 4th Bedfordshire Regt.
He joined in 1916, and was drafted to the Western Front in the same year. He took part in the severe fighting on the Somme and at Beaumont-Hamel, Passchendaele and Cambrai, and was wounded. He returned home and was discharged on account of his injuries in November 1918, holding the General Service and Victory Medals.
45, Windsor Road, Callowland, Watford. X2936.

FOSTER, E., Private, 11th Essex Regiment.
Joining in June 1916, he was shortly afterwards drafted to the Western Front, where he took part in numerous engagements of importance, including those of the Somme, Arras, Ypres and the Retreat of 1918. He was killed in action on March 22nd, 1918, and was entitled to the General Service and Victory Medals.
14, Albert Street, St. Albans. X2937.

FOSTER, E. F. (M.M.), Corporal, 6th Suffolk and North Staffordshire Regiments.
He joined in January 1916, and after his training served on important duties with his unit until June 1918, when he was drafted to France. He took part in many battles in the Retreat and Advance of that year, including those of Cambrai and Ypres, and was twice wounded. He was awarded the Military Medal for conspicuous bravery in the Field, and also holds the General Service and Victory Medals. He was demobilised in February 1919.
10, Kenilworth Road, Luton. 2938.

FOSTER, E. W., Leading Seaman, R.N.D.
He volunteered in August 1914, and in the following year was sent to the Dardanelles, where he saw much service. He was afterwards transferred to the Western Front, and took part in numerous engagements of importance, and was wounded. He was killed in action near Arras on April 23rd, 1917, and was entitled to the 1914-15 Star, and the General Service and Victory Medals.
4, Lowestoft Road, Watford. X2946/C.

FOSTER, G., L/Sergeant, 2nd Worcestershire Regiment.
He was serving at the outbreak of war and was shortly afterwards sent to France. He took part in the severe fighting in the Retreat from Mons and in the Battles of the Marne, Festubert, and Loos, where he was wounded. He was invalided home and discharged, owing to his wounds, in 1916. He holds the Mons Star, and the General Service and Victory Medals.
King's Street, Potton. Z2939.

FOSTER, J., Private, 5th Bedfordshire Regiment.
He was mobilised in August 1914, and in the following year was sent to the Dardanelles, where he was in action at Anzac and Suvla Bay. In December of the same year he was transferred to Egypt, and after fighting in the Canal zone, took part in the Palestine campaign in the battles before Gaza, Haifa and Beyrout. During his service he was wounded on one occasion. He was demobilised in June 1919, after his return home, and holds the 1914-15 Star, and the General Service and Victory Medals.
68, Bury Park Road, Luton. 2940.

FOSTER, J., Private, R.A.V.C.
He volunteered in July 1915, and in the same year was drafted to the Western Front. He was engaged in various sectors, until hostilities ceased, in attending to sick and wounded horses and on transport duties. He was demobilised in January 1919 after returning to England, and holds the 1914-15 Star, and the General Service and Victory Medals.
47, Cardiff Road, Watford. X2941/B.

FOSTER, J. C., Private, 3rd Bedfordshire Regt.
Volunteering in June 1915, he went through his course of training, and was afterwards drafted to the Western Front, where he took part in numerous engagements of importance, including those of the Somme, Arras, Ypres and Cambrai, and was gassed. He was demobilised in March 1919, and holds the General Service and Victory Medals.
Leavesden Green, Watford. X2942.

FOSTER, J. W., Sergeant, 53rd Bedfordshire Regiment.
Joining in October 1917, he was engaged in training and other important duties with his unit until June of the following year, when he was sent to France. While there he took part in the severe fighting at Albert, Amiens and St. Quentin, and was wounded. He was demobilised in March 1920, and holds the General Service and Victory Medals.
47, Cardiff Road, Watford. X2941/A.

FOSTER, P. C., Private, Bedfordshire Regiment.
He volunteered in September 1914, and was shortly afterwards drafted to the Western Front, where he took part in many of the early engagements of the war. He was killed in action on December 19th, 1915, and was entitled to the 1914 Star, and the General Service and Victory Medals.
89, Fearnley Street, Watford. X2943.

FOSTER, R. D., Air Mechanic, Royal Air Force (late Royal Naval Air Service).
He joined in November 1917, and after his training was engaged at Farnborough and Blandford on important duties as an aero-engine fitter with his squadron. He showed a high degree of technical skill and rendered valuable services, but was not successful in obtaining his transfer overseas before the cessation of hostilities. He was demobilised in January 1919.
96, Ashton Road, Luton. 2944.

FOSTER, R. R., Private, Bedfordshire Lancers.
Joining in January 1916, he was sent to France in August of the following year. He took part in numerous important engagements until hostilities ended, including those of the Somme, Arras, Ypres and St. Quentin. He afterwards proceeded with the Army of Occupation to Germany, and on his return home was demobilised in November 1919, holding the General Service and Victory Medals.
46, Lyndhurst Road, Luton. 2945/A.

FOSTER, W. A., Leading Stoker, R.N., H.M.S. " Dartmouth."

He was serving at the outbreak of hostilities and throughout the war was engaged on many important duties. He served in various waters and was in action in the Dardanelles in 1915. He was still serving in 1920, and holds the 1914-15 Star, and the General Service and Victory Medals.
4, Lowestoft Road, Watford. X2946/B.

FOSTER, W. C., Sapper, Royal Engineers.

Volunteering in February 1915, he was drafted to France in the same year. He took a prominent part in maintaining telegraphic communication in the Battles of Loos, the Somme, Arras, Ypres and Cambrai, and was wounded. He was demobilised in February 1919, and afterwards died of illness arising out of his service. He was entitled to the 1914-15 Star, and the General Service and Victory Medals.
11, Thorp's Yard, Queen's Street, Hitchin. 2947.

FOSTER, W. S., Rifleman, 15th London Regiment (Civil Service Rifles).

He volunteered in November 1915, and in August of the following year, on the conclusion of his course of training, was drafted to France, where he saw much service until November. He was then transferred to Salonika, and at a later date proceeded to Egypt. While in the East he did good work in the Palestine campaign, and in April 1918 returned to France in time to take part in the Retreat and Advance of that year. He was invalided home owing to illness in September, and was demobilised in February 1919, holding the General Service and Victory Medals.
46. Lyndhurst Road, Luton. 2945/B.

FOUNTAIN, A., Private, Bedfordshire Lancers.

Volunteering in September 1915, he was drafted to France in June of the following year. He took part in much severe fighting in the Somme Offensive of 1916, and at Arras, Bullecourt, Ypres and Cambrai. He also did good service in the Retreat and Advance of 1918. He was demobilised in 1919 after returning home, and holds the General Service and Victory Medals.
St. John's Yard, Eaton Bray, Dunstable. 2948.

FOUNTAIN, A. W., L/Corporal, Military Mounted Police.

He joined in April 1915, and in the following year, after completing his training, was sent to France. He was engaged at Le Havre and Rouen on important duties with his unit until after fighting ceased, and rendered valuable services. He was demobilised in July 1919, and holds the General Service and Victory Medals.
King's Street, Potton. Z2949.

FOUNTAIN, B., Gunner, Royal Garrison Artillery.

Joining in May 1916, he was drafted to France in December of the same year. He took part in the heavy fighting at the Battles of Arras, Ypres, Cambrai and the Somme, and was wounded. He was demobilised in February 1919 after returning to England, and holds the General Service and Victory Medals.
20, Back Street, Luton. 2950.

FOUNTAIN, B. C., Private, 2nd Cheshire Regt.

He volunteered in November 1915, and in September of the following year, after completing his training, was sent to Salonika, where he was engaged on the Struma and other fronts. He returned home in May 1919, and was demobilised in January 1919, holding the General Service and Victory Medals. 30, Cardiff Road, Watford. X2951.

FOUNTAIN, C., Driver, Royal Engineers.

He was mobilised in August 1914, and in the following month was drafted to the Western Front. He was engaged in the transport of Royal Engineers' stores to the various fronts, and rendered valuable services until hostilities ceased. He was demobilised in March 1919, and holds the 1914 Star, and the General Service and Victory Medals.
58, Union Street, Dunstable. 2952.

FOUNTAIN, E., Rifleman, Rifle Brigade.

He volunteered at the outbreak of war, and was immediately drafted to France. He rendered valuable service in the Retreat from Mons and in the Battle of Ypres, and was wounded. He was discharged in 1916 in consequence of his service, and holds the Mons Star, and the General Service and Victory Medals.
20, Banbury Street, Watford. X659/B.

FOUNTAIN, E., Private, R.A.O.C.

He volunteered in January 1915, and in the following year was sent to the Western Front. He was engaged at Boulogne, Calais, Rouen and Le Havre on important duties in connection with the stores supply department, and rendered valuable service. Having contracted dysentery while abroad he was invalided home and was discharged as medically unfit for further service in March 1919. He holds the General Service and Victory Medals.
52, Church Street, Leighton Buzzard. 2953/B.

FOUNTAIN, E. A. G., Sapper, Royal Engineers.

Joining in April 1917, after his training he was sent to India in July of the same year. In December 1917 he was transferred to Salonika, where he was engaged on various important duties. In 1918 he proceeded with the Army of Occupation to Constantinople. He returned home and was demobilised in December 1919, and holds the General Service and Victory Medals.
94, Rushbymead, Letchworth. 2954/A.

FOUNTAIN, H., Sapper, Royal Marine Engineers.

He joined in April 1917, but after his training was found to be physically unfit for foreign service. He was, however, engaged on duties of an important nature at Dover, Chatham and other docks, and did much valuable work until he was demobilised in 1919.
Stewkley Road, Wing, Leighton Buzzard. 1615.

FOUNTAIN, H., L/Corporal, East Surrey Regt.

He joined in February 1917, and at the conclusion of his training in the following June was drafted to the Western Front. His service in this theatre of war lasted for two years, during which time he fought in the Battles of Ypres, Passchendaele and Cambrai, and in the Retreat and Advance of 1918. At Cambrai in 1918 he was wounded, but was able to rejoin his unit after treatment. He was demobilised on his return to England in February 1919, and holds the General Service and Victory Medals.
1, Bower Lane, Eaton Bray, Dunstable. 2955.

FOUNTAIN, H. W., Private, Durham Light Infantry.

He joined in 1916, and after his training was drafted in the same year to France, where he saw considerable service. He was in action as a Lewis gunner at Arras and Cambrai, and in various engagements in the Retreat and Advance of 1918. He was demobilised in 1919 after returning home, and holds the General Service and Victory Medals.
112, Cotterell's Road, Hemel Hempstead. 296/A.

FOUNTAIN, J., Sapper, Royal Engineers.

He joined in March 1917, and after completing his training in the same year, was drafted to the Western Front. During his service in this theatre of war he did valuable work in connection with making barbed-wire entanglements and railway construction, and was present at many important engagements, notably those at Arras, Messines and Passchendaele Ridge. He was demobilised on his return to England in 1919, and holds the General Service and Victory Medals.
High Street, Westoning, Ampthill. 2957.

FOUNTAIN, J., Private, Essex Regiment.

He joined in June 1916, and after his training was engaged on duties of an important nature at various stations. Owing to physical unfitness he was unable to secure his transfer overseas, but did valuable work in many capacities until February 1918, when he was invalided out of the Service.
High Street, Eaton Bray, Dunstable. 2956.

FOUNTAIN, M. G., Gunner, R.F.A.

Joining in March 1916, he was drafted to the Western Front at the conclusion of his training, and after only a short period of service there was killed in action on August 24th of that year. He was entitled to the General Service and Victory Medals.
52, St. Saviour's Crescent, Luton. 2958.

FOUNTAIN, S., C.S.M., Bedfordshire Regiment.

He joined in January 1916, and on the completion of his training was drafted to France. Whilst in this theatre of war he took a prominent part in many notable engagements until hostilities ceased, and on one occasion was wounded and gassed. He remained overseas until after the close of the war, and on his return to England in September 1919, was demobilised. He holds the General Service and Victory Medals.
85, Waterlow Road, Dunstable. 2959.

FOUNTAIN, S. G., Private, R.M.L.I.

He joined in February 1918, and after his training was engaged on important duties with his unit. He served at Scapa Flow, and although he was not successful in obtaining his transfer to a theatre of war while fighting continued, did valuable work until he was demobilised in February 1919.
94, Rushbymead, Letchworth. 2954/B.

FOUNTAIN, T., Corporal, 4th Bedfordshire Regt.

He volunteered in December 1914, and until 1916, when he was sent to France, was engaged on important duties at various stations. His service overseas lasted for three years, during which period he took an active part in many important engagements, including those at the Somme, Arras, Ypres, Bapaume and Cambrai. He was demobilised after his return to England in January 1919, and holds the General Service and Victory Medals.
95, Oak Road, Luton. 2960.

FOUNTAIN, V. (Mrs.), Private, Forage Corps.
She joined in 1916, and rendered valuable services in various parts of the country, being engaged on important agricultural and transport duties with the Royal Army Service Corps. She was demobilised in February 1919.
52, Church Street, Leighton Buzzard.   2953/A.

FOWLER, A. W., Private, Royal Air Force.
He joined in July 1917, and on the conclusion of his training was retained with his squadron for important duties, which called for much technical knowledge and skill. He was unable to secure his transfer to a theatre of war before hostilities ceased, but did valuable work until demobilised in 1919.
109, Ridge Street, Callowland, Watford.   X2962/B.

FOWLER, B., Private, Machine Gun Corps.
Joining in March 1917, he was sent to France in the following December. In the capacity of gunner, he served in the Battles of Cambrai and the Somme, and after taking part in many other operations in the Retreat and Advance of 1918, proceeded to Germany with the Army of Occupation. He was demobilised after his return to England in September 1919, and holds the General Service and Victory Medals.
17, Dane Road, Luton.   2963/A.

FOWLER, G., Private, Labour Corps.
He joined in October 1916, and at the conclusion of his training was sent to the Western Front. Owing to ill-health, he was unfit for service in a fighting area, but did valuable work in various capacities until November 1917, when he returned to England and was invalided out of the Service owing to heart trouble. He holds the General Service and Victory Medals.
28, Church Street, Ridgmont.   Z2965/A.

FOWLER, G., Sapper, Royal Engineers.
He volunteered at the commencement of war, and after being retained for a time on important duties, was afterwards drafted to the Western Front. Whilst in this theatre of war he served with a field company on important trenching and wiring work in the forward areas, and was present at several engagements, including that at Cambrai. He holds the General Service and Victory Medals, and was demobilised on his return to England in March 1919.
19, Loates Lane, Watford.   X2964/A.

FOWLER, H., Bombardier, R.F.A.
Volunteering in August 1914, he was sent to France three months later. He was engaged in the fighting at Ypres, Loos, Arras, the Somme, Cambrai and in many other important operations, and throughout his service overseas, which lasted for over four years, did excellent work with his unit. He holds the 1914–15 Star, and the General Service and Victory Medals, and was demobilised in March 1919.
Upper Sundon, near Dunstable.   2966.

FOWLER, H. G., Driver, R.A.S.C.
He volunteered in August 1915, and at the conclusion of his training was sent to the Western Front. Throughout his service overseas he was engaged on important transport duties in the forward areas, and did excellent work in this capacity, frequently being under shell fire. Early in 1918 he returned to England in consequence of ill-health, and in May of that year was invalided out of the Service. He holds the 1914–15 Star, and the General Service and Victory Medals.
109, Ridge Street, Callowland, Watford.   X2962/A.

FOWLER, N. J., Sapper, Royal Engineers.
Volunteering in August 1914, he was sent to the Western Front after finishing his course of training. While there he was engaged on duties of an important nature in the forward areas, and after having been wounded, was killed in action on April 21st, 1915. He was entitled to the 1914–15 Star, and the General Service and Victory Medals.
Grove Road, Harpenden.   2967/A.

FOWLER, S., Sergeant, Military Foot Police.
He volunteered in August 1915, and on completing his training early in the following year was sent to Mesopotamia. Throughout his service in this theatre of war, he was engaged on important duties with the Military Foot Police, and did valuable work until 1919, when he returned to England. He was demobilised in December of that year, and holds the General Service and Victory Medals.
28, Weymouth Street, Apsley End.   X2968.

FOWLER, T., Private, Grenadier Guards.
He joined in March 1917, but in the course of his training became seriously ill, and was in hospital for nine months. He was discharged in May 1918 as medically unfit for further military service.
28, Church Street, Ridgmont.   Z2965/B.

FOWLER, W. J., Private, R.A.M.C.
Volunteering in September 1915, he was drafted to France in the following January. He was stationed chiefly at Rouen, where he was engaged on important duties in attendance on the wounded, but also served for a time in the forward areas, and was wounded. He was demobilised after his return to England in May 1919, and holds the General Service and Victory Medals.
32, Hagden Lane, Watford.   X2969.

FOX, A., Rifleman, Royal Irish Rifles.
He volunteered in August 1914, and in the following year was drafted to the Dardanelles, where he took an active part in the landing at Gallipoli, and the Battle of Cape Helles. After leaving the Peninsula, he was sent to the Western Front, and fought at Loos, Vimy Ridge, the Somme, Arras, Cambrai, and in the Retreat and Advance of 1918. During his service overseas he was wounded on four occasions. He was demobilised in February 1919, and holds the 1914–15 Star, and the General Service and Victory Medals.
108, Selbourne Road, Luton.   2970/A.

FOX, A. G., Corporal, East Yorkshire Regt.
He volunteered in 1915, and after the completion of his training proceeded to the Western Front, where he took an active part in many important battles, including those of Ypres, Arras and Cambrai, and was gassed. He holds the General Service and Victory Medals, and was demobilised on his return to England in January 1919.
53, Cromer Road, Watford.   X2971.

FOX, B., Private, Bedfordshire Regiment.
Volunteering in August 1914, he was afterwards drafted to the Western Front, where he took an active part in the engagements at Hill 60, Ypres, the Somme, Arras, Cambrai and Péronne. During his service overseas, which lasted for four years, he was wounded on three occasions, but after treatment returned to the lines. He holds the 1914–15 Star, and the General Service and Victory Medals, and was demobilised in March 1919.
3, Harpenden Lane, Redbourn.   2972/A.

FOX, F. W., Private, 3rd Bedfordshire Regiment.
He volunteered at the commencement of hostilities, and served on the Western Front from early in 1915 until 1917. During this time he took an active part in many engagements, including those of Hill 60, Givenchy, and Arras. He then returned to England in consequence of ill-health, and was discharged as medically unfit for further duty. He holds the 1914–15 Star, and the General Service and Victory Medals.
26, Fearnley Street, Watford.   X2973/A.

FOX, J., Private, R.A.S.C. (M.T.)
A serving soldier, who enlisted in May 1914, he was mobilised and sent to France immediately upon the outbreak of war. He served throughout the Retreat from Mons, and many of the subsequent engagements, including those at the Aisne, Ypres, the Somme and Arras, and did important work in connection with the transport of supplies until the termination of hostilities. He was discharged in December 1918, and holds the Mons Star, and the General Service and Victory Medals.
180, Harwood Road, Watford.   X2974.

FOX, J. A., Private, 9th Royal Fusiliers.
He joined in June 1916, and in November of the same year was drafted to the Western Front, where he took part in various engagements of great importance, including that at Delville Wood. He returned home in 1917, and after being retained on important duties, was demobilised in August 1919. He holds the General Service and Victory Medals.
8, Francis Place, Watford.   X2975.

FOX, L., Private, Bedfordshire Regiment.
He volunteered in September 1914, and early in the following year was sent to the Western Front, where he took an active part in the Battles of Hill 60 and Ypres. He then served for a time at Salonika, where he did valuable work in several engagements. Returning to France in 1916 he fought in the engagements at Langemarck and Arras, and in other operations until the close of hostilities. During his service he was wounded on two occasions. He was demobilised after his return to England in December 1919, and holds the 1914–15 Star, and the General Service and Victory Medals.
3, Harpenden Lane, Redbourn.   2972/B.

FOX, L. H., Sapper, Royal Engineers.
Joining in April 1916, he was drafted to France on the completion of his training in September of the same year. He did valuable service in maintaining communications in the Battles of the Ancre, the Somme, the Marne, Ypres and Cambrai. He returned home and was demobilised in September 1919, and holds the General Service and Victory Medals.
56, Milton Road, Luton.   2976.

FOX, P., Gunner, Royal Field Artillery.

He joined in March 1916, and after his training was engaged on duties of an important nature at Winchester, Romsey, Forest Row and other camps. He was unable to secure his transfer to a theatre of war before the cessation of hostilities, but did valuable work until his demobilisation in October 1919.

3, Harpenden Lane, Redbourn.   2972/C.

FOX, R. A., Air Mechanic, Royal Air Force.

He joined in March 1917, and after his training served as an engine fitter at various stations on important duties, which demanded a high degree of technical skill. He carried out his work in an efficient manner, and rendered valuable services, but was not successful in obtaining his transfer overseas before the cessation of hostilities owing to medical unfitness. He was demobilised in February 1919.

Olive House, New Dalton Street, St. Albans.   X2977.

FOX, W. C., Private, Duke of Cornwall's Light Infantry.

He was serving at the outbreak of war, and shortly afterwards was drafted to the Western Front, where he took part in the Battles of the Aisne, Hill 60, Ypres, Festubert and the Somme. He was killed in action on July 19th, 1916, and was entitled to the 1914 Star, and the General Service and Victory Medals.

8, Francis Place, Watford.   X2975/B.

FOX, W. E., A.B., Royal Navy.

He joined in October 1916, and after his training was posted to H.M.S. "Lion." During his three years' service on board this vessel she was engaged in conveying food to and escorting troopships to and from France, and also on submarine patrol work. He rendered valuable service until December 1919, when he returned to his Base and was demobilised. He holds the General Service and Victory Medals.

108, Selbourne Road, Luton.   2970/B.

FOXEN, J. W., Private, 1st Hertfordshire Regt.

Joining in August 1916, he was sent to France in December of the same year. He did valuable service on the Somme front until June 1917, when he was invalided home owing to septic poisoning and fever. He was discharged in February 1918 as medically unfit for further military service, and holds the General Service and Victory Medals.

49, George Street, Leighton Buzzard.   2978.

FRANCIS, S., Private, 5th Royal Inniskilling Fusiliers.

He joined in July 1916, and in the following year was drafted to Salonika and thence to Egypt and Palestine, where he took part in numerous important engagements. He returned home and was demobilised in February 1919, and holds the General Service and Victory Medals.

35, Cowfair Lands, Biggleswade.   Z2979.

FRANCIS, T. A., L/Corporal, Rifle Brigade.

He enlisted in May 1908, and was serving in India on the outbreak of hostilities, and from there was drafted to the Western Front in December 1914. He took part in severe fighting at Ypres and in many other engagements, and was killed in action at Arras on April 9th, 1917. He was entitled to the 1914–15 Star, and the General Service and Victory Medals.

109, St. James' Road, Watford.   X584/B.

FRANCIS, W., Private, South Wales Borderers.

He joined in February 1916, but in the course of his training was found to be medically unfit for military service, and was discharged in the following June.

Chapel Place, Biggleswade.   Z2980.

FRANKLIN, A., Sapper, Royal Engineers.

He volunteered in 1915, and after a course of training proceeded in 1917 to Egypt and Palestine, where he took part in numerous engagements, including those at Gaza, Medjil, Haifa, Damascus and Aleppo. He was demobilised in 1919, and holds the General Service and Victory Medals.

14, High Street, Redbourn.   2987/C.

FRANKLIN, A., Private, Oxfordshire and Buckinghamshire Light Infantry.

After joining in June 1916, he was sent to India and thence to Mesopotamia in November of the same year. He took part in various engagements, including those at Baghdad, Tekrit and Mosul, and after the conclusion of hostilities, returned home and was demobilised in October 1919. He holds the General Service and Victory Medals.

3, Athol Cottages, Colney Street West, St. Albans.   X2981.

FRANKLIN, A. (M.M.), Corporal, 7th Bedfordshire Regiment.

He volunteered in 1914, and in the following year was sent to France, where he took part in severe fighting in numerous engagements, and was awarded the Military Medal for bravery in the Field. He died in hospital at Rouen on October 30th, 1918, and in addition to holding the Military Medal, was entitled to the 1914–15 Star, and the General Service and Victory Medals.

26, High Street, Redbourn.   2983/A.

FRANKLIN, A. L., Private, R.A.S.C. (M.T.)

After joining in May 1916, he was sent to France in September of the same year, and served in various engagements, including those on the Somme and at Arras and Cambrai. He was demobilised in October 1919, and holds the General Service and Victory Medals.

50, Cardiff Road, Watford.   X2984/B.

FRANKLIN, F., Gunner, R.G.A.

He joined in April 1916, and in the following July was drafted to the Western Front, where he took part in heavy fighting at the Battles of Arras, Ypres and Cambrai, and was wounded. He was demobilised in September 1919, and holds the General Service and Victory Medals.

30, Frogmore, near St. Albans.   X2985

FRANKLIN, H., Private, Duke of Wellington's (West Riding Regiment).

He joined in February 1917, and was drafted to France in January of the following year. He took part in important engagements, including those at St. Quentin and Cambrai, and was killed in action near Rheims on July 20th, 1918. He was entitled to the General Service and Victory Medals.

Gas Street, Toddington.   2986/A.

FRANKLIN, H. (M.M.), Private, Bedfordshire Regiment.

He volunteered in September 1914, and in the following year was drafted to the Western Front, where he took part in the Battles of Loos, the Somme and Arras, and was awarded the Military Medal for conspicuous gallantry. He was killed in action near Cambrai in March 1918, and in addition to holding the Military Medal, was entitled to the 1914–15 Star, and the General Service and Victory Medals.

4, Alma Cut, St. Albans.   X2982/C.

FRANKLIN, H., Gunner, Royal Field Artillery.

After volunteering in 1914, he served on important duties with his battery until 1916, when he was drafted to the Western Front, where he took part in numerous engagements, including those at Arras, Ypres, Passchendaele, Cambrai, Givenchy, Lens and the Somme. He was demobilised in 1919, and holds the General Service and Victory Medals.

14, High Street, Redbourn.   2987/B

FRANKLIN, H. R. A., Private, M.G.C.

He joined in 1916, and proceeded to France in the same year, and took part in various engagements, including those on the Somme and at Ypres, and was gassed. In 1917 he was transferred to Egypt and Palestine, and served at Gaza, Haïfa, Medjil and Aleppo. He was demobilised in 1920, and holds the General Service and Victory Medals.

14, High Street, Redbourn.   2987/A.

FRANKLIN, R. A., Private, Northumberland Fusiliers.

He volunteered in August 1915, and was drafted to France in August of the following year. He took part in the Battles of the Somme, Arras, Ypres and other important engagements, and was wounded near Cambrai in April 1918. He was demobilised in April 1919 and holds the General Service and Victory Medals.

50, Cardiff Road, Watford.   X2984/A.

FRANKLIN, S., Private, Royal Fusiliers.

He volunteered in August 1914, and proceeded in the following year to the Western Front, where he took part in severe fighting at Festubert, Loos and Arras. Later, contracting tuberculosis, he was invalided home, and was discharged as medically unfit for further service in June 1917, and has since died. He was entitled to the 1914–15 Star, and the General Service and Victory Medals.

1, Franklin's Row, Potton.   Z2988.

FRANKLIN, W. G., Private, 6th Royal Berkshire Regiment.

Volunteering in 1915, he was sent to France in the following year. He took part in severe fighting in many important engagements, and was killed in action at Ypres on August 16th, 1917, and was entitled to the General Service and Victory Medals.

26, High Street, Redbourn.   2983/B.

FRANKLIN, W. J., Private, King's (Liverpool Regiment).
After joining in May 1916, he was drafted in March of the following year to Salonika, and served on the Vardar front. In February 1918 he was transferred to France, where he took part in various engagements, including those at St. Quentin and Cambrai. He was demobilised in February 1919, and holds the General Service and Victory Medals.
Gas Street, Toddington.   2986/B:

FRASER, T., Corporal, R.A.S.C.
Volunteering in January 1915, he was drafted to Egypt in the following month. Later he was sent to the Dardanelles and took part in the landing at Suvla Bay. In December 1915 he was transferred to Salonika, where he was present at numerous engagements during the Balkan campaign. After the cessation of hostilities he returned to England, and in March 1919 was demobilised, holding the 1914–15 Star, and the General Service and Victory Medals.
50, Sandringham Road, Watford.   X2989.

FREEMAN, A. E., Private, Grenadier Guards.
Having volunteered in August 1914, he was sent to France immediately afterwards. He took part in severe fighting in the Retreat from Mons, and at Ypres, Neuve Chapelle, the Somme, Arras and Cambrai, and was wounded. He was demobilised in December 1919, and holds the Mons Star, and the General Service and Victory Medals.
6, Garden Road, Abbotts Langley.   X2990/A.

FREEMAN, B. T., Sapper, Royal Engineers.
He joined in June 1916, and after his training served on important duties with his unit until January 1918, when he was drafted to the Western Front. He was engaged on special wireless intelligence duty, and rendered valuable services until he was demobilised in January 1919. He holds the General Service and Victory Medals.
13, Kershaws Hill, Hitchin.   2991.

FREEMAN, C. C., Gunner, R.F.A.
Joining in 1915 he was sent in the same year to France, where he took part in the Battle of Ypres. Later he was transferred to Palestine, and was in action at Gaza, Jaffa and Aleppo. He was demobilised in 1919, and holds the 1914–15 Star, and the General Service and Victory Medals.
6, Garden Road, Abbotts Langley.   X2990/C.

FREEMAN, D., Private, R.A.S.C.
Having joined in April 1917, he proceeded in the following September to the Western Front, where he served at Arras and Cambrai on transport duties. He was wounded near Cambrai in April 1918 and invalided home, and was discharged in June of the same year as medically unfit for further service. He holds the General Service and Victory Medals.
7, Albion Street, Dunstable.   2992.

FREEMAN, E. E., L/Corporal, Royal Fusiliers.
Volunteering in 1914, he was, after completing his training, sent to the Western Front, where he took part in various important engagements. In 1917 he was transferred to Mesopotamia and served at Kut and Mosul. After the Armistice he was sent to Germany with the Army of Occupation, with which he was still serving in 1920. He holds the General Service and Victory Medals.
194, Fishpool Street, St. Albans.   2993/B.

FREEMAN, E. J., Sapper, Royal Engineers.
He joined in 1916, and after his training served on important duties with his unit until 1918, when, after the signing of the Armistice, he proceeded to East Prussia, where he was engaged in the Secret Service. He was still serving in 1920.
High Street, Hailtorn, near Cambridge.   2993/A.

FREEMAN, F., Private, Labour Corps.
He joined in March 1916, and in the same year was drafted to the Western Front, where he served in various engagements, including those on the Somme and at Ypres and Cambrai, and was gassed, from the effects of which he died on May 23rd, 1918. He was entitled to the General Service and Victory Medals.
42, Ebury Road, Watford.   X2994/A.

FREEMAN, F. C., Corporal, Hertfordshire Regt.
He joined in 1916, and in the same year was drafted to the Western Front, where he took part in numerous engagements, including those at Arras, Ypres, Cambrai and the Somme, and was wounded at St. Julien. He was demobilised in 1919, and holds the General Service and Victory Medals.
6, Garden Road, Abbots Langley.   X2990/B.

FREEMAN, G., Sergeant, Royal Field Artillery.
He volunteered in October 1914, and proceeded to France in the following year, and took part in the heavy fighting at Neuve Chapelle, Hill 60 and Ypres, and was wounded. He returned home and was demobilised in March 1919, and holds the 1914–15 Star, and the General Service and Victory Medals.
15, Albion Road, St. Albans.   X2995.

FREEMAN, H. A., Private, Duke of Wellington's (West Riding Regiment).
Volunteering in May 1915, he was sent to France in the same year, and took part in many important engagements, including those on the Somme and at Arras, Ypres, Cambrai and St. Julien. He was demobilised in January 1919, and holds the 1914–15 Star, and the General Service and Victory Medals.
12, Piccotts End, Hemel Hempstead.   X2193/A.

FREEMAN, J. K., Rifleman, King's Royal Rifle Corps.
Joining in June 1918, he was afterwards drafted to India, where he was engaged on important duties with his unit and rendered valuable services. He was still serving in 1920, and holds the General Service and Victory Medals.
52, Clifford Street, Watford.   X2996/B.

FREEMAN, L., Drummer, 1st Bedfordshire Regt.
Called up from the Reserve at the outbreak of hostilities, he was immediately drafted to the Western Front, where he was killed in action during the Retreat from Mons. He was entitled to the Mons Star and the General Service and Victory Medals.
6a, Brache Street, Luton.   4759/B.

FREEMAN, T. R., Private, Sherwood Foresters.
He joined in April 1916, and after his training was sent in the same year to Egypt and Palestine, where he took part in numerous engagements, including those at Gaza and Jaffa. He returned home and was demobilised in July 1919, and holds the 1914–15 Star, and the General Service and Victory Medals.
52, Clifford Street, Watford.   X2996/A.

FREEMAN, W., Private, Labour Corps.
He joined in 1917, and proceeded in the same year to the Western Front, where he served in many important engagements, including those at Ypres and the Somme. He returned home and was demobilised in 1919, and holds the General Service and Victory Medals.
10, Cassio Bridge Road, Watford.   X2997.

FREESTONE, H. F., Bombardier, R.G.A.
He volunteered in November 1915, and in July of the following year proceeded to Salonika and was in action on the Vardar, Struma and Doiran Fronts. During his service in the East he suffered from malaria, and after the conclusion of hostilities returned home and was demobilised in March 1919. He holds the General Service and Victory Medals.
Sun Street, Potton.   Z2998/B.

FREESTONE, H. M., Private, M.G.C.
Having joined in February 1917, he proceeded in October of the same year to the Western Front, where he took part in numerous engagements, including those at Passchendaele Ridge, Cambrai and Albert. He also served in the Retreat and Advance of 1918, and was killed in action on September 19th of that year. He was entitled to the General Service and Victory Medals.
Sun Street, Potton.   Z2998/A.

FREESTONE, T., Corporal, Duke of Wellington's (West Riding Regiment).
After volunteering in November 1914, he was in 1915 drafted to the Western Front, where he took part in the heavy fighting at Ypres, the Somme, Arras and Cambrai, and was twice wounded. He was invalided home and discharged, owing to his wounds, in December 1918 and holds the 1914–15 Star, and the General Service and Victory Medals.
39, Florence Street, Hitchin.   2999.

FRENCH, A., Private, Loyal North Lancashire Regiment.
He volunteered in January 1915, and after serving at various stations was drafted overseas in the following year. He took part in the fighting on the Somme, and at Arras, Ypres, Passchendaele and Cambrai, and in the engagements which followed, until the cessation of hostilities. After the Armistice he proceeded to Germany with the Army of Occupation, and was stationed on the Rhine until August 1919, when he returned home and was demobilised. He holds the General Service and Victory Medals.
100, Nightingale Road, Hitchin.   3000.

FRENCH, A., Private, Cheshire Regiment.
He volunteered in April 1915, and in the same year was drafted to France and took part in the Battles of Ypres and was wounded. After his recovery he fought at Messines Ridge and Passchendaele, and in the second Battle of the Marne. He was demobilised in January 1919, and holds the 1914–15 Star, and the General Service and Victory Medals.
4, St. Andrew's Street, Hitchin.   3001.

FRENCH, A., C.Q.M.S., 1/5th Buffs (East Kent Regiment.)
He had previously enlisted in March 1903, and was mobilised at the outbreak of war, and in February 1916 was sent to Mesopotamia. Whilst in this theatre of war he fought in the offensive on Kut-el-Amara and took part in the capture of Baghdad and the engagements that followed. He contracted malaria, and after some time in hospital was sent to India, and thence returned home and was demobilised in January 1920. He holds the General Service and Victory Medals.
11, St. Andrew's Place, Hitchin. 3002.

FRENCH, A. C., Pte., Somerset Light Infantry.
He volunteered in 1915, and in the following year was drafted to France, where he fought on the Somme and at Albert, Arras, Ypres and Cambrai. He was taken prisoner on March 21st, 1918, and was held in captivity until after the Armistice, when he was released and repatriated. He was demobilised in 1919, and holds the General Service and Victory Medals.
6, Bancroft, Hitchin. 3003.

FRENCH, B. G., Sergt., Hertfordshire Dragoons.
He was mobilised at the outbreak of war, and saw much varied service in Gallipoli, Mesopotamia, Egypt and Russia, and on each of these fronts took an active part in many engagements. After the conclusion of hostilities he returned to England and was demobilised in February 1919, holding the 1914-15 Star, and the General Service and Victory Medals.
2, Ash Road, Luton. 3004/B.

FRENCH, C., Stoker, R.N., H.M.S. " Osprey."
He joined in March 1918, and after his training was posted to H.M.S. " Osprey." Whilst in this vessel he served off the coasts of Ireland and Scotland, and was engaged on important and dangerous duties. He was demobilised in February 1919, and holds the General Service and Victory Medals.
Grove Mill, Hitchin. 3006/A.

FRENCH, C., Private, Buffs (East Kent Regt.) and 2nd Bedfordshire Regiment.
He joined in November 1914, and in the following June was drafted to the Western Front, where he was severely wounded in action at Loos on September 25th, 1915, and invalided home to hospital. After his recovery he was drafted to Mesopotamia in February of the succeeding year, and whilst in this theatre of war took part in the fighting at Kut-el-Amara, Basra and Baghdad, and in November 1919 he returned home and was demobilised, holding the 1914-15 Star, and the General Service and Victory Medals.
12, Telegraph Place, Hitchin. 3005/A.

FRENCH, C. S., Private, 14th London Regiment (London Scottish).
He joined in November 1917, and was drafted to the Western Front. During his service in France he took part in many notable engagements, including those at Bullecourt and Passchendaele, and was gassed in action. After his recovery he served in various subsequent operations in the Retreat and Advance, and was finally demobilised in October 1919. He holds the General Service and Victory Medals.
" Clinton," Ambrose Lane, Harpenden. 3007.

FRENCH, F. A., Private, R.M.L.I.
He joined in July 1917, and after his training was drafted to Ireland, where he served for two years on important duties at Dublin Barracks, attached to the Harbour Guard. In 1920 he was still serving.
Batford Cottages, Lower Luton Road, Harpenden. 3011/C.

FRENCH, G. H., Private, 9th Royal Welch Fusiliers.
He volunteered in January 1915, and in the following July was sent to the Western Front. Two months later he was killed in action in an engagement near Ypres on September 25th, 1915. He was entitled to the 1914-15 Star, and the General Service and Victory Medals.
Oak Dene, Kershaw's Hill, Hitchin. 1856/B.

FRENCH, H., Private, 2nd Bedfordshire and Hertfordshire Regiments.
Volunteering at the outbreak of war, he was drafted to France in the following year, and during his service on the Western Front fought at Festubert, the Somme, Albert, Ypres, St. Quentin and Bullecourt, and in subsequent engagements until the cessation of hostilities. In September 1919 he proceeded to India, and was still serving there in the following year. He holds the 1914-15 Star, and the General Service and Victory Medals.
47, Bancroft, Hitchin 3010.

FRENCH, H., Private, Bedfordshire and Hertfordshire Regiments.
He volunteered in September 1914, and in the following year was drafted to the Western Front. During his service in France he took part in the fighting at Ypres, Loos, the Somme, Albert, Arras, and Cambrai, and was wounded on three occasions. He was demobilised after his return to England in March 1919, and holds the General Service and Victory Medals.
48, Bancroft, Hitchin. 3009.

FRENCH, H., Private, 13th Middlesex Regiment.
He joined in March 1916, and in the same year was drafted to the Western Front, where he took part in the fighting on the Somme and at Arras, and was wounded in the third Battle of Ypres. After his recovery he was again in action at Cambrai and in the engagements which followed until the conclusion of hostilities. He was demobilised in 1919, and holds the General Service and Victory Medals.
The Folly, Luton Road, Wheathampstead. 3008.

FRENCH, H., Private, 6th Bedfordshire Regt.
He volunteered in September 1914, and in the following July was drafted to France. During his service on the Western Front he fought at Loos and in the Battle of the Somme, where he was wounded. Later he died of his injuries on November 25th, 1916, and was entitled to the 1914-15 Star, and the General Service and Victory Medals.
12, Telegraph Place, Hitchin. 3005/C.

FRENCH, J., Private, 6th Bedfordshire Regt.
He volunteered in September 1914, and in the following August was drafted to France, where he served in the Battles of Loos and the Somme, and was severely wounded on July 1st, 1916. He was invalided home to hospital and was under treatment for about three months, and then returned to his unit in France. On April 23rd, 1917, whilst fighting at Arras, he was killed in action, and was entitled to the 1914-15 Star, and the General Service and Victory Medals.
12, Telegraph Place, Hitchin, 3005/B.

FRENCH, J., Private, 3rd Bedfordshire Regt.
He volunteered in November 1914, and during the course of his training was found to be unfit for military service and was consequently discharged in the following month.
22, Periwinkle Lane, Hitchin. 3012/B.

FRENCH, J., Private, Bedfordshire Regiment.
He volunteered in October 1914, and after his training served at various stations on important duties with his unit. He rendered valuable services until May 1915, when he was discharged as medically unfit for further service.
Batford Cottages, Lower Luton Road, Harpenden. 3011/B.

FRENCH, J. E., Sapper, Royal Engineers.
He joined in November 1916, and in the same year was drafted to France, where he served on important signalling duties at Rouen and elsewhere. He was demobilised in February 1919, and holds the General Service and Victory Medals.
The Folly Field, Wheathampstead. 3033.

FRENCH, R., Corporal, Royal Field Artillery.
He had previously enlisted in 1900, and was mobilised at the outbreak of war. He was drafted to the Western Front and took part in the Retreat from Mons, and was also in action at the Battles of the Marne, Ypres and the Somme, where he was gassed. Later he was drafted to Italy and served on the Piave, and in subsequent engagements until the conclusion of hostilities. He was demobilised in May 1919, and holds the Mons Star, and the General Service and Victory Medals.
18, Saulbury Road, Linslade, near Leighton Buzzard. 3013.

FRENCH, W., Sergeant, 1st Lincolnshire Regt.
He volunteered in August 1914, and in the following month was drafted to France, where he took part in numerous engagements, including those at Mons, La Bassée, Ypres, the Somme, Arras and Cambrai. He also served in India for a time, and was still serving in 1920. He holds the Mons Star, and the General Service and Victory Medals.
8, Hockliffe Road, Leighton Buzzard. 1294/A.

FRENCH, W., Cadet, R.A.F.
He joined in July 1918, and was in training as a pilot in the Royal Air Force when the signing of the Armistice brought hostilities to a conclusion. He was demobilised in December 1918.
Grove Mill, Hitchin. 3006/B.

FRESHWATER, C., Corporal, M.G.C.
He joined in August 1916, and in the same year was drafted to France. During his service on the Western Front he took part in the Battles of the Somme, Arras, Ypres and Cambrai, and in subsequent engagements, until the cessation of hostilities. He was demobilised in January 1919, and holds the General Service and Victory Medals.
6, Portland Road, Luton. 3014.

FRIPP, W., Private, 8th Bedfordshire Regiment.
He joined in June 1916, and in the same year was drafted to France. After taking part in several minor engagements he was killed in action at Vimy Ridge on April 19th, 1917, and was entitled to the General Service and Victory Medals.
21, Ashbey Road, North Watford.   X3015.

FROST, A. A., Sapper, Royal Engineers.
He volunteered at the outbreak of war, and in the following March was drafted to France, where he was engaged on important duties in connection with the operations and was frequently in the forward areas. He was killed in action at St. Quentin on June 24th, 1915, and was entitled to the 1914–15 Star, and the General Service and Victory Medals.
82, Park Road West, Luton.   3016/B.

FROST, B., Sapper, Royal Engineers.
He volunteered in April 1915, and in the following July was drafted to Gallipoli, where he was engaged on important duties in connection with the operations, and was present at the landing at Suvla Bay, and in the subsequent engagements until the evacuation of the Peninsula. He was then sent to Egypt and served in the Canal zone, and in 1917 took part in the offensive on Palestine with General Allenby's Forces, and was in action at Gaza, Haïfa and Beyrout. He was finally demobilised in August 1919 after his return to England, and holds the General Service and Victory Medals.
82, Park Road West, Luton.   3016/A.

FROST, F. H., Private, Northamptonshire Regt.
He volunteered in July 1915, and in the following January was drafted to France, where he served for 3½ years. He was present at the Battles of the Somme, Arras, Ypres, Cambrai and St. Quentin, and in the final operations of the war, and after the conclusion of hostilities returned to England and was demobilised in January 1919, holding the General Service and Victory Medals.
82, Park Road West, Luton.   3016/C.

FROST, G., A.B., R.N., H.M.S. " Doon."
He volunteered in 1915, and after his training was posted to H.M.S. " Doon " and sent in this vessel to the North Sea. Throughout his service, which lasted four years, he was engaged on important duties in the Baltic, and various other seas. He was demobilised in 1919, and holds the General Service and Victory Medals.
105, Ridge Street, Callowland, near Watford.   X3017/A.

FROST, J., Bombardier, Royal Garrison Artillery.
He joined in July 1916, and in the following year was drafted to Egypt and served with the British Forces under General Allenby in the Advance through Palestine. He fought at Gaza, Haïfa and Acre, and was present at the fall of Jerusalem, and was also in action at Aleppo and Beyrout, and returned to Egypt and was stationed at Cairo until August 1919, when he was sent home and demobilised. He holds the General Service and Victory Medals.
142, Ridgway Road, Luton.   3018.

FROST, J. S., Gunner, Royal Marine Artillery.
He joined in 1916, and after his training was engaged on important duties in the North Sea and the Baltic, and in various other waters. He also took part in the Battle of Jutland, and during his service was shipwrecked, and was fortunately rescued. In 1920 he was still serving, and holds the General Service and Victory Medals.
105, Ridge Street, Callowland, Watford.   X3017/B.

FROY, E., Private, Middlesex Regiment and Labour Corps.
He joined in October 1916, and after his training served at various stations on important duties with his unit, being engaged on work connected with aerodromes. He rendered valuable services, but was not successful in obtaining his transfer overseas before the cessation of hostilities, and was demobilised in January 1919.
36, Hitchin Hill, Hitchin.   3019/B.

FROY, F., Private, South Wales Borderers.
He joined in April 1916, and after his training was completed was sent to France in the following March. After only a month's service overseas he was killed in the heavy fighting at Arras on April 13th, 1917. He was entitled to the General Service and Victory Medals.
38, Hitchin Hill, Hitchin.   3019/A.

FROY, J., Private, The Welch Regiment.
He joined in July 1916, and after his training was completed was drafted to France. During his service on the Western Front he took part in the fighting in the third Battle of Ypres, and in subsequent engagements. On April 11th, 1918, he died of wounds, and was entitled to the General Service and Victory Medals.
49, Dacre Road, Hitchin.   3020.

FRYER, F., Gunner, Royal Garrison Artillery.
He joined in May 1917, and after his training served at his depôt on important clerical duties. He rendered valuable service, but on medical grounds was unable to secure his transfer overseas, and was discharged as unfit for further military duty in January 1918.
The Dairy, Mount Pleasant, Aspley Guise.   Z3021/B.

FRYER, H. J., Private, Royal Sussex Regiment.
He joined in June 1918, and after his training served at various stations on important duties with his unit. He did excellent work, but was not successful in obtaining his transfer abroad before the termination of hostilities, and was demobilised in January 1919.
The Dairy, Mount Pleasant, Aspley Guise.   Z3021/A.

FUFF, E., Private, R.A.V.C.
He volunteered in January 1915, and in the following June was drafted to France. During his service on the Western Front he was engaged on important veterinary duties, attending to the sick and wounded horses. He was frequently in the forward areas, notably on the Somme, and at Ypres and Cambrai, and rendered valuable services throughout. He was demobilised after his return to England in February 1919, and holds the 1914–15 Star, and the General Service and Victory Medals.
High Street, Eaton Bray, Dunstable.   3022/B.

FULCHER, A. V., Private, Labour Corps.
He joined in November 1917, and after his training served at various stations on important coastal defence duties, and was also engaged in agricultural work. He rendered valuable services, but was not successful in obtaining a transfer overseas, and was demobilised in January 1919.
49, Old Bedford Road, Luton.   3023.

FULCHER, J., Corporal, Bedfordshire Regiment.
Volunteering in September 1914, he served at various depôts on important guard duties until after the cessation of hostilities in November 1918. He then proceeded to Germany with the Army of Occupation, and was stationed at Cologne for four months. He returned home and was demobilised in March 1919.
132, Rushbymead South, Letchworth.   3024/B.

FULCHER, W. J., Rifleman, King's Royal Rifle Corps.
He joined in February 1917, and after his training served at various stations until he was drafted to France in May 1918. Whilst overseas he took part in the fighting in the second Battle of Cambrai, and in the final operations of the war. He was demobilised after his return home in October 1919, and holds the General Service and Victory Medals.
132, Rushbymead South, Letchworth.   3024/A.

FULLARTON, G., Private, 2nd Essex and Bedfordshire Regiments.
He joined in June 1917, and after his training was engaged on duties of a special nature at various stations with his unit. He was not successful in obtaining his transfer overseas before the termination of hostilities, but nevertheless rendered valuable services until he was demobilised in October 1919.
45, Frederic Street, Luton.   1581/B.

FULLER, E. G., Driver, R.A.S.C.
He volunteered in January 1915, and after his training served on the Western Front for three years. During this time he did valuable work as a transport driver in many important sectors, including those of the Somme, Ypres and Cambrai. He holds the General Service and Victory Medals, and was demobilised after his return to England in May 1919.
12, Sandringham Road, Watford.   X3025.

FULLER, S. J., Gunner (Signaller), R.F.A.
Joining in May 1916, he was sent to the Western Front at the conclusion of his training. In the capacity of signaller he took part in numerous engagements, notably those at Ypres, Passchendaele, Arras and Cambrai, and was wounded in action during the Advance in October 1918. He was demobilised on his return to England in March 1919, and holds the General Service and Victory Medals.
95, Highbury Road, Luton.   3026.

FULLER, W. J., Sapper, Royal Engineers.
He volunteered in April 1915, and at the conclusion of his training was sent to France, where he was subsequently engaged for nearly four years on important duties in connection with the Inland Water Transport. He was demobilised on his return to England in February 1919, and holds the 1914–15 Star, and the General Service and Victory Medals.
15, Stanmore Road, Watford.   X3027.

FUNGE, E., Private, R.A.S.C.

Volunteering at the commencement of hostilities, he was sent to the Western Front at the conclusion of his training. Whilst in this theatre of war he was present at many engagements, including those at Ypres and Arras, and was also engaged for a time on important duties at 7th Divisional Headquarters. Later he served on the Italian front, and did valuable work during operations on the Piave. He returned to England and was demobilised in 1919, and holds the 1914–15 Star, and the General Service and Victory Medals.
21, Capell Road, Oxhey, Watford. X3028.

FUNGE, W., Driver, R.A.S.C. (M.T.)

He joined in June 1917, and on completing his training was sent to Egypt. He was subsequently engaged on important transport work during the Palestine campaign, and was present at several battles, notably that of Gaza. He was demobilised after his return to England in February 1920, and holds the General Service and Victory Medals.
51, Cardiff Road, Watford. X3029.

FURNESS, E., Leading Telegraphist, Royal Navy, H.M.S. "Emperor of India."

He volunteered in February 1915, and was posted for duty with the destroyer flotilla in the North Sea. Later he served in H.M.S. "Emperor of India" on escort duties between the Shetland Islands and Denmark. Finally he was with H.M.S. "Iron Duke," engaged in mine-laying. He holds the 1914–15 Star, and the General Service and Victory Medals, and was demobilised in August 1919.
125, Herkomer Road, Bushey. X3030/B.

FURNESS, G. W., Private, 6th Yorkshire Regt.

He joined in September 1916, and after having completed his training was engaged at various stations on important duties with his unit until September 1918, when he was drafted to North Russia. He served in the campaign against the Bolshevists, and was in action in numerous engagements on the Archangel front. He was demobilised in November 1919, and holds the General Service and Victory Medals.
125, Herkomer Road, Bushey. X3030/A.

FURR, A., Rifleman, K.R.R.C.

He joined in April 1918, and after his training was engaged on duties of an important nature with his unit. He was unable to obtain his transfer overseas before the cessation of hostilities, but afterwards was sent with the Army of Occupation to Cologne, where he served for nearly a year. He was demobilised on his return to England in October 1919.
454, Hitchin Road, Luton. 3032/A.

FURR, C., Private, 2/9th Durham Light Infantry.

He joined in 1916, and after his training was sent to Salonika. He fought in many important engagements during his service in this theatre of war, notably in the Advance across the Struma Plain, and on one occasion was wounded. He was demobilised after his return to England in June 1919, and holds the General Service and Victory Medals.
Hillford End, Shillington, Beds. 3031.

FURR, E. W., Private, 7th Bedfordshire Regt.

He volunteered in 1914, and at the conclusion of his training was sent to the Western Front. Subsequently he took an active part in many notable engagements, including those at Neuve Chapelle, Hill 60, Ypres and Arras, and was killed in action on September 27th, 1916. He was entitled to the 1914–15 Star, and the General Service and Victory Medals.
454, Hitchin Road, Luton. 3032/B.

G

GADSBY, W. E. (M.M.), 2nd Lieutenant, 4th York and Lancaster Regiment.

He volunteered in November 1914, and proceeded to France in June of the following year. He took part in severe fighting at Loos and on the Somme, and was wounded and invalided home. On his recovery he returned to France and was engaged at Passchendaele, Cambrai and Ypres, and was again wounded. He was awarded the Military Medal for bravery in the Field, and also holds the 1914–15 Star, and the General Service and Victory Medals, and was demobilised in January 1919.
Old Marford, Wheathamstead. 3034.

GADSDEN, H., Private, 3rd Bedfo-dshire Regt.

Volunteering in September 1914, he proceeded to France in December of the same year. He took part in heavy fighting at Ypres, Neuve Chapelle and Hill 60, where he was severely gassed. After his recovery he was retained on various important duties with his unit, and rendered valuable services. He was discharged in December 1918, and holds the 1914–15 Star, and the General Service and Victory Medals.
Houghton Conquest, near Ampthill. Z3035/A.

GADSDEN, J., Private, Machine Gun Corps.

He joined in 1916, and in the following year was drafted to the Western Front, where he took part in numerous engagements, including those at Arras, Vimy Ridge, Ypres, the Somme and Cambrai. He was employed as Brigade Runner and rendered valuable services. He was demobilised in March 1919 after returning home, and holds the General Service and Victory Medals.
Houghton Conquest, near Ampthill. Z3035/B.

GADSDEN, W., Private, 11th Royal Sussex Regt.

After joining in 1916 he went through a course of training and was then engaged on important duties with his unit until 1918, when he was sent to France. He took part in the severe fighting on the Somme in March 1918, and was wounded. Being invalided home he was discharged owing to his injuries in October 1919, and holds the General Service and Victory Medals.
Houghton Conquest, near Ampthill. Z3035/C.

GADSDEN, W., Private, 124th Labour Company.

He joined in February 1916, and in the following June was drafted to France, where he was engaged in various sectors on important duties in the construction of roads and trenches, and rendered valuable services. He was demobilised in January 1919 after returning home, and holds the General Service and Victory Medals.
High Street, Eaton Bray, Dunstable. 3036.

GADSDEN, W., Private, R.A.V.C.

He joined in June 1916, and after his training served on important duties with his unit. He was engaged in attending to sick and wounded horses, and rendered valuable services, but was not successful in obtaining his transfer overseas before the cessation of hostilities, owing to his medical unfitness for active service. He was demobilised in August 1919.
18, Manchester Place, Dunstable. 3037.

GADSDEN, W. J., Corporal, Bedfordshire Regt.

Joining in June 1916, he was drafted to France at the close of his training in the December following. He took part in severe fighting at Arras, Vimy Ridge, Ypres and Passchendaele, and was killed in action near the latter place on October 6th, 1917. He was entitled to the General Service and Victory Medals.
3, Chapel Yard, Eaton Bray, Dunstable. 3038.

GALBRAITH, A. A., Flight-Lieutenant, R.F.C.

He joined in April 1917, and in September of the same year proceeded to Egypt. During his service overseas he was engaged on various important duties with his squadron, and rendered valuable services. He was accidently killed whilst flying at Abbassia on February 24th, 1918, and was buried at Ismalia. He was entitled to the General Service and Victory Medals. 69, Chapel Street, Luton. 3039.

GALE, W., Gunner, Royal Field Artillery.

He joined in February 1918, and after his training served on important duties with his unit. He rendered valuable services, but was not successful in obtaining his transfer overseas before the cessation of hostilities on account of his medical unfitness. He was demobilised in 1919.
New Marford, Wheathampstead. 3040.

GALER, A. J., Sapper, Royal Engineers.

Volunteering in 1915, he was drafted to France in the same year, and was present at the Battles of Hill 60 and Ypres. He was later in the same year transferred to Mesopotamia, where he rendered valuable service at Kut, Baghdad and Mosul. He returned home and was demobilised in January 1919, and holds the 1914–15 Star, and the General Service and Victory Medals.
22, Windmill Street, Luton. 3041.

GALLAGHER, J. C. (M.M.), Sergeant, R.F.A.

He volunteered in September 1914, and after his training was drafted to the Western Front, where he took part in severe fighting at Ypres, the Somme, Arras, Passchendaele, Cambrai and in other later engagements. During his service he was wounded, and was awarded the Military Medal for great bravery in the Field. He also holds the 1914–15 Star, and the General Service and Victory Medals. He was demobilised in April 1919.
Flamstead, near Dunstable. 3042/A.

GAMBLE, B., C.S.M., 1st Bedfordshire Regiment.

He was serving at the outbreak of war and shortly afterwards was sent to France, where he took part in the Retreat from Mons and other early engagements. He was severely wounded on December 10th, 1914, and died three days later from the effects of his injuries. He was entitled to the Mons Star, and the General Service and Victory Medals.
2, Austins Lane, Ampthill. 3043.

GAME, L. C., Corporal, 8th Bedfordshire Regt.

He volunteered in October 1914, and proceeded to France in September of the following year. He took part in numerous engagements, including those at Ypres and the Somme, where he was wounded in September 1916. He returned home and was discharged in November 1917 owing to his injuries. He holds the 1914-15 Star, and the General Service and Victory Medals.

The Hill, Welwyn. 3044.

GAME, W. G., Private, 4th Bedfordshire Regt.

Joining in November 1916, he went through his course of training and was drafted to France in February of the following year. He took part in much severe fighting at the Somme, Ypres, Albert, Arras, Cambrai and the Aisne, and other engagements until hostilities ceased. He was demobilised in February 1919, and holds the General Service and Victory Medals.

4, Queen's Road, Harpenden. 3045.

GAMMAGE, F. H., Private, Queen's Own (Royal West Kent Regiment), and Labour Corps.

He joined in April 1916, and proceeded to France in the following December. He took part in the heavy fighting at Ypres, Arras, Sanctuary Wood, Bapaume and other engagements, and was wounded. He was demobilised in January 1919, and holds the General Service and Victory Medals.

16, Beech Road, Luton. 3046/A.

GAMMONS, H. J. (M.M.), L/Corporal, 7th Bedfordshire Regiment.

He volunteered in September 1914, and in the following year, after completing his course of training, was drafted to the Western Front, where he took part in important engagements, including those at Neuve Chapelle, Hill 60, Ypres, Festubert, Vimy Ridge and the Somme. He was killed in action on August 10th, 1917, on the Somme. He was awarded the Military Medal for conspicuous bravery and devotion to duty on the Field, and was also entitled to the 1914-15 Star, and the General Service and Victory Medals.

Beeston Green, near Sandy. Z3047/A.

GAMMONS, S., Private, 23rd Royal Fusiliers.

He volunteered in November 1914, and after his training was retained on important duties with his unit until drafted to France in 1916. During his service on the Western Front he took part in the fighting at Beaumont-Hamel, Arras, Vimy Ridge, Messines and Passchendaele. He was reported missing after an engagement on October 26th, 1917, and was later presumed to have been killed in action on that date. He was entitled to the General Service and Victory Medals.

Beeston Green, near Sandy. Z3047/B.

GANDER, A. J., C.Q.M.S., Royal Engineers (Signal Section).

He volunteered in September 1915, and after being retained on important duties with his unit was drafted to Palestine, where he served with the British Forces under General Allenby. He was engaged on important duties in the forward areas whilst operations were in progress, notably at Gaza and Jaffa. He was present at the entry into Jerusalem, and afterwards served at Beyrout. He was mentioned in Despatches for his excellent work, and holds the General Service and Victory Medals. He was demobilised after his return to England in August 1919.

104, Clarendon Road, Luton. 3048.

GANDER, T., Private, R.A.O.C.

He volunteered in March 1915, and in the same year was drafted to France, where he rendered valuable service for four years. He was engaged on important duties as a saddler throughout this period, and was stationed at Le Havre. In May 1919 he returned home and was demobilised, holding the 1914-15 Star, and the General Service and Victory Medals.

Batchworth Hill, Rickmansworth. X3049.

GARDNER, W. J., Gunner, Royal Garrison Artillery ; and Private, Labour Corps.

He joined in November 1917, and after his training was retained for important agricultural duties. He did excellent work, but was not successful in obtaining a transfer overseas before the cessation of hostilities. He was demobilised in March 1919.

17, Talbot Road, Rickmansworth. X3050.

GARMENT, C. H., Pte., 1st Hertfordshire Regt.

He volunteered in April 1915, and in the same year was drafted to the Western Front, where he saw considerable service. He was in action at Ypres and the Somme, and was wounded. After his recovery, he took part in an engagement at St. Julien, where he was killed on July 31st, 1917. He was entitled to the 1914-15 Star, and the General Service and Victory Medals.

37, Bernard Street, St. Albans. X3051/A.

GARMENT, L. C., 2nd Lieutenant, A/Captain, Hertfordshire Regt. & Lancashire Fusiliers.

He volunteered in May 1915, and in the same year was drafted to France, where he saw much heavy fighting. He took part in the Battles of Ypres, the Somme and Arras, and was wounded. After his recovery he fought at St. Quentin, and was killed in action on March 21st, 1918. He was entitled to the 1914-15 Star, and the General Service and Victory Medals.

37, Bernard Street, St. Albans. X3051/B.

GARNER, A. E., Private, Bedfordshire Regiment.

He volunteered in June 1915, and after his training proceeded to France in the following January. Whilst in this theatre of war he was wounded in the Battle of the Somme, and was for a short time in hospital. Later he took part in the engagements at Arras and Cambrai, and was again wounded in March 1918, at the commencement of the Allied Retreat. He returned home and was demobilised in March 1919, holding the General Service and Victory Medals.

Watling Street, Hockliffe, near Leighton Buzzard. 1612/B.

GARNER, B. S., L/Corporal, 6th Bedfordshire and 1st Hertfordshire Regiments.

He joined in February 1916, and on the completion of his training was drafted to France in the same year. He served at Arras, Vimy Ridge, Messines, Ypres, Lens and Cambrai, and was chiefly engaged as a sniper. He was demobilised in December 1919 after returning to England, and holds the General Service and Victory Medals.

The Green, Ickwell, near Biggleswade. 3052/A.

GARNER, E., Corporal, R.A.S.C.

He joined in November 1917, and in the following April was drafted to France, where he was engaged on the Cambrai front on important transport duties, conveying supplies up to the fighting line. After the Armistice he joined the Army of Occupation in Germany, and did much valuable work at Cologne. He returned home and was demobilised in October 1919, holding the General Service and Victory Medals.

12, Bedford Street, Leighton Buzzard. 3053.

GARNER, F., Private, Bedfordshire Regiment.

He volunteered in June 1915, and in the following November was drafted to France, where he was engaged in guarding German prisoners at various internment camps. He saw much service at Arras, Ypres, Cambrai and on the Somme, and in subsequent engagements until the cessation of hostilities. Returning home he was demobilised in March 1919, and holds the General Service and Victory Medals.

Oddfellows Cottages, High Street, Toddington. 3054.

GARNER, F. C., Private, Duke of Wellington's (West Riding Regiment).

He volunteered in August 1914, and after serving at various stations on important duties was drafted to the Western Front in 1917. After taking part in the fighting in several engagements he was killed in action at Valenciennes on October 24th, 1918. He was entitled to the General Service and Victory Medals.

3, Union Square, Hemel Hempstead. X3055.

GARNER, F. J., Private, 4th Bedfordshire Regt.

He volunteered in 1915, and in the following year was drafted to the Western Front, where he took part in the fighting at Arras, Bullecourt, Ypres and Passchendaele. He was severely gassed in action at the second Battle of the Somme in March 1918, and after his recovery served at Cambrai, and was present at Mons on Armistice Day, November 11th, 1918. He was demobilised in the following March, and holds the General Service and Victory Medals.

The Green, Ickwell, near Biggleswade. 3052/B.

GARNER, G., Private, 1st Bedfordshire Regt.

He volunteered in September 1914, and in the same year was drafted to the Western Front, where he took part in many notable battles, including those of Ypres and the Somme, and was wounded. He was later killed in action at Menin Road in October 1917, and was entitled to the 1914 Star, and the General Service and Victory Medals.

Rose Cottage, Puller Road, Boxmoor. X2924/B.

GARNER, G., A.B., Royal Navy.

He volunteered for service in the Navy in 1914, and after a period of training was posted to H.M.S. "Repulse." He took part in the Battle of Jutland, and was also engaged on important patrol duties in the North Sea and in various other waters. He returned home and was demobilised in 1919, and holds the General Service (with Clasp, Jutland, May 31st, 1916), and Victory Medals.

3, Back Street, Biggleswade. Z1535/D—Z1536/D.

GARNER, H. R., Private, Essex Regiment.

Volunteering at the outbreak of war, he proceeded to France in the following January and took part in the Battle of the Somme, where he was wounded in July 1916. He was invalided home, and after his recovery was drafted to Egypt in January 1917. While in the East he fought at Gaza, and in the engagements which followed until the cessation of hostilities. He returned home and was demobilised in March 1919, and holds the General Service and Victory Medals.
Watling Street, Hockliffe, Leighton Buzzard. 1612 /C.

GARNER, S., Private, Queen's Own (Royal West Kent Regiment).

He joined in May 1916, and in the following October was sent overseas. During his service in France he fought in· the Battles of the Somme, Arras, Vimy Ridge and Ypres, and was wounded and taken prisoner in an engagement near Cambrai on October 26th, 1917. He was held in captivity in Germany for many months, and after his release was demobilised in April 1919. He holds the General Servi⸱e and Victory Medals.
99, Heath Road, Leighton Buzzard. 3056.

GARNER, W. G., Rifleman, 5th London Regiment and London Rifle Brigade.

He was mobilised at the commencement of hostilities, and was almost immediately drafted to France, where he fought in the Retreat from Mons and the Battles of La Bassée, Festubert, the Somme, Arras, Passchendaele, Cambrai and in many other engagements. He was discharged on account of his wounds in December 1918, and holds the Mons Star, and the General Service and Victory Medals.
15, Villier Street, Leamington Spa. Z3057 /C.

GARNETT, W., Sergeant, 5th Bedfordshire Regt.

He volunteered in August 1914, and was retained on important duties at his depôt, where he was principally engaged in the instruction of recruits in musketry drill and guard duties. He also did much good work in the East Coast defence. He rendered valuable services, but was unable on medical grounds to secure a transfer abroad, and was discharged in 1915.
27, Plantation Road, Leighton Buzzard. 3226 /B.

GARNETT, W., Private, Machine Gun Corps.

He joined in June 1916, and in the following November was drafted to France, where he took an active part in the Battles of the Somme, Arras, Bullecourt, Ypres, Cambrai and the second engagement on the Somme. He was killed in action near Cambrai in the Retreat of 1918, and was entitled to the General Service and Victory Medals.
27, Plantation Road, Leighton Buzzard. 3226 /A.

GARNHAM, R., L/Corporal, Royal Fusiliers and Royal Warwickshire Regiment.

He volunteered in 1915, and in the same year was drafted to Salonika, where he served in many important operations on the Balkan front for about two years. In 1917 he was sent to France, and fought at Ypres, the Somme, and in the engagements which followed until the cessation of hostilities. He was demobilised after his return home in March 1919, and holds the 1914-15 Star, and the General Service and Victory Medals.
25, Hatfield Road, Watford. X827.

GARRETT, F., Private, 2/1st Royal Sussex Regt.

He joined in April 1917, and after his training served at various stations on important duties with his unit. He was not successful in securing his transfer overseas, and falling ill, died on December 1st in the same year.
84, Queen's Street, Luton. 3058 /B.

GARRETT, F. E., Sapper, Royal Engineers.

He volunteered in 1915, and in January of the following year was drafted to France. While there he was engaged on important duties in connection with the operations and was frequently in the forward areas, notably at the Somme, Ypres and Cambrai. During his service overseas he was gassed. He was demobilised in January 1919, and holds the General Service and Victory Medals.
84, Queen's Street, Luton. 3058 /A.

GARRETT, S. S., Sapper, Royal Engineers.

He volunteered in April 1915, and after the conclusion of his training was drafted to the Western Front in September 1917. During his service in France he was engaged on important duties in various sectors whilst operations were in progress, including those of Ypres, the Somme and Passchendaele. He was demobilised in March 1919 after returning home, and holds the General Service and Victory Medals.
The Heath, Breachwood Green, near Welwyn. 3060.

GARRETT, W. S., Private, 5th Bedfordshire Regt.

Volunteering in September 1914, he was drafted to Gallipoli in the following July and took part in the landing at Suvla Bay and in various subsequent operations. In November 1915 he was sent to Palestine, and whilst fighting in the Battles of Gaza, Jaffa and other engagements, was wounded seven times. He was demobilised in July 1919 after his return to England, and holds the 1914-15 Star, and the General Service and Victory Medals.
82, New Town Street, Luton. 3061.

GASCOYNE, F., Pte., York and Lancaster Regt.

He volunteered in September 1914, and in the following February was drafted to France, where, after serving in various engagements, he was severely wounded and gassed at Loos in September 1915. He was invalided home, and after several months' treatment was discharged as medically unfit for further duty in April 1916. He holds the 1914-15 Star, and the General Service and Victory Medals.
130, Heath Road, Leighton Buzzard. 3062.

GASH, A. C., Private, Berkshire Regiment (Signalling Section).

He volunteered in November 1915, and in the following year was drafted to the Western Front. During his service in France he took part in the fighting at Thiepval and in the Battle of the Ancre, and was wounded on March 25th, 1918, on the Somme. He was reported missing after this engagement, and has not been heard of since that date. He was entitled to the General Service and Victory Medals.
13, Cotterell's Road, Hemel Hempstead. X3063 /A.

GASH, R. W., Private, Machine Gun Corps.

He volunteered in August 1914, and on the completion of his training was drafted to France in the following year. After taking part in various earlier engagements he was killed in action in the Ypres sector in September 1917. He was entitled to the 1914-15 Star, and the General Service and Victory Medals.
13, Cotterell's Road, Hemel Hempstead. X3063 /B.

GATEHOUSE, W. S., Private, R.A.S.C.

He volunteered in March 1915, and in the following July was drafted to France, where he served on important transport and shoeing-smith's duties in various sectors, including those of Loos, the Somme, Arras, Ypres and Albert, and rendered valuable services. He was demobilised in February 1919 after returning home, and holds the 1914-15 Star, and the General Service and Victory Medals.
24, Highbury Road, Hitchin. 3064.

GATES, E., Private, Tank Corps.

He joined in January 1917, and after his training served at various stations on important duties with his unit. He rendered valuable services, but was not successful in obtaining a transfer overseas before hostilities ceased, and was demobilised in September 1919.
5, Heath Terrace, Landridge Road, St. Albans. X3066 /A.

GATES, E. E., Sergeant, 2nd London Regiment (Royal Fusiliers).

He joined in October 1916, and in the same year was drafted to France, where he took part in the Battles at Arras, Ypres and Cambrai, and was taken prisoner at Armentières. After his captivity in Germany, which lasted for ten months, he was repatriated, and in 1919 was demobilised, holding the General Service and Victory Medals.
London Road, Woburn. Z3065.

GATES, E. J., Private, 9th Cheshire Regiment.

He joined in December 1916, and in the following March was drafted to France. During his service on the Western Front he took part in the Battles of Arras, Passchendaele and Cambrai, and in many engagements in the Retreat and Advance of 1918. He was severely wounded near Cambrai in that year, and after his recovery was demobilised in the following February. He holds the General Service and Victory Medals.
Littleworth, Wing, near Leighton Buzzard. 3067 /B.

GATES, F., Sapper, Royal Engineers.

He volunteered in November 1915, and after his training was drafted to Egypt in April 1917. He afterwards served with the British Forces under General Allenby in the Advance through Palestine. He was engaged on important duties in connection with the operations, and was frequently in the advanced areas, notably at Gaza and Jaffa, and was present at the fall of Jerusalem. He was demobilised after his return home in August 1919, and holds the General Service and Victory Medals.
22, George Street, Markyate, near Dunstable. 3070 /A.

GATES, F. W., Driver, Royal Field Artillery.
He volunteered at the outbreak of war, and in the following year was drafted to France, where he took part in many important engagements. In January 1916 he was sent to Egypt, and served in the Offensive in Palestine, at Gaza, Haifa, Damascus and Aleppo. He returned home, and on July 5th, 1919, died from fever which he had contracted in the East. He was entitled to the 1914-15 Star, and the General Service and Victory Medals.
5, Heath Terrace, Landridge Road, St. Albans.   X3066/B.

GATES, H. J., Private, 13th East Surrey Regt.
He volunteered in November 1915, and in the following year, on completing his training, was sent overseas. During his service in France he took part in the Battles of the Somme and Ypres and in other engagements, and was killed in action at Bourlon Wood on November 27th, 1917. He was entitled to the General Service and Victory Medals.
5, Heath Terrace, Landridge Road, St. Albans.   X3066/C.

GATES, J., Private, R.A.V.C.
Joining in May 1917, he went through his course of training, and in the following June proceeded to the Western Front. During his service in France, which lasted two years, he was engaged on important duties in connection with his unit at Ypres, Amiens and other bases. He was demobilised in May 1919 after returning to England, and holds the General Service and Victory Medals.
4, West Alley, Hitchin.   3068.

GATES, S., Trooper, Bedfordshire Lancers.
He volunteered in October 1914, and in the following June was drafted to France. During his service on the Western Front he took part in the fighting at Ypres, the Somme, Arras, Cambrai, and in subsequent engagements until the cessation of hostilities. He was demobilised in March 1919, holding the 1914-15 Star, and the General Service and Victory Medals.
28, Waterloo Road, Linslade.   3069.

GATES, S., Sapper, Royal Engineers.
He joined in February 1917, and in the next month was drafted to France, where he was engaged on important telegraphic duties in connection with the operations on the Arras, Cambrai and Somme fronts. In September of the same year he proceeded to Egypt, and served there until December 1918, when he was sent to Palestine, where in 1920 he was still serving. He holds the General Service and Victory Medals.
22, George Street, Markyate.   3070/B.

GATES, W., Gunner, Royal Field Artillery.
He volunteered in May 1915, and after completing his training in the following October was drafted to Mesopotamia, where he took part in many engagements, including the Battles of Kut and the capture of Baghdad. The remainder of his service was in France until the close of hostilities. He was demobilised in August 1919, and holds the 1914-15 Star, and the General Service and Victory Medals.
Littlewood, Wing, near Leighton Buzzard.   3067/A.

GATES, W. H., Private, 2nd East Surrey Regt.
He volunteered in September 1914, and on the completion of his training was drafted to France in March of the succeeding year. A few weeks later he fought in the Battle of Hill 60, and was killed in action there on April 25th, 1915. He was buried at Zonnebeke, and was entitled to the 1914-15 Star, and the General Service and Victory Medals.
Vine Cottage, King Street, Potton.   Z3071.

GATHARD, A., Private, 5th Bedfordshire Regt.
He volunteered in August 1914, and in the following August was sent to the Dardanelles, where he took part in the landing at Suvla Bay, and Chocolate Hill, and in other engagements until the Evacuation of the Peninsula. He was then drafted to Mudros and afterwards to Egypt, where he served in the defence of the Suez Canal. In February 1917 he joined in the Advance into Palestine and was engaged at El Arish, in all the Battles of Gaza, and at Haifa, Beyrout and Aleppo. He returned home and was demobilised in March 1920, and holds the 1914-15 Star, and the General Service and Victory Medals.
14, Ridgway Road, Luton.   3072.

GATWARD, E., Private, 1st Northamptonshire Regiment.
He joined in March 1916, and in the following October was drafted to the Western Front. After serving in several minor engagements he was wounded on the Somme in February 1917. After his recovery he again took part in the fighting near Passchendaele Ridge, where he was killed in action on November 15th of the same year. He was entitled to the General Service and Victory Medals.
61, Hartley Road, Luton.   3075/C—3074/C—3073/C.

GATWARD, F., Gunner, H.A.C.
He joined in July 1918, and after his training was stationed at his depôt on important duties in connection with the aerial defence of London. He did excellent work, but was unable to secure his transfer to a fighting front before the close of the war. He was demobilised in February 1919.
61, Hartley Road, Luton.   3075/D—3074/D—3073/D.

GATWARD, H., Gunner, R.G.A.
He volunteered in December 1915, and after his training was retained at various depôts on important duties with his unit. In February 1918 he was drafted to France, and was gassed in action near Poelcappelle on April 3rd. After his recovery he took part in several further engagements until the conclusion of hostilities. He was demobilised in February 1919, after his return home, and holds the General Service and Victory Medals.
61, Hartley Road, Luton.   3073/A—3074/A—3075/A.

GATWARD, S., Driver, Royal Field Artillery.
Volunteering in September 1914, he was drafted to France in the following February. During his service on the Western Front he fought in the Battles of Ypres, Arras, Passchendaele Ridge and the second Battle of the Somme. He was severely wounded at Château Thierry in July 1918, and was in consequence invalided home. In May of the following year he was demobilised, and holds the 1914-15 Star, and the General Service and Victory Medals.
61, Hartley Road, Luton.   3073/B—3074/B—3075/B.

GATWOOD, H. C., Corporal, 5th Bedfordshire Regiment.
He joined in January 1916, and in the following December was drafted to Egypt. After doing much valuable work there he joined the British Advance into Palestine under General Allenby, and took part in many important engagements. In August 1919 he returned home and was demobilised, holding the General Service and Victory Medals.
5, Bolton's Road, Luton.   3076.

GAZELEY, E., Private, Machine Gun Corps.
He joined in 1916, and after the completion of his training was drafted to Salonika in 1917. Whilst in this theatre of war he took part in the General Offensive by the Allies on the Doiran front, and also fought in the first and second Battles of Vardar. He was demobilised in October 1919, after his return to England, and holds the General Service and Victory Medals.
57, Old Park Road, Hitchin.   3077.

GAZELEY, G., Sergeant, Bedfordshire Regiment.
Volunteering in August 1914, he was sent to the Western Front early in the following year. During his service overseas he was engaged in the fighting at Hill 60, Festubert, Loos and in many other sectors, and was wounded five times and gassed. He returned to England in consequence, and in April 1919 was invalided out of the service. He holds the 1914-15 Star, and the General Service and Victory Medals.
Ashley Cottages, High Street, Westoning.   3078.

GAZELEY, G., Private, R.A.M.C.
He volunteered in March 1915, and after his training, in consequence of physical disability, was retained for Home service. He did valuable work as an orderly at various hospitals until September 1918, when he was discharged on medical grounds.
88, Sopwell Lane, St. Albans.   X3079.

GAZELEY, H., Private, Labour Corps.
He volunteered in April 1915, and after his training was sent to Egypt and thence to Palestine. Throughout the campaign on this front he was engaged on road-making and other important duties, and saw service at Ludd, Mejdil Yaba and Jerusalem. He later contracted a severe form of malaria, of which he died on January 14th, 1919. He was entitled to the General Service and Victory Medals.
47, Sopwell Lane, St. Albans.   X3080/B.

GAZELEY, H. G., Private, Bedfordshire Regiment and Machine Gun Corps.
He joined the Bedfordshire Regiment in 1916, and was later transferred to the Machine Gun Corps. After his training he was drafted to the Western Front, where in the capacity of gunner he did valuable work during operations at Albert, the Somme, Bullecourt and Passchendaele. On one occasion he was gassed, but afterwards rejoined his unit and remained in France until the cessation of hostilities. He was demobilised in February 1919, and holds the General Service and Victory Medals.
Ivy Cottage, Westoning, Ampthill.   3081.

GAZELEY, J., Private, 1st Devonshire Regiment.
He was mobilised at the commencement of hostilities, and soon afterwards was sent to France. After taking part in several engagements on this front, including those at Mons and Ypres, he was killed in action at Arras on October 4th, 1917. He was entitled to the Mons Star, and the General Service and Victory Medals.
47, Sopwell Lane, St. Albans.   X3080/C.

GAZELEY, L., Sergeant, Sherwood Foresters.
He volunteered in September 1915, and after having completed his training served with his unit at various stations on important duties. He rendered valuable service, but was not successful in obtaining his transfer overseas prior to the cessation of hostilities. On February 13th, 1920, he died of an illness contracted during his service.
31, Dale Road, Luton. 3082.

GAZELEY, R., Sapper, Royal Engineers.
He volunteered in 1915, and during his service in France, which lasted for over three years, was engaged on duties of an important nature at Calais, Rouen, Arras and other forward areas until hostilities ceased. He holds the General Service and Victory Medals, and was demobilised after his return to England in February 1920.
5, Coventry Cottages, Westoning, Ampthill. 3083.

GAZELEY, T., Private, Suffolk Regiment.
He joined in February 1917, and after the conclusion of his training was engaged on important duties with his unit. Owing to physical unfitness he was unable to secure his transfer to a theatre of war, and after doing much good work in the East Coast defences was invalided out of the Service in January 1918.
33, Heyfield Terrace, St. Albans. X3084.

GAZELEY, W., Corporal, R.A.S.C.
He volunteered in April 1915, and at the conclusion of his training in the following year was sent to France. Two months later he was drafted to Salonika, and subsequently saw service on the Vardar, Doiran and Struma fronts, where he was engaged on important transport duties in connection with the Field bakery. Whilst in this theatre of war he contracted malaria, and was in consequence for some time in hospital. He was demobilised after his return to England in February 1919, and holds the 1914–15 Star, and the General Service and Victory Medals.
48, Orchard Road, Walsworth. 3085.

GAZELEY, W. W., Sergeant, R.A.S.C.
Volunteering in August 1915, he was engaged on special duties with his unit until January 1918, when he was sent to Mesopotamia. He did valuable work in this theatre of war at Basra, Baghdad and Tekrit, and remained overseas until after the cessation of hostilities. Returning to England he was demobilised in June 1919, and holds the General Service and Victory Medals.
New Houses, Caddington. 3086.

GAZLEY, T., Gunner, Royal Field Artillery.
He volunteered at the commencement of hostilities, and after his training was engaged on duties of an important nature with his Battery at various depôts. Owing to ill-health he was unable to obtain his transfer overseas while hostilities continued, but rendered valuable services until demobilised in January 1919.
3, Hope Cottages, Old Park Road, Hitchin. 3087.

GEARY, J., Driver, R.A.S.C.
Volunteering in August 1914, after completing his training, he was engaged on important duties transporting mules to Egypt. He continued this work until 1916, when in consequence of ill-health he returned to England, and in August of that year was invalided out of the Service. He holds the 1914–15 Star, and the General Service and Victory Medals.
7, Meeting Alley, Watford. X3088/B.

GEE, W. H., Private, 1st Royal Sussex Regiment.
Joining in November 1916, he was drafted to France early in the following year, and took part in several engagements, including that at Ypres. Later he was sent to the Italian front, where he was in action in the Trentino sector, and was wounded. He was demobilised after his return to England in January 1919, and holds the General Service and Victory Medals.
19, Hartley Road, Luton. 3089.

GEESON, E. J., Private, 3rd Essex Regiment.
He volunteered in December 1915, and on the completion of his training in the following June was drafted to France. Whilst in this theatre of war he fought at Albert and the Somme, and was subsequently wounded at Arras in April 1917. He was invalided home, and after his recovery was engaged on special duties at his depôt until his demobilisation, which took place in April 1919. He holds the General Service and Victory Medals.
Arthur Street, Ampthill. 3090/A.

GENTLE, E., Gunner, Royal Garrison Artillery.
He volunteered in December 1915, and after his training was engaged on important work with the anti-aircraft section. In 1918 he was drafted to the Western Front, where he did valuable work during operations in many important sectors, notably that of Ypres, and was also engaged on the lines of communication. He holds the General Service and Victory Medals, and was demobilised after his return to England in February 1919.
13, Holly Walk, Luton. 3091

GENTLE, H., Private, 1st Bedfordshire Regiment.
Volunteering in August 1914, he was quickly drafted to the Western Front, where he served in the Retreat from Mons and in many of the engagements which followed. He was killed in action on November 15th, 1915, and was entitled to the Mons Star, and the General Service and Victory Medals.
13, Church Street, Slip End, Luton. 3092.

GENTLE, T., Private, Royal Army Medical Corps.
He joined in 1916, and after his training was engaged at the Napsbury Military Hospital as an orderly, in which capacity he did excellent work. Owing to physical unfitness he was unable to secure his transfer to a theatre of war, but rendered valuable services until he was demobilised in December 1919.
28, Camp View Road, St. Albans. X3093/B.

GENTLE, W. (M.M.), L/Corporal, Royal Army Medical Corps.
Called up from the Reserve at the outbreak of war, he was quickly drafted to the Western Front, where he served in the Retreat from Mons and in the subsequent engagements. On March 21st, 1918, he was mentioned in Despatches for his splendid work in tending the wounded, and was also awarded the Military Medal for an act of distinguished gallantry. He was killed in action near Ypres on April 14th, 1918, and was entitled to the Mons Star, and the General Service and Victory Medals.
11, Holly Walk, Luton. 3094.

GEORGE, A. W., Sapper, Royal Engineers.
He was serving when war broke out, and was immediately drafted to France, where he was in action in the Retreat from Mons and the heavy fighting that followed. He was afterwards sent to Salonika, and in the Balkan theatre of war took part in the general Retreat of the Serbians. From Salonika he was sent to Egypt, where he did valuable service till his return home for demobilisation in May 1919. He holds the Mons Star, and the General Service and Victory Medals.
Princess Street, Toddington. 99/A.

GEORGE, F., Sergeant, 4th Bedfordshire Regt.
He volunteered in November 1915, and in the following July was sent to the Western Front, where he remained until November 1918. During his service he fought in many important engagements, including those at Albert, Cambrai, Arras and Passchendaele, and was wounded. He was demobilised after his return to England in February 1919, and holds the General Service and Victory Medals.
High Street, Toddington, Beds. 3095.

GEORGE, F. J., Sapper, Royal Engineers.
A serving soldier, having enlisted in May 1914, he was sent to France immediately upon the outbreak of war, and did valuable work during the Retreat from Mons. He also served in many other important sectors, and was wounded and gassed. Returning to England he was demobilised in February 1919, and holds the Mons Star, and the General Service and Victory Medals.
36, Lea Road, Luton. 3096.

GEORGE, H., Private, Royal Army Medical Corps.
He volunteered in October 1915, and after his training was sent to the Western Front, where he served for three years. During this time he was engaged on important duties tending the wounded in the forward areas, and was present during the Battles of the Somme, Ypres and Cambrai. In 1918 he was wounded at St. Martin, but rejoined his unit after being treated at the Base. He was demobilised on his return to England in February 1919, and holds the General Service and Victory Medals.
3, Astley Road, Hemel Hempstead. X3097.

GEORGE, S., Gunner, Royal Field Artillery.
Volunteering at the commencement of hostilities, he was quickly sent to the Western Front, and took part in the Retreat from Mons and the Battle of Ypres. Later he was sent to Egypt and thence to Mesopotamia, where he served in the Advance on Baghdad. Afterwards he was, for a time, on garrison duty in India. He holds the Mons Star, and the General Service and Victory Medals, and was demobilised after his return to England in February 1919.
5, Duke Street, Watford. X3098.

GEORGE, S. G., Private, 23rd Royal Fusiliers.
He joined in April 1918, and three months later was drafted to France, where he was subsequently killed in action on September 7th, during the Advance of that year. He was entitled to the General Service and Victory Medals.
7, High Street, Luton. 3099.

GEORGE, S. W., Sapper, Royal Engineers.
He volunteered in August 1914, and in the following July was drafted to the Dardanelles, subsequently being engaged on important duties during the landing at Suvla Bay and the engagements which followed. After the Evacuation of the Peninsula he was sent to Egypt, where he saw service in the Canal zone, and later proceeded to Palestine. He was present at the Battle of Gaza, the capture of Haïfa, Acre and Damascus, and at the occupation of Beyrout, and throughout his service overseas, which lasted for over three years, did valuable work with his unit. He was demobilised in 1919, and holds the 1914-15 Star, and the General Service and Victory Medals.
454, Hitchin Road, Luton. 3100.

GEORGE, W. A., Private, Labour Corps.
He joined in 1916, and after his training was engaged on important agricultural duties at various stations. Owing to ill-health he was unable to secure his transfer overseas, but nevertheless did valuable work until his demobilisation, which took place in January 1919.
35, Greatham Road, Bushey, Watford. X3101.

GERMAINE, E., Corporal, R.G.A.
Having enlisted in 1911, he was mobilised at the outbreak of hostilities, and shortly after was sent to India. In 1915 he was drafted to France, where he served for nearly four years, taking part in many important engagements, notably those at Ypres and the Somme. He holds the 1914-15 Star, and the General Service and Victory Medals. and was demobilised in October 1919.
21, Manchester Place, Dunstable. 3102.

GETHING, C., Sergeant, 1/5th Bedfordshire Regt.
Having previously served with the Territorials, he was mobilised at the outbreak of war, and in July 1915 was sent to the Dardanelles. He took part in the landing at Suvla Bay and in the engagements which followed, and after the Evacuation of the Peninsula was sent to Egypt and thence to Palestine, where he fought throughout the campaign on that front. After four years' active service he returned to England, and in August 1919 was demobilised. He holds the 1914-15 Star, and the General Service and Victory Medals.
4, Alfred Street, Luton. 3103/B.

GETHING, W., Private, 1/5th Bedfordshire Regt.
Mobilised with the Territorials at the outbreak of war, he was later drafted to Egypt, where he served until the commencement of operations in Palestine. He subsequently fought throughout that campaign, and did excellent work with his unit until the cessation of hostilities. Returning to England he was demobilised in August 1919, and holds the General Service and Victory Medals.
4, Alfred Street, Luton. 3103/A.

GETTENS, W. A., Gunner, R.H.A.
He joined in May 1917, and at the conclusion of his training was sent to India, where he was engaged on important duties at various hill stations, including Rawal Pindi. He was demobilised after his return to England in December 1919, and holds the General Service and Victory Medals.
8, Jubilee Road, North Watford. X3104/A.

GIBBARD, R. E., Corporal, Military Foot Police.
He joined in 1916, and after his training was engaged on important duties at various depôts. He was unable to secure his transfer overseas before the termination of hostilities, but nevertheless rendered services of a valuable nature until he was demobilised in 1920.
11, Bernard Street, St. Albans. X3105.

GIBBONS, C. B., 1st Air Mechanic, R.F.C.
He joined in March 1917, and after his training was engaged on important duties and rendered valuable service until January 1918, when he died of pneumonia.
"One Ash," Crescent Road, Luton. 3107/B.

GIBBONS, D. (Miss), Member, V.A.D.
This lady volunteered early in 1916, and was subsequently engaged at the American Hospital, Paignton. Throughout her service she worked zealously to relieve the sufferings of the sick and wounded under her charge, and continued her work until December 1917, when she was discharged.
"One Ash," Crescent Road, Luton. 3107/A.

GIBBONS, E., A.B., Royal Navy.
He joined in June 1917, and after his training was posted to H.M.S. "Swiftsure," later being transferred to H.M.S. "Garth." His ship took part in several Naval actions in the Heligoland Bight, and also served with the North Sea Patrol and off the coast of Russia. He was demobilised on returning to his base in February 1919, and holds the General Service and Victory Medals.
2, Athol Cottage, Colney Street, St. Albans. X3106/A.

GIBBONS, F., A.B., Royal Naval Division.
He joined in June 1918, having previously been engaged on work of National importance. He subsequently served at his depôt on important duties, and although he was not successful in obtaining his transfer overseas before the termination of hostilities, did valuable work until he was demobilised in April 1919.
143, High Street, Houghton Regis. 3108.

GIBBONS, T. M., Private, 8th Buffs (East Kent Regiment).
He joined in April 1917, and in the following July was drafted to the Western Front. He served in the Ypres sector, and on August 5th, 1917, died of wounds received in action two days previously. He was entitled to the General Service and Victory Medals.
2, Athol Cottages, Colney Street, St. Albans. X3106/B.

GIBBONS, W., Sapper, Royal Engineers.
He joined in October 1916, and was drafted to the Western Front at the conclusion of his training in the following January. Throughout his service overseas he was engaged in constructing and wiring trenches, bridge-building and other important duties in connection with operations in the forward areas, and was present during engagements at Arras, Ypres and the Somme. He was demobilised after his return to England in February 1919, and holds the General Service and Victory Medals.
82, Bassett Street, Leighton Buzzard. 3109.

GIBBS, C. W., Private, Labour Corps.
He joined in March 1917, and after his training was drafted to the Western Front, where he served until after the cessation of hostilities. During this time he was engaged on important duties with his unit whilst operations were in progress at Ypres, the Somme, Cambrai and Vimy Ridge, and did valuable work throughout. He holds the General Service and Victory Medals, and was demobilised after his return to England in February 1919.
7, Hillside Road, Luton. 3110.

GIBBS, F. E., Private, Middlesex Regiment.
He joined in 1916, and during his service on the Western Front, which lasted for three years, took an active part in many engagements, including those at Ypres and the Somme. He holds the General Service and Victory Medals, and was demobilised on returning to England in January 1919.
457, Whippendell Road, Watford. X3111.

GIBBS, W. E., Private, R.A.M.C.
He volunteered in September 1915, and during the course of his training was stationed in Dublin. In 1916 he crossed to France, and subsequently proceeded to Vimy Ridge, where operations were then in progress. He also fought on the Somme and the Ancre, and in the following year was drafted to Egypt. Later he took part in the Palestine campaign, during which he was in action at Gaza, Haïfa, Damascus and Beyrout. He was demobilised after his return to England in January 1919, and holds the General Service and Victory Medals.
17, Gardenia Avenue, Leagrave, Luton. 3112/A.

GIBBS, W. G., Private, R.A.M.C.
He volunteered in May 1915, and at the conclusion of his training was drafted to the Western Front. Whilst in this theatre of war he did valuable work as an orderly in various Base hospitals, and was for some time stationed at Boulogne. He was demobilised in February 1919, and holds the General Service and Victory Medals.
17, Gardenia Avenue, Leagrave, Luton. 3112/B.

GIDDENS, W. J., Rifleman, 10th King's Royal Rifle Corps.
He volunteered in May 1915, and after his training was engaged on duties of a special nature until he was drafted to France in August 1916. He was subsequently engaged in the fighting on the Somme, at Albert, Ypres, Passchendaele Ridge and Cambrai, and did valuable work with his unit overseas until December 1918. In the following February he was demobilised, and holds the General Service and Victory Medals.
Hillside, Welwyn, Herts. 3121.

GIDDINGS, C., Gunner, Royal Field Artillery.
Volunteering in 1915, he was sent to France on completing his training. He fought in many important engagements, including those at Ypres, Hill 60, the Somme and Lens, and did excellent work with his unit throughout his service. Returning to England after the cessation of hostilities, he was demobilised in March 1919, and holds the 1914-15 Star, and the General Service and Victory Medals.
11, Cross Street North, St. Albans. X3113.

GIDDINGS, E. H., Air Mechanic, R.A.F. (late Royal Flying Corps).

He volunteered in 1914, and at the conclusion of his training early in the following year was sent to Egypt. Later he served in the Palestine campaign, during which he was engaged on important duties which called for a high degree of technical knowledge and skill. He returned to England in 1919, when he was demobilised, and holds the 1914–15 Star, and the General Service and Victory Medals.

75, Church Street, St. Albans. X3115.

GIDDINGS, F., Private, 4th East Lancashire Regiment.

He volunteered in September 1914, but during the course of his training was found to be medically unfit for military service, and on these grounds was discharged in the following month.

Royston Street, Potton, Beds. Z3116.

GIDDINGS, J., Private, Royal Berkshire Regt.

He volunteered in January 1915, and after a short course of training was drafted to France. Subsequently he fought at Hill 60, Ypres and Loos, and was killed in action during the Somme Offensive on September 15th, 1916. He was entitled to the 1914–15 Star, and the General Service and Victory Medals.

Ayot Green, near Welwyn, Herts. 3118/B.

GIDDINGS, R. H., L/Corporal, 1st Norfolk Regt.

Joining in February 1916, he was sent to the Western Front in the same year, and after taking part in several engagements, including that at Ypres, was transferred to Italy. Here he fought on the Piave and in other sectors of the front, and later returned to France, where he served during the concluding stages of the war. He was demobilised after his return to England in February 1919, and holds the General Service and Victory Medals.

Orsett Villa, King Street, Potton. Z3119.

GIDDINS, C., Sergeant, 3rd Bedfordshire and 1st Hertfordshire Regiments.

Volunteering in September 1914, he served, on the completion of his training on important clerical duties at his depôt until October 1917, when he was drafted to France. He there took part in the fighting at Cambrai and in the second Battle of the Somme, and was severely wounded and invalided to hospital at Étaples. After his recovery he served in various engagements until the conclusion of hostilities, and was demobilised in February 1919. He holds the General Service and Victory Medals.

35, Lamb Lane, Redbourn, Herts. 3114.

GIDDINS, H., Private, R.A.M.C.

He joined in May 1918, and three months later was sent to the Western Front. Here he served on important duties in various engagements, notably at Le Cateau and Cambrai. He remained in France until November 1919, when he returned home and was demobilised, and holds the General Service and Victory Medals.

29, Camp Road, St. Albans. X3117.

GIDDINS, W., Private, Hampshire Regiment.

He joined in February 1915, and in July of the same year was sent to Salonika, where he took part in numerous engagements until fighting ceased, including the Vardar Ridge. He returned home and was demobilised in March 1919, and holds the 1914–15 Star, and the General Service and Victory Medals.

52, Inkerman Road, St. Albans. X3120.

GILBERT, A., Private, 5th Bedfordshire Regt.

He volunteered in August 1914, and after his training served at various stations on important duties with his unit. He rendered valuable services, but was not successful in obtaining his transfer overseas owing to his medical unfitness for active service. He was discharged in 1916.

Brookfield Cottage, Plantation Road, Leighton Buzzard. 3123/C.

GILBERT, A., Private, Highland Light Infantry.

Volunteering in November 1914, he proceeded to the Western Front in April of the following year. He took part in numerous engagements, including those at Neuve Chapelle, Hill 60, Ypres and various other places, and was wounded. He was demobilised in March 1919, and holds the 1914–15 Star, and the General Service and Victory Medals.

4, Muriel Avenue, Watford. X3124/A.

GILBERT, A. E., Gunner, Royal Garrison Artillery ; and Sapper, Royal Engineers.

He joined in June 1916, and after his training was engaged on important duties in connection with the transport of guns to France from Richborough, Southampton and Folkestone. He holds the General Service and Victory Medals, and was demobilised in March 1919.

Batchworth Hill, Rickmansworth. X3125.

GILBERT, A. R., Private, Bedfordshire Regt.

Being a Territorial, he was mobilised on the outbreak of hostilities, but his health broke down under the strain of military training, and he was discharged in October of the same year as medically unfit for further service.

49, Benskin Road, Watford. X3122.

GILBERT, A. T., Private, R.M.L.I.

He joined in May 1916, and on the conclusion of his training proceeded to France in the following year. He took part in much severe fighting at Passchendaele, Cambrai and other important engagements until the war ended, and was wounded. He was demobilised in April 1919 after returning home, and holds the General Service and Victory Medals.

Batford Mill Cottages, Lower Luton Road, Harpenden. 3126.

GILBERT, C. G., Sergeant, 6th Essex Regiment.

He was mobilised with the Territorials in August 1914, and was drafted to Egypt in January 1916. He took part in numerous engagements in the subsequent campaign in Palestine, including those at Gaza and in the Advance to Jerusalem. After the close of the war he returned home and was demobilised in August 1919, holding the General Service and Victory Medals.

3, Lyndhurst Road, Luton. 3127/A.

GILBERT, C. J., Private, 6th Essex Regiment.

Being mobilised with the Territorials on the outbreak of the war, he was in the following year drafted to Gallipoli, where he took part in the landing at Suvla Bay and later engagements until the Evacuation. In 1916 he was transferred to Egypt, and afterwards served in many operations in Palestine, including those at Gaza and preceding the capture of Jerusalem. He was demobilised in February 1919, and holds the 1914–15 Star, and the General Service and Victory Medals.

3, Lyndhurst Road, Luton. 3127/B.

GILBERT, F., Private, 5th Bedfordshire Regt.

He volunteered in August 1914, and in the following month was sent to the Western Front, where he took part in many important engagements, including those at La Bassée, Festubert, the Somme, Ypres, Cambrai and the Retreat and Advance of 1918, and was wounded. He was demobilised in March 1919 after returning home, and holds the 1914 Star, and the General Service and Victory Medals.

Brookfield Cottage, Plantation Road, Leighton Buzzard. 3123/A.

GILBERT, H., Sergeant, 5th Bedfordshire Regt.

Volunteering in August 1914, he was sent to the Dardanelles in March of the following year, and took part in the landing at Gallipoli, the Battle of Krithia, and the later operations at Suvla Bay. During his service he was wounded. He was demobilised in March 1919, and holds the 1914–15 Star, and the General Service and Victory Medals.

Brookfield Cottage, Plantation Road, Leighton Buzzard. 3123/B.

GILBERT, J., Private, Grenadier Guards.

He joined in November 1916, and after completing his training was drafted to France in June of the following year. He took part in many important engagements, including those at Ypres and Cambrai, and being afterwards invalided home was discharged in August of the following year as unfit for further military duty. He holds the General Service and Victory Medals.

School Lane, Welwyn. 3152.

GILBERT, J. A., Private, 2nd Bedfordshire Regt.

After volunteering in November 1914, he was sent to France in July of the following year. He took part in severe fighting at Ypres, Cambrai, Albert, Arras and other engagements, and was wounded and three times gassed. He was demobilised in March 1919, and holds the 1914–15 Star, and the General Service and Victory Medals.

4, Muriel Avenue, Watford. X3124/B.

GILBERT, O. W., Private, 4th Duke of Wellington's (West Riding Regiment).

He was mobilised in August 1914, and was retained on important duties with his unit until August 1916, when he was drafted to the Western Front. He afterwards took part in many important engagements, including those at the Somme, Arras and Ypres, and was killed in action on October 9th, 1917. He was buried at Poperinghe cemetery. He was entitled to the General Service and Victory Medals.

51, King's Road, Hitchin. 3128.

GILBERT, S., Private, The Queen's (Royal West Surrey Regiment).

He joined in September 1918, and not having completed his training before the Armistice, was unable to obtain his transfer overseas prior to the cessation of hostilities. In April 1919 he was drafted to Germany, and served with the Army of Occupation on the Rhine until April 1920, when he returned to England and was demobilised.

4, Muriel Avenue, Watford. X3124/C.

GILBERT, W., Private, 3rd York and Lancaster Regiment.

He was mobilised from the Reserve in August 1914, and in the following December was sent to the Western Front, where he took part in numerous engagements, including those at Ypres and Loos, and was wounded. He was invalided home in consequence and discharged owing to his injuries in February 1916 as unfit for further duty. He holds the 1914–15 Star, and the General Service and Victory Medals.
28, Shott Lane, Letchworth. 3129.

GILBERT, W., Private, R.A.V.C.

He joined in August 1916, and was sent to France in the following month. He was engaged in the Somme sector in attending to sick and wounded horses, and rendered valuable service. Being invalided home in January 1917 suffering from shell-shock, he was discharged as medically unfit for further service in the following July. He holds the General Service and Victory Medals.
Chapel Yard, Potton. Z3130.

GILBEY, V. G., Gnr. Fitter, R.G.A. (1st London T.F.)

He volunteered in February 1915, and after the completion of his training was sent to France in February of the following year. He took part in the heavy fighting at the Somme, Arras, Cambrai and other important engagements until hostilities ceased, and was demobilised in March 1919, holding the General Service and Victory Medals.
8, St. Peter's Road, Dunstable. 3131.

GILKS, C. E., A.B., R.N., H.M.S. " Undaunted."

He was serving at the outbreak of war, and was in H.M.S. " Undaunted " when she sank four enemy destroyers off the Coast of Holland. He also took part in the Battles of Jutland and Heligoland. He was serving at Constantinople in 1920, and holds the 1914–15 Star, and the General Service and Victory Medals.
39, Husbourne Crawley, Aspley Guise. Z3057/B.

GILKS, F. C., Private, North Staffordshire and Middlesex Regiments.

He joined in June 1916, and after completing his training at Aldershot was in the following year drafted to the Western Front, where he took part in numerous engagements to the end of the war, including those at Ypres, Passchendaele, Cambrai, the Somme and Albert. He was demobilised in February 1919 after returning home, and holds the General Service and Victory Medals.
59, Leighton Street, Woburn. Z3132.

GILKS, G. W., L/Corporal, 6th Bedfordshire Regt.

He volunteered in October 1914, and was sent to France in July of the following year. He took part in the severe fighting at Festubert and Loos, and was killed in action on the Somme on July 15th, 1916. He was entitled to the 1914–15 Star, and the General Service and Victory Medals.
Woodside Cottage, Aspley Hill, Woburn Sands. Z3133.

GILKS, J. F., Private, Bedfordshire and Hertfordshire Regiments.

He joined in May 1918, and after his training in Scotland was engaged on important duties with his unit. He rendered valuable services, but was not successful in obtaining his transfer overseas before the cessation of hostilities. He was serving in Ireland in 1920.
39, Husbourne Crawley, Aspley Guise. Z3057/A.

GILKS, J. W., Private, 7th Bedfordshire Regt.

After volunteering in October 1914, he was sent to France in the following year. He took part in numerous engagements of importance, including those at Loos, the Somme, Bullecourt, Ypres, Arras and Albert. He was invalided home in 1918 through illness contracted while on service, and was discharged in December of that year as unfit for further duty. He holds the 1914–15 Star, and the General Service and Victory Medals.
22, Leighton Street, Woburn. Z3134/A.

GILKS, T. E., Driver, Royal Field Artillery.

Mobilised in August 1914, he was sent to France in the same month. He took part in the severe fighting at Mons, Neuve Chapelle, Ypres, Loos, Arras and Cambrai, and during his service in France met with a serious accident. He was demobilised in January 1919, and holds the Mons Star, and the General Service and Victory Medals.
2, Hardwick Place, Woburn Sands. Z3135/A.

GILKS, W. H., Private, 8th Bedfordshire Regt.

He volunteered in June 1915, and on the completion of his training a year later was drafted to the Western Front, where he took part in the early stages of the Somme Offensive, and was killed in action on July 15th, 1916. He was entitled to the General Service and Victory Medals.
22, Leighton Street, Woburn. Z3134/B.

GILL, A. W., Private, Royal Fusiliers.

Joining in February 1916, he was drafted to the Western Front later in the same year, and took part in the heavy fighting at Messines Ridge and Cambrai. He was taken prisoner during the Advance of 1918, and released in January of the following year. He was demobilised in August 1919, and holds the General Service and Victory Medals.
Lower Caldecote, Biggleswade. Z3137.

GILL, C., Private, Bedfordshire Regiment.

He volunteered in August 1914, and in the following year was drafted to the Western Front, where he took part in many important engagements, including those at Ypres, Arras, Passchendaele and Cambrai, and was wounded. He was invalided home in 1918, and afterwards discharged as medically unfit for further service. He holds the 1914–15 Star, and the General Service and Victory Medals.
43, Church Road, Watford. X3136/A.

GILLILAND, W. (M.M.), Driver, R.E.

Volunteering in 1915, he was sent to France in the following year, after the completion of his training. He took part in numerous engagements, including those at the Somme, Arras, Vimy Ridge, Cambrai and Albert, and was awarded the Military Medal for conspicuous bravery in the Field. He also holds the General Service and Victory Medals, and was demobilised in May 1919, after returning to England.
23, St. John's Street, Biggleswade. Z3138.

GILLINGHAM, F., Gunner, R.G.A.

He joined in April 1916, and in the same year proceeded to the Western Front, where he took part in the severe fighting at the Somme, Arras, Vimy Ridge and Ypres, and was gassed. In 1918 he was transferred to Italy and was stationed at Taranto. He was demobilised in August 1919 after returning home, and holds the General Service and Victory Medals.
246, Chester Road, Watford. X3139/A.

GILLINGHAM, J., Private, Bedfordshire Regt.

Volunteering in November 1914, in the following year he was drafted to the Western Front, where he took part in the Battles of Ypres, the Somme, Arras and Cambrai, and was wounded. He was afterwards invalided home, and discharged as medically unfit for further service. He holds the 1914–15 Star, and the General Service and Victory Medals.
246, Chester Road, Watford. X3139/B.

GILLINGWATER, E. H. R. (M.M.), Gunner, Royal Field Artillery.

He was called up from the Reserve at the outbreak of war, and was almost immediately drafted to the Western Front. He took part in the Retreat from Mons, and also served at Ypres, the Somme, Cambrai and many other engagements up to the signing of the Armistice in 1918. He was wounded during his service, and won the Military Medal for distinguished gallantry in the Field. He also holds the Mons Star, and the General Service and Victory Medals, and was demobilised in February 1919.
27, Cobden Street, Luton. 628/A.

GILLIS, G., Corporal, 3rd King's Royal Rifle Corps.

Volunteering in January 1915, he was sent to France in the following June and took part in the fighting at Loos and other important engagements. In November 1915 he was transferred to Salonika and did good service on the Struma, Vardar and Doiran fronts. Having contracted malaria while in the East he was invalided home in March 1918, and after recovery did clerical work at Colchester. He was demobilised in March 1919, and holds the 1914–15 Star, and the General Service and Victory Medals.
6, Victoria Place, Biggleswade. Z3140.

GILTROW, D., Private, South Wales Borderers.

He volunteered in 1914, and in the following year proceeded to Mesopotamia, where he took part in various engagements, including those at Kut-el-Amara, the Jordan and Baghdad. During his period of service in this theatre of war he suffered greatly from sunstroke, and after his recovery acted as canteen manager. He was demobilised in 1919, and holds the 1914–15 Star, and the General Service and Victory Medals.
Chapel Street, Woburn. Z3141/C.

GILTROW, E., Private, South Wales Borderers.

Volunteering in 1915 he was drafted in the following year to France, where he took part in the severe fighting at the Somme, Arras and Cambrai. He was afterwards transferred to Mesopotamia and subsequently to India, where he was engaged at Poona on important duties with his unit. He was demobilised in 1919, after his return to England, and holds the General Service and Victory Medals.
Chapel Street, Woburn. Z3141/A.

GILTROW, G. J., Gunner, Royal Field Artillery.
Volunteering in 1915 he proceeded to the Western Front later in the same year. He took part in numerous engagements until hostilities ceased, including those at Loos, the Somme, Arras, Messines and Cambrai. He was demobilised in 1919, and holds the 1914-15 Star, and the General Service and Victory Medals.
Chapel Street, Woburn. Z3141/B.

GILTROW, P., Private, 5th Royal Sussex Regt.
He joined in June 1918 on attaining military age, and after his training proceeded to Italy, where he was engaged on the Piave front on important guard and salvage duties for four months, and rendered valuable services. He was demobilised in February 1919 after returning home, and holds the General Service and Victory Medals.
Watling Street, Hockliffe, Leighton Buzzard. 3142.

GINGER, A., Private, 3rd Essex Regiment.
Volunteering in November 1914 he completed his course of training and was afterwards retained for important duties with his unit until 1916, when he was drafted to the Western Front. He took part in much severe fighting at the Somme, Arras, Ypres, Cambrai and St. Quentin, and was wounded. He returned home and was discharged, owing to his injuries, in November 1918, holding the General Service and Victory Medals.
59, Piccotts End, Hemel Hempstead. X3143.

GINGER, F., Private, Bedfordshire Regiment.
He joined in 1916, and in the same year, after finishing his course of training, was drafted to the Western Front, where he took part in the severe fighting at the Battles of Arras, Ypres, Cambrai and the Somme, and was gassed. Returning to England after the cessation of hostilities he was demobilised in 1919, and holds the General Service and Victory Medals.
31, Adrian Road, Abbots Langley. X3144.

GINGER, G., Corporal, R.A.S.C. (M.T.)
He was serving at the outbreak of war, and afterwards was engaged at various stations on important duties with his unit. He rendered valuable transport services, but was not successful in obtaining his transfer overseas before the cessation of hostilities. He was demobilised in December 1919.
1, Tavistock Crescent, Luton. 3146.

GINGER, J., Sergeant, 7th Bedfordshire Regt.
He volunteered in September 1914, and in January of the following year was sent to the Western Front, where he took part in numerous important engagements, including those at Hill 60, Festubert and Loos. He was killed in action at the Somme on July 1st, 1916, and was entitled to the 1914-15 Star, and the General Service and Victory Medals.
31, Dudley Street, Leighton Buzzard. 3147.

GINGER, J. W., Rifleman, Royal Irish Rifles.
After being mobilised in August 1914, he proceeded to France in the following month. He took part in the severe fighting at La Bassée, Ypres, Festubert, the Somme and Arras. He was killed in action in the third Battle of Ypres in July 1917, and was entitled to the 1914-15 Star, and the General Service and Victory Medals.
64, Edward Street, Dunstable. 3145/A.

GINGER, R. W., Private, Queen's (Royal West Surrey Regiment).
He joined in December 1917, and after his training served at various stations on important duties with his unit. He rendered valuable services, but was not successful in obtaining his transfer overseas before the cessation of hostilities. He afterwards proceeded with the Army of Occupation to Germany, and on his return home was demobilised in January 1920.
64, Edward Street, Dunstable. 3145/B.

GINN, F. W., Gunner, Royal Field Artillery.
After joining in January 1917 he went through his course of training, and in October of the same year was drafted to the Western Front, where he took part in the severe fighting at Cambrai. He was killed in action near Kemmel Hill on April 25th, 1918, and was entitled to the General Service and Victory Medals.
Royston Street, Potton. Z3148.

GINN, J. H., Sergeant, R.A.M.C.
He volunteered in September 1915, and in the same year was drafted to Egypt. After doing much valuable service there he was transferred to France in March 1916, and served at the Somme, Arras, Ypres and Cambrai, and at other engagements until the cessation of hostilities. He was demobilised in July 1919, and holds the 1914-15 Star, and the General Service and Victory Medals.
30, Frederick Street, Luton. 3149.

GIRLING, J. (M.M.), Corporal, R.A.M.C.
Mobilised in August 1914, he was immediately afterwards sent to the Western Front, where he served in the Retreat from Mons and the Battle of the Marne. He was awarded the Military Medal for great bravery in the Field. He was, at a later date transferred to Russia, where he did excellent service for 15 months. While overseas he acted not only as a stretcher-bearer in the Field, in which service he was wounded several times, but also as a nursing-orderly in hospital. He returned home and was demobilised in August 1919, and holds in addition to the Military Medal, the Mons Star, and the General Service and Victory Medals.
Mill Lane, Biggleswade. Z3150.

GIVENS, J., Driver, Royal Field Artillery.
He was mobilised in 1914, and in January of the following year was sent to France, and served on the Somme, and at Arras, Ypres and Cambrai. During his service he was engaged in moving guns into position and transporting supplies. Whilst in action on the Somme he was wounded, and was invalided home and discharged in April 1918, holding the 1914-15 Star, and the General Service and Victory Medals.
11, Standbridge Road, Leighton Buzzard. 3151.

GLADWELL, F. J., Private, R.A.M.C.
He volunteered in September 1914, and in the following year was sent to the Dardanelles, where he served in various actions and was wounded. In 1916 he was transferred to Palestine, and was engaged at Gaza and Jerusalem. Later he proceeded to France, where he served until January 1919, when he returned home and was demobilised, holding the 1914-15 Star, and the General Service and Victory Medals.
8, Salisbury Road, Luton. 3153.

GLANFIELD, W., Bedfordshire Regiment.
Volunteering in August 1914, he was drafted to France in July of the following year. He took part in severe fighting at Ypres, Vimy Ridge, the Somme, Arras, Passchendaele and Cambrai, and was wounded. He was demobilised in April 1919, and holds the 1914-15 Star, and the General Service and Victory Medals.
12, Camp View Road, St. Albans. X3158.

GLANVILLE, H. (D.C.M.), Sergeant, Manchester Regiment.
He was serving at the outbreak of war, and was shortly afterwards sent to France, where he took part in severe fighting in the Retreat from Mons and at Hill 60, Ypres, Vimy Ridge, Arras and Cambrai, and was wounded. He was awarded the Distinguished Conduct Medal for bravery in the Field, and also holds the Mons Star and the General Service and Victory Medals, and was demobilised in February 1919.
24, Lammas Road, Watford. X3276/A.

GLENISTER, A., Private, 5th Bedfordshire and Essex Regiments.
He was mobilised with the Territorials in August 1914, and in 1916 was drafted to the Western Front, where he took part in various engagements. He was killed in action at Ypres on November 14th, 1916, and was entitled to the General Service and Victory Medals.
29, Norman Road, Luton. 3156/C.

GLENISTER, E., Corporal, R.A.S.C. (M.T.)
He joined in March 1916, and in the following year was drafted to the Western Front. He was engaged as a motor driver on various fronts, including those of Ypres, Arras, the Somme and Cambrai, and rendered valuable services. He was demobilised in September 1919, and holds the General Service and Victory Medals.
45, London Road, Markyate. 3156/B.

GLENISTER, F. A. (M.M.), Gunner, R.F.A.
He was mobilised in August 1914, and proceeded to France immediately afterwards. He took part in the Retreat from Mons and the Battles of Ypres, Arras and Cambrai, and was awarded the Military Medal for bravery in the Field. In addition he holds the Mons Star, and the General Service and Victory Medals, and was demobilised in 1919.
16, Herbert Street, Watford. X3159/A.

GLENISTER, G., Private, 4th Bedfordshire Regt.
He joined in May 1916, and after serving on important duties at several stations was drafted to France in March 1918. He took part in the second Battle of the Somme, and in various other engagements, and was for a time on transport duties. He was severely wounded on September 1st, 1918, and has been missing since that date, and is presumed to have died. He was entitled to the General Service and Victory Medals.
65, Dane Road, Luton. 3155.

GLENISTER, H. W., Private, Argyll and Suther-land Highlanders.

He volunteered in November 1915, and in the following January was sent out to France. During his service on the Western Front he took part in the Battles of the Somme, Arras and Ypres, and was severely wounded and taken prisoner near Cambrai in March 1918. After being held in captivity until after the Armistice, he was repatriated and demobilised in January 1919. He holds the General Service and Victory Medals.

Sear Farm, Sundon, near Dunstable   3154.

GLENISTER, J., Sapper, Royal Engineers.

He volunteered in August 1915, and shortly afterwards was drafted to Gallipoli, where he served in the engagements at Suvla Bay and Chocolate Hill, and in the subsequent operations until the Evacuation of the Peninsula. He then proceeded to Egypt and did good service at Port Said, Ismalia and Kantara, and later proceeded into Palestine, where he was engaged on important duties in connection with the campaign, notably at Gaza, Jaffa, Ludd, Haifa and Beyrout. He was demobilised after his return to England in August 1919, and holds the 1914-15 Star, and the General Service and Victory Medals.

22, Smart Street, Luton.   3160.

GLENISTER, W., Private, West Kent (Queen's Own) Hussars.

He volunteered in June 1915, and on the completion of his training was drafted to France, where he took part in the fighting at Ypres, Arras and Cambrai, and was wounded in action. After his recovery he again served in various engagements in the Retreat and Advance of 1918, and was demobilised in September of the following year. He holds the General Service and Victory Medals.

16, Herbert Street, Watford.   X3159/B.

GLENISTER, W., Private, 11th Suffolk Regt.

He joined in February 1916, and in the following June was drafted to France, where he took part in several important battles. He was reported missing after an engagement on April 9th, 1918, and was afterwards found to have been taken prisoner, and to have died in a German Field Hospital. He was entitled to the General Service and Victory Medals.

74, Saxon Road, Luton.   3156/A.

GLOVER, A. S., Private, Bedfordshire Regiment and Royal Irish Fusiliers.

A serving soldier, he came over with his regiment from South Africa and arrived in England in November 1914 He was immediately drafted to France, and took part in many early engagements. He was transferred to the Royal Irish Fusiliers in 1915, and afterwards did good service in Salonika, Malta and Egypt. In October 1918 he returned to the Western Front, and was present at the final entry into Mons on November 11th. He was demobilised in February 1919 after his return home, and holds the 1914 Star, and the General Service and Victory Medals.

36, Kimpton Road, Luton.   3157/B.

GLOVER, F. J., Driver, Royal Engineers.

He volunteered in 1915, and in the following year was drafted to France, where he was engaged throughout his service in the Ypres sector on important duties in connection with the operations. He was frequently in the front lines, and was wounded and suffered from severe shell-shock. He was discharged for causes due to his service in 1918, and holds the General Service and Victory Medals.

36, Kimpton Road, Luton.   3157/A.

GLOVER, W. G., Private, 2nd Norfolk Regt.

He volunteered in 1915, and in the same year was sent to the Western Front, where he did good service for some time. Later he was drafted to Egypt, and served there until the cessation of hostilities. He then went to India and was stationed at Lucknow, and in 1920 was serving on the Afghan Frontier in the British Forces against the Waziri. He holds the General Service and Victory Medals.

36, Kimpton Road, Luton.   3157/C.

GLOYNES, W. T., Sapper, Royal Engineers.

He joined in March 1918, and later in the year was sent to France, where he was engaged on important duties at Boulogne and Calais. He was also employed in the Inland Water Transport Service and did excellent work. He was demobilised in December 1919 after returning home, and holds the General Service and Victory Medals.

84, Benskin Road, Watford.   X682/A.

GOBBY, F. A., Private, 6th Northamptonshire Regiment.

He joined in January 1916, and in the following July was drafted to France, where he took part in the fighting on the Somme and was wounded. After his recovery he served at Arras, Ypres, Passchendaele and Cambrai, and was again severely wounded in 1917. He was demobilised in September 1919 after returning to England, and holds the General Service and Victory Medals.

Pretoria Cottages, Harlington.   3205/A.

GOBBY, T., Bombardier, R.F.A.

He volunteered in August 1914, and after being retained on important duties with his Battery, was drafted to France in 1916. During his service on that front he took part in the Battles of Vimy Ridge, the Somme and Cambrai, and in many subsequent engagements until the cessation of hostilities. He was demobilised in July 1919, and holds the General Service and Victory Medals.

Letchworth Road, Limbury, near Luton.   3217.

GOBEY, G., Private, Machine Gun Corps.

He volunteered in November 1915, and being drafted to France in the following year, served at Albert, the Somme and Ypres. He was severely wounded at Cambrai in November 1917, and was sent for treatment to England. On his recovery he returned to the Western Front, and was soon afterwards gassed in action in March 1918. He was demobilised in March of the following year, and holds the General Service and Victory Medals.

High Street, Clophill, Ampthill.   3185.

GODBEHERE, E. L., Private, Bedfordshire and Essex Regiments.

He joined in 1917, and in March of the following year, on the completion of his training, was drafted to France. After only a few weeks' service on the Western Front he was killed in action near Ypres on May 22nd, 1918. He was entitled to the General Service and Victory Medals

452, Hitchin Road, Luton.   3201/A.

GODBEHERE, W., Private, Bedfordshire Regt.

He volunteered in October 1914, and in the following year was sent to Mesopotamia. Whilst in this theatre of war, until the close of operations, he took part in the engagements at Kut, in the capture of Baghdad, and was present at the occupation of Mosul. After 3½ years' service on this front he was demobilised on his return to England in November 1919, and holds the 1914-15 Star, and the General Service and Victory Medals.

452, Hitchin Road, Luton.   3201/B.

GODFREY, A., Private, 3rd Bedfordshire Regt.

He was mobilised at the commencement of hostilities and was soon sent to France. During his short service on the Western Front he fought in the first Battle of Ypres, and was reported missing after the engagement on November 9th, 1914. He was later presumed to have been killed on that date, and was entitled to the 1914 Star, and the General Service and Victory Medals.

32, St. Saviour's Crescent, Luton   3224/A.

GODFREY, C., Private, Leicestershire Regiment and Royal Defence Corps.

He joined in June 1916, and in the following August was drafted to the Western Front, where he took part in many important engagements, including those in the Somme offensive of 1916. He was wounded at Vaulx in April 1917, and invalided home. On his recovery he was transferred to the Royal Defence Corps, and was engaged in guarding railways, munition works and prisoners, until he was demobilised in March 1919. He holds the General Service and Victory Medals.

32, Back Street, Luton.   206.

GODFREY, E. A., Private, Royal Fusiliers.

Joining in June 1916, he proceeded to France in October of the same year, after the completion of his training. After taking part in several engagements and being wounded, he was killed in action near Beaumont-Hamel on April 29th, 1917. He was entitled to the General Service and Victory Medals.

10, Granville Road, Luton.   3177.

GODFREY, E. C., Private, 5th Bedfordshire Regt.

Volunteering in February 1915, he proceeded to France in the July following. He took part in the severe fighting on the Somme in 1916, and was badly wounded on the Ancre front in February 1917. After a long period in hospital under treatment, he was discharged in March 1919 as medically unfit for further service, holding the General Service and Victory Medals.

4, Campton, Shefford.   Z3176/B.

GODFREY, F. W., Pte., 5th Bedfordshire Regt.
He volunteered in September 1914, and in January of the following year was sent to Egypt. After valuable service at Cairo and Alexandria, he took part in the Palestine campaign in various engagements, including those at Jaffa and preceding the entry into Jerusalem. He was demobilised in June 1919 after returning home, and holds the 1914-15 Star, and the General Service and Victory Medals.
4, Campton, Shefford. Z3176/A.

GODFREY, G., Private, 5th Sherwood Foresters.
He joined in October 1916, and in February of the following year proceeded to the Western Front, where he took part in the heavy fighting at Ypres and the Somme area, and was badly wounded. He returned home in consequence, and was discharged owing to his injuries in May 1918. He holds the General Service and Victory Medals.
92, Cobden Street, Luton. 3223.

GODFREY, G., Sapper, Royal Engineers.
He joined in March 1917, and after his training was engaged at various stations on important building operations. He rendered valuable services, but owing to medical unfitness was not successful in obtaining his transfer overseas before the cessation of hostilities. He was demobilised in March 1919.
Caddington, near Luton. 3220.

GODFREY, G. S., Private, Labour Corps.
Joining in February 1915, he proceeded to France in July of the same year, where he was engaged in various sectors (including those of Ypres, Hill 60 and Vimy Ridge) on important duties with his unit. He rendered valuable services until after the close of hostilities, and was demobilised in February 1919, holding the 1914-15 Star, and the General Service and Victory Medals.
42, Cobden Street, Luton. 3172.

GODFREY, H., Private, R.A.M.C.
He volunteered in October 1914, and in July of the following year, after concluding his training, was drafted to the Dardanelles, where he did excellent work in the landing at Suvla Bay. After his return home he was discharged in May 1916 in consequence of his service, and holds the 1914-15 Star and the General Service and Victory Medals.
63, Chapel Street, Luton. 3161.

GODFREY, J. S., Private, Bedfordshire Regt.
He joined in May 1916, and was drafted to France in December of the same year. He took part in the severe fighting at Arras and Bullecourt, and after being reported missing is believed to have been killed in action in March 1917. He was entitled to the General Service and Victory Medals.
4, Campton, Shefford. Z3176/C.

GODFREY, R. M., Sapper, Royal Engineers.
Joining in July 1917, he was drafted to France in August of the same year. He did much valuable work in numerous engagements until hostilities ceased, including those at Cambrai, St. Quentin, Ypres and the Somme. He was demobilised in February 1919 after returning home, and holds the General Service and Victory Medals.
46, Clarendon Road, Luton. 3171.

GODLEMAN, W. J., Private, R.A.V.C.
He volunteered in October 1914, and was engaged at various depôts on important duties with his unit. He was engaged in attending to sick and wounded horses and mules, and rendered valuable services, but was not successful in obtaining his transfer overseas. He was discharged in April 1915 in consequence of his service.
5, Albion Road, Luton. 3178.

GODLIMAN, F., Private, Labour Corps.
He volunteered in August 1914, and afterwards was engaged at various stations on important duties with his unit. He rendered valuable services, but was not successful in obtaining his transfer overseas before the cessation of hostilities. In March 1919 he was sent to France, where he was engaged on internment duties until the following November, when he returned home and was demobilised.
31, Lamb Lane, Redbourn. 3209.

GODMAN, F. C., A.B., R.N., H.M.S. "Erebus."
He joined in 1917. During his period of war service he was engaged in the Baltic Sea, the Persian Gulf and other waters on important patrol and escort duties, and rendered valuable services in protecting food and troopships. He was still serving in 1920, and holds the General Service and Victory Medals.
40, Prospect Road, St. Albans. X3211/A.

GODMAN, H., Private, R.A.M.C.
Joining in November 1917, he was drafted to France in January of the following year. He did valuable work as a stretcher-bearer at Cambrai and Amiens, and was also engaged in hospital duties. He was demobilised in March 1919 after returning home, and holds the General Service and Victory Medals.
53, Waterside, King's Langley. 3208/A.

GODMAN, J., Private, R.A.S.C. (M.T.)
He volunteered in October 1915, and in February of the following year was sent to France. He served in various sectors until hostilities ceased, and was engaged with the Field Ambulance in conveying wounded from the field. He was demobilised in September 1919 after returning home, and holds the General Service and Victory Medals.
2, Water Lane, King's Langley. 3208/B.

GODMAN, T. A., Private, R.A.V.C.
Joining in July 1916, he proceeded to Salonika in August of the same year and did valuable service on the Vardar front in attending to sick and wounded horses. In June 1918 he was transferred to France, where he was employed on similar duties until after fighting ceased. He was demobilised in April 1919, and holds the General Service and Victory Medals.
Church End, Hockliffe. 3227.

GODMAN, W. A., Air Mechanic, R.A.F.
Joining in April 1918, in the following July he was sent to France, where he was engaged in many sectors on aircraft work of various kinds. His duties demanded a high degree of technical skill and were carried out with great efficiency. He was demobilised in September 1919, and holds the General Service and Victory Medals.
40, Prospect Road, St. Albans. X3211/B.

GODWIN, A., C.Q.M.S., R.E. (R.O.D.)
He was mobilised in August 1914, and was sent to France in the following month. He was engaged throughout the war in railroad construction and in the transport of troops and supplies to the various fronts, including those of the Somme, Ypres, Arras and Cambrai. During his service he was wounded on one occasion. He was demobilised in March 1919, and holds the 1914 Star, and the General Service and Victory Medals.
48, Hatfield Road, North Watford. X3188.

GOLDING, G., Private, R.A.M.C.
He joined in 1917, and after his training was engaged at various hospitals, where he rendered valuable services. He was not successful in obtaining his transfer overseas before the cessation of hostilities, owing to his medical unfitness, and was demobilised in January 1920.
6, Longmire Road, St. Albans. X3200.

GOLDING, W., Private, King's (Liverpool Regt.)
Joining in June 1916, he went through a course of training and was afterwards sent to the Western Front. After taking part in numerous important engagements he was taken prisoner at Cambrai in March 1918. On his release he returned home and was demobilised in December 1919, holding the General Service and Victory Medals.
37, Longmire Road, St. Albans. X3164/D—3165/D.

GOLDSMITH, O., Private, Labour Corps.
He joined in October 1916, and in the following year was drafted to the Western Front. He was engaged on the Ypres, Arras, Somme and Cambrai sectors in the repair of roads and trenches, and rendered valuable services. He was demobilised in April 1919 after returning to England, and holds the General Service and Victory Medals.
17, Dane Road, Luton. 2963/B.

GOMME, W., Sapper, Royal Engineers.
He joined in June 1917, and after his training was engaged on duties of an important nature in Ireland. Although unable to secure his transfer to a theatre of war before the termination of hostilities, he did valuable work until his demobilisation, which took place in November 1919.
9, Smith Street, Watford. X3195.

GOOCH, C., Sergeant, 2nd Bedfordshire Regt.
He volunteered in April 1918, and after his training was drafted to India. At a later date he was transferred to Russia, where he was engaged on duties of an important nature, and was still serving in 1920. He holds the General Service and Victory Medals.
5, New Street, Luton. 3203/A.

GOOCH, E. T., Private, Gloucestershire Regt.
He joined in May 1916, and until March 1918, when he was drafted to the Western Front, was retained on special duties at his depôt. He took part in the Battles of the Somme and in the second Battle of the Marne, and was subsequently killed in action on the Scarpe on September 6th, 1918. He was entitled to the General Service and Victory Medals.
5, New Street, Luton. 3203/B.

GOOCH, R., Private, 4th Norfolk Regiment.
Volunteering in April 1915, he was drafted to the Dardanelles after his course of training, and was later severely wounded during the heavy fighting on the Peninsula. Returning to England he was invalided out of the Service in October 1916, and holds the 1914–15 Star, and the General Service and Victory Medals.
Leavesden Green, Herts. X3168.

GOOD, J., Gunner, Royal Field Artillery.
He volunteered in August 1914, and in the following January was drafted overseas. Whilst in France he fought in several engagements and was severely wounded at Ypres, in consequence of which he died on April 27th, 1915. He was entitled to the 1914–15 Star, and the General Service and Victory Medals.
7, Talbot Road, Rickmansworth. X3190.

GOODAIR, C., Private, Hertfordshire Regiment.
Volunteering in March 1915, he was quickly drafted overseas. During his service on the Western Front he fought in numerous engagements, notably those at Hill 60, Ypres, Givenchy, Arras and Passchendaele, and was subsequently wounded and taken prisoner at Cambrai in May 1918, being held captive until after the Armistice. He was demobilised after his return to England in 1919, and holds the 1914–15 Star, and the General Service and Victory Medals.
105, Norfolk Road, Rickmansworth. X3191/B.

GOODAIR, H., Private, R.M.L.I.
He was serving on the outbreak of war, and was drafted to the Dardanelles early in 1915, and took part in the landing at Gallipoli. Later he was engaged in escorting food and troopships from Canada to France, and also on patrol duties. He did excellent work until his demobilisation, which took place in 1919, and holds the 1914–15 Star, and the General Service and Victory Medals.
105, Norfolk Road, Rickmansworth. X3192.

GOODAIR, H. (jun.), Private, R.M.L.I
He was serving on the declaration of war, and was posted for duty on board H.M.S. " Antrim," in which he subsequently lost his life, when she was torpedoed and sunk in the North Sea on October 16th, 1914. He was entitled to the 1914–15 Star, and the General Service and Victory Medals.
105, Norfolk Road, Rickmansworth. X3191/A.

GOODCHILD, S. C., Sapper, R.E. (R.O.D.)
He joined in August 1916, and at the conclusion of his training was drafted to Salonika, where he was engaged on duties of an important nature in the forward areas. Later he saw service in South Russia, and did valuable work there until 1919. He was demobilised after his return to England in October 1919, and holds the General Service and Victory Medals. 81, Regent Street, North Watford. X3187.

GOODE, A. E., C.Q.M.S., South Wales Borderers.
Joining in December 1916, he served in India for 3½ years. during which time he was engaged on duties of an important nature. He was demobilised on his return to England in February 1920, and holds the General Service and Victory Medals.
13, Lower Paxton Road, St. Albans. X3167.

GOODE, J. H., Private, 5th Bedfordshire Regt. and Royal Army Service Corps.
He volunteered in September 1914, and in March of the following year was drafted to the Western Front. He took an active part in the heavy fighting at Ypres, Arras, the Somme and Passchendaele, and was twice wounded. He was invalided home in consequence, and after later service in Ireland was discharged as medically unfit for further duty in January 1918. He holds the 1914–15 Star, and the General Service and Victory Medals.
74, Dane Road, Luton. 62/C.

GOODE, T. A., L/Corporal, King's Own Royal Lancaster Regiment.
He joined in 1916, and at the conclusion of his training was drafted to Mesopotamia. Whilst in this theatre of war he took part in several engagements, including the capture of Amara, and was with the forces in their attempt to relieve Kut. During his service overseas, which lasted for over three years, he did excellent work with his unit, and was demobilised after his return to England in September 1919. He holds the General Service and Victory Medals.
High Street, Westoning, Ampthill. 3180.

GOODENOUGH, J., Sergeant, The Cameronians (Scottish Rifles).
Joining in April 1916, he was drafted overseas at the conclusion of his training. Whilst in France he fought in many notable engagements, including those on the Somme and at Passchendaele and Cambrai, and quickly gained promotion for his efficient work in the Field. He holds the General Service and Victory Medals, and was demobilised after his return to England in November 1919.
119, Cotterell Road, Hemel Hempstead. X3175.

GOODERHAM, E., 1st Air Mechanic, R.A.F.
He joined in August 1918, and after his training served with his squadron on important duties which called for a high degree of technical skill. He was unable to secure his transfer overseas before the termination of hostilities, but nevertheless rendered valuable services until he was demobilised in February 1919.
4, Norton Road, Leagrave, Luton. 3218.

GOODGE, C. W., Private, 4th Bedfordshire Regt.
Joining in January 1916, he was drafted to France in the following year. He was subsequently engaged in the fighting in many important sectors, and was killed in action at Arras on April 23rd, 1917. He was entitled to the General Service and Victory Medals.
Lilley, near Luton. 3162.

GOODHALL, J. H., Petty Officer, Royal Navy.
He was already in the Navy, and from the commencement of hostilities served on board the " Don Artero." This vessel was engaged in conveying food supplies to and from the United States, Egypt and India, and frequently had to pass through mine-infested areas. He holds the General Service and Victory Medals, and was still serving in 1920.
Laurel Cottage, Fish Street, Redbourn. 3210.

GOODMAN, A. R., Pte., 4th Bedfordshire Regt.
He joined in June 1916, and at the conclusion of his training early in the following year was sent to France. Whilst in this theatre of war he was engaged in fighting in the Arras sector, and in consequence of a severe illness was for some time in hospital. He was demobilised after his return to England in September 1919, and holds the General Service and Victory Medals.
Falda Road, Barton. 3186.

GOODMAN, C., Private, 1st King's Shropshire Light Infantry ; and Gunner, R.F.A.
He volunteered in September 1915, and in the following January was sent to India, where he was engaged on special duties at various garrison outposts. He served also in the same capacity on the Gold Coast in West Africa, and was finally demobilised in June 1919. He holds the General Service and Victory Medals.
18, Church Street, Dunstable. 3214.

GOODMAN, H., Private, Royal Defence Corps.
He volunteered in May 1915, and served at various stations on important guard duties with his unit. He rendered valuable services until March 1919, when he was demobilised.
12, Millbrook, near Ampthill. 3181/B.

GOODMAN, H., Private, Norfolk Regiment.
Joining in June 1918, he was drafted to the Western Front after a short course of training. He subsequently served in the Advance, during which he was severely wounded and gassed. Returning to England after the cessation of hostilities, he was demobilised in January 1919, and holds the General Service and Victory Medals.
21, Talbot Road, Rickmansworth. X3189/B.

GOODMAN, J., A.B., Royal Navy.
He joined the Royal Navy in 1912 and at the outbreak of hostilities was posted to H.M.S. " Empress of India." This vessel was engaged with the North Sea patrol, and also took part in several naval engagements, notably the Battle of Jutland on May 31st, 1916. He did valuable work in his ship until July 1917, when in consequence of ill-health he was invalided out of the Service. He holds the 1914–15 Star, and the General Service and Victory Medals.
25, John Street, Luton. 3219.

GOODMAN, J., A.B., Royal Navy.
He was already in the Navy when war broke out, and was posted to H.M.S. " Goliath." During 1914 this vessel was engaged in conveying troops to and from East Africa, but on May 13th, 1915 was torpedoed off Gallipoli, whilst protecting the French flank inside the Straits, and he was drowned. He was entitled to the 1914–15 Star, and the General Service and Victory Medals.
London Road, Batchworth, Rickmansworth. X3193.

GOODMAN, J. (D.C.M.), Corporal, 1st Bedfordshire Regiment.
Called up from the Reserve at the outbreak of hostilities, he was immediately drafted to the Western Front, and took part in the Retreat from Mons. He subsequently served in other important engagements, including that at Ypres, and was wounded in action at Neuve Chapelle. On October 29th, 1914, he was mentioned in Despatches, and was awarded the Distinguished Conduct Medal for an act of conspicuous bravery whilst exposed to heavy shell-fire. Later he was drafted to India, where on November 30th, 1918, he died, after having undergone an operation. In addition to holding the Distinguished Conduct Medal, he was entitled to the Mons Star, and the General Service and Victory Medals.
21, Talbot Road, Rickmansworth. X3189/A.

GOODMAN, M., Private, Welch Regiment.

He joined in November 1916, and after his training saw service in France and Italy. On each of these fronts he took an active part in many important engagements, and after the termination of hostilities was sent with the Army of Occupation to Germany, where he was engaged on special guard duties. He was demobilised after his return to England in November 1919, and holds the General Service and Victory Medals. 97, Chester Road, Watford. X3202.

GOODMAN, S. J., Corporal, 11th Royal Fusiliers.

He volunteered in September 1914, and in the following year was drafted to France, and fought in the second Battle of Ypres, and was twice wounded on the Somme. After his recovery he served at Arras and Cambrai, and was taken prisoner at St. Quentin on March 21st, 1918. He was held in captivity in Germany until his release in the following April, when he was sent home and demobilised. He holds the 1914–15 Star, and the General Service and Victory Medals. 11, Winlock Street, Luton. 3222.

GOODMAN, W. J., Gnr., Royal Horse Artillery.

He joined in February 1916, and in the same year was drafted to France. During his service on the Western Front he took part in the Battle of the Somme and in various subsequent engagements, and in 1918 was wounded in the fighting at Cambrai. He was demobilised in October 1919, and holds the General Service and Victory Medals. 40, Ebury Road, Watford. X2994/C.

GOODSHIP, F. H., Private, 1/5th Bedfordshire Regiment.

He volunteered at the outbreak of war, and in the following July was drafted to the Dardanelles. Whilst in this theatre of war he took part in the landing at Suvla Bay, and in December 1915 was invalided to England suffering from dysentery, contracted during his service. He was under treatment in hospital for 12 months, and after his recovery proceeded to France in January 1917, and fought in various important engagements. Subsequently he was killed in action at Kemmel on April 15th, 1918, and was entitled to the 1914–15 Star, and the General Service and Victory Medals. Rose Cottage, Ramridge End, Stopsley, Beds. 3207/B.

GOODSHIP, H., Private, 1/5th Bedfordshire Regt

He was mobilised at the declaration of war, and in the following July was sent to the Dardanelles. A month later he was killed at the landing at Suvla Bay on August 16th, 1915. He was entitled to the 1914–15 Star, and the General Service and Victory Medals. Ramridge End, Stopsley, Beds. 3207/C.

GOODSHIP, W. J., Pte., 7th Lincolnshire Regt.

He volunteered in October 1915, and in the following year, on the completion of his training was drafted to France, where he saw considerable service. He took part in the Battles of Ypres, Cambra, St. Quentin, and La Bassée, and was wounded. In April 1919, after returning home, he was demobilised, and holds the General Service and Victory Medals. 133, Park Street, Luton. 262/B.

GOODSON, H. A., Air Mechanic, Royal Flying Corps; and Private, London Regiment (Royal Fusiliers).

He joined in October 1917, but owing to being physically unfit for service at the Front, was unable to procure his transfer to a theatre of war. He rendered valuable services at various stations until February 1918, when he was discharged. 16, Waterloo Road, Linslade. 3183/B.

GOODSON, H. J., Private, R.A.S.C.

He joined in June 1918, on the attainment of military age, and after his training served at his depôt on important transport duties. He did excellent work, but owing to the conclusion of war was unable to obtain his transfer overseas. He was demobilised in March 1919. 16, Waterloo Road, Linslade, Bucks. 3183/A.

GOODWIN, H. C., Private, Oxfordshire and Buckinghamshire Regiment.

Volunteering in September 1914, he was drafted to France in the following year, and whilst in this theatre of war fought at Ypres, the Somme, Arras and Cambrai. Later he proceeded to Italy, where he served in the campaign against the Austrians, and was wounded. In April 1919 he was demobilised after his return to England, and holds the 1914–15 Star, and the General Service and Victory Medals. 35, Dudley Street, Leighton Buzzard. 3194/A.

GOODWIN, R., Private, Machine Gun Corps.

He joined in 1917, and in the same year was drafted to France, and took part in the fighting at Arras, Ypres and Cambrai. In March 1918 he was taken prisoner at Béthune, and was held in captivity in Germany until after the Armistice, when he was released, and rejoining his unit, served until December 1919, when he was demobilised, holding the General Service and Victory Medals. 26, Ridgway Road, Luton. 3170/A.

GOODWIN, R. T., A.B., Royal Navy.

He had enlisted in the Navy in December 1908, and at the outbreak of war was posted for duty in H.M. Submarine " E.4." He served continuously throughout the war, and took part in the Battle of Jutland and in the raid on Zeebrugge, and in many other important naval operations. He was finally demobilised in December 1919, and holds the 1914–15 Star, and the General Service and Victory Medals. 35, Dudley Street, Leighton Buzzard. 3194/B.

GOODWIN, S., Air Mechanic, Royal Air Force.

He joined in July 1918, and was almost immediately drafted to France. During his service on the Western Front he was engaged on important duties and was stationed at Dunkirk until July 1919, when he returned home and was demobilised. He holds the General Service and Victory Medals. 26, Ridgway Road, Luton. 3170/B.

GOODWIN, S. W., Pte., 5th Bedfordshire Regt.

He joined in May 1917, and in the following October proceeded to France and fought in various engagements in the Cambrai sector. He also took part in the Retreat and Advance of 1918, and after the Armistice served with the Army of Occupation at Cologne until May 1920, when he was demobilised on returning to England. He holds the General Service and Victory Medals. 35, Dudley Street, Leighton Buzzard. 3228.

GOODYEAR, E. P., Private, 16th York and Lancaster Regiment.

He volunteered in August 1915, and in March of the succeeding year was drafted to France. In this theatre of war he took part in the Battles of the Somme and Arras, and was wounded at Passchendaele Ridge and in another engagement, and also suffered from fever. After a period in hospital he was finally demobilised in February 1919, and holds the General Service and Victory Medals. 11, Dalton Street, St. Albans. 3166.

GOODYER, W., Private, R.A.S.C.

He joined in September 1916, and in the following year was drafted to Egypt, and served with the British forces under General Allenby in the Advance through Palestine. He was engaged on important duties at El Arish, Rafa and Ramleh, and was present at the Battles of Gaza, Haïfa and Beyrout. In September 1919 he returned home and was demobilised, and holds the General Service and Victory Medals. 16, Highbury Road, Luton. 3197.

GOOSE, C., 2nd Air Mechanic, Royal Air Force.

He joined in January 1917, and after his training served at various depôts on important duties which demanded a high degree of technical skill. He did excellent work, but was not able to secure a transfer overseas before the cessation of hostilities, and was demobilised in December 1919. 65, Cardiff Road, Watford. X3198/A.

GOOSE, S. R., Rifleman, 2nd Rifle Brigade.

A serving soldier, he was drafted from India at the outbreak of war, and arrived in France in November 1914. He took part in the first Battle of Ypres and was severely wounded at Neuve Chapelle on March 10th, 1915. He was invalided to hospital in England, and in the following July was discharged as medically unfit, holding the 1914 Star, and the General Service and Victory Medals. 65, Cardiff Road, Watford. X3198/B.

GORE, T., Private, Bedfordshire Regiment.

He volunteered in 1915, and in June of the following year was drafted to France on the completion of his training. During his service on the Western Front he took part in the fighting in the Battles of the Somme, Arras and Bullecourt, and was reported missing after an engagement at Ypres on April 23rd, 1917, and is presumed to have been killed in action on that date. He was entitled to the General Service and Victory Medals. Clifton Road, Shefford. Z3173.

GORE, W., Sergt.-Instructor, Bedfordshire Regt.

A serving soldier, he was mobilised at the outbreak of war, and was engaged on important duties in the instruction of recruits in musketry and drilling until 1917, when he was drafted to France. Here he fought at Ypres, and was taken prisoner at Cambrai, and kept in captivity in Germany until after the Armistice. He was finally demobilised in March 1919, and holds the General Service and Victory Medals. 10, Langley Place, Luton. 3204.

GORING, G., Private, Training Reserve.

He volunteered in May 1915, and after his training served at various stations on important duties in the Training Reserve Battalion. Owing to medical reasons he was discharged in February 1918 as unfit for further military duty. 1a, Bedford Street, Watford. X3163

GOSS, A. W., Bombardier, R.H.A.

He volunteered in August 1914, and was soon sent to the Western Front. Here he took part in the fighting at Ypres, Neuve Chapelle, the Somme and Arras, and was wounded. He was invalided home and discharged in consequence of service in August 1918, and holds the 1914 Star, and the General Service and Victory Medals.

72, Highbury Road, Luton. 3199.

GOSS, R., Sergeant, 1/5th Bedfordshire and 2nd Dorsetshire Regiments.

He volunteered in August 1914, and after his training was drafted to the Dardanelles in August 1915, and in the following December was invalided home in consequence of ill-health. He was in hospital for about two years, and was then sent to Mesopotamia with the Dorsetshire Regiment, and took part in various operations until the conclusion of hostilities. He was demobilised after his return to England early in March 1919, but re-enlisted at the end of the month and proceeded to India, and in 1920 was stationed at Bangalore. He holds the 1914–15 Star, and the General Service and Victory Medals.

New Road, Clifton, Shefford. Z3213/A.

GOSS, S., Private, 2/5th Manchester Regt.

He joined in January 1917, and after his training was completed was drafted to France. He served at Arras and Ypres, and was subsequently killed in action on October 8th of the same year. He was entitled to the General Service and Victory Medals.

Beeston, Sandy, Beds. Z3179.

GOST, E. J., Private, Queen's (Royal West Surrey Regiment).

He volunteered in 1915, and in the same year was drafted to the Western Front. Whilst in this theatre of war he was engaged in the fighting at Ypres and on the Somme and in various subsequent battles, and later served in the Balkan campaign against the Bulgarians. He returned home and was demobilised in July 1919, and holds the 1914–15 Star, and the General Service and Victory Medals.

29, Cherry Bounce, Hemel Hempstead. X3215.

GOUGH, R. (M.M.), L/Sergeant, 1st Hertfordshire Regiment.

Volunteering in August 1914, he was sent immediately afterwards to the Western Front, where he took part in severe fighting at Mons, Ypres, Hill 60, Verdun, the Somme, Arras, Cambrai and St. Julien. He was twice wounded and gassed, and was awarded the Military Medal for bravery in the Field. In addition to the Military Medal he also holds the Mons Star, and the General Service and Victory Medals, and was demobilised in April 1919.

64, Harwood Road, Watford. X3284.

GOULD, A., Corporal, 7th Middlesex Regiment.

He joined in June 1916, and was drafted to France in October of the same year. He took part in numerous engagements, including those on the Somme and at Arras, Ypres, Cambrai, Albert, Fricourt and Bullecourt, and was four times wounded. He was demobilised in March 1919, and holds the General Service and Victory Medals.

86, Sotheron Road, Watford. X3196.

GOULD, W., Sapper, Royal Engineers.

He was mobilised at the outbreak of hostilities, and in October 1915, after being retained on coastal defence duties of an important nature, was drafted to Salonika. Durng his service on the Balkan front he rendered valuable services on the lines of communication and in wiring and trenching in the forward areas, and also took an active part in several engagements in the Vardar and Doiran sectors. After returning to England he was demobilised in April 1919, and holds the General Service and Victory Medals.

44, Cannon Street, St. Albans. 3221/A.

GOURLAY, D. J., Sapper, Royal Engineers.

He volunteered in September 1914, and in July of the following year was drafted to the Dardanelles, where he was in action at Suvla Bay and Chocolate Hill. Later in the same year he was transferred to Egypt and Palestine and served in the Canal zone, and at Gaza, Mejdil, Haifa, Acre and Beyrout. He was demobilised in July 1919. He holds the 1914–15 Star, and the General Service and Victory Medals.

8, Smart Street, Luton. 3174.

GOWER, E., Private, 1st Bedfordshire Regt.

He volunteered in September 1914, and was sent to France in the same year. He took part in severe fighting at Ypres, Hill 60, Lens and other important engagements, and was wounded. He was invalided home and was discharged in May 1916 as medically unfit, holding the 1914 Star, and the General Service and Victory Medals.

40, Tilehouse Street, Hitchin. 3184.

GOWER, F. W., Private, R.A.V.C.

Joining in August 1916, he proceeded to France in the same year, and served on the Somme, Ypres, Albert and Cambrai Fronts. He was engaged in attending to sick and wounded horses, and rendered valuable services. He was demobilised in February 1919, and holds the General Service and Victory Medals.

15, Alameda, Ampthill. 3182

GOWER, H., Pte., 1st Bedfordshire Regiment; and Riflmn., The Cameronians (Scottish Rifles).

Volunteering in January 1915, he was sent to France in the following May. He took part in heavy fighting at Hill 60, Ypres, the Somme and other important engagements, and returning to England was demobilised in March 1919. He holds the 1914–15 Star, and the General Service and Victory Medals.

29, Stanmore Road, Watford. X3169.

GOWERS, W. G., Sapper, Royal Engineers.

He joined in February 1917, and in the following month proceeded to the Western Front, where he took part in numerous engagements, including those on the Somme and at Arras and Cambrai. He returned home and was demobilised in November 1919, and holds the General Service and Victory Medals.

72, Estcourt Road, Watford. X3229.

GRACE, A., Private, 1st South Wales Borderers.

Volunteering in June 1915, he was drafted to France in June of the following year. He took part in severe fighting on the Somme, and at Arras, Ypres, Passchendaele, Cambrai and in many other engagements. He was demobilised in February 1919, and holds the General Service and Victory Medals.

4, Aley Green, near Luton. 3277.

GRACE, C. H., Private, South Wales Borderers.

He volunteered in June 1915, and was sent to France in June of the following year. He took part in various important engagements, including those on the Somme, and was killed in action on August 13th, 1916. He was entitled to the General Service and Victory Medals.

Lower Woodside, near Luton. 3247.

GRACE, E. S., Private, Suffolk Regiment.

He joined in June 1918, and proceeded to France in the same year and took part in heavy fighting on the Somme, and in other important engagements. He was afterwards transferred to Egypt, but returning to England in March 1920 was demobilised, holding the General Service and Victory Medals.

8, Shakespeare Street North, Watford. X3255.

GRACE, H., Private, 1st Manchester Regiment.

Volunteering in 1915, he was drafted to the Western Front in the same year. He took part in numerous engagements, including that at Passchendaele, and was later transferred to Italy, where he was again in action and was wounded. He was invalided home and was discharged as medically unfit in November 1919, holding the 1914–15 Star, and the General Service and Victory Medals.

37, Greatham Road, Bushey, Watford. 3273/B.

GRACE, J., Private, R.A.S.C.

He volunteered in August 1914, and was immediately afterwards sent to France, where he served in the Retreat from Mons and the Battles of the Marne and Festubert. Later he was invalided home owing to ill-health, and was discharged as medically unfit for further service in November 1915, holding the Mons Star, and the General Service and Victory Medals.

Station Road, Woburn Sands. Z3316.

GRACE, S. F. J., Private, Queen's (Royal West Surrey Regiment).

He joined in February 1917, and in the same month was drafted to the Western Front. He was attached to the Labour Coy., and was engaged on the Ypres, Arras and Albert fronts, road-making and digging trenches. Whilst serving in the Cambrai sector he was gassed. He was demobilised in March 1919, and holds the General Service and Victory Medals.

Mount Pleasant, Aspley Guise. Z3301.

GRACE, W., Private, 6th Bedfordshire Regiment.

He volunteered in September 1914, and was afterwards drafted to the Western Front, where he took part in numerous engagements, including that at Ypres, and was wounded. He was invalided home and discharged as medically unfit for further service in December 1917, and holds the General Service and Victory Medals.

37, Greatham Road, Bushey, Watford. 3273/A.

GRANGE, A., Private, 9th Loyal North Lancashire Regiment.
He joined in December 1916, and in September of the following year was drafted to the Western Front. Whilst in this theatre of war he took part in much severe fighting, and lost his right arm in consequence of wounds received in an engagement near Cambrai in March 1918. After much hospital treatment he was demobilised in June 1919, holding the General Service and Victory Medals.
41, Cardiff Road, Watford. X794/A.

GRANT, H. M., Rifleman (Signaller), 24th Canadian Infantry (Victoria Rifles).
He volunteered in 1914, and was sent to France in the following year. He took part in severe fighting at Neuve Chapelle, Loos, Ypres and Vimy Ridge, and was twice wounded. He was demobilised in January 1919, and holds the 1914-15 Star, and the General Service and Victory Medals.
10, Clifford Street, Watford. X3311/C.

GRANTHAM, W. A., Q.M.S., Royal Defence Corps.
He volunteered in October 1914, and served at various stations on important duties with his unit. He was engaged in guarding Government stores and rendered valuable services. He was demobilised in July 1919.
223, Chester Road, Watford. X3230.

GRAVES, E., Corporal, Machine Gun Corps.
Volunteering in October 1915, he was sent to Mesopotamia in October of the following year, and thence to India. He was engaged at various stations on important duties with his unit, and rendered valuable services. He returned home and was demobilised in March 1919, and holds the General Service and Victory Medals.
26, Bailey Street, Luton. 3297/A.

GRAVES, H., Private, 7th Bedfordshire Regt.
He volunteered in March 1915, and in the same year was drafted to the Western Front, where he took part in severe fighting at Hill 60, Ypres, Givenchy and Arras. He was killed in action on the Somme on July 1st, 1916, and was entitled to the 1914-15 Star, and the General Service and Victory Medals.
Breachwood Green, near Welwyn. 3318.

GRAVESTOCK, H. W., Private, 7th Bedfordshire Regiment.
Joining in June 1916, he was drafted to France in September of the same year. He took part in numerous engagements, including those on the Somme and at Ypres and St. Julien, and was gassed. He was demobilised in September 1919, and holds the General Service and Victory Medals.
Thorne House, Park Street, Dunstable. 3322.

GRAVESTOCK, J., Private, 2nd Border Regt.
He volunteered in September 1914, and after his training was drafted to the Western Front, where he took part in severe fighting at Arras, Ypres and Cambrai, and was wounded. He was invalided home and discharged as medically unfit in 1917, and holds the General Service and Victory Medals.
41, Clifford Street, Watford. X821/B.

GRAVESTOCK, R. H., Private, R.A.S.C.
Volunteering in December 1915, he went through a course of training, and afterwards served on important duties with his unit. He rendered valuable services, but was not successful in obtaining his transfer overseas owing to his being under age for duty abroad, and was discharged for the same reason in November 1916.
2, Back Lane, Leighton Buzzard. 3227/B.

GRAVESTOCK, S. A., L/Corporal, Royal Sussex Regiment.
He volunteered in August 1914, and in the following September, was drafted to the Western Front, where he took part in numerous engagements, including those at La Bassée, Loos, the Somme and Arras. He was wounded and taken prisoner near Arras in July 1917. On his release he returned home and was demobilised in December 1919, and holds the 1914-15 Star, and the General Service and Victory Medals.
2, Back Lane, Leighton Buzzard. 3327/A.

GRAVESTOCK, W. (M.M.), Sergeant, Royal Engineers (Signals).
Volunteering in December 1914, he was sent to France in June of the following year. He took part in numerous important engagements, including those at Festubert, the Somme, Arras, Ypres, Cambrai and Albert. He was awarded the Military Medal for bravery in the Field, and also holds the 1914-15 Star, and the General Service and Victory Medals. He was demobilised in January 1919,
118, Liverpool Road, Watford. X3261.

GRAY, A., Private, R.A.S.C. (M.T.)
He joined in 1916, and in the same year was drafted to the Western Front, where he served in many important engagements. He was employed in the transport of ammunition and supplies on the various fronts, including those of the Somme, Ypres, Albert and Cambrai. After the Armistice he proceeded with the Army of Occupation to Germany, where he served until September 1919, when he returned to England and was demobilised, holding the General Service and Victory Medals.
Ickleford Common, Ickleford, Hitchin. 3331/A.

GRAY, A., Gunner, Royal Field Artillery.
Joining in 1916, he was in the same year sent to France, where he took part in various engagements. In 1917 he was transferred to India and served on the Frontier and at various stations on important duties with his Battery, and rendered valuable services. He was demobilised in September 1919, and holds the General Service and Victory Medals.
20, Grange Street, St. Albans. X3314.

GRAY, A. J., Gunner, Royal Field Artillery.
He joined in May 1918, and in the following October was drafted to the Western Front, and was engaged on important duties with his Battery until 1919, when he proceeded to Germany and served with the Army of Occupation. He was demobilised in March 1920, and holds the General Service and Victory Medals.
Southill, Beds. Z3246.

GRAY, C. F., 1st Class Stoker, R.N., H.M.S. "Swiftsure."
He was serving at the outbreak of war, and was engaged in the Suez Canal. In June 1915, he proceeded to the Dardanelles, where he was in action at Sedd-el-Bahr and Suvla Bay, and was afterwards employed on patrol duties in the Mediterranean. He was discharged in consequence of his service in March 1916, and holds the 1914-15 Star, and the General Service and Victory Medals, and the Naval General Service Medal with Persian Gulf Clasp.
27, Hitchin Hill, Hitchin. 3330.

GRAY, C. O., Gunner, Royal Field Artillery.
He joined in August 1916, and in April of the following year was sent to France, where he took part in numerous engagements, including those on the Somme and at Arras, Ypres, Cambrai, and was wounded. He was demobilised in May 1919, and holds the General Service and Victory Medals.
5, Cannons Gardens, Hitchin. 3287.

GRAY, E., Telegraphist, R.N., H.M.S. "Dragon."
He volunteered in 1915, and was posted to H.M.S. "Dragon," and in the same year proceeded to the Mediterranean and later to the Baltic. He was engaged on patrol and escort duties and rendered valuable services. He was still serving in 1920, and holds the 1914-15 Star, and the General Service and Victory Medals.
6, Alexandra Road, Hitchin. 3329/C.

GRAY, E. D., A.B., R.N., H.M.S. "Natal."
He was serving at the outbreak of war, and was engaged on patrol duty in the North Sea and Eastern Mediterranean and rendered valuable services. He also took part in the Battle of Jutland. He was still serving in 1920, and holds the 1914-15 Star, and the General Service and Victory Medals.
25, Harley Street, St. Albans. 3303/B.

GRAY, E. J., Bombardier, R.F.A.
He enlisted in 1904, and in August 1914 proceeded to the Western Front. He took part in severe fighting during the Retreat from Mons and on the Marne, La Bassée, Festubert and Ypres, and was wounded. He was discharged owing to wounds, in September 1916, and holds the Mons Star, and the General Service and Victory Medals.
4 Taylor's Cottages, Old Park Road, Hitchin. 3295.

GRAY, E. J., Gunner, Royal Field Artillery.
He volunteered in October 1915, and was drafted to the Western Front, where he was engaged on important duties with his Battery. He was invalided home and discharged as medically unfit for further service in July 1916, and holds the General Service and Victory Medals.
25, Harley Street, St. Albans. 3303/A.

GRAY, E. S., Trooper, Herts Dragoons.
Volunteering in November 1915, he was drafted to France in the same year, and thence in 1916 to Egypt and Palestine, where he took part in many important engagements, including that at Gaza. He returned home and was demobilised in May 1919, and holds the 1914-15 Star, and the General Service and Victory Medals.
88, Victoria Street, St. Albans. X3271.

GRAY, F., Sapper, Royal Engineers.
He joined in March 1917, and in the following November was sent to Mesopotamia, where he took part in various engagements, including those at Baghdad and Amara. In February 1918 he was transferred to India, where he was employed on important duties with his unit. He was still serving in 1920, and holds the General Service and Victory Medals.
6, Alexandra Road, Hitchin.   3329/B.

GRAY, H., Gunner, R.G.A.
Joining in September 1916, he was drafted to France in the same month. He took part in heavy fighting on the Somme and at Arras, Cambrai and St. Quentin, and was gassed. He was demobilised in February 1919, and holds the General Service and Victory Medals.
82, Boyle Street, Luton.   3319.

GRAY, H. C., Sapper, Royal Engineers.
Volunteering in May 1915, he went through a course of training and afterwards served on important duties with his unit until 1917, when he was drafted to the Western Front. He was engaged on railway work in the transport of supplies to the various fronts, including those of the Somme, Arras, Ypres, Cambrai and Albert, and rendered valuable services. He was demobilised in May 1919, and holds the General Service and Victory Medals.
6, Alexandra Road, Hitchin.   3329/A.

GRAY, J., Private, 1st Hertfordshire Regiment.
Volunteering in June 1915, he was sent to France in the following year. He took part in various important engagements, including that on the Somme. He was killed in action at Ypres on November 13th, 1917, and was entitled to the General Service and Victory Medals.
7, Hatfield Road, North Watford.   X3283/A.

GRAY, J. H., Sergeant, Bedfordshire and Suffolk Regiments.
He volunteered in September 1914, and served on important duties as an Instructor with his unit until 1918, when he was sent to France. He took part in various engagements, including those at Ypres, Armentières and Amiens. He was demobilised in March 1919, and holds the General Service and Victory Medals.
Summerley's, Eaton Bray, near Dunstable.   Z3286.

GRAY, L. S., Private, Machine Gun Corps.
He joined in 1917, and was drafted to France in the following year. He took part in severe fighting at Havrincourt, Cambrai and Ypres, and after the cessation of hostilities returned home and was demobilised in February 1919, holding the General Service and Victory Medals.
25, Longmore Road, St. Albans.   X1950/B.

GRAY, P., Private, Queen's (Royal West Surrey Regiment).
He joined in March 1916, and in the same year was drafted to the Western Front, where he took part in numerous engagements, including those on the Somme and at Arras, Ypres and St. Quentin, and was twice wounded. He was demobilised in March 1919, and holds the General Service and Victory Medals.
6, Lower Paxton Road, St Albans.   X3270.

GRAY, S. M., Corporal, R.F.A.
Volunteering in August 1914, he was in the following year drafted to the Western Front, where he took part in numerous engagements, including those at Arras, Ypres and Cambrai. He was severely wounded on the Somme in 1918, having his hand blown off, and has since suffered the amputation of an arm. He was invalided home and discharged, owing to wounds, in February 1919, and holds the 1914–15 Star, and the General Service and Victory Medals.
Ireland, Shefford.   Z3281.

GRAY, W., L/Corporal, Labour Corps.
He joined in February 1917, and in the following April was sent to France, where he served for two years. He was engaged at Rouen on important duties connected with the Army Postal Service, and did valuable work until after hostilities ceased. He was demobilised in March 1919 after returning home, and holds the General Service and Victory Medals.
19, York Street, Luton.   300/A.

GRAY, W., Private, Royal Army Medical Corps.
Joining in March 1916, he was drafted to Salonika in the same year. He was engaged on the Struma and Doiran fronts on important hospital duties and rendered valuable services. He returned home and was discharged in March 1918, and holds the General Service and Victory Medals.
8, Anderson's Row, Florence Street, Hitchin.   3291.

GRAY, W., Private, 2nd Bedfordshire Regiment.
He volunteered in December 1914, and after his training served at various stations on important duties with his unit. He rendered valuable services, but was not successful in obtaining his transfer overseas before the cessation of hostilities. He was demobilised in January 1919.
45, Sunnyside, Hitchin.   3325.

GRAY, W., Private, Cambridgeshire Regiment.
Joining in 1918, he went through a course of training and was afterwards sent to the Western Front, where he took part in various engagements, including those at Ypres, the Somme and Cambrai. He was demobilised in November 1919, and holds the General Service and Victory Medals.
7, Hatfield Road, North Watford.   X3283/B.

GRAY, W. S., Gunner, R.G.A.
He joined in June 1917, and in the following October was drafted to France, where he took part in severe fighting at Ypres, Passchendaele, Cambrai and many other engagements. He was demobilised in November 1919, and holds the General Service and Victory Medals.
15, Old Park Road, Hitchin.   3289.

GREAVES, T. H., Private, 10th (Prince of Wales' Own Royal) Hussars.
He enlisted in February 1911, and shortly after the outbreak of war was sent to the Western Front, where he took part in the severe fighting in many engagements, and was wounded at Ypres. He returned home and was discharged in May 1917 in consequence of his service, holding the Mons Star, and the General Service and Victory Medals.
3, Cross Street South, St. Albans.   X3296.

GREEN, A. G. (Mrs.), Charge Nurse, Q.A.I.M.N.S.
This lady was engaged as Charge Nurse at Belmont Military Hospital, Liverpool, from September 1916 to December 1918. Her duties, which were of a most responsible nature, were carried out with great care and efficiency, and she rendered valuable services.
Derwent House, Alfred Street, Dunstable.   3320/B.

GREEN, A. J., Sergeant, South Wales Borderers.
He was mobilised in August 1914, and was sent shortly afterwards to the Western Front, where he took part in the severe fighting at Mons, Ypres and many other important engagements of 1914–15. He was demobilised in March 1919, and holds the Mons Star, and the General Service and Victory Medals and the Territorial Efficiency Medal.
22, New Dalton Street, St. Albans.   X3269.

GREEN, E. E., Bombardier, R.F.A.
Volunteering in September 1914, he was sent to France after completing his training in February of the following year. While there he took part in numerous engagements of importance until hostilities ceased, including those at Ypres, Lens, Loos, Béthune, St. Quentin, the Somme and Cambrai, and for his gallantry was recommended for the Croix de Guerre. He was demobilised in March 1919, and holds the 1914–15 Star, and the General Service and Victory Medals.
78, Reginald Street, Luton.   3274.

GREEN, F. J., Private, Norfolk Regiment.
He joined in August 1917, and after his training was retained at several stations on important duties with his unit. In October 1919 he was drafted to India, and was engaged on garrison duties at Lucknow, where in 1920 he was still serving.
56, Fishpool Street, St. Albans.   X3250/A.

GREEN, F. J, Driver, Royal Field Artillery.
He joined in April 1917, and in the following July proceeded to the Western Front. During his service in France he was in action at Ypres, Passchendaele and Lens, and in numerous later engagements, until the conclusion of hostilities. He was demobilised in October 1919, and holds the General Service and Victory Medals.
41, Periwinkle Lane, Hitchin.   3288.

GREEN, F. T., Corporal, 21st Middlesex Regt.
He volunteered in March 1915, and after training and serving at various depôts on important duties, was drafted to France in January 1917. He was engaged at the Somme and St. Quentin, and was severely wounded in action. He was invalided to hospital, and after protracted treatment was demobilised in January 1919. He holds the General Service and Victory Medals.
Derwent House, Alfred Street, Dunstable.   3320/A.

GREEN, F. T., L/Corporal, Military Police.
He joined in November 1917, and in the following March was sent to France, where he was stationed at Rouen, Boulogne and Calais. He also served with the Military Police at Cambrai. In 1920 he was serving in India, and holds the General Service and Victory Medals.
2, Stanbridge Road, Leighton Buzzard.   3285

GREEN, G., Sapper, Royal Engineers.
He joined in December 1916, and after his training served at various stations, including Aberdeen, on important duties which demanded much skill. He did excellent work with his unit, but was not successful in obtaining his transfer overseas before the conclusion of hostilities. He was demobilised in 1919.
4, Bedford Road, Hitchin.   3326.

GREEN, G., Corporal, Tank Corps.
He volunteered in September 1914, and on the completion of his training was drafted to France in 1916. During his service on the Western Front he was in action in many important engagements until the Armistice was signed, and did much valuable work. He returned home and was demobilised in April 1919, holding the General Service and Victory Medals.
16, Cassio Bridge Road, Watford.   X3231.

GREEN, G. W., Pioneer, Royal Engineers.
He volunteered in November 1915, and after his training was sent to France, where he was engaged on important duties in connection with the operations, and was frequently in the forward areas, notably at Cambrai. During his service he was attached to the Gas Company, and did good work in various sectors. He was demobilised in March 1919, and holds the General Service and Victory Medals.
New Town, Hatfield.   X3232.

GREEN, H. A., Rifleman, 1st Cameronians (Scottish Rifles).
He joined in May 1917, and after his training served on important duties at several stations, including Dublin. He rendered valuable services, but was not able to secure his transfer overseas before the cessation of hostilities. He was demobilised in September 1919.
Elizabeth Cottages, Princess Street, Toddington.   3272.

GREEN, H. J., Private, Royal Air Force.
Volunteering in 1915, he was sent to France in December of the following year. During his service on the Western Front he was engaged in the repair and general upkeep of aeroplanes, chiefly at Arras, Ypres, Passchendaele, Cambrai and the Somme. After the Armistice he proceeded to Germany, and was stationed at Cologne with the Army of Occupation until February 1919, when he was demobilised. He holds the General Service and Victory Medals.
Clifton Fields Green, Shefford.   Z3313.

GREEN, J., Private, Middlesex Regiment.
He joined in June 1916, and was drafted to France on the completion of his training, He fought in the Battle of the Somme, and was killed in action near Arras on April 9th, 1917. He was entitled to the General Service and Victory Medals.
26, Clifford Street, Watford.   X3312.

GREEN, J., Driver, Royal Army Service Corps.
He volunteered in March 1915, and in the same month was drafted to France, where he was engaged on important transport duties with his unit in the Ypres, Loos, Somme and Lens sectors. In April 1917 he was sent to Italy, where he did good work in various engagements until the following December, when he was redrafted to France. Here he served throughout the Retreat and Advance of 1918, and was demobilised in April of the succeeding year. He holds the 1914–15 Star, and the General Service and Victory Medals.
71, Sotheron Road, Watford.   X3323.

GREEN, J., Corporal, Royal Army Service Corps.
Volunteering in January 1915, he was drafted in the following March to the Western Front, and served at Ypres, Festubert, Vimy Ridge and Arras on important duties with his unit. He was present also at various subsequent engagements, and was demobilised after four years' service in 1919. He holds the 1914–15 Star, and the General Service and Victory Medals.
56, Fishpool Street, St. Albans.   X3250/B.

GREEN, R. V., Driver, Royal Field Artillery.
He joined in February 1917, and four months later was sent overseas. During his service in France he took part in the engagements at Ypres, Vimy Ridge, Passchendaele and in various operations which followed until the conclusion of hostilities. He was demobilised in May 1919 after returning home, and holds the General Service and Victory Medals.
Dell Farm, Bidwell, Dunstable.   3321.

GREEN, W. F., Private, R.A.S.C.
Volunteering in August 1915, he proceeded to the Western Front in the same year, and was engaged on important transport duties with his unit at Arras. Later he was drafted to Italy, where he was present at numerous battles, and was wounded. On October 28th, 1918, he died at the 9th Casualty Clearing Station of illness contracted during his service, and was buried at Gravera. He was entitled to the 1914–15 Star, and the General Service and Victory Medals.
72, Sotheron Road, Watford.   X3324.

GREENAWAY, S., Sergeant, Bedfordshire Regt.
He joined in June 1916, and after his training was completed was drafted to the Western Front. Here he took part in the Battles of Arras, Ypres and Cambrai, and many subsequent engagements, and was twice severely wounded. He was demobilised in November 1919, and holds the General Service and Victory Medals.
33, New England Street, St. Albans.   3292.

GREENHAM, F. H. J., Sapper, Royal Engineers.
He volunteered in August 1915, and in the following April was drafted to France, where he was engaged on important duties in connection with the operations, and was frequently in the fighting lines, especially in the Somme and Ypres sectors. In March 1917 he was invalided home, but after a time returned to the Western Front, where he rendered valuable service until killed in action on July 3rd, 1918. He was entitled to the General Service and Victory Medals.
22, Inkerman Road, St. Albans.   X3267.

GREENHOOD, C., Pte., 10th Hampshire Regt.
He volunteered in 1915, and on the completion of his training was drafted to Salonika, where he did much valuable work in several important engagements against the Bulgarians. He was killed whilst fighting there on December 7th, 1915, and was entitled to the 1914–15 Star, and the General Service and Victory Medals.
15, San Remo Road, Aspley Guise.   Z3237/B.

GREENHOOD, H. E. G., Private, Bedfordshire Lancers.
He volunteered in May 1915, and in the same year was drafted to France. Here he took part in numerous important engagements, and on one occasion narrowly escaped being killed when his horse was shot under him. He was in action at Arras, Ypres, Cambrai and on the Somme, and after the cessation of hostilities served on the Rhine with the Army of Occupation. In February 1919 he returned home and was demobilised. He holds the 1914–15 Star, and the General Service and Victory Medals.
15, San Remo Road, Aspley Guise.   Z3237/A.

GREENHOOD, W. J., Rifleman, K.R.R.C.
He joined in December 1916, and in the follow ng year was drafted to France, where he took part in the fighting at Arras, Ypres, Cambrai, the Somme and other engagements in the Retreat and Advance of 1918. After the conclusion of hostilities he proceeded to Germany with the Army of Occupation, and was stationed on the Rhine. In January 1920, after he returned home, he was demobilised, holding the General Service and Victory Medals.
15, San Remo Road, Aspley Guise .   Z3237/C.

GREENING, C. W., Private, 26th Royal Fusiliers.
He joined in February 1916, and in the following September was drafted to France, where he served in numerous important engagements, including those at the Somme, Ypres and Passchendaele, and was also in action in the Retreat and Advance of 1918. He holds the General Service and Victory Medals, and was demobilised in November 1918.
23, George Street, Leighton Buzzard.   3304.

GREENING, G. S., Private, R.A.S.C.
After volunteering in May 1915, he proceeded in the following January to Egypt, where he served for three months. In April 1916 he was drafted to France, and was present at the Battles of the Somme, Arras and Passchendaele, and in the engagements which followed, until the conclusion of hostilities. He returned home and was demobilised in February 1919, and holds the General Service and Victory Medals.
14, Brixton Road, Watford.   X3280/A.

GREGORY, A. J., Private, King's Shropshire Light Infantry.
He joined in June 1916, and in the following November was drafted to the Western Front, where he took part in the Battles of Arras and Vimy Ridge, and was wounded near Bapaume in August 1917. He was invalided home and was discharged as unfit for further service in July 1918. He holds the General Service and Victory Medals.
Campton, Shefford.   Z3293.

GREGORY, F. F., Sergeant, R.A.M.C.
He was mobilised with the Territorials in 1914, and in September of the following year was sent to Gallipoli, where he did excellent service. In November of the same year he was transferred to Egypt, and afterwards went through the Palestine campaign. He was attached to the Royal Air Force at Aboukir as a cadet in 1918, but rejoined the Royal Army Medical Corps in January 1919. He was demobilised in July 1919, and holds the 1914–15 Star, and the General Service and Victory Medals.
9, Leagrave Road, Luton.   3234.

GREGORY, F. M., Sergt., 26th Royal Fusiliers.

He joined in May 1916, and two months later was drafted to the Western Front. He took a prominent part in the Battles of the Somme and Ypres, and was wounded. He returned to England in consequence, but on his recovery again crossed to France. After further valuable service there for a year he was transferred to Italy, where he did very good work until the cessation of hostilities. After coming home he was demobilised in September 1919, and holds the General Service and Victory Medals.
98, Ashton Road, Luton.   3257/A.

GREGORY, H. C., Private, 1st Hertfordshire Regiment.

He volunteered in August 1914, and in 1916, after being retained on important duties with his unit, was drafted to the Western Front. He took part in much severe fighting in various important engagements, and was wounded. He died of his injuries on September 16th, 1917 and was buried near Ypres. He was entitled to the General Service and Victory Medals.
Souldern Street, Watford.   X3262/A.

GREGORY, J., Private, 5th Bedfordshire Regt.

Volunteering in June 1915, he was sent in the following year to France, where he took part in many important engagements until fighting ceased, including those of the Somme, Arras, Ypres, Passchendaele and Cambrai. He was demobilised in March 1919, after returning home, and holds the General Service and Victory Medals.
22, Spring Place, Luton.   3242.

GREGORY, J. F., Sergeant, R.A.V.C.

Joining in November 1917, he proceeded to France in the following year. He was engaged at Rouen, Boulogne and Calais in attending to sick and wounded horses, and rendered valuable services. He was demobilised in June 1919, and holds the General Service and Victory Medals.
45, Spencer Road, Luton.   3248.

GREGORY, R. W., Cpl., Royal Engineers; and Flight Cadet, Royal Air Force.

Volunteering in December 1914, he went through his course of training, and in July 1915 was drafted to the Dardanelles. After valuable service there, in which he was wounded, he was transferred to Egypt in the following December. He subsequently took part in the Palestine campaign and fought at Gaza, and in other later engagements. He was transferred to the Royal Air Force in July 1918. On his return home in April 1919 he was demobilised, and holds the 1914–15 Star, and the General Service and Victory Medals.
98, Ashton Road, Luton.   3257/B.

GREGORY, T., Driver, R.A.S.C.

He volunteered in December 1914, and in July of the following year was drafted to the Western Front, where he did valuable transport work in important engagements until hostilities ceased, including those on the Somme, at Arras, Ypres, Cambrai, Albert and St. Quentin. He was demobilised in July 1919, and holds the 1914–15 Star, and the General Service and Victory Medals.
Oliver Street, Ampthill.   3235.

GRIDLEY, F. D., Corporal, Royal Air Force (late Royal Naval Air Service).

He volunteered in November 1914, and after his training did valuable work at Salonika, and at stations in the Ægean as an airship fitter. In February 1918 he was drafted to Russia, where he rendered valuable services until November of the following year, when he was demobilised after his return to England. He holds the General Service and Victory Medals.
91, High Street, Markyate.   3238.

GRIFFIN, A., Rifleman, K.R.R.C.

He joined in September 1917, and after his training was completed was drafted to France in the following year. He was in action on the Somme and at Cambrai, and in many subsequent engagements until the close of fighting, and remained overseas until August 1919, when he returned home. Two months later he proceeded to India, where he was still serving at Quetta in 1920. He holds the General Service and Victory Medals.
94, Norfolk Road, Rickmansworth.   X3278.

GRIFFIN, A. L., Rifleman, 16th London Regt. (Queen's Westminster Rifles).

He volunteered in February 1915, and after the conclusion of his training was drafted to France. During his service on the Western Front he took part in many important engagements, and was severely wounded in October 1915. He was invalided home in 1918, and demobilised in March of the following year. He holds the 1914–15 Star, and the General Service and Victory Medals.
119, Estcourt Road, Watford.   X3275/A.

GRIFFIN, A. P., Private, Oxfordshire and Buckinghamshire Light Infantry.

A serving soldier, he was immediately drafted to France at the outbreak of war. He took part in the Retreat from Mons, and was wounded in the Battle of the Marne. After a period of treatment at home he returned to the Western Front, and was again in action at Festubert. In 1915 he was again sent home to hospital, and in 1916 was invalided out of the Service. He holds the Mons Star, and the General Service and Victory Medals.
Aspley Hill, Woburn Sands.   Z3300.

GRIFFIN, D., Private, Bedfordshire Regiment.

He volunteered in November 1914, and on the completion of his training served at various stations on important duties with his unit, including those of a Military Policeman. He did excellent work, but was not successful in obtaining his transfer abroad before the cessation of hostilities, and was demobilised in March 1919.
Aspley Hill, Woburn Sands.   Z3302/A.

GRIFFIN, E., Private, Suffolk Regiment.

He volunteered in August 1915, and in July 1917, after being retained on important duties with his unit, was drafted to France. Whilst in this theatre of war he took part in the Battles of Arras, Cambrai and the Somme, and was gassed. He was demobilised in May 1919 after his return home, and holds the General Service and Victory Medals.
24, Merton Road, Watford.   X3254/A.

GRIFFIN, G. E., 2nd Corporal, R.E. (E.A.)

He enlisted on July 30th, 1914, and after doing much valuable service with his unit, was in February 1916 drafted to Egypt. He did good work in the Canal zone, and subsequently joining the Expedition into Palestine, was present at the engagements at El Arish, Rafa, Gaza, Haifa, Damascus and Beyrout. After his return home he was demobilised in June 1919, and holds the General Service and Victory Medals.
60, Claremont Road, Luton.   3245/B.

GRIFFIN, G. W., A.B., R.N., H.M.S. "Hawkins."

He joined the Navy in March 1916, and was posted to H.M.S. "Hawkins," and whilst in this ship served on important and dangerous duties in all seas. He cruised in the North Sea, the Baltic, off the coasts of Japan, and took part in the engagement in the Heligoland Bight in 1918. In 1920 he was still serving, and holds the General Service and Victory Medals.
24, Merton Road, Watford.   3256/B.

GRIFFIN, J., Private, King's Own Scottish Borderers.

He volunteered in September 1914, and a year later was drafted to the Western Front. During his service in France he fought at Festubert and Loos, and was wounded on the Somme in 1916. He was again wounded in the Ypres sector in May of the following year, and for the third time at Cambrai in December 1917. On September 30th, 1918, he was reported missing after an engagement in the Advance, and was later presumed to have been killed in action on that date. He was entitled to the 1914–15 Star, and the General Service and Victory Medals.
Aspley Hill, Woburn Sands.   Z3302/B.

GRIFFIN, J., Private, 5th Bedfordshire Regt.

He volunteered in August 1914, and after his training was drafted to Mesopotamia in the following year. He served in several engagements, but after suffering severely from dysentery was invalided home, and discharged as unfit for further duty in September 1916. He died from the effects of his illness on November 1st, 1918. He was entitled to the 1914–15 Star, and the General Service and Victory Medals.
2, Hardwick Place, Woburn Sands.   Z3135/B.

GRIFFIN, L., Private, 3rd East Surrey Regiment.

Although under age for military service, he joined in May 1918, and after his training was engaged at many different stations on important duties with his unit. He was unable to secure his transfer overseas before the termination of hostilities, but nevertheless rendered valuable services until demobilised in February 1919.
60, Claremont Road, Luton.   3245/A.

GRIFFIN, N., Rifleman, 16th London Regiment (Queen's Westminster Rifles).

Mobilised at the commencement of hostilities, he was quickly drafted to France, and took part in the Battles of the Marne, La Bassée, Festubert and Ypres. He was killed in action at Poperinghe in October 1915. He was entitled to the 1914 Star, and the General Service and Victory Medals.
119, Estcourt Road, Watford.   X3275/B.

GRIFFIN, R. J., Private, Northamptonshire Regt.

Joining in August 1916, he was sent overseas immediately on completing his training. During his service in France he was engaged in the Battles of the Somme, Arras and Ypres, and was subsequently killed in action at Cambrai on September 9th, 1918. He was entitled to the General Service and Victory Medals.

45, Yarmouth Road, Callowland. X3279.

GRIFFIN, W., Driver, Royal Army Service Corps.

Volunteering in September 1915, he proceeded to the Western Front in the December following. He did valuable work as a transport driver until hostilities ceased, in many important sectors, chiefly those of Arras, Cambrai and Ypres, and in discharging these duties often under heavy fire, was on two occasions wounded. He holds the 1914-15 Star, and the General Service and Victory Medals, and was demobilised in February 1919.

24, Merton Road, Watford. 3256/A.

GRIFFIN, W. J., Sapper, Royal Engineers.

He joined in June 1916, and at the conclusion of his training was engaged on duties of an important nature with his unit. Although unable to secure his transfer to a theatre of war before the cessation of hostilities, he did valuable work at Portsmouth and other depôts until after the termination of hostilities, and was demobilised in February 1919.

24, Merton Road, Watford. X3254/B.

GRIFFITHS, C. D., Private, Royal Air Force and Hertfordshire Regiment.

He volunteered in September 1914, and at the conclusion of his training in the following year was sent to France. Whilst in this theatre of war he fought in many engagements, notably those at Arras, Ypres and Cambrai, and suffered from severe shell-shock. He holds the 1914-15 Star, and the General Service and Victory Medals, and was demobilised in 1919.

82, Holywell Road, Watford. X3259.

GRIFFITHS, F. E., Steward, Royal Navy.

He joined in 1917, and after his training was posted to H.M.S. "Boadicea," which vessel was engaged on special duties off the coast of Scotland and in various other waters. He holds the General Service and Victory Medals, and in 1920 was still serving.

82, Holywell Road, Watford. X3258/B.

GRIFFITHS, H. T., Aircraftsman, R.A.F.

He joined the Royal Fusiliers in March 1917, and was later transferred to the Royal Air Force. He saw much service on the Western Front, and was engaged at Abbeville on important duties which called for much technical knowledge and skill. He was demobilised after his return to England in January 1920, and holds the General Service and Victory Medals.

82, Holywell Road, Watford. X3258/A.

GRIFFITHS, L. D., A.B., Royal Navy, H.M.S. "Ganges."

He joined in July 1918, and after his training at Harwich, was engaged on important work in connection with submarine nets. He did much good work, but was discharged through causes due to his service in July 1919.

7, Meeting Alley, Watford. X3088/C.

GRIFFITHS, P. J., Private, 3rd Bedfordshire Regiment.

He volunteered in 1914, and during his training met with an accident in which he was badly injured. After being for some time in hospital he rejoined his unit, and was subsequently run over by a railway engine and killed at Batford Station.

42, Back Street, Biggleswade. Z3308.

GRIFFITHS, T. A., Rifleman, King's Royal Rifle Corps and Rifle Brigade.

He joined in January 1916, and after his training served at various depôts on important duties with his unit. He was unsuccessful in obtaining his transfer overseas before hostilities ceased, owing to ill-health, but rendered valuable services until his demobilisation in January 1919.

67, Edward Street, Dunstable. 3233.

GRIFFITHS, W. A., Private, 6th Royal Warwickshire Regiment.

Volunteering in June 1915, he was sent to France at the conclusion of his training. Whilst overseas he took an active part in several engagements, and after taking part in the fighting near Albert, was reported missing on August 18th, 1916. He was later presumed to have been killed in action on that date. He was entitled to the General Service and Victory Medals.

7, Meeting Alley, Watford. X3088/A.

GRIGG, L. B., Sergeant-Instructor, R.E.

Having previously served with the Territorials, he was mobilised at the outbreak of war. Owing to physical weakness he was not drafted overseas, but he did valuable work during the period of hostilities as an Instructor of physical training and bayonet fighting. He was discharged in October 1918.

1, Spencer Road, Luton. 3249.

GRIMSDALE, G. B., Private, R.M.L.I.

Volunteering in September 1914, he was sent to the Dardanelles in the following May. He took part in the severe fighting which ensued on the Peninsula, and lost his left hand owing to a serious wound. In October 1915 he returned to England, and after protracted hospital treatment was invalided out of the Service in February 1917. He holds the 1914-15 Star, and the General Service and Victory Medals.

71, Cowper Street, Luton. 3260/A.

GRIMSDALE, S. G., A.B., 63rd Royal Naval Division.

Volunteering in November 1915, he was drafted to France in the following August on the conclusion of his training. After taking part in several important engagements, he was reported missing on April 23rd, 1917, and was later presumed to have been killed in action on that date. He was entitled to the General Service and Victory Medals.

71, Cowper Street, Luton. 3260/B.

GRINDROD, W., Gunner, R.F.A.

Volunteering in January 1915, he was sent to the Western Front in the following July, and was subsequently engaged in the fighting at Loos, Vimy Ridge, the Somme and Arras. In 1917 he returned to England suffering from tuberculosis, and after protracted treatment at Cambridge, was invalided out of the service in February 1919. He holds the 1914-15 Star, and the General Service and Victory Medals.

Trowley Bottom, Flamstead. X3305.

GRISTWOOD, J., Sergeant, 2nd Highland L.I.

A serving soldier, he was drafted to the Western Front after the outbreak of hostilities, and took part in many important engagements, including those near Ypres and Beaumont-Hamel. He was killed in action on November 13th, 1916, and was buried in the British cemetery, Beaumont-Hamel. He was entitled to the General Service and Victory Medals.

37, Leavesden Road, Watford. X3264/B—X3265/B.

GRIVES, A. W., Private, R.A.S.C.

Volunteering in April 1915, he was sent to the Western Front in January 1916, after having been engaged on special duties at his depôt. Throughout his overseas service, which lasted over three years, he did valuable work with his unit in many important sectors, chiefly on the Somme, at Arras, Ypres and Cambrai, and frequently carried out his duties under fire. He holds the General Service and Victory Medals, and was demobilised after his return to England in June 1919.

173, Sandringham Road, Watford. X3253.

GRIVES, W. S., Sergeant-Major, R.A.S.C. (M.T.)

He volunteered in August 1914, and three weeks later was sent to the Western Front, where he did valuable service in the Retreat from Mons and the Battles of Ypres, the Somme, Arras and Cambrai. In February 1915, he was wounded, but after treatment was able to rejoin his unit and remained in France until June 1919. He was demobilised in the following December, and holds the Mons Star, and the General Service and Victory Medals.

173, Sandringham Road, Watford. X3266.

GROOM, A., Sergeant-Instructor, 5th Bedfordshire Regiment.

An ex-soldier, with a previous record of 12 years' service with the Colours, he volunteered in September 1914. Throughout the war he served at various stations as an Instuctor of musketry, and although unable to secure his transfer overseas, did most valuable work until February 1919, when he was demobilised. 48, Highbury Road, Luton. 3317.

GROOM, E. W. T., Private, 2nd Bedfordshire Regiment.

He joined in January 1916, and was drafted to the Western Front in the following May. Two months later, on July 11th, 1916, he was reported missing after an engagement at Trônes Wood, and is believed to have been killed in action on that date. He was entitled to the General Service and Victory Medals.

61, Marsh Road, Leagrave. 3282.

GROOM, F., Bandsman, 15th Welch Regiment.

Joining in October 1916, he was sent to the Western Front in the following January, after the completion of his training. His service overseas lasted for two years, during which time he was present at many important engagements, including those at Arras, Ypres (where he was wounded), Cambrai, the Somme and Armentières. He was demobilised after his return to England in March 1919, and holds the General Service and Victory Medals.

7, George Street, Leighton Buzzard. 3310.

GROOM, F., Private, 4th Suffolk Regiment.

He joined in August 1916, and after his training was drafted to the Western Front, where he served for three years. During this time he fought in several engagements, including those at Ypres and Cambrai, and did valuable work until hostilities ceased. He was demobilised after his return to England in 1919, and holds the General Service and Victory Medals.

7, Union Street, Hemel Hempstead.   X3239.

GROOM, F. S., Private, R.A.S.C.

He joined in April 1917, and in the following month was drafted to France. Whilst in this theatre of war he served on important transport and supply duties to the lines, and was present at Arras, Cambrai, the Somme and in many subsequent engagements until the conclusion of the war. He was demobilised after his return home in November 1919, and holds the General Service and Victory Medals.

18, George Street, Markyate.   3240/A.

GROOM, G., Private, Bedfordshire Regiment.

Volunteering at the outbreak of war he was soon drafted to France, and took part in many important engagements, including that at Ypres. During his service he was wounded and suffered from severe shell-shock. He was discharged as unfit for further military duty in July 1915, and died from the effects of shell-shock on November 24th, 1919. He was entitled to the 1914-15 Star, and the General Service and Victory Medals.

9, Cherry Bounce, Hemel Hempstead.   X3315/B.

GROOM, J., Private, Royal Sussex Regiment.

He joined in March 1916, and in the same year was drafted to France, where he fought in numerous important battles, including those on the Somme, at Arras, Ypres and Cambrai. He served also throughout the Retreat and Advance of 1918, and was demobilised in the following year. He holds the General Service and Victory Medals.

9, Cherry Bounce, Hemel Hempstead.   X3315/A.

GROOM, J. A., Air Mechanic, Royal Air Force.

He joined in 1917, and after his training served at various stations on important duties which demanded considerable technical skill. He rendered valuable services, but was not successful in obtaining his transfer overseas before the cessation of hostilities, and was demobilised in March 1919.

123, Lower Paddock Road, Oxhey.   X3236/B.

GROOM, S. W., Private, Duke of Cornwall's L.I.

He joined in April 1917, and in the following March was drafted overseas. During his service in France he fought in numerous important engagements in the Retreat and Advance of 1918, including those at Cambrai and Ypres. He was demobilised after his return to England in September 1919, and holds the General Service and Victory Medals.

24, Inkerman Road, St. Albans.   X3268.

GROOM, T., Driver, Royal Engineers.

He volunteered in April 1915, and after being retained on important duties, was in April 1917 drafted to France. During his service on the Western Front he was engaged on special work in connection with the operations, and served at Cambrai, the Somme and St. Quentin. He was demobilised in June 1919 after his return to England, and holds the General Service and Victory Medals.

39, Essex Street, Luton.   3244/A.

GROOM T. A., 1st Air Mechanic, R.A.F.

He joined in June 1917, and after his training was finished was engaged at the Plymouth air station on important duties in connection with the fitting and testing of aeroplanes. He did skilled work, but was unable to secure his transfer abroad before the cessation of hostilities. He was demobilised in February 1919.

123, Lower Paddock Road, Oxhey.   X3236/A.

GROOM, V., Private, East Surrey Regiment.

He joined in January 1917, and in the following June was drafted to France, where he took part in the fighting at Ypres and the Somme, and was wounded. After his recovery he served in subsequent engagements until the cessation of hostilities. After the Armistice was signed he advanced into Germany with the Army of Occupation, and remained there until October 1919, when he returned home and was demobilised. He holds the General Service and Victory Medals.

39, Essex Street, Luton.   3244/B.

GROOM, W., Private, 2nd Queen's (Royal West Surrey Regiment).

He joined in June 1916, and after his training was retained at various stations on important duties with his unit. In December 1918 he proceeded to Germany with the Army of Occupation, and did valuable work at Cologne for a year. He returned home and was demobilised in December 1919, holding the General Service and Victory Medals.

22, Queen's Square, Luton.   3243.

GROOM, W. G., Air Mechanic, Royal Air Force.

He joined in December 1917, and after his training was retained on important duties which demanded a high degree of technical skill. He was chiefly engaged as a fitter and tester in the aeroplane shops at Farnborough and Blandford, and did excellent work, but was not able to secure his transfer to a fighting front before the war ceased. He was demobilised in February 1919.

16, George Street, Markyate.   3241.

GROOM, W. H., Private, 5th Bedfordshire Regt.

He joined in October 1918, and during his training served at various stations on important duties with his unit. He was rejected for overseas service on medical grounds, and was demobilised in February 1919.

18, George Street, Markyate.   3240/B.

GROVER, F., Private, R.A.S.C.

He volunteered in May 1915, and in the same year was sent to France, where he served for nearly four years. He was engaged on important duties in connection with the transport of supplies to the troops, and was present at Ypres, the Somme, Cambrai and St. Quentin, and in the engagements which followed until the cessation of hostilities. He was demobilised after his return home in April 1919, and holds the 1914-15 Star, and the General Service and Victory Medals.

119, Judge Street, Watford.   X3252.

GROVER, G. E. V., Corporal, R.A.F.

He volunteered in August 1914, and after his training in the Bedfordshire Regiment served at several depôts on important duties. Later he was transferred to the Royal Air Force, and was retained at a training school, where he gave instruction in acetylene welding. He was medically unfit for trench warfare, but rendered valuable services until his demobilisation in February 1919.

21, Church Street, Leighton Buzzard.   3328.

GROVES, A., Driver, R.A.S.C.

Volunteering in August 1914, he saw much varied service. He was first drafted to France, where he was engaged on important transport duties with his unit until 1915, when he was sent to Salonika, and served there for two years. In 1917 he proceeded to Palestine, and was present at all the engagements until the campaign ended. He was still serving in 1920, and holds the 1914 Star, and the General Service and Victory Medals.

6, Ashwell Street, Leighton Buzzard.   3309/B.

GROVES, F., Private, Middlesex Regiment.

He volunteered in 1915, and in the same year was drafted to France. While there he took part in many important engagements during his three years' service overseas, and was killed in action in September 1918. He was entitled to the 1914-15 Star, and the General Service and Victory Medals.

6, Ashwell Street, Leighton Buzzard.   3309/A.

GROVES, R. J., 1st Air Mechanic, R.A.F.

He joined in June 1916, and in the same year was drafted to France, where he was engaged at Etaples and Berck Plage air-stations on important duties which demanded a high degree of technical skill. He rendered valuable services there for three years, and was demobilised in May 1919, holding the General Service and Victory Medals.

8, Brightwell Road, Watford.   X3263.

GRUBB, H., L/Corporal, Gloucestershire Regt.

After much valuable recruiting work all over the country he joined in 1917, and was subsequently retained for important munition duties in a factory at Hitchin, where he did excellent service until his demobilisation in December 1919.

Tilehouse Street, Hitchin.   3290.

GRUMMITT, A. E., Private, Bedfordshire and Suffolk Regiments.

Volunteering in September 1914, he was sent to France shortly afterwards. He took part in the severe fighting at Loos, the Somme, Arras, Ypres and Cambrai, and was wounded. After the Armistice he proceeded to Germany with the Army of Occupation. He was demobilised in 1920, and holds the 1914 Star, and the General Service and Victory Medals.

New Town, Biggleswade.   Z3306.

GRUMMITT, F. C., Private, 7th Bedfordshire Regiment.

Joining in January 1918, he was drafted to the Western Front in June of the same year. He took part in much severe fighting in the Allied Retreat, and was killed by shell-fire on July 18th, 1918. He was entitled to the General Service and Victory Medals.

7, St. John's Street, Biggleswade.   Z3298.

GRUMMITT, H., Private, 3rd Bedfordshire Regt.
He volunteered in 1915, and proceeded to France in the following year after the completion of his training. He took part in many important engagements, including those of the Somme and Arras, and was killed in action on the Arras front on May 23rd, 1917. He was entitled to the General Service and Victory Medals.
Sun Street, Biggleswade. Z3307/B.

GRUMMITT, M., Private, Royal Sussex Regt.
Joining in May 1917, he was drafted to France in the same year. He took part in the severe fighting at Arras and the Somme, and was badly wounded in the Advance in August 1918. After being invalided home he was discharged in 1919 as medically unfit for further service. He holds the General Service and Victory Medals.
Sun Street, Biggleswade. Z3307/C.

GRUMMITT, R., Pte., 5th Lancashire Fusiliers.
He joined in 1916, and in the same year proceeded to the Western Front, where he took part in numerous engagements, including those of the Somme, Arras and Cambrai. Being severely wounded he was invalided home, and had a leg amputated. He was discharged owing to his injuries in 1919, and holds the General Service and Victory Medals.
Sun Street, Biggleswade. Z3307/A.

GRUMMITT, R., Private, Bedfordshire and Loyal North Lancashire Regiments.
He volunteered in 1915, and was retained on important duties until 1917, when he was drafted to the Western Front. While there he took part in much severe fighting in the Arras and Ypres sectors, and was wounded near Dickebusch. After considerable hospital treatment he was demobilised in February 1919, and holds the General Service and Victory Medals.
19, Chapel Fields, Biggleswade. Z3299.

GUDGEON, E., Sergeant, Royal Engineers.
He joined in June 1916, and was afterwards drafted to German East Africa, where he was engaged on important work in connection with bridge-building and field works. He carried out his duties, which were of a responsible nature, with great efficiency, and rendered valuable services. He was demobilised in March 1919, after his return to England, and holds the General Service and Victory Medals.
26, Oswald Road, St. Albans. X3357.

GUDGEON, H., Private, Labour Corps.
Joining in June 1916, he proceeded to France in the following year. He was engaged in many sectors, including Messines, Ypres, Passchendaele, Cambrai and the Somme on the up-keep of roads and trenches, and rendered valuable services. He was demobilised in January 1919, and holds the General Service and Victory Medals.
34, Alma Street, Luton. 3346.

GUDGIN, A. E., Drummer, 5th Bedfordshire Regt.
He joined in September 1917, and after his training served at various stations on important duties with his unit. He rendered valuable services, but was not successful in obtaining his transfer overseas before the cessation of hostilities. He was demobilised in February 1919.
4, Salisbury Road, Luton. 3349/A—3348/A.

GUDGIN, G., Private, 4th South Wales Borderers.
Joining in March 1916, he was drafted to Mesopotamia in June of the same year. He took part in numerous engagements until the cessation of hostilities, including those at Kut and Baghdad, and was wounded. He returned home and was demobilised in April 1919, and holds the General Service and Victory Medals.
The Strand, Clophill, Ampthill. 3343.

GUDGIN, H. G., Private, 19th Middlesex Regt.
He joined in October 1917, and in February of the following year was drafted to the Western Front, where he took part in the Retreat and Advance of that year. After the Armistice he proceeded with the Army of Occupation to Germany, and did good service at Cologne. He was demobilised in February 1920, after returning home, and holds the General Service and Victory Medals.
4, Salisbury Road, Luton. 3348/B—3349/B.

GUDGIN, P. H., Private, King's Own (Royal Lancaster Regiment) and Labour Corps.
He joined in June 1916, and was drafted to Salonika in November of the same year. He served in the Advance on the Doiran front and also at Vardar, and throughout rendered valuable services. During his period of service in this theatre of war he was wounded. He was demobilised in April 1919, and holds the General Service and Victory Medals.
Little Lane, Clophill, Ampthill. 3368.

GUESS, A. G., Private, R.A.M.C.
He joined in June 1916, and in October of the same year was drafted to France, where he did valuable service in many engagements, including those at Arras, Ypres and Cambrai, and was wounded. In January 1918 he was transferred to Salonika, where he served until hostilities ceased. He was demobilised in November 1919 after his return to England, and holds the General Service and Victory Medals.
Westoning Road, Harlington. 3342.

GUESS, G., Private, South Wales Borderers; and Sapper, Royal Engineers.
Joining in April 1916 in the South Wales Borderers, he was later transferred to the Royal Engineers. He was drafted to Mesopotamia in September 1916, and was engaged on the Amara and Kut fronts on important bridge and trench duties with his branch of the Service. He afterwards served in India, and was demobilised in April 1920 after returning home. He holds the General Service and Victory Medals.
18, Back Lane, Leighton Buzzard. 3338/A.

GUESS, G. A., Private, Essex Regiment and Royal Army Medical Corps.
He volunteered in April 1915, and in the same year was drafted to the Western Front, where he did valuable work at Arras and Ypres, and was wounded. He afterwards proceeded to Salonika and thence to Russia. He was demobilised in December 1919 after returning home, and holds the 1914-15 Star, and the General Service and Victory Medals.
Mill Lane, Greenfield, near Ampthill. 3361.

GUESS, T., Private, Northamptonshire Regiment.
Volunteering in May 1915, he proceeded to Egypt in November of the same year. He did good service afterwards in Palestine, where he took part in various engagements, including those at Gaza. In 1917 he was transferred to Salonika, and was in action on the Vardar front. He was demobilised in April 1919 after returning to England, and holds the 1914-15 Star, and the General Service and Victory Medals.
18, Back Lane, Leighton Buzzard. 3338/B.

GUESS, T., Corporal, 5th Bedfordshire Regiment.
He was mobilised in August 1914, and was afterwards drafted to Gallipoli, where he took part in the severe fighting at Anzac and in the landing at Suvla Bay. He returned home and was discharged in 1917 in consequence of his service, holding the 1914-15 Star, and the General Service and Victory Medals.
73, Ash Road, Luton. 3332.

GUESS, W. (M.M.), L/Corporal 2nd Bedfordshire Regiment.
Volunteering in September 1914, he went through his course of training and was drafted to France in August 1915. While there he took part in engagements in the Loos and Ypres sectors, and was wounded. In February 1917 he was transferred to India, where he was engaged on important garrison duties and acted as sergeant for nearly six months. He was awarded the Military Medal for his great gallantry in action in December 1915, and also holds the 1914-15 Star, and the General Service and Victory Medals. After his return home he was demobilised in November 1919.
82, St. Andrew's Street, Leighton Buzzard. 3339.

GUIVER, R., Gunner, Royal Garrison Artillery.
He volunteered in August 1914, and in the same year was drafted to the Western Front, where he took part in numerous engagements until hostilities ceased, including those of the Marne, Festubert, Loos, the Somme, Arras, Ypres and Cambrai, and was wounded. He also served in the Retreat and Advance of 1918. He was demobilised in 1919, and holds the 1914-15 Star, and the General Service and Victory Medals.
72, Ridge Avenue, Letchworth. 3334.

GUNDRY, H. C., Warrant Officer, R.N., H.M.S. " Vernon."
He was serving at the outbreak of war. As chief torpedo-instructor he did excellent work, and was also engaged in mine-laying off the Scottish coast and in other waters. He rendered valuable services throughout until demobilised in August 1919, and holds the General Service and Victory Medals.
64, Grove Road, Hitchin. 3366.

GUNN, H., Private, 2nd Bedfordshire Regiment.
He volunteered in August 1914, and in the same year was drafted to France. He took part in the severe fighting at Ypres, the Somme, Arras, Cambrai and many later engagements, and on one occasion was buried through a shell explosion. He was demobilised in March 1919 after his return home, and holds the 1914 Star, and the General Service and Victory Medals.
118, Harwood Road, Watford. X3362.

GUNN, J., Private, Queen's (Royal West Surrey Regiment).
Joining in March 1917, he went through a course of training and was afterwards drafted to the Western Front. He was principally engaged on railway constructional work on the Messines front, and carried out his duties in an efficient manner. He returned home suffering from shell-shock, and was discharged as medically unfit for further service in October 1918. He holds the General Service and Victory Medals.
33, Longmire Road, St. Albans. X3358.

GUNN, R. S., Sapper, Royal Engineers.
Volunteering in February 1915, he was retained after his training on important duties with his unit until February 1917, when he was drafted to Egypt. In the subsequent Palestine campaign he took part in numerous engagements, including those at El Arish, Gaza, Jaffa, Mejdil, Haifa, Damascus and Aleppo. He was demobilised in February 1919, and holds the General Service and Victory Medals.
27, New Street, Luton. 3341.

GUNNING, S. T., L/Corporal, Leicestershire Regt.
Volunteering in September 1915, he went through a course of training, and afterwards served at various stations on important duties with his unit. He rendered valuable services, but owing to medical unfitness was not successful in obtaining his transfer overseas while hostilities continued. He was discharged in April 1917.
Cranham, Luton Road, Harpenden. 3340.

GURDLER, A., Corporal, Prince of Wales' Leinster Regiment.
He volunteered in August 1914, and in the same year proceeded to the Western Front. He took part in severe fighting at the Marne, the Aisne, Ypres, Hill 60, the Somme, Passchendaele, Cambrai and St. Quentin, and was killed in action on March 22nd, 1918. He was entitled to the 1914 Star, and the General Service and Victory Medals.
107, Norfolk Road, Rickmansworth. X3335/B.

GURDLER, H., Private, Tank Corps.
Joining in 1916, he was drafted to France in the same year on the completion of his training. During his service overseas he was engaged as a gunner on Tanks and took part in numerous engagements with the 8th Division. He contracted an illness from which he died on November 11th, 1918, and was entitled to the General Service and Victory Medals.
107, Norfolk Road, Rickmansworth. X3335/C.

GURDLER, W., Private, 2nd Bedfordshire Regt.
He was serving at the outbreak of war, and was immediately sent to the Western Front. He took part in the severe fighting during the Retreat from Mons and at the Battles of Ypres, Hill 60, Givenchy, Vimy Ridge, the Somme, Arras and Cambrai, and was wounded. He was reported missing, and was believed to have been killed in action on March 28th, 1918. He was entitled to the Mons Star, and the General Service and Victory Medals.
107, Norfolk Road, Rickmansworth. X3335/A.

GURNEY, A., Private, 10th Hampshire Regt.
Volunteering in June 1915, he was drafted in October of the same year to Salonika, where he served until May 1919. During his stay in this theatre of war he took part in various engagements and did much valuable service. He returned home and was demobilised in May 1919, and holds the 1914-15 Star, and the General Service and Victory Medals.
Old Farm Cottage, Park Street, near St. Albans. X3336/B.

GURNEY, A., Private, Bedfordshire Regiment.
He was serving at the outbreak of war, and was immediately afterwards sent to France. He took part in many important engagements, including those of Mons, Ypres, Neuve Chapelle, Hill 60 and the Somme, and was wounded. He returned home, and was discharged owing to his injuries in February 1917, and holds the Mons Star, and the General Service and Victory Medals.
11, Butcher's Yard, Watford. X3363/B.

GURNEY, A., Private, King's Shropshire L.I.
He joined in July 1916, and proceeded to France in August of the same year. He took part in the severe fighting on the Somme in 1916, and in June 1917 was invalided home with trench fever. He was discharged as medically unfit for further service in October 1918, and holds the General Service and Victory Medals.
50, Union Street, Dunstable. 3345.

GURNEY, A. F., Private, R.A.S.C.
He volunteered in December 1914, and after his training was drafted to the Western Front. He was engaged on the transport of ammunition and supplies to the various fronts, and rendered valuable services until the close of the war. He returned home and was demobilised in January 1919, and holds the General Service and Victory Medals.
College Cottage, Leavesden Green, Watford. X3359/B.

GURNEY, A. H., Corporal, Dorsetshire Regt.
He volunteered in April 1915, and after his training was drafted to Salonika. After valuable service there he was transferred to the Western Front, where he took part in the severe fighting at Cambrai and Albert, and was wounded. He was demobilised in January 1919, and holds the General Service and Victory Medals.
College Cottage, Leavesden Green, Watford. X3359/A.

GURNEY, A. R., Private, Grenadier Guards.
He joined in April 1917, and after his training was retained on important duties with his unit. He rendered valuable services, but owing to physical disability was not successful in obtaining his transfer overseas before the cessation of hostilities. He was demobilised in November 1919.
78, Hitchin Road, Luton. 3337.

GURNEY, B. J., Private, Queen's (Royal West Surrey Regiment).
Joining in August 1917, he was drafted to the Western Front in June of the following year. He took part in various engagements in the final operations of the war, including those on the Marne and at Amiens, Bapaume, the Somme and Cambrai, and was wounded. He was demobilised in October 1919 after returning home, and holds the General Service and Victory Medals.
96, Ash Road, Luton. 3347/C.

GURNEY, E., Private, Machine Gun Corps.
Joining in February 1916, he was sent to France in the following July. He took part in much severe fighting in the Somme Offensive and at Ypres, Cambrai and many other important engagements. During his service he was wounded and gassed near Cambrai. He was demobilised in January 1919, and holds the General Service and Victory Medals.
Green Farm, Tilsworth. 3333/B.

GURNEY, E., Corporal, 8th Bedfordshire Regt.
He volunteered in September 1914, and in August of the following year was drafted to the Western Front, where he took part in numerous engagements almost until hostilities ceased, including those at Loos, the Somme, Ypres and Cambrai. He was demobilised in February 1919, and holds the 1914-15 Star, and the General Service and Victory Medals.
61, Park Street, St. Albans. X3356.

GURNEY, E. C., Private, 12th Suffolk Regiment.
Joining in June 1916, he was soon drafted to France. He took part in the severe fighting at the Somme, Arras and Passchendaele, and was killed in action at Cambrai. He was entitled to the General Service and Victory Medals.
34, North Common, Redbourn. 1357/B.

GURNEY, F., Private, 7th Bedfordshire Regt.
He volunteered in October 1914, and in July of the following year was drafted to the Western Front. He took an active part in various engagements, including those at Ypres, Loos and Vimy Ridge, and was killed in action on the Somme on July 5th, 1916. He was entitled to the 1914-15 Star, and the General Service and Victory Medals.
Old Farm Cottage, Park Street, near St. Albans. X3336/C.

GURNEY, F., L/Corporal, 4th Bedfordshire Regt.
Volunteering in September 1914, he proceeded to France in February of the following year. He took part in the severe fighting at Loos, the Somme, Arras and Passchendaele, and also did good service in the Retreat and Advance of 1918. He was gassed on the Somme. He was demobilised in February 1919, after returning home, and holds the 1914-15 Star, and the General Service and Victory Medals.
Green Farm, Tilsworth. 3333/A.

GURNEY, F. G., Rifleman, Cameronians (Scottish Rifles).
He joined in June 1917, and after his training was engaged on important duties with his unit. He rendered valuable services, but on medical grounds was not successful in obtaining his transfer overseas. He was discharged as unfit for further service in August 1918.
96, Ash Road, Luton. 3347/B.

GURNEY, G. (M.M.), Sergeant, 2nd Bedfordshire Regiment.
He was serving in South Africa at the outbreak of war and shortly afterwards reached France. He took part in the Retreat from Mons and many important engagements up to the last year of the war, when he was killed in action on March 22nd, 1918. He was awarded the Military Medal for conspicuous bravery in the Field, and was also entitled to the Mons Star, and the General Service and Victory Medals.
Mill Lane, Biggleswade. Z3364.

GURNEY, G., Private, R.A.V.C.
Volunteering in 1914, he was drafted in the same year to Egypt and Palestine, where he did valuable work in many important engagements. He afterwards proceeded to Salonika and was engaged on important duties with his unit until the close of the war. He was demobilised in April 1919 after returning home, and holds the 1914–15 Star, and the General Service and Victory Medals.
18, Banbury Street, Watford. X3354.

GURNEY, J., Gunner, Royal Field Artillery.
He joined in November 1916, and after his training was drafted to the Western Front, where he took part in many engagements of importance until fighting ceased, including those at Ypres and Cambrai. He returned home and was demobilised in March 1919, and holds the General Service and Victory Medals.
2, Escort Road, Watford. X3353.

GURNEY, J. T., Private, Bedfordshire Regiment.
Mobilised in August 1914, he was sent immediately afterwards to the Western Front, where he took part in the severe fighting in the Retreat from Mons and at Ypres, Hill 60, Arras and Cambrai, and was wounded. He was demobilised in February 1919, after coming back to England, and holds the Mons Star, and the General Service and Victory Medals.
11, Butchers Yard, Watford. X3363/A.

GURNEY, P. J., Private, Bedfordshire Lancers.
He was mobilised in August 1914, and in June of the following year was drafted to the Western Front, where he took part in numerous engagements of importance, including those at Vimy Ridge, the Somme, Ypres, Arras and Cambrai, and was wounded. After the Armistice he served in Germany with the Army of Occupation. He was demobilised in March 1919, and holds the 1914–15 Star and the General Service and Victory Medals.
96, Ash Road, Luton. 3347/A.

GURNEY, S. J., Quartermaster-Sergt., R.F.A.
He joined in June 1915, and in the following March was drafted to the Western Front, where he took a prominent part in numerous important engagements until hostilities ceased, including those at the Somme, Ypres, Passchendaele Ridge and Cambrai. He was demobilised in July 1919, after his return home, and holds the General Service and Victory Medals.
69, Portland Street, St. Albans. 3355.

GUTTERIDGE, C., Private, Manchester Regt.
He volunteered in August 1915, and in the following February was sent to India, where he was engaged on important garrison duties with his unit at Delhi, Rawal Pindi and Poona. In 1918 he was transferred to Hong Kong. After much valuable service there he returned home and was demobilised in June 1919, holding the General Service and Victory Medals.
26, Milton Road, Luton. 3350.

GUTTERIDGE, F., Private, M.G.C.
Volunteering in October 1915, he was drafted to France in the following year. He took part in much severe fighting in many engagements of importance, including those at St. Quentin, where he was killed in action on March 21st, 1918. He was entitled to the General Service and Victory Medals.
Hexton Road, Barton, near Ampthill. 3344.

GUTTERIDGE, F. J., Private, Duke of Cornwall's Light Infantry.
He joined in January 1917, and after his training was retained at various stations on important duties with his unit. He rendered valuable services, but was not successful in obtaining his transfer overseas before the cessation of hostilities. He was demobilised in January 1919.
Howard House, Marsh Road, Leagrave. 3351.

GUTTERIDGE, H., Private, 2nd Suffolk Regt.
He enlisted in 1903, and in August 1914, was drafted to France, where he took part in the Retreat from Mons, and in the Battles of the Marne, Givenchy, Ypres, Loos, the Somme, Cambrai, Albert and Amiens. He was wounded at the Somme in 1916 and invalided home, but on his recovery he returned to France and was again in action. He was demobilised in April 1919, and holds the Mons Star, and the General Service and Victory Medals.
Garden Cottage, Rear 40, Old Park Road, Hitchin. 3367.

GUTTERIDGE, H. D., Private, Royal Fusiliers.
Joining in April 1916, he was drafted to France in September of the same year. He took part in several engagements and was wounded at Beaumont-Hamel. He was reported wounded and missing on February 5th, 1917, and is presumed to have been killed in action on that date. He was entitled to the General Service and Victory Medals.
8, Holly Walk, Luton. 3360.

GUTTERIDGE, W., L/Cpl., Bedfordshire Regt.
He volunteered in August 1914, and proceeded to France in July of the following year. He took part in much severe fighting in the Somme area until February 1916, when he returned home owing to illness, and was discharged in March as unfit for further military service. He holds the 1914–15 Star, and the General Service and Victory Medals.
Clipstone Cottages, High Street, Barton. 3352.

H

HACK, A., Sapper, Royal Engineers.
Volunteering at the outbreak of hostilities he was drafted to the Western Front in the following January. During his service in France he was engaged on important duties, such as wiring, trenching and road-making, and was frequently in the forward areas while hostilities continued. He was demobilised in January 1919, and holds the 1914–15 Star, and the General Service and Victory Medals.
19, Mill Road, Leighton Buzzard. 3369.

HACKERMAN, G., Private, Bedfordshire Regt.
He volunteered in November 1915, and after his training was retained at various depôts on important duties with his unit. He did good work during his service, but owing to illness he was discharged as medically unfit for further duty in August 1916.
Regent Street, Leighton Buzzard. 3370.

HACKMAN, E. F., Sergt., 6th Bedfordshire Regt.
Volunteering in August 1914, he was drafted to the Western Front in the following January. He took part in the Battle of the Somme, and was severely wounded in July 1916 and invalided home. On his recovery he returned to France, and in 1917 was again wounded near Ypres, and sent to hospital in England. Later he returned to the Front, and was gassed at the Battle of Amiens, after which he was engaged as an instructor until July 1919, when he was demobilised. He holds the 1914–15 Star, and the General Service and Victory Medals.
76, Brightwell Road, Watford. X3371/A.

HADDON, W. J., Private, 6th Bedfordshire Regt.
Volunteering in December 1914, he was drafted to the Western Front in the following May. Whilst in this theatre of war he served at Ypres and Festubert, and was wounded at Loos in September 1915. After his recovery he was in action at the Somme, Albert and Messines, where he was gassed. He was demobilised in March 1919 after his return to England, and holds the 1914–15 Star, and the General Service and Victory Medals.
23, Leighton Street, Woburn. Z3375.

HADDOW, A. G., L/Corporal, 1st Herts. Regt.
He volunteered at the outbreak of war, and after his training was drafted to Egypt. He afterwards took part in the Offensive in Palestine under General Allenby, and fought at Gaza, Haïfa and Beyrout, and in other important operations throughout the campaign. He was demobilised after his return to England in June 1919, and holds the General Service and Victory Medals.
43, Upper Heath Road, St. Albans. X3372/A.

HADDOW, B. B. A., Private, Northamptonshire Regiment.
He joined in October 1916, and in the following year was drafted to France after previously serving on important coast defence duties. During his service on the Western Front he fought at Ypres, Cambrai and the Somme, and in the engagements which followed until the cessation of hostilities. He was demobilised in October 1919, after three years' service with the Colours, and holds the General Service and Victory Medals.
88, Hitchin Street, Biggleswade. Z3373/A.

HADDOW, E. R., L/Corporal, Middlesex Regt.
He volunteered at the outbreak of war, and in the following year was drafted to the Western Front. During his service in France he was in action at Ypres, the Somme and Cambrai, and was wounded four times. He was killed in action near Arras on August 6th, 1918, and was entitled to the 1914–15 Star, and the General Service and Victory Medals.
43, Upper Heath Road, St. Albans. X3372/B.

HADDOW, P. J. (M.M.), Sapper, R.E.
He volunteered in February 1915, and in the same year was sent overseas. During his service in France he was frequently engaged in the front areas whilst operations were in progress, notably at Havrincourt, Ypres, the Somme and the Aisne. He was twice wounded in action, and in May 1918 was awarded the Military Medal for distinguished gallantry and devotion to duty on the Field. He holds in addition to the Military Medal the 1914–15 Star, and the General Service and Victory Medals, and was demobilised in March 1919.
3, College Place, St. Albans. 3374.

HADDOW, S., Private, Middlesex Regiment.
He joined in March 1916, and in the same year was drafted to France, where he was severely wounded in the following October at Givenchy. After some time in hospital he was again in action at Arras, Ypres, Cambrai and the Somme, and in subsequent engagements until the conclusion of hostilities. He was demobilised in August 1919, and holds the General Service and Victory Medals. •
88, Hitchin Street, Biggleswade.   Z3373/B.

HADFIELD, E., Private, Sherwood Foresters.
A serving soldier, he was for a time retained on important duties at various stations, and was later drafted to France. He there took part in the fighting at Arras, Ypres and St. Quentin, and in the engagements which followed in the Retreat and Advance of 1918, and was gassed during his service. He was demobilised in December 1919 after returning home, and holds the General Service and Victory Medals.
Luton Road, Harpenden.   3376.

HAGGER, G. D., Corporal, 8th Hampshire Regt.
He volunteered in August 1914, and in the following year was drafted to the Dardanelles. While fighting there he was severely wounded on August 12th, 1915, and was invalided to the military hospital at Cairo. After his recovery he took part in the Advance through Palestine, and was in action at Gaza and Haïfa, and was again wounded. He was demobilised after his return home in June 1919, and holds the 1914–15 Star, and the General Service and Victory Medals.
3, Dacre Road, Hitchin.   3377/A.

HAGGER, H. C., Private, Queen's Own (Royal West Kent Regiment).
He volunteered in June 1915, and was sent to the Western Front in the same year. After earlier operations in which he was once wounded he fought in the Battle of the Somme, and was reported missing after the engagement at Thiepval Wood on July 1st, 1916. He was later presumed to have been killed in action on that date, and was entitled to the 1914–15 Star, and the General Service and Victory Medals.
3, Dacre Road, Hitchin.   3377/B.

HAGGIE, G. G., Corporal, R.A.P.C. and R.G.A.
He joined in February 1917, and in August of the following year was drafted to France. Here he was engaged on important duties as a gunnery instructor, and rendered valuable services. He was discharged in October 1919 for causes due to his service, and holds the General Service and Victory Medals.
11, Newcombe Road, Luton.   3378.

HAILEY, C., Private, King's Own (Royal Lancaster Regiment).
He joined in June 1916, and in the following December was drafted to Salonika. Whilst in this theatre of war he saw much service in the engagements on the Struma, Doiran and Vardar fronts, and was wounded in action. He was demobilised after his return to England in February 1919, and holds the General Service and Victory Medals.
23, Portmill Lane, Hitchin.   3379.

HAILEY, H. J., Private, Royal Fusiliers and Labour Corps.
He joined in 1916, and in the same year was drafted to France. During his service on the Western Front, he did valuable work at the Somme, Arras, Cambrai and St. Quentin, and was present at the entry into Mons on Armistice Day, 1918. He was demobilised in the following January, and holds the General Service and Victory Medals.
4, Queen's Street, Hitchin.   3380.

HAINES, R., Private, Bedfordshire Regiment.
He joined in June 1916, and after his training served at various stations on important duties with his unit. He did much valuable work, but was unable to secure his transfer overseas before the cessation of hostilities, and was demobilised in April 1919.
126, Cravells Road, Harpenden.   3381.

HALE, G. G., Private, Royal Fusiliers.
He joined in July 1918, and after the completion of his training was engaged at various stations on important duties with his unit. Owing to ill-health he could not secure his transfer to a fighting front, and was discharged on medical grounds in March 1919.
32, Reginald Street, Luton.   3382.

HALE, J. G., Private, 1st Hertfordshire Regt.
He volunteered in 1915, and in the following year was drafted to France, where he was in action in many important battles. He fought at the Somme and Arras, where he was wounded, and after his recovery was in action at Cambrai, and in subsequent engagements in the Retreat and Advance of 1918. He was demobilised in the following February, and holds the General Service and Victory Medals.
46, Southern Street, Watford.   X3262/B.

HALE, O., Private, Middlesex Regiment.
He volunteered in July 1915, and after his training was engaged with his unit on important Military Police duties. He was unable to secure his transfer overseas, and was discharged as medically unfit for further duty in 1917. He then volunteered for munition work and rendered valuable services until after hostilities ceased.
2, Mullingar Terrace, London Colney, near St. Albans.
X3383.

HALE, P., Private, Bedfordshire Regiment.
He volunteered in September 1914, and in the following year was drafted overseas. During his service in France he fought at Ypres, the Somme and Arras, and was twice wounded. He also took part in many engagements throughout the Retreat and Advance of 1918. He holds the 1914–15 Star, and the General Service and Victory Medals, and was demobilised in March 1920.
Lower Luton Road, Batford, Harpenden.   3384.

HALES, E., Gunner, Royal Field Artillery.
Volunteering in October 1915, he was drafted to Egypt on the completion of his training and served in the Canal zone. Later he took part in the Palestine campaign and was in action at Gaza, Jaffa, Haïfa and Aleppo. Returning to England he was demobilised in July 1919, holding the General Service and Victory Medals.
9, New Kent Road, St. Albans.   X3385/B.

HALES, F. H., Sergeant, Middlesex Regiment.
He joined in October 1918, and proceeded to Germany with the Army of Occupation in the following month. He was stationed at Cologne, where he was engaged on important guard duties for a year, and was demobilised after his return home in November 1919.
21, Portland Road, Luton.   3386/B.

HALES, J., Corporal, Royal Army Service Corps.
He volunteered in November 1915, and in the following January was drafted to France. After only a short period of service he was severely wounded and suffered from shell-shock, and, being sent home, was invalided out of the Service in February 1916. He holds the General Service and Victory Medals.   21, Portland Road, Luton.   3386/A.

HALES, W., L/Corporal, Herts. Dragoons.
He volunteered in May 1915, and in the same year was drafted to Mesopotamia, where he took part in the campaign against the Turks. He was present at the capture of Baghdad and Mosul, and after the termination of hostilities returned to England and was demobilised in April 1919, holding the 1914–15 Star, and the General Service and Victory Medals.
9, New Kent Road, St. Albans.   X3385/A.

HALES, W., Sergeant, R.A.V.C.
He volunteered in October 1915, and in the following May was drafted to France. Whilst on the Western Front he was engaged, until the close of the war, on important veterinary duties, attending to sick and wounded horses. After the conclusion of hostilities he proceeded to Germany with the Army of Occupation, and was stationed at Cologne until May 1919. He was then demobilised after his return home, and holds the General Service and Victory Medals.
40, Union Street, Leighton Buzzard.   3387.

HALFORD, J., Driver, R.A.S.C. (M.T.)
He joined in 1919, and after his training was sent to Ireland, where he did much valuable service in various capacities with his unit at Belfast. He was demobilised in 1920.
8, Winson Cottages, Rickmansworth.   X3388/A.

HALFPENNY, A. (M.M.), Private, 5th Bedfordshire Regiment.
He volunteered at the outbreak of war, and in the following July was sent to Gallipoli, where he took part in the operations at Suvla Bay and Chocolate Hill, and in the subsequent operations until the Evacuation of the Peninsula. He then proceeded to Egypt and did much good work in the Canal zone and the Sinai Peninsula until 1917, when he proceeded to Palestine. In this theatre of war he fought at Gaza, Haïfa, Acre, and Beyrout, and in all the engagements of the campaign. During his service overseas he was wounded, and was awarded the Military Medal in July 1917 for conspicuous bravery in the Field in signalling under heavy fire. He holds, in addition to the Military Medal, the 1914–15 Star, and the General Service and Victory Medals, and was demobilised after his return to England in June 1919.
29, York Street, Luton.   3389/A.

HALFPENNY, A. C., Driver, R.F.A.
He volunteered in May 1915, and after being retained on important duties at various stations was drafted to France in February 1917. During his service on the Western Front he was engaged in the Battles of Arras, Ypres and the Somme, and in later operations in the Retreat and Advance of 1918. He was demobilised in July of the following year after his return to England, and holds the General Service and Victory Medals.   19, Back Street, Luton.   3390/B.

HALFPENNY, C., Private, Bedfordshire Regt.
Volunteering in August 1914, he was drafted to Gallipoli in the succeeding year, and took part in the engagements at Suvla Bay and Chocolate Hill, where he was wounded. In July 1916 he was sent to the Western Front, where after serving at the Somme, Arras and Ypres, he was killed in the heavy fighting at Passchendaele in August 1917. He was entitled to the 1914-15 Star, and the General Service and Victory Medals.
29, York Street, Luton. 3389/C.

HALFPENNY, G., Driver, R.F.A.
He volunteered in April 1915, and in August 1916 was drafted to France. Whilst in this theatre of war he did good work as a driver for his Battery in the Battles of the Somme, Arras, Ypres and Cambrai. After the Armistice was signed he proceeded to Germany with the Army of Occupation, and was stationed at Cologne until June 1919, when he was demobilised after his return home. He holds the General Service and Victory Medals.
29, York Street, Luton. 3389/B.

HALFPENNY, H. C., Bombardier, R.F.A.
He volunteered at the outbreak of war, and on the completion of his training served at various stations on important duties until September 1916, when he was sent to Mesopotamia. Whilst in this theatre of war he was in action at Kut and at the capture of Baghdad, and in many subsequent engagements until the cessation of hostilities. He afterwards saw service in Afghanistan. He was demobilised in October 1919 after his return to England, and holds the General Service and Victory Medals.
10, Dumfries Street, Luton. 3391.

HALFPENNY, P., Private, 6th Northamptonshire Regiment.
He joined in December 1917, and in the following April was drafted to France. During his service on the Western Front he fought at Villers-Bretonneux, the Somme and Cambrai, and was severely wounded at Combles on August 31st, 1918. He was demobilised in November 1919 after returning to England, and holds the General Service and Victory Medals.
19, Back Street, Luton. 3390/A.

HALL, A., Private, 10th Bedfordshire Regiment.
He joined in October 1916, and in the same year was drafted to France. Whilst in this theatre of war he took part in the Battles of the Somme, Ypres and Cambrai, and was also engaged on important duties at general headquarters. He was demobilised in June 1919, and holds the General Service and Victory Medals.
88, High Street, Markyate. 3392.

HALL, A. C. (M.S.M.), Pte., R.A.S.C. (M.T.)
He joined in May 1917, and in the same year was sent to France, where he was engaged on important transport duties, conveying rations and supplies up to the front lines. He was present at the Battles of Ypres, Cambrai and the Somme, and was awarded the Meritorious Service Medal for his consistently good work. He holds, in addition to the Meritorious Service Medal, the General Service and Victory Medals, and was demobilised in March 1919.
Flamstead, near Dunstable. X3394.

HALL, A. E., Sergeant, 1st Hertfordshire Regt.
He was mobilised in 1914, and in the same year was drafted to France, where he fought in the Battles of Ypres, and in many subsequent engagements up to the close of the war, including those at Arras and Cambrai. He was demobilised in April 1919, after nearly five years' service overseas, and holds the 1914 Star, and the General Service and Victory Medals.
35, Carey Place, Watford. 3393.

HALL, C., Private, 5th Wiltshire Regiment.
He volunteered at the outbreak of war, and in the same year was drafted to France. During his service on the Western Front he fought in the Battle of Ypres, and was wounded. Later he was reported missing after an engagement in 1915, and was afterwards presumed to have been killed in action at that time. He was entitled to the 1914-15 Star, and the General Service and Victory Medals.
30, York Street, Watford. X3395/A.

HALL, C. C., Private, 27th Lincolnshire Regt.
He joined in February 1917, and later in the same year was drafted to the Western Front, where he took part in several engagements, and was twice wounded in action. On October 17th, 1918, he was killed in the fighting at Ramicourt in the Advance of the Allies. He was entitled to the General Service and Victory Medals.
Southill, Beds. 3396/B.

HALL, C. W., Private, 9th Norfolk Regiment.
He joined in January 1917, and after completing his course of training was sent to France in the following June. He took part in the Battles of Messines, Ypres, and the second Battle of the Somme, and was killed in action near Cambrai on March 21st, 1918. He was entitled to the General Service and Victory Medals.
7, Bolton Road, Luton. 3397/A.

HALL, E. G., Private, Grenadier Guards.
He volunteered at the commencement of hostilities, and after finishing his training was drafted to the Western Front. During his service he was wounded on January 2nd, 1916, and was sent to hospital, but after returning to the lines at his own request before he was fully recovered, he was killed in action two days later on January 4th. He was entitled to the 1914-15 Star, and the General Service and Victory Medals. Southill, Beds. Z3396/A.

HALL, E. H., Rifleman, 1st K.R.R.C.
Volunteering at the outbreak of war he was drafted to the Western Front in November 1914. He took part in the first Battle of Ypres, and was killed in action at Neuve Chapelle on March 10th, 1915. He was entitled to the 1914 Star, and the General Service and Victory Medals.
7, Bolton Road, Luton. 3397/B.

HALL, F., Private, King's Shropshire Light Infantry and Royal Army Medical Corps.
He volunteered in March 1915, and in the following September was sent to Malta, where he was engaged on important duties in various hospitals. In January 1917 he was drafted to Salonika, and whilst in this theatre of war did excellent work on the Field attending to the wounded and as Doctor's Orderly. He was demobilised in April 1919, after over four years' service, and holds the 1914-15 Star, and the General Service and Victory Medals.
94, High Street, Markyate. 3398.

HALL, F., Gunner, Royal Horse Artillery.
He volunteered in August 1914, and in the following January was drafted to the Western Front. While on this front he was engaged in many battles until the end of the fighting, including those of Ypres, the Somme, Arras and Cambrai. After the Armistice he proceeded into Germany with the Army of Occupation, and was stationed at Cologne until April 1919, when he was demobilised on his return to England. He holds the 1914-15 Star, and the General Service and Victory Medals. 47, Summer Street, Slip End. 3399.

HALL, F. J., Rifleman, 16th London Regiment (Queen's Westminster Rifles).
Joining in September 1916, he was first drafted to Salonika, and then to Egypt in January of the following year. He took part in the British Offensive on Palestine and fought at Gaza. Owing to illness he was invalided home, but on his recovery was afterwards drafted to France, where he took part in many important engagements in the last year of the war. He was demobilised in November 1919, and holds the General Service and Victory Medals.
5, Fishpond Road, Hitchin. 3400.

HALL, G., Sapper, Royal Engineers.
He joined in January 1916, and in the same year was drafted to France. During his service on the Western Front he was frequently engaged in the forward areas whilst operations were in progress, especially at Albert and Vimy Ridge. In 1917 he was sent to Egypt, and served with the British forces under General Allenby in the Advance through Palestine, where he was present at the Battles of Gaza and Haifa, and in subsequent engagements until the conclusion of hostilities. He was wounded during his service overseas, and was demobilised in August 1919 after his return to England. He holds the General Service and Victory Medals.
Leyton Road, Harpenden. 3401.

HALL, G., Leading Seaman, R.N., H.M.S. "Duke of Edinburgh."
He joined the Navy in 1894, and at the outbreak of war was posted to H.M.S. "Duke of Edinburgh." Whilst in this ship he was engaged on important and highly dangerous duties in patrolling the seas, and chasing enemy submarines in the Mediterranean, North Sea, and in Russian waters. He also fought in the Battle of Jutland in 1916, and in the Red Sea. He was discharged in September 1919, and holds the 1914-15 Star, and the General Service and Victory Medals. 22, Regent Street, Leighton Buzzard. 3402.

HALL, G., Driver, Royal Field Artillery.
Volunteering in December 1914 he was retained for a time on important duties with his unit. He was sent to Mesopotamia in February 1916, and took part in the Relief of Kut. In the following November he was drafted to India, where he served for two months, and in April of the succeeding year he was discharged in consequence of his service. He holds the General Service and Victory Medals.
10, Milton Road, Luton. 3403.

HALL, G., Gunner, Royal Horse Artillery.
Joining in November 1916, he was drafted to France in the following March, and took part in the third Battle of Ypres, where he was severely wounded in 1917. He was invalided home, but returned to the Western Front in February of the following year in time for the Battles of the Somme and Cambrai and other engagements in the last year of the war. After the Armistice he proceeded to Germany with the Army of Occupation, and returning in October 1919, was demobilised in the following month. He holds the General Service and Victory Medals.
14, Langley Road, Watford.   X3404.

HALL, H., L/Corporal, 21st Bedfordshire and 7th Leicestershire Regiments.
He volunteered in September 1914, and in 1916 was drafted to France. During his service on the Western Front he took part in the Battles of Arras, Ypres and Cambrai, and was wounded. He was taken prisoner in the Retreat in May 1918, and held in captivity until after the Armistice was signed. He was demobilised in March 1919, and holds the General Service and Victory Medals.
Southill, Beds.   Z3405.

HALL, H., Private, Bedfordshire Regiment.
He joined in March 1917, and in the following June, after completing his training, was drafted to France. During his service overseas he fought in the Battles of Ypres, Cambrai, the Somme and Amiens, and other engagements until hostilities ceased. He was demobilised in March 1919 after two years' service with the colours, and holds the General Service and Victory Medals.
4, Yarmouth Road, Callowland, near Watford.   X3406.

HALL, H. A., Rifleman, King's Royal Rifle Corps.
He volunteered in 1915, and on completing his training was drafted to the Western Front. Subsequently he fought at Ypres and the Somme, where he is believed to have been killed in action in 1916. He was entitled to the General Service and Victory Medals.
75, Cecil Street, North Watford.   X3407.

HALL, H. J., Private, 4th Norfolk Regiment.
He joined in April 1917, and on the conclusion of his training was sent to Egypt and thence to Palestine. During the campaign on this front he fought in many important battles, notably that of Gaza, and did valuable work with his unit. He was demobilised after his return to England in March 1920, and holds the General Service and Victory Medals.
60, St. Mary's Road, Watford.   X3408.

HALL, L. W., Private, Queen's (Royal West Surrey Regiment).
Volunteering in 1914, he was sent to France in 1916, after being retained on important duties with his unit, and served in various engagements, including those at Ypres and Arras. He was twice wounded in action, but after his recovery took part in the final operations of the war. He was demobilised in 1919, and holds the General Service and Victory Medals.
19, Belgrave Avenue, Watford.   X1445/A.

HALL, N. A., Private, Machine Gun Corps.
He volunteered in August 1914, and at the conclusion of his training early in the following year was sent to France. Whilst in this theatre of war he was engaged in the fighting at Festubert, Loos, Albert, Vimy Ridge and the Somme, and did excellent work with his unit throughout his overseas service, which lasted for over three years. He was demobilised on his return to England in June 1919, and holds the 1914-15 Star, and the General Service and Victory Medals.
Moggerhanger, Sandy.   Z3414.

HALL, P., Corporal, West Yorkshire Regiment and Highland Light Infantry.
Volunteering in March 1915, he joined the West Yorkshire Regiment and later served in the Highland Light Infantry. At the conclusion of his training he was drafted to the Western Front, where he took part in several important engagements, including those at Armentières, the Somme and Cambrai, and was wounded. He was taken prisoner during the German Offensive in April 1918, and was held in captivity until the following December, when he returned to England. He was demobilised a year later, and holds the 1914-15 Star, and the General Service and Victory Medals.
21, Dunstable Place, Luton.   2862/B.

HALL, S. L., Private, Bedfordshire Lancers.
Volunteering in 1915, he was sent to the Western Front early in the following year. Whilst in this theatre of war he took an active part in many notable battles while fighting continued, and after the termination of hostilities advanced into Germany with the Army of Occupation. He holds the General Service and Victory Medals, and was demobilised in February 1919 after his returning to England.
Southill, Beds.   Z3409/A.

HALL, T. W., Rifleman, 9th K.R.R.C.
Volunteering in September 1914, he served at various stations on important duties with his unit until July 1916, when he was drafted to France. While there he took part in the Battles of the Somme and Beaumont-Hamel, and on April 9th, 1917, was killed in action at Arras. He was entitled to the General Service and Victory Medals.
7, Bolton Road, Luton.   3397/C.

HALL, W., Private, Royal Air Force.
Volunteering in 1915, he was sent to India at the conclusion of this training. Throughout his service overseas he was engaged on important duties, which called for much technical knowledge and skill, and did valuable work with his Squadron. Returning to England in August 1918, he was demobilised in the following January, and holds the General Service and Victory Medals.
24, Dorset Road, Luton.   3413.

HALL, W., Private, Queen's (Royal West Surrey Regiment).
Joining in May 1916, he was drafted to France immediately upon the completion of his training. He fought in the Battles of the Somme and Arras, and was wounded, and on June 29th, 1917, was killed in action at Fontaine-lez-Croiselles. He was buried at St. Léger, and was entitled to the General Service and Victory Medals.
13, Puller Road, Boxmoor.   X3412/A.

HALL, W., Sapper, Royal Engineers.
He was serving when war broke out, but owing to physical unfitness was retained for important duties in connection with Inland Transport. He also did valuable work in many other capacities until the cessation of hostilities, and was demobilised in January 1919.
1, Midland Terrace, St. Albans.   X3411.

HALL, W., Private, Royal Army Service Corps.
He volunteered early in 1915, and after a course of training was drafted to France. His service in this theatre of war lasted for over three years, during which time he was engaged on various important transport duties and acted as a guard for prisoners of war. He was demobilised on his return to England in April 1919, and holds the 1914-15 Star, and the General Service and Victory Medals.
New Marford, Wheathampstead.   3410.

HALL, W. J., Sapper, Royal Engineers.
Volunteering at the commencement of hostilities, he was quickly drafted to the Western Front, and took part in the Retreat from Mons. He subsequently served at Ypres, Hill 60, Vimy Ridge, the Somme, Arras and Cambrai, and for 2½ years was engaged in mine-laying operations in these areas. He holds the Mons Star, and the General Service and Victory Medals, and was demobilised after his return to England in January 1920.
Southill, Beds.   Z3409/B.

HALL, W. L., Private, 6th Essex Regiment.
He volunteered in December 1915, and in the following May was sent to the Western Front, where he fought at Ypres and was wounded. In April 1917 he was transferred to Egypt and thence to Palestine, where he took part in the engagements at Gaza and Mejdil. He was demobilised on his return to England in September 1919, and holds the General Service and Victory Medals.
"Corner House," Arthur Street, Ampthill.   3415.

HALLSEY, T. G., Sergeant, R.A.V.C.
Volunteering at the commencement of hostilities, he was quickly sent to the Western Front. He did valuable service in the Retreat from Mons, and in many other important engagements, including that at Ypres, and was for some time engaged on important duties at the hospital for horses at Le Havre. He holds the Mons Star, and the General Service and Victory Medals, and was demobilised on his return to England in 1919.
135, Judge Street, Callowland, Watford.   X3416.

HALLYBONE, A., Private, 2nd Bedfordshire Regiment.
Being mobilised at the outbreak of war, he was sent to France in October 1914, and fought at La Bassée, Ypres, Hill 60, Loos, the Somme, Passchendaele Ridge and Cambrai, and was wounded. In January 1918 he was invalided home suffering from shell-shock, and after being under treatment in hospital for some time, was transferred to the Labour Corps. He was afterwards engaged on important agricultural duties at Sutton, and did valuable work in this capacity until he was demobilised in March 1919. He holds the 1914 Star, and the General Service and Victory Medals.
1, Gladstone Terrace, Biggleswade.   Z3417.

HALLWORTH, W. R., 1st Northamptonshire Regiment.

Joining in April 1916, he was sent to the Western Front on completing his training. After taking part in several important engagements, including that at Ypres, he was killed in action near Nieuport on July 8th, 1917. He was entitled to the General Service and Victory Medals.

5, Banbury Street, Watford.   X3504/B.

HALSEY, A., Private, 7th Norfolk Regiment.

He volunteered in August 1914, and during his service on the Western Front, took part in many important engagements, including those at Arras, Cambrai and Ypres, and was wounded three times. He holds the General Service and Victory Medals, and was demobilised after his return to England in March 1919.

31, Lowestoft Road, Watford.   X3418/A.

HALSEY, C., Private, Gloucestershire Regt.

He joined in May 1917, and five months later was drafted to the Western Front. During his service overseas he fought in the Battles of Cambrai and the Somme, and was killed in action during the German Offensive on April 13th, 1918. He was entitled to the General Service and Victory Medals.

52, Church Street, Dunstable.   3419.

HALSEY, C. R., Stoker, Royal Navy.

Joining in 1917, he was posted after his training to H.M.S. "Osea," in which vessel he was engaged on Channel patrol duties throughout the remaining period of hostilities. He did valuable work until his demobilisation in 1920, and holds the General Service and Victory Medals.

50, Hatfield Road, North Watford.   X3420.

HALSEY, E. C., Private, Queen's (Royal West Surrey Regiment).

He joined in February 1917, and on completing his training was engaged on special duties until the following November, when he crossed to France. After taking part in several engagements on this front, including that at Albert, he was killed in action near Cambrai on January 12th, 1918. He was entitled to the General Service and Victory Medals.

31, Grove Road, Hitchin.   3421/C.

HALSEY, E. J., L/Corporal, Royal Engineers.

He volunteered in 1915, and upon completing his training was sent overseas. During his service in France he fought at Hill 60, Ypres and the Somme, and was killed in action at High Wood on August 27th, 1916. He was entitled to the 1914-15 Star, and the General Service and Victory Medals.

37, Temperance Street, St. Albans.   3422/A.

HALSEY, G., Private, Bedfordshire Regiment.

Joining in March 1916, he was drafted to France at the conclusion of his training. He was engaged in the fighting at Arras, and at Ypres, where he received a serious wound, of which he subsequently died in hospital at Stockport. He was entitled to the General Service and Victory Medals.

72, Sopwell Lane, St. Albans.   X3423.

HALSEY, G. T., Gunner, R.G.A.

He volunteered in June 1915, and after his training was sent to the Western Front. During his service in this theatre of war, he fought in many important engagements until hostilities ceased, notably those of Hill 60, Ypres and Vimy Ridge, and did valuable work with his unit. He holds the 1914-15 Star, and the General Service and Victory Medals, and was demobilised in February 1919.

1, Holly Villa, Luton Road, Harpenden.   3424.

HALSEY, J., Private, M.G.C. (Cavalry).

He volunteered in February 1915, and until he was sent to France in January 1918, was retained on special duties. He took part in the Retreat and Advance of that year, during which he did valuable work with his unit, and after the cessation of hostilities served with the Army of Occupation in Germany. He was demobilised after his return to England in April 1919, and holds the General Service and Victory Medals.

31, Grove Road, Hitchin.   3421/A.

HALSEY, J. T. W., Sapper, Royal Engineers.

Volunteering in February 1915, he was sent to France in October, and was engaged on important duties at Loos and in other sectors until he was sent to Salonika in January 1916. He subsequently served on the Vardar, Doiran and Struma fronts, being employed chiefly on bridge building, and did valuable work with his unit until after the cessation of hostilities. He was demobilised in April 1919, and holds the 1914-15 Star, and the General Service and Victory Medals.

31, Grove Road, Hitchin.   3421/B.

HALSEY, R., 2nd Corporal, Royal Engineers.

He joined in April 1917, and after his training was sent to the Western Front, where he did excellent work as a blacksmith with his unit in many important sectors, including that of Cambrai. He was demobilised on returning to England in July 1919, and holds the General Service and Victory Medals.

55, Leavesden Road, Watford.   X3418/C.

HAMMERTON, S., Private, 4th Bedfordshire Regiment; and Stoker, Royal Navy.

He volunteered in September 1914, and after his training was sent to the Western Front, where he took part in several engagements, and was wounded. Returning to England he was invalided out of the Service in December 1915. In the following March, he joined the Royal Navy, and subsequently served as a stoker on board H.M.S. "Cameleon" which was engaged on special duties in the North Sea, Atlantic, Mediterranean and other waters. He holds the 1914-15 Star, and the General Service and Victory Medals.

28, Hampstead Road, Watford.   X3425.

HAMMOND, G., Sergeant, R.A.V.C.

He volunteered in August 1914, and after his training was engaged on special duties at various stations. Being in Ireland during the Sinn Fein riots of May 1916, he rendered valuable services. Later he was drafted to France, and did excellent work in attendance on the wounded and sick horses until after the cessation of hostilities. He was demobilised in December 1918, and holds the General Service and Victory Medals.

31, Ashton Street, Luton.   3426.

HAMMOND, T., Private, R.A.S.C.

He joined in June 1916, and a month later was drafted to France. Whilst in this theatre of war, he did valuable transport work with his unit in many important sectors, including those of Arras, the Somme and Cambrai, and remained overseas until 1919. He was demobilised in September of that year, and holds the General Service and Victory Medals.   101, Lower Paddock Road, Oxhey. X3427.

HAMPSHIRE, W. T., Private, R.A.V.C.

Volunteering in 1915, he went to France on completing his training. His service in this theatre of war lasted for over three years, during which time he did important work in the forward areas, and was present at many battles, including those of Ypres, the Somme and Cambrai. After the cessation of hostilities he served for a time with the Army of Occupation in Germany. He was demobilised in May 1919, and holds the 1914-15 Star, and the General Service and Victory Medals.

68, St. Peter's Street, St Albans.   X3428.

HANCE, C. (M.M.), Driver, R.F.A.

He volunteered in December 1914, and on the completion of his training was drafted to France in the following year. While overseas he took an active part with his Battery in many engagements of importance until the close of the war, including those of the Somme, Ypres, Passchendaele, Kemmel and Armentières, and was wounded. He was awarded the Military Medal for conspicuous gallantry in the Field, and also holds the 1914-15 Star, and the General Service and Victory Medals. He was demobilised in February 1919.

58, Upper Paddock Road, Oxhey.   X3429.

HANCOCK, W. J., Air Mechanic, R.A.F.

He joined in July 1916, and after serving for a time in a line regiment, was transferred to the Royal Air Force. At the conclusion of his training in March 1917 he was sent to the Western Front, where he took an active part in the engagements at Albert, Thiepval Wood, Arras and Armentières, and was engaged on important duties which demanded much technical knowledge and skill. He was demobilised on his return to England in May 1919, and holds the General Service and Victory Medals.   11, Fishpond Road, Hitchin.   3430.

HANCOCK, W. R., Stoker, R.N., H.M.S. "Polyanthus."

He volunteered in August 1914, and after a period of training was posted to H.M.S. "Polyanthus." Whilst in this vessel he was engaged on important patrol duties of a highly dangerous nature in the North Sea, this ship being torpedoed on three occasions. He also served for a time with the "Mystery" ships. He was finally demobilised in February 1919, and holds the 1914-15 Star, and the General Service and Victory Medals.

49, Copsewood Road, Watford.   563/C.

HANDLEY, J., Corporal, Border Regiment.

He volunteered in August 1914, and in the following year was drafted to Egypt, where he saw much valuable service. In April 1916 he was sent to the Western Front, and subsequently fought at Vimy Ridge, the Somme, Ypres and Arras. During his service he was wounded and gassed, and also suffered from fever. He holds the 1914-15 Star, and the General Service and Victory Medals, and was demobilised in April 1919.   Mimram Road, Welwyn.   3431.

HANDSCOMBE, J., Sapper, Royal Engineers.
He volunteered in November 1915, joining in the Bedfordshire Regiment, and in the course of his service was transferred to the Machine Gun Corps and the Royal Engineers. During 1916 and 1917 he served on the Western Front, taking part in engagements round Loos and Ypres, and in 1918 was drafted to Italy where, during operations on the Piave, he did valuable work with his unit. He was demobilised on his return to England in February 1919, and holds the General Service and Victory Medals.
10, Cemetery Street, Biggleswade.   Z3432.

HANKINS, A., Private, 19th London Regiment.
He joined in April 1917, and was drafted to Egypt after the conclusion of his training. Subsequently he served in the Palestine campaign, in which he took an active part in much heavy fighting, and was twice wounded. He was demobilised after his return to England in January 1920, and holds the General Service and Victory Medals.
7, Dordans Road, Leagrave, Luton.   3433/A.

HANKINS, R. (Mrs.), Special War Worker.
During the war this lady was engaged on work of National importance at a munition factory in Church End, Luton, where she served for three years. During this period she was employed in the fuse department on important duties, which she carried out in a thoroughly capable and efficient manner until her resignation in December 1918.
7, Dordans Road, Luton.   3433/B.

HANNAH, J. C., Sergeant, Royal Fusiliers.
Volunteering in February 1915, he was sent to France before the end of the year. He fought in a number of important battles, including those of the Somme, Ypres, Cambrai and Albert, but in 1918 returned to England in consequence of ill-health. He was invalided out of the Service in February of that year, and holds the 1914-15 Star, and the General Service and Victory Medals.
9, Broughton Hill, Letchworth.   3434.

HARBER, A., Rifleman, Rifle Brigade.
Volunteering in October 1914, he joined the Hertfordshire Regiment, and was later transferred to the Rifle Brigade. After completing his training, he was retained on important duties until 1916, when he was drafted to India, where he did much valuable work. On returning to England in July 1918 he was discharged through causes due to his service, and holds the General Service and Victory Medals.
12, Beechen Grove, Watford.   X3482.

HARDEN, A. L., Sergeant, R.F.A.
Volunteering in 1915, he was retained on important duties until drafted to France in March 1917. He fought in many notable engagements during his service in this theatre of war, including those of the Somme, Ypres and Arras, and did excellent work with his Battery throughout. Returning to England after the cessation of hostilities, he was demobilised in January 1919, and holds the General Service and Victory Medals.
44, Westbourne Road, Luton.   3483/B.

HARDEN, O. G. (Mrs.), Member, V.A.D.
This lady volunteered in 1915, and for three years served as a cook at Wardown Hospital, Luton. In this capacity she rendered most valuable services, and her help was greatly appreciated.
44, Westbourne Road, Luton.   3483/A.

HARDING, C. E., Private, Machine Gun Corps.
He joined in April 1917, and later in the year proceeded to France. During his two years' service there he took part in several battles of importance until fighting ceased, including that of the Somme. Returning to England after the cessation of hostilities, he was demobilised in November 1919, and holds the General Service and Victory Medals.
Leavesden Green, Watford.   X3451/A.

HARDING, F. A., L/Corporal, 13th Welch Regt.
Volunteering in 1915, he was drafted to France in June of the following year. He subsequently fought at Arras, Cambrai and Ypres, and was in action almost continuously until he was killed at Delville Wood on August 27th, 1916, during the Advance of that year. He was entitled to the General Service and Victory Medals.
109, Norfolk Road, Rickmansworth.   X3503/A.

HARDING, F. J., Private, 4th Bedfordshire Regt.
He volunteered in 1915, and before the end of that year was drafted to France. Whilst in this theatre of war he fought at Givenchy, the Somme, Arras and Cambrai, and, being severely gassed, was invalided home in consequence. He was discharged in December as unfit for further military duties, and holds the 1914-15 Star, and the General Service and Victory Medals.
36, Rushby Mead, Letchford.   3473.

HARDING, F. S., Special War Worker,
Rejected from the Army owing to physical disability, he obtained work of National importance with the Commercial Car Company, where he served throughout the war. He held a responsible post, and carried out his duties in a thoroughly efficient and satisfactory manner.
13, Althorpe Road, Luton.   3449.

HARDING, G. F. E., Trooper, Herts. Dragoons.
He volunteered in December 1915, and after his training was drafted to France, where he fought in several engagements. Later he proceeded to Egypt and subsequently served in the Palestine campaign, during which he took part in many battles, and did much valuable work with his unit. He was demobilised on his return to England in April 1919, and holds the 1914-15 Star, and the General Service and Victory Medals.
New Marford, Wheathampstead.   3448.

HARDING, H., Gunner, R.G.A.
Joining in January 1916, he was sent to France five months later. Subsequently as a gunner he took an active part in many important engagements, notably those at Arras, Ypres and Passchendaele, and did excellent work with his battery until after the cessation of hostilities. He was demobilised in January 1919, and holds the General Service and Victory Medals.
109, Norfolk Road, Rickmansworth.   X3503/B.

HARDING, P. A., Private, Bedfordshire Regt.
He joined the Hertfordshire Regiment in March 1918, and was later transferred to the Bedfordshire Regiment. After his training he was engaged upon duties of an important nature with his unit, and although unable to secure his transfer overseas before the termination of hostilities, he did valuable work until demobilised in March 1920.
109, Norfolk Road, Rickmansworth.   X3503/C.

HARDWICK, F. T., Private, R.A.F.
He joined in August 1918, and was sent to France immediately upon completing his training. After serving in the concluding stages of the Advance of that year, he was sent with the Army of Occupation to Germany, where he was engaged on important duties with his Squadron. He was demobilised in August 1919, and holds the General Service and Victory Medals.
20, Yarmouth Road, Callowland.   X3450/B.

HARDWICK, H., Gunner, R.F.A.
Volunteering in October 1915, he was sent to the Western Front in the same year. Whilst in this theatre of war he fought in many important engagements, and was killed in action on August 2nd, 1918, during the Advance of that year. He was entitled to the 1914-15 Star, and the General Service and Victory Medals.
20, Yarmouth Road, Callowland.   X3450/A.

HARDWICK, H. S., Sapper, Royal Engineers.
He volunteered in October 1915, and on the completion of his course of training was engaged on important duties with his unit. Owing to physical disability he was not successful in securing his transfer overseas before the cessation of hostilities, but rendered valuable services until demobilised in February 1919.
20, Yarmouth Road, Callowland.   X3450/C.

HARDY, C., Rifleman, The Cameronians (Scottish Rifles).
He joined in May 1916, and after his training served at various stations on important duties with his unit. He rendered valuable services, but was not successful in obtaining his transfer overseas before the cessation of hostilities. He was discharged in May 1918.
33, Meeting Alley, Watford, Herts.   X373/A.

HARE, R. E., Private, 1st Middlesex Regiment.
He volunteered in June 1915, and after his training was sent to the Western Front. While overseas he fought in many engagements, including that of Ypres, and was severely wounded in 1916. Returning to England, he was invalided out of the Service in October of that year, and holds the 1914-15 Star, and the General Service and Victory Medals.
5, Banbury Street, Watford.   X3504/A.

HARE, W., Private, Somerset Light Infantry.
He joined in April 1917, and after his training was stationed in Ireland, where he was engaged on duties of an important nature with his unit. He was unable to secure his transfer overseas before the cessation of hostilities, but rendered valuable services until his demobilisation in September 1919.
"Primrose Cottage," Letchworth Road, Limbury, Luton.
                                           3460.

HARKNESS, D., A.B., Royal Navy.

He joined in August 1916, and after his training was posted to H.M.T.B.D. " Wrestler," which was engaged on important patrol and escort duties in the Baltic and the North Sea. He was demobilised in October 1919, and holds the General Service and Victory Medals.

" Fairlight," New Dalton Street, St. Albans. X3466.

HARLEY, G. A. (M.M.), 2nd Corporal, R.E.

He volunteered in April 1915, and after his training was drafted to the Western Front, where he took part in various engagements, including that at St.Quentin, and was wounded. He was awarded the Military Medal for bravery in the Field, and also holds the General Service and Victory Medals, and was demobilised in January 1919.

Rookery Cottages, Offley. 3478.

HARLOW, A., Corporal, R.F.A.

He volunteered in August 1915, and after his training served at various stations on important duties with his battery. He rendered valuable service, but was not successful in obtaining his transfer overseas before the cessation of hostilities. He was demobilised in February 1919.

43, May Street, Luton. 3447.

HARMAN, G. (M.M.), Private, Coldstream Guards.

He volunteered in August 1914, and afterwards proceeded to the Western Front, where he took part in severe fighting at Arras, Ypres and Cambrai and was wounded. He was awarded the Military Medal for bravery in the Field, and also holds the General Service and Victory Medals. He was still serving in 1920.

Halls Yard, Hatfield. X3960/B.

HARMAN, L., Private, 2nd Royal Sussex Regt.

He was mobilised in August 1914, and in the following month was sent to the Western Front. He took part in severe fighting at La Bassée, Hill 60, Festubert and the Somme, and was wounded. He also served in the Retreat and Advance of 1918. He was demobilised in June 1919, and holds the 1914 Star, and the General Service and Victory Medals.

37, Plantation Road, Leighton Buzzard. 3502.

HARMSWORTH, F. W., Private, Northumberland Fusiliers.

He volunteered in January 1915, and in the same year was drafted to India,where he served until 1916,when he was sent to Mesopotamia. He took part in the campaign against the Turks, and was in action at Kut, Baghdad and Mosul, and after the cessation of hostilities returned to England and was demobilised in September 1919, holding the 1914-15 Star, and the General Service and Victory Medals.

93, St. John's Road, Boxmoor. X487/B.

HARPER, H. J., Sapper, R.E. (Postal Service).

He volunteered in November 1915, and in June of the following year was drafted to the Western Front, and served on the Somme. During his service he suffered from shell-shock and contracted dysentery. He afterwards proceeded to Salonika, and thence in 1917 to Palestine, where he took part in various engagements, including those at Gaza and Jerusalem. He returned home, but was again sent to France, where he was employed on postal duties. He was demobilised in July 1919, and holds the General Service and Victory Medals.

17, Grove Road, Hitchin. 3471/B.

HARPER, R. C., Private, 1st Bedfordshire Regt.

Volunteering in June 1915, he was drafted to the Western Front in the following year. He took part in heavy fighting on the Somme and at Arras, Ypres, St. Quentin and was four times wounded, and was invalided home. On his recovery he was engaged on important duties with his unit until April 1919, when he was demobilised. He holds the General Service and Victory Medals.

17, Grove Road, Hitchin. 3471/A.

HARPER, W., Corporal, Machine Gun Corps.

He volunteered in 1915, and in the same year was sent to Mesopotamia and took part in various engagements, including those at Kut, Baghdad and Mosul. He returned home and was demobilised in March 1919, and holds the 1914-15 Star, and the General Service and Victory Medals.

1a, Langley Place, Luton. 3436.

HARPER, W. C., Sergeant, 1st Hertfordshire Regiment.

He volunteered in August 1914, and was sent to France in November of the same year. He took part in severe fighting in the Retreat from Mons at Neuve Chapelle, St. Julien, Arras, Passchendaele, and was twice wounded. He died of wounds at Rouen on April 11th, 1918, and was entitled to the Mons Star, and the General Service and Victory Medals.

17, Grove Road, Hitchin. 3471/C.

HARRIS, A., Sergeant, Fort Garry Horse.

Volunteering in May 1915, he was sent in the following October to the Western Front, where he took part in important engagements, including those on the Somme and at Arras, Ypres and Cambrai. He also served in the Retreat and Advance of 1918. He was demobilised in June 1919, and holds the 1914-15 Star, and the General Service and Victory Medals.

66, King Street, Dunstable. 3454.

HARRIS, A., Rifleman, K.R.R.C.

He joined in May 1917, and in June of the same year was drafted to France, where he took part in various engagements, including those at Cambrai and Amiens. He was demobilised in December 1919, and holds the General Service and Victory Medals.

Church Lane, King's Langley. X1514/A.

HARRIS, A., Private, Queen's Own (Royal West Kent Regiment).

He joined in 1916, and was sent to France in the same year. He took part in severe fighting at Arras, the Somme and Ypres, and was twice wounded. He was demobilised in December 1919, and holds the General Service and Victory Medals.

58, Lilley, near Luton. 3498.

HARRIS, A., Private, Northumberland Fusiliers.

Volunteering in August 1914 he was afterwards sent to the Western Front, where he took part in numerous engagements, including those at Arras, Cambrai and St. Quentin, and was wounded. He was demobilised in June 1919, and holds the General Service and Victory Medals.

8, Front Street, Slip End. 3456.

HARRIS, A. E., L/Corporal, 16th K.R.R.C.

He joined in May 1917, and in January of the following year was drafted to the Western Front, where he took part in severe fighting on the Somme and at Cambrai, Albert and other engagements. He was demobilised in December 1919, and holds the General Service and Victory Medals.

Hall End, Maulden, Ampthill. 3485.

HARRIS, C. H., Private, 7th Bedfordshire Regt.

He volunteered in September 1914, and in July of the following year was sent to France. where he took part in various engagements, including those at Ypres and the Somme, and was wounded during the Retreat of 1918. He was invalided home and was discharged in November 1918, holding the 1914-15 Star, and the General Service and Victory Medals.

Sandon Road, Harlington, near Dunstable. 3492A.

HARRIS, E., Private, South Wales Borderers.

He volunteered in May 1915, and after his training served at various stations on important duties with his unit. He rendered valuable services,but was not successful in obtaining his transfer overseas before the cessation of hostilities. He was demobilised in December 1919.

Lower Woodside, near Luton. 3452/A.

HARRIS, E., Sapper, Royal Engineers.

Joining in July 1916, he was sent to France in the same year. He took part in numerous engagements, including those on the Somme and at Arras and Cambrai. He returned home, and was discharged as medically unfit for further service in March 1918, and holds the General Service and Victory Medals.

3, Penns Yard, Queen Street, Hitchin. 3470.

HARRIS, E., Gunner, Royal Field Artillery.

He enlisted in March 1912, and after the outbreak of war was drafted to the Western Front, and thence to Egypt and Palestine, where he took part in important engagements, including those at Gaza, Jaffa and elsewhere. He was demobilised in August 1919, and holds the 1914-15 Star, and the General Service and Victory Medals.

32, Leavesden Road, Watford. X3505/A.

HARRIS, E. F., Private, 2nd Bedfordshire Regt.

He volunteered in August 1914, and was sent to France in April of the following year. He took part in the Battle of Festubert, where he was killed in action on May 17th, 1915, and was entitled to the 1914-15 Star, and the General Service and Victory Medals.

Sandon Road, Harlington, near Dunstable. 3491/B.

HARRIS, E. J., Sergeant, 10th Sherwood Foresters.

Volunteering in August 1914, he was sent to France in the following month. He took part in severe fighting at La Bassée, Festubert, Loos, the Somme and Arras. He also served in the Retreat and Advance of 1918, and was killed in action near Cambrai on September 22nd, 1918. He was entitled to the 1914 Star, and the General Service and Victory Medals.

40, Stanbridge Road, Leighton Buzzard. 3464.

HARRIS, F., Private, City of London (Rough Riders) Lancers.
He volunteered in 1915, and in the same year was sent to Egypt and Palestine, where he served on the Canal zone. He afterwards took part in various engagements, including those at el Arish, Gaza, Beersheba, and others. He was demobilised in March 1919, and holds the 1914-15 Star, and the General Service and Victory Medals.
66, Boyle Street, Luton. 3495/B.

HARRIS, F., Sapper, Royal Engineers.
He joined in May 1916, and in April of the following year was sent to India where he was engaged on the North West Frontier, and lines of communication on various important duties with his unit, and rendered valuable services. He was demobilised in December 1919, and holds the General Service and Victory Medals.
7, Paynes Park, Hitchin. 3472.

HARRIS, F., Private, The Queen's (Royal West Surrey Regiment) (Labour Battalion), and Suffolk Regiment.
He joined in February 1917, and was sent to France in the same year and took part in numerous engagements, including those at Arras, Bullecourt, Ypres, Cambrai and the Somme. He was demobilised in 1919, and holds the General Service and Victory Medals.
4, Ridgway Road, Luton. 3467.

HARRIS, F. W., Private, R.A.M.C.
He joined in May 1916, and after his training served at various stations on important hospital duties with his unit. He rendered valuable services, but was not successful in obtaining his transfer overseas before the cessation of hostilities. He was demobilised in August 1919.
9, Cavendish Road, St. Albans. X3479.

HARRIS, G., Gunner, Royal Field Artillery.
He volunteered in August 1914, and in the following year was drafted to Egypt and Palestine, where he took part in severe fighting at Gaza, Haifa and Aleppo. He was demobilised in April 1919, and holds the 1914-15 Star, and the General Service and Victory Medals.
5, Charles Street, Hemel Hempstead. X3468.

HARRIS, G. W., Private, 1st East Surrey Regt.
Joining in March 1918, he was sent to France in August of the same year and was engaged at Achiet-le-Grand. He afterwards proceeded with the Army of Occupation to Germany. He was demobilised in March 1919, and holds the General Service and Victory Medals.
Sandon Road, Harlington, near Dunstable. 3492/B.

HARRIS, H., Private, 1st Bedfordshire Regt.
Volunteering in December 1914, he went through a course of training and afterwards served on important duties with his unit until August 1916, when he was sent to France, where he took part in severe fighting at Ypres, the Somme and Vimy Ridge, where he was taken prisoner. On his release he returned home and was demobilised in May 1919, and holds the General Service and Victory Medals.
Jacques Lane, Clophill, Ampthill. 3486.

HARRIS, J., Private, R.A.S.C.
He volunteered in June 1915, and after his training was drafted to the Western Front. He was engaged on the railways transporting ammunition and supplies to the various fronts, and rendered valuable services. He was discharged in May 1916, and holds the General Service and Victory Medals.
32, Leavesden Road, Watford. 3505/B.

HARRIS, J., Private, 5th Bedfordshire Regt.
He volunteered in June 1915, and in February of the following year was sent to Egypt and Palestine, where he took part various engagements, including that at Gaza. He contracted pneumonia from which he died in Cairo on January 25th, 1919, and was entitled to the General Service and Victory Medals.
Sandon Road, Harlington, near Dunstable. 3492/C.

HARRIS, J., Sergeant, Cameronians (Scottish Rifles).
Volunteering in August 1914, he was sent in the following month to the Western Front, where he took part in numerous engagements, including those at Mons, Hill 60, Loos, the Somme, Arras, Ypres and Cambrai, and was three times wounded. He was demobilised in March 1919, and holds the Mons Star, and the General Service and Victory Medals.
Adelaide Cottages, Harlington. 3490.

HARRIS, J., Private, 19th London Regiment.
He was mobilised in 1914, and in the following year was sent to France and took part in severe fighting at Ypres. In 1916 he was transferred to Salonika and thence to Egypt and Palestine, where he was again in action and was wounded at Jerusalem. He was demobilised in July 1919, and holds the 1914-15 Star, and the General Service and Victory Medals.
111, Lower Paddock Road, Oxhey. X3458.

HARRIS, J. D., Sapper, Royal Engineers.
Joining in 1918, he was sent to France in the same year and took part in various engagements, including those at Havrincourt and Ypres. He was still serving in 1920, and holds the General Service and Victory Medals.
23, Jubilee Road, North Watford. X3455.

HARRIS, L., Private, Labour Corps.
He volunteered in August 1914, and was afterwards sent to the Dardanelles, where he served at Anzac Cove. He was engaged as a stretcher-bearer and on other important duties with his unit, and rendered valuable services. He was demobilised in June 1919, and holds the 1914-15 Star, and the General Service and Victory Medals.
26, Bun Street, Luton. 3459.

HARRIS, L., Corporal, South African Infantry.
He joined in 1917, and was sent to France in January of the following year. He took part in severe fighting on the Somme and at Ypres, and was twice wounded. He was demobilised in November 1919, and holds the General Service and Victory Medals.
63, Dacre Road, Hitchin. 3453/A.

HARRIS, P. J., Sapper, R.E. (Signals).
He joined in April 1915, and after his training served on important duties with his unit until January 1917, when he was drafted to Egypt and Palestine. He served on the Gaza front and lines of communication, and rendered valuable services. He was demobilised in August 1919, and holds the General Service and Victory Medals.
Sandon Road, Harlington, near Dunstable. 3491/A.

HARRIS, T., L/Corporal, R.D.C.
He joined in 1916, and was engaged in guarding munition works and on many other important duties with his unit, and rendered valuable services. He was demobilised in March 1919.
High Street, Clophill, Ampthill. 3477.

HARRIS, W., Shoeing Smith, R.F.A.
He volunteered in March 1916, and in the following January was drafted to the Western Front, where he served on the Somme and at Arras, Ypres and Cambrai. After the cessation of hostilities he returned to England, and in May 1919 was demobilised, holding the General Service and Victory Medals.
5, William Street, Markyate. 3461.

HARRIS, W., Rifleman, K.R.R.C.
He joined in May 1916, and having completed his training was drafted to France in the following October. He took part in the Battles of the Somme, Arras, Ypres and Cambrai, and was twice wounded, and also served in the Retreat and Advance of 1918. After the Armistice he proceeded to Germany with the Army of Occupation with which he remained until October 1919, when he returned to England and was demobilised, holding the General Service and Victory Medals.
Near Church, Harlington, near Dunstable. 3489.

HARRIS, W. (M.M.), Private, R.A.M.C.
He volunteered in 1915, and after having completed his training was drafted to the Western Front. In 1917 he was mentioned in Despatches for bravery, and was awarded the Military Medal for conspicuous gallantry in carrying wounded under heavy shell-fire, although he himself was injured. During his service overseas he was gassed three times, and in 1918 returning to England was demobilised, holding in addition to the Military Medal, the General Service and Victory Medals.
66, Boyle Street, Luton. 3495/A.

HARRIS, W., Private, 4th Norfolk Regiment.
He joined in May 1916, and after his training was drafted to Egypt. He took part in the Palestine campaign and was in action at Gaza and Jaffa, and was wounded. After the conclusion of hostilities he returned to England, and in October 1919 was demobilised, holding the General Service and Victory Medals.
32, Leavesden Road, Watford. X3505/C.

HARRIS, W., Driver, Royal Engineers.
He volunteered in September 1914, and was engaged on important duties with his unit at various stations until March 1917, when he was drafted to France. After being in action in several engagements he was killed on June 19th, 1917, and was entitled to the General Service and Victory Medals.
106, Judge Street, North Watford. X3506/A.

HARRIS, W. J., Private, Labour Corps.
He joined in June 1916, and in the following September was drafted to France, where shortly after his arrival he was wounded during the Battle of the Somme. He was invalided home and on his recovery served on important duties until March 1919, when he was demobilised, holding the General Service and Victory Medals.
3, The Rookery, Watford. X3499.

HARRISON, B. A., Pte., 14th London Regiment (London Scottish).
He joined in February 1916, and in the following July was drafted to the Western Front, where he was in action on the Somme and at Albert, Ypres and Cambrai. He also served in the Advance of 1918, and after the conclusion of hostilities returned to England and was demobilised, holding the General Service and Victory Medals.
119, Whinbush Road, Hitchin. 3480/B.

HARRISON, J. W., Private, 4th Bedfordshire Regiment.
He joined in July 1917, and in the following March was drafted to the Western Front, where he was in action at Arras, Ypres and Vimy Ridge. He was reported missing after an engagement on May 25th, 1918, and is believed to have been killed on that date. He was entitled to the General Service and Victory Medals.
106, North Street, Luton. 3493/A.

HARRISON, W., Private, Sherwood Foresters.
He volunteered in July 1915, and on completing his training was drafted to the Western Front. In this theatre of war he took part in several important engagements in various sectors, and was once wounded. At the conclusion of hostilities he returned to England for demobilisation in 1919. He holds the General Service and Victory Medals.
99, Regent Street, North Watford, Herts. X154/B.

HARRISON, W., Private, East Surrey Regiment.
He joined in February 1917, and in the following July was drafted to the Western Front, where he was in action at Ypres, St. Julien and Arras, and was twice wounded. He was taken prisoner at Cambrai in February 1918, and was held in captivity until after the Armistice, when he was released, and returning to England was demobilised in July 1919, holding the General Service and Victory Medals.
102, Clarendon Road, Luton 3493/B.

HARRISS, F. G., Private, Machine Gun Corps.
He joined in April 1917, and in the same year was drafted to France, where he was in action at Arras, Ypres, Cambrai and the Somme. After the cessation of hostilities he served with the Army of Occupation in Germany until 1919, when he returned to England and was demobilised, holding the General Service and Victory Medals.
East End, Flitwick. 3462.

HARRISS, T. H., Sergeant, R.A.S.C. (M.T.)
Volunteering in August 1914, he was drafted to France in the same year and was in action at Ypres, Cambrai, St. Quentin and Arras. After the cessation of hostilities he returned to England, and in March 1919 was demobilised, holding the 1914 Star, and the General Service and Victory Medals.
7, Pinner Road, Oxhey. X3457/A.

HARROLD, A. H., Air Mechanic, R.A.F.
Joining in January 1918 he was, after having completed his training, engaged on important duties which required a high degree of technical skill. He rendered valuable service, but was not successful in procuring his transfer overseas prior to the cessation of hostilities.
86, Princess Street, Dunstable. 3484.

HARRUP, F. (M.C.), 2nd Lieut., Royal Fusiliers.
Volunteering in March 1915, he was drafted to France in the following September and took part in the Battle of the Somme and the Retreat of 1918. He was awarded the Military Cross for conspicuous gallantry in the Field, and on September 21st, 1918, was killed in action at Epéhy. In addition to holding the Military Cross, he was entitled to the 1914-15 Star, and the General Service and Victory Medals.
Tilsworth, near Leighton Buzzard. 3476.

HART, A., Sergeant, 2nd Bedfordshire Regiment.
Volunteering in December 1914 he was engaged on important duties at various stations until January 1917, when he was drafted to the Western Front. He was severely wounded at the Battle of Arras and was invalided home and in January 1919 discharged as medically unfit for further service. He holds the General Service and Victory Medals.
11, Princess Street, Toddington. 3488.

HART, A. J., Private, 7th Norfolk Regiment.
Joining in January 1917, he was drafted to France in the following May, and took part in the Battle of Ypres. Later he was wounded at Arras and was in hospital for a time, after which he returned to the firing line, and was in action at Cambrai. He holds the General Service and Victory Medals, and was demobilised in November 1919.
Woodside, near Luton. 3440/B.

HART, C., Sapper, Royal Engineers.
Volunteering in 1915, he was drafted to France in the following year, and was in action on the Somme. He holds the General Service and Victory Medals, and was demobilised in 1919.
11, Breakspeare Road, Abbots Langley. X3443.

HART, C. W., 1st Air Mechanic, R.A.F.
He joined in February 1917, and after his training was engaged on important duties which required a high degree of technical skill. He rendered valuable service, but was unable to procure his transfer to a theatre of war before the termination of hostilities. He was still serving in 1920.
Princess Street, Toddington. 3496/A—3497/A.

HART, F., Pte., 2nd Bedfordshire Regiment.
Volunteering in November 1914, he was drafted to France in the following June, and was in action at the Battles of Loos, Arras, Ypres, Armentières, and St. Quentin. During his service overseas he was twice wounded and gassed, and in September 1918 was invalided home. He was discharged in the following November, and holds the 1914-15 Star, and the General Service and Victory Medals.
112, St. Andrew's Street, Leighton Buzzard. 3501.

HART, G., 2nd Lieutenant, Royal East Kent Hussars (The Duke of Connaught's Own Mounted Rifles).
Volunteering as a private in November 1914, he was later promoted to commissioned rank and proceeded to the Western Front. He took part in the Battles of Arras, Ypres and Cambrai, and also served in the Retreat and Advance of 1918, and after the conclusion of hostilities returned to England and was demobilised in October 1919, holding the General Service and Victory Medals.
Princess Street, Toddington. 3496/B—3497/B.

HART, H. G. H., 1st Air Mechanic, R.F.C.
He volunteered in November 1915, and after his training proceeded to the Western Front, where he was engaged on important duties which required a high degree of technical skill. He was present at the Battles of the Somme and Ypres, and was gassed and was invalided home. In March 1918 he was discharged, and holds the General Service and Victory Medals.
53, Estcourt Road, Watford. X3500.

HART, J. F., Private, 3rd Queen's (Royal West Surrey Regiment).
He joined in May 1917, and in the following October was drafted to France, where he was in action at Cambrai, the Somme and Ypres, and served in the Retreat and Advance of 1918. After the cessation of hostilities he returned to England, and in March 1919 was demobilised, holding the General Service and Victory Medals.
6, Stanbridge Road, Leighton Buzzard. 3469.

HART, L. S., Private, Tank Corps.
Joining in June 1918, he was drafted to France on the completion of his training, and was in action at Arras. After the cessation of hostilities he returned home, and in March 1919 was demobilised, holding the General Service and Victory Medals.
6, Bedford Road, Hitchin. 3474.

HART, R. D., Private, 7th Bedfordshire Regt.
Volunteering in November 1914, he was drafted to France in the following July and was in action at the Battle of Loos and in the Somme sector. In June 1916 he was invalided home owing to ill-health, and was discharged as medically unfit. Later he died on June 28th, 1917, and was entitled to the General Service and Victory Medals.
Princess Street, Toddington. 3496/C—3497/C.

HART, R. J., Driver, Royal Engineers.
Volunteering in January 1915, he was drafted to the Dardanelles in the following July and took part in the Gallipoli campaign, being in action at the landing at Suvla Bay. Later he was sent to the Western Front, where he was engaged on important transport duties in the Cambrai sector. He returned home and was demobilised in November 1919, and holds the 1914-15 Star, and the General Service and Victory Medals.
Woodside, near Luton. 3440/A.

HART, T. B., Private, 11th Royal Fusiliers.
He was mobilised on the outbreak of hostilities, and proceeded to the Western Front in 1914. He took part in the Retreat from Mons and the Battles of La Bassée, Ypres, and Festubert, and was killed in action near Messines on June 26th, 1916. He was entitled to the Mons Star, and the General Service and Victory Medals.
The Grove, Station Road, Woburn Sands.   Z3444/A.

HART, T. F., Corporal, 7th Bedfordshire Regt.
Volunteering in October 1915, he was drafted to the Western Front in the following June, and took part in the Battle of the Somme. Later he was wounded in action near Arras, and was invalided home and discharged in October 1916. He holds the General Service and Victory Medals.
28, Lattimore Road, St. Albans.   X3465.

HART, T. G., Gunner, Royal Field Artillery.
Volunteering in August 1914, he was drafted to France in the same year and took part in the Retreat from Mons and the Battles of La Bassée, Festubert, the Somme, Arras and Cambrai. He holds the Mons Star, and the General Service and Victory Medals, and was demobilised in December 1919.
The Grove, Station Road, Woburn Sands.   Z3444/B.

HART, W., Corporal, Northamptonshire Regt.
Volunteering in October 1914, he was drafted to the Western Front in the following January, and took part in the engagements at Ypres, Loos, the Somme, Arras, and Cambrai. He was killed in action on October 2nd, 1918, and was entitled to the 1914-15 Star and the General Service and Victory Medals.
Woodside, near Luton.   3440/C.

HART, W., Private, 2nd Bedfordshire Regiment.
He volunteered in November 1914, and in the following June was drafted to the Western Front, where he took part in numerous engagements, and was in action in the Arras, Ypres and Armentières sectors. On October 15th, 1916, he died of wounds received in action, and was entitled to the 1914-15 Star, and the General Service and Victory Medals
112, St. Andrew's Street, Leighton Buzzard.   3494.

HART, W. B. (M.S.M.), Private, 14th London Regiment (London Scottish), and 21st London Regiment (The Queen's).
He volunteered in August 1914, and in the following year was drafted to the Western Front, where he took part in the Battles of Ypres and the Somme, and was wounded. He was awarded the Meritorious Service Medal for consistent good work, and in addition holds the 1914-15 Star, and the General Service and Victory Medals. He was demobilised in March 1919.
8, Albert Street, St. Albans.   X3441.

HART, W. G., Sapper, Royal Engineers.
Volunteering in August 1915, he was after his training drafted to Salonika, where he took part in the Balkan campaign. Later he served in Egypt and Malta, and returning to England was discharged in September 1916 in consequence of his service.
69, Park Road West, Luton.   3446/A.

HART, W. J., L/Corporal, R.A.O.C.
He joined in June 1916, and later in the same year proceeded to Ireland, where he served for a time on important duties. In 1917 he was drafted to France, and was stationed at Paris until August 1919, when he returned to England and was demobilised, holding the General Service and Victory Medals.
19, Breakspeare Road, Abbots Langley.   X3442.

HARTLEY, C. J., Private, R.A.S.C. (M.T.)
He joined in July 1915, and having completed his training was drafted to France in the following year. He was present at the engagements on the Somme and at Arras, Ypres and Cambrai, and after the Armistice proceeded to Germany with the Army of Occupation. In July 1919 he returned to England and was demobilised, holding the General Service and Victory Medals.
106, Pinner Road, Oxhey.   X3445.

HARTT, P. W., Driver, Royal Horse Artillery.
He was serving in Egypt on the outbreak of hostilities, and rendered valuable services until, contracting malaria, he was invalided to hospital at Cairo and died on September 29th, 1915. He was entitled to the General Service and Victory Medals.
4, Chambers Lane, Ickleford, Hitchin.   3475.

HARVEY, A., Private, 3rd Hertfordshire Regt.
He joined in June 1916, and after his training was engaged on important duties with his unit at various stations. He rendered valuable service, but was not successful in obtaining his transfer overseas prior to the cessation of hostilities. He was demobilised in October 1919.
38, Portland Street, St. Albans.   3439/A

HARVEY, E. G., Private, Bedfordshire Regt.
He volunteered in August 1914, and in the same year was drafted to the Western Front, where he was in action during the Retreat from Mons, and took part in the Battles of Ypres and Hill 60. He was killed on May 17th, 1915, and was entitled to the Mons Star, and the General Service and Victory Medals.
67, Tilhouse Street, Hitchin.   3463.

HARVEY, W., Private, 1st Bedfordshire Regt.
He was mobilised in August 1914, and in the same month proceeded to the Western Front. In September he was captured during the Retreat from Mons, and was a prisoner of war in Germany until after the Armistice, when he was released, and returning to England was demobilised. He holds the Mons Star, and the General Service and Victory Medals.
38, Portland Street, St. Albans.   3439/B.

HARVEY, W. H., Private, 1/4th Essex Regt.
He volunteered in September 1915, and in the following November was drafted to Mesopotamia, where he took part in the campaign against the Turks, and was in action at Kut-el-Amara. On May 11th, 1916, he died of dysentery, and was entitled to the 1914-15 Star, and the General Service and Victory Medals.
5, Dalton Street, St. Albans.   3437.

HARWOOD, A. G., Private, 1st East Surrey Regt.
He volunteered in December 1915, and in the following year was drafted to France, where he took part in engagements on the Somme and at Arras. Returning to England he was discharged in consequence of his service in July 1917.
113, Lower Paddock Road, Oxhey.   X3438.

HATHAWAY, H., Private, 7th Suffolk Regt.
He joined in April 1916, and in the following October was drafted to France, where after taking part in numerous engagements, he was killed in action near Arras on April 29th, 1917. He was entitled to the General Service and Victory Medals.
43, Arthur Road, St. Albans.   X3507.

HATHAWAY, J., Private, Royal Fusiliers; and Sapper, Royal Engineers.
He volunteered in July 1915, and after having completed his training was drafted to France, where he was engaged on important duties in connection with the railways, and served in the Cambrai and Ypres sectors. He holds the General Service and Victory Medals, and was demobilised in June 1919.
16, Chapman's Yard, Watford   X3508.

HATHAWAY, J., Private, Bedfordshire Regt.
He volunteered in January 1915, and after having completed his training was drafted to Egypt. He served in the Palestine campaign and was in action at Gaza, Haifa, Jaffa and Beyrout, and after the cessation of hostilities returned to England and was demobilised, holding the 1914-15 Star, and the General Service and Victory Medals.
23, Grange Street, St. Albans.   X3510.

HATHRILL, R., Gunner, R.F.A.
He volunteered in December 1915, and was drafted to France in the following July, and took part in the Battles of the Somme, Arras and the Ancre. In November 1917 he was transferred to Italy, and served in the campaign against the Austrians. Returning to France in March 1918, he served in the Retreat and Advance of that year, being in action on the Marne and at Cambrai. He holds the General Service and Victory Medals, and was demobilised in September 1919.
54, John Street, Luton.   3509.

HATTON, A., Private, Bedfordshire and Essex Regiments and Labour Corps.
He joined in May 1916, and in the same year was drafted to France, where he was engaged on important duties in connection with the construction of roads. He was in action on the Somme and at Cambrai, and after the cessation of hostilities returned home and was demobilised in February 1919.
Southill, Beds.   Z3511.

HATTON, C., Sergeant, 3rd Bedfordshire Regt.
He volunteered in August 1914, and during the course of his training was found to be physically unfit for military service. He was consequently discharged in 1915.
14, New Town, Biggleswade.   Z3512.

HATTON, F. H., Private, East Surrey Regiment.
Joining in May 1916, he was drafted to the Western Front in the same year, and was in action on the Somme and at Arras, Ypres and Cambrai, and was three times wounded. He holds the General Service and Victory Medals, and was demobilised in February 1919.
Southill, Beds.   Z3513.

HATTON, S., Sapper, Royal Engineers.
He joined in 1916, and having completed his training was drafted to France in the following year. While in this theatre of war he rendered valuable services with the Royal Engineers for a period of three years, and was in action at Ypres and Bullecourt, and was wounded. Returning home after the Armistice, he was demobilised in April 1919, and holds the General Service and Victory Medals.
94, Judge Street, North Watford. X620/C

HAVELL, W. S., Corporal, R.A.S.C.
He volunteered in August 1914, and in the following June was sent to the Western Front, but shortly afterwards was transferred to Salonika, where he was present at numerous engagements during the Balkan campaign and returning to England was demobilised in March 1919. He holds the 1914–15 Star, and the General Service and Victory Medals.
21, Grange Street, St. Albans. X3514.

HAWES, A., Rifleman, 13th Royal Irish Rifles.
He volunteered in August 1914, and in the following year was drafted to Egypt, where he was stationed at Alexandria. Later he was transferred to the Western Front, where he was in action at Ypres and Arras. He was reported missing on August 16th, 1916, after the Battle of the Somme, and is presumed to have been killed on that date. He was entitled to the 1914–15 Star, and the General Service and Victory Medals.
18, Dudley Street, Luton. 3517.

HAWES, C. W., Gunner, Royal Field Artillery.
He volunteered in 1915, and in the same year was drafted to France, where he was in action at Hill 60, Ypres, the Somme, Arras and Cambrai. After the Armistice he proceeded to Germany with the Army of Occupation, with which he served until September 1919, when he was demobilised, holding the 1914–15 Star, and the General Service and Victory Medals.
63, Piccotts End, Hemel Hempstead. X3524/B.

HAWES, F. C., Gunner, R.N., H.M.S. " Crescent."
He volunteered in October 1914, and was posted for duty with H.M.S. " Crescent," with which vessel he served with the Grand Fleet in the North Sea, and took part in the Battle of Jutland. Later he was engaged on important patrol duties in the Baltic. He holds the 1914–15 Star, and the General Service and Victory Medals, and was still serving in 1920.
9, Spencer Road, Luton. 3525/A.

HAWES, J. J., Private, 1st Hertfordshire Regt.
He volunteered in August 1914, and at the conclusion of his training early in the following year was drafted to the Western Front. His service in this theatre of war lasted for over three years, during which time he fought at Hill 60, Ypres, St. Julien, Festubert, Givenchy, Cambrai and St. Quentin, and was wounded. He was demobilised in February 1919, and holds the 1914–15 Star, and the General Service and Victory Medals.
63, Piccotts End, Hemel Hempstead. X3524/A.

HAWES, O. B., Private, 1st Bedfordshire Regt.
He joined in September 1916, and after his training, owing to his being under age for foreign service, was engaged on important duties at various stations in England. He did valuable work until the cessation of hostilities, and was demobilised in September 1919.
9, Spencer Road, Luton. 3525/B.

HAWES, W., Private, R.A.S.C. (M.T.)
He volunteered in August 1915, and in the following January was sent to the Western Front, where he served for three years, and did valuable work in connection with the transport of supplies to the forward areas in the Somme, Ypres and Cambrai sectors. He was demobilised in June 1919 after returning home, and holds the General Service and Victory Medals.
40, King's Road, St. Albans. 3543.

HAWKES, A. A., Sapper, Royal Engineers.
Joining in March 1916, he was sent to the Western Front after completing his training. He served on important duties with his unit in many sectors, and did valuable work, notably at Messines Ridge, Arras, Ypres, the Somme and Cambrai, where he was wounded in 1918. Returning to England, he was discharged as unfit for further service in October of that year, and holds the General Service and Victory Medals.
23, North Street, Luton. 3518.

HAWKES, A. F., Sapper, Royal Engineers.
Volunteering in February 1915, he was drafted to France in the following August, and did much good work with his unit. He was sent to Egypt in November 1917 and afterwards served in the Palestine campaign, during which he was chiefly engaged in testing the drinking water on the line of march of our troops. He was present at the Battles of Gaza and the Occupation of Haifa and Damascus. On returning to England in May 1919 he was demobilised, and holds the 1914–15 Star, and the General Service and Victory Medals.
28, Liverpool Road, Watford. X3542/A.

HAWKES, A. F., Gunner, R.H.A.
He joined in February 1917, and after his training was sent to France. In this theatre of war he fought in many important engagements, including those at Cambrai and the Somme, and after the termination of hostilities proceeded to Germany with the Army of Occupation. He was demobilised in November 1919 after returning home, and holds the General Service and Victory Medals.
42, Watson's Walk, St. Albans. X3532.

HAWKES, A. S., Sapper, Royal Engineers.
Joining in June 1916, he was sent overseas six months later. Whilst in France he was engaged on duties of an important nature in the forward areas, and was present at various engagements, including those at Arras, Ypres, the Somme and Cambrai. He was demobilised on his return to England in March 1919, and holds the General Service and Victory Medals.
23, Tavistock Street, Luton. 3527.

HAWKES, F., Private, 2nd London Regiment (Royal Fusiliers).
He volunteered in September 1914, and after his training served on the Western Front for three years. During this period he took an active part in many of the principal battles, including those of the Somme, Arras and Ypres, and was wounded. On returning to England in February 1919 he was demobilised, and holds the General Service and Victory Medals.
102, Albert Road, Luton. 3538.

HAWKES, H. C., Sergeant, 4th Essex Regiment.
He volunteered in September 1914, and until January 1916, when he was drafted to Egypt, was retained on duties of an important nature He subsequently served in the Palestine campaign, and was wounded and taken prisoner at Gaza in March 1917. Returning to England after his release at the cessation of hostilities, he was demobilised in February 1919, and holds the General Service and Victory Medals
Hoo Lane Cottages, Offley. 3530.

HAWKES, J., Private, R.A.S.C. (M.T.)
Joining in June 1917, he was sent to Egypt in the following December, and later was engaged on important duties in connection with the transport of supplies to the forward areas during the Palestine campaign. He was demobilised on his return to England in March 1920, and holds the General Service and Victory Medals.
32, Victoria Road, North Watford. X3519.

HAWKES, J. L., Private, R.A.M.C
Volunteering in September 1914, he was sent to the Dardanelles in July of the following year, and took part in the landing at Suvla Bay and the subsequent engagements. After the Evacuation of the Peninsula he was drafted to the Western Front, where he again rendered valuable service in many battles, including those of Ypres, Armentières and Kemmel Hill. He was demobilised in January 1919, and holds the 1914–15 Star, and the General Service and Victory Medals.
32, Hartley Road, Luton. 3535.

HAWKES, S. R., Private, R.A.S.C. (M.T.)
He joined in April 1917, and after his training saw much service in Mesopotamia, Persia, Russia, and Salonika, where he was engaged in the transport of supplies to the forward areas. He was demobilised on his return to England in August 1919, and holds the General Service and Victory Medals.
41, Althorp Road, Luton. 3536.

HAWKES, S. W., Corporal, Royal Army Pay Corps.
He joined in July 1917, and after his training was engaged on important clerical duties at his depôt. He was not successful in obtaining his transfer overseas before the termination of hostilities, but did valuable work until demobilised in January 1919.
28, Liverpool Road, Watford. X3542/B.

HAWKINS, B. (M.M.), Private, Bedfordshire Regiment and Machine Gun Corps.
He volunteered in July 1915, and on the completion of his training served on the Western Front, where he took a prominent part in the fighting at Arras, Ypres, Bullecourt, Cambrai and Albert, and was wounded. He was awarded the Military Medal for conspicuous gallantry on the Field in October 1917, and in addition holds the General Service and Victory Medals, being demobilised in January 1919.
24, Albert Road, Luton. 3537.

HAWKINS, C. H. G., Sapper, Royal Engineers.
He joined in July 1917, and after his training served on important garrison duties at several stations. In 1918 he was sent to Germany with the Army of Occupation, and was stationed on the Rhine until October in the following year, when he was sent home and demobilised.
30, Water Lane, Watford. X3540.

HAWKINS, F., Air Mechanic, Royal Air Force (late Royal Flying Corps).

He joined in May 1916, and in the same year was drafted to France and stationed at Rouen, where he was engaged on important duties which demanded a high degree of technical skill. He was demobilised in February 1919, and holds the General Service and Victory Medals.
160, Upper Cravell's Road, Harpenden.   3541.

HAWKINS, F., Private, 2nd Essex Regiment.

He was serving at the outbreak of war, and was almost immediately drafted to the Western Front and took part in the Retreat from Mons and in the first Battle of Ypres. He was killed in action at St. Jean on May 13th, 1915, and was entitled to the Mons Star, and the General Service and Victory Medals.
27, Newcombe Road, Luton.   .   3516/C.

HAWKINS, F., Private, 3rd Bedfordshire Regt.

He volunteered in October 1914, and was drafted to France and served at Ypres and Hill 60, where he was wounded. After his recovery he took part in the fighting at Passchendaele, St. Julien, Cambrai and St. Quentin, and was gassed. He was demobilised in 1919, and holds the 1914–15 Star, and the General Service and Victory Medals.
The Folly, Wheathampstead.   3520.

HAWKINS, F., Rifleman, Rifle Brigade.

He joined in August 1918, and after his training was drafted to Germany with the Army of Occupation. He was stationed at Cologne on important duties until March 1920, when he was demobilised after his return to England.
Wheathampstead Road, Harpenden.   3522/B.

HAWKINS, F. E., Private, 5th Bedfordshire Regt.

He joined in October 1916, and during the course of his training was found to be unfit for military service and was discharged in March 1917.
52, King's Road, Luton.   3534.

HAWKINS, F. J., Private, 4th Essex Regiment.

He volunteered in 1914, and on the completion of his training was drafted to Egypt in the following year. During his service in the Offensive on Palestine he fought at Gaza and in numerous other engagements during the campaign, and was wounded. In February 1919 he was demobilised, and holds the General Service and Victory Medals.
Wheathampstead Road, Harpenden.   3522/A.

HAWKINS, G., Air Mechanic, Royal Air Force.

He joined in 1916, and in the same year was drafted to Palestine, where he served in the Battles of Gaza on important duties with his section. Owing to ill-health he was invalided home and discharged in September 1917. He holds the General Service and Victory Medals.
133, Bearton Road, Hitchin.   3531.

HAWKINS, H., Gunner, Royal Field Artillery.

He volunteered in May 1915, and after his training served on important duties at various stations until 1918, when he was drafted to France. Here he took part in many of the later engagements of the war, and was wounded. He was demobilised in April 1919, and holds the General Service and Victory Medals.
65, Farley Hill, Luton.   3526.

HAWKINS, H., Air Mechanic, Royal Air Force.

He joined in October 1917, and in the same year was drafted to France. Whilst in this theatre of war he was engaged on important duties in connection with aircraft, and served at Arras, Cambrai and St. Quentin, and was gassed   He was demobilised in March 1919, and holds the General Service and Victory Medals.
Wheathampstead Road, Harpenden.   3523.

HAWKINS, J. A., Private, Machine Gun Corps.

Volunteering in 1915, in the following year he was drafted to France, where he took part in various important engagements, including those of Ypres and Lens. He was taken prisoner at Cambrai in November 1917, and was held in captivity in Germany for about a year. In May 1919 he was demobilised, and holds the General Service and Victory Medals.   10, Capell Road, Oxhey, near Watford.   X3515.

HAWKINS, R. A., Private, R.A.S.C. (M.T.)

He volunteered in November 1914, and in August 1916 was drafted to the Western Front. Here he served on important duties in connection with the transport, and was present at various notable engagements, including those of the Somme and Ypres. He returned home in February 1920, and was demobilised in the following month, and holds the General Service and Victory Medals.
66, Spencer Road, Luton.   3533.

HAWKINS, W. E., Private, 6th South Staffordshire Regiment.

He volunteered in June 1915, and in February 1917 was sent overseas. During his service on the Western Front he took part in various important engagements, and was severely gassed in action. He died from gas-poisoning on December 8th, 1917, and was entitled to the General Service and Victory Medals.
57, Portland Street, St. Albans.   3544/A.

HAWKINS, W. E., Bombardier, R.F.A.

He volunteered in April 1915, and after serving at various stations on important duties was drafted to Mesopotamia in 1917. On this front he served in the capture of Baghdad, and in all subsequent engagements up to the Occupation of Mosul. He returned home and was demobilised in March 1919, and holds the General Service and Victory Medals.
57, Portland Street, St. Albans.   3544/B

HAWKINS, W. F., A.B., R.N., H.M.S. "Dauntless."

He joined the Navy in January 1918, and was posted to H.M.S "Dauntless." Whilst in this ship he served on important and dangerous patrol duties in the North Sea and off the coast of Russia. He took part with his vessel in the raid on Zeebrugge in 1918, and was wounded in action. He holds the General Service and Victory Medals, and in 1920 was still serving.
16, West Street, Watford.   3521.

HAWKINS, W. F., Private, R.A.S.C.

He joined in 1916, and in the same year was drafted to France. During his service on the Western Front he was engaged on duties of an important nature in connection with the maintenance of supplies for the front line troops. He was demobilised in January 1920, and holds the General Service and Victory Medals.
29, Princess Street, Dunstable.   3529.

HAWKSWORTH, C. P., Air Mechanic, R.A.F.

He joined in June 1918, and after his training served at various aerodromes on important duties in connection with aero-engines. He did excellent work, but owing to the cessation of hostilities was unable to proceed overseas. He was demobilised in February 1919.
51, Buxton Road, Luton.   3528/B.

HAWKSWORTH, P. C., Driver, R.F.A.

He volunteered in April 1915, and in the following February was drafted to France, where he served for exactly two years. During this period he was present at engagements at Arras, Ypres, Cambrai and Lens, and after the cessation of hostilities returned home and was demobilised in February 1919, holding the General Service and Victory Medals.
51, Buxton Road, Luton.   3528/A.

HAWLEY, H., Private, R.M.L.I.

He volunteered in August 1914, and was stationed at various places on the East Coast engaged on important guard duties. He rendered valuable services, but owing to being medically unfit for active service was unable to obtain his transfer overseas, and was demobilised in May 1919.
23, Hockcliffe Road, Leighton Buzzard.   1293/A.

HAWTHORN, G., Private, 1st Somerset Light Infantry.

A serving soldier, he was drafted to France with the original Expeditionary Force, and took part in the Retreat from Mons. On August 23rd, 1914, he was taken prisoner, and was held in captivity in Germany for 4½ years. After his release he was sent home and discharged in February 1919, and holds the Mons Star, and the General Service and Victory Medals.
35, Cannon Road, Watford.   X3539/B.

HAYDEN, J. E., Private, Labour Corps.

He joined in February 1917, and was drafted to France in the same month. During his service on the Western Front he was engaged on important duties in connection with road repairs, and was present at engagements at Arras, Vimy Ridge and Cambrai. He was demobilised in November 1919, and holds the General Service and Victory Medals.
13, Orchard Road, Walsworth, Hitchin.   3550.

HAYES, A. J., Private, Queen's (Royal West Surrey Regiment).

He joined in 1916, and in the same year was drafted to the Western Front. During his service in France he fought on the Somme, and at Ypres and Cambrai, and was wounded in action. He was invalided home and discharged on account of his injuries in September 1918, and holds the General Service and Victory Medals.
69, Grover Road, Oxhey, Herts.   X3554.

HAYFIELD, C., Private, Bedfordshire Regt.
Volunteering in 1915, he was rejected on medical grounds for overseas service, and after his training was engaged at various stations on important duties. He rendered valuable services, and was demobilised in 1919
Town Yard, Barton, Beds. 3551.

HAYLEY., W. A., Driver, R.A.S.C.
Volunteering early in September 1914, he was drafted to the Western Front in the following February. Whilst in this theatre of war he served at Neuve Chapelle, Ypres, Loos and Lens, and was wounded and gassed in action and in January 1916 was sent to Egypt. Remaining there, for only two months he returned to France, and was present at the Battles of the Somme and St. Quentin, and in many subsequent engagements until the conclusion of hostilities. He holds the 1914–15 Star, and the General Service and Victory Medals, and was demobilised in June 1919.
72, Hartley Road, Luton. 3546.

HAYNES, F. W., Private, R.A.S.C.
He volunteered in February 1915, and in the same year was drafted to France. During his service he was stationed at Boulogne on important duties in connection with the food supplies for the troops. He did excellent work for four years, and was demobilised in April 1919, and holds the 1914–15 Star, and the General Service and Victory Medals.
Westoning, Ampthill. 3549.

HAYNES, H. A., Air Mechanic, R.A.F.
He joined in 1916, and after his training served at various depôts on important duties which required a high degree of technical skill. He rendered valuable services, but was not successful in obtaining a transfer overseas before the cessation of hostilities, and was demobilised in February 1919.
9, Bury Lane, Rickmansworth. X3555.

HAYWARD, F. J., L/Corporal, 1st Dorsetshire Regiment.
He joined in November 1916, and after his training was completed was sent overseas. During his service in France he took part in many important engagements, including that of Ypres. On August 11th, 1918, he was killed in action during the Advance, and was entitled to the General Service and Victory Medals.
6, Hatfield Road, St. Albans. X3547.

HAYWARD, G., Private, Labour Corps.
He joined in June 1917, and in the following July was drafted to France, where he served on important duties at various stations, including Dunkirk. He was present at the engagements at Albert, Amiens and Étricourt, and in many others subsequently. In October 1919 he returned home and was demobilised, and holds the General Service, and Victory Medals.
8, Duke Street, Luton. 3553.

HAYWARD, L. C., Private, Royal Berkshire Regiment.
He volunteered in August 1915, and was drafted to France on the completion of his training. Whilst serving on the Western Front he took part in various important engagements. He was accidentally killed in the trenches at Albert by the explosion of one of our own bombs on March 22nd, 1917, and was entitled to the General Service and Victory Medals. 58, Arthur Street, Luton. 3548/A.

HAYWARD, P., Private, R.A.S.C.
He volunteered in October 1915, and was drafted in the same month to France. Here he was engaged on important duties in loading and unloading the shipping at Le Havre. In September 1917 he was sent to Ireland, and stationed at Curragh camp until March in the following year, when he was discharged through causes due to his service. He holds the 1914–15 Star, and the General Service and Victory Medals.
58, Arthur Street, Luton. 3548/B.

HAZEL, W. J., L/Corporal, Middlesex Regiment.
Joining in May 1916, he was drafted to France in January of the following year. He took part in severe fighting at Arras, Bullecourt, Passchendaele, Cambrai and Ypres, and was recommended for the Military Medal for conspicuous gallantry. He was demobilised in September 1919, and holds the General Service and Victory Medals.
192, Wallow Road, Luton. 3556.

HEAD, F. W., Air Mechanic, Royal Air Force.
Joining in September 1916, he was drafted to the Western Front in the following year. He was engaged on important work connected with aeroplanes n various sectors. His duties, which demanded a high degree of technical skill, were carried out with great efficiency, and he rendered valuable services. During his service overseas he was gassed. He was demobilised in November 1918, and holds the General Service and Victory Medals.
99, Liverpool Road, Watford. X3715/B.

HEADING, A. E., Private, Suffolk Regiment.
He joined in 1916, and was drafted to France in the same year, where he took part in severe fighting on the Somme and at Beaumont-Hamel, and was wounded. In 1917 he was transferred to Italy, and served on the Piave and Asiago fronts. He was demobilised in March 1919, and holds the General Service and Victory Medals.
68, Bernard Street, St. Albans. X3728/A.

HEADING, L., Private, Queen's Own (Royal West Kent Regiment).
Jo ning in 1918, he was sent to France in the same year. He took part in many important engagements, including that at Cambrai, and was wounded. He returned home and was demobilised in 1919, and holds the General Service and Victory Medals.
68, Bernard Street, St. Albans. X3728/B.

HEALEY, A. H., Driver, Royal Field Artillery.
He volunteered in August 1915, and was drafted to France in December of the following year and took part in various engagements, including those at Vimy Ridge, Ypres and Cambrai. He was also awarded the Croix de Guerre for conspicuous gallantry, and in addition holds the General Service and Victory Medals. He was demobilised in July 1919.
6, Brixton Road, Watford. X3694.

HEALEY, T., Corporal, 11th Middlesex Regt.
He was serving at the outbreak of war, and was drafted to the Western Front, where he took part in severe fighting at Ypres and in many other important engagements. He was killed in action on May 24th, 1915, and was entitled to the 1914–15 Star, and the General Service and Victory Medals
26, Water Lane, Watford. X3693/A.

HEARN, F., Sapper, Royal Engineers.
He joined in April 1916, and in the same year was drafted to France, where he took part in many engagements, including those at Poperinghe, Arras and Cambrai. He was demobilised in April 1919, and holds the General Service and Victory Medals.
19, Bedford Road, St. Albans. X3736.

HEARN, G., Corporal, Royal Field Artillery.
Volunteering in August 1914, he was sent to France immediately afterwards. He took part in severe fighting at Mons, Ypres, the Somme, Cambrai and in many other engagements, and was wounded. He was still serving in 1920, and holds the Mons Star, and the General Service and Victory Medals.
55, Bermack Row, Apsley End. X3705.

HEARN, H., Private, Hertfordshire Regiment.
He volunteered in August 1914, and having completed his training was sent to the Western Front. He saw much fighting in several engagements, including those of Arras and Cambrai, and after the Armistice returned home and was demobilised in February 1919, holding the General Service and Victory Medals.
Bowman's Green Cottages, London Colney, near St. Albans.
X1077/A.

HEARN, W. G., Corporal, Hertfordshire Regt.
He volunteered in August 1914, and having completed his training was sent to France. While overseas he saw much fighting at Arras, Cambrai and Ypres, and was wounded. On his return home he was demobilised in February 1919, holding the General Service and Victory Medals.
Bowman's Green Cottages, London Colney, near St. Albans.
X1077/C.

HEASMAN, A., Pte., 4th Royal Berkshire Regt.
He joined in June 1916, and was drafted to France in October of the same year. He took part in severe fighting on the Somme and at Albert, and was severely wounded near Péronne, losing the sight of his right eye. He was invalided home and discharged as medically unfit in October 1917, and holds the General Service and Victory Medals.
56, Springfield Road, Linslade, near Leighton Buzzard. 3731.

HEATH, F. G., Corporal, 22nd London Regiment (The Queen's).
He was mobilised in August 1914, and served on important duties with his unit until June 1916, when he was drafted to France, where he took part in severe fighting on the Somme and at Arras. In December of the same year he was transferred to Salonika, and served on the Doiran and Vardar fronts. In June 1917 he was sent to Egypt and Palestine, where he was again in action. He was demobilised in June 1919, and holds the General Service and Victory Medals.
27, Lattimore Road, St. Albans. X3718.

HEATH, J. H., Sergeant, Royal Field Artillery.
He volunteered in February 1915, and in the following year was drafted to Mesopotamia and took part in the Relief of Kut. He contracted malaria and was invalided home. On his recovery he was sent to France, where he was in action on the Somme and at Arras. He was demobilised in December 1918, and holds the General Service and Victory Medals.
Charlton, Moggerhanger, Sandy, Beds.   Z3721.

HEATHFIELD, F. C., Sergeant, 3rd Grenadier Guards.
He was mobilised in August 1914, and served on important duties with his unit until July 1917, when he was drafted to Egypt and Palestine, where he took part in various engagements, including those at Gaza and Jericho. He was killed in action near Gaza on June 4th, 1918, and was entitled to the General Service and Victory Medals.
Bedford Road, Shefford.   Z3737.

HEATHFIELD, G., Private, Bedfordshire Regt.
He was mobilised in August 1914, and was sent immediately afterwards to the Western Front, where he took part in heavy fighting during the Retreat from Mons and at Neuve Chapelle, Festubert and Loos. He was taken prisoner on the Somme in 1916, and employed on farm work in Germany. On his release he returned home and was demobilised in February 1919, and holds the Mons Star, and the General Service and Victory Medals.
7, North Bridge Street, Shefford.   Z3702/A.

HEDGE, C., Private, 6th Bedfordshire Regt.
Volunteering in August 1914, he was afterwards drafted to the Western Front, where he took part in numerous engagements, including those on the Somme, at Arras and Ypres, and was gassed. He was demobilised in February 1919, and holds the 1914-15 Star, and the General Service and Victory Medals.
49, Ivy Road, Luton.   3713.

HEDGE, C. J., Rifleman, King's Royal Rifle Corps.
He joined in September 1916, and after his training served at various stations on important duties with his unit. He rendered valuable services, but was not successful in obtaining his transfer overseas before the cessation of hostilities on account of his medical unfitness. He was demobilised in March 1919.
34, Cardiff Road, Watford.   X3743/A.

HEDGE, S., Corporal, Royal Sussex Regiment
Volunteering in September 1914, he was drafted to France in the following year. He took part in severe fighting at Ypres, the Somme, Arras, Cambrai and in many other important engagements. He was demobilised in January 1919, and holds the 1914-15 Star, and the General Service and Victory Medals.
34, Cardiff Road, Watford.   X3743/B.

HEDGECOCK, C., Corporal, King's Own (Yorkshire Light Infantry).
Volunteering in January 1915, after his training was drafted to the Western Front in the same year and took part in severe fighting at Ypres and on the Somme. He was reported missing, and is presumed to have been killed in action in July 1916. He was entitled to the 1914-15 Star, and the General Service and Victory Medals.
42, Shaftesbury Road, Watford   X3943/C—3944/C.

HEDGES, A., Private, Bedfordshire Regiment.
He volunteered in September 1914, and was drafted to France in the same year. He took part in numerous engagements, including those at Hill 60, Givenchy, Ypres, the Somme and Cambrai, and was wounded. He was demobilised in 1919, and holds the 1914 Star, and the General Service and Victory Medals.
3, Bell Terrace, Redbourn.   3741.

HEDGES, A. E., Private, 8th Norfolk Regiment.
Joining in 1916, he was drafted to France in the same year. He took part in numerous engagements, including those on the Somme, at Arras and Ypres, and was wounded near Cambrai in March 1918. He was demobilised in February 1919, and holds the General Service and Victory Medals.
21, Beaudesert, Leighton Buzzard.   3730.

HEDGES, C. E., Private, Hertfordshire Regt. and Oxfordshire and Buckinghamshire Light Infantry.
He volunteered in 1914, and served on important duties with his unit until 1916, when he was drafted to the Western Front, where he took part in severe fighting on the Somme and at Ypres, Cambrai and St. Quentin, and was twice wounded. He was demobilised in 1919, and holds the General Service and Victory Medals.
78, Holywell Road, Watford.   X3732/B.

HEDGES, F., Private, Bedfordshire and Middlesex Regiments
He volunteered in October 1914, and after his training served at various stations on important duties with his unit. He rendered valuable services, but was not successful in obtaining his transfer overseas. He was discharged in October 1916.
78, Holywell Road, Watford.   X3732/A.

HEDGES, F., Driver, Royal Field Artillery.
He volunteered in October 1915, and early in the following year was sent to Mesopotamia, where he took part in fighting at Kut and in the Occupation of Mosul. Throughout his service overseas, which lasted for three years, he did valuable work with his Battery, and was demobilised on his return to England in February 1919. He holds the General Service and Victory Medals.
54, Inkerman Road, St. Albans.   X3710.

HEDGES, J., Private, 5th Bedfordshire Regt.
Volunteering in August 1914, he was sent to France a month later, and served in the Battles of La Bassée and Ypres. In March 1915 he was drafted to the Dardanelles, and subsequently took part in the landing at Gallipoli, and was wounded. After the Evacuation of the Peninsula he proceeded to Malta, where he served for the remaining period of hostilities engaged on special duties. He was demobilised in March 1919, and holds the 1914 Star, and the General Service and Victory Medals.
128, Heath Road, Leighton Buzzard.   3720.

HEFFER, J., Private, 1/5th Bedfordshire Regt.
He volunteered in July 1915, and in the following January was sent to Egypt, where he took part in several minor engagements, including the destruction of the Turkish camp at Jiffjaffa on April 13th, 1916. He also served in the Palestine campaign, during which he participated in the Battles of Gaza and in the capture of Aleppo and Jerusalem. Returning to England in March 1919, he was demobilised a month later, and holds the General Service and Victory Medals.
41, Arthur Road, St. Albans.   X3711.

HEIGHTON, A. G., Sergeant, R.F.A.
Called up from the Reserve at the outbreak of hostilities, he was for some time engaged on special duties. In September 1917, however, he was drafted to India, where he was engaged on garrison duties until October 1919. He was demobilised in the following December, and holds the General Service and Victory Medals.
6, Kimberley Road, Fleetville, St. Albans.   X3700.

HEIGHTON, G. E., Sergeant, 1st Life Guards.
He volunteered in August 1914, and after his training served in France for three years. During this time he fought in many important battles, notably those of Ypres, Arras and Cambrai, and did excellent work with his unit. He holds the 1914-15 Star, and the General Service and Victory Medals, and was demobilised in January 1919.
25, Norman Road, Luton.   3699.

HEMBURY, H. J., Gunner, R.G.A.
Volunteering in October 1915, he completed his training and afterwards served on the Western Front for three years. During this period he was engaged in the fighting on the Somme, at Ypres and Cambrai, and also served in the Retreat and Advance of 1918. He was demobilised in March 1919, and holds the General Service and Victory Medals.
Robin Hood Cottage, New Town, Hatfield.   X3707.

HEMLEY, F. G., Air Mechanic, R.A.F.
He volunteered in 1915, and at the conclusion of his training was engaged on important duties with his unit at various stations. Owing to physical disability he was unable to secure his transfer to a theatre of war, but nevertheless did valuable work until he was demobilised in 1919.
10, Hagden Lane, Watford.   X3733/A.

HEMLEY, H. W., Private, R.A.V.C.
He volunteered in 1916, and on completing his training was engaged on duties of an important nature with his unit. He was unsuccessful in obtaining his transfer overseas before the cessation of hostilities, but nevertheless rendered valuable services until his demobilisation, which took place in 1919.
10, Hagden Lane, Watford.   X3733/B.

HEMLEY, W., Private, Northamptonshire and Bedfordshire Regiments.
He volunteered at the commencement of hostilities, and was quickly sent to France, where he served in the Retreat from Mons and the Battle of Ypres. Early in 1915 he was drafted to the Dardanelles, and was severely wounded during the fighting on the Peninsula. Returning to England in consequence, he was invalided out of the Service in June 1917, and holds the Mons Star, and the General Service and Victory Medals.
East Weymouth Street, Apsley End.   X3722.

HEMMING, A. L., Corporal, R. E. (Signal Section).
He volunteered in 1915, and after his training was drafted to the Western Front, where he was engaged on duties of an important nature in the forward areas. After the termination of hostilities he advanced with the Army of Occupation into Germany, and was demobilised on his return to England in October 1919. He holds the General Service and Victory Medals.
23, Cromer Road, Watford. X3717/A.

HEMMING, V., Staff-Sergeant, Royal Army Cyclist Corps.
Volunteering in September 1914, he joined in the Hampshire Regiment and was later transferred to the Royal Army Cyclist Corps. Early in 1915 he was drafted to the Dardanelles and subsequently fought in several engagements until the Evacuation of the Peninsula. He was afterwards engaged on duties of an important nature until his demobilisation, which took place in March 1919, and holds the 1914-15 Star, and the General Service and Victory Medals.
18, Bradshaw Road, Watford. X3717/B.

HENDERSON, A. V., Special War Worker.
During the war he held an important position at the Commercial Cars Factory, Luton, where he was engaged on responsible work in connection with the supply of motor transport to the War Office. The manner in which he carried out his arduous duties was worthy of the highest commendation.
25, Saxon Road, Luton. 3698.

HENDERSON, W. J., Private, Queen's (Royal West Surrey Regiment).
He joined in June 1918, and at the conclusion of his training was engaged on duties of an important nature with his unit. Owing to the fact that he was under age for military service he was unable to secure his transfer overseas, but nevertheless did valuable work until he was demobilised in March 1919.
5, Copsewood Road, North Watford. X3740.

HENDIN, C., Private, R.A.M.C.
Volunteering in October 1915, he was sent to France at the conclusion of his training and served at Ypres, the Somme, Arras and St. Quentin, later being drafted to the Italian Front. Throughout his service overseas he did excellent work with his unit, and on one occasion was wounded. He holds the General Service and Victory Medals, and was demobilised after his return to England in September 1919.
103, Cotterell's Road, Hemel Hempstead. - X3706.

HENLEY, E., Sapper, Royal Engineers.
He joined in June 1916, and a month later was drafted to the Western Front, where he was engaged upon duties of an important nature, principally in the Somme and Cambrai sectors. In 1918, in consequence of ill-health, he was invalided to a hospital in Leeds, and was under treatment for about a year. He was demobilised in March 1919, and holds the General Service and Victory Medals.
Sandy Lane, Woburn Sands. Z3723.

HENLEY, H., Private, 10th London Regiment.
He volunteered in July 1915, and was sent to Egypt at the conclusion of his training. After taking part in several minor engagements on this front he returned to England on leave, and was afterwards drafted to France. He fought in many important battles whilst in this theatre of war, and was severely gassed and invalided home. He was discharged as medically unfit in September 1919, and holds the 1914-15 Star, and the General Service and Victory Medals.
Royston Street, Potton, Beds. Z3729.

HENMAN, A., Rifleman, King's Royal Rifle Corps.
He joined in May 1916, and after his training was sent to France in February of the following year. He took part in much severe fighting at the Battles of Arras, Ypres, the Somme and Cambrai, and was gassed and wounded. He was demobilised in February 1919 after his return home, and holds the General Service and Victory Medals.
21, Henry Street, Luton. 3709.

HENMAN, A., Private, Bedfordshire Regiment.
He was mobilised in August 1914, and was sent to France in the same month. He took part in many important engagements, including the Retreat from Mons and the Battles of the Marne and the Aisne, and was taken prisoner near Ypres in October 1914. On his release he returned home and was demobilised in February 1919, and holds the Mons Star, and the General Service and Victory Medals.
Hillside, Lidlington. Z3725.

HENMAN, E. (Mrs.), Special War Worker.
This lady was engaged on work of National importance at Messrs. Kent's Factory and the Diamond Foundry, Luton, for a year. She was employed in making detonators and hand-grenades, and carried out her responsible duties with care and efficiency.
21, Wood Street, Luton. 3696.

HENMAN, F., Private, Bedfordshire Regiment.
He volunteered in May 1915, and was soon drafted to the Western Front, where he took part in the severe fighting at Festubert, Loos and the Somme, and was wounded. Being invalided home, he was afterwards transferred to the Labour Corps, and was engaged in guarding prisoners of war. He was demobilised in March 1919, and holds the 1914-15 Star, and the General Service and Victory Medals.
Hillside, Lidlington. Z3724.

HENSON, E. F., Private, 1st Hertfordshire Regt.
Volunteering in August 1914, he was sent to France immediately afterwards. He took part in numerous engagements, including those at Mons, Ypres, Arras and the Somme, and was severely wounded. He died of his injuries on November 16th, 1917, and was entitled to the Mons Star, and the General Service and Victory Medals.
2, Cape Road, St. Albans. X3719.

HENSON, P. E., Rifleman, King's Royal Rifle Corps.
He volunteered in November 1914, and was drafted to France in the same year. He took part in severe fighting at Ypres, Neuve Chapelle, the Somme, Arras and Cambrai, and after the Armistice proceeded with the Army of Occupation to Germany. He was demobilised in February 1919 after his return home, and holds the 1914-15 Star, and the General Service and Victory Medals.
121, Park Street, Luton. 3697.

HERBERT, E. A., Private, 6th Leicestershire Regiment.
After being mobilised in August 1914, he was retained on important duties with his unit until November 1916, when he was drafted to the Western Front. While overseas he took part in numerous engagements, and was wounded and taken prisoner near Cambrai. He died in captivity on March 31st, 1918, and was entitled to the General Service and Victory Medals.
Mill Lane, Clophill, Ampthill. 3739/A.

HERBERT, R. G., Pte., 4th Bedfordshire Regt.
He volunteered in November 1915, and was drafted to France in July of the following year. He took part in the severe fighting on the Somme and in many other engagements, and was wounded at Gavrelle in April 1917. He was in consequence invalided home, and afterwards discharged owing to his injuries in October 1917, holding the General Service and Victory Medals.
Mill Lane, Clophill, Ampthill. 3739/B.

HERBERT, S. G., Sapper, Royal Engineers.
He volunteered in August 1914, and after his training was engaged at various stations on important duties with his unit. He rendered valuable services, but owing to medical unfitness was not successful in obtaining his transfer overseas before the cessation of hostilities. He was demobilised in February 1919.
Stanhurst, Grove Road, Dunstable. 3703.

HERRIDGE, W. H., Gunner, R.F.A.
He joined in 1916, and proceeded to France in the same year. He took part in much severe fighting in the Battles of the Somme, Ypres, Cambrai, St. Quentin and in many other engagements. He afterwards served with the Army of Occupation in Germany. He was demobilised in January 1920 after his return home, and holds the General Service and Victory Medals.
46, Lower Church Street, Rickmansworth. X3727.

HERRIDGE, W. T., Sapper, Royal Engineers.
Joining in October 1917, he was drafted to the Western Front in the following year. He was principally engaged on water transport duties until the cessation of hostilities, and rendered valuable services. He was demobilised in January 1919, and holds the General Service and Victory Medals.
54, Lower Church Street, Rickmansworth. X3726.

HESTER, A. G., Gunner, R.G.A.
He volunteered in June 1915, and in January of the following year was drafted to the Western Front, where he took part in numerous engagements, including those of the Somme, Arras, Ypres and Cambrai, and was gassed. He was invalided home in consequence, and demobilised in January 1919, holding the General Service and Victory Medals.
4, Sotheron Road, Watford. X3716.

HESTER, G. E., Private, 17th Royal Welsh Fusiliers.
Volunteering in October 1915, he was sent to France in June of the following year. He took part in the severe fighting at Arras, Ypres and many other engagements, and was killed in action at St. Julien on July 1st, 1917. He was entitled to the General Service and Victory Medals.
36, Prospect Road, St. Albans.   X3701.

HESTER, H., Sapper, Royal Engineers.
He joined in June 1918, and after his training was retained at various stations on important duties with his unit. He rendered valuable services, but was not successful in obtaining his transfer overseas before the cessation of hostilities, and was demobilised in December 1918.
35, Jubilee Street, Luton.   3742/B.

HESTER, S. G., Private, Bedfordshire Regt.
He joined in May 1918, and after his training was engaged on important duties with his unit until December of the same year, when he was drafted to the Army of Occupation in Germany. He rendered valuable services on the Rhine until March 1920, when he returned to England and was demobilised.
35, Jubilee Street, Luton.   3742/A.

HEWITT, A., Private, Hertfordshire Regiment.
He volunteered in January 1915, and in the same year, after completing his training, was drafted to the Western Front, where he took part in numerous engagements, including those at Arras, Ypres and Cambrai. He was taken prisoner during the Retreat in March 1918, and after his release was demobilised in March 1919. He holds the 1914–15 Star, and the General Service and Victory Medals.
2, Upper Culver Road, St. Albans.   X3735.

HEWITT, H. G., Sapper, Royal Engineers.
Volunteering in April 1915, he proceeded to France in February of the following year. He did valuable work in many important engagements until hostilities ceased, including those of Vimy Ridge, the Somme, Arras and Cambrai. He was demobilised in January 1919 after returning home, and holds the General Service and Victory Medals.
28, St. Saviour's Crescent, Luton.   3708.

HEWITT, W., Private, Norfolk Regiment.
He volunteered in August 1914, and was afterwards sent to the Western Front, where he took part in the fierce fighting at Arras, Ypres, Passchendaele and Cambrai, and acted as runner for his company. He was afterwards drafted to Italy, and did good service there. While overseas he was wounded and gassed. He was demobilised in March 1919, and holds the General Service and Victory Medals.
67, Copsewood Road, Watford.   X3714/B.

HEWITT, W. F., Corporal, R.A.V.C.
Joining in February 1917, he was sent to Egypt and subsequently to Palestine in the same year. He did much valuable service in many important engagements there, including those at Gaza and Jaffa. He returned home and was demobilised in November 1919, holding the General Service and Victory Medals.
Grove Road, Harpenden.   3692.

HEWITT, W. J., Sergeant, Royal Engineers.
He joined in October 1917, and shortly afterwards proceeded to France. He was engaged on the Ypres, Passchendaele, Roulers and Messines fronts on railway construction work, and rendered valuable services. He was demobilised in May 1919, after coming back to England, and holds the General Service and Victory Medals.
67, Copsewood Road, Watford.   X3714/A.

HEWLETT, G. W., Sergeant, 5th Bedfordshire Regiment.
He volunteered in September 1914, and in the following July was drafted to the Dardanelles, where he took part in the landing at Suvla Bay, and in the subsequent engagements until the Evacuation of the Peninsula. In 1917 he was sent to Palestine and fought in the Battles of Gaza, Mejdil Yaba, Haïfa and Acre, and after the cessation of hostilities was stationed at Cairo during the riots. He was demobilised in June 1919 after his return home, and holds the 1914–15 Star, and the General Service and Victory Medals.
3, Grange Road, Luton.   3695/B.

HEWLETT, H. W., Sergeant, 5th East Surrey Regiment.
He volunteered in November 1914, and in June of the following year was sent to India, where he served on the Frontier until September 1916, when he was drafted to Mesopotamia. Here he took part in various operations against the Turks until the conclusion of hostilities. He was sent home and demobilised in September 1919, holding the 1914–15 Star, and the General Service and Victory Medals.
3, Grange Road, Luton.   3695/A.

HEWSON, A., Sapper, Royal Engineers.
He volunteered in November 1914, and in the same year was drafted to France, where he was engaged on important duties in connection with the operations, and was frequently in the forward areas at Vimy Ridge, Cambrai, Kemmel Hill, and Ypres. After the Armistice was signed he advanced into Germany with the Army of Occupation, and remained there until May 1919, when he was demobilised after his return to England. He holds the 1914–15 Star, and the General Service and Victory Medals.
19, Bury Park Road, Luton.   3712.

HEWSON, A., Private, 1st Bedfordshire Regt.
He volunteered in August 1914, and in the following year was drafted to the Western Front. During his service in France he fought in the Battles of Hill 60 and Ypres, and was wounded and gassed at Vimy Ridge. After his recovery he took part in the Battle of Arras, and in the engagements which followed until the cessation of hostilities. He was demobilised in February 1920, and holds the 1914–15 Star, and the General Service and Victory Medals.
The Hill, Wheathampstead.   3734/A.

HEWSON, A. F., Sergeant, Royal Engineers.
He joined in 1916, and in the following year was drafted to France. In this theatre of war he was engaged, until hostilities ceased, on important duties in connection with operations which were in progress, notably at Ypres, Arras and Givenchy. He was demobilised in November 1919 after returning home, and holds the General Service and Victory Medals.
The Hill, Wheathampstead.   3734/B.

HIBBERT, F., Corporal, Leicestershire Regt.
He joined in October 1916, and in the same year was drafted to France, where he took part in the Battle of the Somme, and was wounded. After his recovery he was again wounded at Arras, but later was in action at Ypres and Passchendaele, and in various engagements in the Retreat and Advance of 1918. He was demobilised in November 1919, and holds the General Service and Victory Medals.
120, London Road, St. Albans.   X3796.

HIBBERT, G. W., (D.C.M.), Corporal, Hertfordshire Regiment.
He volunteered in 1915, and in the same year was drafted overseas. During his service in France he fought in numerous important engagements until hostilities ceased, including those of the Somme, Arras, Ypres, Cambrai and the Aisne. He was awarded the Distinguished Conduct Medal for gallantry in action and devotion to duty at Cambrai, and holds in addition the 1914–15 Star, and the General Service and Victory Medals. He was demobilised in February 1919.
109, Lower Paddock Road, Oxhey   X3767.

HIBBERT, H., Corporal, Royal Engineers.
Volunteering in August 1915, he completed his training, and in the same year was drafted to France. While overseas he was frequently engaged in the forward areas whilst operations were in progress, especially at Ypres, Lens, the Somme, and Cambrai, and was wounded. He was demobilised in 1919, after returning to England, and holds the 1914–15 Star, and the General Service and Victory Medals.
70, Bernard Street, St. Albans.   X3801.

HIBBERT, M. F. R., Private, Labour Corps.
He joined in July 1916, and after his training was engaged on important agricultural duties in Essex. He rendered valuable services, but was not able to secure his transfer overseas before the cessation of hostilities, and was demobilised after over three years' service in August 1919.
6, Grove Cottages, Falconer Road, Bushey.   3761/A.

HIBBITT, A. E., Private, R.A.O.C.
He volunteered in September 1914, and on the conclusion of his training was engaged for a time on highly important work at Woolwich Arsenal. He afterwards went to France, where he rendered valuable services at Rouen as a gun-repairer. Owing to dysentery he was invalided to England, and was discharged in November 1917, as unfit for further military duty. He holds the General Service and Victory Medals.
65, Grange Road, Luton.   3791.

HICKINGBOTTOM, C. G., Private, Queen's Own (Royal West Kent Regiment).
He joined in October 1917, and after his training was completed, was drafted to France in the following April. During his service he acted as stretcher-bearer on the Field during engagements in the Retreat and Advance of the Allies, and was killed on the Cambrai front on October 23rd, 1918. He was entitled to the General Service and Victory Medals.
11, Bedford Road, Houghton Regis, Dunstable.   3819.

HICKLIN, F., Gunner, Royal Garrison Artillery.
He joined in March 1916, and in the same year was drafted to India, where he was engaged on special duties at various garrison stations, including Poona and Rawal Pindi. He was demobilised in June 1919 after his return to England, and holds the General Service and Victory Medals.
14, Weymouth Street, Apsley End. X3793.

HICKMAN, H., Driver, Royal Field Artillery.
He was mobilised at the outbreak of hostilities, and for two years was engaged on important duties at various home stations. In October 1916 he was sent to France, and took an active part in many important battles, including those at Arras, Ypres, Cambrai and the Somme, and was wounded in action. He returned to England and was demobilised in January 1919, holding the General Service and Victory Medals.
27, Wimborne Road, Luton. 3778.

HICKS, F., Private, 13th London Regiment (Kensingtons).
He joined in 1917, and in the same year was drafted to Egypt. He afterwards served with the British Forces under General Allenby in their Advance through Palestine, and took part in numerous important engagements throughout the campaign, and was wounded in action. In January 1920 he was demobilised on his return home, after 2½ years' service in the East, and holds the General Service and Victory Medals.
98, Cotterell's Road, Hemel Hempstead. X3788.

HICKS, W. J., Corporal, 13th Royal Sussex Regt.
He volunteered in 1914, and in 1916 after being retained on important duties was sent overseas. During his services on the Western Front he fought in numerous important battles, including those of the Somme, Ypres and Cambrai. He was killed in action in an engagement on April 2nd, 1918, and was entitled to the General Service and Victory Medals.
32, Brightwell Road, Watford. X3811.

HICKS, W. J., L/Corporal, 5th Royal Fusiliers.
Volunteering at the outbreak of war, he was soon drafted to the Western Front, where he saw much service for over 4½ years. He fought at Ypres, the Somme and Arras, and in other engagements until the close of the war, and was wounded in action. In February 1919 he was demobilised after his return to England, and holds the 1914-15 Star, and the General Service and Victory Medals.
34, Albert Street, St. Albans. X3803.

HIGGINS, A., Private, R.A.M.C.
He volunteered in September 1915, and in the same month was drafted to France, where he served as a stretcher-bearer in numerous engagements. Later he acted as an orderly in a hospital at Rouen until June 1919, when he returned to England and was demobilised. He holds the 1914-15 Star, and the General Service and Victory Medals.
3, Bury Park Road, Luton. 3759/A.

HIGGINS, H., Private, Bedfordshire Regiment and Labour Corps.
He joined in June 1916, and in the following November was drafted to the Western Front. During his service in France he did excellent work at Albert, the Somme and Ypres, and in other operations until hostilities ceased. He was demobilised in February 1919, and holds the General Service and Victory Medals.
2, College Place, St. Albans. 3795.

HIGGINS, H. T., A.B., R.N., H.M.S. "Queen."
He joined in July 1917, and was posted for duty with H.M.S. "Queen." He served in the North, Baltic and Ægean Seas, being engaged on important patrol and escort duties. He holds the General Service and Victory Medals, and was demobilised in May 1919.
3, Bury Park Road, Luton. 3759/B.

HIGGINS, S. G., Private, 8th Bedfordshire Regt.
He volunteered in February 1915, and after his training was completed was drafted to France. After taking part in several engagements he was severely wounded at Poperinghe on April 25th, 1916, and died of his injuries on the same day. He was buried in Boeschepe Military Cemetery, and was entitled to the 1914-15 Star, and the General Service and Victory Medals.
38, Stanley Street, Luton. 3809.

HIGGINS, W. F., Corporal, R.A.F. (late R.N.A.S.)
He volunteered in 1915, and after his training served on important duties with the Solent Seaplane Squadron. He was engaged on the Channel Air Defences, and did excellent work, but was not successful in obtaining a transfer overseas before the cessation of hostilities. He was demobilised in January 1919.
33, Temperance Street, St. Albans. 3797.

HIGGS, A., Private, 3rd Leicestershire Regiment.
He joined in February 1916, and in the following September was drafted to France, where he fought at Arras, Vimy Ridge and Ypres. He was severely wounded at St. Quentin, and taken prisoner on September 24th, 1918, and held in captivity in Germany until the following December. After his return home he was demobilised in September 1919, and holds the General Service and Victory Medals.
Chapel Row, Caddington. 3798/B.

HIGGS, C. E., Stoker, Royal Navy, H.M.S. "Indomitable."
He volunteered in November 1915, and was posted to H.M.S. "Indomitable." Whilst in this ship he was continuously engaged on important and dangerous duties, and took part in the Battle of Jutland. He was afterwards gassed at the Zeebrugge landing. He was discharged on account of his service in February 1918, and holds the 1914-15 Star, and the General Service and Victory Medals.
13, Alfred Street, Luton. 1242/B.

HIGGS, C. E. (M.M.), L/Corporal, Bedfordshire Regiment.
He volunteered in May 1915, and was drafted to France in August of the following year. He took part in the Battle of the Somme, and was awarded the Military Medal for conspicuous gallantry. Later he was wounded at Vimy Ridge in April 1917, and was invalided home. He was discharged as medically unfit for further service in October 1918, and holds the General Service and Victory Medals.
16, The Camp View, St. Albans. X3812.

HIGGS, C. R., Private, R.A.S.C. (M.T.)
He joined in 1916, and in the same year was drafted to France, where he was in action at Arras, Ypres and Béthune. After the Armistice he proceeded to Germany with the Army of Occupation, with which he served until February 1919, when he was demobilised, holding the General Service and Victory Medals.
Flitwick Road, Westoning, Ampthill, Beds. 3816.

HIGGS, E., Private, Queen's Own (Royal West Kent Regiment).
He joined in July 1916, and in the following year was drafted to France. He took part in numerous engagements until November 1917, when he died of wounds received in action on the Somme. He was entitled to the General Service and Victory Medals.
92, Bassett Road, Leighton Buzzard. 3752/C.

HIGGS, F. R., Private, Cheshire Regiment.
He joined in February 1917, and in the following November was drafted to the Western Front, where he took part in the Battle of Ypres. After the cessation of hostilities he returned to England, and in December 1919 was demobilised, holding the General Service and Victory Medals.
Chapel Row, Caddington, Luton. 3798/A.

HIGGS, H., L/Corporal, Royal Engineers.
He joined in February 1917, and after his training was engaged as a despatch rider at various stations. He rendered valuable service, but owing to being medically unfit for duty abroad was unable to secure his transfer to a theatre of war prior to the termination of hostilities. He was demobilised in November 1919.
230, Wellington Street, Luton. 3790.

HIGGS, H., Private, 8th Bedfordshire Regiment.
He volunteered in March 1915, and in the following August was drafted to the Western Front, where he took part in the Battle of Loos. During his service overseas he was gassed at Ypres, and severely wounded on the Somme. He was invalided home, and in August 1917 was discharged as medically unfit for further service. He holds the 1914-15 Star, and the General Service and Victory Medals.
105, High Street, Houghton Regis, near Dunstable. 3760.

HIGGS, R., Sapper, Royal Engineers.
He volunteered in April 1915, and in May of the following year was drafted to France, where he was engaged on important duties constructing bridges. He holds the General Service and Victory Medals, and was demobilised in 1919.
2, Local Board Road, Watford. X3799.

HIGGS, R. C., A.B., R.N., H.M.S. "Boadicea."
He volunteered in March 1915, and was posted for duty with H.M.S. "Boadicea." He served on important patrol duties in the North Sea and the Baltic until after the cessation of hostilities, when he returned to his base and was demobilised in May 1919, holding the General Service and Victory Medals.
Westoning, near Ampthill. 3744.

HIGGS, S., Private, Bedfordshire and Hertfordshire Regiments.
He joined in July 1918, and on completion of his training was drafted to France in the following November. After the cessation of hostilities he proceeded to Germany, where he served with the Army of Occupation until March 1920, when he was demobilised, holding the General Service and Victory Medals.
105, High Street, Houghton Regis, Dunstable.   3758/B.

HIGGS, S. J., Sapper, Royal Engineers.
He was mobilised in August 1914, and in the following July was drafted to the Dardanelles, where he took part in the landing at Suvla Bay. After the Evacuation of Gallipoli he was transferred to Egypt and served in the Palestine campaign, being in action at Gaza. He returned to England in June 1919 and was demobilised, holding the 1914–15 Star, and the General Service and Victory Medals.
105, High Street, Houghton Regis.   3758/A.

HIGGS, S. W., Corporal, Royal Sussex Regiment.
He volunteered in December 1914, and was engaged on important duties with his unit until July 1917 when he was drafted to the Western Front. He was in action at Ypres, St. Julien and the Somme, and returning to England in September 1918, was demobilised in the following March, holding the General Service and Victory Medals.
3, Local Board Road, High Street, Watford.   X3800.

HIGGS, W. T., Private, 2nd Bedfordshire Regt.
He volunteered in December 1914, and was sent to the Western Front in the following August. He was wounded at the Battle of the Somme in July 1916, and was gassed at Ypres in the following year. In March 1918 he was taken prisoner at St. Quentin, and was held in captivity until the following December, when he was released, and returning to England was demobilised in March 1919, holding the 1914–15 Star, and the General Service and Victory Medals.
64, High Street, Houghton Regis, near Dunstable.   3817.

HILL, A., Sapper, Royal Engineers.
He joined in June 1917, and after having completed his training was drafted to the Western Front, where he was engaged on important duties on the railways. He was in action on the Somme and at Arras, Cambrai and Ypres, and after the cessation of hostilities returned to England and was demobilised in February 1919, holding the General Service and Victory Medals.
13, Dacre Road, Hitchin.   3751/A.

HILL, A., Private, Berkshire Regiment.
He volunteered in 1915, and was drafted to the Western Front on the completion of his training. He took part in the Battles of Arras and Ypres, and was wounded and in hospital for some time. He holds the General Service and Victory Medals, and was demobilised in 1919.
82, Sopwell Lane, St. Albans.   X3781.

HILL, A., Sergeant, Royal Scots Fusiliers.
He enlisted in August 1909, and on the outbreak of war was drafted to the Western Front, where he took part in the Retreat from Mons and the Battles of the Marne, the Aisne, Hill 60 and Arras, and was wounded eight times. He holds the Mons Star, and the General Service and Victory Medals, and was demobilised in March 1919.
33, Fearnley Street, Watford.   X3815.

HILL, A. E., Rifleman, King's Royal Rifle Corps.
He joined in March 1917, and having completed his training was drafted to France in the following January. He was reported missing after an engagement near Cambrai on March 21st, 1918, and is presumed to have been killed on that date. He was entitled to the General Service and Victory Medals.
38, Liverpool Road, Watford.   X3762.

HILL, A. E., Private, 5th Bedfordshire Regiment.
He volunteered in August 1914, and in the following year was drafted to the Dardanelles, where he took part in the landing at Suvla Bay. Later he was drafted to Egypt, and served in the Palestine campaign. On November 3rd, 1917, he died of wounds received in action at the Battle of Gaza, and was entitled to the 1914–15 Star, and the General Service and Victory Medals.
38, Cowper Street, Luton.   835/B.

HILL, A. H., Corporal, Royal Air Force.
He joined in April 1917, and after his training was engaged on important duties which required a high degree of technical skill. He rendered valuable service, but was not successful in procuring his transfer to a theatre of war prior to the termination of hostilities. He was demobilised in March 1919.
Primrose Hill, King's Langley.   X3770.

HILL, A. P., Private, Labour Corps.
He joined in July 1916, and in the following month was drafted to France, where he was engaged on important duties in the Ypres sector. In March 1919 he returned to England, and in the following month was demobilised, holding the General Service and Victory Medals.
5, Hartley Road, Luton.   3775.

HILL, D., Private, 1st Hertfordshire Regiment.
He was mobilised in August 1914, and was engaged on important duties with his unit until March 1916, when he was posted for special duty in connection with the output of munitions. He was engaged on this vitally important work until January 1918, when he was discharged.
7, Walsworth Villas, Walsworth, Hitchin.   3748.

HILL, E., Private, 7th Bedfordshire Regiment.
He volunteered in May 1915, and in the same year was drafted to France. He took part in the Battle of Loos, and in the fighting at Vimy Ridge, and was wounded. Later he was killed in action at Beaumont-Hamel on September 29th, 1916, and was entitled to the General Service and Victory Medals
High Street, Barton.   4012.

HILL, E., Private, 5th Bedfordshire Regiment.
He volunteered in 1914, and in the following year was drafted to the Dardanelles, where he took part in the landing at Suvla Bay Later he was sent to Egypt and took part in the Palestine campaign, being in action at the Battle of Gaza. Finally he was transferred to the Western Front, where he served until the cessation of hostilities. During his service overseas he was wounded, and returning to England in April 1919 was demobilised, holding the 1914–15 Star, and the General Service and Victory Medals.
6, Langley Place, Luton.   3777.

HILL, E. A., Corporal, Machine Gun Corps.
He volunteered in August 1914, and was immediately drafted to the Western Front, where he took part in the Retreat from Mons and the Battles of Arras, Ypres and Cambrai, and was gassed. He holds the Mons Star, and the General Service and Victory Medals, and was demobilised in January 1919.
33, Liverpool Road, St. Albans.   X3814.

HILL, E. J., Private, Seaforth Highlanders.
He volunteered in September 1914, and in the following year was drafted to France, where he took part in the Battles of Loos, the Somme, Arras and Ypres, and was wounded. On April 23rd, 1918, he was taken prisoner during the Retreat, and was held in captivity until after the Armistice, when he was released. He holds the 1914–15 Star, and the General Service and Victory Medals, and was demobilised in December 1919.
26, Grover Road, Oxhey.   X3820.

HILL, E. J., Corporal, Military Foot Police.
He volunteered in October 1914, and after having completed his training was drafted to the Western Front. He served at St. Omer, Hazebrouck, Dunkirk, La Bassée, the Somme and Ypres, and after the conclusion of hostilities returned to England and was demobilised in March 1919, holding the 1914–15 Star, and the General Service and Victory Medals.
45, Cowper Road, Boxmoor.   X3792.

HILL, F., Private, 6th Queen's Own (Royal West Kent Regiment).
He joined in March 1916, and in the same year was drafted to the Western Front, where he was in action on the Somme and at Ypres, and was wounded at Cambrai in March 1918. He was invalided home, and in the following August was discharged as medically unfit for further service, holding the General Service and Victory Medals.
75, Dane Road, Luton.   3787.

HILL, G., Gunner, Royal Garrison Artillery.
He joined in July 1916, and in the following January was drafted to the Western Front, where he took part in the Battle of Arras. Later he was killed in action at Ypres on October 3rd, 1917, and was entitled to the General Service and Victory Medals.
17, King's Road, Luton.   3773.

HILL, G., Gunner, Royal Field Artillery.
He was serving at the outbreak of war and was drafted to Egypt. Later he took part in the Palestine campaign, and was in action at Gaza and present at the capture of Jerusalem. During his service in the East he was wounded, and after the termination of hostilities returned to England and was demobilised in August 1919, holding the General Service and Victory Medals.
Lowbell Lane, London Colney, St. Albans.   X938/B.

HILL, H., Private, Royal Army Medical Corps.
He joined in July 1916, and in the same year was drafted to the Western Front, where he was present at the Battles of the Somme, Ypres and Cambrai. Returning to England in 1919 he was demobilised, and holds the General Service and Victory Medals.
8, Puller Road, Boxmoor. X3785.

HILL, H. A., Private, 4th Bedfordshire Regiment.
He joined in January 1917, and in the following April was drafted to the Western Front, where he was in action at Ypres and the Somme, and was twice wounded and gassed. He was invalided to hospital in England, but returning to France in June 1918 served in the Cambrai sector. After the termination of hostilities he proceeded to Germany with the Army of Occupation, and served on the Rhine until March 1919 when he returned home and was demobilised, holding the General Service and Victory Medals.
Sharpenhoe Road, Barton. 3745.

HILL, H. S., A.B., R.N., H.M.S. " Turbulent."
He volunteered in November 1914, and was posted for duty with H.M.S. " Turbulent " in the North Sea. His vessel was sunk during the Battle of Jutland, but he was rescued by an enemy ship and made prisoner. He was held in captivity until after the Armistice, when he was released. He holds the 1914–15 Star, and the General Service and Victory Medals, and was demobilised in December 1919.
94, Cobden Street, Luton. 3756/A.

HILL, J., Private, 4th Bedfordshire Regiment.
He joined in July 1916, and in the following November was drafted to France, where he was in action at Beaumont-Hamel and the Ancre. Later he died at Boulogne on February 14th, 1917, of wounds received in action. He was entitled to the General Service and Victory Medals.
13, Kimberley Road, Fleetville. X3779.

HILL, J. W. J., Corporal, Royal Army Medical Corps.
He volunteered in August 1914, and in the same year was sent to the Western Front, where he was in action at the Battles of Ypres, Festubert, Loos, Givenchy, the Somme and Cambrai. Later he was transferred to Italy, and was present at the engagements on the Piave. After the Armistice he served with the Army of Occupation in Austria, until his return to England in January 1920, when he was demobilised, holding the 1914 Star, and the General Service and Victory Medals.
45, Grover Road, Watford. X3763.

HILL, P., Bombardier, Royal Field Artillery.
He volunteered in September 1914, and in the following year was drafted to Mesopotamia, where he took part in the campaign against the Turks. He was in action at Kut-el-Amara, Baghdad and Tekrit, and was present at the capture of Mosul. He returned to England in February 1919 and was demobilised, holding the 1914–15 Star, and the General Service and Victory Medals.
Lowbell Lane, London Colney, near St. Albans. X938/A.

HILL, R., Corporal, Royal Army Service Corps.
He was called up from the Reserve on the outbreak of war, having previously served in the South African campaign, and was immediately drafted to the Western Front, where he was present during the Retreat from Mons and at the Battles of the Marne and Neuve Chapelle. Seriously wounded in action he was invalided home, and in June 1915 was discharged as medically unfit for further service. He holds the Queen's and King's South African Medals, and the Mons Star, and the General Service and Victory Medals.
25, Shott Lane, Letchworth. 3755.

HILL, W., Private, Royal Army Medical Corps.
He joined in May 1917, and after his training served as an orderly at various hospitals. He rendered valuable service, but was not successful in procuring his transfer overseas prior to the termination of hostilities. He was demobilised in May 1919.
14, Ramridge Road, Luton. 3757.

HILL, W., Corporal, 2nd Bedfordshire Regiment.
He volunteered in December 1914, and in the following November was drafted to France, where he was in action on the Somme and at Armentières. He was mentioned in Despatches in November 1917, for conspicuous gallantry and devotion to duty at Montauban. Later he was severely wounded and suffered the amputation of a leg. He was discharged in January 1919, and holds the 1914–15 Star, and the General Service and Victory Medals.
28, Cardigan Street, Luton. 3772.

HILL, W. A., Sergeant, 1st Hertfordshire Regt.
He volunteered in August 1914, and in the following July was sent to France. Serving in several sectors he took an important part in many battles, including those on the Somme, at Ypres, Arras and Cambrai, and was wounded and sent to hospital. On recovery he rejoined his unit in the Field, and was killed in action on July 11th, 1918. He was entitled to the 1914–15 Star, and the General Service and Victory Medals.
7, Union Lane, New Town, Hatfield. X1156/B.

HILL, W. H., Private, Bedfordshire Regiment.
He volunteered in September 1914, and in the following year was drafted to the Dardanelles, where he took part in the Gallipoli campaign and was severely wounded. He was invalided home, and in April 1916 was discharged as medically unfit for further service, holding the 1914–15 Star, and the General Service and Victory Medals.
17, Brache Street, Luton. 3774.

HILLIARD, C., Private, 4th Bedfordshire Regt.
He volunteered in November 1914, and in the following year was drafted to France. During his service on the Western Front he took part in the fighting at Ypres, the Somme and Arras, and in many subsequent engagements until the conclusion of hostilities. He was demobilised in February 1919, and holds the 1914–15 Star, and the General Service and Victory Medals.
6, Alfred Street, Luton. 3808/A.

HILLIARD, P., L/Corporal, York and Lancaster Regiment.
He joined in April 1916, and in the following August was drafted overseas. During his service in France he fought in the Battles of the Somme and Ypres, and was wounded in action. After his recovery he served in many engagements until the cessation of hostilities. He was demobilised in January 1919 after returning home, and holds the General Service and Victory Medals.
6, Alfred Street, Luton. 3808/B.

HILLIARD, R., L/Corporal, 18th London Regt. (London Irish Rifles).
He volunteered in April 1915, and in the following year, being drafted to France, took part in the Battle of Ypres. In 1917 he was sent to Egypt, and served with the British Forces in Palestine, where he fought at Gaza, Jaffa, Haifa, Damascus and Aleppo. During his service overseas he was wounded in action. He returned home and was demobilised in May 1919, and holds the General Service and Victory Medals.
44, Cavendish Road, St. Albans. X3805.

HILLIARD, W., Private, 4th Oxfordshire and Buckinghamshire Light Infantry.
He was mobilised with the Hertfordshire Territorials at the outbreak of war, and in June 1915 was sent to France. Whilst in this theatre of war he served in the Battle of the Somme, and was taken prisoner in a later engagement in February 1917. He was held in captivity in Germany for nearly two years, and was demobilised after his release in February 1919. He holds the 1914–15 Star, and the General Service and Victory Medals.
6, Alfred Street, Luton. 3807.

HILLIARD, W. H., C.S.M., 1st Bedfordshire Regt.
He volunteered at the commencement of hostilities and was quickly sent to the Western Front. During his service in France he was in action at Mons, Ypres and Hill 60, and was wounded in the Battle of the Somme, but after his recovery was again in action at Arras. In 1917 he was drafted to Palestine and served in various operations in the campaign there. He was again wounded and suffered also from malaria. He returned home and was demobilised in April 1919, and holds the Mons Star, and the General Service and Victory Medals.
57, Sopwell Lane, St. Albans. X3782.

HILLS, C., Private, Royal Defence Corps.
He was mobilised in February 1915, after six years' former service in the Army, and having been rejected for overseas service on medical grounds, was engaged on important duties with the Royal Defence Corps at various home stations. In the course of his service he was invalided to hospital, and in July 1917 was discharged as physically unfit for further duty. He afterwards died.
Campton, Shefford, near Bedford. Z3771.

HILLS, O. O. O., Gunner, R.F.A.
He volunteered in May 1915, and in the following year was drafted to France. Whilst in this theatre of war he did good work as a gunner in the Battles of the Somme and Arras, and was wounded in the heavy fighting at Ypres. He was demobilised in May 1919, after four years' service with the Colours, and holds the General Service and Victory Medals.
128, Hartley Road, Luton. 3776.

HILLS, R., L/Corporal, 1st Cambridgeshire Regt.
Volunteering in October 1914, he was retained at first on important duties at several stations. In May 1916 he proceeded to France and fought in the Battles of the Somme, Arras, Givenchy and Ypres, and was severely wounded at Passchendaele on September 26th, 1917. He was invalided home in consequence, and was demobilised in March 1919. He holds the General Service and Victory Medals.
28, King's Road, Hitchin.   3749.

HILLS, W. O., Private, 3rd Machine Gun Corps.
Volunteering in November 1914, he was sent to Mesopotamia in October 1916, and in the following year took part in the capture of Kut-el-Amara and Baghdad. In May 1918 he was drafted to Palestine, where he did valuable work for about a year. He returned home and was demobilised in May 1919, and holds the General Service and Victory Medals.
13, Bolton Road, Luton.   3806.

HILLSDON, J., Sergeant, 4th Bedfordshire Regt.
He joined in October 1916, and was soon drafted to France, where he saw much service. He was in action in the Battles of the Somme, Albert, Vimy Ridge, Ypres and Cambrai, and was wounded in March 1918. After his recovery he fought in various engagements in the Retreat and Advance. He was demobilised in February 1919 after returning home, and holds the General Service and Victory Medals.
9, The Cottages, Napsbury.   X3794.

HILLYARD, J., Private, Bedfordshire Regiment.
He volunteered in 1915, and in the same year was drafted to France, where he fought in the Battles of Ypres and the Somme. He was killed in action on July 26th, 1916, and was entitled to the 1914-15 Star, and the General Service and Victory Medals.
White's Cottages, Westoning, Ampthill.   3804.

HILLYARD, T. J., Private, 14th (King's) Hussars.
Volunteering in September 1914, he was drafted to Mesopotamia in the following year, and served there for nearly 3½ years. He took part in the attacks on Kut-el-Amara and in the subsequent offensive along the Tigris. In September 1919 he returned home and was demobilised, holding the 1914-15 Star, and the General Service and Victory Medals.
Church Street, Westoning, Ampthill.   3746.

HILSDEN, A. C., Private, Bedfordshire Regt.
He volunteered in November 1915, and in July of the following year was sent to France, where he was engaged on important duties with the transport section. He served in the Somme, Albert, Ypres, Arras and Cambrai sectors, and was gassed in action in 1917. He returned home and was demobilised in March 1919, and holds the General Service and Victory Medals.
2, Anderson's Row, Florence Street, Hitchin.   3750.

HILTON, F., Private, 3rd North Staffordshire Regiment.
He joined in March 1916, and was drafted to France in the following May. During his service on the Western Front he fought in the Battles of the Somme, Albert and Arras, and was wounded at Ypres in 1917. After his recovery he was again wounded in action in November of the same year. Returning home in December 1919 he was demobilised in the following January, and holds the General Service and Victory Medals.
40, Aldenham Road, Bushey.   X3810/A.

HILTON, F. W., Pte., Northumberland Fusiliers.
Volunteering in March 1915, he was drafted to France in the same year, after the completion of his course of training. After serving in many engagements he was killed in action on November 14th, 1916, and was entitled to the 1914–15 Star, and the General Service and Victory Medals.
26, Old Park Road, Hitchin.   3747/B.

HILTON, W. A., Private, Queen's (Royal West Surrey Regiment)
He joined in 1916, and after his training was engaged at his depôt on important duties with his unit. He rendered valuable services, but was not successful in obtaining his transfer overseas before the cessation of hostilities, and was demobilised in October 1919.
16, Jubilee Road, North Watford.   X3764.

HILTON, W. H., Private, Royal Fusiliers.
He joined in 1916, and in the same year was drafted overseas. Whilst on the Western Front he served in the Battles of the Somme, Arras, Cambrai and St. Quentin and in subsequent engagements until the cessation of hostilities. He was demobilised in March 1920 after returning to England, and holds the General Service and Victory Medals.
26, Old Park Road, Hitchin.   3747/A.

HILTON, W. J., Corporal, 1st Hertfordshire Regt.
He was mobilised in August 1914, and in the following July was drafted to France. During his service overseas he fought at Loos, the Somme, Lens, Ypres and Cambrai, and was gassed on four occasions. He returned home in December 1918, and was demobilised in the following month, holding the 1914-15 Star, and the General Service and Victory Medals.
40, Aldenham Road, Bushey.   X3810/B.

HINDE, R., Private, Bedfordshire Regiment.
A serving soldier, he came from South Africa at the declaration of war, and on October 2nd, 1914, landed at Zeebrugge with the 7th Division. He took part in the Battles of Ypres, Neuve Chapelle, Festubert, Loos, Givenchy, the Somme and Arras. He was invalided home in 1917, but returned to France in the same year, and was wounded in action near Bapaume on August 23rd, 1918. He holds the 1914 Star, and the General Service and Victory Medals, and was demobilised in March 1919.
Chapel Lane, Wilshamstead.   Z3783.

HINDLEY, J. P., Gunner, R.G.A.
He joined in March 1918, and after completing his training was drafted to France in the same year. He did good work as a gunner in various engagements in the final operations, notably at the fourth Battle of Ypres. In December 1919 he was demobilised after his return home, and holds the General Service and Victory Medals.
11, Fearnley Street, Watford.   X3813.

HINDS, T., Sergeant, Royal Field Artillery.
He volunteered in September 1914, and early in the following year was drafted to France, where he fought in several engagements of importance. In 1916 he was sent to Egypt, and in the following year joined the Palestine campaign, during which he took part in the Battles of Gaza and Jaffa, and in the capture of Haïfa, Aleppo and Damascus. He was demobilised on his return to England in June 1919, and holds the 1914-15 Star, and the General Service and Victory Medals.
30, Hagden Lane, Watford.   X3768.

HINGE, W. J., L/Corporal, Essex Regiment.
He joined the Bedfordshire Regiment in July 1916, and was later transferred to the Essex Regiment. After his training he was drafted to the Western Front, where he was engaged in the fighting at Lens, Cambrai and in other important battles. Owing to ill-health he returned to England early in 1918, and was for some time under treatment in hospital. He was demobilised in February 1919, and holds the General Service and Victory Medals.
Hillford End, Shillington.   3754.

HINKS, J., Private, R.A.S.C.
He volunteered in November 1914, and served on the Western Front for 4½ years. During this period he did excellent work with his unit in connection with the transport of supplies to the forward areas, including the Somme, Arras, Loos and Ypres. On one occasion he was gassed, but after being treated at the base, rejoined his unit. He holds the 1914 Star, and the General Service and Victory Medals, and was demobilised in July 1919.
25, Dane Road, Luton.   3780.

HIPPERSON, C. F. (M.S.M.), R.Q.M.S., R.E.
A serving soldier, he was sent to the Western Front immediately upon the outbreak of hostilities, and fought in the Retreat from Mons and many subsequent engagements. A year later, however, he returned to England suffering from severe shell-shock, from the effects of which he died on January 17th, 1919. He was awarded the Meritorious Service Medal for consistently good work in the Field, and was entitled to the Mons Star, and the General Service and Victory Medals.
5, Queen Street, Houghton Regis, Dunstable.   3818.

HIRDLE, W., 1st Class Stoker, Royal Navy.
Joining in 1917, he obtained his training at Chatham, and afterwards saw much service with the Grand Fleet in the North Sea, and on aeroplane-carrying ships. He did valuable work until after the close of the war, and was demobilised in 1919, holding the General Service and Victory Medals.
Station Road, Ridgmont.   Z3784.

HIRONS, C. A., Private, R.A.S.C. (M.T.)
Joining in September 1916, he was drafted to the Western Front in the following March. During his service overseas he was engaged on important transport work in various sectors, including those of Ypres, the Somme, Cambrai, Albert, Arras and Péronne, and was frequently under heavy fire. He was demobilised on his return to England in October 1919, and holds the General Service and Victory Medals.
23, Stanmore Road, Watford.   X3766.

HISCOCK, T. G., Private, Norfolk Regiment.
Joining in August 1916, he was sent to the Western Front
on the conclusion of his training, and after taking part in
several engagements was killed at Vimy Ridge on April
23rd, 1917. He was entitled to the General Service and
Victory Medals.
15, Ashby Road, North Watford.   X3765.

HISCOCK, W., Rifleman, King's Royal Rifle Corps.
Volunteering at the outbreak of hostilities, he was sent to
France in 1914, and served on that front for over four years.
During this time he took part in the Battles of Ypres, Arras,
Cambrai and the Somme, and in many other important
engagements, and did valuable work with his unit throughout.
He holds the 1914 Star, and the General Service and Victory
Medals, and was demobilised in 1919.
23, Grover Goad, Oxhey.   X3769.

HISEMAN, H., Private, Queen's Own (Royal West Kent Regiment).
Joining in April 1916, he was sent to the Western Front on
completing his training. Whilst in this theatre of war he
fought in many important engagements, including those of
the Somme, Arras and Ypres, and was wounded at Cambrai
during the German Offensive in March 1918. He was
demobilised in August 1919, and holds the General Service
and Victory Medals.
226, High Street, Watford.   X1393/B.

HISKETT, A. W., Private, 22nd Royal Fusiliers.
Volunteering in 1914, he was sent to the Western Front in
October. He was subsequently engaged in the fighting at
La Bassée, Ypres, Hill 60, Festubert, Loos and the Somme,
and was severely wounded in action at Delville Wood in
July 1916. Returning to England he underwent protracted
hospital treatment, and in December 1917 was invalided
out of the Service. He holds the 1914 Star, and the General
Service and Victory Medals.
20, Arthur Road, St. Albans.   X3753/B.

HISKETT, F., (M.M.), Corporal, Royal Engineers.
Joining in April 1916, he was sent to France in the November
following. His service in this theatre of war lasted for three
years, during which time he was engaged on important
duties in the forward areas. He was present at the Battles
of the Somme, Arras and Ypres, and was gassed and wounded
at Cambrai during the German Offensive in March 1918.
In addition to the Military Medal, which was awarded to him
for conspicuous gallantry in the Field, he holds the General
Service and Victory Medals, and was demobilised in March
1919.
27, Lattimore Road, St. Albans.   X3802/A.

HISKETT, F. J., Private, 5th Bedfordshire Regt.
He volunteered in August 1914, and until sent to Egypt in
September 1915, was retained upon duties of a special nature.
After taking part in several engagements on that front, and
having been severely wounded, he returned to England
on leave, during which he died from causes arising out of his
service. He was entitled to the 1914–15 Star, and the
General Service and Victory Medals.
20, Arthur Road, St. Albans.   X3753/A.

HISKETT, H., L/Cpl., 8th Bedfordshire Regt.
Joining in January 1916, he was sent to France in the following December, on the conclusion of his training. After
taking part in several important engagements he was killed
in action at Ypres on July 21st, 1917. He was entitled to
the General Service and Victory Medals.
27, Lattimore Road, St. Albans.   X3802/B.

HITCHCOCK, C. J., Sapper, Royal Engineers.
He joined in June 1916, and after his training was engaged
on duties of an important nature at various stations. Whilst
on the way home from Ireland on board the mail boat
"Leinster," she was torpedoed by a submarine between
Kingstown and Holyhead on October 10th, 1918, and he
was drowned.
25, Astley Hill, Hemel Hempstead.   X3786/B.

HITCHCOCK, F. W., Driver, R.F.A.
He volunteered in 1915, and after the completion of his training was sent to Egypt, where he fought in several minor
engagements. Later he served in the Palestine campaign,
and took part in the Battle of Gaza, and in the occupation of
Haifa and Damascus. Whilst in this theatre of war he contracted fever, of which he subsequently died in hospital at
Alexandria on November 25th, 1918. He was entitled
to the General Service and Victory Medals.
25, Astley Hill, Hemel Hempstead.   X3786/A.

HITE, C. J., A.B., Royal Navy.
He volunteered in August 1914, and after his training was
posted to H.M.S "Offa." On board this vessel, he served
on submarine patrol duties in the North Sea and in the Baltic,
and was also engaged in escorting food and troopships to
and from the United States, France and Russia. He holds
the General Service and Victory Medals, and was demobilised
in March 1919.
6, Letchworth Road, Leagrave, near Luton.   3789/B.

HITE, W. J., Corporal, South Wales Borderers.
He joined in May 1916, and after his training was sent to
India, where he served at various stations, including Poona,
Bangalore and Rawal Pindi. Later he was transferred to
Mesopotamia, and took part in the fighting at Kut-el-Amara,
Baghdad and Ramadieh, and in the occupation of Mosul.
Returning to England after the cessation of hostilities he
was demobilised in December 1919, and holds the General
Service and Victory Medals.
6, Letchworth Road, Leagrave, near Luton.   3789/A.

HOAR, F., Private, Bedfordshire Regiment.
Volunteering in September 1914, he was sent to France in
the same year. He took part in severe fighting on the Somme
and at Arras, Ypres and numerous other important engagements, and was wounded and gassed in February 1919, and
holds the 1914–15 Star, and the General Service and Victory
Medals.
13, Union Street, Hemel Hempstead.   X3901.

HOAR, M., Private, Royal Defence Corps.
He volunteered in October 1914, and was engaged in guarding
bridges and military stores, and other important duties.
He rendered valuable services until he was demobilised in
March 1919.
6, Victoria Terrace, Hemel Hempstead.   X3919.

HOAR, S., Private, 5th Bedfordshire Regiment.
He volunteered in November 1915, and after his training
served at various stations on important duties with his unit.
He rendered valuable services, but was not successful in
obtaining his transfer overseas. He was discharged in June
1916.
39, Dordans Road, Leagrave.   3834.

HOARE, H., Sergeant-Farrier, Royal Field Artillery.
Volunteering in March 1915, he was drafted to France in the
same year, and was present at numerous engagements, including those at Arras, Ypres and Cambrai. He returned home
and was demobilised in September 1919, and holds the
1914–15 Star, and the General Service and Victory Medals.
5, Earl Street, Watford.   X3863/C.

HOARE, H., Private, Bedfordshire Regiment.
He joined in June 1915, and in the following year was drafted
to India. He was engaged at Poona, Rawal Pindi, Bangalore,
and on the North West Frontier on important duties with
his unit, and rendered valuable services. He was demobilised in February 1919, and holds the General Service and
Victory Medals.
42, Ash Road, Luton.   3950.

HOARE, W., Gunner, Royal Field Artillery.
He was mobilised in August 1914, and served on important
duties at various stations until November of the following
year, when he was drafted to the Western Front, where he
took part in heavy fighting at Ypres and Cambrai. He was
later transferred to Palestine, where he was again in action.
He was demobilised in March 1919, and holds the 1914–15
Star, and the General Service and Victory Medals.
9, Arthur Road, Fleetville St. Albans.   X3927/B.

HOBBS, C., Private, Royal Marine Light Infantry.
Volunteering in August 1914, in the same year he was drafted
to the Western Front, where he took part in severe fighting
at Arras, Ypres and the Somme, and was wounded at the
latter place. In 1917 he was transferred to Palestine, and
was in action at Gaza. He was demobilised in April 1919,
and holds the 1914 Star, and the General Service and Victory
Medals.
11, Longmire Road, St. Albans.   X3915/C.

HOBBS, C. P., Private, 5th Canadian Infantry.
Volunteering in August 1914, he was afterwards sent to the
Western Front, where he took part in severe fighting at
Ypres and Festubert and in other important engagements,
and was wounded and gassed. He was discharged in Novem-
ber 1915 owing to his wounds, and holds the 1914–15 Star,
and the General Service and Victory Medals.
Witherington House, High Street, Toddington.   3838/C.

HOBBS, F. B. (M.C.), Captain, 5th Bedfordshire Regiment.

He was serving at the outbreak of war, and in July 1915 proceeded to Gallipoli, where he was engaged at Anzac, Suvla Bay and Chocolate Hill. In December of the same year he was transferred to Egypt, and served in the Canal zone. In 1917 he was sent to Palestine, where he took part in various engagements, including those at El Arish, Gaza, Haifa and Beyrout. During his service overseas he was wounded, and was mentioned in Despatches and awarded the Military Cross for gallantry in the Field. He also holds the 1914-15 Star, and the General Service and Victory Medals, and was demobilised in March 1919.

Kentville, Conway Road, Luton.   3833.

HOBBS, F. C., Chief Petty Officer, R.N., H.M.S. " Magnificent " and " Canopus."

He volunteered in August 1914, and was stationed in the South Atlantic, patrolling near the Falkland Islands. He was engaged on important duties and rendered valuable services until May 1918, when he returned home and was discharged as medically unfit for further service. He holds the 1914-15 Star, and the General Service and Victory Medals.

33, Granville Road, Luton.   3843.

HOBBS, F. J., Trooper, Herts Dragoons.

Volunteering in December 1915, he went through a course of training and afterwards served on important duties with his unit until 1917, when he was drafted to India. He was engaged on various garrison duties, and rendered valuable services until February 1919, when he returned home and was demobilised, holding the General Service and Victory Medals.

The Bridge, King's Langley.   X3887/A.

HOBBS, F. W., Corporal, Machine Gun Corps.

He volunteered in August 1914, and in the same year was sent to the Western Front, where he took part in severe fighting at Ypres, Arras and Cambrai, and in many other engagements. He was killed in action on the Somme on March 21st, 1918, and was entitled to the 1914-15 Star, and the General Service and Victory Medals.

63, Church Street, St. Albans.   X3845—3910/A.

HOBBS, G., Private, Queen's (Royal West Surrey Regiment).

Volunteering in 1915, he went through a course of training and afterwards served at various stations on important duties with his unit. He rendered valuable services, but was not successful in obtaining his transfer overseas before the cessation of hostilities. He was demobilised in 1919.

41, Souldern Street, Watford.   X3905/B.

HOBBS, G. G., Driver, R.A.S.C.

He joined in June 1918, and was engaged on important agricultural duties. He rendered valuable services, but owing to being medically unfit for duty abroad was unable to obtain his transfer overseas. He was demobilised in March 1919.

Princess Street, Toddington, Beds.   577/C.

HOBBS, G. W. A., Sergeant, 8th, Somerset Light Infantry.

He volunteered in 1915, and was drafted to France in the same year. He took part in severe fighting at Loos, the Somme, Arras, Ypres and in many other engagements, and was twice wounded. He was demobilised in December 1919, and holds the 1914-15 Star, and the General Service and Victory Medals.

41, Souldern Street, Watford.   X3905/A.

HOBBS, H. F., Private, Middlesex Regiment.

Joining in May 1917, he was shortly afterwards drafted to the Western Front, where he took part in severe fighting at St. Quentin and Arras. He was later engaged on Military Police duties, and rendered valuable services. He was demobilised in March 1919, and holds the General Service and Victory Medals.

Witherington House, High Street, Toddington.   3838/B.

HOBBS, J., Private, Bedfordshire Regiment; and Sapper, Royal Engineers.

He volunteered in March 1915, and after his training served on important duties with his unit until the following year, when he was drafted to France. During his service overseas he took part in severe fighting at Ypres and Passchendaele, and in various other engagements. He was demobilised in March 1919, and holds the General Service and Victory Medals.

6, Willow Lane, Watford.   X3884.

HOBBS, R. V., L/Corporal, Sherwood Foresters.

Joining in February 1917, he went through a course of training and was afterwards sent to France, where he took part in various engagements, including. those at Albert, Arras, Mount Kemmel and St. Quentin, and was twice wounded. He was demobilised in February 1919, and holds the General Service and Victory Medals.

Corner House, Dunstable Road, Toddington.   3839.

HOBBS, S. R., Private, R.A.O.C.

He volunteered in 1915, and after his training was drafted to the Western Front. He served in various sectors on important duties with his unit, and rendered valuable services. Later he contracted influenza, from which he died on February 5th, 1919. He was entitled to the General Service and Victory Medals.

11, Longmire Road, St. Albans.   X3915/B.

HOBBS, T. E., Private, 10th Essex Regiment.

Joining in April 1916, he was drafted to France in December of the same year. He took part in severe fighting on the Somme and at Messines, Arras, Ypres and Passchendaele, and was wounded. He was invalided home and discharged as medically unfit for further service in May 1918, and holds the General Service and Victory Medals.

12, North Common, Redbourn.   3926.

HOBBS, W. E., Corporal, 6th London Regiment (Rifles).

He volunteered in April 1915, and in February of the following year was drafted to the Western Front, where he took part in numerous engagements, including those on the Somme and at Arras, Bullecourt and Cambrai, and was twice wounded and gassed. He was demobilised in February 1919, and holds the General Service and Victory Medals.

The Bridge, King's Langley.   X3887/B.

HOBBS, W. G., Corporal, 188th Canadian Regt.

He volunteered in January 1915, and was afterwards sent to the Western Front, where he took part in severe fighting at Arras, Ypres, Cambrai, St. Quentin and in various other engagements, and was three times wounded. He was demobilised in February 1919, and holds the General Service and Victory Medals.

Witherington House, Toddington.   3838/A.

HOBBS, W. H., L/Corporal, Machine Gun Corps.

Volunteering in August 1915, in the same year he was sent to France, where he took part in various important engagements, and was afterwards killed in action. He was entitled to the 1914-15 Star, and the General Service and Victory Medals.

34, Castle Road, Fleetville, St. Albans.   X3910/B.

HOCKLEY, S., Private, 16th (The Queen's) Lancers.

He volunteered in September 1914, and served in Ireland on important duties with his unit. He rendered valuable services, but was not successful in obtaining his transfer overseas before the cessation of hostilities. In November 1919 he proceeded to Egypt, where he was still serving in 1920.

26, King's Road, Luton.   1125/A.

HODBY, W., Private, Labour Corps.

He volunteered in August 1915, and after his training served in France for three years, during which period he was engaged on important duties in connection with the light railways in the forward areas. He holds the General Service and Victory Medals, and was demobilised after his return to England in February 1919.

76, Beech Road, Luton.   3860.

HODGE, G., Private, 2nd Bedfordshire Regiment and Labour Corps.

Volunteering in October 1914, he was sent to the Western Front at the conclusion of his training. He was engaged in the fighting at Hill 60, Givenchy, Arras and the Somme, where in November 1917 he was wounded, and after his recovery was transferred to the Labour Corps. He holds the 1914-15 Star, and the General Service and Victory Medals, and was demobilised in February 1919.

128, Cravell's Road, Harpenden.   3916.

HODGE, H., Private, 2nd Essex Regiment.

He joined in June 1917, and after his training was drafted to India, where he served for two years, during which time he was stationed at Rawal Pindi, Poona and Delhi, engaged on duties of an important nature. He was demobilised after his return to England in January 1920, and holds the General Service and Victory Medals.

49, Hibbert Street, Luton.   3953.

HODGES, F. R., Private, R.A.M.C. and Labour Corps.

He joined in April 1916, and after his training was engaged on important duties with his unit at various stations. He was unable to secure his transfer to a theatre of war before hostilities ceased, but nevertheless rendered valuable services until he was demobilised in July 1920.
27, Keyfield Terrace, St. Albans. X3897.

HODGKISS, E. J., Private, R.A.S.C. (M.T.)

Joining in 1916, he was sent to the Italian front at the conclusion of his training. Whilst in this theatre of war he served principally at Taranto, where he was engaged on important duties in connection with the transport of rations for the troops. He was demobilised after his return to England in February 1919, and holds the General Service and Victory Medals.
62, Acme Road, North Watford. X3911.

HODGSON, E. C., Gunner, R.G.A.

He volunteered in 1915, and at the conclusion of his training was sent overseas. During his service on the Western Front he fought at Ypres, the Somme, Arras and Cambrai, and in April 1918 was severely gassed. He holds the 1914–15 Star, and the General Service and Victory Medals, and was still serving in 1920.
3, Church Road, Watford. X3941.

HODSDEN, W. E., Gunner, R.G.A.

Joining in April 1916, he was sent to the Western Front in May 1917, but two months later was invalided home in consequence of ill-health. On his recovery, however, he returned to France and fought in several important engagements, including those at Ypres and the Somme, and after the cessation of hostilities advanced into Germany with the Army of Occupation. He was demobilised in September 1919, and holds the General Service and Victory Medals.
25, North Common, Redbourn. 3854.

HODSON, W. E., Gunner, R.H.A.

He joined in 1916, and shortly afterwards was drafted to France, where he served at Ypres and on the Somme front. Later he was sent to Italy and was in action on the Piave. On the cessation of hostilities he was attached to the Army of Occupation, and proceeded to Germany. He was sent home and demobilised in March 1919, and holds the General Service and Victory Medals.
4, Church Street, Wheathampstead. 124/A.

HOFFMAN, A. E., Gunner, R.G.A.

He joined in December 1914, and after his training was engaged on special duties until he was sent to France in March 1916. He fought on the Somme (where in June 1917 he was wounded), at Arras, Ypres and Cambrai, and did valuable work with his unit until February 1919. On his return to England he was demobilised, and holds the General Service and Victory Medals.
1, Purwell Cottages, Walsworth, Hitchin. 3870.

HOFFMAN, P., Sapper, R.E. (Signal Section).

He volunteered in January 1915, and until he was sent to France in April 1917, was engaged on special work at his depôt. Subsequently he served on important duties in the forward areas, and was present at many engagements, including those at Ypres, Albert, Arras and Cambrai, and was wounded. After the termination of hostilities he advanced into Germany with the Army of Occupation, and was stationed at Cologne. He was demobilised in June 1919, and holds the General Service and Victory Medals.
60, Dacre Road, Hitchin. 3875.

HOLDER, R., Private, 9th Essex Regiment.

He joined in 1916, and after his training was sent to the Western Front, where he fought in several engagements, including that at Ypres. Whilst in action at Arras, he received a severe wound, of which he died on August 15th, 1917, at the 19th Casualty Clearing Station. He was entitled to the General Service and Victory Medals.
39, Albert Street, St. Albans. X3898.

HOLDSTOCK, C., Private, Labour Corps.

He joined in the Royal Field Artillery in June 1916, and was later transferred to the Labour Corps. After his training he served on important duties with his unit at various stations, and although he was unable to secure his transfer overseas before hostilities ceased, did valuable work until he was demobilised in January 1919.
68, Arthur Street, Luton. 3829.

HOLDSTOCK, E. A., Private, Bedfordshire and Hertfordshire Regiments.

He joined in May 1918, and at the conclusion of his training was engaged on duties of a special nature. He was not successful in obtaining his transfer to a theatre of war before the termination of hostilities, but afterwards was sent with the Army of Occupation to Cologne, where in 1920 he was still serving.
43, Reginald Street, Luton 3947.

HOLDSTOCK, F. J., Sapper, Royal Engineers.

He was mobilised at the outbreak of hostilities, and afterwards engaged on duties of an important nature at various stations. Owing to physical disability he was unable to secure his transfer to a theatre of war, and in August 1915 was invalided out of the Service.
130, Hartley Road, Luton. 3949.

HOLDSTOCK, O. S., Sergeant, 5th Bedfordshire and Suffolk Regiments.

He joined the 1/5th Bedfordshire Regiment in October 1916, and in the course of his training was transferred to the Suffolk Regiment. In 1917 he was sent to Egypt, and thence to Palestine, where he took part in many engagements, notably the Battles of Gaza, and the occupation of Haifa and Beyrout. Before returning to England he was stationed for a time in Cairo, and was demobilised in August 1919. He holds the General Service and Victory Medals.
83, Lea Road, Luton. 3956.

HOLDSTOCK, W. J., Private, R.A.M.C.

He joined in 1916, and during his service on the Western Front did valuable work with the Navy and Army Canteen Board, to which he was attached in consequence of physical unfitness for work in a fighting area. Returning to England in 1918, he was invalided out of the Service in September of that year, and holds the General Service and Victory Medals.
2, Ivy Road, Luton. 3946.

HOLLAND, A., Air Mechanic, R.A.F. (late Royal Naval Air Service).

He volunteered in 1915, and after his training served in France for over three years. During this time he was engaged on duties of an important nature which demanded much technical knowledge and skill, and served in aerodromes at Le Havre, Albert and Ypres. He was demobilised on his return to England in 1919, and holds the 1914–15 Star, and the General Service and Victory Medals.
53, Benskin Road, Watford. X1570/B.

HOLLAND, G., Private, 8th Bedfordshire Regt.

He volunteered in August 1914, and after his training served on the Western Front for two years. During this period he fought at Arras, Cambrai, Loos and Ypres, and was twice severely wounded. Returning to England he was invalided out of the Service in October 1917, and holds the General Service and Victory Medals.
44, Dane Road, Luton. 3895.

HOLLAND, H., Private, Scots Guards.

He volunteered in 1915, and after his training was engaged on important duties at various stations. He was not successful in obtaining his transfer overseas before the termination of hostilities, but nevertheless rendered valuable services until he was demobilised in 1919.
53, Benskin Road, Watford. X1570/A.

HOLLAND, H. V., Private, Middlesex Regiment.

He volunteered at the commencement of hostilities, and early in 1915 was drafted to Salonika, where he fought on the Doiran and Vardar fronts. After the cessation of hostilities he served for a time in Constantinople, and was demobilised on his return to England in the latter part of 1919. He holds the 1914–15 Star, and the General Service and Victory Medals.
10, Florence Street, Hitchin. 3877.

HOLLANDS, A. C., Private, R.A.S.C.

He volunteered in August 1914, and at the conclusion of his training was sent to the Western Front. His service in this theatre of war lasted for nearly four years, during which time he was engaged on important duties in the forward areas, and was present at the Battles of Ypres, the Somme and Arras. He holds the 1914–15 Star, and the General Service and Victory Medals, and was demobilised on returning to England in 1919.
7, Cassio Bridge Road, Watford. X3936.

HOLLICK, J., Gunner, Royal Field Artillery.

Volunteering in January 1915, he was drafted to Egypt at the conclusion of his training. He later did valuable work during operations in Palestine, and took part in the Battles of Gaza, and in the capture of Haifa and Aleppo. He holds the 1914–15 Star, and the General Service and Victory Medals, and was demobilised in March 1919.
45a, Puller Road, Boxmoor. X3828.

HOLLIMAN, J., L/Corporal, King's Own Yorkshire Light Infantry.

He volunteered in September 1914, and after his training was for a time engaged on important home duties. In August 1915 he was drafted to the Western Front, where he took part in the fighting at Loos, and on July 1st, 1916, was killed in action on the Somme. He was entitled to the 1914–15 Star, and the General Service and Victory Medals.
San Remo Road, Aspley Guise. Z3922.

HOLLINGSWORTH, W., Rifleman, K.R.R.C.
Volunteering in September 1914, he was quickly sent to the
Western Front, and after taking part in several engagements,
including that at Ypres, was severely wounded near Arras
on April 1st, 1916. Returning to England he underwent
protracted hospital treatment, and in September 1917 was
invalided out of the Service. He holds the 1914 Star, and the
General Service and Victory Medals.
84, Sopwell Lane, St. Albans.   X3920—X3921.

**HOLLIS, E. H., Bandsman, 1/5th Bedfordshire
Regiment.**
Mobilised at the commencement of hostilities, he was engaged
on duties of an important nature until he was sent to Egypt
in 1916. Later he served in the Palestine campaign during
which he took part in the Battle of Gaza, and the capture of
Beyrout and Damascus. He was demobilised on his return
to England in April 1919, and holds the General Service,
Victory, and Long Service and Good Conduct Medals.
9, Cobden Street, Luton.   3756/B.

**HOLLIS, H. C., Private, Queen's (Royal West
Surrey Regiment).**
He joined in June 1918, and was still in training when hostilities ceased. Afterwards, however, he was sent with the
Army of Occupation to Germany, where he was engaged on
duties of an important nature, and was demobilised on his
return to England in April 1920.
2, Chambers Lane, Ickleford, Hitchin   3872.

HOLLMAN, F. W., Private, Bedfordshire Regt.
He volunteered in August 1914, and in the following month
was drafted to France, and fought in the Battles of Ypres
(where he was wounded), Festubert and Loos. He was killed
in action on the Somme on August 14th, 1916, and was entitled
to the 1914 Star, and the General Service and Victory Medals.
19, Capron Road, Dunstable.   3852/B.

HOLLMAN, J., Gunner, Royal Field Artillery.
He volunteered at the outbreak of war, and in the following
month was drafted to France. He did good work as a Gunner
at La Bassée, the first and second Battles of Ypres, and on the
Somme, and was killed in action near Arras on May 4th,
1917. He was entitled to the 1914 Star, and the General
Service and Victory Medals.
19, Capron Road, Dunstable.   3852/A.

HOLLMAN, P., Private, 5th Bedfordshire Regt.
Volunteering at the outbreak of war, he was drafted to
Mesopotamia in July 1915. He took part in the campaign
against the Turks, and was wounded, and later was killed in
action near Kut in September 1915. He was entitled to the
1914-15 Star, and the General Service and Victory Medals.
19, Capron Road, Dunstable.   3852/C.

HOLLOWAY, R., Private, Bedfordshire Regt.
He volunteered in 1915, and after his training was engaged
on important duties with his unit at various stations. He
rendered valuable services, but owing to being medically
unfit for duty abroad was unable to secure his transfer overseas, and was demobilised in May 1919 after about four
years with the Colours.
458, Hitchin Road, Luton.   3907.

**HOLMES, C., Private, 3rd York and Lancaster
Regiment.**
He joined in June 1916, and in the following January was
drafted to France. During his service on the Western
Front he fought in the third Battle of Ypres, and was severely
wounded near Bullecourt in 1917. He was sent home and
admitted to hospital, and after a period of treatment was
invalided out of the Service in February 1918. He holds the
General Service and Victory Medals.
South Street, Leighton Buzzard.   3931.

HOLMES, C. P., Private, Labour Corps.
He joined in September 1916, and in the following March
was drafted to the Western Front, where he was engaged on
important duties in trench-digging and road construction.
He served in the vicinities of Ypres, Arras and Cambrai
until the cessation of hostilities, after which he returned home
and was demobilised in October 1919, holding the General
Service and Victory Medals.
89, Spencer Road, Luton.   3844.

**HOLMES, H., 2nd Lieutenant, Berkshire
(Hungerford) Dragoons and R.A.F.**
He volunteered in March 1915, and in the following November
was drafted to France, where he served on the Somme and at
Ypres with the Berkshire Yeomanry. In 1918 he was
transferred to the Royal Air Force, with which he saw much
flying service. He was demobilised in May 1919, and holds
the 1914-15 Star, and the General Service and Victory Medals.
5, Grove Road, Dunstable.   3900.

HOLMES, P. W., Gunner, R.F.A.
He volunteered in September 1914, and in the following
January was drafted to France. During his service on the
Western Front he did excellent work as a gunner, and took
part in most of the important battles. He was demobilised
in March 1919, and holds the General Service and Victory
Medals.
27, Ship Road, Linslade, near Leighton Buzzard.   3874/B.

HOLMES, W., L/Corporal, R.A.S.C. (M.T.)
He joined in 1916, and in the same year was drafted to France,
where he served on important duties in connection with the
transport, on the Somme and at Ypres and Cambrai. He was
demobilised in October 1919, and holds the General Service
and Victory Medals.
21, St. Margaret's Street, Ipswich.   X3862.

HOLMES, W. A., Private, R.A.M.C.
He joined in 1916, and in the same year was drafted to
France. During his service on the Western Front he was
engaged on important duties with his unit at Arras, Ypres and
Cambrai, and in the engagements which followed until the
cessation of hostilities. He was demobilised in September
1919, and holds the General Service and Victory Medals.
48, Burmack Row, Apsley End.   X3902.

HOLMES, W. J., Private, 7th Bedfordshire Regt.
Volunteering in March 1915, he was drafted to the Western
Front in the following February. Whilst serving in France
he fought in various engagements, including those on the
Somme and at Thiépval and Trônes Wood. He returned
home and was demobilised in March 1919, and holds the
General Service and Victory Medals.
51, Old Bedford Road, Luton.   3934.

HOLT, B. J., Trooper, 1st Bedfordshire Lancers.
He volunteered in September 1914, and in March 1915 was
drafted to France, where he served for four years. He fought
in the engagements at Loos, the Somme, Arras, Ypres and
Cambrai, and in the Retreat and Advance of 1918. After
the Armistice was signed he proceeded into Germany with
the Army of Occupation, and was stationed at Cologne until
March 1919, when he was demobilised on returning to
England. He holds the 1914-15 Star, and the General
Service and Victory Medals.
108, High Street South, Dunstable.   3850/A—3851/A.

HOLT, H., Private, Essex Regiment.
He joined in April 1916, and in the following November
was sent overseas. Whilst in France he fought on the
Somme and at Arras, and Cambrai, and in various
engagements in the Retreat and Advance of 1918. He was
demobilised in April 1919, after exactly three years' service,
and holds the General Service and Victory Medals.
108, High Street South, Dunstable.   3850/C—3851/C.

HOLT, H., Private, Royal Fusiliers.
He volunteered in 1915, and after his training was completed
was drafted to France, where he served for four years.
During this period he took part in many important engage-
ments, and was twice wounded in action. He holds the
General Service and Victory Medals, and was demobilised
in 1919.
St. Elmo, Brampton Park Road, Hitchin.   3823.

HOLT, H., Private, 2nd Bedfordshire Regiment.
He volunteered in November 1914, and early in the following
year was drafted to France. Whilst in this theatre of
war he fought in the Battles of Neuve Chapelle and Festubert,
and was severely wounded at Richebourg. He was sent
home to hospital and invalided out of the Service in January
1916. He holds the 1914-15 Star, and the General Service
and Victory Medals.
10, High Street, Redbourn.   3958/B.

HOLT, J., Private, Royal Inniskilling Fusiliers.
Volunteering in September 1914, he was sent to the Western
Front in April of the following year, and fought in the Battles
of Ypres, Messines and Passchendaele, and was twice
wounded in action. On recovery he took part in many
subsequent engagements until the conclusion of hostilities,
and was demobilised in January 1919. He holds the
1914-15 Star, and the General Service and Victory Medals.
1, Francis Street, Luton.   3889.

HOLT, W., Private, Royal Army Service Corps.
Volunteering in August 1914, he was drafted to France in
the following October. During his service on the Western
Front he was engaged on important transport duties in
connection with supplies for the troops, and was present in
various sectors, including those of the Somme, Arras, Ypres
and Cambrai. He was demobilised on returning home in
March 1919, and holds the 1914 Star, and the General Service
and Victory Medals.
108, High Street South, Dunstable.   3850/D—3851/D.

HOLT, W., Private, Northamptonshire Regt.
He volunteered in April 1915, and in the following year was drafted to France. Here he took part in various important engagements, including those of the Somme, Arras, Ypres and Cambrai, and was wounded. He was demobilised in December 1919, and holds the General Service and Victory Medals.
10, High Street, Redbourn, Herts.   3958/A.

HOLT, W., Private, 2nd Essex Regiment.
He joined in February 1917, and in the same year was drafted to France, where he saw much service. He fought at Arras and Passchendaele, and was gassed at St. Quentin in 1918, and later was severely wounded at Metz, sustaining the loss of a leg. He was invalided to hospital and afterwards demobilised in September 1919, holding the General Service and Victory Medals.
9, Biggin Lane, Hitchin.   3822.

HOLZMEYER, J. J., Private, Bedfordshire Regt.
He volunteered in August 1914, and after his training was completed was drafted to Salonika and served in various operations in the Balkan campaign. He was killed in action in an engagement on December 7th, 1915, and was entitled to the General Service and Victory Medals.
Summer Cottages, Waterside, London Colney, near St. Albans.
X3866/A.

HOMANS, A. G., Rifleman, Rifle Brigade.
He volunteered in November 1915, and in the following year was drafted to the Western Front, where he served in various sectors. He was invalided home suffering from shell-shock, and was discharged as medically unfit for further service in August 1916, and holds the General Service and Victory Medals.
High Street, Woburn Sands.   Z3923.

HONE, G., Private, 5th Bedfordshire Regiment.
He was mobilised with the Territorials in August 1914, and sent to the Dardanelles in July of the following year. He took part in the landing at Suvla Bay, and on the Evacuation of the Peninsula was transferred to Egypt, and served in the Palestine campaign, being present at the Battle of Gaza and other important engagements. During his service overseas he contracted malaria and was in hospital at Alexandria for some time. After the termination of hostilities he returned to England, and in August 1919 was demobilised, holding the 1914–15 Star, and the General Service and Victory Medals.
Austin's Lane, Ampthill.   3871/B.

HONE, J., Sapper, Royal Engineers.
He volunteered in 1915, and proceeded to France in the following year. He took part in numerous engagements, including those on the Somme and the Ancre and at Arras and Cambrai, and was wounded. He was demobilised in November 1919, and holds the General Service and Victory Medals.
Austin's Lane, Ampthill.   3871/C.

HONEY, G., Corporal, Royal Warwickshire Regt.
He joined in August 1917, and after his training served at various stations on important duties with his unit. He rendered valuable services, but was not successful in obtaining his transfer overseas before the cessation of hostilities. He was demobilised in March 1919.
3, Essex Street, Luton.   1126/C.

HONLEY, A., Seaman, R.N., H.M.S. "Queen Mary."
He joined in January 1916, and was posted to H.M.S. "Queen Mary," and served in the North Sea. He took part in the Battle of Jutland and went down with his vessel when it was sunk on May 31st, 1916. He was entitled to the General Service and Victory Medals
32, Hibbert Street, Luton.   3952/A.

HONLEY, S., Private, Bedfordshire Regiment.
Volunteering in August 1915, he was drafted to France in the following year, and took part in severe fighting at Vimy Ridge, the Somme, Passchendaele, Cambrai and in various other engagements. He was demobilised in December 1918, and holds the General Service and Victory Medals.
32, Hibbert Street, Luton.   3952/B.

HOOKER, A., Private, R.A.M.C.
He volunteered in July 1915, and in the same year was drafted to the Western Front, and served on the Somme and at Albert. Later in the same year he was transferred to Salonika, and was engaged on the Doiran front. He was demobilised in September 1919, and holds the 1914–15 Star, and the General Service and Victory Medals.
29, Puller Road, Boxmoor.   X3830.

HOOKER, B., Sapper, Royal Engineers (E.A.)
He volunteered in January 1915, and was drafted to Egypt in the following year. Later he served in the Palestine campaign, and took part in numerous engagements, including those at Gaza, Haifa and Damascus. He was demobilised in July 1919, and holds the General Service and Victory Medals.
32, Bury Park Road, Luton.   3908/A.

HOOKER, E., Chief Petty Officer, Royal Navy.
He joined in January 1918, and throughout his service was stationed at Chatham, where he was engaged on important work. His exceptional abilities and the efficient manner in which he performed his duties won him rapid promotion, and before his demobilisation, which took place in March 1919, he had attained the rank of Chief Petty Officer with only 15 months' service.
4, Alma Cut, St. Albans.   X2982/B.

HOOKER, W., Private, 5th Bedfordshire Regt.
He volunteered in November 1915, and in the following year was sent to France. He took part in severe fighting on the Somme and at Arras, Ypres and Cambrai, and was three times wounded. He was taken prisoner at St. Quentin in May 1918, and was held in captivity until after the Armistice, when he was released and returned home and was demobilised in February 1919. He holds the General Service and Victory Medals.
32, Bury Park Road, Luton.   3908/B.

HOOKER, W. C., Private, Bedfordshire Regt.
Volunteering in September 1914, he was drafted to the Western Front in the following year and took part in severe fighting at Arras and in many other engagements, and was wounded. He was killed in action in 1916, and was entitled to the 1914–15 Star, and the General Service and Victory Medals.
4, Alma Cut, St. Albans.   X2982/A

HOOKHAM, F. A. (M.M.), Private, Duke of Wellington's (West Riding Regiment).
He volunteered in 1915, and in the following year was drafted to the Western Front, where he took part in numerous engagements, including those on the Somme and at Arras, Ypres, Passchendaele and the Marne. During his service overseas he was wounded and was awarded the Military Medal for bravery in the Field. He also holds the General Service and Victory Medals, and was demobilised in February 1919.
6, Bury Lane, Rickmansworth.   X3924/B.

HOOKHAM, G. H., Private, Bedfordshire Regt.
He volunteered in August 1914, and in the following March was sent to France. He took part in severe fighting in various engagements, and was killed in action at Hill 60 on April 18th, 1915. He was entitled to the 1914–15 Star, and the General Service and Victory Medals.
6, Bury Lane, Rickmansworth.   X3924/A.

HOOKHAM, T. B., Trooper, Herts. Dragoons.
Volunteering in August 1914, he was later drafted to the Dardanelles, where he was engaged at Anzac, Suvla Bay and Chocolate Hill. He returned home and was demobilised in February 1919, and holds the 1914–15 Star, and the General Service and Victory Medals.
105, Cecil Street, North Watford.   X3914.

HOOPER, E. W., Private, Royal Air Force.
He joined in 1916, and in the same year proceeded to the Western Front and served in various sectors, including those of Arras, Ypres and the Somme. He was engaged on important duties with his Squadron as a rigger and rendered valuable services. After the Armistice he served with the Army of Occupation at Cologne until August 1919, when he returned home and was demobilised, holding the General Service and Victory Medals.
26, Bury Hill, Hemel Hempstead.   X3906.

HOPE, B., Private, Bedfordshire Regiment.
He volunteered in August 1914, and served on important duties with his unit until August of the following year, when he was sent to France. He took part in severe fighting at Ypres, the Somme, Cambrai and Armentières, and was gassed. He was demobilised in February 1919, and holds the 1914–15 Star, and the General Service and Victory Medals.
22, Arthur Road, St. Albans.   X3865.

HOPE, J., Sapper, Royal Engineers.
Joining in May 1916, he proceeded to France in the same year, and took part in numerous engagements, including those on the Somme and at Arras and Cambrai. He returned home and was demobilised in August 1919, and holds the General Service and Victory Medals.
Hillford End, Shillington.   3879.

HOPKINS, A., Sergeant, Royal Field Artillery.
He was serving at the outbreak of war and proceeded immediately afterwards to France, where he took part in heavy fighting during the Retreat from Mons and at Ypres, Arras and Cambrai, and was wounded. He was invalided home and discharged owing to his wounds in July 1918, and holds the Mons Star, and the General Service and Victory Medals.
Franklin's Cottage, Flitwick. 3846.

HOPKINS, A. J., Sapper, Royal Engineers.
He volunteered in October 1915, and after his training served on important duties with his unit. He rendered valuable services, but was not successful in obtaining his transfer overseas. He was discharged as medically unfit for further service in January 1918.
28, Church Street, Leighton Buzzard. 3825.

HOPKINS, A. E., Private, Bedfordshire Regt. and South Wales Borderers.
He joined in October 1916, and after his training was sent to France, where he took part in severe fighting at Ypres and in other engagements, and was twice wounded. He was invalided home and discharged owing to his wounds in January 1918, and holds the General Service and Victory Medals.
121, Oak Road, Luton. 3858.

HOPKINS, G., Private, Bedfordshire Regiment.
He joined in April 1918, and after his training served on important duties with his unit until November 1918, when he was sent to France and thence with the Army of Occupation to Germany. He was demobilised in December 1919.
Saunder's Piece, Ampthill. 3869.

HOPKINS, G. R., Sapper, Royal Engineers.
Volunteering in June 1915, he was drafted to France in the following year. He took part in various engagements, including those at Arras, Ypres and Albert, and after the cessation of hostilities returned home and was demobilised in June 1919, holding the General Service and Victory Medals.
Primmets Cottages, Ickleford, Hitchin. 3826.

HOPKINS, H., Sergeant, R.A.V.C.
He joined in August 1916, and in the same year was drafted to Salonika. He was engaged in attending to sick and wounded horses and also on instructional duties, and rendered valuable services. He was demobilised in July 1919, and holds the General Service and Victory Medals.
43, Liverpool Road, Watford. X3913.

HOPKINS, H. G., Private, R.A.S.C.
Joining in March 1917, he was drafted to France in the same month. He served in various sectors on important duties with his unit and rendered valuable services. He was invalided home and discharged as medically unfit for further service in May 1918, and holds the General Service and Victory Medals.
24, King's Road, Luton. 3891.

HOPKINS, R., Sapper, Royal Engineers.
He volunteered in 1915, and in the following year was drafted to France. He took part in numerous engagements, including those on the Somme and at Ypres, and was taken prisoner. On his release he returned home and was demobilised in December 1919, and holds the General Service and Victory Medals.
1, Common View, Letchworth. 3827/C.

HOPKINS, R. G., Sapper, Royal Engineers.
Volunteering in November 1915, he proceeded to the Western Front in September of the following year. During his service overseas he took part in many important engagements. He was demobilised in December 1918, and holds the General Service and Victory Medals.
24, Landridge Road, St. Albans. X3937.

HOPKINS, T. L., Private, Seaforth Highlanders.
He volunteered in August 1914, and in the following year was drafted to the Western Front. He took part in severe fighting at Hill 60, Ypres, Loos, Vimy Ridge, the Somme, Arras, Messines, Passchendaele and Cambrai, and after the cessation of hostilities returned home and was demobilised in April 1919, holding the 1914-15 Star, and the General Service and Victory Medals.
37, St. John's Street, Biggleswade. Z3933.

HORLEY, F. W., Private, The Welch Regiment.
He joined early in December 1916, and was almost immediately drafted to Salonika, where he took part in the recapture of Monastir and in the Advance on the Vardar. He suffered severely from malaria during his service, and was discharged on that account in March 1919. He holds the General Service and Victory Medals.
69, Cambridge Street, Luton. 3832.

HORLEY, H. W., Private, 1st Suffolk Regiment.
He volunteered in February 1915, and after his training served at various stations on important duties with his unit. He was chiefly engaged on guard duty at the German prisoners' camps, and rendered valuable services, but he was not able to secure his transfer abroad during hostilities, and was demobilised in January 1919.
35, Henry Street, Luton. 3837/A.

HORLEY, L. I. (Miss), Special War Worker.
In October 1915 this lady accepted an important appointment at the Vauxhall Munition Factory, Luton. She held a responsible position in the fuse department, and the value of her work in this connection cannot be over-estimated. She continued to serve her country with untiring energy until after the termination of hostilities, when she relinquished her appointment.
35, Henry Street, Luton. 3837/C.

HORLEY, T. H. W., L/Corporal, Suffolk Regt.
He joined in April 1918, and in August of the same year was drafted to France. Whilst in this theatre of war he fought in the second Battle of Cambrai and in the final operations until the cessation of hostilities. He was sent home in June 1919, and proceeded to Ireland, where in 1920 he was still serving. He holds the General Service and Victory Medals.
35, Henry Street, Luton. 3837/B.

HORN, J., 20th Hussars.
He had originally joined the Army in 1906, and was drafted to France soon after the declaration of war. During his service on the Western Front he fought at Loos, Ypres, the Somme, Arras and Cambrai, and in the subsequent engagements until the conclusion of hostilities. He was demobilised in March 1919, and holds the 1914 Star, and the General Service and Victory Medals.
34, Ivy Road, Luton. 3859.

HORN, V., Trooper, Hertfordshire Dragoons.
He joined in 1916, and in the same year was sent to the Western Front. During his service in France he fought in the engagements on the Somme and at at Arras, Ypres and Cambrai and in various battles in the Retreat and Advance of 1918. He was demobilised in March 1919, and holds the General Service and Victory Medals.
112, Ridgway Road, Luton. 3945.

HORNE, A., Private, Royal Defence Corps.
He volunteered in October 1914, and was engaged on important duties guarding prisoners of war at various stations. He rendered valuable service until March 1919, when he was demobilised.
128, Cotterell's Road, Hemel Hempstead. X609/A.

HORNE, A., Private, 6th Bedfordshire Regiment.
He volunteered in October 1915, and in the following January was drafted to France, where he served until the termination of hostilities. During this time he fought at Ypres, the Somme, Arras and Cambrai where he was badly gassed, and after the signing of the Armistice advanced into Germany with the Army of Occupation. He was demobilised in February 1919, and holds the General Service and Victory Medals. 13, Bower Lane, Eaton Bray, Dunstable. 3940.

HORNE, A., Private, Machine Gun Corps.
He joined in July 1917, and after his training was engaged on duties of an important nature at various stations. He was unable to secure his transfer overseas before the termination of hostilities, but nevertheless did valuable work until he was demobilised in February 1919.
56, Cromer Road, Watford. X3935/B.

HORNE, G. T., Private, Bedfordshire Regiment.
Volunteering in May 1915, he was sent to France on completing his training and subsequently fought at Ypres, Hill 60, the Somme, Arras and Cambrai. Later he was drafted to the Italian front, where he remained for a year. During his service he was wounded three times, but was able to rejoin his unit on each occasion, after being treated at the base. He was demobilised in January 1919, and holds the 1914-15 Star, and the General Service and Victory Medals.
78, Norfolk Road ,Rickmansworth. X3888/A.

HORNE, H., Private, R.A.S.C.
He joined in June 1916, and after his training served on important transport duties with his unit. He was not successful in securing his transfer to a theatre of war before hostilities ceased, but rendered valuable services, and was demobilised in April 1919.
22, Bedford Road, St. Albans. X3857.

HORNE, J., Private, 1st Bedfordshire Regiment.
He volunteered in August 1914, and was quickly drafted to the Western Front, where he fought in the Retreat from Mons and the Battles of La Bassée, Festubert and Loos. He was killed in action during the Somme Offensive on September 27th, 1916, and was entitled to the Mons Star, and the General Service and Victory Medals.
33, South Street, Leighton Buzzard. 3928.

HORNE, J. W., Private, Queen's (Royal West Surrey Regiment).
He joined in August 1918, but had not completed his training when hostilities ceased. Afterwards, however, he was sent with the Army of Occupation to Germany, where he was engaged on duties of an important nature, and was demobilised on his return to England in February 1920.
56, Cromer Road, Watford. X3935/A.

HORNE, S., Private, 26th Royal Fusiliers.
He joined in June 1916, and was later drafted overseas. He served on the Western Front, taking part in the engagements on the Somme and at Arras and Passchendaele, and was in action during the Retreat and Advance of 1918. He was demobilised in March 1919, and holds the General Service and Victory Medals
114, Long Row, Vandyke Road, Leighton Buzzard. 1585/A.

HORNEY, W., 1st Air Mechanic, R.A.F.
He joined in November 1917, and after his training served at various stations on important duties with his Squadron. He was engaged as a fitter and tester. His work, which demanded a high degree of technical skill, was carried out with great efficiency, and he rendered valuable services. He was not successful in obtaining his transfer overseas before the cessation of hostilities, owing to his medical unfitness for active service. He was demobilised in November 1919.
42, Adelaide Street, St. Albans. X3929.

HORSFALL, A., Private, 399th Employment Coy.
He volunteered in January 1915, and after his training served at various stations on important duties with his unit. He rendered valuable services, but was not successful in obtaining his transfer overseas before the cessation of hostilities, owing to his medical unfitness for active service. He was demobilised in July 1919.
12, Church Street, Leighton Buzzard. 3824.

HORSLER, G. S., Private, 10th Queen's (Royal West Surrey Regiment).
Joining in May 1917, he was drafted to France in the following September. He took part in severe fighting at Ypres and Cambrai, and also served in the Retreat and Advance of 1918. He afterwards proceeded with the Army of Occupation to Germany, there he served until he was demobilised in November 1919, holding the General Service and Victory Medals.
Upper Sundon, West Dunstable. 3955.

HORSLER, R. R. G., Private, R.M.L.I.
He joined in June 1917, and after his training was drafted to Russia. He was in action on the Volga and was wounded. He afterwards served on important duties in Ireland and rendered valuable services. He holds the General Service and Victory Medals, and was still serving in 1920.
111, Albert Road, Luton. 3840.

HORTON, A. B., 1st Air Mechanic, R.A.F.
He joined in April 1918, and after his training was engaged in the repair shops on important work with his Squadron. His duties, which demanded a high degree of technical skill, were carried out in a most efficient manner and he rendered valuable services, but was not successful in obtaining his transfer overseas before the cessation of hostilities. He was demobilised in April 1919.
42, Langley Street, Luton. 3893.

HORTON, F., Private, Queen's (Royal West Surrey Regiment).
Joining in July 1917, he was afterwards drafted to the Western Front, where he took part in severe fighting at Albert, Arras and in many other engagements. He was demobilised in December 1918, and holds the General Service and Victory Medals.
5, Baker Street, Luton. 3894.

HORTON, J., Sergeant, East Surrey Regiment.
He joined in January 1917, and in the same year proceeded to the Western Front, where he took part in numerous engagements, including those at Arras, Ypres, Cambrai and the Somme, and was wounded. He was demobilised in November 1919, and holds the General Service and Victory Medals.
Ampthill Road, Flitwick. 3868.

HORTON, P., Private, 11th Queen's (Royal West Surrey Regiment).
He joined in May 1918, and after his training was engaged on important duties with his unit. He was not successful in obtaining his transfer overseas before the cessation of hostilities, but after the Armistice proceeded to Germany, where he served with the Army of Occupation until January 1920, when he returned home and was demobilised.
28, Winlock Street, Luton. 3942.

HORWOOD, H. G., Private, Worcestershire Regt.
He volunteered in June 1915, and in the following year was drafted to the Western Front, where he took part in severe fighting at Messines and in other engagements. In 1917 he was transferred to Egypt, and later served in Palestine and was in action at Gaza and Jaffa. He was demobilised in December 1919, and holds the General Service and Victory Medals.
Hoo Lane Cottages, Offley. 3821/A.

HORWOOD, V., Private, Royal Fusiliers.
Volunteering in May 1915, he was drafted to the Western Front in the following year. He took part in numerous engagements, including those on the Somme and at Passchendaele, Cambrai and St. Quentin, and after the Armistice proceeded to Germany, where he served with the Army of Occupation until September 1919, when he returned to England and was demobilised, holding the General Service and Victory Medals.
Hoo Lane Cottages, Offley. 3821/B.

HOSIER, B., Private, R.A.S.C.
He volunteered in 1915, and after his training was engaged on important duties with his unit. Later he met with a severe accident, which rendered him unfit for further military service, and he was consequently discharged in March 1916.
59, Weyouth Street, Apsley. X3853.

HOSIER, G., Private, Royal Defence Corps.
He volunteered in November 1914, and served at various stations on important duties with his unit. He was engaged on work in connection with the railways and in guard duties at prisoners of war camps, and rendered valuable services. He was demobilised in March 1919.
57, Chapel Street, Hemel Hempstead. X3904.

HOSIER, P., Private, Queen's Own (Royal West Kent Regiment).
Joining in October 1917, he was sent to France in the same year. He took part in severe fighting on the Somme and at Amiens and Cambrai, and was gassed. He returned home and was demobilised in February 1919, and holds the General Service and Victory Medals.
59, Weymouth Street, Apsley. X3853/B.

HOSIER, W. G., L/Corporal, 1st Bedfordshire Regiment.
He was serving at the outbreak of war, and was immediately afterwards sent to the Western Front, where he took part in numerous engagements, including those at Mons, the Marne, Ypres and Hill 60, and was twice wounded. He was invalided home and discharged owing to his wounds in April 1916, and holds the Mons Star, and the General Service and Victory Medals.
47, Vale Road, Bushey, Watford. X3918.

HOUSDEN, G. R. T., Private, 22nd London Regt. (The Queen's).
He joined in July 1917, and in May of the following year was drafted to the Western Front, where he took part in severe fighting at Cambrai and Albert. He was killed in action during the Advance from Amiens on August 8th, 1918, and was entitled to the General Service and Victory Medals.
39, New Town, Biggleswade. Z3932/B.

HOUSE, A. J., Trooper, 2nd Life Guards.
Volunteering in November 1914, he was drafted to France in July of the following year. He took part in severe fighting in numerous engagements during his period of service overseas, and was twice wounded. He was demobilised in March 1919, and holds the 1914-15 Star, and the General Service and Victory Medals.
40, Bedford Street, Watford. X3864.

HOUSE, C. E., A.B., Royal Navy, T.B. 18.
He volunteered in March 1915, and served in the North Sea and at Scapa Flow, where he was engaged in chasing enemy submarines. He also took part in the bombardment of the Dardanelles. He was demobilised in February 1919, and holds the General Service and Victory Medals.
46, Waterlow Road, Dunstable. 3951/B.

HOUSE, H., Private, 5th Bedfordshire Regiment.
Volunteering in August 1914, he went through a course of training and afterwards served on important duties with his unit until August of the following year, when he was sent to the Dardanelles and was in action at Anzac and Suvla Bay. In December of the same year he was transferred to Egypt, and served on the Canal zone. In 1917 he proceeded to Palestine and was engaged at El Arish, Gaza, Haifa, Acre, Umbrella Hill and Damascus. He was demobilised in July 1919, and holds the 1914-15 Star, and the General Service and Victory Medals.
38, Warwick Road, Luton. 3849.

HOUSE, T., Private, Northumberland Fusiliers.
Volunteering in November 1914, he was drafted to France
in March of the following year. He took part in severe
fighting on the Somme and at Arras, and was reported missing
and is presumed to have been killed in action near Passchendaele on October 23rd, 1917. He was entitled to the
1914–15 Star, and the General Service and Victory Medals.
46, Waterlow Road, Dunstable.   3951/A.

HOUGH, T. E., Private, Royal Berkshire Regt.
He volunteered in January 1915, and in the following year
was drafted to France. During his service on the Western
Front he was wounded in the Battle of the Somme, and after
his recovery fought in the early days of the Retreat, and was
killed in action near Cambrai on March 22nd, 1918. He was
entitled to the General Service and Victory Medals.
32, Longmire Road, St. Albans.   X3855.

HOUGHTON, W., Private, Bedfordshire Regt.
A serving soldier, he had previously joined in 1913, and in
December 1914 was drafted to France. During his service
on the Western Front he took part in the fighting at Neuve
Chapelle, Hill 60 and Festubert, and was severely wounded
on the Ypres front in July 1915. He was invalided home
to hospital and discharged as unfit for further military duty
in June 1916. He holds the 1914–15 Star, and the General
Service and Victory Medals.
8, Penn's Yard, Queen Street, Hitchin.   3876.

HOW, F., Private, Tank Corps.
He volunteered in September 1915, and in the same month
was drafted to the Dardanelles, and was wounded in Gallipoli
in the following December. In 1916 he proceeded to France,
and served on the Somme, at Arras, Ypres, Passchendaele
and Cambrai and in the subsequent engagements until the
cessation of hostilities. He was demobilised in March 1919,
and holds the 1914–15 Star, and the General Service and
Victory Medals.
10, Midland Road, Luton.   3948/A.

HOW, G., Private, 2nd Bedfordshire Regiment.
He joined in 1916, and in the same year was drafted to
France, where he served in the Anti-aircraft Section on the
Somme. He was killed in action at Arras in September
1917, and was entitled to the General Service and Victory
Medals.
56, High Street, Markyate, near Dunstable.   3841.

HOW, H. G., Sapper, Royal Engineers.
He joined in 1916, and in the same year was drafted to the
Western Front. During his service in France he was engaged
on important duties in connection with the operations, and
was frequently in the forward areas. He was killed in action
in the Retreat on April 11th, 1918, and holds the General
Service and Victory Medals.
13, Bernard Street, St. Albans.   X3867.

**HOW, H. G., Ordinary Seaman, R.N., H.M.S.
   "Vulcan" and "Erebus."**
He joined in February 1918, and was posted to H.M.S.
"Vulcan," and whilst in this vessel was engaged on patrol
duties of an important nature. He served in the Pacific
Ocean, the Black Sea and the Sea of Marmora, and during this
period was transferred to a submarine. He holds the General
Service and Victory Medals, and in 1920 was still serving.
10, Midland Road, Luton.   3948/B.

HOW, W., Private, Cheshire Regiment.
He joined in June 1916, and after his training was drafted
to France, where he took part in numerous important
engagements, notably those on the Somme and at Cambrai.
He was twice wounded in action, and was demobilised in
March 1919, and holds the General Service and Victory
Medals.
6, Union Street, Hemel Hempstead.   X3903.

HOW, W. B., Private, Hertfordshire Regiment.
He was mobilised in September 1914, and served on important
duties at various stations until August 1918, when he was
drafted to France. Here he was in action at Amiens, Havrincourt, Cambrai and Ypres and in the engagements which
followed the conclusion of hostilities. He was demobilised in January 1919, and holds the General Service and
Victory Medals.
29, Ashton Road, Luton.   T3831/A.

HOW, W. J., Private, R.A.S.C. (M.T.)
He joined in October 1916, and after his training was completed served on important motor transport duties at his
depôt. He rendered valuable services until, meeting with a
serious accident, he was rendered unfit for further military
duty and was discharged in March 1918.
42, Henry Street, Luton.   3954.

HOWARD, A., Sapper, Royal Engineers.
Volunteering in November 1914, he served on important
duties at various Home stations until 1917, when he was
drafted to Egypt and advanced with the British Forces into
Palestine. Here he was engaged in the forward areas whilst
operations were in progress, and was wounded in April 1918.
He was demobilised after his return to England in June
1919, and holds the General Service and Victory Medals.
21, Bolton Road, Luton.   3925.

HOWARD, A., Private, 4th Bedfordshire Regt.
He volunteered in 1915, and after his training was completed
was engaged on important duties in Home defence until
July 1918, when he was drafted to France. Here he served
in various engagements in the final operations, and was
wounded in action. Later he was present at the entry into
Mons in November 1918. After the cessation of hostilities
he returned to England and was demobilised in the following
March He holds the General Service and Victory Medals.
24, Edward Street, Dunstable.   3835/A.

**HOWARD, C., Private, 18th (Queen Mary's
   Own) Hussars.**
He was serving at the outbreak of war, and was almost imme-
diately drafted to the Western Front, where he fought in the
Retreat from Mons, and was wounded. After his recovery
he was in action again at Ypres, and later was sent home and
discharged on account of his service in September 1915. He
holds the Mons Star, and the General Service and Victory
Medals.
Pasconi, West Parade, Dunstable.   3909.

HOWARD, F. G., Private, Labour Corps.
He volunteered in January 1915, and after his training served
at various stations on important duties with his unit. He
rendered valuable service, but was not successful in obtaining his transfer overseas before the cessation of hostilities,
and was discharged through causes due to his service in May
1918.
60, Hampton Road, Luton.   3847/A.

HOWARD, G., Private, Sherwood Foresters.
He joined in August 1916, and in the following March was
drafted to France. During his service on the Western
Front he took part in the fighting at Ypres, the Somme,
Albert, St. Quentin and Le Cateau. He was demobilised
in February 1919, and holds the General Service and Victory
Medals.
57, Cardiff Road, Watford.   X3939.

HOWARD, H., Sergeant, 3rd Bedfordshire Regt.
He was mobilised at the outbreak of war, and in August 1914
was drafted to France and took part in various early engagements, including the Battle of Hill 60, where he was wounded.
He also served at Ypres, the Somme and Arras, and was
wounded on three further occasions. In February 1919 he
was demobilised, after over 4½ years' service, and holds the
1914 Star, and the General Service and Victory Medals.
24, Edward Street, Dunstable.   3835/B.

HOWARD, S., Private, Machine Gun Corps.
Volunteering in November 1915, he was drafted to France
in the following year. Whilst in this theatre of war he
fought in the Battles of the Somme, Arras, Ypres and Cambrai, and in various engagements during the Retreat and
Advance of 1918. He holds the General Service and Victory
Medals, and was demobilised in January 1919.
100, Victoria Road, Luton.   3957/A.

HOWARD, W. H., Rifleman, Rifle Brigade.
He joined in April 1916, and in September of the following
year was drafted to Mesopotamia. Whilst in this theatre of
war he fought in the engagements at Kut-el-Amara and at
the capture of Baghdad, and was present at the occupation
of Mosul. He holds the General Service and Victory Medals,
and in 1920 was still serving in Mesopotamia.
104, Nightingale Road, Hitchin.   3878.

HOWE, A., Trooper, Hertfordshire Dragoons.
Volunteering in September 1914, he was sent to Egypt and
served with the British Forces under General Allenby in the
Advance on Palestine. where he took part in various operations throughout the campaign. He also served for a time
in France, and was demobilised in March 1919. He holds
the General Service and Victory Medals.
10, Leavesden Road, Watford.   X3861/C.

**HOWE, A. V., Private, Oxfordshire and Bucking-
   hamshire Light Infantry.**
Joining in August 1916, he proceeded overseas in the following December. During his service in France he fought in the
Somme sector and in the Battle of Arras, and was reported
missing after an engagement near Bullecourt on May 3rd,
1917. He was afterwards presumed to have been killed in
action on that date, and was entitled to the General Service
and Victory Medals.
24, Waterloo Road, Linslade, Bucks.   3873/C.

HOWE, F. W., Private, Bedfordshire Regiment.

He joined in 1916, and in the same year was drafted to the Western Front. Whilst in France he fought in the Battles of the Somme, Arras, Cambrai and in many subsequent engagements until the cessation of hostilities. He was demobilised in February 1919, and holds the General Service and Victory Medals.
98, Fishpool Street, St. Albans. X3856.

HOWE, F. W., Corporal, Bedfordshire Regiment and Royal Air Force.

Volunteering at the outbreak of war, he was sent to France in 1914, and fought in various important early engagements, notably at Ypres, and later on the Somme and at Arras. He was four times wounded during his service overseas, and was twice invalided home, returning to the field of action after his recovery. He was demobilised in March 1919, and holds the 1914 Star, and the General Service and Victory Medals. He was afterwards engaged on important work with the War Graves Commission.
51, Sotheron Road, Watford. 3880/A.

HOWE, G., Sergeant, 5th Essex Regiment.

He had joined the Army in 1911, and in 1914 was sent to India and later to the Dardanelles. He returned wounded to England in the following year, after taking part in the landing at Suvla Bay, and on his recovery was drafted to France and fought in the Battle of Ypres. Later he proceeded to Egypt, where he served in many important battles, including those of Gaza, and was again wounded. He was demobilised in June 1919 after his return to England, and holds the 1914-15 Star, and the General Service and Victory Medals.
Austin's Lane, Ampthill. 3848.

HOWE, G. H., L/Corporal, East Yorkshire Regt.

Volunteering in August 1914, he was soon drafted to the Western Front, and fought in various early engagements and later in the Battle of the Somme. He was killed in action on September 26th, 1917, and was entitled to the 1914 Star, and the General Service and Victory Medals.
24, Spring Place, Luton. 3885/A.

HOWE, H. C., Private, Buffs (East Kent Regt.)

He joined in June 1916, and in the following October was drafted to France. He fought in the Battles of the Somme and at Ypres, and in 1918 was taken prisoner at St. Quentin. He was held in captivity in Germany until after the Armistice, when he was released, and was demobilised in December 1919. He holds the General Service and Victory Medals.
62, Kenilworth Road, Luton. 3912.

HOWE, J., Private, Labour Corps.

He volunteered in October 1915, and after his training served on important guard duties at his depôt. He did excellent work, but was not able to secure his transfer overseas before the conclusion of hostilities. He was demobilised in March 1919.
49, Bermack Row, Apsley End, Herts. 1410/B.

HOWE, J. W., Sergeant, 1st Hertfordshire Regt.

He volunteered in November 1915, and was drafted to France, where he served in the Battle of the Somme and at Ypres and Cambrai, and was wounded. After his recovery he fought in various engagements until the conclusion of hostilities, and was demobilised in September 1919. He holds the General Service and Victory Medals.
10, Leavesden Road, Watford. X3861/A.

HOWE, S. E., Private, Machine Gun Corps.

He joined in June 1917, and in the following April proceeded to France. He fought on the Somme front and was reported missing after an engagement in the second Battle of the Somme in May 1918. He was subsequently presumed to have been killed in action at that time, and was entitled to the General Service and Victory Medals.
24, Waterloo Road, Linslade, Bucks. 3873/B.

HOWE, S. G., Private, Labour Corps.

He volunteered in November 1915, and in the following year was sent to France. During his service in this theatre of war he was engaged on important duties in road construction, and was present at engagements at Arras, Amiens and Cambrai. He was demobilised in April 1919, and holds the General Service and Victory Medals.
4, Marsh Road, Leagrave. 3836.

HOWE, W., Private, Bedfordshire Regiment.

Volunteering in August 1914, he was almost immediately drafted to France and took part in the Retreat from Mons. He was buried by the explosion of a shell and was severely wounded and gassed. Invalided to hospital in England, he was discharged as medically unfit for further service in 1915, and holds the Mons Star, and the General Service and Victory Medals.
24, Spring Place, Luton. 3885/B.

HOWE, W., Private, R.A.M.C.

Volunteering in January 1915, he was drafted to Salonika in July of the following year. Whilst in this theatre of war he was engaged on important duties in attending the wounded on the Field and as a stretcher-bearer, and also acted as hospital orderly. He was present at all the engagements on the Vardar front. In 1917 he was sent to Italy, where he served in the same capacities in the Piave sector until the conclusion of hostilities. He was demobilised in June 1919, and holds the General Service and Victory Medals.
24, Waterloo Road, Linslade. 3873/A.

HOWELL, W. A., Private, R.A.S.C. and Essex Regiment.

He volunteered in February 1915, and was drafted to France in the same year and took part in various engagements, including those at Neuve Chapelle and Arras. In 1918 he was transferred to Palestine and served at Haifa and Jaffa. He was demobilised in August 1919, and holds the 1914-15 Star, and the General Service and Victory Medals.
Heath Road, Harpenden. 3917.

HOWLAND, S., Sergeant, Buffs (East Kent Regt.).

He was mobilised in 1914, and was sent immediately afterwards to the Western Front, where he took part in severe fighting during the Retreat from Mons and at Ypres, Arras, Cambrai and Bullecourt, and was three times wounded. He was demobilised in April 1919, but has since re-enlisted in the Royal Engineers, and in 1920 was serving in Ireland. He holds the Mons Star, and the General Service and Victory Medals.
42, Shaftesbury Road, Watford. X3943/A—X3944/A.

HOWLETT, F. T., Sapper, Royal Engineers.

He volunteered in June 1915, and in January of the following year was drafted to Egypt and later served in Palestine. He took part in various engagements, and was wounded at Gaza in March 1917. He returned home and was demobilised in July 1919, and holds the General Service and Victory Medals.
95, Park Street West, St. Albans. X3938.

HOWLETT, F. W., Signalman, Royal Navy, H.M.S. "Nestor."

He was serving at the outbreak of war and was engaged on patrol duty on the Dogger Bank. He afterwards took part in the Battle of Jutland, where his vessel, H.M.S. "Nestor," was sunk, and he was taken prisoner. On his release he returned home and was demobilised in April 1919, and holds the 1914-15 Star, and the General Service and Victory Medals.
High Street, King's Langley. X3886.

HOWLETT, G. (D.C.M.), 2nd Lieutenant, Bedfordshire Regiment and Queen's Own (Royal West Kent Regiment).

He volunteered in December 1914, and in the following month was drafted to France, where he took part in severe fighting at Vimy Ridge, the Somme, Arras and St. Quentin. He was awarded the Distinguished Conduct Medal for bravery at Delville Wood, and was later gazetted to a commission, but afterwards resigned in March 1918. In addition to the Distinguished Conduct Medal he holds the 1914-15 Star, and the General Service and Victory Medals.
3, Shirley Road, Luton. 3842/B.

HOWLETT, P. J., Pte., 1st King's (Liverpool) Regiment.

He joined in March 1916, and was drafted to the Western Front in January of the following year. While in this theatre of war he fought in numerous engagements, including those at Arras, Bullecourt, Cambrai, Ypres and the Somme. After the Armistice he returned home and was demobilised in March 1919, holding the General Service and Victory Medals.
61, West Street, Dunstable. 1110/B.

HOWLETT, W., Private, Bedfordshire Lancers.

He volunteered in September 1914, and having completed his training was drafted to France in June of the following year. While overseas he saw much fighting on the Somme and at Arras, Ypres and Cambrai, and also served in the Retreat and Advance of 1918. Returning home after the cessation of hostilities, he was demobilised in December 1919, holding the 1914-15 Star, and General Service and Victory Medals. 61, West Street, Dunstable. 1110/A.

HOWLETT, W. A., Private, Middlesex Regiment.

He joined in January 1918, and after his training served on important duties with his unit and rendered valuable services. He was later drafted to Egypt, where he was still serving in 1920.
5, Frogmore Cottages, near St. Albans. X3896.

HOWSDEN, T., Private, Bedfordshire Regiment.
He volunteered in August 1914, and proceeded to France in the same month. He took part in severe fighting at Mons, Ypres, the Somme and in many other important engagements, and was killed in action on August 8th, 1917. He was entitled to the Mons Star, and the General Service and Victory Medals.
28, Back Street, Biggleswade. Z3930.

HOY, A. G., Sapper, Royal Engineers (Signals).
Volunteering in August 1914, he afterwards proceeded to the Dardanelles and was engaged at Anzac and Suvla Bay, and was wounded. He was later transferred to Malta and thence to Egypt, where he was employed on various important duties. He returned home and was discharged in January 1918 in consequence of his services. He holds the 1914-15 Star, and the General Service and Victory Medals.
2, Willow Lane, Watford. X3883.

HOY, R. H., Private, Middlesex Regiment.
He joined in 1916, and in the same year was drafted to the Western Front, where he took part in numerous engagements, including those on the Somme and at Arras and Cambrai, and was wounded. He was demobilised in March 1919, and holds the General Service and Victory Medals.
16, Willow Lane, Watford. X3882/B.

HOY, W. R., Rifleman, 1st K.R.R.C.
He was serving at the outbreak of war, and was immediately afterwards sent to the Western Front. He took part in severe fighting during the Retreat from Mons and in the Battles of the Somme, Arras and Cambrai, and in many other engagements, and was wounded. He was demobilised in March 1919, and holds the Mons Star, and the General Service and Victory Medals.
16, Willow Lane, Watford. X3881.

HOYLAND, H. J., Private, Bedfordshire Regt.
He joined in July 1918, and after his training served on the East Coast on various important duties with his unit until the following September, when he was discharged. He afterwards re-enlisted in the Royal Marine Light Infantry, and was posted to H.M.S. " Warspite," with which he was still serving in 1920.
12, Houghton Road, Dunstable. 3899/A.

HOYLAND, J., L/Corporal, Royal Engineers.
Volunteering in December 1914, he went through a course of training and afterwards served on important duties with his unit until June 1916, when he was drafted to France. He took part in numerous engagements, including those on the Somme and at Cambrai, and after the cessation of hostilities returned to England and was demobilised in March 1919, holding the General Service and Victory Medals.
12, Houghton Road, Dunstable. 3899/B.

HUBBARD, G. H. (D.C.M.), Corporal, 1st Northamptonshire Regiment.
He was serving at the outbreak of war, and was drafted to France in the same month. He took part in severe fighting in many important engagements, was wounded and was awarded the Distinguished Conduct Medal for conspicuous gallantry in carrying messages through heavy fire. On July 31st, 1917, he was killed in action, and in addition to holding the Distinguished Conduct Medal and Order of St. George was entitled to the Mons Star, and the General Service and Victory Medals.
Tinwell, Stamford, Lincs. 3004/A.

HUBBARD, H., L/Corporal, Bedfordshire Regt.
He volunteered in September 1914, and was drafted to France in the same month. He took part in severe fighting on the Marne and at Albert, Festubert, Loos, the Somme, Arras and Cambrai, and was killed in action at Ypres on July 21st, 1918. He was entitled to the 1914 Star, and the General Service and Victory Medals.
7, Queen Street, Hitchin. 4021/B.

HUCKLE, E. J., 1st Air Mechanic, Royal Air Force (late Royal Naval Air Service).
He volunteered in June 1915, and after his training served on important duties with a Handley Page Bombing Squadron until 1917, when he was sent to France, where he served until the end of the war and rendered valuable services. He was demobilised in October 1919, and holds the General Service and Victory Medals.
Sharpenhoe Road, Barton. 4016.

HUCKLE, H., Private, Suffolk Regiment.
He joined in September 1918, and after his training served at various stations on important duties with his unit. He rendered valuable services, but was not successful in obtaining his transfer overseas before the cessation of hostilities. He was demobilised in February 1919.
59, Hitchin Street, Biggleswade. Z4011.

HUCKLE, H., Gunner, Royal Garrison Artillery.
He volunteered in June 1915, and in the following year was drafted to France, where he took part in severe fighting on the Somme and at Arras, Passchendaele and in numerous other engagements, and was wounded. He returned home and was demobilised in March 1919, and holds the General Service and Victory Medals.
204, Wellington Street, Luton. 3988.

HUCKLE, H. C., Private, 7th Australian Infantry.
He volunteered in June 1915, and in the same year proceeded to France, where he took part in severe fighting and was wounded at Pozières. He was later transferred to Egypt, but returned to France shortly afterwards. He was discharged owing to his wounds in July 1916, and holds the 1914-15 Star, and the General Service and Victory Medals.
Southill, Beds. Z3991.

HUCKLE, W., Private, Royal Scots (Lothian Regiment) and Royal Defence Corps.
He volunteered in November 1914, and after his training served on important duties with his unit until 1916, when he was sent to France, where he took part in severe fighting and was wounded. He was invalided home and was later transferred to the Royal Defence Corps. He was demobilised in February 1919, and holds the General Service and Victory Medals.
Southill, Beds. Z3990.

HUCKLESBY, A., Sapper, Royal Engineers.
He joined in June 1918, and after his training served on important duties with his unit until the following December, when he was drafted to Salonika. He returned home and was demobilised in April 1919.
52, Lyndhurst Road, Luton. 4002.

HUCKLESBY, A. L., Trooper, Herts. Dragoons.
He volunteered in 1915, and was afterwards drafted to the Western Front, where he took part in various engagements, including that at Ypres. He returned home and was demobilised in December 1918, and holds the General Service and Victory Medals.
East Common, Harpenden. 4006/A.

HUCKLESBY, J., Sergeant, Bedfordshire Regt.
He volunteered in December 1914, and was drafted to the Western Front in March of the following year. He took part in severe fighting at Loos, Arras, Cambrai, St. Quentin, Albert and the Somme, and was twice wounded. He was demobilised in March 1919, and holds the 1914-15 Star, and the General Service and Victory Medals.
Dunstable Road, Toddington. 3977.

HUCKLESBY, S., Private, 23rd Middlesex Regt.
He joined in October 1918, and after his training was drafted with the Army of Occupation to Germany, where he remained on important duties until March 1920, when he returned home and was demobilised.
East Common, Harpenden. 4006/B.

HUCKLESBY, W., Gunner, R.F.A.
He joined in January 1918, and in the following month was drafted to the Western Front, where he took part in various engagements, and was gassed near St. Quentin. He afterwards proceeded to Russia, where he served on important duties. He was demobilised in June 1919, and holds the General Service and Victory Medals.
Luton Road, Toddington. 3978.

HUDDLE, G. R., A.B., Mercantile Marine.
He joined in 1917, and during the rest of the war was engaged in the S.S. " Virginian " transporting troops between England and France. He rendered valuable services until February 1919, when he was discharged, holding the Mercantile Marine War Medal and the General Service Medal.
11, Sotheron Road, Watford. X3986.

HUDSON, A. F., 1st Air Mechanic, R.A.F.
He joined in February 1916, and on the completion of his course of training was drafted to the Western Front, where he was engaged at Abbeville and Dunkirk on responsible duties which demanded much technical knowledge and skill. After his return to England he was demobilised in February 1919 holding the General Service Medals.
107, Stuart Street, Luton. 3962.

HUDSON, W., Private, Bedfordshire and Suffolk Regiments.
Volunteering in 1915, he went through his training at Landguard, and in 1916 was drafted to France. During his service overseas he fought in the Somme Offensive and at Beaucourt, and was wounded. After his recovery he went back to the fighting line and was in action at Arras, Lens, Cambrai and other important engagements until hostilities ceased. He returned home and was demobilised in March 1919, holding the General Service and Victory Medals.
31, Cowfair Land, Biggleswade. Z3969.

HUFFER, P., Private, R.A.S.C. (M.T.)

He volunteered in August 1915, and in the following month proceeded to the Western Front, where he did valuable transport service until the close of the war in connection with many engagements, including those of Loos, the Somme, Arras, Vimy Ridge, Passchendaele and Cambrai. He was demobilised in August 1919, after his return to England, and holds the 1914-15 Star, and the General Service and Victory Medals.

73, Marsh Road, Leagrave.   2891/A.

HUFFER, W., Private, Bedfordshire Regiment.

After volunteering in 1914, he went through his course of training and was drafted to France in 1915. While overseas he took an active part in many engagements while hostilities continued, including those of the Somme, Arras and Cambrai, and after the Armistice was engaged for a year in agricultural work at Sandy. He was demobilised in 1919, and holds the 1914-15 Star, and the General Service and Victory Medals.

Beeston Green, Sandy.   Z4013.

HUGGARD, L. S., C.Q.M.S., Coldstream Guards.

He was mobilised on the outbreak of hostilities, and was soon afterwards sent to France, where he took a distinguished part in many important engagements until fighting ceased, including those of Ypres, the Somme, Arras, Cambrai and the Aisne, and was twice wounded. After returning to England he was demobilised in October 1919, and holds the 1914 Star, and the General Service and Victory Medals.

73, Grover Road, Oxhey.   X933/B.

HUGGETT, H. J., Driver, R.A.S.C.

He volunteered in January 1915, and on the completion of his training was engaged on important duties with his unit. Owing to physical unfitness he was unable to secure his transfer overseas while hostilities continued, but he rendered valuable transport services until his discharge on medical grounds in June 1916.

137, Herkomer Road, Bushey.   X3985.

HUGGINS, G., A.B., R.N., H.M.S. "Mars."

He was mobilised in August 1914, and was posted to H.M.S. "Hogue," in which he was serving when she was torpedoed in action in the North Sea on September 22nd, 1914. He afterwards rendered valuable service in the Dardanelles in H.M.S. "Star" and in various other waters. He was discharged in April 1917 in consequence of his service, and holds the 1914-15 Star, and the General Service and Victory Medals.

24, Cannon Road, Watford.   X3987.

HUGHMAN, S., Driver, R.H.A.

He volunteered in 1914, and after finishing his training was retained on important duties with his Battery until 1916, when he was drafted to France. During the following three years he did much valuable work in the Battles of the Somme, Ypres, Cambrai and the Retreat and Advance of 1918, and was wounded. He was demobilised in April 1919, after his return home, and holds the General Service and Victory Medals.

9, Pickford Road, Markyate.   4000.

HULATT, P. C. E., Corporal, Royal Warwickshire Regiment.

He joined in February 1917, and after training in the Buffs proceeded to France in the following September. While overseas he was transferred to the Royal Warwickshire Regiment and took part in many important operations until December 1917, when he proceeded to Italy. During his service there he did much valuable work on the Piave front until June 15th, 1918, when he was killed in action. He was buried in the British Cemetery at Magna Boschi, and was entitled to the General Service and Victory Medals.

28, Dacre Road, Hitchin.   4017.

HULETT, W., Private, Queen's (Royal West Surrey Regiment).

Volunteering in 1915, he went through his training and proceeded to France in the following year. He took an active part in the Battles of the Somme, Arras, Ypres, Cambrai and the Retreat and Advance of 1918, and was wounded and gassed during his service. He was also on service in Ireland during the rebellion. He was demobilised in January 1919, and holds the General Service and Victory Medals.

41, Vale Road, Bushey.   X4010/B.

HULL, A., Private, Bedfordshire Regiment.

He joined in October 1916, and in the following January was drafted to the Western Front, where he was in action at the Battle of Arras, and was wounded. He was invalided home and on his recovery was sent to Egypt, where he was stationed at Kantara and was engaged on important transport duties. Returning to England, he was demobilised in December 1919, holding the General Service and Victory Medals.

17, Lower Paxton Road, St. Albans.

X3975/A—X3964/A.

HULL, A., Private, Rifle Brigade.

He joined in September 1916, and after completing his training was drafted to France in January 1917. Subsequently he took part in many important battles, including those of Arras, Ypres and Cambrai, in the last of which he was badly gassed. After long hospital treatment in consequence he was discharged in May 1919, and holds the General Service and Victory Medals.

Upper Sundon, near Dunstable.   3984/A.

HULL, D. A., Gunner, Royal Field Artillery.

He volunteered in September 1915, and having completed his training proceeded to France in June 1916. On this front he took part in many engagements of importance until hostilities ceased, including those of the Somme, Ypres, and the Retreat and Advance of 1918, and was wounded on two occasions. After his return home he was demobilised in June 1919, and holds the General Service and Victory Medals.

82, Althorp Road, Luton   4005.

HULL, E., Sapper, Royal Engineers.

After joining in June 1916, he completed his course of training and was engaged with his unit in the Isle of Sheppey on highly important duties. Being medically unfit for overseas service, he could not secure his transfer to a fighting front, but he rendered valuable services until his demobilisation in January 1919. Upper Sundon, near Dunstable.   3982/A.

HULL, F., Private, Sherwood Foresters.

He volunteered in January 1916, and on the conclusion of his training in July proceeded to France, where he took an active part in many engagements of importance until the close of the war, including those of Arras, Vimy Ridge, Ypres, Cambrai and the Retreat and Advance of 1918. He was demobilised in December 1919, after returning to England, and holds the General Service and Victory Medals.

Upper Sundon, near Dunstable.   3981/A.

HULL, G. S., Sergeant, R.A.S.C.

He joined in October 1916, and was at once drafted to France, where he rendered valuable services in connection with the transport of supplies to various fronts until the cessation of hostilities. He was also present in the engagements at Poperinghe, Péronne and Ham. He returned home and was demobilised in February 1919, holding the General Service and Victory Medals.

46, Stanley Street, Luton.   3963.

HULL, G. T., Private, Labour Corps.

He joined in 1916, and in the same year proceeded to France, where he was engaged until 1919 on important duties with his unit, particularly in connection with the transport of supplies of all kinds in the Somme, Arras and Cambrai sectors. He rendered much valuable service until he returned home, and was demobilised in March 1919, holding the General Service and Victory Medals.

39, King's Road, Hitchin.   4022/C.

HULL, H., Private, Bedfordshire Regiment.

Volunteering in November 1915, he was drafted to the Western Front on the completion of his training in February 1916. While there he took an active part in many important battles, including those of the Somme, Arras, Cambrai and the Retreat and Advance of 1918, and was killed in action on the Cambrai front on August 23rd, 1918. He was entitled to the General Service and Victory Medals.

Upper Sundon, near Dunstable.   3982/C.

HULL, H., Gunner, Royal Field Artillery.

He volunteered in May 1915, and in the following year proceeded to the Western Front. While there he was engaged until the cessation of hostilities on important duties as a shoeing-smith, and in this capacity served in various sectors with his Battery. He returned home in December 1918, and was demobilised in the following February, holding the General Service and Victory Medals.

Victoria Road, Leagrave.   3961.

HULL, H. J., Private, 22nd Manchester Regt.

Joining in January 1918 on attaining military age, he was drafted to France in the following April, and took part in many important engagements in the Retreat and Advance of that year, especially on the Cambrai front. In December 1918 he went to the East, and was afterwards engaged on important guard duties in Egypt and Palestine. He returned home and was demobilised in April 1920, holding the General Service and Victory Medals.

Upper Sundon, near Dunstable.   3983.

HULL, J., Private, 7th Bedfordshire Regiment.

Volunteering in September 1914, he was drafted to France in the following January on the completion of his training. While there he took part in many important engagements, including those of Hill 60, Ypres, Loos, Vimy Ridge and the Somme, and was killed in action near Arras on April 9th, 1917. He was entitled to the 1914-15 Star, and the General Service and Victory Medals.

Upper Sundon, near Dunstable.   3981/B.

HULL, J., Private, Machine Gun Corps.
He volunteered in August 1914, and in the same month was drafted to France, where he fought in the Retreat from Mons, and the Battles of the Marne, Ypres and Festubert. He was wounded on the Somme in July 1916, and later was killed in action near Arras in April 1917. He was entitled to the Mons Star, and the General Service and Victory Medals.
39, King's Road, Hitchin.   4022/A.

HULL, J., L/Cpl., 1st Gordon Highlanders.
He was mobilised on the outbreak of war, and in June 1915 proceeded to the Western Front, where he took part in the Battle of the Somme and was wounded at Ypres in 1917. On his recovery he fought at Cambrai, and in March 1918 was wounded during the Retreat on the Somme and invalided home. Later he returned to France and was wounded for the third time, at Ypres. He was sent to hospital in England, and on his recovery was drafted to Turkey with the Army of Occupation, with which he was still serving in 1920. He holds the 1914-15 Star, and the General Service and Victory Medals. 39, King's Road, Hitchin.   4022/B.

HULL, S., A.B., Royal Navy.
He volunteered in September 1915, and during the remainder of the war-period saw varied service in both near and distant waters. He was engaged on patrolling duties in the North Sea, Persian Gulf, Indian Ocean, Red Sea and Mediterranean, and took part in the Battle of Jutland. After returning home he was demobilised in March 1919, holding the 1914-15 Star, and the General Service and Victory Medals.
Upper Sundon, near Dunstable.   3984/B.

HULL, V., Rifleman, King's Royal Rifle Corps.
He joined in March 1917, and on the completion of his course of training was engaged on important guard duties with his unit. Being physically unfit for service overseas, he could not obtain his transfer to a fighting area, but he did much valuable work until demobilised in 1919.
Upper Sundon, near Dunstable.   3982/B.

HULL, W., Private, Middlesex Regiment.
He joined in May 1917, and on the completion of his training was drafted in the same year to the Western Front. While overseas he took an active part in many engagements, including those of Cambrai and the Somme and other operations in the Retreat and Advance of 1918. After returning home he was demobilised in February 1919, and holds the General Service and Victory Medals.
34, New Kent Road, St. Albans.   X3997.

HULL, W. J., Private, Royal Warwickshire Regt.
He volunteered in December 1915, and proceeded to France in the following year. He took an active part in the great Somme Offensive, where he was wounded and taken prisoner in August 1916. After the Armistice he was repatriated, and was demobilised in January 1919, holding the General Service and Victory Medals.
Beeston, Sandy.   Z4014.

HUM, P., Gunner, Royal Garrison Artillery.
Joining in 1917, his service in France commenced later in the same year, and continued until after the termination of hostilities. During this time he fought in various engagements, including that at Ypres, and also served in the Retreat and Advance of 1918. He was demobilised after his return to England in 1920, and holds the General Service and Victory Medals.
18, Bury Hill, Hemel Hempstead.   X3998.

HUMBLES, F. C., Private, Bedfordshire Regt.
Mobilised at the outbreak of war, he was drafted to France in September 1914, and subsequently fought at La Bassée, Festubert, Loos and the Somme. In 1917 he was severely wounded in action near Arras, and returning to England in consequence, was invalided out of the Service in October of that year. He holds the 1914 Star, and the General Service and Victory Medals
16, Barrow Path, Leighton Buzzard.   3967.

HUMBLES, W., Private, King's (Liverpool Regt.)
He joined the King's Royal Rifle Corps in March 1916, and in the course of his training was transferred to the King's (Liverpool Regiment). Later he was sent to the Western Front, and served in the Somme Offensive, the Battles of Arras, Bullecourt, Ypres and Cambrai, and in the Retreat and Advance of 1918. He was demobilised after his return to England in February 1919, and holds the General Service and Victory Medals.
30, Plantation Road, Leighton Buzzard.   3966.

HUMPHREY, A., 1st Class Steward's Boy, R.N.M.B.R.
He joined in June 1917, and was posted for duty with the Motor Boat Reserve, being engaged on important patrol work in the Channel. On one occasion his ship was torpedoed, but fortunately he escaped uninjured. He holds the General Service and Victory Medals, and was demobilised in March 1919.
35, Merton Road, Watford.   X3976/C.

HUMPHREY, A., Pte., Bedfordshire Regiment.
He volunteered in September 1914, and after his training, which he obtained at Felixstowe, was sent to France in January 1915. During his service overseas he fought at Ypres, the Somme and Arras, and in 1917 was severely gassed. He was invalided to a hospital in Oxford, and after his recovery was retained for home duties until he was demobilised in February 1919. He holds the 1914-15 Star, and the General Service and Victory Medals.
35, Merton Road, Watford.   X3976/A.

HUMPHREY, A., Private, 11th Welch Regiment.
Joining in 1916, he was sent to Salonika at the conclusion of his training. He fought in several important engagements on this front and was in action almost continuously until he was taken prisoner at Vardar Ridge in 1918. Returning to England on being released after the cessation of hostilities, he was demobilised in October 1919, and holds the General Service and Victory Medals.
104, Norfolk Road, Rickmansworth.   X3989/C.

HUMPHREY, A., Corporal, 9th (Queen's Royal) Lancers.
A serving soldier, he was drafted to the Western Front at the outbreak of war, and was severely wounded during the Retreat from Mons on August 23rd, 1914. He returned to England, and two years later, after protracted treatment in hospital, was invalided out of the Service. He holds the Mons Star, and the General Service and Victory Medals.
44, Selbourne Road, Luton.   3999.

HUMPHREY, E. C., Private, Machine Gun Corps.
He joined in August 1917, and at the conclusion of his training early in the following year was drafted to the Western Front, where he was taken prisoner during the German Offensive in March 1918. Rejoining his unit on his release after the cessation of hostilities, he was demobilised in September 1919, and holds the General Service and Victory Medals.
43, Church Road, Watford.   X3136/B.

HUMPHREY, F. G., Private, Buffs (East Kent Regiment).
He joined in 1917, and during his service on the Western Front, which lasted for two years, took an active part in several important engagements, notably those at Arras, Cambrai and the Somme, where he was wounded. He was demobilised on his return to England in February 1919, and holds the General Service and Victory Medals.
104, Norfolk Road, Rickmansworth.   X3989/A.

HUMPHREY, L., Private, Royal Fusiliers.
He volunteered in 1915, and after his training served on the Western Front for nearly four years. During this period he was engaged in the fighting at Ypres, Hill 60, Arras, Cambrai and Amiens, and did most valuable work with his unit. He holds the 1914-15 Star, and the General Service and Victory Medals, and was demobilised on his return to England in October 1919.
The Hill, Wheathampstead.   3974/B.

HUMPHREY, O., Private, Bedfordshire Regiment.
Volunteering in 1915, he was sent to France on completing his training, and fought at Ypres, Hill 60 and Givenchy. Later he was transferred to the Italian front and saw service on the Piave. On three occasions whilst overseas he was wounded, but was able to rejoin his unit after being treated at the Base. He holds the 1914-15 Star, and the General Service and Victory Medals, and was demobilised after his return to England in February 1919.
The Hill, Wheathampstead.   3974/A.

HUMPHREY, R., Private, 6th Royal Berkshire Regiment.
Joining in November 1916, he was sent to France in the following year, after training at Halton Camp. Whilst overseas he took an active part in several engagements, including that at Arras, where he was severely wounded, and in consequence suffered the amputation of a leg. He was discharged in October 1917, and holds the General Service and Victory Medals.
35, Merton Road, Watford.   X3976/B.

HUMPHREY, W., Private, 1st Hertfordshire Regiment.
He volunteered in 1914, and after his training was sent to France. Whilst in this theatre of war he took an active part in the Battles of Neuve Chapelle, Ypres, the Somme, Arras, and Cambrai, and was killed in action during the German Offensive on April 28th, 1918. He was entitled to the 1914-15 Star, and the General Service and Victory Medals.
104, Norfolk Road, Rickmansworth.   X3989/B.

HUMPHREY, W. G., Rifleman, 9th London Regt. (Queen Victoria's Rifles).
He volunteered in November 1915, and until February 1917, when he was sent to the Western Front, was engaged upon duties of a special nature. He fought at Messines Ridge, Bullecourt, the Somme and Ypres, where he was severely wounded, losing an eye. Returning to England, he underwent treatment in hospital, and after his recovery served on important duties at his depôt until he was demobilised in January 1919. He holds the General Service and Victory Medals.
38, Reginald Street, Luton. 3992.

HUMPHREY, W. J. J., Gunner, R.F.A.
He volunteered in July 1915, and on completing his training was drafted to Egypt, where he fought in some minor engagements. Later he served in the Palestine campaign, during which he took part in the Battles of Gaza and the capture of Jerusalem. He holds the 1914-15 Star, and the General Service and Victory Medals, and was demobilised in March 1919.
83, Leavesden Road, Watford. X4008.

HUMPHREYS, A., Private, 1st and 5th Lincolnshire Regiment.
Volunteering in August 1914, he was sent to France in the following January, and in July was severely wounded in action at Ypres. He was invalided home to hospital, but after his recovery in 1916 returned to the Western Front and fought at Arras, Ypres and Cambrai, and in the Retreat and Advance of 1918. He was demobilised in February 1919, and holds the 1914-15 Star, and the General Service and Victory Medals.
51, Grange Road, Luton. 4001.

HUMPHREYS, O. (Miss), Special War Worker.
This lady volunteered for war service in 1915, and was engaged at the Vauxhall Motor Co., Ltd. Her work was in connection with the production of fuses, and she carried out these important duties for three years, during which time she attained a high degree of efficiency.
Trowley Bottom, Flampstead, Beds. 3965/B.

HUMPHREYS, O., Private, 3rd Bedfordshire Regiment.
Volunteering in January 1915, he was sent to the Western Front six months later. He subsequently fought at Loos, Vimy Ridge, the Somme—where he was wounded—and at Arras, and also served throughout the Retreat and Advance of 1918. Returning to England after the cessation of hostilities, he was demobilised in February 1919, and holds the 1914-15 Star, and the General Service and Victory Medals.
Trowley Bottom, Flampstead. 3965/A.

HUMPHREYS, W., Private, Hertfordshire Regt.
A serving soldier, having enlisted in February 1914, he was engaged on important Home duties for some time after the outbreak of hostilities. Later he was sent to the Western Front, where he was subsequently engaged in the fighting at Neuve Chapelle, Loos, Festubert, Arras and Cambrai. During his service he was wounded four times, but rejoined his unit on each occasion after being treated at the Base. He holds the 1914-15 Star, and the General Service and Victory Medals, and was demobilised after his return to England in February 1919.
Wall's Yard, Hatfield. X3960/A.

HUMPHRIES, C. C., Private, Royal Army Cyclist Corps.
He joined in June 1918, and was still in training when hostilities ceased. Afterwards, however, he was sent with the Army of Occupation to Germany, where he was engaged on duties of an important nature for seven months. He was demobilised on his return to England in November 1919.
Water End, Maulden, Ampthill. 4004.

HUNT, B., Quartermaster-Sergeant, R.G.A.
He volunteered at the outbreak of war, and in May 1916 was drafted to the Western Front. During his service in France he was in action at Gommecourt, the Somme, Vimy Ridge, Arras, Ypres, Lens, Béthune, and Merville, and was wounded in June 1918, and also gassed. Returning home in 1918 after the Armistice was signed, he was demobilised in the following January, and holds the General Service and Victory Medals.
13, Queen Street, Hitchin. 4020/B.

HUNT, C. H., Private, Machine Gun Corps.
He joined in February 1916, and in the following year proceeded to the Western Front. Whilst serving in France he took part in the third Battle of Ypres, and subsequently was killed in action near Cambrai during the Retreat on March 21st, 1918. He was entitled to the General Service and Victory Medals.
13, Beaston Road, Hitchin. 4019/B

HUNT, F. J., Private, 11th Middlesex Regiment.
Volunteering in November 1914, he was sent to France on the completion of his training, and served in many notable engagements, including those at Cambrai and Ypres. He was severely wounded and invalided home to hospital and was later discharged as medically unfit for further duty in August 1917. He holds the General Service and Victory Medals. 8, Dane Road, Luton. 3996.

HUNT, F. T., Sergeant, Royal Air Force.
He joined in July 1916, and after his training served at various stations on important duties with his Squadron. He rendered valuable services, but owing to being medically unfit for trench warfare was not able to secure his transfer overseas. He was demobilised in October 1919.
Brampton Park Road, Hitchin. 4015.

HUNT, F. W., Gunner, Royal Field Artillery.
He was mobilised at the outbreak of war, and immediately proceeded to the Western Front, where he took part in the Retreat from Mons and in the engagements on the Marne and at Ypres, Loos, the Somme, Arras and Cambrai, and was wounded. After the cessation of hostilities he returned to England and in 1919 was demobilised, holding the 1914 Star, and the General Service and Victory Medals.
16, The Leys, Woburn Sands. Z410/B.

HUNT, G. E., Private, Royal Army Medical Corps.
He joined in April 1917, and being medically unfit for service overseas, was engaged on important hospital duties at various stations. He acted as hospital orderly, and was also attached to the Royal Flying Corps as doctor's orderly, and rendered valuable service for two years. He was demobilised in March 1919.
27, Bedford Road, Houghton Regis, Dunstable. 3979.

HUNT, P. F., Private, Bedfordshire Regiment.
Volunteering in September 1914, he was sent to France in the following April and fought at Festubert and Loos, and was severely wounded in the Battle of the Somme in September 1916. He was invalided home to hospital and returned to the Western Front after his recovery in March 1917. He then took part in the engagements at Arras, Ypres and Cambrai, and on May 8th, 1918, was taken prisoner. He was held in captivity in Germany until January 1919, when he was demobilised after his return to England. He holds the 1914-15 Star, and the General Service and Victory Medals.
119, Whinbush Road, Hitchin. 3480/A.

HUNT, R. A., Private, 7th Bedfordshire Regiment.
Volunteering in September 1914, he was drafted to France in the following year, and served with the Signal Section of the Bedfordshire Regiment. He took part in the Battles of Loos, the Somme, Arras, Ypres and Cambrai, where he was severely wounded in action. He was invalided home to hospital and after a period of treatment was sent to the Landguard Camp at Felixstowe. He was demobilised in March 1919, and holds the 1914-15 Star, and the General Service and Victory Medals.
9, Thorp's Yard, Queen Street, Hitchin. 4020.

HUNT, S. W., Gunner, Royal Field Artillery.
He volunteered at the outbreak of hostilities, and in the following year was drafted to France, where he served for four years. He took part in the Battles of Arras, Cambrai, the Somme, Albert, Ypres and St. Quentin and in the engagements which followed until the cessation of hostilities. After the Armistice he proceeded to Germany with the Army of Occupation, and was stationed at Cologne until June 1919, when he was demobilised after his return to England. He holds the 1914-15 Star, and the General Service and Victory Medals. 13, Beaston Road, Hitchin. 4019/A.

HUNTLEY, C., Private, East Surrey Regiment.
He volunteered in 1915, and in the same year was drafted to the Western Front, where he served for four years. He fought at Loos, the Somme, Ypres, Arras, Albert, St. Quentin and Cambrai and in the engagements which followed until the cessation of hostilities. He was demobilised in 1919, and holds the 1914-15 Star, and the General Service and Victory Medals. 39, Bancroft, Hitchin. 4018/A.

HUNTLEY, F. J., A.B., Royal Navy.
He volunteered for the Navy in 1915, and served on important and dangerous patrol and escort duties for three years. He cruised with his ship in the Mediterranean Sea, the Suez Canal and in Egyptian and Chinese waters until 1919, when he returned to England and was demobilised in November of that year. He holds the General Service and Victory Medals. 39, Bancroft, Hitchin. 4018/B.

HUNTLEY, H. G., Private, Norfolk Regiment.
He volunteered in 1915, and in the following year was sent to India, where he was engaged on special garrison duties of an important nature at Bangalore and at various outposts on the North West Frontier. He returned home and was demobilised in 1919, after four years' service, and holds the General Service and Victory Medals.
39, Bancroft, Hitchin. 4018/C.

HURD, L., Private, 5th Bedfordshire Regiment.
He was mobilised with the Territorials at the outbreak of war, and in July 1915 was drafted to the Dardanelles. He served only five days in Gallipoli, and after being in action at Suvla Bay was killed by a sniper on August 15th, 1915. He was entitled to the 1914-15 Star, and the General Service and Victory Medals.
32, Beech Road, Luton.   3980.

HURLEY, C. F., Flight-Sergeant, R.A.F.
He volunteered in April 1915, and was attached to the Grand Fleet and served on scouting duties off the coast of Scotland and the Orkney and Shetland Isles. He was mentioned in Despatches in June 1919 for consistent good work, and holds the General Service and Victory Medals.
45, Old Road, Linslade, near Leighton Buzzard. 2784/A.

HUTCHINGS, A., Stoker, R.N., H.M.S. " Vivid."
He volunteered in November 1915, and on the completion of his course of training was engaged on highly important patrol and anti-submarine duties in the North Sea and the Atlantic until the cessation of hostilities. He was demobilised in February 1919, after over three years' service, and holds the General Service and Victory Medals.
3a, Kirby Road, Dunstable.   4003.

HUTCHINGS, A., Pioneer, Royal Engineers.
Joining in 1916, he crossed to France later in the year, and during the remainder of the war was engaged on highly important duties with his unit in many sectors of the front, particularly the Somme, Arras, Ypres, Cambrai and the Aisne. He rendered valuable services until his demobilisation in 1919, and holds the General Service and Victory Medals. 2, Sydney Road, Watford. X3973.

HUTCHINS, W., Private, Oxfordshire and Buckinghamshire Light Infantry.
He was mobilised at the outbreak of hostilities, annd immediately crossed to the Western Front, where he took part in the Retreat from Mons and the Battle of Hill 60 and other engagements. He returned home and was discharged in consequence of his service in February 1916, holding the Mons Star, and the General Service and Victory Medals.
75, Salisbury Road, Luton.   4009.

HUTCHINSON, F. A., Private, Duke of Cornwall's Light Infantry.
He was serving in the Army when war broke out, and crossing immediately to the Western Front, took part in the Retreat from Mons. He was severely wounded in the Battle of the Aisne in September 1914, and was discharged in the following December as medically unfit for further service. He holds the Mons Star, and the General Service and Victory Medals.
White House, The Rookery, Watford. X3959.

HUTCHINSON, H., Private, Bedfordshire Regt.
He joined in 1917, and after his training was engaged on important duties with his unit at various stations. He was not successful in securing his transfer to a fighting front while hostilities continued, but after the Armistice went into Germany with the Army of Occupation. After much valuable service at Cologne he returned to England, and was demobilised in April 1920.
12, Biggleswade Road, Potton. Z3970.

HUTCHINSON, H., Sapper, Royal Engineers; and Private, Royal Fusiliers.
He joined in November 1916, and after the completion of his training was drafted to France in the following year. He took part in many severe engagements in the Arras, Cambrai and Ypres sectors, and was badly wounded. After protracted hospital treatment he was discharged in October 1918 as medically unfit for further service. He holds the General Service and Victory Medals.
Chapel Street, Potton.   Z3968.

HUTCHINSON, L., Driver, R.F.A. (1st City of London Battery).
He volunteered in May 1915, and after his training was retained on important duties with his Battery until May 1917, when he was drafted to France. He took part in many important engagements, including those of Ypres and Cambrai, and was invalided home in November 1918, and holds the General Service and Victory Medals.
110, Estcourt Road, Watford. X3972.

HUTSON, F. B., L/Corporal, Royal Engineers.
He volunteered in April 1915, and on the completion of his training in the following autumn was drafted to France, where he did valuable service in the Field Survey Company in the Ypres, Somme, Arras, Cambrai and Amiens sectors, and was present in many engagements. He returned home and was demobilised in April 1919, after four years' service, holding the 1914-15 Star, and the General Service and Victory Medals.
52, Dale Road, Luton.   3995.

HUTTON, G. H., Private, R.A.V.C.
After volunteering in August 1915, he completed his course of training and in January 1916 was drafted to the Western Front. He did much valuable work in attendance upon sick and wounded horses at Le Havre and when crossing from France to England. He returned to England and was discharged as medically unfit for further duty in May 1917. He holds the General Service and Victory Medals.
11, Lowestoft Road, Watford. X3971.

HYDE, A., Sapper, Royal Engineers.
He volunteered in March 1915, and after completing his training was retained on important duties with his unit until February 1917. He was then drafted to the Western Front, where he did much valuable work at St. Quentin, Ypres, Amiens and other engagements until hostilities ceased. He returned home and was demobilised in April 1919, holding the General Service and Victory Medals.
" Tremayne," Marsh Road, Leagrave. 4024.

HYDE, B., Private, 5th Royal Sussex Regiment.
He joined in November 1916, and on the completion of his training proceeded to the Western Front early in February 1918. While overseas he took part in the Battles of the Somme and Kemmel Hill, and was badly wounded. After considerable treatment in hospital in France he returned home in January 1920, and was demobilised. He holds the General Service and Victory Medals.
28, Vandyke Road, Leighton Buzzard. 4025/C.

HYDE, G. R., Private, 13th London Regiment (Kensingtons).
He was mobilised on the outbreak of the war and crossed to the Western Front a few months later. After taking part in the Battles of La Bassée and Ypres and being wounded, he was killed in action at Neuve Chapelle on March 12th, 1915. He was entitled to the 1914 Star, and the General Service and Victory Medals.
New Marford, Wheathampstead. 4026.

HYDE, J. B. (M.M.), Sergeant, R.A.M.C.
He volunteered in October 1914, and in the following month proceeded to France. He took part in many important engagements until hostilities ceased, including those of Ypres, the Somme, Arras, St. Quentin and Cambrai, and acted as stretcher-bearer on the field. He was awarded the Military Medal and the Croix de Guerre for great gallantry in rescuing the wounded under fire, and also holds the 1914 Star, and the General Service and Victory Medals. He was demobilised in February 1920.
Leighton Road, Toddington. 4027.

HYDE, J. E., Corporal, 2nd Bedfordshire Regt.
He had previously joined the Army in April 1914, and in the same year, at the outbreak of war, was drafted to France, where he took part in the Retreat from Mons. He also fought at Ypres and in the Battle of the Somme, and was severely wounded in action. He succumbed to his injuries in Rouen Hospital on October 19th, 1916, and was entitled to the Mons Star, and the General Service and Victory Medals.
18, Spencer Street, St. Albans. X4028.

HYDE, J. W., Sapper, Royal Engineers.
He joined in February 1916, and after his training served with his unit on important guard duties. On account of ill-health he was unfit for overseas service, and was invalided out of the Army in April 1916.
22, Church Street, Leighton Buzzard. 4030/B.

HYDE, J. W., Private, Labour Corps.
He joined in July 1916, and in the same year was drafted to France. Whilst in this theatre of war he took part in the fighting at Arras, Ypres and St. Quentin, and was gassed, and also suffered from severe shell-shock. He was demobilised in February 1919, and holds the General Service and Victory Medals.
32, Ridgway Road, Luton. 4023.

HYDE, N. V., Sapper, Royal Engineers.
He joined in October 1916, and in the following March was drafted to the Western Front. Here he was engaged on important duties in connection with the operations and was frequently in the front lines, notably at La Bassée, Ypres, Messines Ridge, Passchendaele and Givenchy. He was demobilised in December 1919, and holds the General Service and Victory Medals.
1, Salisbury Road, Leagrave. 4029.

HYDE, P., Private, Royal Army Ordnance Corps.
He joined in April 1916, and after his training was drafted to Palestine in the following June and was present at the Battles of Gaza. He was then sent to Mesopotamia and was in action at Baghdad, and later proceeded to France. In January 1920 he was demobilised, and holds the General Service and Victory Medals.
Waterloo Terrace, Hitchin Street, Biggleswade. Z4032.

HYDE, P., L/Corporal, Royal Engineers.
Volunteering in May 1915, he was drafted to France in the same year. He served in various engagements on important duties in connection with the operations and was frequently in the forward areas, notably at Ypres, Arras and the Somme, and was wounded at Cambrai. He was demobilised in February 1919, and holds the 1914–15 Star, and the General Service and Victory Medals.
85, Bury Park Road, Luton.   4031.

HYDE, R. J., Private, 5th Bedfordshire Regiment.
He volunteered in November 1914, and after his training served for a short time on important duties on the East Coast. He was physically unfit for service overseas, and died of an illness contracted during his training on January 9th, 1915.
28, Vandyke Road, Leighton Buzzard.   4025/B.

HYDE, T., Private, 8th Middlesex Regiment.
He joined in July 1916, and in the following January was drafted to the Western Front. Whilst in this theatre of war he fought in the Battles of Arras, Vimy Ridge and Ypres and in many engagements in the Retreat of 1918, and was wounded. He was killed in action near Cambrai on November 8th, 1918, and was entitled to the General Service and Victory Medals.
28, East Street, Leighton Buzzard.   4033/B.

HYDE, W., Private, Canadian M.G.C.
He volunteered in July 1915, and was sent to France in August of the following year. He took part in heavy fighting on the Somme and at Ypres, Passchendaele, Cambrai and in many other engagements, and was wounded. He was demobilised in February 1919, and holds the General Service and Victory Medals.
28, Vandyke Road, Leighton Buzzard.   4025/A.

HYDE, W. G., Private, 2nd Queen's (Royal West Surrey Regiment).
He joined in May 1916, and in the same year was sent to France, where he took part in the severe fighting on the Somme and at Ypres. In 1917 he was transferred to Italy, where he was again in action. Returning to France in 1918, he was engaged at Cambrai, where he was wounded. He was invalided home and discharged in 1918 owing to his wounds, and holds the General Service and Victory Medals.
22, Church Street, Leighton Buzzard.   4030/A.

HYDE, W. J., Sapper, Royal Engineers.
He volunteered in November 1915, and in March of the following year was sent to Mesopotamia. He served at Kut and Amara, and was engaged on important duties with his unit and rendered valuable services. He was demobilised in November 1919, and holds the General Service and Victory Medals.
28, East Street, Leighton Buzzard.   4033/A.

HYLTON, R., Sapper, Royal Engineers.
He volunteered in August 1915, and in the same month was drafted to the Western Front, where he took part in various engagements, including those on the Somme and at Arras, Ypres and Cambrai, and was gassed. He was demobilised in January 1919, and holds the 1914–15 Star, and the General Service and Victory Medals.
29, York Road, Watford.   X4034.

HYMES, J. H., Corporal, Royal Engineers (E.A.)
He volunteered in March 1915, and in the following July proceeded to Gallipoli. In August 1916 he was transferred to France, where he took part in various engagements, including those at Arras, Ypres, Passchendaele and elsewhere. He was demobilised in April 1919, and holds the 1914–15 Star, and the General Service and Victory Medals.
Gas Street, Toddington.   4035.

HYND, W., Private, King's Own Scottish Borderers.
He volunteered in August 1914, and served at various stations on important duties with his unit. He rendered valuable services, but was not successful in obtaining his transfer overseas. He was discharged as medically unfit for further service in March 1915.
63, Warwick Road, Luton.   4036.

I

ILES, F. C. A., Sapper, Royal Engineers (2nd Inland Survey Company).
He volunteered in April 1915, and in the following September was drafted to the Western Front, where he took part in various engagements, including those on the Somme and at Arras, Ypres, and Cambrai, and was twice wounded. He was still serving in 1920, and holds the 1914–15 Star, and the General Service and Victory Medals.
51, Park Street, St. Albans.   X3587.

ILES, J. W., Private, Northumberland Fusiliers.
He volunteered in September 1914, and in the following August was drafted to the Western Front, where he took part in severe fighting on the Somme and at Arras, Ypres and Bourlon Wood. He was killed in action near Cambrai on April 11th, 1918, and was entitled to the 1914–15 Star, and the General Service and Victory Medals.
82, Liverpool Road, Watford.   X3579.

ILETT, A., Corporal, Royal Garrison Artillery.
He volunteered in September 1914, and served at various stations on important duties with his unit. He rendered valuable services, but was not successful in obtaining his transfer overseas, owing to medical unfitness. He was discharged in February 1915.
40, York Street, Luton.   3584.

ILOTT, A. E., L/Corporal, Royal Engineers.
Volunteering in May 1915, he proceeded to France in October of the same year, and took part in numerous engagements, including those on the Somme and at Arras, Ypres and Cambrai. He was demobilised in March 1919, and holds the 1914–15 Star, and the General Service and Victory Medals.
9, Arthur Road, St. Albans.   X3927/A.

IMPEY, A., Private, 2nd Bedfordshire Regiment.
Volunteering in December 1914, he proceeded to France in August of the following year. He took part in severe fighting at Vimy Ridge, Arras, Ypres, Cambrai and in many other important engagements, and was gassed. He was demobilised in January 1919, and holds the 1914–15 Star, and the General Service and Victory Medals.
64, St. Andrew's Street, Leighton Buzzard.   3575.

IMPEY, C., Private, R.A.S.C. (attached to Devonshire Regiment).
He joined in September 1916, and after his training served at various stations on important duties with his unit. He rendered valuable services, but was not successful in obtaining his transfer overseas before the cessation of hostilities. He was demobilised in April 1919.
54, Ashton Road, Luton.   3597.

IMPEY, H., Private, 5th Bedfordshire Regiment.
He joined in October 1916, and in April of the following year was drafted to Egypt, and later to Palestine. He took part in many important engagements, including those at Rafa, Gaza, Haifa, Acre and Beyrout, and was wounded. He was demobilised in September 1919, and holds the General Service and Victory Medals.
53, Cowper Street, Luton.   3596/B.

IMPEY, J., Private, 4th South Staffordshire Regt.
He joined in July 1916, and after his training was drafted to the Western Front, where he took part in severe fighting in many important engagements. He was killed in action on May 30th, 1918, and was entitled to the General Service and Victory Medals.
70, Pondswick Road, Luton.   3603.

IMPEY, S. T. G., Private, 7th Leicestershire Regt.
Joining in March 1916, he was drafted to France in July of the same year. He took part in numerous engagements and was killed in action on October 8th, 1917. He was entitled to the General Service and Victory Medals.
43, Bailey Street, Luton.   3598.

IMPEY, W., Private, Bedfordshire Regiment.
He volunteered in 1914, and in the same year was drafted to the Western Front, where he took part in numerous engagements, and was wounded. On October 12th, 1916, he was killed in action on the Somme, and was entitled to the 1914 Star, and the General Service and Victory Medals.
448, Hitchin Road, Luton.   721/B.

IMPEY, W., Private, 6th Northamptonshire Regt.
He joined in February 1916, and in the following July was drafted to the Western Front, where he took part in severe fighting on the Somme and at Beaumont-Hamel. He was killed in action at Albert on February 17th, 1917, and was entitled to the General Service and Victory Medals.
53, Cooper Street, Luton.   3596/A.

INDGE, B., Private, 6th Northamptonshire Regt.
Joining in April 1916, he was drafted to France in July of the same year, and took part in heavy fighting on the Somme, and at Arras and Beaumont-Hamel. He was killed in action near Vimy Ridge on February 17th, 1917, and was entitled to the General Service and Victory Medals.
24, Leighton Street, Woburn.   Z3577/B.

INDGE, H. R., Private, 5th Bedfordshire Regt.

He was mobilised with the Territorials in August 1914, and served at various stations on important duties with his unit. He rendered valuable service, but was not successful in obtaining his transfer overseas, owing to being medically unfit for duty abroad. He was discharged in September 1917.
158, Dunstable Road, Luton. 3595.

INDGE, T., Private, Labour Corps.

He volunteered in November 1914, and in the following year was drafted to the Western Front. He served in various engagements, including those at Loos, the Somme, Arras, Messines and Ypres, and was three times wounded. He was demobilised in February 1919, and holds the 1914-15 Star, and the General Service and Victory Medals.
24, Leighton Street, Woburn. Z3577/A.

INGRAM, A. C. M., Corporal, 3rd York and Lancaster Regiment.

He joined in May 1916, and was sent to France in September of the same year, and took part in various engagements, including those at Arras, Cambrai and Delville Wood. In October 1916 he was invalided home with trench fever, and was afterwards attached to the Labour Corps. He was demobilised in September 1919, and holds the General Service and Victory Medals.
Fernleigh, Alexandra Road, King's Langley. X3600.

INGRAM, W. H., L/Corporal, Military Foot Police.

He joined in January 1916, and after his training was drafted to the Western Front, where he was present at numerous engagements, and was gassed. During his service overseas he was engaged on important duties with his unit and rendered valuable services. He was demobilised in October 1919, and holds the General Service and Victory Medals.
Hillford End, Shillington. 3561.

INGREY, A. H., Sergeant, R.G.A.

He was serving at the outbreak of war, and was engaged on important duties with his unit until March 1916, when he was drafted to France. He took part in severe fighting on the Somme and at Passchendaele and in many other engagements, and was wounded in October 1918. He was invalided home and was discharged as medically unfit for further service in April 1919, holding the General Service and Victory Medals.
16, Banks Road, Biggleswade. Z3570.

INNS, E. G., Corporal, R.A.M.C.

He was mobilised in August 1914, and was sent to France in the same month and served in the Retreat from Mons and the Battles of the Marne, Ypres, the Somme and Arras. After the Armistice he proceeded with the Army of Occupation to Germany, where he served until demobilised in May 1919. He holds the Mons Star, and the General Service and Victory Medals.
1, Dudley Street, Leighton Buzzard. 3573.

INSKIP, A., L/Corporal, Bedfordshire Regiment.

He joined in February 1916, and proceeded to France in June of the same year. He took part in severe fighting on the Somme and at Arras, Ypres and Cambrai and was wounded. He was demobilised in February 1919, and holds the General Service and Victory Medals.
28, Lyndhurst Road, Luton. 3601/A.

INSKIP, B. W., Private, Bedfordshire Regiment and Royal Sussex Regiment.

He volunteered in January 1915, and after his training served on important duties with his unit until August of the following year, when he was drafted to the Western Front. He took part in various engagements, and was killed in action on the Somme on September 9th, 1916. He was entitled to the General Service and Victory Medals.
Station Road, Potton. Z3572.

INSKIP, G., A/Sergeant, Essex Regiment.

Joining in February 1916, he was drafted to Egypt in July of the same year and later to Palestine. He took part in severe fighting at Gaza and in various other engagements, and was demobilised in August 1919, holding the General Service and Victory Medals.
28, Lyndhurst Road, Luton. 3601/B.

INSKIP, J., Sapper, Royal Engineers.

He joined in May 1917, and in November of the same year was drafted to the Western Front. He served in various sectors, including the Somme and Ypres, and was engaged on important railway duties and rendered valuable services. He was demobilised in May 1919, and holds the General Service and Victory Medals.
9, Water Lane, Hitchin. 3569.

INSKIP, P. W., L/Corporal, Royal Engineers.

He volunteered in 1915, and after his training served on important duties with his unit. He was engaged on transport and cable laying work in various stations and rendered valuable services, but was not successful in obtaining his transfer overseas before the cessation of hostilities. He was demobilised in 1919.
King Street, Potton. 3571.

INWARDS, B., Private, 3rd Bedfordshire and 8th Leicestershire Regiments and Labour Corps.

He volunteered in November 1914, and after his training served on important duties with his unit at various stations until October 1916, when he was drafted to the Western Front. He took part in the Battles of Arras and Ypres, and was three times wounded. In March 1918 he was severely gassed and suffered the loss of his sight for six days. Fortunately he recovered later and continued to serve until April 1919, when he returned to England and was demobilised. He holds the General Service and Victory Medals.
6, Bedford Street, Leighton Buzzard. 3574.

INWOOD, H. W., Corporal, R.A.S.C.

He volunteered in 1915, and was first drafted to Egypt, and later to France. He served for four years on important duties in various sectors of these fronts, and was demobilised in 1919. He holds the General Service and Victory Medals.
23, Buckingham Road, Callow Land, near Watford. X3590/B

INWOOD, R. E. (Miss), Special War Worker.

For three years during the war this lady held a responsible position in the National Filling Factory at Watford. She was engaged on important and dangerous duties filling shells and bombs, and carried out her work with great care and efficiency. She continued to render valuable services until the cessation of hostilities.
23, Buckingham Road, Callow Land, near Watford. X3593.

INWOOD, W. S., L/Corporal, Royal Fusiliers.

He joined in February 1916, and after his training was drafted to France and fought in several engagements. On November 14th of the same year he was killed in the heavy fighting at Beaumont-Hamel, and was entitled to the General Service and Victory Medals.
23, Buckingham Road, Callow Land, near Watford. X3590/A.

IRELAND, A. E., Private, 1st Essex Regiment.

He joined in April 1916, and in the following October was drafted to France. Whilst in this theatre of war he fought on the Ancre and at Vimy Ridge and Arras. He was reported missing and was later presumed to have been killed in action at Bullecourt on April 14th, 1917. He was entitled to the General Service and Victory Medals.
Shefford, Beds. Z3586.

IRELAND, W. G., Sergeant, Royal Air Force.

Volunteering in September 1914, he was sent to the Dardanelles in the following July, and saw much varied service. He took part in the Gallipoli campaign, and after the Evacuation of the Peninsula was drafted to Egypt, where he was in action on the Suez Canal, and served throughout the British Advance in Palestine. During his service overseas he was wounded, and on the termination of hostilities returned to England and was demobilised in March 1919, holding the 1914-15 Star, and the General Service and Victory Medals.
60, Beech Road, Luton. 3594.

IRONS, A., L/Corporal, Royal Engineers.

Volunteering in September 1914, he was drafted in the following year to the Western Front. During his service in France he was engaged on important duties in connection with the operations and was frequently in the forward areas, notably at Loos, the Somme and Arras. He was later killed in action at Passchendaele Ridge on October 11th, 1917. He was entitled to the 1914-15 Star, and the General Service and Victory Medals.
3, Chambers Lane, Ickleford, Hitchin. 3560.

IRONS, C. A., Private, 7th Royal Fusiliers.

He joined in March 1917, and in the following January was drafted to France, and during his service on the Western Front fought at Ypres and in the Battle of the Somme. He was severely wounded on September 30th, 1918, in the second Battle of Cambrai, and was invalided to hospital in England. On his recovery he was demobilised in the following April. He holds the General Service and Victory Medals.
72, Waterlow Road, Dunstable. 3582.

IRONS, R. C., Petty Officer, R.M.L.I.

He joined in April 1918, and was in training at Chatham until the following January, when he was drafted to Mudros, where he was engaged on important duties until April 1920, when he returned to England and was demobilised.
77, Waterlow Road, Dunstable. 3580.

ISAACS, C. W., Rifleman, 18th K.R.R.C.

He joined in April 1918, and after completing his training served at various stations on important duties with his unit. He rendered valuable service, but was not able to secure his transfer overseas before the conclusion of hostilities, and was demobilised in February 1920.

43, King's Road, Luton. 3602.

ISHAM, A., Shoeing Smith, R.A.S.C.

He volunteered in September 1915, and after completing his training served at various stations on important duties with his unit. Although not able to secure his transfer overseas he did good work until July 1916, when he was discharged in consequence of his service.

14, Cecil Street, North Watford. X3591.

IVES, C. H., Corporal, Bedfordshire Regiment.

Volunteering in August 1914, he was drafted to France in the following December. Whilst in this theatre of war he fought at Hill 60, Ypres and Cambrai, and was gassed. After his recovery he took part in various important engagements in the Retreat and Advance of 1918, and was demobilised in the following January. He holds the 1914 Star, and the General Service and Victory Medals.

19, Queen Street, St. Albans. 3588.

IVES, E. W., Private, R.A.S.C.

Volunteering in 1914, he was drafted to France in the following January, and during his service on the Western Front was engaged on important duties at Hill 60 and in the second Battle of Ypres. He did excellent work, but owing to ill-health was invalided home in August 1915, and discharged as unfit for further military duty in the following December. He holds the 1914-15 Star, and the General Service and Victory Medals.

Mill Cottages, Lower Luton Road, Harpenden. 3599/A.

IVES, H., Corporal, Royal Engineers.

He was mobilised at the outbreak of war, and in the following October was drafted to France. Here he was engaged on important duties in connection with the operations and was frequently in the forward areas, notably at Neuve Chapelle, where he was severely wounded. He was invalided home to hospital and was discharged as physically unfit for further military duty in April 1916. He holds the 1914 Star, and the General Service and Victory Medals.

5, Grove Road, Dunstable. 3581.

IVES, P. (D.C.M.), Sergeant, 3rd Canadian Grenadier Guards.

Volunteering at the outbreak of war, he was drafted to the Western Front in January 1915. After only two months' active service in France he was taken prisoner in an engagement near Ypres. Later he died on April 15th, 1915, as a result of the ill-treatment which he received at the hands of the enemy. He was awarded the Distinguished Conduct Medal for conspicuous bravery and devotion to duty on the Field, and was entitled also to the 1914-15 Star, and the General Service and Victory Medals.

Downs Villa, Great Northern Road, Dunstable. 3585/A.

IVES, S. D., Sergeant, 1st East Surrey Regiment.

Volunteering in September 1914, he was drafted overseas in June, 1917. During his service on the Western Front he fought at Messines, Ypres and Merville, and was afterwards sent to Italy, where he served in the Trentino until the conclusion of hostilities. He was demobilised in January 1919, after his return to England, and holds the General Service and Victory Medals.

Downs Villa, Great Northern Road, Dunstable. 3585/B.

IVES, T., Driver, Royal Engineers.

Volunteering in 1915, he served for three years in France on important duties and was frequently in the forward areas whilst operations were in progress, notably on the Somme and at Arras and Ypres. He was demobilised in 1919, and holds the General Service and Victory Medals.

7, Queen's Road, Harpenden. 3604.

IVORY, A. W., Pte., Oxfordshire and Buckinghamshire Light Infantry ; and Air Mechanic, Royal Air Force.

Volunteering in August 1914, he served at first in the Oxfordshire and Buckinghamshire Light Infantry, and was drafted to France in the following year. During his service he was transferred to the Royal Air Force and was in action at Ypres and Arras, and was gassed and wounded. He was subsequently demobilised in February 1919, and holds the 1914-15 Star, and the General Service and Victory Medals.

77, Lea Road, Luton. 3576.

IVORY, L. R., Pte., 4th Gloucestershire Regt.

Joining in October 1916, he was drafted to France in the following June, and served in the Ypres sector. In November 1917 he was transferred to Italy and took part in the campaign against the Austrians, being in action on the Piave front. In November 1918 he returned to England, and was stationed at Plymouth until September 1919, when he was demobilised, holding the General Service and Victory Medals.

" Windermere," Brampton Park Road, Hitchin. 3565/B.

IVORY, S. W., Pte., 4th Gloucestershire Regt.

He joined in October 1916, and in the following June was drafted to the Western Front, where he took part in the Battle of Ypres and was wounded in October 1917. He was invalided to England and in July 1918 was discharged as medically unfit for further service, holding the General Service and Victory Medals.

" Windermere," Brampton Park Road, Hitchin. 3565/C.

IVORY, W. F., Private, Machine Gun Corps.

He joined in January 1917, and in the following April was drafted to the Western Front, where he was in action at Arras, Ypres and Cambrai, and also served in the Retreat and Advance of 1918. In September 1919 he was sent to Egypt and thence to Palestine, where he remained until April 1920, when he returned to England and was demobilised. He holds the General Service and Victory Medals.

Brampton Park Road, Hitchin. 3565/A.

IZZARD, A. W., Bombardier, R.F.A.

He volunteered in 1915, and in November of that year was drafted to Egypt, where he fought in several minor engagements. In 1916, however, he was invalided home in consequence of ill-health, and in May of the following year was discharged. He holds the 1914-15 Star, and the General Service and Victory Medals.

8, Dalton Street, St. Albans. 3589.

IZZARD, B. G., Air Mechanic, Royal Air Force.

He volunteered in September 1914, and after his training, served on the Western Front for over three years. During this time he was engaged in repairing and keeping in order aeroplanes ready for flight, and in this way was present at engagements at Ypres, Arras, the Somme and Cambrai. He was severely wounded in the German Offensive of 1918, and was in consequence invalided home and discharged in May of that year. He holds the 1914 Star, and the General Service and Victory Medals.

Lower Green, Ickleford, Hitchin. 3558.

IZZARD, E., Rifleman, The Cameronians (Scottish Rifles).

Joining in 1917, he was sent to France on completing his training in November of that year. He subsequently fought at Albert, Cambrai, Amiens and in the Retreat and Advance of 1918, remaining overseas until March 1919. Returning to England he was demobilised two months later, and holds the General Service and Victory Medals.

Near Church, Ickleford, Hitchin. 3557.

IZZARD, E. B., Stoker, Royal Navy.

He joined in March 1918, and after his training was posted to H.M.S. " Valiant," in which he saw service in the North Sea and off the coast of Scotland. On board this ship he was also present at the surrender of the German Fleet. He holds the General Service and Victory Medals, and in 1920 he was serving in H.M.S. " Commonwealth."

41, Upper Heath Road, St. Albans. X3592/B.

IZZARD, F., Private, 1st Hertfordshire Regiment.

Volunteering at the commencement of hostilities, he was quickly drafted to the Western Front and took part in the Retreat from Mons. He also served in many of the engagements which followed, notably those at La Bassée, Festubert, the Somme, Arras and Cambrai, and remained overseas for over four years. He holds the Mons Star, and the General Service and Victory Medals, and was demobilised on his return to England in March 1919.

14, Barnard's Yard, Hitchin. 3563.

IZZARD, F., Private, 4th Bedfordshire Regiment.

He volunteered in August 1914, and after his training was sent to the Western Front, where he served for over three years. During this time he was engaged in the fighting at Ypres, Festubert, Loos, Albert, Arras and Cambrai, and was wounded at the third Battle of Ypres in 1917. He holds the 1914-15 Star, and the General Service and Victory Medals, and was demobilised in February 1919.

Lower Green, Ickleford. 3559.

IZZARD, H., L/Corporal, Duke of Wellington's (West Riding Regiment).
Volunteering in August 1914, he joined the Hertfordshire Regiment, and was later transferred to the Duke of Wellington's (West Riding Regiment). After a short course of training he was drafted to the Western Front, where he fought in many of the principal engagements, including those at Ypres, Arras, Armentières and the second Battle of the Marne, and was wounded. Later he died in Rouen Hospital in August 1919, and was entitled to the 1914 Star, and the General Service and Victory Medals.
"The Follies," Wheathampstead.   3578.

IZZARD, L., Private, 3rd Bedfordshire Regiment.
He volunteered in February 1915, and until he was sent to France in December of the following year was engaged on important Home duties. Whilst overseas he fought at Ypres, where he was wounded, and in many other important engagements, including that at Cambrai, where he was again wounded and gassed in March 1918. In April of that year he was invalided home, and after protracted hospital treatment was demobilised in January 1919. He holds the General Service and Victory Medals.
"The Nook," High Street, Clophill, Ampthill.   3605.

IZZARD, P. G., Private, 1st Hertfordshire Regt.
Volunteering at the commencement of hostilities, he was sent to France in November 1914. After taking part in many of the principal engagements he was killed in action at Ypres on November 13th, 1916. He was entitled to the 1914 Star, and the General Service and Victory Medals.
41, Upper Heath Road, St. Albans.   X3592/A.

IZZARD, R., Sapper, Royal Engineers.
He joined in February 1916, and served on the Western Front from September of the following year until after the cessation of hostilities. During this period he was engaged on duties of an important nature in the forward areas, and was present at engagements at Ypres, Arras, Albert, the Somme and Cambrai, where in March 1918 he was wounded. After the cessation of hostilities he was stationed at Cologne for a time with the Army of Occupation. He was demobilised on his return to England in June 1919, and holds the General Service and Victory Medals.
22, King's Road, Hitchin.   3564.

IZZARD, S. B., L/Corporal, 4th Bedfordshire Regiment.
Volunteering in November 1915, he was drafted to the Western Front in the following July. Subsequently he took part in several engagements, including that of Ypres, and was killed in action during the final stages of the Somme Offensive on November 13th, 1916. He was entitled to the General Service and Victory Medals.
Hall End, Maulden, Ampthill.   3562.

J

JACK, A. R., Private, Machine Gun Corps.
He joined in July 1917, and in the same year was drafted to the Western Front, where, after serving in numerous engagements, he was taken prisoner in March 1918. In the following December he was released, and returning to England was demobilised, holding the General Service and Victory Medals.
461, Whippendell Road, Watford.   X3625.

JACKMAN, W., Private, 1st Hertfordshire Regt.
He volunteered in March 1915, and in the following year was drafted to France, where he took part in the Battles of the Somme, Arras and Ypres, and was wounded at St. Julien. He holds the General Service and Victory Medals, and was demobilised in 1919.
24, Mill Street, Apsley End, Hemel Hempstead.   X3608.

JACKSON, A., Private, Bedfordshire Regiment.
He volunteered in September 1914, and in the following June was drafted to the Western Front, where he fought at Loos and the Somme. On April 23rd, 1917, he was killed in action at Arras, and was entitled to the 1914-15 Star, and the General Service and Victory Medals.
High Street, Eaton Bray, Dunstable.   3624.

JACKSON, A., Private, 9th Royal Fusiliers and Essex Regiment.
He volunteered in April 1915, and after having completed his training was drafted to France in the following February. He took part in the engagements on the Somme and at Arras, Vimy Ridge, Ypres, Passchendaele and Cambrai, and was twice wounded. He was invalided home and was discharged as medically unfit for further service in February 1918.
26, Stuart Street, Luton.   3612.

JACKSON, E. A., Corporal, R.A.P.C.
He joined in October 1917, and was engaged on important duties in the Pay Office. He rendered valuable service, but owing to being medically unfit for duty abroad was unable to obtain his transfer to a theatre of war. He was demobilised in February 1919.
Primrose Hill, King's Langley.   X365/C.

JACKSON, E. B. (D.C.M., M.M.), L/Sergeant, 2nd Royal Fusiliers.
He was serving on the outbreak of war, and in June 1915 was drafted to the Dardanelles, where he was in action at Suvla Bay and was awarded the Distinguished Conduct Medal for conspicuous gallantry and was mentioned in Despatches. On the Evacuation of Gallipoli he was sent to France, where he took part in numerous engagements and won the Military Medal for bravery. He holds in addition to the Distinguished Conduct Medal and Military Medal, the 1914-15 Star, and the General Service and Victory Medals, and was demobilised in May 1919.
13, Stanmore Road, Watford.   X3609/A.

JACKSON, F. W., Driver, Royal Field Artillery.
He joined in August 1918, and had not completed his training when the Armistice was signed. He was in consequence unable to secure his transfer overseas, and was demobilised in February 1919.
31, Leys Terrace, Woburn Sands.   Z3638.

JACKSON, G., Private, 8th Bedfordshire Regt.
He volunteered in 1915, and in the following year was drafted to France, where he was killed in action at the Battle of the Somme on September 15th, 1916. He was entitled to the General Service and Victory Medals.
26, Cowfairlands, Biggleswade.   Z3641.

JACKSON, P., Driver, Royal Horse Artillery.
He volunteered in December 1914, and after having completed his training was engaged on important duties at various stations until August 1916, when he was drafted to Egypt. He took part in the Palestine campaign and was in action at Gaza and Beyrout, and in June 1919 returned to England and was demobilised, holding the General Service and Victory Medals.
10, Buckwood Road, Markyate.   3607.

JACKSON, R., Private, East Surrey Regiment and Hampshire Regiment.
He was mobilised on the declaration of war, and was early drafted to the Western Front, where he was in action at Mons and in subsequent battles until he was wounded at Ypres. Invalided home for treatment, he was sent on recovery to Gallipoli and thence to Salonika, where he served until the end of hostilities. He was demobilised in May 1919, and holds the Mons Star, and the General Service and Victory Medals.
The Bridge, King's Langley.   X365/B.

JACKSON, W., Private, Middlesex Regiment.
He joined in March 1916, and in the following June was drafted to the Western Front, where he took part in numerous engagements. On August 7th, 1917, he died of wounds received in action at Ypres, and was entitled to the General Service and Victory Medals.
17, Marsh Road, Leagrave.   3615.

JACKSON, W., Private, 12th Middlesex Regiment.
He joined in March 1917, and in the following May was drafted to the Western Front, where he took part in the Battle of Arras. On August 8th, 1917, he died of wounds received in action at Ypres, and was entitled to the General Service and Victory Medals.
78, Frederick Street, Luton.   3614.

JACKSON, W., Leading Seaman, R.N., H.M.S. "Cæsar."
He was serving at the outbreak of war and was posted for duty with H.M.S. "Cæsar" in the Mediterranean. He served in the Dardanelles during the Gallipoli operations and was wounded. He holds the 1914-15 Star, and the General Service and Victory Medals, and was still serving in 1920.
51, Brighton Road, Watford.   X3610.

JAGGARD, A. E., Private, Bedfordshire Regt.
Volunteering in August 1914, he was immediately drafted to the Western Front, where he took part in the Retreat from Mons and the Battles of Hill 60, the Somme, Arras, Ypres and Cambrai, and was wounded. He holds the Mons Star, and the General Service and Victory Medals, and in February 1919 was demobilised.
32a, Prospect Cottage, Pinner Road, Oxhey.   X3626/A.

JAGGARD, C. (D.C.M., M.M.), Sergeant, 2nd Royal Scots.

He enlisted in 1909, and on the outbreak of war was drafted to the Western Front, where he took part in the Retreat from Mons and the Battles of the Marne, Ypres, the Somme and Cambrai. He was twice wounded and on each occasion was invalided to England, but on his recovery returned to the front. For conspicuous gallantry he was awarded the Distinguished Conduct Medal, and also won the Military Medal for bravery. After the Armistice he proceeded to Germany and served with the Army of Occupation on the Rhine until March 1920, when he returned to England and was demobilised. In addition to the Distinguished Conduct Medal and Military Medal, he holds the Mons Star, and the General Service and Victory Medals.

3, Neal Street, Watford. X3611/A.

JAGGARD, D., Private, Bedfordshire Regiment.

He joined in 1916, and in the same year was drafted to France, where he took part in the Battles of the Somme and Arras. After the termination of hostilities he returned to England and in October 1919 was demobilised, holding the General Service and Victory Medals.

32a, Prospect Cottage, Pinner Road, Oxhey. X3626/B.

JAGGARD, R., Private, Queen's (Royal West Surrey Regiment).

He joined in May 1917, and after having completed his training was drafted to France in the following April, and took part in numerous engagements. After the Armistice he served with the Army of Occupation in Germany until November 1919, when he returned to England and was demobilised, holding the General Service and Victory Medals.

3, Neal Street, Watford. X3611/B.

JAGGER, C., Sapper, Royal Engineers.

He joined in 1917, and after having completed his training served on important duties with his unit at various stations. He rendered valuable service, but owing to being medically unfit for duty abroad was unable to secure his transfer to a theatre of war. He was demobilised in 1919.

8, Russell Place, Boxmoor. X3640.

JAKINS, W. E., Private, 9th Middlesex Regiment.

He joined in May 1916, and after completing his training was drafted in the following November to the East, where he did much valuable service. While in India he was engaged on important garrison duties in Bangalore, and in Mesopotamia took part in the operations before Kut and the capture of Baghdad and Mosul. He returned home and was demobilised in February 1920, and holds the General Service and Victory Medals.

90, Baker Street, Luton. 3618.

JAMES, A. E., Private, 9th (Queen's Royal) Lancers.

He volunteered in August 1914, and after the completion of his training was engaged on important duties with his unit at various stations. He was not successful in securing his transfer overseas while hostilities continued, but rendered valuable services until his demobilisation in August 1918.

63, Pretoria Road, Watford. X3622.

JAMES, C. W., Sergeant, Royal Field Artillery.

He was mobilised at the outbreak of hostilities and was at once drafted to the Western Front, where he did excellent service until 1917 in many important battles, including those of Mons, the Marne, Festubert, the Somme, Arras, Ypres and Cambrai, and was buried by a shell explosion and twice wounded. In 1917 he returned to England and subsequently was retained as Riding Instructor at Biscot Camp, Luton. He was demobilised in February 1919, and holds the Mons Star, and the General Service and Victory Medals.

37, Broughton Hill, Letchworth. 3646.

JAMES, S., Corporal, 17th Middlesex Regiment.

He volunteered in 1915, and having completed his training was in the same year drafted to France. Whilst serving overseas he took part in numerous engagements, including the Battle of the Somme, and was wounded and buried by the explosion of a shell. He holds the 1914-15 Star, and the General Service and Victory Medals, and was demobilised in 1919.

123, Regent Street, North Watford. 421/A.

JAMES, W., Private, Bedfordshire and Hertfordshire Regiments.

After his enlistment in 1919 he went through his course of training and was engaged at various stations on important duties with his unit. He did not take part in the hostilities abroad, but rendered valuable service in Ireland, where in 1920 he was still serving.

52, St. Andrew's Street, Leighton Buzzard. 3645/A.

JAMES, W., Private, Labour Corps.

Volunteering in September 1914, he crossed to France soon afterwards and rendered valuable services with his unit in many sectors until the cessation of hostilities. He was gassed at Ypres and wounded in the Somme Offensive in 1916. After his return home he was demobilised in November 1919, and holds the 1914 Star, and the General Service and Victory Medals.

3, Wood Yard, Woburn Road, Ampthill. 3606.

JANES, A. J., Corporal, Expeditionary Force Canteens.

He joined in September 1917, and soon afterwards proceeded to the Western Front, where he did much valuable work in the Army canteens at Boulogne, Calais and Rouen and in the Somme area. He was unfit for trench warfare, but did excellent service until his return to England for demobilisation in September 1919. He holds the General Service and Victory Medals.

16, Billington Road, Leighton Buzzard. 3630.

JANES, C., Driver, R.A.S.C.

He joined in 1916, and in the same year crossed to the Western Front, where he rendered excellent service in the transport of supplies in the Somme, Arras, Vimy Ridge, Lens and Cambrai sectors until the cessation of hostilities. He returned to England and was demobilised in 1919, holding the General Service and Victory Medals.

High Street, Eddlesborough, near Dunstable. Z3642/A.

JANES, E., Private, York and Lancaster Regt.

Volunteering in May 1915, he went through his training and in 1916 proceeded to France. He took part in the Battle of Vimy Ridge and was taken prisoner in the Somme Offensive in July 1916. He was released in December 1918, and demobilised in the following February, holding the General Service and Victory Medals.

5, South Place, Dunstable. 3631/A.

JANES, E., Sergeant, R.A.O.C. and Norfolk Regt.

He joined in August 1916, and after the completion of his training was drafted to France in the following year. While overseas he took part in many important engagements, including those of Ypres, Cambrai, the Somme and the Retreat and Advance of 1918. After the Armistice he went into Germany with the Army of Occupation and did valuable service at Cologne until his return home for demobilisation in September 1919. He holds the General Service and Victory Medals.

6, Oxford Terrace, West Street, Dunstable. 3616.

JANES, F., Private, Northamptonshire Regiment.

After joining in June 1916, he went through his course of training and was engaged at various stations on important duties. Owing to physical unfitness he did not secure his transfer to a fighting front while hostilities continued, but he did much valuable agricultural work until demobilised in February 1919.

55, Cardiff Road, Watford. X3635/B.

JANES, F., Private, 2nd Essex Regiment.

Volunteering in September 1914, he was drafted to France in the following February. His service in this theatre of war lasted for over three years, during which time he fought in many important engagements, including that of Neuve Chapelle. In May 1915 he was wounded in action at Festubert, but after receiving treatment was able to rejoin his unit. He holds the 1914-15 Star, and the General Service and Victory Medals, and was demobilised after his return to England in February 1919.

22, Alfred Street, Dunstable. 3634.

JANES, F. G., Driver, Royal Engineers.

He enlisted in October 1912, and during the recent war saw service from November 1914 in France, Egypt, Mesopotamia and India. On each of these fronts he was engaged on important duties, and did much valuable work with his unit. He was demobilised in November 1919, and holds the 1914 Star, and the General Service and Victory Medals.

4, Ash Road, Luton. 3621.

JANES, F. H., Sapper, R.E. (Signal Section).

He joined in March 1918, and after his training was drafted in October to the Western Front, where during the Advance of that year he was engaged on important work in connection with the line of communication in the Cambrai sector. After the termination of hostilities he advanced into Germany with the Army of Occupation. He was demobilised on his return to England in March 1920, and holds the General Service and Victory Medals.

Millview, West Parade, Dunstable. 3617.

JANES, F. W., Driver, Royal Field Artillery.
He volunteered in June 1915, and during his service on the Western Front, which lasted for two years, fought in many important battles, notably those of Vimy Ridge, the Somme, Bullecourt, Arras and Cambrai. After the cessation of hostilities he served for some time in Germany with the Army of Occupation. He holds the General Service and Victory Medals, and was demobilised in April 1920.
Laurel Cottage, March Road, Leagrave. 3620/A.

JANES, H., Private, 8th Leicestershire Regt.
Called from the Reserve at the outbreak of war, he was immediately sent to France and took part in the Retreat from Mons. He also fought at Ypres, Festubert, Loos and the Somme, and was killed in action near the Menin Road on October 7th, 1917. He was buried at Ypres, and was entitled to the Mons Star, and the General Service and Victory Medals.
34, Soulbury Road, Linslade, near Leighton Buzzard. 3644.

JANES, H., Private, 5th Bedfordshire Regiment.
Volunteering in May 1915, he was sent to Egypt in the following February. Later he served in the Palestine campaign, during which he fought in many important engagements, including those at Gaza and Aleppo. He was demobilised on his return to England in August 1919, and holds the General Service and Victory Medals.
5, South Place, Dunstable. 3631/B.

JANES, H., Private, Bedfordshire Regiment.
He volunteered at the age of 14 in 1914, and after his training was engaged with his unit at various stations. He did valuable work until November 1917, when he was discharged as being under age for military service.
111, Boyle Street, Luton. 3627.

JANES, J., Corporal, Royal Engineers.
Volunteering in November 1915, he was engaged on special duties until he was sent to the Western Front in February 1917. During his service overseas, which lasted for two years, he was engaged on important work in the forward areas, and was present at the Battles of Arras, Ypres, the Somme and Cambrai. He was demobilised after his return to England in February 1919, and holds the General Service and Victory Medals.
" St. Omere," Cumberland Street, Houghton Regis. 3633.

JANES, J. W., Private, 5th Bedfordshire Regt.
Volunteering in August 1914, he was drafted to the Dardanelles in the following July, and served at Suvla Bay and Chocolate Hill and the engagements which followed. In September 1915 he was sent to Salonika, and in the following year was transferred to France, where he fought in the Battles of Vimy Ridge, the Somme, Ypres, Passchendaele and Cambrai. He holds the 1914-15 Star, and the General Service and Victory Medals, and was demobilised on his return to England in March 1919.
" Laurel Cottage," Marsh Road, Leagrave. 3620/B.

JANES, L., Corporal, 2nd Northamptonshire Regt.
He volunteered in April 1915, and three months later was sent to France, where he served for over two years. During this time he was engaged in the fighting in many important sectors, including those of the Somme, Ypres and Passchendaele, and was severely wounded in December 1917. He was invalided home. and after his recovery was retained on important Home duties until he was demobilised in March 1919. He holds the 1914-15 Star, and the General Service and Victory Medals. 55, Cardiff Road, Watford. X3635/A.

JANES, L., Private, 1st Royal Fusiliers and Labour Corps.
He joined in July 1916, and after his training served on the Western Front, where he fought in numerous important battles, including those of Vimy Ridge and Cambrai, and was wounded. After his recovery he was transferred to the Labour Corps, in which he did valuable work until after the cessation of hostilities. He was demobilised on his return to England in April 1919, and holds the General Service and Victory Medals. 28, Bun Street, Luton. 3613.

JANES, R. W., 2nd Corporal, Royal Engineers.
He joined in 1917, and after his training was drafted in January 1918 to Italy, where he did valuable work with his unit during operations on the Piave. He returned to England in March 1919, when he was demobilised, and holds the General Service and Victory Medals.
119, New Town Street, Luton. 3628.

JANES, S. E., Driver, Royal Horse Artillery.
He joined in 1916, and on the completion of his training at Woolwich was drafted to the Western Front. In this theatre of war he fought on the Ancre, at Lens and Cambrai, and also did excellent work with the signal section of his Battery during the concluding stages of the war. He was demobilised in 1919, and holds the General Service and Victory Medals.
High Street, Eddlesborough, near Dunstable. Z3642/B.

JANES, W. B., Private, R.A.S.C. and Royal Fusiliers.
He joined in September 1918, but had not completed his training when hostilities ceased. Afterwards, however, he was sent with the Army of Occupation to Germany, where he was engaged at Cologne on important duties with his unit, and in 1920 was still serving.
108, Maple Road, Luton. 3629.

JANES, W. T. G., Private, 4th Bedfordshire Regt.
He volunteered in December 1915, and during his service on the Western Front fought in many important engagements, including those at Arras, Ypres, Passchendaele, Cambrai and the Somme. During his service abroad he was wounded. Returning to England, he was invalided out of the Service in September 1918, and holds the General Service and Victory Medals. 4, Salisbury Road, Luton. 3619.

JANEWAY, E., Private, Bedfordshire Lancers and 15th (The King's) Hussars.
He volunteered in August 1914, and was sent to France in the following year. He took part in severe fighting at Loos, Vimy Ridge, the Somme and in other engagements, and is believed to have been killed in action near the Somme on March 30th, 1918. He was entitled to the 1914-15 Star, and the General Service and Victory Medals.
Manor Road, Barton, near Ampthill. 3643/B.

JANEWAY, W., Private, Machine Gun Corps.
He joined in 1916, and in the following year proceeded to the Western Front, where he took part in numerous important engagements, including those on the Somme and at Cambrai. He returned home and was demobilised in February 1919, and holds the General Service and Victory Medals.
Manor Road, Barton, near Ampthill. 3643A.

JAPP, G., Private, The Prince of Wales' Leinster Regiment.
He joined in September 1916, and was afterwards sent to France and thence to Palestine, where he took part in severe fighting at Gaza and Aleppo and in many other important engagements, and was wounded and suffered from shell-shock. He was invalided home and discharged in May 1919, and holds the General Service and Victory Medals.
69, Stanley Street, Luton. 3639

JARDINE, A., Private, Royal Fusiliers.
Joining in May 1917, he went through a course of training and afterwards proceeded to France, where he took part in various actions, including that at Cambrai, and was gassed. After the Armistice he proceeded to Germany with the Army of Occupation, with which he served until he was demobilised in September 1919, holding the General Service and Victory Medals.
7, Clifford Street, Watford. X3637/C.

JARDINE, A. H., Driver, R.F.A.
He volunteered in August 1914, and was later drafted to Egypt and thence to Palestine, where he took part in numerous important engagements, including that of Gaza. He returned home and was demobilised in July 1919, and holds the General Service and Victory Medals.
7, Clifford Street, Watford. X3637/A.

JARDINE, W., Private, Royal Fusiliers.
He was serving at the outbreak of war, and was immediately afterwards sent to France, where he took part in various engagements. He was reported missing, and is believed to have been killed in action on November 11th, 1914, and was entitled to the 1914 Star, and the General Service and Victory Medals.
7, Clifford Street, Watford. X3637/B.

JARMUN, B., Private, Machine Gun Corps.
He joined in November 1918, but owing to being medically unfit for duty abroad, was unable to obtain his transfer overseas, and was demobilised in February 1919.
Well Cottages, Walsworth, Hitchin. 3648/A.

JARMUN, P., Corporal, 6th Bedfordshire Regt.
He volunteered in August 1914, and in the following year was drafted to the Western Front, where he took part in severe fighting at Albert, Loos, the Somme, Arras, Ypres and Cambrai. He also served in the Retreat and Advance of 1918, and was gassed. He was demobilised in July 1919, and holds the 1914-15 Star, and the General Service and Victory Medals.
Well Cottages, Walsworth, Hitchin. 3648/B.

JARVIS, A. E., Private, Buffs (East Kent Regt.)
He volunteered in August 1914, but was shortly afterwards discharged. He rejoined in June 1915, and in the following year was drafted to India and thence to Mesopotamia. In 1917 he was sent to Palestine, where he served in various engagements, and was afterwards transferred to France. He was demobilised in October 1919, and holds the General Service and Victory Medals.
3, Heath Terrace, Landridge Road, St. Albans. X3636/B.

JARVIS, F., L/Corporal, R.E. (E.A.)
Volunteering in December 1914, he was drafted to France in March of the following year. He was engaged on the Somme, Arras, Ypres and Cambrai fronts on important duties, and rendered valuable services. He was demobilised in January 1919, and holds the 1914–15 Star, and the General Service and Victory Medals.
Dunstable Road, Toddington. 3623.

JARVIS, F. W., Private, 23rd Queen's (Royal West Surrey Regiment).
He joined in March 1917, and was sent to France in the same month. He took part in severe fighting at Arras, Ypres, Cambrai, the Somme and the Aisne, and in various other engagements, and after the Armistice proceeded with the Army of Occupation to Germany, where he served until demobilised in February 1920. He holds the General Service and Victory Medals.
3, Heath Terrace, Landridge Road, St. Albans. X3636/A.

JARVIS, W. G., Private, Royal Fusiliers.
He joined in April 1916, and in the same year was drafted to the Western Front, where he took part in various engagements including those on the Somme and at Arras, Ypres and Cambrai, and was wounded. He was demobilised in February 1919, and holds the General Service and Victory Medals.
176, Fishpool Street, St. Albans. 1498/B.

JASPER, S., Private, 8th Bedfordshire Regiment.
He volunteered in September 1914, and after his training served on important duties with his unit until December of the following year, when he was sent to France. He took part in severe fighting on the Somme, and at Arras, Ypres and Armentières, and was three times wounded. He was demobilised in January 1919, and holds the 1914–15 Star, and the General Service and Victory Medals.
61, Waterlow Road, Dunstable. 3632.

JEAKINGS, C. S., Private, Army Cyclist Corps.
He enlisted in July 1914, and after his training served on important duties with his unit until the following year, when he was sent to Gallipoli, where he took part in the landing at Suvla Bay. He was later transferred to Egypt and thence to Palestine and was engaged at Gaza, Haifa, Acre and Beyrout. He was demobilised in March 1919, and holds the 1914–15 Star, and the General Service and Victory Medals.
3, Highbury Road, Luton. 3651/C.

JEAKINGS, E., Private, R.A.V.C.
He joined in April 1916, and after his training served at various stations on important duties with his unit. He was engaged in attending to sick horses, and rendered valuable services, but was not successful in obtaining his transfer overseas before the cessation of hostilities. In June 1919 he was drafted to Germany and served with the Army of the Rhine until the following October, when he returned to England and was demobilised.
Ayot Green, near Welwyn. 3673.

JEAKINGS, H., Sapper, Royal Engineers.
Volunteering in September 1915, he was sent to Egypt in the following year. In February 1917 he was transferred to Palestine, where he took part in various engagements, including those at El Arish, Rafa and Gaza, and was killed in action at the last place on April 4th, 1917. He was entitled to the General Service and Victory Medals.
3, Highbury Road, Luton. 3651/B.

JEAKINGS, H. J., Private, Essex Regiment.
He joined in December 1916, and after his training served at various stations in Ireland on important duties with his unit. He rendered valuable services, but was not successful in obtaining his transfer overseas before the cessation of hostilities. He was demobilised in November 1919.
9, Tavistock Street, Luton. 3666.

JEAKINGS, W., Private, 22nd Northumberland Fusiliers.
Joining in February 1916, he was afterwards drafted to the Western Front, where he took part in severe fighting at Arras and Bullecourt. He was wounded and taken prisoner at the latter place and held in captivity until after the Armistice, when he was released, and returning home was demobilised in August 1919, holding the General Service and Victory Medals.
3, Highbury Road, Luton. 3651/A.

JEEVES, F. H., Bombardier, R.F.A.
He joined in March 1916, and was later drafted to the Western Front. During his 3½ years' service overseas he took part in severe fighting in many engagements, including those at Arras and Cambrai. He was demobilised in September 1919, and holds the General Service and Victory Medals.
9, Park Road West, Luton. 3655.

JEEVES, W. J., Private, Bedfordshire Regiment.
He was mobilised on the outbreak of war, but owing to being medically unfit for duty abroad was unable to procure his transfer to the Front. He rendered valuable services, being engaged on important duties with his unit at various stations, until October 1919, when he was demobilised.
1, Foundry Lane, Biggleswade. Z1527/B.

JEFFCOAT, C., Private, Suffolk Regiment.
Joining in July 1917, he was drafted to France in November of the same year, and took part in severe fighting at Arras, Ypres and the Somme, and was wounded. He also served in the Retreat and Advance of 1918. He was demobilised in March 1919, and holds the General Service and Victory Medals. 10, Baker Street, Leighton Buzzard. 3683.

JEFFCOATE, W., Corporal, Northamptonshire Regiment.
He volunteered in August 1914, and in January of the following year was drafted to the Western Front, where he took part in numerous engagements, including those on the Somme and at Arras and Cambrai. He also served in the Retreat and Advance of 1918, and was demobilised in March 1919, holding the 1914–15 Star, and the General Service and Victory Medals.
2, Baker Street, Leighton Buzzard. 3681.

JEFFERIS, N., Gunner, Royal Field Artillery.
Volunteering in August 1914, he was sent to France in the following month, and took part in heavy fighting at Ypres and Loos. In November 1915 he was transferred to the Macedonian Front and was engaged in the Balkan campaign. During his service overseas he was mentioned in Despatches for conspicuous gallantry, and was three times wounded. He was demobilised in March 1919, and holds the 1914–15 Star, and the General Service and Victory Medals.
33, Essex Street, Luton. 3656.

JEFFERSON, A. R., Private, The Welch Regt.
He volunteered in April 1915, and was sent to France, where he served in numerous important engagements, including those at Ypres, the Somme, Bourlon Wood and the Ancre, and was twice wounded and gassed. He was subsequently demobilised in January 1919, and holds the General Service and Victory Medals.
13, Duke Street, Luton. 3654/B.

JEFFERSON, J., Gunner, R.F.A.
He volunteered in May 1915, and in January 1917 was drafted to the Western Front. During his service in France he did good work as a Gunner at Arras, Ypres, Cambrai and on the Somme and in subsequent engagements, until the cessation of hostilities. After the Armistice he proceeded to Germany with the Army of Occupation, and was stationed at Cologne until May 1919, when he returned home and was demobilised. He holds the General Service and Victory Medals. 13, Duke Street, Luton. 3678/B.

JEFFERSON, W., Private, 5th Bedfordshire Regt
Volunteering in August 1914, he was drafted to Gallipoli in the following year and after taking part in the landing at Suvla Bay, was severely wounded in action at Chocolate Hill on August 15th, 1915. He was invalided home to hospital, and after protracted treatment was discharged as medically unfit for further duty in March 1917. He holds the 1914/15 Star, and the General Service and Victory Medals. 13 Duke Street, Luton. 3678/A.

JEFFERSON, W., Private, Bedfordshire Regt.
Volunteering in August 1914, he was drafted to the Western Front, and served in many important engagements in various sectors, including those of the Somme, Arras and Ypres. He was taken prisoner in an engagement in September 1918 and held in captivity for several months. On his release he returned to England and was demobilised in March 1919, holding the General Service and Victory Medals.
13, Duke Street, Luton. 3654/A.

JEFFERY, H., Private, 4th Essex Regiment.
He volunteered in March 1915, and in October of the following year was drafted to Egypt, and served in the offensive on Palestine under General Allenby. He fought in various important engagements, and was present at the taking of Jerusalem, and later returned to Egypt and was stationed at Cairo. He was demobilised after his return to England in August 1919, and holds the General Service and Victory Medals. Meppershall Road, Shefford. Z3672.

JEFFORD, C. V., Sergeant-Major, R.A.M.C.
He enlisted in June 1905, and after the outbreak of war was drafted to German South-West Africa, where he was present at numerous engagements, including that at Duala. Later he was transferred to Egypt and thence to Mesopotamia, where he served in the campaign against the Turks. Finally he was sent to India. He holds the 1914–15 Star, and the General Service and Victory Medals, and was still serving in 1920.
Myrtle House, Icknield Road, Leagrave. 3657.

JEFFREY, A., Private, Bedfordshire and North-amptonshire Regiments.
He volunteered in September 1914, and on completion of his training was drafted to India, where he served on important duties with his unit at various stations until May 1919, when he returned to England and was demobilised. He holds the General Service and Victory Medals.
High Street, Clophill, Ampthill. 3568 /C.

JEFFREY, P., Private, East Surrey Regiment.
He joined in June 1918, and in the following October was drafted to France. He fought at Cambrai and Ypres, and was present at the entry into Mons at dawn on Armistice Day. He was demobilised in August 1919, and holds the General Service and Victory Medals.
High Street, Clophill, Ampthill. 3568 /B.

JEFFREY, W., Private, Labour Corps.
Volunteering in February 1915, he served on important agricultural duties after his training was completed. He did excellent work at his station, but was not successful in obtaining a transfer overseas before the cessation of hostilities, and was demobilised in January 1919 after four years' service.
High Street, Clophill, Ampthill. 3568 /A.

JEFFREYS, J., Rflmn., 11th London Regt. (Rifles)
He joined in October 1916, and in December of the following year was sent to Egypt and served with the British forces in the Advance through Palestine. He fought at Mejdil, Haifa, Acre and Damascus, and in all engagements until the cessation of hostilities. He was demobilised in March 1920 on his return to England, and holds the General Service and Victory Medals. 4, Beechwood Road, Leagrave. 3658.

JEFFRIES, F. W., Private, 2nd London Regiment (Royal Fusiliers).
Volunteering in October 1914, he served at various stations on important duties with his unit until July 1917, when he was drafted to France. He served in the third Battle of Ypres, and was killed in action on October 26th, 1917. He was entitled to the General Service and Victory Medals.
11, Shott Lane, Letchworth. 3685.

JEFFRIES, H. R., Corporal, Hertfordshire Regt.
He joined in April 1916, and in the following year was drafted to the Western Front, where he took part in the Battle of Ypres. He was severely wounded in 23 places at Cambrai, and was sent home and later invalided out of the Service on account of his injuries in 1918. He holds the General Service and Victory Medals. 9, Pageant Road, St. Albans. X3650 /A.

JEFFRIES, L., Private, 10th Hampshire Regt.
Volunteering in May 1915, he was drafted to Salonika in the following October and served on the Struma and at the recapture of Monastir. He also took part in the engagements on the Doiran and Vardar fronts until the conclusion of hostilities. He holds the 1914-15 Star, and the General Service and Victory Medals, and was demobilised after his return to England in March 1919.
26, Lower Dagnell Street, St. Albans. 3680 /A.

JEFFRIES, W., L/Corporal, 11th East Surrey Regiment and Rifle Brigade.
He volunteered in September 1914, and after his training served at various stations on important duties with his unit. He rendered valuable service, but was unable to procure his transfer overseas prior to the cessation of hostilities. He was demobilised in February 1919.
Brook End, Potton. Z2934 /B.

JEFFS, A. J., Gunner, Royal Garrison Artillery.
He joined in May 1918, and in the following August proceeded to France, where he did excellent work as a gunner on the Cambrai front and in the final operations of the war. After the Armistice was concluded he advanced into Germany with the Army of Occupation and was stationed at Cologne until February 1920, when he was demobilised after his return to England. He holds the General Service and Victory Medals. Horner's Corner, Wing, Leighton Buzzard. 3691.

JEFFS, H. G., Signaller, R.E. (Signal Section).
He volunteered in November 1914, and in the following year was drafted to France. Whilst in this theatre of war he was frequently engaged in the forward areas on important duties whilst operations were in progress, and was present at many engagements until the conclusion of hostilities. He was demobilised in July 1919, and holds the 1914-15 Star. and the General Service and Victory Medals.
99, Ash Road, Luton. 3675 /B.

JEFFS, J., Private, Labour Corps.
He volunteered in January 1915, and in the following July was drafted to France, where he served in various sectors. He was engaged on important duties in the upkeep of roads, in conveying ammunition to the troops, and also in burying the dead. In 1920 he was still serving, and holds the General Service and Victory Medals.
68, St. Andrew's Street, Leighton Buzzard. 3682.

JEFFS, J., Private, Machine Gun Corps.
He volunteered in December 1915, and in the following year was drafted to France. During his service on the Western Front he fought for 18 months in the Ypres sector and was in action at Arras and on the Somme, and suffered from shell-shock. He was demobilised in February 1919, and holds the General Service and Victory Medals.
30, Merton Road, Watford. X3669.

JEFFS, T. R., Sapper, Royal Engineers (E.A.)
He was mobilised in August 1914, and was later drafted to the Dardanelles, where he was engaged at Anzac and Suvla Bay. He was afterwards transferred to Palestine, and served at Gaza, Mejdil, Haifa, Acre and Beyrout. He was demobilised in June 1919, and holds the 1914-15 Star, and the General Service and Victory Medals.
99, Ash Road, Luton. 3675 /A.

JELLEY, W., Private, 4th King's Shropshire Light Infantry.
Joining in July 1916, he was sent to the Western Front in the November following. Subsequently he fought in several important engagements, and was killed in action near Arras on March 18th, 1917, during the German Offensive. He was entitled to the General Service and Victory Medals.
Primrose Hill, King's Langley. X3676.

JELLIS, J., Private, 8th Bedfordshire Regiment.
Volunteering in September 1914, he was sent to France in the following May, and after taking part in the Battle of Festubert, was killed in action at Loos on September 15th, 1915. He was entitled to the 1914-15 Star, and the General Service and Victory Medals.
Luton Road, Toddington, near Dunstable. 3670.

JELLIS, V., Private, 6th Bedfordshire Regiment.
He joined in June 1916, and in December was sent to the Western Front. During his service in this theatre of war he was attached to the Royal Engineers, and did valuable work at Ypres, the Somme, Arras, Cambrai and Albert, and was twice wounded. In June 1918 he returned to England in consequence of ill-health, and four months later was invalided out of the Service. He holds the General Service and Victory Medals.
1, Austin's Lane, Ampthill. 3684 /C.

JELLY, F., Private, East Surrey Regiment.
Joining in November 1916, he went through his course of training and in May 1917 was drafted to the Western Front. He took part in the Battles of Ypres, Passchendaele, Lens and Cambrai, and in many engagements during the Retreat and Advance of 1918. After returning to England he was demobilised in January 1919, and holds the General Service and Victory Medals.
High Street, Watford. Q20000.

JENKINS, A., Drummer, 3rd Bedfordshire Regt.
He joined in April 1917, and after his training was engaged upon important duties at various stations with his unit. He was not successful in securing his transfer overseas before the termination of war, but nevertheless did valuable work until he was demobilised in September 1919.
42, Midland Road, Luton. 3679.

JENKINS, A., Gunner, R.F.A.
He volunteered in August 1914, and on completing his training was drafted to Salonika, where he served until he was transferred to France in January 1917. Subsequently he fought in several engagements on that front, including those of Ypres, the Somme and Cambrai. He was demobilised on his return to England in April 1919, and holds the 1914-15 Star, and the General Service and Victory Medals.
Hillford End, Shillington. 3689.

JENKINS, A. D., Private, R.A.M.C.
He volunteered in September 1914, and at the conclusion of his training was engaged on important duties with his unit. He was not successful in obtaining his transfer overseas owing to physical unfitness, but nevertheless did valuable work until he was invalided out of the Service in 1917.
85, Boyle Street, Luton. 3668.

JENKINS, A. F., Sergeant, 5th Cameron Highlanders.
He had previously volunteered for military service, but was rejected in consequence of physical unfitness. In March 1918, however, he was accepted, and on completing his training in the following July was drafted to the Western Front, where he did valuable work with his unit during the Advance of that year, in which he was wounded. He was demobilised after his return to England in October 1919, and holds the General Service and Victory Medals.
79, Church Street, Dunstable. 3662.

JENKINS, B., Private, Bedfordshire Regiment.
Volunteering in 1915, he received his training at Wendover and Bury St. Edmund's. He was drafted to France in 1916, and after taking part in the Battles of Loos, the Somme, Arras, Ypres and Cambrai, was taken prisoner in the following year. After his release at the termination of hostilities, he served for a time with the Army of Occupation at Cologne, and also in Russia. He was demobilised on his return to England in February 1919, and holds the General Service and Victory Medals. Hillford End, Shillington. 3690.

JENKINS, E., Corporal, Royal Engineers.
He volunteered in January 1915, and after his training served in France for over three years. During this period he was engaged on duties of an important nature in the forward areas of the Somme, Cambrai and Arras. He holds the 1914–15 Star, and the General Service and Victory Medals, and was demobilised after his return to England in March 1919. 2, Taylor Cottages, Old Park Road, Hitchin. 3686/A.

JENKINS, E. L., R.S.M., R.E. (Signal Section).
Called up from the Reserve at the outbreak of war, he was engaged on duties of an important nature with his unit at various stations. He was not successful in securing his transfer overseas before the termination of hostilities, but in March 1919 was sent with the Relief Force to Russia, where he did valuable work until the following October. He was demobilised on his return to England a month later, and holds the General Service and Victory Medals. 62, High Street, Houghton Regis. 3671.

JENKINS, F., Sergeant, Royal Irish Fusiliers.
Volunteering at the commencement of hostilities, he was quickly drafted to France, and served in the Retreat from Mons and the Battles of Ypres, Arras and Cambrai. Later he was sent to Egypt and thence to Palestine, where during the campaign on that front he fought at Gaza, Jaffa and Haifa. He was demobilised on his return to England in February 1919, and holds the Mons Star, and the General Service and Victory Medals.
New Street, Shefford. Z3661.

JENKINS, G., A.B., R.N., H.M.S. "Baltic."
He volunteered in August 1914, and throughout the war rendered valuable service in the North Sea and the Baltic. After the Armistice he was engaged in the Black Sea on highly dangerous mine-sweeping duties and remained until 1919. He was demobilised in December 1919, and holds the General Service and Victory Medals.
Maiden Croft Lane, Gosmore, near Hitchin. 2448/B.

JENKINSON, W. H., Private, R.A.V.C.
He volunteered in 1914, and in the following year was drafted to France, where he served for four years. During this period he was engaged on important veterinary duties, and was stationed at Rouen, Boulogne and Ypres, where he rendered valuable services throughout in the hospitals for wounded horses. He was demobilised in March 1919, and holds the 1914–15 Star, and the General Service and Victory Medals. 13, Union Street, Luton. 3664.

JENNER, D. S. J., Signalman, R.N., H.M. Minesweeper "Fareham."
Volunteering at the outbreak of war, he was sent to the North Sea in the following year, and served on important and dangerous duties aboard a mine-sweeper. His ship took part in the Battle of Jutland in May 1916, and he was later again engaged in mine-sweeping in the Mediterranean Sea. He was demobilised in May 1920, and holds the 1914–15 Star, and the General Service and Victory Medals. 18, Cherry Bounce, Hemel Hempstead. X3677/A.

JENNINGS, C., Sapper, Royal Engineers.
He joined in April 1916, and during his training was found to be unfit for military service and was consequently discharged in July of the same year.
30, Puller Road, Boxmoor. 3653/B.

JENNINGS, E., Rifleman, K.R.R.C.
He volunteered in November 1915, and in the following year was drafted to France, where he took part in the engagements at Albert and Vimy Ridge. In 1917 he was sent to Salonika, and served on the Vardar Ridge until the following year, when he was re-drafted to the Western Front in January. He was then in action in the second Battles of the Somme and the Marne, at Amiens and Cambrai, and in the final engagements up to the Armistice. In June 1919 he was demobilised, and holds the General Service and Victory Medals. 8a, Brache Street, Luton. 3667.

JENNINGS, F. C., Pte., 4th Canadian Infantry.
Volunteering in October 1914, he was drafted to France in the following year, and fought in numerous important engagements, including those at the Somme and Arras. He was severely wounded in April 1918 near Cambrai, and was for a time in hospital. In August 1919 he was demobilised, and holds the 1914–15 Star, and the General Service and Victory Medals.
6, Grove Cottages, Falconer Road, Bushey. 3761/B.

JENNINGS, F., Private, 8th Bedfordshire Regt.
He volunteered in October 1914, and in January 1916 was drafted to France. During his service on the Western Front he took part in the Battles of the Somme, Vimy Ridge, Passchendaele and Cambrai, and was severely wounded and invalided home to hospital. In October 1917 he was discharged as medically unfit for further military duty, and holds the General Service and Victory Medals.
43, Dalton Street, St. Albans. X3660.

JENNINGS, G., Driver, Royal Field Artillery.
Volunteering in August 1915, he proceeded to France in the following January, and did excellent work as a driver in the Royal Field Artillery on the Somme and at Arras and Cambrai, and in numerous other engagements. In September 1919 he was demobilised, and holds the General Service and Victory Medals.
50, Wing Road, Leighton Buzzard. 3688.

JENNINGS, P., Private, Queen's (Royal West Surrey Regiment).
He joined in September 1918, and after his training was completed was sent to Germany with the Army of Occupation and was stationed at Cologne, where he served on important duties with his unit. He rendered valuable sevices, and was demobilised on returning to England in 1919. 30, Puller Road, Boxmoor. 3653/A.

JENNINGS, R., A.B., Motor Launch 258.
He volunteered in August 1915, and after his training was posted to H.M. Motor Launch 258 and sent to the North Sea. Later he took part with his ship in the engagement at Zeebrugge, and was in action at Dunkirk. He was demobilised in December 1918, and holds the General Service and Victory Medals. 69, Church Street, St. Albans. X3674.

JENNINGS, T. (D.C.M.), Sergt., 3rd Rifle Brigade.
He volunteered at the outbreak of war, and later in the same month was drafted to France and took part in the memorable Retreat from Mons. He also fought in many later engagements, including the Battles of the Somme, Ypres and Cambrai, and was awarded the Distinguished Conduct Medal for conspicuous bravery. He was killed in action on March 27th, 1918, and in addition to holding the Distinguished Conduct Medal, was entitled also to the Mons Star, and the General Service and Victory Medals.
10, White Lion Street, Apsley, Herts. X3665.

JESSOPP, E., Driver, R.A.S.C. (M.T.) and Tank Corps.
He joined in December 1917, and in the following June was drafted to France, where he was engaged on important duties in connection with the transport of supplies for the troops on the Somme and Cambrai fronts. After the Armistice was signed he served on salvage work for three months, and was demobilised on returning home in February 1919. He holds the General Service and Victory Medals. 90, High Street, Markyate. 3663/B.

JESSOPP, W., Private, 4th Essex Regiment.
He joined in June 1916, and in the same year was sent overseas and fought in the Battles of the Somme, Vimy Ridge and Passchendaele, and later served at Amiens and in the fourth Battle of Ypres. He was demobilised in March 1919, and holds the General Service and Victory Medals. 90, High Street, Markyate. 3663/A.

JOHNSON, D., Sapper, Royal Engineers.
He joined in May 1916, and a year later was sent to the Western Front. Subsequently he was engaged on field duties of an important nature, and was present at the engagements at Passchendaele, Cambrai, the Somme, the Ancre and the Sambre, and at the second Battles of the Aisne and the Marne. He holds the General Service and Victory Medals, and was demobilised after his return to England in June 1919.
45, Dudley Street, Leighton Buzzard. 4061.

JOHNSON, F., L/Corporal, R.A.V.C.
He volunteered in October 1915, and after the conclusion of his training was engaged on important duties in connection with the sick and wounded horses. He was not successful in securing his transfer overseas owing to physical unfitness, but did valuable work until May 1918, when he was invalided out of the Service.
4, Springfield, Linslade, Leighton Buzzard. 4064.

JOHNSON, F., Corporal, R.A.S.C.
Volunteering at the commencement of hostilities, he was sent to France at the conclusion of his training, and served for a time as a baker at the Base. Later he was drafted to Mesopotamia, where he was engaged on important duties in connection with the transport of supplies to the troops in the forward areas. He holds the 1914–15 Star, and the General Service and Victory Medals, and was demobilised after his return to England in June 1919.
27, St. John's Street, Biggleswade. Z4062.

JOHNSON, G., Bombardier, R.G.A.
He was serving in India at the outbreak of war, but returned to England soon afterwards and was drafted to Gallipoli, where he was in action at Suvla Bay. On the Evacuation of the Peninsula he was sent to Egypt, and took part in the Palestine campaign. He was killed in action at Gaza in April 1917, and was entitled to the 1914-15 Star, and the General Service and Victory Medals.
138, St. Alban's Road, Watford.   X4049/B.

JOHNSON, G., Leading Aircraftsman, R.A.F.
Joining in February 1917, he was sent to France after the conclusion of his training. He served in many sectors, including those of Ypres and Messines, and was engaged on important duties which demanded a high degree of technical skill. Whilst overseas he was gassed. After returning to England he was demobilised in October 1919, and holds the General Service and Victory Medals.
1, Shakespeare Street, North Watford.   X4046.

JOHNSON, G. P., Private, 2nd Queen's Own (Royal West Kent Regiment).
He volunteered in November 1915, and in the following May was sent to the Western Front. After taking part in many important engagements, including that at Ypres, he was killed in action in the Somme sector on December 5th, 1917. He was entitled to the General Service and Victory Medals.
2, Dorset Street, Luton.   1512/B.

JOHNSON, J., Pioneer, Royal Engineers.
He volunteered in 1914, and from early in the following year until 1919 served on the Western Front. Whilst in this theatre of war he was attached to a Field Company engaged on important transport duties, and was present during engagements at Loos, the Somme, Albert and Cambrai. He was demobilised in August 1919, and holds the 1914-15 Star, and the General Service and Victory Medals.
57, Balmoral Road, Hitchin.   3566.

JOHNSON, J. C., L/Corporal, 3rd (Prince of Wales') Dragoon Guards.
Volunteering at the outbreak of hostilities, he was quickly drafted to the Western Front, and served in the Retreat from Mons. He also took part in many of the engagements which followed, including those of La Bassée, Ypres, Festubert, the Somme and Arras, and throughout his overseas service, which lasted for over four years, did valuable work with his unit. He holds the Mons Star, and the General Service and Victory Medals, and was demobilised in April 1919.   70, Ridge Avenue, Letchworth.   4065.

JOHNSON, J. F., Private, 6th Bedfordshire Regt.
Volunteering in 1915, he was sent to France on completing his training, and after taking part in several engagements was killed in action at Ypres on August 7th, 1916. He was entitled to the 1914-15 Star, and the General Service and Victory Medals.   16, Willow Lane, Watford.   X3882/A.

JOHNSON, P. A., Sapper, R.E. (R.O.D.)
He joined in March 1917, and three months later was sent to France. Throughout his service overseas he did valuable work with the Railway Operating Department, and was present during engagements on the Somme and at Ypres, Albert and Arras. After the cessation of hostilities he advanced into Germany with the Army of Occupation. He was demobilised on his return to England in November 1919, and holds the General Service and Victory Medals.
5, Sunnyside, Hitchin.   3567.

JOLLIFFE, W. J., Telegraphist, Royal Navy.
He joined in 1918, and after his training saw service with his ship in the Mediterranean and in Russian waters during the blockade. He holds the General Service and Victory Medals, and in 1920 was still serving
43, Bedford Road, St. Albans.   X4043—X4044.

JONES, A. C., Pte., R.A.S.C. and Expeditionary Force Canteens.
Joining in July 1916, he was sent to France a month later Owing to physical unfitness for duty in the firing line, he served with the Expeditionary Force Canteens whilst overseas, and did valuable work at Rouen and Arras, but in consequence of continued ill-health he returned to England in 1917, and in March of that year was invalided out of the Service. He holds the General Service and Victory Medals.
65, Harcourt Street, Luton.   4052.

JONES, A. H., Lieut. and Q.M., 10th K.R.R.C., 3rd King's Liverpool Regiment and R.D.C.
He volunteered in September 1914, having previously served, and was drafted to France in the following July. Whilst on the Western Front he was in action at Laventie, Armentières and Ypres, and in May 1916 returned to England. He then served at various stations until May 1919, when he was demobilised, holding the India General Service Medal (with Clasps), the 1914-15 Star, and the General Service and Victory Medals, and Long Service and Good Conduct Medals.
King of the Belgian's Inn, Hertford.   Z5751.

JONES, A. L. (Miss), Special War Worker.
During the war this lady held an important position at a munition factory in Luton, where she did valuable work for a period of two years. The manner in which she carried out the arduous duties allotted to her was worthy of the highest commendation.
5, Wright's Yard, Houghton Regis.   4056.

JONES, A. L., Corporal, 23rd London Regiment.
He volunteered in September 1914, and during his service in France, took part in several of the principal engagements, and was wounded Returning to England, he was invalided out of the Service in January 1918, and holds the General Service and Victory Medals.
50, Catherine Street, St. Albans.   X4045.

JONES, A. L., Private, Royal Army Service Corps.
He joined in June 1917, and after his training was drafted to France. He was engaged on important duties in connection with the issue of rations to our troops, and was stationed principally at Marseilles. He holds the General Service and Victory Medals, and was demobilised on his return to England in December 1918.
80, Baker Street, Luton.   4041.

JONES, B. M. (Miss), Special War Worker.
This lady volunteered for work of National importance in July 1917, and for two years rendered valuable services at a munition factory in Luton.
5, Wright's Yard, Houghton Regis.   4057.

JONES, C., L/Corporal, Oxfordshire and Buckinghamshire Light Infantry.
Volunteering at the commencement of hostilities, he was quickly sent to France, and fought in the Retreat from Mons and in the Battles of La Bassée, Ypres, Festubert and Loos, where in 1915 he was wounded. In the following year he was drafted to Mesopotamia, and on April 8th, 1916, was killed in action at Kut. He was entitled to the Mons Star, and the General Service and Victory Medals.
"Omrah," Gardenia Avenue, Leagrave.   4042/A.

JONES, C. G., Special War Worker.
Being under age for military service, he obtained work of National importance at a high explosive factory in Luton, and for a period of two years did valuable work in the fuse-filling department.
5, Wright's Yard, Houghton Regis, Dunstable.   4055/B.

JONES, C. J., Private, 18th Middlesex Regiment.
Joining in August 1916, he was sent to France a month later. For nearly three years he did valuable work with his unit in many important sectors, and fought on the Somme, and at Cambrai, Passchendaele Ridge, Messines and Ypres. He was demobilised in February 1919, and holds the General Service and Victory Medals.
5, Wright's Yard, Houghton Regis, Dunstable.   4055/A.

JONES, E. A., Driver, Royal Army Service Corps.
He volunteered in March 1915, and in the same year was drafted to France, where he was engaged on important duties, and was present at the Battles of the Somme, Arras, Ypres and Cambrai. Returning to England, he was demobilised in March 1919, holding the 1914-15 Star, and the General Service and Victory Medals.
5, Pinner Road, Oxhey.   X4050.

JONES, F., Private, 2nd Oxfordshire and Buckinghamshire Light Infantry.
He volunteered in August 1914, and after his training was sent to India and thence to Mesopotamia, where he took part in engagements at Kut and Baghdad and was wounded. In 1917 he was drafted to France, and after taking part in fighting at Messines, Ypres and Bapaume, was killed in action at Havrincourt on September 11th, 1918. He was entitled to the 1914-15 Star, and the General Service and Victory Medals.
"Omrah," Gardenia Avenue, Leagrave.   4042/B.

JONES, E., Private, East Surrey Regiment.
Joining in May 1916, he trained at Aldershot and Northampton, and was sent to France in the following December. Whilst overseas he fought in many important engagements, notably that at Ypres, and was wounded at Hollebeke in November 1917. He was invalided home, and after being for a long time under treatment in Portsmouth Hospital, was engaged on land work until his demobilisation, which took place in March 1919. He holds the General Service and Victory Medals.
Campton Turn, Shefford.   Z4039.

JONES, F., Private, 5th Bedfordshire Regiment.
He volunteered in December 1914, and after his training, which he received at Ampthill, was drafted to the Western Front. Subsequently he fought in many notable engagements, including those at Ypres, Loos and the Somme, and was severely wounded in action at Cambrai in October 1917. He was then invalided home, and after undergoing protracted treatment in hospital at Birmingham was engaged on important agricultural work until he was demobilised in March 1919. He holds the 1914–15 Star, and the General Service and Victory Medals.
33, Cowfair Lands, Biggleswade. Z4060.

JONES, H. G., Sergeant, Royal Field Artillery.
He volunteered in November 1914, and in the following March was sent to the Western Front, later in the same year being drafted to Salonika, where he served in important operations. Afterwards he returned to the Western Front and subsequently fought in several engagements, including those at Ypres, Cambrai and Albert. He holds the 1914–15 Star, and the General Service and Victory Medals, and was demobilised in February 1920.
The Knoll, Maulden, Beds. 4047.

JONES, J., Sapper, Royal Engineers.
He volunteered in December 1915, and after his training was sent to the Western Front. During his service overseas he did valuable work with his unit in the forward areas, and was present at operations on the Somme, at Bellenglise and St. Quentin. He was demobilised in April 1919, and holds the General Service and Victory Medals.
76, Church Street, Luton. 4037/A.

JONES, J., Staff-Sergeant, R.F.A.
He was mobilised with the Territorials at the commencement of hostilities, and was afterwards engaged on important duties as a saddler with his unit. He was unable to secure his transfer to a fighting area before the termination of hostilities, but nevertheless did valuable work until he was demobilised in February 1919.
88, Harwood Road, Watford. X4038.

JONES, J. S., Corporal, R.A.M.C.
He was mobilised at the outbreak of hostilities, and in July 1915 was drafted to the Dardanelles and took part in the landing at Suvla Bay and the engagements which followed. After the Evacuation of the Peninsula he was sent to France, where he fought in many battles, notably those of Ypres, the Somme and Cambrai, and was twice wounded. He holds the 1914–15 Star, and the General Service and Victory Medals, and was demobilised in July 1919.
" The Rising Sun," High Street, Clophill. 4053.

JONES, K., Private, 1st Norfolk Regiment.
He joined in May 1918, and after a short period of training was sent to the Western Front. Whilst in this theatre of war he fought in several engagements, including those at Vimy Ridge, Cambrai and the Somme, and was wounded in action at Gouzeaucourt on three occasions. He was demobilised on his return to England in March 1919, and holds the General Service and Victory Medals.
76, Church Street, Luton. 4037/B.

JONES, P. W., Sapper, R.E. (Signal Section).
He joined in June 1916, and six months later was sent to France, where he served on important duties in the forward areas for two years, and was twice wounded. After the cessation of hostilities he was sent to Salonika, and was for some time engaged on special work with his unit in the Balkans. He holds the General Service and Victory Medals, and was demobilised on his return to England in February 1919.
5, Cranbourne Terrace, Hatfield. X4048/A.

JONES, S. J., Sergeant, K.R.R.C.
Volunteering at the commencement of hostilities, he was sent to the Western Front, and after taking part in the Retreat from Mons and the Battle of the Marne was killed in action at La Bassée on October 31st, 1914. He was entitled to the Mons Star, and the General Service and Victory Medals.
123, West Street, Dunstable. 4040.

JONES, T. W., Bandsman, 2nd Oxfordshire and Buckinghamshire Light Infantry.
He volunteered in August 1914, and was quickly drafted to the Western Front, where he fought in the Retreat from Mons and many of the subsequent engagements, notably those on the Somme and at Arras. On one occasion he was wounded. He was demobilised in April 1919, and holds the Mons Star, and the General Service and Victory Medals.
" Omrah," Gardenia Avenue, Leagrave, Luton. 4042/C.

JONES, W. O., Corporal, 1/5th Manchester Regt.
Called up from the Reserve at the outbreak of war, he was sent to the Dardanelles in April 1915, and took part in the landing at Gallipoli and the Battle of Cape Helles. After the Evacuation of the Peninsula he was sent to Egypt and thence to Palestine, where he fought in engagements at El Arish, Gaza, Mejdil Yarba and the Nablus Road, and was also present at the capture of Damascus. During his service he was wounded. He was demobilised in February 1919, and holds the 1914–15 Star, and the General Service, Victory, and Long Service and Good Conduct Medals.
37a, Tennyson Road, Luton. 4058.

JORDAN, E. G., Private, King's Own Yorkshire Light Infantry.
He joined in January 1916, and in the same year was drafted to the Western Front, where he took part in numerous engagements, including those at Vimy Ridge, Givenchy, the Somme, Cambrai and St. Quentin, and was wounded and gassed. He was demobilised in February 1919, and holds the General Service and Victory Medals.
2, Aylesbury Road, Leighton Buzzard. 4066/A.

JORDAN, H. A., Private, Royal Air Force.
He joined in July 1918, and after his training served on important duties with his unit. He rendered valuable services, but was not successful in obtaining his transfer overseas before the cessation of hostilities on account of his medical unfitness. He was demobilised in February 1919.
Rothschilds Road, Wing, Leighton Buzzard. 4066/C.

JORDAN, J., Private, 23rd Middlesex Regiment.
Joining in March 1916, he was sent to Hong Kong in August of the same year, his vessel being torpedoed on the voyage out. After valuable garrison services there he was drafted in March 1918 to North Russia, where he took part in various engagements. He was demobilised in January 1920 after his return home, and holds the General Service and Victory Medals.
C/o Bunkers, Chalk Hill, Dunstable. 873/A.

JORDAN, J. A., Private, Machine Gun Corps.
He volunteered in 1914, and in the following year, after the completion of his training, was drafted to the Western Front, where he took part in the severe fighting at Hill 60, Ypres, Givenchy, the Somme, Cambrai and other engagements until hostilities ceased. He returned home and was demobilised in April 1919, and holds the 1914–15 Star, and the General Service and Victory Medals.
Rothschilds Road, Wing, Leighton Buzzard. 4066/B.

JOSLIN, W. D., Lieutenant, R.A.S.C.
He joined in February 1916, and proceeded to France in October of the same year. He was present at numerous engagements of importance, including those at the Somme, Messines, Ypres and Cambrai. He was demobilised in July 1919 after returning to England, and holds the General Service and Victory Medals.
26, King's Road, Luton. 4051/B.

JOY, H. J., 1st Class Stoker, R.N., H.M.S. " Vanguard " and " Shark."
He was serving at the outbreak of war, and was engaged with the Grand Fleet in the North Sea on highly important mine-sweeping duties. He took part in the Battle of Jutland, and in the bombardment of Zeebrugge and Ostend, and was wounded. During the war he also rendered valuable service off the coasts of Russia and Turkey and in the Persian Gulf. In 1920 he was serving at Portsmouth, and holds the 1914–15 Star, and the General Service and Victory Medals.
87, Plummer's Lane, Haynes, near Bedford. Z4059.

JOY, J., Private, Tank Corps.
He joined in June 1918, and after his training was engaged on important duties at various stations with his unit. He rendered valuable services, but was not successful in obtaining his transfer overseas before the cessation of hostilities, and was demobilised in January 1919.
Bedford Street, Ampthill. 4063.

JOYCE, J., Private, Labour Corps.
Joining in March 1917, he went through a course of training and afterwards served at various stations with his unit. He rendered valuable services, but was not successful in obtaining his transfer overseas before the cessation of hostilities. He was demobilised in 1919.
16, Brunswick Street, Luton. 4054.

JUDGE, F. W., Private, R.A.M.C.
He volunteered in September 1915, and in the following year was sent to France, where he rendered valuable medical services at the Somme, Ypres, St. Quentin and other engagements until fighting ceased, and was three times wounded and gassed. He was demobilised in December 1919 after returning to England, and holds the General Service and Victory Medals.
49, Cecil Street, North Watford. X4068.

JUDKINS, F. (M.S.M.), Sergeant, R.F.A.
He was serving at the outbreak of war, and was immediately afterwards sent to France, where he took part in the heavy fighting at Mons, Ypres, Hill 60, the Somme and Arras, and was wounded. In November 1917 he was transferred to Italy, and did excellent service on the Piave and in the General Advance. He was awarded the Meritorious Service Medal for consistently good work and devotion to duty, and also holds the Mons Star, and the General Service and Victory Medals. He was demobilised in January 1920.
10, Oak Road, Luton.   4069/B.

K

KATON, A. E., Private, Seaforth Highlanders.
He joined in 1916, and began his service in France in the following year. After taking part in several important engagements he was reported missing after a battle in August 1917, and was afterwards presumed to have been killed in action at that time. He was entitled to the General Service and Victory Medals.
4, Symington Street, Harpenden.   4072/C.

KAY, R., Private, Royal Air Force.
After previous service as an accountant for the Ministry of Munitions he joined in 1916, and after his training was engaged at various stations on important duties with his unit. He was not able to secure his transfer overseas on medical grounds, and after doing much valuable work was demobilised in July 1919. Woodlands, Harpenden.   4071.

KEALEY, O. F., Pte., 9th (Queen's Royal) Lancers
Volunteering in August 1914, he began his overseas service in the following June, and remained in France for nearly four years. During this period he fought in numerous engagements, including Ypres, and was wounded near Cambrai in April 1918. He was demobilised in February of the succeeding year, and holds the 1914-15 Star, and the General Service and Victory Medals.
Hall End, Maulden, Ampthill.   4073/A.

KEALEY, S. J., 1st Class Petty Officer, R.N., E.1 (Submarine).
He was serving in the Navy at the outbreak of war, and was engaged on important and dangerous patrol duties in the Baltic Sea and off the coasts of Russia. In the course of his service he was in H.M.S. "Calgarian" when she was torpedoed off the North Coast of Ireland, but was saved. In 1920 he was still serving with the Navy, and holds the 1914-15 Star, the Russian Medal of St. George, and the General Service and Victory Medals.
Hall End, Maulden, Ampthill.   4073/B.

KEELER, E. J., Private, 5th Norfolk Regiment.
He was mobilised at the outbreak of war, and in the following year was drafted to the East, where he served for four years. He took part in the British Offensive in Palestine and fought in the Battle of Gaza. After being present at the fall of Jerusalem he served in many subsequent engagements until the cessation of hostilities. He was demobilised after his return to England in February 1919, and holds the 1914-15 Star, and the General Service and Victory Medals.
14, Shaftesbury Road, Watford.   972/E—973/E.

KEEN, C., Private, Royal Warwickshire Regt.
He joined in November 1916, and in the following July was drafted to India, where he was engaged on important garrison duties at Poona, Rawal Pindi and Bangalore. After 18 months' service he returned to England, and was demobilised in March 1919, holding the General Service and Victory Medals. 73, Highbury Road, Luton.   4074.

KEEN, G. L., L/Corporal, Royal Scots Fusiliers.
He was mobilised at the outbreak of hostilities, and being shortly afterwards drafted to France with his Regiment, took part in the Retreat from Mons. He served also at La Bassée and at Ypres, where he was killed in action on November 11th, 1914. He was entitled to the Mons Star, and the General Service and Victory Medals.
Littleworth, Wing, near Leighton Buzzard.   4097/B.

KEEN, G., L/Corporal, Labour Corps.
He joined in June 1916, but was unfit for service overseas on account of his health. He rendered valuable services at various stations on important duties in connection with food supplies until his demobilisation in March 1919. He had previously fought in the South African War.
28, Back Street, Luton.   4075.

KEENS, W., Air Mechanic, Royal Air Force.
He was mobilised with the Bedfordshire Territorial Force at the outbreak of war, but was unfit on medical grounds for service overseas. He rendered valuable services at various stations, and was engaged as an engine-fitter on important duties which demanded a high degree of technical skill. He was demobilised in February 1919, after 4½ years' service with the Colours.
2, Cambridge Street, Luton.   4080.

KEFFORD, F., Driver, Royal Field Artillery.
Volunteering in January 1915, he was drafted later in the same year to the Dardanelles and took part in the landing at Suvla Bay and in the subsequent engagements until the Evacuation of the Peninsula. In 1916 he was drafted to Salonika, where he served for a year, and then proceeded to the Western Front, and whilst in this theatre of war fought at Ypres, the Somme, Bapaume and in the engagements which followed up to the cessation of hostilities. He was demobilised in February 1919, and holds the 1914-15 Star, and the General Service and Victory Medals.
Green End, Shillington.   4098.

KEFFORD, H., Gunner, R.G.A.
He volunteered in December 1914, and began his service in France in the following year. Whilst in this theatre of war he did excellent work as a gunner at Bapaume, Givenchy and Festubert. In 1916 he was drafted to Salonika, where he served against the Bulgarians during their retreat and in many important engagements on the Balkan front. He holds the 1914-15 Star, and the General Service and Victory Medals, and was demobilised in February 1919.
Summer Leyes, Eaton Bray, near Dunstable.   Z4095.

KEFFORD, W., Private, Machine Gun Corps.
He joined in 1916, and later in the same year was drafted to France, where he fought in many important engagements, including those at Arras, Ypres, Cambrai and the Somme, and was gassed. After three years' service with the Colours he was demobilised in 1919, and holds the General Service and Victory Medals. Coronation Road, Potton.   Z4091.

KELVEY, F. C., L/Corporal, Royal Engineers.
He volunteered in October 1915, and after his training served at various stations on important duties with his unit. Owing to his special abilities in horsemanship he was engaged in training cadets, and rendered valuable services. He was demobilised in February 1919, after over 3½ years with the Colours. New Marford, Wheathampstead.   4078/B.

KEMPSON, G., Private, Labour Corps.
He was mobilised at the outbreak of war, and was almost immediately drafted to France, where he was present at the Retreat from Mons and the Battles of Hill 60 and Ypres. After his return from France in September 1915 he was retained for important duties with his unit. He was demobilised in April 1919, and holds the Mons Star, and the General Service and Victory Medals.
The Knoll, Maulden, near Ampthill.   4084.

KEMPSTER, C., Private, 1st Bedfordshire Regt.
Volunteering in August 1914, he was drafted to the Western Front in September of the following year. During his service in France he took part in many important battles, and being wounded on the Somme, was invalided home for a time. In January 1920 he was demobilised after his return to England, and holds the 1914-15 Star, and the General Service and Victory Medals.
26, Chapel Path, Leighton Buzzard.   4093.

KEMPSTER, D., Private, Bedfordshire Regt.
Volunteering in August 1914, he was soon afterwards drafted to France and took part in the first Battle of Ypres and many subsequent engagements. In 1917 he was sent to Palestine and fought at Kantara, in the three Battles of Gaza, the two engagements at Umbrella Hill, and at Mejdil, Haïfa and Aleppo. He returned to Egypt, and after being stationed at Cairo for a time was demobilised in March 1919, on his return to England. He holds the 1914 Star, and the General Service and Victory Medals.
59, Chapel Street, Hemel Hempstead.   4088/B.

KEMPSTER, E., Private, Royal Fusiliers.
He joined in 1917, and later in the same year, after finishing his training, served on the Western Front. While there he was in action at Messines Ridge, Ypres, Passchendaele and many subsequent engagements until hostilities ceased, and was wounded. He holds the General Service and Victory Medals, and was demobilised in March 1919, after his return to England. 59, Chapel Street, Hemel Hempstead. X3888/B.

KEMPSTER, J., Rifleman, Rifle Brigade.
He joined in June 1918, and on the completion of his training was drafted to Germany with the Army of Occupation, where he rendered much valuable service. After his return home he was demobilised in March 1920.
78, Norfolk Road, Rickmansworth.   X3888/B.

KEMPSTER, L. H., A.B., Royal Navy.
He volunteered in 1915, and after his training was engaged on important and hazardous duties in His Majesty's destroyers and cruisers. His vessel was in action in the Dardanelles, and cruised in the Mediterranean Sea and off the coasts of India and Turkey. H.M.S. "Weymouth," in which he was serving, was torpedoed, but he was saved, and in 1920 was still with his ship off the coast of Ireland. He holds the 1914-15 Star, and the General Service and Victory Medals.
14, Alma Road, Hemel Hempstead.   X981/A—X982/A.

KEMPSTER, T., Private, 1st Bedfordshire Regt.
He volunteered in September 1914, and in the following
January was drafted overseas. During his service in France
he fought at Loos, the Somme (where he was gassed), Arras,
Ypres, Cambrai and in many engagements in the Retreat
and Advance of 1918. He was demobilised in February of
the following year, and holds the 1914-15 Star, and the
General Service and Victory Medals.
4, Barrow Path, Leighton Buzzard.   4086

KEMPSTER, W., Private, Labour Corps.
He volunteered in November 1915, and in the same year
proceeded to France, where he was engaged on important
duties with his company in various sectors of the Western
Front, including the Somme, Arras and Ypres. He was
demobilised in November 1919, after four years' service with
the Colours, and holds the 1914-15 Star, and the General
Service and Victory Medals.
6, Yarmouth Road, Callowland.   X4081.

KEMSLEY, N. G., Driver, Royal Field Artillery.
Volunteering in November 1915, he was drafted to France
on the completion of his training in December of the following year. During his service on the Western Front he fought
at Arras, Bullecourt and in other engagements, and was killed
in action in the Battle of the Aisne on May 7th, 1918. He
was entitled to the General Service and Victory Medals.
25, Sandringham Road, Watford.   X4089/B.

KEMSLEY, V., Driver, R.F.A.
He was mobilised in August 1916, and in the following July
was sent overseas. During his service in France he took
part in the engagements at Ypres, Vimy Ridge, Cambrai and
in the operations which followed until the cessation of hostilities. He was demobilised in March 1919 after his return
home, and holds the General Service and Victory Medals.
25, Sandringham Road, Watford.   X4089/A.

**KEMPSON, F., Rifleman, 17th London Regiment
(Rifles).**
He volunteered in September 1914, and after completing his
training was drafted to France. He took an active part in
the engagements near La Bassée, Lens, Armentières, Givenchy and Vimy Ridge, where he was severely wounded. He
was discharged in April 1918 as medically unfit for further
military duty, and holds the 1914-15 Star, and the General
Service and Victory Medals.
47, Cambridge Street, Luton.   4077.

KENDALL, F. E., Gunner, R.G.A.
Joining in November 1916, he went through his course of
training and was soon drafted to the Western Front, where
he took part in many important engagements until hostilities
ceased, including those at Arras, Ypres and the Somme. He
was afterwards invalided home, and in January 1919 was
demobilised, holding the General Service and Victory Medals.
110, Victoria Street, St. Albans.   X4094.

**KENDALL, F. W. H., Private, R.A.O.C. and
Royal Air Force.**
He joined in August 1916, and after the completion of his
training was drafted in the following year to the Western
Front, where he did much valuable work until after the
cessation of hostilities as a pattern-maker in the aeroplane
workshops. He was demobilised in May 1919 after his return
home, and holds the General Service and Victory Medals.
96, Waterlow Road, Dunstable.   4085.

KENDALL, W. J., L/Sergeant, Grenadier Guards.
He was mobilised at the outbreak of hostilities, and was
quickly drafted to France. He took part in the Retreat from
Mons and in many later engagements, including those at
Ypres and the Somme, and was wounded. He was killed in
action on September 25th, 1918, near Deniecourt, and was
entitled to the Mons Star, and the General Service and
Victory Medals.
117, St. James' Road, Watford.   X4076.

**KENT, A., Private, Queen's (Royal West Surrey
Regiment).**
He volunteered in November 1914, and after the completion
of his training proceeded to the Dardanelles in July 1915.
In the landing at Suvla Bay in August he was badly wounded,
and was invalided to Egypt in consequence. After his
recovery he rendered valuable service for a time on the Gaza
front, and was subsequently drafted to France, where he was
in action in the Retreat and Advance of 1918, chiefly in the
Cambrai sector. After his return home he was demobilised
in 1919, holding the 1914-15 Star, and the General Service
and Victory Medals.
58, Stanbridge Road, Leighton Buzzard.   4092.

**KENT, F., Private, Oxfordshire and Buckingham-
shire Light Infantry.**
He joined in January 1917, and after his training proceeded
to India in the following July. At the close of his service
there he was drafted in the same year to Salonika, where he
did valuable work for six months on the Vardar front. In
March 1918 he crossed to Egypt, and subsequently took an
active part in the Palestine campaign until hostilities there
ceased. After his return home he was demobilised in October
1919, holding the General Service and Victory Medals.
High Street, Wing.   4096.

KENTISH, H. B., Gunner, R.G.A.
He joined in February 1917, and on the completion of his
training was engaged on important duties with his unit at
various stations. He was not successful in obtaining his
transfer overseas before the close of hostilities, but rendered
valuable services until his demobilisation in February 1919.
27, Beecher Grove, Watford.   X3863/A.

KEOUGH, H. W., Sergeant, Border Regiment.
He was mobilised at the outbreak of hostilities, and afterwards crossed to France, where he took an active part in
many engagements of great importance, including those at
Ypres and Arras, and was wounded. He returned home
in consequence of his injuries, and was discharged in 1917 as
unfit for further military duty. He holds the General
Service and Victory Medals.
74, Ridge Avenue, Letchworth.   4099.

KERR, A. S., Private, Royal Fusiliers.
He joined in 1916, and after completing his training was sent
to France, where he took an active part in many important
operations, and was killed in action on May 15th, 1917. He
was entitled to the General Service and Victory Medals.
86, St. John's Road, Boxmoor.   X489/B.

KERRIDGE, F. G., C.S.M., 10th Royal Fusiliers.
He was mobilised at the outbreak of hostilities, and was
immediately drafted to the Western Front. He took a
distinguished part in many battles until the end of the war,
including those of Mons, Ypres, Arras and the Somme, and
was wounded at La Bassée and gassed at Kemmel. He was
mentioned in Despatches by Sir Douglas Haig for his consistently good work in October 1917. After his return home
he was demobilised in November 1919, and holds the Mons
Star, and the General Service and Victory Medals.
            X4082.

KERRISON, G., Sergeant, Hertfordshire Regt.
He was mobilised in August 1914, and crossing at once to
France, took part in the Retreat from Mons. He afterwards
took a leading part in the Battles of Ypres—where he was
wounded—Arras, Passchendaele, Cambrai, the Somme and
other engagements until the close of hostilities. During his
service he was wounded on four occasions. He returned
home and was demobilised in March 1919, holding the Mons
Star, and the General Service and Victory Medals.
Lea Cottages, High Street, Wheathampstead.   4087.

KERRISON, L. W., Sergeant, R.F.A.
He volunteered in August 1914, and was retained on important duties with his unit until 1916, when he was drafted to
Mesopotamia. He did much valuable work in this theatre
of operations until the close of hostilities, and fought at Kut-
el-Amara, Baghdad and other places on the Tigris. After
his return home he was demobilised in 1919, holding the
General Service and Victory Medals.
6, Bernard Street, St. Albans.   X4090/A.

**KESNER, H. B., Sergeant, Queen's (Royal West
Surrey Regiment).**
Volunteering in January 1915, he went through his course
of training and later in the year proceeded to France, where
he remained until the war was over. He took part in many
important battles, including those at the Somme, Arras and
Cambrai, and rendered much valuable service. After
returning home he was demobilised in October 1919, and holds
the 1914-15 Star, and the General Service and Victory Medals.
10, Weymouth Street, Apsley End.   X4079.

KEYS, E., Corporal, Royal Field Artillery.
After being mobilised in August 1914, he was drafted to
France in the following month and fought in the Battles of
Mons, Hill 60 and Ypres. In July 1915 he proceeded to
Egypt, where he remained for nearly four years. While in
the East he took an active part in many important engage-
ments in the Palestine campaign, including those at Gaza.
After returning to England he was demobilised in February
1919, and holds the Mons Star, and the General Service and
Victory Medals.
54, Portland Street, St. Albans.   4083.

KIFF, C. D., L/Corporal, Bedfordshire Regiment.
He volunteered in 1914, and on the conclusion of his training
was drafted to France, where he took part in many engagements of importance until hostilities ceased, including those
at the Somme, Arras and Ypres, and was wounded and gassed.
He returned to England and was demobilised in 1918, holding the General Service and Victory Medals.
11, Hatfield Road, St. Albans.　　　　　　　X4117.

KIFF, E., Sergeant, 4th Bedfordshire Regiment.
He was mobilised in August 1914, and being medically unfit
for service overseas was retained at Colchester on important
duties with his unit. He was engaged in the training of
recruits and rendered valuable services, particularly as a
Musketry Instructor, until June 1917, when he was discharged. 2, Grove Cottages, London Colney.　　X4134.

KIFF, H. S., L/Corporal, Royal Marine Engineers.
He joined in April 1918, and after his training was engaged
on important duties. He was not successful in securing his
transfer to a fighting unit while hostilities continued, but he
rendered valuable services at Gosport, Dover and other
stations as an Instructor and in the construction of jetties
and bridges. He was demobilised in February 1919.
33, Castle Road, Fleetville, St. Albans.　　　　X4135.

KIFF, P., Private, Royal Army Service Corps.
He volunteered in March 1915, and quickly proceeded to
France, where he did much valuable work at Rouen. He
was, however, physically unfit to bear the strain of military
duties, and after five months' service was discharged in
August 1915. He holds the 1914–15 Star, and the General
Service and Victory Medals.
67, Cecil Street, North Watford.　　　　　　X4116.

KILBY, E. G., Gunner, Royal Field Artillery.
He volunteered in December 1914, and in the following June,
on the conclusion of his training, was drafted to France. He
took part in many important engagements until the cessation
of hostilities, including those at the Somme, Arras, Ypres
and Cambrai, and rendered much valuable service. He was
demobilised in February 1919 after his return to England,
and holds the 1914–15 Star, and the General Service and
Victory Medals. 3, Bolton Road, Luton.　　　4140/B.

KILBY, F. J., Trooper, Royal Bucks Hussars.
Volunteering in November 1915, he was drafted to the
Western Front a year later. While there he took part in the
Battles of the Somme, Ypres and Cambrai, but returned to
England on account of wounds in March 1918. He was de-
mobilised in February 1919, and holds the General Service
and Victory Medals.
60, Clarendon Road, Luton.　　　　　　　　4109.

KILBY, H. J., Private, R.A.S.C.
Joining in June 1916, he proceeded to France in the following
year, and from that date until after hostilities ceased did
excellent work in the transport of supplies of all kinds at
Boulogne, Etaples and other bases. He was demobilised in
May 1919 after his return home, and holds the General Service
and Victory Medals.
"The Tank," Marsh Road, Leagrave.　　　　4110.

KILBY, P. S., Corporal, Machine Gun Corps.
He joined in March 1918, and on the completion of his training was drafted to France in the following June. He took an
active part in many of the final engagements of the war,
especially in the Somme and Ypres sectors, and after the
Armistice proceeded to Germany, where he is still serving.
He holds the General Service and Victory Medals.
3, Bolton Road, Luton.　　　　　　　　　4140/A.

KILBY, W. S., Gunner, Royal Field Artillery.
Joining in June 1916, he went through a course of training,
and in the following August was drafted to the Western
Front. While overseas he fought at the Somme, Ypres and
other important engagements, but was invalided home in
February 1918 owing to ill-health. He was afterwards
demobilised in January 1919, holding the General Service
and Victory Medals.
19, Moor Street, Luton.　　　　　　　　　4137.

KILLICK, A. G., Private, Buffs (East Kent Regiment).
He joined in June 1917, and was drafted to France in the
following year. He took part in severe fighting at Ypres,
Passchendaele and the Somme, and was wounded, and
returning home was demobilised in September 1919, holding
the General Service and Victory Medals.
14, Piccotts End, Hemel Hempstead.　　　　X4101.

KIMBLE, L. T., C.S.M., 1st Bedfordshire Regt.
He volunteered in August 1914, and was drafted to France
immediately afterwards. He took part in severe fighting in
many important engagements, including the Retreat from
Mons, and was killed in action at La Bassée on October 14th,
1914. He was entitled to the Mons Star, and the General
Service and Victory Medals.
79, High Street South, Dunstable.　　　　　4100.

KIMPTON, G., Sergeant, Mounted Military Police.
Volunteering in October 1915, he was drafted to the Western
Front in June of the following year, and served in various
engagements, including those on the Somme and at Arras,
Cambrai, Armentières and Mount Kemmel. He was
demobilised in April 1920, and holds the General Service and
Victory Medals.
1, Primrose Cottages, Hatfield.　　　　　　X4126.

KIMPTON, J., Driver, Royal Field Artillery.
He volunteered in September 1914, and in the following year
was drafted to India, where he served on important duties
with his Battery until 1917, when he was transferred to
Mesopotamia. He took part in various engagements, including those at Kut, Mosul and Hit, and returning to England
was demobilised in August 1919, holding the General Service
and Victory Medals.
56, Adrian Road, Abbots Langley.　　　　　X4138.

KING, A., Private, Machine Gun Corps.
He joined in November 1916, and after his training was transferred to the Western Front, where he took part in various
engagements, including that at Arras. He was killed in
action in August 1917, and was entitled to the General
Service and Victory Medals.
37, Dumfries Street, Luton.　　　　　　　928/B.

KING, A., Private, Essex Regiment.
Having volunteered in September 1914, he was drafted to
France in January of the following year. He took part in
various important engagements, including those at Ypres,
Loos, the Somme, Arras and Cambrai, and was wounded.
He was demobilised in March 1919, and holds the 1914–15
Star, and the General Service and Victory Medals.
32, Princess Street, Dunstable.　　　　　　4111.

KING, A., Private, Royal Air Force.
He volunteered in September 1914, and after his training
served at various stations on important duties with his
Squadron. He was engaged as a carpenter in the aeroplane
shops and rendered valuable services, but was not successful
in obtaining his transfer overseas on account of his medical
unfitness for active service. He was discharged in April
1918, owing to his physical disabilities.
15, High Street, Houghton Regis, near Dunstable.　4120.

KING, A., Sapper, Royal Engineers.
He volunteered in 1914, and in the following year was sent
to France. He served at Festubert, Loos, the Somme, Arras
and Cambrai, and was engaged on important duties with his
unit and rendered valuable services. During his period of
service overseas he was wounded. He was demobilised in
1919, and holds the 1914–15 Star, and the General Service
and Victory Medals.
Barnard Yard, Queen Street, Hitchin.　　　4021/C.

KING, A., Private, Bedfordshire Regiment.
He volunteered in 1915, and in the following year was drafted
to India, where he served on the North West Frontier at
various stations on important duties with his unit. Contracting dysentery, he was invalided home, and in 1919 was
demobilised, holding the General Service and Victory Medals.
19, Barnard's Yard, Queen Street, Hitchin.　　4021/A.

KING, A., Private, Labour Corps.
He joined in 1917, and was drafted to France in the same
year and served in various important engagements, including those at Ypres, Cambrai, the Somme and the Aisne. He
was demobilised in June 1919, and holds the General Service
and Victory Medals.
2, Willow Lane, Watford.　　　　　　　　X4102.

KING, A., Private, Labour Corps.
He volunteered in 1915, and was sent to the Western Front
in the same year and served in many important engagements,
including those on the Somme and at Arras, Ypres and
Cambrai. He was demobilised in 1919, and holds the
1914–15 Star, and the General Service and Victory Medals.
9, Bell Terrace, Redbourn.　　　　　　　4131/B.

KING, A. E., Private, 8th Somersetshire Light Infantry.
He volunteered in September 1914, having served in the
Army, and was engaged on important duties with his unit
until August of the following year, when he was sent to
France, where he took part in many important engagements,
including the Battle of the Somme, in which he was wounded.
He was invalided home and discharged as medically unfit for
further service in October 1916, and holds the 1914–15 Star,
and the General Service and Victory Medals.
6, Dudley Street, Leighton Buzzard.　　　　4151.

KING, A. E., Private, York and Lancaster Regt.
and Royal Army Medical Corps.
Joining in January 1916, he was drafted to France in May of
the same year. He took part in severe fighting on the
Somme and at Arras, Ypres, and in other important engagements, and was afterwards transferred to the Royal Army
Medical Corps. He was demobilised in March 1919, and
holds the General Service and Victory Medals.
14, College Street, St. Albans.   4118.

KING, A. J., Private, 6th Royal Berkshire Regt.
He volunteered in December 1914, and after his training
served on various important duties with his unit until July
1916, when he was drafted to the Western Front. Later,
on October 14th, 1916, he died of wounds received in action
at Thiepval, and was entitled to the General Service and
Victory Medals.
High Street, Welwyn.   4129/B.

KING, A. J., Sergeant, Royal Horse Artillery.
Volunteering in August 1914, he was drafted to France in
February of the following year. He took part in severe
fighting on the Somme, at Arras, Ypres and Cambrai, and
also served in the Retreat and Advance of 1918. He was
demobilised in February 1919, and holds the 1914–15 Star,
and the General Service and Victory Medals.
123, West Street, Dunstable.   4113.

KING, A. W., Private, 2nd Bedfordshire Regiment.
He volunteered in August 1914, and in February of the
following year was sent to the Western Front, where he took
part in various important engagements, including Hill 60
and Ypres. He was killed in action in subsequent fighting
at the latter place in September 1915, and was entitled to
the 1914–15 Star, and the General Service and Victory
Medals. Tilsworth, near Leighton Buzzard.   4153./B

KING, C. E., Corporal, Middlesex Regiment and
65th Labour Company.
Joining in October 1916, he was drafted to France in the
same year. He was engaged in road-making and trench
digging, also in the transport by rail of ammunition and
supplies to the various fronts, including those of Ypres, the
Somme, Kemmel and Arras. He was demobilised in October
1919, and holds the General Service and Victory Medals.
London Road, Woburn.   Z4139.

KING, E., 2nd Lieutenant, Sherwood Foresters.
He joined in December 1917, and in March of the following
year was drafted to the Western Front. He took part in
severe fighting during the Retreat and Advance of 1918, and
was wounded at Oppy Wood in August of that year. He
was demobilised in April 1919, and holds the General Service
and Victory Medals.
31, Waterlow Road, Dunstable.   4125.

KING, E., Sapper (Despatch Rider), R.E. (Signals).
He joined in August 1917, and after his training served at
various stations on important duties with his unit. He was
later sent to Germany, where he was still serving in 1920 at
Cologne, as a Despatch Rider for the Signal Service.
Tilsworth, Leighton Buzzard.   4153/A.

KING, E. D., Private, R.A.M.C. (M.T.)
Joining in February 1916, he was drafted to France in the
same year and served on various fronts, including those of
Arras, Cambrai, Ypres, Loos and Albert. He was engaged
in the transport of ammunition and supplies, and rendered
valuable services. He was demobilised in September 1919,
and holds the General Service and Victory Medals.
c/o Mrs. Hunt, 116, Bearton Road, Hitchin.   4152.

KING, E. W., Private, Royal Fusiliers.
He joined in March 1917, and after his training served on
important duties with his unit until the following year,
when he was drafted to the Western Front. He took part
in heavy fighting during the Retreat and Advance of 1918,
and was severely wounded. He was invalided home, and
was still under medical treatment in hospital in 1920, and
holds the General Service and Victory Medals.
14, Grove Road, Dunstable.   4133/A.

KING, F., Sapper, Royal Engineers.
He volunteered in May 1915, and after a course of training
served on important duties with his unit until September
1917, when he was drafted to the Western Front, where he
took part in various engagements, including those at Ypres,
Cambrai, the Somme and Arras. He was demobilised in
January 1919, and holds the General Service and Victory
Medals. 26, Albion Road, Luton.   4141.

KING, F. J., Private, 1st Bedfordshire Regiment.
He volunteered in September 1914, and in May of the follow-
ing year was sent to the Western Front. He took part in
severe fighting in various engagements, including those at
Loos and the Somme. He was killed in action at Delville
Wood on August 27th, 1916, and was entitled to the 1914–15
Star, and the General Service and Victory Medals.
24, St. Andrew's Street, Leighton Buzzard.   4145.

KING, G., Private, 9th (Queen's Royal) Lancers.
He was in the Army at the outbreak of war, and in September
1914 was drafted to the Western Front, where he took part
in many important engagements, including the Retreat from
Mons and the Battles of the Aisne, Ypres and the Somme,
and was gassed. He was demobilised in April 1919, and
holds the Mons Star, and the General Service and Victory
Medals.
Sharpenhoe Road, Barton, Bedfordshire.   60/B.

KING, G., Private, Queen's Own (Royal West
Kent Regiment).
Volunteering in 1915, he was drafted to France in the same
year and took part in severe fighting at Givenchy, Hill 60,
the Somme, Arras, Ypres, Passchendaele, Cambrai and St.
Julien. He was demobilised in January 1919, and holds
the 1914–15 Star and the General Service and Victory Medals.
55, London Road, Boxmoor.   X4108.

KING, H., Private, Bedfordshire Regiment.
He volunteered in August 1914, and was shortly afterwards
sent to France, where he took part in numerous engagements,
including those at Ypres, Hill 60, Givenchy and elsewhere.
He was killed in action on March 13th, 1918, and was entitled
to the 1914–15 Star, and the General Service and Victory
Medals.
9, Bell Terrace, Redbourn.   4131/A.

KING, H., Sapper, R.E. (R.O.D.)
He volunteered in June 1915, and was drafted to France in
the same year. He was engaged in many sectors on important railway duties with his unit, and rendered valuable
services. He returned home and was demobilised in June
1919, and holds the 1914–15 Star, and the General Service
and Victory Medals.
48, Brightwell Road, Watford.   X4122/A.

KING, H. A., Private, 4th Essex Regiment.
He joined in March 1917, and in the following October was
drafted to Egypt, and took part with the British Forces in the
Advance through Palestine. He fought at Gaza and
Beyrout, and in many other engagements until the conclusion
of hostilities, and was demobilised after his return to England
in January 1920. He holds the General Service and Victory
Medals.
14, Grove Road, Dunstable.   4133/B.

KING, H. T., Private, 1st Bedfordshire Regiment.
He volunteered in August 1914, and in the following February
was drafted to France, where he took part in the Battle of
Neuve Chapelle, and was wounded in an engagement near
Festubert in April 1915. Later he was killed in action at
Hill 60 on May 5th, 1915, and was entitled to the 1914 Star,
and the General Service and Victory Medals.
Tilsworth, Leighton Buzzard.   4153/C.

KING, I., Gunner, Royal Field Artillery.
He joined in July 1916, and in the following June was sent
overseas. During his service in France he did excellent
work as a gunner at Arras, Ypres and Cambrai, and in many
subsequent engagements in the Retreat and Advance of
1918. He was demobilised in May 1919, and holds the
General Service and Victory Medals.
47, Union Street, Dunstable.   4112.

KING, J., Private, 2nd Bedfordshire Regiment.
He joined in June 1916, and in November of the same year
commenced his service in France. He fought at Arras and
Cambrai, and in the second Battle of the Somme, where he
was severely wounded. Later he succumbed to his injuries
on March 21st, 1918, at a casualty clearing station in France,
and was entitled to the General Service and Victory Medals.
25, Mill Road, Leighton Buzzard.   2461/B.

KING, J., Private, 1st Hertfordshire Regiment.
He volunteered at the outbreak of war, and was almost
immediately drafted to France, and took part in the Retreat
from Mons. He also saw service in the Battles of the Marne,
La Bassée, St. Eloi, and Ypres, where he was severely
wounded in 1915. He was invalided home to hospital, and
subsequently discharged as unfit for further military service
in July 1916. He holds the Mons Star, and the General
Service and Victory Medals.
Church Path, Ickleford, Hitchin.   4155.

KING, J., Private, Middlesex Regiment.
He volunteered in April 1915, and in the same year was
drafted to France, where he served for four years. He was
engaged on important duties connected with the interment
of the dead in numerous sectors of the Western Front. He
was demobilised in 1919, and holds the General Service and
Victory Medals.
48, Brightwell Road, Watford.   X4122/C.

KING, J. H., Air Mechanic, Royal Air Force.
He volunteered in 1914, and after his training served at various stations on important duties with his Squadron. Owing to being medically unfit for duty abroad he was unable to secure his transfer overseas, but rendered valuable services until he was demobilised in February 1919.
85, Judge Street, North Watford.   X4130/B.

KING, J. H., Sergeant, R.G.A.
He was mobilised at the outbreak of war, and in the following April was drafted to France and taken prisoner in his first engagement at Ypres on April 21st, 1915. He was held in captivity in Germany for over three years, and was then sent to Holland in June 1918, and interned there until April of the following year, when he was repatriated and demobilised. He holds the 1914-15 Star, and the General Service and Victory Medals.
48, Waterside, King's Langley.   X4127.

KING, J. T., Private, 6th Buffs (East Kent Regt.)
He joined in May 1916, and in the following October was drafted to France. During his service on the Western Front he fought in the Battle of the Somme, and at Vimy Ridge, Bullecourt and Ypres, where he was gassed in action. After his recovery he served in various engagements in the Retreat and Advance of 1918, and was demobilised after the cessation of hostilities in February 1919. He holds the General Service and Victory Medals.
64, Bassett Road, Leighton Buzzard.   4144.

KING, R., Driver, Royal Field Artillery.
Volunteering in January 1915, he was drafted to France in the following year, and did excellent work as a driver for the Royal Field Artillery on the Somme, and at Arras, Ypres and Cambrai, and in the engagements which followed until the conclusion of hostilities. He was demobilised in June 1919, and holds the General Service and Victory Medals.
33, Lamb Lane, Redbourn.   4128.

KING, R. H., Private, 8th Bedfordshire Regt.
He volunteered in September 1914, and in August of the following year was drafted to France. Whilst in this theatre of war he fought at Ypres, and was severely wounded in action in April 1916, and invalided home in the following month. After prolonged treatment in hospital he was discharged as medically unfit for further duty in August 1917. He holds the 1914-15 Star, and the General Service and Victory Medals.
56, Ridgeway Road, Luton.   4123.

KING, S. J., Sergeant, R.A.S.C. (M.T.)
He volunteered in June 1915, and later in the same year was drafted to France, where he served on important duties as a motor transport driver, and was engaged in the conveyance of supplies for the troops. In 1917 he was sent to Italy, where he acted in the same capacity during the operations on the Piave front. He was demobilised after his return to England in February 1919, and holds the 1914-15 Star, and the General Service and Victory Medals.
16, Ashwell Street, Leighton Buzzard.   4147.

KING, T., Private, Middlesex Regiment.
He volunteered in August 1915, and in the following October was drafted to Salonika. During his service in this theatre of war he fought in the general offensive by the Allies on the Doiran front and in the Advance across the Struma. He was demobilised in August 1919 on his return to England, and holds the 1914-15 Star, and the General Service and Victory Medals.
96, Whinbush Road, Hitchin.   4150.

KING, W., Private, Royal Army Service Corps.
He joined in January 1917, and was drafted to France, where he was engaged on important duties in connection with the supplies for the troops. During his service on the Western Front he was stationed at Le Havre and Rouen, and after the Armistice was signed, proceeded to Germany with the Army of Occupation and served in Cologne until June 1920, when he returned home and was demobilised. He holds the General Service and Victory Medals.
5, Bridge Place, Watford.   X4136.

KING, W., Sergeant, 1st Hertfordshire Regiment.
He was mobilised in December 1914, and in the following year was drafted to France. During his service overseas he fought at Loos, Arras, Cambrai and St. Quentin, and was three times wounded and in hospital. He was demobilised in February 1919, and holds the 1914-15 Star, and the General Service and Victory Medals.
High Street, Welwyn.   4129/A.

KING, W., Private, Essex Regiment.
He joined in April 1917, and in the following August was sent to France, where he took part in many important engagements, including those at Ypres and Cambrai. He was severely wounded on September 2nd, 1918, on the Somme front, and was invalided home to hospital, and was demobilised in June of the succeeding year. He holds the General Service and Victory Medals.
Old Farm Cottage, Park Street, St. Albans.   X4119.

KING, W. F. (M.M.), Driver, R.A.S.C. (M.T.)
He joined in April 1916, and in the following September was drafted overseas. During his service in France he was engaged on the Somme and Cambrai fronts on important transport duties conveying supplies of food and ammunition to the lines. He was awarded the Military Medal for distinguished gallantry in taking supplies through under exceptionally heavy shell-fire. After the Armistice was signed he advanced into Germany with the Army of Occupation in November 1918, and was stationed at Cologne until September in the following year, when he was demobilised after his return to England. He holds in addition to the Military Medal, the General Service and Victory Medals.
4, Victoria Road, Linslade, Bucks.   4148.

KINGHAM, A., Private, 7th Bedfordshire Regt.
He volunteered in August 1914, and proceeded immediately afterwards to France, where he took part in many important engagements, including those in the Retreat from Mons and the Battles of Ypres, Arras and Cambrai. He was killed in action at Thiepval on September 28th, 1916, and was entitled to the 1914 Star, and the General Service and Victory Medals.
High Street, Toddington, Beds.   1128/B.

KINGHAM, A., Private, Grenadier Guards.
He volunteered in August 1914, and after his training served on duties of an important nature with his unit. Owing to physical unfitness he was unable to secure his transfer overseas, but he rendered valuable services until April 1916, when he was discharged.
88, Cromwell Road, Luton.   4132/B.

KINGHAM, A. H., Driver, R.F.A.
He volunteered in October 1915, and after his training was engaged on important duties until he was sent to Salonika in November 1916. Whilst in this theatre of war he fought on the Struma, Vardar and Doiran fronts, and in the recapture of Monastir, and did valuable work until the cessation of hostilities. In April 1919 he was drafted to Russia with the Relief Force and served there for four months. During his service he suffered from malaria. He was demobilised in September 1919, and holds the General Service and Victory Medals.
High Street, King's Langley.   X4103/B—X4104/B.

KINGHAM, G. W., Private, 3rd Leicestershire Regiment.
Volunteering in September 1915, he was sent to France four months later. His service overseas lasted for three years, during which time he fought at Vimy Ridge, Messines, Bullecourt (where he was wounded), and the Somme, where he was wounded a second time in March 1918. He holds the General Service and Victory Medals, and was demobilised in December 1918.
Wellington Terrace, Luton Road, Toddington.   4121.

KINGHAM, J., Shoeing Smith, R.F.A.
He volunteered in October 1915, and for a considerable period was engaged at Salisbury Plain in training and shoeing horses. In 1918 he was sent to India, where he served on important garrison duties until December 1919. He was demobilised on his return to England, and holds the General Service and Victory Medals.
"The Bridge," King's Langley.   X4107.

KINGHAM, S. D. V., Gunner, R.G.A.
Joining in October 1916, he was sent to Egypt a year later, and subsequently served in the Palestine campaign, during which he fought at Gaza, Jaffa and Haifa. Later he contracted dysentery, of which he died in hospital at Cairo on November 18th, 1918. He was entitled to the General Service and Victory Medals.
88, Cromwell Road, Luton.   4132/A.

KINGHAM, S. P., Private, 9th Norfolk Regt.
He joined in December 1917, and in the following May was sent to the Western Front. In this theatre of war he fought at the Somme, Albert and Ypres, and was gassed. After the termination of hostilities he was drafted into Germany with the Army of Occupation. He was demobilised after his return to England in April 1920, and holds the General Service and Victory Medals.
High Street, King's Langley.   X4104/A—X4103/A.

KINGSLEY, F., Private, 5th Bedfordshire Regt.
Volunteering in February 1915, he was sent to France upon completing his training, and fought in the Battles of Loos, the Somme, Arras and Ypres. In 1917 he was drafted to Egypt and afterwards to Palestine, where he took part in the engagements near Gaza, Jerusalem and the River Jordan. Throughout his overseas service, which lasted for over three years, he did valuable work with his unit, and was demobilised after his return to England in July 1919. He holds the 1914-15 Star, and the General Service and Victory Medals.
8, Bearton Road, Hitchin.   4154/B.

KINGSLEY, J., Private, 7th Bedfordshire Regt.
He volunteered in February 1915, and eight months later was drafted to the Western Front. Subsequently he fought at Loos, the Somme and Ypres, and was reported missing on October 18th, 1917, after taking part in an engagement at Passchendaele Ridge. He was later presumed to have been killed in that battle, and was entitled to the 1914-15 Star, and the General Service and Victory Medals.
8, Bearton Road, Hitchin.   4154/A.

KINGSLEY, W., Private, 8th Bedfordshire Regt.
Volunteering in December 1914, he was sent to France a year later, and after taking part in the engagements at Ypres, Festubert and Loos, was killed during the Somme offensive on August 21st, 1916. He was entitled to the 1914-15 Star, and the General Service and Victory Medals.
16, Sunnyside, Hitchin.   4149.

KIRBY, B. R., Private, Royal Sussex Regiment.
He joined in October 1916, and after his training was engaged on important duties with his unit. He was unable to secure his transfer overseas before the termination of hostilities, but rendered valuable services, especially as a guard of German prisoners, until he was demobilised in January 1919.
41, St. Albans Road, Watford.   X4105.

KIRBY, G., Private, Royal Marine Labour Corps.
He volunteered in October 1915, and in the same month was sent to France. Here he was engaged upon duties of an important nature with his unit, and was present at the Battles of Hill 60, Loos and the Somme. Later he contracted pneumonia, of which he died in hospital on April 30th, 1917. He was entitled to the 1914-15 Star, and the General Service and Victory Medals.
1, Keyfield Terrace, St. Albans.   X4115.

KIRK, J., Steward, Royal Navy.
He volunteered in August 1914, and in the course of his service was engaged on important duties as canteen manager in H.M.S. "Yarmouth," "Royalist" and "Cambrian." He took part in many Naval engagements, notably the Battles of Jutland and Heligoland Bight, and did excellent work until he was discharged through causes due to his service. He holds the 1914-15 Star, and the General Service and Victory Medals.
9, Stuart Street, Luton.   4106.

KITCHENER, G., Private, 1st Lincolnshire Regt.
Joining in August 1917, he was sent to the Western Front on completing his training in the following April. He fought at Aveluy Wood and the Somme, where he was severely wounded in May 1918, and a month later returned to England. He was demobilised in November 1919, and holds the General Service and Victory Medals.
9, Barker's Cottages, Hitchin Hill, Hitchin.   4146.

KITCHENER, H. C., Private (Signaller), 5th Bedfordshire Regiment.
He volunteered in November 1914, and in the following July was drafted to the Dardanelles, where he took part in the landing at Suvla Bay and the engagements which followed. After the Evacuation of the Peninsula he was sent to Egypt, where he saw much service in the Canal zone. He also fought in many engagements during the Palestine campaign, including those at Haifa, Acre and Beyrout, and did valuable work with his unit overseas until 1919. He was demobilised on his return to England in April of that year, and holds the 1914-15 Star, and the General Service and Victory Medals.
92, Hitchin Road, Luton.   4124/B.

KITCHENER, J., Private, Labour Corps.
Joining in March 1916, he was engaged on important home duties at Aldershot until he was sent to France in 1918. Whilst overseas he was engaged in trench digging and road-making, principally on the Cambrai and Somme fronts, and during his service contracted pneumonia, of which he died in hospital on November 3rd, 1918. He was entitled to the General Service and Victory Medals.
39, New Town, Biggleswade.   Z3932/A—Z4142/B.

KITCHENER, L., Private, Bedfordshire Regt.
He volunteered in December 1915, and after his training was drafted to France, where he served for over three years. During this time he fought in many important battles, notably those of the Somme, Arras and Ypres, and did excellent work with his unit throughout. He was demobilised after his return to England in April 1919, and holds the General Service and Victory Medals.
65, Cowper Road, Boxmoor.   X4114.

KITCHENER, M., Private, Royal Air Force.
He joined in June 1916, and after his training served with his unit at various stations on important engine repairing duties, which demanded much technical knowledge and skill. Although unable to secure his transfer overseas before the cessation of hostilities, he did valuable work until his demobilisation, which took place in February 1919.
Coronation Road, Potton.   Z4143/A.

KITCHENER, S., Private, Sherwood Foresters.
He volunteered in March 1915, and was sent to the Western Front in July 1916. During his service overseas he fought in many important battles, including those of the Somme and Arras, and in March 1917 was severely gassed at Gommecourt. He was sent to a hospital in Gloucester, and in September of the same year was invalided out of the Service. He holds the General Service and Victory Medals.
Station Road, Potton.   Z4142/A.

KITCHENER, W. S., 1st Class Aircraftsman, Royal Air Force.
He was mobilised at the outbreak of hostilities. After crossing to France he served in the Retreat from Mons, and many of the engagements which followed, including those at Ypres, the Somme, Arras, and Cambrai, and was wounded four times. In 1917 he returned to England, and was subsequently engaged on various important duties until his demobilisation in June 1919. He holds the Mons Star, and the General Service and Victory Medals.
92, Hitchin Road, Luton.   4124/A.

KNEE, A. E., Sergeant, Herts. Dragoons.
He volunteered in August 1914, and was immediately afterwards sent to France. He took part in severe fighting during the Retreat from Mons and at Ypres, the Somme and many other engagements, and was wounded. In 1918 he proceeded to Africa, where he remained until March 1919, when he returned home and was demobilised, holding the Mons Star, and the General Service and Victory Medals.
5, Inkerman Road, St. Albans.   X4163/A.

KNEE, B., Lieutenant, Royal Air Force.
He volunteered in August 1914, and shortly afterwards proceeded to the Western Front, where he served with the Royal Army Service Corps at Mons, Ypres, the Somme and Arras. He was afterwards transferred to the Royal Air Force, and was wounded in action whilst flying. He was demobilised in March 1919, and holds the Mons Star, and the General Service and Victory Medals.
5, Inkerman Street, St. Albans.   X4163/B.

KNIGHT, A., Gunner, Royal Field Artillery.
He was serving at the outbreak of war, and was sent to France immediately afterwards. He took part in severe fighting during the Retreat from Mons, and was wounded. He afterwards proceeded to Egypt, and thence to Palestine, where he served in various engagements, including that at Gaza. He was demobilised in March 1919, and holds the Mons Star, and the General Service and Victory Medals.
near School, Walsworth, Hitchin.   4172.

KNIGHT, A., Private, Northamptonshire Regt.
Volunteering in August 1914, he proceeded to France immediately afterwards. He took part in severe fighting at Mons, Ypres and many other important engagements, and was killed in action on May 6th, 1915. He was entitled to the Mons Star, and the General Service and Victory Medals.
8, Aldenhall Road, Oxhey, Watford.   X4165.

KNIGHT, A. H., Rifleman, Rifle Brigade ; and Private, Labour Corps.
He volunteered in September 1914, and was drafted to France in March of the following year. He took part in severe fighting at Hill 60 and in other engagements, and was wounded at La Bassée in May 1916. He was invalided home, and afterwards transferred to the Labour Corps. He was discharged in June 1917 owing to wounds, and holds the 1914-15 Star, and the General Service and Victory Medals.
15, Park Road, Bushey.   X4159/A.

KNIGHT, B., Driver, Royal Field Artillery.
He joined in May 1916, and was shortly afterwards drafted to the Western Front, where he took part in various engagements, including those on the Somme and at Péronne, Rheims, Cambrai and Arras. He was demobilised in February 1920, and holds the General Service and Victory Medals.
Glenmore, Letchworth Road, Leagrave.   4170.

KNIGHT, C. H., Private, North Staffordshire Regiment.
He joined in 1917, and after his training served at various stations on important duties with his unit. He rendered valuable services, but was not successful in obtaining his transfer overseas before the cessation of hostilities. He was demobilised in September 1919.
Flitwick Road, Westoning, Ampthill.   4171/B.

KNIGHT, F., Private, 6th Bedfordshire Regt.
He volunteered in September 1914, and in the following year was drafted to the Western Front and took part in heavy fighting in many engagements. He was killed in action at Ypres on July 15th, 1916, and was entitled to the 1914–15 Star, and the General Service and Victory Medals.
40, Brightwell Road, Watford.   X275/A.

KNIGHT, G., Private, Hertfordshire Volunteers.
He joined in 1916, and was engaged in guarding railways, bridges and Government property, and in many other important duties. He rendered valuable services until demobilised in 1919.
9, Grange Street, St. Albans.   X4169/A.

KNIGHT, G. A., Sapper, Royal Engineers.
He volunteered in August 1914, and was shortly afterwards sent to France, where he took part in numerous engagements, including the Retreat from Mons and the Battles of Albert, Festubert and Loos, and was wounded near Roy. He was invalided home, and was discharged in 1917 as medically unfit for further service, and holds the Mons Star, and the General Service and Victory Medals.
17, Portmill Lane, Hitchin.   4174.

KNIGHT, G. H. W., Sergeant, Royal Engineers.
He volunteered in August 1914 and served on various important duties with his unit until December of the following year, when he was sent to German East Africa. He was attached to the Brigade Signal Station at Kilwa, where he was engaged on important duties, and rendered valuable services. He was still serving in 1920, and holds the 1914–15 Star, and the General Service and Victory Medals.
68, Church Street, Leighton Buzzard.   4176/A—4175/A.

KNIGHT, G. W., Private, 1st Bedfordshire Regt.
Volunteering in September 1914, he was drafted to France in the following year. He took part in severe fighting on the Somme and at Ypres and Cambrai. He was taken prisoner in March 1918, and on his release returned home and was demobilised in March 1919, holding the 1914–15 Star, and the General Service and Victory Medals.
9, Grange Road, St. Albans.   X4169/C.

KNIGHT, H., Petty Officer, Royal Navy.
He volunteered in August 1914, and served with the Grand Fleet in the North Sea and in various other waters. He took part in the Battle of Jutland, where he was killed in action on May 31st, 1916, and was entitled to the 1914–15 Star, and the General Service and Victory Medals.
25, Piccotts End, Hemel Hempstead.   X4161.

KNIGHT, H. G., Gunner, Royal Field Artillery.
Volunteering in September 1914, he was afterwards drafted to Egypt and thence to Palestine, where he took part in many important engagements, including those at Gaza and Haifa. He returned home and was demobilised in 1919, and holds the General Service and Victory Medals.
61, Regent Street North, Watford.   X4156.

KNIGHT, H. R., Air Mechanic, Royal Air Force (late Royal Flying Corps).
He joined in 1917, and after his training served at various stations on important duties with his Squadron. He was engaged as a painter, and rendered valuable services, but was not successful in obtaining his transfer overseas before the cessation of hostilities owing to his medical unfitness for active service. He was demobilised in March 1919.
15, Alexandra Road, St. Albans.   X4157.

KNIGHT, H. S. C., Private, Royal Fusiliers and Royal Air Force.
He joined in 1916, and after his training proceeded to the Western Front, where he took part in various important engagements. After the Armistice he was sent to Germany with the Army of Occupation. He was demobilised in May 1920, and holds the General Service and Victory Medals.
9, Grange Street, St. Albans.   X4169/B.

KNIGHT, J., 2nd Lieutenant, 2nd Bedfordshire Regiment.
He volunteered in September 1914, and in the following year proceeded to the Western Front, where he took part in numerous engagements, including those at Hill 60, Ypres and St. Quentin, and was wounded and gassed. He was demobilised in January 1919, and holds the 1914–15 Star, and the General Service and Victory Medals.
116, Marlowes, Hemel Hempstead.   X4168.

KNIGHT, J., Sapper, Royal Engineers.
Joining in October 1916, he was sent to France in the following year, where he took part in various engagements, including that at Amiens. After the Armistice he proceeded with the Army of Occupation to Germany. He was demobilised in May 1919, and holds the General Service and Victory Medals.
4, Grover Road, Oxhey.   X4164.

KNIGHT, J. V., 1st Air Mechanic, R.A.F.
Joining in 1916, he was drafted to France in the same year. He served in various sectors, including Ypres and the Somme, and was engaged as an aero-engine fitter. His duties, which demanded a high degree of technical skill, were carried out with great care and efficiency, and he rendered valuable services. He was demobilised in February 1919, and holds the General Service and Victory Medals.
116, Fishpool Street, St. Albans.   4158.

KNIGHT, P. S., Private, 2nd Bedfordshire Regt.
He was serving at the outbreak of war, and was immediately afterwards sent to France. He took part in severe fighting in the Retreat from Mons and at Ypres, Hill 60, Vimy Ridge and the Somme, and was wounded. He later proceeded to Russia, where he served for 12 months. He was demobilised in October 1919, and holds the 1914–15 Star, and the General Service and Victory Medals.
38, Warwick Road, Luton.   4162.

KNIGHT, R., Private, Canadian Scottish.
He volunteered in 1915, and was sent to France in the same year. He took part in numerous engagements, including those on the Somme, and was wounded. He was killed in action on October 19th, 1917, and was entitled to the 1914–15 Star, and the General Service and Victory Medals.
54, Cobden Street, Luton.   820/C.

KNIGHT, W., Private, Bedfordshire Regiment.
He volunteered in 1915, and in the same year was drafted to France, where he took part in heavy fighting at Hill 60, Loos and Vimy Ridge, and was wounded. In 1917 he was transferred to Egypt, and thence to Palestine, where he served in various engagements, including that at Gaza and those leading up to, and in the taking of, Jerusalem. He was demobilised in August 1919, and holds the 1914–15 Star, and the General Service and Victory Medals.
Flitwick Road, Westoning, Ampthill.   4171/A.

KNIGHT, W., Private, Yorkshire Regiment.
He joined in 1917, and was sent to Italy in the same year. He took part in various engagements on the Piave front, and also served on important duties in Taranto. He returned home and was demobilised in 1919, and holds the General Service and Victory Medals.
2, Lower Paddock Road, Oxhey, Watford.   X4167.

KNIGHT, W., Private, 8th Bedfordshire Regt.
He joined in March 1916, and in February of the following year was drafted to the Western Front, where he served in the Somme sector. He was reported missing on April 29th, 1917, and is believed to have been killed in action on that date. He was entitled to the General Service and Victory Medals.
15, Park Road, Bushey.   X4159/B.

KNIGHT, W. G., Private, 1st Hertfordshire Regt.
He volunteered in July 1915, and after the completion of his training was drafted to France in April 1917. After having taken part in several engagements, he was reported missing after the engagement at St. Julien in July 1917, and is believed to have been killed in action. He was entitled to the General Service and Victory Medals.
c/o Mrs. Bertha Chapman, 4, St. Michael's Mount, Hitchin.   1606/A.

KNIGHTLEY, P. E., 2nd Air Mechanic, R.F.C.
He joined in August 1916, and in the following October was drafted to the Western Front, where he served in many sectors. He was killed in action whilst flying near Poperinghe on February 14th, 1917, and was entitled to the General Service and Victory Medals.
35, Waterloo Road, Linslade.   4173.

KNIGHTS, P. C. H., Driver, R.F.A.
He volunteered in October 1915, and after his training was drafted to the Western Front. He was later transferred to Salonika and thence to Egypt, and finally to Palestine, where he took part in various engagements, including that at Gaza. Later he died on October 13th, 1918, and was entitled to the General Service and Victory Medals.
61, Loates Lane, Watford.   X4166.

KRIMHOLTZ, R., Private, Labour Corps.
He joined in September 1918, and was drafted to the Western Front, where he served in various engagements in the Ypres, Somme and Cambrai sectors. He returned home and was demobilised in May 1919, and holds the General Service and Victory Medals.
2, Camp View Road, St. Albans.   X4177.

L

LACEY, F. J., Sapper, R.E. (Signal Section).

Volunteering at the commencement of hostilities, he was quickly drafted to the Western Front, and served in the Retreat from Mons and the Battles of La Bassée, Ypres, Vimy Ridge and the Somme. In 1916 he was sent to Egypt, and in the following year took part in the Palestine Campaign with General Allenby's forces. He did excellent work with his unit in many important sectors, notably at Gaza, Beersheba, the Jordan, Jerusalem and Jericho, and remained overseas until June 1919. He was demobilised a month later, and holds the Mons Star, and the General Service and Victory Medals.
13, Albert Street, Markyate, Herts.   1617.

LACEY, J., Driver, Royal Field Artillery.

He volunteered in November 1914, and at the conclusion of his training in the following July was sent to France. Subsequently, he took an active part in numerous important engagements, including those on the Somme, at Arras, Ypres and in the Retreat and Advance of 1918, being severely wounded in October of that year. He returned to England, and in the following month was invalided out of the Service. He holds the 1914-15 Star, and the General Service and Victory Medals.
31, Friday Street, Leighton Buzzard.   1618/A.

LACK, E. W., L/Cpl., Northamptonshire Regt.

He volunteered in September 1914, and during his service on the Western Front took part in a number of important battles, notably those of Ypres and the Somme. On two occasions he was severely wounded and gassed, but remained in France until 1919. He was demobilised in April of that year, and holds the 1914-15 Star, and the General Service and Victory Medals.
31, Louldem Street, Watford.   1620.

LACK, S., Private, Royal Scots Fusiliers.

Volunteering in November 1914, he was sent to the Dardanelles at the conclusion of his training in the following July. He took part in the Landing at Suvla Bay and the Battle of Sari Bair, during which he did excellent work with his unit, and remained on the Peninsula until the Evacuation. From August 1917 until the cessation of hostilities he served in France, and fought in the Battles of Cambrai and the Somme, and in the Retreat and Advance of 1918. Returning to England he was demobilised in February 1919, and holds the 1914-15 Star, and the General Service and Victory Medals.
9, Back Street, Luton.   1621.

LAIN, A. F., Sapper, Royal Engineers.

He volunteered in January 1915, and after training was drafted to the Western Front, where he was engaged on important duties in connection with the construction of railways in various sectors during heavy fighting. He did excellent work throughout his service, and returned home on the conclusion of hostilities. He was demobilised in December 1919, and holds the General Service and Victory Medals.
37, Leavesden Road, Watford.   X3264/A, X3265/A.

LAIRD, F. H., Corporal, 1st Bedfordshire Regt.

He was mobilised on the outbreak of war, and almost immediately proceeded to France, where he fought in the Retreat from Mons and in subsequent engagements on the Marne, in which he was wounded and sent to a Base Hospital. Recovering from the effects of his wounds he returned to his unit, and took part in the Battles of La Bassée and Ypres, and was killed in action near Ypres on December 11th, 1914. He was entitled to the Mons Star, and the General Service and Victory Medals.
18, High Street, Silsoe, Beds.   1863.

LAKE, A. E., Corporal, Queen's (Royal West Surrey Regiment).

He joined in February 1917, and in the following month proceeded overseas. Whilst on the Western Front he fought in numerous battles and engagements, including those at Ypres and on the Somme and the subsequent fighting until the signing of the Armistice. He was demobilised in March 1919, and holds the General Service and Victory Medals.
68, Shott Lane, Letchworth.   4070.

LAKE, T. H., Corporal, R.A.S.C.

He volunteered early in 1915, and after his training was engaged on special duties until drafted to France in the following year. During his overseas service he was engaged in conveying supplies of food and ammunition to the forward areas, and was present at many of the principal engagements, notably those of Ypres and Vimy Ridge, and was severely wounded. He holds the General Service and Victory Medals, and in 1920 was still serving.
4, Maple Road, Luton.   1622.

LAMB, A. W., Air Mechanic, Royal Air Force.

Joining in September 1918, he had not completed his training when hostilities ceased. He was, however, engaged at various aerodromes on important duties, which called for a high degree of technical skill, and did good work as an aero engine fitter until his demobilisation, which took place in March 1919.
36, Ashton Road, Luton.   1624/B.

LAMB, C., Corporal, Bedfordshire Regiment and Rifle Brigade.

He volunteered in September 1914, and early in the following year was drafted to India. During his service there, which lasted for nearly four years, he was engaged on duties of an important nature at various stations, in the Punjab and at Rawal Pindi. He was demobilised on his return to England in November 1919, and holds the General Service and Victory Medals.
10, Queen's Place, Hemel Hempstead, Herts.   1623.

LAMB, F. (M.M.), Sergeant, Royal Engineers.

Volunteering in September 1914, he was sent to the Western Front at the conclusion of his training. Whilst in this theatre of war he served with his unit in many important sectors, notably those of Ypres, Festubert, Loos, Arras and Cambrai. He was awarded the Military Medal for distinguished bravery and devotion to duty, and in addition holds the 1914-15 Star, and the General Service and Victory Medals. He was demobilised after his return to England in February 1919.
"Oxford Villa," Ampthill Road, Flitwick, Beds.
1625/B.

LAMB, J., Private, 8th Lincolnshire Regiment.

Joining in August 1916, he was drafted to France at the conclusion of his training in the following January. He took part in much heavy fighting, and was in action almost continuously until July 29th, 1917, when he was killed at Messines. He was entitled to the General Service and Victory Medals.
36, Ashton Road, Luton.   1624/A.

LAMB, P., Private, Bedfordshire Regiment.

He volunteered in January 1915, and in the following year was drafted to the Western Front. Here he fought in many of the principal engagements, including those on the Somme, at Ypres, Arras, St. Quentin and Cambrai, and in 1917 was severely wounded. After receiving treatment at one of the base hospitals he rejoined his unit and again went into action, taking part in the Retreat and Advance of 1918. He afterwards served with the Army of Occupation in Germany, and was demobilised after his return to England in February 1919, and holds the General Service and Victory Medals.
"Oxford Villa," Ampthill Road, Flitwick, Beds.
1625/A.

LAMB, S., Private, Bedfordshire Regiment.

He volunteered in January 1916, and after his training was sent to France. In this theatre of war he took part in fighting on the Somme, at Arras, Ypres and Neuve Chapelle, and was also engaged on duties of a special nature. After the cessation of hostilities he advanced into Germany with the Army of Occupation, but returned to England for his demobilisation in February 1919. He holds the General Service and Victory Medals.
"Oxford Villa," Ampthill Road, Flitwick, Beds.
1625/C.

LAMB, S., Private, Royal Army Medical Corps.

He volunteered in October 1915, and at the conclusion of his training in the following August was sent to Salonica. Here he served for nearly four years, attached to the 80th Field Ambulance, 26th Division, in which he did excellent work on the Vardar and Doiran Fronts and at Monastir. On one occasion he was severely wounded, but after receiving treatment at the base, was able to rejoin his unit. He was demobilised after his return to England in April 1919, and holds the General Service and Victory Medals.
62, Ash Road, Luton.   1626.

LAMBERT, A. P., Private, 2nd Queen's Own (Royal West Kent Regiment).

He joined in July 1917, and after his training was engaged on duties of an important nature until drafted to France in April 1918. Subsequently he went into action at Cambrai, where he was severely wounded and taken prisoner during the German Offensive in May of that year. After his release at the cessation of hostilities, he rejoined his unit, and in 1920 was still serving. He holds the General Service and Victory Medals.
120, Cassiobury Cottages, St. Albans Road, Watford.
1627/B.

LAMBERT, G. A., Pte., 1/5th Bedfordshire Regt.

He volunteered in September 1914, and at the conclusion of his training in the following year was drafted to the Dardanelles, subsequently taking part in the landing at Suvla Bay and the Battle of Sari Bair. After the Evacuation of the Peninsula he was sent to the Western Front, where he took an active part in many notable battles, including those of the Somme and Ypres, and was wounded. Returning to England he was demobilised in February 1919, and holds the 1914-15 Star, and the General Service and Victor
78, Frederic Street, Luton.   1628.

LAMBERT, J. C., Pte., 2nd Bedfordshire Regt.

Volunteering in August 1914, he was in training until the following January, when he was drafted to the Western Front. Subsequently, he went into action at Hill 60, where he was blown up and severely wounded by a mine explosion. Returning to England he was for some time in hospital, and in December 1915, was invalided out of the service. He holds the 1914-15 Star, and the General Service and Victory Medals.
120, Cassiobury Cottages, St. Albans Road, Watford.
1627/A.

LAMBERT, T., Driver, Royal Field Artillery.

Volunteering in February 1915, he was sent overseas in the following July. During his service in France he was engaged in conveying guns and ammunition to the forward areas and also took an active part in many of the principal engagements, including those of Arras, Ypres, Cambrai, and the Retreat and Advance of 1918, and was severely wounded. He was demobilised in June 1919, and holds the 1914-15 Star, and the General Service and Victory Medals.
" Navda " Cottage, Regent Street, Leighton Buzzard.
1629.

LAMBERT, T. P., Sapper, Royal Engineers.

He joined in December 1916, but after his training was retained for special duties until April 1918, when he was sent to France. Subsequently he served in the Retreat and Advance of that year, during which he did excellent work with his unit, remaining overseas until after the cessation of hostilities. He was demobilised in June 1919, and holds the General Service and Victory Medals.
46, St. Mary's Road, Watford.   1630.

LAMBOURNE, H. W., Private, 1/2nd London Regiment (Royal Fusiliers).

Volunteering in November 1914, he was drafted to the Western Front in the following March. His service in this theatre of war lasted for nearly four years, during which time he took part in many of the principal battles, notably those of Hill 60, Ypres, the Somme and Cambrai. He also fought in the Retreat and Advance of 1918, and returning to England in 1919 was demobilised in March of that year. He holds the General Service and Victory Medals.
22, Union Street, Leighton Buzzard.   2464/A.

LAMPORT, W. J., Private, R.A.M.C.

He joined in March 1917, and in the same year was drafted overseas. During his service on the Western Front he was engaged on important hospital duties in the forward areas, and served at Ypres and Arras. He was also employed on hospital ships, and throughout his service did much good work. He was demobilised in March 1920, and holds the General Service and Victory Medals.
99, Liverpool Road, Watford.   X3715/A.

LANCASTER, A. W., Rifleman, King's Royal Rifle Corps.

Joining in May 1916, he was drafted to the Western Front in the following December. Whilst overseas he took an active part in many of the principal engagements, notably those at Ypres and Cambrai, and did excellent work with his unit throughout. He was demobilised after his return to England in February 1919, and holds the General Service and Victory Medals.
56, Cambridge Street, Luton.   1632/B.

LANCASTER, J., Private, R.A.S.C.

He volunteered at the outbreak of war, and early in 1915 was sent to India. Here he was engaged on important transport work in connection with equipment and supplies for the troops, and in this capacity did much good work. He was demobilised after his return to England in March 1919, and holds the General Service and Victory Medals.
6, Baker Street, Leighton Buzzard.   1640.

LANCASTER, S. A., A.B., Royal Navy.

Joining in 1917 he was posted to H.M.S. "Africa," in which ship he saw service in the Baltic and Mediterranean Seas and other waters throughout the remaining period of war. He holds the General Service and Victory Medals, and in 1920 was still serving.
16, Cecil Street, North Watford.   1633.

LANCASTER, W., Stoker, Merchant Service.

Volunteering in August 1914, he was posted to the " Tiflis," in which ship he was engaged on important transport duties in various waters. His vessel was afterwards sent to Salonica and served in the Mediterranean, carrying stores and supplies for the troops engaged in the Balkans. He was later employed in home waters in the " Duffield," and was rescued when that ship was torpedoed. He was demobilised in January 1919, and holds the General Service and the Mercantile Marine War Medals.
30, York Road, Watford.   X3395/B.

LANCASTER, W. H., Driver, Royal Engineers.

He volunteered in July 1915, and after his training saw service in France and Italy. In both of these theatres of war he did important work in many sectors, and remained overseas until after the cessation of hostilities. He was demobilised in February 1919, and holds the General Service and Victory Medals.
56, Cambridge Street, Luton.   1632/A.

LAND, F. W., Private, 7th Bedfordshire Regt.

Volunteering in November 1915, he was sent to France in the following August. He took part in fighting on the Somme, where he sustained severe wounds, of which he subsequently died in the 2nd General Hospital at Boulogne on October 9th, 1916. He was entitled to the General Service and Victory Medals.
146, Hitchin Street, Biggleswade.   1634.

LAND, J., Private, 1/5 Bedfordshire Regiment.

He volunteered in September 1914, and after his training was drafted to Egypt. After taking part in several minor engagements on that front he fought in the Palestine Campaign under General Allenby, and was severely wounded and also suffered from shell shock Returning to England he was demobilised in April 1919, and holds the General Service and Victory Medals.
3, Gaitskell Row, Luton.   1635.

LANDALE, W. B., Driver, Royal Engineers.

Volunteering in September 1914, he was drafted to the Western Front early in the following year. His service overseas lasted for nearly four years, and during this time he did excellent work with his unit in many important sectors, notably those of Hill 60, Ypres, the Somme and Cambrai. He was demobilised on his return to England in 1919, and holds the 1914-15 Star, and the General Service and Victory Medals.
80, Hagden Lane, Watford.   1636.

LANE, C. D., Air Mechanic, Royal Air Force.

Joining in September 1918, he was drafted to Malta, where he was engaged on important duties, which called for a high degree of technical skill. He rendered valuable services before returning to England for his demobilisation, which took place in November 1919.
22, Chapel Street, Hemel Hempstead.   1637/A.

LANE, J. A., Private, Machine Gun Corps.

Volunteering in February 1916, he was drafted to the Western Front in the following July, when he went into action on the Somme. Subsequently, he fought in many other important sectors, including those of Ypres, Arras and Cambrai, and throughout his service overseas did good work with his unit. He was demobilised in October 1919, and holds the General Service and Victory Medals.
Bute Cottages, Harlington, near Dunstable.   1638.

LANE, W. T., Pte., Royal Marine Light Infantry.

He was mobilised at the outbreak of hostilities, but was unable to secure his transfer overseas. Throughout the war, however, he was engaged upon duties of an important nature and rendered valuable services before he was demobilised in January 1919.
29, Henry Street, Luton.   1639.

LANGDALE, C., Sapper, Royal Engineers.

Volunteering in August 1914, he was drafted to the Western Front, and took part in the Retreat from Mons. He also served in many of the subsequent engagements, including those at Ypres, Arras and Cambrai, and in the Retreat and Advance of 1918. He was demobilised in February 1919, and holds the Mons Star, and the General Service and Victory Medals.
42, York Road, Watford.   1641/A.

LANGFORD, G. R., Sapper, Royal Engineers.

A Territorial, he was in camp in Scotland when war broke out, and was at once mobilised and drafted to the Western Front. Here he served in the Retreat from Mons and the Battles of Ypres, Hill 60 and Festubert, and in 1915 was severely wounded during the second Battle of Ypres. He was invalided home 'o hospital, and after recovery was stationed for a time in Yorkshire. In 1917 he returned to France, and again did good work in many important sectors until the cessation of hostilities, when he was sent to Germany with the Army of Occupation. He holds the Mons Star, and the General Service and Victory Medals, and was demobilised after his return to England in May 1919.
55, Cemetery Street, Biggleswade.   Z1305/A.

LANGLEY, H., Trooper, Hertfordshire Dragoons.

He was serving in the Territorials when war was declared, and was mobilised and drafted to the Dardanelles in the following year. In this theatre of war he was engaged in the fierce fighting at the landing at Suvla Bay and in the subsequent battles until the Evacuation of the Peninsula. He was then sent to Egypt, and was in action in Palestine at the Battles of El Arish, Gaza, Haifa, Damascus and Aleppo. He returned to England and was demobilised in July 1919, and holds the 1914-15 Star, and the General Service and Victory Medals.
114, Harwood Road, Watford, Herts.   X608/A.

LANGLEY, J. J., Private, Bedfordshire Regiment and Essex Regiment.

He joined the Bedfordshire Regiment in June 1916, and was later transferred to the Essex Regiment. In the same year he was sent to France, where he remained until the cessation of hostilities, taking part in many battles, notably those of Arras and Cambrai. He holds the General Service and Victory Medals, and was demobilised in January 1919.
22, Harwood Road, Watford.   1642.

LANGRISH, H. G., Sapper, Royal Engineers.

He volunteered in January 1915, and after a period of training was sent to France. He was engaged on important duties with his unit in connection with operations, and was frequently in the forward areas. He served at the Battles of the Somme and Cambrai, and in the Retreat and Advance of 1918, and was demobilised in February 1919. He holds the General Service and Victory Medals.
23, Weymouth Street, Watford.   1643.

LANGSTON, A. E., Private, Grenadier Guards.

He joined in May 1918, and at the conclusion of his training served at various stations on important duties with his unit. He did good work, but was unable to secure his transfer to a theatre of war before the signing of the Armistice, and was demobilised in November 1919.
59, Regent Street, North Watford.   1644/A.

LANGSTON, C., Private, 6th Bedfordshire Regt.

He volunteered in August 1914, and was shortly afterwards drafted to France, where he served with his battalion and fought at the Battles of Ypres, Arras, and many others and was wounded. On recovery he rejoined his unit, and was in action again until killed at St. Julien on October 8th, 1917. He was entitled to the 1914 Star, and the General Service and Victory Medals.
123, Herkomer Road, Bushey, Herts.   X615/B.

LANGSTON, G. W., Private, Middlesex Regt.

He joined in September 1917, and in the same year was drafted to the Western Front, where he took part in the engagements at Cambrai, Arras, Bullecourt and Albert. He was also employed on guard duties and other important work during his service in France. He was demobilised in December 1919, and holds the General Service and Victory Medals.
123, Herkomer Road, Bushey, Herts.   615/A.

LANGSTON, W. G., Private, 3rd London Regt. (Royal Fusiliers).

He volunteered is September 1914, and in the following December was sent to Malta where he served for a time. He was then drafted to Gallipoli and fought there until the Evacuation of the Peninsula, when he proceeded to Egypt, and in 1917 was drafted to the Western Front. He took part in many engagements is this theatre of war and was killed in action at Arras on May 16th, 1917. He was entitled to the 1914-15 Star, and the General Service and Victory Medals.
59, Regent Street North, Watford.   1644/B.

LANKIN, C. A., 1st Class Stoker, Royal Navy.

Mobilised at the outbreak of war, he was posted to H.M.S. "Aboukir" in which ship he lost his life, when she was torpedoed and sunk off the Hook of Holland on September 22nd, 1914. He was entitled to the 1914-15 Star, and the General Service and Victory Medals.
102, Cobden Street, Luton.   1631/B.

LANT, A., Sapper, Royal Engineers.

He volunteered in September 1914, and after his training was drafted to Gallipoli. He served at Suvla Bay and was present at many other battles. In 1916 he was sent to Egypt, where he was employed on important duties in the forward areas and was in action during the operations at Beersheba, in the Jordan Valley, and at Jerusalem. He returned home and was demobilised in February 1919, and holds the 1914-15 Star, and the General Service and Victory Medals.
30, Midland Road, Luton.   1645.

LARCOMBE, B., Private, Bedfordshire Regiment.

He was mobilised at the outbreak of hostilities and served at various stations on important duties with his unit but owing to ill-health was discharged as medically unfit for further service in October 1914.
136, Harley Road, Luton.   1646.

LARGE, A., Private, Royal Sussex Regiment.

He volunteered in March 1915, and in the following year was drafted to France. He served in many sectors of the Western Front, and was engaged in much heavy fighting and was killed in action in August 1917. He was entitled to the General Service and Victory Medals.
43, Chobham Street, Luton.   1647/A.

LARGE, F. R., Private, Bedfordshire Regiment.

He volunteered in August 1914, and after his training was drafted overseas. He took part in the fighting on the Western Front, and fought in the Battles of Arras, Ypres, Cambrai and in the Retreat and Advance of 1918. He was demobilised in February 1919, and holds the General Service and Victory Medals.
120, Wenlock Street, Luton.   1648.

LARGE, J., A.B., Royal Navy.

He joined in March 1918, and was posted to H.M.S. "Erebus," which vessel was engaged on convoy duties in the English Channel, the Mediterranean, and North Seas. His ship also served at Scapa Flow and escorted His Majesty the King to France on one occasion. He was demobilised in March 1919, and holds the General Service and Victory Medals.
43, Chobham Street, Luton.   1647/B.

LARKINS, T. G., Private, Bedfordshire Regt.

He volunteered in November 1915, and in the following year was sent to Egypt, where he served for nearly three years. During this period he fought at Gaza, Jaffa, Haifa, and in other engagements in the British advance through Palestine until hostilities ceased. He was demobilised in March 1919, and holds the General Service and Victory Medals.
Johnson's Yard, Horslow Street, Potton, Beds. 1649.

LARMAN, E., Private, 12th Suffolk Regiment.

He joined in July 1916, and in the following March was drafted to France. He fought at Bullecourt and Armentières, and was wounded and taken prisoner in April 1917. He was held in captivity until after the cessation of hostilities, when he returned to England and was demobilised in December 1919. He holds the General Service and Victory Medals.
48, Queen Street, Hitchin.   1650.

LASSLETT, C. W., A.B., Royal Navy.

He volunteered in August 1914, and was posted to H.M.S. "Gorgon," which vessel was engaged on convoy duties to and from Canada. His ship also took part in the operations in the North Sea and frequently passed through mine infested areas. He holds the 1914-15 Star, and the General Service and Victory Medals, and was still serving in 1920.
190, Chester Road, Watford.   1651/A.

LASSLETT, H., Private, 5th Royal Fusiliers.

He joined in February 1917, and in the same year was drafted to France, where he served with his battalion and took part in the heavy fighting and was wounded in action at Cambrai. He holds the General Service and Victory Medals, and was demobilised in October 1919.
190, Chester Road, Watford.   1651/B

LAST, P. J., Sergeant, Royal Engineers.
He volunteered in August 1914, and in the following
month was drafted overseas where he served on the Western Front and was employed on important duties in
connection with operations in the forward areas. He
was present at the Battles of Ypres, and was wounded
on the Somme in 1916. He was later in action at Arras,
Cambrai and in other sectors until the close of the
war. He was demobilised in February 1919 and holds
the 1914 Star, and the General Service and Victory
Medals.
80, Victoria Terrace, Victoria Street, Dunstable. 1133/B.

LATCHFORD, A., Driver, Royal Field Artillery.
He volunteered in April 1915, and in the same year
was drafted to France. He was engaged in the fighting
at Ypres, Arras, Givenchy, on the Somme, at Cambrai,
and in the Retreat and Advance of 1918. He was
demobilised in March 1919, and holds the 1914-15 Star,
and the General Service and Victory Medals.
47, Queen's Street, Hemel Hempstead. 1652/A.

LATCHFORD, E., Gunner, Royal Field Artillery.
He volunteered in April 1915, and in the same year
was sent overseas to Salonika. He served on the Vardar
Front and took part in the Battle of Monastir, and later
proceeded with the Relief Force to Russia, and remained
there until 1919 when he returned to England and was
demobilised in July of that year. He holds the 1914-15
Star, and the General Service and Victory Medals.
47, Queen's Street, Hemel Hempstead. 1652/B.

LATCHFORD, H., Private, King's Own (Royal Lancaster Regiment).
Volunteering in 1916, he was drafted overseas in the
same year. Whilst on the Western Front he saw much
service in various sectors and took part in many import-
ant engagements until he was killed in action on
October 11th, 1917 in the vicinity of Neuve Chapelle.
He was entitled to the General Service and Victory
Medals.
Batchworth Hill, Rickmansworth. 1653.

LATCHFORD, H. B., Sergt., Hertfordshire Regt.
Volunteering in 1914, he was sent to France in the
following year. He took part in many engagements on
the Western Front, including those at Ypres, Arras,
Hill 60 and on the Somme, and was gassed. He was
invalided to England, and after receiving hospital treatment was discharged in October 1918. He holds the
1914-15 Star, and the General Service and Victory
Medals.
115, Cotterells Road, Hemel Hempstead. 1654.

LATCHFORD, R. H., Private, South Lancashire Regiment.
Volunteering in May 1915, he was almost immediately
drafted to Egypt, where he completed his training. He
was then sent to the Dardanelles, and was in action at
Suvla Bay and other places until the Evacuation of the
Peninsula. In 1916 he proceeded to Salonika, and during
his service there contracted malaria and was in hospital
for a time. On recovery he was transferred to the
Western Front, and there fought on the Somme and at
Cambrai during the final stages of the war. He was
demobilised in May 1919, and holds the 1914-15 Star, and
the General Service and Victory Medals.
The Folly, Wheathampstead, Herts. 1655.

LATHERON, R., Private, Bedfordshire Regt., and Sapper, Royal Engineers.
He volunteered in November 1914, and served with his
regiment at various stations until September 1916, when
he was drafted overseas. During his service on the
Western Front he took part in the fighting on the Somme
and was wounded. On recovery he was transferred to
the Royal Engineers, Railway Operative Department,
with which unit he was employed until after hostilities
ceased. He was demobilised in May 1919, and holds the
General Service and Victory Medals.
40, Saxon Road, Luton. 1656.

LATHOM, F. W. F. (M.C.), Major, 28th London Regiment (Artists' Rifles).
He was mobilised at the commencement of hostilities
with the 2/5th Bedfordshire Regiment, and later transferred to the Artists Rifles. In 1915 he was drafted to
the Western Front, where he played a distinguished part
in many of the principal battles, and served overseas
for nearly four years, and was mentioned in Despatches
and awarded the Military Cross for conspicuous gallantry
and devotion to duty in the Field. During his service
in France he was severely wounded, and returning to
England in 1919 was invalided out of the service. He
holds the 1914-15 Star, and the General Service and
Victory Medals.
" Durban," London Road, St. Albans. 2466.

LATHWELL, A. T., Gunner, R.F.A.
He volunteered in July 1915, and on completion of his
training served with his Battery on important duties at
various stations. He did much good work but was not
successful in obtaining his transfer overseas owing to
medical unfitness. He was discharged in consequence in
September 1916.
Garden Edge, Leighton Buzzard. 2465.

LATHWELL, A. T., Private, Essex Regiment.
Volunteering in January 1915, he was sent to Salonika
in the following July. He saw much service on the
Vardar Front, and in 1916 was drafted to Egypt and
thence to Palestine, where he was engaged in much
heavy fighting, notably that at Gaza. In January 1917
he was transferred to the Western Front, and again
took an active part in engagements until August 1918,
when he returned to England. Whilst in the East he
contracted fever, from the effects of which he died in
hospital at Aylesbury on March 13th, 1920. He was
entitled to the General Service and Victory Medals.
7, East Street, Leighton Buzzard. 2467/B.

LATHWELL, F., Sapper, Royal Engineers.
He joined in September 1918 on attaining military age,
and at the conclusion of his training served with his
unit on important duties at various stations. He did
much good work but was unable to secure his transfer
overseas before the cessation of hostilities. In March
1919, however, he was drafted to India, where in 1920
he was still serving.
7, East Street, Leighton Buzzard. 2467/A.

LATHWELL, G., Gunner, R.G.A.
He joined in June 1916, and three months later was
drafted to France, where he was in action in various
sectors and took part in many important engagements,
including those on the Somme, at Arras and Cambrai.
He was demobilised in March 1919, and holds the
General Service and Victory Medals.
Rothschild Road, Wing, near Leighton Buzzard. 1657.

LAUD, W., Private, Sherwood Foresters.
He volunteered in January 1915, and was shortly afterwards drafted overseas. He served in many sectors of
the Western Front, and took part in the operations on
the Somme, at Cambrai and other places. He was demobilised in April 1919, and holds the 1914-15 Star, and
the General Service and Victory Medals.
23, Pretoria Road, Watford. 1658/A.

LAUD, W., Private, Suffolk Regiment.
He volunteered in September 1914, and in the following
year was drafted to France. Whilst on the Western
Front he took part in many engagements, including
operations at Cambrai, during which he was taken
prisoner in 1916. He was held in captivity until after
the Armistice, when he was released and returned to
England. He was demobilised in April 1919, and holds
the 1914-15 Star, and the General Service and Victory
Medals.
23, Pretoria Road, Watford. 1658/B.

LAVENDER, E., Private, Yorkshire Regiment.
He joined in 1917, and after completing his training was
stationed at various places in England and Ireland. He
was engaged on important duties with his battalion
and rendered valuable services, but was unable to obtain
a transfer to a theatre of war before the cessation of
hostilities. He was demobilised in 1919.
48, Brightwell Road, Watford. X4122/B.

LAWMAN, J. Z. W. (M.M.), Corporal, 1st Bedfordshire Regiment.
He volunteered in June 1915, and in the following
January was drafted to Egypt. Whilst in this theatre
of war he took part in the Advance through Palestine
under General Allenby, and was in action in several
battles, including those of Haifa, Jaffa, Gaza and Jerusalem, and was wounded. He was awarded the Military
Medal for conspicuous bravery and devotion to duty in
the Field. He also holds the General Service and
Victory Medals, and was demobilised in March 1919.
51, Sunnyside Hitchin. 1872.

LAWMAN, W. G., Private, Labour Corps.
He joined in February 1918, and after completing his
training served at various stations on important duties
with his unit. He did much good work but was unable
to secure his transfer overseas owing to medical unfitness, and was demobilised in December 1919.
Pretoria Cottages, Harlington, Beds. 1659.

LAWRENCE, A., Sapper, Royal Engineers.

He volunteered in March 1915, and six months later was sent overseas. He served on the Western Front, and was engaged on important duties in the forward areas, and was present at the Battles of Ypres, Arras, the Somme, Cambrai, and was gassed. He holds the 1914-15 Star, and the General Service and Victory Medals, and was demobilised in April 1919.

Salisbury Road, Batford, Harpenden. 1660.

LAWRENCE, A., Private, Bedfordshire Regiment.

He volunteered in August 1914, and in the following year was sent to Egypt. During his service in this theatre of war he took part in many important engagements under General Allenby in the Advance through Palestine, and was wounded. He returned to England and was demobilised in 1919, and holds the 1914-15 Star, and the General Service and Victory Medals.

57, Vctoria Road, North Watford. 1661/B.

LAWRENCE, A. C., Private, Suffolk Regiment.

He joined the Volunteer Training Corps in November 1916, as he was ineligible for service with the colours, and served on guard duties until July 1918, when he joined the Suffolk Regiment. After completing his training he served with this unit at various stations on important duties. He did good work but was not able to secure his transfer overseas before the Armistice. He was demobilised in February 1919.

10, Newcombe Road, Luton. 1662.

LAWRENCE, A. E., Driver, Royal Engineers.

He volunteered in March 1915, and after his training served at various stations with his unit until sent to France in 1917. Whilst in this theatre of war he was employed on important duties in connection with operations and was present at many engagements, including those at Cambrai and on the Marne. He was demobilised in May 1919, and holds the General Service and Victory Medals.

129, North Street, Luton. 1663

LAWRENCE, A. P., Gunner, Machine Gun Corps.

He joined in November 1918, and after his training served with his unit at various stations until sent to Egypt in the following May. He was employed at Gaza and other places in Palestine on guard duties until March 1920, when he returned home and was demobilised.

160, Hitchin Road, Luton. 1664.

LAWRENCE, A. W., Private, R.A.S.C. (M.T.)

He joined in April 1916, and was drafted to East Africa in the following March. Landing at Dar-es-Salaam he saw much active service in German East Africa where he was engaged on important duties in connection with the transport of ammunition and supplies to the forward areas. He returned to England in March 1919, and was demobilised in the following June, and holds the General Service and Victory Medals.

"Robin Hood Cottage," New Town, Hatfield. 1665.

LAWRENCE, C., L/Corporal, 4th Bedfordshire Regiment.

He volunteered in January 1915, and in the following June was drafted to the Western Front, where he took part in many important engagements and was severely wounded in action at Beaumont-Hamel. He subsequently died from the effects of his wounds on February 16th, 1917. He was entitled to the 1914-15 Star, and the General Service and Victory Medals.

59, Ashton Road, Luton. 1666/B.

LAWRENCE, E., Sapper, Royal Engineers.

He volunteered in August 1914, and in the following year was sent to Salonika. After serving for a time in this theatre of war, he was drafted to Egypt, where he was employed on important duties in connection with the supplies of water for the troops. On the termination of hostilities he returned to England for demobilisation in April 1919, and holds the 1914-15 Star, and the General Service and Victory Medals.

1, Grove Road, St. Albans. 1667.

LAWRENCE, E. F. (M.M.), Private, Essex Regt.

He volunteered in October 1914, and in the following March was drafted to France Whilst on the Western Front he took part in the fighting at Loos, on the Somme, and at Arras, and in October 1917 was awarded the Military Medal for gallant conduct and devotion to duty in the Field at Poelcappelle. Later at Arras he was gassed and invalided home and after a period of hospital treatment was discharged as medically unfit in March 1919. He holds the 1914-15 Star, and the General Service and Victory Medals.

11, Heath Terrace, Sandridge Road, St. Albans. 1668.

LAWRENCE, E. G., Private, Bedfordshire Regt.

He volunteered in November 1915, and proceeded overseas in the following year. He served on th Western Front and was engaged in the fighting in many battles, including those of the Somme, and Cambrai, until killed in action at Arras on March 25th, 1918. He was entitled to the General Service and Victory Medals.

63, Eversholt Road, Ridgmont, Beds. Z1788/A

LAWRENCE, F. C., Air Mechanic, R.A.F.

He joined in May 1918, and was sent overseas in the following July. Whilst on the Western Front he served with his squadron at various aerodromes and his duties called for a high degree of techical skill. He remained in France until after the Armistice, when he returned to England and was demobilised in February 1920. He holds the General Service and Victory Medals.

43, Vale Road, Bushey, Herts. 1669.

LAWRENCE, F. J., Corporal, Royal Marine Light Infantry.

He was serving in the Army at the outbreak of war, having enlisted in 1892, and being unfit for active service was engaged on important coastal defence duties at various stations. During the latter portion of his service he was employed in the Officers' Mess of his unit, and was demobilised in February 1919.

58, Grove Road, Oxhey, Herts. 1670/A.

LAWRENCE, F. J., Private, Royal Marine Light Infantry.

He joined in 1918, and after a period of training was engaged on important duties with his unit at various stations. He did good work but was unable to obtain his transfer overseas before the cessation of hostilities, and in 1920 was still serving.

58, Grove Road, Oxhey. 1670/B.

LAWRENCE, F. J. P., Sergeant, R.F.A.

Volunteering in August 1914, he was drafted to the Western Front in the following year. Whilst overseas he was in action in several important engagements, including the Battles of Neuve Chapelle, Hill 60, and Ypres, and was taken prisoner during the heavy fighting on the Ancre in March 1917. He was held captive in Germany until after the Armistice when he returned to England and was demobilised in January 1919. He holds the 1914-15 Star, and the General Service and Victory Medals.

4, Queen's Place, Hemel Hempstead. 1671

LAWRENCE, G., Private, 3rd Middlesex Regt.

Volunteering in 1915, he was drafted to Salonika in the same year. In this theatre of war he served with his battalion throughout the Balkan campaign and took part in engagements on the Doiran and Vardar Fronts until the cessation of hostilities. He was demobilised in 1919, and holds the 1914-15 Star, and the General Service and Victory Medals.

57, Victoria Road, North Watford. 1661/A.

LAWRENCE, G., Private, Hertfordshire Regt.

He volunteered in 1914, and was drafted overseas in the following year. Whilst on the Western Front he was engaged in heavy fighting in various sectors. Amongst the important battles in which he took part were those of Hill 60, Ypres, Givenchy, Loos, Albert, Vimy Ridge, and Arras, and he was wounded three times. He was demobilised in 1919, and holds the 1914-15 Star, and the General Service and Victory Medals.

9, Stanley Cottages, Batford Road, Harpenden 1672/A.

LAWRENCE, G. J., Pte., 7th Bedfordshire Regt.

Volunteering in November 1914, he was sent overseas in the following July. Whilst on the Western Front he took part in several important engagements, and was wounded in action on the Somme and invalided home in October 1916. On recovery he rejoined his unit in France and fought at Arras and Armentières, and was again wounded and sent home to hospital, where, after receiving treatment for a considerable time, he was subsequently discharged as medically unfit for further service in August 1918. He holds the 1914-15 Star, and the General Service and Victory Medals.

High Street, Codicote, Herts. 1673.

LAWRENCE, H., Private, Bedfordshire Regiment.

He volunteered in September 1914, and in the following July was sent to France. In this theatre of war he was engaged in several important battles, including those of the Somme, Loos, Arras, Ypres, and Albert, and contracting pneumonia was invalided to hospital at the base. On recovery he returned to his unit, and fought in the concluding stages of the war. He holds the 1914-15 Star, and the General Service and Victory Medals, and was demobilised in January 1919.

63, Eversholt Road, Ridgmont, Beds. 1674.

LAWRENCE, H. W., Private, 3rd Bedfordshire Regiment.

Volunteering in September 1914, he was sent to France in the same year. He saw much service on the Western Front, and took part in the second Battle of Ypres and the Battle of Arras, and was wounded, and invalided to hospital in England, where after receiving treatment was discharged as medically unfit for further active service in March 1916. He holds the 1914-15 Star, and the General Service and Victory Medals.
Salisbury Road, Batford, Harpenden.   1675.

LAWRENCE, J., Bandsman, 22nd London Regt. (The Queen's).

Joining in October 1916, he served with his unit at various stations before proceeding overseas in April 1919. He was sent to Egypt, and there employed on garrison and other duties at Alexandria and Cairo until his return home for demobilisation in December 1919.
57, Cromwell Road, Luton.   1676.

LAWRENCE, J., Private, 17th Essex Regiment, Bandsman, 22nd London Regt. (The Queen's).

Joining in 1916 he was drafted to Salonika in the same served with the Band of that unit, and was subsequently transferred to the 22nd London Regiment. In May 1919 he was drafted to Egypt, and engaged there on garrison and other duties at various depôts, assisted in quelling the riots at Cairo. He returned home in November 1919, and was demobilised in the following January.
57, Cromwell Road, Luton.   1677.

LAWRENCE, J., Private, R.A.S.C., and Bedfordshire Regiment.

Joining in 1916, he was drafted to Salonika in the same year. During his service in this theatre of war he took part in heavy fighting on the Vardar and Doiran Fronts, and contracting malaria was sent to hospital, where he died in November 1917. He was entitled to the General Service and Victory Medals.
9, Stanley Cottages, Batford Road, Harpenden.   1672/B.

LAWRENCE, J. S., Private, Royal Fusiliers.

He joined in October 1916, and in the following year was sent to France. Whilst in this theatre of war he was in action at Arras and Ypres, and was wounded. On recovery he returned to the firing line and fought on the Somme, at Cambrai and in the final operations of the war. After the Armistice he was drafted to Mesopotamia, and in 1920 was still serving there. He holds the General Service and Victory Medals.
63, Eversholt Road, Ridgmont, Beds.   Z1788/B.

LAWRENCE, R. H., Gunner, Tank Corps.

He volunteered in January 1915, and in the same year was drafted to France. Whilst in the Western theatre of war he did good work in various sectors, and was gassed and wounded in the heavy fighting at Ypres. Returning to his unit after hospital treatment he was engaged in several important actions until wounded and taken prisoner at Cambrai in April 1918. He was repatriated after the cessation of hostilities, and demobilised in February 1919. He holds the 1914-15 Star, and the General Service and Victory Medals.
35, Newcombe Road, Luton.   1678.

LAWRENCE, T. J., Private, 4th Yorkshire Regt.

He joined in 1916, and in the following September was sent to France. During his service on the Western Front he was engaged in the fighting in many battles, including those of the Somme and Cambrai, and was severely wounded in action at Arras. He was invalided home, and after spending some time in hospital was discharged in September 1917 as medically unfit for further service. He holds the General Service and Victory Medals.
Ayot Green, near Welwyn.   1679.

LAWRENCE, V. A., Private, Bedfordshire Regt.

He volunteered in September 1914, and was sent overseas early in the following year. During his service on the Western Front he fought in several important battles, including those at Hill 60, Givenchy, Passchendaele, Arras and the Somme. He was wounded in action at Cambrai in 1918 and taken prisoner, and subsequently died from the effects of his wounds on March 3rd, 1919. He was entitled to the 1914-15 Star, and the General Service and Victory Medals.
33, Weymouth Street, Apsley.   1680.

LAWRENCE, W., Driver, Royal Field Artillery.

Volunteering in October 1914, he served at various depôts with his unit until sent to Salonika in 1916. Whilst in this theatre of war he was engaged with his battery in the fighting in various sectors, and took part in operations on the Vardar Front. He proceeded in 1918 to Russia, where he served with the Relief Force for a time. He returned to England and was demobilised in February 1919, and holds the General Service and Victory Medals.
1, Common Lane, Batford Mill, Harpenden.   1681.

LAWRENCE, W., Rifleman, 17th London Regt. (Rifles).

He volunteered in August 1914, and in the following year proceeded overseas. During his service on the Western Front he fought in many engagements, and was wounded in action on the Somme. On recovery he returned to the firing line and took part in the fighting at Ypres, and was again wounded at Arras in 1917. He was invalided to England, and after receiving hospital treatment was discharged as medically unfit for further service in December 1917. He holds the 1914-15 Star, and the General Service and Victory Medals.
7, Queen Street, St. Albans.   1682.

LAWRENCE, W., L/Corporal, 9th (Queen's Royal) Lancers.

He joined in May 1916, and in the following November proceeded to France, where he was engaged in the heavy fighting, and took part in many engagements. He was severely wounded in action, and subsequently died from the effects of his wounds on March 29th, 1918. He was entitled to the General Service and Victory Medals.
59, Ashton Road, Luton.   1666/A.

LAWSON, A. R., Private, Training Reserve Bn.

He joined in September 1918, and after completing his training served with his unit at various stations on important duties. He did good work but was not successful in obtaining his transfer overseas owing to medical unfitness. He was demobilised in February 1919.
64, Eversholt Road, Ridgmont, Beds.   Z1789/C.

LAWSON, A. W. (Senior), Private, Buffs (East Kent Regiment).

He joined in May 1918, and was later drafted to France, where he served with his battalion, and took part in the fighting on the Somme at Cambrai and Le Cateau during the final stages of the war. After the Armistice he remained on the Western Front for a time, and was on parade at Brussels at the inspection of British troops by the King of the Belgians. He holds the General Service and Victory Medals, and was demobilised in October 1919.
64, Eversholt Road, Ridgmont, Beds.   Z1789/B.

LAWSON, A. W., Private, 5th Bedfordshire Regt.

He volunteered in April 1915, and shortly afterwards proceeded to Gallipoli where he was engaged in the fierce fighting at the landing at Suvla Bay. He was also in action in other engagements until severely wounded on September 2nd, 1915. He died from the effects of his wounds three days later, and was entitled to the 1914-15 Star, and the General Service and Victory Medals.
64, Eversholt Road, Ridgmont, Beds.   Z1789/A.

LAWSON, H. S., Private, 1/4th Norfolk Regt.

He volunteered in May 1915, and was drafted to Egypt in the following year. Whilst in this theatre of war he took part in many engagements and was wounded in action in 1916. On recovery he rejoined his battalion and fought in the British Advance through Palestine until killed in the vicinity of Gaza, on December 11th, 1917. He was entitled to the General Service and Victory Medals.
Chaul End, near Luton.   1683/A.

LAWSON, H. W., Private, 52nd Queen's (Royal West Surrey Regiment).

He joined in April 1918 on attaining military age and at the conclusion of his training served with his battalion at various stations on important guard and other duties. He did good work but was not successful in obtaining his transfer overseas before hostilities ceased. He was demobilised in February 1919.
Chaul End, near Luton.   1683/B.

LAWSON, J., Pioneer, Royal Engineers, and Private, Labour Corps.

He volunteered in September 1915, and in the following year was sent to the Western Front, where he was engaged on important duties in various sectors and was present at several battles, including those of Festubert, Loos, and the Somme. He was invalided home suffering from double pneumonia, and after spending some time in hospital, was discharged as medically unfit for further service in July 1916. He holds the 1914-15 Star, and the General Service and Victory Medals.
28, Periwinkle Lane, Hitchin. 1868/B.

LAWSON, T., Private, 1st Hertfordshire Regt.

He joined in January 1917, and six months later proceeded to France. Whilst on the Western Front he fought in various sectors and was in action at the Battles of Arras, Ypres, the Somme, Cambrai and in the Retreat and Advance of 1918. He was demobilised in March 1919, and holds the General Service and Victory Medals.
44, Stanbridge Road, Leighton Buzzard. 1684/B.

LAWSON, W., Private, 6th Bedfordshire Regt.

He volunteered in October 1914, and in the following year was drafted to France, where he took part in many important engagements, including those at Ypres, on the Somme, at Passchendaele, Cambrai, and in the German Offensive and subsequent Allied Advance of 1918. He holds the 1914-15 Star, and the General Service and Victory Medals, and was demobilised in August 1919.
Hockliffe Hill, Leighton Buzzard. 1685.

LAWSON, W. C., Private, 1st Bedfordshire Regt.

He volunteered in September 1914, and was drafted overseas in the following April. During his service on the Western Front he took part in many important engagements and was gassed at the Battle of Hill 60. He subsequently died from the effects of gas poisoning on May 1st, 1915. He was entitled to the 1914-15 Star, and the General Service and Victory Medals.
28, Periwinkle Lane, Hitchin. 1868/A.

LAWTON, J., Private, Suffolk Regiment.

He joined in 1918, and after completing his period of training was employed with his regiment at various stations on special guard duties. He was not able to secure his transfer to a theatre of war before the signing of the Armistice, but he did good work until demobilised in 1919.
119, Chester Road, Watford. 1686.

LAYFIELD, F., Lieutenant, Royal Marine Light Infantry.

He volunteered in August 1914, and in the following year was sent to France. During his service on the Western Front he fought in engagements at Ypres, on the Somme, at Cambrai, and in the Retreat and Advance of 1918, and was gassed. He returned to England after the Armistice and was demobilised in December 1919, and holds the 1914-15 Star, and the General Service and Victory Medals.
4, Cassiobridge Road, Watford. 1687.

LEA, W., Private, Tank Corps.

He volunteered in October 1914, and served at home with his unit on important duties until June 1916 when he was drafted to France. He was in action at the Battles of Vimy Ridge, the Somme and Ypres, and in June 1917 proceeded to Egypt. Whilst in this theatre of war he took part in the British Advance through Palestine, and fought at the Battle of Gaza, and was wounded in August 1917. He returned to England after the Armistice and was discharged, and holds the General Service and Victory Medals.
Bedford Cottage, Bedford Road, Houghton Regis, Beds. 1688.

LEACH, F. A., Private, R.A.S.C.

He joined in 1916 and in the following year was sent to France. During his service on the Western Front he was employed on various duties with his unit in the forward areas and was present at many engagements including those on the Somme and was wounded. He was demobilised in February 1919, and holds the General Service and Victory Medals
107, Cotterells Road, Hemel Hempstead. X1689/A.

LEACH, F. A. (Junior), Private, 1st Hertfordshire Regiment.

He volunteered in 1915, and was shortly afterwards drafted to France, where he was engaged in the heavy fighting and took part in many battles. He was reported missing at the third Battle of Ypres on July 31st, 1917, and was later presumed to have been killed in action on that date. He was entitled to the 1914-15 Star, and the General Service and Victory Medals.
107, Cotterells Road, Hemel Hempstead. 1689/B.

LEACH, J., Sergeant, 2nd Middlesex Regiment.

He joined in June 1916, and in the following November was sent to France He fought on the Somme, at Arras, and Cambrai, and during the German Offensive was wounded and taken prisoner in April 1918. He suffered many hardships whilst in captivity and returned to England after the Armistice and was demobilised in January 1919. He holds the General Service and Victory Medals
48, Stanbridge Road, Leighton Buzzard. 1690.

LEACH, S., Corporal, Royal Engineers.

He volunteered in October 1914, and in the following March was sent overseas. Whilst on the Western Front he acted as a despatch rider and was frequently in the front lines during operations and was present at the Battle of Loos. He was wounded twice and invalided home in November 1915, and subsequently discharged as medically unfit for further service. He holds the 1914-15 Star, and the General Service and Victory Medals.
238, High Town Road, Luton. 1691.

LEACH, S. H., Sapper, Royal Engineers.

He volunteered in August 1915, and after completing his training was employed at home with his unit until April 1917 when he was sent to France. He served in various sectors and was engaged on important duties in the forward areas and was in action at the Battles of Bullecourt and Ypres, where he was killed on September 21st, 1917. He was entitled to the General Service and Victory Medals.
5, Bigthan Road, Dunstable. 1692.

LEADER, F., A.B., Royal Navy.

He was serving in the Navy when war was declared, and aboard H.M.S. " Greenwich " served on important escort duties convoying troopships, and other transports from England to France. His ship frequently had to pass through mine infested areas and had many narrow escapes. In 1920 he was still serving, and holds the 1914-15 Star, and the General Service and Victory Medals.
7, Sotheron Road, Watford. X1693/B.

LEADER, L. A., L/Corporal, 16th Rifle Brigade.

He joined in May 1917, and was drafted to France in the following April. Whilst on the Western Front he fought in the second Battle of Cambrai and in other important engagements during the concluding stages of the war. He was demobilised in November 1919, and holds the General Service and Victory Medals.
7, Sotheron Road, Watford. X1693/C.

LEADER, R., A.B., Royal Navy.

He was serving in the Navy at the outbreak of war, and aboard H.M.S. " Bristol " served on important patrol duties in the North Sea, West Indian and other waters. His ship was also in action in the Battles of Heligoland and Jutland, and had other encounters with the German Fleet. Transferred later to H.M.S. " Dolphin " he did good work in that vessel until the cessation of hostilities. He holds the 1914-15 Star, and the General Service and Victory Medals, and in 1920 was still serving.
7, Sotheron Road, Watford. X1693/A.

LEANY, W. G., Private, Labour Corps.

Volunteering in September 1915, he was sent to the Western Front early in the following year. In the course of his service overseas he was engaged on important duties with his unit, and was frequently in the forward areas during operations. He served at Ypres, on the Somme and at other places. He returned to England for demobilisation in April 1919, and holds the General Service and Victory Medals.
53, Chapel Street, Hemel Hempstead. X1694.

LEAPER, A., Rifleman, The Cameronians (Scot-tish Rifles).

He joined in April 1917, and on conclusion of his training served with his unit at various stations on important duties. He did good work, but owing to medical unfitness was not drafted overseas. He was demobilised in September 1919.

17, Albert Street, Watford.   X1695/B.

LEAPER, R., Sapper, Royal Engineers.

Joining in April 1917, he was drafted to Egypt in the following November. He was engaged on important work in connection with operations in Palestine, and in the course of his service was present at several notable battles, including those of Gaza and Jaffa. He returned to England for demobilisation in March 1920, and holds the General Service and Victory Medals.

17, Albert Street, Watford.   X1695/A.

LEAVER, C. W., Private, 1st Hertfordshire Regt.

He volunteered in December 1915, and in the following year proceeded to France. Whilst on the Western Front he was engaged in several important battles, including those of the Somme, Arras, Ypres and Cambrai, and was wounded. At the conclusion of hostilities he returned to England, and was demobilised in February 1919. He holds the General Service and Victory Medals.

1, Benskin Road, Watford.   X1696.

LEE, A. T., Private, Northamptonshire Regiment.

He joined in August 1917, and in the following January was sent to the Western Front, where he took part in heavy fighting during the Retreat and Advance of 1918. After the signing of the Armistice he went into Germany with the Army of Occupation, and was engaged on garrison and other duties at Cologne. He holds the General Service and Victory Medals, and in 1920 was still serving.

4, Stanbridge Road, Leighton Buzzard.   1697.

LEE, A. W., Corporal, Bedfordshire Regiment.

He volunteered in October 1915, and in the following year was drafted to France. In this theatre of war he was engaged in the fighting during the Somme Offensive, and was gassed at the Battle of Ypres in 1917. Rejoining his unit after hospital treatment, he fought at Arras and Cambrai, and in other engagements until the Armistice. He was demobilised in March 1919, and holds the General Service and Victory Medals.

29, Branch Road, Park Street, St. Albans.   X1698/B.

LEE, C. E., Private, Royal Marine Light Infantry.

He joined in August 1916, and in the same year was sent to the Western Front, where he was engaged in heavy fighting, and fought in engagements at Lens, Cambrai, Ypres and Amiens. After the conclusion of hostilities he was drafted to Turkey, where he served until his demobilisation in November 1919. He holds the General Service and Victory Medals.

81, Cowper Road, Boxmoor.   X1699.

LEE, F. C., Private, Bedfordshire Regiment, and Royal Fusiliers.

Volunteering in September 1914, he was drafted to France in the same year. Whilst on the Western Front he took part in several important battles, including those of the Somme, Arras, Ypres and Cambrai, and at the conclusion of hostilities went with the Army of Occupation into Germany. He returned to England for demobilisation in February 1919, and holds the 1914-15 Star, and the General Service and Victory Medals.

Church Street, Biggleswade.   Z1700.

LEE, H. E. (Miss), Special War Worker.

This lady volunteered her services for the work of National importance, and in 1917 was engaged at one of the N.A.C.B. canteens at Houghton Camp. Later, transferred to a large military camp on the Isle of Sheppey, she rendered valuable services throughout until discharged in February 1919.

8, Sussex Road, Watford.   X5010/F, X5011/F.

LEE, J., Pte., Queen's (Royal West Surrey Regt.)

He joined in December 1917, and six months later proceeded to the Western Front. He fought in many engagements during the Allied Advance of 1918, and was wounded near Cambrai in August 1918. He was invalided to England, where he received hospital treatment, and on recovery was demobilised in February 1919, and holds the General Service and Victory Medals.

37, Puller Road, Boxmoor.   X1701/B.

LEE, R. W., Gunner, Royal Field Artillery.

He joined in May 1915, and was later drafted to Egypt, where he served under General Allenby in the British Advance through Palestine, and took part in the Battles of Gaza, Haifa, Acre and Damascus. He returned home at the conclusion of hostilities, and was demobilised in May 1919. He holds the General Service and Victory Medals.

37, Puller Road, Boxmoor.   X1701/A.

LEE, S. A., Private, Royal Marine Light Infantry.

He joined in June 1918, and after completion of his training was engaged on various important duties at the depôt of his unit. He did good work, but was not successful in securing his transfer overseas before the close of the war. He was demobilised in January 1919.

29, Branch Road, Park Street, St. Albans.   X1698/A.

LEE, W., Private, 1st Hertfordshire Regiment.

He volunteered in August 1914, and was shortly afterwards drafted to France, where he fought in the Retreat from Mons and the subsequent Battles of Ypres, Hill 60, Festubert, the Somme, Cambrai, and many others until hostilities ceased. He was wounded once during his service overseas, and was demobilised in March 1919. He holds the Mons Star, and the General Service and Victory Medals.

31, Cherry Bounce, Hemel Hempstead.   X1702.

LEE, W. H., Sapper, Royal Engineers.

He joined in May 1916, and after serving with his unit at various home stations was drafted overseas in the following year. Whilst on the Western Front he was engaged on important duties in several sectors, and was present at many battles, including those on the Somme, at Ypres, Armentières and Vimy Ridge. On the conclusion of hostilities he accompanied the Army of Occupation into Germany, and was stationed at Cologne and other places on the Rhine until sent home for demobilisation in 1919. He holds the General Service and Victory Medals.

23, Crescent Road, Brentwood.   Z1703.

LEE, W. H., Corporal, R.A.F. (late R.F.C.)

He joined in May 1916, and after completing his training served with his squadron on important duties, which called for a high degree of technical skill. He did good work as a rigger, but was not successful in securing his transfer overseas owing to medical unfitness. He was discharged in consequence in May 1918.

122, Biscot Road, Luton.   1704.

LEE, W. J., Sergeant, 1/22nd London Regiment (The Queen's), and Royal Engineers.

He volunteered at the declaration of war, and in 1915 was sent to the Western Front. He took part in heavy fighting in several sectors, and fought at many battles, including those of Festubert, Givenchy and Vimy Ridge, and was wounded and suffered from shell-shock. Demobilised in May 1919, he holds the 1914-15 Star, and the General Service and Victory Medals.

Trowley Bottom, Flamstead.   X1795.

LEEDS, F. J., Private, 3rd Bedfordshire Regt.

He joined in November 1916, and in the following April proceeded to the Western Front, where he was wounded in the Battle of Arras, and invalided home to hospital. After treatment he was sent to Italy in January 1918, in which theatre of war he served in operations on the Piave. Returning to England he was demobilised in April 1919, and holds the General Service and Victory Medals.

28, Dudley Street, Leighton Buzzard.   1706.

LEEDS, G. W., Private, Machine Gun Corps.

Volunteering in November 1915, he was drafted to the Western Front in the following September. Whilst overseas he was engaged in several important engagements, and was invalided home in consequence of wounds received in the Battle of the Somme. Rejoining his unit in the Field he was again wounded in October 1918, and sent back to England to hospital. On recovery he was demobilised in February 1919, and holds the General Service and Victory Medals.

28, Dudley Street, Leighton Buzzard.   1707.

LEEFE, C. F., Private, 2/6th Essex Regiment.

He joined in May 1916, and after completing his training served with his unit at various depôts on important duties. He did very good work but was unable to obtain a transfer overseas owing to medical unfitness. He was discharged in consequence in January 1918.

Oliver Street, Ampthill.   1708/B.

LEEFE, R. A., Private, R.A.M.C.

He volunteered in September 1914, and on the conclusion of his training served with his unit on important duties until drafted to France in 1916. In this theatre of war he did very valuable work with the Field Ambulance in several important engagements, including those on the Somme, at Ypres and Cambrai. Taken prisoner in March 1918, he was kept in captivity in Germany until the Armistice. He was then released and returned to England and was subsequently demobilised in January 1920, and holds the General Service and Victory Medals.
Oliver Street, Ampthill.   1708/A.

LEES, C., Private, Bedfordshire Regiment.

He volunteered in May 1915, and in the following year was drafted to France where he served with his regiment in many important engagements, including those at Cambrai, Ypres and Arras. After the Armistice he went with the Army of Occupation to Germany and was stationed at Cologne. He was demobilised in 1919, and holds the General Service and Victory Medals.
West Hill, Aspley Guise.   Z1709.

LEGGETT, C. W., Gunner (Gun Layer), R.F.A.

He volunteered in June 1915, and in the following December proceeded to Egypt, where he saw much active service and was engaged in the operations during the British Advance through Palestine. He fought at the Battles of Gaza, Jericho, and Jerusalem, and was wounded. Returning to England at the end of the war, he was demobilised in June 1919, and holds the 1914-15 Star, and the General Service and Victory Medals.
Hazeldene, Highbury, Hitchin.   1865.

LEGGETT, G., Private, Northamptonshire Regt.

He volunteered in June 1915, and six months later was sent overseas. During his service on the Western Front he was engaged in the fighting at the Battles of Ypres, the Somme, Cambrai, and many others, until the cessation of hostilities. He was demobilised in September 1919, and holds the 1914-15 Star, and the General Service and Victory Medals.
39, Elizabeth Street, Luton.   1710/B.

LEGGETT, M. (Mrs.) (O.B.E.), Special War Worker.

During the war this lady offered her services for work of National importance, and was engaged at Kent's Munition Factory, where she operated a capstan lathe and performed other duties to increase the output of munitions. She rendered valuable services throughout.
39, Elizabeth Street, Luton   1710/A.

LEGGETT, P., Air Mechanic, R.A.F. (late R.N.A.S.)

He volunteered in July 1915, and in the following year was drafted to France where he served with his squadron at various aerodromes on duties which called for a high degree of technical skill. He was in action at Ypres, Cambrai, Arras and was gassed at Albert. Owing to ill-health he was invalided home and after receiving hospital treatment was discharged as medically unfit for further service in September 1918. He holds the General Service and Victory Medals.
16, Albert Street, St. Albans.   X1711.

LENTON, H., Private, Bedfordshire Regiment.

He volunteered in December 1914, and in the following year was sent to France, where he took part in the Battles of Ypres, Arras, the Somme, Albert, Hill 60 and Vimy Ridge. He was severely wounded in action on the Somme Front and was invalided to hospital in Birmingham. He was subsequently discharged from the service in consequence of his wounds in 1919, and holds the 1914-15 Star, and the General Service and Victory Medals.
Brook End, Potton, Beds   Z1712.

LENTON, H., Private, Duke of Wellington's (West Riding Regiment).

He joined in July 1917, and in the same year was drafted overseas. Whilst on the Western Front he served in many sectors and fought in the Battles of Ypres, Cambrai, the Somme, and was wounded at Arras in March 1918. He was demobilised in 1919, and holds the General Service and Victory Medals.
2, Sandy Road, Potton, Beds.   Z1713.

LENTON, W. H., Private, 2nd Bedfordshire Regt.

He joined in June 1916, and in the following November was sent to France. During his service on the Western Front he took part in many engagements, including those of Loos, and the Somme where he was wounded in action in January 1917. He returned to England and after receiving hospital treatment was transferred to the Royal Defence Corps, with which unit he served until demobilised in February 1919. He holds the General Service and Victory Medals.
Wagstaff Terrace, Potton, Beds.   Z1714

LEONARD, L., Shoeing Smith, R.F.A.

He joined in July 1916, and in the following November was sent to France. He served in many sectors of the Western Front, and was in action on the Somme, at Arras and Douai. He returned to England in April 1919, and was demobilised in the following month, and holds the General Service and Victory Medals.
22, Elizabeth Street, Luton.   1715.

LESLEY, A., Private, Leicestershire Regiment.

He volunteered in November 1915, and in the following year was sent to France, where he took part in many important engagements, including those at Ypres and on the Somme. He was killed in action during the Battle of Cambrai on March 21st, 1918, and was entitled to the General Service and Victory Medals.
6, Herbert Street, Watford.   X1716.

LEVETT, F., Private, Buffs (East Kent Regt.)

He volunteered in August 1915, and for a time served with his unit on various duties. In December 1916 he was sent to France, and was engaged in the heavy fighting at Albert, on the Somme, and was severely wounded at Ypres in 1917. He was invalided to England and after protracted hospital treatment was retained at home where he did good work until demobilised in February 1919. He holds the General Service and Victory Medals.
Meeting Lane, Potton, Beds   Z1717.

LEVIN, A., Private, 5th Bedfordshire Regiment.

He volunteered in October 1916, and in the following year was sent to Egypt. Here he was engaged in heavy fighting in the Advance through Palestine and took part in engagements at Jaffa and Gaza, and was twice wounded. He returned home at the end of the war and was demobilised in September 1919, and holds the General Service and Victory Medals.
27, Leavensden Road, Watford.   X165/A.

LEVIN, F., C.Q.M.S., 4th Bedfordshire Regt.

He volunteered at the outbreak of war, and in the following year was drafted to France. He served in this theatre of war for nearly four years, during which period he took part in engagements at Festubert, on the Somme, at Arras, Passchendaele, and Ypres. He was demobilised in June 1919, and holds the 1914-15 Star, and the General Service and Victory Medals.
27, Brixton Road, Watford.   X1718/A.

LEVIN, J., Private, Royal Marine Light Infantry.

He volunteered in June 1915, and in the following year was drafted to East Africa. He was in action in the Advance into German East Africa, and took part in many engagements, including that preceding the surrender of Dar-es-Salaam. He returned to England in 1918, and was still serving in 1920. He holds the General Service and Victory Medals.
27, Brixton Road, Watford.   X1718/C.

LEVIN, L., A.B., Royal Navy.

He was mobilised at the outbreak of hostilities and served in H.M.S. "Barham," which vessel was engaged on important patrol duties, chiefly in the North Sea. His ship was also in action at the Battle of Jutland in 1916, and had other encounters with the German Fleet. He was demobilised in February 1919, and holds the 1914-15 Star, and the General Service and Victory Medals.
27, Brixton Road, Watford.   X1718/B.

LEWIN, A., Private, 6th Bedfordshire Regiment.

He volunteered in November 1914, and early in the following year was drafted to the Western Front. He was engaged in several important battles in various sectors, including those at Ypres, and Arras, and was killed in action on April 3rd, 1918 during the second Battle of the Somme. He was entitled to the 1914-15 Star, and the General Service and Victory Medals.
Grove Road, Harpenden, Herts.   109/A.

LEWIN, D. W., Private, R.A.M.C.

He joined in February 1918, and after completing his training served at various hospitals on important duties with his unit. He did good work as an orderly but was unable to obtain his transfer overseas before the cessation of hostilities, and was demobilised in February 1919.
10, Edward Street, Luton.   1720

LEWIN, F. H., Private, 1/5th Bedfordshire Regt.

He volunteered in January 1915, and was later sent to Egypt, where he served with his battalion on important guard duties and fought in various engagements in the Canal Zone. Owing to ill-health he was sent to hospital and after a short illness died in September 1916. He was entitled to the General Service and Victory Medals.
33, Brunswick Street, Luton.   1719/A.

LEWIS, A., Corporal, Royal Field Artillery.

He volunteered in November 1914, and in the following year was sent to France. He served in many sectors of the Western Front and fought in the engagements at Hill 60, Ypres, Vimy Ridge, on the Somme, at Arras, on the Marne, at Cambrai, and was wounded four times. He was discharged in March 1918, and holds the 1914-15 Star, and the General Service and Victory Medals.
44, Pondswick Road, Luton   1721/A.

LEWIS, E. J., L/Corporal, 1st Hertfordshire Regt.

He was serving at the outbreak of hostilities and in the following year was drafted to France remaining in this theatre of war for three years. During this period he fought in many battles, including those on the Somme, at Ypres, Arras, and on the Marne (1918), and was gassed and twice wounded. He was demobilised in February 1919, and holds the 1914-15 Star, and the General Service and Victory Medals.
423, Whippendale Road, Watford.   X1722/A.

LEWIS, H., Sapper, Royal Engineers.

He volunteered in October 1914, and in the following year was drafted to France where he was employed on various duties in the forward areas. He was present during the heavy fighting at Festubert, Loos, on the Somme, at Ypres, Arras and Cambrai, and suffered from shell-shock. He was demobilised in April 1919, and holds the 1914-15 Star, and the General Service and Victory Medals.
24, Lower Dagnell Street, St. Albans.   1726

LEWIS, H., Private, Bedfordshire Regiment.

A serving soldier, he was immediately drafted to France at the declaration of war He was engaged in the fighting in the Retreat from Mons and in the Battle of Ypres, and was wounded in December 1914. On recovery he was sent to Egypt where he was in action in many engagements, including those at Gaza, Haifa, and Aleppo. He was demobilised in March 1919, on returning to England, and holds the Mons Star, and the General Service and Victory Medals.
12, Harpenden Lane, Harpenden.   1725.

LEWIS, H., Private, 1st Bedfordshire Regiment.

He volunteered in January 1915, and in the same year was drafted overseas. He took part in many engagements on the Western Front and was killed in action at Delville Wood on July 27th, 1916. He was entitled to the 1914-15 Star, and the General Service and Victory Medals.
4, Hatfield Road, St. Albans.   1724

LEWIS, H., Corporal, 28th London Regiment (Artists' Rifles).

He joined in November 1917, and was sent in the same year to the Western Front, where he served with his unit in several sectors. He took part in heavy fighting in many important engagements, including those on the Somme and at Arras, and contracting illness was invalided to hospital in England, and on recovery was demobilised in 1919. He holds the 1914-15 Star, and the General Service and Victory Medals.
8, Verulam Road, Hitchin.   1867/A.

LEWIS, H. J., L/Corporal, 1/7th Durham Light Infantry.

He joined in June 1916, and in the following October was sent to France. He fought in many engagements on the Western Front, including those at Ypres and on the Somme, and was wounded and invalided home in December 1917. In the following April he returned to the firing line, and during the fighting at Cambrai was reported missing on May 27th, 1918. He was later presumed to have been killed in action on that date, and was entitled to the General Service and Victory Medals.
3, West Alley, Hitchin.   1727.

LEWIS, H. J., Private, Durham Light Infantry.

He volunteered in 1915, and in the same year was drafted to the Western Front, where he was in action in several of the principal battles, including those of Loos, Ypres and Albert, and was wounded. Rejoining his unit on recovery he took part in heavy fighting on the Somme, and was killed in action on May 27th, 1918. He was entitled to the 1914-15 Star, and the General Service and Victory Medals.
2, Leicester Cottages, Nightingale Road, Hitchin.
                                                                       1869/B.

LEWIS, J., Sapper, Royal Engineers.

He volunteered in August 1914, and after training was employed with his unit at various stations on important duties until drafted to Mesopotamia in 1918. In this theatre of war he did excellent work in connection with operations in the forward areas, and was present at engagements during the concluding stages of the war. Contracting illness whilst on service he was invalided home to hospital, and subsequently discharged as medically unfit for further active service in September 1919. He holds the General Service and Victory Medals.
8, Verulam Road, Hitchin.   1867/B.

LEWIS, J. W., Private, Duke of Cornwall's Light Infantry.

He was mobilised at the outbreak of war, and drafted to France with the First Expeditionary Force, fought' in the Retreat from Mons, and in the subsequent Battles of the Marne, Albert, Ypres and the Somme. He was sent to Italy in November 1917, and took part in the operations on the Piave and at Trentino. In March 1918 he returned to the Western Front, and there was engaged in the fighting in the Retreat and Advance of that year, and was wounded twice. He holds the Mons Star, and the General Service and Victory Medals, and was demobilised in September 1919.
2, Leicester Cottages, Nightingale Road, Hitchin.
                                                                       1869/A.

LEWIS, S. A., Private, Labour Corps.

He joined in March 1917, and in the same month was sent to France, where he remained for over two years. During this period he served at Ypres, on the Somme and at Cambrai, and was employed on special duties with his unit. He was demobilised in November 1919, and holds the General Service and Victory Medals.
40, Stanmore Road, Watford.   X1728.

LEWIS, W. H., Private, 2nd Essex Regiment.

He was serving at the outbreak of war, and was immediately drafted to France. He was in action in the Retreat from Mons, and in the subsequent Battles of Ypres, Arras, Cambrai, Albert, and many others until the signing of the Armistice. He was demobilised in February 1919, and holds the Mons Star, and the General Service and Victory Medals.
112, Wenlock Street, Luton.   1723/B

LIGHTFOOT, S. R., Private, South Staffordshire Regiment.

He volunteered in September 1914, and served at various stations with his unit until drafted to France in 1916. He was engaged in many sectors and at the base on important duties until after the cessation of hostilities. He then returned to England, and was demobilised in January 1919. He holds the General Service and Victory Medals.
6, Stockwood Crescent, Luton.   1729.

LILLY, W. J., Private, R.A.S.C.

Volunteering in 1915, he was shortly afterwards sent to Salonika. He served in this theatre of war for nearly three years, and was present during many engagements. He was then drafted to the Western Front, and was employed on various duties in the forward areas whilst operations were in progress on the Somme and at Cambrai, in the Retreat and Advance of 1918. He was demobilised in March 1919, and holds the 1914-15 Star, and the General Service and Victory Medals.
51, Pinner Road, Oxhey, Herts.   X1730.

LIMBREY, W. A. P., Pte., 6th Middlesex Regt.

He joined in June 1916, and after completing a course of training proceeded to France. There he served in several sectors, and was engaged on important duties at various detention camps until sent with the Army of Occupation into Germany, where he was employed on guard and other duties at Cologne. He returned to England for demobilisation in December 1919, and holds the General Service and Victory Medals.
25, Grove Road, Hitchin.   1871.

LINCOLN, H. G., Gunner, Royal Field Artillery.

He joined in April 1916, and at the conclusion of his training served at various stations on important duties with his battery. He did good work, but was unable to secure his transfer overseas, and was demobilised in September 1919.

Lower Coldecote, Biggleswade. Z1731.

LINCOLN, H. J., Gunner, Royal Field Artillery.

Serving in India at the outbreak of war he was drafted to England and sent to France in January 1915. He took part in the fierce fighting at Neuve Chapelle, Ypres, and Festubert, and was wounded. On recovery he rejoined his battery and fought in the operations on the Somme, and was again wounded at Arras. He later returned to the firing line and was wounded a third time at Cambrai during the Advance of 1918, as a result of which he subsequently died on June 17th, 1918. He was entitled to the 1914-15 Star, and the General Service and Victory Medals, and had been recommended for the Distinguished Conduct Medal for conspicuous bravery and devotion to duty in the Field.

Mill Lane, Campton, Shefford. Z1732.

LINCOLN, J., Rifleman, The Cameronians (Scottish Rifles).

He volunteered in June 1915 and in the same year was drafted to France. He fought in the Battle of the Somme and was severely wounded and invalided home. On recovery he returned to the Western Front and took part in the fighting at Arras and Cambrai, and was again wounded. This resulted in the partial amputation of his foot and he was discharged as physically unfit for further service in March 1919. He holds the 1914-15 Star, and the General Service and Victory Medals.

Cowfairlands, Biggleswade. Z1733.

LINDGREN, J. T., Sapper, Royal Engineers.

He volunteered in March 1915, and after his training was employed at various stations on important duties with his unit until after the cessation of hostilities He was then drafted with the Army of Occupation to Germany, serving for twelve months at Cologne. He was demobilised in November 1919.

11, Chapel Walk, Dunstable. 1734

LINDGREN, J. W., Private, 4th (Queen's Own) Hussars.

He was serving at the outbreak of war, and was immediately drafted to France. He took part in the fierce fighting in the Retreat from Mons, and in the subsequent Battles of Ypres, Arras, the Somme and during the Retreat and Advance of 1918, and was wounded. He holds the Mons Star, and the General Service and Victory Medals, and was demobilised in November 1919.

11, Chapel Walk, Dunstable. 1735.

LINE, A., Private, Labour Corps.

He joined in June 1916, and after his training served at various stations on important duties with his unit. He did good work, but owing to medical unfitness was unable to obtain his transfer overseas and was demobilised in February 1919.

East End, Flitwick, Beds. 1736

LINES, G., Shoeing Smith, R.A.V.C.

He volunteered in June 1915, and in the following month proceeded to the Western Front. He was engaged as a shoeing smith and in attending to the sick and wounded horses and in this capacity did much good work. He was invalided home in December 1915, and after receiving hospital treatment was discharged in July 1916, and holds the 1914-15 Star, and the General Service and Victory Medals.

Primrose Hill, King's Langley, Herts. X399/C.

LINES, R., Cpl., 1st York and Lancaster Regt.

He was serving at the outbreak of war and was sent to France in January 1915. He took part in the Battles of Ypres and Loos and was wounded. He was later drafted to Salonika and was in action in the Advance on the Struma and at the Battle of Monastir. He returned home and was demobilised in April 1919, and holds the 1914-15 Star, and the General Service and Victory Medals.

Primrose Hill, King's Langley, Herts X399/B.

LINES, W., Private, Suffolk Regiment.

He joined in February 1916, and after completing his training was stationed at various places engaged on important duties with his unit. He rendered valuable services but owing to ill-health was not successful in securing his transfer overseas and he was discharged as medically unfit for further service in July of the same year.

The Folly, Wheathampstead. 1737.

LINES, W. H., Private, Royal Fusiliers.

He joined in June 1916, and in the following September was drafted to France. Whilst in this theatre of war he served in various sectors with his battalion and took part in various engagements and was wounded. He returned to England after hostilities ceased and was demobilised in February 1919, and holds the General Service and Victory Medals.

Oliver Street, Ampthill. 1738.

LINGER, E. J., Lance-Corporal, Royal Fusiliers.

He joined in April 1916, and at the conclusion of his training was sent to France. During his service in this theatre of war he served in many sectors and took part in many battles, including those of Arras and Cambrai, and was reported missing on November 30th, 1917. He was later presumed to have been killed in action on that date, and was entitled to the General Service and Victory Medals.

20, Curzon Road, Luton. 1739.

LINGER, P. F., Private, 24th London Regiment (Queen's).

He volunteered in September 1914, and in the following March was drafted to France. He was engaged in much heavy fighting on the Western Front and fought at Ypres and Festubert and was killed in action on May 26th, 1915. He was entitled to the 1914-15 Star, and the General Service and Victory Medals.

6, Lyndhurst Road, Luton. 1740.

LINNEY, E. G., Bombardier, Royal Field Artillery.

He volunteered in November 1915, and in the following year was sent to France. He was engaged in the fighting on the Western Front and was wounded near Ypres in 1917. On recovery he returned to the firing line and during the Allied Advance of 1918 was again wounded near Cambrai. He later rejoined his unit and took part in the final operations of the war. He was demobilised in April 1919, and holds the General Service and Victory Medals.

75, Park Street, St. Albans. X1741.

LINNEY, F., Sapper, Royal Engineers.

Volunteering in October 1914, he was drafted overseas in the following March. He served on the Western Front and was engaged on important duties in the forward areas and was present at the Battle of Ypres and was wounded in October 1915 and again on the Somme in June 1917. On recovery he rejoined his unit and remained in France until April 1919, when he returned home and was demobilised. He holds the 1914-15 Star, and the General Service and Victory Medals.

20, Bedford Street, Leighton Buzzard. 1742.

LINNEY, F. W., Private, Royal Fusiliers.

He joined in June 1916, and at the conclusion of his training was engaged at various stations on important duties with his unit. He did much useful work but was unable to secure his transfer to a theatre of war on account of medical unfitness and was discharged in consequence in October 1918.

3, Watland Place, Frogmore, St. Albans. X1743.

LINNEY, H. A., Pte., 10th Queen's (Royal West Surrey Regiment).

He joined in July 1918, and after his training was engaged on important duties with his unit at various stations but was unsuccessful in obtaining his transfer overseas until after the signing of the Armistice. He was drafted to Germany in March 1919, and served with the Army of Occupation on the Rhine for twelve months. He returned home and was demobilised in March 1920.

28. Bedford Street, Leighton Buzzard. 1744/A.

LINNEY, J., Private, Labour Corps.

He joined in February 1917, and in the following month was drafted to France. He was engaged on important duties in the forward areas, and was present at the Battles of Festubert and Ypres, and was wounded in August 1917. He returned home, and on recovery remained in England on special duties until March 1919, when he was demobilised. He holds the General Service and Victory Medals.

" Ascania," Alfred Street, Dunstable. 1745.

LINNEY, J., Sapper, Royal Engineers.

He joined in March 1918, and in the following August was drafted to Salonika. In this theatre of war he was engaged with his unit on special duties in connection with operations in the Struma Valley, and remained on this front until March 1919, when he returned home and was demobilised. He holds the General Service and Victory Medals.

42, Essex Street, Luton.   1746.

LINNEY, S., Lance-Corporal, Machine Gun Corps.

He joined in September 1916, and in the following February proceeded overseas. During his service on the Western Front he was engaged in the fighting at Ypres, Arras and on the Somme, and was gassed during the German Offensive in March 1918. He returned home and was demobilised in August 1919, and holds the General Service and Victory Medals.

28, Bedford Street, Leighton Buzzard.   1744/B.

LINNEY, S. L., Private, Bedfordshire Regiment.

Volunteering in August 1914, he proceeded overseas in the following January. He was engaged on special transport duties during his service on the Western Front, and served at Ypres, Arras, on the Somme and at Cambrai. He was demobilised in January 1919, and holds the 1914-15 Star, and the General Service and Victory Medals.

38, Bedford Street, Leighton Buzzard.   1747.

LISLES, J., Private, 8th Bedfordshire Regiment.

He volunteered in September 1914, and was sent overseas in the following year. Whilst on the Western Front he fought in the Battles of Ypres (II.) and Loos, and in the offensive operations on the Somme, during which he was severely wounded. Invalided home to hospital at Bristol, he died from the effects of his wounds on September 29th, 1916. He was entitled to the 1914-15 Star, and the General Service and Victory Medals.

8, Brampton Park Road, Hitchin.   1866.

LISTER, D. W., Private, Machine Gun Corps.

He was serving in the Army when war broke out, having enlisted in 1912, and after doing good work with his unit at various stations on guard and other duties was drafted overseas in 1917. During his service on the Western Front he was engaged in heavy fighting in several sectors, and took part in the Battles of the Somme, Cambrai and St. Quentin. He was demobilised in March 1919, and holds the General Service and Victory Medals.

19, Boyle Street, Luton.   2155.

LITCHFIELD, A., Pte., Northamptonshire Regt.

He joined in July 1918, and was shortly afterwards sent to France. He was in action at Ypres, Bapaume, Cambrai, on the Marne and at Le Cateau during the final stages of the war. After the signing of the Armistice he proceeded to Germany with the Army of Occupation and was stationed on the Rhine. He returned home, and was demobilised in December 1919, and holds the General Service and Victory Medals.

Armours Yard, Clifton Road, Shefford.   Z1748.

LITCHFIELD, G. W., Private, Royal Warwickshire Regiment.

He joined in October 1916, and at the conclusion of his training proceeded to France. During his service on the Western Front he fought in the Battle of Ypres, and was later sent to Egypt, where he served for a time. He was then sent to Italy, and took part in operations on the Piave. After the Armistice he returned home and was demobilised in December 1919, and holds the General Service and Victory Medals.

4, Wood Street, Luton.   1749.

LITCHFIELD, P. W., Gunner, R.F.A.

He volunteered in December 1915, and after a period of training was sent to Mesopotamia in the following September. He took an active part in the operations in this theatre of war, and was wounded during the Advance on Baghdad in February 1917. He was invalided to India, and remained there after recovery until he returned to England for demobilisation in February 1919. He holds the General Service and Victory Medals.

5, Malvern Road, Luton.   1750.

LITTLECHILDS, T., Private, Essex Regiment.

He volunteered in June 1915, and in the following January was drafted to Egypt, and a month later to Palestine. Here he took part in much heavy fighting, and in March 1917 was severely wounded at Gaza, and after receiving treatment at one of the base hospitals rejoined his unit. He was demobilised after his return to England in February 1919, and holds the General Service and Victory Medals.

83, Park Street, near St. Albans.   X1751.

LITTLEJOHN, E. (Miss), Special War Worker.

This lady offered her services for work of National importance during the war, and was engaged at No. 1 Filling Factory, Watford, in filling shells and packing cartridges from January 1916 until the following May. She was then employed at Boxmoor at a munition factory, and did good work in making tents and other Army equipment. Her duties were carried out in a highly satisfactory manner throughout.

8b, Chapel Street, Hemel Hempstead.   X1752/B.

LITTLEJOHN, S. H., Gunner, R.F.A.

He volunteered in September 1914, and in the following month was drafted to India, where he served on important garrison duties with his Battery at Lahore and other stations until March 1916. He then returned to England, and was engaged on special work with the Anti-aircraft guns until demobilised in March 1919. He holds the General Service and Victory Medals.

8b, Chapel Street, Hemel Hempstead.   X1752/A.

LIVESEY, J., 1st Class Stoker, Royal Navy.

Mobilised at the outbreak of war, he was posted to H.M.S. " Euryalus " and later served in H.M.S. "Queen Elizabeth." Throughout the period of hostilities his ship was engaged on duties of an important nature and also took part in several naval engagements, including the bombardment of the Dardanelles Forts and the Battles of Heligoland Bight. He was demobilised in January 1919, and holds the 1914-15 Star, and the General Service and Victory Medals.

10, Weymouth Street, Watford.   X1753.

LLOYD, G. W., Private, 13th East Surrey Regt.

He volunteered in August 1915, and in the following June was drafted to the Western Front. Whilst overseas he took part in many important engagements, notably those on the Somme, at Ypres and Cambrai, and was subsequently wounded and taken prisoner near Albert during the German Offensive in April 1918. Released in November of that year, he returned to England, and in February 1919 was demobilised. He holds the General Service and Victory Medals.

3, Shaftesbury Road, Watford   X1754/B, X1755/B.

LLOYD, H. R., Rifleman, 11th King's Royal Rifle Corps.

Joining in June 1917, he was sent to France in the following December. Subsequently he fought in many important engagements, including those at Arras and Cambrai, and was gassed whilst in action at Lens in September 1918. He remained on the Western Front until February 1919, when he returned to England and a month later was demobilised. He holds the General Service and Victory Medals.

3, Shaftesbury Road, Watford.   X1754/C, X1755/C.

LLOYD, L. F., Corporal, King's Royal Rifle Corps.

He volunteered in April 1915, and in the following August was drafted to France. Here he took an active part in many battles, notably those of Ypres, where he was severely wounded, Loos and the Somme, and after the cessation of hostilities served with the Army of Occupation in Germany until April 1919. Returning to England he was demobilised a month later, and holds the 1914-15 Star, and the General Service and Victory Medals.

3, Shaftesbury Road, Watford.   X1754/A, X1755/A.

LLOYD, R. S., Air Mechanic, Royal Air Force.

Although under age for military service, he joined the R.A.F. in March 1918, but was unable to secure his transfer overseas before the termination of war. He was, however, engaged on important duties, which called for a high degree of technical knowledge and skill, and rendered services of a valuable nature, however, until February 1919, when he was demobilised.

3, Shaftesbury Road, Watford.   X1754/D, X1755/D.

LOCKER, W., Private, Royal Munster Fusiliers.

Volunteering in September 1914, he obtained his training at various home stations, and was subsequently drafted to the Dardanelles. He was killed in action at Suvla Bay on August 16th, 1915, and was entitled to the 1914-15 Star, and the General Service and Victory Medals.

London Road, Rickmansworth.   X1756.

LOCKEY, W. R., Flight Cadet, Royal Air Force.

He joined in April 1918, but had not completed his training for an officer when hostilities ceased. He rendered services of a valuable nature, however, until February 1919, when he was demobilised.
10, Pondwicks Road, Luton. 1757.

LOCKYER, E., Private, Suffolk Regiment.

He volunteered in 1915, and at the conclusion of his training was drafted to the Western Front. Here he served for nearly four years, during which time he took part in many important engagements, notably those at Ypres, the Somme, and Arras, and was wounded. Returning to England after the cessation of hostilities, he was demobilised in January 1919, and holds the 1914-15 Star, and the General Service and Victory Medals.
1, Cotterall's Hill, Hemel Hempstead. X1374/B.

LODGE, A. Private, East Surrey Regiment.

He volunteered at the commencement of hostilities and in June 1915 was sent to the Western Front. Here he served for nearly four years, during which time he took part in many of the principal engagements, notably those on the Somme, at Ypres, Passchendaele, Arras and Cambrai. One one occasion he was severely wounded but after receiving treatment at one of the base hospitals, was able to rejoin his unit. He was demobilised on his return to England in February 1919, and holds the 1914-15 Star, and the General Service and Victory Medals.
Watland Place, Park Street, near St. Albans. X1758/A.

LODGE, W., Private, 10th Bedfordshire Regt.

He volunteered in August 1914, and after his training was drafted to France. Here he served for nearly two years, taking part in numerous engagements, including those at Loos and the Somme. In May 1917 he was transferred to Egypt, and thence to Palestine, and on November 25th of the same year, was killed in action at Gaza. He was entitled to the 1914-15 Star, and the General Service and Victory Medals.
Watland Place, Park Street, near St. Albans. X1758/B.

LOMAX, V., Private, Northamptonshire Regt.

He joined in June 1916, and after a course of training was drafted to the Western Front. He took part in the heavy fighting at Ypres, Arras and Cambrai, and was twice wounded. He returned home and was demobilised in February 1919, and holds the General Service and Victory Medals.
103, High Street, Silsoe, Beds. 63/E, 64/E.

LONG, A., Driver, Royal Field Artillery.

Volunteering in August 1914, he was drafted to Egypt at the conclusion of his training and served there until May 1917, when he was transferred to France. Here he took part in fighting at Arras and in the Somme sector, and was killed in action at Vlamerlinghe on October 5th, 1917. He was entitled to the 1914-15 Star, and the General Service and Victory Medals.
38, Adelaide Street, St. Albans. X1759.

LONG, A. D., Chief Petty Officer, Royal Navy.

Joining in November 1917, he was posted to H.M.S. "Phaeton." This vessel was engaged on special patrol duties in the North Sea, and later helped to escort the surrendered German Fleet to Scapa Flow. Throughout his service, which lasted until January 1919, he did valuable work, and holds the General Service and Victory Medals.
8, Park Road West, Luton. 1760.

LONG, G., Sergeant, Royal Engineers.

He volunteered in September 1914, and after his training was drafted to the Western Front. Throughout his service overseas he was engaged on duties of an important nature in the forward areas, and did excellent work, notably at Lens, Loos and Arras, and was severely gassed. He was demobilised after his return to England in March 1919, and holds the General Service and Victory Medals.
14, Adelaide Road, Luton. 1762.

LONG, G. (Miss), Special War Worker.

For a considerable period of the war, this lady served at Messrs. Kent and Co.'s, Ltd., Luton, where she was engaged on important work in connection with fuses. She carried out her duties in a thoroughly capable manner and proved in every way a most efficient worker.
88, Ashton Road, Luton. 1764/B.

LONG, H. G., Gunner, Royal Garrison Artillery.

Joining in September 1916, he served for a year on the Western Front, where he did excellent work during many important engagements, notably those at Arras, and Ypres Returning to England he was discharged in February 1918, from causes due to his service. He holds the General Service and Victory Medals.
129, Lower Paddock Road, Oxhey, Herts. X1763.

LONG, M. E. (Miss), Special War Worker.

This lady was engaged for three years during the war in the clerical department of a munition works at Luton, where she held a responsible post and carried out the duties thus entailed in a commendable manner. She afterwards served for nine months as a land worker in Wales, Lincolnshire and Nottinghamshire, and in this capacity again did valuable work
88, Ashton Road, Luton. 1764/A.

LONG, P. R., Aircraftsman, Royal Air Force.

Joining in October 1917, he was drafted to the Western Front early in the following year. During his service overseas, he was engaged on duties of an important nature, which called for much technical knowledge and skill and did most valuable work until after the cessation of hostilities. He holds the General Service and Victory Medals, and was demobilised in October 1919.
88, Ashton Road, Luton. 1764/C.

LONG, R., Rifleman, 8th London Regiment (Post Office Rifles).

Volunteering at the outbreak of war, he joined the 5th Middlesex Regiment, and was later transferred to the 8th London Regiment. After his training he was sent to France, where he saw service in many sectors, notably those of Ypres and the Somme, and was also engaged on special duties. Returning to England in 1919, he was demobilised in September of that year and holds the General Service and Victory Medals.
10, Wensum Cottages, High Street, Rickmansworth X1765.

LONG, T., Private, Bedfordshire Regiment.

He volunteered in June 1915, but owing to medical unfitness was unable to secure his transfer overseas. He was entrusted with special duties, however, which he carried out in a commendable manner until 1916, when he was invalided out of the service.
1, Cross Street West, Dunstable. 1761/B.

LONG, W., Private, 8th Lincolnshire Regiment, and Labour Corps.

He joined in the Durham Light Infantry in November 1916, and was later transferred to the 8th Lincolnshire Regiment. After his training he was drafted to the Western Front, where he served principally at Armentières until October 1918, when he was wounded and invalided home. On being discharged from hospital he was transferred to the Labour Corps, with which unit he did valuable work until his demobilisation, which took place in February 1919. He holds the General Service and Victory Medals.
88, Ashton Road, Luton. 1766.

LONGHURST, E., Private, Bedfordshire Regt., and Royal Army Service Corps.

He volunteered in November 1914, and after his training was drafted to the Western Front, where he took part in many engagements, notably those at Ypres, Arras and Cambrai. In November 1917 he was severely wounded whilst in action at Beaumont-Hamel, and after treatment in hospital was transferred to the R.A.S.C. Later, however, owing to his wound he was sent to England, and in March 1918 was invalided out of the service. He holds the 1914-15 Star, and the General Service and Victory Medals.
Southill, Beds. Z1767/B.

LONGHURST, P., Leading Stoker, Royal Navy.

Volunteering at the outbreak of war, he was posted to H.M.S "Birmingham." Aboard this ship he served in the North and Mediterranean Seas, and took part in several naval engagements, including the Battles of Heligoland Bight and Jutland. He was also present at the surrender of the German Fleet at Scapa Flow. He holds the 1914-15 Star, and the General Service and Victory Medals, and was serving in 1920.
Southill, Beds. Z1767/A.

LONNON, W. G., Sapper, Royal Engineers.

He volunteered in May 1915, and in the following year was drafted to France. Here he served for three years, during which time he did valuable work in many important sectors, notably those of Hill 60 and the Somme. On one occasion he was wounded, but after treatment at the base was able to rejoin his unit. He was demobilised in May 1919, and holds the General Service and Victory Medals.
62, Jubilee Road, North Watford. X1768.

LOOMES, E., Sapper, Royal Engineers.
Joining in December 1916, he was sent to France six months later. Subsequently he saw service in many important sectors, including those of Ypres, Messines, Arras and Cambrai. He was also engaged on transport work in the forward areas, and after the cessation of hostilities advanced into Germany with the Army of Occupation. He holds the General Service and Victory Medals, and was demobilised on his return to England in September 1919.
Saunders Piece, Ampthill.   1769.

LOUGHTON, W., Pte., 1/5th Bedfordshire Regt.
He volunteered in August 1914, and at the conclusion of his training in December 1915 was drafted to Egypt, where he saw service in the Canal Zone. Subsequently, he was sent on to Palestine, and with General Allenby's Forces took part in many important engagements on that front, notably that at Gaza. Whilst in this theatre of war he contracted a severe illness, from which he died at En Saret on November 14th, 1917. He was entitled to the 1914-15 Star, and the General Service and Victory Medals.
42, May Street, Luton.   1770.

LOVATT, A. W., Pte., 7th Bedfordshire Regt.
He volunteered in March 1915, and was drafted to France in the following January. During his service in this theatre of war he served with his battalion in various sectors, and was engaged in the fighting on the Somme, in which he was killed on July 1st, 1916. He was entitled to the General Service and Victory Medals.
5, Bedford Street, Hitchin.   1771.

LOVEGROVE, R., Gunner, R.G.A.
Joining in January 1916, he was drafted to the Western Front after training at various stations in England. He was subsequently in action in many important sectors, notably those of the Somme, Arras, Ypres and Cambrai, and did valuable work with his battery. On one occasion he was severely gassed, but on his recovery was able to rejoin his unit. He holds the General Service and Victory Medals, and was demobilised in January 1919.
58, Union Street, Dunstable.   1772.

LOVEJOY, C. T., L/Corporal, Oxfordshire and Buckinghamshire Light Infantry.
Volunteering at the commencement of hostilities, he was quickly drafted to the Western Front, and took part in the Retreat from Mons and many of the subsequent engagements. He was killed in action at Menin Road on July 30th, 1915, after having been severely wounded. He was entitled to the Mons Star, and the General Service and Victory Medals.
244, Chester Road, Watford.   X1773.

LOVEJOY, R. J., Private, 1st Hertfordshire Regt.
He volunteered in August 1914, and after completing his training was engaged at various stations with his unit. He did much good work on guard and other duties, but was not able to secure his transfer to a theatre of war owing to medical unfitness, and he was demobilised in 1919.
Back Street, Hatfield.   X1774.

LOVELL, F. E., Private, R.A.M.C.
He volunteered in January 1915, and in the following November was drafted to East Africa. Here he served for nearly four years, during which time he did excellent work with his unit in tending the sick and wounded troops. Returning to England in 1919, he was demobilised in April of that year, and holds the 1914-15 Star, and the General Service and Victory Medals.
Rothschild's Road, Wing, Leighton Buzzard.   1775.

LOVELL, H., Private, 16th Middlesex Regiment.
He joined in June 1917, and was sent to the Western Front in the following November. Subsequently, he took an active part in many engagements, notably those at Arras, Cambrai and the Somme, and was almost continuously in action until March 1918, when, owing to ill-health, he returned to England. He was invalided out of the service in June of that year, and holds the General Service and Victory Medals.
20, Alfred Street, Dunstable.   1776.

LOVELL, H., L/Corporal, R.A.V.C.
Volunteering in November 1915, he was sent to France in the following January. During his service overseas he was engaged in removing sick and wounded horses from the forward areas, and in otherwise tending them, in which capacity he did excellent work until after the cessation of hostilities. He was demobilised in April 1919, and holds the General Service and Victory Medals.
"Littleworth," Wing, Leighton Buzzard.   1777.

LOVELL, H., Driver, Royal Field Artillery.
He volunteered in August 1914, and in the following year was drafted to the Western Front. Serving with his battery in several sectors, he was engaged in heavy fighting in many of the principal battles, including those of Ypres, Arras, Loos, Lens and Cambrai. He was demobilised in 1919, and holds the 1914-15 Star, and the General Service and Victory Medals.
153, Lower Marlowes, Hemel Hempstead.   X874/A.

LOVELL, W., Sergeant, 2nd Bedfordshire Regt.
Volunteering in August 1914, he was quickly drafted to France, and subsequently took part in the Retreat from Mons and many of the engagements which followed, including those at Arras and Cambrai. On two occasions he was severely wounded, but after receiving treatment rejoined his unit. He holds the Mons Star, and the General Service and Victory Medals, and in 1920 was still serving.
9, Lowestoft Road, Watford.   X1778.

LOVELOCK, B., Private, Labour Corps.
Joining in 1916, he was drafted to the Western Front at the conclusion of his training. His service overseas lasted for three years, during which time he did important work with his unit in many sectors, notably those of Ypres, Cambrai and the Somme. He was demobilised after his return to England in November 1919, and holds the General Service and Victory Medals.
1, Prospect Place, Chalk Hill, Oxhey, Herts.   X1779.

LOVELOCK, C. S., Private, Hertfordshire Regt., and Bedfordshire Regiment.
He joined in 1916, and in the same year was sent to the Western Front, where he served in various sectors with his regiment, and took part in many important engagements until killed in action on March 27th, 1917. He was entitled to the General Service and Victory Medals.
8, Park Gate Road, Callowland, Watford.   X1780/A.

LOVELOCK, E. A., Sapper, Royal Engineers.
He volunteered in 1914, and after his training was drafted to the Western Front. During his service in this theatre of war he was engaged on duties of an important nature in the forward areas, and was present at many important engagements, including those at Ypres, the Somme, Arras and Cambrai. He holds the General Service and Victory Medals, and in 1920 was still serving.
8, Park Gate Road, Callowland, Watford.   X1780/B.

LOVERIDGE, J., Corporal, 2nd South Lancashire Regiment.
A serving soldier, he was drafted to the Western Front immediately upon the outbreak of hostilities, and took part in the Retreat from Mons and many of the subsequent engagements, and was wounded three times. In July 1915 he was sent to the Dardanelles, and was again wounded during the landing at Suvla Bay. After the Evacuation of the Peninsula he was transferred to India, where he served for a time, and returned to England for his discharge, which took place in May 1916. He holds the Mons Star, and the General Service and Victory Medals.
"Single House," Pond Head, Toddington, Beds.   1781.

LOVERIDGE, J., L/Corporal, York and Lancaster Regiment.
He was mobilised in August 1914, and almost immediately proceeded to France. He was engaged in the fighting during the Retreat from Mons, and in the subsequent Battles of La Bassée, Festubert, Neuve Chapelle and Arras. He was killed in action on April 20th, 1916, and was entitled to the Mons Star and the General Service and Victory Medals.
24, Back Street, Biggleswade.   Z1577/A.

LOVERIDGE, L., Pte., 7th Bedfordshire Regt.
He volunteered in May 1915, and after his training was engaged for some time on various duties with his unit. In November 1916 he was drafted to the Western Front, where he took part in many battles, notably those of Ypres, Passchendaele and Cambrai, and on February 12th, 1918, was killed in action at Langemarck, having previously been wounded. He was entitled to the General Service and Victory Medals.
"Single House," Pond End, Toddington, Beds.   1782.

LOVETT, A., Private, 52nd Canadian Independent Corps.

Volunteering in September 1914, he was sent to the Western Front on completing his training early in the following year. He took part in the Battles of Festubert and Loos, and was killed whilst acting as stretcher bearer in the Somme sector on September 18th, 1916. He was entitled to the 1914-15 Star, and the General Service and Victory Medals.
63, Sun Street, Biggleswade.   Z1783/B.

LOVETT, H., Pte., 2nd Northamptonshire Regt.

He joined in August 1917, and in the following April was sent to France. Whilst in this theatre of war he served in several sectors during the German Offensive, and fought at Albert and St. Quentin. He was killed in action in the vicinity of Cambrai on May 27th, 1918. He was entitled to the General Service and Victory Medals.
68, Sun Street, Biggleswade.   Z1783/C.

LOVETT, R., Private, 8th Bedfordshire Regiment.

He volunteered in August 1915, and in the following March was drafted to France. Subsequently, he fought at Bullecourt, Gommecourt and in other important engagements, and until his death, which occurred during the Somme Offensive on September 15th, 1916, was in action almost continuously. He was entitled to the General Service and Victory Medals.
68, Sun Street, Biggleswade.   Z1783/A.

LOWE, A. A., Private, Norfolk Regiment.

He joined in May 1918, and in the same year was drafted overseas. He served in several sectors of the Western Front during the concluding stages of the war, and after the signing of the Armistice was sent into Germany with the Army of Occupation, and was stationed at Cologne. He returned home for demobilisation in February 1919, and holds the General Service and Victory Medals.
15, St. John's Road, Maggerhanger, Sandy.   Z1862/B.

LOWE, A. G., Pte., 7th Bedfordshire Regiment.

Joining in November 1916, he was drafted overseas early in the following year. Whilst on the Western Front he took part in many important operations, and was reported missing on May 3rd, 1917, during the Battle of Arras. He was afterwards presumed to have been killed in action on that date, and was entitled to the General Service and Victory Medals.
15, St. John's Road, Maggerhanger, Sandy.   Z1862/A.

LOWE, A. T., Private, Essex Regiment.

He joined in 1916, and after his training saw service in Egypt, Palestine and France. On each of these fronts he took part in many important engagements and with his unit did valuable work throughout, and during his service overseas was severely wounded. He holds the General Service and Victory Medals, and was demobilised in March 1920.
35, Longmire Road, St. Albans.   X3164/A, X3165/A.

LOWE, F. J., Corporal, 2nd Lincolnshire Regt.

Joining in March 1916, he was drafted to France the following August. He saw much service on the Western Front, where he took part in many engagements, including the Battle of the Somme, and was wounded in September 1916. Rejoining his unit after hospital treatment he was engaged in heavy fighting, and was killed in action near Ypres on August 16th, 1917. He was entitled to the General Service and Victory Medals.
2, Alexandra Road, King's Langley.   X1785.

LOWE, G., Leading Seaman, Royal Navy.

He was serving in the Navy when war broke out, and aboard H.M.S. " Pactolus " served in the North Sea until 1915 when his ship was sent to the Dardanelles, and took part in the naval operations there until the Evacuation of the Peninsula. He then served in Italian waters, and in 1917 was engaged on mine-sweeping duties in various waters until the cessation of hostilities. He holds the 1914-15 Star, and the General Service and Victory Medals, and was demobilised in May 1919.
31, Church Road, Watford.   X1786.

LOWE, H., Private, Bedfordshire Regiment.

He joined in 1917, and after his training was drafted to the Western Front Here he took an active part in several notable engagements, including those at Arras, Ypres and Cambrai, and was subsequently killed in action during the German Offensive on April 5th, 1918. He was entitled to the General Service and Victory Medals.
35, Longmire Road, St. Albans.   X3164/C, X3165/C.

LOWE, J. W., Gunner, Royal Garrison Artillery.

He volunteered in January 1915, and during his service on the Western Front served in several engagements, including those of Arras and Cambrai, and was wounded three times. He was demobilised after his return to England in February 1919, and holds the General Service and Victory Medals.
35, Longmire Road, St. Albans.   X3164/B, X3165/B.

LOWE, W. W., Sergeant, Machine Gun Corps.

He volunteered in March 1915, and was drafted to the Western Front in the following January. Whilst in this theatre of war he took part in heavy fighting in several sectors, and fought in the Battles of the Somme, Arras, and in the Retreat and Advance of 1918. Returning to England at the end of the war, he was demobilised in March 1919, and holds the 1914-15 Star, and the General Service and Victory Medals.
79, Waterside, King's Langley.   X1781.

LUCAS, W. W., Special War Worker.

Volunteering for work of National importance soon after the declaration of war he was for a time engaged at a Y.M.C.A. Hut in London. Subsequently as a special constable at Harpenden he was employed on various duties and did excellent work during the air raids until the end of the war
Fonthill, Cowper Road, Harpenden.   1790.

LUCCHESI, F., Rflmn., King's Royal Rifle Corps.

He was serving in the Army at the outbreak of war, and was almost immediately drafted to France. There he took part in the Retreat from Mons and subsequent engagements of Ypres, Arras and Cambrai and was then sent to the Middle East. During his service in Mesopotamia, he was frequently in action and fought in the Battle of Baghdad. He also served in Salonika where he remained until the close of the war. He holds the Mons Star, and the General Service and Victory Medals, and was demobilised in March 1919.
14, Wells Yard, Watford.   1791/A.

LUCK, A., Private, 1st Hertfordshire Regiment.

He joined in June 1916, and in the same year was drafted overseas. Whilst on the Western Front he saw much service and took part in many important engagements. He was killed in action at the Battle of the Somme on November 13th, 1916, and was entitled to the General Service and Victory Medals.
121, Marlowes, Hemel Hempstead.   X1792

LUCK, A. W., Private, 19th Middlesex Regiment.

He joined in July 1917, and after completing his training served with his unit at various stations. He did good work but was not successful in obtaining his transfer overseas before the Armistice. In December 1918, however, he was drafted to Germany to the Army of Occupation and was stationed at Cologne, where he was engaged on important duties until his return to England for demobilisation in March 1920.
46, Cannon Street, St. Albans.   1793

LUDERS, A., Corporal, R.E. (Signal Section).

He volunteered in July 1915, and in the following year was drafted overseas. He served in several sectors of the Western Front and was engaged on important duties during heavy fighting on the Somme, at Ypres, Arras, Albert, St. Quentin, and other places. Returning to England after the signing of the Armistice, he was demobilised in July 1919, and holds the General Service and Victory Medals.
23, New England Street, St. Albans.   1795.

LUDFORD, A., Private, 1st Bedfordshire Regt.

He volunteered in August 1914, and was sent to France in the following year. Whilst on the Western Front he served with his battalion in various sectors and took part in many engagements until killed in action at Hill 60 on April 21st, 1915 He was entitled to the 1914-15 Star, and the General Service and Victory Medals
Queen Street, Hitchin.   1864

LUDFORD, G. W., Pte., 1st Hertfordshire Regt

He volunteered in August 1914, and in the following year was drafted to the Western Front. During his service in this theatre of war, he served in various sectors and fought in the Battles of Ypres, Arras, the Somme, St. Quentin and Cambrai and was wounded three times. He was demobilised in May 1919, and holds the 1914-15 Star, and the General Service and Victory Medals.
5, Anderson's Row, Florence Street, Hitchin.   1870.

LUDFORD, H., Private, 1st Hertfordshire Regt.

He volunteered at the outbreak of war and after his training served at various stations on important duties with his unit. He was not successful in obtaining his transfer overseas owing to medical unfitness. He was discharged in consequence in October 1914.
52, Balmoral Road, Hitchin.   1796.

LUGSDEN, E., Private, 26th Royal Fusiliers.

He volunteered in November 1915, and in the following February proceeded to the Western Front. Whilst in this theatre of war he was engaged in the Offensive operations on the Somme, where he was wounded in July 1916, and invalided home to hospital. He was later drafted to Italy and there took part in the operations on the Piave. He was demobilised in January 1919, after returning to England, and holds the General Service and Victory Medals.
10, Friday Street, Leighton Buzzard.   1797.

LUMM, G., Private, 4th Bedfordshire Regiment.

He volunteered in September 1914, and was drafted overseas in the following April. He saw much active service on the Western Front and was engaged in several important battles, including those of the Somme, Arras, Ypres, Cambrai and St Quentin, and was twice wounded. He was invalided home in March 1918, and after recovery was demobilised in March 1919. He holds the 1914-15 Star, and the General Service and Victory Medals.
139, Herkomer Road, Bushey.   X1798/A.

LUMM, J. R., Private, 4th Bedfordshire Regiment.

Volunteering in January 1915, he completed his training and was engaged with his unit on important duties at various stations until sent overseas in July of the following year. He served on the Western Front in several sectors and fought in many battles, including those of the Somme, Ypres, Arras and Cambrai, and was wounded on September 3rd, 1918. He died from the effects of his wounds eight days later, and was entitled to the General Service and Victory Medals.
19, Park Road, Bushey.   X1798/B.

LUNDIE, A. H., Private, 16th Middlesex Regt.

He joined in May 1916, and was sent to France in the following October. In this theatre of war he took part in many important engagements, including the Battle of the Somme and was killed in action on July 19th, 1917. He was entitled to the General Service and Victory Medals.
38, Clifton Road, Luton.   1800.

LUNNON, C., Private, Royal Fusiliers.

He volunteered in January 1916, and was sent to the Western Front in the following July. Whilst in this theatre of war he took part in the Offensive operations on the Somme and in many other important engagements until the termination of the war. He was demobilised in March 1920, and holds the General Service and Victory Medals.
Hockcliffe, near Leighton Buzzard.   1801/B.

LUNNON, E. W., Driver, Royal Field Artillery.

He was mobilised at the outbreak of hostilities, and almost immediately drafted to France, where he was engaged in the fierce fighting in the Retreat from Mons and in the subsequent battles, including those of Arras, Ypres and the Somme. He was later drafted to Egypt, and there was employed on important transport duties during the Advance, under General Allenby, through Palestine. He also served at the Battle of Gaza and the capture of Jerusalem. At the termination of the war he returned to England and was demobilised in June 1919, and holds the 1914-15 Star, and the General Service and Victory Medals.
5, Jones Yard, St. Albans.   1802.

LUNNON, P., Private, Bedfordshire Regiment and Hertfordshire Regiment.

He joined in October 1918 on attaining military age, and on completion of his training was engaged with his unit on guard and other duties. He did good work, but was not able to secure his transfer overseas before the cessation of hostilities and was demobilised in April 1920.
Hockcliffe, near Leighton Buzzard.   1801/A.

LUSHER, C. J., Corporal, Royal Field Artillery.

Mobilised when war was declared, he was shortly afterwards drafted to France, where he fought in the Retreat from Mons and in the Battles of Ypres and the Somme, and was wounded. Returning to his Battery from hospital he served in many other sectors during the concluding stages of the war. He was demobilised in 1919, and holds the Mons Star, and the General Service and Victory Medals.
73, Acme Road, North Watford.   X1803.

LYNES, E. R., Pte., R.A.S.C., and Labour Corps.

He joined in November 1917, and in the same year was drafted to the Western Front, where he was engaged on important transport duties in several sectors, and was present at the Battles of Arras, Ypres and Passchendaele. He was gassed and suffered from shell-shock, and on recovery was transferred to the Labour Corps, with which unit he was employed on important duties until the cessation of hostilities. He was demobilised in October 1919, and holds the General Service and Victory Medals.
25, Watson Row, St. Albans.   X1804.

LYON, A., Sapper, Royal Engineers.

Volunteering in January 1915, he was drafted to the Dardanelles in the following July. He saw much service in Gallipoli, from the landing at Suvla Bay until the Evacuation of the Peninsula, after which he was sent to Egypt. In this seat of war he was employed on important duties in connection with operations during General Allenby's Advance through Palestine, and was present at the Battle of Gaza and other engagements until the end of the war. He was demobilised in December 1919 after returning to England, and holds the 1914-15 Star, and the General Service and Victory Medals.
29, Wimbourne Road, Luton.   1805/B.

LYON, H., Pte., Essex Regt. (Cyclist Battalion).

Volunteering in September 1914, he was drafted to Gallipoli in the following August. He was engaged in heavy fighting at the landing at Suvla Bay and in other operations which followed until the Evacuation of the Peninsula. He then proceeded to France, acting as a despatch rider, was present at several important engagements, including those on the Somme, at Ypres, Arras and Cambrai. He was demobilised in February 1919, and holds the 1914-15 Star, and the General Service and Victory Medals.
29, Wimbourne Road, Luton.   1805/C.

LYON, H., Private, 2nd Bedfordshire Regiment.

He was mobilised on the declaration of war, and almost immediately drafted to France. He fought in the Retreat from Mons and in the subsequent heavy fighting in the Battles of the Aisne, Ypres and Festubert, during which he was killed in action on June 16th, 1915. He was entitled to the Mons Star, and the General Service and Victory Medals.
29, Wimbourne Road, Luton.   1805/A.

M

MABBITT, F., L/Corporal, 1/5th Bedfordshire Regiment.

He volunteered in November 1914, and in the following February was drafted overseas. Whilst serving on the Western Front he took an active part in the operations at Loos and at the Battle of the Somme, where he was wounded. On recovery he rejoined his battalion, and fought at Arras and during the Retreat and Advance of 1918. He was demobilised in January 1919, and holds the 1914-15 Star, and the General Service and Victory Medals.
1, Cross Street West, Dunstable.   1761/B.

MABBITT, H., Private, 1st Hertfordshire Regt.

He was mobilised at the outbreak of war, and in November 1914 proceeded overseas. During his service on the Western Front he was engaged in the fighting at Neuve Chapelle, Ypres, Givenchy, Arras and on the Somme, and was wounded. He returned to England after the cessation of hostilities, and was demobilised in March 1919. He holds the 1914 Star, and the General Service and Victory Medals.
31, Shott Lane, Letchworth.   1873/A.

MABBITT, W., Cpl., Military Mounted Police.
He volunteered in 1915, and in the same year was drafted to France. Whilst on the Western Front he served in various sectors, including that of Ypres. He was severely wounded on the Somme and invalided home, but subsequently died from the effects of his wounds on January 2nd, 1918. He was entitled to the 1914-15 Star, and the General Service and Victory Medals.
31, Shott Lane, Letchworth. 1873/B.

MABBOTT, A. T., Private, Bedfordshire Regt.
Volunteering in August 1914, he was almost immediately drafted overseas. During his service on the Western Front he took part in the fierce fighting in the Retreat from Mons and at the Battles of the Marne and the Aisne, and was severely wounded at La Bassée and invalided home. He was subsequently discharged, in consequence of his wounds, in November of the same year. He holds the Mons Star, and the General Service and Victory Medals.
Clifton Fields, Shefford. Z1874/A.

MABBOTT, B. E., Private, Bedfordshire Regt.
He was serving at the outbreak of war, and in 1915 was drafted to Egypt. He took part in the operations in Palestine and fought in many engagements, including those at Jaffa and Haifa. He contracted pneumonia, and subsequently died from the effects in November 1918. He was entitled to the 1914-15 Star, and the General Service and Victory Medals.
Clifton Fields, Shefford. Z1874/B.

MABBOTT, G. W., Private., Bedfordshire Regt.
He volunteered in March 1915, and on the conclusion of his training served at various stations on important duties with his unit. He did valuable work, but was unable to secure a transfer overseas before the signing of the Armistice on account of medical unfitness. He was demobilised in June 1919.
Clifton Fields, Shefford. Z1874/C.

MABBOTT, R., Pte., 6th Bedfordshire Regiment.
Volunteering in September 1914, he was in the following year drafted to the Western Front, but after a short period in this theatre of war he was invalided home. Later he returned to France, and took part in the fighting at Ypres and Arras. On November 16th, 1916, during the Battle of the Somme he was killed in action. He was entitled to the 1914-15 Star, and the General Service and Victory Medals.
4, Austin's Lane, Ampthill. 1875.

MABLEY, W., Private, Canadian Infantry.
Volunteering in Canada in 1915, he was drafted to England, and in the following year proceeded to the Western Front. During his service in this theatre of war he was in action at the Battle of the Somme, Vimy Ridge, and also took part in many other notable engagements, being severely wounded at Ypres. He was invalided to England and after a lengthy stay in hospital was finally discharged in August 1919, being medically unfit for further service. He holds the General Service and Victory Medals.
Salford Road, Aspley Guise. Z1876/A.

McCORMICK, R., Sergeant, 1/5th Bedfordshire Regiment.
He was mobilised at the outbreak of war, and in July 1915 was drafted to the Dardanelles. He took part in the fighting during the landing at Suvla Bay, and in the subsequent engagements until the Evacuation of the Peninsula. He suffered ill-health, was transferred to Egypt, invalided to hospital, and subsequently died on July 16th, 1916. He was entitled to the 1914-15 Star, and the General Service and Victory Medals.
"Salisbury Arms," Wellington Street, Luton. 1877.

McDONALD, F., Private, Suffolk Regiment.
Volunteering in August 1914, he went through a course of training and was later drafted overseas. During his service on the Western Front he took part in many notable engagements, and was wounded at Loos. On recovery he rejoined his battalion, and was in action during the final stages of the war. He was demobilised in March 1919, and holds the General Service and Victory Medals.
113, Ash Road, Luton. 1878.

McDONNEL, A., Private, R.A.S.C.
He joined in July 1916, and after a period of training was drafted to Egypt, where he was stationed at Kantara and Alexandria. He subsequently joined in the British Advance through Palestine under General Allenby, and was present at the entry into Jerusalem. He returned to England after the cessation of hostilities, and was demobilised in March 1919, holding the General Service and Victory Medals.
17, Lea Road, Luton. 1879.

McGRATH, J. C., Private, R.A.S.C. (M.T.)
He volunteered in 1916, and after training served at various stations on important duties. Disabled from active service by a fractured knee cap, he was employed on the depôt staff, and after doing good work for three years was demobilised in February 1919.
26, High Street, Redbourne. 2983/C.

MACGREGOR, F. (Mrs.), Special War Worker.
During the war this lady offered her services for work of National importance, and from September 1915 until November 1918 was engaged at the Explosive Works, Chaul End, Luton. Engaged on the inspecting staff, she carried out her responsible duties in a thoroughly efficient manner throughout her period of service.
9, Bedford Road, Houghton Regis, Dunstable. 908-9-10/B.

McKEE, S., Gunner, Royal Field Artillery.
He joined in May 1916, and six months later was drafted overseas to France. Whilst on the Western Front he was engaged in the heavy fighting on the Somme, at Arras, Ypres and the Retreat, and subsequent Advance of the Allies into Germany. He returned to England, and was demobilised in April 1919. He holds the General Service and Victory Medals.
46, Ashton Road, Luton. 1880.

MACKEY, T., Pte., 27th Durham Light Infantry.
He joined in November 1916, and after his training was engaged on important coast defence duties at various stations with his unit. Owing to physical disability he was unable to secure his transfer to a theatre of war, but rendered valuable services until March 1919, when he was demobilised.
"The Piggeries," Tilsworth, Beds. 2477.

McMILLEN, R., Sapper, Royal Engineers (E.A.)
Volunteering in September 1914, he served at various stations on important duties with his unit until drafted overseas. He was engaged on the Western Front, and was employed on special duties in many notable engagements until after the signing of the Armistice. During his overseas service he was wounded. He was demobilised in March 1919, and holds the General Service and Victory Medals.
26, Dane Road, Luton. 1881.

McNEILL, H. B., Private, R.A.S.C., and 23rd Middlesex Regiment.
He volunteered in June 1915, and was later sent to Ireland, where he served during the Dublin Riots. He subsequently went to the Western Front, and was engaged in the fighting on the Somme, and in the Retreat and Advance of 1918. After the signing of the Armistice he was stationed at Cologne with the Army of Occupation on the Rhine. He was demobilised in July 1919, and holds the General Service and Victory Medals.
35, Cromwell Road, Luton. 1882/B.

McNEILL, W. J., Private, Machine Gun Corps.
He joined in August 1916, and was later sent to France. He took part in the heavy fighting on the Somme, and in the Retreat and subsequent Allied Advance at Cambrai in 1918. He afterwards proceeded with the Army of Occupation into Germany, and remained there until he was demobilised in October 1919. He holds the General Service and Victory Medals.
86, Ash Road, Luton. 1882/A.

McPHEAT, J., Sergeant, 2nd Bedfordshire Regt.
Volunteering in August 1914, he was drafted to the Dardanelles in the following year and was present at the landing at Suvla Bay and the subsequent engagements until the Evacuation of the Peninsula. He was later transferred to the Western Front and took part in the engagements at Ypres and Messines, until he was unfortunately killed in action on June 7th, 1917. He was entitled to the 1914-15 Star, and the General Service and Victory Medals.
33, John Street, Luton. 1883/A.

McPHEAT, M., A.B., Royal Navy.
Volunteering in May 1915, he joined the 10th Cruiser Squadron and was engaged on blockade duties from September 1915 till June 1916. His ship was then employed on convoy duties from Canada, the United States, Brazil, and Africa to England and France. He was demobilised in January 1919, and holds the 1914-15 Star, and the General Service and Victory Medals.
33, John Street, Luton. 1883/B.

McVEY, J. (Miss), Special War Worker.
For a period of nearly four years this lady was engaged on work of National importance at Messrs. George Kent's munition factory, Luton. She carried out her duties, which were in connection with the inspection of fuses, with great skill and efficiency, and she was much appreciated for her services.
151, Dallow Road, Luton. 1884/B.

McVEY, A., Corporal, 11th Queen's (Royal West Surrey Regiment).
He joined in August 1918 on attaining military age and after completing his training was drafted overseas after the signing of the Armistice. He served with the Army of Occupation at Cologne on important garrison duties until demobilised in March 1920, after returning to England.
151, Dallow Road, Luton.   1885/C.

McVEY, M. (Miss), Special War Worker.
During the war, for a period of eighteen months, this lady was engaged on important work at Messrs. George Kent's factory, Luton. Her duties, which were in connection with the gauging of fuses, were carried out with great care and skill and she received high commendation for the services she rendered.
151, Dallow Road, Luton.   1884/A.

McVEY, T. N., L/Corporal, 1/5th Bedfordshire Regiment, and 1/4th Dorsetshire Regiment.
He volunteered at the outbreak of war and was employed on various duties with his regiment until January 1916, when he was sent overseas He served in Mesopotamia for a time, and owing to ill-health was invalided to Bombay in December 1917. On recovery he was drafted to Salonika and there was engaged in the fighting on the Vardar Front. He returned to England and was demobilised in March 1919, and holds the General Service and Victory Medals.
151, Dallow Road, Luton.   1885/A.

McVEY, W. M., Private, R.A.M.C.
He volunteered in October 1915, and in the following June was drafted to France. In this theatre of war he was engaged on important ambulance duties in the forward areas, and was present at the Battles of Ypres, Cambrai, Arras and on the Somme. He was demobilised in May 1919, and holds the General Service and Victory Medals.
151, Dallow Road, Luton   1885/B.

MADDAMS, W., Sergeant, Bedfordshire Regt., attached Machine Gun Corps.
He volunteered in September 1914, and after serving at various stations with his unit was sent to the Western Front in January 1916. Whilst overseas he fought at Arras, Ypres, and Merville, and was wounded at Havrincourt in April 1916. After hospital treatment he returned to France in December 1916, and was in action in many important engagements until the close of the war. He was demobilised in February 1919, and holds the General Service and Victory Medals.
36, Florence Street, Hitchin.   1886.

MADDOX, H., Private, R.A.S.C.
He joined in 1916, and after completing his training was engaged with his unit on various duties at several stations. He was unable to obtain his transfer overseas owing to unfitness for active service, and was demobilised in April 1919.
7, Inkerman Road, St. Albans.   X1887.

MADDOX, J. R., Private, R.A.S.C. (M.T.)
He volunteered in October 1914, and in the same month was drafted to France, where he was engaged with his unit in several sectors while heavy fighting was in progress. He was employed in the transport of ammunition and supplies to the forward areas and was present at the Battles of Ypres, Arras, Cambrai and La Bassée. He was demobilised in May 1919, and holds the 1914-15 Star, and the General Service and Victory Medals.
18, Brixton Road, Watford.   X1888.

MAGEE, W., Flight-Sergeant, Royal Air Force.
He was mobilised on the outbreak of war and after his training served with his Squadron at Chingford on important duties which called for great technical skill. He did good work, but was not successful in obtaining his transfer overseas owing to medical unfitness. He was demobilised in June 1919.
18, St. Mary's Road, Watford.   X1889.

MAHONEY, A., Private, Royal Irish Fusiliers.
He was mobilised on the declaration of war, and in September 1914 was drafted to France, where he took part in heavy fighting and was twice wounded. He was later sent to Salonika and was in action in several engagements, and was again wounded. In October 1918, he was taken prisoner and sent to Philippopolis. When released from captivity, on the termination of hostilities, he returned to England and was demobilised in June 1919, holding the 1914 Star, and the General Service and Victory Medals.
31, Sun Street, Biggleswade.   Z1890.

MAIDMENT, A. H., Private, Royal Defence Corps.
He volunteered in August 1915, and being unfit for active service was posted to the Royal Defence Corps, in which he did good work on guard, and other important duties, at various stations until he was demobilised in 1919.
The Green, Ickwell, near Biggleswade.   Z1891/A.

MAILES, J., Private, Lancashire Fusiliers.
Joining in March 1917, he was sent in the following September to the Western Front. He fought in the first Battle of Cambrai and in the second Battle of the Somme, where he was wounded and sent to hospital at Boulogne. On his recovery he rejoined his unit and took part in the Retreat and Advance of 1918. He was demobilised in March 1919, and holds the General Service and Victory Medals.
59, High Street, Markyate.   1344/A.

MAILING, A. P., Private, Bedfordshire Regt. and Lancashire Fusiliers.
He volunteered in September 1914, and was engaged on important duties with his unit at various stations until drafted to France in 1917. He served in many sectors of the Western Front and fought in several important battles, including those of Ypres, the Somme, Passchendaele and Cambrai, and was once wounded. Returning to England at the end of the war he was demobilised in January 1919, and holds the General Service and Victory Medals.
7, Bun Street, Luton.   1892, 1893.

MAIR, A. W., Private, R.A.S.C.
He joined in April 1917, and in the following October was sent to the Western Front. There he was engaged with his unit on important transport duties in various sectors and was present among other actions at the Battle of Ypres. He returned to England on the cessation of hostilities, and was demobilised in November 1919. He holds the General Service and Victory Medals
82, Ashton Road, Luton.   1894.

MAJOR, H., Chief Petty Officer, Royal Navy.
Joining in June 1918, he was posted to the Motor Boat Service, and employed on important patrol duties in various waters. After serving in the Mediterranean, and at Turkish and other stations he was demobilised in December 1919, and holds the General Service and Victory Medals.
6, Pondswick Road, Luton.   1895.

MAJOR, L. W., Private, 7th Bedfordshire Regt.
He volunteered in September 1914, and in the following February was drafted to the Western Front. In this theatre of war he took part in heavy fighting on the Somme and at Arras. He was unfortunately wounded and taken prisoner in April 1917. He was released from captivity in Germany shortly after the conclusion of hostilities and was demobilised in March 1919, holding the 1914-15 Star, and the General Service and Victory Medals.
24, Regent Street, Leighton Buzzard.   1896.

MAJOR, T., Sergeant, 2/5th Suffolk Regiment.
He volunteered in September 1914, but at the conclusion of his training was found to be physically unfit for overseas service. For nearly three years, however, he was engaged on duties of a special nature with his unit at various stations, and during this time was promoted to the rank of Sergeant for his efficient work. He was invalided out of the service in September 1917.
39, Church Street, Leighton Buzzard.   2475.

MAJOR, T., Sapper, Royal Engineers.
Volunteering in August 1914, he was drafted in the following January to the Western Front, where he did useful work in the forward areas. He was engaged with his unit in road construction and trench digging, and was present at the Battles of the Somme, Arras, Ypres and Cambrai. He returned to England for demobilisation in March 1919, and holds the 1914-15 Star, and the General Service and Victory Medals.
8, Chapel Path, Leighton Buzzard.   1897.

MAKEPEACE, C., Staff-Sergeant, R.A.S.C.(M.T.)
He joined in July 1916, and in the following December was drafted to Mesopotamia. He did most useful work in this theatre of war in connection with the transport of supplies and ammunition to the forward areas, and was present at the Battles of Ramadieh, Shahraban and the occupation of Mosul. He returned to England in September 1919, and was demobilised in the following January. He holds the General Service and Victory Medals.
14, Cardiff Road, Watford.   X1898/B.

MAKEPEACE, A., 1st Air Mechanic, R.A.F.
He joined in July 1918, and in the following month was sent to Egypt. There he was engaged upon engine repairs at the aerodromes at Abalka, Alexandria and Helouan, near Cairo. He returned to England for demobilisation in April 1919, and holds the General Service and Victory Medals.
14, Cardiff Road, Watford. X1898/A.

MALACRIDA, A., Rifleman, Royal Irish Rifles.
He joined in 1917, and in the same year was sent to France. He served with his unit in various sectors, and was in action in several important engagements, including those on the Somme, at Arras and Cambrai, and was wounded. He returned to England for demobilisation in January 1919, and holds the General Service and Victory Medals.
15, Greatham Road, Bushey. X1899/B.

MALACRIDA, P., Corporal, 7th London Regt. (Labour Corps).
Volunteering in September 1914, in the following March he was drafted to the Western Front, where he took part in heavy fighting around Ypres, and was wounded at Festubert. Rejoining his unit after hospital treatment he was engaged on important duties at Ypres and in other sectors until the termination of the war. He was demobilised in January 1919, and holds the 1914-15 Star, and the General Service and Victory Medals.
15, Greatham Road, Bushey. X1899/A.

MALES, F., Corporal, Bedfordshire Regiment.
Mobilised in August 1914, he was shortly afterwards drafted to the Western Front, where he fought in the Retreat from Mons and in the Battles of La Bassée, Ypres, Hill 60, and was wounded. Returning to his unit on recovery, he took part in heavy fighting at Vimy Ridge, Cambrai and in other sectors. During this period he was again wounded. On the cessation of hostilities he returned to England, was demobilised in November 1919, and holds the Mons Star, and the General Service and Victory Medals.
Batford Cottages, Lower Luton Road, Harpenden.
3011/A.

MALES, H., Private, 1st Duke of Cornwall's Light Infantry.
He volunteered in April 1915, and shortly afterwards was drafted to the Western Front, where he took part in many engagements in various sectors. During the fighting at Hill 60 he was severely wounded, and as a result invalided home. After several months in hospital he was finally discharged on June 28th, 1916, being medically unfit for further service. He holds the 1914-15 Star, and the General Service and Victory Medals.
2, Bedford Street, Hitchin. 1900.

MALES, L., Private, 17th South Lancashire Regt.
He joined in September 1917, but owing to physical disability was on completion of his training retained on important transport duties. In this capacity he was stationed at various places in England and rendered services of a valuable nature until February 1919, when he was demobilised.
35, Highbury Road, Hitchin. 2472.

MALEY, D., Private, Royal Fusiliers.
He volunteered in January 1916, and in the same year was drafted overseas. During his service on the Western Front he took part in heavy fighting in several engagements, and was reported missing on February 7th, 1917. He was later presumed to have been killed in action on that date, and was entitled to the General Service and Victory Medals.
26, Water Lane, Watford. X3693/B.

MALONE, G., Corporal, Royal Engineers.
Volunteering in August 1914, he was engaged on important duties in connection with the East Coast defence, where he rendered valuable services. Owing to ill-health he was unable to secure his transfer overseas, and in October 1916 was discharged as medically unfit for further service.
158, Dallow Road, Luton. 1901.

MALONEY, C. A., Private, Royal Fusiliers.
Volunteering at the outbreak of war, he was sent to France in January 1915, and took part in various engagements, and was wounded at Ypres in March. On recovery, drafted to Gallipoli he was in action at the landing at Suvla Bay and in the subsequent actions until wounded. After hospital treatment at Malta he returned to France, and saw much fighting, and was wounded a third time at Cambrai in March 1918. Invalided to England he received hospital treatment, and was demobilised in January 1919. He holds the 1914-15 Star, and the General Service and Victory Medals.
17, New England Street, St. Albans. 1902.

MALTBY, R., Private, Labour Corps.
He volunteered in May 1915, and after training was drafted to France in September of the following year. He was engaged on important duties in the forward areas in several sectors of the Western Front, and was present at the Battles of the Somme, Arras, Vimy Ridge, Bullecourt, Amiens and Cambrai. He was demobilised in January 1919 on his return to England, and holds the General Service and Victory Medals.
3, Stanley Street, Luton. 1903.

MANGER, T. H., Sergeant, R.A.S.C.
He joined in 1916 and after completing his training was engaged at Chatham on important clerical duties with his unit. He was not sent overseas before the cessation of hostilities, and in 1920 was still serving, carrying out responsible duties at the regimental depôt.
28, Cavendish Road, St. Albans. X1904.

MANN, F. C., Private, R.A.M.C.
An old soldier who had fought in the South African Campaign, he volunteered in November 1914, and being unfit for active service was posted to the R.A.M.C. He was employed on important postal duties at Blackpool, and did good work until his demobilisation in February 1919. He holds the South African Medals (with two clasps for the Relief of Mafeking and Ladysmith).
207, Park Street, Luton. 1905.

MANN, H., Private, 2nd Leicester Regiment.
He joined in 1916, and was drafted to India where he took part in several actions against the rebel tribes on the North-West Frontier. In 1917 he was sent to Mesopotamia and from there to Egypt and Palestine. He fought in many of the principal engagements of the Advance under General Allenby, and on the termination of hostilities returned to England for demobilisation in 1919. He holds the General Service and Victory Medals.
Hexton Road, Barton, near Ampthill. 1906.

MANNING, A. E., Sapper, Royal Engineers.
Volunteering in November 1914, he was drafted to the Western Front in the following year and was engaged on important duties in many sectors. He was employed with his unit in the forward areas while heavy fighting was in progress, and was present, amongst other actions, at the Battles of the Somme, Ypres, Arras, and Cambrai. Demobilised in February 1919, on his return to England, he holds the 1914-15 Star, and the General Service and Victory Medals.
127, Ridgeway Road, Luton. 1907.

MANNING, C., Private, 2nd Royal Inniskilling Fusiliers.
He enlisted in 1912, and at the outbreak of hostilities was sent overseas. He was present during the fighting in the Retreat from Mons, and at the Battles of the Marne, Ypres, Festubert, Loos, Albert, the Somme, and in the fighting during the German Offensive and Allied Advance of 1918. He is still serving and holds the Mons Star, the General Service and Victory Medals.
8, Bethel Lane, Hitchin, Herts. 2471/A.

MANNING, H. G., Private, 9th Cheshire Regt.
Volunteering in April 1915, he was engaged on important duties with his unit at various stations until drafted to France in December of the following year. He took part in various engagements, including those on the Somme, at Ypres, Arras, and Cambrai, and was wounded and invalided home to hospital in April 1918. After treatment he was demobilised in March 1919, and holds the General Service and Victory Medals.
34, Hastings Street, Luton. 1908.

MANNING, J. H., Private, Bedfordshire Regiment.
Mobilised at the outbreak of war, he was engaged on duties of an important nature until January 1915, when he was drafted to Egypt. Here, he took part in several minor engagements, and later was sent to Palestine, where, with General Allenby's forces, he fought at Gaza, Jaffa, and on the Jordan, also taking part in the capture of Jerusalem. On one occasion he was badly wounded, but after receiving treatment at the base, was able to rejoin his unit. He holds the 1914-15 Star, and the General Service and Victory Medals, and in 1920 was still serving.
8, Bethel Lane, Hitchin, Herts. 2471/C.

MANNING, L., Private, 1st Hertfordshire Regt.
He volunteered in September 1914, and after his training served with his battalion and was stationed at various depôts employed on important duties. He rendered valuable services and was later transferred to the Labour Corps, but owing to medical unfitness was unable to obtain his transfer overseas. He was discharged in consequence in July 1918.
8, Bethel Lane, Hitchin, Herts. 2471/B.

MANNING, S., Private, 11th Essex Regiment.
He volunteered in January 1916, and after his training was sent to France. In that theatre of war he was engaged in heavy fighting in several sectors and was, unfortunately, killed in action at the Battle of St. Quentin on September 18th, 1918. He was entitled to the General Service and Victory Medals.
2, Balmoral Road, Hitchin. 1909/A.

MANNING, S., Private, Grenadier Guards.
He volunteered in May 1915, and after completing a course of training was drafted to the Western Front, where he served with his unit in various sectors. He fought in the Battles of Arras, Cambrai, St. Quentin, and in many other engagements of the final stages of the war. He was demobilised in February 1919, on returning to England, and holds the General Service and Victory Medals.
2, Balmoral Road, Hitchin. 1909/B.

MANNING, W., Private, 3rd Bedfordshire Regt., and 2nd South Wales Borderers.
He volunteered in July 1915, and in the following year was drafted to the Western Front. He saw much service in this theatre of war, and took part in several engagements, including those at Arras and Ypres, and was wounded. Returning to England on account of wounds, he was under medical treatment for a time, and discharged as unfit for further service in July 1918. He holds the General Service and Victory Medals.
2, Nursery Cottages, Old Bedford Road, Luton.
1407/A.

MANNING, W., Sergt., 1/5th Lincolnshire Regt.
Volunteering in September 1914, in the following year he was sent to France. There he was in action in several important engagements, including those of Arras, Ypres and Cambrai, and was three times wounded and gassed. Sent home on account of his wounds and gas-poisoning, he was under medical treatment for a considerable time and was discharged unfit for further service in December 1918, and holds the 1914-15 Star, and the General Service and Victory Medals.
19, Dordans Road, Leagrave. 1910.

MANNING, W. G., Pioneer, Royal Engineers.
He volunteered in June 1915, and in the following March was sent to the Western Front, where he was engaged on important duties in the forward areas. He took part in heavy fighting at Ypres and Messines amongst other important battles, and returned to England on the cessation of hostilities. He was demobilised in February 1919, and holds the General Service and Victory Medals.
64, Frederic Street, Luton. 1911.

MANSFIELD, L. M., 2nd Lieut., Labour Corps.
He volunteered in October 1914, and in the following January was drafted to France. During his service on the Western Front he took part in many important engagements and was granted a commission in the Labour Corps after its inception in 1917. He was placed in charge of a company engaged in making roads and railway tracks in the Somme, Arras and Cambrai sectors, and rendered valuable services. He was demobilised in May 1919, and holds the Long Service and Good Conduct Medal, also the 1914-15 Star, and the General Service and Victory Medals.
1, Houghton Road, Dunstable. 1912.

MANTELL, G. B., Private, 17th (Duke of Cambridge's Own) Lancers.
He joined in July 1918, and after a period of training served with his unit on important duties at various stations until February 1919, when he was drafted to Germany to the Army of Occupation and was stationed at Cologne. He returned home in November 1919, and was demobilised.
82, Oak Road, Luton. 1913.

MANTON, S., L/Corporal, 25th Middlesex Regt.
He volunteered in July 1915, and in the following year was drafted overseas. During his service on the Western Front he took part in the fighting at Loos, Ypres and on the Somme, and was wounded. He was later sent with the Relief Force to Russia, where he served until 1919. He returned home and was demobilised in November of that year, and holds the General Service and Victory Medals.
34, Dumfries Street, Luton. 1914.

MAPP, E. G., 1st Class Stoker, Royal Navy.
He joined in December 1917, and was posted to H.M.S. "Valentine," which ship was engaged in the North and Baltic Seas on important patrol duties. His ship was also employed in chasing enemy submarines, and had other encounters with the German Fleet. He was demobilised in July 1919, and holds the General Service and Victory Medals.
8, Park Road, Bushey, Herts. X1915.

MARCH, F., Sergeant, 29th Middlesex Regiment.
He volunteered in October 1914, having previously served in the South African War, and was engaged at various stations on important duties with his unit. He did good work, but was unsuccessful in obtaining his transfer overseas on account of ill-health. He was invalided to hospital, and subsequently died on April 14th, 1917.
82, Estcourt Road, Watford. X1916.

MARCH, F. (Miss), Private, Q.M.A.A.C.
She joined in June 1917, and was engaged at various stations on important clerical duties with her unit. She rendered valuable services but was unable to secure a transfer abroad, and was demobilised in January 1920.
38, Stuart Street, Luton. 1917/A.

MARCH, F. J., Private, Oxfordshire and Buckinghamshire Light Infantry.
He was serving at the outbreak of war, and in March 1915 was drafted to France. During his service in this theatre of war he fought at Ypres, Loos and on the Somme, and was twice wounded. He was later transferred to the R.A.S.C. (M.T.), with which unit he served on the Western Front until April 1919 when he returned home and was demobilised. He holds the 1914-15 Star, and the General Service and Victory Medals.
38, Stuart Street, Luton. 1917/B.

MARCH, S., Private, R.A.S.C.
He volunteered in November 1914, and in the following month was sent to France. He served in many sectors of the Western Front, and was present at engagements at Ypres, Neuve Chapelle, Loos, Vimy Ridge, Albert, the Ancre, Messines, Cambrai, and on the Somme. He returned to England, and was demobilised in March 1919, and holds the 1914-15 Star, and the General Service and Victory Medals.
17, Liverpool Road, Luton. 1918/C.

MARCHANT, H. W., Private, Hertfordshire Regt.
Volunteering at the outbreak of war, he was shortly afterwards sent to France. He took part in the heavy fighting at Arras, on the Somme, at Cambrai, Ypres and the subsequent engagements, until killed in action at Cambrai on March 22nd, 1918. He was entitled to the 1914 Star, and the General Service and Victory Medals.
52, Ratcliffe Road, Hitchin, Herts. 1919.

MARDEL, A. E., Private, 2nd Suffolk Regiment.
He volunteered in January 1915, and in the same year was drafted to France. During his service on the Western Front he fought in many battles, including those at Ypres and Arras. He was killed in action on the Aisne on April 21st, 1918, and was entitled to the 1914-15 Star, and the General Service and Victory Medals.
Myrtle Cottage, London Colney. X1920, X1921.

MARDELL, H., Sergeant, R.A.S.C.
He joined in March 1916, and in the following month proceeded overseas. He was engaged on important duties with his unit in many sectors of the Western Front, including that of Poperinghe, and he remained in this theatre of war until 1919. He returned home, and was demobilised in October of the same year, and holds the General Service and Victory Medals.
The Odd Fellows' Arms, Dunstable Place, Luton. 1922.

MARDELL, S. L., Gunner, R.G.A.
He volunteered in 1914, and in the following year was drafted to France. During his service on the Western Front he took part in much heavy fighting at Ypres, Arras, Vimy Ridge, Passchendaele, Cambrai, and in the Retreat and Advance of 1918, and was wounded. He was demobilised in 1919, and holds the 1914-15 Star, and the General Service and Victory Medals.
19, Bernard Street, St. Albans. X1923.

MARDELL, W., Private, 3rd Bedfordshire Regt.
He volunteered in September 1914, and in the following year proceeded to France. He fought in the Battles of Arras, Ypres, Armentières, and in 1917 was transferred to Egypt. He served in the British Advance through Palestine under General Allenby, and was in action in the Battle of Gaza. He returned to England and was demobilised in July 1919, and holds the 1914-15 Star, and the General Service and Victory Medals.
15, Mimram Road, Welwyn. 1924.

MARDLE, A. G., Driver, Royal Field Artillery.
He joined in April 1916, and in the following year proceeded to the Western Front. He served in many sectors, and took part in much heavy fighting in this theatre of war and was severely burnt by liquid fire. He was invalided to hospital in England, and after some months of hospital treatment was discharged on account of service in December 1918, and holds the General Service and Victory Medals.
18, Althorpe Road, Luton. 1925.

MARDLE, H., Private, 3rd Essex Regiment.
He joined in August 1918, and after his training served at various stations on important guard and other duties with his unit. He did good work, but was unable to secure a transfer overseas before the cessation of hostilities, and was demobilised in March 1919.
38, Alexandra Road, St. Albans. X1926.

MARDLE, H., Pte., 28th Durham Light Infantry.
He joined in September 1916, and at the conclusion of his training served at various stations on important coastal patrol duties with his unit, chiefly on the East Coast. He rendered valuable services, but was unsuccessful in obtaining his transfer to a theatre of war, and was demobilised in February 1919.
71, Cambridge Street, Luton. 1927.

MARDLE, W., Private, 2nd Essex Regiment.
He joined in June 1916, and in the following October proceeded to France. Whilst on the Western Front he fought at Ypres, and the subsequent Battle of the Somme, and many other engagements until the cessation of hostilities. He was demobilised in March 1919, and holds the General Service and Victory Medals.
2, Buxton Road, Luton. 1928.

MARDLIN, W., Gunner, Royal Garrison Artillery.
He joined in March 1918, and after his training served at various stations on general home service duties with his unit. He was unable to secure a transfer overseas on account of medical unfitness, but he did good work until demobilised in March 1919.
37, Heath Road, Leighton Buzzard. 1929.

MARDLING, T. E., Private, 4th Middlesex Regt.
Volunteering at the outbreak of war he was almost immediately drafted to France, where he fought in the Retreat from Mons and was wounded and taken prisoner. He suffered many hardships during his long captivity in Germany, and was released after the signing of the Armistice and returning to England was demobilised in April 1919. He holds the Mons Star, and the General Service and Victory Medals.
7, Chapman Terrace, Hatfield. X1930.

MARKS, A., L/Corporal, Bedfordshire Regiment, and Labour Corps.
He volunteered in September 1914, and in the following year proceeded to France. He was engaged on important duties at various stations on the Western Front, as he was over age for service in the trenches. He was demobilised in May 1919, and holds the 1914-15 Star, and the General Service and Victory Medals.
23, Chequer Street, Luton. 1931 A.

MARKS, A. F., L/Cpl., 1/5th Bedfordshire Regt.
He was serving at the outbreak of war, having enlisted in January 1913, and in 1915 was drafted to the Dardanelles. He took part in the fighting at the landing at Suvla Bay and the subsequent engagements until the Evacuation of the Peninsula. He was then sent to France and fought on the Somme, and at Cambrai, and during the final stages of the war. He was demobilised in February 1919, and holds the 1914-15 Star, and the General Service and Victory Medals.
23, Chequer Street, Luton. 1931/B.

MARKS, H., Sergeant, Royal Field Artillery.
Volunteering in August 1914, he was almost immediately drafted to France. He fought in the Retreat from Mons and the Battles of the Marne and Ypres. He was sent to Salonica in 1915, and in this theatre of war was engaged in the fighting on the Vardar and Doiran Fronts and in the Battle of Monastir. He was demobilised in May 1919, and holds the Mons Star, and the General Service and Victory Medals.
Thatch Cottages, Cumberland Road, Leagrave. 1932.

MARLOW, A. C., Pte., 2/4th Hampshire Regt.
He volunteered in September 1914, and in the following September proceeded to Salonika. He took part in much heavy fighting on the Macedonian Front and was wounded. He was later transferred to the Western Front and fought in various engagements until killed in action at Arras, on August 30th. 1918. He was entitled to the 1914-15 Star, and the General Service and Victory Medals.
Chestnut Row, Lilley, near Luton. 1933.

MARLOW, C., Private, Bedfordshire Regiment.
He volunteered in June 1915, and in the following November proceeded to France. During his service on the Western Front he fought in various engagements, including those on the Somme, at Ypres, Arras, Passchendaele, and in the German Offensive and subsequent Allied Advance of 1918. He was demobilised in February 1919, and holds the 1914-15 Star, and the General Service and Victory Medals.
Upper Sundon, near Dunstable. 1937/B.

MARLOW, G., Cpl., 1/5th Bedfordshire Regt.
He volunteered in September 1914, and in the following July was drafted to the Dardanelles. He took part in the fighting at the landing at Suvla Bay and the subsequent engagements until the Evacuation of the Peninsula. He was later sent to Egypt, and served under General Allenby in the Advance through Palestine, and fought at Gaza, El Arish, Haifa and Aleppo, and was wounded. He was discharged on account of service in May 1919, and holds the 1914-15 Star, and the General Service and Victory Medals.
86, Reginald Street, Luton. 1934/B.

MARLOW, H., Private, 5th Bedfordshire Regt.
He volunteered in September 1914, and in the following year was drafted to the Dardanelles. He fought at the landing at Suvla Bay, and was severely wounded in action at Chocolate Hill. He was invalided home and after receiving hospital treatment was discharged as medically unfit for further service in May 1916. He holds the 1914-15 Star, and the General Service and Victory Medals.
15, Cavendish Road, Luton. 1935.

MARLOW, J., Private, 9th King's Own (Royal Lancaster Regiment).
He volunteered in September 1914, and after his training was employed on important duties at various stations until drafted to Salonika in 1917. He took part in the heavy fighting in the operations on the Vardar front until February 1918. He then returned to England where he served until demobilised in December of that year. He holds the General Service and Victory Medals.
62, Hartley Road, Luton. 1936.

MARLOW, S., Private, 1/4th Essex Regiment.
He volunteered in May 1915, and in the following July was drafted to Egypt. Here he served with his battalion and was engaged in the British Advance through Palestine under General Allenby until killed in action at the Battle of Gaza on October 29th, 1917. He was entitled to the 1914-15 Star, and the General Service and Victory Medals.
Upper Sundon, near Dunstable. 1937/A.

MARLOW, W. C. (M.M.), C.S.M., 1/5th Bedfordshire Regiment.
He volunteered in September 1914, and in the following August was sent to Gallipoli. In this theatre of war he fought at the landing at Suvla Bay and the operations which followed. He was later sent to Egypt where he was in action at El Arish, Gaza, Mejdel, Haifa, Damascus and Beyrout, and was mentioned in Despatches and awarded the Military Medal for conspicuous bravery and devotion to duty in the Field. He also holds the 1914-15 Star, and the General Service and Victory Medals, and was demobilised in April 1919.
86, Reginald Street, Luton. 1934/C.

MARLOW, W. G., Driver, Royal Engineers.
He volunteered in November 1915, and served at various stations until drafted to France in March 1917. In this theatre of war he was engaged on important duties in connection with operations and served on the Somme, and was severely wounded at Albert in July 1918. He was invalided home to hospital, where he remained for a time, and on recovery was demobilised in January 1919. He holds the General Service and Victory Medals.
8, Bailey Street, Luton. 1938.

MARLOW, W. H., L/Corporal, 8th West Yorkshire Regiment
He volunteered in September 1914, and after his training served at various stations until drafted to France in 1917. During his service on the Western Front he fought on the Somme, at Cambrai, St. Quentin and in the Retreat and Advance of 1918, and after the cessation of hostilities proceeded with the Army of Occupation to Germany and was stationed at Cologne. He returned home and was demobilised in March 1919, and holds the General Service and Victory Medals.
86, Reginald Street, Luton. 1934/A.

MARRIOTT, C. T., Private, Loyal North Lancashire Regiment.
He volunteered in November 1915, and in the following January proceeded to France. Whilst in this theatre of war he was in action in numerous engagements, including those during the Somme Offensive in 1916, and was wounded. After recovery he rejoined his battalion and fought at Arras, Cambrai, and in the German Offensive and subsequent Allied Advance of 1918, and was again wounded. He afterwards served with the Army of Occupation and was stationed at Cologne until March 1919, when he returned home and was demobilised. He holds the General Service and Victory Medals.
Rushmere, near Leighton Buzzard. 2095/A.

MARRIOTT, A. E., Cpl., 1st Hertfordshire Regt.
He volunteered in September 1914, and in the following August proceeded to France. During his service on the Western Front he took part in the heavy fighting at Ypres, Loos, on the Somme, at Arras, Albert and in the Retreat and Advance of 1918. He was demobilised in February 1919, and holds the 1914-15 Star, and the General Service and Victory Medals.
3, Sutton Road, Watford.   X1939.

MARRIOTT, F., Pte., Royal Army Cyclist Corps.
He volunteered in November 1915, and in the following March proceeded to Salonica, where he fought in numerous engagements on the Vardar and Struma Fronts, and was twice wounded and also suffered from malaria. After hostilities ceased he returned to England, and was demobilised in 1919, and holds the General Service and Victory Medals.
147, New Colony Road, New Town, Dartford, Kent.
     2095/B.

MARRIS, J. P., Private, R.A.S.C.
He volunteered in November 1915, and was later drafted to Egypt. He was engaged on important duties with his unit in the forward areas during the British Advance through Palestine, and served at the Battle of Gaza, and in the fighting near Jerusalem. He was demobilised in August 1919, and holds the General and Victory Medals.
39, Ridge Road, Letchworth.   1940.

MARSDEN, F., Sergeant, Essex Regiment.
He volunteered in May 1915, and on completion of his training was drafted to the Western Front. Here he fought in several important engagements, notably those at Albert and Cambrai, and was in action almost continuously until he contracted a severe form of influenza, of which he subsequently died at the 66th Clearing Station, on November 2nd, 1918. He was entitled to the General Service and Victory Medals.
Nosellen Cottages, Landy Road, Potton, Beds.   Z1941.

MARSH, C. J., Private, 1st Hertfordshire Regt.
He volunteered in November 1915, and after his training was engaged on duties of an important nature until he was sent to the Western Front in March 1917. His service overseas lasted for two years, and during this time he took part in many notable battles, including those of Arras, Ypres and Passchendaele Ridge. Returning to England, he was demobilised in March 1919, and holds the General Service and Victory Medals.
13, Lower Dagnall Street, St. Albans.   X1942.

MARSH, R., Private, Royal Scots.
He volunteered in August 1914, and was almost immediately drafted to the Western Front. He took part in the fighting in the Retreat from Mons, and the subsequent Battles of Ypres, Arras, Hill 60 and Loos, and was wounded. He returned home in December 1915, and served at various stations with his battalion until after the signing of the Armistice. He was demobilised in February 1919, and holds the Mons Star, and the General Service and Victory Medals.
85, Judge Street, Watford.   X4130/A.

MARSH, W., Private, 1st Bedfordshire Regiment.
He was mobilised on the outbreak of war, and almost immediately sent to France. There he took part in the Retreat from Mons, and in the heavy fighting which followed. He was also engaged in the Battles of Neuve Chapelle, Arras, Bullecourt, Cambrai, and in other actions until the end of the war. He was demobilised in February 1919, on his return to England, and holds the Mons Star, and the General Service and Victory Medals.
42, Ebury Road, Watford.   X2994/B.

MARSHALL, A., Private, 14th Welch Regiment.
He was mobilised at the declaration of war, and until January 1917 served on home duties with his battalion at various stations. He was then drafted to France, and took part in many engagements and was twice wounded. He later fought on the Somme, where he was killed in action in August 1918. He was entitled to the General Service and Victory Medals.
10, Queen Square, Luton.   593/A.

MARSHALL, B., Private, Bedfordshire Regiment.
Volunteering in August 1915, he joined the Worcestershire Regiment, and served in France from June 1916 until the following December, when on his return to England he was discharged as under age. In December 1917, however, he re-joined, and was again sent to the Western Front, where he fought in many important engagements, including those at Cambrai, St. Quentin and the Somme, and in the Retreat and Advance of 1918, after which he went to Germany with the Army of Occupation. Later he was transferred to India, where in 1920 he was still serving. He holds the General Service and Victory Medals.
31, Park Road West, Luton.   1943.

MARSHALL, F. G., Bombardier, R.F.A.
Joining in April 1916, he was drafted to France in the following December. He there took part in many important engagements, and was severely wounded in October 1917. The following year he returned to France, and served in the Retreat and Advance of 1918, during which action he took part in much heavy fighting. In September 1919 he returned to England, and was demobilised the following month. He holds the General Service and Victory Medals.
33, Spencer Road, Luton.   1944.

MARSHALL, F. J., Private, Bedfordshire Regt., and Hertfordshire Regiment.
He joined in September 1917, and shortly afterwards was sent to the Western Front, where he took part in several important engagements during the Retreat and Advance of 1918, notably the actions at Cambrai and on the Somme. After the Armistice he was drafted to India, and was stationed at Poona and Rawal-Pindi. In 1920 he was still serving in India, and holds the General Service and Victory Medals.
42, Park Road West, Luton.   1945/A.

MARSHALL, G., Pte., 1/5th Bedfordshire Regt.
He volunteered in August 1914, and in the following year was sent to Gallipoli, where he was engaged in the fighting at the landing at Suvla Bay and the engagements which followed until the Evacuation of the Peninsula. He was then drafted to Egypt, and was in action in the operations in Palestine, including the Battles of Gaza, Mejdel and Haifa. He was demobilised in April 1919, and holds the 1914-15 Star, and the General Service and Victory Medals.
18, Brache Street, Luton.   285/C.

MARSHALL, G., Pte., 1/5th Bedfordshire Regt.
He volunteered in August 1914, and during his service in Egypt and Palestine, which lasted for four years, took part in many engagements, and did excellent work with his unit. He was demobilised after his return to England in April 1919, and holds the 1914-15 Star, and the General Service and Victory Medals.
42, Park Road West, Luton.   1945/C.

MARSHALL, G. M., A.B., Royal Navy.
Joining in December 1917, he was first posted to H.M.S. " Floral " and afterwards to H.M.S. " Swordsman " and " Renown." On board these vessels he saw service in the North Sea and in various other waters, and was engaged on special patrol duties until after the cessation of hostilities. He holds the General Service and Victory Medals, and was serving in 1920.
28, Hampton Road, Luton.   1947/A.

MARSHALL, H. (M.M.), L/Corporal, M.G.C.
He joined in May 1916, and at the conclusion of his training was drafted to France. Here he took an active part in many important engagements, notably those at Ypres and the Somme, and in September 1917 was mentioned in Despatches. He was also awarded the Military Medal for an act of distinguished gallantry and devotion to duty in the Field. Later he served in Italy, and after the Armistice was sent to Germany with the Army of Occupation. In addition to the decoration won on the Field, he holds the General Service and Victory Medals, and was demobilised in September 1919.
1, Dorset Street, Luton.   1946.

MARSHALL, J., Bombardier, R.F.A.
Joining in April 1917, he was sent to India on the completion of his training. He was subsequently engaged on duties of a special nature at stations in the Punjab and at Rawal Pindi and Delhi. He was still serving in India in 1920, and holds the General Service and Victory Medals.
28, Hampton Road, Luton.   1947/B.

MARSHALL, J., Private, Machine Gun Corps.
Although under age for military service, he joined in April 1918, but was unable to secure his transfer overseas before the cessation of hostilities. He was, however, engaged on duties of a special nature, and rendered valuable services until his demobilisation, which took place in January 1919.
42, Park Road West, Luton.   1945/B.

MARSHALL, W. C., Sapper, Royal Engineers.
He volunteered in August 1914, and after his training was retained for some time on important duties. In July 1918 he was drafted to German East Africa, where he rendered valuable services as a signaller whilst operations were in progress, but in the following December was invalided home suffering from malarial fever. He was demobilised in February 1919, and holds the General Service and Victory Medals.
16, Beale Street, Dunstable.   1948.

MARSOM, J., Corporal, Rifle Brigade.
Mobilised at the outbreak of war, he was immediately drafted to France and took part in the Retreat from Mons. He also fought in many of the subsequent engagements, notably those at Albert, Armentières, the Somme, Ypres, Passchendaele, Langemarck and Delville Wood, and was severely wounded on three occasions. Throughout his overseas service, which lasted for nearly five years, he did excellent work with his unit, and holds the Mons Star, and the General Service and Victory Medals. He was demobilised after his return to England in February 1919.
4, Buck Fields, Hitchin Hill, Hitchin. 1949.

MARTIN, A. J., Private, 25th King's (Liverpool Regiment).
He joined in October 1916, and after his training was engaged on duties of an important nature until early in 1918, when he was drafted to France. Subsequently he served in the Advance of that year, when he fought on the Somme and in the Battles of Cambrai and St. Quentin. He holds the General Service and Victory Medals and was demobilised in January 1919.
25, Longmere Road, St. Albans. X1950/A.

MARTIN, C., Rifleman, Rifle Brigade.
He volunteered in August 1914, and after his training was drafted to France. There he took part in numerous battles, notably those of Ypres (1916), Arras and Loos, and was in action almost continuously until his death, which occurred in 1916. He was entitled to the 1914-15 Star, and the General Service and Victory Medals. His memory is cherished with pride.
High Street, Barton, near Ampthill. 1951.

MARTIN, C. W., Private, 2nd Bedfordshire Regt.
He volunteered in August 1914, and almost immediately proceeded to France. He took part in the fighting during the Retreat from Mons, and was engaged in the Battles of the Marne, La Bassée, Ypres, St. Eloi, Neuve Chapelle, the Somme, Albert and St. Quentin, and was gassed in 1917. Returning to France he was engaged in the fighting in the German Offensive and subsequent Allied Advance of 1918. He was demobilised in February 1919, and holds the Mons Star, and the General Service and Victory Medals
Back of Church, Ickleford, Hitchin, Herts. 2469.

MARTIN, F., Air Mechanic, Royal Air Force.
He joined in December 1917, and at the conclusion of his training was engaged on duties which called for great technical knowledge and skill. He was unable to secure his transfer overseas before the termination of the war, but rendered valuable services in connection with the fitting of seaplane engines, until his demobilisation, which took place in April 1919.
15, Dane Road, Luton. 1952.

MARTIN, F., Private, Machine Gun Corps.
Volunteering in December 1914, he received his training at various stations, and was afterwards engaged on duties of an important nature until January 1917, when he was sent to the Western Front. He subsequently took part in fighting and was taken prisoner in the Ypres sector in March 1917. He was demobilised on his return to England in December 1918, and holds the General Service and Victory Medals.
2, Cavendish Road, St. Albans. X1953.

MARTIN, F. W. (M.S.M.), Sergeant, 2/8th Sherwood Foresters.
Mobilised as a Territorial at the outbreak of war, he was retained in England on important duties until 1916, when he was drafted to the Western Front. Here he took part in many important battles, notably those of Ypres, the Somme and Cambrai, and was wounded. He was subsequently taken prisoner during the German Offensive on March 21st, 1918, and died in the enemy's lines on the same day. He was awarded the Meritorious Service Medal for his efficient work in the field and was also entitled to the General Service and Victory Medals.
90, Estcourt Road, Watford. X1954.

MARTIN, H. J., Private, 1st Border Regiment.
Joining in September 1916, he was drafted to the Western Front in the following December. Subsequently he participated in fighting at Loos, Ypres and Arras, and was wounded. In December 1917, he was again wounded, and was taken prisoner at Cambrai, remaining a captive in Germany until after the cessation of hostilities. He was demobilised after his return to England in March 1919, and holds the General Service and Victory Medals.
29, Beech Road, Luton. 1955.

MARTIN, H. J., Sergeant, R.A.M.C.
Volunteering in August 1914, he was almost immediately sent to the Western Front, where he served in the Retreat from Mons, and in many of the subsequent engagements, notably that at Ypres. Later he was drafted to East Africa. During this long period of service he was wounded. He was demobilised after his return to England in April 1919, and holds the Mons Star, and the General Service and Victory Medals.
17, Alexandra Road, St. Albans. X1956.

MARTIN, J., Private, Leicestershire Regiment.
He volunteered in March 1915, and was sent to the Western Front in the same year. Subsequently he fought in many engagements, notably those at Ypres, the Somme and Arras, and was killed in action on October 20th, 1917. He was entitled to the 1914-15 Star, and the General Service and Victory Medals.
Town Yard, Barton, Ampthill. 1959/B.

MARTIN, J., Sergeant, Royal Field Artillery.
He volunteered in October 1914, and after his training was sent to the Western Front. Here he took part in a number of important battles, including those of Ypres and Dixmude, and was gassed whilst in action at Noyon. He was demobilised in May 1919, and holds 1914-15 Star, and the General Service and Victory Medals.
4, Adrian Road, Abbots Langley, Herts. X1957.

MARTIN, J. H., Stoker, Petty Officer, Royal Navy.
Volunteering in August 1914, he was posted to H.M.S. "Osprey." Aboard this vessel he saw service with the North Sea patrol, and was also engaged on special duties and in submarine chasing in the Baltic, frequently being in action with enemy craft. Throughout the period of hostilities, he did excellent work, and holds the 1914-15 Star, and the General Service and Victory Medals. He was demobilised in February 1920.
Trowley Bottom, Flamstead, near Dunstable. X1960.

MARTIN, L. W., L/Corporal, Royal Engineers.
He volunteered in September 1914, and three months later was drafted to France. Here he was engaged on duties of an important nature in the forward areas, and was present at many engagements, notably those at Ypres, Arras, Vimy Ridge and Beaumont-Hamel. Whilst overseas he contracted fever and in March 1918 was invalided home. He was demobilised in February 1919, and holds the 1914-15 Star, and the General Service and and Victory Medals.
16, Castle Road, St. Albans. X1958.

MARTIN, P., Private, Gloucestershire Regiment.
He joined in March 1918, and after his training served for the remaining period of hostilities on the Western Front, where he was engaged on special duties and did most valuable work. Returning to England in 1920, he was demobilised in March of that year, and holds the General Service and Victory Medals.
Town Yard, Barton, Ampthill. 1959/A.

MARTIN, P. A., Private, Grenadier Guards.
He volunteered in November 1915, and was drafted to the Western Front. In this theatre of war he took part in numerous engagements, including those on the Somme and at Ypres. He was also wounded and contracted fever, but after treatment at the base rejoined his unit, and remained in France until March 1919, when, returning to England, he was demobilised. He holds the 1914-15 Star, and the General Service and Victory Medals.
5, Athol Cottages, Colney Street, near St. Albans. X1961.

MARTIN, P. S., Private, 4th Bedfordshire Regt.
Volunteering in December 1915, he was sent to France at the conclusion of his training in the following July. Subsequently, he took part in much heavy fighting on the Somme, and was killed in action near Arras on November 13th, 1916. He was entitled to the General Service and Victory Medals.
23, Back Street, Luton. 1962/A.

MARTIN, W., Private, Bedfordshire Regiment.
He volunteered at the outbreak of war, and on completion of his training was drafted to the Western Front, where he took part in the heavy fighting at Ypres, Arras, Hill 60, Verdun, and was severely wounded. He was invalided home and subsequently discharged as medically unfit for further service in 1916. He holds the 1914-15 Star, and the General Service and Victory Medals.
53, Sopwell Lane, St. Albans. X541/A.

MARTINDALE, E., Rifleman, 17th Cameronians (Scottish Rifles).
He joined in 1916, and on completion of his training served with his unit at various stations. He was engaged on guard and other duties and did good work, but was not successful in securing his transfer overseas. He was demobilised in 1919.
4, Brightwell Road, Watford. X197/B.

MARTINDALE, A., Private, 9th Royal Warwickshire Regiment.
He joined in March 1917, and in the same year was drafted to India. He was stationed at various places on the North-Western Frontier, where he was engaged on garrison and other duties until 1919. He returned to England and was demobilised in February 1920, and holds the General Service and Victory Medals.
55, Old London Road, St. Albans.   1963.

MARTINDALE, A. J. (M.M.), Corporal, Canadian Infantry, and Machine Gun Corps.
He volunteered in August 1914, and was later sent to France. He took part in many engagements, including those of Passchendaele, Cambrai and Lens, and was awarded the Military Medal and subsequently a Bar to that medal for conspicuous bravery and devotion to duty in the Field. After the cessation of hostilities he proceeded with the Army of Occupation into Germany, and was stationed on the Rhine. He was demobilised in March 1919, and in addition to the Military Medal holds the General Service and Victory Medals.
42, Brighton Road, Watford.   1964.

MARTINDALE, W., Gunner, R.F.A.
He joined in January 1916, and was shortly afterwards drafted to Egypt. He saw active service on the Palestine Front, and fought in the first, second and third battles of Gaza, the engagements of Medjel, the subsequent capture of Jerusalem, and in the British Offensive of September 1918. He returned to England, and was demobilised in October 1919, and holds the General Service and Victory Medals.
32, Bedford Road, St. Albans.   1965.

MARTINDALE, W. (M.M.), Bombardier, R.F.A.
He was mobilised in August 1914, and in the following January was sent to France. He took part in many engagements, including those of the Aisne, the Marne, Ypres, the Ancre, Festubert, Loos, Givenchy, Albert, Cambrai, Bapaume, and saw heavy fighting during the German Offensive and subsequent Allied Advance of 1918. He was awarded the Military Medal for conspicuous bravery in the Field. He was demobilised in March 1919, and also holds the General Service and Victory Medals.
8a, The Rookery, Watford, Herts.   1966.

MARTINDALE, W. J., Trooper, 1st (King's) Dragoon Guards.
He enlisted in H.M. Forces in 1906, and on the outbreak of hostilities proceeded to France. He fought in the Retreat from Mons and in the Battles of the Aisne, Ypres and Arras, and other engagements. Owing to ill-health he was invalided to England and after receiving hospital treatment was discharged on account of medical unfitness in March 1915. He holds the Mons Star, and the General Service and Victory Medals.
66, Albert Street, St. Albans.   1967.

MASKELL, W. M., Private, Bedfordshire Regt.
He volunteered in September 1914, and in August of the following year was sent to France. He saw active service in many parts of the Western Front, and served in the Battles of Arras, Ypres, the Somme, Cambrai, and was wounded in 1917 and later gassed. He was discharged on medical grounds in March 1919, and holds the 1914-15 Star, and the General Service and Victory Medals.
43, St. John's Street, Biggleswade.   1968.

MASON, W., Driver, Royal Field Artillery.
He joined in April 1915, and in the following November embarked for France. He was engaged in heavy fighting in many sectors of the Western Front, and fought in the Battles of Ypres, the Somme, Kemmel Hill, Messines Ridge, and in the Retreat and Advance of 1918. He was demobilised in December 1918, and holds the 1914-15 Star, and the General Service and Victory Medals.
77, Buxton Road, Luton.   1969.

MASON, Wm., Private, 2/5th Bedfordshire Regt.
He volunteered in December 1914, and in the following year was sent to France. He served in many sectors of the Western Front, and fought in the Battles of Ypres, the Somme, Cambrai and other engagements, and was wounded. He was invalided to England after receiving hospital treatment, and was discharged as medically unfit for further service in May 1916. He holds the 1914-15 Star, and the General Service and Victory Medals.
48, Hampton Road, Luton.   1970.

MATHEWS, A., Private, Suffolk Regiment.
Mobilised in August 1914, he was drafted to the Western Front early in the following year. He was engaged in heavy fighting at Ypres, Arras, and on the Somme, and was taken prisoner at the Battle of Festubert in May 1915. He was kept in captivity in Germany until after the signing of the Armistice. He then returned to England, and was demobilised in February 1919. He holds the 1914-15 Star, and the General Service and Victory Medals.
Station Road, Woburn Sands.   Z366/A.

MATHEWS, G. A., Gunner, R.G.A.
He joined in July 1916, and in the following year embarked for France. Whilst overseas he was engaged in the heavy fighting on the Western Front, and took part in the Battles of the Somme, Arras and in the Retreat and Advance of 1918. He was demobilised in July 1919 and holds the General Service and Victory Medals.
35, Ashwell Street, Leighton Buzzard.   1971.

MATSON, A. M. (Miss), Special War Worker.
This lady volunteered her services for work of National importance during the war, and from October 1915 until December 1918 worked in a munition factory. She held the important post of inspector over a fuse-making department, and throughout rendered very valuable services.
73, Ivy Road, Luton.   2077/B.

MATSON, C., Private, Northamptonshire Regt. and 6th Cheshire Regiment.
He volunteered in February 1915, and was later drafted to France. He served in many sectors of the Western Front and fought in the Battles of the Somme, Ypres, Passchendaele and during the German Offensive and subsequent Allied Advance in 1918. During his service in France he was twice wounded. He was demobilised in March 1919, and holds the General Service and Victory Medals.
73, Ivy Road, Luton.   2077/A.

MATTHEWS, B., Private, Middlesex Regiment, and East Surrey Regiment.
Joining in May 1916, he was drafted to France in the same year and saw much service in many sectors. He took part in several important engagements, including the Battles of Arras, and Ypres, and on the cessation of hostilities returned to England. He was demobilised in January 1919, and holds the General Service and Victory Medals.
12, Brightwell Road, Watford.   X1972.

MATTHEWS, C. G., Private, 1/5th Bedfordshire Regiment.
Volunteering in November 1915, he was sent to Egypt early in the following year. Engaged with his unit in garrison and other duties at Cairo, he was afterwards in action in the Canal Zone. He also fought in the Battles of Gaza, Haifa, Acre, Beyrout, and other important engagements of General Allenby's Advance through Palestine, and returned to England on the termination of hostilities. Demobilised in March 1919, he holds the General Service and Victory Medals.
27, Charles Street, Luton.   1973.

MATTHEWS, E. R., C.S.M., Suffolk Regiment.
He volunteered in August 1914, and in the following month was drafted to the Western Front, where he took a prominent part in heavy fighting in various sectors. He fought in several important battles, including those of Loos, the Somme (I.), Arras (I.), Ypres (III.) and Cambrai, and was killed in action near Ypres in October 1918. He was entitled to the 1914 Star, and the General Service and Victory Medals.
11, Barrow Path, Leighton Buzzard.   1974.

MATTHEWS, F. G., Private, Labour Corps.
He joined in June 1916, and in the following January was sent to France. He served with his unit on important duties in various sectors while heavy fighting was in progress. He also fought at Cambrai, and in other important engagements. At the end of the war he returned to England, and was demobilised in March 1919. He holds the General Service and Victory Medals.
2, Dalton Street, St. Albans.   1975.

MATTHEWS, H. J., Private, Royal Fusiliers.
He joined in May 1916, and in July of the same year was drafted to the Western Front. Whilst in this theatre of war he took part in heavy fighting in several sectors. He was unfortunately killed in action in October 1917 during offensive operations prior to the first Battle of Cambrai. He was entitled to the General Service and Victory Medals.
43, King Street, Dunstable.   1976/A.

MATTHEWS, W., C.Q.M.S., Royal Engineers.

He was serving in the Army at the outbreak of hostilities, and was almost immediately drafted to France, where he fought in the Retreat from Mons and in many subsequent battles, including those of Ypres and Neuve Chapelle. He did excellent work with his unit until the signing of the Armistice, when he returned to England He was discharged on the termination of his engagement in February 1920, and holds the Mons Star, and the General Service and Victory Medals.
39, Clifford Street, Watford. X1977/A.

MATTHEWS, W. C., Driver, Royal Engineers.

Volunteering in November 1914, he was drafted in the following July to Egypt. He did good work in the Eastern theatre of war during the Advance under General Allenby through Syria and Palestine, and amongst other important engagements was present at the Battle of Gaza. He returned to England for demobilisation in March 1919, and holds the 1914-15 Star, and the General Service and Victory Medals.
43, King Street, Dunstable. 1976/B.

MAXWELL, G., Corporal, 1st Bedfordshire Regt.

Mobilised on the declaration of war, he was shortly afterwards drafted to France, where he was engaged in heavy fighting in the Retreat from Mons, and at the Battles of Arras, Ypres and Passchendaele. He was twice wounded and invalided to hospital, and on recovery rejoined his unit in the field until captured by the enemy. He was repatriated in January 1919, and in 1920 was still serving. He holds the Mons Star, and the General Service and Victory Medals.
32, Cherry Bounce, Hemel Hempstead. X1978.

MAY, C. H., Private, R.A.M.C.

Volunteering in September 1914, he did duty with his unit at various stations until drafted overseas in February 1916. Serving with a field ambulance in France, he did excellent work during the offensive operations on the Somme. He was then sent to Salonika, and was employed in the Vardar and Struma sectors as a stretcher bearer, and later as an orderly in various hospitals. He was demobilised in June 1919, and holds the General Service and Victory Medals.
1, Edward Street, Dunstable. 1979.

MAY, E. G., Rifleman, Rifle Brigade.

Joining in August 1918, he was engaged with his unit on important duties at various depôts until sent with the Army of Occupation into Germany, where he was employed on guard and other duties. He returned to England, and was demobilised in March 1920.
7, Station Terrace, Park Street, St. Albans. X1980.

MAY, J. J., Corporal, Royal Air Force.

He volunteered in May 1915, and after training was engaged at Falkirk on aero-engine testing and other work requiring a high degree of technical skill. He carried out his important duties with considerable success, but was unable to obtain a transfer overseas before the cessation of hostilities, and was demobilised in January 1919.
16, Hagden Lane, Watford. X1981.

MAY, J. J. W., 1st Air Mechanic, Royal Air Force.

Volunteering in November 1915, he was shortly afterwards drafted to Egypt, where he was engaged at aerodromes at Aboukir, Heluan and Cairo in aero-engine fitting and other duties calling for a high standard of technical knowledge and skill. After doing excellent work for over three years he returned to England on the termination of hostilities, and was demobilised in March 1919. He holds the General Service and Victory Medals.
28, Princess Street, Luton. 1982.

MAY, P. E., L/Corporal, Royal Scots Fusiliers.

He volunteered in June 1915, and proceeded to the Western Front in April 1917, and saw considerable service in many sectors. He was wounded in September 1917, and on recovery returned to the front lines and fought throughout the Retreat and Advance of 1918. He holds the General Service and Victory Medals, and was demobilised in February 1919.
1, Edward Street, Luton. 1983.

MAYER, W. H., L/Cpl., 1st Hertfordshire Regt.

He volunteered in September 1914, and being drafted to France shortly afterwards took part in heavy fighting at Hill 60, Ypres and Loos, and was gassed and wounded. On recovery he rejoined his unit, and was engaged in several important battles until he was unfortunately killed in action at St. Julien on July 31st, 1917. He was entitled to the 1914-15 Star, and the General Service and Victory Medals.
13, Albion Road, St. Albans. X1985.

MAYBANK, E., Private, R.A.M.C.

He joined in March 1916, and after a course of training was employed at a large military hospital on ambulance and other duties. He did good work, but was unable to obtain his transfer overseas, and was demobilised in August 1919.
Oak Cottage, Shenley Lane, London Colney. X1984.

MAYES, A., Private, 1st Bedfordshire Regiment.

He was mobilised on the outbreak of hostilities, and was shortly afterwards drafted to France, where he was engaged in fierce fighting in the Retreat from Mons. He also fought in the Battles of Ypres and Hill 60, where he was severely wounded. He was subsequently discharged in March 1916 as medically unfit for further military service. He holds the Mons Star, and the General Service and Victory Medals.
17, Brighton Road, Watford. X1986.

MAYHO, G., Private, R.A.S.C.

Volunteering in October 1915, he was drafted to Salonika in the same month. He served with his unit in the Near East, and was engaged on important duties in connection with the transport of ammunition and supplies to the forward areas, and was present at heavy fighting on the Vardar and Doiran fronts in the Advance across the Struma and at Monastir. Returning to England on the conclusion of hostilities, he was demobilised in February 1919, and holds the 1914-15 Star, and the General Service and Victory Medals.
14, Brixton Road, Watford. X3280/B.

MAYLES, C., Gunner, Royal Field Artillery.

Joining in April 1916, he was drafted overseas in the following August. Serving with his battery on the Western Front he took part in several notable battles, including those of Ypres, Passchendaele, Messines, and the Retreat and Advance of 1918. On the conclusion of hostilities he was sent with the Army of Occupation into Germany, where he served until returned to England for demobilisation in September 1919. He holds the General Service and Victory Medals.
113, Frederic Street, Luton. 1990.

MAYLES, H. C., L/Corporal, Bedfordshire Regt., and Machine Gun Corps.

He joined in May 1916, and after training was sent to the Western Front. Whilst in this theatre of war he served with his unit in various sectors, and took part in heavy fighting until he was unfortunately killed in action near Ypres on September 20th, 1917. He was entitled to the General Service and Victory Medals.
14, Wood Street, Luton. 1987.

MAYLIN, G., Private, Bedfordshire Regiment.

He was mobilised on the declaration of war, and almost immediately drafted to France, where he was in action in the Retreat from Mons and in several other important battles. He was wounded in February 1915, and invalided home, and was subsequently discharged as unfit for further military service in August 1916. He holds the Mons Star, and the General Service and Victory Medals.
"Hope Villa," Kershaws Hill, Hitchin. 1988.

MAYLING, J. N., Private, Norfolk Regiment.

He joined in January 1917, and after training was drafted to France in the following September. He fought in the first Battle of Cambrai and in other engagements, and was severely wounded in heavy fighting in the Retreat of 1918. Invalided to Roehampton Hospital, he was under treatment until discharged unfit for further service, owing to the loss of a leg, in 1919. He holds the General Service and Victory Medals.
120, Hitchin Road, Luton. 1989/B.

MAYNARD, F., Private, 2nd Bedfordshire Regt.

He volunteered in August 1914, and soon afterwards embarked for France. He took part in the heavy fighting at Ypres and in many other parts of the Western Front, and was wounded. After recovery he was sent to the Dardanelles, and was again wounded during the heavy fighting in this theatre of war. He later rejoined his unit and was drafted to France, and fought in the Battles of the Somme, Arras, Cambrai, and in the Retreat and Advance of 1918. He was demobilised in 1919, and holds the 1914-15 Star, and the General Service and Victory Medals.
Aspley Guise. 1991/A.

MAYNARD, J., Private, 2nd Bedfordshire Regt.

He volunteered in August 1914, and in the following July was sent to the Dardanelles. He took part in the heavy fighting on the Peninsula, and was killed in action on September 13th, 1915. He was entitled to the 1914-15 Star, and the General Service and Victory Medals.
Aspley Guise. 1991/B.

MAYLING, H., Rifleman, 7th King's Royal Rifle Corps.
A serving soldier, he was mobilised at the outbreak of war, and sent to the Western Front in September 1914. He fought in many important engagements, including those at Ypres and Hill 60, where he was wounded. Invalided to England, he received hospital treatment, and was subsequently discharged unfit for further service in 1917. He holds the 1914 Star, and the General Service and Victory Medals.
120, Hitchin Road, Luton.   1989/A.

MAYNE, J., Private, R.A.S.C.
He volunteered in December 1914, and in the following February was sent to France, where he was engaged on important duties with his unit. He served in many battles on the Western Front, including those of Hill 60, Ypres, Arras, Passchendaele and Albert. He returned to England and was discharged in September 1918 on account of his service, and holds the 1914-15 Star, and the General Service and Victory Medals.
8, Yarmouth Road, Callowland, Herts.   1992/A.

MAYNE, R. J., Driver, Royal Field Artillery.
He volunteered in November 1914, and in the same year proceeded to France. He fought in many engagements on the Western Front, including those of Ypres, Arras, Passchendaele and Cambrai. After the cessation of hostilities he was sent to Germany with the Army of Occupation, and was stationed on the Rhine. He was demobilised in May 1919, and holds the 1914-15 Star, and the General Service and Victory Medals.
8, Yarmouth Road, Callowland, Herts.   1992/B.

MAYS, H., Stoker, 1st Class, Royal Navy.
He joined in February 1918, and was posted to H.M.S. " Superb." During his period of service his ship was on duty in the Mediterranean Sea, later in November 1918 with the Allied Fleet at Constantinople, and afterwards on duty in the Black Sea assisting in the Blockade of Russia. He was demobilised in March 1919, and holds the General Service and Victory Medals.
176, Chester Road, Watford.   1993.

MEACHAM, J., Corporal, Royal Marine Light Infantry.
He volunteered in January 1915, and later in the same year embarked for France. He fought in many sectors, and took part in the Battles of the Somme, Cambrai, St. Quentin, and in the Retreat and Advance of 1918, and was wounded. He was demobilised in January 1919, and holds the 1914-15 Star, and the General Service and Victory Medals.
30, Ebury Road, Watford.   1994.

MEAD, A., Private, R.A.M.C., and Labour Corps.
He volunteered in October 1914, and after serving with his unit on important duties at various stations was drafted to France in 1917. He did useful work in various sectors, and was present at the Battle of Ypres and other important engagements. At the termination of the war he went with the Army of Occupation into Germany and was stationed at Cologne. He returned to England for demobilisation in April 1919, and holds the General Service and Victory Medals.
16, Beech Road, Luton.   3046/B.

MEAD, A., C.S.M., 4th Bedfordshire Regiment.
He volunteered in January 1915, and in June of that year was sent to France. Whilst on the Western Front he fought at the Battles of the Somme, Cambrai, Passchendaele, Ypres, and in the German Offensive and subsequent Allied Advance in 1918. He was wounded twice whilst on active service, and demobilised in March 1919, and holds the 1914-15 Star, and the General Service and Victory Medals.
26, Cobden Street, Luton.   1995.

MEAD, A., Gunner, Royal Field Artillery.
He enlisted in H.M. Forces in 1903, and on the outbreak of war was drafted overseas. He was in action during the Retreat from Mons, and in the Battles of the Aisne, the Marne, Givenchy, Ypres, Arras, and many other engagements. In January 1917 he was invalided to England owing to ill-health, and after receiving hospital treatment was engaged on home service until July 1919, when he was discharged. He holds the Mons Star, and the General Service and Victory Medals.
12, George Street, Markyate, Herts.   1996.

MEAD, A. C., Driver, Royal Field Artillery.
He joined in 1916, and later in that year proceeded to the Western Front. He fought at the Battles of the Somme, Ypres and many others, and experienced heavy fighting during the German Offensive and subsequent Allied Advance of 1918. He was demobilised in April 1919, and holds the General Service and Victory Medals.
25, Elizabeth Street, Luton.   1997.

MEAD, A. H., Corporal, Royal Welch Fusiliers.
He volunteered in May 1915, and later in the same year was drafted to France. He was actively engaged in many sectors of the Western Front, and fought in the Battles of Ypres, the Somme and Arras, and was wounded. He returned to England in 1918, and was demobilised in March 1919, and holds the 1914-15 Star, and the General Service and Victory Medals.
120, Estcourt Road, Watford.   1998.

MEAD, A. J., Corporal, Royal Engineers (R.O.D.)
He volunteered in February 1916, and was sent to France in the following month. From that time until the cessation of hostilities he was engaged upon railway construction in the forward areas, and served at Ypres, Arras, Cambrai and on the Somme. After the Armistice he went into Germany with the Army of Occupation, and was stationed at Cologne. He was demobilised in May 1919, and holds the General Service and Victory Medals.
100, Norfolk Road, Rickmansworth.   1999.

MEAD, A. W, Sergeant, Bedfordshire Regiment.
He volunteered in September 1914, and proceeded to the Dardanelles in July of the following year, and served at Suvla Bay and in other engagements until the Evacuation of the Peninsula. He was then sent to Egypt, and stationed there for some time, and was invalided to England on account of ill-health. On recovery he was drafted to France, and fought in the Retreat and Advance of 1918, until killed in action on the Bapaume Road on August 26th, 1918. He was entitled to the 1914-15 Star, and the General Service and Victory Medals.
82, Edward Street, Dunstable.   2000.

MEAD, C., Private, 3rd Bedfordshire Regiment.
Volunteering in August 1914, he was sent to France in the following month, and took part in the final stages of the Retreat from Mons and the subsequent engagements at La Bassée, Ypres and Hill 60. In 1915 he was severely wounded at the second Battle of Ypres, and in consequence was invalided to a hospital in Liverpool, where he was under treatment for six months. On his recovery he returned to France, and towards the end of 1916 was again wounded in action at Loos, but after receiving treatment in a hospital at Boulogne, rejoined his unit and served at Cambrai. Shortly after, however, he returned to England, and in August 1917 was invalided out of the service. He holds the 1914 Star, and the General Service and Victory Medals.
46, Baker Street, Leighton Buzzard.   2476.

MEAD, D., Private, Middlesex Regiment.
He joined in 1917, and in the same year proceeded to France. He saw active service on the Western Front, and was present at the Battles of Arras and Messines. He was wounded at Ypres in the same year. On recovery he was again in action, and in 1918 was wounded at Cambrai after taking part in the fighting during the German Offensive of that year. He was demobilised in 1919, and holds the General Service and Victory Medals.
Lower Green, Ickleford, Herts.   2470/A.

MEAD, E. Sergeant, Yorkshire Regiment.
He enlisted in H.M. Forces in 1910, and upon the declaration of war was drafted to India. During his service there he was stationed at various places on the North-Western Frontier, where he later saw active service. He returned to England in 1919, and in the following year was still serving with his regiment. He holds the General Service and Victory Medals, and the Indian General Service Medal (with clasp Afghanistan, N.W. Frontier 1919).
27, Bernard Street, St. Albans.   2008/A.

MEAD, E., Bombardier, Royal Field Artillery.
He volunteered in June 1915, and six months later was drafted to France. During his service on the Western Front he took part in heavy fighting at the Battles of the Somme, Arras, Ypres, Cambrai, and in the Retreat and subsequent Advance of 1918. He was demobilised in June 1919, and holds the General Service and Victory Medals.
9, William Street, Markyate, Herts.   2002.

MEAD, E., Gunner, R.F.A.
He joined in June 1916, and later was drafted to the Western Front, where he served on the Somme Front for six months, and was in action almost continuously. Transferred to Salonika he saw active service on the Vardar front, and was then sent with the British Expeditionary Force to Russia, where he fought in many engagements. He returned to England and was demobilised in March 1919, and holds the General Service and Victory Medals.
15, Two Water Road, Hemel Hempstead.   X2001.

MEAD, E., Private, 5th Bedfordshire Regiment.
He volunteered in September 1915, and in the following May proceeded to Egypt. In this theatre of war he served in many engagements in Palestine under General Allenby and fought at the Battle of Gaza, and was present at the entry into Jerusalem. He returned home in March 1919, and was demobilised in the following month. He holds the General Service and Victory Medals.
9, George Street, Markyate, Herts. 2003.

MEAD, F., Private, Royal Fusiliers.
He joined in January 1918, and after his training was employed on important duties at various stations with his unit. He did good work but was unable to secure a transfer overseas until after the signing of the Armistice, when he was sent with the Army of Occupation to Germany, and was stationed at Cologne. He was demobilised in November 1919.
65, Spenser Road, Luton. 2009.

MEAD, F. (D.C.M.), C.S.M., 1st Bedfordshire Regiment.
Volunteering in August 1914, he was drafted to France in the following month. During his service on the Western Front he was engaged in heavy fighting at Ypres, Hill 60, Arras, and was twice wounded on the Somme. He also served in the Retreat and subsequent Advance at Cambrai in 1918. He was awarded the Distinguished Conduct Medal for conspicuous bravery and devotion to duty in the Field. He also holds the 1914 Star, and the General Service and Victory Medals, and was still serving in 1920.
6, Albion Street, Dunstable. 2010/A.

MEAD, F., Private, 4th Bedfordshire Regiment.
Volunteering in November 1914, he was sent to the Western Front in the following June, and saw much service there. He fought at the Battles of the Somme, Arras and Ypres, where he was wounded in April 1917. He returned to England, and after receiving hospital treatment was invalided out of the service in October 1917, and holds the 1914-15 Star, and the General Service and Victory Medals.
3, Buckwood Road, Markyate. 2004/A.

MEAD, G., Sergeant, Tank Corps.
He volunteered in August 1914, and at the conclusion of his training served with his unit at various stations on important duties. He did much good work, but was not able to secure his transfer overseas owing to medical unfitness. He was demobilised in November 1919.
30, St. Mary's Street, Dunstable. 1029/A.

MEAD, G., Sergeant, 6th Bedfordshire Regiment.
Volunteering at the outbreak of war, he was drafted to the Dardanelles in March 1915, and took part in the fighting at the first landing at Gallipoli and the subsequent battles which followed. He was later transferred to Egypt, and in this theatre of war served with his battalion in many engagements until killed in action at the Battle of Gaza on April 17th, 1917. He was entitled to the 1914-15 Star, and the General Service and Victory Medals.
6, Albion Street, Dunstable. 2010/B

MEAD, H., Driver, Royal Field Artillery.
He joined in April 1916, and in the same year was drafted to France. During his service on the Western Front he took part in the fighting at Ypres, on the Somme, at Arras and Cambrai. After the signing of the Armistice he proceeded to Turkey, where he served for a time. In October 1919 he returned home, and was demobilised, and holds the General Service and Victory Medals.
25, Elizabeth Street, Luton. 1997/C.

MEAD, H., Private, Bedfordshire Regiment.
He volunteered in August 1914, and was almost immediately drafted to France. He took part in the fierce fighting in the Retreat from Mons and the subsequent engagements which followed, and was wounded. He later returned to the firing line, and was killed at Ypres in February 1915. He was entitled to the Mons Star, and the General Service and Victory Medals.
66, Piccott's End, Hemel Hempstead, Herts. X2005/A.

MEAD, H., Gunner, Royal Field Artillery.
He volunteered in December 1915, and six months later proceeded overseas. Whilst on the Western Front he took part in the Battles of the Somme, Ypres III. and Cambrai, and in the German Offensive and subsequent Allied Advance of 1918. He was demobilised in March 1919, and holds the General Service and Victory Medals.
7, Hicks Road, Markyate. 2006.

MEAD, H. A., Gunner, Royal Horse Artillery.
He joined in April 1916, and in the same year was drafted to Mesopotamia, where he saw active service and fought in many engagements, including those of Kut and Baghdad. He was later sent to India, and there took part in the fighting on the North-Western Frontier. He returned to England and was demobilised in 1920, and holds the General Service and Victory Medals, and the Indian General Service Medal (with clasp Afghanistan, N.W. Frontier 1919).
Laburnum Cottage, Soulbury, Bucks. 2468/A.

MEAD, H., Sergeant, 5th Bedfordshire Regt.
He volunteered in June 1915, and after his training served at various stations as an Instructor in drill and bombing. He rendered excellent service, but was unable to secure his transfer overseas, and was demobilised in February 1919.
2, Waterlow Road, Dunstable. 2007/B.

MEAD, H. E., Corporal, 1st Hertfordshire Regt.
Volunteering in September 1914, he was drafted to France in the following year. He was engaged in much heavy fighting at Ypres, Festubert and Arras, and in the Retreat and Advance (1918), when he was severely wounded. He was invalided to hospital, and subsequently died from the effects of his wounds on November 16th, 1918. He was entitled to the 1914-15 Star, and the General Service and Victory Medals.
27, Bernard Street, St. Albans. X2008/B.

MEAD, J., Private, 1st Bedfordshire Regiment, and 1st Lincolnshire Regiment.
He volunteered in November 1915, and in the following June was drafted to France. He took part in the Battle of the Somme, and was wounded and invalided home. On recovery he returned to France, and was engaged in the fighting at Arras, and was again wounded. He later rejoined his battalion and served in the engagements at Cambrai, being wounded a third time and again invalided home. After hospital treatment he returned to the firing line, and in September 1918 was unfortunately killed in action near Havrincourt. He was entitled to the General Service and Victory Medals.
5, Buckwood Road, Markyate. 2004/C.

MEAD, L., Private, Royal Army Medical Corps.
Volunteering in November 1915, he was drafted to France in the following year. He was engaged in the Battles of Ypres, the Somme and Cambrai, and in the German Offensive and subsequent Allied Advance of 1918. After the signing of the Armistice he proceeded to Germany with the Army of Occupation, remaining there until August 1919, when he returned home and was demobilised. He holds the General Service and Victory Medals.
25, Elizabeth Street, Luton. 1997/B.

MEAD, P., Rifleman, 2/15th King's Royal Rifle Corps.
He volunteered in 1915, and proceeded to France in the following year. He took part in much heavy fighting at Ypres, Arras and Vimy Ridge, where he was severely wounded. He subsequently died from the effects of his wounds at the 17th Casualty Clearing Station on October 17th, 1918. He was entitled to the General Service and Victory Medals.
32, Dorset Street, Luton. 941/B.

MEAD, P., Private, Hampshire Regiment.
He volunteered in August 1915, and was shortly afterwards drafted to France. During his service on the Western Front he took part in much heavy fighting during numerous engagements until he was unfortunately killed in action at Delville Wood on July 14th, 1916. He was entitled to the 1914-15 Star, and the General Service and Victory Medals.
66, Piccott's End, Hemel Hempstead. X2005/B.

MEAD, V. J., Private, Bedfordshire Regiment.
He volunteered in August 1914, and in the same month was drafted to France. He took part in the Retreat from Mons and the subsequent Battles of the Marne, Neuve Chapelle and Ypres. He was killed in action in April 1915 at Hill 60, and was entitled to the Mons Star, and the General Service and Victory Medals.
Lower Green, Ickleford, Herts. 2470/B.

MEAD, W., Corporal, 2nd Bedfordshire Regiment.
He was serving at the outbreak of war, and in September 1914 was drafted to France. Whilst on the Western Front he took part in much heavy fighting at Ypres, on the Somme and at Arras. He was wounded and taken prisoner at Cambrai in May 1918. He suffered many hardships during his long captivity until he was released after the signing of the Armistice. He was demobilised in March 1919, and holds the 1914-15 Star, and the General Service and Victory Medals.
5, Buckwood Road, Markyate. 2004/B.

MEAD, W. H., Private, Royal Fusiliers.

He joined in July 1916, and in the following November proceeded to France. Whilst on the Western Front he fought at Arras, on the Somme and the Marne, at Bapaume, and also at Cambrai in the final operations of the war. He was gassed during the Battle of Arras. He was demobilised in March 1919, and holds the General Service and Victory Medals.
64, Tavistock Street, Luton. 2012.

MEAD, W., Private, Bedfordshire Regiment.

He volunteered in 1914, and at the conclusion of his training served at various stations on important duties with his unit. He was, however, unsuccessful in obtaining his transfer to a theatre of war, and was demobilised in 1919.
15, Millbrook, near Ampthill. 2011.

MEAD, W. J., L/Corporal, 69th Field Co., R.E.

Volunteering in September 1914, he was drafted to France in July 1917. Whilst on the Western Front he fought at Ypres, Arras, on the Somme, at Lens and Cambrai. He was demobilised in July 1919, and holds the General Service and Victory Medals.
16, Elizabeth Street, Luton. 2013.

MEALING, H. W., Pte., 2nd Bedfordshire Regt.

He joined in May 1916, and in the following July was drafted to France. Whilst on the Western Front he took part in the heavy fighting at the Battle of the Somme, and was severely wounded in October 1916, and invalided home. After hospital treatment he was discharged in June 1917 as medically unfit for further service. He holds the General Service and Victory Medals.
8, Kimberley Road, Fleetville, Eastwood, St. Albans. 2014.

MEALING, J. E., Sergeant, 1st Hertfordshire Regt.

He volunteered in 1915, and at the conclusion of his training served at various stations on important duties with his unit until 1917, when he embarked for Egypt aboard the "Aragon." This vessel was sunk in the Mediterranean Sea on December 30th, 1917, and he was unfortunately drowned. He was entitled to the General Service and Victory Medals.
8, Kimberley Road, Fleetville, St. Albans. 2015.

MEDCALF, H. J., Pte., 1/5th Bedfordshire Regt.

Volunteering in September 1914, he was sent in the following year to the Dardanelles. He took part in the heavy fighting there, and later was drafted to Egypt. He joined in the British Advance through Palestine and fought in the Battle of Gaza, where he was wounded. He was demobilised in July 1919, and holds the 1914-15 Star, and the General Service and Victory Medals.
33, Ashton Street, Luton. 2016/A.

MEDCALF, S., Private, 1/4th Norfolk Regiment.

He joined in February 1917, and was shortly afterwards drafted to Egypt. He took part in the British Advance in Palestine under General Allenby, but was unfortunately killed in action near Jerusalem on December 16th, 1917. He was reburied on June 27th, 1919, at Ramleh Military Cemetery, near Jaffa. He was entitled to the General Service and Victory Medals.
33, Ashton Street, Luton. 2016/B.

MEDCALF, T. W., Stoker, Royal Navy.

He joined in July 1918, and after training was posted to H.M.S. "Crescent," which ship was engaged on patrol and other important duties off the coast of Scotland. In 1920 he was still serving, and holds the General and Victory Medals.
33, Ashton Street, Luton. 2106/C.

MEDHURST, E. R., Driver, Royal Field Artillery.

He volunteered in May 1915, and in July of the following year was drafted to Mesopotamia. Whilst in this theatre of war, he took part in much heavy fighting, and was in action at Baghdad and Aya. After this long period of service he returned to England in October 1919, and was demobilised a month later. He holds the General Service and Victory Medals.
63, Liverpool Road, Watford. X2017.

MEDHURST, W. H., Private, Bedfordshire Regiment.

He volunteered in March 1915, and after his training was drafted overseas. Whilst on the Western Front he was in action in the Battle of the Somme, and at Arras, Ypres and Cambrai. He took part also in the Retreat and Advance of 1918. He was demobilised in 1919, and holds the General Service and Victory Medals.
24, Shakespeare Street, North Watford. 2018.

MEECH, J. H., Air Mechanic, Royal Air Force.

Joining in December 1916, he served at the conclusion of his training at various aerodromes on the East Coast and elsewhere. He was partly engaged upon engine fitting, which work called for a high degree of technical skill. He also undertook the dangerous duties of an observer. He was, however, unable to secure his transfer to a theatre of war, and was demobilised in April 1920.
Church Street, Hatfield. 2019.

MEEKS, F., Private, 1/5th Bedfordshire Regt.

He volunteered in November 1915, and after his training was stationed at various stations on important duties with his battalion. For a period he was employed as an Instructor of Musketry. He did good work, but on account of medical unfitness was unable to obtain a transfer overseas. He was demobilised in April 1919.
Clifton, Shefford. Z2020/A.

MEEKS, J. A., Private, 2nd Bedfordshire Regt.

As a Reservist he was called up in August 1914, and after his training served at various stations on special duties until drafted to France in March 1916. Whilst on the Western Front he served as a signaller in many important engagements, including those on the Somme, at Ypres, Arras and Cambrai. He was wounded and gassed shortly before the signing of the Armistice and invalided home. He was demobilised in March 1919, and holds the General Service and Victory Medals.
Campton, Shefford. Z2021/A.

MEEKS, O., Private, Norfolk Regiment.

He joined in 1916, and after his training served at various stations in England and Ireland, being principally engaged upon guard duties. He rendered good service, but was unable to obtain a transfer to a theatre of war, being under military age. He was demobilised in November 1919.
Clifton, Shefford. Z2020/B.

MEEKS, P., Private, Bedfordshire Regiment.

Called up from the Reserve in August 1914, he was sent in the following July to the Dardanelles. He took part in the landing at Gallipoli, and was wounded. He was later sent to Egypt, and during the Campaign in Palestine was in action at Gaza and Jaffa. He was also present when Jerusalem was taken. He was demobilised in March 1919, and holds the 1914-15 Star, and the General Service and Victory Medals.
Clifton, Shefford. Z2020/C.

MEHIGAN, J., Sergeant, Royal Engineers.

He was serving at the outbreak of war, and was immediately drafted to France. He was engaged on important duties in the forward areas during the fierce fighting in the Retreat from Mons, and was later sent to the Balkans. He served at Salonika and on the Vardar front until January 1919, when he returned to England. He holds the Mons Star, and the General Service and Victory Medals, and was still serving in 1920.
41, High Street, Houghton Regis, Dunstable. 2022.

MEIKLE, J. A., Gunner, Royal Field Artillery.

He volunteered in August 1914, and in October of the following year was sent to the Western Front, where he fought in several battles. He afterwards proceeded to Egypt, and took part in heavy fighting at Gaza and other engagements, including those leading up to the taking of Jerusalem and Damascus. He returned home and was demobilised in June 1919, and holds the 1914-15 Star, and the General Service and Victory Medals.
13, Sotheron Road, Watford. X400/A.

MELTON, G. A., Corporal, Bedfordshire Regt.

He volunteered in 1914, and was immediately drafted to France. He took part in the fierce fighting in the Retreat from Mons, at Ypres, Hill 60, Vimy Ridge and many other subsequent engagements on the Western Front. On one occasion during his long period of service he was wounded. He was demobilised in 1919, and holds the Mons Star, and the General Service and Victory Medals.
132, St. James' Road, Watford. X2023.

MEREDITH, H. J., Pte., 2nd Bedfordshire Regt.

He volunteered in September 1914, and after his training served at various stations with his unit until drafted to France in November 1916. During his service on the Western Front he fought at Arras, Hill 60, St. Quentin, on the Somme and at Ypres, remaining in this theatre of war until February 1919. He then returned home, and was demobilised in the next month. He holds the General Service and Victory Medals.
10, Bailey Street, Luton. 2024.

MERRIFIELD, A., Bombardier, R.F.A.
He volunteered in September 1915, and in the following year was drafted to France. He was in action on the Western Front, and served at Arras, Cambrai, Lens, Le Cateau, and in the Retreat and Advance of 1918, and was gassed at Armentières in May 1916. He was demobilised in July 1919, and holds the General Service and Victory Medals.
11, Carey Place, Watford. X2015.

MERRIFIELD, A., Corporal, 12th (Prince of Wales' Royal) Lancers.
He volunteered in August 1914, and in the following year was drafted to France. Whilst on the Western Front he was engaged in the fighting at Ypres, on the Somme, at Festubert, Loos and at Cambrai, where he was wounded in March 1918. On recovery he rejoined his unit, and remained on the Western Front until March 1919, when he returned home and was demobilised. He holds the 1914-15 Star, and the General Service and Victory Medals.
11, Carey Place, Watford. X2025.

MERRIFIELD, G., Gunner, Royal Field Artillery.
He was mobilised at the outbreak of war, and in November 1915 was drafted to Egypt. He took part in operations in Palestine, including the engagements at Gaza, Jaffa and Aleppo, and remained in this theatre of war until March 1919. He then returned home, and was demobilised in the following month, and holds the 1914-15 Star, and the General Service and Victory Medals.
11, Carey Place, Watford. X2027.

MERRIFIELD, G., Corporal, R.G.A.
He volunteered in August 1914, and after his training was stationed at various depôts employed on important duties with his battery. He rendered excellent services, but was unable to secure his transfer to a theatre of war as he was too old for service overseas, and was discharged in March 1918.
11, Carey Place, Watford. X2028/A.

MERRIFIELD, H., Rifleman, 7th Rifle Brigade.
He joined in May 1917, and in the following August was drafted to France. Whilst on the Western Front he took part in the heavy fighting at Ypres, and was killed in action at Passchendaele Ridge on December 25th, 1917. He was entitled to the General Service and Victory Medals.
11, Carey Place, Watford. X2028/B.

MERRIMAN, C. H., Gunner, Royal Field Artillery.
He volunteered in April 1915, and in the following year was drafted to the Western Front. Whilst in France he served on the Somme and at Ypres, and during the German Offensive in March 1918 was taken prisoner. He suffered many hardships during his captivity in Germany, and was released after the cessation of hostilities and returned to England. He was demobilised in March 1919, and holds the 1914-15 Star, and the General Service and Victory Medals.
31, Souldern Street, Watford. X2029.

MERRY, A., L/Corporal, Royal Sussex Regiment.
He volunteered in August 1914, and after his training served at various stations on special duties until drafted to France in 1916. Whilst in action on the Somme he was buried by the explosion of a shell. He later took part in the fighting at Ypres, Arras, Messines and Cambrai, and also served with the Salvage Corps. He was demobilised in March 1919, and holds the General Service and Victory Medals
2, North Bridge Street, Shefford. Z2031/C.

MERRY, C., Private, Duke of Wellington's (West Riding Regiment).
He joined in January 1917, and in March of the following year was drafted overseas. He took part in the fighting in the German Offensive and subsequent Allied Advance at Cambrai, and was wounded in the Somme sector in September 1918. He returned home and was demobilised in July 1919, and holds the General Service and Victory Medals.
2, North Bridge Street, Shefford. Z2031/A.

MERRY, F. W., Private, 2nd Bedfordshire Regt.
He was serving at the outbreak of war, and in the following month was sent to France. He took part in the fierce fighting in the Battle of Ypres, where he was wounded and taken prisoner. After receiving treatment in various hospitals in Germany he was interned in Switzerland in May 1916, and there received further medical treatment, and in September of the following year returned to England and was invalided out of the service. He holds the Mons Star, and the General Service and Victory Medals.
2, North Bridge Street, Shefford. Z2031/B.

MERRITT, W. G., Corporal, R.G.A.
He volunteered in April 1915, and in the following May was drafted overseas. He was engaged in heavy fighting in many sectors of the Western Front, and fought in the engagements at Ypres and Cambrai. In July 1917 he returned to England, and was employed on special duties until his demobilisation in January 1919. He holds the General Service and Victory Medals.
208, Dallow Road, Luton. 2030.

MESSENGER, A., Sapper, Royal Engineers.
He joined in September 1916, and in the following March proceeded overseas. He shortly afterwards returned home through ill-health, and on recovery rejoined his unit on the Western Front in February 1918. He was engaged on important duties in the forward areas of the Somme, Marne and Amiens sectors, and was wounded. He returned to England in October 1918, and was demobilised in the following March. He holds the General Service and Victory Medals.
1, Pleasant Side, Harpenden. 2032.

MESSENGER, A. (M.M.), Private, 1st Hertfordshire Regiment.
He was mobilised at the outbreak of war, and immediately drafted to France. He served in the Retreat from Mons, and at the Battles of Hill 60, Ypres, the Somme, Arras and Cambrai, and was awarded the Military Medal for conspicuous gallantry and devotion to duty in the Field. He also holds the Mons Star, and the General Service and Victory Medals, and was demobilised in February 1919.
38, King's Road, St. Albans. 2033/A.

MESSENGER, A., Private, Machine Gun Corps.
A serving soldier, he was immediately sent to France at the outbreak of hostilities. He took part in the fighting during the Retreat from Mons and the engagements at Hill 60, on the Somme, at Arras, Ypres, Cambrai, and was wounded in April 1918. He was invalided home, and after spending some time in hospital was demobilised in July 1919. He holds the Mons Star, and the General Service and Victory Medals.
38, King's Road, St. Albans. 2033/B.

MESSENGER, J. G., Cpl., 5th Bedfordshire Regt.
He was serving at the outbreak of war, and was drafted at once to the Western Front. He fought in the Retreat from Mons, and served in various sectors, and was engaged in the fighting in many battles until the cessation of hostilities. During his service overseas he was wounded and gassed. He was demobilised in February 1919, and holds the Mons Star, and the General Service and Victory Medals.
130, Wenlock Street, Luton. 2034/B.

MESSENGER, W., Pte., 1st Bedfordshire Regt., and Hertfordshire Regiment.
He was mobilised at the outbreak of war, and immediately drafted to France, where he was engaged in heavy fighting in the Retreat from Mons, and was wounded. On recovery he was again in action, and fought at Hill 60 and on the Somme. In 1916 he proceeded to Egypt and served in engagements at Gaza and the subsequent battles until the Fall of Jerusalem. He was demobilised in May 1920, and holds the Mons Star, and the General Service and Victory Medals.
38, King's Road, St. Albans. 2033/C.

MESSENGER, W., Drummer, 1/5th Bedfordshire Regiment.
A serving soldier he was immediately drafted to France at the outbreak of war. He took part in the fierce fighting in the Retreat from Mons, and was severely wounded. He was invalided home and later discharged from the service in consequence of his wounds in June 1915. He holds the Mons Star, and the General Service and Victory Medals.
130, Wenlock Street, Luton. 2034/A.

METCALF, C. G., Private, 1st Norfolk Regiment.
On attaining military age he joined H.M. Forces in August 1918, and after completing his period of training was in the following January drafted to Ireland, where he served on important guard and other duties. He did excellent work during the riots, and was still serving in 1920.
6, Queen's Terrace, Church Street, Dunstable. 2035.

METCRAFT, H., Sapper, Royal Engineers.
He volunteered in May 1915, and after his training was engaged on duties of an important nature with his unit at various stations on the East Coast. He was chiefly engaged in wiring and trenching on the 1st Line of Defence. He was unable to secure his transfer overseas, owing to physical disability, but rendered valuable services until his demobilisation, which took place in February 1919.
6, Bigtham Road, Dunstable. 2036.

MEYERS, W., L/Corporal, Bedfordshire Regt.
Called up from the Reserve at the outbreak of hostilities, he was immediately drafted to the Western Front, where he took part in the Retreat from Mons and the subsequent Battles of the Marne, the Aisne and Hill 60. In 1915, he returned to England in consequence of ill-health, and was invalided out of the service in July of that year. He holds the Mons Star, and the General Service and Victory Medals.
9, Longmire Road, St. Albans.   X2037.

MICHEL, G. F., Rflmn., King's Royal Rifle Corps.
He volunteered at the commencement of hostilities and was quickly drafted to the Western Front, where he served in the Retreat from Mons and many of the engagements which followed. He was unfortunately killed in action at Loos on September 26th, 1915. He was entitled to the Mons Star, and the General Service and Victory Medals.
69, Judge Street, North Watford.   X2038/A.

MIDDLETON, C., Pte., 1/5th Bedfordshire Regt.
He volunteered in May 1915, and whilst training at Halton Camp for foreign service met with an accident and sustained severe injuries. After being for some time under treatment in hospital, he was discharged in May 1916 as physically unfit for further service.
28, Prosperous Row, Dunstable.   2039.

MIDDLETON, G., Pte., 2/5th Yorkshire Regt., and Labour Corps.
He volunteered in July 1915, and after his training was engaged upon duties of an important nature at various stations with his unit. Although unsuccessful in obtaining his transfer overseas, he rendered valuable service until his demobilisation, which took place in July 1919.
20, Shakespeare Street, North Watford.   X2040.

MIDDLETON, J. H., Private, Royal Fusiliers, and Labour Corps.
He volunteered in June 1915, and after his training was drafted to France. Here he took part in many engagements, notably those on the Somme, at Ypres, Hill 60, St. Quentin and Cambrai, and was wounded. He was demobilised in 1919, and holds the 1914-15 Star, and the General Service and Victory Medals.
22, Shakespeare Street, North Watford.   X2041.

MILES, M. G., Sergeant, 4th Bedfordshire Regt.
Volunteering in 1915, he was sent to the Western Front in the following year. Subsequently, he took part in many of the principal engagements, including those at Ypres and Beaumont-Hamel, where in 1917 he was severely wounded and taken prisoner. He was interned in Hanover until after the cessation of hostilities. He returned to England in March 1919, when he was demobilised. He holds the General Service and Victory Medals.
Garden Road, Abbots Langley, Herts.   X2042.

MILES, R., Pte., 1/8th Somerset Light Infantry.
He volunteered in June 1915, and at the conclusion of his training was drafted to the Western Front. Subsequently he took part in much heavy fighting, notably in the Battle of the Somme, and at Arras and Passchendaele. He was unfortunately killed in action near Cambrai on October 15th, 1917. He was entitled to the 1914-15 Star, and the General Service and Victory Medals.
24, Plantation Road, Leighton Buzzard.   2043.

MILES, W., Sergeant, R.A.V.C.
He volunteered in September 1914, and on completion of his training in the following February was drafted to Egypt. After serving there for some time he was sent on to Palestine, where throughout that campaign he did valuable work with his unit and was present at many engagements, notably that at Beersheba. Returning to England in June 1919, he was demobilised a month later, holding the 1914-15 Star, and the General Service and Victory Medals.
56, Inkerman Road, St. Albans.   X2044.

MILES, W. F. A., Private, Bedfordshire Regiment.
Called from the Reserve at the outbreak of war, he was immediately drafted to France, and took part in the Retreat from Mons. Subsequently he served in the Battles of Ypres, the Somme, Arras and Cambrai, and was wounded four times, but on each occasion, after receiving treatment, was able to rejoin his unit. He remained on the Western Front until after the cessation of hostilities. He was demobilised in February 1919, and holds the Mons Star, and the General Service and Victory Medals.
69, Breakspeare Road, Abbots Langley.   X2045.

MILLARD, D. D., Private, R.A.S.C.
Mobilised at the outbreak of war, he was engaged with his unit on duties of an important nature at various stations. He was unable to secure his transfer overseas before the termination of hostilities, but did valuable work until he was discharged through ill-health in February 1917. He died on December 6th, 1918, from causes due to his service.
26, Upper Culver Road, St. Albans.   X2047/B.

MILLARD, H., Trooper, 1st (King's) Dragoon Guards.
He joined in May 1916, and at the conclusion of his training was engaged on duties of an important nature at various stations with his unit. He was unable to secure his transfer overseas before the termination of war, but rendered valuable services until his demobilisation, which took place in May 1919.
Near School, Greenfield, near Ampthill.   2048.

MILLARD, J., Private, 1/1st Oxfordshire and Buckinghamshire Light Infantry.
Mobilised at the outbreak of war, he was for a time engaged upon duties of an important nature, and in March 1915 was sent to France. Here he took part in numerous important engagements, notably those at Ypres (1915), the Somme, St. Quentin and Albert, and was in action almost continuously until November 1917, when, in consequence of ill-health, he was invalided home. He was discharged as physically unfit in March 1918, and holds the 1914-15 Star, and the General Service and Victory Medals.
26, Upper Culver Street, St. Albans.   X2047/A.

MILLARD, W. D., Trooper, Machine Gun Corps (Cavalry).
He volunteered in February 1915, but owing to physical disability was unable to obtain his transfer to a theatre of war. At the conclusion of his training, however, he was engaged on duties of an important nature at various stations with his unit, and rendered valuable service in various capacities until he was demobilised in February 1919.
54, Queen's Street, Hitchin.   2049.

MILLER, A. H. J., Captain, attached R.A.M.C.
He volunteered in August 1915, and in the same month was drafted to the Western Front. Here, in the capacity of Dental Surgeon, he served with the R.A.M.C. in many important sectors, including that of the Somme, and for a period of nearly four years did valuable work overseas. From the cessation of hostilities until October 1919, he was with the Army of Occupation in Germany, and was demobilised on his return to England. He holds the 1914-15 Star, and the General Service and Victory Medals.
Church Green, Harpenden, Herts.   2051.

MILLER, A. T., Sapper, Royal Engineers.
He volunteered in June 1915, and on completing his training in the following December was drafted to the Western Front and thence to Egypt. Here he was engaged on important duties until 1917, when he was transferred to Palestine, where he served at Haifa, Beyrout, Gaza, Jaffa and Jerusalem. He was demobilised after his return to England in March 1919, and holds the 1914-15 Star, and the General Service and Victory Medals.
5, Plantation Road, Leighton Buzzard.   2052.

MILLER, A. V., Gunner, Royal Garrison Artillery.
He volunteered in July 1915, and at the conclusion of his training was drafted to the Western Front. Here he served for eighteen months, during which time he did valuable work as a gunner in many important sectors, notably those of Ypres, the Somme, Arras and Passchendaele. In June 1918 he was transferred to Italy, where he fought on the Piave. He was later stationed at Taranto. Returning to England he was demobilised in April 1919, and holds the General Service and Victory Medals.
58, Warwick Road, Luton.   2050.

MILLER, F., Private, R.A.M.C., and M.G.C.
He volunteered in September 1914, and after his training was engaged on duties of a special nature until 1917, when he was drafted to France. Here he fought in many important engagements, including those on the Somme and at Cambrai, and was taken prisoner during the German Offensive in March 1918. Released after the cessation of hostilities, he returned to England, and in February 1919 was demobilised. He holds the General Service and Victory Medals.
13, Boyle Street, Luton.   2054/A.

MILLER, F., Private, 1st Bedfordshire Regiment.

Volunteering in September 1914, he was drafted to France at the conclusion of his training. He fought in many battles, notably at Ypres and Hill 60, where on May 2nd, 1915, he was unfortunately killed in action, having previously been gassed. He was entitled to the 1914-15 Star, and the General Service and Victory Medals. His memory is cherished with pride.

60, Victoria Road, Lower Watford. X2053/A.

MILLER, J., Private, Bedfordshire Regiment.

He joined in 1917, and after his training was engaged on duties of an important nature with his unit at various stations. He was unable to secure his transfer overseas before the cessation of hostilities, but in December 1918 was sent to Germany, where he served with the Army of Occupation for some months. He was demobilised after his return to England in November 1919.

13, Boyle Street, Luton. 2054/B.

MILLER, J. T., Private, Royal Sussex Regiment.

He joined in February 1917, and was drafted to France at the conclusion of his training. Subsequently he took part in many of the principal engagements, including those at Ypres, Arras and Cambrai, and was wounded. Upon his recovery he rejoined his unit and remained on the Western Front until 1919. He was demobilised in October of that year, and holds the General Service and Victory Medals.

60, Victoria Road, North Watford. X2053/B.

MILLER, T., Air Mechanic, R.A.F. (late R.N.A.S.)

He volunteered in October 1915, and a year later was sent to the Western Front. Here he served in many sectors, being engaged upon important duties which demanded a high degree of technical knowledge and skill. He did much valuable work until after the cessation of hostilities, being demobilised in February 1919. He holds the General Service and Victory Medals.

61, Oak Road, Luton. 2055.

MILLER, W. J., Private, 1st Lancashire Fusiliers.

Volunteering in August 1914, he was drafted to Gallipoli in the following year on the completion of his training. He was unfortunately killed in the Landing at Cape Helles on April 25th, 1915. He was entitled to the 1914-15 Star, and the General Service and Victory Medals.

60, Chapel Street, Hemel Hempstead. X2056.

MILLINGTON, J., A/Sergeant, East Surrey Regt.

He volunteered in August 1914, and in the following year embarked for France. He fought in the engagements at Serre, Arras, Cambrai, Béthune, Amiens and in the Retreat and subsequent Allied Advance of 1918, and was wounded. He was demobilised in 1919, and holds the 1914-15 Star, and the General Service and Victory Medals.

3, Queen's Place, Hemel Hempstead. 2057/A

MILLINGTON, J., Private, Bedfordshire Regt.

He volunteered in August 1914, and was sent to France in May of the following year, and served in many parts of the Western Front, where severe fighting was in progress. He was wounded in March 1918 during the German Offensive, and, invalided to England, received hospital treatment and was discharged unfit for further service in November 1918. He holds the 1914-15 Star, and the General Service and Victory Medals.

3, Queen's Place, Hemel Hempstead. X2057/B.

MILLS, A., Private, Bedfordshire Regiment.

He volunteered in August 1914, and in the following November was drafted to France. He took part in the Battles of La Bassée, Neuve Chapelle, Loos, Ypres and the first Battle of the Somme, in which engagement he was gassed. After receiving hospital treatment he fought in the Retreat and Advance of 1918, and was demobilised in March 1919. He holds the 1914-15 Star, and the General Service and Victory Medals.

30, Chapel Path, Leighton Buzzard. 2061/B.

MILLS, J., Corporal, R.A.M.C.

He joined in April 1917, and later in the year was drafted to Salonika, where he served for a time. He was then sent to Egypt, and in Palestine was engaged on ambulance duties in the forward areas during operations, and was present at the Battles of Gaza, Haifa and Aleppo, afterwards serving with the Army of Occupation in Constantinople. He returned to England, and was demobilised in May 1920, and holds the General Service and Victory Medals.

27, Acme Road, Watford. 2060.

MILLS, A. S., A.B., Royal Navy.

He volunteered in August 1914, and was posted to H.M.S. "Harrier," afterwards serving in H.M.S. "Shakespeare." During the course of the war his ships served in the North, Mediterranean and Baltic Seas on important patrol and other duties until hostilities ceased. He was still serving in 1920, and holds the 1914-15 Star, and the General Service and Victory Medals.

40, Princes Street, Dunstable. 2058.

MILLS, F., Gunner, Royal Garrison Artillery.

He joined in June 1916, and in the following year was sent to France. In this theatre of war he fought in many engagements, including the Battle of the Somme, and during his service overseas he was stationed at Etaples for some time. He was discharged in May 1918 on account of service, and holds the General Service and Victory Medals.

71, Salisbury Road, Luton. 2059.

MILLS, J., Private, Norfolk Regiment.

He volunteered in January 1915, and in the following July embarked for France. He served in many sectors of the Western Front, and fought in the first and second Battles of the Somme, the Battles of Vimy Ridge, Bullecourt, Passchendaele, and was wounded at the Battle of Ypres in 1917. He later rejoined his unit, and took part in the heavy fighting during the German Offensive and subsequent Allied Advance in 1918. He was demobilised in January 1919, and holds the 1914-15 Star, and the General Service and Victory Medals.

30, Chapel Path, Leighton Buzzard. 2061/A.

MILLS, R., Private, R.A.M.C.

He joined in September 1916, and after his training served at various military hospitals on important ambulance and other duties. He rendered valuable services, but was not successful in obtaining his transfer overseas owing to medical unfitness. He was demobilised in February 1919.

Caddington, near Luton. 2062.

MILLS, S., Driver, Royal Engineers.

He volunteered in 1914 and later in the same year proceeded to France, where he served in many engagements, including those of Ypres, Arras, Cambrai and the Somme. In 1917 he was sent to Italy, and was employed on important duties in connection with the battles on the Piave and Trentino fronts. He returned to England, and was demobilised in February 1919, and holds the 1914-15 Star, and the General Service and Victory Medals.

31, Balmoral Road, Hitchin. 2063

MILLS, W. J., Private, Machine Gun Corps.

He volunteered in September 1914, and after training was engaged on important duties with his unit until drafted overseas in July 1916. Serving on the Western Front he took part in many important battles, including those of the Somme, Ypres, Passchendaele, Cambrai and Givenchy, and was seriously wounded and invalided home in August 1918. He was demobilised in March 1919, and holds the General Service and Victory Medals.

Sun Street, Potton. Z2064.

MILTON, H. A. (Miss), Special War Worker.

During the war this lady offered her services for work of National importance, and was engaged as a "viewer" in the Engine Section A.I.D. Her duties, which called for a high standard of technical knowledge and skill, were carried out in a careful and efficient manner until after the cessation of hostilities.

85, Cardiff Road, Watford. X2065/A.

MILTON, S. H., Petty Officer, Royal Navy.

He was mobilised on the declaration of war and posted to H.M.S. "Queen," aboard which vessel he was engaged on patrol and other duties in the North Sea. His ship took part in the bombardment of the forts in the Dardanelles, and subsequently had several encounters with the German Fleet in the North Sea and the Baltic. He was still serving in 1920, and holds the 1914-15 Star, and the General Service and Victory Medals.

62, Holywell Road, Watford. X2066.

MINALL, G., Private, 1st Hertfordshire Regiment.

He volunteered in November 1914, and after training was drafted to France in the following year. He served with his unit in several sectors, and fought at Ypres and in many operations during the Offensive on the Somme and was wounded. Rejoining his unit he took part in further heavy fighting, and was killed in action at St. Julien in April 1917. He was entitled to the 1914-15 Star, and the General Service and Victory Medals.

New Farm, Station Road, Harpenden. 2067/B.

MINALL, W., Private, 1st Hertfordshire Regt.
Volunteering in September 1914, he was drafted overseas in the following year. He proceeded to the Western Front, where he served in several sectors, and took part in heavy fighting at Hill 60, Ypres and Albert. He was later despatched to Egypt, and in the Eastern theatre of war was in action in the Canal Zone and in the Battles of Romani, Gaza, Haifa and Aleppo, in the Advance through Palestine under General Allenby. He was twice wounded during his service abroad, and was demobilised on his return to England in December 1918. He holds the 1914-15 Star, and the General Service and Victory Medals.
New Farm, Station Road, Harpenden.   2067/A.

MINCHIN, T. G., Corporal, R.A.M.C.
He volunteered in August 1915, and was shortly afterwards posted to the "Aquitania." This vessel was engaged in bringing sick and wounded soldiers from the fighting fronts to England and Canada. He also rendered good service in the "Braemar Castle," and was demobilised in August 1919. He holds the General Service and Victory Medals.
22, Sotheran Road, Watford.   X4049/A.

MING, W. J., Driver, R.A.S.C. (M.T.)
Volunteering in 1915, in the same year he was drafted to Salonika. He did excellent work in the Balkans, where he was engaged on important duties in connection with the transport of ammunition and supplies during the Advance on the Struma and on Monastir. On the termination of hostilities he returned to England, and was demobilised in February 1919. He holds the 1914-15 Star, and the General Service and Victory Medals.
25, Pinner Road, Oxhey, Watford.   X2068.

MINGAY, H., Private, Bedfordshire Regiment.
He volunteered in September 1914, and was later drafted to France. During his service on the Western Front he took part in much heavy fighting, and was wounded at Hill 60. He was invalided home, and subsequently discharged as medically unfit for further service in 1916. He holds the 1914-15 Star, and the General Service and Victory Medals.
16, Cambridge Street, Luton.   3892/B.

MINGAY, H., Private, R.A.M.C.
He was mobilised at the outbreak of war, and was almost immediately drafted overseas. He was in action in many sectors of the Western Front, and served at the Battles of Ypres, the Somme and Hill 60. Owing to ill-health he was invalided home in June 1918, and was subsequently demobilised in the following March. He holds the 1914 Star, and the General Service and Victory Medals.
16, Cambridge Street, Luton.   3892/C.

MINGAY, J. T., Sergt., Royal Garrison Artillery.
He was mobilised in August 1914, and served at various stations with his Battery until drafted to France in August 1916. He was in action in many engagements, including those on the Somme, at Ypres, Cambrai, and in the German Offensive and subsequent Allied Advance of 1918. He was demobilised in April 1919, and holds the General Service and Victory Medals.
72, Collins Road, Southsea.   3892/A.

MINNEY, O., Private, Northamptonshire Regt.
He was serving in the Army when war was declared, and was shortly afterwards sent to France, where he was in action in the Retreat from Mons and other important battles. He was later drafted to Salonika and then to Egypt, where he saw much active service. He took part in General Allenby's Advance through Palestine, and among other engagements fought in the Battles of Jaffa and Haifa. He was transferred to the Royal Inniskilling Fusiliers, and discharged on completion of service in March 1919. He holds the Mons Star, and the General Service and Victory Medals.
High Street, Woburn Sands.   2069.

MINNEY, W. T., Pte., Volunteer Training Corps.
Unfit for active service he joined the second Luton Volunteer Battalion in February 1918, and after training was engaged on important duties at various stations on the East Coast, and later in guarding munition factories and railway communications. He did good and useful work, and was demobilised in January 1919.
Brickhill, Chaul End Lane, Caddington.   2070.

MINNS, E. F. C., A.B., Royal Navy.
He volunteered in April 1915, and trained at Chatham and later at Malta. He then served with his ship on important patrol and other duties in the North Sea until the cessation of hostilities. Owing to an accident he was invalided to hospital, and after receiving treatment was discharged from the Service in January 1919. He holds the General Service and Victory Medals.
Beeston Green, Sandy.   Z2073.

MINNIS, A. W., Private, 3rd Bedfordshire Regt.
He joined in July 1916, and in the following October was drafted to France. There he took part in the offensive operations on the Somme, and in heavy fighting at Arras until he was invalided home. On recovery he was proceeding to Egypt when the transport was torpedoed on December 30th, 1917, and he was amongst those who were lost. He was entitled to the General Service and Victory Medals.
8, Providence Row, St. Andrew's Place, Hitchin.   2071.

MINNIS, F., Private, Essex Regiment.
He volunteered in November 1915, and after training was engaged on various duties with his unit until drafted in December of the following year to the Western Front. He took part in heavy fighting in the Battles of the Somme, Arras, Ypres and Cambrai, and was wounded in the Retreat of 1918. He was demobilised in 1919, on returning to England, and holds the General Service and Victory Medals.
7, Penns Yard, St. Andrew's Street, Hitchin.   2072.

MITCHELL, A. E., Private, 1/5th Bedfordshire Regiment.
He volunteered in September 1914, and being drafted to Gallipoli took part in the landing at Suvla Bay and in other engagements in the Peninsula until killed in action at Anafarta in September 1915. He was entitled to the 1914-15 Star, and the General Service and Victory Medals.
8, Peach Road, Luton.   2074.

MITCHELL, A. J., A.B., Royal Navy.
He was serving in the Navy when war broke out, having enlisted in 1911, and in H.M.S. "Cressy" was engaged on patrol and other duties in the North Sea. He was drowned on September 22nd, 1914, when his vessel was torpedoed off the Hook of Holland. He was entitled to the 1914-15 Star, and the General Service and Victory Medals.
Ampthill Road, Flitwick.   2075.

MITCHELL, F. A., Sergeant, Royal Engineers.
He joined in 1917, and was drafted overseas in the same year. He served with his unit in the Egyptian theatre of war, and was engaged on important duties in the Advance under General Allenby into Palestine. Amongst the important battles at which he was present were those of Gaza, Jaffa, Aleppo and Damascus. He was demobilised in March 1920, on his return to England, and holds the General Service and Victory Medals.
82, Breakspeare Road, Abbots Langley.   X2076.

MITCHELL, G., Pte., 1/5th Bedfordshire Regt.
He volunteered at the commencement of hostilities, but after his training was found to be unfit for foreign service, owing to physical disability, and was retained for important duties. He was subsequently stationed on the East Coast and at various other places, and was engaged on guard and instructional duties until March 1918, when he was invalided out of the service.
116, Long Row, Vandyate, Leighton Buzzard.   2474.

MOBLEY, W. G., Private, 2nd Bedfordshire Regt.
Volunteering in September 1914, in the following November he was drafted to France. There he took part in heavy fighting in several sectors, and was engaged at Ypres, Loos, and in several of the offensive operations on the Somme. He was killed in action on the Somme on October 12th, 1916, and was entitled to the 1914 Star, and the General Service and Victory Medals.
13, Albert Road, Houghton Regis.   2078.

MOCKRIDGE, J. T., Pte., 29th Middlesex Regt., and 8th Labour Corps.
He joined the 29th Middlesex Regiment in March 1917, and being found unfit for active service owing to physical disability was transferred to the Labour Corps. Serving with this unit at various stations he did good work until his demobilisation in March 1919.
Hampton Cottage, Leyton Road, Harpenden.   2079.

MONEY, G., Sergeant, 4th Bedfordshire Regt.
He volunteered in 1914, and after undergoing a course of training was engaged with his unit on important duties at various depôts until drafted to the Western Front in June 1916. Proceeding from the base to the trenches he took a prominent part in several important battles, including those on the Somme and at Ypres. He was killed in action near Arras on May 29th, 1917, and was entitled to the General Service and Victory Medals.
26, Bedford Street, Ampthill.   2081/A.

MONEY, J., Private, 6th Bedfordshire Regiment.
Volunteering in 1915, after training he served with his unit at various stations and was drafted overseas in September 1917. Almost immediately on reaching the Western Front he was sent to the firing line and took part in heavy fighting in the Ypres sector. He was killed in action on Passchendaele Ridge on October 9th, 1917, and was entitled to the General Service and Victory Medals.
26, Bedford Street, Ampthill. 2081/B.

MONGER, W., Corporal, R.A.V.C.
He volunteered in August 1914, and in the following September was sent to the Western Front. He served at Rouen, Calais, Arras, Ypres and Cambrai and did excellent work attending to sick and wounded horses and mules during the course of the war. He returned to England and was demobilised in 1919, and holds the 1914 Star, and the General Service and Victory Medals.
9, Hicks Road, Markyate. 2080.

MONK, A., Private, 1st Bedfordshire Regiment.
He volunteered in September 1914, and in the following year was sent to France. There he served in many sectors and was in action at Arras, Ypres, Cambrai, St. Quentin and on the Somme, and was wounded and gassed. Rejoining his unit on recovery, he took part in the closing stages of the war, and returned to England for demobilisation in January 1919. He holds the 1914-15 Star, and the General Service and Victory Medals.
Garden Fields, Offley 2705/A,

MONK, A. J., Sapper, Royal Engineers.
He volunteered in November 1914, and in August of the following year was sent to the Dardanelles where he took part in the landing at Suvla Bay and the subsequent fighting until the Evacuation of the Peninsula. He was then drafted to Egypt, where he saw active service on the Palestine front and in the British Offensive under General Allenby in 1918. He returned to England and was demobilised in March 1919, and holds the 1914-15 Star, and the General Service and Victory Medals.
65, Frederic Street, Luton. 2082.

MONK, J., Private, Bedfordshire Regiment.
He volunteered in September 1914, and in the following year was drafted to the Western Front in several sectors of which he took part in heavy fighting. He fought in the Battles of Arras and Ypres, and was killed in action in the Ypres sector on October 15th, 1917. He was entitled to the 1914-15 Star, and the General Service and Victory Medals.
Garden Fields, Offley 2705/B.

MONKMAN, F., Private, 4th Bedfordshire Regt.
He joined in 1916, and in the same year embarked for France, where he saw active service in many parts of the Western Front. He fought in the Battles of Arras, Ypres, Cambrai, and the Somme, and was later invalided home. After hospital treatment he returned to France and served with his unit until killed in action on July 10th, 1918, during the German Offensive. He was entitled to the General Service and Victory Medals.
Potton, Beds. 2083/A.

MONKMAN, F. T., Sapper, Royal Engineers.
He volunteered in August 1914, and proceeded to France in the following year, and served at the Battles of the Somme, Arras, Ypres, Festubert; afterwards he was transferred to the Italian theatre of war and served at the Battles of the Piave. During his service overseas he was engaged upon important engineering and constructional work. He returned to England and was demobilised in February 1919, and holds the 1914-15 Star, and the General Service and Victory Medals
Potton, Beds. Z2083/B.

MONTAGUE, A. H., Sergeant, 2/13th London Regiment (Kensingtons).
He volunteered in February 1915, and in the same year proceeded to France where he saw active service in many sectors. He was afterwards transferred to the Macedonian theatre of war and served on the Vardar and Struma fronts. Later he was sent to Egypt and took part in the fighting and British Offensive in Palestine in 1918 until hostilities ceased. He then served with the Allied Army of Occupation in Asia Minor and Turkey. He returned to England and was demobilised in February 1920, and holds the 1914-15 Star, and the General Service and Victory Medals.
73, Elfrida Road, Watford. X2084.

MONTGOMERY, S. B., Gnr. (Signaller), R.F.A.
He joined in April 1917, and after his training served at various stations on important duties with his unit. He rendered valuable services and had passed out as a first-class signaller, but, owing to injuries received in the course of his duties, was unable to obtain his transfer overseas before the cessation of hostilities. He was demobilised in November 1919.
48, Periwinkle Lane, Hitchin. 2085.

MOODY, F., Private, 1st Bedfordshire Regiment.
He volunteered in June 1915, and was drafted to France, where he served in many engagements, including those of Arras and Ypres, and during his service in this theatre of war was wounded twice. He was later sent to the Italian Front, and took part in the fighting on the Trentino. He returned to England and was demobilised in February 1919, and holds the General Service and Victory Medals.
81, Ridgeway Road, Luton. 2086.

MOONEY, E. C., Private, R.A.S.C.
He volunteered in June 1915, and in the same year was sent to France. In this theatre of war he served with his unit in several sectors and was present during many engagements, including those of Ypres, the Somme and Arras. He was demobilised in April 1919, and holds the 1914-15 Star, and the General Service and Victory Medals.
2, Union Street, Hemel Hempstead X2087/A.

MOONEY, M. (Miss), Special War Worker.
This lady volunteered her services for work of National importance, and from January 1915 until December 1915 was employed at Messrs. Eley's munition works, Edmonton. Her duties were in connection with the filling of cartridges and she did very good work. She was afterwards engaged in the production of bricks at the Brick Yards, Hemel Hempstead, for a time and her services were greatly appreciated.
2, Union Street, Hemel Hempstead 2087/B.

MOONEY, T., Pte., 1st King's (Liverpool Regt.)
He was serving in H.M. Forces at the outbreak of hostilities and proceeded to France in August 1914. He served throughout the fighting in the Retreat from Mons and in the Battles of the Aisne, the Marne, Ypres, Loos, Festubert, the Somme, Cambrai, Albert, and in many other engagements. He was discharged in March 1919 on account of service, and holds the Mons Star, and the General Service and Victory Medals.
14, Carey Place, Watford. 2088.

MOONEY, W., L/Corporal, Sherwood Foresters.
He volunteered in August 1914, and in the following July was drafted to France, where he was engaged in the fighting in the Battles of the Somme, Arras, Ypres, and other major engagements. He was killed in action at Poperinghe on July 15th, 1918, during the German Offensive, and was entitled to the 1914-15 Star, and the General Service and Victory Medals.
48, King Street, Dunstable. 2089.

MOORE, C. H., Private, 6th Bedfordshire Regt.
He volunteered in October 1914, and in June of the following year embarked for France. He was almost continually in action in many sectors of the Western Front, and on July 15th, 1916, was reported wounded and missing, but was afterwards believed to have been killed in action on that date at Pozières. He was entitled to the 1914-15 Star, and the General Service and Victory Medals.
77, Liverpool Road, Watford. 2090/A.

MOORE, E., Sapper, Royal Engineers (R.O.D.)
He joined in November 1916, and after his training was drafted to Egypt, where he was engaged on duties of a technical nature in the forward areas. He also served in a similar capacity during the Palestine campaign. He holds the General Service and Victory Medals, and was demobilised in September 1919.
65, Leavesden Road, Watford. X2091.

MOORE, E. G., Corporal, 8th Oxfordshire and Buckinghamshire Light Infantry.
Volunteering in September 1914, he was sent to the Western Front a year later and subsequently took part in several engagements, including that on the Somme. In September 1917, he was drafted to Salonika, where he did excellent work with his unit, notably on the Vardar front, and served there until March 1919. He was demobilised after his return to England in the following month, and holds the 1914-15 Star, and the General Service and Victory Medals.
62, New Road, Linsdale, Bucks. 2092.

MOORE, F., Private, East Surrey Regiment.
He volunteered in September 1914, and early in the following year proceeded to the Western Front. He was engaged in the heavy fighting at the Battle of Ypres and was severely wounded and gassed. He was invalided home and after receiving hospital treatment was discharged as medically unfit for further service in February 1916. He later died from the effects of gas poisoning, and was entitled to the 1914-15 Star, and the General Service and Victory Medals.
Coronation Road, Potton, Beds.   Z4143/B.

MOORE, H., Air Mechanic, Royal Air Force.
Joining in November 1916, he was drafted to the Western Front two months later and was employed in the workshops of the 9th Squadron until the cessation of hostilities, when he was sent with the Army of Occupation to Germany. In 1919 he was transferred to Mesopotamia, where in the following year he was still serving, being engaged on duties which called for a high degree of technical knowledge and skill. He holds the General Service and Victory Medals.
33, Newcombe Road, Luton.   2093.

MOORE, J., Private, R.A.S.C.
He volunteered in June 1915, and after his training served at various stations on important duties with his unit. He rendered valuable services, but was not successful in obtaining his transfer overseas before the cessation of hostilities. He was demobilised in February 1919.
77, Liverpool Road, Watford.   2090/B.

MOORE, J. E., Private, Bedfordshire Regiment.
He joined in February 1918, and after his training was drafted to the Western Front, where he served in the Advance of that year. He took part in the fighting on the Marne and at Amiens and Bapaume, and was wounded. He holds the General Service and Victory Medals, and was demobilised in February 1919.
45, Jubilee Road, North Watford.   X2094/A.

MOORE, T. A., Gunner, Royal Garrison Artillery.
Volunteering in December 1914, he was drafted to Egypt early in the following year, and subsequently took part in several minor engagements. He also fought in the Palestine Campaign under General Allenby, remaining on this front until early in 1918, when he was sent to France and served in the final stages of the war. Whilst in the East he contracted malaria, and was in consequence for some time in hospital. He was demobilised after his return to England in June 1919, and holds the 1914-15 Star, and the General Service and Victory Medals.
5, Three Crown Passage, High Street, Watford.   X2096.

MOORE, W., Private, R.A.S.C.
He volunteered in November 1915, and in the same year was drafted to Salonika. He served with his unit in several sectors of the Balkan Front, and was engaged on important transport duties in the front lines whilst heavy fighting was in progress. He was in action at many of the principal engagements, notably those on the Vardar and at Monastir. He contracted malaria in the course of his service, and was discharged in consequence as medically unfit for further military service in August 1919. He holds the 1914-15 Star, and the General Service and Victory Medals.
28, Camp View Road, St. Albans.   X3093/A.

MOORE, W. H., Private, Bedfordshire Regiment.
He joined in 1917, and after his training was engaged on duties of an important nature at various stations with his unit. For a period he was engaged upon work on the land. He was unable to secure his transfer overseas, but nevertheless did valuable work until his demobilisation, which took place in February 1919.
45, Jubilee Road, North Watford.   X2094/B.

MOORHEAD, F. J., Private, 11th Middlesex Regt.
Joining in June 1916, he was quickly drafted to the Western Front, where he took part in heavy fighting in the Somme sector. He was subsequently killed in action at Arras on May 4th, 1917. He was entitled to the General Service and Victory Medals.
25, Stockwood Crescent, Luton.   2098.

MOORING, A. G., Private, Coldstream Guards.
Mobilised on the outbreak of war, he was almost immediately drafted to France, where he fought in the Retreat from Mons and in many of the subsequent battles until he was killed in action at Lillers on October 9th, 1915. He was entitled to the Mons Star, and the General Service and Victory Medals.
65, High Street, Markyate.   1472/B.

MOORING, S., Sapper, Royal Engineers.
He volunteered in May 1915, and after his training proceeded to France in 1917. He served with his unit in many engagements on the Western Front, and was killed in action on the Somme at the commencement of the German Offensive on March 21st, 1918. He was entitled to the General Service and Victory Medals.
7, St. Paul's Road, Luton.   2764/A.

MOORING, S. F., Private, East Yorkshire Regt.
Called up from the Reserve on the outbreak of hostilities, he was quickly sent to France, where he took part in the Retreat from Mons and the Battles of Ypres and La Bassée. He was unfortunately killed in action at Neuve Chapelle on March 10th, 1915. He was entitled to the Mons Star, and the General Service and Victory Medals.
30, Pondswick Road, Luton.   900/A.

MORECRAFT, J., Corporal, Hertfordshire Regt.
A serving soldier, he was drafted to France in November 1914, and subsequently took part in engagements at Ypres, Givenchy, Festubert and Hill 60. He also took part in the Battle of the Somme, and on one occasion was wounded and gassed. He returned to England, and was discharged as time expired in April 1916, holding the 1914 Star, and the General Service and Victory Medals.
7, Verulam Road, Hitchin.   2099.

MORETON, J., Corporal, 6th Bedfordshire Regt.
He volunteered in August 1914, and in January of the following year was sent to France. Here he took part in several engagements, including those at Ypres and the Somme, and was subsequently killed in action at Arras on April 9th, 1917. He was entitled to the 1914-15 Star, and the General Service and Victory Medals.
22, Liverpool Road, Watford.   X2100/A.

MORETON, T., Royal Air Force.
He joined in June 1917, and after his training served at various aerodromes as an observer on important duties. He did good work, but was not successful in obtaining his transfer overseas before the cessation of hostilities. He was, however, sent with the Army of Occupation into Germany, and was stationed at Cologne. He was demobilised in November 1919.
22, Liverpool Road, Watford.   X2100/B.

MORGAN, A., Driver, R.E. (Signal Section).
He volunteered in October 1915, and at the conclusion of his training was sent to Salonika. Here he served for nearly three years, during which time he did valuable work with his unit in the forward areas, chiefly on the Doiran front. He was demobilised after his return to England in June 1919, and holds the General Service and Victory Medals.
29, Silsoe, near Ampthill.   2101.

MORGAN, A., L/Corporal, Queen's (Royal West Surrey Regiment).
Volunteering in 1915, he joined the Royal Fusiliers, and was later transferred to the "Queen's." After his training, he was engaged on duties of a special nature at various stations, and although unable to secure his transfer to a theatre of war before the cessation of hostilities, rendered valuable services until his demobilisation, which took place in September 1919.
27, Fearnley Street, Watford.   X2102.

MORGAN, F. C., Private, Norfolk Regiment.
He volunteered in February 1915, and was shortly afterwards drafted to the Western Front. He fought in many engagements, including those on the Somme, at Arras and Ypres, where he was severely wounded in 1916. He was invalided home and subsequently discharged in consequence of his wounds in July 1916. He holds the 1914-15 Star, and the General Service and Victory Medals.
1, Common View, Letchworth.   3827/B.

MORGAN, H., Private, 4th Norfolk Regiment.
He joined in April 1917, and after completing his training was sent to Egypt. He was engaged in heavy fighting in Palestine, where he was killed in action on December 11th of the same year. He was entitled to the General Service and Victory Medals.
29, Lowestoft Road, Watford.   X2105/A.

MORGAN, H. J., Sergt., 51st Royal Sussex Regt.
He joined in July 1917, and after his training was engaged on duties of an important nature at various stations with his unit. He was unable to secure his transfer overseas before the cessation of hostilities, but in December 1918 was sent with the Army of Occupation to Germany, where he served at Cologne for a time. He was demobilised on his return to England in March 1920.
2, Waterlow Road, Dunstable.   2007/A.

MORGAN, H., Driver, Royal Field Artillery.

He volunteered in 1915, and was sent to France in the same year. During his service in this theatre of war he was attached to the Ammunition Flying Column and took part in many of the principal engagements, notably those at Ypres, Hill 60, Vimy Ridge, the Somme, Arras and Passchendaele. After the cessation of hostilities, he served with the Army of Occupation in Germany, and was demobilised on his return to England in June 1919. He holds the 1914-15 Star, and the General Service and Victory Medals.

14, Austin's Place, Hemel Hempstead. X2103.

MORGAN, H., L/Cpl., 13th Royal Irish Rifles.

He volunteered in September 1914, and in the following year was drafted to the Dardanelles, subsequently taking part in the landing at Suvla Bay and in fighting at Anzac. After the evacuation of the Peninsula, he was transferred to France, where he served in several engagements, including those at Ypres and Arras, and was killed in action on August 16th, 1917. He was entitled to the 1914-15 Star, and the General Service and Victory Medals.

8, Peach Street, Luton. 2104.

MORGAN, H. W., Sergeant, 1st Bedfordshire Regiment, and Hertfordshire Regiment.

He enlisted in December 1904, and was mobilised at the outbreak of hostilities, subsequently being drafted to France. He fought in many of the principal engagements, notably those on the Somme, where he was severely wounded, at Arras and Monchy. After his return to England at the termination of the war, he was demobilised, but in March 1919 rejoined for a further period of service. He holds the 1914-15 Star, and the General Service and Victory Medals.

10, Albion Road, Luton 2106.

MORGAN, J., Private, 3rd Bedfordshire Regt.

He was mobilised at the outbreak of war, but owing to medical unfitness was unable to secure his transfer overseas. He was engaged on important duties and rendered valuable services until demobilised in April 1919.

102, Hartley Road, Luton. 2107.

MORGAN, J. L., Driver, Royal Engineers.

He volunteered in February 1915, and after his training served at various stations until drafted to France in 1917. He was engaged in many sectors of the Western Front on important duties in connection with railroad repairing and was frequently under heavy fire. He served at the Battles of the Somme, the Marne, Arras and Vimy Ridge. He was demobilised in June 1919, and holds the General Service and Victory Medals.

1, Common View, Letchworth. 3827/A.

MORGAN, W., Private, R.A.S.C. (M.T.)

He volunteered in April 1915, and was later drafted to the Western Front. Here he was engaged on important transport work in the forward areas and was present at several engagements, notably those at Ypres and Cambrai. He holds the General Service and Victory Medals, and was demobilised after his return to England in July 1919.

29, Lowestoft Road, Watford. X2105/B.

MORLEY, A., Private, Middlesex Regiment.

He joined in May 1916, and in the following July was on active service on the Western Front. There he fought in several important engagements, including the Battles of the Somme, Arras and Messines, and was killed in action at Ypres on August 16th, 1917. He was entitled to the General Service and Victory Medals.

22, Periwinkle Lane, Hitchin 3012/A.

MORLEY, E. S., Officers' Cook, Royal Navy.

Joining in September 1917, he was posted to H.M.S. "Rameses," which vessel was engaged on special patrol duties in the North Sea and off the Coast of Scotland. Later he was transferred to H.M.S. "Shamrock," in which, in 1920, he was still serving in the Baltic. He holds the General Service and Victory Medals.

15, Southwold Road, Callowland, Watford. X2108.

MORLEY, L., Private, Middlesex Regiment.

He joined in February 1916, and in the same year was drafted to the Western Front. In this theatre of war he took part in the Battles of the Somme, and Arras, in which he was severely wounded. After receiving treatment at the base, however, he rejoined his unit and again served in engagements, including those at Ypres. He was demobilised after his return to England in 1919, and holds the General Service and Victory Medals.

15, Southwold Road, Callowland, Watford. X2109/B.

MORLEY, H., Private, Suffolk Regiment.

He joined in 1917, and after his training was engaged upon duties of an important nature at various stations with his unit. He was unsuccessful in obtaining his transfer to a theatre of war, but nevertheless rendered valuable services until his demobilisation, which took place in 1919.

15, Southwold Road, Callowland, Watford. X2109/A.

MORLEY, W. G., Cpl., 4th Bedfordshire Regt.

He volunteered in November 1914, and was sent to the Western Front in February 1916. He served in many sectors of this Front and fought in the Battles of Ypres, the Somme, Arras and other engagements, and was wounded early in 1918. He returned to England, and was subsequently discharged in consequence of his wounds, in May of that year. He holds the General Service and Victory Medals.

90, Clarendon Road, Luton. 2110

MORRIS, A. T., Gunner, R.G.A.

He joined in March 1917, and later in the same year was drafted to France. He was in action in many engagements and fought during the German Offensive in 1918, and was killed in action near Arras on 2nd September 1918, during the subsequent Allied Advance. He was entitled to the General Service and Victory Medals.

22, Cumberland Street, Luton. 2111.

MORRIS, C., Private, London Regiment.

He joined in July 1917, and was sent to France in the same year. In this theatre of war he fought in the Battles of Ypres, the Somme and during the German Offensive and Allied Advance of 1918, and was gassed. He was demobilised in December 1919, and holds the General Service and Victory Medals.

12, Park Street, Dunstable. 2112.

MORRIS, C. W., C.S.M., Royal Scots Fusiliers.

Volunteering in September 1914, he completed his training with the Scottish Rifles, and proceeded to France in November of the following year, and was there transferred to the Royal Scots Fusiliers. He saw much fighting during his service on the Western Front and was drafted to Salonika in 1916, and served on the Vardar front until invalided to England in October of the same year. He was unfit for further service overseas, and was stationed in Scotland training recruits for the New Armies until demobilised in December 1919. He holds the 1914-15 Star, and the General Service and Victory Medals.

11, Greatham Road, Bushey. X2113.

MORRIS, H., Private, 3rd Bedfordshire Regiment.

He volunteered in August 1914, and in the same year was sent to India, where he served at various stations on garrison duties until 1916. He was then transferred to the Palestine Front and fought in the Battles of Romani and Gaza, and was present at the subsequent taking of Haifa, Aleppo and Damascus. He returned to England and was demobilised in July 1919, and holds the General Service and Victory Medals.

63, Ivy Road, Luton. 2114

MORRIS, J., Sapper, Royal Engineers.

Volunteering in November 1914, he served with his unit at various depôts until drafted to the Western Front. He served with his unit on important constructional work in the forward areas and was present at several notable engagements, including those of Arras, Ypres and Cambrai. Returning to England on the conclusion of hostilities he was demobilised in March 1919, and holds the General Service and Victory Medals.

32, St. Saviour's Crescent, Luton. 3224/B.

MORRIS, J. T., Air Mechanic, Royal Air Force.

He volunteered in 1914, and in September of the same year was sent to France. He served with his squadron at various aerodromes, including those in the Ypres salient and on the Loos, Somme, Arras and Cambrai fronts, and did much good work. He was demobilised in March 1919, and holds the 1914 Star, and the General Service and Victory Medals.

Church End, Harlington. 2115.

MORTIMER, H., Private, 17th Middlesex Regt.

He volunteered in September 1915, and in the following year proceeded to the Western Front. He was in action in many engagements, including those of Arras and the first Battle of the Somme, and was killed in action on April 27th, 1917, at the Battle of Vimy Ridge. He was entitled to the General Service and Victory Medals.

5, Holy Walk, Luton. 2116.

MORTON, G. W., Trooper, Hertfordshire Dragoons.

He volunteered in 1915, and was drafted to the Western Front in the same year. While in this theatre of war he fought in the Battle of Ypres and other engagements. In 1917 he joined the Egyptian Expeditionary Force and served under General Allenby in the Advance through Palestine. He returned to England and was demobilised in 1919, and holds the 1914-15 Star, and the General Service and Victory Medals.
Slate Corner, Flamstead, Dunstable.   X2117.

MOSS, A. W., Private, Lincolnshire Regiment.

He volunteered in April 1915, and after his training served at various stations on important duties with his unit. He rendered valuable services, but was not successful in obtaining his transfer overseas before the cessation of hostilities owing to medical unfitness. He was invalided out of the service in March 1918.
79, Chapel Street, Luton.   2118.

MOSS, T. J., Private, 1st Norfolk Regiment.

He joined in May 1918, and in the following August was drafted to France, where he took part in the Allied Advance of 1918, and was in action at Amiens, Bapaume, and was wounded on the Somme in September. He returned to England, and, after hospital treatment, was demobilised in January 1919. He holds the General Service and Victory Medals.
202, Wellington Street, Luton.   2119.

MOTLEY, J. W., Private, Royal Defence Corps.

He joined in 1916, and being unfit for active service was posted to the Royal Defence Corps. After training he was engaged at various stations on guard and other important duties, and did valuable service until his discharge in 1918.
63, Dacre Road, Hitchin.   3453/C.

MOTLEY, W. J., Pioneer, R.E. (R.O.D.)

Joining in March 1917, in the following month he was sent to France. He served with his unit on special duties in the forward areas in various sectors, and was present at many important engagements, including those of Ypres, Arras and Cambrai. On the termination of hostilities he was sent with the Army of Occupation to Germany and was stationed at Cologne until his return to England for demobilisation in November 1919. He holds the General Service and Victory Medals.
63, Dacre Road, Hitchin.   3453/B.

MOTT, A., Corporal, King's Royal Rifle Corps.

He volunteered in August 1914, and in the following month embarked for France, where he served in many parts of the Western Front. He fought in the Battles of the Marne, Festubert, Loos, Vimy Ridge, Messines and other engagements of note. He was demobilised in February 1919, and holds the 1914 Star, and the General Service and Victory Medals.
13, Millbrook, Ampthill.   2120.

MOULDEN, H. C., Private, Queen's (Royal West Surrey Regiment).

He joined in February 1917, and in the same year was drafted to France, where he was attached to the Labour Corps. He served with this unit in the forward areas of the Somme, Ypres, Cambrai, St. Quentin, and throughout the German Offensive and subsequent Allied Advance in 1918. He was demobilised in April 1919, and holds the General Service and Victory Medals.
37, Fillhouse Street, Hitchin.   2121.

MOULDER, T. H., Private, R.A.V.C.

He volunteered in February 1916, and in the following April embarked for Salonika, where he served with his unit until 1919. During this period he was engaged on important duties in attending to sick and wounded horses, and in this capacity did excellent work. He returned to England and was demobilised in August 1919, and holds the General Service and Victory Medals.
27, Albert Street, Watford.   X1090/B, X1091/B.

MOULDER, W. J., Private, Royal Fusiliers.

He volunteered in September 1914, and early in the following year proceeded to the Western Front, where he served in various sectors. He fought in the Battles of Arras and Ypres, and was twice wounded during his service overseas. He was discharged in August 1916, on account of wounds received, and holds the 1914-15 Star, and the General Service and Victory Medals.
7, Albert Street, Watford.   X1090/C, X1091/C.

MOULES, W., Air Mechanic, Royal Air Force.

He joined in June 1918, and after his training served at various stations on important duties with his squadron. He rendered valuable services, but on account of medical unfitness was unable to obtain his transfer overseas prior to the signing of the Armistice. He was demobilised in May 1919.
11, Keyfield Terrace, St. Albans   2123.

MOULES, A., Trooper, Royal Buckinghamshire Hussars.

Volunteering in September 1914, he completed his training and served at various stations on the East Coast until drafted to France in January 1916. He was in action in many battles, including that of the Somme, and was wounded. On recovery he returned to the front lines, and fought in the Retreat and Advance of 1918. He was demobilised in March 1919, and holds the General Service and Victory Medals.
3, Thorps Yard, Queen Street, Hitchin.   2122/B.

MOULES, G., Private, Royal Berkshire Regiment.

He joined in October 1916, and in the following July was sent to France, where he served in the Battles of Arras, Ypres, and was wounded in action on the Somme Front in February 1918. He was invalided to England, and after receiving hospital treatment was engaged on home service until demobilised in April 1919. He holds the General Service and Victory Medals.
3, Thorps Yard, Queen Street, Hitchin.   2122/A.

MUCKFORD, H. J., Corporal, Royal Warwickshire Regiment.

He volunteered on the outbreak of war, and was almost immediately drafted to France, where he took part in the fierce fighting during the Retreat from Mons and the Battle of Ypres, and was wounded. Rejoining his unit on recovery, he was engaged at the Battle of Loos and in the first British Offensive on the Somme, and was killed in action on September 24th, 1916. He was entitled to the Mons Star, and the General Service and Victory Medals.
79, Waterlow Road, Dunstable.   2137.

MUCKLESTON, H., Sapper, Royal Engineers.

He volunteered in November 1914, and in June 1915, was drafted to France. He was in action at Ypres, Laventie, Armentières and many other engagements. He was killed in action on October 7th, 1916, in the course of the first Battle of the Somme. He was entitled to the 1914-15 Star, and the General Service and Victory Medals.
High Street, Toddington.   2125.

MUCKLESTON, W., L/Sergeant, Suffolk Regt.

He volunteered in August 1915, and in the following January was sent to the Western Front. There he took part in much heavy fighting, and was in action at the Battles of the Somme, Arras, Ypres, Passchendaele, Cambrai and in the Retreat and Advance of 1918. On the termination of the war he returned to England, and was demobilised in March 1919. He holds the General Service and Victory Medals.
Upper Sundon, near Dunstable.   2133.

MUIR, E. H., L/Corporal, Royal Fusiliers.

Volunteering in 1914, he was drafted in the same year to the Western Front, in several sectors of which he served with his unit. He saw much heavy fighting and amongst other important actions took part in the Battles of the Somme and Ypres, and was wounded. He returned to England in 1919, and was demobilised in February of the following year, and holds the 1914-15 Star, and the General Service and Victory Medals.
10, Willow Lane, Watford.   2713/A.

MULLETT, F. G., Gunner, Royal Field Artillery.

He joined in May 1917, and in the following November proceeded to the Western Front, where he served in various engagements, including the Battles of Ypres, Passchendaele, the Somme, Cambrai, St. Quentin, and throughout the German Offensive and subsequent Allied Advance in 1918. He was demobilised in January 1919, and holds the General Service and Victory Medals.
25, Kenilworth Road, Luton.   2126.

MULLIS, A., Private, 8th Bedfordshire Regiment.

He joined in March 1916, and in the following September was drafted to the Western Front, where he was in action in the first Battle of the Somme, during the course of which he was wounded. On recovery he rejoined his unit and was again wounded in an engagement near Loos in May 1917, and was invalided to hospital in England, and in consequence of his wounds one of his legs had to be amputated He was subsequently discharged in October 1918, and holds the General Service and Victory Medals.
101, High Street, Markyate.   2146.

MULLIS, S., Air Mechanic, Royal Air Force.

He joined the Royal Air Force in June 1917, and was attached to the Kite Balloon Section. He was employed at various stations on important duties which required a high degree of technical skill, but was not successful in obtaining his transfer overseas before the cessation of hostilities. He was demobilised in April 1919.
30, Pickfords Hill, Markyate.   2147.

MUNDAY, A., L/Corporal, Oxfordshire and Buckinghamshire Light Infantry.

He volunteered on the outbreak of war, and was shortly afterwards drafted to France, where he fought in the Retreat from Mons, in the Battles of Ypres and the Somme, and other important actions until wounded in 1917. He was invalided home and was subsequently discharged on account of service in that year, and holds the Mons Star, and the General Service and Victory Medals.
125, Regent Street, North Watford. X2149.

MUNDAY, C., Corporal, 17th (Duke of Cambridge's Own) Lancers.

He joined in March 1916, and in the following October was sent overseas. He saw much service on the Western Front, where he fought in many important engagements, including those on the Somme, at Arras and Bullecourt. He was taken prisoner during heavy fighting near Ypres in 1917, and was repatriated to England on the signing of the Armistice. He was demobilised in 1919, and holds the General Service and Victory Medals.
69, Edward Street, Dunstable. 2134/A.

MUNDAY, E., Private, Gloucestershire Regiment.

Volunteering in September 1914, he completed his training and in the following year was drafted to France where he saw much service. He was in action in several engagements, including the Battles of the Somme, Ypres, Messines, Cambrai and St. Julien, and was wounded. He was invalided to England and after hosp'tal treatment ws discharged as medically unfit for further service in December 1918. He holds the 1914-15 Star, and the General Service and Victory Medals.
Belmont Cottages, Lower Luton Road, Harpenden 2132/A.

MUNDAY, H., Private, 1st Hertfordshire Regt.

He volunteered in 1915, and later in the year embarked for France, where he fought in many engagements, including those of Ypres and the Somme. He was wounded at Givenchy, and after receiving hospital treatment rejoined his unit and served throughout the German Offensive and Allied Advance of 1918. He was demobilised in August 1919, and holds the 1914-15 Star, and the General Service and Victory Medals.
33, Ashby Road, Watford. 2139/A.

MUNDAY, H., Driver, R.A.S.C.

He volunteered in May 1915, and was drafted to France in March of the following year. Whilst in this theatre of war he served in the forward areas in many sectors and was present at the Battles of Ypres and the Somme, and during the fighting in the Retreat and Advance of 1918. He was demobilised in July 1919, and holds the General Service and Victory Medals.
33, Ashby Road, Watford. 2139/C.

MUNDAY, J., Gunner, Royal Field Artillery.

He volunteered in January 1915, and in the following year was drafted overseas. Serving with his battery on the Western Front, he was in action in several sectors and took part in many important battles, including those of the Somme, Vimy Ridge, Ypres, Passchendaele, and Messines. He was wounded in the course of his services and on recovery rejoined his unit and served until the conclusion of hostilities. He was demobilised in April 1919, and holds the General Service and Victory Medals.
Belmont Cottages, Lower Luton Road, Harpenden. 2132/B

MUNDAY, J., Rifleman, The Cameronians (Scottish Rifles).

He joined in April 1917, and on completion of his training served at various stations on important duties with his unit. He rendered valuable services but was not successful in obtaining his transfer overseas before the close of the war. He was demobilised in November 1919.
33, Ashby Road, Watford. 2139/B.

MUNDAY, M. (Mrs.), Special War Worker.

This lady offered her services for work of National importance, and from 1915 until 1917 was employed at Chaul End munition factory, where she was engaged in filling fuses. From 1917 until January 1919 she worked on the manufacture of cordite at Waltham Cross munition works, and her work throughout gave every satisfaction.
Belmont Cottages, Lower Luton Road, Harpenden. 2127

MUNNS, A. T., Private, Royal Sussex Regiment.

A Reservist, he was mobilised on the outbreak of war, and underwent a course of training, afterwards serving with his unit at various stations on important duties until August 1917, when he was drafted to the Western Front. Here he took part in heavy fighting at Ypres, Passchendaele and other notable battles until wounded near Cambrai in January 1918. Invalided home on account of wounds he received hospital treatment and was subsequently discharged in September 1918. He holds the General Service and Victory Medals.
7, New Town, Potton. Z2152.

MUNNS, H., Air Mechanic, Royal Air Force.

He joined in November 1917, and was sent to France in the same year. In this theatre of war he served at various aerodromes with his squadron, where he was engaged as a carpenter and rigger. His duties called for a high degree of technical skill and he did much good work. He was demobilised in September 1919, and holds the General Service and Victory Medals.
3, Cross Street North, St. Albans. X2141.

MUNT, A., Private, Machine Gun Corps.

He joined in February 1917, on attaining military age, and was drafted to France in March of the following year. In this theatre of war he was in action throughout the German Offensive and Allied Advance of 1918, and after hostilities ceased returned to England and was demobilised in February 1919, and holds the General Service and Victory Medals.
10, Balford Road, Harpenden. 2128.

MUNT, A. G., Driver, Royal Field Artillery.

He volunteered in 1915, and after training served with his unit at various stations until drafted to Mesopotamia in June 1917. He served with his regiment in many important engagements, and took part in the campaign which resulted in the capture of Baghdad. Returning to England on the cessation of hostilities he was demobilised in February 1919, and holds the General Service and Victory Medals.
20, New Dalton Street, St. Albans. X2150.

MUNT, A. J., Gunner, Royal Field Artillery.

Volunteering in 1915, he was drafted to Mesopotamia in the same year. He saw much service in this theatre of war and was engaged in heavy fighting in the attempts to relieve Kut. On the cessation of hostilities he returned to England and was demobilised in April 1919, and holds the General Service and Victory Medals.
59, Breakspeare Road, Abbots Langley. X2145.

MUNT, H., Private, Duke of Cornwall's Light Infantry.

He joined in April 1916, and in the following month embarked for France. He was in action at the first Battle of the Somme, and at Arras, Ypres, Cambrai and St. Quentin. He was later transferred to the Labour Corps and served with this unit in many sectors until the Armistice. He was demobilised in February 1919, and holds the General Service and Victory Medals.
81, Breakspeare Road, Abbots Langley. X2143.

MUNT, R., L/Corporal, Cambridgeshire Regt.

He volunteered in September 1914, and after his training was retained for duties of an important nature until January 1916, when he was sent to France. Here he served until the cessation of hostilities and took part in many of the principal battles, notably those of Ypres, the Somme and Arras, and also fought in the Retreat and Advance of 1918. He was wounded at Neuve Chapelle, but after being treated at the base was able to rejoin his unit. He was demobilised on his return to England in November 1918, and holds the General Service and Victory Medals.
13, Cannon Cottage, Hitchin. 2473/A.

MUNT, T. R., Corporal, Royal Engineers.

Mobilised on the outbreak of hostilities, he was drafted to the Western Front in November 1914. His service in this theatre of war lasted for over four years, during which time he did excellent work in many important sectors, notably those of Ypres, Arras, Passchendaele and the Somme. Whilst overseas he contracted an illness, of which he died after his return to England on April 11th, 1919. He was entitled to the 1914 Star, and the General Service and Victory Medals.
13, "Cannon Cottage," Hitchin. 2473/B.

MURPHY, T. E., Sergeant, 1st West Yorkshire Regiment.
Volunteering on the outbreak of hostilities he was shortly afterwards drafted to France, where he took part in the heavy fighting at the Battles of Ypres and the Marne, and in many other important engagements until seriously wounded in 1917. He was invalided to England, and after being in hospital for a considerable time was subsequently discharged as medically unfit for further service in August 1917. He holds the 1914-15 Star, and the General Service and Victory Medals.
66, Harwood Road, Watford.   X2130.

MURPHY, T. G., Sapper, Royal Engineers.
Volunteering in September 1914, in the following year he was drafted to Gallipoli, where he served until the Evacuation of the Peninsula, and then proceeded to Egypt. He did excellent work during the British Advance through Sinai, Palestine and Syria, and was present at heavy fighting in several important engagements, including the Battle of Gaza. On the conclusion of hostilities he returned to England for demobilisation in July 1919, and holds the 1914-15 Star, and the General Service and Victory Medals.
10, Ferndale Road, Luton.   2136.

MURRAY, P., Private, Norfolk Regiment, and Leicestershire Regiment.
He volunteered in August 1915, and later in the same year was sent to India, where he was engaged on important garrison duties at various stations, including Poona, Karachi and Quetta. He also served in Egypt and was stationed at Alexandria. He returned home, and was demobilised in December 1919, and holds the General Service and Victory Medals.
74, Dane Road, Luton.   62/B.

MUSK, A., Rifleman, Rifle Brigade, and Private, R.A.S.C.
He volunteered in March 1915, and on completion of his training proceeded to the Western Front, where he served with his unit in various sectors and took part in many of the principal battles, including those at Ypres. He was twice wounded in the course of his service, which extended for over four years and was demobilised on his return to England in April 1919. He holds the 1914-15 Star, and the General Service and Victory Medals.
5, Leith Cottages, Wharf Lane, Rickmansworth.   X2144.

MUSKETT, F., L/Corporal, Loyal North Lancashire Regiment.
Volunteering in August 1914, he was drafted after training overseas in the following May. He served on the Western Front, and was in action in several sectors, taking part in the Battles of Arras, Ypres and Armentières. Wounded and suffering from gas poisoning, he was invalided to hospital in England in September 1918, and after medical treatment was demobilised in the following February. He holds the 1914-15 Star, and the General Service and Victory Medals.
30, High Street, Houghton Regis.   ,   2138.

MUSKETT, G., Gunner, Royal Garrison Artillery.
He joined in 1916, and in the same year proceeded to France, where he fought in many engagements, including those of Ypres, Arras, Hill 60, and the Somme, and throughout the German Offensive and Allied Advance of 1918. He returned to England and was demobilised in 1919, and holds the General Service and Victory Medals.
77, Breakspeare Road, Abbots Langley.   X2140.

MUSKETT, G., L/Corporal, 4th Suffolk Regt.
Joining in July 1916, in the same year he was drafted to the Western Front, and saw much service in many sectors. He took part in important engagements, and was wounded near Passchendaele in April 1917. Rejoining his unit after medical treatment he was in action at Arras, Ypres and on the Somme, and was wounded a second time at Cambrai during the German Offensive in 1918. He was demobilised in January 1919, and holds the General Service and Victory Medals.
50, Hartley Road, Luton.   2151.

MUSKETT, H., Sergeant, R.A.V.C.
He volunteered in October 1914, and after training was stationed at various depôts until drafted overseas. He served for a time on the Western Front, where he did excellent work during heavy fighting at Vimy Ridge and on the Somme. He was then sent to Salonika, and in this theatre of war carried out responsible duties in connection with the treatment of sick and wounded horses in the forward areas, and was in action in the advance across the Vardar and the Struma. He returned to England and was demobilised in June 1919, and holds the General Service and Victory Medals.
11, Roberts Road, Watford.   X2131.

MUSKETT, P., Private, Machine Gun Corps.
He joined in March 1917, and after training was drafted overseas in the following June. He served with his unit in various parts of the Western Front, and fought in many notable battles, including that of Cambrai, and was wounded. After receiving medical treatment he returned to his unit, and served during the concluding stages of the war. He was demobilised in May 1919, and holds the General Service and Victory Medals.
Downsview, Borough Road, Dunstable.   2135/B.

MUSKETT, W., Private, 100th Bn. Canadian Infantry.
He joined in June 1916, and in the following year proceeded to France, where he was in action in many major engagements. He was reported missing on May 3rd, 1917, and later was presumed to have been killed in action at Vimy Ridge on that date. He was entitled to the General Service and Victory Medals.
83, Breakspeare Road, Abbots Langley.   X2142.

MUSKETT, W., Private, Royal Marine Engineers.
He joined in April 1918, and was employed on important duties in connection with the manufacture of brick and stone work for government use. He rendered valuable services, but was unable to obtain a transfer overseas prior to the cessation of hostilities, and was demobilised in February 1919.
2, Cambridge Street, Luton.   2148.

MUSSINO, H., Private, Machine Gun Corps.
Volunteering in January 1915, he completed his training and was engaged on important duties with his unit at various stations until drafted to the Western Front. There he served in various sectors and took part in many important battles, including those of Arras, Ypres and Bullecourt, and was taken prisoner in the German Offensive on March 21st, 1918. He was demobilised in February 1919, on his repatriation to England, and holds the General Service and Victory Medals.
15, Percy Road, Watford.   X2129.

MYERS, W., Gunner, Royal Garrison Artillery.
Volunteering in October 1915, he was in action in France in the following year. He saw much service in various sectors, and was engaged in heavy fighting on the Ancre, at Vimy Ridge, Bullecourt, and was unfortunately killed in action in the vicinity of Arras on June 25th, 1917. He was entitled to the General Service and Victory Medals.
3, Lindum Cottages, Alma Cut, St. Albans.   2154/B.

MYNARD, F. E., Sergeant, Machine Gun Corps.
He volunteered in March 1915, and after training was drafted overseas in the following August. Whilst on the Western Front he took part in heavy fighting in various sectors until gassed near Loos in February 1916. He was invalided home and was in hospital under treatment for gas poisoning for many months, and was discharged as medically unfit for further service in January 1919. He holds the 1914-15 Star, and the General Service and Victory Medals.
13, Vernon Road, Luton.   2153.

McCRAE, K., Captain, Queen's Own Cameron Highlanders.
Volunteering in October 1914, he was sent to France shortly afterwards and served in various sectors fighting at the Battles of Loos, Arras, Cambrai, Ypres, Albert and many other important engagements. He was mentioned in Dispatches for conspicuous gallantry and devotion to duty in the Field, and during his period of service was gassed twice. Returning to England he was demobilised in January 1919, and holds the General Service and Victory Medals.
94, St. Mary's Road, Watford.   X1448/B.

MONEY, T., Private, 6th Bedfordshire Regiment.
He volunteered in 1915, and was sent to the Western Front in September 1917. He was fighting almost continuously during his service overseas, and was unfortunately killed in action on October 9th of the same year at Passchendaele Ridge. He was entitled to the General Service and Victory Medals.
26, Bedford Street, Ampthill.   2081/B.

N

NAPIER, J. J., Sergeant-Major, R.G.A.
A serving soldier, he was drafted to France in September 1914, and took part in the final stages of the Retreat from Mons. He fought in many other engagements, notably those at Loos, Beaumont-Hamel (where he was wounded), the Somme, Passchendaele, Arras and Cambrai, and remained on the Western Front for some months after the cessation of hostilities. He was discharged in March 1919, and holds the Mons Star, and the General Service, Victory, and Long Service and Good Conduct Medals.
9, High Street, Houghton Regis.   2156.

NARROWAY, F. W., Pte., Machine Gun Corps.
Volunteering in 1915, he was sent to France early in the following year. He fought in many of the principal engagements, including those at Ypres, the Somme and Cambrai (where he was gassed), and Arras. He was demobilised after his return to England in February 1919, and holds the General Service and Victory Medals.
115, Lower Paddock Road, Oxhey. X2157.

NASH, A., A.B., Royal Navy.
Joining in January 1917, he was posted to H.M.S. "Suffolk." His ship was engaged with the North Sea Patrol and also served in Russian and Japanese waters. During his services his ship frequently passed through mine infested areas in the discharge of her duties. He was demobilised in April 1919, and holds the General Service and Victory Medals.
19, Curzon Road, Luton. 2158.

NASH, A. G., Private, Bedfordshire Regiment.
He joined in February 1917, and during his service in France, which lasted for nearly two years, was in action in many engagements, including those at Arras, Cambrai and the Somme. Returning to England he was demobilised in 1919, and holds the General Service and Victory Medals.
1, Caroline Cottages, Capel Road, Oxhey, Herts. X2165/B.

NASH, A. G., Gunner (Signaller), R.F.A.
He volunteered in May 1915, and was stationed in Ireland, where he served during the Sinn Fein riots of May 1916. In July of that year he was sent to France and took part in many important engagements, notably those on the Somme, at Arras, Ypres and Cambrai, and was twice wounded. He was demobilised after his return to England in June 1919, and holds the General Service and Victory Medals.
22, Salisbury Road, Luton. 2159.

NASH, A. H., Gunner, Royal Garrison Artillery.
He joined in 1917, and after his training was engaged on important duties with his unit at various stations. He was unable to secure his transfer overseas before the termination of the war, and rendered services of a valuable nature until his demobilisation in November 1919.
131, Lower Marlowes, Hemel Hempstead. X2160.

NASH, D. E., Gunner, Royal Field Artillery.
He volunteered in June 1915, and was later drafted to Mesopotamia, where he participated in much heavy fighting, notably in that at Baghdad. He afterwards served at various garrison stations in India, remaining there until after the cessation of hostilities. He returned to England and was demobilised in April 1919, and holds the General Service and Victory Medals.
23, Primrose Cottages, Hatfield, Herts. X2161/A.

NASH, G. W., Private, Bedfordshire Regiment.
He volunteered in 1914, and owing to medical unfitness was retained for home service. He served at various stations with his unit on important duties, and rendered valuable services throughout. He was invalided out of the service in 1917.
29, Ebenezer Street, Luton. 2543/B.

NASH, G. W., Private, Bedfordshire Regiment.
Joining in July 1916, he was sent to France in the same year and fought in the Battles of Ypres, the Somme and Arras. In 1918 he was severely wounded, and in consequence was invalided home and discharged in April of that year. He holds the General Service and Victory Medals.
23, Primrose Cottages, Hatfield, Herts. X2161/B.

NASH, H. C., Leading Seaman, Royal Navy.
Mobilised in July 1914, he was first posted to H.M.S. "Himalaya," which was engaged in the Battle of the Narrows in the following March. Subsequently he saw service in H.M.S. "River Clyde" and "Albion," off the East Coast of Africa, and on one occasion was wounded. He holds the 1914-15 Star, and the General Service and Victory Medals, and was demobilised in February 1919.
3, Field Terrace, Watford. X2162.

NASH, J., Private, Bedfordshire Regiment, and Rifleman, Royal Irish Rifles.
He joined in the Bedfordshire Regiment in January 1917, and was later transferred to the Royal Irish Rifles. After his training he served at various stations on important duties with his unit but was unable to secure his transfer overseas. He did valuable work until demobilised in November 1919.
58, Fearnley Street, Watford. X2163.

NASH, J. A., Gunner, Royal Field Artillery.
He joined in November 1917, and in the following year was sent to the Western Front, where he participated in much heavy fighting, during the Retreat and Advance of 1918. After the cessation of hostilities he went into Germany with the Army of Occupation, and was demobilised in April 1919. He holds the General Service and Victory Medals.
2, Common Lane, Batford, Harpenden. 2164.

NASH, T., Sergeant, Rifle Brigade.
He volunteered in August 1914, and was quickly drafted to France, where he took part in the Retreat from Mons, and many other engagements, including those of Ypres, Arras and Cambrai. He was wounded at Beaumont-Hamel in 1916, but after receiving medical treatment returned to the front line and served on the Western Front until after the cessation of hostilities. Returning to England, he was demobilised in March 1919, and holds the Mons Star, and the General Service and Victory Medals.
1, Caroline Cottages, Capel Road, Oxhey, Herts. X2165/A.

NASH, T., Private, 1/5th Essex Regiment.
He joined in January 1917, and in the following July was sent to Egypt and thence to Palestine. In November of that year he was severely wounded during operations resulting in the capture of Gaza, but after being treated in hospital for four months, served in the British Advance through Palestine and Syria and was present at the Occupation of Aleppo. He was demobilised after his return to England in December 1919, and holds the General Service and Victory Medals.
48, Clarence Road, Leighton Buzzard 2166.

NASH, T., Private, Royal Fusiliers.
He joined in March 1917, and was drafted to France later in the year. He took part in several engagements, and was in action almost continuously until March 1918, when he was taken prisoner on the Somme. After his release he returned to England and was demobilised in November 1919. He holds the General Service and Victory Medals.
23, Primrose Cottages, Hatfield, Herts. X2161/C.

NASH, W., Private, R.A.S.C.
Joining in 1916, he was sent to France in the same year, and was engaged on important duties in the forward areas. He was present at the Battles of Loos, Arras and Cambrai, and on one occasion was severely wounded. On recovery he rejoined his unit and remained on the Western Front until after the cessation of hostilities. He was demobilised in September 1919, and holds the General Service and Victory Medals.
210, Harwood Road, Watford. X2167.

NEAL, A., 1st Air Mechanic, Royal Air Force.
Joining in July 1916, he was engaged, upon duties which called for a high degree of technical knowledge and skill. He was unsuccessful in obtaining his transfer to a theatre of war, but rendered valuable services until his demobilisation, which took place in January 1919.
15, Albert Street, Markyate, Herts. 2177.

NEAL, C. (M.M.), Bombardier, R.F.A.
Volunteering at the commencement of hostilities, he was drafted to France early in 1915, and took an active part in many important engagements, notably those at Ypres, the Somme and Delville Wood. On four occasions he was wounded, and after being treated at a Base Hospital rejoined his unit and remained overseas until after the cessation of hostilities. He was awarded the Military Medal for distinguished gallantry in the Field, and in addition holds the 1914-15 Star, and the General Service and Victory Medals. He was still serving in 1920.
82, Brightwell Road, Watford X2168/A.

NEAL, E., Private, Royal Defence Corps.
Being ineligible for service with the Colours, he joined the Royal Defence Corps in October 1914. Throughout the period of hostilities he was engaged in important guard and other duties at various stations, and did valuable work until his discharge in March 1919.
31, Common View Square, Letchworth. 2185

NEALE, J., Private, R.A.M.C.
He joined in October 1916, but after his training, in consequence of medical unfitness, was retained for service at home. He was engaged as stretcher-bearer and in other capacities at various hospitals, and did valuable work until his demobilisation, which took place in July 1919.
59, Spencer Road, Luton. 2186.

NEALE, M., Private, 6th Royal Berkshire Regt.
He joined early in 1916, and was drafted to the Western Front in the same year. On his arrival at this theatre of war he was sent to the Somme sector, where operations were then in progress, during the course of which he sustained a serious wound and died in hospital on October 7th, 1916. He was entitled to the General Service and Victory Medals.
18, Sydney Road, Watford.   2187.

NEALE, W., Sapper, Royal Engineers.
He volunteered in September 1915, and a month later was sent to France. Here he served for nearly four years, and was engaged on duties of an important nature in the forward areas. He was present at many battles, including those of Ypres, Arras, the Somme, Cambrai and Passchendaele. He holds the 1914-15 Star, and the General Service and Victory Medals, and was demobilised in February 1919.
29, Husbourne Crawley, Aspley Guise, Beds.   Z2171.

NEEDLE, C., Private, 9th Middlesex Regiment.
He volunteered in August 1914, and at the conclusion of his training was drafted to India, where for the remaining period of hostilities, he was engaged on duties of an important nature. He was demobilised after his return to England in May 1919, and holds the General Service and Victory Medals.
96, Leavesden Road, Watford.   X2172/A.

NEEDLE, F., 1st Class Stoker, Royal Navy.
He was already in the Navy, and for a year after the outbreak of war served with the North Sea patrol in H.M.S. "Paragon." This vessel was afterwards engaged in convoying troops to Salonika until March 18th, 1917, on which date she was torpedoed and sunk in the Straits of Dover, and he was drowned. He was entitled to the 1914-15 Star, and the General Service and Victory Medals.
96, Leavesden Road, Watford.   X2172/C.

NEEDLE, H. J., Private, R.A.S.C.
He volunteered in June 1915, and in the following January was sent to Egypt and thence to Palestine. In this theatre of war, he did valuable work, and was severely wounded during operations at Gaza in March 1917. He was able to rejoin his unit after treatment, however, and remained overseas until July 1919. He returned to England and was demobilised a month later, and holds the General Service and Victory Medals.
96, Leavesden Road, Watford.   X2172/B.

NEGUS, A., Corporal, Norfolk Regiment.
He volunteered at the commencement of hostilities, and was sent to France in the following year and took part in fighting at Festubert and Loos. Later he was transferred to Mesopotamia, and in 1917 was taken prisoner at Kut. During his captivity he contracted a severe illness, of which he died in June 1918. He was entitled to the 1914-15 Star, and the General Service and Victory Medals.
13, Dacre Road, Hitchin.   3751/B.

NEGUS, A. E., L/Corporal, 2nd Norfolk Regt.
A serving soldier he was stationed in England for a time, and early in 1915 was sent to Mesopotamia. In this theatre of war he took part in several engagements, and during the Siege of Kut contracted fever of which he died on February 2nd, 1917. He was entitled to the 1914-15 Star, and the General Service and Victory Medals.
1, Taylor's Cottages, Old Park Road, Hitchin.   2188.

NEGUS, G., L/Corporal, 1st Bedfordshire Regt.
He volunteered in August 1914, and from the following June until March 1919 served on the Western Front. During this time he took part in several of the principal engagements, notably those at Cambrai and Ypres, where he was wounded in 1917. He rejoined his unit after being treated at a base hospital, and was demobilised on his return to England. He holds the 1914-15 Star, and the General Service and Victory Medals.
Saunders Piece, Park Hill.   2184/A.

NEGUS, G., Corporal, Bedfordshire Regiment.
Volunteering in August 1914, he was sent to the Western Front in the following year. He was engaged in the fighting at Festubert, Loos and Arras, and was unfortunately killed in action at Cambrai in December 1917. He was entitled to the 1914-15 Star, and the General Service and Victory Medals.
13, Dacre Road, Hitchin.   3751/C.

NEGUS, S., Private, 51st Royal Sussex Regiment.
Joining in June 1918, he had not completed his training when hostilities ceased. In the following January he was sent to the Army of Occupation in Germany, where he served at various stations on the Rhine until March 1920, when he returned to England and was demobilised.
Saunders Piece, Ampthill.   2184/B.

NEGUS, R. J., Private, 2nd Bedfordshire Regt.
He volunteered in November 1914, and was sent to the Western Front in the following June. His service overseas lasted for nearly four years, during which time he was engaged in the fighting in many sectors, notably at Loos, the Somme, Arras, Ypres, Passchendaele Ridge and Cambrai, and did excellent work with his unit. He holds the 1914-15 Star, and the General Service and Victory Medals, and was demobilised in February 1919.
Park Hill, Ampthill.   2183.

NEIGHBOUR, A. C., Private, Canadian Mounted Rifles.
He volunteered in 1914, and was sent to the Western Front in 1916. During his overseas service, which lasted for three years, he was engaged in the fighting at Ypres, on the Somme, at Arras and Cambrai, and did valuable work with his unit throughout. He was demobilised after his return to England in March 1919, and holds the General Service and Victory Medals.
74, Church Street, Rickmansworth.   2189.

NELSON, P., Corporal, Royal Engineers.
He volunteered in August 1914, and was drafted to France in the following June. He was engaged on important duties in the forward areas, and was present at many engagements, including those at Ypres, Arras, the Somme and Cambrai and did excellent work with his unit. He was demobilised in September 1919, and holds the 1914-15 Star, and the General Service and Victory Medals.
19, May Street, Luton.   2181/A.

NELSON, R. G., Driver, Royal Engineers.
Volunteering in March 1915, he was sent to France at the conclusion of his training. He saw service in many important sectors of the Western Front, notably those of the Somme, Ypres and Cambrai, but in 1918, in consequence of an injury received, returned to England, and in October of that year was invalided out of the service. He holds the General Service and Victory Medals.
8, Duke Street, Luton.   2190.

NEVILLE, C., Private, Royal Army Cyclist Corps.
Volunteering in August 1914, he saw much service of a varied nature. In 1915 he was sent to the Dardanelles, where he took part in the campaign in that theatre of war until the evacuation of the Peninsula. He was then drafted to Egypt and served on the Palestine Front during the operations preceding and during the British Advance of 1917. Finally proceeding to France he was in action in many engagements during the latter months of the war. He was demobilised in July 1919, and holds the General Service and Victory Medals.
101, Highbury Road, Luton.   695/B.

NEVILLE, W. G., Private, R.A.S.C., and 1/8th Hampshire Regiment.
He volunteered in August 1914, and early in the following year embarked for the Dardanelles and took part in all engagements until the Evacuation of the Peninsula. He was then transferred to Egypt and thence to Palestine, where he fought at Gaza, Jaffa and Haifa, and remained on this front until the cessation of hostilities. He was demobilised in June 1919, and holds the 1914-15 Star, and the General Service and Victory Medals.
6, Fearnley Street, Watford.   X2169.

NEW, R. H., Sapper, Royal Engineers.
He enlisted in H.M Forces prior to the outbreak of war and embarked for France in August 1914. He served with his unit through many engagements, including those of Arras, the Somme, and Passchendaele During his service overseas he was wounded, and returned to England in 1918. He was still serving in 1920, and holds the 1914 Star, and the General Service and Victory Medals.
15, King Street, Houghton Regis.   2175.

NEWBERY, A. W., Flight-Sergeant, R.A.F.
He joined in January 1918, and after training was stationed at various aerodromes with his squadron and engaged on important duties which called for a high degree of technical skill. He had many flights to France with bombing machines and rendered valuable services, and was demobilised in January 1919. He holds the General Service and Victory Medals.
21, Alfred Street, Luton.   2194

NEWBOLT, G. W., Air Mechanic, R.A.F.
He joined in August 1917, and on completion of his training was drafted to France in August of the following year. Whilst in this theatre of war he served at various aerodromes and was engaged on important duties which called for a high degree of technical skill. He rendered valuable services and returned to England in 1919, and was demobilised in March of the same year. He holds the General Service and Victory Medals.
10, Surrey Street, Luton.   641/A.

NEWBURY, A., Driver (Farrier), R.A.S.C. (H.T.)
He joined in November 1916, and in the following January proceeded to the Western Front. He served in many sectors and was present at the Battles of Ypres, Somme, Cambrai, St. Quentin, and was in action in the Retreat and Advance of 1918. He was demobilised in June 1919, and holds the General Service and Victory Medals.
34, Saxon Road, Luton. 2191.

NEWBURY, A., Private, Bedfordshire Regiment.
He volunteered in 1915, and in the same year was sent to the Western Front, where he was in action in the Battles of Loos, Ypres, Arras, Cambrai and Albert, and throughout the Retreat and Advance of 1918. He returned to England and was demobilised in 1919, and holds the 1914-15 Star, and the General Service and Victory Medals.
Lower Green, Ickleford, Hitchin. 4186.

NEWBURY, A. G., Private, R.A.S.C.
He volunteered in April 1915, and in the following year was sent to France, where he was engaged on the transport of ammunition and supplies in the advanced areas, and was frequently under fire. He served at the Battles of Ypres, the Somme, Cambrai and Albert, and was demobilised in May 1919. He holds the General Service and Victory Medals.
14, Leighton Street, Woburn. Z2192/B.

NEWBURY, A. J., Private, Bedfordshire Regt., and Loyal North Lancashire Regiment.
He volunteered in July 1915, and after his training served at various stations on important duties with his unit. He rendered valuable services, but, owing to ill-health, was not passed as medically fit for service overseas, and for this reason he was discharged in October 1917.
65, Ash Road, Luton. 2180.

NEWBURY, E. A., Private, Dorsetshire Regiment.
He joined in November 1916, and proceeded to France where he was in action with his regiment in many engagements, until unfortunately killed on August 11th, 1918, during the Allied Advance. He was entitled to the General Service and Victory Medals.
New Marford, Wheathampstead. 2182/B.

NEWBURY, F. J., Private, Royal Fusiliers.
On attaining military age he joined in March 1918, and after his training embarked for France two months later and was in action throughout the German Offensive and subsequent Allied Advance. In December of the same year he was sent to Mesopotamia and was stationed at Baghdad and Amara on garrison duties. He was still serving in 1920, and holds the General Service and Victory Medals.
80, Orchard Road, Walworth. 2407/B.

NEWBURY, H. J., Private, Machine Gun Corps.
He joined in June 1918, and served with his unit at various stations in England. He was unsuccessful in obtaining his transfer overseas prior to the cessation of hostilities, but soon afterwards was sent with the Army of Occupation into Germany and was stationed at various places on the Rhine on garrison duties. On his return to England he was transferred to Ireland and served there until demobilised in March 1920.
New Marford, Wheathampstead 2182/A.

NEWBURY, J. G., Private, Loyal North Lancashire Regiment.
Volunteering in November 1914, he proceeded to France three months later and was engaged in many important battles, including those of Loos, Vimy Ridge and the Somme. He was in action almost continuously until 1917, when he was invalided to England owing to ill-health, and, after a protracted illness, died on July 29th, 1918. He was entitled to the 1914-15 Star, and the General Service and Victory Medals.
45, South Street, Leighton Buzzard. 2195.

NEWBURY, W., Private, Lancashire Fusiliers, and Bedfordshire Regiment.
He volunteered in August 1914, and was sent to France almost immediately. He saw heavy fighting throughout the Retreat from Mons and in the Battles of the Marne, St. Eloi, Loos, the Somme, Arras, Ypres, and other engagements. He was killed in action at Passchendaele on September 5th, 1917, and was entitled to the Mons Star, and the General Service and Victory Medals.
Ickleford Common, Ickleford, Hitchin. 3331/B.

NEWBURY, J. R., Corporal, Machine Gun Corps.
He volunteered in February 1916, and later in the year embarked for France and in this theatre of war fought in many engagements, including the Battle of Passchendaele. He was killed in action on the Menin Road, in November 1917, and was entitled to the General Service and Victory Medals.
14, Leighton Street, Woburn. Z2192/C.

NEWBURY, W. F., Pte., 4th Bedfordshire Regt., and Royal Naval Division.
He volunteered in January 1916, and in the following March proceeded overseas to the Western Front, where he was almost continually in action, fighting on the Somme and in other engagements until killed in action at Beaumont-Hamel in November of the same year. He was entitled to the General Service and Victory Medals
14, Leighton Street, Woburn. Z2192/A.

NEWELL, A., Private, R.A.S.C.
He volunteered in August 1915, and in the following year embarked for France, where he served with his unit in many advanced sectors. He was under fire at the Battles of the Somme, Vimy Ridge and Beaumont-Hamel, and was gassed. He was demobilised in March 1919, and holds the General Service and Victory Medals.
51, Souldern Street, Watford. X2196/A.

NEWELL, C. H., Sapper, Royal Engineers.
He joined in August 1916, and in January of the following year was drafted to Salonika, where he served on the Doiran Front with his regiment until 1919. Whilst in this theatre of war he was present at the fighting on the Struma and the Vardar and also at Monastir. After the signing of the Armistice he was engaged on garrison duties with the Army of Occupation in Turkey. He returned to England and was demobilised in December 1919, and holds the General Service and Victory Medals.
Chaul End, Luton. 2179.

NEWELL, E. J., S.M., South Wales Borderers.
A serving soldier, he was mobilised at the outbreak of war, and on account of his qualifications and experience served at various stations as Instructor to the New Armies. He rendered very valuable services, but was unable to obtain his transfer overseas. He was discharged in February 1919.
21, Alexandra Road, Hitchin. 4185.

NEWELL, G., Sergeant, Royal Field Artillery.
He volunteered in September 1914, and in the following year proceeded to the Western Front. He fought at the Battles of the Aisne, Ypres, Arras, St. Julien, Hill 60, Cambrai and throughout the Retreat and Advance of 1918. During his service overseas he was wounded and gassed. He was demobilised in February 1919, and holds the 1914-15 Star, and the General Service and Victory Medals.
25, Westbourne Terrace, St. Albans. X2176.

NEWELL, W. A., Boy 1st Class, Royal Navy.
He joined the Service in March 1914, and was posted to H.M.S. "Vanguard." His ship during the war served in home and foreign waters, and was in action at the Battle of Jutland, and was also engaged on patrol work, frequently passing through mine-infested areas. He was killed when H.M.S. "Vanguard" was sunk at Scapa Flow by an internal explosion on July 9th, 1917. He was entitled to the 1914-15 Star, and the General Service and Victory Medals.
51, Souldern Street, Watford. X2196/B.

NEWENS, A., Leading Stoker, Royal Navy.
He joined the Navy prior to the outbreak of hostilities, and was posted to H.M.S. "Vulcan," in which ship he served throughout the war engaged on the coastal patrol against the submarine menace, and on the blockade of Germany. He was discharged in January 1920, and holds the 1914-15 Star, and the General Service and Victory Medals.
34, Saxon Road, Luton. 2197

NEWITT, H. J., Private, 23rd Middlesex Regt.
Joining in June 1917, he proceeded to the Western Front in January of the following year, and was in action with his regiment at the Battles of the Somme, Cambrai and in the German Offensive of 1918. He was killed in action at Ypres on October 1st, 1918, during the Allied Advance, and was entitled to the General Service and Victory Medals.
Upper Sundon, Dunstable. 2174/A.

NEWITT, R. C., Private, Gloucestershire Regt.
He joined in March 1918, on attaining military age, and on completing his training was drafted to India, where he served with his unit on garrison and other important duties at various stations. He was still serving in 1920.
Upper Sundon, Dunstable. 2174/B.

NEWLYN, S. G., Private, Middlesex Regiment.

He joined the Forces in 1916, and later in the year embarked for France. He served in many sectors on this front fighting in the Battles of the Somme, Arras, Cambrai, and throughout the Retreat and Advance of 1918, and remained in this theatre of war until after the cessation of hostilities. He returned to England, and was demobilised in 1919, and holds the General Service and Victory Medals.

5, Souldern Street, Watford.   X2170.

NEWMAN, C., Private, 1/5th Bedfordshire Regt.

Volunteering in June 1915, he left England for the Near East in the following February, and served with the Egyptian Expeditionary Force in the Advance through Palestine and Syria. He was in action at Gaza, and in the vicinity of Jaffa. He returned to England and was demobilised in August 1919, and holds the General Service and Victory Medals.

Campton, Shefford.   2198.

NEWMAN, F., Corporal, Royal Engineers.

Joining in March 1916, he embarked for Egypt six months later. Engaged on important constructional duties, he served in many advanced areas and was present at the Battles of Gaza and the operations during the Advance through Palestine and Syria. He returned to England, and was demobilised in October 1919, and holds the General Service and Victory Medals.

82, Shortmead Street, Biggleswade.   Z2199.

NEWMAN, F. J., Private, Bedfordshire Regiment.

He volunteered in September 1914, and proceeded to France in the same year. Whilst in this theatre of war he served in many engagements, including those of Festubert and Loos, and was killed in action in September 1916. He was entitled to the 1914 Star, and the General Service and Victory Medals.

34, Hitchin Street, Biggleswade.   Z2200.

NEWMAN, G. T., L/Cpl., Machine Gun Corps.

Joining H.M. Forces in February 1917, he was sent to the Western Front in the following August and served with his regiment in the Battles of Ypres, Passchendaele, until wounded at Cambrai in April 1918, during the German Offensive. He was demobilised in January 1919, and holds the General Service and Victory Medals.

101, Sun Street, Biggleswade.   Z2201/B.

NEWMAN, H. A., Private, Oxfordshire and Buckinghamshire Light Infantry.

He volunteered in January 1916, and in October of the same year embarked for the Macedonian theatre of war, where he was attached to the R.A.M.C., and with this branch of the service served on the Struma and Vardar fronts and in the vicinity of Lake Doiran on important hospital duties. He returned to England, and was demobilised in March 1919, and holds the General Service and Victory Medals.

101, Sun Street, Biggleswade.   Z2201/A.

NEWMAN, R., Royal Army Ordnance Corps.

He joined in February 1918, and shortly afterwards proceeded to France, where he served in the forward areas in the vicinity of Amiens and Cambrai, and in other sectors throughout the German Offensive and subsequent Allied Advance of 1918. On the cessation of hostilities he was sent into Germany with the Army of Occupation, and was stationed at various places on the Rhine. He was demobilised in March 1920, and holds the General Service and Victory Medals.

40, Bolton Road, Luton.   2178/B.

NEWMAN, R. W., Sapper, Royal Engineers.

Joining in March 1916, he underwent a course of training, and on its completion served with his unit at various stations on important duties, connected with constructional work. Owing to medical unfitness he was not able to obtain his transfer overseas. He rendered valuable services throughout, and was demobilised in August 1919.

80, Shortmead Street, Biggleswade.   2202.

NEWMAN, W. C., Private, Labour Corps.

He volunteered in May 1915, and in the following year embarked for the Western Front, where he fought with his regiment in many engagements of note until wounded in the Ypres salient in 1917. After hospital treatment he returned to France and was transferred to the Labour Corps. With this unit he served in many advanced areas, and was under fire at the Battles of Albert, Vimy Ridge, the Somme, Ypres, Cambrai, and during the Retreat and Advance of 1918. He was demobilised in July 1920, and holds the General Service and Victory Medals.

40, Bolton Road, Luton.   2178/A.

NEWMAN, S., Private, Lancashire Fusiliers.

He volunteered in December 1915, and in the following year was drafted to the Western Front. Whilst overseas he fought in the Battles of Vimy Ridge, the Somme, and in the third Battle of Ypres. In the last-named battle he was severely wounded, and was invalided to England. After receiving hospital treatment he was discharged on account of his service in March 1918, and holds the General Service and Victory Medals.

North Bridge Street, Shefford.   Z735/A.

NEWSON, G., Private, 2nd Black Watch.

He volunteered in November 1915, and in the following May was drafted to Mesopotamia. He took part in heavy fighting at Sunna-i-Yat, and in various engagements in the attempts to relieve Kut, and was severely wounded. Invalided home in December 1916, he was discharged as medically unfit for further service in the following September, and holds the General Service and Victory Medals.

2, Symington Street, Harpenden.   2203/B.

NEWSON, R., Sergeant, 32nd Middlesex Regt.

He joined in June 1916, and after his training was engaged as Instructor of Musketry at an important military school. He carried out his responsible duties in a thorough and efficient manner, but was not successful in obtaining a transfer overseas before the cessation of hostilities. He was demobilised in April 1919.

2, Symington Street, Harpenden.   2203/C.

NEWTON, D. G., Private, Royal Sussex Regt.

He joined in 1916, and after a period of training was drafted overseas in the same year. He saw much service in various sectors of the Western Front, and fought in many important engagements until he fell in action in 1917. He was entitled to the General Service and Victory Medals.

9, Grosvenor Terrace, Boxmoor   X2173/B.

NEWTON, G. T., Gunner, R.G.A.

Joining in 1916, he was very soon afterwards drafted to the Western Front, in several sectors of which he was engaged with his battery in heavy fighting. He took part in the Battles of Ypres, Amiens and other important engagements until the cessation of hostilities, and returning to England was demobilised in 1919. He holds the General Service and Victory Medals.

9, Grosvenor Terrace, Boxmoor.   X2173/A.

NEWTON, J. E. R., Private, R.A.M.C.

He joined in August 1917, and after a period of training was drafted to the Western Front. He served at a large Casualty Clearing Station, and besides attending to the sick and wounded acted as postman until the conclusion of hostilities. Demobilised in December 1919 on his return to England, he holds the General Service and Victory Medals.

1, Anchor Cottages, Walsworth, Hitchin.   2204.

NICHOLAS, A., Corporal, Dragoon Guards, and Royal Engineers.

He was serving in the Army when war was declared, and, drafted to France, took part in the Retreat from Mons and in several subsequent engagements, including the Battles of Ypres, Arras and Cambrai, and was wounded. Rejoining his unit on recovery he was shortly afterwards transferred to the Royal Engineers, and served in that Corps until his return home for demobilisation in March 1919. He holds the Mons Star, and the General Service and Victory Medals.

46, St. Mary Street, Dunstable.   1120/A.

NICHOLAS, E. F., Private, 4th Norfolk Regiment.

Joining in 1916, he was drafted to Mesopotamia in the same year, and in that theatre of war saw much service. He took part in heavy fighting in the Advance on Baghdad, was present at the capture of that town, and fought in several subsequent engagements until the cessation of hostilities. Returning to England, he was demobilised in March 1919, and holds the General Service and Victory Medals.

10, Sotheron Road, Watford.   X2205/A.

NICHOLLS, A. G., Private, Royal Defence Corps.

He volunteered in December 1914, in a regiment of the line, and in the following July proceeded to France. There he served in several sectors and took part in heavy fighting in the operations on the Somme and in other important battles, including those of Arras and Vimy Ridge, and was wounded on April 23rd, 1917. He was invalided home, and on recovery was posted to the Royal Defence Corps, and was demobilised in February 1919. He holds the 1914-15 Star, and the General Service and Victory Medals.

23, Bolton Road, Luton.   2207.

NICHOLAS, S. J., Private, Labour Corps.

He joined in 1917, and in the same year was drafted overseas. Serving with his unit on the Western Front, he was engaged on important operations in various forward areas whilst heavy fighting was in progress, and was present at the Battles of the Somme, Arras, Cambrai and other engagements. On returning to England he was demobilised in October 1919, and holds the General Service and Victory Medals.
10, Sotheron Road, Watford.   X2205/B.

NICHOLLS, A., Private, 4th Norfolk Regiment.

He joined in May 1916, and shortly afterwards proceeded to the Western Front, where he was almost continually in action and was wounded near Ypres in May 1917. On recovery, he rejoined his unit and took part in the Battles of Passchendaele, Cambrai, the Somme and other important engagements until the signing of the Armistice. He was demobilised in December 1918, and holds the General Service and Victory Medals.
Chaul End, near Luton.   2206.

NICHOLLS, C., Private, 1/4th Duke of Cornwall's Light Infantry.

He joined in 1916, and after his training was sent to Mesopotamia in the following year. He took part in heavy fighting in the Advance on Damascus, being in action at Gaza, Haifa and Aleppo. On the cessation of hostilities he returned to England for demobilisation in June 1919, and holds the General Service and Victory Medals.
170, Chester Road, Watford.   2208.

NICHOLLS, E. (Mrs.), Special War Worker.

Volunteering for work of National importance, this lady accepted a position at the factory of Messrs. Geo. Kent, Ltd., Luton, in February 1916, and was engaged as an Inspector of Fuses. She carried out her responsible duties in a thorough and efficient manner, and to the entire satisfaction of her employers, until her discharge in January 1920.
204, Dallon Road, Luton.   2212/B.

NICHOLLS, J., Private, Labour Corps.

He joined in 1918, and was engaged at various stations on important work in connection with agriculture and the food supply of the country. He did excellent work, but was not successful in obtaining his transfer overseas before the cessation of hostilities, and was demobilised in 1919.
30, Souldern Street, Watford.   2209.

NICHOLLS, J., Private, North Staffordshire Regt.

He volunteered in August 1914, and after being was engaged with his unit on important duties at various stations until drafted overseas in 1917. Whilst on the Western Front he served in several sectors, and fought in the Battles of Arras, the Somme, Cambrai and other important engagements, and was wounded. He returned to England on the conclusion of hostilities, and was demobilised in February 1919. He holds the General Service and Victory Medals.
69, Cecil Street, North Watford.   X2210/A.

NICHOLLS, S., Corporal, Royal Army Pay Corps.

Volunteering in February 1916, he was posted to Woolwich, and was engaged on important clerical duties with his unit. He did excellent work, but was unsuccessful in obtaining a transfer overseas before the cessation of hostilities, and was demobilised in December 1919.
Grasmere, Westbourne Road, Luton.   2211.

NICHOLLS, W., Private, Manchester Regiment.

He volunteered in August 1914, and was engaged on important duties with his unit until drafted overseas in 1917. His regiment was sent to Italy and there he saw much service, taking part in heavy fighting in various offensive operations on the Piave and in other sectors. Returning to England at the end of the war he died on March 4th, 1919, from the effects of illness contracted whilst on service. He was entitled to the General Service and Victory Medals.
69, Cecil Street, North Watford.   X2210/B.

NICHOLLS, W. C., Sapper, Royal Engineers.

He volunteered in February 1916, and after a period of service at various depôts proceeded to Egypt in June 1917. He was engaged on important duties in the forward areas whilst heavy fighting was in progress and was present at the Battles of Gaza and Jaffa, and the Fall of Jerusalem, and other engagements during General Allenby's Advance through Palestine. He was demobilised in October 1919, and holds the General Service and Victory Medals.
204, Dallow Road, Luton.   2212/A.

NICHOLS, H., Private, R.A.M.C.

He volunteered in July 1915, and in the following year embarked for France, where he served as a hospital orderly and stretcher-bearer with the Field Ambulance in various sectors. He did excellent work during heavy fighting on the Somme, at Arras, Cambrai, Albert and other places, until the cessation of hostilities. He was demobilised in February 1919, and holds the General Service and Victory Medals.
Brampton Park Road, Hitchin.   2213.

NICHOLS, R. J., Air Mechanic, Royal Air Force.

He joined in June 1916, and in the following January was sent to France where he was engaged at various aerodromes as a fitter and tester of aeroplanes. He carried out his duties, which called for a very high standard of technical knowledge and skill, until the cessation of hostilities, when he returned to England for demobilisation in February 1919. He holds the General Service and Victory Medals.
Artville, West Parade, Dunstable.   2214.

NICHOLS, R. S., Sapper, Royal Engineers.

He joined in March 1916, and in the same year was drafted to France. He was engaged on important duties during heavy fighting at Vimy Ridge and Ypres, and was later transferred to Italy. In this theatre of war he served on the Asiago Plateau and in the offensive on the Piave. He returned to England and was demobilised in October 1919, and holds the General Service and Victory Medals.
13, Liverpool Road, Luton.   1918/B.

NICHOLS, W., Corporal, R.A.S.C.

He volunteered in September 1914, and was almost immediately sent to France. He took part in the fierce fighting in the Retreat from Mons, and in the Battles of Ypres, Hill 60, Loos, Vimy Ridge, the Ancre, Messines, the Somme and in the final operations of the war, and was present at the entry into Mons at dawn on November 11th, 1918. He was demobilised in April 1919, and holds the Mons Star, and the General Service and Victory Medals.
13, Liverpool Road, Luton.   1918/A.

NICHOLSON, G. O., Private, Bedfordshire Regt.

He volunteered in 1915, and in the same year was sent to the Western Front. Serving with the Lewis Gun section of his unit, he was in almost continuous action in various sectors, and took part in many important battles, including those of Ypres, Arras and Cambrai, and was four times wounded. He returned to England on the cessation of hostilities and was demobilised in 1919. He holds the 1914-15 Star, and the General Service and Victory Medals.
106, Judge Street, North Watford.   X3506/B.

NOAH, A., Sergeant, Royal Garrison Artillery.

Volunteering on the outbreak of war he was drafted to France with the First Expeditionary Force, and fought in the Retreat from Mons and at the first Battle of Ypres. He took part in the Battles of the Somme, Cambrai and in the Retreat and Advance of 1918. He was twice wounded in the course of his service and at the end of hostilities went into Germany with the Army of Occupation. He was demobilised in January 1919, and holds the Mons Star, and the General Service and Victory Medals.
11, Russell Place, Boxmoor.   X2215.

NOBBS, E., A.B., Royal Navy.

He joined in July 1918, and after completing his training was stationed at Chatham, where he was engaged on important duties. He did good work but contracting illness died on September 7th of the same year.
40, Hagden Lane, Watford.   X2217.

NOBBS, G., Private, R.A.S.C. (M.T.)

Volunteering in December 1915, he was sent overseas in the following year. He served on the Western Front and was engaged on important duties in connection with the transport of ammunition and supplies to the forward areas during the progress of operations, and was present at many important battles, including those of Ypres and St. Quentin. He was demobilised in December 1919, and holds the General Service and Victory Medals.
14, Hagden Lane, Watford.   X2216.

NOBLE, G. H., Private, 2/5th Yorkshire Regt.

He joined in July 1916, and was drafted to the Western Front in the following March. Whilst in this theatre of war he served in several sectors and took part in almost continuous fighting until severely wounded in action. He was invalided to hospital at Etaples, where he died from the effects of his wounds on April 26th, 1917. He was entitled to the General Service and Victory Medals.
3, Lyndhurst Road, Luton.   2218.

NOLDER, A. P., Private, 26th Royal Fusiliers.
Joining in 1916, he was drafted overseas in the same year and saw much service in various sectors of the Western Front. He took part in several engagements, including the Battles of Messines and Ypres and was seriously wounded. Invalided home he received hospital treatment, and on recovery was discharged as medically unfit for further military service in June 1918. He holds the General Service and Victory Medals.
49, Pinner Road, Oxhey. X2219.

NOON, C. F., Corporal, Queen's (Royal West Surrey Regiment).
Volunteering in August 1914, he shortly afterwards embarked for France. He saw much service in several sectors and was engaged in many important battles, including those of Neuve Chapelle and the Somme. He was later sent to Italy in which theatre of war he served with his unit until the cessation of hostilities. He was awarded the Belgian Croix de Guerre for gallant conduct in the Field, and also holds the 1914-15 Star, and the General Service and Victory Medals. In 1920 he was still serving.
68, Edward Street, Dunstable. 2220.

NOON, G., Private, Sherwood Foresters.
He volunteered in August 1914, and in the following year was in action on the Western Front in the Battles of Neuve Chapelle, Ypres, Loos, and in other important engagements, and was wounded. On recovery he rejoined his unit and fought in various actions until captured in the second Battle of the Somme in March 1918. Released on the signing of the Armistice, he was repatriated to England and subsequently demobilised in December 1918. He holds the 1914-15 Star, and the General Service and Victory Medals.
114, Norfolk Road, Rickmansworth. X2221.

NORGAN, B., L/Corporal, R.A.V.C.
He joined in July 1916, and in the following month was drafted to the Western Front. There he served in various sectors and was engaged on important transport duties and in attending to sick and wounded horses. He was present at heavy fighting on the Somme, at Ypres, Albert, and other places until the end of hostilities. He was demobilised in September 1919, on his return to England, and holds the General Service and Victory Medals.
3, Gaping Lane, Hitchin. 2222.

NORGAN, H., Private, East Surrey Regiment.
He volunteered in August 1914, and in the following year proceeded overseas. He saw active service on the Western Front, where he took part in heavy fighting in various sectors until wounded at Ypres. Later serving with his unit he was again wounded on the Somme, and on recovery was sent to Egypt, and was in action there until June 1918, when he returned to England. He was demobilised in September 1919, and holds the 1914-15 Star, and the General Service and Victory Medals.
30, Hitchin Hill, Hitchin. 2223/B.

NORMAN, A. E., Private, Suffolk Regiment.
He volunteered in December 1915, and in the following October was drafted to France. Whilst in this theatre of war he saw service in several sectors and took part in many important battles, including that of Cambrai, where he was wounded. Returning to his unit on recovery, he was in action in several engagements until wounded again near Albert in March 1918. He was invalided home and after receiving hospital treatment was demobilised in April 1919, and holds the General Service and Victory Medals.
22, Brixton Road, Watford. X2224.

NORMAN, D., Driver, Royal Field Artillery.
He volunteered in August 1914, and was engaged with his unit on important duties at various stations until drafted overseas in November of the following year. He served with his battery in several sectors of the Western Front, and took part in many important engagements before he was sent to Egypt in March 1916. He was in action during the Advance through Palestine and amongst other important battles fought at Gaza. On the conclusion of hostilities he returned to England for demobilisation in March 1919, and holds the 1914-15 Star, and the General Service and Victory Medals.
Arm and Sword Yard, Hatfield. X2225.

NORMAN, F. J., Private, Norfolk Regiment.
Joining in December 1915, he completed his training and was engaged with his unit at various stations on important duties. He did good work guarding large munition factories and was on duty at various detention camps in which German prisoners were confined. He was unable to procure his transfer overseas before the cessation of hostilities, and was demobilised in March 1919.
32, Puller Road, Boxmoor. X2226.

NORMAN, A. W., Private, Bedfordshire Regt.
He volunteered in January 1915, and after training served at various stations with his unit on important duties. He rendered valuable services throughout, but was not sent overseas owing to his being medically unfit for active service, and was demobilised in April 1919.
Mount Pleasant, Aspley Guise. Z560/B.

NORMAN, G. T., Sergeant, Bedfordshire Regt.
Volunteering in September 1914, he was drafted to the Western Front shortly afterwards and took part in many battles, fighting at Arras, Cambrai, Ypres and in many other engagements of note. During his service overseas he was wounded, and, invalided to England, was discharged in consequence of injuries received in August 1918.
8, Sussex Road, Watford. X5010/E, X5011/E.

NORMAN, H., Air Mechanic, Royal Air Force.
He joined in September 1917, and was drafted to the Western Front, where he served in the vicinity of Lille, Cambrai and Ypres on important work connected with aeroplanes. His duties demanded a high degree of technical knowledge and skill, and he did good work until the end of the war. He returned to England for demobilisation in May 1919, and holds the General Service and Victory Medals.
22, Arthur Street, Luton. 2227.

NORMAN, R., Driver, Royal Field Artillery.
He volunteered in March 1915, and in the same year was drafted to the Western Front, where he was engaged on important duties in connection with the transport of ammunition to his battery in the forward areas, and was present at the Battles of the Somme and Cambrai, and was gassed. He was later sent to Italy, and served there for nearly three years. He was demobilised in February 1919 after returning home, and holds the 1914-15 Star, and the General Service and Victory Medals.
Hockliffe, Leighton Buzzard. 2228.

NORRIS, L., Drummer, 3rd Hertfordshire Regt.
He volunteered in October 1914, and after training at the depôt of his unit was engaged on important guard and other duties at various stations on the East Coast. Owing to his being under military age he was unable to obtain a transfer overseas before the cessation of hostilities, and was demobilised in February 1919.
79, Copsewood Road, Watford. X2229.

NORRIS, P. W., Private, Labour Corps.
He joined in February 1917, and in the following month was drafted to the Western Front, where he served with his unit in the front lines in many sectors. He was engaged on important duties during heavy fighting, and was present at many of the principal battles, including those of the Somme, Ypres, Lens, Poperinghe and Menin Road. He was demobilised in March 1919, and holds the General Service and Victory Medals.
84, Spenser Road, Luton. 2230.

NORRIS, S. J., Sapper, Royal Engineers.
He volunteered in October 1914, and after training was engaged with his unit on important duties at various stations. He rendered valuable services throughout, but was unable to obtain his transfer overseas before the cessation of hostilities, and was demobilised in March 1919.
46, Ridgway Road, Luton. 2231.

NORRIS, W., Private, 1st Bedfordshire Regiment.
Volunteering on the outbreak of war, he was soon afterwards sent to France with the First Expeditionary Force, and was engaged in fierce fighting in the Retreat from Mons, and the Battles of Ypres and Hill 60. He also took part in several engagements during the Somme Offensive and in the operations that ended with the capture of Vimy Ridge, where he was severely wounded. He was invalided home and after receiving hospital treatment was subsequently discharged, totally disabled in November 1917. He holds the Mons Star, and the General Service and Victory Medals.
26, Fearnley Street, Watford. X2973/B.

NORTH, E., Private, R.A.S.C., and Loyal North Lancashire Regiment.
He volunteered in March 1915, and later in the same year was drafted to the Western Front, where he took part in several important engagements, including the Battles of Arras, Ypres and Cambrai. He rendered valuable services and returning to England on the cessation of hostilities, was demobilised in June 1919, and holds the 1914-15 Star, and the General Service and Victory Medals.
26, Albert Street, Watford. X2232.

NORTH, F. G., Corporal, West Yorkshire Regt.
Already serving at the outbreak of war, he at once proceeded overseas, and took an important part in the Retreat from Mons, and in the Battles of Neuve Chapelle and Loos, and was twice wounded. Invalided home, he was discharged on account of his service in June 1917, and holds the Mons Star and the General Service and Victory Medals.
47, Leavesden Road, Watford, Herts.   X2233/A.

NORTH, G. T., Rifleman, 8th London Regiment (Post Office Rifles).
He volunteered in December 1915, and after a period of training was drafted overseas. He saw service on the Western Front, and took part in several engagements, including the Battles of Ypres Bullecourt and St. Quentin. Returning to England on the cessation of hostilities, he was demobilised in February 1919, and holds the General Service and Victory Medals.
28, Upper Paddock Road, Oxhey, Herts.   X2234.

NORTH, L. A., Gunner, Royal Field Artillery.
He volunteered in January 1915, and, after a period of training proceeded to the Western Front. He took part in several engagements, including the Battles of Arras, Ypres and Cambrai, and returning to England on the cessation of hostilities was demobilised in February 1919. He holds the General Service and Victory Medals.
47, Leavesden Road, Watford, Herts.   X2233/B.

NORTH, S. E., Sapper, Royal Engineers.
He joined in 1917, and, on the completion of his training was drafted to Salonika, where he did valuable work with his unit until the cessation of hostilities. He subsequently contracted fever, and died at Salonika on December 30th, 1918. He was entitled to the General Service and Victory Medals.
53, Lower Paddock Road, Oxhey, Watford, Herts.
X2235/A.

NORTH, W. V., Private, 6th Suffolk Regiment.
He volunteered in 1915, and after his training served at various stations on important duties with his unit. He rendered valuable services, and was drafted to France in April 1917, but was shortly invalided home and died on April 7th, 1918. He was entitled to the General Service and Victory Medals.
53, Lower Paddock Road, Oxhey, Watford, Herts.
X2235/B.

NORTHWOOD, G., Private, Labour Corps.
Volunteering in February 1915, he was medically unfit for service overseas. He joined the Labour Corps on its formation and was engaged entirely on agricultural work until the cessation of hostilities. He carried out his duties in a thorough and conscientious manner and was demobilised in March 1919.
Magpie Row, George Street, Maulden, Ampthill, Berks.
2236.

NORTHWOOD, H., Private, Labour Corps.
He joined in 1916, and served at various stations on important duties with his unit. Proceeding overseas in March 1917, he was engaged on the Arras, Ypres and Cambrai fronts in the making of roads and railways, and in the transport of ammunition to the forward areas. He returned home and was demobilised in February 1919, and holds the General Service and Victory Medals.
55, Chapel Walk, Dunstable.   2237.

NORTHWOOD, J. T., Pte., Hertfordshire Regt., and Air Mechanic, Royal Air Force.
He joined in August 1916, and was drafted to France in January of the following year. He took part in several engagements, including the Battle of Arras. Returning to England in July 1917, he was transferred to the Royal Air Force, and served with that branch until his demobilisation in February 1919. He holds the General Service and Victory Medals.
78, Spenser Road, Luton.   2238.

NORTHWOOD, P., Private, 3rd Bedfordshire Regiment, and Hertfordshire Regiment.
He joined in March 1916, and in the following December was drafted to France. He did valuable work in the Battles of Arras, Ypres III, Passchendaele and Cambrai, and was wounded in the Retreat of 1918. He was later gassed and returning to England was demobilised in August 1919, and holds the General Service and Victory Medals.
The Strand, Clophill, near Ampthill.   2239.

NORTON, L., Sgt., Royal Marine Light Infantry.
Mobilised on the outbreak of war, he saw much varied service in the North Sea, the South Atlantic, and the Pacific Ocean. He took a prominent part in the Battle of the Falkland Islands, and rendered valuable services with his unit throughout the campaign. He holds the 1914-15 Star, and the General Service and Victory Medals, and was demobilised in February 1919.
5, Cross Street North, Dunstable.   2240.

NOTTINGHAM, H. G., Corporal, 4th Bedfordshire Regiment.
He joined in 1916, and after a period of training was drafted to the Western Front, where he took part in several important engagements, including the Battles of Vimy Ridge, the Somme, Arras and Cambrai. He was gassed on the Somme, and returning home on the cessation of hostilities, was demobilised in July 1919, and holds the General Service and Victory Medals.
12, Portmill Lane, Hitchin.   2241.

NOTTINGHAM, J. E., Private, R.A.M.C.
Already serving at the outbreak of war, he was drafted to the Western Front in December 1914, and took part in the Battles of St. Eloi, Hill 60, and Ypres II. He subsequently saw service in Italy and Salonika, and, invalided home with malaria in August 1918, was demobilised in the following March. He holds the 1914-15 Star, and the General Service and Victory Medals.
4, William Road, Walsworth, Hitchin.   2242.

NOVELL, W., Driver, Royal Engineers.
He volunteered in January 1915, and after his training served at various stations on important duties with his unit. He rendered valuable services, and in 1916 was drafted to Egypt, where he took part in engagements at Gaza and Jerusalem. Returning home he was demobilised in July 1919, and holds the General Service and Victory Medals.
101, Stores Yard, Silsoe, Ampthill.   2243.

NUNN, S. R., Private, Middlesex Regiment.
He volunteered in June 1915, and after his training served at various stations on important duties with his unit. Proceeding overseas in May 1916, he took part in the Battles of St. Quentin, Arras and Cambrai. He returned home on the cessation of hostilities and was demobilised in February 1919, and holds the General Service and Victory Medals.
Watling Street, Hockliffe.   2244.

NUNN, W., Private, 3rd Bedfordshire Regiment.
He joined in 1916, and after a period of training was drafted to the Western Front, where he took part in several engagements, including the battles of the Somme Arras, and Ypres. He subsequently saw service in Italy, and returning home was demobilised in February 1919, and holds the General Service and Victory Medals.
11, Sheppards Row, Redbourn.   2245.

NURSALL, C. A., Private, 3rd Bedfordshire Regt.
Volunteering in August 1914, he was shortly drafted to the Western Front, where he took part in several important engagements, including the Battles of Ypres, Neuve Chapelle, Loos and Arras. He was taken prisoner at the commencement of the Retreat of 1918, and returning home after the Armistice was demobilised early in 1919, and holds the 1914-15 Star, and the General Service and Victory Medals.
Sandy Lane, Woburn Sands.   2247.

NURSALL, H. J., Bombardier, R.F.A
He joined in October 1916, and in the following year was drafted to France, where he took part in several important engagements, including the Battles of Arras, Ypres, Cambrai and the Somme, and was gassed. Returning to England, he was demobilised in September 1919, and holds the General Service and Victory Medals.
40, Bedford Street, Woburn.   2246.

NUTT, B. A., Private, Northumberland Fusiliers.
Mobilised on the outbreak of hostilities, he was shortly afterwards drafted to the Western Front, where he took part in the Battles of Neuve Chapelle, Ypres, Loos, the Somme, Arras, and in the Retreat and Advance of 1918. He returned to England after the signing of the Armistice, and was demobilised in February 1919, and holds the 1914 Star, and the General Service and Victory Medals.
196, Dallow Road, Luton.   2249/A.

NUTT, C. M. (Mrs.), Special War Worker.
This lady offered her services, and was given an important position at the Diamond Foundry. She carried out her responsible duties in a thorough and efficient manner and gave entire satisfaction to her employers.
196, Dallow Road, Luton.   2249/B.

NUTTALL, E., Private, Machine Gun Corps.
He volunteered in May 1915, and after his training served at various stations on important duties with his unit. Proceeding to France in February 1917, he took a prominent part in the Battles of Cambrai and the Somme, and was twice wounded. He returned home, and was demobilised in March 1919, and holds the General Service and Victory Medals.
36, Wellbeck Street, East Kirkby.   2250.

O

OAKLEY, W. R., Private, Middlesex Regiment.
He joined in 1916, but was retained on important duties with his unit at various stations. Although unable to obtain his transfer overseas before the cessation of hostilities, he rendered valuable services in many ways, and was demobilised in 1919.
78, Ridgway Road, Luton, Beds.   2251.

O'BRIEN, F., Lieutenant, Bedfordshire Regiment.
Volunteering in 1914, he was drafted to France in the same year and took part in heavy fighting in several sectors. He was in almost continuous action, and was actively engaged at Hill 60, Ypres, Festubert, Loos, the Somme, Cambrai and during the Retreat and Advance of 1918. Returning to England on the conclusion of hostilities, he was demobilised in April 1919, and holds the 1914 Star, and the General Service and Victory Medals.
15, Common View Square, Letchworth.   4187.

O'BRIEN, T., Driver, Royal Field Artillery.
He joined in February 1917, and, after a short period of training, was drafted to India, where he served on important duties in various stations. Transferred in 1918 to Mesopotamia he did good work on that front, taking part in several engagements, until he again proceeded to India, and, afterwards, Persia. On his return home he was demobilised in the latter part of 1919, and holds the General Service and Victory Medals.
Bedford Road, Shefford, Beds.   Z2252.

O'DELL, A., Private, Labour Corps.
Joining in February 1916, he was immediately drafted to the Western Front, where, for some time, he was engaged on the construction of railways and in the carrying of ammunition for the fighting line. He saw service in various sectors, and took part in the Battles of Arras and Ypres, in both of which he was wounded. On his return home he was demobilised in December 1918, and holds the General Service and Victory Medals.
8, Spring Place, Luton, Beds.   2253.

O'DELL, A. W., Corporal, Labour Corps.
Upon his joining in December 1916, he was appointed to the Labour Corps for duty on the Western Front, and in that area saw some heavy fighting, including the Battle of Ypres. He performed important duties of a varied character until his return home for demobilisation in October 1919, and holds the General Service and Victory Medals.
57, Grange Road, Luton, Beds.   2254.

O'DELL, A. W., Private, Hertfordshire Regiment.
Volunteering in 1915, at the end of his training, he proceeded to France. In this theatre of war he did much good work, and with his unit took part in many important engagements, including the Battle of Ypres. After rendering services of a valuable nature he was unfortunately killed in action, the exact locality not being known, in 1917. He was entitled to the General Service and Victory Medals.
Folly Field, Wheathampstead, Herts.   2255/B.

O'DELL, B., Special War Worker.
Soon after the outbreak of hostilities, this lady volunteered for work of National importance, and proceeded to Messrs. Kents', Ltd., Luton, where she was engaged on the output of munitions. Her service extended to the cessation of hostilities, and she did work of a very valuable nature, giving complete satisfaction to her employers.
112, Clarendon Road, Luton, Beds.   2256/B.

O'DELL, B., Private, South Staffordshire Regt.
Volunteering in August 1914, he was drafted to France in the following year and took part with his unit in many of the most severe engagements, including the Battles of Arras, Ypres and Cambrai, in each of which he was wounded. Taken prisoner in 1917 he was, on his release, transferred to the Bedfordshire Regiment, in which he was still serving in India in 1920. He holds the 1914-15 Star, and the General Service and Victory Medals.
Saracen's Head, New Street, Shefford, Beds.   Z2257/B.

O'DELL, C., Sergeant, Queen's (Royal West Surrey Regiment).
He volunteered in September 1914, but was retained on important duties with his unit at various stations. Although unable to obtain his transfer overseas before the cessation of hostilities, he rendered valuable services as Sergeant-Cook, and was demobilised in March 1919.
Manor Road, Barton, Ampthill, Beds.   2258.

O'DELL, C., Special War Worker.
This lady volunteered soon after the outbreak of hostilities, and for the whole period of her service, which extended to the duration of the war, was employed in work of National importance at Messrs. Kents', Ltd., Luton. She rendered services of great value, and gave complete satisfaction to her employers.
112, Clarendon Road, Luton, Beds.   2256/C.

O'DELL, E., Special War Worker.
Volunteering in June 1915, this lady was engaged on work of National importance at Messrs. Kents', Ltd., Luton, until December 1919. Employed in the output of munitions, she did valuable work as Inspector in the Fuse Department, and was of great assistance to her firm.
90, Dane Road, Luton, Beds.   2259/B.

O'DELL, E. E., Sapper, Royal Engineers.
He volunteered in June 1915, and after a short term of training proceeded to France. In that theatre of war he rendered good service with his unit in many different sectors and took part in many important engagements, including the Battles of Loos, Vimy Ridge, the Somme, Messines, Passchendaele and Cambrai. He formed part of the Army of Occupation in Germany until his demobilisation in June 1919, and holds the General Service and Victory Medals.
43, Ash Road, Luton, Beds.   2260.

O'DELL, F. C., Pte., Northumberland Fusiliers.
After volunteering in September 1914, he saw service both in France and at the Dardanelles, rendering excellent services with his unit in many engagements. On the Western Front he took part in much heavy fighting, including the Battles of the Somme, Arras and Ypres, and was taken prisoner at the Battle of the Marne. On his return home he was demobilised in March 1919, and holds the General Service and Victory Medals.
Upper Sundon, Dunstable, Beds.   2261.

O'DELL, F. E., Private, Machine Gun Corps.
He joined in 1916, and after a short period of training was drafted to the Western Front, where until 1918 he was engaged with his unit in many important sectors and took part in much heavy fighting, including the Battles of Ypres, Arras and the Somme. At a later period he was employed with the Graves Concentration Unit in reburying the dead. After doing good work in many ways he returned home for demobilisation in 1919, and holds the General Service and Victory Medals.
Folly Field, Wheathampstead, Herts.   2255/A.

O'DELL, G., Private, Hampshire Regiment.
He volunteered in August 1915, and was quickly drafted to Salonika for the Balkan front, where he played an important part with his unit in the retirement through Serbia. Being unfortunately wounded and taken prisoner by the Bulgarians, he succumbed to his injuries in January 1916. He was entitled to the General Service and Victory Medals.
Ampthill Road, Shefford, Beds.   Z1321/C.

O'DELL, G. T., Corporal, Bedfordshire Regiment, and Military Mounted Police.
A time-serving soldier at the beginning of the war, he was drafted to the Western Front in 1915, and was soon engaged with his unit in some of the heavy fighting and rendered good service (being mentioned in Despatches), in the Battles of the Somme, Arras and Ypres. Transferred later to the Italian scene of operations, he took part in the Battle of Fiume. On his return home he was demobilised in March 1919, and holds the 1914-15 Star, and the General Service and Victory Medals.
36, Beech Road, Luton.   2262.

O'DELL, G. W., Warrant Officer, Royal Navy.
He volunteered in August 1914, and was attached to the Grand Fleet, operating in the North Sea. Throughout his war service he cruised in many different and dangerous waters, and took a prominent part with his ship in many naval engagements, including the Battles of Jutland and Heligoland Bight. He rendered services of great value, and was still at sea in 1920, and holds the 1914-15 Star, and the General Service and Victory Medals.
Saracen's Head, New Street, Shefford, Beds.   Z2257/A.

O'DELL, H., 1st Air Mechanic, Royal Air Force.
He volunteered in January 1915, and after a period of training proceeded to Egypt for service in the Palestine theatre of war. For more than three years he rendered excellent services under conditions which required a high degree of technical skill and knowledge. Returning home he was demobilised in March 1919, and holds the General Service and Victory Medals.
25, Hitchin Hill, Herts.   2263/A.

O'DELL, H., Private, Bedfordshire Regiment.
He volunteered in 1915, and in the same year was drafted to the Western Front. There he served with his unit in various sectors and took part in many important battles, including those of the Somme, Arras and Ypres. He was killed in action on April 11th, 1917, at the Battle of Vimy Ridge, and was entitled to the 1914-15 Star, and the General Service and Victory Medals.
Saracen's Head, New Street, Shefford.   Z2257/C.

O'DELL, H., Private, Middlesex Regiment, and Labour Corps.
Joining in October 1916, he completed his training and was engaged with his unit at various stations on important duties. He was later transferred to the Labour Corps and employed at several rest camps on general duties, rendering excellent service, but was unsuccessful in obtaining a transfer overseas, and was demobilised in December 1918.
4, Mimram Road, Welwyn.   2264.

ODELL, H. A., Private, 3rd Bedfordshire Regt. and Labour Corps.
He joined in 1916, and was engaged on important duties with his regiment at various stations until August 1918, when he was drafted to the Western Front. There he took part in heavy fighting at Havrincourt and Ypres, and was wounded in an engagement in the Somme sector. Recovering from the effects of his wounds, he rejoined his unit and was sent with the Army of Occupation into Germany and was stationed at Cologne. He was discharged on account of service in November 1919, and holds the General Service and Victory Medals.
Campton, Shefford.   Z2265.

ODELL, H. S., Gunner (Signaller), R.G.A.
Joining in September 1917, in the following February he was sent to France. He saw much service on the Western Front and was engaged in heavy fighting in the Battles of the Somme, the Marne, Amiens, Cambrai and in other important actions during the closing operations of the war. He returned to England for demobilisation in January 1919, and holds the General Service and Victory Medals.
50, Ashburnham Road, Luton.   2266.

ODELL, J., Sapper, Royal Engineers.
Volunteering in November 1914, in the following May he was serving with his unit on the Western Front, in various sectors of which he was engaged on important duties whilst heavy fighting was in progress. He was present at many important battles, including those at Ypres, on the Somme, and during the Advance of 1918, and was wounded. He returned home for demobilisation in January 1919, and holds the 1914-15 Star, and the General Service and Victory Medals.
51, Spenser Road, Luton.   2267.

O'DELL, J. B. (D.C.M.), L/Corporal, 9th Seaforth Highlanders.
He volunteered in August 1914, and in the following May was drafted to the Western Front. There he served in many sectors, and was engaged in heavy fighting at Ypres until wounded in April 1916. He was invalided home, and on recovery returned to the firing line in the following November, and took part in the Battle of the Somme and other important engagements. He was awarded the Distinguished Conduct Medal for conspicuous gallantry and devotion to duty in the Field, and was again wounded. He also holds the 1914-15 Star, and the General Service and Victory Medals, and was demobilised in March 1919.
Oliver Street, Ampthill.   2268/A.

ODELL, J. H., A.B., Royal Navy.
He was serving in the Navy when war was declared, and aboard H.M.S. "Sandhurst" was engaged in important patrol duties in home and foreign waters. His ship took part in the Battle of Jutland and had several other encounters with the German Fleet. He was demobilised in June 1919, and holds the 1914-15 Star, and the General Service and Victory Medals.
Oliver Street, Ampthill.   2268/B.

ODELL, P. W., Rifleman, 1st King's Royal Rifle Corps.
He joined in January 1917, and was drafted to France in February of the following year. He was engaged in heavy fighting in many engagements, and was wounded and taken prisoner at Cambrai in March 1918. Released from captivity after the signing of the Armistice, he returned to England in December 1918, and was demobilised in the following October. He holds the General Service and Victory Medals.
George Street, Maulden, near Ampthill.   2269.

O'DELL, R., Private, 1/3rd Hertfordshire Regt.
He volunteered in April 1915, and after training was engaged at various stations with his unit on important guard and other home defence duties. He was unable to obtain a transfer overseas owing to medical unfitness, but did excellent work until demobilised in March 1919.
29, Dalton Street, St. Albans.   2270.

ODELL, R., L/Corporal, Bedfordshire Regiment.
He volunteered in 1914, and being medically unfit for service overseas was engaged on important duties at various home stations. He was afterwards transferred to the Military Police, and rendered valuable services at several depôts until demobilised in March 1919.
New Street, Shefford.   Z2271.

O'DELL, R. M., 1st Class Stoker, Royal Navy.
He joined the Navy in 1912, and was posted to H.M.S. "Formidable." Aboard this vessel he was engaged during the war on important duties in the English Channel, and was drowned when his ship was torpedoed and sunk on January 1st, 1915. He was entitled to the 1914-15 Star, and the General Service and Victory Medals.
25, Hitchin Hill, Hitchin.   2263/B.

O'DELL, W., Private, Labour Corps.
Joining in June 1917, he completed his training, and was engaged on important agricultural work for nearly two years. He was drafted to France in May 1919, and did excellent work at Etaples and other places, where he was employed on special duties with his unit. He returned to England for demobilisation in March 1920.
46, Ashton Road, Luton.   2272.

O'DELL, W., Pte., Loyal North Lancashire Regt.
He joined in July 1916, and in the following January was drafted to Egypt. He saw much service in this theatre of war, and taking part in the Advance through Palestine under General Allenby was in action at Gaza, Jaffa, Haifa, Damascus and other important engagements until the end of hostilities. Returning home, he was demobilised in August 1919, and holds the General Service and Victory Medals.
Seymour House, Limbury Road, Leagrave.   2273.

O'DELL, W., Private, Bedfordshire Regiment.
He joined at the outbreak of war and was almost immediately drafted to France, where he fought in the Retreat from Mons and in many subsequent battles. He was twice wounded in the course of his service overseas, and, invalided home on account of his wounds, was discharged in January 1916 as medically unfit for further military service. He holds the Mons Star, and the General Service and Victory Medals.
82, Althorp Road, Luton.   2274.

O'DELL, W. H., Gunner (Signaller), R.G.A.
He joined in April 1917, and in the following August was sent to the Western Front, and was in action at the Battles of Ypres and Passchendaele, during which he was severely wounded in September 1917. Invalided home he received hospital treatment, and on recovery was engaged on important coastal defence duties until the end of the war. He was demobilised in October 1919, and holds the General Service and Victory Medals.
84, Grove Road, Hitchin.   2275.

O'DELL, W. J., Private, 8th Norfolk Regiment.
Joining in January 1917, he was drafted to the Western Front in the following April. He served with his unit in various sectors, and took part in many important engagements until killed in action on November 6th, 1917, in the third Battle of Ypres. He was entitled to the General Service and Victory Medals.
56, Hitchin Hill, Hitchin.   2276.

O'DELL, W. J., Sapper, Royal Engineers.
He volunteered in October 1915, and was drafted to France in April 1917. There he served in various sectors on duties in connection with operations in the forward areas, and was present at the Battles of the Somme and Ypres and other important engagements. He was demobilised after returning to England in January 1919, and holds the General Service and Victory Medals.
112, Clarendon Road, Luton.   2256/A.

O'DELL, W. R., Private, Bedfordshire Regiment, and 17th Lancashire Fusiliers.
He joined in June 1916, and in April of the following year was drafted to the Western Front, where he served in various sectors and fought in several notable battles, and was gassed. Returning to England on the conclusion of hostilities, he was demobilised in October 1919, and holds the General Service and Victory Medals.
90, Dane Road, Luton.   2259/A.

OFFER, F. E., Drummer, 2/4th Wiltshire Regt.
He volunteered in September 1914, and in the same year
was drafted to India, where he was engaged on important guard and other duties at Rawal Pindi and other
stations. He returned to England for demobilisation in
November 1919, and holds the General Service and
Victory Medals.
1, Liden Terrace, Church Walk, Devizes.   2277.

OLDMEADOW, C. J., Private, R.A.S.C.
He volunteered in May 1915, and after training was
engaged on important transport duties with his unit.
He did valuable work, but was unable to obtain a
transfer overseas owing to medical unfitness, and was
discharged in consequence in February 1919.
25, Loates Lane, Watford.   X2278.

OLIVER, F. W., Private, Royal Irish Fusiliers.
He was mobilised on the outbreak of war, and shortly
afterwards drafted to France, where he was engaged in
heavy fighting in the Retreat from Mons and the first
Battle of Ypres. He was sent to Egypt in 1915, and
there took part in many important engagements in the
British Advance through Palestine, and was wounded.
Returning home at the close of hostilities, he was discharged on account of service in 1918, and holds the
Mons Star, and the General Service and Victory Medals.
58, Grover Road, Oxhey, Watford.   X2279.

OLIVER, F. W., Private, Sherwood Foresters.
He joined in April 1917, and in the following July was
drafted to the Western Front. Whilst in France he saw
much service with his unit in various sectors and took
part in several important engagements, including the
Battles of Ypres, the Marne II., Amiens, Cambrai, and
was wounded. He holds the General Service and Victory Medals, and was demobilised, on his return to
England, in January 1919.
42, St. Saviour's Crescent, Luton.   2280.

OLIVER, G., Private, R.A.V.C.
He joined in April 1916, and in the same month was
drafted to France. There he was engaged on important
duties in connection with the treatment of sick and
wounded horses, and did excellent work for three years.
Sent with the Army of Occupation into Germany, he
remained there until his return to England for demobilisation in September 1919. He holds the General
Service and Victory Medals.
George Street, Maulden, near Ampthill.   2281.

OLIVER, G., Gunner, Royal Garrison Artillery.
He joined in November 1917, and was drafted overseas
in April of the following year. Serving on the Western
Front he was in action in several sectors, and took part
in the engagements on the Somme, at Cambrai and
Albert. Returning to England at the end of hostilities,
he was demobilised in July 1919, and holds the General
Service and Victory Medals.
17, High Street, Lilley.   646/B.

OLIVER, H., Private, 1st Hertfordshire Regiment.
He volunteered in January 1915, and in the following
year embarked for the Western Front, in which theatre
of war he saw much service. He took part in heavy
fighting, and was in action in many important engagements until wounded in the Battle of Arras. He was
invalided home, and receiving medical treatment was
subsequently discharged as medically unfit for further
service in December 1917. He holds the General Service
and Victory Medals.
8, Dolphin Yard, St. Albans.   X4564.

**OLIVER, W., Private, Queen's Own (Royal West
Kent Regiment)**
Joining in May 1918, he was shortly afterwards sent
overseas. Whilst on the Western Front he served with
his unit in several sectors and took part in the Battles
of Cambrai and Ypres, and other important engagements until the cessation of hostilities. He holds the
General Service and Victory Medals, and was demobilised in February 1919 on his return to England.
18, High Street, Lilley.   2282.

OLNEY, A. C., Private, 12th Middlesex Regt.
He joined in May 1916, and in the following August
was sent to the Western Front. There he saw active
service in several sectors, and was in almost continuous
action until severely wounded in the Battle of the Somme
in September 1916. He was invalided to England, and
in consequence of his wounds one of his legs had to be
amputated. He was discharged in January 1918 as
medically unfit for further service, and holds the General
Service and Victory Medals.
2, Symington Street, Harpenden.   2203/A.

OLNEY, A. C., Private, 6th Middlesex Regiment.
Joining in May 1916, in the following August he embarked for service in France. In that theatre of war
he took part in heavy fighting in various sectors until
wounded at Thiepval. He was sent home and after prolonged hospital treatment was discharged as medically
unfit for further military service in January 1918. He
holds the General Service and Victory Medals.
2, Ashton Road, Luton.   2283.

OLNEY, S., Corporal, 5th Royal Welch Fusiliers.
He volunteered in November 1914, and almost immediately sailed for the Western Front, and took part in
many important engagements until sent to Egypt. There
he was engaged in offensive operations in several sectors
and was despatched to Mesopotamia, in which
theatre of war he served with his unit until the cessation
of hostilities. He was wounded three times whilst overseas, and returning to England was demobilised in
March 1919. He holds the 1914-15 Star, and the General
Service and Victory Medals.
The Green, Ickleford, Hitchin.   2284.

OLNEY, W., A.B., Royal Navy.
He volunteered in August 1914, and was engaged on
important patrol duties in the North Sea during the
early part of the war and later served in various ships,
which were employed in convoying troops to France,
Egypt and Russia. He was demobilised in June 1919,
and holds the 1914-15 Star, and the General Service and
Victory Medals
27a, Plantation Road, Leighton Buzzard.   3226/C.

**ORCHARD, H., Private, Royal Fusiliers, and
R.A.O.C.**
He joined in June 1917, and after training was drafted
to France in the same year. He was employed at Le
Havre and other bases on important duties in connection
with the storage and despatch to the forward areas of
ammunition and other military stores. He was demobilised in July 1919, and holds the General Service and
Victory Medals.
58, Cecil Street, North Watford.   X2285.

ORCHARD, L., Corporal, Royal Welch Fusiliers.
He volunteered in February 1915, and in the following
July was sent to the Western Front. There he served
in several sectors and amongst other engagements took
part in the Battles of Loos, the Somme, Ypres, Cambrai,
and in the Retreat and Advance of 1918. He was gassed
and three times wounded in the course of his service,
and returning to England on the conclusion of hostilities was demobilised in June 1919. He holds the
1914-15 Star, and the General Service and Victory Medals.
Rose Cottage, Stanbridge.   2286.

ORCHARD, P., Private, R.A.S.C.
He volunteered in 1915, and in the same year was drafted
to the Western Front. There he served in various
sectors on important duties in connection with the transport of supplies and was present at many important engagements, including those on the Somme, at Arras,
Ypres and Passchendaele. He was demobilised in May
1919, and holds the 1914-15 Star, and the General Service
and Victory Medals.
8, White Lion Street, Aspley End, Herts.   X67/A.

ORCHARD, W. T., Private, Royal Defence Corps.
He volunteered in August 1915, and after training was
engaged on important guard duties with his unit at
various stations on the South-East Coast. He did excellent work for nearly four years, and was demobilised in
March 1919.
256, Chester Road, Watford.   X2287.

ORME, H., Sergeant, R.A.S.C.
He joined in October 1916, and was drafted to the
Western Front in the following year. There he was
attached to the Indian Army, and employed on important
transport work in various sectors and was present at
many notable battles, including those of the Aisne,
Arras, Messines and Cambrai. Returning to England on
the cessation of hostilities, he was demobilised in March
1919, and holds the General Service and Victory Medals.
124, Biscot Road, Luton.   2288.

ORSMAN, A. B., Private, Middlesex Regiment.
He volunteered in 1915, and was drafted overseas in the
same year. On the Western Front he served with his
unit in several sectors and took part in many important
engagements. He was reported missing on April 28th,
1917, whilst the Battle of Arras was in progress, and
was later presumed to have been killed on that date.
He was entitled to the 1914-15 Star, and the General
Service and Victory Medals.
9, Verulam Road, Hitchin.   2289/B.

ORSMAN, W. S., Private, Bedfordshire Regiment.
Volunteering in September 1914, he was drafted overseas in the following year. He saw much service on the Western Front and was in action at Festubert, Loos, Albert and Delville Wood, where he was severely wounded. Rejoining his unit on recovery he was sent to Italy, and after a short period of service there returned to France and was engaged in heavy fighting on the Somme, at Arras, Cambrai and other places during the final operations of the war. He was demobilised in May 1919, and holds the 1914-15 Star, and the General Service and Victory Medals.
9, Verulam Road, Hitchin.   2289/A.

OSBORN, A., Private, 7th Bedfordshire Regt.
He volunteered in September 1914, and was drafted to the Western Front in 1916 and there took part in many important engagements, including the Battles of the Somme, Bullecourt, Delville Wood, and was killed in action at Arras on May 3rd, 1917. He was entitled to the General Service and Victory Medals.
Upper Green, Ickleford, Hitchin.   4188.

OSBORN, A. C., Corporal, Royal Air Force.
He joined in December 1917, and on completing his training was engaged at various aerodromes on important duties. His work, which demanded a high standard of technical knowledge and skill was efficiently carried out, but he was unable to obtain a transfer overseas before the cessation of hostilities, and was demobilised in January 1919.
5, Cranbourne Terrace, Hatfield.   X4048/B.

OSBORN, C. G., Air Mechanic, Royal Air Force.
He volunteered in January 1916, and was later drafted to the Western Front. There he served on special duties at Le Havre, Dunkirk and other important aerodromes in this theatre of war. Returning to England on the conclusion of hostilities, he was demobilised in December 1919, and holds the General Service and Victory Medals.
Flitton.   2291/C.

OSBORN, P. J., Trooper, Canadian Light Horse.
He volunteered in August 1914, and after training was engaged on important duties with the Canadian Contingent at various stations. He did excellent work but was not sent overseas owing to medical unfitness, and was discharged in consequence in June 1919.
Flitton.   2291/A.

OSBORN, R. E., Captain, Canadian Infantry.
He volunteered in August 1914, and was engaged at various depôts on important duties with the Canadian Forces. He did excellent work, but was unsuccessful in obtaining his transfer overseas before the cessation of hostilities owing to medical unfitness for active service, and was demobilised in June 1919.
Flitton.   2291/B.

OSBORN, S. H. (D.C.M.), Sergeant, 1st Hertfordshire Regiment.
Mobilised on the outbreak of hostilities, he was shortly afterwards drafted to France. He fought in the Retreat from Mons and in the Battle of Ypres and took part in several other important engagements, including those on the Somme, at Ypres, Passchendaele, Vimy Ridge and St. Julien. He was awarded the Distinguished Conduct Medal for conspicuous bravery and devotion to duty in the Field at St. Julien in July 1917. He was killed in action on October 28th, 1917, in the third Battle of Ypres. He was also entitled to the Mons Star, and the General Service and Victory Medals.
1, Chapman's Terrace, Hatfield.   X2295.

OSBORNE, A., Rfimn., King's Royal Rifle Corps.
He joined in March 1917, and was drafted to the Western Front in the following February. He was in action in many engagements, and was captured at Cambrai on March 21st, 1918, during the Retreat. Repatriated to England after the signing of the Armistice he was demobilised in January 1919, but re-enlisted for a further term of service, and was sent to India, where he was still serving in 1920. He holds the General Service and Victory Medals.
Saunders Piece, Ampthill.   2290/A.

OSBORNE, H. T., Air Mechanic, R.A.F., and A.B., Royal Navy.
He joined in October 1917, and after training was engaged on important duties at various stations. He was later transferred to the Royal Navy and posted to H.M.S. " Tyne," aboard which vessel he served on the North Sea on patrol duties. He was still in the service in 1920.
53, Marsh Road, Leagrave, near Luton.   2292/A.

OSBORNE, A. G. R., Cpl., Devonshire Regiment.
He joined in May 1918, on attaining military age, and after training was engaged on important duties at various stations on the East Coast, and did excellent work. He was unsuccessful in obtaining a transfer overseas before the conclusion of hostilities, and was demobilised in February 1919.
38, Baker Street, Leighton Buzzard.   2812/C.

OSBORNE, J., Private, 23rd Middlesex Regt.
He joined in October 1918, and after completing his training served at various stations on important duties with his battalion until the following year. He was then sent to Germany with the Army of Occupation and served there until 1920, when he returned to England and was demobilised in April of that year.
57, Shaftesbury Road, Watford.   X2293.

OSBORNE, J. (M.M.), Sapper, R.E.
He volunteered in May 1915, and in the following December was drafted to the Western Front. There he saw much service in several sectors, and took part in heavy fighting at Givenchy, and was wounded on the Somme in 1916. Returning to the front lines he fought at Arras, Ypres, Messines and in other important battles until hostilities ceased. He was awarded the Military Medal for conspicuous bravery and devotion to duty in the Field, and holds, in addition, the 1914-15 Star, and the General Service and Victory Medals, and was demobilised in June 1920.
59, Shaftesbury Road, Watford.   X2294.

OSBORNE, J. T., Pte., 8th Bedfordshire Regt.
He volunteered in August 1914, and in the following month proceeded overseas. Whilst on the Western Front he was in almost continuous action in various sectors, and amongst other important battles took part in those of La Bassée, the Somme and Ypres. Severely wounded in an engagement in the Ypres sector during the Allied Advance of 1918, he was invalided to hospital in England and died there from the effects of his wounds on September 11th, 1918. He was entitled to the 1914-15 Star, and the General Service and Victory Medals.
38, Baker Street, Leighton Buzzard.   2812/A.

OSBORNE, L. J., L/Cpl., 1/20th London Regt.
Volunteering in January 1916, he was drafted to the Western Front early in the following year. There he took part in heavy fighting at Arras, Ypres, Messines, Cambrai and other notable battles, and died on March 24th, 1918, from the effects of wounds received in action near Albert. He was entitled to the General Service and Victory Medals.
Saunders Piece, Ampthill.   2290/B.

OSBORNE, T. H., Private, Royal Defence Corps.
He volunteered in March 1915, and served with his unit at various stations in England. He was engaged on special work at large docks on the Thames, and did valuable work on guard and other important duties until discharged as unfit for further service in February 1918.
58, Marsh Road, Leagrave.   2292/B

OSGERBY, J. W., A.B., Royal Navy.
He joined in 1918, and served with his ship on important patrol duties in the North and Baltic Seas and in other waters. His ship took part in several engagements with the German Fleet, and on the cessation of hostilities he was demobilised in February 1919. He holds the General Service and Victory Medals.
50, Regent Street, North Watford.   X2296.

OSGOOD, H. J., Gunner (Fitter), R.F.A.
Joining in July 1916, on the completion of his training he was sent overseas. He served with his battery in several sectors of the Western Front until invalided home suffering from fever and heart trouble. He was subsequently discharged unfit for further military service in February 1919, and holds the General Service and Victory Medals.
2, Union Road, Hitchin.   4189.

OSMAN, J. T., Corporal, R.A.S.C. (M.T.).
Volunteering in November 1915, he shortly afterwards was drafted to France, where he was engaged on important duties in the transport of ammunition, rations and other supplies to the front lines. He was present at several of the principal battles, including those of Ypres, Arras and Passchendaele, and on the cessation of hostilities went into Germany with the Army of Occupation. He returned to England for demobilisation in May 1919, and holds the General Service and Victory Medals.
47, Sopwell Lane, St. Albans.   X3080/A.

OVERTHROW, A. E., Private, 2nd Devonshire Regiment.
He joined in 1916, and in the same year was sent overseas. He saw much service on the Western Front in various sectors of which he was engaged in heavy fighting. He was wounded and taken prisoner on March 23rd, 1918, during the second Battle of the Somme, and held in captivity in Germany until repatriated after the signing of the Armistice. He was demobilised in 1919, and holds the General Service and Victory Medals.
160, Ridgway Road, Luton.						2297.

OVERTON, W. G., L/Corporal, 1st Hertfordshire Regiment.
Volunteering in 1914, he was drafted to France in 1916. He saw much service in various sectors and took part in several important battles, including those at Ypres and on the Somme, and was unfortunately killed in action on February 11th, 1918. He was entitled to the General Service and Victory Medals.
88, Hagden Lane, Watford.						X2298.

OWEN, A., Sergeant, R.G.A.
He volunteered in 1915, and in the same year was on active service on the Western Front. In this theatre of war he fought with his battery in many notable engagements, including those on the Somme, the Aisne, at Vimy Ridge, Ypres, Messines, Passchendaele and Cambrai. He was gassed and wounded three times in the course of his service overseas, and was demobilised in 1919. He holds the General Service and Victory Medals.
5, Talbot Road, Rickmansworth.						X2299.

OWEN, A. E., Private, 7th Bedfordshire Regt.
He volunteered in November 1914, and in the same year proceeded to the Western Front. There he served with his unit in various sectors and fought in several important engagements including the second Battle of Ypres. He was killed in action in the Albert sector on April 7th, 1916, and was buried at Carnay. He was entitled to the 1914 Star, and the General Service and Victory Medals.
8, Bury Hill, Hemel Hempstead.						X2300.

OWEN, S., Private, Royal Sussex Regiment.
Joining in 1918, he completed his training and was engaged at the depôt of his unit on important duties until the cessation of hostilities, when he was sent with the Army of Occupation into Germany. There he served at Cologne and other towns on the Rhine, and returning to England was demobilised in March 1920.
72, Bury Road, Hemel Hempstead.						X2302/B.

OWEN, W. S., Private, 1st Hertfordshire Regt.
He joined in 1916, and on completion of his training was sent to the Western Front in the same year, where he saw much service. He took part in heavy fighting, and amongst other important engagements fought in the Battles of Arras, Cambrai and the Somme. Returning to England on the cessation of hostilities he was demobilised in February 1919, and holds the General Service and Victory Medals.
72, Bury Road, Hemel Hempstead.						X2302/A.

OWENS, J., Private, R.A.S.C.
He volunteered in 1915, and was drafted overseas in the same year. Serving with his unit on the Western Front he was engaged on important transport duties in various sectors, in which heavy fighting was in progress. He was present at many important battles, including those of the Somme, Ypres, Bullecourt, Cambrai and St. Quentin. He was demobilised in February 1919, and holds the General Service and Victory Medals.
21, Astley Road, Hemel Hempstead.						X2301.

P

PACKER, J., Driver, R.F.A.
He volunteered in November 1915, and, after a period of training, was drafted to the Western Front. There he took part in many important engagements, including the Battles of the Somme, Ypres and Cambrai, and was wounded. Later he was transferred to Italy, and was in action during the fighting on the Piave. He returned home and was demobilised in May 1919, and holds the General Service and Victory Medals.
82, Norfolk Road, Rickmansworth.						X2303.

PACKHAM, R., Private, Royal Sussex Regiment.
He volunteered in November 1914, and was engaged on important duties at home until drafted overseas. During his service on the Western Front, he took part in the Battles of Arras, Cambrai, the Somme and St. Quentin, and was wounded. He was killed in action on August 8th, 1918, and was entitled to the General Service and Victory Medals.
71, Lancaster Road, Hitchin.						1823/C.

PACKHAM, C., Corporal, Royal Sussex Regiment.
He volunteered in November 1914, and, after a period of training was drafted to France, where he served as a pioneer in various sectors of the Front. He also took part in many important engagements whilst in this theatre of war, including those at St. Quentin, and was twice wounded in action. He was demobilised in February 1919, and holds the General Service and Victory Medals.
71, Lancaster Road, Hitchin.						1823/B.

PAGE, A., Corporal, Royal Inniskilling Fusiliers.
He volunteered in January 1916, and in the following July was drafted to the Western Front. In this theatre of war he took part in the Battles of the Somme, was wounded in action and spent six months in hospital in England. On recovery he was sent to Egypt, where he saw much active service, and later fought in Palestine at the Battles of Gaza and the capture of Jerusalem. He returned home and was demobilised in March 1919, holding the General Service and Victory Medals.
28, Wing Road, Leighton Buzzard.						2304/C.

PAGE, A. W., Seaman, R.N., Submarine "E.26."
He was in the Navy at the outbreak of hostilities, and served in Submarine "E.26" on the high seas. This boat was engaged on important patrol duties in the North Sea and Baltic Sea and also in chasing enemy submarines. He lost his life when she went down in 1916, and was entitled to the 1914-15 Star, and the General Service and Victory Medals.
28, Wing Road, Leighton Buzzard.						2304/A.

PAGE, C. H., Private, 1st Bedfordshire Regt.
He volunteered in August 1914, and was shortly afterwards drafted to the Western Front. Whilst in this theatre of war he took part in many engagements, including that of Ypres, and was wounded on two occasions. He was invalided home and discharged in January 1916, and holds the 1914 Star, and the General Service and Victory Medals.
32, Curzon Road, Luton.						2306.

PAGE, D., Private, Royal Marine Light Infantry.
He was mobilised in August 1914, and was posted to H.M.S. "Aboukir," losing his life when this vessel was torpedoed by a German submarine off the Hook of Holland on September 22nd, 1914. He was entitled to the 1914-15 Star, and the General Service and Victory Medals.
6, Union Lane, New Town, Hatfield.						4405/B.

PAGE, F. E., Sapper, Royal Engineers.
He joined in July 1916, and, after a period of training served at various stations on important duties with his unit. He was not successful in obtaining a transfer overseas, but rendered valuable service at home until his demobilisation in January 1919.
Selford Road, Aspley Guise.						Z1876/B.

PAGE, G., Private, R.A.S.C.
He joined in 1917, and after a period of training served at various stations on important duties with his unit. Owing to the early cessation of hostilities he was not successful in obtaining a transfer overseas, but rendered valuable services at home. He was demobilised in June 1919.
Batchworth Hill, Rickmansworth.						X2307.

PAGE, H., Corporal, Royal Warwickshire Regt.
He joined in January 1917, and was sent for training to Ireland. Later he was drafted to France and took part in many engagements, including those of Ypres (III.), Cambrai, the second Battle of the Somme, and the Retreat and Advance of 1918. After the cessation of hostilities he went into Germany with the Army of Occupation until his demobilisation in March 1919. He holds the General Service and Victory Medals.
28, Wing Road, Leighton Buzzard.						2304/B.

PAGE, H. H., Private, 4th Bedfordshire Regt.
He joined in July 1917, and later in the same year was drafted to France. There he took part in many important engagements, including those of Cambrai, the second Battle of the Somme and Arras, and was wounded in action. He served on the Western Front until his demobilisation in 1919, and holds the General Service and Victory Medals.
44, Nightingale Road, Hitchin.						2308.

PAGE, J., Private, Bedfordshire Regiment, attached R.A.S.C.
He volunteered in August 1914, and after a period of training served at various stations on important duties. He was not successful in obtaining a transfer overseas, owing to his being medically unfit, but rendered valuable services in connection with agricultural work throughout the whole period of the war. He was demobilised in August 1919.
Beeston, Sandy, Beds.						Z2309.

PAGE, J., Private, Royal Warwickshire Regt.

He volunteered in September 1914, and in the following year was drafted to France. In this seat of war he took part in many engagements, including the Battles of Loos, the Somme, Arras, Ypres and Cambrai, and was wounded in action. After the cessation of hostilities he went into Germany with the Army of Occupation, where he served until his demobilisation in 1919. He holds the 1914-15 Star, and the General Service and Victory Medals

14, Sanremo Road, Aspley Guise. Z863/B.

PAGE, L., Corporal, Bedfordshire Regiment.

He volunteered in August 1914, and on completing his training in the following year, was drafted to France. During his four years' service on the Western Front he took part in many important engagements, including the Battles of Hill 60, Ypres and the Somme, and was twice wounded in action. He was demobilised in January 1919, holding the 1914-15 Star, and the General Service and Victory Medals.

13, Heath Terrace, Sandridge Road, St. Albans. X2310.

PAGE, W. L., Private, 11th Middlesex Regiment.

He volunteered in August 1914, and in the following year was drafted to the Western Front. There he took part in many important engagements, including the Battles of Ypres, Festubert and the Somme, where he was severely wounded. He died from the effects of his wounds two months later on November 19th, 1916. He was entitled to the 1914-15 Star, and the General Service and Victory Medals.

27, Cannon Road, Watford. X2311.

PAIN, C., Private, 6th Royal Berkshire Regt.

He joined in July 1917, and later in the same year proceeded to the Western Front. In this seat of war he took part in many important battles, including those of Cambrai, Ypres and Arras. He returned home and was demobilised in 1919, holding the General Service and Victory Medals.

85, Regent Street, North Watford. X2312/B.

PAINE, G. J., Gunner, R.G.A.

He joined in October 1916, and on completing his training in the following year was drafted to France. There he took part in many battles, including those of Ypres, Cambrai, the Somme (II.) and the Marne (II.). He served in France until February 1919, when he returned home and was demobilised in the following month. He holds the General Service and Victory Medals.

9, Waterside, King's Langley. X2313.

PAINTER, H. J., Private, Grenadier Guards.

Volunteering in November 1915, he proceeded to the Western Front shortly after. He took part in much severe fighting in this theatre of war, served through the Battles of Arras, Ypres and Cambrai, and was wounded in action. He was demobilised in March 1919, and holds the General Service and Victory Medals.

31, Lowestoft Road, Watford. X3418/B.

PAINTON, A., 2nd Corporal, R.M.E.

He was serving in August 1914, and was shortly afterwards drafted to France. Whilst on the Western Front he took part in several engagements, including the Battles of Hill 60, Ypres, the Somme and Arras, and was wounded three times. He returned home in 1917, and served on various important duties until his discharge in July 1919. He holds the 1914 Star, and the General Service and Victory Medals.

19, Upper Paddock Road, Oxhey. X2314.

PAKES, A. F., L/Corporal, R.E. (Signal Section).

He volunteered in September 1914, and in the following year was drafted to the Dardanelles, where he took part in the landing at Suvla Bay and other engagements. After the Evacuation of the Gallipoli Peninsula, he was transferred to Palestine and was in action during many battles in this seat of war and was wounded. In 1919 he returned home, was demobilised in April of that year, and holds the 1914-15 Star, and the General Service and Victory Medals.

31, Malvern Road, Luton. 2315.

PAKES, E., A.B., R.N., H.M.S. "Lord Clyde."

He joined the Navy in 1909, and at the outbreak of war was drafted to France with the Naval Brigade. There he was in action at Antwerp, Ypres and Arras. Later he was engaged on board H.M.S. "Lord Clyde," and took part in bombarding the Belgium coast, and was again in action during the raid on Zeebrugge. In 1920 he was still serving, and holds the 1914 Star, and the General Service and Victory Medals.

8, Whitby Road, Luton. 2316.

PAKES, C. G., Private, M.G.C.

He volunteered in September 1914, and after completing his training was drafted to France. There he took part in many important engagements, including those of the Somme, Givenchy, Lens, Passchendaele, Hill 70, Bullecourt and Cambrai, and was wounded in action. He was demobilised in July 1919, and holds the General Service and Victory Medals.

1, Oak Road, Luton, Beds. 2317.

PALFREY, A., Private, R.A.S.C., and Gunner, R.F.A.

He volunteered in July 1915, and proceeded to France in the following year. During his service on the Western Front he was in action in many engagements, including the Battles of the Somme, Arras, Ypres and Cambrai, where he was wounded. He was invalided home in 1917, and served on various duties until his demobilisation in February 1920. He holds the General Service and Victory Medals.

14, Terrace Gardens, St. Albans Road, Watford. X2318.

PALFREY, D. D. (Mrs.), Head Cook, V.A.D.

She joined in May 1916, and was engaged at the 1st Southern General Hospital, Mony Hill Section, for about three years. She rendered very valuable services, and carried out her important duties in a highly commendable manner. She was demobilised in July 1919.

14, Waddington Road, St. Albans. 2319/B.

PALFREY, R. E., Private, 10th and 12th London Regiment, and R.A.M.C.

He volunteered in August 1914, and in the following year was drafted to the Dardanelles, where he was in action during the landing at Suvla Bay and other engagements. After the Evacuation of the Gallipoli Peninsula he was transferred to France, and took part in the Battles of the Somme and Ypres, and was wounded. In 1919 he returned home for his demobilisation, and holds the 1914-15 Star, and the General Service and Victory Medals.

14, Waddington Road, St. Albans. 2319/A.

PALLETT, E. W., Pte., 6th Bedfordshire Regt.

He volunteered in August 1914, and in the following year was drafted to France. In this theatre of war he took part in many engagements, including those of Ypres, the Somme, Arras, Albert and Cambrai, and was twice badly wounded in action. He died from the effects of his wounds on May 20th, 1919, and was entitled to the 1914-15 Star, and the General Service and Victory Medals.

7, St. Michael's Mount, Hitchin. 2320.

PALLETT, H. C., Driver, R.H.A.

He joined in January 1918, and after completing his training served at various stations on important duties with his Battery. Owing to the early cessation of hostilities he was unable to obtain a transfer overseas, but did consistent good work at home. He was demobilised in 1919.

4, Chapman Terrace, Hatfield. 2321.

PALMER, A. C. H., L/Corporal, Royal Warwickshire Regiment.

He joined in May 1917, and in the following year was drafted to France. There he took part in many engagements, including the second Battle of the Somme, and the Retreat and Advance of 1918. He was demobilised in April 1919, and holds the General Service and Victory Medals.

"Blenheim," Stanbridge Road, Leighton Buzzard. 2322

PALMER, A. J. G., Sergeant, R.A.F.

He volunteered in September 1914 and proceeded to France in the following year. During his service on the Western Front he was engaged on important flying duties and for nearly two years acted as a Sergeant Observer in the Somme sector. In March 1919 he returned home and was demobilised, holding the 1914-15 Star, and the General Service and Victory Medals.

33, Vernon Road, Luton. 2323.

PALMER, E. R., Private, Bedfordshire Regt.

He joined in July 1918, and in the following October was drafted to France, where he was employed in guarding German prisoners at Abbeville and Calais. During his service he was transferred to the Suffolk Regiment, and after the cessation of hostilities went into Germany with the Army of Occupation. He returned home and was demobilised in January 1920, holding the General Service and Victory Medals.

15, Primrose Cottages, Hatfield. X2324.

PALMER, A. J., Private, Bedfordshire Regiment.
He volunteered in August 1914, and after his training was engaged on important duties at various stations. Owing to ill-health he was unable to obtain his transfer overseas, and in December 1914 was invalided out of the service.
Chequers Lane, Preston, Herts. 2328.

PALMER, F., L/Corporal, 9th Suffolk Regiment.
He joined in June 1916, and in December of that year was drafted to the Western Front, where he saw much active service. After taking part in the Battles of Cambrai and Hulluch, he was invalided to hospital in April 1917. He was discharged as medically unfit in September of the same year, and holds the General Service and Victory Medals.
52, Claremont Road, Luton. 2325.

PALMER, F. W., Private, 1st Bedfordshire Regt.
Volunteering in September 1914, he was sent to the Western Front in the following year. He took part in many important engagements, including the Battles of Ypres and Arras, and on October 26th, 1918, was killed in action. He was entitled to the 1914-15 Star, and the General Service and Victory Medals.
43, Spencer Street, St. Albans. X2326/A.

PALMER, G. (M.M.), Corporal, 1st Hertfordshire Regiment.
He joined in February 1917, and shortly afterwards proceeded to France, where he saw much active service. He played a prominent part in many engagements, including the Battles of Arras, Ypres, St. Quentin, Cambrai and the Somme, and was awarded the Military Medal for conspicuous bravery and devotion to duty in the Field. He holds also the General Service and Victory Medals, and in February 1919 was demobilised.
East End, Flitwick. 2327/A.

PALMER, J. A., Staff-Sergeant, R.A.M.C.
He volunteered in May 1915, and in 1917 was drafted to the Western Front. There he was engaged on important duties at Etaples Hospital, and also took an active part in the Battle of Ypres. After the cessation of hostilities, he was sent with the Army of Occupation into Germany, where he was stationed at Cologne. He holds the General Service and Victory Medals, and in 1920 was still with his unit.
Laurel Dean, Kingston Street, Luton. 2329.

PALMER, J. C., Pioneer, Royal Engineers.
He volunteered in May 1915, and shortly after was sent to France. Whilst in this theatre of war he was engaged on signalling, wiring and dispatch-riding duties in various sectors of the front, and saw service at Ypres and Amiens. He was demobilised in March 1919, and holds the 1914-15 Star, and the General Service and Victory Medals
5, St. Mary's Road, Watford. X2330.

PALMER, L., L/Corporal, Hertfordshire Regt.
Volunteering in June 1915, he sailed for France in September of the same year and fought in the engagements at Ypres, Loos and the Somme, where he was wounded during the British Offensive in 1916. On recovery he returned to the Front, and was in action almost continuously until taken prisoner in March 1918 at St. Quentin in the German Advance. Repatriated, after hostilities ceased he was demobilised in March 1919, and holds the 1914-15 Star, and the General Service and Victory Medals.
43, Spencer Street, St. Albans. X2326/B

PALMER, S., Driver, R.F.A.
He volunteered in July 1915, and, on completing his training in the following March was drafted to the Western Front. There he took part in the Battles of the Somme and Ypres, and also served through severe fighting at Bullecourt, Passchendaele and many other places. He was demobilised in February 1919, and holds the General Service and Victory Medals.
9, Havelock Road, Luton. 2331.

PALMER, S., Private, Northamptonshire Regt.
He joined in August 1917, and shortly afterwards proceeded to the Western Front, where he saw much active service. He took part in many important engagements, including the Battles of Cambrai, the Somme and Ypres, was in action also at Messines and Passchendaele, and was gassed. In September 1919 he was demobilised, holding the General Service and Victory Medals.
37, Wenlock Street, Luton. 2332.

PAMMENT, C., Private, Duke of Cornwall's Light Infantry.
He volunteered in August 1914, and in the same year was drafted to France, where he took part in the Battles of Ypres and many other important engagements. In January 1916 he was transferred to Salonika, and there saw active service on the Macedonian front until the cessation of hostilities. He was wounded in action whilst overseas and on his return home in September 1919 was demobilised, holding the 1914-15 Star, and the General Service and Victory Medals.
67, Benskin Road, Watford. X2333.

PAMPALONI, W. R., Sapper, R.E.
He volunteered in December 1914, and in July of the following year was drafted to the Dardanelles. He took part in the severe fighting at Suvla Bay whilst in Gallipoli, and on the Evacuation of the Peninsula in December 1915 was transferred to Egypt. There he was again in action, and, taking part in the Advance into Palestine, fought in the three Battles of Gaza and at the capture of Jaffa. He returned to England for demobilisation in July 1919, and holds the 1914-15 Star, and the General Service and Victory Medals.
79, Havelock Road, Luton. 2334.

PANGBOURNE, P., Private, Royal Marine Light Infantry.
He volunteered in August 1914, and served in various ships in many waters. He was engaged on important duties with the Grand Fleet in the North Sea and also in the Baltic, and took part in the Battles of Heligoland Bight and Jutland and many minor engagements. He was demobilised in 1919, and holds the 1914-15 Star, and the General Service and Victory Medals.
10, Lower Paxton Road, St. Albans. 2335.

PANTLING, A. C., L/Corporal, M.G.C.
He volunteered in December 1915, and in the following February was sent to the Western Front. There he took part in the fighting in various sectors, and served through the Battles of the Somme, Ypres and Cambrai, and was wounded in action. He was demobilised in March 1919, and holds the General Service and Victory Medals.
14, Hockliffe Road, Leighton Buzzard. 2336.

PANTLING, A. P., Pte., 7th Bedfordshire Regt.
He volunteered in August 1914, and in the following March was sent to France, where he saw much severe fighting until wounded in action on the Somme in 1916. He was invalided home, but returned to the Western Front on his recovery and again took part in many important engagements. He was wounded a second time at the Battle of Cambrai in 1918 and again returned to England. He was demobilised in March 1919, and holds the 1914-15 Star, and the General Service and Victory Medals.
14, Union Street, Leighton Buzzard. 2338.

PANTLING, A., Private, Bedfordshire Regiment.
Volunteering in August 1914, he was drafted to the Western Front in September of the same year. He took part in many important engagements whilst in this theatre of war, including the Battles of La Bassée, Ypres and Hill 60, and was severely wounded in action on the Somme. He returned to England, and after being for a time in hospital was invalided from the Army in February 1917. He holds the 1914 Star, and the General Service and Victory Medals.
20, East Street, Leighton Buzzard. 2337.

PANTLING, B., Private, Royal Scots.
He joined in March 1917, and in October of the same year proceeded to North Russia. There he took part in important operations at various places until his return to England in August 1919. He was then demobilised, holding the General Service and Victory Medals.
48, Plantation Road, Leighton Buzzard. 2339/A.

PANTLING, F., Private, 1/5th Bedfordshire Regiment.
He was mobilised in August 1914, and served at various stations in England until July 1916, when he was sent overseas. During his service on the Western Front he took part in the Battles of Arras, Ypres and the Somme and many other engagements, and was gassed near Bapaume in August 1918. He was discharged in March 1919, and holds the General Service and Victory Medals.
12, St. Andrew's Street, Leighton Buzzard. 2340.

PANTLING, H., Private, 7th Middlesex Regt.
He volunteered in October 1914, and after completing a period of training served with his unit at various stations. He was unable to obtain his transfer overseas on account of ill-health, but rendered valuable services until March 1917, when he was invalided from the Army.
34, Chapel Yard, Leighton Buzzard. 2413.

PANTLING, H. J., Private, Loyal North Lancashire Regiment.

He joined in May 1916, was sent to France in November of the same year and there saw much heavy fighting. He took part in engagements on the Somme and at various other places, and was killed in action on April 28th, 1917, in the first Battle of Arras. He was entitled to the General Service and Victory Medals.

48, Plantation Road, Leighton Buzzard. 2339/B.

PANTLING, W. C., Private, Norfolk Regiment.

He enlisted in March 1914, and in August of the following year was drafted to the Western Front, where he saw much active service. He took part in the Battles of Loos, the Somme, Arras and Cambrai, and also fought in the Retreat and Advance of 1918. In November 1919 he was discharged, holding the 1914-15 Star, and the General Service and Victory Medals.

39, Mill Road, Leighton Buzzard. 2341.

PAPWORTH, W. C., Gunner, R.F.A.

He volunteered in January 1915, and was shortly afterwards drafted to France, where he saw much active service. Later he was transferred to Salonika, and took part in the heavy fighting in the Balkans. He was invalided home in March 1918, and served until hostilities ceased at Messrs. Loftus', Cleveland Anti-Aircraft Works, Yorkshire. He was demobilised in February 1919, holding the 1914-15 Star, and the General Service and Victory Medals.

4, Florence Street, Hitchin. 2342.

PARIS, S. F., Private, Labour Corps (338th Works Company).

He joined in September 1916, and after a period of training served at various stations on important duties with his unit. He was not successful in obtaining a transfer overseas owing to his being medically unfit, but rendered valuable services at home. He was demobilised in January 1919.

27, Garfield Street, Watford. X2343.

PARKER, A., A/Q.M.S., Bedfordshire Regt.

He joined in 1916, and after a period of training was drafted to France, where he saw active service in various sectors of the front. He took a prominent part in many engagements, including the Battles of the Somme, Messines and Ypres, and was wounded in action. He was invalided home, and after his recovery acted as an Instructor at various stations in England until August 1919, when he was demobilised. He holds the General Service and Victory Medals.

Rose Cottage, Aspley Hill, Woburn Sands. Z2344.

PARKER, A., Private, R.A.S.C.

Volunteering in October 1915, he was immediately sent to France, where he saw much active service. He was chiefly engaged on transport duties, conveying ammunition and supplies to the forward areas in the Loos, Somme, Ypres and Albert sectors. He returned home in August 1917, and in November of that year was invalided from the Army owing to injuries received whilst overseas. He holds the 1914-15 Star, and the General Service and Victory Medals.

1, Barker's Cottages, Hitchin Hill, Hitchin. 2345/B.

PARKER, C. H., Private, Royal Marine Light Infantry.

He volunteered in August 1915, and in the following year proceeded to France, where he took part in much severe fighting. He served through important engagements in various sectors of the Front and was wounded in action at Arras in 1917. He was invalided home, and in the following year was sent to the East and served at Constantinople until June 1919. He then returned home and was demobilised, holding the General Service and Victory Medals.

5, Court 3, Meeting Alley, Watford. X2346/C.

PARKER, H. W., Private, Middlesex Regiment.

He volunteered in February 1915, and after a period of training was drafted to the Western Front, where he saw much severe fighting. He took part in the Battles of Ypres, Arras and Cambrai, and in many other engagements, until the cessation of hostilities, and in February 1919 was demobilised. He holds the General Service and Victory Medals.

14, Longmire Road, St. Albans. X2364.

PARKER, J. A., Driver, R.A.S.C.

He volunteered in June 1915, and shortly afterwards was sent to the Western Front. There he served on various sectors and took an active part in the Battles of the Somme, Ypres and Cambrai. He was demobilised on his return home in February 1919, and holds the 1914-15 Star, and the General Service and Victory Medals.

5, Court 3, Meeting Alley, Watford. X2346/B.

PARKER, J. (M.M.), Sergeant, R.F.A.

He volunteered in June 1915, and in the following November was drafted to the Western Front. There he took part in many important engagements in various sectors, including the Battles of the Somme, Arras and Cambrai, and was wounded in action. After the signing of the Armistice he was sent into Germany with the Army of Occupation, remaining until May 1919, when he returned home for demobilisation. He was awarded the Military Medal for distinguished gallantry on the Field at Bullecourt in October 1917, and holds also the 1914-15 Star, and the General Service and Victory Medals.

58, Upper Paddock Road, Oxhey, Watford. X2347.

PARKER, L. J., Corporal, 2/5th Gloucestershire Regiment.

He volunteered in 1914, and in the following year was drafted to France. There he took part in many engagements, including those of the Somme, Arras and Ypres. He returned home in October 1918, and was discharged as medically unfit for further service. He holds the General Service and Victory Medals.

25, Bedford Road, St. Albans. X618 B.

PARKER, S., Private, Labour Corps.

Joining in October 1916, he was sent to the Western Front in the following January. He was engaged on important duties in various sectors whilst in this theatre of war, and was present at the Battles of Ypres and Cambrai. He was demobilised in May 1919, and holds the General Service and Victory Medals.

65, Queen's Street, Luton. 2348.

PARKER, S. R., Private, Royal Marine Light Infantry.

He joined in March 1918, and after completing a period of training, was engaged on important duties at Chatham and other stations. Owing to the early cessation of hostilities, he was unable to obtain his transfer to the Front, but, nevertheless, rendered valuable services with his unit until his demobilisation in June 1919.

5, Court 3, Meeting Alley, Watford. X2346/A.

PARKER, T., Private, 52nd Royal Fusiliers.

He joined in February 1917, and after his training served at various stations, where he was engaged on important duties with his unit. He was unable to obtain his transfer overseas and on August 1st, 1918, died at No. 1 Eastern General Hospital.

5, Arthur Street, Luton. 2349.

PARKER, T., Gunner, R.F.A.

He enlisted in April 1912, and in April 1915 was sent to Egypt and was stationed at Alexandria until the following October, when he was drafted to Salonika. Here he served on the Vardar and Struma fronts, and in the vicinity of Monastir. In August 1916 he embarked for Egypt and served throughout the Advance through Sinai, Palestine and Syria, and returning to England, was demobilised in February 1919. He holds the 1914-15 Star, and the General Service and Victory Medals.

339, High Town Road, Luton. 5172/A.

PARKER, T. A., Private, M.G.C.

He joined in July 1917, and shortly afterwards was drafted to the Western Front, where he served through much severe fighting. He took part in the Battles of Ypres and Cambrai, and was also in action at Arras, Loos, St. Quentin, and many other places. He was demobilised in March 1919, and holds the General Service and Victory Medals.

45, St. Saviour's Crescent, Luton. 2350.

PARKER, W. C., Private, 5th Middlesex Regt.

He joined in October 1916, and in the same year was drafted to France, where he served in various sectors of the Front. He took part in the Battle of Ypres, and many other important engagements, and was wounded in action near Mons shortly before the signing of the Armistice. He was demobilised in 1919, and holds the General Service and Victory Medals.

21, Cassio Bridge Road, Watford. X2351.

PARKER, W. H., Sapper, R.E.

He joined in October 1916, and in August of the following year proceeded to the Western Front. There he took an active part in the Battles of the Somme, Ypres and Albert, and many other engagements, and was gassed and wounded in action at Cambrai in March 1918. After the cessation of hostilities, he was drafted to India, where he was still with his unit in 1920, and holds the General Service and Victory Medals.

1, Barker's Cottages, Hitchin Hill, Hitchin. 2345/A.

PARKER, W. J., Private, Guards Machine Gun Regiment.

He joined in June 1918, and after completing a term of training served with his unit at various stations. He was unable to obtain his transfer overseas owing to the early cessation of hostilities, but, whilst engaged on important duties, rendered very valuable services until demobilised in March 1919.
47, Sunnyside, Hitchin. 2412.

PARKIN, C., Sergeant, Machine Gun Corps.

Volunteering in November 1914, he was drafted to the Western Front in the following year. He took part in much severe fighting in this theatre of war, served through the Battles of Ypres, Arras and Cambrai, and was wounded in the first Battle of the Somme. He was demobilised in March 1919, and holds the 1914-15 Star, and the General Service and Victory Medals.
1, Sunny Side, Cowper Road, Harpenden. 2353.

PARKINS, A. J., Sergeant, Royal Fusiliers.

He volunteered in December 1915, and in November of the following year was sent to France. There he took part in the fighting in various sectors of the front, served through the Battles of Arras and Ypres, and was wounded in action at Monchy in August 1917. He was demobilised in February 1919, and holds the General Service and Victory Medals.
55, Park Street, St. Albans. X2354/B.

PARKINS, B. W., Private, Bedfordshire Regt.

He joined in July 1916, and in the following December was sent to the Western Front. There he took part in many important engagements, and, after being wounded, was killed in action at Loos on June 26th, 1917. He was entitled to the General Service and Victory Medals.
6a, Chapel Street, Hemel Hempstead. 2352.

PARKINS, C. F., Corporal, Grenadier Guards.

He joined in April 1918, and after his training was engaged on important guard duties at various stations. Owing to the early cessation of hostilities, he was unable to obtain his transfer to the Front, but did useful work with his unit until his demobilisation in December 1919.
55, Park Street, St. Albans. X2354/A.

PARKINS, E. W., Private, 1st Suffolk Regiment.

He joined in November 1916, and in the following January was drafted to the East. After serving for a short time in Egypt, he proceeded into Palestine, where he took part in many important engagements, including the Battles of Gaza and the capture of Jerusalem and Aleppo. He was demobilised on his return home in October 1919, and holds the General Service and Victory Medals.
36, Edward Street, Dunstable, Luton. 2355/A.

PARKINS, F. G., Private, 23rd Royal Fusiliers.

He volunteered in December 1915, and after a period of training was drafted to France. In this theatre of war he took part in many important engagements, including those of Cambrai and Deniecourt, where he was wounded in action and invalided home. He was demobilised in January 1919, holding the General Service and Victory Medals.
26, Bailey Street, Luton. 3297/B.

PARKINS, F. W., Private, Coldstream Guards.

He was already in the Army when the war broke out in August 1914, and was immediately drafted to the Western Front. There he served through the Retreat from Mons and later took part in the Battles of Hill 60, Ypres and Arras, and was wounded in action on the Somme. He was invalided home in 1917, and in January 1919 was discharged, holding the Mons Star, and the General Service and Victory Medals.
39, Bailey Street, Luton. 2356/A.

PARKINS, J., Private, Labour Corps.

He was already serving on the outbreak of war in August 1914, and in 1915 proceeded to France. There he fought in the Battles of Hill 60, Ypres, Festubert, Loos and Arras, and many other engagements until September 17th, 1917, when he was killed in action at Lens. He was entitled to the 1914-15 Star, and the General Service and Victory Medals.
39, Bailey Street, Luton. 2356/B.

PARKINS, L. C., Private, M.G.C.

He joined in April 1916, and shortly afterwards proceeded to Egypt, where he served at various stations. Later he was transferred to the Western Front and there took part in the Battles of Arras, Cambrai and the Somme, and was gassed and taken prisoner. He was held in captivity in Germany until the cessation of hostilities, and in April 1920 was demobilised, holding the General Service and Victory Medals.
Upper Green, Ickleford, Hitchin. 2414/A.

PARKINS, F. J., Private, Suffolk and Royal Warwickshire Regiments.

He volunteered in 1915, and in the following year was sent to the Western Front, where he took part in many engagements, including the Battles of Albert, the Somme, Arras, Ypres and Passchendaele. In November 1917 he was transferred to Italy and saw active service in this theatre of war until March 1918, when he returned to France. There, after taking part in the second Battle of Cambrai and Le Cateau, he was killed in action in the Amiens sector on October 10th, 1918. He was entitled to the General Service and Victory Medals.
Upper Green, Ickleford, Hitchin. 2414/C.

PARKINS, L. G., Sergeant, R.F.A.

He volunteered in April 1915, and in November proceeded to France, where he saw much severe fighting. He took part in the Battles of the Somme, Ypres and Cambrai and many other engagements until transferred to Italy in 1917. He saw active service on the Piave and Trentino whilst in this theatre of war, and in March 1918 returned to the Western Front in time to fight in the Retreat and Advance of 1918. He was demobilised in April of the following year and holds the 1914-15 Star, and the General Service and Victory Medals.
55, Park Street, St. Albans. X2354/C.

PARKINS, P. W., Private, R.A.O.C.

He joined in May 1918, and after a period of training was engaged on important duties at various stations. Owing to the early cessation of hostilities, he was unable to obtain his transfer overseas, but nevertheless rendered valuable services with his unit until demobilised in December 1919.
Upper Green, Ickleford, Hitchin. 2414/B.

PARKINS, S. G., Private, Bedfordshire Regiment.

He joined in June 1918, and was immediately sent to France, where he saw active service in various sectors of the Front. He took part in the Battle of Cambrai and many other engagements until the cessation of hostilities, when he proceeded to Germany. There he was stationed at Cologne until March 1920, and then returned home for demobilisation. He holds the General Service and Victory Medals.
5, Duke Street, Luton. 2357.

PARKINS, W. G., L/Corporal, 1st Essex Regt.

He joined in March 1916, and in November of that year was drafted to the Western Front. There, after taking part in many important engagements, he was reported missing and, afterwards, as killed in action in the Battle of Arras on April 14th, 1917. He was entitled to the General Service and Victory Medals.
36, Edward Street, Dunstable, Luton. 2355/B.

PARKINSON, G., Sergeant, Rifle Brigade.

He volunteered in October 1914, and in the following year was drafted to India. There he saw active service on the North-West Frontier, and was also engaged on garrison duties at Rawal Pirdi and various other places. He was demobilised on his return home in April 1919, and holds the General Service and Victory Medals.
61, Fearnley Street, Watford. X2358.

PARKS, F. J., Private, Royal Defence Corps.

He volunteered in October 1914, and after completing a period of training served at various stations, where he was engaged on important duties with his unit. He did much useful work until demobilised in May 1919.
33, Union Street, Luton. 2359.

PARLES, B. (M.S.M.), Corporal, 7th Bedfordshire Regiment.

He volunteered in September 1914, and in the following year was sent to France, where he served in various sectors of the Front. After taking part in many important engagements, he was wounded in action on April 5th, 1918, and died on the following day at Abbeville. He had been awarded the Meritorious Service Medal for his continuously good work, and was also entitled to the 1914-15 Star, and the General Service and Victory Medals.
69, Sopwell Lane, St. Albans. X2361/B.

PARLES, G. H., Private, 22nd London Regiment (Queen's Bermondsey).

He volunteered in 1915, and in the same year proceeded to the Western Front, where he took part in the Battle of Ypres and other engagements. In 1916 he was transferred to Salonika, whence he was sent in 1917 to Palestine. There he took part in the fighting at Haifa, Damascus and Aleppo and other places until the cessation of hostilities. He returned home for demobilisation in 1919, and holds the 1914-15 Star, and the General Service and Victory Medals.
69, Sopwell Lane, St. Albans. X2361/A.

PARNELL, H., Private, Hertfordshire Regiment.
He joined in 1916, and later in the same year was drafted to the Western Front. Whilst in this seat of war he took part in many important battles, including those of the Somme, Albert and Messines, and was invalided home. He was discharged as medically unfit for further service in July 1917, and holds the General Service and Victory Medals.
6, Cross Street, Ware, Herts. 4072/A.

PARNELL, J., Private, Essex Regiment.
He volunteered in 1915, and later in the same year was drafted to France. There he took part in many engagements and was reported missing in September 1915, and is now presumed to have been killed in action. He was entitled to the 1914-15 Star, and the General Service and Victory Medals.
6, Cross Street, Ware, Herts. 4072/B.

PARRIS, W., Private, 1st Hertfordshire Regt.
He volunteered in September 1914, and after completing a term of training served at various stations, where he was engaged on various important duties with his unit. He was not successful in his efforts to obtain his transfer to the front, but, nevertheless, rendered valuable services until his demobilisation in 1919.
83, Fearnley Street, Watford. X2362.

PARROTT, A., Private, Labour Corps.
He joined in February 1917, and in March proceeded to France, where he was engaged in making roads and on other important duties in various sectors of the Front. He served at Lille and the Vimy Ridge and many other places until his return home for demobilisation in March 1919. He holds the General Service and Victory Medals.
42, Newcombe Road, Luton. 2363.

PARROTT, C. E., Private, 7th Royal Fusiliers.
He volunteered in November 1915, and in the following September was drafted to the Western Front. There he took part in the Battles of the Somme, Messines Ridge and Ypres, and many other engagements until transferred to Italy in November 1917. After seeing much active service on the Piave, he returned to France and was again in action at Nieuport and Cambrai. He was demobilised in February 1919, and holds the General Service and Victory Medals.
9, Albert Cottages, Houghton Conquest, near Ampthill. Z2365.

PARROTT, F., Private, R.A.S.C.
He joined in December 1916, and during his service on the Western Front was engaged or important duties with an ammunition column in various sectors. After the cessation of hostilities he was sent with the Army of Occupation into Germany, where he remained until October 1919. He then returned home for demobilisation and holds the General Service and Victory Medals.
Park Street, Hatfield. X2366/B.

PARROTT, G. H., Private, 7th Royal Fusiliers.
Joining in June 1916, he was sent to the Western Front in November of the same year. He took part in many important engagements in this theatre of war, including the Battles of Passchendaele, the Marne and Amiens, and was wounded in action at Arras in April 1917. He was demobilised in February 1919, and holds the General Service and Victory Medals.
10, Glebe Cottages, Hatfield. X2367.

PARROTT, J. W., Private, 3rd Northamptonshire Regiment.
He joined in 1917, and shortly afterwards proceeded to France, where he saw much service in various sectors of the Front. He took part in the Battles of Arras and Cambrai and the heavy fighting at Neuve Chapelle, and was wounded in action at Ypres. After the cessation of hostilities, he was sent into Germany, where he served with the Army of Occupation until June 1919. He then returned home and was demobilised, holding the General Service and Victory Medals.
High Street, Ridgmont. Z2369.

PARROTT, W. J., Sapper, R.E.
He volunteered in August 1914, and shortly afterwards proceeded to France, where he took an active part in the fighting in various sectors of the Front. He was blown up and wounded by an explosion at Hill 60, was invalided home, and on June 8th, 1915, died of wounds at St. Thomas' Hospital, London. He was entitled to the 1914 Star, and the General Service and Victory Medals.
Hall's Yard, Park Street, Hatfield. X2366/A.

PARROTT, J. A. C., Private, Tank Corps.
He joined in November 1917, and on completing his training in the following March was drafted to the Western Front. There he took part in many important engagements, and also served through the Retreat and Advance of 1918. He holds the General Service and Victory Medals, and in 1920 was still with his unit.
32, Bassett Road, Leighton Buzzard. 2368.

PARSONS, A. E. W., Private, Royal Berkshire Regiment.
Volunteering in September 1914, he was drafted overseas in the following January. During his service on the Western Front, he took part in several important engagements, including the Battles of Ypres and the Somme. He was wounded in action and suffered severely from shell-shock, as a result of which he was discharged in September 1916 as medically unfit for further service. He holds the 1914-15 Star, and the General Service and Victory Medals.
"Rosemere," Icknield Road, Leagrave. 2373/B.

PARSONS, A. J., Cook's Mate, R.N., H.M.S. "Repulse."
He joined in 1916, and was posted to H.M.S. "Repulse," with which ship he was engaged in important Naval operations in many waters. He saw much active service off the coasts of Scotland, and was demobilised in 1919, holding the General Service and Victory Medals.
72, Queen Street, Hitchin. 2380/B.

PARSONS, F., Private, R.A.S.C. (M.T.).
He joined in May 1917, and in the following August was drafted to the Western Front, in which seat of war he was engaged on important transport duties with his unit. He was present at the Battles of Ypres, the Somme, Arras, Bapaume and Cambrai, and returned home in May 1919. He was then demobilised, and holds the General Service and Victory Medals.
33, Stanmore Road, Watford. X2370.

PARSONS, F., Private, Sherwood Foresters.
Volunteering in April 1915, he was drafted to France later in the same year. Whilst in this theatre of war he took part in the Battles of the Somme, Ypres and Cambrai and also served throughout the Retreat and Advance of 1918. He was wounded in action and on his return home was demobilised in March 1919, holding the 1914-15 Star, and the General Service and Victory Medals.
60, Plantation Road, Leighton Buzzard. 2371.

PARSONS, F. G., Private, Labour Corps.
Having volunteered in October 1915, he was sent to France in the following January, and was engaged on important duties in the forward areas. Apart from making and repairing roads and light railways, he carried rations and ammunition to the troops in the line and was wounded during the Retreat of 1918. He was demobilised in December 1919, and holds the General Service and Victory Medals.
40, Baker Street, Leighton Buzzard. 2374.

PARSONS, F. H., Sergeant, R.F.A.
He volunteered in November 1915, and was drafted to France in the following July. Whilst on the Western Front he served with distinction in the A/84 Battery, R.F.A. Brigade, and took part in the Battles of the Somme, Arras, Messines, Ypres, Merville and Béthune. He returned home in July 1918 and was demobilised in March of the following year, holding the General Service and Victory Medals.
53, Chatsworth Road, Luton. 2375.

PARSONS, F. H., A.B., R.N.
He was mobilised in August 1914, and saw much active service in the Mediterranean Sea, off the coast of Palestine, and in the Canal zone in Egypt. He took part in the landing of troops on the Gallipoli Peninsula and assisted in the attacks on Jaffa and Gaza. In November 1918 he was invalided from the service, and holds the 1914-15 Star, and the General Service and Victory Medals.
64, St. Peter's Street, St. Albans. X2376.

PARSONS, H., Staff-Sergeant, R.A.S.C.
After having volunteered in September 1914, he was drafted to the Western Front in the following year. Whilst in this theatre of war he served with distinction in the forward areas, was present at the Battles of the Somme, Arras, and Cambrai, and was wounded in action. He was awarded the Divisional Parchment Certificate for devotion to duty in the Field, and holds the 1914-15 Star, and the General Service and Victory Medals. He was demobilised in March 1919.
76, Hagden Lane, Watford. X2378.

PARSONS, G., Special War Worker.
He took up work of National importance in June 1915 at Messrs. Fricker's Metal Works. His duties were in connection with the manufacture of fuses and were carried out in a very skilful manner. He rendered valuable services until the cessation of hostilities, when he relinquished his duties.
42, Clifton Road, Luton.   2372.

PARSONS, H., 1st Air Mechanic, R.A.F.
He volunteered in April 1915, and after qualifying as a first-class air mechanic, was retained on important duties which demanded a high degree of technical knowledge and skill. He rendered valuable services at various aerodromes, but was unsuccessful in his efforts to obtain his transfer overseas. He was demobilised in March 1919.
35, St. Mary's Road, Watford.   X2377.

PARSONS, H. T. (M.M.), L/Corporal, Buff s (East Kent Regt.) and 3rd Middlesex Regt.
Volunteering in October 1914, he was sent to France in December of the following year. He fought with distinction in several engagements and was wounded in action near Albert during the Battle of the Somme in July 1916. After a period of hospital treatment in England, he returned to the Western Front six months later and took part in the Battles of Arras, Passchendaele, Lens, Cambrai, the Somme (II), Bapaume and Mons (II). He was awarded the Military Medal for conspicuous bravery and disregard of his own safety in rescuing two wounded officers from No Man's Land under heavy shell fire in August 1917. He also holds the 1914-15 Star, and the General Service and Victory Medals, and in 1920 was serving with the Army of Occupation in Germany.
Bedford Road, Shefford, Beds.   Z2379.

PARSONS, J., Sergeant, R.F.A.
Volunteering in September 1914, he first saw active service at the landing on the Gallipoli Peninsula, where he was wounded in action. He returned to England for treatment and on his recovery was sent to France in 1916. After a period of heavy fighting on the Western Front, he was transferred to Italy and was stationed at the base as a Farrier Sergeant Instructor. He was demobilised in March 1919, and holds the 1914-15 Star, and the General Service and Victory Medals.
72, Queen Street, Hitchin.   2380/A.

PARSONS, N. A., Private, R.A.S.C.
He joined in 1916, and was drafted overseas at a later date. He saw much active service in France and Italy, and was transferred to the infantry. Whilst on the Western Front, he took part in many engagements, including the Battle of Cambrai, and was wounded in action. He was demobilised in January 1919, and holds the General Service and Victory Medals.
5, Greenfield Terrace, London Colney.   X2381.

PARSONS, S. C. P., L/Corporal, Gloucestershire Regiment.
Joining in May 1917, he was retained on important duties at Sittingbourne and Catterick Camp. Although unable to obtain his transfer overseas, he rendered valuable services with his unit until his demobilisation in October 1919.
" Rosemere," Icknield Road, Leagrove.   2373/A.

PARSONS, W., Private, 8th Bedfordshire Regt.
Volunteering in June 1915, he was drafted to France later in the same year. During his service on the Western Front, he took part in many engagements, including the Battle of the Somme, and was twice wounded and invalided home. After his return to France for the third time, he was killed in action at the Battle of Arras, on April 14th, 1917. He was entitled to the 1914-15 Star, and the General Service and Victory Medals.
14, Chapel Path, Leighton Buzzard.   2382.

PARSONS, W. H., Private, East Surrey Regt.
He joined in 1916, and after a period of training was drafted to France. During his service on the Western Front, he fought in several important engagements, including that near Arras in 1916, and was killed in action at Ypres on April 10th, 1917. He was buried at Dickebusch, and was entitled to the General Service and Victory Medals.
163, Whippendell Road, Watford.   X2383.

PARSONS, W. H., Private, R.A.S.C.
He joined in May 1916, and in the following August was sent to France. After a short period of service on the Western Front, during which he was engaged on important transport duties, he was invalided home suffering from fever, in December 1916. He died in hospital at Cambridge on the 24th of the same month, and was entitled to the General Service and Victory Medals.
102, Crawley Road, Luton.   2384.

PASMORE, A. J., Gunner, R.F.A. (T.F.).
He volunteered in October 1914, and in the following year was drafted to France. After a period of service there, he was transferred to Egypt and was on the Canal defences for some time. He then went on to Palestine and was in action at Haifa, Medjul Yarba and Gaza. In March 1919, he was demobilised, and holds the 1914-15 Star, and the General Service and Victory Medals.
423, Whippendell Road, Watford.   X1722/B.

PATEMAN, C., Private, 2nd Bedfordshire Regt.
Volunteering in October 1914, he was sent to France in the following March. Whilst on the Western Front he was employed as a stretcher bearer and took part in the Battles of Festubert, Loos, the Somme, Arras, Ypres and Albert. He was demobilised in July 1919, and holds the 1914-15 Star, and the General Service and Victory Medals.
1, Thorpe's Yard, Hitchin.   2385.

PATEMAN, L. M., Pte., Royal Berkshire Regt.
He joined in November 1916, and was almost immediately drafted to the Western Front. In this seat of war he took part in important engagements and was killed in action at Delville Wood on February 17th, 1917. He was entitled to the General Service and Victory Medals.
13, Barnard's Yard, Hitchin.   2388/B.

PATEMAN, M., Private, 1st Bedfordshire Regt.
He volunteered in August 1914, and was drafted to France in the following March. He took part in the Battle of Neuve Chapelle and was gassed shortly after. On his recovery he returned to the line, fought at the Battles of the Somme, Arras, Ypres and Cambrai, and was killed in action at Achiet-le-Petit on August 23rd, 1918. He was entitled to the 1914-15 Star, and the General Service and Victory Medals.
Luton Road, Toddington, Beds.   2386/B.

PATEMAN, W., Private, 11th Suffolk Regiment.
Joining in January 1917, he was drafted to France four months later and took part in much severe fighting. He was in action at the Battles of Ypres and Passchendaele, and was killed at Hargicourt on August 26th, 1917. He was entitled to the General Service and Victory Medals.
Luton Road, Toddington, Beds.   2386/A.

PATEMAN, W., Driver, R.A.S.C.
He joined in January 1918, and was quickly sent to France, where he was engaged on important transport duties in the forward areas, particularly in the Cambrai sector. After the Armistice he carried out special salvage work until his return home for demobilisation in February 1920. He holds the General Service and Victory Medals.
4, Union Street, Dunstable.   2387.

PATEMAN, W. S., Private, Wiltshire Regiment.
He joined in March 1917, and was almost immediately drafted to France. He was in action during our advance on the Somme in the same year and was taken prisoner of war. He was held in captivity in Germany at the camp at Fredrichsfeld and suffered many privations until his release after the Armistice. He returned home and was demobilised in September 1919, holding the General Service and Victory Medals.
13, Barnard's Yard, Hitchin.   2388/A.

PATES, H. C., Private, 7th The King's (Liverpool Regiment).
He volunteered in April 1915, and after a period of training was drafted to France. Whilst in this seat of war he took part in several engagements, including those of Lens and Cambrai, and was badly wounded in action and sent home. He was invalided out of the service in February 1918, and holds the General Service and Victory Medals.
The Green, Ickwell, near Biggleswade, Beds.   Z2389.

PATES, S. A., Saddler, R.A.S.C.
He volunteered in December 1915, and in the following year was drafted to France. In this theatre of war he was engaged on important duties connected with his trade and rendered valuable services. He returned home and was demobilised in August 1919, holding the General Service and Victory Medals.
St. John's Street, Biggleswade, Beds.   Z2390.

PAVEY, H., Private, Canadian Overseas Forces.
Volunteering in August 1914, he was drafted to the Western Front twelve months later. In this theatre of war he saw much active service and took part in the Battles of the Somme, Arras, Ypres and Cambrai, and many other important engagements. He was demobilised in May 1919, and holds the 1914-15 Star, and the General Service and Victory Medals.
58, Liverpool Road, Watford.   X2391/B.

PAVEY, B., Private, 1st Hertfordshire Regiment.
He volunteered in September 1914, and early in the following year was drafted to France. There he took part in many important engagements, including those of Festubert, the Somme, Ypres and Cambrai. He served on the Western Front until after the cessation of hostilities, when he returned home for his demobilisation in March 1919. He holds 'the 1914-15 Star, and the General Service and Victory Medals.
58, Liverpool Road, Watford.   X2391/A.

PAXTON, A. W., Gunner, R.F.A.
He volunteered in May 1915, and in September proceeded to France, where he saw much severe fighting. After taking part in many important engagements, including the Battles of Loos and the Somme, he was killed in action near Arras in May 1917. He was entitled to the 1914-15 Star, and the General Service and Victory Medals.
Oakley Cottage, Wing, near Leighton Buzzard.   2411.

PAXTON, J., L/Cpl., 2nd Worcestershire Regt.
He was mobilised in August 1914, and was immediately drafted to France, where he took part in the Retreat from Mons. He also fought through the Battle of the Marne, and was killed in action on September 14th, 1914. He was entitled to the Mons Star, and the General Service and Victory Medals.
High Street, Wing, near Leighton Buzzard.   2392.

PAYNE, A., Corporal, Royal Engineers.
He joined in June 1918, and after a short period of training was sent to the Western Front. There he took part in the Advance of 1918, serving through the second Battle of Le Cateau and many other important engagements. He was demobilised on his return home in February 1919, and holds the General Service and Victory Medals.
35, Arthur Road, St. Albans.   X2393.

PAYNE, A., Private, 1st and 1/5th Bedfordshire Regiments.
He joined in May 1916, and in March of the following year was drafted to the Western Front. He took part in heavy fighting at Loos, and also in the Battles of Ypres and Passchendaele, where he was wounded in action in September 1917. In January 1918 he went to Italy and fought on the Piave and the Trentino. He was demobilised in January 1919, and holds the General Service and Victory Medals.
10, Kimberley Road, Fleetville, St. Albans.   X2394.

PAYNE, A. E., Private, R.A.O.C.
He joined in December 1917, and after a period of training was drafted to France. He was stationed at the Base Depôt, Rouen, and rendered valuable services whilst engaged on the repair of rifles and guns. After the Armistice he was sent to Germany with the Army of Occupation and served at Cologne. In 1920 he was still with his unit, and holds the General Service and Victory Medals.
77, Beech Road, Luton.   2395.

PAYNE, A. W., Private, Labour Corps.
He joined in June 1917, and was retained on important agricultural work in various districts. Owing to his being medically unfit he was not successful in obtaining his transfer overseas, but rendered valuable services with his unit until his demobilisation in August 1919.
4, Parker Street, Watford.   X2396.

PAYNE, A. W., Private, Queen's (Royal West Surrey Regiment).
He joined in February 1918 on attaining military age, and whilst undergoing his training was taken seriously ill. He unfortunately died in hospital at Cambridge in May of the same year.
Station Road, Harpenden.   2397.

PAYNE, B., Private, Bedfordshire Regiment.
He joined in 1917, and after a period of training was engaged on important duties in connection with agricultural work. He was not sent overseas until after the cessation of hostilities, and was then drafted to the Army of Occupation in Germany. He served at Cologne until his demobilisation in 1919.
Horslow Street, Potton, Beds.   2398/B.

PAYNE, C., Private, East Surrey Regiment.
Volunteering in September 1914, he was speedily drafted to France, and took part in the Battles of the Marne, Festubert and the Somme. He was then wounded in action and invalided home. On his recovery he was sent to Salonika, where he was engaged on important duties. He contracted malaria in a severe form, and was in hospital on seven different occasions. He was demobilised in March 1919, and holds the 1914 Star, and the General Service and Victory Medals.
Horslow Street, Potton, Beds.   2398/A.

PAYNE, C. E., Private, Royal Defence Corps.
He volunteered in November 1914, and after a period of training served at various stations on important duties with his unit. He rendered very valuable service throughout hostilities, and carried out his work in a highly commendable way. He died on November 11th, 1918, through ill-health brought about by war service.
98, Baker Street, Luton.   2803/B.

PAYNE, E. C., Sergeant, Bedfordshire Regiment.
He volunteered in August 1914, and after a period of duty in England was sent to France. Whilst in this theatre of war he served with distinction at the Battles of the Somme, Albert, Vimy Ridge, Passchendaele and Cambrai, and was wounded in action. He also suffered from trench feet, and in March 1919 was demobilised. He holds the General Service and Victory Medals.
59, Turner's Road, Luton   2399.

PAYNE, E. S., Sapper, R.E. (Postal Section).
After having volunteered in March 1915 he was drafted to East Africa, where he was engaged on important duties with the Postal Section. On the fall of Dar-es-Salaam he was stationed there for some time and carried out consistently good work. He was demobilised in April 1919, and holds the 1914-15 Star, and the General Service and Victory Medals.
113, Norfolk Road, Rickmansworth.   X2404/B.

PAYNE, F., Private, 10th Queen's Own (Royal West Kent Regiment).
He volunteered in 1914, and in the following year was drafted to France. During his service on the Western Front he took part in many important engagements, including the Battles of Ypres, the Somme, Cambrai and the Marne. After the Armistice he was sent with the Army of Occupation to Germany, where he served until his demobilisation in 1919. He holds the 1914-15 Star, and the General Service and Victory Medals.
73, Fearnley Street, Watford.   2401/A.

PAYNE, F. W., (M.M.), King's Corporal, Bedfordshire Regiment.
He was mobilised in August 1914, and immediately drafted to France. During his service on the Western Front, he took part in the Retreat from Mons and the Battles of the Marne, Festubert, Loos, the Somme and Arras. He was awarded the Military Medal and appointed King's Corporal for conspicuous bravery and devotion to duty in the Field. He was twice wounded in action, and as a result was discharged in December 1919 as medically unfit for further service, holding also the Mons Star, and the General Service and Victory Medals.
Lower Caldicote, near Biggleswade.   Z2400.

PAYNE, G. B., Private, Bedfordshire Regiment.
He volunteered in 1914, and on completion of his training was engaged with his unit on important duties at various stations. He was unsuccessful in obtaining his transfer overseas before hostilities ceased, but after the Armistice was sent with the Army of Occupation to the Rhine. He was stationed at Cologne until his demobilisation in 1919.
113, Norfolk Road, Rickmansworth.   X2404/C.

PAYNE, H., Private, Bedfordshire and Northamptonshire Regiments.
He volunteered in September 1914, and first saw active service in the Dardanelles, where he took part in the landing at Suvla Bay and in heavy fighting at Anzac. On the Evacuation of the Gallipoli Peninsula he was sent to Egypt, and was stationed at Cairo with a Labour Battalion for twelve months. He then went on to Palestine, and whilst with General Allenby's Forces fought at Gaza, Haifa and other places. He was demobilised on his return home in February 1919, and holds the 1914-15 Star, and the General Service and Victory Medals.
119, Marlowes, Hemel Hempstead.   X2402.

PAYNE, J., Driver, R.A.S.C.
Volunteering in December 1915, he was retained on important duties owing to his being medically unfit for transfer overseas. He rendered valuable services with his unit throughout the whole period of hostilities, and was demobilised in June 1919.
47, Bun Street, Luton.   2403.

PAYNE, J., L/Corporal, R.E. (Postal Section).
Having volunteered in February 1915, he was drafted to Salonika in the same year. Whilst in this theatre of war he rendered valuable services with the Postal Section at General Headquarters. He remained overseas until his demobilisation in February 1919, and holds the 1914-15 Star, and the General Service and Victory Medals.
113, Norfolk Road, Rickmansworth.   X2404/A.

PAYNE, J. A., L/Cpl., 12th East Surrey Regt.
Joining in June 1916, he was sent to France in the following September. He served on the Western Front for fifteen months, and during this time fought at the Battles of Bapaume, Messines Ridge and Ypres. He went to Italy in November 1917, and saw heavy fighting on the Piave until March 1918, when he returned to France and took part in many engagements during the Retreat and Advance of that year. During his service overseas he was wounded in action at Tournai. He was demobilised in October 1919, and holds the General Service and Victory Medals.
3, Grove Road, St. Albans.   X2405.

PAYNE, M., Pte., 1st South Staffordshire Regt.
Having volunteered in 1914, he was sent overseas in the following year. During his service on the Western Front he took part in the Battles of Ypres, the Somme, Arras and St. Quentin and other minor engagements. He also saw much severe fighting in Italy, and was demobilised in March 1919. He holds the 1914-15 Star, and the General Service and Victory Medals.
73, Fearnley Street, Watford.   2401/B.

PAYNE, S. C., B.S.M., R.F.A.
He volunteered in August 1914, and was drafted overseas in the following year. Whilst on the Western Front he played a prominent part in the Battles of Arras, Ypres and Cambrai and other important engagements. He also served with distinction in Egypt, and was demobilised on his return home in January 1919. He holds the 1914-15 Star, and the General Service and Victory Medals.
25, West View Road, St. Albans.   X2406.

PAYNE, S. T. J., Private, Queen's (Royal West Surrey Regiment).
He joined in August 1917, and after a period of training was drafted to the Western Front in the following April. Whilst in this theatre of war he saw much severe fighting, and was killed in action in the Cambrai sector on May 31st, 1918. He was entitled to the General Service and Victory Medals.
81, Sotheron Road, Watford.   X2407.

PAYNE, T., Private, Bedfordshire Regiment.
Volunteering at the outbreak of war, he was sent to France in May of the following year. Whilst in this theatre of war he took part in many important engagements, and was killed in action in August 1915. He was entitled to the 1914-15 Star, and the General Service and Victory Medals.
73, Fearnley Street, Watford.   2401/C.

PAYNE, V., Private, 11th Queen's (Royal West Surrey Regiment).
He joined in May 1917, and on completion of his training was drafted to the Western Front. In this theatre of war he took part in much severe fighting in various sectors, and was in action at the Battle of Cambrai. He was demobilised in January 1920, and holds the General Service and Victory Medals.
48, Dane Road, Luton.   2408/A.

PAYNE, W. F., Corporal, Royal Engineers.
Joining in August 1917, he was quickly drafted to the Western Front, where he was engaged on important duties with his unit. He was also present at the Battles of the Somme and Cambrai, and in heavy fighting at Armentières. He was demobilised in February 1919, and holds the General Service and Victory Medals.
110, Baker Street, Luton.   2409.

PAYNE, W. H., Gunner, R.G.A.
Joining in November 1916, he was retained on important duties with his unit owing to his age. He was later posted to an anti-aircraft section, and served on the aerial defences of the Forth Bridge, Scotland. He rendered valuable services until his demobilisation in March 1919.
35, Brache Street, Luton.   2410.

PEACH, W. H., Private, 11th (Prince Albert's Own) Hussars.
He joined the Army in April 1913, and at the outbreak of hostilities was immediately drafted to France. There he was in action during many important battles, including those of Mons, Ypres, Loos, the Somme, Arras, and was killed in action at St. Quentin on February 17th, 1918. He was entitled to the Mons Star, and the General Service and Victory Medals.
Pretoria Cottages Harlington, Beds.   3205/B.

PEACHEY, J. H., Pte., 4th Bedfordshire Regt.
Having volunteered in August 1915, he was drafted to France in July of the following year. He took part in the Battle of the Somme, was wounded in action, and was killed at Angres, near Lens, on November 16th, 1916. He was entitled to the General Service and Victory Medals.
26, Elfridge Road, Watford.   X2415.

PEACOCK, A. E., Private, Worcestershire Regt.
Volunteering in August 1914, he was sent to France in the following year. During his service on the Western Front, he took part in many engagements, including the Battles of Ypres, Arras and Passchendaele, and was killed in action on the Somme on July 3rd, 1917. He was entitled to the 1914-15 Star, and the General Service and Victory Medals.
72, High Street, Redbourne.   2416/B.

PEACOCK, A. J., Trooper, Hertfordshire Dragoons.
He volunteered in November 1915, and after completing his training served at various stations on important duties with his unit. He was not successful in obtaining a transfer overseas, but rendered valuable services at home throughout the war. He was demobilised in January 1919.
86, Victoria Street, St. Albans.   1372/B.

PEACOCK, E. C., Pte., 1/5th Bedfordshire Regt.
Mobilised in August 1914, he first saw active service in the Dardanelles, where he took part in the landing at Suvla Bay, and in heavy fighting at Anzac. On the Evacuation of the Gallipoli Peninsula, he was sent to Egypt, and after a period of service there, went on to Palestine. In this theatre of war he fought in many engagements with General Allenby's Forces and was mentioned in Despatches in June 1917 for conspicuous bravery at the Battle of Gaza. On his return home in March 1919, he was discharged, and holds the 1914-15 Star, and the General Service and Victory Medals.
Brookside, Potton, Beds.   Z2417.

PEACOCK, F. J., Pte., 4th Bedfordshire Regt.
He volunteered in January 1916, and later in the same year was drafted to the Western Front. He took part in engagements at Ypres and Hill 60, and was killed in action at Gavrelle, near Arras, in April 1917. He was entitled to the General Service and Victory Medals.
1, College Place, St. Albans.   2418/B.

PEACOCK, G., A.B., R.N., H.M.S. "Princess Irene."
He was mobilised in August 1914, and immediately proceeded to sea on board H.M.S. "Princess Irene," with which ship he saw much active service in the Mediterranean and North Sea. He was killed in action on May 27th, 1916, and was entitled to the 1914-15 Star, and the General Service and Victory Medals.
1, College Place, St. Albans.   2418/A.

PEACOCK, H., Private, 13th Essex Regiment.
He joined in 1916, and later in the same year was drafted to the Western Front. In this theatre of war he took part in several engagements, including that of Albert, and was reported missing at Oppy Wood, and afterwards presumed killed on April 28th, 1917. He was entitled to the General Service and Victory Medals.
86, Victoria Street, St. Albans.   X1372/A.

PEACOCK, J. (M.M.), Sergt., Bedfordshire Regt.
Volunteering in August 1914, he was first retained on important duties at home. Later, he was drafted to the Western Front and was in action in several engagements. He served with distinction at the Battles of Arras, Ypres and Cambrai, and was awarded the Military Medal for conspicuous bravery and devotion to duty in the Field. He was gassed in action, was demobilised in March 1919, and holds, also, the General Service and Victory Medals.
3, Alma Cut, St. Albans.   2454/A.

PEACOCK, S., Private, Bedfordshire Regiment.
Volunteering in September 1914, he was sent to France in the following year, took part in the Battles of Hill 60, Ypres, Loos, Arras and Lens, and was gassed in action. In 1917 he was transferred to the Royal Air Force, and rendered valuable services as a rigger at Rouen. He was demobilised in March 1919, and holds the 1914-15 Star, and the General Service and Victory Medals.
72, High Street, Redbourne.   2416/A.

PEACOCK, S. C. W., Driver, R.F.A.
He was mobilised in August 1914, and a month later was drafted to the Western Front. Whilst in this theatre of war he saw much severe fighting and took part in the Battles of Ypres, the Somme, Arras, and Cambrai. On his return home in April 1919, he was demobilised, and holds the 1914 Star, and the General Service and Victory Medals.
Bury Road, Stopsley.   2419/A.

PEACOCK, W., Private, Suffolk Regiment.
He joined in August 1918, on attaining military age, and, after his training was engaged on guard duty at prisoner of war camps at various stations. He rendered valuable services until his demobilisation in November 1919.
4, Beaconsfield Terrace, Hatfield.   X2420.

PEARCE, A. E., A.B., R.N., H.M.S. "Indomitable."
Already serving in August 1914, he proceeded to sea in H.M.S. "Indomitable." He took part in the Battle of the Dogger Bank, the naval operations in the Dardanelles, and the Battle of Jutland, and was wounded in action. He received his discharge in November 1919, and holds the 1914-15 Star, and the General Service and Victory Medals.
13, Duke Street, Watford. 2427/B.

PEARCE, A. G. E., Trumpeter, R.A.S.C.
He volunteered in 1914, although under military age, and was stationed at Aldershot and Barking, where he underwent his training. He rendered valuable services later whilst engaged on important duties, and was discharged as medically unfit in April 1917.
6, Clifton Street, St. Albans. X2421.

PEARCE, C., Sergeant, Bedfordshire Regiment.
He volunteered in September 1914, and in the following year was drafted to the Western Front. He served with distinction at the Battles of Hill 60, Ypres, Givenchy, the Somme, Cambrai and St. Quentin, and was wounded in action in 1916 and 1917. He was demobilised in February 1919, and holds the 1914-15 Star, and the General Service and Victory Medals.
17, John Street, Luton. 2422/B.

PEARCE, C. W., Private, Labour Corps.
He joined in 1917, and owing to his being medically unfit for transfer overseas, was retained on important agricultural work at various stations. He rendered valuable services in this capacity until his discharge in March 1919.
17, Husbourne, Crawley, Aspley Guise, Beds. Z2423.

PEARCE, E., Private, 1st Bedfordshire Regiment.
He joined in July 1917, and was shortly afterwards sent to France. In this theatre of war he took part in the fighting at Ypres, Arras and on the Somme. He was then drafted to Italy, where he was in action on the Asiago Plateau, until killed in August 1918. He was entitled to the General Service and Victory Medals.
17, Lower Paxton Road, St. Albans. X3964/B.

PEARCE, E. B., Private, R.A.V.C.
Volunteering in September 1914, he was engaged on important duties in connection with the treatment of sick horses at the R.A.V.C. Hospital, St. Albans. Although unable to obtain a transfer overseas owing to medical unfitness, he rendered valuable services until his discharge in April 1918.
Salisbury Road, Batford, Harpenden. 2424/B.

PEARCE, F., Corporal, Hertfordshire Regiment.
Volunteering in 1914, he was retained on important duties with his unit at various stations. Although unsuccessful in obtaining his transfer overseas, he rendered valuable services on guard duties at prisoner of war camps and was demobilised in 1919.
24, Arthur Road, St. Albans. X2426/C.

PEARCE, F. J., Shoeing Smith, R.A.V.C.
Joining in February 1916, he was retained on important duties at Longmore Camp, where he was engaged in the shoeing of horses. He was unsuccessful in obtaining his transfer overseas, but rendered valuable services with his unit until his demobilisation in December 1918.
1, Salisbury Road, Batford, Harpenden. 2424/A.

PEARCE, F. J., Private, Royal Marine Light Infantry.
He was already serving when war broke out in August 1914, and was drafted to the East. He was first stationed for a time in Egypt, but later went on to Palestine, and took part in the Battles of Gaza and the capture of Jerusalem. He received his discharge in April 1919, and holds the 1914-15 Star, the General Service and Victory and Long Service and Good Conduct Medals.
13, Duke Street, Watford. 2427/A.

PEARCE, G. T., Private, 1st Hertfordshire Regt.
He volunteered in August 1915, and later in the same year was drafted to France. He took part in heavy fighting at Hill 60 and Festubert, and also in other important engagements, and was wounded in action. He was demobilised in 1918, and holds the 1914-15 Star, and the General Service and Victory Medals.
Salisbury Road, Batford, Harpenden. 2430/A.

PEARCE, H. E., Private, Royal Fusiliers.
He volunteered in April 1915, and in the same year was drafted to the Western Front. During his service in France he was engaged in the fierce fighting at the Battle of Ypres and was killed in action on the Somme on April 14th, 1916. He was entitled to the 1914-15 Star, and the General Service and Victory Medals.
Angel Cottages, Offley, Herts. 2433.

PEARCE, H. J., Sergeant, R.A.F. (late R.N.A.S.).
He was mobilised with the 13th London (Kensington) Territorials in August 1914, and was sent to France in November 1915. Whilst on the Western Front he played a prominent part in the Battles of the Somme, Ypres and Amiens and was wounded in action. On his return home in February 1919, he was demobilised, and holds the 1914-15 Star, and the General Service and Victory Medals.
Hill View, Ferndale Road, Luton. 2425/A.

PEARCE, J., Rifleman, King's Royal Rifle Corps.
Joining in May 1918 on attaining military age, he was unable to obtain his transfer overseas owing to the early cessation of hostilities. He, however, rendered valuable services with his unit and in 1920 was still in the Army.
24, Arthur Road, St. Albans. X2426/B.

PEARCE, J., Private, Queen's (Royal West Surrey Regiment).
He joined in 1917, and in September of the same year proceeded to the Western Front. Whilst in this theatre of war he fought on the Somme, the Aisne and the Marne, and was seriously wounded at the Battle of Amiens in August 1918. As a result he was discharged as medically unfit for further service in the following October, and holds the General Service and Victory Medals.
17, John Street, Luton. 2422/A.

PEARCE, J., Private, Bedfordshire Regiment.
Volunteering in 1914, he was retained on important guard duties at Felixstowe owing to his being too old for transfer overseas. He rendered valuable services with his unit until his demobilisation in 1919.
51, Grange Street, St. Albans. 2428.

PEARCE, J. H. (Jnr.), Sergeant, 13th London Regiment (Kensingtons).
He was mobilised with his unit in August 1914, and was sent to France in the following November. After a period of heavy fighting he was wounded in action and returned home in February 1915. On his recovery in August of the same year he returned to the Western Front, took part in the Battles of Ypres, the Somme and Arras, and was again wounded in action in July 1917. He was invalided home and after some time in hospital was discharged in July 1918 as medically unfit for further service. He holds the 1914 Star, and the General Service and Victory Medals.
Hill View, Ferndale Road, Luton. 2425/B.

PEARCE, J. R., Private, Queen's (Royal West Surrey Regiment).
He joined in April 1918, and was drafted to France in time to take part in the Advance of that year. He fought at Albert, St. Quentin and Cambrai, and was badly wounded in the last-named engagement. He was demobilised in January 1919, and holds the General Service and Victory Medals.
Folly Field, Wheathampstead, Herts. 2429.

PEARCE, L. E., Driver, R.A.S.C. (M.T.).
He volunteered in May 1915, and was quickly drafted overseas. During his service on the Western Front he was engaged on important duties conveying munitions and stores to the forward areas during the Somme, Arras and Cambrai Battles. He returned to England in June 1918, and was demobilised in the following January, holding the 1914-15 Star, and the General Service and Victory Medals.
93, Nightingale Road, Hitchin. 2431.

PEARCE, R. F., Pte., Australian Light Infantry.
Volunteering in March 1915, he was drafted to the Western Front after a period of training. During his service in this theatre of war he took part in many important engagements, including the Battles of the Somme, Arras and Cambrai, and was wounded in action. As a result he was discharged in September 1918 as medically unfit for further service, and holds the General Service and Victory Medals.
24, Arthur Road, St. Albans. X2426/A.

PEARCE, W., Private, Bedfordshire Regiment.
He joined in January 1917, and after his training was drafted to France, where he took part in the Battle of Ypres. He was later transferred to Palestine, and fought at the Battle of Gaza, and in other important engagements during the Advance with General Allenby's Forces. He was stationed at Cairo from the cessation of hostilities until his demobilisation in April 1920, and holds the General Service and Victory Medals.
13, Cross Street, St. Albans. 2432/A.

PEARCE, T., Private, Bedfordshire Regiment.
He volunteered in August 1914, and was eventually drafted to the Western Front. In this theatre of war he took part in much heavy fighting in various sectors, and was three times wounded in action. He unfortunately died whilst on service, and was entitled to the General Service and Victory Medals.
13, Cross Street, North St. Albans.   2432/B.

PEARMAN, J., Private, Coldstream Guards.
He volunteered in 1915, and in the same year was drafted to France, and was engaged in the fighting at Messines Ridge, Arras, Ypres, Bullecourt, and in the Retreat and the subsequent Advance of 1918. He holds the 1914-15 Star, and the General Service and Victory Medals, and was still serving at Ribecourt, France, in 1920.
The Hill, Wheathampstead.   3734/C.

PEARMAN, T. C., Private, Labour Corps.
He volunteered in October 1915, and was drafted to France in the following year. During his service overseas he was engaged on important duties with his unit at Calais and other places until after the signing of the Armistice. He was demobilised in February 1919, and holds the General Service and Victory Medals.
26, Lower Dagnell Street, St. Albans.   3680/B.

PEASE, F., Private, R.A.S.C.
He joined in July 1916, and after his training served at various stations on important duties with his unit. He did excellent work in connection with the transport of supplies to the Forces overseas, but owing to medical unfitness was unable to secure his transfer to a theatre of war, and was demobilised in July 1919.
High Street, Wing, Bucks.   2478.

PEASE, W., Private, 1/4th Oxfordshire and Buckinghamshire Light Infantry.
He joined in March 1916, and two months later proceeded overseas. Whilst on the Western Front he fought in various sectors, and was engaged in the fighting at the Battle of the Somme in July of that year. He was later killed in action on August 14th, 1916, and was entitled to the General Service and Victory Medals.
Church Street, Wing, Bucks.   2479.

PEARSON, A. A., Trooper, 10th (Australian) Light Horse.
He volunteered in August 1914, and was sent to Gallipoli in July of the following year. He fought at the landing at Suvla Bay and in the subsequent engagements until killed in action at Walkers Ridge on August 7th, 1915. He was entitled to the 1914-15 Star, and the General Service and Victory Medals.
12, Dudley Street, Leighton Buzzard.   2480/A.

PEARSON, C. W., Pte., 1st Hertfordshire Regt.
He volunteered in September 1914 and in the following July proceeded to the Dardanelles, and was wounded during the fighting at the landing at Suvla Bay. On recovery he rejoined his battalion and was sent to France in October 1916, and in this theatre of war took part in many engagements, including those on the Somme, at Ypres and Cambrai. He was demobilised in March 1919, and holds the 1914-15 Star, and the General Service and Victory Medals.
1, King's Road, Luton.   2434.

PEARSON, F. C., Rifleman, 15th London Regiment (Civil Service Rifles).
He joined in December 1917, and six months later was drafted to France. During his service on the Western Front he was engaged in the Allied Advance, and was severely wounded near Cambrai in July 1918. He was sent home and after treatment in hospital was invalided out of the service in January 1919. He holds the General Service and Victory Medals.
25, Copsewood Road, Watford.   X2463/A.

PEARSON, W. W., Corporal, Royal Fusiliers.
He volunteered in 1915, and later in the same year was drafted to the Western Front, where he served with the Sportsman's Battalion of the Royal Fusiliers. He took a prominent part in the Battles of Ypres, the Somme, Arras and Cambrai, and fought through the Retreat and Advance of 1918. In all engagements he was in charge of a bombing squad and did splendid work. He holds the 1914-15 Star, and the General Service and Victory Medals, and was demobilised in April 1919.
12, Dudley Street, Leighton Buzzard.   2480/B.

PEAT, D., Driver, Royal Engineers.
He joined in 1916, and on conclusion of his training served at various stations on important duties with his unit. He rendered valuable services throughout, but was not successful in obtaining his transfer overseas, and was demobilised in 1919.
Lower Caldicote, Biggleswade.   Z2483.

PEAT, A. S., Signalman, Royal Navy.
He joined the service in January 1917, and was posted to H.M.S. "Calypso," in which ship he served in the North and Baltic Seas. He was in action against the Bolshevik Naval Forces at Reval in December 1918, and in other engagements, and was wounded. He was invalided out of the service in July 1919, and holds the General Service and Victory Medals.
High Street, Clophill, Beds.   2481.

PEAT, C. W., Private, Royal Warwickshire Regt.
Joining in June 1916, he proceeded overseas two months later and saw active service in many sectors of the Western Front. On May 3rd, 1917, he was reported missing during the operations on the Somme, and later was presumed to have been killed in action on that date. He was entitled to the General Service and Victory Medals.
24, Cobden Street, Luton.   2482.

PEAT, J., Private, 5th Bedfordshire Regiment.
Volunteering at the outbreak of war he was sent to the Dardanelles, and took part in the fighting at Suvla Bay and the subsequent engagements until the Evacuation of the Peninsula. He was later sent to Egypt, and served in the British Advance through Palestine, and was in action at Gaza, Jaffa, Haifa and Beyrout. He was demobilised in June 1919, and holds the 1914-15 Star, and the General Service and Victory Medals.
17, Gardenia Avenue, Leagrave, Luton.   3112/C.

PEAT, J. T., Private, 1/5th Bedfordshire Regt.
Volunteering in 1915, he embarked for Egypt in the following year, and took part in various engagements, including the Battles of Gaza and Mejdel. He served during the Advance on the Palestine front, and was present at the occupation of Haifa, Acre and Beyrout. He returned to England and was demobilised in June 1919, and holds the General Service and Victory Medals.
Hope Villa, Gardenia Avenue, Leagrave.   2484.

PECK, A. H., Private, 9th Cheshire Regiment
He volunteered in April 1915, and at the conclusion of his training proceeded to France. Whilst on the Western Front he was in action at Hill 60, Ypres, Arras and on the Somme, and was severely wounded at Ypres III. He was invalided home and subsequently discharged as medically unfit for further service in May 1918, and holds the General Service and Victory Medals.
39, Essex Street, Luton.   3244/C.

PECK, H. R., Private, 7th Bedfordshire Regt.
He volunteered in June 1915, and on completing his training served with his unit at various stations on important duties in connection with road construction. He was unable to obtain his transfer overseas on account of ill-health, and was invalided out of the service in May 1916.
134, Hartley Road, Luton.   2485.

PECK, S., Private, Royal Sussex Regiment and Labour Corps.
He joined in November 1916, and served with his unit at various stations. He was later transferred to the Labour Corps, and owing to medical unfitness did not obtain his transfer overseas, and was engaged on important duties in connection with food production until March 1919, when he was demobilised.
13, Dordans Road, Leagrave, Beds.   2406/B.

PECK, S. C., Private, 2nd Bedfordshire Regiment.
He volunteered in October 1915, and was drafted to the Egyptian Expeditionary Force in the following year, and served in many engagements, including that at Gaza. He was subsequently killed in action on November 2nd, 1917, and was entitled to the General Service and Victory Medals.
66, Oak Road, Luton.   2487/B.

PECK, W., Private, 2nd Bedfordshire Regiment.
Volunteering in August 1914, he was later drafted overseas. He was in action almost continuously on the Western Front until July 27th, 1917, on which date he was killed in the fighting at Ypres. He was entitled to the 1914 Star, and the General Service and Victory Medals.
13, Dordans Road, Leagrave, Beds.   2486/A.

PECK, W. G., Private, 1/5th Sherwood Foresters.
A serving soldier, he proceeded to France at the commencement of hostilities, and fought in the Retreat from Mons, and the Battles of Ypres, Arras, Lens and Loos. He was reported missing during the fighting on the Somme front on July 7th, 1916, and was later presumed to have been killed in action on that date. He was entitled to the Mons Star, and the General Service and Victory Medals.
66, Oak Road, Luton.   2487/A.

PECK, W. S., Private, 8th Leicestershire Regt.
Volunteering in October 1915, he embarked for the Western Front in October of the following year. In this theatre of war he fought in many sectors, and was actively engaged at the Battle of Passchendaele. He was unfortunately killed on the Somme front on October 1st, 1917, and was entitled to the General Service and Victory Medals.
66, Oak Road, Luton.   2487/C.

PECKS, L., Trooper, Bedfordshire Lancers.
Mobilised in August 1914, he was sent overseas in the following month, and took part in heavy fighting, both in France and Flanders. He was in action at the Battles of Loos, Arras, Ypres, Cambrai and was wounded on the Somme. He was demobilised in January 1919, and holds the 1914 Star, and the General Service and Victory Medals.
47, Church Street, Dunstable.   2488.

PEDDER, C., Private, Bedfordshire Regiment.
He volunteered in August 1914, and was drafted almost immediately to France. Here he saw active service in many sectors, and fought during the Retreat from Mons, and in many other engagements which followed. Whilst on the Western Front he contracted fever and was invalided to England and died in hospital on September 9th, 1916. He was entitled to the Mons Star, and the General Service and Victory Medals.
Trowley Bottom, Flamstead.   2493/A.

PEDDER, D. M. (Miss), Special War Worker.
This lady volunteered her services for work of National importance in the early days of the war and from February 1915 until September 1917 was employed at Messrs. Vauxhall's Fuse Depôt. Relinquishing this work she was engaged on important duties on the land from June 1918 until the following October.
48, Cambridge Street, Luton.   2489/B.

PEDDER, G. M., Sapper, Royal Engineers.
He joined in January 1917, and on completion of his training served at various depôts on important duties. He rendered valuable services, but owing to ill-health was unsuccessful in obtaining his transfer overseas. He was demobilised in November 1919.
48, Cambridge Street, Luton.   2489/A.

PEDDER, G. W., Private, 4th Bedfordshire Regt.
Volunteering in December 1915, he was drafted to France in July of the following year. Here he served in various engagements, including the Battle of Beaumont-Hamel, and was wounded in February 1917. On recovery he embarked for Egypt and, with the forces in Palestine, fought at Gaza, and took part in the advance through the Holy Land and Syria. He was demobilised in August 1919 on his return to England, and holds the General Service and Victory Medals.
Flitton.   2490.

PEDDER, H., Private, Northamptonshire Regt.
He joined in April 1918, and after completing his training was stationed at various depôts with his unit on important duties. He rendered valuable services but was unable to obtain his transfer overseas before the cessation of hostilities, and was demobilised in February 1919.
Trowley Bottom, Flamstead.   2493/C.

PEDDER, H., Private, Bedfordshire Regiment.
Volunteering in December 1914, he embarked for the Western Front in the following year, and was in action almost continuously for three years. During this period he fought at the Battles of Cambrai, the Somme, and was unfortunately killed in action at Ypres in April 1918 during the German offensive. He was entitled to the 1914-15 Star, and the General Service and Victory Medals.
Trowley Bottom, Flamstead.   2493/B.

PEDDER, H., Private, Bedfordshire Regiment.
He joined in 1916, and was later drafted to the Western Front, where he was engaged in many battles, including those of Loos, Arras and the Somme. Transferred to Italy, he served throughout the campaign in this theatre of war. He was twice wounded during the course of his service, and was demobilised on his return to England in February 1919. He holds the General Service and Victory Medals.
26, Hampton Road, Luton.   2491.

PEDDER, H. W., Private, Bedfordshire Regt.
Volunteering in 1915, he proceeded to Egypt in the following year, and served on the Eastern Front during the advance through Palestine subsequent to the third Battle of Gaza. He was wounded in the vicinity of Rafa prior to the final British offensive, in the course of which he was present at the capture of Haifa. He returned to England and was demobilised in 1919 and holds the General Service and Victory Medals.
Station Road, Toddington.   2492.

PEDLEY, L. O., Sergeant, Royal Engineers.
Volunteering in September 1915, he served with his unit at various stations on important duties. He rendered valuable services as Sergeant-Instructor in Field work, but was unable to obtain his transfer overseas. He was demobilised in October 1919.
30, Reginald Street, Luton.   2494.

PEDRICK, H. J., Gunner, R.F.A.
He volunteered in March 1916, and in April of the succeeding year embarked for France, where he was in action with his battery at Messines Ridge, and in the Ypres salient, and was wounded in August 1917. Invalided to England he received hospital treatment and was subsequently discharged on account of his service in April 1918. He holds the General Service and Victory Medals.
77, Spenser Road, Luton.   2495.

PEERS, W., Private, Yorkshire Regiment and Labour Corps.
He joined in 1916, and completing his training, served with his regiment at various stations on important duties. He was later transferred to the Labour Corps and with this unit rendered valuable services until 1919, when he was demobilised.
9, Southwold Road, Callowland, Watford.   X2496.

PEGRAM, W. R., Private, R.A.O.C.
He volunteered in 1915, and after his training served at various stations on important duties with his unit. He did good work but owing to medical unfitness was unable to obtain his transfer overseas. Owing to ill-health he was invalided to Bute Hospital where he subsequently died on December 1st, 1916.
Myrtle Cottage, London Colney.   2497.

PELLOW, L., Sister, Q.A.I.M.N.S. (Reserve).
A trained nurse, this lady was stationed at the Military Hospital, Devonport, for a time, and was drafted to Macedonia on June 1st, 1917. She rendered excellent services in the nursing of Serbian sick and wounded troops, and was frequently under shell fire. She carried on her much appreciated work until November 1918, when she returned to England and was discharged in May of the following year. She holds the General Service and Victory Medals.
220, Beech Hill, Luton.   2498/B.

PELLOWES, E. A., Private, Bedfordshire Regt.
He joined in September 1917, and at the conclusion of his training was stationed at various places on important duties with his battalion. He did excellent work, but on account of medical unfitness was unable to secure his transfer to a theatre of war, and was demobilised in September 1919.
220, Beech Hill, Luton.   2498/A.

PEMBERTON, G. R., A.B., Royal Navy.
At the outbreak of hostilities he was serving at Portsmouth in H.M.S. "Victory," and during the war served aboard a mine sweeper, which vessel was employed on mine sweeping duties in the North and Black Seas. His ship had several encounters with enemy craft and had many narrow escapes. He was discharged in January 1919, and holds the General Service and Victory Medals.
17, King Street, Houghton Regis.   2499.

PENNELL, C., Sergeant, Middlesex Regiment.
He volunteered at the outbreak of war and was shortly after drafted to France. He fought in the Retreat from Mons and the subsequent Battles of the Marne, Festubert and Arras. He was killed in action on the Somme on July 1st, 1916, and was entitled to the Mons Star, and the General Service and Victory Medals.
57, Ratcliffe Road, Hitchin.   2500/B.

PENNELL, W., Corporal, 1st Hertfordshire Regt.
Volunteering in August 1914, he was immediately drafted to France, and fought in the Retreat from Mons and was wounded. He later rejoined his unit and was engaged in the fighting at Ypres and again wounded. On recovery he returned to his battalion in the firing line and took part in the fierce fighting on the Somme, and was wounded a third time and invalided home. He was subsequently discharged in consequence of his wounds in December 1918, and holds the Mons Star, and the General Service and Victory Medals.
57, Ratcliffe Road, Hitchin.   2500/A.

PENNY, A., Private, R.A.M.C.
He joined in October 1916, and after his training was drafted to France. He was engaged with his unit on important duties at Boulogne and other base hospitals in nursing and attending to the wounded, remaining in this theatre of war until December 1919, when he returned home and was demobilised. He holds the General Service and Victory Medals.
28, Harley Street, St. Albans.   2552.

PENNY, A. J., Private, 1/5th East Surrey Regt.
He volunteered in January 1916, and in the same year was drafted to India, where he was engaged on guard and other duties until the following year. He was then sent to Mesopotamia and was actively engaged in the operations there until the cessation of hostilities. He returned to England and was demobilised in 1920, and holds the General Service and Victory Medals.
42, Shakespeare Street, North Watford. 2501.

PENNY, C., Private, Bedfordshire Regiment.
He volunteered in September 1914, and in the following year was drafted overseas. Whilst on the Western Front he fought in many engagements, including those at Ypres, Arras and the Retreat and subsequent Advance of 1918. He was later sent to Salonika and after the signing of the Armistice returned home and was demobilised in 1919. He holds the 1914-15 Star, and the General Service and Victory Medals.
67, Fearnley Street, Watford. X2502/C.

PENNY, F., Trooper, 1st County of London Yeomanry (Middlesex, Duke of Cambridge's Hussars).
He volunteered in December 1914, and in the following September was drafted to Egypt. He took part in the British advance through Palestine and was in action at Gaza, Haifa, Damascus and Aleppo, and also served at Cairo during the riots there in March 1918. He returned to England after the cessation of hostilities, and was demobilised in January 1919. He holds the 1914-15 Star, and the General Service and Victory Medals.
67, Fearnley Street, Watford. X2502/B.

PENNY, H., Private, Oxfordshire and Buckinghamshire Light Infantry.
He joined in November 1916, and in the following year was drafted to France. During his service on the Western Front he took part in many engagements, including those at Ypres, on the Somme, at Arras and St. Quentin. He was demobilised in March 1919, and holds the General Service and Victory Medals.
67, Fearnley Street, Watford. X2502/A.

PENTLING, F. A., Corporal, R.A.S.C.
He volunteered in August 1914, and was drafted to France in the following year. During his service on the Western Front he was engaged in the fighting at Arras, Ypres, on the Somme, at Cambrai, and in the Allied Advance of 1918, afterwards proceeding to Cologne with the Army of Occupation. He was demobilised in September 1919, and holds the 1914-15 Star, and the General Service and Victory Medals.
26, Duke Street, Luton. 2503.

PEPPER, B., Private, 1st Bedfordshire Regiment.
He joined in March 1918, and at the conclusion of his training served at various stations on important duties with his battalion. He rendered valuable services but was unable to secure his transfer overseas and was still serving in 1920.
1, Austin Lane, Ampthill. 3684/B.

PEPPER, F., Sapper, R.E.
He volunteered in February 1915, and served with his unit at various stations until drafted to France in 1916. Whilst on the Western Front he was engaged on important duties in connection with operations and was frequently in the front lines during the fighting on the Somme and at Arras, where he was badly wounded. He was removed to hospital in England and in consequence of his wounds his injured leg had to be amputated. He was invalided out of the Service in September 1918, and holds the General Service and Victory Medals.
70, Hitchin Street, Biggleswade. Z2505/B.

PEPPER, F., Private, Queen's Own (Royal West Kent Regiment).
He volunteered in 1915, and on the completion of his training was stationed at various places on important duties with his battalion. He did excellent work but owing to medical unfitness was unable to obtain his transfer to a theatre of war, and was demobilised in March 1919.
50, Chapel House, Cowfair Lands, Biggleswade. Z2505/A.

PEPPER, H. J., Driver, Royal Engineers.
He was mobilised in August 1914, and was immediately sent to France. He was engaged on special transport duties with his unit and was frequently under heavy shell fire. He served in the Retreat from Mons, and in the Battles of the Somme, Arras, Armentières, Albert and Ypres. He was demobilised in February 1919, and holds the Mons Star, and the General Service and Victory Medals.
8, Orchard Road, Walsworth, near Hitchin. 2507/A.

PEPPER, E. (M.M.), Sergeant, 2nd Bedfordshire Regiment.
A serving soldier, he was drafted to France shortly after the outbreak of war and fought in the Battle of Ypres, and was wounded on October 22nd, 1914. On recovery he returned to his unit and was again wounded at Festubert in May 1915. He rejoined his battalion and during the fighting at Loos on September 29th, 1915, displayed conspicuous bravery and devotion to duty in the Field, for which he was mentioned in Despatches and awarded the Military Medal. He returned to England after the signing of the Armistice and was demobilised in November 1919, and also holds the 1914 Star, and the General Service and Victory Medals.
c/o Mr. H. Fossey, Bedford Street, Ampthill. 2504.

PEPPER, H., Private, Bedfordshire Regiment.
He volunteered in November 1914, and in the following year was drafted to the Western Front. In this theatre of war he fought in many engagements, including those at Arras, Ypres, on the Somme, at Cambrai, until taken prisoner during the fierce conflict at Kemmel Hill in May 1918. He was held in captivity until after the cessation of hostilities when he was repatriated and demobilised in 1919. He holds the 1914-15 Star, and the General Service and Victory Medals.
5, High Street, Ridgmont, Beds. 2506/A.

PEPPER, M. W. (Miss), Member, W.R.A.F.
She joined in 1917, and was stationed at the Henlow Aircraft Works with her squadron. She was employed on important duties in connection with the making of aeroplane wings and for a time was engaged on clerical work. She carried out her several duties in a highly satisfactory manner, and was demobilised in 1919.
50, Chapel House, Cowfair Lands, Biggleswade. Z2505/C.

PEPPER, W. (M.M.), L/Corporal, Military Mounted Police.
He was mobilised in August 1914, and was shortly afterwards sent to France. He took part in the fighting at Arras and on the Somme, and was wounded. On recovery he rejoined his unit and during the fighting at Passchendaele was awarded the Military Medal for conspicuous bravery and devotion to duty in the Field. He was subsequently killed in action near Doullons on June 29th, 1918, and was entitled to the 1914 Star, and the General Service and Victory Medals.
39, Periwinkle Lane, Hitchin. 2508.

PEPPER, W. J., L/Corporal, Bedfordshire Regt.
He joined in May 1916, and in the following November proceeded overseas. He took part in the fighting on the Somme and was wounded. On recovery he returned to the front line trenches and fought at Arras, Passchendaele, Ypres and Cambrai. He was demobilised in August 1919, and holds the General Service and Victory Medals.
26, Church Street, Ridgmont, Beds. Z2509.

PEPPER, W. T., Private, 4th Bedfordshire Regt.
He volunteered in November 1915, and in the following July proceeded overseas. He fought in many sectors of the Western Front, including the engagements on the Somme, at Ypres and Arras and was wounded in April 1917. He was invalided home, and in consequence of his wounds lost the use of his right arm, and was invalided out of the service in April of the following year. He holds the General Service and Victory Medals.
1, Austin Lane, Ampthill. 3684/A.

PEPPIATT, D., Private, Leicestershire Regt.
He joined in March 1916, and in the same year proceeded overseas. During his service on the Western Front he fought in the Battles of the Somme and Arras, where he was taken prisoner on May 3rd, 1917. He was held in captivity until after the cessation of hostilities and was then repatriated and demobilised in April 1919, and holds the General Service and Victory Medals.
8, Lammas Walk, Leighton Buzzard. 2510.

PEPPIATT, V., Leading Stoker, R.N.
He was mobilised at the outbreak of war, and served in H.M.S. "Wellington," which vessel took part in the fighting during the Naval operations at the Dardanelles. His ship was later engaged on patrol and mine-sweeping duties in the North Sea until the cessation of hostilities. He was demobilised in February 1919, and holds the 1914-15 Star, and the General Service and Victory Medals.
1, Park Cottages, Westoning, Ampthill. 2511.

PERFECT, H., Sergeant, Sherwood Foresters.
He volunteered in September 1914, and in the following year was drafted to France. Whilst in this theatre of war he was engaged in the fighting at Ypres, on the Somme, and at Cambrai, and was twice wounded. He was demobilised in December 1918 and holds the General Service and Victory Medals.
110, Sandringham Road, Watford. X2513.

PERCIVAL, C., Corporal, 1st Essex Regiment.
He was mobilised at the outbreak of war and drafted to France in the following year. During his service on the Western Front he took part in the fierce fighting at the Battle of Ypres and, reported missing on August 16th, 1917, was later presumed to have been killed on that date. He was entitled to the 1914-15 Star, and the General Service and Victory Medals.
38, Denmark Street, Watford.　　X2512.

PERHAM, C., Pte., 22nd London Regt. (Queen's).
He volunteered in April 1915, and in July of the following year proceeded to the Western Front. Whilst in France he served with his battalion and took part in the fierce fighting during the Battle of the Somme, wherein he was killed in action on September 16th, 1916. He was entitled to the General Service and Victory Medals.
9, Pageant Road, St. Albans.　　X3650/B.

PERKINS, B., Private, R.A.M.C.
Joining in June 1917, he completed a course of training and in the same year was drafted to Italy. There he was engaged on hospital work at Taranto and Naples, and later with the field ambulance did excellent work during the British offensive operations on the Piave. He holds the General Service and Victory Medals.
76, Pondwicks Road, Luton.　　2514.

PERKINS, C. J., Engine Room Artificer, Royal Navy.
He joined in April 1918, and was posted to H.M. Torpedo Boat Destroyer No. 32, in which ship he was engaged on important duties in various waters until the cessation of hostilities. He was demobilised in January 1919, and holds the General Service and Victory Medals.
6, Coventry Cottages, Westoning, Ampthill.　　2515.

PERKINS, F. C., Private, R.A.S.C. (M.T.).
He joined in April 1916, and on the conclusion of his training was drafted to France. There he served in several sectors and was engaged on important transport duties in the forward areas at Cambrai, Ypres, the Somme and was wounded during the Battle of Ypres. He was demobilised in October 1919, and holds the General Service and Victory Medals.
54, Pondwicks Road, Luton.　　2516.

PERKINS, P. G., Pte., Northamptonshire Regt.
He joined in July 1918, and in the following September was drafted overseas. Serving with his unit on the Western Front, he took part in heavy fighting on the Somme, at St. Quentin, Cambrai and Ypres, and in other important battles until the cessation of hostilities. He was then sent with the Army of Occupation into Germany where he was employed on guard and other duties at Cologne. On returning to England he was demobilised in February 1919, and holds the General Service and Victory Medals.
17, York Street, Luton.　　2517.

PERKINS, W., Driver, R.F.A.
He volunteered in September 1914, and in the following year was sent to Egypt, in which theatre of war he took part in several important engagements. Attached to the forces, which, under General Allenby advanced through Palestine, he fought with his battery at Gaza, Haifa, Aleppo and in other notable battles, until the end of hostilities. He returned to England for demobilisation in 1919 and holds the 1914-15 Star, and the General Service and Victory Medals.
46, Shakespeare Street, North Watford.　　2518.

PERRIN, P. J., Gunner, R.G.A.
He joined in November 1916, and at the conclusion of his training was drafted to France. During his service in this theatre of war he was engaged in the heavy fighting on the Somme, and during the Allied Advance was seriously wounded. He was sent to hospital in England and died from the effects of his wounds on October 6th, 1918. He was entitled to the General Service and Victory Medals.
12, Cassiobridge Road, Watford.　　2709/B.

PERRIN, W., Private, R.A.S.C.
He volunteered in 1915, and in the same year was sent to Salonika where he saw much service and was in action in various engagements during the course of the Balkan campaign. In 1918 he was sent to Russia with the British Relief Force, with which unit he served until his return to England for demobilisation in July 1919. He holds the 1914-15 Star, and the General Service and Victory Medals.
21, Bernard Street, St. Albans.　　X2519.

PERRY, A., Private, Queen's (Royal West Surrey Regiment).
He volunteered in September 1914, and after training was sent overseas in the following January. Whilst on the Western Front he served in several sectors and was engaged in heavy fighting at the Battles of Loos, the Somme, Arras, Vimy Ridge, Ypres and Cambrai. He was killed in action in the vicinity of Cambrai on October 25th, 1918, and was entitled to the 1914-15 Star, and the General Service and Victory Medals.
Westoning Road, Harlington.　　2520/A.

PERRY, A. B., Private, Grenadier Guards.
He volunteered in November 1914, and in the following year was on active service on the Western Front. Severely wounded in the Battle of Loos in 1915, he was invalided home, and on recovery rejoined his unit in the Field. He was again in action in several important engagements, including the Battles of the Somme, Arras and Ypres, and was sent home suffering from shell-shock. Returning to France he saw further action at Cambrai during the concluding operations of the war, and was demobilised in March 1919. He holds the 1914-15 Star, and the General Service and Victory Medals.
38, Wenlock Street, Luton.　　2521/A.

PERRY, C. H., Private, Wiltshire Regiment.
Volunteering in June 1915, he completed his training and was drafted overseas. He saw service on the Western Front, in several sectors of which he was engaged in the fighting during the Battle of Cambrai and other important engagements, and was wounded. He was afterwards sent to Salonika, and in that theatre of war did excellent work on transport duties until the cessation of hostilities. He was demobilised in March 1919, and holds the General Service and Victory Medals.
9, Ladysmith Road, St. Albans.　　X2523/A.

PERRY, F., Private, Middlesex Regiment.
Joining in January 1917, on completion of his training he was engaged with his unit on special duties at various stations. He did excellent work, but was unable to secure his transfer overseas before the cessation of hostilities owing to medical unfitness for general service, and was discharged in consequence on May 30th 1917.
38 Wenlock Street, Luton.　　2521/B.

PERRY, F. H., Private, 2nd Middlesex Regiment and Air Mechanic, R.A.F.
Volunteering in September 1915, he was drafted overseas in the following November. He was in action on the Somme, at Arras, Loos and Ypres, where he was wounded in May 1917. On recovery he served through the Retreat and Advance of 1918, and was again wounded. He was demobilised in February 1919, and holds the 1914-15 Star, and the General Service and Victory Medals.
2, Bury Dell Lane, Park Street, St. Albans.　　213/B.

PERRY, G., Gunner, R.F.A.
He joined in May 1915, and shortly afterwards was serving with his battery on the Western Front. He was in action in heavy fighting, and was engaged in the Battles of the Somme, Arras, Ypres and other important engagements until the termination of the war. Returning to England, he was demobilised in March 1919, and holds the 1914-15 Star, and the General Service and Victory Medals.
50, Bradshaw Road, Callowland, Herts.　　2525/A.

PERRY, G., Private, 4th Bedfordshire Regiment.
He volunteered in September 1914, and in the following July was sent to France. In this theatre of war he was engaged in almost continuous fighting in various sectors and took part in many notable battles, including those of Arras and the Somme, and was gassed and wounded. He also did good with his battalion until the conclusion of hostilities and returning to England was demobilised in January 1919. He holds the 1914-15 Star, and the General Service and Victory Medals.
36, Chapel Street, Hemel Hempstead.　　X2524.

PERRY, G. T., Private, Essex Regiment.
Joining in August 1916, he was shortly afterwards drafted to the Western Front, where he served with his battalion in several sectors. He took part in the Battles of the Somme, Ypres and Cambrai, amongst other important engagements, and was killed in action in the Somme sector on April 11th, 1918. He was entitled to the General Service and Victory Medals.
42, Chapel Street, Hemel Hempstead.　　X2522.

PERRY, H., Sapper, Royal Engineers.
He joined in June 1916, and after training was drafted overseas. He served on the Western Front and was present at many important engagements, including the Battles of the Somme and Arras. and was killed in action on July 27th, 1917, in the vicinity of Arras. He was entitled to the General Service and Victory Medals.
45, Boyle Street, Luton.　　2528.

PERRY, H.. Corporal, Royal Engineers.
He was mobilised on the outbreak of hostilities and after a course of training was engaged at various stations on important duties until June 1918, when he was sent to Salonika. In this theatre of war he was engaged in wiring, pontoon bridge building, and other work during operations in the advance on the Vardar and Struma fronts. He holds the General Service and Victory Medals, and was demobilised in April 1919.
9, Cumberland Street,, Houghton Regis.   2526.

PERRY, H., Private, East Surrey Regiment.
He joined in June 1917, and in the following October was despatched to Mesopotamia. In this theatre of war he took part in heavy fighting in the operations on the Tigris and Euphrates until contracting severe illness he was invalided to India. He died in hospital on July 20th, 1919, and was entitled to the General Service and Victory Medals.
49, Ashton Road, Luton.   2527.

PERRY, P. A., Private, Northamptonshire Regt.
He joined in March 1918, and after training was engaged at various stations on important duties in connection with coastal defence work. Owing to medical unfitness for general service he was not sent overseas, and after rendering valuable services with his unit was demobilised in January 1919.
56, King Street, Dunstable.   2529.

PERRY, P. A., Private, M.G.C.
He joined in March 1917, and, on the conclusion of his training was drafted overseas in the same year. Serving with his unit on the Western Front he was actively engaged in many important battles, including those of Ypres, Albert and Cambrai, and was wounded. He returned to England for demobilisation in October 1919, and holds the General Service and Victory Medals.
50, Broadshaw Road, Callowland.   2525/B.

PERRY, T. R., Flight-Sergeant, R.A.F.
He volunteered in September 1914, and on completion of his training was engaged as a Sergeant-Instructor at various aerodromes. He did excellent work in the training of recruits and the testing of aero engines, but was unable to secure his transfer overseas before the cessation of hostilities, owing to medical unfitness, and in 1920 he was still serving.
Bury Road, Stopsley.   2530.

PERRY, W. F., Private, Bedfordshire Regiment.
Volunteering in September 1915, he was drafted to Egypt in the following January, and saw much service in this theatre of war. He was engaged in heavy fighting in the British Advance through Palestine, and fought at the Battle of Gaza, and other important engagements. He was unfortunately killed in action on July 20th, 1917, and was entitled to the General Service and Victory Medals.
Westoning Road, Harlington.   2520/B.

PERRY, W. R., Driver, R.F.A.
He joined in May 1916, and after serving with his battery at various stations was drafted overseas in the following May. He saw much service on the Western Front and was in action in the Battles of the Somme, Ypres and Cambrai, and other important engagements until the conclusion of hostilities. He was demobilised in October 1919 and holds the General Service and Victory Medals.
15, Wellclose Street, St. Albans.   2531.

PERTON, A. T., Private, Middlesex Regiment.
Volunteering in 1914, in the following year he was drafted to France, and served with his unit in various sectors. He fought at St. Eloi, Ypres, Loos, and in various offensive operations on the Somme, and was severely wounded on August 8th, 1916. Invalided home on account of his wounds, he was ultimately discharged as medically unfit for further service in 1917, and holds the 1914-15 Star, and the General Service and Victory Medals.
2, Flowerdale, Markyate.   2532.

PESTELL, A. B., Private, Bedfordshire Regt.
He volunteered in October 1914, and on the conclusion of his training was engaged on important coastal defence duties at various stations on the East Coast. He was not sent overseas owing to medical unfitness for service and was invalided out of the service on August 8th, 1917.
15, Spring Place, Luton.   2533.

PESTELL, C. E., Private, Queen's (Royal West Surrey Regiment).
Joining in June 1918, in the following August he was drafted to the Western Front, and in this theatre of war was engaged in heavy fighting at Cambrai and other places during the final operations of the war. Returning to England for demobilisation in January 1919, he holds the General Service and Victory Medals.
23, Gardenia Avenue, Leagrave, near Luton.   2535/A.

PESTELL, F. R., Private, Essex Regiment.
He joined in March 1917, and after serving with his unit at various stations was drafted overseas in April of the following year. He was in action on the Western Front in several important engagements, including those of Amiens, Cambrai and Ypres, and on the conclusion of hostilities returned to England. He was demobilised in November 1919, and holds the General Service and Victory Medals.
28, Gardenia Avenue, Leagrave, near Luton.   2535/B.

PESTELL, F. R., Bombardier (251st Siege Battery), R.G.A.
He joined in March 1917, and in the following June was on active service in France. Engaged with his battery in various sectors, he took part in several important battles, including those of Arras, Ypres and Cambrai. He returned to England for demobilisation in February 1919, and holds the General Service and Victory Medals.
79, Spencer Road, Luton.   2537.

PESTELL, H. G., Gunner, R.F.A.
He volunteered in 1915, and in the same year was drafted overseas. Serving with his battery in Egypt, he took part in the British advance through Palestine and fought at Gaza, Haifa, and in other important battles, until discharged on account of service in September 1918. He holds the 1914-15 Star, and the General Service and Victory Medals.
37, Balmoral Road, Hitchin.   2534.

PETERS, C., Sergeant, R.F.A.
He volunteered in August 1914, and in the following year was sent to the Western Front. There he took part in many important battles, including those of Ypres, the Somme and Cambrai, until the cessation of hostilities, and was demobilised after returning to England in June 1919. He holds the 1914-15 Star, and the General Service and Victory Medals.
28, Alexandra Road, St. Albans.   X2536.

PETERS, D. (Miss), Special War Worker.
This lady offered her services for work of National importance, and from October 1916 until February 1919 was employed at the Davis Gas Stove Company's Works, Luton, on important work in connection with the manufacture of shell cases. She rendered valuable services throughout.
Flint Cottage, Biscot.   2538.

PETERS, E. M., Driver, R.F.A.
He joined in April 1916, and in the following year was despatched overseas. Sent to Salonika he served with his battery and was engaged in heavy fighting in the advance on the Doiran and Vardar fronts, and in other operations in this theatre of war. He was demobilised on returning to England in May 1919, and holds the General Service and Victory Medals.
51, New England Street, St. Albans.   2539.

PETERS, F., Gunner, R.F.A.
He joined in 1916, and in the same year was sent to Mesopotamia, where he was engaged in many important battles, including those on the Tigris, at Kut-el-Amara, Baghdad and Mosul. He returned to England in December 1919, and was demobilised in the following month. He holds the General Service and Victory Medals.
3, St. Michael's Street, St. Albans.   2540.

PETERS, H., Band Sergeant, Hertfordshire Regt.
He volunteered in August 1914, and in the same year drafted to the Western Front, in several sectors of which he was engaged in heavy fighting. He was wounded in action and sent to hospital and returning to the Field served with his unit until the cessation of hostilities. He holds the 1914 Star, and the General Service and Victory Medals.
5, Moira Cottages, Letchworth.   2551.

PETERS, H. G., Pte., 1st Buffs (East Kent Regt.
Joining in January 1916, he proceeded to France in the following July, and was stationed at Rouen and Calais on guard and other important duties at various detention camps. He rendered excellent services throughout and was demobilised in November 1919, and holds the General Service and Victory Medals.
5, Holly Cottages, Preston, Herts.   2541/A.

PETERS, J., L/Cpl., 17th London Regt. (Rifles).
Volunteering in August 1914, he was engaged on various duties with his unit until drafted overseas in the following year. Serving on the Western Front he took part in the Battles of Ypres, Festubert, Cambrai, the Somme, Passchendaele, Amiens, and in most of the principal engagements during the concluding operations of the war. He holds the 1914-15 Star, and the General Service and Victory Medals, and was demobilised in January 1919.
3, Bloomfield Cottages, Hatfield.   2542.

PETERS, L. H., Pte., 12th Royal Sussex Regt.
Volunteering in May 1915, in the same year he saw active service on the Western Front. Whilst in this theatre of war he fought in the Battles of Ypres, Festubert, the Somme, Albert Cambrai and other important engagements until the cessation of hostilities. He was discharged on account of service in March 1919, and holds the 1914-15 Star, and the General Service and Victory Medals.
Chequers Lane, Preston, Herts. 2541/C.

PETERS, W. C., Gunner, R.F.A.
He volunteered in January 1915, and in the same year was sent to France. He took part in heavy fighting in several important engagements, including the Battles of Ypres, Loos, Arras and Cambrai, and was wounded Rejoining his regiment he saw much service, and on the termination of hostilities returned to England and was demobilised in March 1920. He holds the 1914-15 Star, and the General Service and Victory Medals.
5, Holly Cottages, Preston, Herts. 2541/B.

PETERSON, P., Driver, R.F.A.
He volunteered in 1915, and in February of the following year was sent to the Western Front, where he saw much service. He was in action in many important engagements, and amongst other battles, took part in those on the Somme, at Arras, Ypres and Cambrai, and was wounded. He returned to England for demobilisation in February 1919, and holds the General Service and Victory Medals.
29, Ebenezer Street, Luton. 2543/A.

PETT, S. G., Shoeing Smith, R.A.S.C.
Volunteering in November 1915, he was engaged on important duties with his unit at various stations until April 1917, when he was sent to Salonika. He did excellent work in various sectors of the Balkan front whilst heavy fighting was in progress on the Struma. He also served in the Persian Gulf. He returned to England for demobilisaion in May 1919, and holds the General Service and Victory Medals.
Princess Street, Toddington. 2544.

PETTIFAR, F., Private, Royal Munster Fusiliers.
Volunteering in August 1914, in the following year he was sent to Gallipoli, where he took part in heavy fighting at the landing on the Peninsula. Later, in 1915, drafted to France, he was in action in several important engagements, including those at Loos, Albert, Messines, and on the Somme, and on the termination of hostilities returned to England. Demobilised in February 1919, he holds the 1914-15 Star and the General Service and Victory Medals
Moggerhanger, Sandy, Beds. Z1816/B.

PETTIFER, A., Private, Royal Berkshire Regt.
He volunteered in September 1914, and in December of the following year was drafted to the Western Front. There he served in several sectors and was engaged in the Battles of Loos, Albert, Vimy Ridge, and in various operations on the Somme. Severely wounded in an engagement in the Somme Offensive, he was invalided to hospital in England and unfortunately died from the effects of his wounds on July 20th, 1916. He was entitled to the 1914-15 Star, and the General Service and Victory Medals.
Garden Cottage, New Street, Shefford. Z2545.

PETTIFER, H., Private, 1/7th Middlesex Regt.
Volunteering at the outbreak of war he was drafted to Egypt in 1915, and served on important duties with his battalion. He was also in action in the British advance through Palestine, and fought at Gaza and Jaffa. He was later transferred to the Western Front and was actively engaged on the Ancre, at Vimy Ridge, Ypres, Lens and on the Marne. He was demobilised in 1919, and holds the 1914-15 Star, and the General Service and Victory Medals.
New Street, Shefford. Z2815/B.

PETTIT, A. J., Gunner, R.G.A.
Joining in March 1917, on the conclusion of his training he was engaged with his battery on important duties in connection with coastal defence work. He rendered valuable services at various stations, but was not sent overseas owing to medical unfitness, and was invalided out of the service in March 1919.
London Road, Woburn, Beds. Z2547.

PETTIT, E., Rifleman, Rifle Brigade.
He volunteered in August 1914, and was shortly afterwards drafted overseas. He saw much service in France and Flanders and took part in many important engagements. He was killed in action on March 24th, 1915, and was entitled to the 1914-15 Star, and the General Service and Victory Medals.
28, Cotterel's Road, Hemel Hempstead. X2546.

PETTY, J., Private, Middlesex Regiment and Labour Corps.
He joined in July 1916, and after training served with his unit at various stations on important duties. Found unfit for general service he was engaged as boot repairer at a large military depôt and did excellent work until his demobilisation in March 1919.
33, Lowestoft Road, Watford. 2548/A.

PETTY, S. J. E., Private, R.A.S.C.
He joined in April 1918, and on the conclusion of his training served with his unit on important duties at various stations. He was engaged in the regimental bakery, and did excellent work, but was unsuccessful in obtaining a transfer overseas before the cessation of hostilities, and was demobilised in March 1920.
146, Sandringham Road, Watford. X2549.

PETTY, V. (Miss), Special War Worker.
During the war this lady offered her services for work of National importance and was employed at the Perivale Munition Factory. Engaged there on the Inspection Staff in the Fuse Department, she discharged the duties of her responsible position in a thoroughly efficient manner from January 1916 until December 1919.
33, Lowestoft Road, Watford. 2548/B.

PEVREALL, A., Corporal, R.E. (I.W.T.).
Volunteering in August 1914, he served with his unit at various stations until sent to India on completing his training. He was afterwards drafted to Mesopotamia, in which theatre of war he was engaged on important duties in connection with operations in the forward areas, and was present at several battles, including that of Deli-Abbas. Returning to England on the termination of hostilities, he was demobilised in July 1919, and holds the General Service and Victory Medals.
5, Normanhurst, Grosvenor Road East, St. Albans.
X2550.

PHEASANT, A., Private, Machine Gun Corps.
He joined in October 1916, and in the following year was drafted to the Western Front. Whilst overseas he was engaged in heavy fighting in several important battles, including those of the Somme, Amiens and Bapaume. He served until the Armistice, and returned to England for demobilisation in December 1918. He holds the General Service and Victory Medals.
High Street, Barton, Ampthill. 2553.

PHILIPS, F. W., Private, Machine Gun Corps.
He joined in 1916, and later in the same year was drafted to France where he fought in many engagements, including the Battle of Ypres. In 1917 he left the Western Front for Salonika, and was in action on the Vardar. In the following year he was transferred to the Italian theatre of war and served on the Piave, and returned to England and was demobilised in January 1919. He holds the General Service and Victory Medals.
41, Albert Street, St. Albans. 783/B.

PHILLIPS, W. F., Private, Royal Berkshire Regt.
Mobilised on the outbreak of hostilities he was almost immediately drafted to France and fought in the Retreat from Mons, and in the Battles of La Bassée and Festubert. He was reported missing on May 17th, 1915, and was later presumed to have been killed in action on that date at Festubert. He was entitled to the Mons Star, and the General Service and Victory Medals.
Ivy Cottage, Church Street, Westoning. 2554.

PHILLIPS, W. H., Sergeant, R.A.V.C.
He volunteered in November 1915, and in the following May was serving on the Western Front. Engaged on special duties he did excellent work with his corps in several sectors and was present at many important battles, including those on the Marne, at Ypres, and St. Quentin. On the cessation of hostilities he went with the Army of Occupation into Germany, and was stationed at Cologne. He returned to England for demobilisation in June 1919, and holds the General Service and Victory Medals.
East Hall Farm, Paul's Waldron, Hitchin. 2555.

PHILPOTT, F. T., L/Corporal, 6th Queen's Own (Royal West Kent Regiment).
He joined in October 1916, and after serving at various stations was drafted overseas in July 1918. He served in France in the heavy fighting at Bullecourt, Passchendaele and Arras, in the Allied Advance of that year, and was reported missing on September 21st. He was later presumed to have been killed in action on that date, and was entitled to the General Service and Victory Medals.
10, Oak Road, Luton. 4069/A.

PHILPOTT, A. W., Private, East Surrey Regt.
He joined in June 1916, and in the following February proceeded overseas. During his service on the Western Front he fought at Arras, Bullecourt, Passchendaele, Bapaume, on the Somme, and at Cambrai, and was four times wounded. He was demobilised in October 1919, and holds the General Service and Victory Medals.
42, May Street, Luton. 2556.

PHILPOTT, H. C., Sapper, Royal Engineers.
He volunteered in April 1915, and served at various stations with his unit until drafted to France in September 1917. Whilst on the Western Front, he was engaged in the forward areas and was frequently under heavy shell fire during the operations at Beaucourt and Passchendaele Ridge. He was demobilised in February 1919, and holds the General Service and Victory Medals.
35, Hartley Road, Luton. 2557.

PICKERING, D. G., Bandmaster, Royal Navy.
He joined in November 1916, and was posted to H.M.S. "Avoca." His ship was engaged on important patrol and other duties in the North Sea and various other waters during the whole period of the war, and frequently passed through mine-infested areas. He was demobilised in March 1919, and holds the General Service and Victory Medals.
19, Dallow Road, Luton. 2604.

PICKERING, F., Rifleman, 16th King's Royal Rifle Corps.
He volunteered in November 1915, and in the following year was drafted to France. In this theatre of war he was engaged in the fighting on the Somme and various other battles. He was killed in action at Delville Wood on July 15th, 1916, and was entitled to the General Service and Victory Medals.
Littleworth, Wing, Bucks. 2559.

PICKERING, J. E., Sergeant, Royal Engineers.
He joined in 1916, and in the same year was drafted overseas. He was engaged on important duties with his unit in various sectors of the Western Front, including those of Ypres, the Somme and Cambrai, and was frequently in the firing line. He was demobilised in February 1919, and holds the General Service and Victory Medals.
20, Victoria Road, North Watford. X2560.

PICKERING, J. F., Sergeant, R.A.V.C.
He volunteered in June 1915, and was drafted to France in the following year. During his service on the Western Front he was engaged on special duties and was in action in the forward areas in the Somme and Albert sectors, and was wounded and suffered from shellshock. He was demobilised in May 1919, and holds the General Service and Victory Medals.
High Street, Wing, Bucks. 2561.

PICKIN, D. (Senr.), Corporal, West Yorkshire Regiment.
He volunteered in October 1914, and was sent overseas in the following year. Whilst on the Western Front he served in many sectors and fought at Arras, Ypres, Cambrai, Loos, Lille and on the Somme. He was discharged in March 1918 on account of service, and holds the 1914-15 Star, and the General Service and Victory Medals.
14, London Road, Woburn. Z2562/B.

PICKIN, D., 1st Air Mechanic, Royal Air Force.
He joined in March 1918, and after his training served at various stations with his squadron on important duties which called for a high degree of technical skill. He rendered good service as a mechanic and fitter, but was unable to secure his transfer to a theatre of war, and was demobilised in February 1920.
14, London Road, Woburn, Beds. Z2562/A.

PICTON, A., Driver, R.A.S.C.
He volunteered in October 1914, and in the following February proceeded overseas. He was engaged on many important duties during his service in France and was in the front lines during heavy fire at Arras, Ypres and Cambrai. He was demobilised in March 1919, and holds the 1914-15 Star, and the General Service and Victory Medals.
10, Russell Place, Boxmoor, Herts. X2563.

PICTON, B., Private, 2nd East Surrey Regiment.
Volunteering in August 1914, he was shortly afterwards sent to France. In this theatre of war he took part in much heavy fighting at Loos, where he was gassed, and at Ypres was severely wounded in action. He was sent to England and in consequence of his wounds his injured arm had to be amputated. He was invalided out of the Service in 1918, and holds the 1914 Star, and the General Service and Victory Medals.
36, Ebben Road, Apsley End, Herts. 2564/A.

PICTON, C., Private, Queen's (Royal West Surrey Regiment).
He joined in 1916, and was later drafted to the Western Front. He took part in various engagements and was in action at Ypres, on the Somme, at Arras, and was twice wounded. He was discharged on account of service in May 1918, and holds the General Service and Victory Medals.
77, Cowper Road, Boxmoor. X2565.

PICTON, G. G., Air Mechanic, Royal Air Force.
He volunteered in April 1915, and at the conclusion of training served at various aerodromes on important duties which called for a high degree of technical skill. He did excellent work as a rigger, but owing to medical unfitness was unable to obtain his transfer to a theatre of war and was discharged on account of service in November 1918.
4, Russel Place, Boxmoor. X2566.

PICTON, H., Private, Bedfordshire Regiment.
Having served with the colours previous to the outbreak of war in 1914, he volunteered in June 1915, and was later sent to France. He was engaged in the fighting on the Somme, at Arras, and in many other sectors and was wounded three times and twice gassed. He returned to England and was invalided out of the service in November 1918, and holds the General Service and Victory Medals.
27, Cherry Bounce, Hemel Hempstead. X2567.

PICTON, H., Private, Royal Field Artillery.
He volunteered in 1915, and at the conclusion of his training was drafted to France. During his service on the Western Front he was engaged in almost continuous fighting at Ypres and on the Somme until December 1917 when he was wounded. He returned home and on recovery remained in England until demobilised in March 1919. He holds the General Service and Victory Medals.
99, Fearnley Street, Watford. X2884/A.

PICTON, S., Private, 2nd Bedfordshire Regiment.
Volunteering in August 1914, he was immediately drafted to France and was actively engaged in many battles, including those of Loos, Givenchy, Hill 60, and Ypres. He was killed in action in 1917 at the third Battle of Ypres, and was entitled to the 1914 Star, and the General Service and Victory Medals.
Aston Villa, Hemel Hempstead. 2564/B.

PICTON, W., Private, Labour Corps.
He volunteered in August 1914, and in the following year proceeded to Egypt. He was engaged with his unit on important duties chiefly in connection with irrigation and rendered very valuable services. He returned to England in 1919, and was demobilised in November of that year, and holds the 1914-15 Star, and the General Service and Victory Medals.
5, Russel Place, Boxmoor. X2568.

PIERCE, W. E., A/Sergeant, 2nd Essex Regt.
He joined in June 1917, and in November of that year was drafted to India. He was engaged at various stations with his unit on special guard and other duties until the end of 1919. He then returned to England and was demobilised in January 1920. He holds the General Service and Victory Medals.
25, Copsewood Road, Watford. X2569.

PIGGOTT, A., Private, 6th Bedfordshire Regt.
He volunteered in September 1914, and in the following July proceeded to France. He served in many sectors of the Western Front and fought at the battles of Loos, the Somme, Ypres, Albert, Beaumont Hamel and many others. He suffered from shell-shock and invalided home in November 1918, was demobilised in February of the following year. He holds the 1914-15 Star, and the General Service and Victory Medals.
King Street, Potton, Beds. Z2571/A.

PIGGOTT, F., Private, Bedfordshire Regiment.
He joined in March 1916, and in the following August was sent to France. He was engaged in the fighting on the Somme, at Arras and Cambrai, and in the Retreat and subsequent Advance of 1918. He returned to England after the cessation of hostilities, and was demobilised in December 1918. He holds the General Service and Victory Medals.
Tilsworth, near Leighton Buzzard. 2572.

PIGGOTT, H., Private, 8th Tank Corps.
He joined in February 1917, and in the following August proceeded overseas. Whilst on the Western Front he was engaged on important duties in the forward areas whilst operations were in progress in the Arras, Ypres and Cambrai sectors. He was demobilised in March 1919, and holds the General Service and Victory Medals.
Tilsworth, near Leighton Buzzard. 2573/B.

PIGGOTT, E., Rifleman, 13th King's Royal Rifle Corps.
He volunteered in 1915, and in the following year proceeded overseas. Whilst on the Western Front he took part in many engagements, including those at Ypres, on the Somme, and at Beaumont-Hamel. He was twice wounded during the conflicts and returning to England was eventually discharged as medically unfit for further service in 1919. He holds the General Service and Victory Medals.
Tilsworth, near Leighton Buzzard. 2570.

PIGGOTT, J., Private, 6th Bedfordshire Regt.
Joining in February 1916, he completed his training and embarked for the Western Front in the following August, and, serving with his battalion in various parts of the line, fought in many important engagements. He was unfortunately killed in action at Gavrelle on April 24th, 1917, and was entitled to the General Service and Victory Medals.
Tilsworth, Leighton Buzzard. 2573/A.

PIGGOTT, R. B., Private, Labour Corps.
He joined in August 1916, and in the following March was drafted to France. He served in many sectors of the Western Front on important road repair work with his battalion at Arras, the Somme, Messines, Ypres and Cambrai. He was demobilised in March 1919, and holds the General Service and Victory Medals.
119, Highbury Road, Luton. 2574.

PIKE, F., Sapper, Royal Engineers.
He volunteered at the outbreak of war and served with his unit at various stations until drafted to France in 1916. He was engaged on important duties in the front lines at Ypres, Arras, Cambrai and the Somme, until the signing of the Armistice. He then proceeded with the Army of Occupation to Germany, and was stationed at Cologne. He returned to England in April 1919, and was demobilised, and holds the General Service and Victory Medals.
138, Ridgway Road, Luton. 2575.

PIKE, J. W. K., Private, 9th Essex Regiment.
He volunteered in January 1915, and was later drafted to the Western Front. In this theatre of war he took part in much heavy fighting at Arras and Cambrai, and was taken prisoner during the German offensive in March 1918. He was held in captivity until after the signing of the Armistice, and then returned home and was demobilised in March 1919. He holds the General Service and Victory Medals.
12, Ebury Road, Watford. X2576.

PILCHER, H. G., Sergeant, R.A.V.C.
Volunteering in November 1914, he was drafted to the Western Front in the same month, and served in many advanced areas on duties connected with the care of sick and wounded horses. In December 1915, he was transferred to Mesopotamia, and saw active service in this theatre of war until 1918, when he was sent to Egypt. He returned to England in February 1919, and was demobilised in the following month, and holds the 1914-15 Star, and the General Service and Victory Medals.
16, Brixton Road, Watford. X2591.

PILGRIM, C., Corporal, R.A.M.C.
He volunteered in September 1914, and embarked for Egypt in the following year. Here he served at various base hospitals and in forward areas on important duties, in attending to sick and wounded troops. He rendered valuable services and on his return to England was demobilised in 1919, and holds the 1914-15 Star, and the General Service and Victory Medals.
5, High Street, Ridgmont. 2506/B.

PILGRIM, H., Sapper, Royal Engineers (R.O.D.).
He volunteered in April 1915, and later in the year was sent overseas. Whilst on the Western Front he was engaged on important work as a railway fireman, and served in many advanced areas, including those of Arras, Ypres, Albert, Festubert, and was wounded at Delville Wood during heavy fighting on the Somme front. He was demobilised in 1919, and holds the 1914-15 Star, and the General Service and Victory Medals.
69, Eversholt Road, Ridgmont. Z2577.

PILGRIM, W. G., Private, Bedfordshire Regiment and Highland Light Infantry.
Volunteering in June 1915, he was drafted to France in the following year. He saw active service in many parts of the Western Front, and fought in the Battles of Arras, Cambrai, the Somme, Messines, Ypres, Albert, and in the Retreat and Advance of 1918. Returning to England he was demobilised in December 1918, and holds the General Service and Victory Medals.
Station Road, Ridgmont. Z2578.

PILGRIM, A. G. (M.M.), Private, Welch Regt.
Volunteering in February 1916, he proceeded to the Western Front in the following July. In this theatre of war he was engaged at the Battles of Ypres, Cambrai, Arras, and the Somme, where he was wounded. On recovery he was drafted to Italy in January 1918, and saw active service there until the following September. He was awarded the Military Medal for devotion to duty and gallantry in the Field. He returned to France and was wounded in the Allied Advance. Invalided to Boulogne hospital, he died of wounds received in action on October 4th, 1918. He was entitled to the General Service and Victory Medals.
15, Stoke Road, Linslade, Leighton Buzzard. 2468/B.

PIMM, W. F., Private, Buffs (East Kent Regt.).
He joined in August 1918, and was stationed at various depôts with his regiment on completing his training. He was unable to secure his transfer overseas before the cessation of hostilities, and was engaged on guard and other duties of an important nature until demobilised in February 1919. He had previously served from August 1915, until June 1916 in the 3rd Bedfordshire Regiment.
27, Watford Fields, Watford. X2579/B.

PIMM, W. J., Private, 1st Hertfordshire Regiment and Royal Defence Corps.
He volunteered in May 1915, and on completion of his training served at various stations on important work with his unit. He was over age for service overseas, and was later transferred to the Royal Defence Corps, and rendered valuable services whilst guarding prisoners of war at different detention camps. He was demobilised in April 1919.
27, Watford Fields, Watford. X2579/A.

PINE, W. H. T., Private, R.A.M.C.
Joining the Forces in 1916, he embarked for the Western Front later in the same year. Here he served as hospital orderly, attending the sick and wounded troops, on a hospital train, and later at various Casualty Clearing Stations, and also at Base Hospitals. After the signing of the Armistice he returned to England and was demobilised in March 1920, and holds the General Service and Victory Medals.
70, Harwood Road, Watford. X2580.

PING, F. G., Rifleman, 11th Rifle Brigade.
He joined in May 1918, and shortly afterwards proceeded to France, where he took part in the fighting in the later stages of the German Offensive and in the subsequent Allied Advance. He was in action at the Battles of Cambrai, Albert, and on the Somme, and on the cessation of hostilities was sent into Germany with the Army of Occupation and stationed at Coblenz. He was demobilised in December 1919, and holds the General Service and Victory Medals.
27, Leighton Street, Woburn. Z2581.

PINNEY, J., Private, R.A.S.C.
Volunteering in August 1914, he was sent overseas in the same month. Whilst in France he was engaged on important duties in connection with the transport of ammunition and supplies to the front lines. He was constantly under fire in the fighting in the Retreat from Mons, and in the advanced areas of the Ypres salient, Arras, the Somme, and Cambrai, and during the Retreat and Advance of 1918. Returning to England in January 1919, he was demobilised in the following month, and holds the Mons Star, and the General Service and Victory Medals.
50, Portland Street, St. Albans. 2582.

PINNEY, W., Private, Bedfordshire Regiment.
He volunteered in August 1914, and in the following March sailed for Egypt. In this theatre of war he was engaged in the heavy fighting in the advance through Sinai, Palestine and Syria. He fought at the Battle of Gaza, where he was wounded, and in the operations prior to the capture of Jerusalem. Returning to England he was demobilised in June 1919, and holds the 1914-15 Star, and the General Service and Victory Medals.
Upper Sundon, Dunstable. 2583.

PINNOCK, A. F., 1st Air Mechanic, R.A.F.
He joined in January 1917, and on completion of his training served at various aerodromes on important duties connected with the fitting and testing of aero engines. Unable to obtain his transfer overseas, he rendered valuable services until his demobilisation in March 1920.
42, Prospect Road, St. Albans. X2584/B.

PINNOCK, C. S., 3rd Worcestershire Regiment.
He volunteered in August 1914, and in the same month was sent to France, where he fought in the Retreat from Mons and in the engagement at Ypres. He was unfortunately killed in action on October 24th, 1914 whilst heavy fighting was in progress, and was entitled to the Mons Star, and the General Service and Victory Medals.
13, College Place, St. Albans. 2585.

PINNOCK, L. D., Sapper, Royal Engineers.
Joining in September 1917, he completed his training and was stationed at various depôts with his unit. Engaged on important duties in connection with the construction of railways and work in the docks, he rendered valuable services. Owing to medical unfitness he was unable to obtain his transfer overseas, and was demobilised in March 1920.
42, Prospect Road, St. Albans.   X2584/A.

PINNOCK, P. G., Sergeant, R.F.A.
Volunteering in April 1915, he was drafted to France in the succeeding year, and served with his battery in many engagements, including those at Ypres, Cambrai, Festubert, Loos, Vimy Ridge, the Somme, and during the Retreat and Advance of 1918. Returning to England, he was demobilised in December 1918, and holds the General Service and Victory Medals.
46, Highbury Road, Luton.   2586.

PINOCK, P. J., 2nd Class Stoker, Royal Navy.
He joined the service on August 4th, 1914, and was posted to H.M.S. "Amphion." His ship was attached to the North Sea Patrol, and he was unfortunately drowned on August 6th of the same year, when his ship was sunk by a mine off Gt. Yarmouth. He was entitled to the 1914-15 Star, and the General Service and Victory Medals.
29, Boyle Street, Luton.   2587.

PIPKIN, F., Gunner, R.G.A.
Joining in July 1916, he was drafted overseas in April of the following year. He served in many sectors of the Western Front with his battery, and was wounded in action at Arras, and later at Ypres, and fought throughout the Retreat and Advance of 1918. He was demobilised in December of the same year, and holds the General Service and Victory Medals.
22, Russel Rise, Luton.   2588.

PIPKIN, J., Driver, R.F.A.
He volunteered in December 1915, and was sent to the Western Front in the following year, and fought in the Battles of the Somme, Ypres, Arras, Cambrai, St. Quentin and during the German Offensive and subsequent Allied Advance of 1918. On return to England he was demobilised in April 1919, and holds the General Service and Victory Medals.
41, Oak Road, Luton.   2589.

PIPKIN, J., Private, 3rd Northamptonshire Regt.
Joining in July 1917, he embarked for France in June of the following year, and was engaged at many battles during the Retreat and Advance of 1918, including those at the Somme, the Marne, and Cambrai, where he was wounded in September 1918. Invalided to England, he received hospital treatment and was demobilised in March 1919, and holds the General Service and Victory Medals.
St. Giles Yard, Eaton Bray, Dunstable.   2590.

PITCHER, W., Seaman, Merchant Service.
He was in the Merchant Service prior to the outbreak of hostilities, and throughout the war served on the "Panama," which ship was engaged in transporting troops to various theatres of war. During his period of service his ship was present at the Evacuation of the Gallipoli Peninsula, and frequently passed through mine infested waters and areas where the U-boat menace was particularly active. He holds the General Service and Merchant Marine War Medals, and in 1920 was serving in the Merchant Service.
20, Dale Road, Luton.   2592.

PITKIN, E., Driver, R.A.S.C.
He joined in 1916, and embarked for France later in the same year, and served in the advanced areas of Ypres, Cambrai, and on the Somme, and in many other sectors. He was engaged on important duties connected with the transport of ammunition and supplies and was constantly under heavy fire during the German Offensive and subsequent Allied Advance of 1918. He was demobilised in January 1919, and holds the General Service and Victory Medals.
27, Oxhey Street, Oxhey.   X2593/B.

PITKIN, G. C., Gunner, R.F.A.
Volunteering in August 1914, he proceeded to the Western Front in the following November and was in action at the Battles of Ypres, Hill 60, Messines, Passchendaele, Arras, Cambrai, the Somme, and in the Retreat and Advance of 1918. He returned to England after the signing of the Armistice and was demobilised in January 1919, and holds the 1914 Star, and the General Service and Victory Medals.
27, Oxhey Street, Oxhey.   X2593/A.

PITTS, W. J., Rifleman, 5th Rifle Brigade.
He joined in April 1917, and proceeded to the Western Front later in the same year. In this theatre of war he was engaged in heavy fighting and fought at the Battles of the Somme, St. Quentin, and during the Retreat and Advance of 1918, and was wounded. He was demobilised in 1919, and holds the General Service and Victory Medals.
Midland Cottage, Ickleford, Hitchin.   2594.

PLANT, G., Corporal, Sherwood Foresters.
Volunteering in August 1914, he was almost immediately drafted to France and was in action in the Retreat from Mons, and at the Battles of Ypres, Cambrai, Passchendaele, and in many other sectors where heavy fighting was in progress, and was twice wounded and gassed. Returning to England he was demobilised in February 1919, and holds the Mons Star, and the General Service and Victory Medals.
12, New Road, Watford.   X2595.

PLATER, C. B., Private, 2nd Queen's (Royal West Surrey Regiment).
He joined in November 1916, and was later drafted to France. He fought on the Western Front in many engagements, and in December 1917 was sent to Italy. In this theatre of war he took part in the fighting on the Piave, where he was killed in action on October 29th, 1918. He was entitled to the General Service and Victory Medals.
27, Newcombe Road, Luton.   3516/B.

PLATER, W. F., Private, 12th Norfolk Regt.
He volunteered in January 1916, and was sent to Ireland on important duties until drafted to France in 1917. During his service on the Western Front he was twice wounded, gassed and buried alive by the explosion of a shell. He was invalided home in September 1918, and on recovery served in England until demobilised in September 1919. He holds the General Service and Victory Medals.
27, Newcombe Road, Luton.   3516/A.

PLATT, J., Sapper, Royal Engineers.
He volunteered in August 1914, and proceeded overseas in the following year. He served in the front lines in many parts of the Western Front, engaged on important constructional duties, and was present at the Battles of the Somme, Cambrai, Arras and Ypres. He was demobilised in March 1919, and holds the 1914-15 Star, and the General Service and Victory Medals.
Strand, Clophill, Ampthill.   2596.

PLEASANTS, R., Pte., 2nd Bedfordshire Regt.
He volunteered in December 1914, and was sent to France in the following April. Here he saw much active service and fought in the Battles of Ypres, the Somme, Arras, and Cambrai, where he was taken prisoner. He was held in captivity until after the Armistice, and was then repatriated and subsequently demobilised in February 1919, and holds the 1914-15 Star, and the General Service and Victory Medals.
36, Denmark Street, Watford.   X2597.

PLESTER, J. G., Private, R.M.L.I.
Volunteering in 1915, he was sent to the Western Front in June of the same year, and took part in many engagements, including those at Festubert, Loos, the Somme, the Ancre, Ypres and Cambrai. Owing to ill-health, he returned to England and after receiving hospital treatment was invalided out of the Service in January 1918. He holds the 1914-15 Star, and the General Service and Victory Medals.
74, New Town Street, Luton.   2598.

PLUCK, W. J., Private, Essex Regiment and South Staffordshire Regiment.
He joined in 1916, and on completion of his training proceeded to France, where he was in action in many parts of this theatre of war. He was unfortunately killed in action at Messines Ridge on April 26th, 1918, during the German offensive. He was entitled to the General Service and Victory Medals.
4, Rushby Mead, Letchworth.   2599.

PLUMB, A. R., Driver, R.A.S.C.
He volunteered in October 1914, and embarked for France in the following year and served in the Ypres salient until 1917 on important duties connected with the transport of ammunition and supplies and was constantly under fire. He was then transferred to Italy and was stationed at Taranto on similar duties until 1919. He was mentioned in Despatches for consistent good work and devotion to duty in the Field. Returning to England he was demobilised in March 1919, and holds the 1914-15 Star, and the General Service and Victory Medals.
"Frambesa," Symington Street, Harpenden.   2601.

PLUM, W., Private, Essex Regiment.
Volunteering in June 1915, he was drafted overseas in the following year, and during his service on the Western Front fought in many of the principal engagements, including those at Ypres, Arras, the Somme, Cambrai and in the second Battle of the Marne, during the Retreat of 1918. He was demobilised in 1919, and holds the General Service and Victory Medals.
19, Cherry Bounce, Hemel Hempstead. 2600.

PLUMLEY, J. O., Private, Labour Corps.
Volunteering in June 1915, he completed his training and served with his unit at various stations on important duties. He was transferred to the Labour Corps on its formation and rendered valuable services. Unfit for general service he was unable to obtain his transfer overseas and was discharged in October 1918.
10, Birds Hill, Letchworth. 2602.

PLUMMER, E., Private, Bedfordshire Regiment.
He volunteered in November 1915, and later proceeded to the Western Front. Here he saw a considerable amount of fighting in many sectors and was wounded at the Battle of Arras, and later at the Battle of the Somme. He was demobilised in January 1919, and holds the General Service and Victory Medals.
31, Milton Road, Luton. 2603.

POCOCK, B. J. J., Armourer's Crew, Royal Navy.
He joined in May 1918, and was stationed at Chatham aboard H.M.S. "Pembroke." He was engaged on important duties with his ship and did excellent work until after the cessation of hostilities. He was demobilised in January 1919.
36, Kimpton Road, Luton. 2605.

POCOCK, H., Sergeant, 1st Hertfordshire Regt.
He volunteered at the outbreak of war and in November 1914 was drafted overseas. Whilst on the Western Front he was engaged in the fighting at Ypres, Arras, on the Somme, and in the Retreat and Advance at Cambrai in 1918. He returned to England after the cessation of hostilities and was demobilised in February 1919. He holds the 1914 Star, and the General Service and Victory Medals.
68, Albert Street, St. Albans. X2606.

POCOCK, W. H., Sergeant, 1st Somerset Light Infantry.
He was serving at the outbreak of war and was sent at once to France. He served in the fierce fighting in the Retreat from Mons, and at the Battle of Hill 60, and was badly wounded. He was invalided home and subsequently discharged as medically unfit for further service in December 1915. He holds the Mons Star, and the General Service and Victory Medals.
30, Milton Road, Luton. 2607.

POINTER, W. A. E., Boy 1st Class, Royal Navy.
He volunteered in June 1915, and was posted to H.M.S. "Ganges," which vessel was engaged on important patrol duties in the North Sea, and off the East Coast, until after the signing of the Armistice. He was demobilised in February 1919, and holds the General Service and Victory Medals.
8, Sussex Road, Watford. X5010/D, X5011/D.

POLLARD, A., Pte., 1/5th Bedfordshire Regt.
He volunteered in September 1914, and in the following July was drafted to the Dardanelles. He fought at the landing at Suvla Bay, and was wounded. On recovery he rejoined his battalion and proceeded to Palestine and was in action during the operations in the British advance and was again wounded. He returned to England after the cessation of hostilities and was demobilised in September 1919. He holds the 1914-15 Star, and the General Service and Victory Medals.
44, Jubilee Street, Luton. 2608.

POLLARD, C., Private, Oxfordshire and Buckinghamshire Light Infantry.
He joined in October 1916, and in the following March proceeded overseas. During his service on the Western Front he was in action at Arras, on the Somme, and in other sectors and was taken seriously ill. He was invalided home and subsequently discharged as medically unfit for further service in July 1918. He holds the General Service and Victory Medals.
High Street, Wing, Bucks. 2609/B.

POLLARD, E., Sergeant-Farrier, Royal Buckinghamshire Hussars.
He volunteered at the outbreak of war and in March 1915 proceeded to Egypt. He was engaged on special duties whilst operations were in progress and was constantly under heavy shell fire. He was killed in action at Gaza in August 1917, and was entitled to the 1914-15 Star, and the General Service and Victory Medals.
High Street, Wing, near Leighton Buzzard. 2609/A.

POLLARD, J. W., Private, Essex Regiment.
He volunteered in January 1916, and was later drafted to France. Whilst in this theatre of war he was in action at Arras, Passchendaele and Cambrai, and was wounded. He returned to England after the signing of the Armistice, and was demobilised in February 1919. He holds the General Service and Victory Medals.
Gray Cottage, Garston Lane, Leavesden.
X2610/C, X2611/C.

POLLARD, W., Private, Oxfordshire and Buckinghamshire Light Infantry.
He volunteered in December 1914, and in the following month proceeded to France. He served in many engagements on the Western Front, including those at Hill 60, Ypres, Vimy Ridge, Arras, on the Somme, and at Cambrai, and in 1916 was transferred to Italy, where he was in action on the Piave front, and during his service overseas was three times wounded. He was demobilised in May 1919, and holds the 1914-15 Star, and the General Service and Victory Medals.
Lily Crescent, Leighton Road, Wing, Bucks. 2612/A.

POOLEY, A. E., Air Mechanic, R.A.F.
He joined in 1916, and in November of the same year was drafted to Italy. In this theatre of war he was engaged on important duties with his squadron, and was in the forward areas whilst operations were in progress on the Piave and Trentino. He was demobilised in May 1919, and holds the General Service and Victory Medals.
9, Cassiobridge Road, Watford. X2613.

POPE, C., Stoker, Royal Navy.
He was serving at the outbreak of war aboard H.M.S. "Barham," which vessel was engaged in the fighting at the Battle of Jutland and the naval operations at Zeebrugge and the Dardanelles, and he was wounded. He holds the 1914-15 Star, and the General Service and Victory Medals, and was still serving in 1920.
47, Herkomer Road, Bushey. X2615/B.

POPE, E. C., Private, R.A.M.C.
He volunteered in 1914, and in the following year proceeded to France, where he served for a time and was later transferred to Salonika. Whilst on the Macedonian front he was engaged with his unit on various duties, and was constantly in the front lines attending to the sick and wounded. He suffered from malaria, was wounded, and, invalided home, was subsequently discharged in September 1919. He holds the 1914-15 Star, and the General Service and Victory Medals.
19, St. John Street, Biggleswade. Z2614.

POPE, J., Officer's Cook, Royal Navy.
He was serving at the outbreak of war in H.M.S. "Carysfort." His ship was engaged off the coasts of France and Russia, in the North Sea, and the Dardanelles, on important patrol duties, and in chasing submarines. He was still serving in 1920, and holds the 1914-15 Star, and the General Service and Victory Medals.
47, Herkomer Road, Bushey. X2615/A.

PORTER, C., Gunner, R.F.A., and Private, Bedfordshire Regiment.
He volunteered in October 1915, and in the following May proceeded overseas. He fought in many engagements on the Western Front, including those at Ypres, Arras, Passchendaele, and owing to ill-health was sent home. After receiving hospital treatment he was later discharged as medically unfit for further service in May 1917. He holds the General Service and Victory Medals.
123, Marlowes, Hemel Hempstead. X2616.

PORTER, G., Sapper, Royal Engineers.
He joined in January 1917, and in the following month proceeded overseas. Whilst in France he was engaged on special road constructing duties, and was frequently in the forward areas whilst operations were in progress, in the Ypres, Somme and Cambrai sectors. He was demobilised in October 1919, and holds the General Service and Victory Medals.
The Grove, Woodside, near Luton. 2852/B.

PORTER, H. W., C.S.M., R.A.S.C. (M.T.).
He volunteered in August 1914, and was immediately drafted overseas. He fought in the Retreat from Mons, and the subsequent Battles at Hill 60, Ypres, Arras, the Somme, Cambrai, and in the final operations during the Allied Advance of 1918. He was demobilised in April 1920, and holds the 1914-15 Star, and the General Service and Victory Medals.
78, Grover Road, Oxhey, Herts. X2617.

POTTER, D. W., Leading Seaman, Royal Navy.
He was serving at the outbreak of war, having enlisted
in January 1911, and aboard H.M.S. "Tralee," was engaged in the operations in the North Sea, and took
part in the fighting at Heligoland Bight and the Battle
of Jutland in May 1916. He was demobilised in March
1920, and holds the 1914-15 Star, and the General Service
and Victory Medals.
5, White Hill, Hitchin, Herts.   2618.

POTTER, E., Corporal, 2nd Rifle Brigade.
A serving soldier, he was immediately drafted to France
at the outbreak of hostilities. He fought in the Retreat
from Mons, the Battle of Ypres, and the subsequent engagements in various sectors of the Western Front until
July 1st, 1916, when he was unfortunately killed in action
at the first Battle of the Somme. He was entitled
to the Mons Star, and the General Service and Victory
Medals.
32, Elfrida Road, Watford.   X2619/A.

**POTTER, E. W. (M.S.M.), Farrier Q.M.S.,
Royal Field Artillery.**
Enlisting in 1896, he served in the South African War
and in August 1914, was stationed with his battery in
India. He was drafted to Gallipoli in 1915, and fought
at the landing on the Peninsula, and many subsequent
engagements, and was wounded, and in consequence lost
the sight of an eye. He was awarded the Meritorious
Service Medal for consistent good work and devotion
to duty in the Field. He also holds the Queen's and
King's South African Medals, the 1914-15 Star, the General Service and Victory Medals, and the Long Service
and Good Conduct Medals. He was discharged in December 1918.
73, Crawley Road, Luton.   2620.

POTTER, G., Sapper, Royal Engineers.
He volunteered in June 1915, and served at various
stations with his unit until drafted to France. Whilst
on the Western Front he was engaged on important duties
in the forward areas whilst operations were in progress
at Ypres, Arras, and many other places. He returned
to England after the cessation of hostilities, and was
demobilised in February 1919. He holds the General
Service and Victory Medals.
17, May Street, Luton.   2621.

POTTER, J., Corporal, Bedfordshire Regiment.
He volunteered at the outbreak of war, and was sent
to France. During his service on the Western Front
he was in action in the Retreat from Mons, the Battles
of Ypres, Cambrai and the Somme. He was killed during
the fierce fighting at Arras on August 28th, 1917, and was
entitled to the Mons Star, and the General Service
and Victory Medals.
32, Elfrida Road, Watford.   X2619/B.

POTTON, A., Private, Bedfordshire Regiment.
He volunteered in 1915, and in the following year was
drafted to France. In this theatre of war he took part
in the fighting at Arras, Ypres, Cambrai, and in the
German Offensive and subsequent Allied Advance of
1918, and was wounded. He was demobilised in 1919,
and holds the General Service and Victory Medals.
Trowley Bottom, Flamstead, Dunstable.   X2622.

POTTON, A. J., Private, Machine Gun Corps.
He volunteered in August 1915, and was sent to France
in the following year. During his service on the Western Front he was engaged in the heavy fighting in various
sectors and took part in many fierce conflicts and was
wounded. He returned to England after the signing of
the Armistice, and was demobilised in March 1919. He
holds the General Service and Victory Medals.
Trowley Bottom, Flamstead, Dunstable.   4444.

POTTON, R. (M.M.), Sergt., Machine Gun Corps.
He joined in August 1916, and in the following February
proceeded overseas. Whilst on the Western Front he was
in action in the fighting at Ypres and Poelcapelle, and
was awarded the Military Medal for conspicuous gallantry and devotion to duty in the Field. He was demobilised in January 1919, and holds the Military Service and Victory Medals.
10, King Street, Markyate.   2623.

POTTON, W. A., Sapper, Royal Engineers.
He volunteered in October 1915, and in the following
year proceeded to Egypt. He was engaged on important duties with his unit in the forward areas whilst
operations were in progress during the British Advance
through Palestine, and was present at the Battles of
Gaza, Haifa and Beyrout. After the signing of the
Armistice he was stationed at Kantara on garrison
duties, and was still serving in 1920. He holds the
General Service and Victory Medals.
New Cottage, High Street, Markyate.   4444/B.

POTTON, W. H., Sergeant, Royal Engineers.
He joined in 1916, and in the same year was sent to
France. Whilst in this theatre of war he was in action
in many sectors, and was present during the fighting
on the Somme, at Arras, Cambrai, and in the final
operations of the war. He was demobilised in February
1919, and holds the General Service and Victory Medals.
54, Alexandra Road, St. Albans.   X/2624.

**POTTS, A. J., Sapper, 2nd Field Company,
Canadian Engineers.**
He volunteered in June 1916 at Toronto, Ontario, and
served with his unit at various stations on important
duties. He did excellent work but owing to medical
unfitness was unable to secure his transfer to a theatre
of war, and was demobilised in May 1919.
Aspley Hill, Woburn Sands.   Z/2625.

POTTS, E. W., Pte., 1/5th Bedfordshire Regt.
He was mobilised at the outbreak of war, and in
August 1915 proceeded to the Dardanelles. He fought
at the landing at Suvla Bay and was wounded, and
during a subsequent engagement on the Peninsula was
again wounded. On recovery he was drafted with his
battalion to France in 1916, and took part in the
fighting on the Somme, and was wounded a third time,
but was able to rejoin his unit and fight at Ypres and
in the Allied Advance of 1918. He returned home after
the signing of the Armistice, and was demobilised in
January 1919. He holds the 1914-15 Star, and the
General Service and Victory Medals.
90, Langley Road, Luton.   2626.

POTTS, S. G., Private, South Wales Borderers.
He volunteered in October 1915, and in the following
January proceeded to Mesopotamia. He took part in
many engagements in this theatre of war, and was
unfortunately killed in action near Kut on January 25th,
1917. He was entitled to the General Service and
Victory Medals.
The Poplars, Toddington, Beds.   2627.

POULSON, C. A., Private, 14th King's Hussars.
Volunteering at the outbreak of war, he was immediately drafted overseas and fought in the Retreat from
Mons and the subsequent engagements until transferred
to the Dardanelles in 1915. He was engaged in the
fighting on the Peninsula for a time, and was later
sent to Mesopotamia, where he served and was in action
at Baghdad. He was demobilised in February 1919,
and holds the Mons Star, and the General Service and
Victory Medals.
68, Church Street, Leighton Buzzard.   4175/C, 4176/C.

POULTER, P. R., Air Mechanic, R.A.F.
He joined in March 1916, and in the same year was
drafted to the Western Front. Engaged on important
duties with his squadron at various aerodromes, he
was often under heavy shell fire, and was in action at
Passchendaele, Cambrai, Albert, and was gassed and
twice wounded. He holds the General Service and
Victory Medals, and was demobilised in February 1919.
10, Napier Road, Luton.   2628.

**POULTON, F., Private, 19th (Queen Alexandra's
Own) Hussars.**
He enlisted in December 1909, and on the declaration
of war was drafted to France in September 1914. He
was in action in many important engagements and was
fighting almost continuously until the termination of the
war, and was wounded. He was discharged on account
of service in February 1919, and holds the 1914 Star,
and the General Service and Victory Medals.
1, Limbury Road, Leagrave, Luton.   2629.

POWELL, E. G., Private, 1st Dorsetshire Regt.
He joined in December 1916, and shortly afterwards
proceeded to the Western Front. In this theatre of
war he served in several sectors, and took part in
heavy fighting in the Battle of Ypres. He was severely
wounded in an engagement near St. Quentin and was
invalided home to hospital, and after hospital treatment
was discharged as medically unfit for further service in
November 1917. He holds the General Service and
Victory Medals.
50, Cobden Street, Luton.   2631.

POWELL, E. R., Gunner, R.F.A.
He volunteered in 1914, and in the following year was
sent overseas. Serving with his battery on the Western
Front he was in action in several important engagements, including the Battles of Arras, Ypres and
Passchendaele. He was wounded and received hospital treatment, and rejoining his battery took part in
the Battles of the Somme and the Marne. Returning
to England on the termination of hostilities, he was
demobilised in September 1919, and holds the 1914-15
Star, and the General Service and Victory Medals.
Wheathampstead Road, Harpenden.   2632.

POWELL, A. S. W., Private, R.A.M.C.

In the Territorials he was mobilised in August 1914, and in the following July was drafted overseas. He saw much service in Gallipoli, taking part in the landing at Suvla Bay, and on the Evacuation of the Peninsula was sent to Egypt in December 1915. Attached to the forces which advanced through Palestine under General Allenby, he did excellent work with the field ambulance and was present at the Battle of Gaza. In July 1918 he was despatched to the Western Front, where he served during the final operations of the war. He was wounded in the course of his service abroad, and was demobilised in January 1919. He holds the 1914-15 Star, and the General Service and Victory Medals.

100, Cambridge Street, Luton. 2630.

POWELL, F., Sapper, Royal Engineers.

Volunteering in August 1914, he was sent to Gallipoli in the following year and served on important duties in the operations there from the landing at Suvla Bay until the Evacuation of the Peninsula. Sent to Egypt in December 1915, he was engaged on special work whilst heavy fighting was in progress in the Sinai desert and in the British Advance through Palestine, and was present at the Battles of Romani, Gaza, Haifa, Acre, at the capture of Beyrout and Aleppo, and was wounded. He was demobilised on returning to England in April 1919, and holds the 1914-15 Star, and the General Service and Victory Medals.

8, Graville Road, Luton. 2633.

POWELL, H. W., Private, 9th Essex Regiment.

He joined in 1916, and in the same year was drafted to France. In this theatre of war he was in action at Ypres, on the Somme, at Cambrai, and in the German Offensive and subsequent Allied Advance of 1918. He was demobilised in 1919, and holds the General Service and Victory Medals.

4, Lower Luton Road, Harpenden. 3599/B.

POWELL, J. T., Pioneer, Royal Engineers.

He joined in March 1917, and in the same year was drafted overseas. Serving with his unit on the Western Front he was engaged on important duties in the forward areas during heavy fighting, and was present at the Battles of Armentières, Passchendaele, Vimy Ridge and Messines. He holds the General Service and Victory Medals, and was demobilised in November 1919.

3, Queen's Road, Harpenden. 5182/B.

POWELL, J. T., Private, Queen's Own (Royal West Kent Regiment).

He attested in November 1915, and was called up for service in April 1917 and was later drafted to India, where he served at various stations on garrison and other duties of an important nature. Returning to England he was stationed in Ireland until demobilised in October 1919, and holds the General Service and Victory Medals.

34, Albert Street, St. Albans. X2634.

POWELL, S. F., Private, Essex Regiment.

He joined in April 1916, and in the following September embarked for the Western Front. There he served with his unit in various sectors, and took part in heavy fighting in the Battles of the Somme, Arras and Cambrai. Severely wounded in an engagement near Cambrai in 1918, he was invalided home to hospital, and subsequently discharged as medically unfit for further service in December 1918. He holds the General Service and Victory Medals.

52, Regent Street, Leighton Buzzard. 2635/B.

POWLEY, J. E., Private, Machine Gun Corps.

He volunteered in September 1914, and served on various duties with his unit at several stations until he proceeded overseas in February 1916. Whilst on the Western Front he fought in many important engagements, including those in the first British Offensive on the Somme, where he was killed in action on November 3rd, 1916. He was entitled to the General Service and Victory Medals.

Mill Cottages, Ickleford, Hitchin. 2636.

PRATT, A. W., Private, 6th Bedfordshire Regt.

He volunteered in February 1916, and in July of the same year was sent to France. He was engaged in fierce fighting on the Somme, at Beaumont-Hamel and Vimy Ridge and was wounded near Arras in April 1917. Rejoining his unit he took part in several engagements and was very severely wounded in the Ypres sector on December 16th, 1917, and consequently both his legs had to be amputated. He was sent to England in the following March and invalided out of the Service in May 1919. He holds the General Service and Victory Medals.

King Street, Potton. Z1281/A, Z1282/A.

PRATT, A. W., Private, R.A.S.C., and Sapper, Royal Engineers.

Volunteering in February 1915, in the same year he embarked for Gallipoli, and served there from the landing at Suvla Bay until the Evacuation of the Peninsula. He was then drafted to Egypt and was engaged on important duties during General Allenby's advance through Palestine, and was present at the Battle of Gaza. He returned to England for demobilisation in June 1919, and holds the 1914-15 Star, and the General Service and Victory Medals.

20, Stanmore Road, Watford. X2637.

PRATT, C., Driver, Royal Engineers.

He volunteered in April 1915, and was later drafted to Egypt, where he served with his unit in the front lines, and was present at the Battles of Gaza. He served in the British advance through Palestine and Syria, and was unfortunately killed in action in the vicinity of Damascus on October 14th, 1918. He was entitled to the General Service and Victory Medals.

103, High Street, Luton. 63/D, 64/D.

PRATT, E., Private, 4th Bedfordshire Regiment.

Volunteering in August 1914, in the following month he was sent to France. Severely wounded during the Battle of La Bassée in October of the same year, he was invalided home. He returned to the Western Front in January 1915, and was in action in several important engagements until again sent to England on account of wounds received at Zillebeke in 1916. Rejoining his unit in December he was wounded a third time in the course of severe fighting in 1917, and was sent home for hospital treatment. In the following year he was again engaged in France during the final operations of the war. He was demobilised in February 1919, and holds the 1914-15 Star, and the General Service and Victory Medals.

19, Husbourne Crawley, Aspley Guise Z2643/B.

PRATT, E., A.B., Royal Navy.

He was serving in the Royal Navy when war was declared and was engaged on patrol duties in the North Sea aboard H.M.S. "Idaho." Later his ship was employed in the Irish Sea on mine sweeping and other duties, and was twice torpedoed. He holds the General Service and Victory Medals, and was discharged on September 25th, 1919.

49, Dordans Road, Leagrave. 2641/B, 2642/B.

PRATT, E. G., Private, East Surrey Regiment.

He joined in 1917, and on the conclusion of his training was engaged at various stations on important duties with his unit. He rendered valuable services but was unsuccessful in obtaining a transfer overseas before the cessation of hostilities, and was demobilised in March 1919.

Warden View, Letchworth Road, Limbury, Luton. 2640.

PRATT, F., Private, Bedfordshire Regiment.

He volunteered in September 1914, and after training was engaged on various duties at the depôt of his unit. He was not sent overseas owing to medical unfitness, and was discharged in consequence in November 1914.

42, Mill Road, Leighton Buzzard. 2644.

PRATT, F. J., Air Mechanic, R.A.F. (late R.N.A.S.).

He joined in December 1916, and after training was drafted overseas. Serving with his squadron in Italy, he was engaged on special duties at various aerodromes and did excellent work. He was afterwards stationed at Malta, and returned to England for demobilisation in January 1919. He holds the General Service and Victory Medals.

2, Pretoria Road, Watford. X2638.

PRATT, G., Sergeant, Rifle Brigade.

He was serving in the Army when war broke out and almost immediately proceeded to France. There he took part in the Retreat from Mons and in the Battle of Ypres. Severely wounded at Armentières he was invalided home, and after receiving hospital treatment was subsequently discharged as medically unfit for further service in February 1916, and holds the Mons Star, and the General Service and Victory Medals.

4, England Lane, Dunstable. 2645.

PRATT, H., Gunner, Royal Field Artillery.

He volunteered in April 1915, and in the following October was sent to the Western Front. He was wounded in the Battle of the Somme in 1916, and on recovery returned to the front line and fought in several important engagements, including those of Arras, Ypres and Cambrai. On the termination of hostilities he went with the Army of Occupation into Germany and was stationed at Cologne. He returned to England for demobilisation in December 1919, and holds the 1914-15 Star, and the General Service and Victory Medals.

41, Great Northern Road, Dunstable. 2646.

PRATT, G., Private, 3rd Norfolk Regiment.
Volunteering in December 1915, on the completion of
his training he was employed on important guard duties
with his regiment and rendered valuable services. He
was not sent to a theatre of war on account of ill-health,
and was invalided out of the service in June 1916.
King Street, Potton.   Z1281/B, Z1282/B.

PRATT, G. C., Private, 26th Royal Fusiliers.
He joined in December 1916, and in the following year
embarked for France. He served in various sectors of
the Western Front and took part in many important
engagements, including the Battles of Ypres, Arras,
Messines Ridge and Cambrai, and was twice wounded.
On the termination of hostilities he returned to England for demobilisation in February 1919, and holds the
General Service and Victory Medals.
63, The Green, Silsoe.   2639/A.

PRATT, H., Private, Bedfordshire Regiment.
Joining in February 1917, he was drafted overseas in
the following December, and was engaged in severe
fighting in the Arras sector. He took part in the Battles
of Cambrai, the Somme, Ypres, and in other important
actions until the close of the war, and was demobilised
in February 1919. Rejoining the Army for a further
period of service in May of the same year, he was
drafted to India, where he was still serving in 1920. He
holds the General Service and Victory Medals.
19, Husbourne Crawley, Aspley Guise.   Z2643/C.

PRATT, H. G. M., Private, R.M.L.I.
He joined in July 1917, and in the following October
was posted to H.M.S. "Dublin," which vessel was engaged in the blockade of Russia for several months.
In February 1919 he was sent into Turkey with the
Army of Occupation and was engaged on important
duties at Constantinople. He was still serving in 1920,
and holds the General Service and Victory Medals.
49, Dordans Road, Leagrave.   2641/A, 2642/A.

**PRATT, J., Private, Queen's (Royal West
Surrey Regiment.).**
He joined in June 1916, and in the following September
was drafted to France. Serving with his unit in several
sectors he took part in many important engagements,
including the first Battle of the Somme. He was killed
in action near Beaumont Hamel in January 1917, and
was entitled to the General Service and Victory Medals.
71, Victoria Street, Dunstable.   2647/B.

**PRATT, J. W., Rifleman, King's Royal Rifle
Corps.**
He joined in October 1916, and after training was engaged with his unit on important duties at various
stations. He did excellent work but was not sent overseas
owing to medical unfitness, and was discharged in consequence in June 1917.
63, The Green, Silsoe.   2639/B.

PRATT, M. E. (Miss), Special War Worker.
During the war this lady volunteered for work of National
importance, and was employed at a large aeroplane
factory at Leagrave. where she was engaged in making
aeroplane wings, from June 1916 until December 1918.
Throughout the period of her service she rendered
valuable services.
63, The Green, Silsoe.   2639/C.

PRATT, R., 1st Class Air Mechanic, R.A.F.
He volunteered in September 1914, and in the following
January was sent to the Western Front. Stationed at
Rouen, Boulogne, Calais, and other aerodromes, he was
engaged on important duties in connection with the
fitting and testing of aero engines. He was demobilised
in March 1919, and holds the 1914-15 Star, and the
General Service and Victory Medals.
31, Plantation Road, Leighton Buzzard.   2649.

**PRATT, R., Trooper, Royal Buckinghamshire
Hussars.**
He volunteered in August 1914, and in the same year
was drafted overseas. He saw much service on the
Western Front and was in action at the Battles of Ypres,
Arras, Cambrai, and other important engagements. He
was killed in action in 1917, and holds the 1914 Star,
and the General Service and Victory Medals.
41, Puller Road, Boxmoor.   X2648.

PRATT, S. H., Corporal, Bedfordshire Lancers.
He volunteered in August 1914, and in the following
month was drafted overseas. He served with his unit
in several sectors of the Western Front, and was engaged in many notable actions, including the Battles
of the Somme, Arras, Ypres, and Cambrai. Owing to
ill-health he returned to England and was invalided
out of the Service in March 1916, and holds the 1914-15
Star, and the General Service and Victory Medals.
61, Plantation Road, Leighton Buzzard.   2651.

PRATT, R., Driver, Royal Field Artillery.
He joined in June 1917, on attaining military age, and
served at various stations on important duties with
his battery. He did excellent work, but was unable to
secure a transfer to a theatre of war before hostilities
ceased, and was still serving in 1920.
52, St. Andrew's Street, Leighton Buzzard.   3645/B.

PRATT, S., Private, 7th Bedfordshire Regiment.
He joined in May 1916, and was sent to France in the
following October and fought in many parts of the
Western Front. He was engaged in the fighting during
the Battles of the Somme and Ypres, and was killed in
action at Mametz on July 1st, 1917. He was entitled to
the General Service and Victory Medals.
43, Astley Road, Hemel Hempstead.   X2650.

PRATT, V. W., Private, 2nd Bedfordshire Regt.
Volunteering in December 1914, he was sent to the Western Front in the following March, and saw much service
in various sectors. He was in action at the Battles of
Loos, the Somme, Béthune, Arras, Ypres, Cambrai, and in
other notable actions, until the close of the war. He was
demobilised in February 1919, and holds the 1914-15 Star,
and the General Service and Victory Medals.
"Peace Cottage," Plantation Road, Leighton Buzzard.
                                                   2652.

PRATT, W., Private, 4th Bedfordshire Regt.
He volunteered in April 1915, and in the following year
proceeded to France and fought on the Somme, and was
wounded on March 2nd, 1916. On recovery he returned
to the front lines and was again wounded in action
on the Ancre, losing the sight of an eye. He was taken
prisoner on February 11th, 1917, and held in captivity
until after the signing of the Armistice. He then returned to England and was demobilised in April 1919,
and holds the 1914-15 Star, and the General Service and
Victory Medals.
71, Waterlow Road, Dunstable.   2653.

PRATT, W., Private, 6th Northamptonshire Regt.
He joined in May 1916, and in September of the same
year was drafted to France. There he saw much service in many sectors and was in action in many important
engagements, including the Battles of the Somme and
Ypres. He was severely wounded on August 8th, 1917,
at Ypres and invalided home to hospital. He was discharged in December 1918 as medically unfit for further
service, and holds the General Service and Victory
Medals.
46, Bunyan Road, Hitchin.   2654.

**PRATT, W. (M.M.), Corporal, 1/5th Bedford-
shire Regiment.**
He volunteered in September 1914, and in the following
year was serving with his unit in France. He was in
action in several important actions and was severely
wounded at Festubert. Invalided to hospital he returned
to his regiment and was sent to Egypt in 1916, and
during General Allenby's advance through Palestine
took part in the Battles of Gaza, Jaffa, and Haifa. He
was awarded the Military Medal for gallantry in the
Field and devotion to duty, and in addition holds the
1914-15 Star, and the General Service and Victory
Medals. He was demobilised in June 1919.
19, Husbourne Crawley, Aspley Guise.   Z2643/A.

PREBBLE, E., Private, Royal Irish Fusiliers.
He volunteered in September 1914, and in the following
July was drafted to the Dardanelles. He was engaged
in the fighting at the landing at Suvla Bay and many
subsequent engagements until transferred to Salonika in
October 1915. He was in action at Monastir, where in
December of the same year he was reported missing,
and later presumed to have been unfortunately killed on
that date. He was entitled to the 1914-15 Star, and the
General Service and Victory Medals.
29, Ashton Road, Luton.   T3831/B.

PREECE, A. C., Private, East Surrey Regiment.
Volunteering in January 1915, on completion of his
training he was stationed at various depôts with his
unit on guard and other important duties. Owing to
medical unfitness he was unable to obtain his transfer
overseas prior to the cessation of hostilities, and after
several months in hospital was discharged in March 1919.
21, Queen Street, St. Albans.   2655.

PREECE, S. J., Private, R.M.L.I.
A serving soldier, he was mobilised and drafted to
France on the outbreak of hostilities. He fought in the
Retreat from Mons and at the Battles of Ypres, Arras,
the Somme and many others. He was wounded in
March 1918 during the German Offensive, and returned
to England. After receiving hospital treatment he was
invalided out of the service in November 1918, and holds
the Mons Star, and the General Service and Victory
Medals.
Summer Cottages, Waterside, London Colney. X3866/B.

PREIS, A. E., Private, 3rd Queen's (Royal West Surrey Regiment).

He volunteered in 1915, and in the same year proceeded to France. Here he was in action in many important engagements, including those in the vicinity of Ypres. Transferred to Italy in 1916 he served throughout the campaign in this theatre of war. He returned to England and was demobilised in February 1919, and holds the 1914-15 Star, and the General Service and Victory Medals.
95, Fearnley Street, Watford. X2656.

PRESSLAND, A. F., Private, Bedfordshire Regt.

Volunteering in September 1914, he was drafted to the Western Front in January 1917, and was almost continuously in action until the following April, when he was invalided to England owing to ill-health. On recovery he was again sent to France in January 1918 and fought in many engagements during the German Offensive, and was wounded in April at Ypres. After receiving hospital treatment he was discharged on account of his wounds in April 1919, and holds the General Service and Victory Medals.
Hall End, Maulden, Ampthill. 2657.

PRICE, C. A., Driver, R.A.S.C. (H.T.)

He joined in April 1918, and on conclusion of his training served at various stations with his unit on important transport and other duties. Medically unfit, he was unable to obtain his transfer to any theatre of war prior to the cessation of hostilities, but did good work and continued his service until December 1919 when he was demobilised.
14, Kimpton Road, Luton. 2658.

PRICE, H., L/Corporal, Royal Engineers.

A serving soldier, he was drafted to the Western Front at the outbreak of war, and served throughout the heavy fighting during the Retreat from Mons and in the subsequent Battle of Ypres. In 1915 he was transferred to the Macedonian front, and there was engaged on important duties connected with pontooning, and wiring and entrenching the forward areas on the Vardar and Struma fronts. Returning to England he was demobilised in March 1919, and holds the Mons Star, and the General Service and Victory Medals.
77, High Street, Houghton Regis. 2659.

PRICE, J., Private, 1/5th Bedfordshire Regiment.

Volunteering in June 1915, he proceeded to Egypt in November of the same year. Here he saw considerable service on the Palestine front, fighting at the Battles of Gaza, and in the operations prior to the capture of Jerusalem and in the Jordan Valley. He returned to England and was demobilised in April 1919, and holds the 1914-15 Star, and the General Service and Victory Medals.
85, Sun Street, Biggleswade. Z2660.

PRICKETT, A. C., A.B., Royal Navy.

He joined the service in August 1914, and was posted to H.M.S. "Yarmouth." His ship was engaged at the Battles of the Falkland Islands and Jutland, and served in many waters on important patrol and scouting duties. He was discharged in July 1919, and holds the 1914-15 Star, and the General Service and Victory Medals.
94, Regent Street, North Watford. X2661/C.

PRICKETT, C., Private, Oxfordshire and Buckinghamshire Light Infantry.

He volunteered in August 1914, and embarked for India in the following year. Here he served at various garrison towns on important duties with his regiment until 1919, when he returned to England and was demobilised in November of that year. He holds the General Service and Victory Medals.
94, Regent Street, North Watford. X2661/A.

PRICKETT, H. H., Sapper, R.E. (R.O.D.).

Joining in 1917, he embarked for France later in the same year, and there experienced much fighting on all parts of the Western Front. He was engaged on important constructional work in many advanced areas and rendered excellent services throughout. He was demobilised in September 1919, and holds the General Service and Victory Medals.
29, Hatfield Road, Watford. X2662.

PRICKETT, R., Private, Royal Marines.

He volunteered in August 1914, and was posted to one of the ships then engaged on the Irish Sea patrol. In these waters he was engaged on important duties, his ship frequently passing through mine-infested areas. He was unfortunately drowned in April 1915, and was entitled to the 1914-15 Star, and the General Service and Victory Medals.
94, Regent Street, North Watford. X2661/B.

PRIME, S., Sergeant, Royal Engineers.

Volunteering in August 1914, he proceeded to the Western Front two months later, and served in various advanced areas until March 1915, when he was wounded at Ypres. On recovery he was drafted to Egypt in January of the following year and served on the Sinai front, and was again wounded in July 1916 at Katia. He was invalided to England in December of the same year, and returned to France in June 1917, and was present at important engagements. He was sent back to England in January 1918, where he remained until demobilised in February 1919, but re-enlisted in the same regiment in April, and served until discharged on account of service in May 1920. He holds the 1914 Star, and the General Service and Victory Medals.
30, Smart Street, Luton. 2663.

PRIMETT, C., Private, 2nd Bedfordshire Regt.

A Reservist, he was mobilised at the declaration of war, and sent to France in September 1914. Here he fought at the Battles of La Bassée, Ypres, Hill 60 and Loos. He was killed in action on the Somme on October 12th, 1916, and was entitled to the 1914 Star, and the General Service and Victory Medals.
18, Spencer Road, Luton. 2664/A.

PRIMETT, F., Corporal, 8th Bedfordshire Regt.

A Territorial, he was mobilised in August 1914, and in the following month proceeded to France, where he was engaged in heavy fighting and fought at the Battles of Ypres, Neuve Chapelle, Hill 60 and Festubert. He was unfortunately killed in action on the Somme in 1916, and was entitled to the 1914 Star, and the General Service and Victory Medals.
18, Spencer Road, Luton. 2664/B.

PRIMETT, H. T., Gunner (Signaller), R.F.A.

He volunteered in November 1915, and later in the same year proceeded to the Western Front, and fought at the Battles of Festubert, Loos, Albert, the Somme, Ypres, Cambrai and Vimy Ridge, and was gassed in 1917. Later, transferred to Mesopotamia, he was in action in the concluding operations of the campaign in this theatre of war. He returned to England and was demobilised in April 1919, and holds the 1914-15 Star, and the General Service and Victory Medals.
2, Tilehouse Street, Hitchin. 2665.

PRIMMETT, H., Private, Bedfordshire Regiment.

Joining in May 1918, on completing his training he served with his unit at various stations on important guard and other duties. He rendered valuable services but was unable to obtain his transfer overseas before the cessation of hostilities, and was demobilised in April 1919.
Vine Cottages, Ickleford, Hitchin. 2666.

PRINCE, W. G., Rifleman, 15th London Regiment (Civil Service Rifles).

He joined in February 1917, and proceeded to France in the following July, and was almost continuously in action in sectors where heavy fighting was in progress. He was unfortunately killed in action at Passchendaele on September 9th, 1917, and was entitled to the General Service and Victory Medals.
6, St. Mary's Road, Watford. X2667.

PRITTY, C., Sapper, Royal Engineers.

On attaining military age he joined in May 1918, and at the conclusion of his training served with his unit at many stations on important constructional work. He was unsuccessful in obtaining his transfer overseas before the Armistice was signed, and was demobilised in January 1919.
Laburnum Villa, King Street, Dunstable. 2668.

PROCTER, J. A., Private, Suffolk Regiment.

He joined in July 1917, and after his training was stationed with his battalion at various depôts on guard and other important duties. He did good work, but unfortunately died on November 7th of the same year from illness contracted whilst on service.
13, Mill Road, Leighton Buzzard. 2672/A.

PROCTER, J. A., Driver, R.A.S.C.

He volunteered in June 1915, and on the conclusion of his training served at various stations on important transport duties with his unit. Too old for active service he did good work, but was unable to obtain his transfer overseas, and was demobilised in March 1919.
13, Mill Road, Leighton Buzzard. 2672/B.

PROCTER, W. T., Private, Suffolk Regiment.

He joined in April 1919, and was stationed at various depôts after a course of training, and was engaged on guard and other important duties. Medically unfit, he was unable to obtain his transfer abroad to the Armies of Occupation, and was demobilised in March 1920.
13, Mill Road, Leighton Buzzard. 2672/C.

PROCTOR, A., Private, 8th Northumberland Fusiliers.
Joining in June 1917, he was drafted to France later in the same year, and fought in many of the principal engagements and in various parts of the Western Front. He was taken prisoner near Cambrai in March 1918 in the opening phases of the German Offensive. Repatriated after the cessation of hostilities, he was demobilised in November 1919, and holds the General Service and Victory Medals.
8, Water Lane, Hitchin.   2669.

PROCTOR, A. C., Corporal, Royal Engineers.
Volunteering in October 1915, he embarked for the Western Front in November of the following year. Here he served in the forward areas of Ypres, the Somme, Cambrai, Albert and Amiens, and was continuously under fire. Owing to ill-health he was invalided home in June 1917, and on recovery returned to France in November 1918, and was stationed at various depôts until, returning to England, he was demobilised in October 1919. He holds the General Service and Victory Medals.
33, Alexandra Road, Hitchin.   2670.

PROCTOR, F., L/Corporal, 2/5th Bedfordshire Regiment and Royal Fusiliers.
He volunteered in February 1916, and in September of the same year was sent to France, and was in action at the Battles of Ypres, Passchendaele and Messines Ridge. In 1917 he was transferred to Italy, and served there until early in 1918. Returning to France he fought throughout the German Offensive, and was wounded on September 8th at Ypres in the Allied Advance. Invalided to England he received hospital treatment and was ultimately discharged on account of his wounds in April 1918, and holds the General Service and Victory Medals.
The Green, Eddlesborough, Dunstable.   Z2671/A.

PROCTOR, P., Private, Bedfordshire Regiment.
Volunteering in August 1914, he was drafted to the Western Front almost immediately, and was in action during the Retreat from Mons and in the Battles of Ypres, Hill 60, Arras, the Somme, and was wounded. Returning to England he received hospital treatment, and was invalided out of the service in 1916. He holds the Mons Star, and the General Service and Victory Medals.
10, Woodman's Yard, Watford.   X2673.

PRUDDEN, S. W., Sapper, Royal Engineers.
He volunteered in May 1915, and served with his unit at various stations until drafted to France in January 1917. In this theatre of war he was engaged on special duties in the forward areas, and was wounded at Passchendaele in 1917. He later served on the Somme, and during the German Offensive was taken prisoner at Ploegsteert on April 11th, 1918, and held in captivity until after the signing of the Armistice. Released on November 25th of that year, he was demobilised in January 1919, and holds the General Service and Victory Medals.
18, Hampton Road, Luton.   2674.

PRUDDEN, T. C., Private, 10th Queen's (Royal West Surrey Regiment).
He joined in May 1917, and was later drafted overseas. During his service on the Western Front he took part in various engagements, and was killed in action during the fierce conflict at Kemmel Hill on July 27th, 1918. He was entitled to the General Service and Victory Medals.
65, Old Bedford Road, Luton.   2675.

PRUTTON, W. C., Private, 2nd Cheshire Regt.
He volunteered in December 1915, and in the following September proceeded to France, where he served with his regiment. In November 1916 he was sent to Salonika and was engaged in much fighting in this theatre of war and fought on the Struma and Doiran fronts. He returned to England in December 1918, and was demobilised in the following year. He holds the General Service and Victory Medals.
40, Bancroft, Hitchin.   2676.

PRYOR, A. W., Private, 6th Bedfordshire Regiment and 1st Hertfordshire Regiment.
Volunteering at the outbreak of war he was drafted to the Western Front in the following year. He took part in the operations in various sectors, including those of Arras, Ypres, Hill 60, Passchendaele and in the final operations until the signing of the Armistice. He was demobilised in January 1919, and holds the 1914-15 Star, and the General Service and Victory Medals.
Batchworth Hill, Rickmansworth.   X2677.

PRYOR, W. G., Private, 1/4th Essex Regiment.
He volunteered in December 1915, and in the following July proceeded to Egypt. He was engaged in the fighting in the British Advance through Palestine, and was in action at the Battle of Gaza. He returned to England after the signing of the Armistice, and was demobilised in September 1919. He holds the General Service and Victory Medals.
Mimram Road, Welwyn.   2678.

PUDDEPHATT, A. J., Private, Middlesex Regt.
He joined in 1916, and was shortly afterwards sent to the Western Front. He took part in many engagements, including those at Arras, on the Somme, and was wounded at Cambrai. He returned home and was discharged in February 1918, and holds the General Service and Victory Medals.
41, Pretoria Road, Watford.   X2679.

PUDDEPHATT, H., Corporal, 1/5th Bedfordshire Regiment.
He joined in September 1916, and was later sent to France. Whilst on the Western Front he was in action at Arras, Ypres, Albert, Cambrai, and was wounded. He afterwards proceeded with his battalion to Italy, where he served until hostilities ceased. He returned to England after the signing of the Armistice, and was demobilised in September 1919. He holds the General Service and Victory Medals.
36, Court Road, Luton.   2680/A.

PUDDEPHATT, L. J., Sapper, Royal Engineers (2/2nd Field Company).
He volunteered in May 1915, and after his training proceeded to the Western Front. He was engaged on important duties in connection with operations, and was frequently in the trenches during the fierce fighting at Ypres and Arras. He was unfortunately killed in action at Delville Wood during the Allied Advance on September 1st, 1918. He was entitled to the General Service and Victory Medals.
103, Victoria Street, Dunstable.   3452/B.

PUDDEPHATT, P., Pte., 5th Bedfordshire Regt.
He joined in March 1916, and served with his battalion at various stations until drafted to France. In this theatre of war he was engaged in the fighting at Arras, Cambrai and Messines, and during his service overseas was three times wounded. He was demobilised in February 1919, and holds the General Service and Victory Medals.
36, Court Road, Luton.   2680/B

PUGH, H. J., Private, Suffolk Regiment.
He joined in August 1916, and proceeded to France shortly afterwards. During his service on the Western Front he fought at Ypres, Arras, on the Somme, at Cambrai and St. Quentin, and in the final operations of the war, and was wounded. He was demobilised in 1919, and holds the General Service and Victory Medals.
1, Church Street, St. Albans.   X2681.

PUGH, J., Private, 1/5th Bedfordshire Regiment.
He volunteered at the outbreak of war and at the conclusion of his training served at various stations on important duties with his battalion. He rendered valuable service, but owing to medical unfitness was unable to secure his transfer to a theatre of war, and was discharged as medically unfit for further service with the colours in January 1915.
19, Henry Street, Luton.   2682/A.

PUGH, P. W., Private, Bedfordshire Regiment.
He volunteered in August 1914, and in the following March proceeded to France. Whilst in this theatre of war he fought in many notable engagements, including those on the Somme, at Arras, Abbeville, and in the Retreat and Advance of 1918, and was wounded on September 1st of that year. He holds the 1914-15 Star, the General Service and Victory Medals, and was demobilised in February 1919.
14, Henry Street, Luton.   2683.

PUGH, P. W., Air Mechanic, R.A.F.
He volunteered in August 1914, and was drafted to France in the same year. During his service overseas he was stationed with his squadron at Boulogne and employed on important duties which demanded a high degree of technical skill, and was wounded during a hostile air-raid. He returned to England after the cessation of hostilities and was demobilised in February 1919. He holds the 1914-15 Star, and the General Service and Victory Medals.
19, Henry Street, Luton.   2682/B.

PUGH, S., Sapper, Royal Engineers.
He joined in March 1916, and was sent overseas in the same year. Whilst on the Western Front he fought at the Battles of Ypres, Arras, the Somme, and Cambrai, and in the final Allied Advance into Germany. He returned to England after the signing of the Armistice, and was demobilised in March 1919. He holds the General Service and Victory Medals.
77, Church Street, St. Albans. X2684.

PUGH, W. T., Corporal, R.F.A.
He volunteered in June 1915, and in the following year proceeded to France. In this theatre of war he was in action at Ypres, on the Somme, at Arras and Cambrai, and after the cessation of hostilities proceeded with his battery to Ireland, remaining there until January 1919. He then returned to England and was demobilised. He holds the General Service and Victory Medals.
1, George Street, Markyate. 2685.

PULLEN, L. P., Sapper, R.E. (Signal Section).
He joined in June 1917, and in the following January was sent to France. He was engaged on important duties with his unit in the forward areas, and was constantly under heavy shell fire whilst operations were in progress at Cambrai, Valenciennes, and in the final operations of the war. He was demobilised in January 1919, and holds the General Service and Victory Medals.
19, Althorpe Road, Luton. 2686.

PULLEN, O. H., Private, Wiltshire Regiment.
He volunteered at the outbreak of hostilities and served at various stations on important duties with his unit. He did excellent work but was unable to obtain his transfer overseas on account of medical unfitness and was discharged in consequence in March 1916.
4, Bolton Road, Luton. 2687.

PULLEN, W., Private, Oxfordshire and Buckinghamshire Light Infantry and Wiltshire Regt.
He joined in October 1916, and at the conclusion of his training served at several stations on important duties with his battalion. He did excellent work but was unable to secure his transfer to a theatre of war on account of medical unfitness, and was demobilised in February 1919.
15, Waterloo Road, Linslade, Bucks. 2688.

PURR, E., Corporal, R.A.V.C.
Volunteering at the outbreak of war he was sent to Egypt in 1915. He was engaged on special duties with his unit in attending to sick and wounded horses, and served at Gaza, Jaffa, and Haifa. During his service in this theatre of war he was lost in the desert for three days, and when found was in a precarious condition. He returned to England and was demobilised in August 1919, and holds the 1914-15 Star, and the General Service and Victory Medals.
West Hill, Aspley Guise. Z2689.

PURRETT, W. T., Private, Royal Defence Corps.
He was ineligible for service with the Colours, and joined the Royal Defence Corps in 1915. After completing his training he was engaged on important guard and other duties at various stations. He did good work, but owing to ill-health was discharged as unfit for further service in 1918.
15, Cassiobridge Road, Watford. X2690.

PURSER, W. H., Private, Rifle Brigade.
He joined in November 1918, and after his training served at various stations with his unit on important guard duties. He rendered valuable services but was unable to secure his transfer to a theatre of war before the cessation of hostilities and was demobilised in November 1919.
Pretoria Cottages, Harlington, Beds. 2691.

PURYER, E. G., Private, Middlesex Regiment.
He volunteered in January 1916, and in the following July proceeded to France. During his service in this theatre of war he fought at the first Battle of the Somme, and engagements at Arras, Bullecourt and Ypres. He was killed in action at Bailleul on October 6th, 1917, and was entitled to the General Service and Victory Medals.
1, South Street, Leighton Buzzard. 2692.

PUTLAND, F. J. S., Sapper, Royal Engineers.
He volunteered at the outbreak of war, and at the conclusion of his training served at various stations with his unit on important duties as a despatch rider. He did excellent work, but was unable to secure his transfer overseas, and was demobilised in May 1919.
64, Greatham Road, Bushey, Herts. X2693.

PUTMAN, A., Private, Tank Corps.
He joined in January 1918, and after his training was stationed in the South of England on important duties with his unit. He rendered valuable service, but was unsuccessful in obtaining his transfer overseas, and was demobilised in April 1919.
48, Shakespeare Street, North Watford. X2695.

PUTMAN, T., Private, Oxfordshire and Buckinghamshire Light Infantry.
He joined in June 1916, and three months later proceeded to France. During his service on the Western Front he fought on the Somme, at Arras, Ypres, Cambrai, and in the Retreat and subsequent Advance of 1918, and was wounded. He was demobilised in 1919, and holds the General Service and Victory Medals.
7, Chapel Yard, Eaton Bray, Dunstable 797/B.

PUTT, T. H., Telegraphist, Royal Navy.
He joined in November 1917, and was posted to H.M.S. "Glory," which vessel was engaged on patrol duties in the White Sea, and in the operations off Archangel. His ship also served in Irish waters. He was demobilised in May 1919, and holds the General Service and Victory Medals.
55, Park Road, Luton. 2694.

PUTTERILL, R. W., Private, 6th Royal Berkshire Regiment.
He joined in November 1916, and in the following June proceeded overseas. He fought in many sectors of the Western Front, and during the fierce conflict at St. Julien was killed in action on July 31st, 1917. He was entitled to the General Service and Victory Medals.
6, Primrose Cottages, Hatfield. X2696.

PYPER, F. T., Sergeant, R.A.O.C.
He volunteered in August 1914, and in the following year was drafted to the Dardanelles and was stationed at Mudros, where he was engaged on important duties with his unit. After the Evacuation of the Peninsula he was sent to Egypt, and there served at Alexandria and Cairo until hostilities ceased. He returned home, and in 1920 was still serving at Chatham. He holds the 1914-15 Star, and the General Service and Victory Medals.
23, Grove Road, Luton. 2697/B.

PYPER, J. E., Driver, Royal Field Artillery.
He joined in February 1917 and after his training proceeded overseas. Whilst on the Western Front he was engaged on important work with the guns and in conveying ammunition to the front line trenches whilst operations were in progress. He was demobilised in October 1919, and holds the General Service and Victory Medals.
23, Grove Road, Luton. 2697/A.

Q

QUARMAN, C. E., Private, 1st Highland Light Infantry.
He was serving at the outbreak of war, and proceeded in August 1914 to France. He fought in the Retreat from Mons, the Battles of the Marne, the Aisne and Ypres, and in February 1916 was transferred to Mesopotamia. He was present during the operations at Kut, and was severely wounded. He subsequently died from the effects of his wounds on January 28th, 1917, and was entitled to the Mons Star, and the General Service and Victory Medals.
5, Garden Road, Abbots Langley. X4182/A.

QUARMAN, J. A., Pte., 1st Bedfordshire Regt.
Volunteering in September 1914, he was drafted to France. In this theatre of war he took part in the fighting at La Bassée, Ypres, Hill 60, the second Battle of Ypres, and Loos, and was unfortunately killed in action at Longueval on July 28th, 1916. He was entitled to the 1914 Star, and the General Service and Victory Medals.
Garden Road, Abbots Langley. X4182/B.

QUARMAN, L. S., Pte., 1st Hertfordshire Regt.
He volunteered in September 1914, and in the following year proceeded overseas. Whilst on the Western Front he took part in the heavy fighting at Ypres, Hill 60, Festubert, Cambrai, and the German Offensive and subsequent Allied Advance into Germany, and suffered from shell-shock. He was demobilised in March 1919, and holds the 1914-15 Star, and the General Service and Victory Medals.
Garden Road, Abbots Langley. X4182/C.

QUARMAN, J., Private, 1st Bedfordshire Regt.
He volunteered in September 1914, and in the same
year was sent to France. During his service on the
Western Front he fought at Ypres, Hill 60, and was
killed in action during the battle of the Somme on
July 27th, 1916. He was entitled to the 1914 Star, and
the General Service and Victory Medals.
62, Breakspeare Road, Abbots Langley, Herts. X4183.

QUARTERMAN, S., Rifleman, 24th Rifle Bgde.
He volunteered in 1914, and after his training served at
various stations until drafted to India in 1916. He was
in action on the North West Frontier and during his
service overseas was stationed at Rawal Pindi for some
time. He returned to England after the cessation of
hostilities and was demobilised in April 1919. He holds
the Indian General Service Medal (with Clasp Afghanistan, North West Frontier 1919).
82, Brightwell Road, Watford. X2168/B.

**QUIBELL, E. W., Private, Royal Marine Light
Infantry.**
He volunteered in August 1914, and was posted to
H.M.S. " Weymouth." His ship was engaged on patrol
duties in the North Sea, the Straits of Gibraltar and the
Mediterranean Sea, and frequently passed through
mine-infested areas and had many narrow escapes. He
was discharged on account of his service in January 1915,
and he holds the 1914-15 Star, and the General Service
and Victory Medals.
195, Queen's Road, Watford. X4179.

**QUIBELL, E. W., Private, Royal Marine Light
Infantry.**
He enlisted in the Service in August 1911, and at the
outbreak of war was sent to German East Africa where
he saw active service for a time. His ship was then
engaged on patrolling the Mediterranean Sea and in
escorting troops across the Channel to France. He was
wounded, and was discharged in January 1915 on account of his service, and holds the 1914-15 Star, and the
General Service and Victory Medals.
195, Queen's Road, Watford. X4181.

**QUIBELL, G. A., Rifleman, 9th London Regi-
ment (Queen Victoria's Rifles).**
Volunteering in January 1915, he was drafted overseas
in November 1917, and saw much fighting in various
parts of the Western Front, and was gassed at
Poperinghe in February 1918. On recovery he rejoined
his regiment and fought during the German Offensive,
in the course of which he was wounded at Cambrai in
April. He returned to England and received hospital
treatment, and was stationed in England until demobilised in March 1919. He holds the General Service
and Victory Medals.
115, Ridge Street, Callowland, Watford. X4184/B.

**QUIBELL, S. W., Rifleman, 9th London Regi-
ment (Queen Victoria's Rifles).**
He volunteered in February 1915, and proceeded to
France twelve months later, and was in action in the
Ypres salient and in many other sectors, where heavy
fighting took place. He was reported missing after the
Battle of St. Julien on September 25th, 1917, and later
was presumed to have been killed in action on that
date. He was entitled to the General Service and
Victory Medals.
115, Ridge Street, Callowland, Watford. X4184/A.

QUICK, A. J., Private, R.A.S.C.
Volunteering in 1915, he was later drafted to the
Western Front, where he served in many engagements
and was employed on important transport duties. Later,
transferred to Italy, he saw active service in many parts
of that theatre of war and for some time acted as
interpreter. Returning to England he was demobilised
in May 1919, and holds the General Service and Victory
Medals.
8, Sussex Road, Watford. X5010/A, X5011/A.

QUICK, F., Private, Buffs (East Kent Regiment).
He joined in January 1917, and in the same year was
drafted to France. Whilst on the Western Front he
took part in the heavy fighting on the Somme, and in
the Retreat and Advance of 1918. He was later transferred to India, where he was still serving in 1920. He
holds the General Service and Victory Medals.
92, Bassett Road, Leighton Buzzard. 3752/B.

QUICK, H., Private, 4th Bedfordshire Regiment.
He volunteered in January 1915, and in the following
year proceeded to France. He fought in many engagements, including those at Hill 60, Arras, the Somme,
and was gassed at Cambrai. He returned to England
and was demobilised in March 1919, and holds the
General Service and Victory Medals.
36, Albert Street, St. Albans. X4180/B.

QUICK, E. G., Private, Royal Welch Fusiliers.
He volunteered in January 1915, and in the following
November proceeded overseas. He fought at Ypres, on
the Somme, at Arras, and was wounded and taken
prisoner in May 1918. He suffered many hardships
during his captivity, and upon his release after the
cessation of hostilities was demobilised in February
1919, and holds the 1914-15 Star, and the General Service
and Victory Medals.
36, Albert Street, St. Albans. X4180/A.

QUICK, F. G., Private, Bedfordshire Regiment.
He volunteered in August 1914, and was sent to France
later in the same year. He fought in the Battles of
Arras, Cambrai, Ypres, Passchendaele, Vimy Ridge, and
was wounded in action in the German Offensive of 1918,
and returning to England received hospital treatment
and was invalided out of the service in April 1918. He
holds the 1914-15 Star, and the General Service and
Victory Medals.
8, Sussex Road, Watford. X5010/B, X5011/B.

QUICK, F. J., Private, 3/10th Middlesex Regt.
He volunteered at the outbreak of war and was later
sent to France. He rendered valuable service as a
despatch rider in many sectors of the Western Front,
including those of the Somme and Cambrai, and was
severely wounded in the Retreat in March 1918. He
was taken to hospital in France and died from the
effects of his wounds on March 22nd, 1918. He was
entitled to the General Service and Victory Medals.
92, Bassett Road, Leighton Buzzard. 3752/A.

QUICK, S. R., Sergeant, R.F.A.
He volunteered in September 1914, and after his training
served at various stations on important duties with his
unit until drafted to France in February 1918. During
his service on the Western Front he fought on the
Somme, and was gassed at Ypres during the German
Offensive on April 29th, 1918. He returned home in
May 1920, and was demobilised in the following month,
and holds the General Service and Victory Medals.
58, Cardiff Road, Watford. X2732/B.

QUICK, T. S., Sergeant, R.A.S.C.
He volunteered in September 1914, and was immediately
sent to France. He was engaged on important duties in
the forward areas in the Retreat from Mons, and the
subsequent Battles of Ypres, the Somme and Cambrai,
remaining in this theatre of war for over five years,
and on November 13th, 1916 was mentioned in Despatches
for devotion to duty in the Field. He was demobilised
in November 1919, and holds the Mons Star, and the
General Service and Victory Medals, and also a French
decoration.
36, Albert Street, St. Albans. X4180/C.

QUICK, W. G., Private, Bedfordshire Regiment.
Volunteering in August 1914, he was engaged on important guard and other duties with his unit at various
stations on the East Coast. He rendered excellent
services, but was unable to obtain his transfer overseas
prior to the signing of the Armistice, and was demobilised
in April 1919.
8, Sussex Road, Watford. X5010/C, X5011/C.

QUINT, T. W., Sapper, Royal Engineers.
He joined in June 1916, and six months later proceeded
overseas. Whilst on the Western Front he was engaged
on special duties during operations on the Somme, at
Arras, Ypres, Cambrai, Le Cateau, and saw much heavy
fighting until the cessation of hostilities. He was demobilised in May 1919, and holds the General Service
and Victory Medals.
136, Liverpool Road, Watford. X4178.

R

RACKLEY, E. R., Corporal, 11th Essex Regt.
He volunteered in December 1915, and in the following
year was drafted to the Western Front. He served in
many sectors during much heavy fighting, including the
Battles at Cambrai and St. Quentin, and was three
times wounded. He was sent to England and discharged in February 1918. He holds the General Service
and Victory Medals.
20, Pretoria Road, Watford. X4190.

RACKLEY, W., Corporal, R.A.M.C.
He joined in 1917, and in the same year was drafted to
Salonika, where he was engaged on important duties
at the Base Hospital until after the cessation of hostilities. Later he served with the Army of Occupation
at Constantinople. During his service he contracted
malaria and was invalided home and in January 1919
was demobilised. He holds the General Service and
Victory Medals.
9, Hollywell Road, Watford. X4191.

RACKLEY, W. A., Gunner, R.F.A.
He joined in 1916, and in the same year was drafted overseas. Whilst on the Western Front he was in action during much heavy fighting in various sectors, including the Battle of the Somme, and the Retreat of 1918. He was killed in action during the latter engagement on April 13th, 1918, and was entitled to the General Service and Victory Medals.
106, Judge Street, North Watford. X4192.

RADFORD, A., Gunner, R.G.A.
He volunteered in 1915, and after his training served at various stations on important duties with his unit. Later he was drafted to France and during his service in this theatre of war he was in action on the Somme, Arras, and at Cambrai, being gassed and twice wounded. After the cessation of hostilities he proceeded to Germany with the Army of Occupation. He was demobilised in August 1919, and holds the General Service and Victory Medals.
Chapel Place, Biggleswade. Z4196.

RADFORD, E., Pte., 1/5th Bedfordshire Regt.
He was mobilised at the outbreak of war and in July of the following year proceeded to the Dardanelles. He was in action during the landing at Gallipoli and Suvla Bay and was later sent to Egypt. He took part in the operations during the British Advance into Palestine and the fighting at Gaza until the fall of Jerusalem. He suffered from malaria and dysentery, was invalided home and subsequently died at Kempston Military Hospital from the effects of his illness on June 21st, 1919. He was entitled to the 1914-15 Star, and the General Service and Victory Medals.
13, New Town, Biggleswade. Z4195/B.

RADFORD, E. M. (Miss), Member, W.R.A.F.
She joined in August 1918, and was stationed at Henlow. For a period of nearly twelve months she was engaged on important work in connection with salvage. She rendered excellent service, carried out her duties with great care, and her services were much appreciated. She was demobilised in July 1919.
5, Brittain's Yard, Hitchin Street, Biggleswade. Z4194/A.

RADFORD, F., Private, 2nd London Regiment (Royal Fusiliers).
He was mobilised at the outbreak of war and served at various stations on important duties with his unit until drafted to France in August 1916. Whilst on the Western Front he was engaged in the fighting on the Somme, at Albert, Ypres, and was severely wounded at Arras in March 1917. He was invalided home and after treatment in hospital was discharged on account of his wounds in February 1918. He holds the General Service and Victory Medals.
13, New Town, Biggleswade. Z4195/A.

RADFORD, H. G., Pte., 4th Bedfordshire Regt.
He joined in April 1917, and in March of the following year was drafted to the Western Front where he took part in the heavy fighting during the German Offensive and subsequent Allied Advance at Cambrai, until he was wounded. He was invalided home and after treatment in hospital served in England until demobilised in September 1920. He holds the General Service and Victory Medals.
16, Dudley Street, Leighton Buzzard. 4193.

RADFORD, J. W., Private, 3rd Northamptonshire Regiment.
He joined in July 1918, on attaining military age, and was drafted to Ireland. He served at various stations on important duties with his battalion and did good work, but was unable to secure his transfer to a theatre of war before the cessation of hostilities. He was demobilised in October 1919.
5, Brittain's Yard, Hitchin Street, Biggleswade. Z4194/B.

RADFORD, W. J., Private, Bedfordshire Regt.
He joined in May 1918, and after his training served at various stations on important duties with his unit. He rendered valuable services but was unable to obtain his transfer overseas owing to the cessation of hostilities. He was demobilised in March 1920.
13, New Town, Biggleswade. Z4195/C.

RAINBOW, A., Private, 3rd Bedfordshire Regt.
A serving soldier, he was immediately drafted to France at the outbreak of war. He fought in the Retreat from Mons, at La Bassée, Festubert, Hill 60, Neuve Chapelle, and was severely wounded near Ypres in 1916. He was invalided home, and discharged through the effects of his wounds in October of that year. He holds the Mons Star, and the General Service and Victory Medals.
Clifton Road, Shefford. Z4198/A.

RAINBOW, C., Private, 2nd Bedfordshire Regt.
He was serving at the outbreak of war, and was immediately drafted overseas. During his service on the Western Front he fought in the Retreat from Mons and the Battles of La Bassée, Festubert and Ypres, and was wounded. On recovery he rejoined his battalion, and while fighting at the Battle of the Somme was taken prisoner. During his captivity he suffered greatly from hardships and privations, and in consequence died on November 3rd, 1918, while still a prisoner. He was entitled to the Mons Star, and the General Service and Victory Medals.
Clifton Road, Shefford. Z4199/A.

RAINBOW, G., Private, 2nd Bedfordshire Regt.
He was serving in 1914, and in the following year was sent to Egypt. In this theatre of war he took part in the fighting at Gaza, Jaffa, Aleppo, and in the British Advance through Palestine and the entry into Jerusalem in 1917. He was afterwards sent to India, where he was serving at Secunderabad in 1920. He holds the 1914-15 Star, and the General Service and Victory Medals.
Clifton Road, Shefford. Z4199/B.

RAINBOW, J., Private, 4th Middlesex Regiment.
He joined in June 1916, and six months later proceeded to France. Whilst on the Western Front he fought at Arras, Vimy Ridge and Ypres, being taken prisoner during the last engagement. He suffered many hardships during his captivity, but was released after the signing of the Armistice and rejoined his unit. In 1920 he was serving on garrison duty at Gibraltar, and holds the General Service and Victory Medals.
Clifton Road, Shefford. Z4198/B.

RAINBOW, W. G., Cpl., 1st Bedfordshire Regt.
He was mobilised in August 1914, and was immediately sent to the Western Front, where he took part in the severe fighting during the Retreat from Mons and at Le Cateau, and in the subsequent actions on the Marne and the Aisne, also in the Battles of La Bassée and Neuve Chapelle. He was later killed in action near St. Eloi on March 31st, 1915. He was entitled to the Mons Star, and the General Service and Victory Medals.
15, Albert Street, Watford. X4197/A.

RAINSDEN, E., Private, R.A.S.C. (M.T.).
He volunteered in November 1914, and in the following year was despatched to France. There he was engaged on important duties in connection with the transport of supplies and ammunition to the forward areas in several sectors, and was present at the Battles of Arras and Ypres. Sent to Egypt in 1917, he did excellent transport work with the forces engaged under General Allenby in the Advance through Palestine, and saw heavy fighting at Gaza, Haifa, Aleppo and Damascus. He holds the 1914-15 Star, and the General Service and Victory Medals, and in 1920 was still serving with his unit at Acre.
The Hill, Wheathampstead. 5161/C.

RAINSDEN, F. (M.M.), Sergeant, Hertfordshire Regiment.
He was mobilised on the declaration of war, and almost immediately drafted to France. There he took part in the fighting during the Retreat from Mons and in several other important battles, including those at Ypres, Givenchy, Hill 60 and Passchendaele, and was wounded three times. He did valuable work with his unit, and was awarded the Military Medal for conspicuous gallantry and devotion to duty in the Field. In addition, he holds the 1914-15 Star, and the General Service and Victory Medals, and was demobilised in 1919.
The Hill, Wheathampstead. 5161/A.

RAINSDEN, H., Private, 3rd Bedfordshire Regt.
Volunteering in 1914, he was shortly afterwards drafted to the Western Front, in several sectors of which he saw much service with his unit. He was engaged in heavy fighting at Ypres and in the Arras sector and was severely wounded in 1915, as a result of which he was invalided home. He was discharged as medically unfit for further service in that year, and holds the 1914-15 Star, and the General Service and Victory Medals.
The Hill, Wheathampstead. 5161/B.

RALLEY, W., Sapper, Royal Engineers.
He volunteered in December 1914, and in the following July was drafted to the Dardanelles, where he was engaged on important duties during the landing at Suvla Bay. Later he was transferred to Egypt, and in this theatre of war was present in the forward areas at the Battles of Gaza and during the British Advance through Palestine. He was demobilised in March 1919, and holds the 1914-15 Star, and the General Service and Victory Medals.
160, New Town Street, Luton. 4201.

RALPH, R., Gunner, Royal Field Artillery.
He volunteered in August 1914, and in November of
the following year was drafted to Egypt. During his
service on the Eastern Front he was engaged in the
fighting at the Battles of Gaza, and took part in the
Advance into Palestine. He returned home and was
demobilised in March 1919, and holds the 1914-15 Star,
and the General Service and Victory Medals.
15, Camp Road, St. Albans.   X4202.

RALPH, W., Corporal, Royal Air Force.
He volunteered in September 1914, and after his training
served at various stations until drafted to France in
1916. During his service on the Western Front he was
engaged on important duties which called for a high
degree of technical skill, and served in the Somme
sector and at Arras. After the cessation of hostilities
he returned to England and was demobilised in March
1919. He holds the General Service and Victory Medals.
2, Hedley Road, St. Albans.   X4200.

RANCE, F. G., Private, Labour Corps.
He volunteered in February 1915, and in the same year
proceeded to the Western Front. During his service
overseas he was engaged on work of an important
nature, chiefly in the Arras sector, and was frequently
in the forward areas. He remained in this theatre of
war for a period of four years, and was demobilised on
his return to England in April 1919. He holds the
General Service and Victory Medals.
11, Longmin Road, St. Albans.   X3915/A.

RANCE, F. G., Sergeant, 24th London Regiment.
He volunteered in September 1914, and in the following
year was drafted overseas. He served in many sectors
of the Western Front, and took part in the heavy fighting at Ypres, on the Somme, Arras and Cambrai. He
returned to England after the cessation of hostilities,
and was demobilised in January 1919. He holds the
1914-15 Star, and the General Service and Victory
Medals.
16, Camp View Road, St. Albans   X4203.

RANCE, H., Private, Bedfordshire Regiment.
Volunteering in June 1915, he was drafted to the
Western Front in February of the following year. Here
he was in action in various battles, and was wounded
in July 1916 on the Somme. Returning to England he
was discharged in February 1917, after a protracted
course of hospital treatment and holds the General
Service and Victory Medals.
39, Chapel Street, Hemel Hempstead.   X4209.

RANCE, J., Private, 1/5th Suffolk Regiment.
He volunteered in June 1915, and after his training
served at various stations with his unit until drafted
to the Western Front in January 1917. During his
brief service in this theatre of war he took part in the
heavy fighting at Ypres, Vimy Ridge, on the Somme,
and was reported missing during the Battle of Arras
on April 28th of the same year, and was later presumed
to have been killed in action on that date. He was
entitled to the General Service and Victory Medals.
67, Boyle Street, Luton.   4221.

RANCE, W. G., Private, 7th Bedfordshire Regt.
He volunteered in November 1914, and was sent to
France in 1916. Whilst on the Western Front he took
part in many important engagements, including the
fighting at Kemmel Hill, Ypres and Messines. In
November 1917 he was invalided home, and on recovery
he remained in England on special duties until demo-
bilised in May 1919. He holds the General Service and
Victory Medals.
Poultry Cottages, King's Langley.   X4223.

RANCE, W. H., Driver, R.A.S.C. (M.T.)
He joined in February 1917, and sailed for Mesopotamia in the following August. He served in the forward areas and in various engagements on important
duties connected with the transport of supplies, and
was present at the occupation of Mosul in November
1918. He was demobilised in May 1919 on his return
to England, and holds the General Service and Victory
Medals.
17, Alexandra Road, Hitchin.   4238.

RAND, W. H., Private, Labour Corps.
Volunteering in March 1915, he received his training
at Thetford and was afterwards drafted to France,
where he was subsequently engaged on important duties
in the forward areas. He was present at the Battles of
the Somme and Arras, but later, in consequence of
ill-health was invalided home. On his recovery he was
transferred to the Royal Defence Corps, in which unit
he served until he was demobilised in 1918. He holds
the 1914-15 Star, and the General Service and Victory
Medals.
7, Lyles Row, Hitchin.   4213.

RANDALL, A., Corporal, Royal Field Artillery.
Volunteering in October 1914, he was, on completion
of his training, sent to Egypt, where he served in
several minor engagements, and subsequently took part
in the Palestine Campaign, during which he participated
in heavy fighting at the Battles of Gaza, Jaffa and
Aleppo. He holds the 1914-15 Star, and the General
Service and Victory Medals, and was demobilised in 1919.
58, Bernard Street, St. Albans.   X4090/B.

**RANDALL, A., Private, 2nd Oxfordshire and
Buckinghamshire Light Infantry.**
Joining in July 1916, he was drafted to France in the
following November and subsequently served in the final
stages of the Somme Offensive. He also fought at Ypres
and Cambrai, and in the Retreat and Advance of 1918,
remaining overseas until September 1919. Returning
then to England he was demobilised and holds the
General Service and Victory Medals.
21, Soulbury Road, Linslade, Leighton Buzzard.   4215.

RANDALL, A. G., Sapper, Royal Engineers.
He volunteered in 1915, and after his training was drafted
to the Western Front, where for nearly three years he
was engaged on duties of an important nature in the
forward areas and took part in the actions at Arras
and on the Somme. In 1918 he was sent to Italy and
again did valuable work until the cessation of hostilities.
He was demobilised after his return to England in
April 1919, and holds the General Service and Victory
Medals.
210, Harwood Road, Watford.   X4212/A.

RANDALL, C. G., Private, 12th Royal Fusiliers.
Volunteering in September 1914, he was sent to France
early in the following year and after taking an active
part in several notable battles, was wounded and taken
prisoner at Loos in September 1915. Released at the
signing of the Armistice, he returned to England and
was subsequently demobilised in December 1919. He
holds the 1914-15 Star, and the General Service and
Victory Medals.
Station Road, Aspley Guise, Beds.   Z4216/A.

RANDALL, D. (Miss), Special War Worker.
This lady volunteered for work of National importance
early in 1915, and was subsequently engaged by Messrs.
G. Kent, of Luton, for important work in connection
with shell filling and testing. Throughout her service
there, which lasted until the cessation of hostilities in
November 1918, she carried out her duties in a thoroughly
capable and efficient manner and proved worthy of high
commendation.
Upper Sundon, near Dunstable.   1937/C.

RANDALL, D., Gunner, Royal Field Artillery.
Joining in September 1916, he was sent to France at the
conclusion of his training in the following January
and subsequently took an active part in numerous important engagements, notably those at Arras and Cambrai. In 1918 he came home on leave and after his
return to the Western Front contracted influenza, of
which he died in November of that year. He was entitled
to the General Service and Victory Medals.
21, Union Street, Leighton Buzzard.   2464/B.

RANDALL, E. J., Private, Middlesex Regiment.
He volunteered in August 1914, and after his training
was engaged for a time on special duties. In the following July he was drafted to France, and was killed in
action during operations subsequent to the Battle of
Loos, on September 28th, 1915. He was entitled to the
1914-15 Star, and the General Service and Victory Medals.
4, Rose Terrace, Littleworth, Leighton Buzzard.   4211.

RANDALL, F. T., Sapper, Royal Engineers.
He volunteered in October 1914, and in the following
year was sent to the Western Front. There he was engaged on special duties in connection with operations
in the advanced areas, and was wounded. Rejoining
his unit on recovery he was severely wounded during
the operations on the Somme, at Delville Wood, and died
from the effects of his wounds on August 28th, 1916. He
was entitled to the 1914-15 Star, and the General Service and Victory Medals.
High Street, Wheathampstead.   4218.

RANDALL, G., Gunner, Royal Field Artillery.
He joined in 1916, and during his service in France, which
lasted for nearly three years, took an active part in several
notable engagements, including those at Messines Ridge,
Vimy Ridge, Arras and Cambrai, and was wounded.
He holds the General Service and Victory Medals, and
was demobilised after his return to England in February
1919.
Beeston Green, Sandy, Beds.   Z4219.

RANDALL, F. J., Cpl., 1/5th Bedfordshire Regt.
He volunteered in August 1914, and a year later took part in the landing at Suvla Bay and the Battle of Sari Bair, remaining on the Peninsula until the Evacuation. He was then sent to Egypt and subsequently served in the Palestine campaign, during which he participated in heavy fighting at Gaza, Jaffa, Haifa and Aleppo, and in the capture of Jerusalem. On one occasion he was wounded, but receiving treatment at the base, remained overseas until 1919. He was demobilised in March of that year and holds the 1914-15 Star, and the General Service and Victory Medals.
35, Woburn Road, Ampthill.   4225/B.

RANDALL, G., Staff-Sergeant, R.F.A.
He volunteered in September 1914, and in the following March was drafted to France, where he took a prominent part in many engagements, notably those on the Somme and at Arras. He holds the 1914-15 Star, and the General Service and Victory Medals, and was demobilised after his return to England in 1918.
Letchworth Road, Limbury, near Luton.   4207.

RANDALL, G. A., Sergeant, Machine Gun Corps.
Volunteering in 1915, he was drafted to the Western Front at the conclusion of his training. Subsequently he served in many important engagements, including those at Ypres, Arras, Cambrai and the Somme, and in 1918 was severely gassed. He returned to England, and in September of that year was invalided out of the Service. He holds the 1914-15 Star, and the General Service and Victory Medal.
1, Beech Road, Luton.   4222.

RANDALL, G. D. (Miss), Special War Worker.
This lady volunteered her services for work of National importance, and from October 1917 until December 1919 was employed in the No. 80, Fuse Department of the Munition Works at Chaul End, and was present when the explosion took place at that factory in February 1918. She rendered valuable services throughout.
2, White Cottages, Limbrey, Leagrave.   4210/A.

RANDALL, H., Private, Bedfordshire Regiment.
He volunteered in January 1915, and in the following January was sent to the Western Front. After a year's service, during which he took part in several battles, including the fighting at Loos, he was severely wounded in action on the Somme, and in consequence was invalided to England, where he was under treatment for six months. On his recovery he was drafted to Egypt and thence to Palestine, subsequently being transferred to Italy where he participated in fighting on the Piave. After the cessation of hostilities, he returned to England and in March 1919, was demobilised. He holds the 1914-15 Star, and the General Service and Victory Medals.
Church Street, Wing, Bucks.   4214.

RANDALL, J. R., Sapper, Royal Engineers.
Joining in 1916, he received his training and afterwards served for three years on the Western Front. During this time he was engaged on important duties in the forward areas, and did excellent work with his unit, notably at Lens and Ypres. He holds the General Service and Victory Medals, and was demobilised in 1919.
210, Harwood Road, Watford.   X4212/B.

RANDALL, J. S., Private, 2nd Welch Regiment.
Volunteering in 1915, in the Royal Engineers, he was afterwards transferred to the 2nd Welch Regiment, and sent to the Western Front in the following year. Serving as Lewis gunner he took part in many important engagements in France and Flanders and was twice wounded in the course of the Battles of Arras, Ypres and Cambrai. On the termination of hostilities he returned to England for demobilisation in December 1918, and holds the General Service and Victory Medals.
Station Road, Aspley Guise.   Z4216/B.

RANDALL, S., Private, 1st Bedfordshire Regt.
He enlisted in May 1914, and after the outbreak of war was sent to France in the following year. He was in action in various sectors and being wounded in an engagement in the Somme sector in 1915 was invalided home. Returning to the Field on recovery, he took part in further fighting on the Somme, and was killed in action on October 6th, 1916. He was entitled to the 1914-15 Star, and the General Service and Victory Medals.
32, High Street, Houghton Regis.   4206.

RANDALL, S. G., Private, Northumberland Fusiliers.
Joining in May 1917, he underwent a course of training and proceeded to France in the following April, and in the same month was reported missing, and later was presumed to have been killed in action during the German Offensive. He was entitled to the General Service and Victory Medals.
220, Wellington Street, Luton.   4224.

RANDALL, S. C., Private, R.A.O.C.
Volunteering in November 1915, he was engaged on important duties with his unit at various stations until drafted to Mesopotamia in 1917. He served in that theatre of war for two years, during which period he was transferred to the Queen's (Royal West Surrey Regiment), the Middlesex and finally to the Yorkshire Regiment. He was later sent to India and was in action in several engagements against the rebel tribes on the North-Western Frontier. Returning to England he was demobilised in September 1919, and holds the General Service and Victory Medals, and the Indian General Service Medal (with clasp, Afghanistan, N.W. Frontier, 1919).
98, Baulk Road, Biggleswade.   Z4220.

RANDALL, T., Private, R.A.S.C.
He joined in September 1916, and on the completion of his training was engaged on special duties with his unit at various stations. He rendered valuable service but was not successful in obtaining a transfer overseas before the cessation of hostilities, owing to medical unfitness for general service. He was demobilised in September 1919.
35, Woburn Road, Ampthill.   4225/A.

RANDALL, W., Private, Labour Corps.
He joined in September 1917, and on conclusion of his training served at various places on agricultural work. He was unable to obtain his transfer overseas prior to the cessation of hostilities on account of medical unfitness and was invalided out of the Army in May 1919.
2, White Cottages, Limbrey, Leagrave.   4210/B.

RANDALL, W. C., Private, King's Own (Yorkshire Light Infantry).
He volunteered in September 1914, and was drafted overseas on the completion of his training. He first saw active service on the Western Front, taking part in various actions at Loos, Albert, Vimy Ridge, the Somme, Arras, Ypres and Cambrai. He was then sent to Italy. In that theatre of war he was engaged in several of the British offensive operations on the Piave and on the Asiago Plateau, and served until the termination of hostilities. He returned to England for demobilisation in December 1918, and holds the General Service and Victory Medals.
Station Road, Aspley Guise.   Z4216/C.

RANDALL, W. G., L/Corporal, 7th Bedfordshire Regiment.
He volunteered in October 1914, and in the following October was sent to the Western Front. There he took part in the severe fighting in the Battles of Loos, the Somme and Arras, and was wounded. Rejoining his unit he fought in the third Battle of Ypres, and was killed in action near Passchendaele on August 16th, 1917. He was entitled to the 1914-15 Star, and the General Service and Victory Medals.
Gas Street, Toddington.   4205.

RANDELL, E. H., L/Corporal, Royal Engineers.
He volunteered in March 1915, but after his training was engaged on special duties until he was drafted to France in March 1918. He there served on the Somme, at Ypres, Arras, and in many other sectors during the final Retreat and Advance, and did excellent work with his unit until March 1919, when he returned to England and was demobilised. He holds the General Service and Victory Medals.
11, King Street, Houghton Regis, Dunstable.   4204.

RANDLE, W. G., Private, 1st Bedfordshire Regt.
He joined in April 1917, and on the conclusion of his training was engaged with his unit on important duties at various stations. He also rendered valuable services at the London Docks where he was employed on special duties in connection with guarding military stores and equipment for shipment overseas. He was unable to obtain a transfer overseas before the termination of hostilities owing to medical unfitness and was demobilised in January 1919.
114, Judge Street, North Watford.   X4217

RANDS, H. G., A.B., Royal Navy.
He was serving in the Royal Navy when war was declared having joined in 1911, and aboard H.M.S. "Ready" was engaged on patrol duties in the North and Mediterranean Seas and other waters. His ship was in action in the Battle of Jutland, and had other encounters with enemy craft and was at Scapa Flow when the surrendered German Fleet was interned. He holds the 1914-15 Star, and the General Service and Victory Medals, and in 1920 was still serving.
The Grove, Lidlington.   Z4208.

RATCLIFFE, F. W. (M.M.), Private, Duke of Cornwall's Light Infantry.

Volunteering in August 1914, in the same year he was sent to the Western Front. He fought in several important engagements, including the Battles of the Somme, Ypres and Cambrai, and was wounded. Rejoining his unit on recovery, he took part in the closing operations of the war, and was awarded the Military Medal for conspicuous bravery and devotion to duty in the Field. In addition he holds the 1914-15 Star, and the General Service and Victory Medals, and was demobilised in January 1919.
Trowley Bottom, Flamstead.   X4226.

RAWLINS, J., Stoker Petty Officer, Royal Navy.

He volunteered in October 1914, and was posted to H.M.S. "Boxer," which ship was engaged on important patrol duties in the Channel and in escorting transports carrying troops and military supplies between the English and French ports. He did valuable work throughout the war and was demobilised in February 1919, and holds the 1914-15 Star, and the General Service and Victory Medals.
21, Chobham Street, Luton.   4227.

RAY, A., Pte., Queen's (Royal West Surrey Regt.)

He joined in 1918, and after training was sent with the Army of Occupation into Germany where he was engaged on important duties at Cologne and other towns on the Rhine. He returned to England and was demobilised in January 1920.
Lea Cottages, Lower Luton Road, Harpenden.   4231/A.

RAY, A. W., Sergeant, R.A.S.C.

He joined in March 1917, and in the following August was drafted to Egypt. He was stationed at Alexandria and Port Said, and later, with the forces engaged under General Allenby in the advance through Palestine, did valuable work in connection with the transport of ammunition and supplies to the front lines. He was present at the Battle of Gaza and the occupation of Jerusalem, and after the signing of the Armistice, returned to England. He was demobilised in March 1920, and holds the General Service and Victory Medals.
46, Stanbridge Road, Leighton Buzzard.   4233.

RAY, F. W., L/Corporal, Bedfordshire Regiment, and Hertfordshire Regiment.

He volunteered in July 1915, and in the following year was drafted overseas. Serving with his unit on the Western Front he was in action in many important engagements, including those of Ypres and Cambrai, and was gassed and wounded three times. On the termination of hostilities he returned to England and was demobilised in March 1919. He holds the General Service and Victory Medals.
48, Alexandra Road, St. Albans.   X4229.

RAY, J. E., L/Corporal, Royal Field Artillery.

Volunteering in August 1914, he was engaged on important duties at several stations until drafted to Mesopotamia. In this theatre of war he served with his battery in many important engagements for nearly two years. Contracting severe illness whilst on service he was removed to hospital where he died on January 15th, 1918. He was entitled to the General Service and Victory Medals.
14, Park Gate Road, Callowland, Watford.   X4228.

RAY, L. W., Private, Queen's (Royal West Surrey Regiment).

He joined in March 1916, and after serving with his unit at various stations was sent to India in April of the following year. Stationed at various military depôts in India he was employed on garrison and other duties until sent to the North-Western front, where he took part in the operations against the Afghans. He returned to England for demobilisation in November 1919. He holds the General Service and Victory Medals, and the Indian General Service Medal (with clasp, Afghanistan, N.W. Frontier, 1919).
86, Fishport Street, St. Albans.   205/B.

RAY, W. R., Sapper, Royal Engineers.

Mobilised on the outbreak of hostilities, he was shortly afterwards sent to France where he was engaged on important duties in connection with operations during the Retreat from Mons, and the Battles of La Bassée, Ypres, the Somme, and Cambrai, and was wounded. He did excellent work in wiring trenches and making roads in the front lines, and was also employed on special duties on the lines of communication. He was demobilised in January 1919, and holds the Mons Star, and the General Service and Victory Medals.
6, Mill Road, Leighton Buzzard.   4236.

RAY, W., Private, Royal Fusiliers.

He joined in 1917, and in April of the following year was dispatched to the Western Front. In this theatre of war he was engaged in heavy fighting in the second Battle of the Somme, and was unfortunately killed in action on April 7th, 1918. He was entitled to the General Service and Victory Medals.
Lea Cottages, Lower Luton Road, Harpenden.   4231/B.

RAYMENT, B. E., Gunner, R.F.A., R.G.A.

He volunteered in November 1914, and served with his battery on important duties until drafted to France in February 1916. He took part in the fighting at the Battle of the Somme and was wounded near Ypres in September ot the same year. He was invalided home and after recovery remained in England until demobilised in March 1919. He holds the General Service and Victory Medals.
54, Spencer Road, Luton.   4234/A.

RAYMENT, E., Private, 2nd Bedfordshire Regt.

He joined in July 1917, and in the same year proceeded overseas. He fought in many engagements on the Western Front, including those on the Somme, at Arras, and in the Allied Advance into Germany, and was wounded. He was demobilised in October 1919, and holds the General Service and Victory Medals.
19, Common View Square, Letchworth.   4237.

RAYNER, F., Private, Bedfordshire Regiment.

A serving soldier, he was mobilised on the declaration of war, and engaged on important duties until drafted to France. There he served in several sectors with his regiment and took part in many of the principal battles and was gassed. Returning to the Field, he was killed in action on October 23rd, 1917. He was entitled to the General Service and Victory Medals.
Bowman's Green Cottages, London Colney.   217/B.

RAYNER, H., Driver, Royal Field Artillery.

He joined in May 1916, and in April of the following year was sent to France. In this theatre of war he was engaged in the operations at Arras, Ypres, the Somme, Neuve Chapelle, Cambrai and in the German Offensive and subsequent Allied Advance of 1918. He was demobilised in 1919, and holds the General Service and Victory Medals.
2, The Terrace, Aspley Guise.   Z4235.

RAYNER, J., Private, 4th Bedfordshire Regiment.

He was mobilised at the outbreak of war and served on important duties with his unit until drafted to France in January 1917. During his service on the Western Front he fought at Vimy Ridge, and was wounded. On recovery he rejoined his battalion and during the fighting near Cambrai was killed in action on January 12th, 1918. He was entitled to the General Service and Victory Medals.
8, East Street, Leighton Buzzard.   4232.

RAYNER, W., Gunner, Royal Garrison Artillery.

He joined in October 1916, and in September of the following year was drafted to Egypt. He took part in the operations in the British Advance through Palestine, and fought in the Battle of Gaza, and was present at the fall of Jerusalem. He remained in this theatre of war until January 1920, when he returned home and was demobilised. He holds the General Service and Victory Medals.
29, Spencer Road, Luton.   4230.

READ, A., Sapper, Royal Engineers.

He joined in March 1916, and was shortly afterwards drafted to the Western Front. In this theatre of war he was engaged during many important operations, including the actions at Ypres and Cambrai, and was frequently under heavy shell fire. He was demobilised in January 1919, and holds the General Service and Victory Medals.
6a, Dane Road, Luton.   4243.

READ, C., Sergeant, Bedfordshire Regiment.

He volunteered in February 1915, and in April of the ensuing year proceeded overseas. During his service on the Western Front he was engaged in the fighting in various sectors, including the Battles of Ypres, the Somme and Cambrai. He suffered from ill-health, returned to England in July 1916, and was invalided out of the Service in September of the same year. He holds the General Service and Victory Medals.
9, Jubilee Street, Luton.   4248.

READ, F., Private, 1st Northamptonshire Regt.
Joining in April 1916, in the following July he was drafted to the Western Front. In this theatre of war he fought in many important battles, including those at Arras, Ypres, Cambrai, and was severely wounded on October 28th, 1918, in the Somme sector. Invalided to hospital in England he received medical treatment, and on recovery was demobilised in February 1919. He holds the General Service and Victory Medals.
3, Wright's Yard, Houghton Regis, Dunstable. 460/B.

READ, H. B., Corporal, Hertfordshire Regiment.
He volunteered in 1915, and served as an Instructor in physical training with his battalion until drafted to France in 1917. In this theatre of war he took part in the fighting at Ypres, Passchendaele, the Somme, and the Retreat and Advance of 1918. He was demobilised in 1919, and holds the General Service and Victory Medals.
"Fern Cottage," Pullers Road, Boxmoor, Herts. X4241.

READ, H. W., Private, R.A.V.C.
He volunteered in July 1915, and in the same year proceeded overseas. He served in France at Rouen on important duties with his unit for a period of four years. His work, which was in connection with tending to sick and wounded horses, was efficiently carried out. He was demobilised in July 1919, and holds the 1914-15 Star, and the General Service and Victory Medals.
Lowbell Lane, London Colney, near St. Albans. X4250/B.

READ, J. M., Private, 2nd Hertfordshire Regt.
He joined in July 1916, and after his training served at various stations with his battalion on important guard duties. He did excellent work, but was unable to secure his transfer overseas, and was demobilised in November 1919.
93, Oak Road, Luton. 4249/A.

READ, S. W., Rifleman, 4th King's Royal Rifle Corps.
He joined in September 1918, and served with his battalion on important duties at various stations, but was unable to secure his transfer overseas until after the signing of the Armistice. He was drafted to India in December of the same year, and was still serving at Poona in 1920.
93, Oak Road, Luton. 4249/B.

READ, W., Private, 1st Bedfordshire Regiment.
He volunteered in November 1914, and in the following year proceeded to France He fought in many engagements, and took part in the Battles of Ypres, the Somme, Arras, Passchendaele, Cambrai and the German Offensive and subsequent Allied Advance of 1918. During his service he was twice wounded. He was demobilised in February 1919, and holds the 1914-15 Star, and the General Service and Victory Medals.
Lowbell Lane, London Colney, St. Albans. X4250/A.

READHEAD, H. S., Private, R.A.M.C.
He joined in February 1917, and at the conclusion of his training was stationed with his unit at various places on special duties. He rendered valuable service, but owing to medical unfitness was unable to obtain his transfer to a theatre of war. He was demobilised in October 1919.
34, Lyndhurst Road, Luton. 4247.

READING, A. E., Corporal, Royal Air Force.
He joined in September 1916, and after his training was stationed at Montrose Aerodrome where he was engaged on important duties which called for a high degree of technical skill. As an engine fitter he rendered valuable services, but was not successful in securing a transfer overseas before the cessation of hostilities. He was demobilised in March 1919.
94, Cambridge Street, Luton. 4246.

READING, P. A., Pte., 6th Northamptonshire Regiment.
He joined in May 1916, and in September of the same year proceeded overseas. During his service on the Western Front he fought in the Battle of the Somme, and took part in other engagements, and was severely wounded during the third Battle of Ypres in July 1917. He was invalided home, and after hospital treatment was discharged medically unfit for further service in December of that year. He holds the General Service and Victory Medals.
48, King's Road, St. Albans. 4251.

READING, W., Private, 5th Yorkshire Regiment.
Volunteering in August 1914, he was drafted to France in the following April, and was there engaged in the fighting at Ypres, Armentières and the Battle of the Somme. He was killed in action in September 1916 at Martinpuich. He was entitled to the 1914-15 Star, and the General Service and Victory Medals.
7, Cleveland Road, Markyate. 4245/A.

READY, W., Private, Cambridgeshire Regiment, and Northamptonshire Regiment.
He joined in October 1916, and in the following year was sent overseas. During his service on the Western Front he was engaged in the fighting at Ypres. Owing to ill-health he was invalided home, and on recovery returned to France and fought in engagements on the Somme, at Amiens and Cambrai. He was demobilised in March 1919, and holds the General Service and Victory Medals.
2, Heath Terrace, Sandridge Road, St. Albans. X4242/B.

REAVELL, L., Gunner, Royal Field Artillery.
He joined in November 1916, and in the succeeding year was drafted to Gibraltar. From there he proceeded to France in March 1918, and in this theatre of war took part in the General Allied Advance from Cambrai into Germany. He was demobilised in February 1919, and holds the General Service and Victory Medals.
35, Camp Road, St. Albans. X4244/B.

REDHEAD, W., Private, Dorsetshire Regiment.
He volunteered in September 1914, and in June of the ensuing year was drafted to France. During his service in this theatre of war he was engaged in the fighting at Ypres, and was killed in action at Voormezeele on August 29th, 1915. He was entitled to the 1914-15 Star, and the General Service and Victory Medals.
22, Stanmore Road, Watford. X4252.

REDMAN, T. W., Private, 2nd Bedfordshire Regt.
He volunteered in January 1915, and in the succeeding September was drafted to the Western Front. He took part in the fighting at Loos, Albert, on the Somme, at Vimy Ridge, Arras, Bapaume and Cambrai, and was twice gassed. He was demobilised in February 1919, and holds the 1914-15 Star, and the General Service and Victory Medals.
New Road, Clifton, Shefford. Z3213/B.

REDMAN, W. C., Private, Bedfordshire Regt.
He joined in August 1918, and at the conclusion of his training was engaged with his battalion on important duties at various stations. He did good work, but owing to medical unfitness was unable to secure a transfer overseas before the cessation of hostilities. He was demobilised in December 1918.
43, Alexandra Terrace, Biggleswade. Z4254.

REDRUP, A., Corporal, R.A.S.C.
Volunteering in October 1915, he proceeded to Salonika later in the same year. Here he was engaged on important duties with his unit throughout the Balkan campaign and did much good work. He returned to England and was demobilised in February 1919, and holds the General Service and Victory Medals.
72, Brighton Road, Watford. X4253.

REDSULL, R. G., Corporal, R.A.S.C.
He volunteered in 1915, and embarked for the Macedonian theatre of war in the same year, and was engaged on important work connected with the transport of ammunition and supplies to the forward areas. In 1918, contracting fever, he was invalided to England and discharged as medically unfit for further service. He holds the General Service and Victory Medals.
120, Judge Street, North Watford. X4255.

REECE, A. H., Gunner, Royal Garrison Artillery.
He joined in June 1916, and was sent to the Western Front in the following January and fought in many engagements, including those of Arras and Ypres, where he was wounded. Invalided to England he received hospital treatment and returned to France in March 1918, and was in action continuously during the German Offensive and subsequent Allied Advance. He was demobilised in March 1919, and holds the General Service and Victory Medals.
Western Villa, Cowper Road, Harpenden. 4259.

REED, C. S., Private, Queen's (Royal West Surrey Regiment).
He joined in 1917, and on the conclusion of his training was stationed at various depôts with his unit engaged on guard and other important duties. He rendered valuable services, but was not successful in obtaining his transfer overseas prior to the cessation of hostilities. He was demobilised in 1919.
72, Norfolk Road, Rickmansworth. X4265.

REED, A. L., Gunner (Signaller), R.G.A.

Joining in 1916, he was drafted to Salonika later in the same year and served there with his battery until 1917. Transferred to Egypt he was in action on all parts of the Palestine front, and was present at the capture of Gaza, Jerusalem, Damascus, Beyrout and Aleppo. He returned to England and was demobilised in November 1919, and holds the General Service and Victory Medals.
72, Norfolk Road, Rickmansworth.   X4267.

REED, C. C., Corporal, Royal Engineers.

Volunteering in August 1914, he proceeded to the Western Front in the following February and was engaged in many battles, including those of Ypres, the Somme and during the Retreat and Advance of 1918, and was twice wounded. He returned to England and was demobilised in April 1919, and holds the 1914-15 Star, and the General Service and Victory Medals.
55, Prospect Road, St. Albans.   X4270.

REED, W. H., Private, 2nd Bedfordshire Regt.

Volunteering in August 1914, he embarked for France in the following November. Here he took part in much heavy fighting, and was engaged at the Battles of Ypres, the Somme, Loos, Neuve Chapelle and Vimy Ridge, and during the Retreat and Advance of 1918, and was wounded five times. He was demobilised in March 1919, and holds the 1914 Star, and the General Service and Victory Medals.
20, North Common, Redbourn.   4258.

REED, W. H. L., Private, Bedfordshire Regiment.

He volunteered in September 1914, and embarked for France in the following year. Whilst in this theatre of war he saw much fighting, and was in action in the Battles of Ypres, Hill 60, Arras, Givenchy, Cambrai, and in the Retreat and Advance of 1918. He was demobilised in March 1919, and holds the General Service and Victory Medals.
72, Norfolk Road, Rickmansworth.   X4266.

REEDER, H. J., Gunner, Royal Garrison Artillery.

He volunteered in September 1915, and was later drafted to the Western Front, where he served with his battery in many engagements, including those at the Somme in 1916, Arras, Messines, and in the Retreat and Advance of 1918. He was demobilised in March 1919 on his return to England, and holds the General Service and Victory Medals.
8, Earl Street, Watford.   X4261.

REEKS, W. J., Driver, Royal Field Artillery.

He volunteered in July 1915, and proceeded to France later in the same year. Here he saw heavy fighting in many sectors, and was engaged at the Battles of Albert and Ypres. During his service overseas he received injuries in action, which resulted in partial loss of sight, and was invalided to England, and after hospital treatment was discharged as unfit for further service in January 1917. He holds the 1914-15 Star, and the General Service and Victory Medals.
2, Grove Road, Harpenden.   4257.

REEVE, A., Sapper, Royal Engineers.

On attaining military age, he joined the Forces in April 1918, and on completing his training was engaged on important constructional work at various stations. He was unable to obtain his transfer overseas before the cessation of hostilities, and was demobilised in February 1919.
117, Upper Union Street, Dunstable.   4262.

REEVE, A. E., Private, R.A.M.C.

Volunteering in 1915, he completed his training and served at various hospitals on important duties connected with the care of sick and wounded troops. He rendered valuable services throughout, but was unsuccessful in procuring his transfer to a theatre of war, and was demobilised in August 1919.
2, Heber Cottages, London Colney.   2935/B.

REEVE, S. L., Corporal, South Wales Borderers.

He joined in March 1916, and was sent to the Western Front in the following September. Here he took part in the severe fighting at the Battles of the Somme, Arras, Cambrai, Ypres, and in the Retreat and Advance of 1918. On his return to England in January 1919 he was demobilised, and holds the General Service and Victory Medals.
155, The Square, Dunstable.   4268.

REEVES, B. H., Pte., 5th Bedfordshire Regt.

Joining in May 1918, on conclusion of his training he served at various stations on important duties with his unit, and after the cessation of hostilities was sent into Germany with the Army of Occupation, and was stationed at Cologne until his return to England for demobilisation in February 1919.
"Home Farm," Sundon Road, Leagrave.   4264/A.

REEVES, C. R., Sapper, Royal Engineers, and Private, 15th Welch Regiment.

He volunteered in May 1915, and proceeded overseas in January 1917. Whilst on the Western Front he was engaged on duties connected with the wiring and entrenching of the front lines and was continuously under fire. He served in the Battles of the Somme, Ypres and Albert, where he was wounded in May 1918 during the German Offensive. He was demobilised in March 1919, and holds the General Service and Victory Medals.
14, Park Street, Dunstable.   4256.

REEVES, D. A., Sapper, Royal Engineers.

Volunteering in January 1916, on completion of his training he served at various stations until drafted to Russia in 1919. He was engaged on important duties connected with railway construction, and in 1917 was transferred to Egypt, and served there until sent to Turkey with the Army of Occupation. He was demobilised in March 1920, and holds the General Service and Victory Medals.
1, Robin Hood, Right of Way, Hatfield.   X4342/A.

REEVES, E. E., Driver, Royal Engineers.

Volunteering in September 1914, he was sent to Egypt in January 1916. There he served throughout the Advance through Sinai, Palestine and Syria, and was present at the Battles of Gaza and Mejdel and the occupation of Haifa, Acre and Beyrout. He returned to England and was demobilised in August 1919, and holds the General Service and Victory Medals.
31, Union Street, Luton.   4263/B.

REEVES, F. A., Private, Queen's (Royal West Surrey Regiment).

He joined in March 1916, and on completing his training was stationed at various depôts with his unit, and was engaged on guard and other important duties. He rendered valuable services, but owing to ill-health was not successful in obtaining his transfer overseas prior to the signing of the Armistice, and was demobilised in September 1919.
"Home Farm," Sundon Road, Leagrave.   4264/B.

REEVES, G., Cpl., Royal Marine Labour Corps.

He volunteered in December 1914, and proceeded to France in May of the following year, and was engaged on important work in many advanced areas, including those of Ypres, Arras, the Somme, Cambrai and St. Quentin whilst heavy fighting was in progress. He also served throughout the Retreat and Advance of 1918, and on his return to England was demobilised in February 1919, and holds the General Service and Victory Medals.
120, Wellington Street, Luton.   4310/B.

REEVES, H., Private, Labour Corps.

Volunteering in 1915, he was drafted to France in the following year and served in the front lines, and was present at the Battles of Ypres and Cambrai. In 1917, owing to ill-health, he was invalided to England, and subsequently discharged unfit for further service. He holds the General Service and Victory Medals.
70, St. James' Road, Watford.   X4269/A.

REEVES, H. G., Private, 2nd King's Own (Yorkshire Light Infantry).

He joined in June 1917, and later was sent to France, where he saw much active service. He fought in many important engagements, including that at Cambrai, and was unfortunately killed in action on October 4th, 1918, during the Allied Advance. He was entitled to the General Service and Victory Medals.
26, Cannon Road, Watford Fields.   X4272.

REEVES, H. W., Sapper, Royal Engineers.

Joining in April 1917, he completed his course of training and served at various stations with his unit. He was engaged on important constructional work and other duties, but was unable to obtain his transfer overseas before the signing of the Armistice, and was demobilised in November 1919.
15, Brixton Road, Watford.   X4260.

REEVES, V. G., Pte., 53rd Bedfordshire Regt.

He joined in June 1916, and embarked for France six months later, and was engaged at the Battles of Arras, Ypres, Passchendaele, and was wounded at Loos in August, 1917. On recovery he returned to the front lines, and was in action on the Somme, at Amiens and Cambrai during the Retreat and Advance of 1918. He was demobilised in September 1919, and holds the General Service and Victory Medals.
"Home Farm," Sundon Road, Leagrave.   4264/C.

REEVES, T., Private, R.A.M.C.
Volunteering in 1914, he was immediately sent to the Western Front, where he was engaged in many battles. He rendered valuable services as a stretcher-bearer in the Battle of Ypres, and in 1915 was invalided to England. After receiving hospital treatment he was discharged unfit for further service, and holds the 1914-15 Star, and the General Service and Victory Medals.
70, St. James Road, Watford.   X4269/B.

REEVES, W. A., Private, Buffs (East Kent Regt.)
He joined in June 1917, and was sent to France in October 1918, and fought at many important engagements on the Cambrai front during the Allied Advance into Germany. He returned to England in the following year, and was eventually demobilised in November 1919, and holds the General Service and Victory Medals.
7, Belmont Cottages, Hatfield.   X4342/B.

REEVES, W. P., Rifleman, 52nd Rifle Brigade.
He joined in July 1918, and, completing his training, was drafted to the Army of Occupation in Germany in March 1919, and stationed on the Rhine, where he served until 1920. Returning to England he was demobilised in April of the same year.
21, Ebury Road, Watford.   X4271.

REGGIE, P., Corporal, King's Royal Rifle Corps.
Joining in March 1917, he proceeded to France later in the same year, and fought in many important engagements, and was in action at the Battles of the Somme, Amiens, and was taken prisoner near Cambrai in October 1918 during the Allied Advance. Repatriated after the Armistice, he was demobilised in October 1919, and holds the General Service and Victory Medals.
19, May Street, Luton.   2181/B.

REID, T. J., Private, 9th Norfolk Regiment.
Joining in January 1917, he embarked for France in September of the same year, and saw heavy fighting in many sectors. He was engaged at the Battle of Cambrai in December 1917, and fought in the opening phases of the Retreat of 1918. He returned to England in March 1918, and was subsequently demobilised in February 1919. He holds the General Service and Victory Medals.
154, North Street, Luton.   4274.

REID, W. A., Sapper, Royal Engineers.
He volunteered in April 1915, and was drafted to Salonika in the following September. Here he served on important constructional duties in the forward areas on the Vardar and Struma fronts until March 1919, when he returned to England and was demobilised in the following month. He holds the 1914-15 Star, and the General Service and Victory Medals.
7, Copse Wood Road, Watford.   X4273.

REYNARD, H., Gunner, Royal Garrison Artillery.
Joining in December 1916, he completed his training, and served at various stations with his unit on important duties. He rendered valuable services, but was unable to obtain his transfer overseas before the cessation of hostilities. He was demobilised in February 1919, and died in the following November from illness contracted on service.
63, Liverpool Road, Watford.   X4277/A.

REYNARD, J., Private, 8th Lincolnshire Regt.
Volunteering in May 1915, he proceeded to France later in the same year, and saw active service in many parts of the Western Front, fighting at the Battles of Ypres, Cambrai and Arras. He was killed in action at Arras on August 18th, 1917, and was entitled to the 1914-15 Star, and the General Service and Victory Medals.
63, Liverpool Road, Watford.   X4277/B.

REYNOLDS, A., L/Cpl., Military Foot Police.
He joined in August 1916, and in the following year embarked for Egypt. He served on the Palestine front and was present at many engagements, including those at Gaza, where he was wounded, and in the Valley of the Jordan. He returned to England and was demobilised in January 1920, and holds the General Service and Victory Medals.
Lower Green, Ickleford, Herts.   4240.

REYNOLDS, C. G., Gunner, R.F.A.
He volunteered in April 1915, and was sent to the Western Front in the following year. He served with his battery in many engagements, and was wounded on the Somme in 1916. Rejoining his unit on recovery he again fought at Arras, Messines, Albert and Ypres, and on August 16th, 1917, was reported missing. He was later presumed to have been killed in action on that date, and was entitled to the General Service and Victory Medals.
119, Whinbush Road, Hitchin.   3481/A.

REYNOLDS, F., Private, Labour Corps.
He joined in March 1916, and proceeded overseas in January of the following year. He served on the Western Front in many advanced areas on important constructional work in connection with roads and railways and in entrenching in the front lines, and was constantly under fire. He was demobilised in October 1919, and holds the General Service and Victory Medals.
Red Lion, Sundon, Beds.   4275/A.

REYNOLDS, F. J., Gunner, Royal Marine Artillery.
He joined in November 1917, and in May of the following year was drafted to the Western Front, where he took part in many important engagements, including those of Cambrai, Lens and in the Retreat and Advance of 1918. He was demobilised in June 1919, and holds the General Service and Victory Medals.
32, Jubilee Road, North Watford.   X4284.

REYNOLDS, G., Gunner, Royal Field Artillery.
Volunteering in November 1914, he proceeded to the Western Front in the following January, and was in action with his battery in many sectors fighting at the Battles of Lens and the Somme, and throughout the German Offensive and subsequent Allied Advance in 1918. He was demobilised in February 1919, and holds the General Service and Victory Medals.
68, Cobden Street, Luton.   4283/A.

REYNOLDS, H., R.A.M.C.
He volunteered in October 1914, and in the following year embarked for the Dardanelles, where he was present at the landing at Suvla Bay and the subsequent fighting until the Evacuation of the Peninsula. He was then drafted to France, where he served in many advanced areas in the Ypres salient and on the Somme front until 1917. Sent to Egypt, he was stationed at Sollum and later was transferred to Palestine, and served at the Battle of Gaza and was present at the Capture of Jerusalem and Haifa. He returned to England and was demobilised in March 1919, and holds the 1914-15 Star, and the General Service and Victory Medals.
84, Biscot Road, Luton.   4276/A, 4279/B, 4278/A.

REYNOLDS, H. W., L/Corporal, 1/1st Bedfordshire Lancers.
A Territorial, he was mobilised at the outbreak of war, and sent to France in May of the following year. Here he fought in many important engagements, including those at the Somme, Loos, Messines, Cambrai and during the Retreat and Advance of 1918. He returned to England, and was demobilised in April 1919, and holds the 1914-15 Star, and the General Service and Victory Medals.
17, Regent Street, Dunstable.   4282.

REYNOLDS, P., Air Mechanic, R.A.F. (late R.N.A.S.)
He joined in December 1917, and after his training served at the R.N.A.S. Base at Calshot on important duties. He rendered excellent services throughout, but was unable to obtain his transfer overseas prior to the cessation of hostilities, and was demobilised in October 1919.
84, Biscot Road, Luton.   4278/B, 4276/B, 4279/C.

REYNOLDS, P. W., Lieutenant, Labour Corps.
He volunteered in August 1914, and in the following year sailed for Gallipoli, where he served throughout the campaign. In 1916 he was drafted to France, and saw active service in many parts of the Western Front. He was granted a commission for exemplary conduct and devotion to duty in the field, and served throughout the Retreat and Advance of 1918 and was wounded. He holds the 1914-15 Star, and the General Service and Victory Medals, and was still serving in 1920.
68, Cobden Street, Luton.   4283/B.

REYNOLDS, T. J., Sergeant, R.E. (R.O.D.)
Joining in May 1917, he embarked for Egypt in the following September, and served on the Palestine front. He was engaged on important work on the railways and in the transport of ammunition and supplies to the front lines. He was under fire at the Battle of Gaza, and was present at the Occupation of Jerusalem and Jaffa. He returned to England and was demobilised in May 1919, and holds the General Service and Victory Medals.
17, Commons Cottages, Hitchin.   4239.

REYNOLDS, W. J., Pte., Royal Defence Corps.
A Reservist, he was mobilised on the outbreak of war, and after his training served with his unit at various stations on guard and other important duties. He rendered excellent services throughout until his demobilisation in January 1919.
68, Cobden Street, Luton.   4283/C.

REYNOLDS, W., C.S.M., 2nd Bedfordshire Regt.
Volunteering in August 1914, he proceeded to France in
1916, and was in action in many engagements of note,
including those at Ypres, the Somme and Arras, and
was wounded. On recovery he returned to the front
lines, and took part in heavy fighting until killed in
action on August 15th, 1918, during the Allied Advance.
He was entitled to the General Service and Victory
Medals.
33, Adelaide Street, St. Albans.   4280.

**REYNOLDS, W. G., Private, Bedfordshire Regt.,
and Prince of Wales' (Leinster Regiment).**
Volunteering in 1914, he was sent to the Western Front
in August of the following year, and fought at the
Battles of Ypres, the Somme and Arras, and was
wounded in July 1916. He was invalided to hospital in
England, and on recovery he returned to the front lines,
and was in action throughout the Retreat and Advance
of 1918. He was demobilised in February 1919, and
holds the 1914-15 Star, and the General Service and
Victory Medals.
Sandon Road, Harlington.   4281.

RHODES, A. V., Sapper, R.E. (I.W.T.)
Joining in September 1916, in the same year he was
drafted to Mesopotamia, where he was engaged on important transport duties on the Tigris and Euphrates. He
rendered valuable services throughout the campaign,
and returned to England after nearly four years' service. He was demobilised in February 1920, and holds
the General Service and Victory Medals.
66, St. Mary's Road, Watford.   X4285.

RHODES, F. W., Private, R.A.S.C. (M.T.)
He joined in May 1917, and in the following month
embarked for France. There he was engaged on important duties in connection with the transport of
ammunition and supplies to the firing lines at Arras,
Ypres, Cambrai and Albert, and was wounded in September 1917 in the third Battle of Ypres. He served
with his unit until the conclusion of hostilities, and
returned to England for demobilisation in December
1919. He holds the General Service and Victory Medals.
12, Smith Street, Watford.   X4286.

RICE, A. G., Driver, Royal Field Artillery.
He volunteered in November 1915, and in the following
May was sent to Mesopotamia. In this theatre of war
he fought in several engagements on the Euphrates, and
was in almost continuous action until the conclusion of
hostilities. Returning to England he was demobilised
in April 1919, and holds the General Service and
Victory Medals.
8, Primrose Cottages, Hatfield.   X4308/A.

RICE, G., Sergeant, Bedfordshire Regiment.
Volunteering in August 1914, he served with his unit at
various stations until drafted overseas in December
1915. He took part in several battles on the Western
Front and did valuable work with his unit and
was wounded in April 1917. He was later in action and
was badly gassed in August 1918. Invalided home he
died in the V.A.D. Hospital at Hatfield from the effects
of gas poisoning in the following month. He was entitled
to the 1914-15 Star, and the General Service and Victory
Medals.
8, Primrose Cottages, Hatfield.   4308/B.

RICHARDS, A., Private, 5th Royal Fusiliers.
He joined in June 1916, and in the following September
was sent to the Western Front. Taking part in engagements in various sectors, including that of the Somme,
he was severely wounded near Bapaume on November
19th, 1916, and invalided home. He was discharged
as medically unfit for further military service in January
1918, and holds the General Service and Victory Medals.
12, Waterlow Road, Dunstable.   4291.

RICHARDS, E. M. (Miss), Worker, Q.M.A.A.C.
She joined in October 1917, and was employed as a cook
at various military camps for over two years. She rendered valuable services and was demobilised in December
1919.
23, Alexandra Terrace, Biggleswade.   Z4290/B.

RICHARDS, W. S., Private, Labour Corps.
He joined in January 1917, and after training served at
various stations until sent overseas in the following
year. Engaged on important duties in connection with
operations on the Western Front he was present at
the fighting at Ypres and the Somme, and owing to the
explosion of an ammunition dump lost the sight of an
eye. He was demobilised in October 1919, and holds
the General Service and Victory Medals.
23, Alexandra Terrace, Biggleswade.   Z4290/A.

RICHARDSON, C., L/Cpl., Grenadier Guards.
Volunteering in March 1915, in the same year he was
drafted to the Western Front. Whilst in France he
served in several sectors and fought in most of the
principal battles, including those of Ypres, Cambrai and
the Somme, and was twice wounded. Returning to
England at the end of hostilities, he was demobilised
in February 1919, and holds the 1914-15 Star, and the
General Service and Victory Medals.
202, Chester Road, Watford.   X4297/A.

RICHARDSON, C. A., Private, Suffolk Regt.
He volunteered in November 1915, and in the following
June was sent to the Western Front. There he fought
in the Battles of the Somme, and Ypres, and was sent
home on account of wounds received in action in August
1917. He returned to France in March 1918, and took
part in the Retreat and Advance of that year. He holds
the General Service and Victory Medals, and was demobilised in April 1919.
9, Dudley Street, Leighton Buzzard.   4288.

RICHARDSON, C. H., Private, M.G.C.
He volunteered in February 1916, and after serving at
various stations, in the following February was drafted
to Palestine. In this theatre of war he saw much service with his unit and fought in several important
battles, including those of Gaza, Haifa, Acre and Beyrout. Returning to England at the conclusion of hos-
tiltities, he was demobilised in March 1919, and holds
the General Service and Victory Medals.
49, Saxon Road, Luton.   4300.

RICHARDSON, E. A., Private, Labour Corps.
He volunteered in May 1915, and in the following year
was sent to the Western Front in several sectors of
which he was engaged on important duties whilst heavy
fighting was in progress. Amongst other notable battles
at which he was present were those of Ypres, Arras,
Cambrai and the Somme. He was demobilised in March
1919, and holds the General Service and Victory Medals.
19, Church Street, St. Albans.   X4307.

RICHARDSON, F., Private, 3rd Suffolk Regt.
Joining in 1916, he was drafted overseas in the same
year and saw much active service on the Western Front.
He fought in several notable engagements, including
those at Arras, Ypres, Cambrai and was taken prisoner
on March 22nd, 1918, in the Battle of the Somme. After
enduring many privations in various detention camps in
Germany he was repatriated on the signing of the
Armistice, and was ultimately demobilised in November
1919. He holds the General Service and Victory Medals.
Horslow Street, Potton.   4293/A.

**RICHARDSON, F., Private, 1st Bedfordshire
Regiment, and Machine Gun Corps.**
He joined in 1916, and in the same year was drafted to
Egypt. He was engaged in the fighting in the British
advance through Palestine and was present at the Fall
of Jerusalem. He was sent to the Western Front in
1918 and fought in the Battles of Ypres and Cambrai,
and was gassed. He returned to England for demobilisation in December 1919, and holds the General Service and
Victory Medals.
2, Chapel Fields, Biggleswade.   Z4294.

**RICHARDSON, F. H. R., Colour-Sergeant, Royal
Marines.**
He volunteered in January 1915, and posted to a mine-
laying squadron was engaged on mine-laying and patrol
duties in the North Sea, and other waters. His ship
was also employed on special duties at Scapa Flow and
at other important naval bases. He was demobilised in
March 1919, and holds the 1914-15 Star, and the General
Service and Victory Medals.
44, Selbourne Road, Luton.   4299.

RICHARDSON, J., Pte., 6th Bedfordshire Regt.
He volunteered in February 1916, and in July of the
same year was despatched to the Western Front. There
he saw much service and was engaged in heavy fighting
at Merville and in the Battles of the Somme and Cambrai.
He served with his unit in several other operations
during the closing stages of the war, and was sent home
for demobilisation in June 1919. He holds the General
Service and Victory Medals.
"The Brache," Maulden, near Ampthill.   4293.

RICHARDSON, K. C., Air Mechanic, R.A.F.
He joined in 1916, and on the conclusion of his training
served with his Squadron at various aerodromes. Engaged on important duties in connection with the fitting
and repairing of aero engines he did very good work,
but was unable to obtain a transfer to a theatre of
war before the cessation of hostilities, and was demobilised in March 1919.
42, Albion Road, Luton.   4303.

RICHARDSON, L. S. E., Private, 2nd Highland Light Infantry.
Volunteering in August 1914, he was almost immediately drafted to France where he fought in the Retreat from Mons and in many subsequent engagements. He was unfortunately killed in action on November 13th, 1914, near Ypres, and was entitled to the Mons Star, and the General Service and Victory Medals.
72, Olympia Cottages, Selby, Yorkshire. 3847/B.

RICHARDSON, O., Private, Bedfordshire Regt.
He volunteered in August 1915, and on the completion of his training was engaged on special duties with his unit at various stations. He was unable to procure his transfer overseas on account of medical unfitness and was invalided out of the Service in May 1916.
4, Wellington Road, St. Albans. X4295.

RICHARDSON, P., Pte., 1st Hertfordshire Regt.
Joining in 1916, he was drafted overseas in the same year. He served on the Western Front and fought in several important engagements until wounded in action at Ypres. Returning to the firing line on recovery he saw much service during the concluding operations of the war. He was demobilised in January 1919, and holds the General Service and Victory Medals.
202, Chester Road, Watford. X4297/B.

RICHARDSON, P., Pte., 2nd Bedfordshire Regt.
Volunteering in August 1914, in the following month he was sent to France. He was in action near Mons and was wounded and taken prisoner on October 30th, 1914. He was held in captivity in various detention camps in Germany and Russia until 1918, when he was released and returned to England. He was demobilised in December of that year, and holds the 1914 Star, and the General Service and Victory Medals.
Horslow Street, Potton. 4293/B.

RICHARDSON, P. G., Corporal, 1st Queen's (Royal West Surrey Regiment).
He volunteered in September 1914 and in the following month was drafted to Mesopotamia. In this theatre of war he was engaged in heavy fighting on the Euphrates, and took part in the Battles of Nasiriyeh, Ramadieh, Khan Baghdadie, and several other important engagements. He was sent to India on the conclusion of hostilities, and returned home for demobilisation in May 1919, and holds the 1914-15 Star, and the General Service and Victory Medals.
96, Spenser Road, Luton. 4301.

RICHARDSON, S., Gunner, R.G.A.
He joined in March 1918, and after training was engaged on important duties with the 8th Hampshire Fire Command at various stations. He did very valuable work but was unable to obtain his transfer overseas on account of medical unfitness. He was demobilised in February 1919.
17, Oliver Street, Ampthill. 4289.

RICHARDSON, W., Pte., 2nd Bedfordshire Regt.
He enlisted in December 1910, and at the outbreak of war was sent to the Western Front in October 1914. During his service in this theatre of war he was in action at Ypres and Neuve Chapelle, and was wounded at Festubert in May 1915. Rejoining his unit he took part in several important engagements, including the Battles of Ypres and Vimy Ridge, and was invalided home on account of wounds received at Dickebusch on June 21st, 1917. After medical treatment he served at the depot of his regiment until his demobilisation in March 1919, and holds the 1914 Star, and the General Service and Victory Medals.
The Strand, Clophill, near Ampthill. 4304.

RICHARDSON, W. F., Private, King's Own (Yorkshire Light Infantry).
He joined in June 1917, and was drafted to the Western Front in the same year. Serving with his unit he fought in many of the principal engagements during the closing stages of the war, including the Battles of Ypres and Cambrai, and was twice wounded. On the conclusion of hostilities he was sent to India and in 1920 he was still serving there. He holds the General Service and Victory Medals.
12, Neal Street, Watford. X4306.

RICHINGS, E., Corporal, Military Foot Police.
He volunteered in March 1915, and at the conclusion of his training was engaged on special duties with his unit at various stations. He rendered valuable service, but owing to medical unfitness was unable to obtain his transfer overseas, and was demobilised in October 1919.
95, Norfolk Road, Rickmansworth. X4296.

RICHMOND, W., Private, 1/7th London Regt.
He joined in March 1916, and in the following August proceeded to France. Whilst on the Western Front he served with his Battalion and took part in the fierce fighting at the Battle of the Somme and was unfortunately killed in action on October 7th, 1916. He was entitled to the General Service and Victory Medals.
3, Keyfield Terrace, St. Albans. 4300.

RICKARD, L., Private, Oxfordshire and Buckinghamshire Light Infantry.
He volunteered in January 1916, and in the following September was sent to Mesopotamia. Serving with his unit he fought in several of the operations in the attempts to relieve Kut and was in action in many important battles, including those of Kut-el-Amara and Khan Baghdadie. He returned to England for demobilisation in March 1920, and holds the General Service and Victory Medals.
Handpost Wing, near Leighton Buzzard. 4287.

RICKARD, T. A. E., Driver, Royal Engineers.
Volunteering in March 1915, when fifteen and a half years of age, he completed his training and was engaged on various duties with his unit at several stations. He was not drafted overseas on account of his age, but did good work until kicked by a mule. He died from the effects of his injuries on May 9th, 1918, and was buried at Luton.
34, North Street, Luton. 4292/A.

RICKARD, T. E., Sapper, Royal Engineers.
He volunteered in July 1915, and on the completion of his training was engaged with his unit at various stations on the East Coast on important duties in connection with coastal defence work. He rendered valuable services, but was unable to obtain a transfer to a theatre of war before the cessation of hostilities. He was demobilised in March 1919.
34, North Street, Luton. 4292/B.

RICKETT, W. J., Private, 1st Essex Regiment.
He volunteered in November 1915, and in the following September was sent overseas. Whilst on the Western Front he served in many sectors, and was in almost continuous action in the offensive operations on the Somme. Owing to illness he was sent home to hospital in February 1917, and after a period of treatment was invalided out of the service in August of the same year. He holds the General Service and Victory Medals.
Fleur-de-Lys, Hockliffe Hill, Leighton Buzzard. 4305.

RIDER, G. W., Corporal, Labour Corps.
He joined in March 1917, and two months later proceeded to France. Whilst in this theatre of war he was engaged on special duties with his Battalion in the forward areas at Ypres and Cambrai, and was constantly under heavy shell fire. He was demobilised in March 1919, and holds the General Service and Victory Medals.
25, Copsewood Road, Watford. X2463/B.

RIDLEY, C. A., Private, Queen's Own (Royal West Kent Regiment).
He joined in May 1917, and in the following October was sent to France. He fought in many engagements on the Western Front, and was severely wounded at the Battle of Arras in April 1918. He was invalided home and discharged from the Service as medically unfit in December of that year. He holds the General Service and Victory Medals.
7, Saxon Road, Luton. 4309.

RIGGS, C., Air Mechanic, Royal Air Force.
He joined in October 1917, and was almost immediately drafted overseas. Whilst on the Western Front he was stationed at St. Omer Aerodrome with his Squadron, and was engaged on special duties as an aero engine fitter until February 1918. He then returned to England and was discharged on account of service in the ensuing April. He holds the General Service and Victory Medals.
120, Wellington Street, Luton. 4310/A.

RILEY, A. G., Sergeant, Royal Air Force.
He joined the Royal Army Pay Corps in June 1917, and served at Woking on important duties with this unit. He did excellent work, but owing to medical unfitness was unable to secure his transfer overseas. He later transferred to the Royal Air Force, and in 1920 was still serving.
26, Portland Street, St. Albans. 4311.

RILEY, F. J., Private, 1st Norfolk Regiment.
He joined in July 1917, and in May of the following year was sent to France. Whilst on the Western Front he served in many engagements and fought on the Somme and during the Retreat and Advance of 1918, and was gassed. He was demobilised in October 1919, and holds the General Service and Victory Medals.
9, Common View Square, Letchworth. 4312.

RINGHAM, A., Driver, Royal Field Artillery.
He joined in May 1916, and was employed with his Battery until December 1917, when he was drafted to France. He fought at Arras, Ypres, Passchendaele, Douai, Poperinghe, Lens, Loos and Cambrai, and in the Retreat and Advance of 1918. He was demobilised in October 1919, and holds the General Service and Victory Medals.
38, Springfield Road, Linslade, Bucks.   4313.

RIPLEY, N., Sapper, Royal Engineers.
Volunteering at the outbreak of war he was drafted to France in the following year. He was engaged on special duties with his unit in many sectors of the Western Front and was wounded. On recovery he was sent to Salonika, and during his service there contracted an illness. He was invalided to hospital and subsequently died on October 3rd, 1918. He was entitled to the 1914-15 Star, and the General Service and Victory Medals.
East End, Flitwick, Beds.   4314.

RITCHIE, J., A.B., Royal Navy.
He was serving in the Royal Navy when the war broke out, and aboard H.M.S. " Blake " was engaged on important patrol duties in the North Sea for over three years. His ship was later sent to the Adriatic, and there employed on similar duties until hostilities ceased. He holds the 1914-15 Star and the General Service and Victory Medals, and in 1920 was still serving.
39, Old Bedford Road, Luton.   142/A.

RIVETT, A., Private, Labour Corps.
He joined in 1916, and was shortly afterwards drafted to the Western Front. In this theatre of war he was engaged on important duties with his battalion at Ypres, Arras, the Aisne, Vimy Ridge, Passchendaele and on the Somme. He was demobilised in 1919, and holds the General Service and Victory Medals.
36, Souldern Street, Watford.   X1237/B.

RIVETT, J. W., Private, Royal Fusiliers.
He volunteered in June 1915, and was later sent to France. During his service on the Western Front he took part in the fighting at Ypres, Passchendaele and Arras. He later returned to England, and was discharged on account of service in 1918, and holds the General Service and Victory Medals.
17, Red Lion Yard, Watford.   X4315.

RIX, L. G., Sapper, Royal Engineers.
He joined in April 1916, and in the same year was drafted to Egypt. He was engaged on important duties with his unit at Cairo and whilst operations were in progress at Jerusalem and Gaza. He was transferred to Salonika in 1918, and there served on the Doiran, Vardar and Struma fronts. He was demobilised in November 1919, and holds the General Service and Victory Medals.
64, Lancaster Road, Hitchin.   4316.

RIX, S. G., Aircraftsman, Royal Air Force.
He joined in August 1917, and at the conclusion of his training served at various aerodromes on important duties, which demanded a high degree of technical skill. He did excellent work with his Squadron as an aero-engine fitter, but was unable to obtain his transfer to a theatre of war, and was demobilised in February 1919.
Norfolk House, Limbury Road, Limbury, Beds.   4317.

RIX, S. J., Private, Royal Marine Light Infantry.
He volunteered in October 1914, and in the following year proceeded to the Dardanelles. He fought at the landing at Suvla Bay and the subsequent engagements until the Evacuation of the Peninsula in December 1915. He then served in Egypt for a time and was sent to France in 1916. In this theatre of war he was in action at Ypres, Ostend and Zeebrugge, and was wounded. He was demobilised in July 1919, and holds the 1914-15 Star, and the General Service and Victory Medals.
61, Manor Road, Luton.   4318.

ROADNIGHT, J. T., Pte., 13th East Surrey Regt.
He volunteered in June 1915, and was shortly afterwards drafted to France. He fought at Ypres, Arras and Passchendaele, and was taken prisoner at Cambrai in April 1918. Held in captivity until after the signing of the Armistice, during which time he suffered many privations, he returned to England and was demobilised in March 1919. He holds the 1914-15 Star, and the General Service and Victory Medals.
45, Copsewood Road, Watford.   X4343/B.

ROADNIGHT, H. G., Pte., 1/5th Bedfordshire Regiment.
He joined in 1916, and was later sent to Egypt. He took part in the operations in the British Advance through Palestine, and the fighting at Gaza and the Occupation of Jerusalem, and was once wounded. He returned to England after the signing of the Armistice, and was demobilised in February 1919. He holds the General Service and Victory Medals.
45, Copsewood Road, Watford.   X4343/A.

ROBERSON, J. W., Pte., Royal Naval Division.
He joined in November 1916, and was later sent overseas. Whilst on the Western Front he served in various sectors and was engaged in much heavy fighting, and was unfortunately killed in action at the Battle of Ypres on October 26th, 1917. He was entitled to the General Service and Victory Medals.
35, Liverpool Road, Watford.   X4394/B.

ROBERSON, T., Stoker, Royal Navy.
He joined in January 1916, and after completing his training was posted to H.M.S. " Danae," which vessel was engaged on important patrol duties in the Pacific Ocean and off the coast of South Africa until hostilities ceased. He was demobilised in June 1919, and holds the General Service and Victory Medals.
35, Liverpool Road, Watford.   X4394/A.

ROBERTS, A. T., Private, Machine Gun Corps.
He volunteered in January 1915, and in the following June was drafted to France. He took part in the fighting at Ypres, St. Quentin, Cambrai, on the Somme, and in the final operations of the war. After the cessation of hostilities he served with the Army of Occupation on the Rhine and was stationed at Cologne. He was demobilised in February 1919, and holds the 1914-15 Star, and the General Service and Victory Medals.
Bury Road, Stopsley.   2419/B.

ROBERTS, B., Trooper, South Nottinghamshire Hussars.
He volunteered in 1915, and served with his squadron at various stations until drafted to France in 1917. In this theatre of war he was engaged in the fighting at Ypres, Arras, Cambrai and other places, and was wounded five times. He was demobilised in January 1919, and holds the General Service and Victory Medals.
26, Villiers Road, Oxhey, Herts.   X4412.

ROBERTS, C., Private, 12th East Surrey Regt.
He joined in June 1916, and twelve months later proceeded to France. During his service on the Western Front he took part in various engagements, and was wounded and taken prisoner at Ypres on August 5th, 1917. During his captivity in Germany he suffered many hardships until released in December 1918. He returned to England and was demobilised in April 1919, and holds the General Service and Victory Medals.
Princess Street, Toddington, Beds.   4351.

ROBERTS, E., Rflmn., King's Royal Rifle Corps.
He joined in January 1917, and later in the same year was drafted to India, where he was stationed at Calcutta and other depôts, and employed on garrison and other duties with his battalion. He was serving at Rawal Pindi in 1920, and holds the General Service and Victory Medals.
Bailey Villas, London Colney.   X4393/C.

ROBERTS, E., Pte., 1/5th Bedfordshire Regt.
He was mobilised at the outbreak of war, and in 1915 was sent to Ireland, where he was engaged on important duties during the riots caused by the Sinn Feiners. He returned to England in January 1916 owing to ill-health and was invalided out of the service in March of that year.
4, Bedford Street, Leighton Buzzard.   4352/B.

ROBERTS, F., Private, R.A.V.C.
He volunteered in November 1915, and in the succeeding year was drafted to France. He served at Rouen, tending sick and wounded horses, until transferred to Egypt in 1917. In this theatre of war he was engaged on special duties with his unit, and was stationed at Ramleh, Ludd and Wilhelmina during the British Advance through Palestine. He was demobilised in April 1919, and holds the General Service and Victory Medals.
Bailey Villas, London Colney.   X4393/A.

ROBERTS, F. C., Private, Canadian Regiment.
He volunteered in August 1915, and was drafted to France in the following year. Whilst on the Western Front he fought on the Somme and was severely wounded. He was invalided to England, and after hospital treatment returned to France and rejoined his unit on the Cambrai front, taking part in the Allied Advance into Germany. He was demobilised in January 1919, and holds the General Service and Victory Medals.
50, Clarence Load, Leighton Buzzard.   4327/A.

ROBERTS, G., Private, 1/7th London Regt.
He volunteered in August 1914, and was posted to the
East Surrey Regiment. He was later transferred to the
London Regiment, with which unit he was sent overseas in the following January. Whilst in France he
fought in many engagements and was wounded, gassed
and suffered from trench fever. Returning to England
he was demobilised in February 1919, and holds the
1914-15 Star, and the General Service and Victory
Medals.
50, Clarence Road, Leighton Buzzard.   4327/B.

ROBERTS, H. P., Pte., 1st Hertfordshire Regt.
A Territorial, he was mobilised at the outbreak of war,
and was sent to the Western Front almost immediately,
and fought in the Retreat from Mons and in the Battles
of Ypres and Hill 60. Transferred to Italy early in
1916 he saw heavy fighting on the Piave and in other
sectors until returning to France in February 1918. He
was in action throughout the Retreat and Advance of
1918, and later proceeded into Germany with the Army
of Occupation and was stationed at Cologne. He was
demobilised in March 1919, and holds the Mons Star,
and the General Service and Victory Medals.
123, Cotterells Road, Hemel Hempstead.   X4366.

**ROBERTS, H. T., Private, Queen's Own (Royal
West Kent Regiment).**
He joined in June 1916, and in the following October
was sent to the Western Front, where he saw much
service. He fought in engagements at Arras, Ypres III.,
Cambrai and in the second Battle of the Somme, and
was twice wounded. He was demobilised in March 1919,
and holds the General Service and Victory Medals.
Rosellen Cottages, Sandy Road, Potton.   Z1285/B.

ROBERTS, J., Private, Coldstream Guards.
He volunteered at the outbreak of war, and was almost
immediately drafted to France. He fought in the
Retreat from Mons and the subsequent Battles of Ypres,
Hill 60, the Somme, Cambrai, and during the German
Offensive and subsequent Allied Advance of 1918. During
his service in this theatre of war he was gassed and
three times wounded. He was demobilised in February
1919, and holds the Mons Star, and the General Service
and Victory Medals.
Littleworth, Wing, Bucks.   4380/B.

ROBERTS, J. F., Private, Royal Fusiliers.
He volunteered in May 1915, and was later drafted overseas. He served on the Western Front and took part
in the fighting during many battles and engagements.
He was unfortunately killed in action at the Battle of
the Somme on July 1st, 1916, and was entitled to the
General Service and Victory Medals.
3, Normanhurst, Grosvenor Road East, St. Albans.
                                              X4361.

ROBERTS, S., Private, Machine Gun Corps.
He volunteered in August 1914, and on completion of
his training was drafted to France. In this theatre of
war he fought at Ypres, Vimy Ridge, Hill 60, and in
many other important engagements. He was killed in
action on July 8th, 1916, in the vicinity of Verdun, and
was entitled to the General Service and Victory Medals.
Bailey Villas, London Colney.   X4393/B.

ROBERTS, S., Private, 1st Bedfordshire Regt.
He volunteered in June 1915, and in the following April
was sent to France. He took part in the fighting near
Vimy Ridge, and was wounded at Vimy Ridge in 1916.
He received hospital treatment and later returned to
the front line trenches, and was again wounded on the
Somme in the same year. On recovery he rejoined his
battalion, and during an engagement at Lens was killed
in action on April 23rd, 1917. He was entitled to the
General Service and Victory Medals.
4, Bedford Street, Leighton Buzzard.   4352/A.

ROBERTS, S. J., Private, Bedfordshire Regt.
A Territorial, he was mobilised at the outbreak of war,
and in September 1914 was sent to France. In this
theatre of war he was engaged in the fighting in many
sectors until March 1915. He was then drafted to
Egypt and was in action in the British Advance through
Palestine, and fought at the Battle of Gaza, and the
occupation of Jerusalem and Aleppo. He was demobilised in March 1919, and holds the 1914 Star, and the
General Service and Victory Medals.
50, Clarence Road, Leighton Buzzard.   4327/C.

ROBERTSON, A. B., A.B., Royal Navy.
He joined in 1918, and posted to H.M.S. "Leader," was
engaged on mine-sweeping and patrol duties in the
North Sea and English Channel until after the signing
of the Armistice. His ship frequently passed through
mine-strewn areas and had many narrow escapes. He
was demobilised in July 1918, and holds the General
Service and Victory Medals.
26, Ashburnham Road, Luton.   4322.

**ROBINS, F. J., Private, 1st Bedfordshire Regt.,
and Hertfordshire Regiment.**
He joined in June 1916, and on completing his training
was engaged on important duties at various stations
in connection with the defences of the South and South-
East Coasts. He was also employed on Military Police
duties and rendered valuable services but was unable
to obtain a transfer overseas before the termination of
hostilities and was demobilised in September 1919.
4, Breakspeare Road, Abbots Langley.   X4363/B.

ROBINS, P. C., Private, Lincolnshire Regiment.
Volunteering in September 1914, he was engaged on
various duties with his battalion until drafted overseas
in 1917. He saw much service on the Western Front
and took part in heavy fighting in the Battles of Arras,
Ypres and other important engagements until the
termination of the war. He holds the General Service
and Victory Medals, and was demobilised in April 1919.
4, Breakspeare Road, Abbots Langley.   X4363/A.

ROBINSON, A., Private, R.A.V.C.
He joined in June 1917, and in the following November embarked for the Western Front. There he was
engaged on important duties in attending to sick and
wounded horses, and was present at the Battles of the
Somme, Ypres and Cambrai. On the cessation of hostilities he returned home for demobilisation in February
1919, and holds the General Service and Victory Medals.
Trowley Bottom, Flamstead, Beds.   X4353.

ROBINSON, A. (M.M.), Pte., Bedfordshire Regt.
Volunteering in February 1916, he was sent to France in
the same year. Whilst overseas he was in action in
several notable battles, including those of the Somme,
Arras, Ypres and Cambrai, and was wounded. He was
awarded the Military Medal for conspicuous bravery and
devotion to duty in the Field, and in addition holds
the General Service and Victory Medals. He was demobilised in November 1918.
30, Woburn Road, Ampthill.   4324/A.

**ROBINSON, A. B., L/Corporal, King's Royal
Rifle Corps.**
He joined in August 1918, on attaining military age
and after completing his training served with his
unit at various stations until the following December
when he was drafted to Germany to the Army of
Occupation and was stationed at Cologne. He was
engaged on guard and other duties and in December
1919 returned to England and was demobilised.
44, Hockcliffe Street, Leighton Buzzard.   4326/A.

ROBINSON, A. G., Sapper, Royal Engineers.
He joined in March 1917, and in the following August
was sent to the Western Front where he was engaged
on important duties in connection with operations
in the front line trenches during heavy fighting at
Arras, Ypres, Cambrai, and in the Retreat and Advance
of 1918. He was killed in action on October 28th, 1918,
near Cambrai, and was entitled to the General Service
and Victory Medals.
14, Hockcliffe Road, Leighton Buzzard.   4325.

**ROBINSON, A. J., Private, King's Own (Royal
Lancaster Regiment).**
Joining in June 1916, he was drafted to Salonika in the
following November. In this theatre of war he fought
in many important engagements in the Allied Advance on
the Doiran front, where he was wounded during stubborn
fighting. He subsequently died from the effects of his
wounds on September 19th, 1918, and was entitled to the
General Service and Victory Medals.
123, New Town Street, Luton.   4371.

ROBINSON, A. W., Gunner, Royal Field Artillery.
He volunteered in August 1914, and in the following
January was sent to France. There he served with his
Battery in many important engagements, including those
of Loos, Vimy Ridge, the Somme and Cambrai, and was
wounded in July 1915. Taken prisoner in June 1918
during the German Offensive on the Somme, he was
kept in captivity in Germany and suffered many hardships and privations, until released after the signing of
the Armistice. He holds the 1914-15 Star, and the General
Service and Victory Medals, and was demobilised in 1919.
Littleworth, Wing, near Leighton Buzzard.   4338.

ROBINSON, C., Gunner, Royal Garrison Artillery.
He was serving in India when war was declared and
was immediately sent to France. He fought in the
Retreat from Mons and in the Battle of Festubert, and
was subsequently taken prisoner in an engagement in
September 1915. He died in captivity in the same month,
and was entitled to the Mons Star, and the General
Service and Victory Medals.
Leighton Street, Woburn.   Z4364.

ROBINSON, B., Private, 1/6th Essex Regiment.

He volunteered in November 1915, and in July of the following year was sent to Egypt. During the Advance through Palestine he fought in several important engagements and was wounded in the Battle of Gaza on March 26th, 1917. On recovery he rejoined his unit and served through the remainder of the Eastern campaign. He returned to England and was demobilised in September 1919, and holds the General Service and Victory Medals.

23, Alfred Street, Dunstable. 4399.

ROBINSON, C., Private, Royal Berkshire Regt.

He volunteered in January 1915, and in the same year embarked for France. Serving with his unit in several sectors he was in action in many important engagements, including the Battle of Ypres. He was taken prisoner during the Battle of the Somme, and during his captivity in Germany received harsh treatment at the hands of the enemy for refusing to work on munitions. He was released after the Armistice and demobilised in February 1919 after returning to England, and holds the 1914-15 Star, and the General Service and Victory Medals.

51, Sotheron Road, Watford. 3880/B.

ROBINSON, C. C., L/Corporal, 7th Bedfordshire Regiment.

He volunteered in September 1914, and in the following June was drafted to the Western Front. Whilst in this theatre of war he fought in several notable engagements, including the Battles of Loos and the Somme. He was killed in action at Achiet-le-Grand on March 15th, 1917, and was entitled to the 1914-15 Star, and the General Service and Victory Medals.

96, Spencer Road, Luton. 4346.

ROBINSON, C. T., Pte., 1st Bedfordshire Regt.

Volunteering in December 1915, in the following February he was sent to France, where he served with his unit and was in action in many important engagements, including the Battles of Arras, St. Quentin and Bapaume, and was gassed. On the termination of hostilities he served with the Army of Occupation in Germany and was stationed at Cologne. He was demobilised in February 1919, and holds the General Service and Victory Medals.

Old Vicarage Cottages, Offley. 4321.

ROBINSON, C. W., Private, R.A.V.C.

He volunteered in September 1914, in the Royal Engineers, and was discharged after serving with this unit for a short time owing to medical unfitness. He later joined the Royal Army Veterinary Corps and in 1916 was drafted to Egypt. In this theatre of war he did valuable work attending to sick and wounded horses in the Advance through Palestine and was present during operations at Gaza, Jaffa and Haifa. He contracted malaria and suffered from shell-shock and returning to England, after receiving hospital treatment, he was invalided out of the Service in June 1919, and holds the General Service and Victory Medals.

Church Lane, Pavenham, Beds. Z4340.

ROBINSON, F., Private, 1st Hertfordshire Regt.

He volunteered in August 1914, and in the following November was drafted overseas. Serving on the Western Front he was in action in many important engagements, including the Battles of Arras and Ypres. He was discharged on account of service in April 1917, and holds the 1914 Star, and the General Service and Victory Medals.

49, Grange Street, St. Albans. X4409.

ROBINSON, F., Gunner, R.G.A., Anti-Aircraft Section.

He joined in April 1916, and after training was engaged on important duties at various stations until drafted to the Western Front in May 1918. Whilst overseas he rendered valuable services in many sectors of France, and was in action at the Battle of Ypres and other important engagements. He was demobilised in February in 1919, and holds the General Service and Victory Medals.

16, Collingdon Street, Luton. 4369.

ROBINSON, F., Private, 2nd Royal Fusiliers.

Volunteering in December 1915, in the following August he was sent to France. In this theatre of war he was in action in the Somme Offensive, the Battles of Beaumont-Hamel, Arras, and was wounded at Ypres in October 1917. Rejoining his unit on recovery, he served in the final operations of the war and returned to England. He was demobilised in April 1919, and holds the General Service and Victory Medals.

73a, Burr Street, Luton. 4373.

ROBINSON, G. W., Private, 3rd Norfolk Regt.

He joined in February 1918, and in the same year embarked for the Western Front. There he saw much active service and fought in several engagements, including those at Albert and St. Quentin during the Retreat and Advance of 1918, and was gassed. He returned to England for demobilisation in June 1919, and holds the General Service and Victory Medals.

Park Hill, Ampthill. 4333/C.

ROBINSON, H. V., Private, West Yorkshire Regt.

He joined in 1916, and in the same year was drafted to the Western Front where he served for three years. During this period he was engaged in the fighting in many important battles, including those of the Somme, Albert, Ypres, Messines, and in the Retreat and Advance of 1918, and was gassed. He returned to England for demobilisation in February 1919, and holds the General Service and Victory Medals.

Park Hill, Ampthill. 4333/A.

ROBINSON, J. F., Sapper, Royal Engineers.

He was mobilised on the outbreak of hostilities and was shortly afterwards drafted to France. In this theatre of war he served in the Retreat from Mons, at Armentières, and in other important engagements. He was discharged on account of service in December 1915, and holds the Mons Star, and the General Service and Victory Medals.

3, New Street, Luton. 4383.

ROBINSON, J. W., L/Corporal, R.A.M.C.

He joined in April 1916, and in the following June was drafted overseas. Sent to Egypt he was engaged on important duties at various base hospitals, and later took part in the British Advance through Palestine. He rendered valuable services with the Field Ambulance at Gaza, Mejdel and other important engagements in the course of the Palestine campaign, and returned home for demobilisation in September 1919. He holds the General Service and Victory Medals.

50, Rothesay Road, Luton. 4375.

ROBINSON, J. W., Private, 13th London Regt. (Kensingtons).

He joined in November 1915, and in the following year was sent to the Western Front. Whilst in this theatre of war he fought in several important engagements, including those on the Somme and at Ypres, and was wounded near Arras in January 1917. Returning to his unit he was killed in action on April 9th of the same year in the first Battle of Arras, and was entitled to the General Service and Victory Medals.

Park Hill, Ampthill. 4333/B.

ROBINSON, M. (Miss), Special War Worker.

This lady volunteered her services for work of National importance in January 1915, and was engaged in the shell filling departments of large munition factories at Watford and Perivale for over three years. She carried out her various duties to the satisfaction of the authorities.

42, Shaftesbury Road, Watford. X3943-4/D.

ROBINSON, P., Private, 7th Northamptonshire Regiment.

He joined in 1917, and on completion of his training was sent to France where he served in several sectors and took part in many important engagements. He was unfortunately killed in action on April 25th, 1918, during the Retreat from Cambrai, and was entitled to the General Service and Victory Medals.

30, Woburn Road, Ampthill. 4324/B.

ROBINSON, P. T., O.S., Royal Navy.

He joined in January 1918, and after completing his training was engaged on important duties at various naval stations. He did valuable work, but was unsuccessful in his efforts to be sent to sea before the termination of hostilities, and was discharged in February 1919.

10, Villa Road, Luton. 4362.

ROBINSON, S., Driver, Royal Engineers.

He volunteered in September 1914, and in the following July proceeded overseas. Sent to Gallipoli, he was employed on important duties in connection with the landing at Suvla Bay and other operations until the Evacuation of the Peninsula. He was sent to Egypt in March 1916, and served with the Forces engaged under General Allenby in the Advance through Palestine. He was present at the Battle of Gaza and other important operations until the cessation of hostilities. He returned to England for demobilisation in June 1919, and holds the 1914-15 Star, and the General Service and Victory Medals.

42, Midland Road, Luton. 4384.

ROBINSON, R. G., Private, Royal Fusiliers.

He joined in May 1916, and on the conclusion of his training was engaged at various stations on the East Coast on guard and other important duties in connection with coastal defence. He rendered valuable services but was not sent overseas owing to medical unfitness for general service, and was demobilised in December 1919.
44, Hockliffe Street, Leighton Buzzard.   4326/B.

ROBINSON, S., Private, Labour Corps.

He joined in March 1917, and two months later was sent to France. Whilst overseas he was engaged in making roads and digging trenches in the front lines, and was present at the Battles of Arras, Ypres, Albert and the Somme. Invalided home in October 1918 on account of illness contracted whilst overseas, he was demobilised in March 1919, and holds the General Service and Victory Medals.
Saunders Piece, Ampthill.   4330.

ROBINSON, T. E., Pte., 1st Bedfordshire Regt.

He volunteered in August 1914, and in the following year was drafted to Gallipoli, where he took part in fierce fighting in the landing at Suvla Bay and the engagements which followed. He was killed in action on September 10th, 1915, and was entitled to the 1914-15 Star, and the General Service and Victory Medals.
30, Millbrook, near Ampthill.   4332.

ROBINSON, V., Private, Queen's (Royal West Surrey Regiment).

He was mobilised on the outbreak of war, and shortly afterwards proceeded to France. He fought in the Retreat from Mons and in several subsequent actions until wounded in May 1915 in the second Battle of Ypres. After medical treatment he returned to the firing line and served in the Battles of Arras, St. Quentin, and other important engagements during the continuance of hostilities. He was demobilised in March 1919, and holds the Mons Star, and the General Service and Victory Medals.
17, Front Street, Slip End.   4347.

ROBINSON, W., Rifleman, 18th King's Royal Rifle Corps.

Volunteering in July 1915, he was sent to the Western Front in the following May and was engaged in heavy fighting until wounded near Ypres in July 1916. Rejoining his unit he fought again, and was killed in action at Hollebeke on June 13th, 1917, and was entitled to the General Service and Victory Medals.
17, High Street, Houghton Regis, Beds.   4398.

ROBINSON, W., Private, 2nd Bedfordshire Regt.

A serving soldier, he was mobilised on the outbreak of hostilities and almost immediately drafted to France. Whilst on the Western Front he took part in heavy fighting in the Retreat from Mons and the Battle of the Marne. He was killed in action in the Battle of La Bassée on October 23rd, 1914, and was entitled to the Mons Star, and the General Service and Victory Medals.
31, Friday Street, Leighton Buzzard.   1618/B.

ROBINSON, W., Gunner, Royal Field Artillery.

He volunteered in June 1915, and in the same year was sent to Egypt, and served overseas for upwards of four years. During this period he was in action in several engagements in the British Advance through Palestine, and fought in the Battles of Gaza and Jaffa, and was present at the Fall of Jerusalem. He returned home for demobilisation in July 1919, and holds the 1914-15 Star, and the General Service and Victory Medals.
42, Shaftesbury Road, Watford.   X3943-4/B.

RODD, C., Sapper, Royal Engineers.

He was mobilised on the declaration of war, and served with his unit at various stations until drafted overseas in August 1916. He was attached to the Anti-aircraft Section, and did excellent work as a gunner in various sectors of the Western Front, and served on the Somme, at Ypres, Cambrai and several other important engagements. He holds the General Service and Victory Medals, and was demobilised in April 1919.
122, Vandyke Road, Leighton Buzzard.   4319.

RODDIS, E. C., Private, R.A.S.C. (M.T.)

He joined in September 1916, and in the following month was despatched to the Western Front. Invalided home on account of illness in December 1916, he returned to the Field in the following April and was attached to the Tank Corps. Serving with this unit he was engaged in the Battles of Messines, Ypres, Cambrai and many others during the closing stages of the war. He was demobilised in October 1919, and holds the General Service and Victory Medals.
The Green, Ickwell, Beds.   Z4344.

ROCKALL, R., Sergeant, Royal Engineers.

He was serving in the Army when war broke out and was shortly afterwards drafted to France. Whilst in this theatre of war he was engaged on important duties in connection with operations at La Bassée and Ypres. Invalided home in May 1915, owing to illness, he was employed as an Instructor of Signallers until sent to Gallipoli in July 1915. He served during the landing at Suvla Bay and other engagements on the Peninsula, and was sent to hospital in the following November suffering from fever. On recovery, he was despatched to Salonika in January 1917, and did good work there until hostilities ceased. He returned to England, and in 1920 was still serving with his unit at Brentwood, and holds the 1914-15 Star, and the General Service and Victory Medals.
High Street, Shefford.   Z4368.

RODELL, A., Private, 1/6th Cheshire Regiment.

He joined in October 1916, and in the following February was sent to France. Whilst in this theatre of war he fought at Arras, Ypres, Vimy Ridge, Passchendaele, on the Somme, the Marne, and in the Retreat and Advance of 1918, and was gassed. He was mentioned in Despatches for conspicuous gallantry in the Field, and after the termination of hostilities returned to England in September 1919. He holds the General Service and Victory Medals, and in 1920 was still serving.
3, Surrey Street, Luton.   4367/B.

RODELL, E., Private, 13th Royal Sussex Regt.

He volunteered in August 1914, and was engaged with his unit on important duties at various stations for two years. Sent to the Western Front in August 1916, he fought in many engagements during the Somme Offensive, and at Arras and Vimy Ridge. He was killed in action on October 18th, 1917, in the vicinity of Cambrai, and was entitled to the General Service and Victory Medals.
3, Surrey Street, Luton.   4367/A.

RODNEY, A. L., Private, R.A.S.C.

Volunteering in October 1915, in the same year he was despatched to Salonika. He served for four years in the Balkans, where he was engaged on important duties in connection with the transport of ammunition and other military supplies to the forward areas. He was present at several engagements in the Advance across the Vardar, and was wounded. He was invalided to England, and after hospital treatment was discharged in January 1918, and holds the 1914-15 Star, and the General Service and Victory Medals.
88a, Judge Street, North Watford.   X4392/A.

RODNEY, S., Seaman, Merchant Service, and Private, 2nd Hampshire Regiment.

At the outbreak of war he joined the Merchant Service, and served in various ships engaged in conveying supplies across the Channel. In September 1917 the ship he was serving in was torpedoed and sunk and he was wounded. He received hospital treatment and on recovery joined the 2nd Hampshire Regiment in March 1918, and after training and a period of home service was drafted to India in March 1919. He was still serving in 1920, and holds the General Service and Mercantile Marine War Medals.
88a, Judge Street, Callowland, Watford.   X4392/B.

RODWELL, E. F., Telegraphist, Royal Navy.

He joined the service in June 1915, and with his ship was engaged on important patrol and escort duties for two and a half years. In January 1916 he was transferred to one of the transports which was engaged in conveying troops to France. In 1920 he was serving in Mediterranean waters, and holds the General Service and Victory Medals.
77, Weymouth Street, Apsley, Herts.   X4345/C.

RODWELL, H. T. (M.M.), Private, 6th Bedfordshire Regiment.

Volunteering in August 1914, he proceeded to France in the following year and saw active service in many sectors, fighting at the Battles of Ypres, Hill 60, Givenchy, Loos, Festubert and Vimy Ridge, where he was wounded. In November 1916 he was awarded the Military Medal for conspicuous bravery and devotion to duty in the Field. He was unfortunately killed in action at Arras on April 17th, 1917, and was entitled to the 1914-15 Star, and the General Service and Victory Medals.
77, Weymouth Street, Apsley, Herts.   X4345/A.

RODWELL, T. B., L/Corporal, 20th Australian Infantry.

Volunteering in March 1915, he was drafted to the Dardanelles in the following year, and took part in the landing at Suvla Bay and the subsequent fighting until the Evacuation of the Peninsula. In May 1916 he was sent to France, and was killed in action on the Somme on July 29th, 1916. He was entitled to the General Service and Victory Medals.

77, Weymouth Street, Apsley, Herts. X4345/B.

ROE, A. W., Private, Lancashire Fusiliers.

Volunteering in August 1914, he proceeded to the Western Front in the following year, and was in action at many important engagements including those at Ypres and Hill 60. In 1916, drafted to India, he was stationed with his Regiment at Rawal Pindi and other garrison towns, and was still serving there in 1920. He holds the 1914-15 Star, and the General Service and Victory Medals.

7, Sopwell Lane, St. Albans. X4341.

ROE, B., Corporal, Sherwood Foresters.

He volunteered in October 1914, and was drafted to France in the following December, and engaged in many sectors where heavy fighting was in progress. Wounded on the Somme in August 1916 he returned to England and underwent a prolonged course of hospital treatment. He was invalided out of the service in March 1917, and holds the 1914-15 Star, and the General Service and Victory Medals.

53, Regent Street, Leighton Buzzard. 2635/A.

ROFFE, A. (Sen.), Sergeant, R.A.S.C.

Volunteering in 1915, he embarked for the Western Front later in the same year, and served on transport and other important duties at Rouen and other places. In 1918, sent into Germany with the Army of Occupation, he was stationed at Cologne until, returning to England, he was demobilised in March 1919, and holds the 1914-15 Star, and the General Service and Victory Medals.

1, Lower Paddock Road, Oxhey. X4388/B.

ROFFE, A., Private, Hertfordshire Regiment, and Gloucestershire Regiment.

He volunteered in May 1915, and proceeded to France later in the same year and saw heavy fighting in various parts of the Western Front. He was in action at the Battles of Ypres, Arras, Cambrai and the Somme, where he was taken prisoner in the British Offensive in 1916. Repatriated to England on the cessation of hostilities he was demobilised in December 1918, and holds the 1914-15 Star, and the General Service and Victory Medals.

1, Lower Paddock Road, Oxhey. X4388/A.

ROFFE, F., Private, Northamptonshire Regiment.

He joined in December 1917, and was later drafted to France where he fought in many engagements, including those at Arras, the Somme, and in the Retreat and Advance of 1918, and was wounded. At the termination of the war he was sent into Germany with the Army of Occupation and stationed at Cologne. He was demobilised in 1919, and holds the General Service and Victory Medals.

Millbrook, Ampthill. 4331.

ROFFE, W., Private, Bedfordshire Regiment.

He volunteered in August 1914, and embarked for France in the following year. He served in many sectors whilst heavy fighting was in progress, and was in action at the Battles of Festubert, Hill 60, Cambrai, Arras and Ypres, where he was wounded. On recovery he was sent to Salonika, and was stationed at the Base. He also saw service in Egypt. Returning to England he was demobilised in April 1919, and holds the 1914-15 Star, and the General Service and Victory Medals.

Millbrook, Ampthill. 4328.

ROGERS, H., Private, 1/5th Bedfordshire Regt., and 5th Dorsetshire Regiment.

He volunteered in September 1914, and in the following August embarked for Gallipoli, and took part in the landing at Suvla Bay and in the subsequent operations until the Evacuation of the Peninsula. Transferred to France, he was in action at the Battles of Ypres, Arras, Cambrai and the Somme, and during the Retreat and Advance of 1918, and was wounded three times. He was demobilised in January 1919, and holds the 1914-15 Star, and the General Service and Victory Medals.

32, Maple Road, Luton. 4377/A.

ROGERS, A., Corporal, 1st Norfolk Regiment.

Volunteering in August 1914, he was later drafted to France, where he saw much heavy fighting and was engaged in the actions at Arras, Cambrai, Armentières and Hulluch, and was wounded. He was later transferred to Italy, and after serving there for a time returned to France and fought throughout the German Offensive and subsequent Allied Advance in 1918, and was demobilised in March 1919, and holds the General Service and Victory Medals.

29, Leavesden Road, Watford. 4408.

ROGERS, H. F., Private, Machine Gun Corps, and 3rd Bedfordshire Regiment.

He volunteered in July 1915, and in the following March was sent to the Western Front. Here he was actively engaged with his unit in many sectors, where heavy fighting took place until taken prisoner at Cambrai. Repatriated after the cessation of hostilities he was demobilised in February 1919, and holds the General Service and Victory Medals.

32, Maple Road, Luton. 4377/C.

ROGERS, J. L., Private, King's Own Scottish Borderers.

Volunteering in November 1915, he was sent to France in the following January and served in many parts of the Western Front, fighting in the Battles of Cambrai, Ypres and in the Retreat and Advance of 1918, and was twice wounded. He returned to England and was demobilised in January 1919, and holds the General Service and Victory Medals.

131, Pinner Road, Oxhey, Herts. X4406/A.

ROGERS, J. S., Private, Royal Fusiliers.

Joining in May 1916, he was drafted to France four months later, and served with his Battalion in various sectors, and engaged in the fighting at the Battles of the Somme, Arras and Cambrai. He was gassed and taken prisoner at St. Quentin on March 25th, 1918. Held in captivity in Germany until after the Armistice he was repatriated and eventually demobilised in October 1919. He holds the General Service and Victory Medals.

Station Road, Toddington. 4359.

ROGERS, M. J., Private, 10th Norfolk Regiment.

Volunteering in December 1915, and completing his training, he served at various stations with his unit engaged on guard and other duties of an important nature. He was unsuccessful in obtaining his transfer overseas through medical unfitness, but rendered valuable services until invalided out of the service in March 1917.

131, Pinner Road, Oxhey. X4406/B.

ROGERS, W., Private, 5th Royal Irish Fusiliers.

Volunteering in August 1914, he was sent to France almost immediately, and fought in the Retreat from Mons, and the Battles at Ypres and Hill 60. Transferred to Gallipoli in 1915, he took part in the landing and the subsequent campaign until the Evacuation of the Peninsula. He was then drafted to Egypt, and served in this theatre of war for some time until returning to France when he was in action during the German Offensive and Allied Advance in 1918, and was gassed and twice wounded. He was demobilised in February 1919, and holds the Mons Star, and the General Service and Victory Medals.

7, Surrey Street, Luton. 4382/A.

ROGERS, W. F., Private, 1st Bedfordshire Regt., and 5th Royal Irish Fusiliers.

He volunteered in August 1914, and proceeding to the Western Front was in action in the Retreat from Mons and the subsequent battles. He was wounded in the Battle at Hill 60 in April 1915, and invalided to England. Drafted to Salonika in the following November, he served in this theatre of war for a time, and was then sent to the Egyptian Expeditionary Force, and fought at the Battle of Gaza and throughout the Advance through the Holy Land, and was four times wounded. He returned to England, and was demobilised in March 1919, and holds the Mons Star, and the General Service and Victory Medals.

32, Maple Road, Luton. 4377/B.

ROGERS, W. G., Private, 4th Bedfordshire Regt.

He volunteered in September 1914, and was sent to the Western Front in 1916, and fought at the Battles of the Somme, Ypres, Cambrai, Arras, the second Battle of the Aisne, and throughout the Retreat and Advance of 1918, and was gassed and wounded. On his return to England he was demobilised in February 1919, and holds the General Service and Victory Medals.

121, Lower Paddock Road, Oxhey. X4387.

ROLFE, F. H., Private, R.A.S.C.

Volunteering in April 1915, he proceeded overseas in the following July and served in many advanced areas of the Western Front on important transport duties and as an ambulance driver. He was continuously under fire, and was present at heavy fighting during the German Offensive and Allied Advance of 1918 and was wounded. He holds the 1914-15 Star, and the General Service and Victory Medals, and was demobilised in January 1919.
289, High Town Road, Luton.   4374.

ROLFE, H. A., Private, R.A.S.C.

He volunteered in October 1915, and was later sent overseas and served on both the Western and Italian Fronts in the repair shops and on important duties connected with the transport of ammunition and supplies. He was frequently in the firing line in the discharge of his duties and returning to England was demobilised in July 1919, and holds the General Service and Victory Medals.
31, St. Mary's Road, Watford.   X4360.

ROLLARTH, D., Gunner, Royal Field Artillery.

A serving soldier, he proceeded to France at the commencement of hostilities, and fought throughout the Retreat from Mons and in the subsequent Battles of the Marne, Festubert, Ypres and the Somme. Transferred to Italy in 1917 he was in action on the Asiago Plateau and on the Piave, and served in this theatre of war until 1919. He returned to England, and was demobilised in March 1919, and re-enlisted in the R.A.F. in May of that year, and was still serving in 1920. He holds the Mons Star, and the General Service and Victory Medals.
Clifton Fields, Shefford.   Z4381.

ROLLINGS, C., Private, 8th Suffolk Regiment.

He joined in April 1917, and was sent to France in the following July, and saw active service in all parts of the Western Front, fighting at the Battles of Passchendaele, Cambrai, the Somme, and during the Retreat and Advance of 1918. He was demobilised in March 1919, and holds the General Service and Victory Medals.
3, Hartwell Grove, Leighton Buzzard.   4334.

ROLLINGS, E. H., Pte., Northamptonshire Regt.

Volunteering in May 1915, he proceeded to the Western Front on completion of his training. Here he was engaged with his Battalion in many sectors, and fought at the Battles of Ypres and Cambrai, and in the German Offensive and Allied Advance in 1918, and was three times wounded. He was demobilised in March 1919, and holds the General Service and Victory Medals.
29, Cromer Road, Watford.   X4403.

ROLLINGS, G. R., Private, 16th Essex Regiment.

He joined in October 1916, and after his training was stationed at various depôts with his unit engaged on guard and other duties. He was unable to obtain his transfer to a theatre of war owing to medical unfitness, but rendered excellent services until his demobilisation in February 1919.
High Street, Eaton Bray, Dunstable.   4356.

ROLLINGS, H., Corporal, Machine Gun Corps.

Volunteering in January 1916, he sailed for Mesopotamia in the following July, and fought at the second Battle of Kut, and in the operations resulting in the capture of Baghdad and the concluding operations in that theatre of war. He returned to England and was demobilised in February 1920, and holds the General Service and Victory Medals.
Hope and Anchor, Eaton Bray, Dunstable.   4354.

ROLLS, C. J., Private, 14th London Regiment (London Scottish).

He joined in September 1914, and later proceeded to the Western Front, where he saw much fighting in all parts of the line, and was severely gassed at Arras in May 1915. Returning to England he received hospital treatment, and was invalided out of the service in the following December, and holds the 1914-15 Star, and the General Service and Victory Medals.
4, St. Ann's Road, Luton.   4349/A.

ROLLS, P. J., Private, Bedfordshire Regiment.

Volunteering in August 1914, he proceeded overseas in the following year, and was in action in many sectors and fought at the Battles of Ypres, Cambrai and Albert, where he was wounded in 1917. On recovery he returned to the front lines, and served throughout the Retreat and Advance of 1918, and was stationed at Brussels after the Armistice was signed. He was demobilised in 1919, and holds the 1914-15 Star, and the General Service and Victory Medals.
4, St. Ann's Road, Luton.   4349/B.

ROLLS, E. G., Private, R.A.V.C.

He volunteered in November 1914, and was drafted to France in the following year, and was engaged on important duties connected with the care of sick and wounded horses until after the signing of the Armistice. Returning to England for demobilisation in December 1919, he holds the 1914-15 Star, and the General Service and Victory Medals.
6, Union Lane, New Town, Hatfield.   4405/A.

ROLLS, G., Private, Bedfordshire Regiment, and Labour Corps.

Volunteering in August 1915, he served at various stations with his unit on guard and other important duties. He was unsuccessful in obtaining his transfer overseas prior to the cessation of hostilities, but did excellent work until demobilised in March 1919.
93, Sotheron Road, Watford.   X4396.

ROLLS, R., Private, 2/5th Bedfordshire Regt.

He volunteered in August 1914, and was drafted to France later in the same year. In this theatre of war he served with his unit, and was engaged in the Battles of Ypres, Arras and in the Retreat and Advance of 1918, and was wounded and suffered from trench fever. He was demobilised in March 1919, and holds the 1914 Star, and the General Service and Victory Medals.
68, Warwick Road, Luton.   4390.

ROLLS, W., Sergeant, Bedfordshire Regiment.

Volunteering at the outbreak of hostilities, he was sent to France, and fought in the Retreat from Mons and in the subsequent Battles of the Aisne, the Marne, Ypres and Cambrai. In 1915, transferred to Gallipoli, he served throughout the campaign there until the Evacuation of the Peninsula and then proceeded to Egypt, where he took part in the Advance through Palestine and Syria. During his service he was wounded and returning to England was demobilised in 1919, and holds the Mons Star, and the General Service and Victory Medals.
3, Caroline Cottages, Oxhey.   4385/B.

ROLPH, A., Private, 33rd Trench Mortar Battery, 2nd Bedfordshire Regiment.

He volunteered in November 1914, and in the following June proceeded overseas. Whilst on the Western Front he was engaged in the fighting at Ypres, on the Somme, at Arras, Cambrai, Le Cateau and in the Allied Advance of 1918. He was demobilised in February 1919 and holds the 1914-15 Star, and the General Service and Victory Medals.
8, Smith Street, Watford.   X4386.

ROLPH, E., Rifleman, King's Royal Rifle Corps.

He joined in October 1918, and at the conclusion of his training served at various stations with his unit. He was unable to obtain his transfer overseas until after the signing of the Armistice. He was then drafted to Germany, and was engaged on important guard duties with the Army of Occupation on the Rhine. He was demobilised in November 1919.
Breachwood Green, Welwyn.   4401/A.

ROLPH, S. H., Private, Bedfordshire Regiment.

He volunteered in March 1915, and in the following year proceeded overseas. During his service on the Western Front he was in action at Ypres, the Somme, Arras, Cambrai, and in the Retreat and subsequent Advance of 1918. He was discharged on account of service in November 1918, and holds the General Service and Victory Medals.
Breachwood Green, Welwyn.   4401/B.

ROLPH, W. E., Driver, Royal Field Artillery.

He joined in January 1916, and was sent to Ireland, where he assisted in quelling the Dublin Riots. In the following year he proceeded to France and fought on the Somme, at Passchendaele and Cambrai. After the signing of the Armistice he served with the Army of Occupation on the Rhine until February 1920, when he was demobilised. He holds the General Service and Victory Medals.
Breachwood Green, Welwyn.   4401/C.

ROLT, E., Private, Bedfordshire Regiment, Sapper, Royal Engineers.

He volunteered in June 1915, and served in Egypt for upwards of four years. During this period he served in Palestine, and was present at the Battle of Gaza, and the occupation of Jerusalem, being engaged on important duties in connection with operations. He returned to England and was demobilised in March 1919, and holds the 1914-15 Star, and the General Service and Victory Medals.
Front Street, Slip End, near Luton.   5167/A.

ROLT, F., Corporal, Duke of Wellington's (West Riding Regiment).

He volunteered in August 1915, and in the following July was drafted to France. During his service on the Western Front he took part in many engagements, including those on the Somme and at Ypres. Owing to ill-health he was invalided to hospital, and subsequently died on June 21st, 1917. He was entitled to the General Service and Victory Medals.
13, Old London Road, St. Albans. X4358.

ROOK, F., Driver, Royal Engineers.

He volunteered in October 1915, and at the conclusion of his training served with his unit in England until drafted to France in 1918. Whilst on the Western Front he was engaged on special duties in the Retreat and Advance, and after the Armistice proceeded with the Army of Occupation to Germany, and was stationed at Cologne. He was demobilised in April 1919, and holds the General Service and Victory Medals.
6, Waterloo Terrace, Hitchin Street, Biggleswade.
Z4329.

ROOK, F. C., Sapper, Royal Engineers.

He volunteered in 1915, and in the following year was drafted to France, where he served for a time. He was then sent to Egypt. Taking part in the Palestine Campaign he was engaged on important duties in connection with operations during the Advance under General Allenby, and was present at the Battles of Gaza, Jaffa, Haifa, Aleppo, and the fall of Jerusalem. He was demobilised in August 1919, and holds the General Service and Victory Medals.
41, Alexandra Terrace, Biggleswade. Z1262/B.

ROOM, P. F., Sapper, Royal Engineers.

He volunteered in February 1915, and in the same year was drafted to Egypt, where he served for a time. In June 1916 he was sent to France, and in this theatre of war was engaged on important duties as a telephone operator on the Somme and Cambrai fronts. He was demobilised in June 1919, and holds the 1914-15 Star, and the General Service and Victory Medals.
116, High Street South, Dunstable. 4369.

ROOM, S. (M.M.), Private, 1/5th Bedfordshire Regiment.

Volunteering in August 1914, he was shortly afterwards drafted to France. He took part in the fighting in the Retreat from Mons and the engagements which followed until the following year when he was transferred to the Dardanelles, where he fought at the landing at Gallipoli and in the subsequent battles. He afterwards served in Italy for a time. During his service overseas he was awarded the Military Medal for conspicuous gallantry and devotion to duty in the Field. He also holds the Mons Star, and the General Service and Victory Medals, and was demobilised in May 1919, after returning to England.
55, Union Street, Dunstable. 4323.

ROOTHAM, H. A., Lieutenant, Tank Corps.

He was mobilised at the outbreak of war, and proceeded to France in September 1914. He fought in the Retreat from Mons and the subsequent engagements at Hill 60, Neuve Chapelle, Ypres and Arras. He returned to England in 1917, and for the remaining period of the war served at home on important duties with his unit. He was demobilised in January 1919, and holds the Mons Star, and the General Service and Victory Medals.
59, Union Street, Dunstable. 4339.

ROPER, E., Private, Tank Corps.

He joined in 1918, on attaining military age, and at the conclusion of his training served at various stations on important duties with his unit. He did good work, but was unable to secure his transfer to a theatre of war before hostilities ceased, and he was demobilised in March 1920.
76, Church Street, Dunstable. 4370.

ROPER, E. F., Corporal, Royal Field Artillery.

He joined in May 1916, and was drafted to France in the same year. During his service in this theatre of war he was engaged in the fierce fighting at Ypres, on the Somme, at Arras, Cambrai and St. Quentin. He returned to England after the cessation of hostilities, and was demobilised in May 1919. He holds the General Service and Victory Medals.
Lily Crescent, Leighton Road, Wing, Bucks. 4379.

ROSE, C. E., Private, R.A.M.C.

He volunteered in July 1915, and later proceeded to Mesopotamia. In this theatre of war he was attached to the Indian Staff of Royal Engineers, and was engaged on important duties in tending the sick and wounded, and was frequently under shell fire. He was demobilised in October 1919, and holds the General Service and Victory Medals.
50, Parker Street, Watford. X4357.

ROSE, G. F., Sergeant, Royal Engineers.

He volunteered in September 1914, and in the following July proceeded overseas. He served for upwards of four years on the Western Front, during which period he was engaged on important duties at Ypres, on the Somme, at Arras, Cambrai, and in the final Allied Advance into Germany. He holds the 1914-15 Star, and the General Service and Victory Medals, and was still serving in 1920.
56, Estcourt Road, Watford. X4407.

ROSHIER, W. A., Private, 3rd Buffs (East Kent Regiment).

He joined in 1916, and in the same year was sent to France. He took part in many engagements, including those at Ypres, Amiens, Arras, Cambrai, and was buried by the explosion of a shell and in consequence suffered from shell-shock. He was demobilised in February 1919, and holds the General Service and Victory Medals.
37, Heath Road, Oxhey, Herts. X4411.

ROSS, V. H. C. F., Private, H.A.C.

He volunteered in June 1915, and in the following March was drafted overseas. Whilst on the Western Front he was engaged in the fighting at Arras, on the Somme, and in many other engagements. He returned to England in March 1919, and was demobilised in the following month, and holds the General Service and Victory Medals.
53, Cardiff Road, Luton. 4376.

ROSS, W. A., L/Cpl., 5th Seaforth Highlanders.

He volunteered in August 1914, and in the following May was sent to France. He fought at Ypres, Festubert, the Somme, and was wounded at Arras in April 1917. On recovery he rejoined his Battalion, and returned to the firing line, and was in action at Cambrai. He returned to England after the cessation of hostilities, and was demobilised in January 1919. He holds the 1914-15 Star, and the General Service and Victory Medals.
84, Liverpool Road, Watford. X4413.

ROSSON, F., Gunner, Royal Field Artillery.

He joined in May 1916, and in November of the same year proceeded overseas. During his service on the Western Front he was engaged in the fighting at Ypres and was wounded. On recovery he returned to his unit and fought at Arras, Vimy Ridge, the Somme, Cambrai and St. Quentin. He was demobilised in December 1919, and holds the General Service and Victory Medals.
97, Highbury Road, Luton. 4397.

ROSSON, H., Private, Leicestershire Regiment.

A serving soldier, he was mobilised at the commencement of hostilities, and proceeded to France in July 1915, and fought at Hill 60, the Somme, Arras and Ypres, where he was wounded in October 1917. Returning to England he underwent a prolonged course of hospital treatment, and was finally invalided out of the service in May 1918. He holds the 1914-15 Star, and the General Service and Victory Medals.
77, Bury Park Road, Luton. 4360.

ROSSON, P. L., Stoker, Royal Navy.

He was serving at the outbreak of war in H.M.S. "Royalist," which vessel was engaged in the fighting at the Battle of Jutland and in other Naval engagements in the North Sea. His ship also served on patrol duties off the coast of Russia and at Scapa Flow. He was demobilised in February 1919, and holds the 1914-15 Star, and the General Service and Victory Medals.
24, Albert Street, Watford. X4410.

ROSSON, W. G., Private (Gunner), M.G.C.

He volunteered in the early part of 1915, and was shortly afterwards sent to France. Whilst on the Western Front he was in action at La Bassée, Hill 60, and was wounded at Albert. On recovery he returned to the firing line and remained on there until the signing of the Armistice. He was demobilised in December 1919, and holds the 1914-15 Star, and the General Service and Victory Medals.
56, Cecil Street, North Watford. X4395.

ROUSE, F., Private, Royal Fusiliers.
He joined in June 1916, and in the following October proceeded to France. During his service in this theatre of war he took part in the fighting on the Somme, at Ypres, Passchendaele, Messines and Cambrai. He was demobilised in April 1919, and holds the General Service and Victory Medals.
39, Whitby Road, Luton. 4378.

ROWE, A. S., Private, R.A.S.C.
He joined in April 1916, and in the following month proceeded overseas. He served on the Western Front and engaged on important duties with his unit was present at the Battles of Ypres, Vimy Ridge, the Somme and Albert. He returned to England in September 1918, and was demobilised in January of the following year. He holds the General Service and Victory Medals.
12, St. Ann's Road, Luton. 4348.

ROWE, C. J., Private, Royal Army Cyclist Corps and R.A.S.C.
Joining in October 1916, he completed his training, and was stationed at various depôts on important duties with his unit. He rendered valuable services, but was unable to obtain his transfer to a theatre of war, and was demobilised in October 1919.
"Singapore," Blundell Road, Leagrave. 4391.

ROWE, F., Private, R.A.M.C.
He volunteered in March 1915, and in the following January was drafted to France. In this theatre of war he served with his unit on important ambulance duties in the Somme, Arras and Ypres sectors, and suffered from shell-shock. He was later sent to Palestine and was engaged as a stretcher bearer in various sectors and during the fighting at Gaza. He also served at Salonika and did good work on the Vardar front. He returned to England after the cessation of hostilities and was demobilised in May 1919, and holds the 1914-15 Star, and the General Service and Victory Medals.
10, Back Lane, Leighton Buzzard. 4320/A.

ROWE, G. F., Private, 51st Royal Sussex Regt.
He joined in July 1918, on attaining military age, and at the conclusion of his training served at various stations with his Battalion. He did good work but was unable to obtain his transfer overseas until after the cessation of hostilities. He was then drafted to Germany with the Army of Occupation and was stationed at Cologne. He returned home and was demobilised in March 1920.
Victoria Terrace, Leighton Buzzard. 4335.

ROWE, G. S., Private, Bedfordshire Regiment.
He volunteered in December 1914, and at the conclusion of his training served at various stations on important guard duties with his Battalion. He did excellent work but was unsuccessful in obtaining his transfer to a theatre of war, and was demobilised in March 1919.
10, Back Lane, Leighton Buzzard. 4320/B.

ROWE, H., Private, 1st Buffs (East Kent Regt.)
He joined in January 1918, and in the following August was drafted to France. Whilst on the Western Front he fought on the Somme, at Ypres, and at Havrincourt Wood, where he was wounded in September. He was demobilised in November 1919, and holds the General Service and Victory Medals.
Wellington Terrace, Luton Road, Toddington. 4355.

ROWE, K. (Mrs.), Special War Worker.
This lady was engaged for a period of over two years during the war on important work at Messrs. George Kent's Munition Factory, Luton. She was engaged as a telephone operator, and carried out her duties in a highly satisfactory manner.
27, Lyndhurst Road, Luton 4372.

ROWE, T., Private, 3rd London Regiment (Royal Fusiliers).
He volunteered in December 1914, and in the following March proceeded to the Dardanelles, where he fought at the first landing at Gallipoli and the engagements which followed. He was drafted to Egypt in 1916, and in this theatre of war was engaged in the operations in the British Advance through Sinai. He returned to England and was discharged on account of service in August 1916, and holds the 1914-15 Star, and the General Service and Victory Medals.
34, Mill Road, Leighton Buzzard. 4337/A.

ROWE, W. V., Private, 12th East Surrey Regt.
He joined in June 1916, and in the following September was drafted to France. He fought at the Battles of the Somme and Arras and was taken prisoner on April 9th, 1917. He suffered many privations during his captivity in Germany and was released in January 1919. He returned to England and was subsequently demobilised in October 1920, and holds the General Service and Victory Medals.
Victoria Terrace, Leedon, Leighton Buzzard. 4336.

ROWLAND, H., Private, Bedfordshire Regiment.
He volunteered in September 1914, and in the following year was sent to the Western Front. Serving with his unit in this theatre of war he took part in many important battles. He was unfortunately killed in action, and was entitled to the 1914-15 Star, and the General Service and Victory Medals.
Waterloo Terrace, Hitchin Street, Biggleswade. Z1574/B.

ROWLAND, W., Private, Bedfordshire Regiment.
He joined in 1916, and was shortly afterwards drafted to France. He served with his regiment in various sectors and fought at Arras, Ypres, Cambrai, and the Neuve Chapelle, and after the signing of the Armistice was sent to Salonika in 1919. He holds the General Service and Victory Medals, and was still serving in Salonika in 1920.
8, Ivel Terrace, Biggleswade. Z1315/B.

ROWLES, E., Private, Bedfordshire Regiment.
He volunteered in 1914, and in the following year proceeded overseas. During his service on the Western Front he took part in the fighting at Ypres, Arras, the Somme, and Cambrai, remaining in this theatre of war until 1919. He holds the 1914-15 Star, and the General Service and Victory Medals, and was still serving in 1920.
3, Caroline Cottages, Capell Road, Oxhey. X4385/A.

ROWLETT, D. (Miss), Member, W.R.A.F.
She joined early in 1918, and was stationed at Henlow, where she was engaged on work in connection with the dismantling of aeroplanes. She did good work and was demobilised in 1919.
32, Sun Street, Biggleswade. 1253/C, 1254/C.

ROWLETT, F., Private, Bedfordshire Regiment.
Mobilised on the outbreak of war and shortly afterwards drafted to France, he fought in the Retreat from Mons, and in other important engagements, including the Battles of the Marne and Festubert. He was killed in action on October 31st, 1914, and was entitled to the Mons Star, and the General Service and Victory Medals.
32, Sun Street, Biggleswade. 1253/E, 1254/E.

ROWLETT, H. M. (Miss), Member, W.R.A.F.
She joined in 1918, and was stationed at Henlow, where she was engaged on important duties in connection with the inspection of aeroplane parts. She was also employed as a waitress in the Officers' Mess, and rendered valuable services throughout. She was demobilised in January 1919.
6, Back Street, Biggleswade. 1253-4/D.

ROWLETT, T., Private, 11th (Prince Albert's Own) Hussars.
Volunteering in August 1914, when sixteen and a half years of age, he was later discharged, being under military age. He re-enlisted in 1917, and in the same year was sent to the Middle East. He saw much service in Mesopotamia and amongst other important engagements fought in those on the Tigris and at Kut-el-Amara. He holds the General Service and Victory Medals, and was demobilised in May 1919.
32, Sun Street, Biggleswade. 1253-4/F.

ROWLEY, A. J., Sapper, Royal Engineers.
He volunteered in December 1914, and in November 1916, was drafted to France, where he was employed on special duties during engagements at Ypres and Passchendaele. He was later transferred to Italy and served with his unit on the Piave and Trentino fronts, and was frequently in the forward areas. He was demobilised in February 1919, and holds the General Service and Victory Medals.
112, Liverpool Road, Watford. X4404.

ROWLEY, H., Rifleman, 53rd Rifle Brigade.
He joined in May 1918, and in the following August was sent to France. He fought in the Allied Advance on the Cambrai front, and after the signing of the Armistice, proceeded into Germany with the Army of Occupation, and was stationed at Cologne. He was demobilised in February 1920, and holds the General Service and Victory Medals.
Franklin Cottage, Harlington. 4402.

ROWLEY, H. F., Private, R.A.M.C.
He volunteered in September 1914, and in the following year proceeded to France. He served on special duties with his unit in many sectors and was engaged on ambulance duties in the front lines whilst operations were in progress at Hill 60, Arras, the Somme, Cambrai, and Ypres, where he was wounded. He was subsequently killed in action at Cambrai on October 11th, 1918, and was buried at Abbeville three days later. He was entitled to the 1914-15 Star, the General Service and Victory Medals.
67, Stanley Street, Luton. 4365.

ROWLEY, S., Private, Bedfordshire Regiment.
He volunteered in August 1914, and was sent to France in the following year. He took part in many engagements, including those at Ypres, on the Somme, at Cambrai, and in the Retreat and Advance of 1918, and was wounded. He was demobilised in February 1919, and holds the 1914-15 Star, and the General Service and Victory Medals.
13, Pullen Road, Boxmoor. X3412/B.

RUDD, E. H., Corporal, Royal Air Force.
He joined in August 1916, and at the conclusion of his training served at various stations with his Squadron on important duties, which called for a high degree of technical skill. He did excellent work as a fitter, but was unsuccessful in obtaining his transfer overseas before hostilities ceased and was still serving in 1920.
16, Lower Paxton Road, St. Albans. X4437/B.

RUDD, L. J., Private, 6th Royal Berkshire Regt.
He volunteered in April 1915, and was later sent overseas. He served with his Battalion in many sectors of the Western Front and fought at the Battle of Ypres, and was later killed in action at Thiepval on October 8th, 1916. He was entitled to the General Service and Victory Medals.
16, Lower Paxton Road, St. Albans. X4437/A.

RUFFETT, C. H., Private, 1st Bedfordshire Regt.
He volunteered in December 1915, and in the following year was sent to France. During his service on the Western Front, he took part in the Battle of the Somme, and was severely wounded in September 1916. He was sent to England, and after treatment in hospital was invalided out of the Service in July 1917. He holds the General Service and Victory Medals.
The Green, Eddlesborough, near Dunstable. Z2671/B.

RUFFETT, D., Private, 6th Queen's (Royal West Surrey Regiment).
He joined in June 1918, on attaining military age, and in the following month was sent to France. He was engaged in the fighting on the Cambrai front during the Allied Advance into Germany. He was demobilised in October 1919, and holds the General Service and Victory Medals.
Bury Road, Stopsley, Luton. 4428/B.

RUFFETT, E., Private, 5th Bedfordshire Regt.
He volunteered in November 1914, and in the following January was sent to France. In this theatre of war he took part in the engagements at Neuve Chapelle, Ypres and Festubert, and was drafted to Egypt in January 1916. He served in the Palestine Campaign and fought at Gaza, and was wounded near Jerusalem in December 1918. He was invalided home and on recovery was demobilised in October 1919. He holds the 1914-15 Star, and the General Service and Victory Medals.
Bury Road, Stopsley, Luton. 4428/A.

RUFFETT, H., Captain, 18th London Regiment (London Irish Rifles).
He volunteered at the outbreak of war, and was almost immediately drafted to France. He fought in the Retreat from Mons and the subsequent battles at Ypres, Arras, the Somme, Cambrai, and in the Retreat and Advance of 1918, and during his service in this theatre of war he was three times wounded. He holds the Mons Star, and the General Service and Victory Medals, and was demobilised in November 1919.
53, Regent Street, North Watford. X4429.

RUFFITT, G., Rifleman, 1st Connaught Rangers.
He volunteered in June 1915, and in the same year was drafted to India, where he served with his unit on garrison and other duties until sent to Egypt. There he took part in the Advance under General Allenby through Palestine and fought in several important engagements, including the Battle of Gaza. On the termination of hostilities he returned to England for demobilisation in May 1919, and holds the General Service and Victory Medals.
12, Chapman's Yard, Watford. X725/A.

RUMBLES J., Air Mechanic, Royal Air Force.
He was mobilised at the outbreak of war, and in September 1914 was sent to France. Whilst on the Western Front he was wounded at Ypres, and on recovery rejoined his Squadron and proceeded to the Persian Gulf, where he was again wounded. He later was sent to Egypt, remaining there until 1919, when he returned home, and was demobilised in March of that year. He holds the 1914 Star, and the General Service and Victory Medals.
17, Back Street, Luton. 4427.

RUMNEY, A. E., Driver, Royal Field Artillery.
He volunteered in November 1915, and was later sent to Mesopotamia. In this theatre of war he was engaged in important work with the guns in the forward areas, and fought at Kut-el-Amara and other places until hostilities ceased. He was demobilised in April 1919, and holds the General Service and Victory Medals.
13, Union Lane, New Town, Hatfield. X4418.

RUMNEY, J., Gunner, Royal Field Artillery.
He was mobilised at the outbreak of war, and was drafted to France in September 1914. Whilst on the Western Front he took part in many engagements until 1916. He was sent to Egypt, where he served in many sectors, and contracting pneumonia died on December 4th, 1918. He was entitled to the 1914 Star, and the General Service and Victory Medals.
3, Bury Dell Lane, Park Street, St. Albans. X4432.

RUNDLE, S., Gunner, Royal Marine Artillery.
He joined in June 1917, and was posted to H.M.S. "Revenge." His ship was engaged on important duties in the North Sea, and off the coasts of Russia and Scotland, and frequently passing through mine infested areas had many narrow escapes. He was demobilised in December 1919, and holds the General Service and Victory Medals.
125, St. James' Road, Watford. X4425.

RUNHAM, C., Corporal, 1st Bedfordshire Regt.
He was serving in the Army when war broke out, and was drafted to France in December 1914. He fought in the Battles of Neuve Chapelle, Hill 60, Festubert and the Somme. He was reported wounded and missing on April 23rd, 1917, at the Battle of Vimy Ridge, but was afterwards presumed to have been killed in action on that date. He was entitled to the 1914-15 Star, and the General Service and Victory Medals.
30, St. John's Street, Biggleswade. Z4436/B.

RUNHAM, S., Private, 6th Bedfordshire Regt.
Volunteering in September 1914, in the following January he was sent to the Western Front. There he fought in several important engagements, including the Battles of Neuve Chapelle, Hill 60 and the Somme. He was killed in action at High Wood on August 3rd, 1916, and was entitled to the 1914-15 Star, and the General Service and Victory Medals.
30, St. John's Street, Biggleswade. Z4436/A.

RUNNACLES, N. G., Sergeant, 3rd (King's Own) Hussars.
A regular soldier, he was mobilised on the declaration of war and almost immediately drafted to France. He was in almost continuous fighting in the Retreat from Mons and the Battles of Ypres, the Somme, Arras and Passchendaele, until the Armistice. He holds the Mons Star, and the General Service and Victory Medals, and in 1920 was still serving.
77, Waterlow Road, Dunstable. 4424.

RUSH, A. T., Sergeant, 9th London Regiment (Queen Victoria's Rifles).
He volunteered in June 1915, and after serving with his unit at various stations was sent overseas in 1917. He saw much service on the Western Front, and was in action on the Somme, at Arras, Ypres, Passchendaele, Cambrai and St. Quentin, and on the conclusion of hostilities went with the Army of Occupation into Germany and was stationed at Cologne. He was demobilised in May 1919, and holds the General Service and Victory Medals.
93, Norfolk Road, Rickmansworth. X4433.

RUSH, E. H., Private, 1st Royal Scots Fusiliers.
Mobilised on the declaration of war, he was shortly afterwards drafted to France and took part in the Retreat from Mons and the Battles of Ypres, Arras and the Aisne, and was twice wounded. He also served through the final operations of the war, and was sent home for demobilisation in 1919. He holds the Mons Star, and the General Service and Victory Medals.
230, Chester Road, Watford. X4419.

RUSH, W. F., Private, 1st Bedfordshire Regt.
He was mobilised when war broke out, and was almost immediately despatched to the Western Front. He was in heavy fighting in the Retreat from Mons and in many subsequent battles, including those of Arras, Ypres and Cambrai, and was wounded four times. He also served in Italy, and did valuable work attached to the Labour Corps whilst in that theatre of war. He was demobilised in February 1919, and holds the Mons Star, and the General Service and Victory Medals.
9, Chater Yard, Watford. X4422-3.

RUSS, H., Private, Middlesex Regiment.

He joined in 1916, and in the same year was drafted overseas. Serving on the Western Front he was in action in various sectors, and took part in the Battles of the Somme, Beaumont-Hamel, Arras, Messines and other important engagements. He returned to England for demobilisation in September 1919, and holds the General Service and Victory Medals.

11, Southwold Road, Callowland, Watford. X4416.

RUSS, J. W., Private, 52nd Bedfordshire Regt.

He joined in May 1918, and after training was engaged on important duties with his unit at various stations. He was unable to obtain a transfer to a theatre of war before the conclusion of hostilities. In December 1918 he was sent to Germany with the Army of Occupation, and was stationed at Cologne and Bonn, employed on special duties until his return to England for demobilisation in March 1920.

92, Ridgway Road, Luton. 4421/B.

RUSS, W. J., Private, 2/5th Yorkshire Regt.; Labour Corps.

He joined in July 1916, and after training was engaged on agricultural work at several stations. He rendered valuable services, but was unable to secure a transfer overseas owing to medical unfitness for general service, and was discharged in consequence in May 1918.

92, Ridgway Road, Luton. 4421/A.

RUSSELL, A. E. (M.M.), Corporal, M.G.C.

He volunteered in November 1915, and in the following February was sent to France. Whilst in this theatre of war he took part in many important engagements, including the Battles of the Somme, Ypres, Cambrai and St. Quentin. He was awarded the Military Medal for conspicuous bravery and devotion to duty in the Field, and in addition holds the General Service and Victory Medals. He was demobilised in April 1919.

Dunstable Road, Toddington. 4431.

RUSSELL, E., Private, 1st Hertfordshire Regt.

Volunteering in July 1915, he was sent overseas in the following May. Whilst on the Western Front he was in action in the Somme Offensive and in the Battles of Albert and Ypres, and was wounded on March 26th, 1918, near Cambrai. Rejoining his unit on recovery he served through the final operations of the war and returned to England for demobilisation in February 1919. He holds the General Service and Victory Medals.

11, Copsewood Road, Watford. X4434/A.

RUSSELL, F., Private, 1st Essex Regiment.

He joined in April 1916, and in October of the same year was despatched to the Western Front. During his service in this theatre of war he took part in heavy fighting until taken prisoner on April 14th, 1917, at the Battle of Arras. He was held in captivity for nearly two years and was repatriated after the signing of the Armistice. Demobilised in February 1919, he holds the General Service and Victory Medals.

11, Copsewood Road, Watford. X4435.

RUSSELL, G. A., Air Mechanic, R.A.F. (late R.N.A.S.)

He volunteered in October 1915, and in the following month was sent to the Western Front. He did valuable work with his Squadron at various aerodromes and was killed on June 27th, 1917, during an hostile air raid on Dunkirk. He was entitled to the 1914-15 Star, and the General Service and Victory Medals.

11, Copsewood Road, Watford. X4415/A.

RUSSELL, H. A., Driver, Royal Field Artillery.

Volunteering in October 1915, he was engaged on special duties at various stations until March 1917, when he was despatched to the Western Front. In this theatre of war he was in action in many important engagements including the Battles of the Somme, Arras, Ypres and St. Quentin. He was demobilised in July 1919, and holds the General Service and Victory Medals.

Primrose Hill, Kings Langley. X4426.

RUSSELL, H. R., Sapper, Royal Engineers.

He volunteered in June 1915, and a year later was drafted overseas. He saw much service on the Western Front where he was engaged on important duties in connection with operations in the forward areas. He was present at the Battles of Ypres, Armentières, the Somme and other notable engagements until the conclusion of hostilities. Demobilised in March 1919, he holds the General Service and Victory Medals.

49, Spenser Road, Luton. 4430.

RUSSELL, H. J., 1st Class Stoker, Royal Navy.

He was serving in the Royal Navy when war broke out and posted to H.M.S. "Aboukir," which vessel was engaged on important patrol duties in the North Sea. He lost his life when his ship was torpedoed and sunk off the Hook of Holland on September 22nd, 1914. He was entitled to the 1914-15 Star, and the General Service and Victory Medals.

11, Copsewood Road, Watford. X4415/B.

RUSSELL, W., Sergt., Australian Light Infantry.

He volunteered in November 1915, and in the following year was despatched to the Western Front. Whilst in France he took part in severe fighting on the Somme, at Albert, Passchendaele, and other places and returned to England in March 1918. He was demobilised in April 1919, and holds the General Service and Victory Medals.

11, Copsewood Road, Watford. 4434/B.

RUSSELL, W. H., Pte., 4th Bedfordshire Regt.

Volunteering in November 1915, he was engaged on important duties with his unit at various stations until drafted overseas in March 1917. Whilst on the Western Front he was in action in many important engagements, including those at Ypres, Passchendaele, Kemmel Hill and on the Somme. He was demobilised in May 1919, and holds the General Service and Victory Medals.

9, Dalton Street, St. Albans. 4420.

RUST, A., Private, Royal Fusiliers.

He joined in July 1916, and in the following October was sent to France. There he saw much service with his unit and fought in several important engagements, including the Battles of Arras and Ypres. He was killed in action on July 31st, 1917, near Passchendaele, and was entitled to the General Service and Victory Medals.

18, Camp View Road, St. Albans. X4438/B.

RUTLAND, F., Private, 23rd Middlesex Regt.

He joined in March 1917, and in the following July was drafted overseas. Serving on the Western Front for a time, he took part in several battles, including those of Passchendaele and Dickebusch. He was sent to Italy in February 1918 and after a period of service on the Italian front returned to France in the following April and fought at Kemmel Hill and was gassed in June. He was demobilised in February 1919, and holds the General Service and Victory Medals.

The Strand, Clophill, near Ampthill 4417.

RUTLAND, H. G., Private, 1st Wiltshire Regt.

Joining in 1917, he was sent overseas after a course of training and saw much service in France. He was in action in many important engagements and was taken prisoner during the Retreat in March 1918. He was made to work behind the German firing lines and owing to starvation and ill-treatment fell ill and was removed to Friedrichsfelde Camp, where he died on November 16th, 1918. He was entitled to the General Service and Victory Medals.

46, Nightingale Road, Hitchin. 4439.

RUTLAND, J. F., Private, 9th Northamptonshire Regiment.

He joined in June 1918, and after training was engaged with his unit on important duties at various stations on the East Coast. He was unsuccessful in obtaining a transfer to a theatre of war before the conclusion of hostilities owing to medical unfitness, and was demobilised in December 1919

30, East Street, Leighton Buzzard. 4414.

RYALL, G., Private, Queen's (Royal West Surrey Regiment).

He joined in October 1918, and contracting influenza whilst training at the regimental depôt was sent to hospital where he died on November 5th of the same year.

49, Bunyan Road, Hitchin. 4443.

RYDER, B. (M.M.), Sergt., 12th Middlesex Regt.

Volunteering in June 1915, three months later he embarked for France. In that theatre of war he took part in the Battles of the Somme and Ypres, and was awarded the Military Medal for conspicuous bravery and devotion to duty in the Field. He was later killed in action on October 17th, 1917, and was entitled to the 1914-15 Star, and the General Service and Victory Medals.

89, Liverpool Road, Watford. X4440/A.

NATIONAL ROLL OF THE GREAT WAR

RYDER, G., Private, R.A.S.C.
He joined in November 1916, and in the following March
was sent to France, where he served for three years.
During this period he was engaged on important duties
in connection with the transport of ammunition and
supplies to the forward areas and was present at the
Battles of the Somme, Ypres, St. Quentin, and other
important engagements. He was demobilised in April
1920, and holds the General Service and Victory Medals.
12, Cross Street, Watford.   X4442.

RYDER, J, Private, 1st Hertfordshire Regiment.
Volunteering in February 1915, five months later he
embarked for the Western Front. Whilst in this theatre
of war he took part in the Somme offensive and the
Battles at Ypres, Arras and Cambrai, and was gassed
in April 1918. Rejoining his unit on recovery he served
through the concluding stages of the war, and returned
to England for demobilisation in March 1919. He holds
the 1914-15 Star, and the General Service and Victory
Medals.
89, Liverpool Road, Watford.   X4440/B.

RYDER, W., Private, 4th Bedfordshire Regiment.
Volunteering in February 1916, he was despatched three
months later to the Western Front and was wounded in
the Battle of the Somme in the following July. On
recovery he returned to the trenches and was in action
in several notable engagements until taken prisoner on
April 22nd, 1918, in the vicinity of Cambrai. He was
repatriated after the signing of the Armistice and
demobilised in December 1918, and holds the General
Service and Victory Medals.
89, Liverpool Road, Watford.   X4440/C.

RYLETT, G., Pte., Buffs (East Kent Regiment).
He volunteered in 1915, and in the same year was
sent overseas. Serving on the Western Front he was in
action at Hill 60, Ypres and Festubert, and was drafted
to Salonika in 1916. In this theatre of war he fought
in many important engagements on the Bulgarian frontier
and on the cessation of hostilities was stationed with
the Army of Occupation in Turkey for a year. He was
demobilised in 1919, and holds the 1914-15 Star, and
the General Service and Victory Medals.
49, Norfolk Road, Rickmansworth.   X4441.

S

SAMM, C. A. (M.C.), 2nd Lieutenant, 2nd North-
    amptonshire Regiment.
He volunteered in December 1914, and shortly afterwards proceeded overseas. He served in many sectors
of the Western Front, fighting in the Battles of Arras,
Vimy Ridge and throughout the German Offensive and
subsequent Allied Advance of 1918. He was awarded
the Military Cross for devotion to duty and gallantry in
the Field, and was twice gassed. He was demobilised
in May 1919, and holds the General Service and Victory
Medals.
Genesta, St. Peter's Road, Dunstable.   4445/A.

SAMM, E. A., Private, Royal Sussex Regiment,
    and 2nd Northamptonshire Regiment.
On attaining military age he joined the Forces in June
1918, and on completion of his training served with his
regiment on important duties until October 1919, when
he was sent to India. Here he was stationed at various
depôts, and employed on garrison duties, and was still
serving in that country in 1920.
Genesta, St. Peter's Road, Dunstable.   4445/B.

SAMMS, H., Private, Royal Defence Corps.
Volunteering in September 1914, he underwent a course
of training and served at various stations on guard and
other important duties. He rendered excellent services
throughout the duration of the war, and was demobilised in March 1919.
8, Chaters Yard, High Street, Watford.   X4484/B.

SAMMS, S. G., Private, Bedfordshire Regiment,
    and Labour Corps.
Joining in July 1916, he embarked for Italy later in the
same year, and saw active service on the Piave and in
other sectors until 1917. Proceeding to the Western
Front he fought at Messines, Ypres, Passchendaele and
Cambrai, and during the German Offensive and Allied
Advance of 1918. He was sent into Germany with the
Army of Occupation, and stationed at Cologne until his
return to England for demobilisation in March 1919. He
holds the General Service and Victory Medals.
7, Highbury Road, Luton.   4474.

SAMPSON, S., Staff-Sergeant, R.A.S.C.
He volunteered in August 1914, and was stationed in
Ireland for two years. Proceeding to France in 1916
he took part in the Battles of Loos, Vimy Ridge, the
Somme, and Cambrai, and was in action during the
Retreat and Advance of 1918. He returned to England
and was demobilised in June 1919, and holds the General
Service and Victory Medals.
2, Alma Street, Luton.   4446.

SAMPSON, W., Private, 6th Sherwood Foresters.
Volunteering in August 1914, he was drafted to France
in the following year and saw much service, fighting at
the Battles of the Somme, Arras, Ypres and Cambrai
and throughout the engagements of the concluding
phases of the war, and was wounded. He was demobilised in December 1918, and holds the 1914-15 Star,
and the General Service and Victory Medals.
49, Arthur Street, Luton.   4454.

SAMUEL, A., Private, Sherwood Foresters.
He joined in March 1916, and embarked for France in
the following September, and took part in heavy fighting
at the Battles of Arras, Bullecourt, Ypres and Lens,
where in August 1917 he received wounds which necessi-
tated the amputation of a leg. He returned to England,
and after prolonged hospital treatment was invalided
out of the service in 1919, and holds the General Service
and Victory Medals.
48, Plantation Road, Leighton Buzzard.   2339/C.

SAMUEL, B. B., Sergeant, Royal Engineers.
He joined in May 1916, and embarked for France two
months later, and was engaged on constructional work
and other duties of an important nature near Calais.
He rendered valuable services and returned to England
for demobilisation in October 1919, and holds the General
Service and Victory Medals.
7, Diamond Road, Watford.   X4461.

SAMUELS, A. P., Private, 7th Bedfordshire Regt.
He volunteered in November 1914, and was sent to the
Western Front in the following year and saw active
service in many parts of the line. He was severely
wounded on the Somme during the British Offensive in
that sector, and subsequently succumbed to his injuries
on April 29th, 1916. He was entitled to the 1914-15 Star,
and the General Service and Victory Medals.
467, Whippenden Road, Watford   4472/B.

SAMUELS, A. P., Pte., Northamptonshire Regt.
Volunteering in November 1914, he completed his training, and proceeded overseas in the following year. In
Egypt and Palestine he served on guard and various
other important duties until 1919, when he returned to
England and was demobilised in June of that year. He
holds the General Service and Victory Medals.
467, Whippenden Road, Watford.   4472/A.

SAMUELS, C. A., Gunner, Royal Marine Artillery.
He joined in October 1916, and was posted to H.M.S.
"Lord Nelson," which ship was engaged on patrol and
scouting work in the Mediterranean Sea, and in the
discharge of her duties frequently passed through areas
where hostile submarines were showing great activity. He
was still serving in 1920, and holds the General Service
and Victory Medals.
27, Bolton Road, Luton.   4489

SAMUELS, E., Private, Northamptonshire Regt.
He volunteered in August 1915, and after training served
at various depôts on guard and other important duties.
He rendered valuable services, but on account of medical
unfitness was not successful in obtaining his transfer
overseas and was invalided out of the service in October
1918.
Southill, Beds.   Z4495/A.

SAMUELS, H., Air Mechanic, Royal Air Force
    (late R.N.A.S.)
Volunteering in June 1915, he completed his training
and served at various aerodromes on important duties
which called for a high degree of technical skill. Owing
to ill-health he was unable to obtain his transfer overseas, and was discharged on account of medical unfitness
in 1918.
Southill, Beds.   Z4495/B.

SAMUELS, H., Sapper, Royal Engineers.
He volunteered in December 1915, and proceeded overseas in April of the following year. Whilst on the
Western Front he was engaged on important work in
connection with the laying of railway tracks and on
transport duties, and served in many advanced areas.
He was invalided to England in March 1918, and discharged on account of his service a month later, and
holds the General Service and Victory Medals.
18, Regent Street, Leighton Buzzard.   4451/B.

SAMUELS, H. C., Sapper, Royal Engineers.
Volunteering in January 1916, he proceeded to Italy in the following July, and served on the Piave front engaged on constructional work and in wiring and entrenching the front lines and was present at many engagements. He rendered valuable services, and returning to England was demobilise in March 1919. He holds the General Service and Victory Medals.
18, Regent Street Leighton Buzzard. 4451/A.

SAMUELS, L., Private, Bedfordshire Regiment.
He volunteered in September 1914, and after serving at various stations was drafted to the Dardanelles in April 1915, and fought in the Battle of Krithia, and the subsequent engagements until the evacuation of the Peninsula. He saw much service in other theatres of war and owing to ill-health was invalided to England early in 1918, and after hospital treatment was discharged from the Service in July of the same year. He holds the 1914-15 Star, and the General Service and Victory Medals.
Southill, Beds. Z4494/A.

SAMUELS, S. J., Private, East Surrey Regiment.
He joined in May 1918, and on conclusion of his training proceeded overseas three months later. During his service in France he saw heavy fighting during the German Offensive and was severely wounded on October 25th, 1918, in the Allied Advance, and subsequently died from the effects of his injuries on November 24th of that year. He was entitled to the General Service and Victory Medals.
Southill, Beds. Z4494/B.

SAMUELS, T., Private, 1st Bedfordshire Regt.
Volunteering in August 1914, he embarked for France almost immediately and fought in the Retreat from Mons and in the Battles of Le Cateau, Lens and La Bassée, where he was wounded and taken prisoner in October 1914. He was repatriated in 1919 and demobilised in January of the following year, and holds the Mons Star, and the General Service and Victory Medals.
3, Waldock Yard, Waller Street, Luton. 4485/A.

SANDERS, A., Private, Bedfordshire Regiment, and Hertfordshire Regiment.
He joined in January 1918, on attaining military age, and after his training was stationed at various depôts with his unit and served on guard and other duties. Whilst on duty he was injured and admitted into hospital, where, after treatment, it was found necessary to amputate one of his legs, and in 1920 was at Roehampton awaiting the fitting of an artificial limb.
3, Stanbridge Road, Leighton Buzzard. 4450/A

SANDERS, F. J., Private, Queen's Own (Royal West Kent Regiment).
He volunteered in August 1914, and proceeded to France almost immediately and fought in the Retreat from Mons. He was reported missing on August 23rd, 1914, and later was presumed to have been killed in action on that date. He was entitled to the Mons Star, and the General Service and Victory Medals.
10, Oxhey Street, Oxhey. X4492.

SANDERS, G., Private, Queen's (Royal West Surrey Regiment).
He joined in May 1918 on attaining military age, and after his training served at various stations on guard and other important duties. In January 1920 he was sent to South Russia, and saw active service there for a time, and was still serving later in 1920.
3, Stanbridge Road, Leighton Buzzard. 4450/B

SANDERS, H. C., Staff-Sergeant, R.A.S.C.
He volunteered in October 1914, and proceeded to the Western Front in the following year, where he was engaged on important duties in the forward areas and was present at the Battles of Ypres, Arras, Passchendaele and the Somme. He also served at the base at Rouen. He returned to England and was demobilised in March 1919, and holds the 1914-15 Star, and the General Service and Victory Medals.
83, Warwick Road, Luton. 4476.

SANDERS, W. J., Sergeant, 2nd Bedfordshire Regiment.
He volunteered in August 1914, and proceeded to France a month later, and took part in the Battles of La Bassée, Ypres, the Somme, Arras, Passchendaele and many other engagements. He was taken prisoner on March 22nd, 1918, at Cambrai during the opening operations of the German Offensive and was held in captivity in Germany. Repatriated in March 1919, he was still serving in 1920, and holds the 1914-15 Star, and the General Service and Victory Medals.
17, Vandyke Road, Leighton Buzzard. 4478.

SANDFORD, G., Private, 8th Oxfordshire and Buckinghamshire Light Infantry.
He joined in October 1916, and on completion of his training was drafted to India, where he served at various garrison stations on important duties. He was sent to Salonika in November 1918, and was there employed on guard duties on the lines of communication until his return to England for demobilisation in January 1920. He holds the General Service and Victory Medals.
68, High Street, Houghton Regis. 4460.

SANDIFER, T., Private, 4th Bedfordshire Regt.
Volunteering in September 1914, he was sent to France in July 1916, and was in action in many sectors, fighting in the Battles of the Somme, and Arras, where he was wounded on April 23rd, 1917. He returned to England and after receiving hospital treatment was invalided out of the Service in July of the same year. He holds the General Service and Victory Medals.
29, High Street, Houghton Regis. 4479.

SANDS, E. S., A.B., Royal Navy.
He was mobilised at the outbreak of hostilities, and was posted to H.M.S. "Hecla," in which vessel he saw service during the bombardment of the Dardanelles Forts in 1915. His ship was also engaged on patrolling duties in the Mediterranean and Black Seas, frequently passing through mine-infested areas. He was discharged in April 1919, and holds the 1914-15 Star, and the General Service and Victory Medals.
115, High Street, Houghton Regis. 4459.

SANSOM, J. T. B., Sergeant, 10th Worcestershire Regiment.
Volunteering in September 1914, he was sent to France later in the same year and took part in heavy fighting during the Battles of the Somme, Arras, Ypres, and many other important engagements. He was killed in action in 1917, and was entitled to the 1914-15 Star, and the General Service and Victory Medals.
Ver House, 23, High Street, Redbourn. 4487/A.

SANSOM, R. J., Private, 3rd Norfolk Regiment.
He joined in 1916, and in the same year was drafted to the Egyptian Expeditionary Force and served throughout the advance through Sinai, Palestine and Syria. He returned to England and died on January 20th, 1919, through an illness contracted on service. He was entitled to the General Service and Victory Medals.
Ver House, 23, High Street, Redbourn. 4487/B.

SANSOME, E. J. O. (M.M.), Captain, R.E.
He volunteered in September 1914, and proceeded to France in the following year and was engaged on important duties at the Battles of Loos, Givenchy, Festubert, Vimy Ridge and Messines, and in 1917 was transferred to Russia where he served for a time and was wounded. He was awarded the Military Medal for devotion to duty and gallantry in the Field and was mentioned in Despatches twice. He was demobilised in April 1919, and holds the 1914-15 Star, and the General Service and Victory Medals.
4, Kingston Road, Luton. 4458.

SAPSED, A. J., Sergeant, 6th Bedfordshire Regt.
Volunteering in August 1914, he embarked for the Western Front in the following year and served in many sectors with his battalion. He fought at the Battles of Loos, the Somme, Ypres and Albert, and was killed in action on April 9th, 1917, at Arras. He was entitled to the 1914-15 Star, and the General Service and Victory Medals.
Well Cottage, Walsworth. 4449.

SAUNDERS, A., Pte., York and Lancaster Regt.
He volunteered in May 1915, and was sent overseas four months later and took part in the engagements at Lens, Ypres, Loos, Arras and many others. In 1917 transferred to Italy he was in action on the Piave front and served in this theatre of war until 1919, when he returned to England and was demobilised in November of that year. He holds the 1914-15 Star, and the General Service and Victory Medals.
17, Cumberland Street, Luton. 4447.

SAUNDERS, A. C., Private, R.A.M.C.
He volunteered in April 1915, and was drafted to France in September of the same year and served as a stretcher bearer in the front lines during the Battles of the Somme, Arras and Cambrai, and was gassed. He also rendered valuable services at various base hospitals, attending to the sick and wounded troops. He was demobilised in February 1919, and holds the 1914-15 Star, and the General Service and Victory Medals.
Pretoria Cottages, Harlington. 4499.

SAUNDERS, A. G., Private, Queen's Own (Royal West Kent Regiment).
Volunteering in September 1914, he proceed to France in 1917, and was engaged in heavy fighting on the Ypres, Somme and Cambrai fronts and during the German offensive and subsequent Allied Advance in 1918. He was demobilised in January 1919, and holds the General Service and Victory Medals.
2, Etna Road, St. Albans.　　　4847/B.

SAUNDERS, A. S., Gunner, R.G.A.
Volunteering in August 1914, he underwent a course of training and served at various depôts on important duties with his unit. In attempting to rescue a child from danger he was killed at Shooters Hill in June 1916, on the day on which he was due for embarkation overseas.
79, Victoria Street, Dunstable.　　　4477/A.

SAUNDERS, B. C., Pte., 1st Hertfordshire Regt.
He volunteered in September 1914, and proceeded to France in January of the following year. He took part in the engagements at Festubert, Loos, Ypres, Givenchy and the Somme. He was reported missing at St. Julien on July 31st, 1917, and was later presumed to have been killed in action on that date. He was entitled to the 1914-15 Star, and the General Service and Victory Medals.
81, Elfrida Road, Watford.　　　X4491.

SAUNDERS, C. E., Sergeant, East Surrey Regt.
Volunteering in August 1914, he completed his training and served at various stations with his unit until he embarked for France in June 1917. He fought at the Battles of Passchendaele, Cambrai and the Somme, and was killed in action on August 2nd, 1918, during the Allied Advance. He was entitled to the General Service and Victory Medals.
44, Edward Street, Dunstable.　　　4498.

SAUNDERS, C. L., 1st Class Stoker, Royal Navy.
He joined the Service in July 1918, and was posted to H.M.S. "Royal Sovereign," which ship was engaged on patrol and other important duties in the North Sea and Scapa Flow. After the Armistice his ship proceeded with the Allied Fleet to Constantinople, where he was still serving in 1920, and holds the General Service and Victory Medals.
28, Brixton Road, Watford.　　　X751/B.

SAUNDERS, E. G., Sapper, Royal Engineers.
Volunteering in June 1915, he embarked for the Western Front in February of the following year and was engaged on important duties in connection with operations in the advanced areas and was present at the Battles of Arras, Ypres, the Somme and Albert. He was demobilised in February 1919, and holds the General Service and Victory Medals.
3a, Bedford Street, Watford.　　　X4483.

SAUNDERS, F., Private, 6th Bedfordshire Regt.
Volunteering in August 1914, he proceeded to France in the same month and was in action in the Retreat from Mons and the subsequent battles. Wounded in December 1914, he received hospital treatment and returned to the Western Front and fought at Hill 60, Arras, Ypres, the Somme, and Passchendaele, and was wounded again in December 1915, and later in March 1918 during the German offensive. He was invalided out of the Service in August 1918 and holds the Mons Star, and the General Service and Victory Medals.
15, Barkers Cottages, Hitchin Hill.　　　4448.

SAUNDERS, F. E., L/Cpl., Royal Defence Corps.
Being ineligible for service with the colours, he joined the Royal Defence Corps in 1915, and after completing his training was stationed at various depôts on guard and other duties. He rendered valuable services until his discharge in 1918.
19, Hastings Street, Luton.　　　4497/B.

SAUNDERS, F. E., Private, Middlesex Regiment.
He joined in April 1918, and on completion of his training served with his unit at various stations. He did not obtain his transfer to a theatre of war before hostilities ceased, but was sent with the Army of Occupation into Germany in December 1918, and was stationed at Cologne. He was still serving in 1920.
79, Victoria Street, Dunstable.　　　4477/B.

SAUNDERS, F. J., R.A.S.C.
He volunteered in September 1915, and was sent to France in the following year. Here he was engaged on the transport of ammunition and supplies to the forward areas and was constantly under fire. He rendered valuable services and returned to England for demobilisation in June 1919. He holds the General Service and Victory Medals.
14, Elfrida Road, Watford.　　　X4463.

SAUNDERS, F. E., A.B., Royal Navy.
He joined the Service in 1912, and was mobilised at the outbreak of war and posted to H.M.S. "Indefatigable," which ship took part in the bombardment of the Dardanelles Forts, and was later engaged on patrol work in the North Sea and was sunk during the Battle of Jutland on May 31st, 1916. He was later posted to H.M.S. "Swiftsure," and was engaged on patrol and other important duties until the cessation of hostilities. He was still serving in South American waters in 1920, and holds the 1914-15 Star, and the General Service and Victory Medals.
19, Hastings Street, Luton.　　　4497/A.

SAUNDERS, G. G., Private, 2nd Bedfordshire Regiment, and Hertfordshire Regiment.
On attaining military age he joined in October 1918 and underwent a course of training, afterwards serving at various depôts on important duties with his unit. In January 1919, he sailed for India and, stationed at various garrison towns, was still serving there in 1920.
10, Brighton Road, Dunstable.　　　4457/A.

SAUNDERS, H. F., Private, Labour Corps.
He joined in March 1916, and proceeded overseas in the same month and served on important duties in the forward areas of Ypres, Passchendaele, Messines, and throughout the Retreat and Advance of 1918. He returned to England and was demobilised in November 1919, and holds the General Service and Victory Medals.
44, Waterloo Road, Dunstable.　　　4473.

SAUNDERS, H. J., Private, Bedfordshire Regt.
He volunteered in August 1914, and was sent to France almost immediately and fought throughout the Mons Retreat and the subsequent Battles of Ypres, Arras, Neuve Chapelle, and many other important engagements, and was gassed. He was also in action during the Retreat and Advance of 1918, and on his return to England was demobilised in March 1919, and holds the Mons Star, and the General Service and Victory Medals.
2, Ottoman Terrace, Watford.　　　X4486.

SAUNDERS, H. W., Pte., 2nd Bedfordshire Regt.
He joined in 1916, and embarked for the Western Front in December of the same year. Here he took part in many important engagements, and saw service in many parts of the line, and was taken prisoner in March 1918 during the German Offensive. Repatriated, he was demobilised in December 1919, and holds the General Service and Victory Medals.
43, Grange Street, St. Albans.　　　X4467.

SAUNDERS, H. W., Pte., 22nd Manchester Regt.
Joining in October 1916, he was drafted overseas in January 1917. During his service on the Western Front he fought in many sectors, and was engaged at the Battles of Arras, Ypres and Cambrai. Early in 1918 he was wounded on the Somme front and returned to England, and after receiving hospital treatment was discharged unfit for further service in May 1918. He holds the General Service and Victory Medals.
"Red Lion," Sundon, Beds.　　　4275/B.

SAUNDERS, H. W., Private, 2/5th Bedfordshire Regiment, and 1st Air Mechanic, R.A.F.
Joining in April 1916, he underwent a course of training and proceeded later to Egypt. He was afterwards transferred to the Royal Air Force, and served at Cairo, Alexandria and Ismailia on important duties which demanded a high degree of technical skill as an engine fitter. He rendered valuable services, and returning to England was demobilised in September 1919. He holds the General Service and Victory Medals.
23, Wood Street, Luton.　　　4462.

SAUNDERS, J., Sapper, Royal Engineers.
Joining in June 1917, he embarked for Egypt later in the same year, and served on the Palestine front on important duties connected with the construction of the railway from Kantara to the Holy Land, and was present at the capture of Gaza and Haifa, and was later stationed at Damascus. He returned to England and was demobilised in February 1920, and holds the General Service and Victory Medals.
4, New Marford, Wheathampstead.　　　4470.

SAUNDERS, J., Private, Machine Gun Corps.
Volunteering in September 1914, he was drafted to the Western Front later in the same year, and took part in many engagements, including those at Cambrai, Arras and the Somme, and was wounded and gassed. He also served throughout the Retreat and Advance of 1918, and was demobilised in June of the following year. He holds the 1914-15 Star, and the General Service and Victory Medals.
21, Sotheron Road, Watford.　　　X4481/A.

SAUNDERS, J. C., Private, 11th Sherwood Foresters.

Volunteering in August 1914, he proceeded overseas in November of the following year and fought at the Battle of Loos, the first Somme Offensive in 1916 and the Battle of Arras, and was almost continuously in action until killed near Ypres on October 16th, 1917. He was entitled to the 1914-15 Star, and the General Service and Victory Medals.
10, Brighton Road, Dunstable. 4457/B.

SAUNDERS, J. J., Private, R.A.S.C.

He volunteered in June 1915, and later in the same year was sent to the Macedonian theatre of war, where he was engaged on important duties in connection with the transport of ammunition and supplies to the forward areas on the Vardar front. He returned to England and was demobilised in April 1919, and holds the 1914-15 Star, and the General Service and Victory Medals.
25, Fearnley Street, Watford. X4482.

SAUNDERS, P. A. G., Driver, R.A.S.C.

He joined in October 1916, and on conclusion of his training served with his unit at various depôts on important clerical duties. Owing to ill-health he was unable to obtain his transfer overseas, and rendered valuable services until demobilised in March 1919.
75, Chapel Street, Luton. 4453.

SAUNDERS, R., Private, Bedfordshire Regiment.

He volunteered in August 1914, and on completing his training was sent overseas in the following year. He saw much service on the Western Front, and was engaged in many important battles, including those of Ypres, Arras and the Somme, and was twice wounded. He holds the 1914-15 Star, and the General Service and Victory Medals, and was demobilised in 1919.
81, Fearnley Street, Watford. X135/B.

SAVAGE, E., Regimental Sergt.-Major, R.A.M.C.

He was serving at the outbreak of war, having entered the Army in 1909. He was engaged at various home stations until March 1917, when he was drafted to France. There he served in hospitals at Aire and Arras, and also acted as Lieutenant Quartermaster for a period extending over two years. He was recommended for a commission in November 1918, but unfortunately did not receive it, since the Armistice was signed shortly afterwards. He was demobilised in July 1919, and holds the General Service and Victory Medals.
178, Dallow Road, Luton. 4464.

SAVAGE, H. J., Private, 8th King's (Liverpool Regiment).

He joined in November 1916, and in the following March was drafted to France. He fought at Ypres, and was wounded and invalided home. On recovery he rejoined his fighting unit, and on September 11th, 1918, was reported missing. He was later presumed to have been killed in action on that date. He was entitled to the General Service and Victory Medals.
305, High Town Road, Luton. 4455.

SAVENER, A. B., Corporal, Labour Corps.

He joined in February 1917, and was shortly afterwards drafted to France. In this theatre of war he was engaged on important duties in connection with the building of roads and railways and for some time was in charge of Chinese labourers. He was demobilised in January 1920, and holds the General Service and Victory Medals.
20, Newcombe Road, Luton. 4456.

SAVILLE, F., Private, R.A.M.C.

Joining in January 1917, he was drafted overseas in the same year. He served on the Western Front, and was engaged on important duties with his unit at Arras, Ypres, on the Somme and at Cambrai. He was demobilised in September 1919, and holds the General Service and Victory Medals.
28, Henry Street, Luton. 4488/B.

SAVILLE, W. H., Private, Queen's (Royal West Surrey Regiment).

He joined in August 1918, and at the conclusion of his training served at various stations with his Battalion, but was unable to secure his transfer overseas until after the cessation of hostilities. He was then sent to Germany and joined the Army of Occupation. He was serving in England in 1920, when he was stationed at Sheffield.
28, Henry Street, Luton. 4488/A.

SAWYER, C., Gunner, Royal Field Artillery.

He volunteered in 1915, and was shortly afterwards drafted overseas. He served on the Western Front, and was engaged in the fighting on the Somme and at Arras, Ypres and Cambrai, and in the Retreat and Advance of 1918. During this long period of service he was gassed. He was demobilised in January 1919, and holds the 1914-15 Star, and the General Service and Victory Medals.
Rose Terrace, Littleworth, near Leighton Buzzard. 4496.

SAWYER, E., Private, 2nd Suffolk Regiment.

He volunteered in December 1915, and in the following year proceeded overseas. He took part in the fighting at Arras, Cambrai and on the Somme. In this battle he was severely wounded and his injuries were of such a nature that his leg was amputated. He was invalided out of the service in October 1919, and holds the General Service and Victory Medals.
Bury Lane, Rickmansworth. X4468.

SAWYER, G. E., Pte., 13th Bedfordshire Regt.

He joined in 1916, and after his training served at various stations in England with his Battalion, being chiefly engaged upon guard duties. He rendered valuable service, but was unsuccessful in obtaining his transfer to a theatre of war. He was demobilised in November 1919.
Seaton Road, London Colney. X4480.

SAWYER, H. R. W., Corporal, Royal Air Force.

Joining in August 1916, he completed his training, and served with his Squadron at various aerodromes engaged on work connected with the repair of aeroplanes and other duties which demanded a high degree of technical skill. He rendered valuable services, but was unable to obtain his transfer to a theatre of war before hostilities ceased. He was demobilised in February 1919.
22, Liverpool Road, Watford. X2100/C.

SAWYER, J., Private, 1st Hertfordshire Regt.

He joined in September 1916, and in the following January proceeded overseas. Whilst on the Western Front he fought at Ypres, on the Somme, at Arras, Messines and Passchendaele. He returned home in July 1917, and served with his Battalion on important duties until demobilised in June 1919. He holds the General Service and Victory Medals.
69, Salisbury Road, Luton. 4490.

SAWYERS, H., Gunner, Royal Garrison Artillery.

He joined in March 1917, and in the following July was sent to France. During his service on the Western Front he fought at Ypres, and took part in the subsequent engagements on the Somme, at Lens and at Arras. He returned home and was demobilised in July 1919, and holds the General Service and Victory Medals.
14, Midland Road, Leagrave, Luton. 4471.

SAYELL, G., Gunner, Royal Garrison Artillery.

Volunteering in November 1915, he was sent overseas on the conclusion of his training. Whilst on the Western Front he took part in the Battles of Ypres, the Somme and Cambrai, and on one occasion was wounded. He was subsequently killed in action near Arras on May 3rd, 1917. He was entitled to the General Service and Victory Medals.
"A valiant soldier,
With undaunted heart he breasted life's last hill."
50, Regent Street, Leighton Buzzard. 4466.

SAYELL, H., Private, Bedfordshire Regiment, and Labour Corps.

He joined in January 1918, and after his training served with his Battalion at various stations on important duties. He did excellent work, but owing to medical unfitness was unable to secure his transfer to a theatre of war, and was demobilised in April 1919.
108, Estcourt Road, Watford. X233/C.

SAYELL, J., Private, 1st Hertfordshire Regiment.

He volunteered in May 1915, and in the following February proceeded overseas. He fought in many sectors of the Western Front, and was engaged in the Battles of the Somme and Bullecourt. He was unhappily killed in action near Albert on October 30th, 1916, and was entitled to the General Service and Victory Medals. His memory is cherished with pride.
27, Copsewood Road, Watford. X4493/B.

SAYELL, S., Private, Northumberland Fusiliers.

Joining in June 1916, he was drafted at the conclusion of his training to the Western Front. Whilst in this theatre of war he was engaged in the fighting at Arras, Cambrai, Ypres and Hargicourt, and also in the Battles of the Marne and the Scarpe. He was demobilised in February 1919, and holds the General Service and Victory Medals.
16, Mentmore Road, Linslade, Bucks. 4465.

SAYELL, W., Sapper, Royal Engineers.
He volunteered in January 1916, and in July of the same year proceeded overseas. He was drafted on the Western Front, where he was engaged in roadmaking, digging trenches and in mining. He also served on lines of communication. He returned home and was demobilised in March 1919, and holds the General Service and Victory Medals.
50, Regent Street, Leighton Buzzard.   4452.

SAYELL, W., Sapper, R.E. (10th Rly. Company).
He joined in May 1918, but was unable to secure his transfer overseas until after the cessation of hostilities. He was sent to France in December 1918, and subsequently proceeded to Germany, where he was engaged on the railroad transport of troops and rations. He returned to England in March 1920, and was demobilised in the following month.
27, Copsewood Road, Watford.   X4493/C.

SAYERS, R., Private, 165th Labour Corps.
Volunteering in May 1915, he proceeded overseas in the same year. During a long period of service on the Western Front, he was engaged at Arras, Ypres, Lens and Cambrai, and for a time served as a Convoy Runner. He was demobilised in February 1919, and holds the 1914-15 Star, and the General Service and Victory Medals.
1, Wharf Lane, Rickmansworth.   X4469.

SCALES, A., Private, R.A.M.C.
He volunteered in September 1914, and in the following year was sent to France. He was engaged on important duties in the forward areas, being in action at the Battles of Ypres and the Somme. He was mortally wounded on August 22nd, 1917, and died on the following day. He was entitled to the 1914-15 Star, and the General Service and Victory Medals.
66, Dudley Street, Luton.   4501.

SCALES, R., Corporal, R.A.S.C.
He volunteered in May 1915, and was shortly afterwards sent to Egypt. He served with Remount Depôts at Gaza, Jaffa, the Jordan and elsewhere in Palestine for a period of upwards of four years. On one occasion he was seriously injured in the performance of his duties. He returned to England and was demobilised in August 1919, and holds the 1914-15 Star, and the General Service and Victory Medals.
The Green, Ickleford, Hitchin.   4517.

SCALES, S., Private, 5th Bedfordshire Regiment.
Volunteering in October 1914, he served at home stations until drafted to France in 1916. Whilst on the Western Front he took part in many notable engagements, and was wounded at Cambrai and at Etaples. He returned to England in December 1917, and served with his Battalion until he was demobilised in March 1919. He holds the General Service and Victory Medals.
142, Hartley Road, Luton.   4512.

SCALES, T., Sergeant, 1/5th Bedfordshre Regt., and Machine Gun Corps.
He volunteered in May 1915, and in January of the following year proceeded to Egypt, where he remained at Cairo for a time. He was later engaged in the operations connected with the British Advance through Palestine, and was present at Gaza, Jaffa, Haifa and Jerusalem, and took part in the capture of Aleppo. He was demobilised in March 1919, and holds the General Service and Victory Medals.
59, Queen Street, Luton.   882/A.

SCARFF, H. G., Private, R.A.S.C.
He volunteered in April 1917, and was shortly afterwards sent to France. During his service on the Western Front he was engaged on special duties as a baker with his unit at Boulogne. After the signing of the Armistice he proceeded with the Army of Occupation to Germany and was stationed at Cologne, where he served until 1920. He returned home and was demobilised in March of that year and holds the General Service and Victory Medals.
22, Chapel Street, Hemel Hempstead.   1637/B.

SCHREIBER, A. C. M., L/Corporal, R.E.
He joined in July 1916, and five months later was sent overseas. He served on the Western Front with the Railway Operative Department, and was engaged on important duties in the forward areas at Ypres, the Somme and Cambrai. He was demobilised in October 1919, and holds the General Service and Victory Medals.
90, Upper Dagnall Street, St. Albans.   X4511.

SCOATS, C. C., Private, R.A.M.C.
He volunteered in October 1915, and at the conclusion of his training embarked for Egypt in April 1916. He lost his life when the ship in which he was sailing was torpedoed and sunk by enemy action in the Mediterranean Sea on April 15th, 1916. He was entitled to the General Service and Victory Medals.
70, Bun Street, Luton.   4506/C.

SCOATS, H. J., Private, Lincolnshire Regiment, and Gunner, Royal Field Artillery.
He volunteered in May 1915, and was later sent overseas. He was engaged in the fighting on the Western Front and fought in many battles, including those of Ypres, Arras, Albert and Cambrai. He returned to England and was demobilised in September 1919, and holds the General Service and Victory Medals.
70, Bun Street, Luton.   4506/A.

SCOATS, H. W., Air Mechanic, Royal Air Force.
He joined in January 1916, and after completing his training was drafted to France with his Squadron. He was engaged at aerodromes in the Ypres sector and at Dunkirk on important duties as an armourer, and did very good work. He was demobilised in October 1919, and holds the General Service and Victory Medals.
70, Bun Street, Luton.   4506/B.

SCOTCHETT, J. W., Private, 2nd Hertfordshire Regiment, and Bombardier, R.F.A.
He was serving at the outbreak of war and for a period of two years was engaged on important duties with his unit. He did excellent work but was unable to secure his transfer to a theatre of war owing to medical unfitness and was discharged in consequence in August 1916.
8, Sutton Road, Watford.   X4509/B.

SCOTCHETT, J. W. (Junr.), Pte., Royal Fusiliers.
He joined in October 1916, and was shortly afterwards sent to France. He fought in many battles on the Western Front, including those on the Somme, and at Cambrai during the final operations of the war, and was wounded. He was demobilised in September 1919, and holds the General Service and Victory Medals.
8, Sutton Road, Watford.   X4509/A.

SCOTCHMER, F. G., Gunner, R.G.A.
He was serving in August 1914, and was almost immediately drafted to Aden, where he served with his Battery until 1916. He was then sent to France and was engaged in the fighting at the Battles of Ypres, St. Julien and Cambrai. He was demobilised in March 1919, and holds the 1914-15 Star, and the General Service and Victory Medals.
New Marford, Wheathampstead.   4503/A.

SCOTCHMER, V. E., Pte., Sherwood Foresters.
He joined in April 1917, and twelve months later was sent to France. Whilst in this theatre of war he took part in many engagements and was wounded during the Allied Advance at Cambrai in September 1918. He was demobilised in February 1919, and holds the General Service and Victory Medals.
New Marford, Wheathampstead.   4503/B.

SCOTT, A. W., Private, Northamptonshire Regt.
He joined in 1917, and was shortly afterwards drafted to France. During his service on the Western Front he was engaged in the fighting at Ypres, Hill 60, Givenchy, on the Somme, and in the Allied Advance of 1918. After the signing of the Armistice he proceeded to Cologne with the Army of Occupation where he served until demobilised in 1919 after returning to England. He holds the General Service and Victory Medals.
82, Weymouth Street, Apsley End, Herts.   X4505.

SCOTT, C. (Mrs.) Special War Worker.
During the war, for a period of over two years, this lady rendered valuable services at Hayes Munition Factory. Her duties, which were in connection with the filling of shells with T.N.T., were carried out in a highly satisfactory manner.
Church Lane, King's Langley.   X1094/B.

SCOTT, F. E., Private, 10th Essex Regiment.
He joined in 1916, and in the following year proceeded to France. Whilst serving on the Western Front he fought at the Battle of the Somme, and the subsequent engagements at Arras and Cambrai. He was killed in action on August 8th, 1918, during the Allied Advance, and was entitled to the General Service and Victory Medals.
36, Rose Terrace, Biggleswade.   Z4515.

SCOTT, F. S., Private, R.A.S.C. (M.T.)
He volunteered in October 1915, and in February of the following year proceeded overseas. During his service on the Western Front, he was engaged at Ypres, Arras, Cambrai and the Somme on important transport duties in the forward areas. He was demobilised in August 1919, and holds the General Service and Victory Medals.
51, Leighton Street, Woburn. Z4510/B.

SCOTT, G. A., Private, Royal Fusiliers.
He volunteered in August 1914, and in the following year was drafted to France. In this theatre of war he served in the fighting at Ypres and other places, and was killed in action on July 28th, 1916. He was entitled to the 1914-15 Star, and the General Service and Victory Medals.
42, Alexandra Road, St. Albans. X4508.

SCOTT, H., Private, Tank Corps.
He volunteered in November 1914, and was drafted to France in the following year. He was employed on special duties with his unit and was engaged in the Battles of the Somme and Cambrai, and was wounded near Arras in November 1917. He was demobilised in March 1919, and holds the 1914-15 Star, and the General Service and Victory Medals.
Church Lane, King's Langley. X1094/A.

SCOTT, H., Private, R.A.S.C., and Labour Corps.
He volunteered in October 1915, and in the following January was sent to France. In this theatre of war he was engaged on important transport work and on his transfer to the Labour Corps was employed on road-making in various sectors. He was demobilised in February 1919, and holds the General Service and Victory Medals.
3, The Bridge, King's Langley. X4502.

SCOTT, H. H., Sergeant, Bedfordshire Regiment, and Royal Air Force.
He volunteered in September 1914, and in the following July was sent to the Dardanelles. He fought at the landing at Suvla Bay and many of the subsequent engagements on the Peninsula until wounded in action. He was invalided home and on recovery was drafted to the Western Front, where he took part in engagements at Ypres and on the Somme. He was demobilised in February 1919, and holds the 1914-15 Star, and the General Service and Victory Medals.
26, Clarendon Road, Luton. 4513/A.

SCOTT, H. J., Stoker, Royal Navy.
He joined in January 1916, and was posted to H.M.S. "Blanche," which vessel was employed on mine laying duties off the Coast of Germany and in the North Sea. His ship was also engaged in escorting the surrendered German Fleet to Scapa Flow. He was demobilised in January 1919, and holds the General Service and Victory Medals.
71, Waterside, King's Langley. X4507.

SCOTT, R. R. F., Private, East Surrey Regiment.
He volunteered at the outbreak of war and in 1915 was drafted to France. He fought at Ypres and Hill 60, and was severely wounded. He was invalided home and after treatment in hospital was discharged as medically unfit for further service in 1916. He holds the 1914-15 Star, and the General Service and Victory Medals.
3, Commerce Avenue, Letchworth. 4516.

SCOTT, S. E., Private, R.A.V.C.
He volunteered in 1915, and at the conclusion of his training served at various depôts on important duties with his unit. He rendered valuable services but was unsuccessful in obtaining his transfer overseas, and was demobilised in August 1919.
7, Beechwood Road, Leagrave. 4500.

SCOTT, W. T., Sapper, Royal Engineers (R.O.D.)
He joined in 1916, and was shortly afterwards sent to Egypt. He served at Alexandria, Cairo and Kantara with his unit on special duties and was frequently in the forward areas at Jaffa, Haifa and Jerusalem, whilst operations were in progress. He was demobilised in March 1919, and holds the General Service and Victory Medals.
102, Villiers Road, Oxhey, Herts. X4514.

SCRIVENER, A. E., Sergeant, 4th Bedfordshire Regiment.
Volunteering in September 1914, he was sent to the Western Front in the following year. Whilst in France he fought in many engagements and was wounded and invalided home. On recovery he served with his regiment for nearly two years and returned to France in 1917. He was killed in action at the Battle of Ypres on April 23rd, 1917, and was entitled to the 1914-15 Star, and the General Service and Victory Medals.
7, Surrey Street, Luton. 4382/B.

SCRIVENER, A. W., Private, 2nd Royal Fusiliers.
He volunteered in August 1914, and was drafted to the Western Front three months later and saw heavy fighting in the Ypres salient and other sectors. Transferred to the Dardanelles in May 1915, he took part in the second Battle of Krithia and was killed in action in June of that year. He was entitled to the 1914 Star, and the General Service and Victory Medals.
3, Waldock Road, Waller Street, Luton. 4485/B.

SCRIVENER, S., Private, R.A.S.C. (M.T.)
He joined in September 1916, and in the same year was drafted overseas. Serving on the Western Front he was engaged on important duties in connection with the transport of ammunition and other military supplies to the forward areas and was present at the Battle of Ypres and other important engagements, until the termination of hostilities. He was then sent with the Army of Occupation into Germany and was stationed at Cologne for over a year. Returning to England he was demobilised in February 1920, and holds the General Service and Victory Medals.
126, Ridgway Road, Luton. 4504.

SEABROOK, A., Cpl., 7th Bedfordshire Regt.
He volunteered in September 1914, and in the following year embarked for the Western Front and took part in many important operations in that theatre of war. He fought in the Battles of Ypres, Arras and other notable engagements, and was wounded at Hill 60, and also at Givenchy. Rejoining his unit, he was killed in action on the Somme on September 23rd, 1918, and was entitled to the 1914-15 Star, and the General Service and Victory Medals.
128, Cravells Road, Harpenden. 4528/A.

SEABROOK, B. H., Pte., 5th Bedfordshire Regt.
He enlisted in May 1914, and after training was engaged on important guard duties at various stations with his Battalion. He did valuable work, but was not sent overseas owing to medical unfitness. He was accidentally killed by a train at Manningtree station whilst on duty on August 27th, 1914.
34, West Street, Dunstable. 4550/A.

SEABROOK, C. R., Private, Middlesex Regiment.
He was mobilised in August 1914, and a month later was despatched to the Western Front. He saw much service in this theatre of war, and was in action in the Battle of Ypres and other important engagements. He returned to England for demobilisation in January 1919, and holds the 1914-15 Star, and the General Service and Victory Medals.
48, Holywell Road, Watford. X2790/B.

SEABROOK, C. W., Private, Lancashire Fusiliers.
He joined in August 1917, and proceeded to France in the following December. During his service overseas he was in action at Amiens, Avesnes and in other important operations until the close of the war. He then proceeded into Germany with the Army of Occupation, and was stationed at various towns on the Rhine. He was demobilised in November 1919, and holds the General Service and Victory Medals.
36, Portland Street, St. Albans. 4534.

SEABROOK, F., Private, R.A.S.C.
He joined in 1918, and after completing his training served at various stations on important duties with his unit. He rendered valuable services, but was not successful in obtaining his transfer overseas before the cessation of hostilities, and was demobilised in 1919.
64, Brightwell Road, Watford, Herts. X375/B.

SEABROOK, F. J., Pte., 7th Bedfordshire Regt.
Joining in November 1917, he was drafted overseas in the same year. Serving with his unit on the Western Front, he took part in various important operations, including the Battles of Ypres, Hill 60, Vimy Ridge, Givenchy, and was wounded in September 1918 during the Allied Advance. He returned to England for demobilisation in January 1919, and holds the General Service and Victory Medals.
128, Cravells Road, Harpenden. 4528/B.

SEABROOK, G. W., Private, R.A.S.C.
He volunteered in 1915, and on the conclusion of his training was engaged with his unit on important duties at various stations. He did excellent work in connection with the transport of military stores, but was unable to obtain a transfer to a theatre of war before the termination of hostilities, and was demobilised in 1919.
72, Brightwell Road, Watford. X4527/A.

SEABROOK, N. W., Private, 1/5th Bedfordshire Regiment.
Volunteering in April 1915, he was sent to Gallipoli in the following July, and took part in the Landing at Suvla Bay and other important operations until the Evacuation of the Peninsula. Drafted to Egypt he fought at Gaza, Haifa, and was present at the fall of Damascus and Beyrout. He was wounded in the course of his service overseas, and returned to England on the conclusion of hostilities. He was demobilised in March 1919, and holds the 1914-15 Star, and the General Service and Victory Medals.
35, Union Street, Luton. 4552.

SEABROOK, R., Sapper, Royal Engineers.
He volunteered in May 1915, and in the same year proceeded to the Western Front. He was engaged on important duties in connection with operations in forward areas, and was present at the Battles of Ypres, Hill 60 and other notable engagements until the termination of the war. He was demobilised in February 1919, and holds the 1914-15 Star, and the General Service and Victory Medals.
44, Upper Paddock Road, Oxhey. X4549/B.

SEABROOK, R. J., Sergeant, Royal Air Force.
Mobilised on the outbreak of hostilities, he embarked for France in 1915, and served overseas for nearly five years. During this period he did most valuable work with his Squadron at various aerodromes on scouting and other duties. He was also engaged in training and instructing recruits, and on the cessation of hostilities returned to England. He was demobilised in May 1919, and holds the 1914-15 Star, and the General Service and Victory Medals.
34, West Street, Dunstable. 4550/B.

SEABROOK, S. H., Pte., 2nd Bedfordshire Regt.
He volunteered in November 1914, and in the following year was drafted overseas. He saw much service on the Western Front, and took part in many important operations. He was killed in action on June 25th, 1916, and was entitled to the 1914-15 Star, and the General Service and Victory Medals.
7, Souldern Street, Watford. X4537.

SEABROOK, W., Private, Royal Fusiliers.
He joined in March 1916, and in the following August proceeded to France. There he fought in the Somme Offensive, and in the Battles of Arras, Ypres and other important engagements. He was killed in action near Bapaume on August 20th, 1918, and was entitled to the General Service and Victory Medals.
69, Edward Street, Dunstable. 2134/B.

SEABROOK, W., Pte., 2nd Bedfordshire Regt.
He volunteered in August 1914, and in the following year was sent to the Western Front. Whilst in this theatre of war he took part in the Battles of Ypres, the Somme, Cambrai and other important operations until hostilities ceased, and was wounded three times. Returning to England he was demobilised in March 1919, and holds the 1914-15 Star, and the General Service and Victory Medals.
Grove Road, Harpenden. 2967/B.

SEABROOK, W., Private, R.A.O.C.
He joined in November 1916, and proceeded overseas later in the same year, and was stationed at Calais. He was engaged on important duties in the wheelwright's department of the Royal Army Ordnance Corps workshops, and rendered excellent services. He returned to England and was demobilised in May 1919, and holds the General Service and Victory Medals.
52, London Road, Hemel Hempstead. X4524.

SEABROOK, W. G., Private, Bedfordshire Regt. Camel Corps.
He volunteered in 1914, and in the following year proceeded to Egypt. In this theatre of war he was engaged in operations in the Canal Zone and in the British Advance through Palestine. Amongst the important battles in which he fought were those of Gaza, and Jaffa; on the conclusion of hostilities he returned to England. He was demobilised in 1919, and holds the 1914-15 Star, and the General Service and Victory Medals.
72, Brightwell Road, Watford. X4527/B.

SEABROOK, W. J., Corporal, R.F.A.
Volunteering in August 1915, in the following year he embarked for France. Serving with his unit in various sectors he was engaged in the Battles of Arras, Ypres, and in the offensive operations on the Somme. He was killed in action on September 21st, 1917, at Poperinghe, and was entitled to the General Service and Victory Medals.
44, Upper Paddock Road, Oxhey, Watford. X4549/A.

SEABORN, A., Corporal, R.F.A.; R.G.A.
He was serving in the Army when war was declared, and was engaged as a Gunnery Instructor at various training depôts, and did valuable work in this capacity. He was unsuccessful in obtaining his transfer to a theatre of war before the cessation of hostilities, and was demobilised in April 1919. He had previously served in the South African War, and holds medals for that campaign.
6, Newcombe Road, Luton. 4548.

SEALE, E., Private, 13th Hussars.
He was serving in the Army when war broke out and in February 1915 was despatched overseas. He saw much service on the Western Front and was in action on the Somme and in the Ypres sector. In July 1916 he was sent to Mesopotamia, where he fought in many engagements in the British advance and was present at the capture of Baghdad. He returned to England in April 1919 and was still serving in 1920. He holds the 1914-15 Star, and the General Service and Victory Medals.
74, Estcourt Road, Watford. X4535/A.

SEALE, T. H., A.B., Royal Naval Division.
He joined in June 1917, and was later drafted to the Western Front, where he did good work with his unit. He was in action in many engagements, including those at Passchendaele and Vimy Ridge, and was wounded. Returning to the Field on recovery he served in operations during the concluding stages of the war and returned to England for demobilisation in January 1919. He holds the General Service and Victory Medals.
22, Gladstone Avenue, Luton. 4521.

SEALEY, A., Gunner, Royal Marine Artillery.
He joined in June 1918, and on the completion of his training was engaged with his Battery at various docks and railway stations on guard and other duties. He was unable to obtain a transfer overseas before the cessation of hostilities, and was discharged in 1919.
101, St. James' Road, Watford. X4531/A.

SEALEY, C., Private, 8th Queen's Own (Royal West Kent Regiment).
Attesting in May 1917, he was called up in the following March and drafted to France. Whilst in this theatre of war he took part in severe fighting at Péronne and other places during the final operations of the war. He was sent with the Army of Occupation into Germany in March 1919, and was stationed on the Rhine for nearly a year. He returned to England for demobilisation in January 1920, and holds the General Service and Victory Medals.
101, St. James' Road, Watford. X4531/C.

SEALEY, F. E., Sergeant, Leicestershire Regt.
He volunteered in September 1914, and after training was engaged on important training and guard duties with his unit at various stations for four years. He was then sent into Germany with the Army of Occupation and stationed at Cologne. Returning to England after two years' service on the Rhine he was demobilised in March 1920.
101, St. James' Road, Watford. X4531/B.

SEALEY, H., Private, Labour Corps.
Joining in May 1916, after training he was engaged on various duties at the depôt of his unit until August 1918. He was then drafted to France and there rendered valuable services on transport duties and in making roads during the closing stages of the war. He holds the General Service and Victory Medals, and was demobilised in February 1919.
13, Cardiff Road, Watford. X4543.

SEAR, A., Private, 4th Bedfordshire Regiment.
He was mobilised when war broke out and after training was engaged on important duties at home until drafted to the Western Front in June 1916. Seriously wounded in the following October in the Battle of the Somme, he was invalided to England and after hospital treatment returned to France in February 1917. He was killed in action near Lens on August 22nd, 1917, and was entitled to the General Service and Victory Medals.
4, Oxford Terrace, Dunstable. 4523/C.

SEAR, A. (Mrs.), Special War Worker.
This lady volunteered for work of National importance, and from April 1917 until the following October was engaged by the Hendon Aircraft Manufacturing Co., in important work in connection with the building of aeroplanes. Her duties called for a high degree of technical knowledge and skill, and were discharged in a careful and efficient manner.
2, St. Mary's Road, Watford. X4545/B.

SEAR, A. J., Sergeant, 5th Bedfordshire Regt.

He enlisted in the Army in April 1914, and was sent to Gallipoli in July 1915. He fought at the landing of Suvla Bay and in several other operations until the evacuation of the Peninsula. In December 1915 he proceeded to Egypt and served in the Canal Zone and at the Battles of Gaza, Haifa, Acre, Beyrout, Aleppo, and other important engagements in General Allenby's advance through Palestine. He was demobilised in May 1919, and holds the 1914-15 Star, and the General Service and Victory Medals.

36, Kenilworth Road, Luton. 5054.

SEAR, A. V. (Miss), Special War Worker.

This lady volunteered her services for work of National importance during the war from June 1915 until December 1918 worked at Chaul End Munition Factory where she was engaged upon the manufacture of the component parts of fuses. She rendered excellent services throughout.

4, Oxford Terrace, Dunstable. 4523/B.

SEAR, C., Corporal, Royal Engineers.

He volunteered in September 1914, and in the following year was drafted to the Western Front. There he was employed on important duties in connection with operations in the advanced areas whilst heavy fighting was in progress and was present at several battles, including those at Arras, Ypres, Messines, Lens and Cambrai, and was gassed. He returned to England for demobilisation in February 1919 and holds the 1914-15 Star, and the General Service and Victory Medals.

The Green, Eddlesborough, near Dunstable. Z4553.

SEAR, F., Drummer, 6th Bedfordshire Regiment.

He volunteered in August 1914, and in the following July proceeded to France. Whilst in this theatre of operations he fought at the Battles of Loos and the Somme, and was killed in action on July 15th, 1916. He was entitled to the 1914-15 Star, and the General Service and Victory Medals.

2, St. Mary's Road, Watford. X4545/A.

SEAR, G. (Miss), Special War Worker.

During the war this lady offered her services for work of National importance, and was employed in the munition factory of Messrs. G. Kent, Ltd., Luton, from June 1916 until December 1918. She was engaged in the Fuse department and during the course of her service discharged her duties in a thoroughly capable and efficient manner.

4, Oxford Terrace, Dunstable. 4523/A.

SEAR, H., Private, Buffs (East Kent Regiment).

He volunteered in January 1915, and in the following April embarked for the Western Front. He took part in the Somme Offensive in 1916, and the Battles of Arras and Passchendaele, and was wounded at Kemmel Hill on June 11th, 1917. On recovery he returned to the firing line, and was again wounded in April 1918 in the Retreat from Cambrai. He was demobilised in March 1919, and holds the General Service and Victory Medals.

28, Cardiff Road, Watford. X4532.

SEAR, H., Private, 2nd Bedfordshire Regiment.

He volunteered in September 1914, and was later sent to France, where he served for over four years. During this period he took part in many operations, and fought in the Battles of Ypres and Cambrai, and was wounded three times. Returning home at the end of the war he was demobilised in 1919, and holds the 1914-15 Star, and the General Service and Victory Medals.

15, Union Street, Hemel Hempstead. X4541/C.

SEAR, H. W., Private, Royal Fusiliers.

Joining in May 1916, he proceeded overseas in the following September. He served with his unit on the Western Front, and whilst there fought in the Battle of the Somme and other important engagements, and was wounded at Arras in May 1917, and invalided home for treatment. He was demobilised in March 1919, and holds the General Service and Victory Medals.

Coffee Tavern, Eaton Bray, near Dunstable. 4547.

SEAR, T., Private, R.A.S.C.

He volunteered in 1915, and in the same year was drafted to France. Serving in various sectors, he did valuable work in connection with the transport of ammunition and supplies to the front line trenches during several important engagements. Amongst other battles he was present at were those of Arras, Ypres, Bullecourt and Cambrai, and on the conclusion of hostilities returned to England. He was demobilised in 1918, and holds the 1914-15 Star, and the General Service and Victory Medals.

15, Union Street, Hemel Hempstead. X4541/B.

SEAR, W., Private, R.A.S.C.

Volunteering in 1915, he was despatched overseas in the same year, and saw much service on the Western Front. He was engaged on important transport duties whilst heavy fighting was in progress and was present at the Battles of Arras, Ypres, and the Somme and other important operations. He was demobilised in May 1919, and holds the 1914-15 Star, and the General Service and Victory Medals.

15, Union Street, Hemel Hempstead. X4541/A.

SEAR, W. J., Gunner (Signaller), R.F.A.

He volunteered in April 1915, and in the following October was sent to France, where he served until drafted to Salonika in April 1916. He was engaged in operations in the Balkan theatre of war for nearly three years, and in April 1919 proceeded to Russia with the Relief Force. Returning to England for demobilisation in October 1919, he holds the 1914-15 Star, and the General Service and Victory Medals.

15, Copsewood Road, Watford. X4540.

SEARLE, A., Private, Somerset Light Infantry, and Suffolk Regiment.

He joined in September 1916, and completing his training was engaged on important patrol duties at several depôts on the East Coast. He did valuable work, but was unable to obtain a transfer overseas owing to medical unfitness for general service, and was demobilised in September 1919.

7, Breadcroft Lane, Harpenden. 4530.

SEARLE, J. H., Pte., 1/5th Seaforth Highlanders.

He volunteered in September 1914, and in the following May embarked for service overseas. Shortly after landing in France he proceeded to the firing line, and was in almost continuous fighting in the Ypres sector. He was killed in action near Ypres on June 15th, 1915, and was entitled to the 1914-15 Star, and the General Service and Victory Medals.

32, Liverpool Road, Watford. X4529/B.

SEARLE, S. J., Private, 1st Bedfordshire Regt.

A regular soldier, he was mobilised on the outbreak of hostilities, and in February 1915 was sent to France. Whilst in this theatre of war he saw much service, and was engaged on severe fighting at Ypres and in various operations on the Somme, and was wounded. He was later killed in action in July 1916 at Delville Wood, and was entitled to the 1914-15 Star, and the General Service and Victory Medals.

74, Estcourt Road, Watford. X4535/B.

SEARLE, S. J. E., Writer, Royal Navy.

He volunteered in August 1914, and was posted to H.M.S. "Montrose," which vessel was engaged on special duties in the North Sea and other waters. His ship was sent to the Black Sea in 1916 to protect British interests there, and he was awarded the Cross of St. George by the Russian Government for meritorious service. In addition he holds the 1914-15 Star, and the General Service and Victory Medals, and in 1920 was still serving.

32, Liverpool Road, Watford. X4529/C.

SEARLE, T. G. (M.C. and M.S.M.), 2nd Lieut., 2nd Bedfordshire Regiment.

A serving soldier, he was mobilised on the outbreak of war, and drafted overseas in December 1914. Whilst on the Western Front he took part in the Battles of Neuve Chapelle, Loos, Ypres and other important engagements, and before obtaining commissioned rank was awarded the Meritorious Service Medal. He was later awarded the Military Cross for conspicuous gallantry and devotion to duty in the Field. He was killed in action at Hollebeke on September 20th, 1917, and was entitled to the 1914-15 Star, and the General Service and Victory Medals.

32, Liverpool Road, Watford. X4529/A.

SEARLE, W. H., Sergeant, 9th (Queen's Royal) Lancers.

He was mobilised on the declaration of war, and sent to the Western Front in 1915. Whilst overseas he was in action in several important engagements, including those at Ypres, Vimy Ridge and the Somme. Seriously wounded in the course of operations in the Somme sector, he was sent home and invalided out of the Service in December 1917. He holds the 1914-15 Star, and the General Service and Victory Medals.

32, Liverpool Road, Watford. 4529/D.

SEARLE, W. A., Sergt., 1st Hertfordshire Regt.
He was mobilised on the outbreak of war, and in
November 1914 was drafted overseas. He served on the
Western Front and fought in many important engagements, including the Battles of Ypres and Festubert.
He was sent home in June 1915 owing to illness, and
in the following October was invalided out of the Service. He holds the 1914 Star, and the General Service
and Victory Medals.
74, Estcourt Road, Watford.   X4535/C.

SEARS, F., Private, Labour Corps.
He joined in March 1917, and was shortly afterwards
sent to France. In this theatre of war he was engaged
on important duties in the forward areas, and was
present at the Battles of the Somme and Cambrai. On
the termination of hostilities he returned to England for
demobilisation in November 1919, and holds the General
Service and Victory Medals
25, Ashby Road, North Watford.   X4519.

SEARS, W., Sapper, Royal Engineers.
He joined in October 1916, and in September of the
following year was drafted overseas. Serving on the
Western Front he took part in several engagements and
was then drafted to Italy, where he served on important
duties in connection with the British Offensive on the
Asiago Plateau. In April 1918 he was invalided home
owing to illness, and was discharged as medically unfit
for further service in August 1918, and holds the General
Service and Victory Medals.
79, Estcourt Road, Watford.   X4533.

SEATON, E. E. (Mrs.), Special War Worker.
Volunteering for work of National importance in August
1916, she was engaged at Messrs Heatley and Gres-
ham's factory, Letchworth, until February 1919. She
was employed in the shell department as a turner, and
throughout the period of her service discharged her
duties in a thoroughly efficient and satisfactory manner.
10, Black Horse Lane, Hitchin.   4555/A.

SEATON, F. J., Sapper, Royal Engineers.
He volunteered in October 1915, and in the following
year was despatched to France. During his service
overseas he was engaged on important duties in connection with operations during the Battles of the Somme,
Arras, Ypres, Passchendaele, Cambrai and other places.
Demobilised in March 1919, he holds the General Service
and Victory Medals.
10, Verulam Road, Hitchin.   4561.

SEATON, W. G., Private, 9th Norfolk Regiment.
He joined in August 1917, and in the following April
embarked for service overseas. Shortly after landing in
France he took part in severe fighting at Ypres and
St. Quentin during the German Offensive and subsequent
Allied Advance. Returning to England at the end of
hostilities, he was demobilised in January 1920, and
holds the General Service and Victory Medals.
10, Black Horse Lane, Hitchin.   4555/B.

SEEAR, A., Private, R.A.M.C.
He joined in 1918, and on the completion of his training
was engaged with his unit in attending to sick and
wounded troops at Blackpool Military Hospital. He
did excellent work, but was unsuccessful in his efforts
to obtain a transfer overseas before the termination of
hostilities, and was demobilised in January 1919.
60, Holywell Road, Watford.   X4520.

SEEAR, G., Private, 9th Border Regiment.
He joined in September 1916, and after serving at the
depot of his unit for a time proceeded overseas. Sent
first to China and then to India, he was afterwards
drafted to Salonika, and in that theatre of war saw
much service. He took part in the advance across the
Struma and in other operations, including the Battle at
Monastir. He returned home for demobilisation in
January 1920, and holds the General Service and Victory
Medals.
4a, York Street, Watford.   1641/B.

SELL, H. C., Petty Officer, Royal Navy.
Volunteering in November 1915, he was detailed for
special duty and sent to the Balkans in the following
year. Serving with the armoured cars he took part in
several important engagements on the Dobrudja and
Galicia fronts, and was later sent to Mesopotamia.
There he did excellent work at Kut, Baghdad and other
places during the British Advance into Persia. He was
afterwards engaged with Commander Locker Lampson's
armoured cars in North Russia, and on one occasion
was icebound at Archangel. He returned to England on
the withdrawal of the forces from that theatre of war
and was demobilised in March 1919, and holds the
1914-15 Star, and the General Service and Victory
Medals.
25, Cromwell Road, Luton.   4505/A.

SELL, A. C., Private, 1st Hertfordshire Regt.
He volunteered in August 1914, and in the following
month was sent to the Western Front, and was in action
on the Marne and in the first Battle of Ypres, and was
later engaged in severe fighting at Givenchy and Loos.
He was severely wounded in the Battle of the Somme,
and in consequence lost the sight of an eye and was
invalided home in 1916. He was discharged as medically
unfit for further military service in November 1917, and
holds the 1914 Star, and the General Service and Victory
Medals.
13, Chapman's Yard, Hitchin.   4560/C.

SELL, C. B., Sergeant, 4th Bedfordshire Regt.
He volunteered in April 1915, and in the same year was
despatched to the Western Front, where he served for
upwards of four years During this period he was in
action in the Battles of Festubert, Loos, the Somme,
Arras, Ypres, Cambrai and other notable engagements
until the signing of the Armistice. He returned home
for demobilisation in January 1919, and holds the 1914-15
Star, and the General Service and Victory Medals.
9, Boscombe Place, Letchworth.   4563.

SELL, L. B., 2nd Lieutenant, Royal Air Force.
He joined in May 1918, and after training was engaged
on important duties at various large aerodromes. He
did valuable work with his squadron, but was unable to
obtain a transfer to a theatre of war before the cessation of hostilities, and was demobilised in February 1919.
25, Cromwell Road, Luton.   4525/B.

SELL, R. D., Private, R.A.S.C.
He joined in April 1917, and in the same year was
despatched to Egypt. Whilst in this theatre of war he
was engaged on important duties in connection with
the transport of ammunition and supplies during the
British Advance through Palestine. He was present at
the Battles of Gaza, Jaffa, and several other notable
engagements, and died whilst on active service on
October 27th, 1919. He was entitled to the General
Service and Victory Medals.
13, Chapman's Yard, Hitchin.   4560/A.

SELL, W. J., Private, 1st Hertfordshire Regiment.
Volunteering in August 1914, he embarked for France
in the following month. During his service in this
theatre of war he fought in the Battles of the Marne,
the Aisne, Festubert, Albert and in the Somme Offensive of 1916. He was wounded and gassed in the
Advance of 1918, and shortly afterwards died from the
effects of his injuries on August 18th. He was entitled
to the 1914 Star, and the General Service and Victory
Medals
13, Chapman's Yard, Hitchin.   4560/B.

SELLEY, W. H., Gunner, Royal Field Artillery.
He joined in April 1916, and in the following December
was drafted overseas. He served in the Balkan Campaign, in the course of which he was in action in
several notable engagements and took part in the
advance into Bulgaria. He was sent to Russia in June
1919, and three months later to Turkey. Returning to
England he was demobilised in November 1919, and
holds the General Service and Victory Medals.
7, Duke's Lane, Hitchin.   4557.

SELLS, A. J., Corporal, R.A.S.C. (M.T.)
He volunteered in January 1915, and in the following
July proceeded to the Western Front where he served
for five years. During this period he was engaged
on important duties in connection with the transport of
troops, ammunition and other military supplies to the
front lines in the Somme, Arras and Cambrai sectors.
He was demobilised in February 1920, and holds the
1914-15 Star, and the General Service and Victory
Medals.
Stanbridge, Leighton Buzzard.   4559/C.

SELLS, A. W., Sapper, Royal Engineers.
He volunteered in June 1915, and was engaged on
important duties at the depot of his unit until drafted
to France in 1917. Whilst overseas he did excellent
work in connection with operations in the forward areas
and was taken prisoner in an engagement at Berry-au-
Bac. Released from captivity on the signing of the
Armistice, he was demobilised in March 1919, and holds
the General Service and Victory Medals.
36, Dane Road, Luton.   4518.

SELLS, H. W. G., Corporal, R.A.S.C.
Mobilised when war broke out, he was shortly afterwards
sent to France and saw much service in that theatre of
operations. He was attached to the Field bakery and
rendered valuable services in the capacity of a baker
in the Somme and other sectors until the termination
of hostilities. He holds the 1914 Star, and the General
Service and Victory Medals, and in 1920 was still
serving.
Stanbridge, Leighton Buzzard   4559/A.

SELLS, H., Private, 2nd Bedfordshire Regiment.
He was mobilised on the outbreak of war and embarked for Gallipoli in 1915. Serving throughout the campaign in this theatre of operations from the landing at Suvla Bay until the evacuation of the Peninsula, he was drafted to Egypt in 1916. He was engaged in the fighting in Palestine and took part in the Battles of Jaffa, Haifa, Gaza and other notable engagements until the cessation of hostilities. He was demobilised on his return to England in November 1919, and holds the 1914-15 Star, and the General Service and Victory Medals.
Clifton Road, Shefford. Z4522.

SELLS, P., Private, R.A.S.C. (M.T.)
He volunteered in 1915, and in the following year proceeded to the Western Front. He was engaged on various duties in connection with the transport of rations and supplies to the front lines during the Battles of Ypres, the Somme, Passchendaele and Cambrai. He did valuable work until the cessation of hostilities and was demobilised in March 1919. He holds the General Service and Victory Medals.
17, Bury Hill, Hemel Hempstead. X4526.

SELLS, W. G., Private, 7th Lincolnshire Regt.
Volunteering in August 1914, he was sent to France in the following month and soon after arrival was in action at the Battles of Loos and Ypres. He took part in several other important engagements and was wounded on the Somme in 1916. He was invalided home and on recovery rejoined his unit in the Field and fought at Cambrai and in the Retreat and Advance of 1918. He was demobilised in March 1919, and holds the 1914 Star, and the General Service and Victory Medals.
Stanbridge, near Leighton Buzzard. 4559/B.

SENIOR, F. J. (D.C.M. and M.M.), Private, Bedfordshire Regiment.
He was mobilised on the declaration of war and shortly afterwards proceeded to France. He was engaged in fierce fighting in the Retreat from Mons and was wounded in the Battle of Ypres. Returning to his unit he took part in the Battles of Festubert, Hill 60 and Loos, and was gassed and twice wounded. He was accorded the Distinguished Conduct Medal and the Military Medal for conspicuous bravery and devotion to duty in the Field, and in addition holds the Mons Star, and the General Service and Victory Medals. He returned to England on the conclusion of hostilities, and was demobilised in March 1919.
Victoria Place, Biggleswade. Z4539/A.

SENIOR, G., Sergt., 2/4th Royal Berkshire Regt.
Volunteering in August 1914, he was engaged with his unit until drafted overseas in 1916. Whilst on the Western Front he took part in operations in various sectors and fought in the Battles of Arras and Ypres. He was killed in action on September 14th, 1917, and was entitled to the General Service and Victory Medals.
Victoria Place, Biggleswade. Z4539/B.

SENIOR, H., Private, 1st Bedfordshire Regiment.
Joining in November 1916, he proceeded overseas in May of the following year. After serving for a time on the Western Front he was sent to Italy in which theatre of war he took part in several engagements and early in 1918 was sent back to France. He was killed in action at Nieuport on May 13th, 1918, and was entitled to the General Service and Victory Medals.
18, Stanmore Road, Watford. X4542/B.

SENIOR, J. R., Sapper, Royal Engineers.
He joined in April 1917, and in the same year was sent to Egypt. Serving with his unit during the Advance through Palestine he was engaged on important duties in connection with operations and was present at many battles until the cessation of hostilities. He returned home, and was demobilised in December 1919, and holds the General Service and Victory Medals.
32, Shakespeare Street, North Watford. X4546.

SENIOR, W. (D.C.M.), Private, 1st Loyal North Lancashire Regiment.
Mobilised from the Army Reserve on the outbreak of war, he was shortly afterwards despatched to France. He fought in the Retreat from Mons and in the subsequent Battles of the Marne, the Aisne, Ypres and the Somme and was wounded. He was awarded the Distinguished Conduct Medal for conspicuous gallantry in delivering despatches under heavy fire. He also holds the Mons Star, and the General Service and Victory Medals, and was demobilised in March 1919.
18, Stanmore Road, Watford. X4542/A.

SENIOR, W., 1st Class Stoker, Royal Navy.
He joined in April 1918, and was posted to H.M.S. "Clio," which vessel was engaged on important duties in the North Sea and other waters until the cessation of hostilities. His ship was also sent to America and India on special duties and in 1920 he was still serving. He holds the General Service and Victory Medals.
Victoria Place, Biggleswade. Z4539/C.

SETCHELL, H., Staff-Sergeant, R.G.A.
He joined in 1917, and was shortly afterwards drafted to France. In this theatre of war he was engaged in the fighting at the Battles of the Somme, Ypres and many other notable engagements until the signing of the Armistice. He then proceeded to Germany with the Army of Occupation and served there until 1919, when he returned home and was demobilised. He holds the General Service and Victory Medals.
23, Chobham Street, Luton. 286/B.

SETCHELL, S., Pte., 6th Northamptonshire Regt.
He joined in July 1918, and at the conclusion of his training was drafted to France. He served with his Battalion at Rouen and other places on special guard duties until October 1919, when he returned home and was demobilised. He holds the General Service and Victory Medals.
44, Arthur Street, Luton. 4551.

SEVERN, F, Saddler, Royal Field Artillery.
He volunteered in February 1915, and in the following October proceeded to the Dardanelles where he fought in many engagements and was severely wounded in action. He died from the effects of his wounds on December 31st of that year, and was entitled to the 1914-15 Star, and the General Service and Victory Medals.
9, Carey Place, Watford. 212/A.

SEVERS, J. H., Rifleman, 1st Rifle Brigade.
He volunteered in August 1915, and four months later was sent to France. Whilst in this theatre of war he fought on the Somme, at Ypres, Aras, Cambrai, Passchendaele Ridge, and in the subsequent operations until the signing of the Armistice. He was demobilised in March 1919, and holds the 1914-15 Star, and the General Service and Victory Medals.
7, Prospect Place, Welwyn. 4538.

SEWELL, A. T., Driver, R.A.S.C.
He volunteered in March 1915, and in the following month was sent to France. During his service on the Western Front he was engaged on special duties with his unit at Ypres, Albert and on the Somme, and after the cessation of hostilities proceeded to Germany with the Army of Occupation and was stationed at Cologne. He was demobilised in June 1919, and holds the 1914-15 Star, and the General Service and Victory Medals.
19, Ickleford Road, Hitchin. 4562.

SEWELL, C., Sergeant, Northamptonshire Regt.
He volunteered in August 1914, and in the following month was drafted to France. He was in action at La Bassée, Ypres, Loos, Passchendaele, and was wounded and taken prisoner at Cambrai in October 1918. He suffered many hardships during his captivity and was released after the signing of the Armistice. He holds the 1914-15 Star, and the General Service and Victory Medals and was still serving in 1920.
54, Regent Street, Leighton Buzzard 4558/B.

SEWELL, J. H., Private, 1st Hertfordshire Regt.
He volunteered in August 1914, and in the succeeding year was drafted overseas. During his service on the Western Front he was engaged in the fighting in various sectors, including those of Ypres and Arras. He was killed in action at St. Julien on July 31st, 1917, and was entitled to the 1914-15 Star, and the General Service and Victory Medals.
50, Ratcliffe Road, Hitchin. 4556.

SEWELL, W. G., Cpl., 2nd Bedfordshire Regt.
He volunteered in September 1914, and in the following January proceeded to France and took part in the Battle of Ypres, and was wounded. He was invalided home and after six months hospital treatment returned to the Western Front and served on the Somme, at Arras, and Cambrai and was again wounded. Returning to England he was demobilised in February 1919, and holds the 1914-15 Star, and the General Service and Victory Medals.
54, Regent Street, Leighton Buzzard. 4558/A

SEXTON, F. G., Private, Queen's (Royal West Surrey Regiment).
He joined in May 1916, and was later drafted overseas. Whilst serving on the Western Front he was engaged in the fighting at Arras and was wounded. He was taken prisoner at Fontaine on April 23rd, 1917, and held in captivity until after the signing of the Armistice. He returned to England and was demobilised in March 1919, and holds the General Service and Victory Medals.
Ganders Ash, Leavesden Green, near Watford.   X4544.

SEYMOUR, P. J., Private, R.A.M.C.
Mobilised at the outbeak or war, he was almost immediately sent to France. He was engaged on important duties with his unit during the Retreat from Mons, and the subsequent engagements in the Ypres, Somme and Cambrai sectors. He was demobilised in February 1919, and holds the Mons Star, and the General Service and Victory Medals.
6, St. Faith's Terrace, Orchard Road,Walsworth, Hitchin.
4554.

SEYMOUR, T., Lieut., Royal Dublin Fusiliers.
He volunteered in October 1914, and in November of the following year served to France. He was engaged in the fighting at Ypres, on the Somme, at Delville Wood and Beaumont-Hamel, and granted a commission in December 1917, proceeded to Egypt in the following March, where he served until hostilities ceased. During his service overseas he was twice wounded. He holds the 1914-15 Star, and the General Service and Victory Medals, and was still serving in 1920.
9, Estcourt Road, Watford.   X4536.

SHADBOLT, E., Sergeant, Queen's Own (Royal West Kent Regiment).
He volunteered in September 1914, and was shortly afterwards drafted to France. Whilst in this theatre of war he was in action at Messines Ridge, Arras, Cambrai and was wounded. He later proceeded to Mesopotamia and India, where he served for a time. He was demobilised in September 1919, and holds the 1914-15 Star, and the General Service and Victory Medals.
11, Blacksmith's Lane, St. Albans.   4601/B.

SHADBOLT, G., Private, Labour Corps.
He joined in May 1917, and in March of the following year was drafted to France. He served with his Battalion on important duties in the forward areas during the German Offensive of 1918. Owing to ill-health he was invalided home in May of that year and was discharged in February 1919. He holds the General Service and Victory Medals.
18, Keyfield West, St. Albans.   X4617.

SHADBOLT, H., Private, Hertfordshire Regiment.
Mobilised at the outbreak of war, he was immediately drafted to France. In this theatre of war he fought in the Retreat from Mons and many subsequent battles on the Western Front until the cessation of hostilities, and was twice wounded. He was demobilised in March 1919, and holds the Mons Star, and the General Service and Victory Medals.
Arm and Sword Yard, Hatfield.   X4595.

SHADBOLT, H. S., Corporal, 20th Hussars.
He volunteered in September 1914, and in June of the following year was sent to France. Whilst on the Western Front he fought on the Somme, at Arras, Cambrai, Loos, and was wounded in the Allied Advance of 1918. He returned to England, and was demobilised in February 1919, and holds the 1914-15 Star, and the General Service and Victory Medals.
5, Lyndhurst Road, Luton.   4615.

SHADBOLT, H. T. (M.M.), Private, Bedfordshire Regiment.
He volunteered in September 1914, and in the following year was sent to France. He fought at Hill 60, Givenchy, Festubert, the Somme, Arras and Cambrai, and was wounded three times. He was awarded the Military Medal for conspicuous gallantry and devotion to duty in the Field, and in April 1918 was invalided out of the Service as a result of wounds. He also holds the 1914-15 Star, and the General Service and Victory Medals.
14, St. George's Cottages, Batford Road, Harpenden.
4578.

SHADBOLT, H. W., Private, 2/4th London Regt. (Royal Fusiliers).
He joined in February 1918, and in the following July proceeded overseas. During his service on the Western Front he fought on the Somme, and was killed in action on August 25th, 1918. He was entitled to the General Service and Victory Medals.
87, Cromwell Road, Luton.   4571/B.

SHADBOLT, P. C., Corporal, Bedfordshire Regt.
He volunteered in September 1914, and was later sent to France. He took part in many engagements, including those at Ypres, Arras, the Somme and Vimy Ridge. He returned to England after the cessation of hostilities, and was demobilised in March 1919. He holds the General Service and Victory Medals.
87, Cromwell Road, Luton.   4571/A.

SHADBOLT, T. (M.M.), L/Corporal, 1st Bedfordshire Regiment.
He volunteered in January 1915, and was shortly afterwards sent to France. He fought at Ypres, Hill 60 and Verdun, and was awarded the Military Medal for distinguished bravery and devotion to duty in the Field. He was demobilised in March 1919, and also holds the 1914-15 Star, and the General Service and Victory Medals.
11, Blacksmith's Lane, St. Albans.   4601/A.

SHAMBROOK, C. D., L/Corporal, 8th Bedfordshire Regiment.
He volunteered in January 1916, and was shortly afterwards drafted to France. He took part in the fierce fighting at Ypres, and was killed in action on the Somme on September 15th, 1916. He was entitled to the General Service and Victory Medals.
53, Fearnley Street, Watford.   X4584.

SHANE, C. H., Private, 1/5th Bedfordshire Regiment, and Military Foot Police.
He volunteered at the outbreak of war, and was sent to the Dardanelles in the following year. He fought at the landing at Suvla Bay, and subsequent engagements until the Evacuation of the Peninsula. He then proceeded to Palestine, and was engaged in the operations at Gaza and Mejdel. Later, drafted to the Western Front, he served on important duties until the cessation of hostilities. He was demobilised in July 1919, and holds the 1914-15 Star, and the General Service and Victory Medals.
12, Langley Place, Luton.   4616.

SHANE, C. H., Sergeant, 2/5th Sussex Regiment.
He volunteered in September 1914, and after his training was engaged on important duties with his unit. He did good work in conducting drafts to France during the whole period of his service. He was discharged on account of service in April 1918, and holds the General Service and Victory Medals.
57, London Road, Luton.   4596.

SHANE, H., Sapper, Royal Engineers.
He volunteered in September 1914, and in the following July was drafted to Egypt, where he was stationed for a time at Cairo and Alexandria. He was later engaged on important duties with his unit in the forward areas during the Advance through Palestine and was wounded. He returned to England in September 1918, and was demobilised in the following February, and holds the General Service and Victory Medals.
10, Gaitskill Row, Luton.   4574.

SHANE, W., Sapper, Royal Engineers.
He volunteered in August 1914, and in the following year was drafted to Egypt. He saw much service on the Eastern Front, and was engaged on important duties during the fighting in the Canal Zone and at Gaza and Haifa. He contracted fever whilst in this theatre of war, and was invalided to hospital in Cairo, and died on November 22nd, 1918. He was entitled to the 1914-15 Star, and the General Service and Victory Medals.
7, Warwick Street, Luton.   1198/B.

SHARMAN, G., Gunner, Royal Field Artillery.
He joined in January 1918, and three months later proceeded overseas. He served on the Western Front with his Battery, and was engaged in the fighting in various sectors and fought at Ploegsteert and many other places during the Retreat and Advance. He was demobilised in January 1919, and holds the General Service and Victory Medals.
3, Alfred Street, Dunstable.   4570.

SHARMAN, J., Private, 5th Bedfordshire Regt., and Dorsetshire Regiment.
He joined in August 1916, and in the following February proceeded to France. In this theatre of war he fought in many battles, including those at Arras, Cambrai and the Somme. He was severely wounded at Ypres in August 1917, and sent home. After treatment in hospital he was invalided out of the Service on account of wounds on December 23rd, 1917. He holds the General Service and Victory Medals.
Jacques Lane, Clophill, Ampthill.   4629/A.

SHARMAN, R., Private, 15th King's Own (Yorkshire Light Infantry).
He volunteered in July 1915, and served with his Battalion at many stations until drafted to France in March 1917. Whilst on the Western Front he was engaged in the fighting at Arras, the Somme, Ypres, Cambrai and Albert. He was demobilised in March 1919, and holds the General Service and Victory Medals.
51, Bedford Street, Hitchin.   4628.

SHARMAN, S., Private, 5th Bedfordshire Regt.
He joined in January 1917, and in the following July was sent to France. Whilst on the Western Front he fought at Ypres, on the Somme and at Cambrai. He was killed in action on October 19th, 1917, and was entitled to the General Service and Victory Medals.
Jacques Lane, Clophill, Ampthill.   4630.

SHARMAN, W., Private, 2nd Bedfordshire Regt.
He volunteered in 1914, and served with his Battalion on important duties until drafted to Egypt in March 1917. Whilst in this theatre of war he took part in the fighting at Gaza during the British Advance through Palestine. After the Armistice he proceeded to India, where in 1920 he was still serving. He holds the General Service and Victory Medals.
Jacques Lane, Clophill, Ampthill.   4629/B.

SHARMAN, W., Private, 4th Bedfordshire Regt.
He volunteered in November 1915, and in the following year was sent to France. During his service on the Western Front he was engaged in the fighting at the Battle of the Somme, and was killed in action on November 13th, 1916. He was entitled to the General Service and Victory Medals.
Biggleswade Road, Potton.   Z4597.

SHARMAN, W., Private, R.A.M.C.
He joined in October 1916, and in the following July was sent to France. Whilst on the Western Front he was engaged on important duties with his unit in various sectors, and was severely wounded at Thiepval in September 1917. Invalided home he received hospital treatment and was demobilised in March 1919, and holds the General Service and Victory Medals.
Jacques Lane, Clophill, Ampthill.   4581.

SHARP, A. B., Lieutenant, 8th Royal Warwickshire Regiment.
He volunteered in February 1915, and was engaged on important coastal defence duties until January 1918. He then proceeded to France and in the following month was sent to Italy, where he served in the operations on the Piave front. He was later invalided home through ill-health, and on recovery was drafted to Germany with the Army of Occupation, and was stationed at Cologne until March 1920. He then returned to England, and was demobilised in the following month, and holds the General Service and Victory Medals.
82, Grove Road, Hitchin.   4624.

SHARP, B., Sapper, Royal Engineers.
He joined in April 1916, and in the same year was sent to Egypt. He served on important duties with his unit during the operations at Gaza and Haifa during the British Advance through Palestine. He was demobilised in August 1919, and holds the General Service and Victory Medals.
3, Balmoral Road, Hitchin.   4627/A.

SHARP, C. H., Gunner (Signaller), R.F.A.
He volunteered in September 1914, and in the following March was sent to Mesopotamia. In this theatre of war he was in action at Baghdad and many other places. He was later drafted to India where he served for a time. He returned to England and was demobilised in April 1919, and holds the 1914-15 Star, and the General Service and Victory Medals.
1, New Kent Road, St. Albans.   X4618.

SHARP, E., Driver, Royal Engineers.
He joined in 1916, and in the same year proceeded overseas. He was engaged with his unit on important transport duties to the front lines in many sectors of the Western Front, including those of the Somme, Arras and Cambrai. He was demobilised in 1919, and holds the General Service and Victory Medals.
3, Balmoral Road, Hitchin.   4627/B.

SHARP, F., A.B., Royal Navy.
He volunteered in August 1915, and was posted to H.M.S. "Royal Oak," which vessel took part in the Battle of Jutland. His ship was also engaged on important patrol duties in the North Sea and other waters. He holds the 1914-15 Star, and the General Service and Victory Medals, and was still serving in 1920.
2, Wright's Buildings, St. Albans Road, Watford.
                                                 X4605.

SHARP, F. T., Private, 8th Bedfordshire Regt.
He volunteered in October 1914, and in September of the following year he was drafted to the Western Front. In this theatre of war he took part in important engagements, including those at Ypres, Messines, Vimy Ridge and was gassed in December 1915. On recovery he returned to the trenches and was killed in action at Ypres on April 19th, 1916, and was entitled to the 1914-15 Star, and the General Service and Victory Medals.
21, Essex Street, Luton.   T466/A.

SHARP, H., Pte., London Regt. (Royal Fusiliers).
He joined in January 1917, and in the following May was drafted to France. He took part in the fighting at Ypres and was killed in action at Poperinghe on September 5th, 1917. He was entitled to the General Service and Victory Medals.
5, Windmill Street, Luton.   282/A.

SHARP, H. E., Private, Grenadier Guards.
He was mobilised at the outbreak of war and sent to France in September 1914. He fought at La Bassée, Ypres, and was almost continuously in action until killed near Neuve Chapelle on February 22nd, 1915. He was entitled to the 1914 Star, and the General Service and Victory Medals.
"Cartref," Alfred Street, Dunstable.   4579.

SHARP, H. S., Stoker, Royal Navy.
He was mobilised at the outbreak of war and served in H.M.S. "Repulse." His ship was engaged in the bombardment of the Dardanelles Forts and was also employed on patrol and other duties in the North Sea, and at Scapa Flow. He lost his life during an hostile air-raid at Chatham on September 3rd, 1917. He was entitled to the 1914-15 Star, and the General Service and Victory Medals.
5, Windmill Street, Luton.   282/B.

SHARP, J., Private, 4th Bedfordshire Regiment.
A Territorial, he was mobilised in August 1914, and was shortly afterwards drafted to France. In this theatre of war he fought at Ypres, Arras, Cambrai, on the Somme and at Hill 60. He was severely wounded in 1916, and sent to hospital at Oxford, where he remained for upwards of two years. He was invalided out of the Service in April 1918, and holds the 1914 Star, and the General Service and Victory Medals.
5, Terrace Gardens, St. Albans Road, Watford.   4611/A.

SHARP, P. E., Corporal, Royal Field Artillery.
He volunteered in March 1915, and in the following year proceeded overseas. He took part in much fighting on the Western Front and fought in the Battles of the Somme, Arras, Cambrai, Albert, Vimy Ridge and Messines. He was demobilised in January 1919, and holds the General Service and Victory Medals.
73, Grove Road, Hitchin.   4625.

SHARP, W., Private, 10th Hampshire Regiment.
He volunteered in August 1914, and in the following year was drafted to the Dardanelles, and was engaged in the fighting on the Peninsula and was later transferred to Salonika. He fought on the Bulgarian Frontier and was taken prisoner on December 7th, 1915, and held in captivity until after the cessation of hostilities. He was demobilised in March 1919, and holds the 1914-15 Star, and the General Service and Victory Medals.
5, Terrace Gardens, St. Albans Road, Watford.   X4610.

SHARP, W. A., Sapper, Royal Engineers.
He joined in March 1916, and in May of the following year proceeded overseas. During his service on the Western Front he was engaged on important duties with his unit, whilst operations were in progress at the Battles of Arras, the Somme, Ypres and in the Allied Advance into Germany. He remained with the Army of Occupation at Cologne until September 1919, when he returned home, and was demobilised. He holds the General Service and Victory Medals.
160, Wellington Street, Luton.   4576.

SHARP, W. G., Private, 7th and 3rd Bedfordshire Regiment.
He joined in February 1917, and in the following June was sent to France. Whilst in this theatre of war he was engaged in the fighting at Ypres, the Somme, Cambrai, and in the German Offensive of 1918. He was wounded in April 1918, and invalided home, and on recovery served with his Battalion until demobilised in September 1919. He holds the General Service and Victory Medals.
68, Shott Lane, Letchworth.   4566.

SHARP, W. T., Sergeant, 2nd Essex Regiment.
He volunteered in December 1915, and in January 1917 was sent to France. During his service on the Western Front he took part in many engagements, including those on the Somme, at Arras, Cambrai, Ypres, Passchendaele Ridge and Messines. He was demobilised in February 1919, and holds the General Service and Victory Medals.
9, Bigthan Road, Dunstable. 4589.

SHARP, W. T., Private, Machine Gun Corps.
He joined in August 1916, and in the folllowing April proceeded to Mesopotamia. In this theatre of war he was engaged in the operations at Kut, Baghdad, and many other places. He returned to England in 1920, and was demobilised in March of that year. He holds the General Service and Victory Medals.
10, Dunstable Place, Luton. 4577.

SHARPE, B., Private, R.A.M.C.
He volunteered in April 1915, and in November of the same year was drafted to Alexandria. He served on important duties at No. 27 General Hospital and did very good work. He was sent to France in July 1918 and was engaged with his unit at the Base Hospital at Etaples. He was demobilised in April 1919, and holds the General Service and Victory Medals.
25, Frederic Street, Luton. 4586/A, 4587/A.

SHARPE, C., Private, Suffolk Regiment.
He volunteered in January 1915, and was later drafted to Egypt. He served in the British Advance through Palestine and took part in the fighting at the first, second and third Battles of Gaza, and other engagements. He was demobilised in July 1919, and holds the General Service and Victory Medals.
52, Warwick Road, Luton. 4569.

SHARPE, G., Corporal, Royal Air Force.
He joined in June 1916, and a year later proceeded overseas. He served on the Western Front and was engaged on important duties with his Squadron in aerodromes in the Ypres and Arras sectors. He was demobilised in April 1919, and holds the General Service and Victory Medals.
2, Brickfields, Hitchin Hill, Hitchin. 4626.

SHARPE, G. E., Private, 3rd Bedfordshire Regt., and R.A.S.C.
He joined in April 1918, and at the conclusion of his training served on important duties with his Battalion at many stations. He rendered valuable services, but was unable to secure his transfer to a theatre of war before hostilities ceased, and was demobilised in December 1919.
68, Cambridge Street, Luton. 4621.

SHARPE, G. H., Pte., 1/6th Sherwood Foresters.
He was mobilised at the outbreak of war and served with his Battalion on important home duties until drafted to France in February 1916. He took part in many engagements and was wounded on the Somme in 1917. On recovery he returned to the firing line and fought at Bullecourt, Arras, Ypres, Albert and Cambrai. He was demobilised in February 1919, and holds the General Service and Victory Medals.
Park Street, Ampthill. 4622.

SHARPE, G. T., Pioneer, Royal Engineers.
Volunteering in October 1914, he was drafted to the Dardanelles in the following July. He was engaged on important duties at the landing at Suvla Bay and in the subsequent engagements on the Peninsula. In December 1915 he was drafted to Egypt and served in the Canal Zone and later at El Arish, Gaza, Haifa and Beyrout, until 1919, when he returned to England and was demobilised in June of that year. He holds the 1914-15 Star, and the General Service and Victory Medals.
198, Wellington Street, Luton. 4620.

SHARPE, J., Private, Labour Corps.
He volunteered in July 1916, and after his training served on important duties with his unit at various places and did very good work. He was also engaged on agricultural work during his service and was demobilised in February 1919.
25, Frederic Street, Luton. 4586/B, 4587/B.

SHARPE, W., Driver, Royal Engineers.
He volunteered in April 1915, and six months later proceeded to Salonika. In this theatre of war he was employed with his unit on important duties in connection with operations and was present at engagements at Monastir and on the Vardar front. He was demobilised in June 1919, and holds the 1914-15 Star, and the General Service and Victory Medals.
7, Holywell Road, Watford. X4575.

SHARPE, W., Private, 1st Bedfordshire Regt.
He volunteered in November 1914, and the following January was sent to France. He took part in the fighting at Ypres, Vimy Ridge and was wounded on the Somme in 1916. On recovery he returned to the firing line and was in action at Arras and was again wounded near Ypres in 1918. He was demobilised in February 1919, and holds the 1914-15 Star, and the General Service and Victory Medals.
High Street, Eaton Bray, near Dunstable. 3022/A.

SHARRATT, A., L/Corporal, Royal Engineers.
He joined in 1916, and in December of the same year proceeded to France. He served with his unit in many sectors, including those on the Somme, at Arras, Ypres and Cambrai, on important duties in connection with wiring, trenching and pontooning. He was demobilised in December 1919, and holds the General Service and Victory Medals.
High Street, Eaton Bray, Dunstable. 4614.

SHARRATT, F. D., Q.M.S., R.G.A.
A serving soldier, he was drafted to France at the outbreak of war, and was engaged in the fierce fighting in the Retreat from Mons, and the subsequent Battles of the Marne, Festubert, the Somme, Arras and Cambrai. He suffered from shell-shock and was invalided home, and later served on home duties until November 1919, when he was discharged, having completed 26 years' service with the Colours. He holds the Mons Star, and the General Service and Victory Medals.
2, Wood Street, Woburn Sands. Z4602.

SHARRATT, S. A., Cpl., R.A.F. (late R.F.C.)
He joined in December 1916, and on completion of his training was drafted to Canada, and was engaged with his Squadron at Texas Aerodrome on important duties as a wireless operator and Instructor in Wireless Telegraphy. He did very good work, but was not successful in obtaining his transfer to a theatre of war before hostilities ceased. He was demobilised in February 1919, and holds the General Service and Victory Medals.
54, Clarence Road, Leighton Buzzard. 4603.

SHAW, A. E., Sapper, Royal Engineers.
He joined in January 1917, and in the following month proceeded to France. In this theatre of war he was engaged on important duties in the front lines whilst severe fighting was in progress, and was in action at the Battles of Ypres, Arras and Cambrai. He returned to England for demobilisation in September 1919, and holds the General Service and Victory Medals.
40, Liverpool Street, Watford. X4582.

SHAW, C., Petty Officer, Royal Navy.
Volunteering in November 1915, on the conclusion of his training he was engaged as an Instructor of recruits at Chatham and other naval stations. He did valuable work, but owing to medical unfitness for active service he was retained on shore, and was discharged in March 1916.
19, Vernon Road, Luton 4591.

SHAW, C. E. S., Private, Bedfordshire Regiment.
Volunteering in November 1915, in the following May he was despatched to the Western Front. Whilst in this theatre of war he was engaged on important duties in various sectors, and fought in the Battles of the Somme, Arras, Bullecourt and other engagements, and was wounded three times. He was demobilised in February 1919, and holds the General Service and Victory Medals.
1, Bolton Road, Luton. 4592-3/B.

SHAW, E. S., Air Mechanic, Royal Air Force.
He joined in August 1918, and after training was engaged with his Squadron at various aerodromes on important duties in connection with aero-engine fitting. His work demanded a high degree of technical knowledge and skill, and he did very good work. He was unsuccessful in obtaining a transfer overseas before hostilities ceased, and in 1920 was still serving.
1, Bolton Road, Luton. 4592/E, 4593/E.

SHAW, J., Sergeant, 17th London Regt. (Rifles).
He volunteered in August 1914, and in the following year was drafted to France. He served in this theatre of war for two years, and took part in the Battles of Ypres, St. Julien and other important engagements, and was then drafted to East Africa. Employed for a time as an Instructor he was afterwards engaged in much heavy fighting, and was killed in action on October 17th, 1917. He was entitled to the 1914-15 Star, and the General Service and Victory Medals.
1, Bolton Road, Luton. 4592-3/D.

SHAW, J. R., L/Corporal, 26th Northumberland Fusiliers.
He volunteered in December 1914, and after serving with his unit for a time was drafted overseas in 1916. Whilst on the Western Front he was engaged in several important battles, including those of Arras, Cambrai and in the German Offensive and subsequent Allied Advance. He returned to England for demobilisation in March 1919, and holds the General Service and Victory Medals.
66, Bassett Road, Leighton Buzzard. 2707/B.

SHAW, L., Private, Labour Corps.
He joined in 1916, and in the same year was sent overseas. He saw much service on the Western Front, and was engaged on trench digging and other duties in the forward areas during the Battle of Cambrai and other important engagements until the termination of the war. He was demobilised in March 1919, and holds the General Service and Victory Medals.
Gosmore, Herts. 4623.

SHAW, S. W., Gunner, Royal Marine Artillery.
He joined in 1917, and was posted to H.M.S. "Collingwood," which vessel was engaged on important patrol and other duties in the North Sea and at Scapa Flow. His ship was afterwards sent to Constantinople to protect British interests, and in 1920 he was still serving. He holds the General Service and Victory Medals.
1, Bolton Road, Luton. 4592-3/C.

SHAW, T. F., Private, 1/5th Bedfordshire Regt.
Volunteering in December 1914, he was drafted to India in the following year, and after serving there for a time was sent to Mesopotamia in 1916. He took part in several operations in the Eastern theatre of war, and fought at Kut and was present at the capture of Baghdad and the occupation of Mosul. He was demobilised in May 1919 on returning to England, and holds the General Service and Victory Medals.
1, Bolton Road, Luton. 4592-3/A.

SHAWYER, C. G., Pte., 4th Bedfordshire Regt.
He joined in January 1917, and in the same year embarked for France, where he served for two years. During this period he took part in many important engagements, including the Battles of Cambrai and the Somme, and was gassed. He holds the General Service and Victory Medals, and was demobilised in October 1919.
36, Alexandra Road, St. Albans. X4585.

SHEATH, E. R., Telegraphist, Royal Navy.
He joined in 1916, and was posted to H.M.S. Submarine "L14." His ship was engaged on important operations in the North Sea, the Irish Channel, off the East Coast, and in other mine-strewn seas until the conclusion of hostilities. He was demobilised in 1920, and holds the General Service and Victory Medals.
65, Benskin Road, Watford. X4608/B.

SHEATH, W. H., Tpr., Hertfordshire Dragoons.
He joined in 1916, and in the same year embarked for Egypt. Taking part in General Allenby's Advance through Palestine, he fought in the Battles of Gaza, Haifa, Aleppo and other operations until the close of the campaign. After the signing of the Armistice he returned home and was demobilised, and holds the General Service and Victory Medals.
65, Benskin Road, Watford. X4608/A.

SHELDRAKE, A. E., Pte., Lancashire Fusiliers.
He volunteered in November 1914, and in the following year proceeded to the Western Front. Whilst in this theatre of war he fought in several important battles, notably those of Arras and Passchendaele, and was taken prisoner at St. Quentin on March 22nd, 1918. He was held in captivity until the signing of the Armistice, and on repatriation was demobilised in February 1919. He holds the 1914-15 Star, and the General Service and Victory Medals.
25, Cannon Road, Watford. 4580/B.

SHELLEY, W., Private, Loyal North Lancashire Regiment.
He volunteered in January 1916, and two months later was despatched to the Western Front. Serving with his unit he took part in the Battles of Arras, Cambrai and the Somme, and was twice wounded. He was engaged with his unit in other operations until the cessation of hostilities, and returned to England for demobilisation in January 1919. He holds the General Service and Victory Medals.
202, Chester Road, Watford. X4612.

SHELDRAKE, G. W., Pte., Lancashire Fusiliers.
Volunteering in November 1914, he was sent overseas in the following year. He saw much active service in France, and amongst other important engagements fought in the Battles of Arras and Passchendaele, and was taken prisoner at St. Quentin on March 22nd, 1918. On the cessation of hostilities he was released and returned to England. He was demobilised in February 1919, and holds the General Service and Victory Medals.
25, Cannon Road, Watford. 4580/A.

SHELTON, A. E., Gunner, R.H.A., and R.G.A.
Joining in October 1916, he was drafted to Mesopotamia in the following year. Whilst in the Eastern theatre of war he served with his Battery in several important engagements, and was present at the capture of Baghdad. He returned home for demobilisation in February 1920, and holds the General Service and Victory Medals.
The Green, Ickwell, near Biggleswade. Z4598/B.

SHELTON, C., Gunner, Royal Field Artillery.
A Territorial, he was mobilised in August 1914, and after serving with his unit at home for two years embarked for the Western Front. There he was in action on the Somme, and at Arras, Ypres, Passchendaele, and several other notable engagements until the signing of the Armistice. He returned to England for demobilisation in January 1919, and holds the General Service and Victory Medals.
The Green, Ickwell, near Biggleswade. Z4598/A.

SHELTON, G. W., Pte., 1/4th Lincolnshire Regt.
He volunteered in 1915, and in June of the following year proceeded to the Western Front. Whilst in this theatre of war he took part in several important engagements, and was unfortunately killed in action on the Somme on September 14th, 1916. He was entitled to the General Service and Victory Medals.
The Green, Ickwell, near Biggleswade. Z4598/C.

SHELTON, H., A.B., Royal Navy.
He joined in June 1916, and was posted to H.M. Torpedo Boat "A16." Aboard this ship he was engaged in the North Sea on important patrol duties and in chasing enemy submarines. Afterwards transferred to H.M. Torpedo Boat "D60," he was employed on special duties in Russian waters until discharged on account of service in June 1918. He had previously served in the 4th and 11th Battalions East Surrey Regiments, and holds the General Service and Victory Medals.
Luton Road, Toddington. 4609.

SHEPHARD, G., Gunner (Signaller), R.F.A.
He joined in October 1916, and in the following May proceeded to the Western Front. Serving with his Battery in various parts of the line, he fought in several important engagements, including that at Courcelles, and was wounded. He returned to England on the cessation of hostilities and was demobilised in November 1919, and holds the General Service and Victory Medals.
244, High Town Road, Luton. 877/B.

SHEPHARD, G., Sergt., 11th Bedfordshire Regt.
He volunteered in January 1915, and in the following year was drafted overseas. He was engaged on important duties in various parts of the Western Front and fought in many of the principal operations of the war, and was wounded. On the termination of hostilities he returned home for demobilisation in February 1919, and holds the General Service and Victory Medals.
10, Park Street, Hitchin. 4567/A.

SHEPHARD, H. G., A.B., Royal Navy.
He joined in April 1918, and was posted to H.M.S. "Sutton," which vessel was engaged in mine-sweeping and other duties in the North Sea and off the coasts of Holland and Scotland, until the end of the war. He was demobilised in December 1919, and holds the General Service and Victory Medals.
21, Mill Street, Apsley End, Hemel Hempstead. X4573.

SHEPHERD, A. H., Gunner, R.G.A.
He joined in March 1917, and on the completion of his training was engaged on important guard and other duties at various stations with his Battery. He did very good work, but was unsuccessful in obtaining a transfer to the theatre of war owing to medical unfitness for general service and was demobilised in December 1919.
Flamstead, near Dunstable. 4613/B.

SHEPHERD, E., Rflmn., King's Royal Rifle Corps.
He joined in April 1917, and in the following September embarked for France. Taking part in heavy fighting soon after landing he was wounded at the Battle of Ypres and buried by the explosion of a shell. Recovering from the effects of his injuries, he returned to the front lines, and fought in the Retreat and Advance of 1918 and the second Battle of Cambrai. He was demobilised in September 1919, and holds the General Service and Victory Medals.
Flamstead, near Dunstable. 4613/A.

SHEPHERD, H., Private, Queen's Own (Royal West Kent Regiment).

Joining in June 1916, he was drafted overseas in the following October. He saw much service on the Western Front and fought in the Battles of Arras and Messines, and was then drafted to Italy. In this theatre of war he took part in several important engagements, including those of the British Offensive on the Piave. He was invalided home on account of severe illness in March 1918, and died on October 15th of the same year. He was entitled to the General Service and Victory Medals.
Princess Street, Toddington. 4590.

SHEPHERD, H. G., Pte., 7th Bedfordshire Regt.

He volunteered in August 1914, and in the following year was sent to the Western Front. Whilst in France he was engaged on important duties in the course of operations and fought at Arras, Cambrai and several other places, and was wounded. Invalided to England on account of his wounds, he was discharged as medically unfit for further military service in May, 1918, and holds the 1914-15 Star, and the General Service and Victory Medals.
27, Church Road, Watford. X4583/B.

SHEPHERD, R., Private, 1st Hertfordshire Regt.

He volunteered in August 1914, and on the completion of his training served with his unit at various depôts and was employed on important duties in connection with home defence work. He rendered valuable services but was unable to obtain a transfer to a theatre of war owing to medical unfitness, and was discharged in consequence in February 1915.
32, Primrose Cottages, Hatfield. X4588.

SHEPHERD, S. A., Tpr., Hertfordshire Dragoons.

Volunteering in August 1914, he was drafted overseas in the following year. Sent to Gallipoli he took part in the landing at Suvla Bay and in many other engagements until the Evacuation of the Peninsula in December 1915. He then proceeded to Egypt, in which theatre of war he was in action in several notable battles, including those at Gaza and Aleppo and was present at the occupation of Damascus. He was demobilised in June 1919, and holds the 1914-15 Star, and the General Service and Victory Medals.
27, Church Road, Watford. X4583/A.

SHEPHERD, W., Corporal, Royal Engineers.

Mobilised on the outbreak of hostilities, he was shortly afterwards drafted to France, and was engaged on important duties in the Retreat from Mons, the first Battle of Ypres and several other important engagements. He was also in action in the Somme Offensive, and was discharged on account of service in February 1917. He holds the Mons Star, and the General Service and Victory Medals.
66, Regent Street, North Watford. X4594.

SHEPHERD, W., Corporal, Hertfordshire Regt.

He volunteered in 1914, and at the conclusion of his training was engaged at the depôt of his unit and other places of military importance on guard and other duties. He did excellent work, but was unsuccessful in procuring a transfer overseas on account of medical unfitness, and was invalided out of the service in March 1915.
20, Cherry Bounce, Hemel Hempstead. X4599.

SHERDEL, G. H., Private, 2nd Northamptonshire Regiment.

Volunteering in October 1914, in the following year he proceeded to the Western Front. Whilst in this theatre of war he was engaged in heavy fighting in the Battles of Festubert and Loos, and in several other operations of importance. He was taken prisoner on the Somme in 1917, and held in captivity in Germany until the signing of the Armistice. He then returned to England and was demobilised in January 1919, and holds the 1914-15 Star, and the General Service and Victory Medals.
25, Common View Square, Letchworth. 4565/B.

SHERING, A. W., L/Corporal, 6th Northamptonshire Regiment.

He volunteered in January 1916, and in the same year embarked for France, where he saw considerable service in many sectors—fighting at the Battles of Ypres, the Somme, Amiens and in the Retreat and Advance of 1918, and was wounded. He returned to England and was demobilised in February 1919, and holds the General Service and Victory Medals.
57, Bury Road, Hemel Hempstead. X4619.

SHORTLAND, A., Private, 1st London Regiment (Royal Fusiliers).

Volunteering in August 1914,' he completed his training and served at various depôts on important home service duties until drafted to the Western Front in July 1918. Here he saw heavy fighting in the Somme and Cambrai sectors. Severely wounded, he subsequently died from the effects of his injuries on September 22nd, 1918, and was buried at Rouen. He was entitled to the General Service and Victory Medals.
5, Diamond Road, Watford. X4600/B.

SHORTLAND, A. E., Private, Loyal North Lancashire Regiment.

He volunteered in 1915, and after completing a course of training served at home for two years with his unit. Embarking for France in 1917, he fought in the Battles of Ypres, Passchendaele, Cambrai, the Somme and various other important engagements during the German Offensive and subsequent Allied Advance in 1918. He was demobilised in March 1919, and holds the General Service and Victory Medals.
30, Boyle Street, Luton. 397/C.

SHORTLAND, A. J., Private, Royal Sussex Regt.

He joined in May 1918, and after completing his training was drafted to Russia and served for eleven months in the Caucasus engaged on guard and other important duties. He returned to England and was demobilised in October 1919, and holds the General Service and Victory Medals.
30, Boyle Street, Luton. 397/B.

SHORTLAND, F., Private, 1st Yorkshire Regt.

He enlisted in December 1909, and was serving in India when war broke out. He was stationed at various garrison towns on guard and other important duties until sent to the North-Western Frontier. He was severely wounded during a raid, and subsequently died of his injuries at Rawal-Pindi hospital on August 22nd, 1917. He was entitled to the General Service and Victory Medals.
5, Diamond Road, Watford. X4600/A.

SHORTLAND, J., Private, East Surrey Regiment.

He volunteered at the outbreak of hostilities, and embarked for the Western Front later in 1914. He saw much service in this theatre of war and was actively engaged at the Battles of Ypres, the Somme, Arras, and during the Retreat and Advance of 1918, and was three times wounded. He was invalided out of the Service in October 1917, and holds the 1914-15 Star, and the General Service and Victory Medals.
5, Diamond Road, Watford. X4607.

SHOTBOLT, E., Private, 2/4th Royal Scots Fusiliers.

He joined in June 1916, and after a course of training served at various stations with his unit on important guard and other duties. Medically unfit, he was unable to obtain his transfer overseas and in consequence of ill-health was invalided out of the Service in March 1918.
Barton Cottages, High Street, Clophill. 4568.

SHOWLER, G., Private, Bedfordshire Regiment.

He volunteered in June 1915, and was sent to France later in the same year, where he saw much service in various sectors of the Western Front. He fought at the Battles of Loos, Arras, Ypres, Cambrai and the Somme, and was wounded three times. He was invalided to England and after hospital treatment was discharged unfit for further service in 1917, and holds the 1914-15 Star, and the General Service and Victory Medals.
57, Leighton Street, Woburn. Z4604.

SHOWLER, W. T., Pte., Buffs (East Kent Regt.)

He joined in 1917, and on completion of his training served on important duties with his unit. Proceeding to France in the following year he was in action at the second Battles of the Marne and the Somme and other notable engagements in the Retreat and Advance of 1918. He was demobilised in 1919, and holds the General Service and Victory Medals.
Leighton Street, Woburn. Z253/B.

SHRIMPTON, F., Private, 5th and 8th Middlesex Regiment.

He volunteered in July 1915, and later was drafted to the Western Front, where he saw active service in many sectors and fought in the engagements at Loos, Arras, Cambrai, Albert, and in the Retreat and Advance of 1918, and was three times wounded. He was still serving in 1920, and holds the 1914-15 Star, and the General Service and Victory Medals.
48, Dane Road, Luton. 2408/B.

SHRIMPTON, R. A., Gunner, R.F.A.
He joined in May 1916, and proceeded overseas later in the same year and took part in the severe fighting in the Battles of Ypres, the Somme, Passchendaele, Cambrai, and many other engagements of note during the Retreat and Advance of 1918, and was twice wounded. He was demobilised in July 1919, and holds the General Service and Victory Medals.
54, Upper Paddock Road, Oxhey.   X4606.

SHUFFILL, W. C., Pte., 1st Bedfordshire Regt.
Volunteering in August 1914, he underwent a course of training and after serving at various stations on important duties was sent overseas in April 1915. On the Western Front he took part in various engagements and was unfortunately killed in action at Hill 60 on May 5th, 1915. He was entitled to the 1914-15 Star, and the General Service and Victory Medals.
28, Willow Lane, Watford.   X4572/B.

SHUFFILL, W. H., Driver, R.A.S.C.
He volunteered in 1915, and, sent to Salonika in the same year, served in various sectors on important transport duties. Transferred to the Egyptian Expeditionary Force in 1917 he saw active service on the Palestine front until 1918, when he was sent to Russia, and was present there at many engagements. He returned to England and was demobilised in September 1919, and holds the 1914-15 Star, and the General Service and Victory Medals.
28, Willow Lane, Watford.   X4572/A.

SIBLEY, B. H., Air Mechanic, Royal Air Force.
He joined in December 1917, and proceeded to France in 1918, and was engaged at Rouen and various aerodromes on important work in connection with the repair of aircraft. His duties called for a high degree of technical skill and he did very good work. Returning to England he was demobilised in 1919, and holds the General Service and Victory Medals.
South View Road, Harpenden.   4638.

SIBLEY, H. J., Bombardier, Royal Field Artillery.
He volunteered in October 1914, and proceeded to France in the following July and took part in the engagements at Ypres and in many others. He was unfortunately killed in action at Dickebusch on March 2nd, 1916, and was entitled to the 1914-15 Star, and the General Service and Victory Medals.
12, Park Street, Dunstable.   4637.

SIBLEY, J. E., Gunner, Royal Field Artillery.
He volunteered in August 1914, and embarked for France in the succeeding month and fought at the Battles of Festubert, Loos, Cambrai, and the Somme, where he was wounded in July 1916. After receiving hospital treatment he rejoined his Battery and served throughout the German Offensive and subsequent Allied Advance in 1918. He was demobilised in January 1919, and holds the 1914 Star, and the General Service and Victory Medals.
30, Hailey Street, St. Albans.   1045/A.

SIBLEY, L. G., Corporal, Oxfordshire and Buckinghamshire Light Infantry.
He joined in May 1917 and embarked for France later in the year. Here he fought in various engagements, including those at Passchendaele and Lens. In November 1917, he was drafted to Egypt and served on the Palestine front taking part in the operations in the Valley of the Jordan and in the Advance through Syria, and was present at the capture of Aleppo. He was still serving in 1920, and holds the General Service and Victory Medals.
Tree Cottage, Salisbury Road, Batford, Harpenden.   4633.

SIBLEY, T., Sapper, Royal Engineers.
Volunteering in September 1915, he was drafted to the Western Front in the following year and saw heavy fighting in various sectors and was in action at Arras, Cambrai, the Somme and throughout the German Offensive and subsequent Allied Advance in 1918. He was demobilised in March 1919, and holds the General Service and Victory Medals.
7, Fish Street, Boxmoor, Herts.   X4658.

SIBLEY, W., Private, Suffolk Regiment.
Joining in January 1917, he embarked for the Western Front six months later and saw much fighting in the Battles of Ypres, Passchendaele, Cambrai and Albert, and was wounded on May 13th, 1918, during the German Offensive. He died whilst on leave on October 29th, 1918 from sickness contracted on service and was entitled to the General Service and Victory Medals.
61, Crow Lane, Husbourne Crawley, Beds.   Z4647/B.

SIBLEY, J., Private, Labour Corps.
Joining in February 1917, on conclusion of his training he proceded to France in the following month. Engaged on trench-digging and road-making, he served on the Arras, Ypres, Albert and Cambrai fronts and was constantly under fire. He rendered excellent services and was demobilised in March 1919, and holds the General Service and Victory Medals.
37, Husbourne, Crawley, Beds.   Z4647/C.

SIBLEY, T. H., Corporal, R.A.O.C.
He joined in June 1916, and shortly afterwards proceeded to France and served at Calais and other bases with his unit on important duties in the stores. He rendered valuable services throughout and on his return to England was demobilised in June 1919, and holds the General Service and Victory Medals.
27, Liverpool Road, St. Albans.   4651.

SILLS, C. G., Private, Royal Fusiliers.
He joined in October 1916, and on conclusion of his training served at various stations on the East Coast with his unit, engaged on guard and other important duties. He was not successful in obtaining his transfer overseas but rendered valuable services until demobilised in 1919.
85, Regent Street, North Watford.   X2312/A.

SILLS, J. H., Private, 6th Dorsetshire Regiment.
He joined in April 1916, and later embarked for France, where he saw considerable service in many sectors of the Western Front and fought at the Battle of the Somme. He was taken prisoner in March 1918, during the German Advance and held in captivity in Germany until the cessation of hostilities. Repatriated, he was demobilised in September 1919, and holds the General Service and Victory Medals.
13, Merton Road, Watford.   X4650.

SILMAN, H. S., Corporal, Royal Engineers.
He volunteered in August 1914, and embarked for Egypt in the following year. He served on important duties connected with the transport of supplies on the Palestine front and was engaged in the building of pontoon bridges at Ghoraniyeh and Hajla Ford on the River Jordan. He was present at the Battle of Gaza and during the advance through the Holy Land. Returning to England he was demobilised in January 1919, and holds the 1914-15 Star, and the General Service and Victory Medals.
Chambers Lane, Ickleford, Hitchin.   4665.

SILSBY, H., Private, 6th Northamptonshire Regt.
He joined in May 1916, and proceeded to France in the following November and was engaged in the fighting on the Somme and the Ancre and in many other important engagements. He was killed in action at Arras on May 3rd, 1917, and was entitled to the General Service and Victory Medals.
44, Pondswicks Road, Luton.   1721/B.

SILVESTER, H., Corporal, Royal Engineers.
He volunteered in March 1915, and proceeded to France later in the same year. Here he served in the forward areas on important duties connected with the maintenance of the lines of communication and was present at the Battles of the Somme, Cambrai and Ypres, and many other engagements in the Retreat and Advance of 1918. He was demobilised in January 1919, and holds the General Service and Victory Medals.
31a, Plantation Road, Leighton Buzzard.   4644.

SIMMONS, E., Private, 4th East Surrey Regt.
Volunteering in September 1914, he was sent to the Western Front in the following year and was engaged at the Battles of Ypres, Hill 60, the Somme, Arras and Cambrai. He also fought at the second Battle of the Marne in the Retreat of 1918, and was in action during the subsequent Allied Advance and was twice wounded. He was demobilised in January 1919, and holds the 1914-15 Star, and the General Service and Victory Medals.
85, Fearnley Street, Watford.   X4645.

SIMMONS, H., Pte., 1/5th West Yorkshire Regt.
Volunteering in September 1914, he embarked for France in the following April, and was in action at Ypres, Neuve Chapelle, and was wounded. He was sent to hospital in England, and on recovery rejoined his unit and fought at Armentières, Messines and in the Retreat and Advance of 1918, and was gassed. Returning to England he received hospital treatment, and was discharged in December 1918. He holds the 1914-15 Star, and the General Service and Victory Medals.
The Grove, Eddlesborough.   Z4660.

SIMMONS, A., Private, Royal Welch Fusiliers.

He volunteered in December 1914, and after his training served on special duties with his regiment for a time. In 1916, transferred to Salonika, he saw active service in various sectors of that theatre of war and fought in many engagements during the Serbian Retreat. He returned to England and was demobilised in March 1919, and holds the General Service and Victory Medals.
Brooke Street, Eddlesborough.   Z4659/A.

SIMMONS, B. W., Driver, Royal Field Artillery.

Volunteering in August 1915, he proceeded to Mesopotamia after service at various stations and was engaged on important duties in connection with the transport of ammunition and supplies to the advanced areas. He was present at the Battle of Kut el Amara, and the capture of Baghdad. Returning to England he was demobilised in April 1919, and holds the General Service and Victory Medals.
15, Telegraph Terrace, Hitchin.   4661.

SIMMONS, L. A., A/C.S.M., East Surrey Regt.

He volunteered in September 1914, and later proceeded to the Western Front, where he saw considerable service in many sectors, fighting at the Battles of Ypres, Arras, Cambrai and Passchendaele. Transferred to Italy he served in many parts of the line in that theatre of war until he returned to England, and was demobilised in March 1919. He holds the General Service and Victory Medals.
23, Loates Lane, Watford.   X4642.

SIMMONS, O., Private, Loyal North Lancashire Regiment.

A serving soldier, he was mobilised at the outbreak of hostilities, and was sent to France almost immediately. He was in action in the Retreat from Mons and in the subsequent battles. He was killed in action on October 28th, 1914, and was entitled to the Mons Star, and the General Service and Victory Medals.
The Square, Toddington, Dunstable.   4631.

SIMMONS, P. A., Driver, R.A.S.C.

He joined in 1916, and embarked for Egypt in the following year, and was engaged on important transport duties on the Palestine front. He was present at the Battle of Gaza and the capture of Jerusalem, and served throughout the Advance through the Holy Land and Syria. He returned to England and was demobilised in March 1920, and holds the General Service and Victory Medals.
Brooke Street, Eddlesborough, Dunstable.   Z4659/B.

SIMMONS, R. H., Corporal, Sherwood Foresters.

Volunteering in May 1915, he underwent a course of training and served at various depôts with his unit until drafted to France in February 1917. He fought in the Battles of the Somme, Ypres, Lens, Cambrai, and throughout the German Offensive and subsequent Allied Advance of 1918, and was wounded. He was demobilised in October 1919, and holds the General Service and Victory Medals.
39, Brook Street, Luton.   4634/B.

SIMMONS, T. L., Pioneer, R.E. (Signal Section).

Joining in October 1916, he was sent to France in November of the following year. Here he was engaged on important work in maintaining the lines of communication in the Field during operations and was present at many important engagements, including those at Ypres and Cambrai. He was demobilised in November 1919, and holds the General Service and Victory Medals.
29, Chalk Hill, Oxhey.   X4632.

SIMMONS, W. C., L/Corporal, M.G.C.

He volunteered in 1915, and was drafted to Mesopotamia in June of the following year. He was in action at the Battle of Kut, and was present at the capture of Baghdad and the occupation of Mosul, and was wounded. He returned to England in October 1918, and was demobilised in the following March, and holds the General Service and Victory Medals.
39, Brook Street, Luton.   4634/A.

SIMMONS, W. H., Air Mechanic, R.A.F.

He joined in January 1918, and proceeded to France later in the same year. He served with his Squadron at various aerodromes in the sectors of the Somme, Ypres and Cambrai, and was also stationed at Dunkirk. He rendered valuable services, and was demobilised in January 1919, and holds the General Service and Victory Medals.
54, Dane Road, Luton.   4657.

SIMPKINS, A., Gunner, Royal Garrison Artillery.

He volunteered in August 1914, and in the following July was sent to Gallipoli, where he took part in the landing at Suvla Bay and in various other operations until the evacuation of the Peninsula. Early in 1916 he proceeded to the Western Front, and was severely wounded on the Somme on June 30th and invalided to hospital in England. He was discharged as medically unfit for further military service in October 1917, and holds the 1914-15 Star, and the General Service and Victory Medals.
71, Chapel Street, Luton.   4641.

SIMPKINS, A. H., Private, Bedfordshire Regt.

He volunteered in November 1914, and after serving at the depôt of his unit embarked for France and was engaged in the heavy fighting in this theatre of war. He took part in many notable battles, including those of Arras and Cambrai, and was wounded. Demobilised in March 1919, he holds the General Service and Victory Medals.
44, Cannon Street, St. Albans.   3221/B.

SIMPKINS, B., Trooper, 3rd (Prince of Wales') Dragoon Guards.

He was serving in the Army in Egypt when war broke out, having enlisted in February 1910, and was sent to the Western Front shortly after the outbreak of war. He fought in the Battles of Ypres, the Somme, Arras and was severely wounded at Vimy Ridge in May 1916. Invalided home on account of wounds he was discharged as medically unfit for further military service in October 1917, and holds the 1914 Star, and the General Service and Victory Medals.
High Street, Barton, near Ampthill.   4662/A.

SIMPKINS, D., Sergeant, 1st Bedfordshire Regt.

He volunteered in August 1914, and in the following year proceeded overseas. Serving on the Western Front he took part in important operations in various sectors, and fought in the Battles of Neuve Chapelle and Ypres, and was twice wounded. He was subsequently killed in action near Vimy Ridge on February 9th, 1918, and was entitled to the 1914-15 Star, and the General Service and Victory Medals.
High Street, Barton, Ampthill.   4662/B.

SIMPKINS, E., Stoker, Petty Officer, R.N.

He was serving in the Royal Navy when war broke out, having joined in January 1909, and aboard H.M.S. "Indomitable" was engaged on important duties in the Mediterranean Sea and in the Indian Ocean. His ship later took part in the operations in the Dardanelles, and was also in action in the Battles of Heligoland Bight and Jutland and in other encounters with the German Fleet. He was demobilised in January 1920, and holds the 1914-15 Star, and the General Service and Victory Medals.
Trevor Cottages, Maulden, near Ampthill.   4654.

SIMPKINS, L., Private, Essex Regiment.

Joining in 1916, he embarked in the same year for the Western Front, and saw much service in that theatre of war for three years. During this period he served in the Battles of the Somme, Arras, Cambrai and St. Quentin, and was twice wounded. He returned to England for demobilisation in February 1919, and holds the General Service and Victory Medals.
Thatch Cottage, Cumberland Road, Leagrave.   4656.

SIMPKINS, R. J., Private, 1/5th Essex Regiment.

He joined in November 1916, and in the following year proceeded to Egypt. In this theatre of war he took part in the British Advance through Palestine and was in action in several important engagements, including the Battles of Gaza and Jaffa. On the conclusion of hostilities he was stationed at Cairo and other garrison towns in Egypt until his return home for demobilisation in October 1919. He holds the General Service and Victory Medals.
The Bull, Offley.   4664.

SIMPSON, C. R., Rifleman, 17th London Regt. (Rifles).

Volunteering in August 1914, he was drafted overseas in the following March. He served with his unit on the Western Front, and fought in the Battle of Loos and other notable engagements. He was severely wounded near La Bassée in February 1916, and sent home for hospital treatment. He was invalided out of the Army in July 1916, and holds the 1914-15 Star, and the General Service and Victory Medals.
4, Upper Culver Road, St. Albans.   X4653.

SIMPSON, A. S., Corporal, 1st Queen's (Royal West Surrey Regiment).

He joined in April 1917, and in the following March was despatched to France, where he saw much service at Albert and Le Cateau. He was also engaged on important clerical duties with the Royal Army Ordnance Corps, General Headquarters, at Wimereux and Boulogne, and did very good work. He was demobilised in April 1920, and holds the General Service and Victory Medals.
High Street, Clophill, near Ampthill.   4635.

SIMPSON, J., Private, Middlesex Regiment.

He joined in 1916, and in the same year was sent to the Western Front. Whilst in this theatre of war he was engaged in the fighting in the Battles of Vimy Ridge, the Somme, Ypres and Messines, and in many other operations until the termination of the war. He was demobilised in 1919, and holds the General Service and Victory Medals.
42, East Common, Redbourn.   4636.

SIMPSON, J. E., L/Cpl., Military Foot Police.

He volunteered in March 1915, and in the same year was sent to Salonika. Serving in the Balkans he was in action in several engagements in that theatre of war and in 1917 was sent to Egypt. There he was employed on important police duties at Alexandria, Cairo and other bases for two years and did excellent work. He returned to England for demobilisation in March 1919, and holds the General Service and Victory Medals.
5, Sydney Road, Watford.   X4639.

SIMPSON, J. F. W., Sergeant, Royal Engineers.

He volunteered in 1914, and served at the depôt of his unit until drafted to France in 1916. He was engaged on important duties in the front lines in connection with operations whilst fierce fighting was in progress and was present at the Battles of Ypres and Cambrai, and other engagements. On the cessation of hostilities he returned to England for demobilisation in 1919, and holds the General Service and Victory Medals.
44, Elizabeth Road, Luton.   4652.

SIMPSON, J. W., Driver, Royal Field Artillery.

He volunteered in August 1914, and in the following year proceeded overseas. He saw much service on the Western Front and fought in the Battle of Ypres and other important engagements until 1917, when he was sent to Egypt. In this theatre of war he was engaged in the advance through Palestine and was in action at Gaza, Haifa, and other places. He holds the 1914-15 Star, and the General Service and Victory Medals, and was demobilised in 1919, after returning to England.
2, Chalk Hill, Oxhey.   X4640.

SIMPSON, S., Private, Middlesex Regiment.

He volunteered in September 1915, and proceeded to India where he served for a time at various military stations. He was then sent to the Balkans and from there to Mesopotamia, in which theatre of war he took part in several engagements. Subsequently drafted to East Africa he saw much service until hostilities ceased. He returned to England and was demobilised in February 1919, and holds the General Service and Victory Medals.
48, Baker Street, Leighton Buzzard.   4649.

SIMPSON, W., Sapper, Royal Engineers.

He volunteered in 1915, and was sent to the Western Front in the following year. He was engaged on important work in connection with the construction of railways in the forward areas, and in the course of his service was gassed three times. On the termination of hostilities he returned to England and was demobilised in August 1919, and holds the General Service and Victory Medals.
18, Cowfairlands, Biggleswade.   Z1255/B.

SIMS, R. L., Leading Seaman, Royal Navy.

He joined the Royal Navy in 1911, and, mobilised on the declaration of war, served aboard H.M.S. "Ness," which ship was engaged on important patrol duties in the North Sea and other waters and in convoying vessels between the Humber and the Shetland Islands. He also served in H.M.S. "Africa," and throughout the war did much valuable work. He was demobilised in September 1919, and holds the 1914-15 Star, and the General Service and Victory Medals.
124, Leagrave Road, Luton.   4643.

SINDEN, C., Private, 4th Bedfordshire Regiment.

He joined in October 1916, and in the following year proceeded to France. Serving on the Western Front he took part in the Battles of Arras, Ypres, Passchendaele, the Somme and Cambrai, and other operations until the cessation of hostilities. He was demobilised in November 1919, and holds the General Service and Victory Medals.
Bedford Road, Aspley Guise.   Z4648.

SINDEN, T. H., Private, R.A.S.C.

He volunteered in May 1915, and was shortly afterwards drafted to France. Serving with his unit he was engaged on important duties in various parts of the line until sent to hospital at Le Havre suffering from pneumonia. He was afterwards removed to the Red Cross Hospital in Dublin and died there on December 28th, 1916. He was entitled to the 1914-15 Star, and the General Service and Victory Medals.
Weathercock Lane, Woburn Sands.   Z4646.

SINFIELD, G. E., L/Corporal, Bedfordshire Regt.

He volunteered in June 1915, and a month later was sent to France where he saw much service. He fought in the Somme Offensive, and in several important engagements in the Arras and Cambrai sectors, and was twice wounded. He was subsequently killed in action at Corbie on August 9th, 1918, and was entitled to the 1914-15 Star, and the General Service and Victory Medals.
Tilesworth, near Leighton Buzzard.   4663.

SINFIELD, H. C., Sergeant, Bedfordshire Regt., and 23rd Cheshire Regiment.

Volunteering in December 1914, he was engaged at the depôt of his regiment in training recruits for the new armies for a time. Drafted to Salonika in November 1916, he did excellent work during the course of the Balkan campaign and fought in many engagements. In May 1917 he was sent to the Western Front where he served in various sectors until the close of the war. He was demobilised in February 1919, and holds the General Service and Victory Medals.
29, Newcombe Road, Luton.   4655.

SKEGGS, A., Sapper, Royal Engineers.

He volunteered in January 1915, and was shortly afterwards drafted to the Western Front. He was engaged on special duties in connection with operations at the Battles of the Somme, Arras, Passchendaele, Cambrai and other important engagements. On the cessation of hostilities he was sent into Germany with the Army of Occupation and was stationed at Cologne. He was demobilised in April 1919, and holds the 1914-15 Star, and the General Service and Victory Medals.
8, Bower Lane, Eaton Bray, Dunstable.   976/C.

SKEGGS, A. E., Private, 6th Bedfordshire Regt.

He volunteered in June 1915, and in the same year embarked for France, where he took part in heavy fighting at Ypres, Albert, Contalmaison and other places. He was reported missing on August 9th, 1916, at Delville Wood, and was later presumed to have been killed in action on that date. He was entitled to the 1914-15 Star, and the General Service and Victory Medals.
24, Primrose Cottages, Hatfield.   X4668.

SKELTON, T., Sapper, Royal Engineers.

He enlisted in September 1914, and in the following year proceeded to France. He was engaged on important duties in connection with operations in various sectors and was in action at Ypres, Cambrai, Arras and on the Somme. At the close of hostilities he returned to England and was demobilised in March 1919, and holds the 1914-15 Star, and the General Service and Victory Medals.
15, Reginald Street, Luton.   X4666.

SKINNER, F. W., A.B., Royal Navy.

Mobilised on the outbreak of hostilities he was posted to H.M.T.B.D. "P23," which vessel was engaged on important patrol duties in the North Sea and other waters. His ship was in action at the Battles of Heligoland and Jutland and also took part in the naval operations at the Dardanelles and he was wounded. He holds the 1914-15 Star, and the General Service and Victory Medals, and in 1920 was still serving.
5, Holly Villas, Harpenden.   4669.

SKINNER, G. F. W., Private, 13th London Regt. (Kensingtons), and 2nd Lieutenant, R.A.F.

A Territorial, he was mobilised when war broke out, and shortly afterwards proceeded to France. Whilst in this theatre of war he fought in the Battles of Ypres, the Somme, Givenchy Passchendaele, Cambrai and other operations, and was gassed. Returning to England on the conclusion of hostilities, he was demobilised in January 1919, and holds the 1914 Star, and the General Service and Victory Medals.
40, Upper Paddock Road, Oxhey.   X4671.

SKINNER, F. G., Sapper, Royal Engineers.
He joined in 1916, and was shortly afterwards drafted overseas. Serving on the Western Front he did excellent work with his unit whilst operations were in progress during the Battle of Ypres, and other important engagements until the end of the war. He was demobilised in 1919, and holds the General Service and Victory Medals.
152, Chester Road, Watford.   X4667.

SKINNER, R., Private, 1/5th Bedfordshire Regt.
Volunteering in September 1914, he proceeded overseas in the following year and served in the Gallipoli campaign. He fought in the landing at Suvla Bay and in many operations on the Peninsula and was severely wounded. Sent to Egypt in 1916, he was in action at Jaffa, Gaza, Acre, Beyrout, and other places in the British advance through Palestine and was again wounded on July 20th, 1917. He was demobilised in April 1920, and holds the 1914-15 Star, and the General Service and Victory Medals.
12, Holly Walk, Luton.   4670/B.

SKINNER, R. F., Private, R.A.S.C. (M.T.)
He joined in June 1916, and in October of the same year was sent to the Western Front. He was attached to the Tank Corps Supply Column, and did very valuable work during the Battles of the Somme, Ypres, Arras, and in the Retreat and Advance of 1918. Returning home on the termination of the war he was discharged on account of service in October 1919, and holds the General Service and Victory Medals.
12, Holly Walk, Luton.   4670/A.

SLADE, A., Gunner, Royal Garrison Artillery.
He joined in May 1916, and was drafted to France in the same year. During his service on the Western Front he took part in the fighting at Ypres, the Somme, Passchendaele, and Cambrai, and in the Retreat and Advance of 1918. He was demobilised in 1919, and holds the General Service and Victory Medals.
39, Pinner Road, Oxhey.   X4673.

SLADE, R. H., Pte., Royal Fusiliers, and M.G.C.
He volunteered in November 1914, and in the following year was sent to France. He fought at Arras, Ypres and Cambrai, and in 1917 was drafted to Egypt. He served in the Palestine campaign and was engaged in the fighting at Gaza, and Jaffa, and was present at the Occupation of Jerusalem. He was later transferred to Salonika and was in action on the Doiran front. He returned to England and was demobilised in March 1919, and holds the 1914-15 Star, and the General Service and Victory Medals.
The Grove, Lidlington, Beds.   Z4683.

SLADE, W. J. A., Stoker, Royal Navy.
He volunteered in August 1914, and was posted to H.M.S. "Royal Arthur," which vessel took part in the fighting at the Battle of the Falkland Islands and later proceeded to the Dardanelles and was engaged in the bombardment of the Peninsula and the forcing of the Narrows. His ship was later employed in the North Sea on patrol duties until after the Armistice. He was demobilised in February 1919, and holds the 1914-15 Star, and the General Service and Victory Medals.
58, Oxford Street, Watford.   X4675.

SLANEY, E. J., Private, 2nd Queen's (Royal West Surrey Regiment).
He joined in March 1918, and in the following August proceeded to France. He took part in the fighting at Bapaume, and was wounded at Kemmel Hill in September 1918, during the Allied Advance. He was demobilised in May 1919, and holds the General Service and Victory Medals.
11, Sandringham Road, Watford.   X4680/A.

SLANEY, W. E., Gunner, Royal Field Artillery.
He volunteered in October 1915, and served with his Battery at various depôts on important duties until drafted to Mesopotamia in August 1917. He was in action at Kut-el-Amara and Baghdad, and was present during the offensive on the Tigris. He was demobilised after returning to England in April 1919, and holds the General Service and Victory Medals.
11, Sandringham Road, Watford.   X4680/B.

SLATER, H., Gunner, Royal Garrison Artillery.
He volunteered in November 1915, and at the conclusion of his training was engaged on important coastal defence duties with his Battery at various stations. He did excellent work, chiefly on the East Coast, but owing to medical unfitness was unable to secure his transfer to a theatre of war, and was demobilised in February 1919.
4, Bedford Street, Hitchin.   4684.

SLAUGHTER, H., Private, Royal Fusiliers.
He volunteered in December 1915, and after serving for a period on home duties was drafted to France in August 1917. During his service on the Western Front he fought at Arras, and was wounded at Ypres in October 1917. He was invalided home and after receiving hospital treatment was subsequently discharged unfit for further service in July 1918. He holds the General Service and Victory Medals.
135, Herkomer Road, Bushey, Herts.   X4674.

SLAUGHTER, N., Private, R.A.S.C. (Remounts).
He volunteered in June 1915, and in the following year proceeded overseas. Whilst on the Western Front he served at Rouen and Havre on important duties in connection with the training of horses for active service. He returned to England after the cessation of hostilities, and was demobilised in March 1919, and holds the General Service and Victory Medals.
35, Old London Road, St. Albans.   X4681/A.

SLEIGHT, E. G., Private, East Surrey Regiment.
He joined in May 1916, and after his training served at various stations on important duties with his Battalion. He did very good work but was unable to secure his transfer to a theatre of war owing to injuries received in an accident whilst on duty. He was invalided out of the Service in May 1917.
26, Clarendon Road, Luton.   4513/B.

SLOPER, C. J., Private, 2nd Queen's (Royal West Surrey Regiment).
He joined in July 1916, and two months later proceeded to Egypt, where he served for a time. In December 1916 he was drafted to Salonika and in this theatre of war took part in the fighting on the Vardar and Struma fronts, and was invalided home with malaria in May 1918. He was demobilised in December of the same year, and holds the General Service and Victory Medals.
73, Shaftesbury Road, Watford.   X4677.

SLOUGH, E., Corporal, R.A.S.C.
He volunteered in January 1915, and later proceeded overseas. Whilst on the Western Front he was engaged on important transport duties with his unit in the Somme, Fesubert and Ypres sectors. He was demobilised in April 1919, and holds the General Service and Victory Medals.
29, Longmire Road, St. Albans.   X4678.

SLOUGH, E. C., Private, 6th Oxfordshire and Buckinghamshire Light Infantry, attached Royal Army Cyclist Corps.
He volunteered in August 1914, and in the following May was drafted to the Western Front. In this theatre of war he took part in many important battles, including those at Arras, Ypres, Cambrai and on the Somme, and was twice wounded and gassed. He returned to England after the cessation of hostilities and was demobilised in January 1919, and holds the 1914-15 Star, and the General Service and Victory Medals.
Old Marford, Wheathampstead.   101/A.

SLOUGH, H. (M.M.), L/Corporal, 1/5th Bedfordshire Regiment.
He volunteered in February 1915, and in the following month was sent to Egypt. He fought in the British advance through Palestine and during the operations at Gaza and was awarded the Military Medal for bravery and devotion to duty in the Field at Umbrella Hill on July 27th, 1917. He was engaged in the subsequent fighting at Mejdel, Haifa, Acre and Beyrout, and returned to England after the signing of the Armistice. He was demobilised in August 1919, and holds the 1914-15 Star, and the General Service and Victory Medals.
30, Old Bedford Road, Luton.   4676.

SLOUGH, H. W., Cpl., Shoeing Smith, R.F.A.
He volunteered in April 1915, and served on important work with his Battery until drafted to India in 1917. He was engaged on garrison duties at Rawal Pindi, Poona and Bangalore, until December 1919, when he returned to England and was demobilised. He holds the General Service and Victory Medals.
33, Stanley Street, Luton.   4672/A.

SLOUGH, J. (M.M.), Private, 4th Bedfordshire Regiment.
He volunteered in November 1915, and was shortly afterwards sent to France. During his service on the Western Front he fought at Arras, Ypres and Cambrai and was gassed and wounded. He was awarded the Military Medal for conspicuous gallantry and devotion to duty in the Field. He also holds the General Service and Victory Medals, and was demobilised in February 1919.
The Follies, Wheathampstead.   4679.

SLOUGH, R. W., Gunner, Royal Marine Artillery.
He volunteered in March 1915, and was posted to H.M.S. "Benbow," which vessel was engaged on patrol duties in the Mediterranean and Baltic Seas. His ship was also employed on important duties in the North Sea, and after the signing of the Armistice served off the Coast of Russia. He holds the 1914-15 Star, and the General Service and Victory Medals, and was still serving in 1920.
33, Stanley Street, Luton. 4672/B.

SLY, A. E., Gunner, Royal Garrison Artillery.
He volunteered in 1915, and in the same year was drafted to France. In this theatre of war he fought at Ypres, on the Somme, at Messines Ridge, Arras and Nieuport, and was wounded. He returned to England, and on recovery served on special home duties until demobilised in 1918. He holds the 1914-15 Star, and the General Service and Victory Medals.
445, Whippendell Road, Watford. X4682.

SMALL, B., Private, Royal Welch Fusiliers.
He volunteered in January 1916, and in the following July proceeded overseas. He fought on the Western Front and was in action at the first Battle of the Somme. He was severely wounded in September of the same year and invalided to England. He remained for several months in hospital at York, but succumbed to his injuries on January 11th, 1917, and was buried at Dunstable. He was entitled to the General Service and Victory Medals.
70, Waterlow Road, Dunstable. 179/A.

SMALLBONES, A., Sapper, Royal Engineers.
He volunteered in March 1915, and five months later was drafted to France. Whilst in this theatre of war he was engaged with his unit wiring trenches, bridge building, pontooning, mining, and other important duties whilst operations were in progress in the Retreat and Advance of 1918. He was demobilised in April 1919, and holds the 1914-15 Star, and the General Service and Victory Medals.
12, Hockliffe Road, Leighton Buzzard. 4741.

SMALLBONES, J., Sergeant, Bedfordshire Regt.
He volunteered in January 1915, and at the conclusion of his training was engaged with his Battalion on important duties as a drill instructor at many stations. He did excellent work, but was unsuccessful in obtaining his transfer to a theatre of war, and was demobilised in March 1919.
50, Plantation Road, Leighton Buzzard. 4789.

SMART, A. F., Private, Northamptonshire Regt.
He volunteered at the outbreak of war, and was almost immediately sent to France. In this theatre of war he was engaged in the fierce fighting in the Retreat from Mons and in the vicinity of Ypres. He was killed in action on October 23rd, 1914, and was entitled to the Mons Star, and the General Service and Victory Medals.
52, Holywell Road, Watford. X152/B.

SMART, E. F., Corporal, 2nd London Regiment (Royal Fusiliers).
He was mobilised at the outbreak of hostilities and served with his Battalion on important duties until drafted overseas in August 1916. During his service on the Western Front he fought at the Battle of the Somme, and was killed in action on the Ancre on February 10th, 1917. He was entitled to the General Service and Victory Medals.
75, Leagrave Road, Luton. 4688/B.

SMART, E. R., Driver, Royal Engineers.
He joined in June 1916, and three months later proceeded to France. Whilst on the Western Front he served on the Somme, Arras, Ypres and Cambrai sectors, on important duties with his unit, and was frequently under heavy shell fire. After the signing of the Armistice he proceeded to Germany with the Army of Occupation and was stationed at Cologne. He was demobilised in September 1919, and holds the General Service and Victory Medals.
New Cottages, High Street, Markyate. 4772/B.

SMART, T. W., Bandsman, 6th Bedfordshire Regiment.
He volunteered in November 1914, and in June of the following year proceeded to France. In this theatre of war he was in action at Ypres, Arras and on the Somme, and was wounded. He was invalided home, and on recovery returned to the Western Front in October 1918, and was engaged in the fighting on the Somme until the cessation of hostilities. He was demobilised in March 1919, and holds the 1914-15 Star, and the General Service and Victory Medals.
High Street, Houghton Conquest, near Ampthill. 4742/B.

SMART, G. S., Private, Machine Gun Corps.
He was mobilised at the outbreak of war and was sent to the Dardanelles in July 1915. He fought at the landing at Gallipoli and the subsequent engagements until the evacuation of the Peninsula. He was later drafted to Egypt, and during the British advance through Palestine was wounded at Gaza. On recovery he rejoined his unit and was in action at Haifa and Beyrout. He holds the 1914-15 Star, and the General Service and Victory Medals, and was still serving in 1920.
75, Leagrave Road, Luton. 4688/A.

SMART, H., Private, Essex Regiment.
He joined in October 1916, and was sent to France in the following May. He was engaged in much fighting and was in action at Ypres, Armentières, Cambrai, and in the German Offensive and subsequent Allied Advance of 1918. He was demobilised in October 1919, and holds the General Service and Victory Medals.
Alma House, Alfred Street, Dunstable. 4706.

SMART, S. J., Private, Machine Gun Corps.
He joined in April 1918, on attaining military age, and at the conclusion of his training was engaged on important duties with his unit. He did very good work but was unable to secure his transfer to a theatre of war before the signing of the Armistice, and was demobilised in September 1919.
New Cottages, Markyate. 4772/A.

SMEE, H. C., Corporal, Queen's (Royal West Surrey Regiment).
He volunteered in May 1915, and in the following December was drafted to France. Whilst on the Western Front he was engaged in much heavy fighting and was severely wounded on the Somme. He was invalided home in February 1917, and subsequently discharged in consequence of the effects of his wounds. He holds the 1914-15 Star, and the General Service and Victory Medals.
8, Westbourne Road, Luton. 4711.

SMITH, A., Private, 2nd Bedfordshire Regiment.
He volunteered in August 1914, and after serving with his unit for a time was drafted to France. Whilst in this theatre of war he saw much service in various parts of the line and was in action in the Battles of Arras, Ypres and Passchendaele. He was killed in action near Cambrai on October 23rd, 1918, and was entitled to the General Service and Victory Medals.
13a, Wells Yard, Watford. X4751/A.

SMITH, A., Private, East Surrey Regiment.
He joined in May 1917, and two months later proceeded to the Western Front where he served with his unit in various sectors. He fought in several important engagements, and was taken prisoner on April 1st, 1918, during the Retreat from Cambrai. Released from captivity on the signing of the Armistice, he was demobilised in November 1919, and holds the General Service and Victory Medals.
10, Limbury Road, Leagrave. 4747.

SMITH, A., Private, R.A.S.C.
He volunteered in September 1915, and shortly afterwards embarked for France. During his service on the Western Front he was engaged on important transport duties in the Battles of the Somme, Arras, Ypres, Cambrai, and was wounded in 1918. Returning to England he was discharged on account of service in April 1919, and holds the 1914-15 Star, and the General Service and Victory Medals.
4, Lambs' Yard, High Street, Watford. X4738.

SMITH, A., Private, Durham Light Infantry.
He volunteered in August 1914, and in the following year was drafted overseas. He saw much service on the Western Front and fought in the Battle of the Somme and other important engagements. He was killed in action in the vicinity of Ypres on October 13th, 1916, and was entitled to the 1914-15 Star, and the General Service and Victory Medals.
Sandy Lane, Woburn Sands. Z4737/A.

SMITH, A., L/Corporal, R.A.M.C.
He volunteered in August 1915, and three months later was sent to the Western Front. Whilst in France he was engaged on special duties at hospitals behind the lines at Loos, Arras, Ypres, Albert, Amiens and on the Somme, and did valuable work as a cook. At the end of hostilities he was sent to Germany with the Army of Occupation and stationed at Cologne. He was demobilised in June 1919, and holds the 1914-15 Star, and the General Service and Victory Medals.
64, Sun Street, Biggleswade. Z4730.

SMITH, A., L/Corporal, Royal Engineers.
He volunteered in November 1914, and on the completion of his training was engaged on important duties with his unit at various stations on the East Coast. He did most useful work, but was unable to obtain a transfer overseas owing to medical unfitness for general service, and was invalided out of the service in April 1916.
170, Dallow Road, Luton.   4729.

SMITH, A., L/Cpl, 2nd Worcestershire Regt.
He joined in 1916, and in August of the same year proceeded to France. Whilst in this theatre of war he was in action in the Battles of the Somme, Arras, Ypres, Cambrai and various other operations until the close of the war. He holds the General Service and Victory Medals, and was demobilised in February 1919.
12, Tasker's Row, Eddlesborough, near Dunstable.
                                                  Z4781/A.

SMITH, A., Private, 1/7th Manchester Regiment.
Volunteering in January 1916, he was shortly afterwards despatched to the Western Front. Whilst overseas he took part in several important engagements and was wounded. Rejoining his unit on recovery, he was killed in action on July 5th, 1918, and was entitled to the General Service and Victory Medals.
11, St. Peter's Cottages, Hatfield.   X4720.

SMITH, A., Trooper, Dragoon Guards.
A serving soldier, he was mobilised on the declaration of war and almost immediately proceeded to France. There he fought in the Retreat from Mons and in the Battles of the Marne, the Aisne and Festubert, and was wounded. Invalided home in consequence of his wounds, he received medical treatment, and was subsequently discharged on account of service in February 1917. He holds the Mons Star, and the General Service and Victory Medals.
79, Cardiff Road, Watford.   4713/A.

SMITH, A. C., Cadet, Royal Air Force.
He joined in August 1918, and was undergoing a course of training prior to obtaining commissioned rank when the Armistice was signed. He did most useful work in connection with aero-engine fitting at various stations, and was eventually discharged in November 1919.
45, Ivy Road, Luton.   4697.

SMITH, A. C., Private, 1st Bedfordshire Regt.
Mobilised from the Army Reserve at the outbreak of war, he proceeded to France in October 1914, and was in action at the Battles of Ypres. Severely wounded, he was sent to England and on recovery returned to the Western Front, and was again wounded and invalided home. Rejoining his unit in the Field he was killed in action on the Somme in May 1917, and was entitled to the 1914 Star, and the General Service and Victory Medals.
25, Buxton Road, Luton.   4696/A.

SMITH, A. E., Driver, Royal Engineers.
He volunteered in 1914, and was engaged on important duties with his unit until despatched to the Western Front in 1918. During the operations of the closing stages of the war he rendered valuable services on the Somme, at Amiens, Cambrai and other places, and returned to England on the conclusion of hostilities. He was demobilised in 1919, and holds the General Service and Victory Medals.
7, Chobham Street, Luton.   4780/B.

SMITH, A. E. (Senior), Gunner, R.F.A.
Volunteering in August 1914, he was drafted to the Dardanelles in the following year. He fought in the landing at Gallipoli and in other operations until the Evacuation of the Peninsula when he was sent to Egypt. There he took part in the British Advance through Palestine, and served with his Battery in many important engagements. He was discharged on account of service in March 1918, and holds the 1914-15 Star, and the General Service and Victory Medals.
64, Grover Road, Oxhey.   X4757/A.

SMITH, A. G., Private, Bedfordshire Regiment.
He volunteered in September 1914, and was drafted to Gallipoli in July of the following year. He was engaged in fierce fighting in the landing at Suvla Bay and in other engagements on the Peninsula until invalided home with fever. On recovery he was sent to France in November 1916, and served with his unit in many important battles until the close of the war. He was demobilised in February 1919, and holds the 1914-15 Star, and the General Service and Victory Medals.
Stopsley Green, Stopsley.   4705/C.

SMITH, A. E. (Junior), Gunner, Royal Navy.
He joined in 1917, and was posted to H.M.S. "Renown," which vessel was engaged on patrol and convoy duties in the North and Baltic Seas and other waters until after hostilities ceased. He also served aboard this ship during H.R.H. the Prince of Wales' visits to Canada and the United States, and later to Australia and New Zealand. In 1920 he was still serving, and holds the General Service and Victory Medals.
64, Grover Road, Oxhey, Herts.   X4757/B.

SMITH, A. E., L/Corporal, Middlesex Regiment.
Volunteering in January 1916, he embarked for Salonika in the following August and saw much service in the Balkans. Amongst other operations he took part in the Advance across the Vardar and in the Battle of Monastir, and after the Armistice was sent to Turkey. He returned to England for demobilisation in March 1919, and holds the General Service and Victory Medals.
11, Norman Road, Luton.   4685/A.

SMITH, A. E., Private, 1/5th Bedfordshire Regt.
He volunteered in September 1915, and in the following year proceeded to Egypt, where he served for a time. He was drafted to France in April 1917, and whilst on the Western Front took part in heavy fighting in engagements in the Somme and Ypres sectors, and was mentioned in Despatches for devotion to duty in the Field, and was twice wounded. He holds the General Service and Victory Medals, and was demobilised in February 1919.
90, Cromwell Road, Luton.   4690.

SMITH, A. G., Sergeant, 1st Lincolnshire Regt.
He volunteered in November 1914, and in the following June was sent to France where he saw much service with his Regiment for three years. During this period he was in almost continuous action in various parts of the line, and fought in the Battles of Arras, Ypres and other operations, and was twice wounded. He was killed in action on April 16th, 1918, during the Retreat from Cambrai, and was entitled to the 1914-15 Star, and the General Service and Victory Medals.
14, Wells Yard, Watford.   X1791/B.

SMITH, A. H., Corporal, 9th Loyal North Lancashire Regt., and 20th Manchester Regt.
He joined in 1916, and in the same year was drafted overseas. Serving with his unit on the Western Front he fought in several important engagements, and was killed in action on the Somme on September 3rd, 1916. He was entitled to the General Service and Victory Medals.
65, Crow Lane, Husbourne Crawley, Aspley Guise.
                                                  Z4774/A.

SMITH, A. J., Private, Oxfordshire and Buckinghamshire Light Infantry.
He volunteered in June 1915, and in the following January embarked for France, and was in action in the Battles of the Somme, Vimy Ridge, Arras, Passchendaele and other important engagements. He was killed in action on the Somme on August 16th, 1917, and was entitled to the General Service and Victory Medals.
6, Plantation Road, Leighton Buzzard.   4754/A.

SMITH, A. J., Gunner, Royal Field Artillery.
Volunteering in November 1914, he embarked for France in the following February. Whilst on the Western Front he fought in several important engagements, including those at Ypres, Arras, Armentières, Bullecourt, Cambrai and on the Somme. Returning to England on the cessation of hostilities, he was demobilised in May 1919, and holds the 1914-15 Star, and the General Service and Victory Medals.
15, Ashton Road, Luton.   4689.

SMITH, A. M., Private, 11th Cheshire Regiment.
He volunteered in September 1914, and four months later proceeded overseas. Whilst in France he took part in the Battles of Hill 60, Festubert, the Somme, Ypres, Arras, and other engagements. He was killed in action on March 23rd, 1918, during the German Offensive, and was entitled to the 1914-15 Star, and the General Service and Victory Medals.
6, Rosebury Terrace, Upper Culver Road, St. Albans.
                                                  X4765/A.

SMITH, A. W., Private, Bedfordshire Regiment.
He joined in 1917, and shortly afterwards proceeded to the Western Front where he served for nearly three years. During this period he saw service in various parts of the line and fought in the Battles of the Somme, Cambrai, and in other important operations until the close of the war. He was demobilised in February 1920, and holds the General Service and Victory Medals.
7, Puller Road, Boxmoor.   X4778.

SMITH, A. W., Private, 1/15th Essex Regiment.
Volunteering in December 1915, on completing his training he was engaged on various duties in connection with coastal defence at various places on the East Coast. He rendered valuable services but was unable to obtain a transfer overseas and was discharged on account of service in March 1918.
44, Naseby Road, Luton. 4760.

SMITH, A. W., Private, 8th Bedfordshire Regt.
He volunteered in November 1915, and in March of the following year was despatched overseas. Serving with his unit on the Western Front he was in action on the Somme, and at Arras and Ypres, and was taken prisoner on March 22nd, 1918, in the Retreat from Cambrai. Repatriated from Germany after the Armistice, he was demobilised in February 1919, and holds the General Service and Victory Medals.
6, Cardiff Road, Watford. X4714.

SMITH, A. W., Corporal, Royal Berkshire Regt.
He volunteered in 1915, and in the following year was drafted overseas. He saw much service on the Western Front, where he fought in the Battle of Arras, and several other important engagements, and was wounded. Later sent to Mesopotamia, he served in that theatre of war and then proceeded to Russia with the Relief Force. On the conclusion of hostilities he was sent to India, where he was still serving in 1920. He holds the General Service and Victory Medals.
10, Leavesden Road, Watford. X3861/B.

SMITH, B. A. (M.M.), Sapper, Royal Engineers.
Volunteering in November 1915, he was sent to France in the following year. Whilst on the Western Front he was engaged on important duties in connection with the maintenance of communication in the forward areas during operations, and was awarded the Military Medal for conspicuous gallantry and devotion to duty in the Field. He was afterwards sent to Italy and did valuable work in that theatre of war until the termination of hostilities. He was demobilised in April 1919, and holds the General Service and Victory Medals.
40, Hockliffe Street, Leighton Buzzard. 4730/A.

SMITH, B. J., Trooper, Bedfordshire Lancers.
He volunteered in 1915, and in the following year was despatched to the Western Front. In this theatre of war he was in action at Albert, Vimy Ridge, and was wounded on the Somme. Returning to his unit he took part in various operations until the conclusion of hostilities. He was demobilised in 1919, and holds the General Service and Victory Medals.
Home Farm, Westoning, Ampthill. 4783/C.

SMITH, C., Private, 5th Middlesex Regiment.
He joined in June 1916, and proceeded to Salonika in the following May. During his service in the Balkans he was in action on the Vardar front, at Monastir and in the Allied advance in September 1918. After the cessation of hostilities he returned to England and was demobilised in March 1919, and holds the General Service and Victory Medals.
41, Burr Street, Luton. 4710.

SMITH, C., Private, 1st Bedfordshire Regiment.
A serving soldier, he was mobilised and sent to France at the outbreak of hostilities, and was in action in the Retreat from Mons and in the Battles of Ypres and Lens, and was wounded in the Ypres salient in 1915. He returned to England and after discharge from hospital was stationed at various depôts as he was unfit for further service overseas. He was invalided out of the Service in 1916, and holds the Mons Star, and the General Service and Victory Medals.
Luton Road, Toddington. 4753.

SMITH, C., Private, R.A.S.C. (M.T.)
Joining in October 1916, he proceeded to the Western Front in the following September and was engaged on important duties connected with the transport of supplies in the forward areas. He was under fire in the Battles of the Somme, Cambrai and Arras, and at many other engagements during the Retreat and Advance of 1918, and after the Armistice was sent into Germany with the Army of Occupation and stationed at Cologne. He was demobilised in July 1919, and holds the General Service and Victory Medals.
11, Boyle Street, Luton. 4703.

SMITH, C. A., Gunner, Royal Garrison Artillery.
He joined in June 1916, and embarked for France in the following January and saw much service in various sectors, fighting at the Battles of Arras, Passchendaele and Cambrai, and was gassed twice. He was also in action throughout the Retreat and Advance of 1918, and returning to England, was demobilised in January 1920. He holds the General Service and Victory Medals.
109, High Street, Markyate, Herts. 4775.

SMITH, C. F., Private, 1st Bedfordshire Regt.
He joined in May 1916, and was drafted to France in the following August. In this theatre of war he was engaged with his Battalion in various sectors and fought in many battles, including those of the Somme, Arras and Cambrai. He was unforunately killed in action on September 25th, 1916, and was entitled to the General Service and Victory Medals.
78, Station Road, Ridgmont, Beds. Z4777.

SMITH, C. G., Private, 2nd Suffolk Regiment.
Joining in April 1918, he completed his training and was stationed at various depôts with his regiment engaged on guard and other important duties. He was unsuccessful in obtaining his transfer overseas prior to the cessation of hostilities, but rendered valuable services until demobilised in February 1919.
15, Cowper Street, Luton. 4779/A.

SMITH, C. H., Trooper, Dragoon Guards.
He volunteered in February 1916, and embarked for the Western Front in the following December, and took part in many engagements, including those on the Somme, at Arras, Cambrai and Passchendaele. He also was in action throughout the German Offensive and Allied Advance. He was demobilised in February 1919, and holds the General Service and Victory Medals.
83, Cardiff Road, Watford. 4713/C.

SMITH, C. J., Sergeant, 5th Suffolk Regiment.
A serving soldier, he was mobilised on the declaration of war and was drafted to the Dardanelles in July 1915, taking part in the landing at Suvla Bay and the subsequent engagements until the Evacuation of the Peninsula. Drafted to Palestine in December 1915, he served in the Advance through Sinai, Palestine and Syria, and fought in the Battles of Gaza and was present at the capture of Jerusalem. He returned to England and was demobilised in August 1919, and holds the 1914-15 Star, and the General Service and Victory Medals.
27, Copsewood Road, Watford. X4493/A.

SMITH, C. J. S., Private, East Yorkshire Regt.
He volunteered in February 1916, and proceeded overseas later in the same year, and saw active service in many parts of the Western Front. He was engaged in many important battles and was unfortunately killed in action on March 31st, 1918, during the opening operations of the German Offensive. He was entitled to the General Service and Victory Medals.
Alemeda, Ampthill. 4725.

SMITH, C. S. B., Private, 1st Seaforth Highlanders.
Volunteering in May 1915, he was drafted to France three months later and was engaged in the fighting in many sectors until December of the same year. Transferred to Mesopotamia he took part in the British advance in that theatre of war and fought at Kut and was present at the capture of Baghdad, and was twice wounded. Returning to England he was demobilised in January 1919, and holds the 1914-15 Star, and the General Service and Victory Medals.
18, Hockliffe Street, Leighton Buzzard. 4730/B.

SMITH, C. W., Private, 42nd Canadian Infantry Regiment.
He volunteered in 1915 in Canada, and shortly afterwards proceeded to England with his Regiment and after receiving training was sent to the Western Front, where he took part in many important engagements, including those at Arras, Cambrai and the Somme. He was killed in action on June 2nd, 1916, and was entitled to the 1914-15 Star, and the General Service and Victory Medals.
25, Bedford Street, Woburn, Beds. Z4740.

SMITH, C. W., Private, 1/6th Essex Regiment.
Volunteering in February 1916, he embarked for Egypt in the following July. He fought in many engagements, including that at Gaza, and in the advance through Palestine and Syria, and was twice wounded. He died at Beyrout from illness contracted on service on November 22nd, 1919. He was entitled to the General Service and Victory Medals.
Sunny Dale, Clophill, Beds. 4709.

SMITH, D. T., 2nd Lieutenant, 2nd London Scottish, and 14th Durham Light Infantry.
He volunteered in November 1915, and was sent to France in the following June. He fought at the Battles of the Somme, Arras, and Ypres, and many other important engagements, and was unfortunately killed in action near Cambrai on December 3rd, 1917. He was entitled to the General Service and Victory Medals.
43, Springfield, Linslade, Leighton Buzzard. 4784.

SMITH, D. E. (Miss), Special War Worker.
This lady volunteered her services for work of National importance during the war and for three years rendered valuable services employed as an inspector in the fuse department at Kent's Munition Factory, Luton, supervising the construction of fuses for every variety of shell.
18, Grove Road, Luton. 4766.

SMITH, E., Gunner, Royal Field Artillery.
Volunteering in March 1915, he embarked for the Western Front in July of the following year and saw much service. He fought at the Battles of the Somme, Arras, Cambrai, Ypres and in the Retreat and Advance of 1918. He returned to England and was demobilised in May 1919, and holds the General Service and Victory Medals.
Wilshampstead, Beds. Z4776.

SMITH, E., Private, 2nd Royal Sussex Regiment.
A serving soldier, mobilised upon the outbreak of hostilities, he proceeded to France immediately and was in action in the Mons Retreat and the subsequent Battle of the Marne, where he was wounded on September 10th, 1914. On recovery he rejoined his unit and fought at Ypres, the Somme, Bapaume and Loos, and was wounded three times more. He returned to England in 1917, and served at home until demobilised in February 1919, as he was unfit for further service overseas. He holds the Mons Star, and the General Service and Victory Medals.
58, Shaftesbury Road, Watford. X4723/A.

SMITH, E., Private, Royal Marines.
He joined in June 1917, and was posted to H.M.S. "Penelope, which ship was engaged on important patrol duties in the English Channel, the North Sea, and other waters, frequently passing through mine-infested areas in the discharge of her duties. He was still serving in 1920, and holds the General Service and Victory Medals.
68, Grover Road, Oxhey. X4722/C.

SMITH, E., Gunner, Royal Garrison Artillery.
He joined in 1916, and on conclusion of his training served at various depôts on guard and other important duties. He also served with the anti-aircraft gun Batteries engaged in the defence of London. He was unable to obtain his transfer overseas owing to ill-health, but rendered valuable services until demobilised in February 1919.
12, Taskers Row, Eddlesborough. Z4781/B.

SMITH, E., Private, Royal Marine Light Infantry.
He enlisted prior to the war and was posted to H.M.S. "Cyclops," which ship was engaged on patrol duties in the North Sea. Later he was attached to the Secret Service and saw much service in France, Italy and Russia. He was still serving in 1920, and holds the 1914-15 Star, and the General Service and Victory Medals.
13a, Wells Yard, Watford. X4751/C.

SMITH, E., Private, 2nd Bedfordshire Regiment.
Volunteering in September 1914, he completed a course of training and was stationed at various depôts on guard and other important duties. Proceeding to France in 1918, he took part in many engagements in the Retreat and Advance of 1918, including those at Albert and Cambrai, and was wounded. He was demobilised in April 1919, and holds the General Service and Victory Medals.
25, Buxton Road, Luton. 4696/B.

SMITH, E. J., Driver, R.A.S.C.
Volunteering in December 1914, he was sent to France in February 1916, and saw active service in many sectors fighting at the Battles of the Somme and Arras. He was killed in action at Ypres on August 18th, 1917, and was entitled to the General Service and Victory Medals.
12, Taskers Road, Eddlesborough, Beds. Z4781/C.

SMITH, E. J., Corporal, Royal Engineers.
He volunteered in October 1914, and embarked for France in the following year, and was engaged on important duties in the advanced areas and was present at many battles, including those of Arras, the Somme, Cambrai and in the Retreat and Advance of 1918, and was gassed. He was demobilised in February 1919, and holds the 1914-15 Star, and the General Service and Victory Medals.
6, Lea Mead, Hatfield. 4719/A.

SMITH, F., Gunner (Fitter), R.G.A.
He volunteered in October 1914, and proceeded to France two months later and saw considerable service in many parts of the Western Front, fighting at the Battles of Ribecourt, Arras and Armentières, and was wounded. In 1917 he was sent to Gibraltar and was engaged there on garrison duties until he returned to England for demobilisation in April 1919. He holds the 1914-15 Star, and the General Service and Victory Medals.
Luton Road, Toddington. 4727.

SMITH, E. C. (Mrs.), Member, W.R.A.F.
Joining in July 1917, she served at various aerodromes with her unit and was engaged on important duties in the sail-maker's shop. She rendered valuable service, and was demobilised in July 1918.
17, Victoria Place, Biggleswade. 4731/B.

SMITH, F., Private, Middlesex Regiment.
He joined in 1916, and proceeded to France later in the same year. He was engaged in many important battles and served in various sectors of the Western Front. He was killed in an air raid in June 1918, and was entitled to the General Service and Victory Medals.
12, Landridge Road, St. Albans. X4746/C.

SMITH, F., Driver, Royal Field Artillery.
Volunteering in October 1915, he was later drafted to Salonika and served there with an anti-aircraft gun Battery at the base. He afterwards saw service on the Black Sea coast. He rendered valuable services, and returning to England, was demobilised in September 1919, and holds the General Service and Victory Medals.
13, Albert Street, St. Albans. X4770.

SMITH, F., Private, Bedfordshire Regiment.
Joining in October 1917, he completed his training and served at various stations with his unit on guard and other important duties. He was unsuccessful in obtaining a transfer to a theatre of war, but rendered excellent services until demobilised in March 1919.
9, Dudley Street, Luton. 4700.

SMITH, F. B., Rifleman, King's Royal Rifle Corps.
He joined in March 1918, and on completion of his training served at various depôts with his unit. On the cessation of hostilities he was sent into Germany with the Army of Occupation and stationed at various places on the Rhine. He was demobilised in October 1919.
49, Kimberley Road, St. Albans. X4764.

SMITH, F. C., Gunner, Royal Field Artillery.
He volunteered in June 1915, and embarked for the Western Front three months later. He was in action in the Battles of Ypres, Arras and the Somme, and many other engagements, and was wounded. On recovery he returned to the trenches and was unfortunately killed in action at Armentières on August 10th, 1917, and was entitled to the 1914-15 Star, and the General Service and Victory Medals.
15, Cowper Street, Luton. 4779/B.

SMITH, F. D., Private, 1/5th Bedfordshire Regt.
Volunteering in September 1914, he was drafted to the Dardanelles in the following July, and took part in the landing at Suvla Bay, and in the subsequent fighting until the Evacuation of the Peninsula. Sent to Egypt, he served in the Canal Zone until February 1917, when he proceeded to the Palestine front and fought in the Battles of Gaza, and was wounded and taken prisoner whilst on patrol on July 24th of the same year. Repatriated, he was demobilised in 1919, and holds the 1914-15 Star, and the General Service and Victory Medals.
7, Chobham Street, Luton. 4780/A.

SMITH, F. G., Driver, Royal Field Artillery.
Joining in November 1916, he was drafted to the Western Front in the following April and fought in the Battles of Arras, Ypres, Bullecourt, and throughout the German Offensive and subsequent Allied Advance of 1918. After the close of the war he was sent into Germany with the Army of Occupation and was stationed at Cologne. He returned to England for demobilisation in February 1920, and holds the General Service and Victory Medals.
52, Old Road, Linslade, Bucks. 4787/B.

SMITH, F. J., Corporal, 8th Suffolk Regiment.
He joined in 1917, and on completion of his training served at various stations with his unit on guard and other important duties. He was medically unfit for active service, and consequently was unable to procure his transfer overseas. He rendered valuable services and was demobilised in October 1919.
40, Victoria Road, North Watford. X4746.

SMITH, F. T. (M.M.), Private, R.A.M.C., 5th Bedfordshire Regiment.
Volunteering in August 1914, he embarked for the Dardanelles in the following July and was in action in the landing at Suvla Bay and in the subsequent fighting until the Evacuation of the Peninsula. Proceeding to the Palestine front he engaged in the Battles of Gaza and Mejdel, and was wounded. He was awarded the Military Medal for devotion to duty and gallantry in the Field. He returned to England and was demobilised in July 1919, and holds the 1914-5 Star, and the General Service and Victory Medals.
110, Ridgway Road, Luton. 4698/B.

SMITH, F. J., Private, Oxfordshire and Buckinghamshire Light Infantry .

He volunteered in August 1915, and proceeded to the Western Front later in the same year and fought in many important engagements, including the Battles of Arras, Cambrai, Ypres and Loos. He was killed in action on October 15th, 1916, and was entitled to the' 1914-15 Star, and the General Service and Victory Medals.
Sandy Lane, Woburn Sands. Z4737/B.

SMITH, F. W., Sapper, Royal Engineers.

He joined in June 1918, and after his training was stationed at various depôts on important duties with his unit. Owing to ill-health he was not successful in obtaining his transfer to a theatre of war, and was invalided out of the Service in December 1918.
Common Cottages, Aspley Guise, Beds. Z4736.

SMITH, F. W., Private, 1/5th Bedfordshire Regt.

Volunteering in September 1914, he embarked for the Dardanelles in the following year and saw much service there until the Evacuation of the Peninsula. Drafted to Egypt in 1916, he served in the advance through Sinai into Palestine, fighting at the Battles of Gaza, and in other important engagements. Owing to ill-health he was invalided to England and discharged unfit for further service in April 1918. He holds the 1914-15 Star, and the General Service and Victory Medals.
28, Midland Road, Luton. 4694.

SMITH, F. W. J., Private, R.A.M.C.

Volunteering in January 1915, he embarked for the Western Front in the following September and served in many sectors. In December of the same year he was transferred to the Macedonian theatre of war and was engaged on important duties in attending to sick and wounded troops. Returning to England he was demobilised in February 1919, and holds the 1914-15 Star, and the General Service and Victory Medals.
11, Norman Road, Luton. 4685/B.

SMITH, G., Sapper, Royal Engineers.

He volunteered in February 1915, and after his training served with his unit on important duties at many stations. He did good work, but was unable to obtain his transfer overseas on account of medical unfitness, and in consequence was discharged from the Service in September 1918.
6a, Brache Street, Luton. 4759/A.

SMITH, G., Private, 4th Middlesex Regiment.

He volunteered in January 1915, and was later drafted overseas. He served on the Western Front, and was in action in many sectors, including those of Ypres, Messines and Wytschaete. He was wounded in action on July 16th, 1917, and was killed shortly afterwards on July 31st. He was entitled to the General Service and Victory Medals.
Puzzle Gardens, Station Road, Toddington. 4728.

SMITH, G., Corporal, Royal Engineers (I.W.T.)

He volunteered in August 1915, and in the following year was drafted to France. In this theatre of war he was engaged on duties of great importance in connection with irrigation in the Arras and other sectors, and was constantly under shell fire. He was demobilised in January 1919, and holds the General Service and Victory Medals.
8, Winsin Cottages, High Street, Rickmansworth.
X3388/B.

SMITH, G., Special War Worker.

Volunteering his services for work of National importance, he worked at Messrs. Kent's Munition Factory from October 1915 until December 1918, engaged on manufacturing gauges for fuses, work which demanded a high degree of technical knowledge, and rendered very valuable services.
19, Saxon Road, Luton. 4767/A.

SMITH, G. E. (Mrs.), Special War Worker.

During the war this lady was engaged on important work at the Diamond Foundry for a period of four years. Her duties, which were in connection with the making of 13 and 18 pounder shells, were carried out in a highly satisfactory manner.
58, John Street, Luton. 4763/B.

SMITH, G. I., Petty Officer, R.A.F. (late R.N.A.S.)

He volunteered in 1915, and at the conclusion of his training served with his unit at many stations until drafted to France in 1918. He was engaged at Dunkirk on important duties which called for a high degree of technical skill, and was mentioned in Despatches for consistently good work with his Squadron. He holds the General Service and Victory Medals, and was demobilised in 1919
Home Farm, Westoning, Ampthill. 4783/B.

SMITH, G. F., R.S.M., Royal Field Artillery.

He was mobilised at the outbreak of war, and served on important duties with his Battery at many stations. He did excellent work but was unable to secure his transfer to a theatre of war, being unfit for service overseas, and was demobilised in February 1919.
83, Benskin Road, Watford. X4717.

SMITH, G. T., Private, Labour Corps.

He joined in July 1916, and on completion of his training served at various stations on important duties with his unit. He rendered valuable services, and was later employed on agricultural work until his demobilisation in March 1919.
Oliver Street, Ampthill. 4782.

SMITH, G. W., Steward, Merchant Service.

He was serving in the Merchant Service at the outbreak of hostilities, and during the war was employed on important duties in S.S. "Dee" and other vessels, which were engaged in transporting troops from England to France, the Dardanelles, Egypt and India. He was demobilised in 1919, and holds the General Service and Mercantile Marine War Medals.
The Gables, Wheathampstead. 4726.

SMITH, G. W., Private, 8th Suffolk Regiment.

He joined in July 1916, and in the following December was sent to France. Whilst in this theatre of war he fought at Ypres, Vimy Ridge, Bullecourt, and was wounded. On recovery he returned to the firing line, and was engaged in the fighting at Passchendaele, the Somme and Cambrai. After the signing of the Armistice he proceeded to Germany with the Army of Occupation and was stationed at Cologne. He holds the General Service and Victory Medals, and was still serving in 1920.
29, Hartley Road, Luton. 4716.

SMITH, G. W., Driver, R.A.S.C. (M.T.)

He joined in March 1916, and in the following month proceeded overseas. He served on the Western Front, and was engaged with his unit on important duties in the Arras, Somme, Ypres, Lens and Cambrai sectors, and was constantly under shell fire. He was demobilised in August 1919, and holds the General Service and Victory Medals.
The Green, Ickwell. Z4734.

SMITH, G. W., Private, 4th Middlesex Regiment.

He joined in June 1916, and six months later was drafted to the Western Front. Whilst in this theatre of war he fought at Ypres, Amiens, Messines, the Somme and Cambrai, and was twice wounded. He was killed in action near Cambrai on October 12th, 1918, and was entitled to the General Service and Victory Medals.
201, North Street, Luton. 4702.

SMITH, G. W., Special War Worker.

During the war this man offered his services for work of National importance, and from June 1917 worked at Messrs. Kent's Munition Works, Luton, engaged on the manufacture of fuse-gauges, and rendered excellent services until December 1918.
19, Saxon Road, Luton. 4767/B.

SMITH, H., Driver, Royal Field Artillery.

He joined in April 1916, and in the same year was sent to France. During his service on the Western Front he was in action in many sectors, including those of Arras, Ypres, the Somme and St. Quentin, and was wounded. He returned to England after the signing of the Armistice, and was demobilised in February 1919. He holds the General Service and Victory Medals.
123, St. James' Road, Watford. X4692.

SMITH, H., Steward, Royal Navy.

He volunteered at the outbreak of war, and was posted to H.M.S. "Undaunted." His ship was engaged on important patrol duties in the North and Baltic Seas until the cessation of hostilities. He was still serving in 1920, and holds the 1914-15 Star, and the General Service and Victory Medals.
3, Harcourt Street, Luton. 1420/B.

SMITH, H., Private, Bedfordshire Regiment, and R.A.S.C.

He volunteered in September 1914, and was drafted to France in the following year. Whilst on the Western Front he fought at Hill 60, and was wounded. He was invalided home, and after a period of hospital treatment was transferred to the R.A.S.C., with which unit he was employed on important transport work until demobilised in February 1919. He holds the 1914-15 Star, and the General Service and Victory Medals.
42, Bancroft Road, Hitchin. 1810/B.

SMITH, H., Private, Queen's Own (Royal West Kent Regiment).

He joined in April 1916, and in the following September was sent to France. He fought on the Somme, at Ypres, Béthune, Cambrai, and in the German Offensive and subsequent Allied Advance of 1918. He holds the General Service and Victory Medals, and was demobilised in June 1919.

75, Church Street, Dunstable.   4769.

SMITH, H., Driver, Royal Field Artillery.

He volunteered in 1915, and in the same year was drafted overseas. He served in Egypt and during the British Advance through Palestine was in action at Gaza, Haifa, Damascus and Jerusalem. He was demobilised in June 1919, and holds the 1914-15 Star, and the General Service and Victory Medals.

66, Souldera Road, Watford.   X1192/A.

SMITH, H., Sergeant, 3rd Bedfordshire Regiment.

He volunteered in August 1914, and in the following year was drafted to France. Whilst in this theatre of war he fought in the engagements at Festubert, Loos, the Somme and Beaumont-Hamel, and was twice wounded. He was demobilised in 1919, and holds the 1914-15 Star, and the General Service and Victory Medals.

Crow Lane, Husbourne Crawley, Aspley Guise. Z4774/B.

SMITH, H., Private, 1st Bedfordshire Regiment.

He joined in 1916, and shortly afterwards proceeded to France. During his service on the Western Front he fought on the Somme and was wounded. On recovery he returned to the firing line, and was engaged in the fighting at Arras, Albert, Loos, and in the Retreat and Advance of 1918. He was demobilised in March 1919, and holds the General Service and Victory Medals.

16, Ratcliffe Road, Hitchin.   4788.

SMITH, H., L/Corporal, 26th Royal Fusiliers.

Volunteering in August 1914, he was drafted to the Dardanelles in the following March and was in action at the first landing at Gallipoli and the subsequent fighting until the Evacuation of the Peninsula. Proceeding to France in 1916, he fought at the Somme and Ypres, and was killed in action at Passchendaele on August 2nd, 1917. He was entitled to the 1914-15 Star, and the General Service and Victory Medals.

34, Lamb Lane, Redbourn, Herts.   4724.

SMITH, H. G., Sergeant, Machine Gun Corps.

He joined in October 1917, and in January of the following year proceeded to France. Whilst on the Western Front he fought on the Somme and at Cambrai, and was wounded during the German Offensive. He returned to his unit after recovery, and took part in the final operations of the war, and after the Armistice went with the Army of Occupation to Germany and was stationed at Cologne. He was demobilised in 1919, and holds the General Service and Victory Medals.

8, Saulbury Road, Linslade, Bucks.   4786.

SMITH, H. J., A.B., Royal Navy.

He joined in November 1917, and after his training was posted to a minesweeper, which vessel was engaged in the North Sea and other waters on minesweeping duties until after the signing of the Armistice. He was demobilised in May 1919, and holds the General Service and Victory Medals.

20, Collingdon Street, Luton.   4686/B.

SMITH, H. K., L/Corporal, Tank Corps.

He volunteered in April 1915, and in November 1917 was sent to France. During his service on the Western Front he was engaged in much heavy fighting, and was severely wounded near Cambrai in March 1918. He was sent to England, and after a period in hospital was invalided out of the service in February 1919. He holds the General Service and Victory Medals.

20, Collingdon Street, Luton.   4686/A.

SMITH, H. M., Rflmn., King's Royal Rifle Corps.

He joined in July 1918, on attaining military age, and at the conclusion of his training was employed at various stations on important duties with his Battalion. He was unable to secure his transfer overseas until after the signing of the Armistice. He was then drafted to Germany in December 1918, and served with the Army of Occupation and was stationed at Cologne. He was demobilised in January 1920.

31, South Street, Leighton Buzzard.   4755.

SMITH, H. V., Gunner, Royal Garrison Artillery.

He joined in 1916, and in the following year was drafted to France. Whilst in this theatre of war he was engaged in the fighting at Messines, Arras, and in the Retreat and Advance of 1918. He was demobilised in February 1919, and holds the General Service and Victory Medals.

15, Chapel Fields, Biggleswade.   Z4733.

SMITH, H. S., Private, Machine Gun Corps, and Bedfordshire Regiment.

He volunteered in May 1915, and in the following November was sent to France. In this theatre of war he was engaged in the fighting on the Somme, and was wounded. He was taken to hospital, where he died from the effects of his wounds on March 22nd, 1917. He was entitled to the 1914-15 Star, and the General Service and Victory Medals.

6, Plantation Road, Leighton Buzzard.   4754/B.

SMITH, H. S., 2nd Lieutenant, 1st Hertfordshire Regiment, and 4th Bedfordshire Regiment.

He was mobilised in August 1914, and was later sent to France. He served on the Western Front and fought in the Battles of Ypres and Cambrai, and after the cessation of hostilities proceeded to Germany with the Army of Occupation, and was stationed at Cologne. He was demobilised in November 1919, and holds the General Service and Victory Medals.

32, Cannon Street, St. Albans.   4715.

SMITH, H. W., Private, 1st Gloucestershire Regt.

A serving soldier, he was mobilised and immediately drafted to France at the outbreak of war. He took part in the fierce fighting in the Retreat from Mons, the Battles of the Marne, the Aisne, Ypres, St. Julien, Armentières, and was then sent to Macedonia in December 1915, where he remained until March 1918. He then returned to the Western Front and was in action during the final operations of the war. He was demobilised in January 1920, and holds the Mons Star, and the General Service and Victory Medals.

58, John Street, Luton.   4762.

SMITH, J., Private, Sherwood Foresters.

He volunteered in January 1915, and was later drafted to the Western Front where he saw much service. Whilst in France he was in action in several important engagements, including the Battles of Arras, Cambrai and the Somme, and was twice wounded. He was invalided home on account of his wounds and was subsequently discharged as medically unfit for further service in December 1917. He holds the General Service and Victory Medals.

4, Dragon Yard, London Colney.   4712/A.

SMITH, J., Private, 1/4th Essex Regiment, and Bedfordshire Regiment.

Volunteering in May 1915, he served with his unit until drafted to Egypt in July of the following year. He took part in several engagements during General Allenby's advance through Palestine and was reported missing on March 26th, 1917, after the Battle of Gaza. He was later presumed to have been killed in action on that date, and was entitled to the General Service and Victory Medals.

17, Victoria Place, Biggleswade.   4731/A.

SMITH, J., Private, R.A.S.C.

He volunteered in June 1915, and three months later proceeded to Salonika. He did valuable work in connection with the transport of ammunition and supplies during the advances across the Vardar and the Struma and in other operations in the Balkan campaign. On the conclusion of hostilities he returned to England for demobilisation in August 1919, and holds the 1914-15 Star, and the General Service and Victory Medals.

18, Plantation Road, Leighton Buzzard.   4758.

SMITH, J., Private, Labour Corps, and Pioneer R.E.

He volunteered in August 1914, and after serving for a time at the depôt of his unit was sent to the Western Front. During his service in this theatre of war he was engaged on important duties in connection with operations in various sectors and was present at the Battle of Cambrai and other notable engagements. He was demobilised in January 1919, and holds the General Service and Victory Medals.

Bowman Green Cottages, London Colney. X268/A, X269/B.

SMITH, J., Private, 2nd Middlesex Regiment.

Volunteering in June 1915, he proceeded to Salonika in the following year. After serving for a time in the Balkans, he was drafted to the Western Front and fought at Arras, Cambrai, and other places, and was wounded. He was reported missing on April 24th, 1918, during the Retreat from Cambrai, and was later presumed to have been killed in action on that date. He was entitled to the General Service and Victory Medals.

13a, Wells Yard, Watford.   X4751/B.

SMITH, J., Rflmn., 5th King's Royal Rifle Corps.
He joined in September 1918, and on the conclusion of his training was engaged on guard and other duties with his unit at various home stations. He did good work, but was unable to secure a transfer overseas before the termination of hostilities, and was demobilised in May 1919.
43, Lattimore Road, St. Albans. X4743.

SMITH, J., L/Corporal, 11th Bedfordshire Regt.
He joined in June 1916, and after completing his training was engaged on important duties in connection with coastal defence measures at Lowestoft and other stations on the East Coast. He did excellent work but was ineligible for service overseas on account of his age. He was demobilised in February 1919.
Malting Cottage, Mount Pleasant, Aspley Guise. Z4771.

SMITH, J., Sapper, Royal Engineers.
Joining in June 1916, he completed his training and served with his unit at various stations on the coast. He rendered valuable services in the construction of railways and other duties in connection with coastal defence, but was unable to obtain a transfer to a theatre of war before the cessation of hostilities, and was demobilised in January 1919.
12, Landridge Road, St. Albans. X4746/A.

SMITH, J., Sergeant, 1st Bedfordshire Regt.
Volunteering in January 1916, he was engaged as physical training Instructor at various depôts with his regiment and did valuable work in that capacity. He was also employed in conducting drafts to the Western Front until the cessation of hostilities. Demobilised in November 1919, he holds the General Service and Victory Medals.
21, Beaconsfield Terrace, Hatfield. X4735.

SMITH, J., Private, Bedfordshire Regiment.
He enlisted in August 1914, and in the following March embarked for France, where he was engaged in heavy fighting at Ypres. He was shortly afterwards killed in action at Loos on September 8th, 1915, and was entitled to the 1914-15 Star, and the General Service and Victory Medals.
70, St. Andrews Street, Leighton Buzzard. 4739/A.

SMITH, J., Private, R.A.S.C., and Labour Corps.
He volunteered in August 1914, and on completing his training was engaged with his unit on important transport duties in various parts of England. He was later transferred to the Labour Corps and did useful work in connection with the production of agricultural products and food supplies, but was unable to secure his transfer overseas before the close of the war, and was demobilised in 1919.
54, Brightwell Road, Watford. X4708.

SMITH, J. D., Private, Royal Sussex Regiment.
He volunteered in April 1915, and in the same year was despatched to France. Whilst on the Western Front he fought in the Battles of Ypres, Cambrai, Amiens, and in many other operations until the close of the war. In the course of his service he was twice wounded and lost a finger of his right hand in consequence. He was demobilised in September 1919, and holds the 1914-15 Star, and the General Service and Victory Medals.
73, Waterside, King's Langley. X4704.

SMITH, J. H., Private, 2nd Oxfordshire and Buckinghamshire Light Infantry, and R.A.S.C.
Mobilised from the Army Reserve on the outbreak of war he proceeded to France and fought in the Retreat from Mons and the Battle of La Bassée, where he was wounded. He was invalided to England and in January 1915, returned to the Western Front and served during the Battles of the Somme, Arras, Ypres, and in the Retreat and Advance of 1918. He was demobilised in May 1919, and holds the Mons Star, and the General Service and Victory Medals.
31, Dudley Street, Leighton Buzzard. 4785.

SMITH, J. H., Private, Suffolk Regiment.
He joined in February 1917, and in January of the following year proceeded overseas. Whilst in France he saw much heavy fighting in the Arras and Ypres sectors and was severely wounded in an engagement near Ypres and invalided to England. After hospital treatment he served at the depôt of his unit until his demobilisation in January 1920. He holds the General Service and Victory Medals.
110, Ridgway Road, Luton. 4698/A.

SMITH, J. H., Special War Worker.
He volunteered his services for work of National importance and from August 1914 to the cessation of hostilities was employed at the Commercial Cars Works on important duties connected with the production of munitions, and rendered valuable services throughout.
78, Saxon Road, Luton. 4768.

SMITH, J. T., Shoeing Smith, Hertfordshire Dragoons.
He was mobilised on the declaration of war and embarked for Egypt later in 1914. After serving at Cairo, Alexandria, and other stations, he took part in the British Advance through Palestine and was in action at Gaza, Haifa, Acre and Damascus. Returning to England for demobilisation in June 1919, he holds the 1914-15 Star, and the General Service and Victory Medals.
12, Landridge Road, St. Albans. X4746/B.

SMITH, J. W., Private, 7th Bedfordshire Regt.
Volunteering in August 1914, he was sent to France in the following August. He saw much service in the Ypres sector and fought in several engagements, including the Battle of Loos. He was unfortunately killed in action in the vicinity of Loos on December 21st, 1915, and was entitled to the 1914-15 Star, and the General Service and Victory Medals.
Fowlers Yard, Toddington. 4752.

SMITH, J. W., Private, R.A.S.C.
He joined in 1916, and was later drafted to the Western Front where he served on important duties at Boulogne and other places. He did good work as a baker for over three years and returned to England for demobilisation in July 1919. He holds the General Service and Victory Medals.
24, Smart Street, Luton. 4701.

SMITH, J. W. R., L/Corporal, 9th West Yorkshire Regiment.
He enlisted in October 1915, and served at his regimental depôt until drafted overseas in February 1917. Sent to the Western Front he was engaged in heavy fighting in various parts of the line and amongst other battles fought in those of Arras, Ypres, and was wounded near Lens in November 1917. He returned to England in March 1918, and was demobilised in the following March, and holds the General Service and Victory Medals.
43, Lattimore Road, St. Albans. X4743/B.

SMITH, L. B., A.B., R.N.V.R.
He joined in January 1918, and after training was engaged on important guard and other duties at the Crystal Palace. He rendered valuable services but was not sent to sea before the conclusion of hostilities, and was demobilised in June 1919.
110, Ridgway Road, Luton. 4698/C.

SMITH, O. R., Private, 1/4th Essex Regiment.
He volunteered in September 1914, and in the following August proceeded overseas. Sent to Egypt he took part in the British advance through Palestine and fought in several engagements and was present at the entry into Jerusalem. On the cessation of hostilities he returned to England for demobilisation in March 1919, and holds the 1914-15 Star, and the General Service and Victory Medals.
22, Chequer Street, Luton. 4756.

SMITH, P., Private, Bedfordshire Regiment.
Volunteering in September 1914, he embarked for Gallipoli in the following July and fought in the landing at Suvla Bay and other engagements until invalided to England with fever. On recovery he was drafted to France in December 1916 and saw much service in that theatre of war. He was in action at Arras, Ypres, Cambrai and other places, until sent back to England and discharged on account of service in June 1918. He holds the 1914-15 Star, and the General Service and Victory Medals.
Stopsley Green, Stopsley. 4705/B.

SMITH, P., Private, 2nd London Regiment (Royal Fusiliers).
He joined in February 1918, on attaining military age, and five months later was drafted to the Western Front and fought in many engagements during the Allied Advance. He was unfortunately killed in action near Bapaume on August 22nd, 1918, and was entitled to the General Service and Victory Medals.
52, Old Road, Linslade, Bucks. 4787/C.

SMITH, R., Sergeant, 7th Bedfordshire Regiment.
He was mobilised at the outbreak of war, and in 1915 was drafted to France. Whilst on the Western Front he fought at the Battle of the Somme, and was wounded. He returned to the firing line after recovery, and was in action at Ypres, Passchendaele and Cambrai, and was again wounded in 1917. He later rejoined his Battalion, and was gassed and taken prisoner in March 1918. He was repatriated after the signing of the Armistice, and demobilised in March 1919. He holds the 1914-15 Star, and the General Service and Victory Medals.
70, Hartley Road, Luton. 4718.

SMITH, P. A., Private, 6th Queen's (Royal West Surrey Regiment).
He joined in June 1918, and four months later was ordered to France. Whilst in this theatre of war he fought in the second Battle of Le Cateau and in various other engagements until the cessation of hostilities. Returning home he was demobilised in October 1919, and holds the General Service and Victory Medals.
83, Cardiff Road, Watford. 4713/B.

SMITH, P. L., Officers' Steward, Royal Navy.
Mobilised on the declaration of war, he was posted to H.M.S. "Pathfinder," which vessel was engaged on important patrol duties in the North Sea. His ship was sunk in an encounter with an enemy submarine off St. Abb's Head on September 5th, 1914, and he was unfortunately drowned. He was entitled to the 1914-15 Star, and the General Service and Victory Medals.
Mount Pleasant, Aspley Guise. Z4773.

SMITH, R., Corporal, Bedfordshire Regiment.
He joined in January 1916, and in the following August proceeded overseas. He fought in many sectors of the Western Front, and was wounded at Arras in April 1917. He was invalided to England, and subsequently discharged as medically unfit for further service in September 1918. He holds the General Service and Victory Medals.
Stopsley Green, near Luton. 4705/A.

SMITH, R., Private, Northamptonshire Regiment.
He joined in March 1916, and in the following June was sent to France. During his service on the Western Front he was engaged in the fighting on the Somme, at Ypres, and Cambrai. Returning to England, on leave, in November 1918, he unfortunately died on the 27th of the same month. He was entitled to the General Service and Victory Medals.
70, St. Andrew's Street, Leighton Buzzard. 4739/B.

SMITH, R., 1st Air Mechanic, Royal Air Force.
He joined in 1918, and at the conclusion of his training served at Farnborough with his Squadron on important duties which called for a high degree of technical skill. He did excellent work in repairing aero-engines, but was unable to secure his transfer overseas before the cessation of hostilities, and was demobilised in 1919.
Home Farm, Westoning, Ampthill. 4783/A.

SMITH, R., Gunner, Royal Field Artillery.
He joined in 1916, and in the same year was drafted overseas. During his long and varied service on the Western Front he was engaged in the fighting on Vimy Ridge and at Messines, Ypres, the Somme and Cambrai, as well as in the Retreat and Advance of 1918. He holds the General Service and Victory Medals, and was demobilised in 1919.
Talbot Road, Luton. 2896/C.

SMITH, R., Private, Machine Gun Corps.
He volunteered in June 1915, and in the same year proceeded overseas. Whilst on the Western Front he fought in many sectors, and was wounded at Arras. He later returned to the firing line, and was engaged in the fighting at Ypres, the Marne, the Somme and Cambrai, being wounded on two other occasions. He was demobilised in April 1919, and holds the 1914-15 Star, and the General Service and Victory Medals.
101, Norfolk Road, Rickmansworth. X4744/A.

SMITH, R. E., Private, 4th Royal Fusiliers.
He volunteered in April 1915, and after his training served with his Battalion at many stations until drafted to France in February 1918. He was in action at Bapaume, and was wounded near Festubert in the following June. He was sent to England, and on recovery was engaged on home duties until demobilised in January 1919. He holds the General Service and Victory Medals.
184, High Town Road, Luton. 4687.

SMITH, S. C., Sergeant, R.A.M.C., and R.A.P.C.
He volunteered in August 1914, and after serving for a time in England was later drafted to France. He was engaged on important duties at the Base Hospital, Rouen, and was frequently under shell fire whilst clearing the wounded from the field. He was demobilised in January 1919, and holds the General Service and Victory Medals.
4, Carey Place, Watford. X4745.

SMITH, S. J., Bombardier, Royal Field Artillery.
A serving soldier, he was drafted to the Western Front at the outbreak of war. He fought in the Retreat from Mons and the subsequent Battles of the Marne, the Aisne, Ypres, La Bassée, Loos, Givenchy, Arras, the Somme, Vimy Ridge and St. Quentin. On one occasion during his long and varied service he was wounded. He was demobilised in February 1919, and holds the Mons Star, and the General Service and Victory Medals.
58, John Street, Luton. 4763/A.

SMITH, S. M., Corporal, Lincolnshire Regiment.
He volunteered in 1915, and in the following year was sent to France. Whilst in this theatre of war he was in action at Ypres. He was subsequently wounded during an engagement on the Somme in 1916. He later rejoined his Battalion and fought at Arras and Cambrai. Returning to England after the cessation of hostilities, he was demobilised in April 1919. He holds the General Service and Victory Medals.
6, Rosebury Terrace, Upper Culver Road, St. Albans. X4765/A.

SMITH, T., Private, 2nd Royal Berkshire Regt.
He volunteered in June 1915, and three months later was sent to France. During his service on the Western Front he fought in the Battles of Arras, the Somme, Ypres, Cambrai, and the German Offensive and subsequent Allied Advance of 1918. He holds the 1914-15 Star, and the General Service and Victory Medals, and was demobilised in February 1919.
25, Cowper Street, Luton. 4721.

SMITH, T. F., Private, 1/1st Leicestershire Regt.
Volunteering in September 1914, he was shortly afterwards drafted overseas. Whilst on the Western Front he fought in many battles, including those of Ypres, the Somme and Cambrai. He also took part in the Retreat and Advance of 1918. He was demobilised in February 1919, and holds the 1914 Star, and the General Service and Victory Medals
Littleworth, Wing, Bucks. 4699.

SMITH, W., Corporal, 1st Queen's Own (Royal West Kent Regiment).
A serving soldier, he was drafted to France at the outbreak of hostilities. He fought in the Retreat from Mons, and also in the Battles of Ypres, Arras and Cambrai. In 1917 he was transferred to the Italian Front. During his long period of service he was wounded. He returned to England after the signing of the Armistice and was demobilised in February 1919. He holds the Mons Star, and the General Service and Victory Medals.
4, Dragon Yard, London Colney, St. Albans. 4712/B.

SMITH, W., Private, Labour Corps.
He volunteered in March 1915, and proceeded overseas in the following August. He served on the Western Front, and was engaged on the important duties of trench digging, transporting ammunition, road construction and the making of railways He also took part in the Retreat and Advance of 1918. He was demobilised in March 1919, and holds the 1914-15 Star, and the General Service and Victory Medals.
74, Bassett Road, Leighton Buzzard. 1301/B.

SMITH, W., Private, Bedfordshire Regiment.
Volunteering in 1915, he was drafted in the same year to the Western Front, where he was engaged in the fighting at Ypres, Loos, the Somme, Arras and Cambrai. He also took part in the Retreat and subsequent Allied Advance of 1918. During his long period of service he was wounded. He was demobilised in 1919, and holds the 1914-15 Star, and the General Service and Victory Medals.
8, Oxhey Street, Oxhey. X4693.

SMITH, W., Private, 7th Bedfordshire Regiment.
He volunteered in January 1915, and was later sent to France. During his service on the Western Front he fought in the Battles of Arras, Ypres, Passchendaele and Cambrai. He returned to England after the signing of the Armistice, and was demobilised in February 1919. He holds the General Service and Victory Medals.
3, Upper Culver Road, St. Albans. X4750.

SMITH, W., Private, 14th Royal Warwickshire Regiment.
He joined in February 1917, and in the following September proceeded to Italy and fought in various engagements on the Piave Front until transferred to France in March 1918. He was in action during the heavy fighting in the German Offensive and was reported missing on April 13th, 1918, and later was presumed to have been killed in action on that date. He was entitled to the General Service and Victory Medals.
52, Old Road, Linslade, Bucks. 4787/A.

SMITH, W. A., Sergeant, Royal Air Force.
Joining in April 1916, he was drafted in the following year to France. Whilst in this theatre of war he was stationed at Dunkirk, where he was engaged upon important duties which called for a high degree of technical skill. He returned to England after the signing of the Armistice, and was demobilised in April 1919. He holds the General Service and Victory Medals.
100, Leavesden Road, Watford. X4749.

SMITH, W. C., L/Corporal, Royal Engineers.

He volunteered in August 1914, and in January of the following year was sent to Alexandria. In the following August he proceeded to the Dardanelles, and was engaged on special duties at Suvla Bay and Anzac. He was then sent back to Egypt, where he was engaged at the Canal zone. Later he joined in the British Advance through Palestine, and served at Gaza, Haifa and Beyrout. He returned to England after the signing of the Armistice, and was demobilised in July 1919. He holds the 1914-15 Star, and the General Service and Victory Medals.

20, Pondwick's Road, Luton.   4707.

SMITH, W. E. M., Pioneer, Royal Engineers.

He volunteered in August 1915, when he was specially enlisted as a pioneer. On the completion of his training he was drafted overseas, where he was engaged in many battles on the Western Front, notably those of the Somme and Cambrai. He was demobilised in March 1919, and holds the General Service and Victory Medals.

106, Chapel Street, Luton.   4695.

SMITH, W. G., Sapper, Royal Engineers.

He joined in 1916, and was stationed at Plymouth, where he received his training. He was chiefly engaged on guard duties, and did excellent work, but was unable to obtain his transfer to a theatre of war owing to medical unfitness. He was demobilised in February 1919.

19, Cassiobridge Road, Watford.   X4761.

SMITH, W. H., Sapper, Royal Engineers.

He joined in March 1916, and in January of the following year was sent to Palestine. Whilst in that theatre of war he was engaged with his unit on important duties in the forward areas during the fighting at Gaza, Haifa, Beyrout, Acre, Damascus and Kantara. He returned to England in September 1919, and was demobilised in the following month. He holds the General Service and Victory Medals.

15, Cowper Street, Luton.   4779/C.

SMITH, W. J., Private, 1st Hertfordshire Regt., and 3rd Bedfordshire Regiment.

He volunteered in September 1914, and in the following year was sent to France. During his long and varied service he fought on the Somme and at Ypres, Hill 60, Givenchy and Cambrai. He was wounded on two occasions. He was demobilised in February 1919, and holds the 1914-15 Star, and the General Service and Victory Medals.

68, Grover Road, Oxhey.   X4722/B.

SMITH, W. J. (Sen.), Private, R.A.V.C.

He joined in 1916, and was shortly afterwards drafted overseas. He served on the Western Front, and was engaged on important duties at various veterinary hospitals, including those on the Somme, at Ypres and Abbeville. He returned to England, and was demobilised in January 1919. He holds the General Service and Victory Medals.

68, Grover Road, Oxhey.   X4722/A.

SMITH, W. M., L/Corporal, Machine Gun Corps.

He joined in 1916, and in the same year was drafted to India. He was engaged with his unit on garrison duties on the North-West Frontier for a period of three years. He returned to England in 1919, and was demobilised in January 1920. He holds the Indian General Service Medal, 1908 (with clasp " Afghanistan, N.W. Frontier, 1919 "), and the General Service and Victory Medals.

6, Rosebury Terrace, Upper Culver Road, St. Albans.   X4765/C.

SMITH, W. T., 1st Air Mechanic, R.A.F.

He joined in September 1916, and at the conclusion of his training was posted to H.M.S. " Pegasus," which vessel was engaged on patrol duties in the North Sea. Whilst serving in this ship he was employed on special work and rendered valuable services. He was demobilised in March 1919.

27, Brighton Road, Watford.   X4691.

SMITH, W. W., Private, R.A.S.C. (M.T.)

He volunteered in October 1915, and after serving with his unit at various stations was sent to France in the following year. He was engaged on important transport duties in the forward areas during operations, and did excellent work until the end of the war. He was demobilised in August 1919, after returning to England, and holds the General Service and Victory Medals.

39, Clifford Street, Watford.   X1977/B.

SNEDDON, T., Corporal, Royal Garrison Artillery.

He volunteered in August 1914, and in May of the following year was sent to the Western Front, where he served for over four years. Throughout the course of hostilities he was engaged as gun layer with his Battery, and fought in the Battles of Arras, Ypres, Cambrai, the Somme and various other operations. He was demobilised in December 1918, and holds the 1914-15 Star, and the General Service and Victory Medals.

6, San Remo Road, Aspley Guise.   Z4791.

SNOW, E., Private, Royal Fusiliers.

He joined in 1916, and in the same year was drafted to France, where he took part in many important engagements, including the Battles of Arras, the Somme and Cambrai. After the Armistice he was sent to Germany with the Army of Occupation, and was stationed at Cologne until his return to England. He was demobilised in April 1919, and holds the General Service and Victory Medals.

1, Hope Cottage, Old Park Road, Hitchin.   4794.

SNOXELL, C. S., Private, 1st Essex Regiment.

He joined in July 1916, and shortly afterwards was ordered to the Western Front. Whilst in this theatre of war he saw much service in various sectors, and took part in the Battles of Beaumont-Hamel, Arras, Vimy Ridge and Ypres. He was reported missing in an engagement in the Ypres sector on August 16th, 1917, and was later presumed to have been killed in action on that date. He was entitled to the General Service and Victory Medals.

32, Whitby Road, Luton.   4790.

SNOXELL, H., Cpl., 1/5th Bedfordshire Regt.

He volunteered in September 1914, and in July of the following year proceeded overseas. He took part in various operations in Gallipoli, from the landing at Suvla Bay up to the Evacuation of the Peninsula and was then sent to Egypt. During his service in this theatre of war he served in General Allenby's Advance through Palestine, and fought in many important engagements. He was killed in action at Gaza on April 19th, 1917. He was entitled to the 1914-15 Star, and the General Service and Victory Medals.

86, Hartley Road, Luton.   4792.

SNOXELL, S., A.B., Royal Naval Division.

He joined in June 1917, and in the following October was sent to the Western Front, where he served with the 63rd Drake Battalion. He took part in many engagements on the Somme, including the Battle of Bapaume, and was killed in action at Achiet-le-Grand on August 21st, 1918. He was entitled to the General Service and Victory Medals.

" Burleigh," Victoria Street, Dunstable.   4793.

SOAL, A. J., Trooper, 2nd Life Guards.

Volunteering in September 1914, in December of the following year he embarked for France and served on the Western Front for nearly four years. He was engaged in heavy fighting in various parts of the line and took part in the actions at Ypres, Cambrai and on the Somme. He returned to England in February 1919, and in 1920 was still serving. He holds the 1914-15 Star, and the General Service and Victory Medals.

14, Langley Road, Watford.   X4800.

SOFFE, G., Private, 6th Bedfordshire Regiment.

He joined in April 1916, and in November of the same year proceeded on active service. He took part in many important engagements on the Western Front, including the actions at Beaucourt and other places on the Ancre, and in the capture of Vimy Ridge. He was killed in action near Cambrai on April 11th, 1917, and was entitled to the General Service and Victory Medals.

57, Park Road West, Luton.   4798/B.

SOFFE, H., Private, Royal Marine Light Infantry.

He volunteered in June 1915, and attached to the Dover Patrol was engaged on important duties in the English Channel and in the North Sea throughout the war. He was afterwards sent to Malta, and in 1920 was still serving. He holds the 1914-15 Star, and the General Service and Victory Medals.

57, Park Road West, Luton.   4798/A.

SOLE, W. H., A.B., Royal Navy.

He joined the Service in March 1915, and was posted to H.M.S. "Chatham," which ship was engaged in escorting transports and food convoys to France and was also employed on important patrol duties in the North and Baltic Seas. He was discharged in January 1919, and holds the 1914-15 Star, and the General Service and Victory Medals.

76, Brightwell Road, Watford.   X3371/E.

SOLE, S. E., Private, 1st Hertfordshire Regt.

Volunteering in November 1914, he completed his training and served with his unit at various stations on guard and other important duties. He was over age for service overseas and rendered excellent services until discharged in May 1916.
64, Brightwell Road, Watford. X3371/C.

SOMMERVILLE, J., Sergeant, Royal Engineers.

Having previously served in the Territorial Force he was mobilised at the outbreak of war and was engaged on important duties as an Instructor in the signal section until drafted to Egypt in August 1918. He saw much service in Palestine where he did valuable work on the lines of communication during General Allenby's campaign. He returned to England for demobilisation in June 1919, and in addition to the Territorial Long Service Medal holds the General Service and Victory Medals.
33, Lancaster Road, Hitchin. 4802.

SOPER, G. W., Private, 1/5th Bedfordshire Regt.

When war broke out he was already serving and in the following year was drafted to Gallipoli. He there took part in the landing at Suvla Bay and in various other actions on the Peninsula. Later he was sent to Malta and in 1916 was sent to the Western Front. In France he was in action during many engagements and was killed in action on April 11th, 1917, during the Battle of Arras. He was entitled to the 1914-15 Star, and the General Service and Victory Medals.
81, Boyle Street, Luton. 4796/C.

SOPER, H., Sapper, Royal Engineers.

He joined in January 1917, and in the following July embarked for France. During his service on the Western Front he was engaged on important duties in connection with operations on the Somme, and at Arras, Ypres, Béthune, and other places, and was wounded. He was demobilised in January 1919, and holds the General Service and Victory Medals.
81, Boyle Street, Luton. 4796/B.

SOPER, W., Private, 1/5th Bedfordshire Regt.

Enlisting in May 1914, he was sent to Gallipoli in the following year and was in action at Suvla Bay and various other engagements until the Evacuation of the Peninsula, and was wounded. Sent to Egypt on recovery he fought at Gaza, Haifa, Beyrout, and other places during the British Advance through Palestine and was again wounded. He returned to England on the conclusion of hostilities, and was demobilised in June 1919, and holds the 1914-15 Star, and the General Service and Victory Medals.
81, Boyle Street, Luton. 4796/A.

SOUSTER, W., Pte., 8th East Lancashire Regt.

He joined in June 1916, and in the following October proceeded to the Western Front. During his service he was engaged on important duties in various parts of the line in France and fought in the Battle of Beaumont-Hamel and other operations on the Ancre. He was severely wounded during the Battle of Arras, and died of the effects of his injuries on May 2nd, 1917. He was entitled to the General Service and Victory Medals.
446, Hitchin Road, Luton. 4797.

SOUTH, F. A., Private, Machine Gun Corps.

He volunteered in 1914, and in the next year was sent to Mesopotamia. Whilst in this theatre of war he was engaged in heavy fighting in operations for the relief of Kut and was present at the capture of Baghdad and the occupation of Mosul. On the cessation of hostilities he proceeded to India and was stationed at Rawal-Pindi until sent home for demobilisation in October 1919. He holds the 1914-15 Star, and the General Service and Victory Medals.
19, Puller Road, Boxmoor, Herts. X4795.

SOUTH, G., Private, 3rd Bedfordshire Regiment.

He volunteered in October 1915, and was drafted overseas in the following year. He saw much service with his unit on the Western Front and fought in the Somme offensive and in the Battles of Arras, Ypres and Passchendaele. During his service he was twice wounded, at Arras and Ypres. He was demobilised in March 1919, and holds the General Service and Victory Medals..
18, New Dalton Street, St. Albans. 4801/A.

SOUTH, G. E., Rifleman, Rifle Brigade.

He volunteered in 1915, and in the following year was drafted to the Western Front. During his service overseas he fought in the Battles of the Somme, Arras and Cambrai, and in many other engagements, and was three times wounded. He was demobilised in March 1919, and holds the General Service and Victory Medals.
1, Queen's Place, Hemel Hempstead. X520/A.

SOUTH, H. G., Pte., R.A.S.C., and Labour Corps.

Volunteering in 1915, he embarked for France in the same year, and was engaged on important duties in the forward areas during the Battles of the Somme, Ypres, St. Quentin and Cambrai. He was later employed in the construction and repair of roads and did valuable work until the termination of hostilities. He holds the 1914-15 Star, and the General Service and Victory Medals, and was demobilised in April 1919.
12, Weymouth Street, Apsley End. X4799.

SOUTH, W., Private, R.A.S.C. (M.T.)

He volunteered in April 1915, and was engaged on important duties in connection with the transportation of supplies until 1918 when he was sent to the Western Front. He there took part in final operations and was engaged at the fourth Battle of Ypres and in the actions at Cambrai and Le Cateau during the Advance of 1918. In February 1919, he returned to England and was demobilised, and holds the General Service and Victory Medals.
18, New Dalton Street, St. Albans. 4801/B.

SPACEY, A., Sergt., 1/5th Bedfordshire Regt.

He enlisted in July 1913, and in 1915 was drafted overseas. He was in action at the landing at Suvla Bay and in various other engagements of the Gallipoli campaign. On the Evacuation of the Peninsula he proceeded to Egypt and there saw much fighting in the Canal zone and during the British advance through Palestine in the course of which he was engaged at Gaza, Beyrout, and other battles, and was wounded. He returned to England for demobilisation in March 1919, and holds the 1914-15 Star, and the General Service and Victory Medals.
8, Alfred Street, Luton. 4835.

SPACEY, A., Corporal, Royal Defence Corps.

He volunteered in October 1914, and on the conclusion of his training was engaged on important guard duties at various aeroplane and seaplane works. He rendered valuable services throughout the whole period of the war and was demobilised in April 1919.
8, Alfred Street, Luton. 4812/B.

SPACEY, A., Sergt., 1/5th Bedfordshire Regt.

He volunteered in August 1914, and in the following year was sent to Gallipoli. There he served in various operations until the withdrawal of the forces from the Peninsula, and was wounded. Sent to Egypt he was in action at Gaza and several other battles during the British advance through Palestine and returned to England at the close of the war in 1918. He was demobilised in April 1919, and holds the 1914-15 Star, and the General Service and Victory Medals.
8, Alfred Street, Luton. 4812/A.

SPACEY, T., L/Corporal, 7th Bedfordshire Regt.

Volunteering in September 1914, he was drafted to France in the following year and fought in the Battles of Hill 60, Givenchy, the Somme, and was wounded in action at Trones Wood. He was invalided to hospital and on recovery returned to the firing line and served at Cambrai and was again wounded in action at Ypres. He was sent home and subsequently invalided out of the Service in May 1918. He holds the 1914-15 Star, and the General Service and Victory Medals.
8, Alfred Street, Luton. 4812/C.

SPACKMAN, F. W., Pte., Buffs (East Kent Regt.)

Volunteering in 1914, he was sent to France in the following year and fought in many parts of the Western Front and was in action at the Battles of Arras, Cambrai, the Somme and Hill 60. In 1917 he returned to England on account of injuries received in action which affected his eyesight and after receiving hospital treatment was invalided out of the Service in 1917. He holds the 1914-15 Star, and the General Service and Victory Medals.
4, Terrace Gardens, St. Albans Road, Watford. X4807.

SPARKSMAN, A., Private, Royal Fusiliers.

Volunteering in August 1914, he was drafted to France on completion of his training and fought in the Battles of Ypres, the Somme and Cambrai and many other important engagements, and was wounded. After the Armistice was signed he was sent into Germany with the Army of Occupation and was still serving there in 1920. He holds the General Service and Victory Medals.
83, Chester Road, Watford. X4815/A.

SPARKSMAN, A. J., Corporal, Royal Engineers.

Volunteering in January 1915, he was sent to France later and served in various sectors on important duties in connection with operations and was wounded and gassed. He rendered excellent services throughout and was demobilised in March 1919, and holds the General Service and Victory Medals.
83, Chester Road, Watford. X4815/B.

SPARROW, T., Private, 4th Bedfordshire Regt.

He volunteered in March 1915, and on conclusion of his training served at various stations with his unit. Later he renderered excellent services working on the land, as he was medically unfit for service overseas. He was demobilised in April 1919.

New Marford, Wheathampstead.   4822.

SPARVELL, A., Gunner, Royal Field Artillery.

He enlisted in March 1914, and was mobilised on the outbreak of war and embarked for France in May 1915. He fought in many important engagements, including those of the Somme, Arras, Armentières, and was wounded in 1915 at Ypres, and later at Vimy Ridge in April 1917. He was in action throughout the Retreat and Advance of 1918, and was demobilised in June 1919, and holds the 1914-15 Star, and the General Service and Victory Medals.

73, Waterlow Road, Dunstable.   4829/A.

SPARVELL, A., Ordinary Seaman, Royal Navy.

He joined the Service in February 1918, and was posted to H.M.S. "Hibernia," which ship was engaged on patrol and other important work in the North Sea, frequently passing through mine-infested areas in the discharge of her duties. He was discharged in January 1919, and holds the General Service and Victory Medals.

73, Waterlow Road, Dunstable.   4829/C.

SPARVELL, C. T., Corporal, R.A.M.C.

He joined in September 1916, and was sent to Italy in the following January, and served on the Piave front as a stretcher-bearer and also was engaged on important duties at the base hospitals. He returned to England and was demobilised in August 1919, and holds the General Service and Victory Medals.

73, Waterlow Road, Dunstable.   4829/B.

SPARVELL, G. A., Corporal, R.A.M.C.

Mobilised in August 1914, he was stationed at various depôts engaged on important duties. Later he was attached to the Suffolk Yeomanry and rendered valuable services. He was unable to obtain his transfer overseas owing to medical unfitness and died in January 1918 from illness contracted on service.

73, Waterlow Road, Dunstable.   4829/D.

SPARY, A. E., Gunner, Royal Field Artillery.

A Reservist, he was mobilised and sent to France on the outbreak of hostilities, and fought in the Retreat from Mons and was wounded in September 1914. Returning to England he received medical treatment and was invalided out of the Service in July 1915. Later he worked on munitions at Woolwich Arsenal and holds the Mons Star, and the General Service and Victory Medals.

93, Norman Road, Luton.   4803/B.

SPARY, F., Private, 2nd Bedfordshire Regiment.

He enlisted in 1910, and was stationed in South Africa at the outbreak of hostilities. He was drafted to France and served with his Battalion in various engagements. He was killed in action at Ypres on October 29th, 1914, and was entitled to the 1914 Star, and the General Service and Victory Medals.

93, Norman Road, Luton.   4803/A.

SPARY, H., Special War Worker.

He volunteered his services for work of National importance, and from January 1915 until December 1919 was engaged in the manufacture of munitions at Woolwich Arsenal, the Vauxhall Factory, and Messrs. Kent's Munitions Works, and rendered valuable services throughout.

17, Saxon Road, Luton.   4827.

SPARY, T., Shoeing Smith, Royal Field Artillery.

Volunteering in January 1915, he embarked for the Western Front two months later. Here he saw active service and was engaged in the Battles of Ypres, the Somme, Arras and Loos and fought throughout the Retreat and Advance of 1918. He was demobilised in February 1919, and holds the 1914-15 Star, and the General Service and Victory Medals.

50, Whitby Road, Luton.   4813.

SPARY, W., Private, Bedfordshire Regiment, and Sapper, Royal Engineers.

A Reservist, he was mobilised at the commencement of the war and was drafted to France and fought in the Retreat from Mons and was wounded. On recovery he returned to the front line and was in action on the Somme, at Ypres, Arras and other important engagements during the Retreat and Advance of 1918. He was demobilised in February 1919, and holds the General Service and Victory Medals.

93, Norman Road, Luton.   4803/C.

SPARY, W., L/Corporal, Royal Engineers.

A serving soldier, he was sent to France at the outbreak of hostilities and served throughout the Retreat from Mons and in the subsequent Battles of Arras, Ypres, Cambrai, Albert and in the Retreat and Advance of 1918. He was mentioned in Despatches for devotion to duty in the Field, and was demobilised in February 1919, and holds the Mons Star, and the General Service and Victory Medals.

84, Hampton Road, Luton.   4804.

SPATCHER, W. F., 1st Air Mechanic, Royal Air Force (late R.N.A.S.)

He joined in August 1917, and after completing his training was posted to the Q-boat H.M.S. "Argus," which vessel was engaged on particular work of a most dangerous nature, in the North Sea, until the cessation of hostilities. He was demobilised in June 1919, and holds the General Service and Victory Medals.

64, Sotheron Road, Watford.   X4809.

SPEAR, A. E. (M.M.), Sergeant, 24th London Regiment (The Queen's).

Volunteering in August 1914, he was drafted to France in the following March and was engaged in many important battles, including those of Arras, the Somme and Ypres, and was twice wounded. He also saw heavy fighting in the Retreat and Advance of 1918, and was awarded the Military Medal for devotion to duty and gallantry in the Field. He was demobilised in April 1919, and holds the 1914-15 Star, and the General Service and Victory Medals.

10, Lower Dagnall Street, St. Albans.   X4814/B.

SPEAR, F. G., Sergeant, Queen's (Royal West Surrey Regiment).

He volunteered in September 1915, and proceeded to the Western Front in the following May and was in action in various parts of the line and was gassed on the Somme in July of the same year. He returned to England for treatment, and on recovery served at various stations until the cessation of hostilities when he was sent into Germany with the Army of Occupation. He was demobilised in August 1919, and holds the General Service and Victory Medals.

10, Lower Dagnall Street, St. Albans.   X4814/A.

SPENCE, F., Private, R.A.S.C.

Volunteering in September 1915, he proceeded to France in the same month and was engaged on important transport duties in the forward areas. In the following December he returned to England in consequence of ill-health and after hospital treatment was invalided out of the Service in April 1916. He holds the 1914-15 Star, and the General Service and Victory Medals.

99, Old London Road, St. Albans.   X4823/A.

SPENCE, F., A.B., Royal Navy.

Joining the Service in January 1915, he was posted to H.M.S. "Napier," and later to H.M.S. "Venturous." In these ships he was engaged on patrol duties and was in action in the Battles of the Dogger Bank, Jutland, and in the Naval engagements in the Battle of Heligoland. He was discharged in February 1920, and holds the 1914-15 Star, and the General Service and Victory Medals.

99, Old London Road, St. Albans.   X4823/C.

SPENCE, R. A., A.B., Royal Navy.

He joined the Service in August 1915, and was posted to H.M.S. "Marne," which ship was engaged on patrol and other important duties in the North Sea. He also served on H.M. Ships "Africa," "Gloucester," and "Blake," and owing to ill-health he was discharged unfit for further service in August 1919, and holds the 1914-15 Star, and the General Service and Victory Medals.

99, Old London Road, St. Albans.   X4823/B.

SPENCER, G., Private, Bedfordshire Regiment.

Volunteering in August 1914, he was drafted to France almost immediately and was engaged in the fighting during the Retreat from Mons and in the Battles of Loos, Ypres and other important engagements and was wounded. He was unfortunately killed in action on May 18th, 1915, and was entitled to the Mons Star, and the General Service and Victory Medals.

23, St. Andrew's Road, Hitchin.   4833.

SPENCER, G. H., Pioneer, Royal Engineers.

Volunteering in January 1915, he proceeded to the Western Front at a later date and served in the forward areas in many parts of the line engaged on important duties. He rendered excellent services throughout and returning to England was demobilised in January 1919, and holds the General Service and Victory Medals.

69, Park Road West, Luton.   3446/B.

SPENCER, H., Sergeant, 1st Bedfordshire Regt.
He volunteered in August 1914, and was drafted to the Western Front where he fought in the Retreat from Mons and in the Battles of the Marne, Ypres, Hill 60, St. Eloi, Givenchy and Loos. Severely wounded in 1916, he became totally blind and it was necessary to amputate one of his arms. He was invalided out of the Service in June 1916, and holds the Mons Star, and the General Service and Victory Medals.
Lower Green, Ickleford, Hitchin. 4841/A.

SPENCER, S. G., Private, Oxfordshire and Buckinghamshire Light Infantry.
A serving soldier, he was sent to France at the outbreak of war, and was in action throughout the Retreat from Mons, and in the Battle of Ypres and other important engagements. He was wounded, and returning to England received medical treatment and was invalided out of the Service in 1915. He holds the Mons Star, and the General Service and Victory Medals.
80, Harwood Road, Watford. X4806.

SPENCER, W. G., Sapper, Royal Engineers.
Joining in December 1916, he completed his training and was stationed at various depôts engaged on important duties with the searchlights in connection with anti-aircraft work with his unit. He was unable to obtain his transfer to a theatre of war but rendered valuable services until demobilised in March 1919.
48, Cecil Street, North Watford. X4818.

SPICER, F., Private, Royal Inniskilling Fusiliers.
Joining in July 1916, he embarked for Salonika three months later and served in various sectors in this theatre of war. Transferred to the Western Front in March 1918, he fought at Cambrai and Albert and in many other engagements during the German Offensive and subsequent Allied Advance. He was demobilised in March 1919, and holds the General Service and Victory Medals.
48, Sunnyside, Hitchin. 1611/B.

SPICER, F., Private, 1/6th Essex Regiment.
Volunteering in February 1916, he was drafted to Egypt in July 1916, and saw considerable service on the Palestine front. He fought at the Battle of Gaza and took part in the Advance through the Holy Land and Syria He returned to England and was demobilised in March 1919, and holds the General Service and Victory Medals.
18, Cannon Cottages, Hitchin, Herts. 4838/B.

SPICER, J., Corporal, 2nd Manchester Regiment.
He joined in March 1917, and proceeded to France later in the same year. During his period of service overseas he fought at the Battles of the Somme, Arras, Ypres, and Cambrai, and in the Retreat and Advance of 1918. He was demobilised in October 1919, and holds the General Service and Victory Medals.
12, Park Street, Hitchin. 4837.

SPICER, J., Private, 1st Hertfordshire Regiment.
Volunteering in April 1915, he was sent overseas on the conclusion of his training and was in action in various sectors of the Western Front. In 1917 he was transferred to Italy and took part in many engagements in this theatre of war and was wounded. He returned to England and was discharged in November 1918 on account of service, and holds the General Service and Victory Medals.
39, Bernard Street, St. Albans. X4816.

SPICER, L., Private, 4th Northamptonshire Regt.
Joining in July 1918, he concluded his training and was stationed at various depôts on guard and other important duties with his unit. Owing to ill-health he was unsuccessful in obtaining his transfer overseas prior to the cessation of hostilities, and was discharged in August 1919.
18, Cannon Cottages, Hitchin. 4838/A.

SPICER, W., Private, Royal Fusiliers.
He volunteered in June 1915, and in November of the following year embarked for the Western Front. Here he was engaged in the Battles of Neuve Chapelle, Arras and Cambrai, and was twice wounded in 1918, in August and October during the Retreat and Advance. Returning to England he received hospital treatment and was discharged on account of his wounds in February 1919, and holds the General Service and Victory Medals.
7, Taylors Cottages, Old Park Road, Hitchin. 4840.

SPIERS, J. R., Private, R.A.S.C. (Remounts).
He volunteered at the outbreak of war and in 1915 was drafted to France, where he served at a Remount Depôt. He was later transferred to Egypt and subsequently served in Palestine. He returned to England and was demobilised in October 1919, and holds the 1914-15 Star, and the General Service and Victory Medals.
21, Meeting Alley, Watford. X4810/D.

SPIERS, E. A., Private, 7th Bedfordshire Regt.
He volunteered in August 1915, and proceeded overseas on the completion of his training. During his service on the Western Front he fought in the Battles of Arras, Passchendaele and Vimy Ridge, and was wounded on two occasions. He was unfortunately killed in action on October 21st, 1918. He was entitled to the General Service and Victory Medals. His memory is cherished with pride.
21, Meeting Alley, Watford. X4810/B.

SPIERS, G. A., Private, Machine Gun Corps.
Volunteering in August 1914, he proceeded overseas in the following year. During his long service on the Western Front he was engaged in much heavy fighting, and was in action at Arras, Ypres and Cambrai. He was wounded on three occasions. He holds the 1914-15 Star, and the General Service and Victory Medals, and was still serving in 1920.
21, Meeting Alley, Watford X4810/A.

SPIERS, J. R. (Junior), Corporal, R.A.S.C.
He volunteered in January 1915, and two months later was drafted overseas. Whilst on the Western Front he was engaged with his unit at Ypres and Cambrai. After the signing of the Armistice he proceeded to Germany with the Army of Occupation and was stationed at Cologne. At one period of his service he was engaged on transport duties in Dublin. He was demobilised in May 1920, holding the 1914-15 Star, and the General Service and Victory Medals.
21, Meeting Alley, Watford. X4810/C.

SPILSBURY, E., Private, 2/5th Yorkshire Regt., and Labour Corps.
He joined in September 1916, and at the conclusion of his training served with his Battalion on special duties. He was subsequently employed on land work for a considerable period, but owing to medical unfitness was unable to obtain his transfer to a theatre of war. He was demobilised in February 1919.
105, Cowper Street, Luton. 4832.

SPINKS, R., Private, 8th East Surrey Regiment.
He joined in June 1916, and three months later was drafted to France. Whilst in this theatre of war he was engaged in the fighting at Albert, Béthune and Arras, where he was wounded. Proceeding subsequently to Egypt he was stationed for a short time at Alexandria. He joined in the British advance through Palestine and fought in the many battles of that campaign. He was demobilised in September 1919, and holds the General Service and Victory Medal.
84, Hagden Lane, Watford. X4824.

SPITTEL, G., Private, 1/4th Essex Regiment.
Volunteering in June 1915, he was sent to Egypt in the succeeding December and served with the advance through Sinai, Palestine and Syria, fighting at the Battles of Gaza, and in many other important engagements. He returned to England and was demobilised in July 1919, and holds the 1914-15 Star, and the General Service and Victory Medals.
19, King Street, Houghton Regis, Beds. 4960.

SPITTLE, W. A., Driver, Royal Field Artillery.
He volunteered in January 1915, and in November of the same year was drafted to France. In this theatre of war he was engaged in the fighting at La Bassée, Ypres, and the Somme and was wounded near Arras on August 28th, 1916. He subsequently fought at Cambrai and in the Retreat and Advance of 1918. Returning to England after the cessation of hostilities, he was demobilised in March 1919. He holds the 1914-15 Star, and the General Service and Victory Medals.
71, Cardiff Road, Watford. X4826.

SPOKES, E. T., Private, 2nd Bedfordshire Regt.
He volunteered in November 1914, and in the succeeding March proceeded to France. Whilst on the Western Front he fought on the Somme and at Arras, and was wounded in April 1917, near Ypres. On recovery he rejoined his Battalion and was engaged in the fighting at Cambrai. He was demobilised in February 1919, and holds the 1914-15 Star, and the General Service and Victory Medals.
23, Branch Road, Park Street, St. Albans X4825.

SPOKES, E. V., Private, 1st Hertfordshire Regt.
He volunteered in January 1915, and served on important duties with his Battalion until drafted to France in June 1918. During his service on the Western Front in the closing stages of the war, he fought at Cambrai, where he was wounded. He returned to England and was demobilised in January 1919. He holds the General Service and Victory Medals.
27, Branch Road, Park Street, St. Albans. X4808.

SPOONER, W., Sergeant, R.A.S.C. (M.T.)
He volunteered in May 1915, and in the following January proceeded overseas. Whilst on the Western Front he was engaged on the transport of ammunition and supplies in the Arras, Somme, Ypres, Albert, St. Quentin and Cambrai sectors. After the signing of the Armistice he served in Cologne with the Army of Occupation. He was demobilised in June 1919, and holds the General Service and Victory Medals.
3, Wootton Terrace, Walsworth, near Hitchin. 4836.

SPRATLEY, A., Private, 27th Norfolk Regiment.
He joined in November 1916, and in the following year was drafted to France. During his service on the Western Front he fought on the Somme, and was wounded at Cambrai on August 2nd, 1918. He returned to England and was demobilised in December 1919, holding the General Service and Victory Medals.
28, Stanmore Road, Watford. X4811.

SPRATLEY, F. C., Private, 3rd Norfolk Regt.
He joined in May 1917, and in the following January was sent to Ireland. He was engaged with his Battalion on important guard duties at the Curragh, and did good work, but owing to ill-health was unable to secure his transfer to a theatre of war. He was demobilised in September 1919.
29a, Langley Street, Luton. 4821.

SPRIGGS, S., Private, R.A.S.C.
He volunteered at the outbreak of war, and at the conclusion of his training served in the forage department of his unit at Hatfield, and in the neighbourhood. He did good work, but on account of medical unfitness was unable to secure his transfer overseas, and was demobilised in May 1919.
5th Right of Way, New Town, Hatfield. X4817/A.

SPRING, E., Private, Royal Defence Corps.
He joined in January 1917, being ineligible for service with the Colours. He did excellent work in guarding German prsoners and also in munition factories. Owing to ill-health he was discharged in November of the same year being medically unfit for service overseas.
21, Garfield Street, Watford. X4828.

SPRITTLES, S. A., Corporal, Royal Garrison Artillery, and 21st Trench Mortar Battery.
A serving soldier, stationed at Gibraltar at the outbreak of hostilities, he was sent to France and fought in the Retreat from Mons, and in many other engagements, including those at La Bassée, Ypres, Hill 60, and in the Retreat and Advance of 1918. He was discharged in February 1919, and holds the Mons Star, and the General Service and Victory Medals.
17, Ship Road, Linslade, Bucks. 4834.

SPROATES, J. T., Private, 2nd Durham Light Infantry.
A serving soldier, he was almost immediately drafted to France at the outbreak of war. He fought in the Retreat from Mons, and in the subsequent Battles of La Bassée, Ypres and the Marne. He was mentioned in Despatches by General French in March 1915, for devotion to duty in the Field. He subsequently fought at Pozières, in the Battle of the Somme, and at Arras, Albert and Cambrai.. In 1917 he was transferred to the Royal Engineers and attached to the Signal Section. He was demobilised in March 1919, and holds the Mons Star, and the General Service and Victory Medals.
3, Fountain Yard, Biggleswade. Z4820/A.

SPUFFORD, A. G., Private, Coldstream Guards.
He joined in April 1918, and two months later was drafted to France. During his service in this theatre of war he fought at Amiens, Ypres and Cambrai. After the cessation of hostilities he proceeded to Germany with the Army of Occupation and was stationed at Cologne. He was demobilised in October 1919, and holds the General Service and Victory Medals.
54, Milton Road, Luton. 4819.

SPURR, G., Private, West Yorkshire Regiment.
Volunteering at the outbreak of war he was shortly afterwards sent to Salonika, where he was engaged in much heavy fighting until 1916. He was then transferred to France and fought in engagements on the Somme and at Cambrai. He was demobilised in 1919, and holds the 1914-15 Star, and the General Service and Victory Medals.
24, Weymouth Street, Apsley End, Herts. X4830/A.

SPURR, S. G., Telegraphist, Royal Navy.
He volunteered in 1915, and was posted to H.M.S. "Isis," which ship was engaged on many important duties in the North and Baltic Seas, and was also employed on patrol duties in the Mediterranean Sea, and many other waters. He holds the General Service and Victory Medals, and was still serving in 1920
24, Weymouth Street, Apsley End. X4830/B.

SPURR, S. B., Bombardier, Royal Field Artillery.
He volunteered in 1915, and in the same year was sent to France. During his service in this theatre of war he took part in much heavy fighting, and served in the engagements at Ypres, the Somme, and Arras, and was wounded. He was demobilised in April 1919, and holds the 1914-15 Star, and the General Service and Victory Medals.
91 St. John's Road, Boxmoor. X4831.

SQUIRE, T. J., Corporal, 2nd Bedfordshire Regt.
He volunteered in 1915, and in the following July was sent to France. Whilst on the Western Front he fought at Loos, Albert, the Somme, Arras and Messines, and was wounded at Ypres in August 1917. He later rejoined his Battalion in the firing line and was again wounded in the fighting at Albert in July 1918. He was sent to England and on recovery served on home duties until demobilised in February 1919. He holds the 1914-15 Star, and the General Service and Victory Medals.
9, North Bridge, Shefford. Z4842.

STACEY, L. W., Private, Queen's (Royal West Surrey Regiment).
He joined in 1916, and at the conclusion of his training was engaged on important duties with his Battalion at various stations. He did very good work, but owing to medical unfitness was unable to secure his transfer to a theatre of war, and was demobilised in 1920.
New Street, Shefford. Z4942.

STACEY, S. W., Tpr., Hertfordshire Dragoons.
He volunteered in 1915, and in the same year was sent to Egypt. He served in the British advance through Palestine, and was engaged in the operations at Gaza, Jaffa, Haifa and Damascus. He returned to England and was demobilised in August 1919, and holds the 1914-15 Star, and the General Service and Victory Medals.
277, High Street, Watford. X4961.

STACEY, W. H., Private, Hertfordshire Regiment, and Royal Defence Corps.
He volunteered at the age of forty-five in October 1914, and was posted to the Hertfordshire Regiment, but on account of his age he was transferred to the Royal Defence Corps. He served on special duties with his unit and rendered very valuable services until discharged in November 1918.
13, Stanmore Road, Watford. X3609/B.

STAFFORD, J. D., Private, Queen's (Royal West Surrey Regiment).
He joined in February 1917, and in the same year proceeded to France. Whilst in this theatre of war he was engaged in the fighting in the Ypres, Somme and Cambrai sectors, and during his service on the Western Front was gassed and suffered from shell-shock. He was demobilised in March 1919, and holds the General Service and Victory Medals.
Trowley Bottom, Flamstead. X4959.

STAGG, W. G., Private, 11th Bedfordshire Regt.
Volunteering in November 1914, he was engaged on important duties with his Battalion at many stations. He did good work but was unsuccessful in obtaining his transfer overseas, and was demobilised in March 1919.
Parkside Cottages, Welwyn. 4888.

STAINES, F., Rifleman, Cameronians (Scottish Rifles).
He volunteered in August 1914, and was almost immediately sent to France. He fought in the Retreat from Mons, and the subsequent engagements at La Bassée and Ypres. Owing to ill-health he was sent to England in January 1915, and after receiving hospital treatment was invalided out of the Service in the following month. He holds the Mons Star, and the General Service and Victory Medals.
St. Margaret's, Stuart Street, Dunstable. 4950.

STAINES, W., Sergt., 4th (Royal Irish) Dragoon Guards.
A serving soldier, he was mobilised and sent to France at the outbreak of war. Whilst on the Western Front he fought in the Retreat from Mons, and the subsequent engagements of the Marne, Albert, Arras, Cambrai and St. Quentin, and was wounded. After the signing of the Armistice he proceeded to Germany with the Army of Occupation and was stationed at Cologne. He was demobilised in May 1919, and holds the Mons Star, and the General Service and Victory Medals.
15, Union Street, Dunstable. 4867.

STAINES, H. J., Bombardier, R.G.A.
He volunteered in 1915, and in the same year was sent to France. During his service in this theatre of war he fought in many engagements, including that of Ypres, and was unfortunately killed in action on July 17th, 1916. He was entitled to the 1914-15 Star, and the General Service and Victory Medals.
George Street, Wing, Bucks.   4947.

STALLAN, H. E. (D.C.M.), Sergeant, 7th Bedfordshire Regiment.
He volunteered in September 1914, and in the succeeding year was sent to France. During his service on the Western Front he was in action in several engagements, including those at Hill 60, Givenchy, Arras, Ypres, Cambrai, the Somme, and was gassed and wounded. He was awarded the Distinguished Conduct Medal for conspicuous gallantry and devotion to duty in the Field, and also holds the 1914-15 Star, and the General Service and Victory Medals, and was demobilised in February 1919.
38, Princess Street, Luton.   4951.

STAMMERS, G. W., Private, 2nd Royal Fusiliers.
He joined in October 1916, and was shortly afterwards drafted overseas. He saw much service on the Western Front and was in action on the Somme, at Ypres, Lens and other places, and was wounded on November 23rd, 1917, in the Battle of Cambrai. He was demobilised in May 1919, and holds the General Service and Victory Medals.
83, Cambridge Street, Luton.   4870.

STANBRIDGE, A. (M.M.), Trooper, 2nd County of London Yeomanry (Westminster Dragoons).
He volunteered in June 1915, and after serving with his unit on important duties embarked for Egypt in June 1917. Whilst in this theatre of war he was engaged in various operations during the advance through Palestine and was in action at Gaza and in the vicinity of Jerusalem. He was sent to France in June 1918, and fought in the Battle of Ypres and other important engagements during the final stages of the war, and was wounded. He was awarded the Military Medal for conspicuous bravery and devotion to duty in the Field. In addition he holds the General Service and Victory Medals, and was demobilised in February 1919.
47, Hampton Road, Luton.   4860.

STANBRIDGE, E., Sapper, Royal Engineers.
He joined in June 1917, and after completing his training was engaged on important duties as a rivetter in the shipbuilding yard at Sandwich. He did valuable work, but was unsuccessful in securing a transfer to a theatre of war before the close of the war, and was demobilised in February 1919.
4, Oak Road, Luton.   4912.

STANBRIDGE, F. A., Private, 1/5th Bedfordshire Regiment.
He volunteered in July 1915, and embarked for Egypt in the following December. He saw much service in the Eastern theatre of operations, and fought in the Battle of Gaza and other important engagements during the Advance through Palestine. He was demobilised in February 1919, and holds the 1914-15 Star, and the General Service and Victory Medals.
168, Wellington Street, Luton.   2740/B.

STANBRIDGE, G., Private, R.A.S.C.
He joined in September 1916, and a month later proceeded to the Western Front. During his service in France he was engaged on important duties in connection with Army remounts in the Arras, Cambrai and other sectors and did good work throughout the war. Returning to England for demobilisation in November 1919, he holds the General Service and Victory Medals.
3, Dunstable Street, Ampthill.   4880.

STANBRIDGE, G. T., Sapper, Royal Engineers.
He volunteered in September 1914, and in the following year embarked for Gallipoli. He rendered valuable services at the landing at Suvla Bay and in other operations on the Peninsula, and was unfortunately killed in action at "Chocolate Hill" on August 15th, 1915. He was entitled to the 1914-15 Star, and the General Service and Victory Medals.
28, Ridgway Road, Luton.   4902.

STANBRIDGE, H. R., Private, West Yorkshire Regiment.
He joined in August 1916, and shortly afterwards embarked for France. Whilst on the Western Front he served with his unit in various parts of the line, and fought in the Battles of Passchendaele, Cambrai, St. Quentin, Kemmel Hill and other important engagements, and was wounded. He holds the General Service and Victory Medals, and was demobilised in October 1919.
Fernville, Flitwick, Beds.   4910.

STANBRIDGE, H. R., Gunner (Signaller), R.G.A.
He joined in August 1918, and after completing his training served at various stations on the South Coast. He did valuable work in connection with coastal defence measures, but was unable to obtain a transfer overseas before the termination of hostilities, and was demobilised in September 1919. For two years before enlistment, he had been employed at a munitions factory and discharged his various duties in a thoroughly efficient and satisfactory manner.
55, Hampton Road, Luton.   4034.

STANBRIDGE, S., Private, East Surrey Regt.
Joining in June 1916, he was sent overseas in the following October. He saw much service on the Western Front, and fought in the Battles of Arras, Vimy Ridge and other operations. He was killed in action in the vicinity of Arras on February 14th, 1917, and was entitled to the General Service and Victory Medals.
Brewery Lane, Ampthill.   4894.

STANFORD, B. S., Bombardier, R.F.A.
He volunteered in December 1914, and in the following month was drafted overseas. Serving with his Battery in various sectors of the Western Front he was in action at Ypres, Arras, Armentières, Passchendaele and various other important engagements, and was twice wounded. He returned to England for demobilisation in March 1919, and holds the 1914-15 Star, and the General Service and Victory Medals.
10, Sunny Side, Hitchin.   4881.

STANFORD, F. A., Private, Machine Gun Corps.
Volunteering in November 1915, he embarked for France in the following year, and saw heavy fighting on the Somme, at Arras, Messines, Ypres and Cambrai, and was killed in action on August 4th, 1918, during the Allied Advance. He was entitled to the General Service and Victory Medals.
71, Leighton Street, Woburn, Beds.   Z4844/A.

STANFORD, J. T., Pte., Durham Light Infantry.
He enlisted in June 1917, and after serving at his regimental depôt was despatched to the Western Front in May of the following year. He was in almost continuous action in the German Offensive, and was taken prisoner in June 1918. He died shortly afterwards in a detention camp in Germany, and was entitled to the General Service and Victory Medals.
71, Leighton Street, Woburn.   Z4844/B.

STANFORD, W., Prvate, 8th Bedfordshire Regt.
Joining in May 1916, he embarked for France in the following January. Whilst on the Western Front he was engaged on important duties with his unit in various sectors, and took part in several notable engagements. He was killed in action on April 18th, 1917, in the course of heavy fighting in the Arras sector, and was entitled to the General Service and Victory Medals.
38, Whitby Road, Luton.   4966.

STANFORD, W. C., L/Corporal, Leicestershire Regiment.
He volunteered in August 1914, and was engaged on important duties with his unit until drafted to the Western Front. Whilst in that theatre of war he saw heavy fighting at Albert and St. Quentin and in many other parts of the line. He was wounded and gassed and invalided home, and after receiving medical treatment was discharged as medically unfit for further service in May 1918. He holds the General Service and Victory Medals.
103a, North Street, Luton.   358/B.

STANLEY, F. T., Sergeant, Royal Defence Corps.
Being ineligible for service with the Colours in consequence of his age he volunteered for service in the Royal Defence Corps, and after completing his training was engaged on important guard duties at Chelmsford Prisoner of War Camp, and rendered valuable services until discharged in March 1919.
No. 3, Court 3, Meeting Alley, Watford.   X4851.

STAPLES, F., Private, Labour Corps.
He joined in 1916, and after completing his training was engaged on important guard and other duties at various depôts. He was also employed on agricultural work in many parts of England and rendered valuable services. He was unable to obtain a transfer overseas before the cessation of hostilities, and was demobilised in December 1918.
4, Langley Place, Luton.   4053.

STAPLES, W. T., Private, Bedfordshire V.T.C.
Joining in July 1918, he was engaged on special duties on the East Coast in connection with coastal defence measures. He did good work until his discharge in the following month.
9, Shirley Road, Luton.   4939.

STAPLETON, A. E., Corporal, Middlesex Regt.

A serving soldier, he was mobilised on the outbreak of war and almost immediately sent to France. He took part in fierce fighting in the Retreat from Mons and was also in action in the Battle of Loos, and was wounded and taken prisoner during the offensive on the Somme in 1916. He was held in captivity in various detention camps in Germany and was repatriated after the signing of the Armistice. He holds the Mons Star, and the General Service and Victory Medals, and in 1920 was still serving.

17, Weymouth Street, Apsley. X4940.

STAPLETON, G., Sergt.-Major, R.A.S.C. (M.T.)

He joined in 1917, and in the same year proceeded to Egypt. With the Egyptian Expeditionary Force he was engaged on important duties in connection with the transport of ammuniton and supplies during operations in the British advance through Palestine. He holds the General Service and Victory Medals, and in 1920 was still serving.

Greenfield, near Ampthill. 4876/A.

STAPLETON, H., 2nd Corporal, Royal Engineers.

Volunteering in April 1915, he was sent to France three months later and served for nearly five years on the Western Front. During this period he was engaged on important duties in the forward areas and was present at the Battles of the Somme, Arras, Ypres, Passchendaele and Cambrai. He returned home for demobilisation in February 1919, and holds the 1914-15 Star, and the General Service and Victory Medals.

Offley Bottom Farm, near Hitchin. 4884.

STAPLETON, J., Pte., King's (Liverpool Regt.)

He enlisted in the Territorials in August 1914, but owing to physical disability was discharged after a year's service. He rejoined in 1916, and in the following year was drafted to France, where he fought in the Battles of Arras, the Somme, Cambrai, and in the Retreat and Advance of 1918. He was demobilised in October 1919, and holds the General Service and Victory Medals.

48, Florence Street, Hitchin. 4891/B.

STAPLETON, P. W., Gunner, R.G.A.

He volunteered in 1915, and embarked for France in the following year. Serving with his Battery in various sectors he was in action at Arras, Albert, Messines, Havrincourt, Cambrai and other battles and was gassed. In 1920, he returned to England for demobilisation, and holds the General Service and Victory Medals.

Falda Road, Barton, Beds. 1578/A.

STAPLETON, R., Rifleman, Rifle Brigade, and Private, Royal Army Ordnance Corps.

He joined the Rifle Brigade in March 1918, and after training served with that unit until transferred to the R.A.O.C. Sent with the Army of Occupation into Germany after the signing of the Armistice, he was engaged on special duties at Cologne for upwards of a year. He returned to England and was demobilised in March 1920.

48, Florence Street, Hitchin. 4891/A.

STAPLETON, S., Trooper, Bedfordshire Lancers.

Volunteering in 1915, he was drafted to the Egyptian Expeditionary Force in the following year. Serving in Egypt he took part in the campaign in Palestine and fought in the Battles of Gaza, Jaffa, Haifa, and other operations. At the end of the war he returned to England, and was demobilised in June 1919, and holds the General Service and Victory Medals.

Greenfield, near Ampthill. 4876/B.

STAPLEY, W. R., 1st Air Mechanic, R.A.F.

Joining in 1916, he was sent to France in the same year and served with his Squadron at various aerodromes in the Ypres and Cambrai sectors on important duties, which called for a high degree of technical skill, until the cessation of hostilities. He returned to England and was demobilised in February 1919, and holds the General Service and Victory Medals.

Potton. Z4918.

STARKINS, F., Private, Bedfordshire Regiment.

He volunteered in September 1914, and in the following year was sent to France. Serving in various sectors for two years, he took part in the Battles of Hill 60, Givenchy, Vimy Ridge, and other important engagements. In 1917 he was drafted to Salonika and was in action in the advance on the Vardar and several other operations until the close of the war. He returned to England for demobilisation in February 1919, and holds the 1914-15 Star, and the General Service and Victory Medals.

1, Heath Road, Harpenden. 4963/B.

STARKINS, J., Driver, R.A.S.C.

Volunteering in October 1915, he served with his unit until despatched to Egypt in 1917. He was engaged in important duties in connection with the transport of ammunition and supplies during the Palestine campaign and was present at El Arish, Jaffa, Gaza, Ramleh, whilst heavy fighting was in progress. He was demobilised in April 1919, on his return to England, and holds the General Service and Victory Medals.

1, Heath Road, Harpenden. 4963/C.

STARLING, T. J., Private, Military Foot Police, and Rifleman, 8th London Regiment (Post Office Rifles).

He volunteered in September 1914, and on the conclusion of his training served with his unit at various depots, on important duties. He rendered valuable services, but was unsuccessful in obtaining a transfer overseas before the cessation of hostilities and was demobilised in July 1919.

64, Acme Road, North Watford. X4938.

STATHAM, A., Sergeant, Royal Marine Artillery.

Mobilised at the declaration of war, he proceeded overseas shortly afterwards and served at Ostend and various other places on the Western Front. He was in action at Jutland in May 1916, and afterwards served at Mudros from 1917 until 1918. He was demobilised in February 1919, and holds the 1914 Star, and the General Service and Victory Medals.

37, Castle Road, St. Albans. X4845/C.

STATHAM, A. J., Private, 3rd East Surrey Regt.

Joining in April 1918, he completed his training and embarked for France in the following August. He took part in the concluding operations of the Allied Advance, and later was sent into Germany with the Army of Occupation and was stationed at Cologne. He was demobilised in October 1919, and holds the General Service and Victory Medals.

37, Castle Road, St. Albans. X4845/A

STATHAM, F. G., Telegraphist, Royal Navy.

He joined the Service in 1917, and was posted to H.M.S. "Benbow," which ship was engaged on patrol work and mine sweeping duties in the North Sea until the cessation of hostilities. He rendered excellent services and was still serving in 1920, and holds the General Service and Victory Medals.

37, Castle Road, St. Albans. X4845/B.

STEABBEN, J. D., Corporal, R.A.M.C., and Lieutenant, Delhi Regiment, Indian Army.

Volunteering in April 1915, he rendered valuable services at various hospitals in England until drafted to India in July 1917. He was stationed in Bombay for a time and was granted a commission in the Delhi Regiment and promoted to Lieutenant in June 1920, and was still serving in India later in that year in command of garrison and Acting Adjutant, and holds the General Service and Victory Medals.

High Street, Shafford. Z4866

STEARN, F., Corporal, Bedfordshire Regiment.

He volunteered in December 1914, and was sent to France in the following May and fought at the Battles of Loos, Vimy Ridge, the Somme, and other important engagements. Proceeding to Italy in 1917, he saw active service in various sectors of the Piave front until the cessation of hostilities. Returning to England he was demobilised in February 1919, and holds the 1914-15 Star, and the General Service and Victory Medals.

42, Great Northern Road, Dunstable. 4954/A.

STEARN, H., Corporal, Royal Welch Fusiliers.

He volunteered in May 1915, and embarked for Mesopotamia in June of the following year. He took part in the operations on the Tigris and was in action at Kut-el-Amara and served throughout the final British advance in that theatre of war. He returned to England and was demobilised in March 1919, and holds the General Service and Victory Medals.

42, Great Northern Road, Luton. 4954/B.

STEDMAN, W., Private, Bedfordshire Regiment.

Volunteering in 1915, he was drafted to Salonika in the following year. During his service in the Macedonian theatre of war he was engaged in many battles on the Doiran and Vardar fronts and was in action during the crossing of the Struma. He was demobilised in June 1919 on returning to England, and holds the General Service and Victory Medals.

116, Nightingale Road, Hitchin. 4892.

STEEDENS, R., Telegraphist, Royal Navy.
He joined in November 1918, and was posted to H.M.S. "Canopus," which ship was engaged on escort and patrol duties in the English Channel and the North Sea. He rendered valuable services and was discharged in February 1919, and holds the General Service and Victory Medals.
66, Park Road West, Luton.   4873/B.

STEEDENS, S., Sergeant, Royal Engineers.
Volunteering in September 1914, he embarked in the following August for the Dardanelles and took part in the landing at Suvla Bay and in the subsequent fighting until the Evacuation of the Peninsula. In 1916, drafted to France, he served in the Battles of Vimy Ridge, the Somme and Arras, engaged on important duties, and was wounded. He was demobilised in February 1919, and holds the 1914-15 Star, and the General Service and Victory Medals.
66, Park Road West, Luton.   4873/A.

STEELE, B., Private, 1st Bedfordshire Regiment, Rifleman, The Cameronians (Scottish Rifles), and Sapper, Royal Engineers.
He enlisted in June 1907, and was sent to France on the outbreak of hostilities and fought in the Retreat from Mons and at Ypres, Messines, Hill 60 and Valenciennes, and was engaged throughout the Retreat and Advance of 1918. He was twice wounded and gassed during his service overseas, and demobilised in June 1919, holds the Mons Star, and the General Service and Victory Medals.
34, Essex Street, Luton.   4857.

STEELE, T. W., Sapper, Royal Engineers.
Volunteering in September 1914, he embarked for Gallipoli in the following July and was present at the landing at Suvla Bay and the subsequent engagements until the Peninsula was evacuated. Drafted to the Egyptian Expeditionary Force, he served in the Canal zone until 1917, and then was sent to the Palestine front. He served throughout the Battles of Gaza and the advance through Palestine and Syria. He was demobilised in June 1919, and holds the 1914-15 Star, and the General Service and Victory Medals.
48, Albert Road, Luton.   4874.

STEELL, G. P., C.M. Mechanic, Royal Naval Motor Boat Reserve.
He joined in March 1918, and was engaged on patrol and other important duties in the North and Baltic Seas, and in the English Channel. He also rendered valuable services in the workshops, fitting and testing engines. He was discharged in November 1919, and holds the General Service and Victory Medals.
Batterdale, Hatfield.   X716/A.

STEER, H., Private, Bedfordshire Regiment.
Joining in September 1916, he was sent to the Western Front in March 1917, and saw heavy fighting in various sectors and was in action at Arras and Vimy Ridge, where he was killed in action on April 23rd, of the same year. He was entitled to the General Service and Victory Medals.
144, Baker Street, Luton.   4871.

STEFF, H. J., L/Corporal, 3rd Suffolk Regiment.
He joined in February 1917, and in the following September was drafted to the Western Front and saw much service in various sectors. He was wounded at Cambrai and returned to England in January 1918. On recovery he was stationed at home until his demobilisation in September 1919. He holds the General Service and Victory Medals.
9, Chequer Street, Luton.   4858/B.

STEFF, M. H., Lieutenant, R.A.F. (late R.N.A.S.)
Volunteering in September 1914, he was engaged on important patrol duties, and served in the Battle of Jutland in H.M.S. "Inflexible." Later he was transferred to the Mediterranean and patrolled the region of the Ægean Islands, and was sent to Constantinople with the Army of Occupation. He was still serving in 1920, and holds the 1914-15 Star, and the General Service and Victory Medals.
9, Chequer Street, Luton.   4858/A.

STEFF, N. P., R.Q.M.S., Bedfordshire Regiment, and Hertfordshire Regiment.
A serving soldier, he was mobilised on the outbreak of war, and served with his unit on special duties at various stations on the East Coast. Medically unfit he was unable to obtain his transfer overseas, but rendered valuable services until discharged in March 1920.
34, Vicarage Street, Luton.   4905.

STENHOUSE, A., Pte., 3/5th Bedfordshire Regt.
Volunteering in May 1915, he completed his training and served at various stations until proceeding to France in March 1917. He took part in various important engagements and was killed in action at Arras in the following month. He was entitled to the General Service and Victory Medals.
36, Clifton Road, Luton.   4917/C.

STENHOUSE, J., Pte., 1/5th Bedfordshire Regt.
Volunteering at the outbreak of hostilities he embarked for the Dardanelles in the following July. He made the supreme sacrifice, being killed in action during the heavy fighting at the landing at Suvla Bay in August 1915. He was entitled to the 1914-15 Star, and the General Service and Victory Medals.
36, Clifton Road, Luton   4917/B.

STENHOUSE, W., Private, 3/5th Bedfordshire Regiment.
He volunteered in November 1915, and embarked for Egypt four months later and served in the Canal zone for some time. Drafted to the Palestine front he was engaged in many battles and was unfortunately killed in action at Gaza in April 1917. He was entitled to the General Service and Victory Medals.
36, Clifton Road, Luton.   4917/A.

STEVANS, H. C., Private, Royal Fusiliers.
He joined in May 1918, and on completion of his training served at various stations with his unit on important guard and other duties. He did not obtain his transfer overseas before hostilities ceased, but was sent into Germany with the Army of Occupation and was stationed at Cologne. He returned to England in 1919, and was demobilised in January of the following year.
2, Whinbush Grove, Hitchin.   4890/B.

STEVANS, J., Private, R.A.M.C.
Volunteering in March 1915, he was drafted to France later in the same year, and served in the front lines on important ambulance duties during the Battles of Somme, Ypres, Cambrai, Givenchy and Armentières, and was gassed in 1916. He returned to England and was demobilised in April 1919, and holds the 1914-15 Star, and the General Service and Victory Medals.
2, Whinbush Grove, Hitchin.   4890/A.

STEVENS, A., Private, Coldstream Guards.
He joined in April 1918, and at the conclusion of his training was engaged on important guard and other duties at his regimental depôt. He did good work, but was unsuccessful in obtaining his transfer overseas before the cessation of hostilities, and was demobilised in February 1919.
54, Clifford Street, Watford.   X4848.

STEVENS, E., Private, 6th Bedfordshire Regt.
He volunteered in February 1915, and shortly afterwards was sent to France. During his service in this theatre of war he was engaged in much heavy fighting, and was reported missing on August 9th, 1915. He was later presumed to have been killed in action on that date, and was entitled to the 1914-15 Star, and the General Service and Victory Medals.
New Street, Shefford.   Z4865.

STEVENS, E., Wheeler, R.A.S.C.
He volunteered in February 1915, and after his training was engaged on important duties as a wheelwright at various stations with his unit. He did excellent work, but owing to medical unfitness was unable to secure his transfer to a theatre of war, and on account of injuries received in an accident was invalided out of the Service in 1918.
1, New Street, Shefford.   Z4909.

STEVENS, F., Leading Stoker, Royal Navy.
Serving in the Royal Navy in East Indian waters prior to the war, his ship sailed for Ireland at the outbreak of hostilities, and was engaged on important patrol duties. He was later posted to H.M.S. "Fawn," which vessel sunk the German submarine U.8, on March 4th, 1915. He also served in H.M.S. "Renown," and was present at Scapa Flow at the surrender of the German Fleet after the signing of the Armistice. He holds the 1914-15 Star, and the General Service and Victory Medals, and in 1920 was serving in H.M.S. "Cornflower," in the Red Sea.
Compton, Shefford.   Z2021/B.

STEVENS, F. W., Private, 29th Middlesex Regt.
He joined in August 1916, and after his training served with his Battalion on important duties at the depôt where his Regiment was stationed. He did good work, but owing to medical unfitness was unable to obtain his transfer overseas, and was eventually discharged as unfit for further service in December of the same year.
53, New Road, Linslade, Bucks.   4886.

STEVENS, F., Private, Duke of Cornwall's Light Infantry.
Volunteering in December 1914, he was employed on special duties until drafted to France in July 1916. After a short period of active service he was killed in action at Grandecourt on September 16th, 1916. He was entitled to the General Service and Victory Medals. His memory is cherished with pride.
51, Thilehouse Street, Hitchin. 4883.

STEVENS, G., Private, R.A.S.C.
He joined in June 1917, and at the conclusion of his training was engaged with his unit on transport duties. He rendered valuable service, but was unsuccessful in obtaining his transfer to a theatre of war on account of medical unfitness, and was demobilised in October 1919.
Hoo Lane Cottages, Offley. 4882.

STEVENS, H., Private, 2/19th London Regt.
He volunteered in December 1915, and embarked for France four months later, and was in action at the Somme, Arras, Cambrai, and was wounded in March 1918 during the offensive. After receiving protracted hospital treatment he was drafted to Ireland and served there until February 1919. He was then sent to Egypt and later proceeded to Asia Minor where he was engaged on important guard duties. He was demobilised in May 1920, and holds the General Service and Victory Medals.
61, Warwick Road, Luton. 4935.

STEVENS, H. J., Gunner, R.G.A.
Volunteering at the outbreak of war, he was almost immediately drafted to the Western Front. He fought in the Retreat from Mons, and was wounded at Ypres. He was later in action on the Somme, at Arras, Cambrai and St. Quentin, and in many other engagements. After so long a period of service he was demobilised in January 1919, and holds the Mons Star, and the General Service and Victory Medals.
4, Luton Road, Markyate. 4869/A.

STEVENS, H. J., Private, 4th Bedfordshire Regt.
He joined in 1916, and in the same year was drafted to France. He fought in the Battle of the Somme, and in the subsequent engagements at Ypres, Arras, Neuve Chapelle and Cambrai. He subsequently took part in the Retreat and Advance of 1918. He was demobilised in 1919, and holds the General Service and Victory Medals.
Gosmore, Hitchin. 4895.

STEVENS, J., Corporal, R.A.S.C. (M.T.)
He volunteered in October 1915, and was shortly afterwards sent to France. There he drove a caterpillar tractor, and served in many sectors, including those of Cambrai, the Somme, Loos, Lille and Neuve Chapelle. Whilst in England he was engaged on anti-aircraft duties. He was demobilised in August 1919, and holds the General Service and Victory Medals.
Merton Cottage, Woburn Sands. Z4843.

STEVENS, J., Private, 1/5th Bedfordshire Regt.
Volunteering at the outbreak of war, he was drafted overseas in 1915. He was engaged in the fighting at Suvla Bay, and was later transferred to Egypt. He served in the Advance through Palestine, and was in action at Gaza, Haifa, Acre and Damascus. During his service he was twice wounded. Returning to England after the signing of the Armistice, he was demobilised in 1919, and holds the 1914-15 Star, and the General Service and Victory Medals.
66, Church Street, Leighton Buzzard 4887/B.

STEVENS, T., Private, 2nd Bedfordshire Regt.
He volunteered in September 1914. and in the following February proceeded to France. During a long term of service he fought in the great battles of the Western Front, being wounded on the Somme in 1916. Later at Arras in 1917 he was again wounded. After his recovery he again returned to the firing line, and at Cambrai, in the closing campaign of the war. was wounded a third time. He was demobilised in February 1919, and holds the 1914-15 Star, and the General Service and Victory Medals.
54, Regent Street, Leighton Buzzard. 4558/C.

STEVENS, W., Private, South Lancashire Regt.
Volunteering in August 1914, he was almost immediately sent overseas. He fought in many battles on the Western Front, including those of La Bassée, Neuve Chapelle, Loos and the Somme. He was unfortunately killed in action near Passchendaele on August 5th, 1917, and was entitled to the 1914 Star, and the General Service and Victory Medals.
66, Church Street, Leighton Buzzard. 4887/C.

STEVENS, W. A., Air Mechanic, Royal Air Force.
Joining in May 1918, he was shortly afterwards sent to France. He was engaged on special duties, fitting and testing aero engines at the aerodromes, where his Squadron was stationed, and on several occasions served on the Cambrai front. After the cessation of hostilities, he proceeded to Germany with the Army of Occupation and was stationed at Cologne. He holds the General Service and Victory Medals, and was still serving in 1920.
4, Luton Road, Markyate. 4869/B.

STEWARD, A., C.S.M., Bedfordshire Regiment.
He volunteered in September 1914, and after his training served at several Schools of Instruction, being engaged as an Instructor of Musketry. He did excellent work and rendered service of great value, but he was unable to secure his transfer overseas, and was demobilised in February 1919.
18, Aldenham Road, Oxhey. X4908.

STEWART, A., Private, 23rd Royal Fusiliers.
He joined in June 1916, and was shortly afterwards sent overseas. He fought in many sectors of the Western Front, including those of Ypres, the Somme, Arras and Cambrai. He was severely wounded and gassed and after having received hospital treatment, was invalided out of the Service in September 1918. He holds the General Service and Victory Medals.
41, Adelaide Street, St. Albans. X4922.

STILLWELL, A. J., Sapper, 109th Canadian Royal Engineers.
He volunteered in August 1915, and served on important duties until drafted to the Western Front in March 1918. He was present with his unit while operations were in progress on the Somme and the Marne, and at Cambrai. Suffering from ill-health, he was invalided to hospital at Etaples, where he died on February 14th, 1919. He was entitled to the General Service and Victory Medals.
108, Ashburnham Road, Luton. 4913/C.

STILLWELL, H., Sapper, R.E. (Signal Section).
He volunteered in 1914, and in the following year proceeded to the Dardanelles. In this theatre of war he was engaged with his unit on special duties at Suvla Bay and Anzac. In the succeeding year he was transferred to the Western Front where he served at Vimy Ridge, the Somme, Arras, Messines and Cambrai He proceeded to Germany, after the Armistice, with the Army of Occupation, and was stationed at Cologne. He was demobilised in March 1919, and holds the 1914-15 Star, and the General Service and Victory Medals.
108, Ashburnham Road, Luton. 4913/B.

STILLWELL, P., Pte., 2/6th Sherwood Foresters.
He joined in June 1917, and in the following April was sent to France. During his brief service on the Western Front he took part in much heavy fighting and was severely wounded at Kemmel Hill in May 1918. His injuries being so serious as to necessitate the amputation of a leg, he was subsequently invalided out of the Service in August 1919. He holds the General Service and Victory Medals.
108, Ashburnham Road, Luton. 4913/A.

STIMPSON, E., Private, 5th Yorkshire Regt.
Volunteering at the outbreak of war he was later drafted to France. At the outset of his long period of service he fought at Ypres, and was wounded. On recovery he returned to the firing line, and took part in the Battles of Arras, Cambrai, Loos and Lille. He was unfortunately killed in action on the Somme on March 28th, 1918. He was entitled to the 1914 Star, and the General Service and Victory Medals.
Ireland, Shefford. Z4941.

STIMPSON, L., Rifleman, 1st King's Royal Rifle Corps.
He volunteered in November 1914, and in the following March proceeded overseas. He took part in almost continuous fighting until he was unfortunately killed in action at the Battle of Festubert on May 15th, 1915. He was entitled to the 1914-15 Star, and the General Service and Victory Medals.
Wellington Terrace, Luton Road, Toddington. 4915.

STIMPSON, S. A., Rifleman, 15th London Regt. (Civil Service Rifles).
He joined in September 1916, and after his training was sent to the Eastern Front. He served at Salonika and in Egypt, and subsequently taking part in the British advance through Palestine, fought at Gaza and Beersheba. He was unhappily killed in action near Jerusalem on December 8th, 1917. He was entitled to the General Service and Victory Medals.
47, St. Mary's Street, Dunstable. 4931.

STIMPSON, A., L/Corporal, Royal Engineers.
He volunteered in May 1915, and in the following month
was sent to the Dardanelles. Whilst in this theatre of
war he was engaged upon important duties with his unit
at Suvla Bay. Contracting fever, he was invalided home
in 1916. On recovery he was drafted to France, where
he served in the Somme, Lens and Cambrai sectors. He
was demobilised in June 1919, and holds the 1914-15 Star,
and the General Service and Victory Medals.
3, Handley's Yard, Shortmead Street, Biggleswade.
Z4878.

STIMSON, A., Corporal, Royal Field Artillery.
He volunteered in October 1915, and in January of the
following year was sent to Salonika. He was engaged
in the fighting on the Vardar and Doiran fronts, and in
the operations during the crossing of the Struma. He
returned to England after the cessation of hostilities,
and was demobilised in 1919. He holds the 1914-15 Star,
and the General Service and Victory Medals.
Lower Green, Ickleford, Hitchin.
4897.

STIMSON, W. G., Private, Bedfordshire Regt.
Volunteering at the outbreak of war he was shortly
afterwards sent to France. He was engaged in the
fighting on the Marne and the Somme, and at Festubert
and Arras. In 1915 he was badly gassed, and in consequence was invalided to England. On his recovery he
returned to the Western Front and was again in action.
He was demobilised in 1919, and holds the 1914-15 Star,
and the General Service and Victory Medals.
11, Ivel Terrace, Biggleswade.
Z4920.

**STOCK, P. G. (M.M.), Sergeant-Major, Northamp-
tonshire Regiment.**
He joined in August 1916, and three months later embarked for France where he served for three years. During this period he took a prominent part in the Battles
of Albert, Ypres, Arras, the Somme, Cambrai, and was
awarded the Military Medal for conspicuous bravery and
devotion to duty in the Field at Amiens. In addition
he holds the General Service and Victory Medals, and
was demobilised in November 1919.
109, Windmill Road, Luton.
4914.

STOCKER, W., Private, Devonshire Regiment.
Joining in February 1917, he was sent to France in the
same year. In the course of his service on the Western
Front he was engaged on important duties in various
parts of the line, and was in action at Arras, Ypres,
Vimy Ridge, and in other operations until the end of
hostilities. He was demobilised in October 1919, and
holds the General Service and Victory Medals.
12, Banbury Street, Watford.
X4898.

STOCKLEY, E. V., 1st Class Stoker, Royal Navy.
Mobilised on the outbreak of war, he was posted to
H.M.S. "Lancaster," and saw much service aboard that
vessel in the North Sea and other waters. His ship
was engaged on important patrol duties until after the
cessation of hostilities. He was demobilised in June
1919, and holds the 1914-15 Star, and the General Service
and Victory Medals.
18, West Street, Watford.
X4907.

STOCKS, F. G., Pioneer, Royal Engineers.
Joining in 1916, he was drafted overseas in the same
year and saw much service on the Western Front. He
was engaged on important work in connection with the
laying of railway tracts in the Ypres and Arras sectors,
and rendered valuable services until discharged on
account of service in June 1917. He holds the General
Service and Victory Medals.
21, Cardiff Road, Watford.
X4853/A.

STOCKS, F. H., Private, 9th East Surrey Regt.
He joined in October 1916, and was shortly afterwards
drafted overseas. In the course of his service on the
Western Front he took part in the Battles of Arras,
Ypres, Cambrai, and other operations until the cessation
of hostilities. He was demobilised in November 1919,
and holds the General Service and Victory Medals.
21, Cardiff Road, Watford.
X4853/B.

STOKES, A., Driver, Royal Field Artillery.
Volunteering in January 1916, he proceeded to India
in the following year and saw much service there until
drafted to France in September 1918. Whilst in the
Western theatre of war he fought in the Battles of
Ypres and Cambrai, and other important engagements
until the signing of the Armistice. He was then sent to
Ireland and was there engaged on garrison and other
duties, until, returning to England, he was demobilised
in September 1919. He holds the General Service and
Victory Medals.
Northill, near Biggleswade.
Z4926/B.

STOKES, F. J., Gunner, Royal Field Artillery.
Joining in November 1916, he proceeded to France in
the following year. He was engaged with his Battery
in various sectors of the Western Front and fought
in the Battles of Arras, Passchendaele, Cambrai, the
Marne, and the Somme. He returned to England in
1919, and holds the General Service and Victory Medals,
and in 1920 was still serving.
"Moordale," Marsh Road, Leagrave.
4933/B.

**STOKES, H., Private, Bedfordshire Regiment, and
Machine Gun Corps.**
He volunteered in December 1915, and in the following
year was sent to France. There he saw much service
in various parts of the line and was in action on the
Somme, the Marne, and at Ypres, Messines and Cambrai.
After the cessation of fighting he returned home for
demobilisation in March 1919, and holds the General
Service and Victory Medals.
Northill, near Biggleswade.
Z4926/A.

STOKES, H. W., Corporal, R.A.S.C. (E.F.C.)
He joined in September 1916, and was almost immediately sent to the Western Front. During his service
overseas he was engaged on important duties with the
Expeditionary Force canteens in the forward areas, and
was in action at Arras and Armentières, and was wounded.
He did valuable work until the end of the war and
was demobilised in November 1919, and holds the General
Service and Victory Medals.
62, Frederic Street, Luton.
4944/A.

STOKES, J., Corporal, R.A.S.C.
Joining in July 1916, on the conclusion of his training
he was engaged on important duties with his unit.
Acting as Sergeant-Cook he rendered valuable services
but was unable to obtain a transfer to a theatre of
war before the cessation of hostilities, and was demobilised in September 1919.
6, Normanhurst, Grosvenor Road East, St. Albans.
X4850.

STOKES, J., Private, 1st Bedfordshire Regiment.
He volunteered in January 1916, and shortly afterwards
embarked for France. Whilst on the Western Front he
fought in the Battles of the Somme, Beaumont-Hamel,
Arras, Ypres, Cambrai, and in the Retreat and Advance
of 1918. He was taken prisoner at St. Quentin, and
held in captivity in Germany until repatriated after
the signing of the Armistice. He was demobilised
in March 1919, and holds the General Service and
Victory Medals.
10, Alfred Street, Luton.
4936/A.

STOKES, P., Private, 1/5th Bedfordshire Regt.
He joined in September 1916, and in the following
January proceeded to Egypt. Whilst in this theatre
of war he was in action at El Arish, Gaza, Haifa,
Acre, Damascus, Beyrout, and other places during the
fighting in Palestine. Returning to England after the
signing of the Armistice he was demobilised in January
1919, and holds the General Service and Victory Medals.
62, Frederic Street, Luton.
4944/B.

**STOKES, R. (M.M.), L/Cpl., 6th Bedfordshire
Regiment.**
He volunteered in August 1914, and in January of the
following year was despatched to the Western Front.
He was engaged in heavy fighting at Ypres, Loos, Vimy
Ridge, and was awarded the Military Medal for conspicuous bravery and devotion to duty in the Field.
He was reported missing on August 9th, 1916, during
the Somme offensive, and was later presumed to have
been killed in action on that date. He was entitled to
the 1914-15 Star, and the General Service and Victory
Medals.
10, Alfred Street, Luton.
4936/B.

STOKES, R., Private, Northamptonshire Regt.
Joining in May 1918, he was shortly afterwards drafted
overseas. Serving on the Western Front he fought in
several important engagements until severely wounded
in action at St. Quentin. He was sent to hospital in
England and after receiving medical treatment for a
considerable time was invalided out of the Army in
July 1919. He holds the General Service and Victory
Medals.
Lower Caldecote, Biggleswade.
Z4885.

STOKES, S., Private, 6th Northamptonshire Regt.
He joined in March 1916, and two months later embarked
for the Western Front where he saw much service and
fought in several important engagements. He was unfortunately killed in action on the Somme on October
25th, 1916, and was entitled to the General Service
and Victory Medals.
10, Alfred Street, Luton.
4936/C.

STOKES, T., Pte., Loyal North Lancashire Regt.
Volunteering in February 1916, he completed his training and was sent overseas in the following July. Shortly after disembarkation in France he proceeded to the front line trenches and was in almost continuous fighting for two months. He was killed in action near Trones Wood on August 29th, 1916, and was entitled to the General Service and Victory Medals.
"Moordale," Marsh Road, Leagrave. 4933/A.

STOKES, W., Private, 8th Bedfordshire Regt.
He joined in October 1916, and served with his unit until drafted to France in December of the following year. He was engaged on important duties in various parts of the Western Front, and fought in several battles, including those at Cambrai and the Somme. Owing to ill-health he was sent home in March 1918, and was discharged as medically unfit for further service in the following June. He holds the General Service and Victory Medals.
"Moordale," Marsh Road, Leagrave. 4933/C.

STONE, A., Sapper, Royal Engineers.
He volunteered in April 1915, and in the following year was drafted to Egypt. He was engaged on important duties in connection with operations during the advance through Palestine and was present at the Battles of Gaza, Haifa, Acre, Aleppo and Damascus, and was wounded. Returning to England on the conclusion of hostilities, he was demobilised in April 1919, and holds the General Service and Victory Medals.
23, Church Street, St. Albans. X4900.

STONE, A., Sergeant, 2nd Bedfordshire Regt.
Volunteering in September 1914, he was drafted to France in November 1915, and served on the Western Front for nearly four years. During this period he did good work in many bombing raids and amongst other operations fought in the Battles of Vimy Ridge, the Somme, Arras, Ypres and Cambrai. He was demobilised in March 1919, and holds the 1914-15 Star, and the General Service and Victory Medals.
26, Prosperous Row, Dunstable. 4948

STONE, A. R., Rflmn., King's Royal Rifle Corps.
He joined in 1916, and in the same year proceeded to the Western Front. During his service in this theatre of war he was engaged in severe fighting on the Somme at Arras, Cambrai, and other places until the close of hostilities. He was demobilised in September 1919, and holds the General Service and Victory Medals.
6, Heath Terrace, Landridge Road, St. Albans. X4849.

STONE, E., L/Corporal, 2nd Royal Sussex Regt.
Joining in February 1917, he proceeded overseas in the following August and saw much service on the Western Front. He was in action at Arras, Ypres, Cambrai, and during the Retreat of 1918. He holds the General Service and Victory Medals, and was demobilised in July 1919.
70, Plantation Road, Leighton Buzzard. 4856.

STONE, G., Private, 2nd Bedfordshire Regiment.
He volunteered in August 1914, and was drafted to France in the following month. He was in action in the final stages of the Retreat from Mons and in many subsequent engagements, including the Battle of Ypres. He was killed in action in the vicinity of Loos on April 23rd, 1915, and was entitled to the Mons Star, and the General Service and Victory Medals.
Sundon Road, Harlington. 4952/A.

STONE, H. C., Sergeant, 3rd Bedfordshire Regt., and Hertfordshire Regiment.
Volunteering in September 1914, in the following month he proceeded to the Western Front. During his service in this theatre of war he took part in the Battles of the Somme and Ypres and various operations in the Cambrai sector, and was wounded at Beaumont-Hamel on November 13th, 1916. Invalided to hospital in England he was subsequently engaged as an Instructor at various depôts until demobilised in February 1919. He holds the 1914-15 Star, and the General Service and Victory Medals.
68, Tavistock Street, Luton. 4872.

STONE, J. D., Private, 4th Bedfordshire Regt.
He volunteered in January 1915, and was sent overseas in the following July. He saw much service on the Western Front and was engaged in severe fighting on the Somme, at Arras, Ypres and Cambrai, and was wounded in July 1917. He was sent to hospital and on recovery rejoined his Battalion in the Field and was subsequently killed in action near Cambrai on August 27th, 1918. He was entitled to the 1914-15 Star, and the General Service and Victory Medals.
Sundon Road, Harlington. 4952/C.

STONE, L., Gunner, Royal Garrison Artillery.
Joining in March 1918, on attaining military age, he embarked for France in the following August. In the course of his service overseas he was engaged on important duties and took part in the fighting at St. Quentin and Cambrai, during the closing operations of the war. He holds the General Service and Victory Medals, and was demobilised in February 1919.
Sundon Road, Harlington. 4952/B.

STONE, T., Private, R.A.S.C. (M.T.)
He joined in 1916, and in the same year was sent to the Western Front. Whilst in this theatre of war he was engaged on important duties in connection with the transport of ammunition and supplies to the front line trenches during the Battles of the Somme, Arras, Ypres, and other operations. He was discharged on account of service in June 1918, and holds the General Service and Victory Medals.
15, Albert Street, Watford. X4197/B.

STONE, W., Gunner (Signaller), R.F.A.
He joined in July 1918, and proceeded to France shortly afterwards. During his service on the Western Front he was in action at the Battle of Ypres, and in other engagements, and was gassed. He returned to England for demobilisation in January 1919, and holds the General Service and Victory Medals.
23, Wimbourne Road, Luton. 4863.

STONE, W. F., Private, 36th Royal Fusiliers.
Joining in June 1916, he embarked for France in the same month. Whilst on the Western Front he fought in the Battles of the Somme, Arras, Ypres, Vimy Ridge, Messines, Cambrai and Le Cateau, and was wounded. He returned to England for demobilisation in March 1919, and holds the General Service and Victory Medals.
4, Parcels Place, Bucklersbury, Hitchin. 4889.

STONEBRIDGE, W., Private, Bedfordshire Regt.
A serving soldier, he was mobilised on the outbreak of war and shortly afterwards proceeded to France. During his service on the Western Front he was in action in the Battles of the Marne, Festubert and Loos, and was severely wounded at Lens in August 1917. He was sent to hospital in Birmingham and subsequently invalided out of the Service in 1918. He holds the 1914 Star, and the General Service and Victory Medals.
Franklins Row, Potton. Z4924.

STORTON, F. H., Private, Bedfordshire Regt.
Joining in May 1916, he was drafted to the Western Front in the following year. During his service overseas he was in action at Arras, Ypres, Cambrai, and the Somme, and was wounded at Bullecourt. Returning to England he received hospital treatment and was invalided out of the Service in July 1918. He holds the General Service and Victory Medals.
32, St. John's Street, Biggleswade. Z4921/A.

STORTON, W. S., Private, Bedfordshire Regt.
Volunteering in August 1914, he embarked for France in the following February and saw service in various sectors of the Western Front and fought at Arras and Ypres. He was killed in action at Neuve Chapelle on March 10th, 1915, and was entitled to the 1914-15 Star, and the General Service and Victory Medals.
32, St. John's Street, Biggleswade. Z4921/B.

STOTEN, A. G., Gunner, Royal Garrison Artillery.
He enlisted in July 1911, and proceeded to the Western Front shortly after the outbreak of war and served in many parts of the line and was in action in the Battles of the Somme, Albert and Armentières. He was wounded and returned to England, and after receiving hospital treatment was discharged unfit for further service in July 1917. He holds the 1914 Star, and the General Service and Victory Medals.
98, Highbury Road, Luton. 4964.

STOTEN, W., Sergeant, Royal Engineers.
He volunteered in April 1915, and in 1916 was sent to Ireland, where he was engaged on special duties during the Sinn Fein Riots. Drafted to the Western Front in 1917, he fought at Ypres, Cambrai, St. Quentin, and through the German Offensive and subsequent Allied Advance of 1918, and was gassed. He was demobilised in May 1919, and holds the General Service and Victory Medals.
Rookery Farm, Offley, Herts 4896.

STOTEN, W., Rflmn., King's Royal Rifle Corps.
A Territorial, he was mobilised at the outbreak of hostilities, and later sent to France. He served in various parts of the line fighting at the Battles of Arras and Ypres. He returned to England owing to ill-health and after hospital treatment was invalided out of the Service in March 1917. He holds the General Service and Victory Medals.
42, Curzon Road, Luton. 4965.

STOW, A. E., Private, Bedfordshire Regiment, and Sherwood Foresters.
Volunteering in November 1914, he embarked for the Western Front in the following July, and saw much service in various sectors, fighting at Ypres, Hill 60, Givenchy, Arras, the Somme and in the Retreat and Advance of 1918, and was twice wounded. He was demobilised in January 1919, and holds the 1914-15 Star, and the General Service and Victory Medals.
67, Bury Park Road, Luton.   4946.

STOXLEY, H., 1st Air Mechanic, Royal Air Force.
He joined in July 1916, and on completing his training was stationed at various aerodromes on important duties in the carpenter's shop, engaged in the construction of aeroplane parts. He did much good work but was unsuccessful in obtaining his transfer overseas before the signing of the Armistice, and was demobilised in May 1919.
54, Waterside, Kings Langley.   X4956.

STRANGE, A., Private, 7th Bedfordshire Regt.
Volunteering in August 1914, he was drafted to France in May 1915, and was engaged in the fighting at the Battles of Hill 60, Ypres, and many other important engagements. He was killed in action on September 2nd, 1915, and was entitled to the 1914-15 Star, and the General Service and Victory Medals.
7, Dunstable Place, Luton.   4932/B.

STRANGE, A. (Mrs.), Special War Worker.
This lady volunteered her services for work of National importance during the war, and from January 1916 until May 1919, rendered valuable services at the V.A.D. Hospital at Wardown Park, Luton, where she was engaged on important secretarial duties.
206, Dunstable Road, Luton.   4916/A.

STRANGE, A., Special Constable.
He volunteered his services as a special constable during the war and from June 1917 until after the cessation of hostilities rendered valuable services generally assisting the police. He was detailed for special duties during air raids and carried out his work in a most efficient and satisfactory manner.
206, Dunstable Road, Luton.   4916/C.

STRANGE, H. H., Corporal, 2nd Wiltshire Regt.
He volunteered in January 1915, and proceeded overseas five months later. During his service in France he fought in many important engagements, including those of Loos, Vimy Ridge and the Somme, and was killed in action at Flers on October 18th, 1916. He was entitled to the 1914-15 Star, and the General Service and Victory Medals.
7, Dunstable Place, Luton.   4932/A.

STRANGE, R. S., 2nd Lieutenant, 1st Bedfordshire Regiment.
Joining in December 1916, he completed his training and served at various depôts until drafted to France in September 1918. He fought on the Somme, Ypres and Cambrai fronts during the Allied Advance and was killed in action at Le Cateau on October 17th, 1918. He was entitled to the General Service and Victory Medals.
206, Dunstable Road, Luton.   4916/B.

STRAPP, J. J., Private, R.A.S.C.
Joining in March 1917, he proceeded to France on completion of his training and rendered excellent services in transporting supplies to the forward areas. He was present at the Battles of Arras, Ypres, Cambrai, and the Somme, and was demobilised in April 1919. He holds the General Service and Victory Medals.
23, Ramridge Road, Luton.   4859.

STRAPP, P., Private, 2nd Gloucestershire Regt.
He joined in October 1918, and after his training was stationed at various depôts with his unit on guard and other important duties until drafted to India in September 1919. There he served at various garrison towns and was still in the Army in 1920.
36, Vernon Road, Luton.   4861/A.

STRAPP, S., Private, 2nd Gloucestershire Regt.
Joining in July 1916, on conclusion of his training he served at various stations with his unit on guard and other important duties. He was unable to procure his transfer to a theatre of war, but rendered excellent services until demobilised in May 1919.
36, Vernon Road, Luton.   4861/B.

STRATFORD, J., Leading Aircraftsman, R.A.F.
A Territorial, he was mobilised on the outbreak of hostilities, and embarked for France in November 1914. He fought at La Bassée, Béthune and Ypres, and many other engagements, and returned to England in December 1915. He was later transferred to the Royal Air Force, and served at various aerodromes engaged on important duties until demobilised in April 1919. He holds the 1914 Star, and the General Service and Victory Medals.
91, Sotheron Road, Watford.   X4903.

STRATFULL, F. P., L/Corporal, R.A.M.C.
Volunteering in August 1914, he proceeded to France almost immediately and was under fire in the Retreat from Mons, and in the Battles of the Aisne, Arras and Ypres, and did excellent work. In 1917, transferred to Italy, he served in the forward areas in many sectors and was wounded. He returned to England and was demobilised in January 1919, and holds the Mons Star, and the General Service and Victory Medals.
21, Greatham Road, Bushey.   X4854.

STRATTON, A., L/Corporal, 34th London Regt. (Rifles).
Volunteering in August 1914, he was drafted to France two months later and fought in many engagements and was wounded. He rejoined his Battalion on recovery and was again in action until wounded a second time at Ypres in March 1917. He was invalided to England and after protracted hospital treatment was discharged as medically unfit for further service in September 1918. He holds the 1914 Star, and the General Service and Victory Medals.
21, Cavendish Road, St. Albans.   X4899.

STRATTON, A. F., Sapper, R.E. (R.O.D.)
He volunteered in February 1916, and embarked for France three months later and saw considerable service in various parts of the Western Front. He fought in engagements of Arras, the Somme, Thiepval, and throughout the Retreat and Advance of 1918. He was demobilised in June 1919, and holds the General Service and Victory Medals.
54, Frederic Street, Luton.   4855.

STRATTON, F. G., Private, R.A.V.C.
Volunteering in 1915, he was drafted to Egypt later in the same year, and served in the advance through Sinai and Palestine, rendering excellent services in attending to sick and wounded horses at various Veterinary Hospitals. In 1917 he returned to England and was discharged from the Service on account of sickness contracted whilst on service. He holds the 1914-15 Star, and the General Service and Victory Medals.
57, Alexandra Road, St. Albans.   X4852.

STRATTON, S. A., Private, Bedfordshire Regt.
Volunteering in August 1914, he was sent to France later in the same year and fought at La Bassée, Lens, Loos, Ypres, and many other engagements and was wounded. He was later killed in action on January 15th, 1915, and was entitled to the 1914 Star, and the General Service and Victory Medals.
67, Cecil Street, North Watford.   X4928.

STRATTON, W. W., Private, Bedfordshire Regt., and Air Mechanic, Royal Air Force.
Volunteering in August 1914, he completed his training and served at various depôts with his unit. Later, transferred to the Royal Air Force, he rendered valuable services at Rouen and other aerodromes engaged as a fitter of aero-engines. He was demobilised in February 1919, and holds the General Service and Victory Medals.
53, Sopwell Lane, St. Albans.   X4864.

STREET, A., Private, 11th Royal Sussex Regt.
He volunteered in October 1914, and proceeded to France in August 1916, after serving at various stations with his unit, and was engaged in the fighting at Ypres, Arras, and many other engagements. He was reported missing but was later found to have been killed in action at Auchon Villiers on October 21st, 1916, and was entitled to the General Service and Victory Medals.
34, Portland Street, St. Albans.   4962/A.

STREET, C. J., Sapper, Royal Engineers.
Joining in May 1917, he embarked for the Western Front in the following October, and was engaged on important duties in establishing and maintaining lines of communication in the forward areas during engagements at Arras, Ypres, Passchendaele, Vimy Ridge, the Somme, and throughout the German Offensive and Allied Advance of 1918. He was demobilised in November 1919, and holds the General Service and Victory Medals.
34, Portland Street, St. Albans.   4962/B.

STREET, E. (Miss), Member, W.R.A.F.

She joined in 1918, and served at Henlow aerodrome, engaged on important duties inspecting the component parts of aeroplanes, work demanding a high degree of technical knowledge and skill. She rendered valuable services throughout, and was demobilised in 1919.
6, Back Street, Biggleswade. 1253/B, 1254/B.

STREET, F. G , Private, 2nd Norfolk Regiment.

He joined in May 1918, and on conclusion of his training served at various stations until drafted to India in September 1919. Later he proceeded to Burma and was engaged on guard and other important duties. He was still serving in 1920.
45, Cowfair Lands, Biggleswade. Z4925/B.

STREET, G. H., Private, Essex Regiment.

Joining in June 1916, he completed his training and served at various depôts on important coastal defence duties. He was unable to obtain his transfer overseas owing to ill-health, and died on July 4th, 1918, through an illness contracted whilst on service.
117, Ridge Street. Callowland, Wat ord. X4927.

STREET, H., Private, Queen's (Royal West Surrey Regiment).

He joined in 1916, and later was sent to the Western Front, where he took part in many important engagements. Owing to ill-health he was admitted into hospital and on recovery he returned to the front lines and after a further period of service was invalided to England and again received hospital treatment. He was discharged as medically unfit for further service in June 1919, and holds the General Service and Victory Medals.
Lower Caldecote, Biggleswade. Z4877.

STREET, J., Sergeant, Bedfordshire Regiment.

A Reservist, he was mobilised at the commencement of hostilities, and was stationed at various depôts acting as Instructor until 1917. Drafted to France, he was in action at Arras and Bullecourt, and other engagements, and was sent to Italy later in the same year and fought on the Piave front. Returning to the Western Front in 1918, he was in action throughout the Retreat and Advance, and was demobilised in February 1919. He holds the General Service and Victory Medals.
61, Cemetery Street, Biggleswade. Z4923.

STREET, W., Private, 2nd Bedfordshire Regt., and Machine Gun Corps.

Volunteering in December 1914, he was sent overseas in September of the following year and saw much service in various parts of the Western Front, fighting at Givenchy, Arras, the Somme, and many other places, and was gassed. On recovery he was transferred to the Labour Corps, and rendered valuable services until demobilised in March 1919. He holds the 1914-15 Star, and the General Service and Victory Medals.
45, Cowfair Lands, Biggleswade. Z4925/A.

STRIDE, P. W., Private, 3rd Middlesex Regiment.

He joined in June 1916, and in the following October was sent to Salonika. He took part in the operations at Monastir in December of that year, and the subsequent engagements on the Doiran and Vardar fronts, and remained in this theatre of war until after the Armistice. He returned home and was demobilised in August 1919, and holds the General Service and Victory Medals.
8, Lower Dagnall Street, St. Albans. X4846.

STRINGER, G. (M.M.), Pte., Bedfordshire Regt.

He volunteered in 1914, and in the following year was sent to France. He fought at Ypres, Cambrai, the Somme and in the Retreat and the subsequent Allied Advance of 1918, and was wounded. He was awarded the Military Medal for bravery and devotion to duty in the Field. He also holds the 1914-15 Star, and the General Service and Victory Medals, and was demobilised in March 1919.
White's Cottages, Westoning. Ampthill 4911

STRINGER, J. W., L/Corporal, Queen's (Royal West Surrey Regiment), and Labour Corps.

He volunteered in 1914, and in October of the following year was sent to Salonika. During his service in this theatre of war he was engaged in the fighting on the Doiran and Struma fronts. He returned to England after the cessation of hostilities and was demobilised in 1919, and holds the 1914-15 Star, and the General Service and Victory Medals.
Church Street. Westoning, Ampthill. 4875.

STRINGER, R. J., Gunner, Royal Field Artillery.

He joined in 1916, and at the conclusion of his training was engaged on important duties with his Battery at various stations. He did very good work but owing to medical unfitness was unable to secure his transfer overseas, and was demobilised in 1919.
Westoning, Ampthill. 4879.

STRINGER, S. T., Private, 1st Norfolk Regiment.

He joined in April 1916, and in the following August was sent to France. During his service on the Western Front he fought in many battles, including those of Ypres, Passchendaele, Givenchy, Guillemont, Neuve Chapelle, and was severely wounded in November 1917. He was invalided home, and on recovery served on home duties until demobilised in January 1919. He holds the General Service and Victory Medals.
40, Beech Road, Luton. 4957.

STRONELL, A. W., Trumpeter, R.F.A.

He volunteered in April 1915, at the age of fifteen years, and was shortly afterwards sent to Ireland. He was engaged with his Battery at Dublin and the Curragh on important duties until his age was discovered, and he was in consequence discharged from the Service in May 1917.
45a, Buxton Road, Luton. 4868.

STRONNELL, W. B., Private, Labour Corps.

Joining in 1917, he was shortly afterwards drafted to France. Whilst on the Western Front he served on special duties in connection with road and railway construction, and was constantly, under shell fire. He was wounded near Ypres in August 1918, and was invalided home. On recovery he was engaged on home duties with his unit until demobilised in February 1919. He holds the General Service and Victory Medals.
Stopsley Green, Stopsley. 4955.

STRUDWICK, H., Gnr., Royal Marine Artillery.

He joined in November 1917, and at the conclusion of his training proceeded overseas after the cessation of hostilities. He was engaged with his Battery on important work in Egypt, Turkey and Russia. In 1920 he was serving in H.M.S. "Marlborough."
51, Wycombe Road, Marlow, Bucks. X4929.

STUART, W., Private, 1st Dorsetshire Regiment.

He volunteered in May 1915, and was later sent to France. During his service on the Western Front he fought in many engagements, including those at Ypres II and St. Quentin, and was wounded. He returned to England after the cessation of hostilities and was demobilised in February 1919. He holds the General Service and Victory Medals.
Upper Woodside, near Luton. 4904.

STUBBING, P. W., Sergeant, Duke of Cornwall's Light Infantry.

He joined in May 1916, and in the following September was sent to France. During his service in this theatre of war he fought at Ypres, the Somme and Arras, and was wounded in September 1917. He was invalided home two months later and on recovery was engaged on special clerical duties at Whitehall until February 1919. He was demobilised in the following month and holds the General Service and Victory Medals.
125, Queen's Road, Watford. X4949/B.

STUBBING, R. J., Private, 1st Australian Light Infantry.

He volunteered in July 1915, and in the following November was sent to Egypt, where he served for a time. In March 1916, he proceeded to France and was engaged in the fighting at Albert, Pozières, Doullens, Poperinghe, and Ypres. He was killed in action at Bullecourt on May 6th, 1917, and was entitled to the 1914-15 Star, and the General Service and Victory Medals.
125, Queen's Road, Watford. X4949/A.

STUDMAN, A. M., L/Corporal, 18th King's Royal Rifle Corps.

He joined in September 1916, and was sent to France in the following March. Whilst on the Western Front he was engaged in the fighting at Ypres and on the Somme, and was wounded at Cambrai in March 1918. He later took part in the Allied Advance into Germany, and returned home after the cessation of hostilities. He was demobilised in January 1919, and holds the General Service and Victory Medals.
5, Prospect Place, Welwyn. 4901.

STUDMAN, W., Private, Labour Corps.

He joined in June 1916, and in the succeeding month was sent to France. During his service in this theatre of war he was employed on special mining duties with the Royal Engineers in the Ypres, Somme and Arras sectors and was constantly under shell fire. He returned to England after the signing of the Armistice, and was demobilised in February 1919, and holds the General Service and Victory Medals
6, Collin Road, Luton. 4945.

STUDMAN, A. V., Rifleman, 15th London Regt. (Civil Service Rifles).

He volunteered in November 1915, and after completing his training, served with his Battalion at various stations on important duties. He did good work, but owing to medical unfitness was unable to secure his transfer overseas, and was subsequently invalided out of the Service in March 1916.

9, Cornwall Road, Harpenden.   4943.

STURGESS, A., Private, Norfolk Regiment.

Joining in April 1916, he proceeded overseas in the following July. Whilst on the Western Front he fought at the Battle of the Somme, and was wounded in September 1916. He was invalided home and after receiving hospital treatment served on home duties at various stations until demobilised in January 1919. He holds the General Service and Victory Medals.

Sharpenhoe Road, Barton, Beds.   4893.

STURGESS, B., Private, R.A.S.C.

He joined in November 1916, and was engaged on special duties as a baker with his unit at various home stations. He was unable to obtain his transfer to a theatre of war until after the signing of the Armistice. He was then sent to Germany with the Army of Occupation and served at Cologne, until demobilised in December 1919, after returning to England.

High Street, Barton, Ampthill.   4919.

STURGESS, G., Sergeant, Bedfordshire Regiment.

He volunteered in 1915, and in the folowing year proceeded overseas. Whilst on the Western Front he fought in many battl-s, including those of Arras, Cambrai, St. Quentin, the Somme, and in the Allied Advance into Germany. He returned home after the cessation of hostilities and was demobilised in January 1919, and holds the General Service and Victory Medals.

Manor Road, Barton, Beds.   4958.

STURMAN, E., Private, Royal Sussex Regiment.

He joined in March 1918, and after completing his training served with his Battalion on important duties at various stations. He did good work, but was unable to secure his transfer overseas before the cessation of hostilities. He then proceeded to Germany with the Army of Occupation and was stationed at Cologne until March 1920, when he returned to England. He was still serving in 1920.

Downsview, Borough Road, Dunstable.   2135/A.

STURMAN, W., Private, Essex Regiment.

Volunteering in March 1915, he was drafted to Egypt in the following August. He took part in the British advance through Palestine, and was wounded at the Battle of Gaza in 1917. He later rejoined his Battalion and was present at the Occupation of Jerusalem. Returning to England after the cessation of hostilities, he was demobilised in February 1919, and holds the General Service and Victory Medals.

Stuart Street, Dunstable.   922/B.

STURTIVANT, G. J., Private, Royal Marine Light Infantry.

He was mobilised at the outbreak of war, and in July 1915, was sent to the Dardanelles. He was engaged in the fighting at the landing at Suvla Bay and the subsequent engagements at Anzac, and other places until the evacuation of that Peninsula. He was afterwards stationed at Corfu on special duties, and returned to England in 1919, and was demobilised in October of that year. He holds the 1914-15 Star, and the General Service and Victory Medals.

3, Etna Road, St. Albans.   4847/A.

STYGALL, G. A., Sergeant, 2nd Bedfordshire V.T.C.

He voluntecred in January 1915, and at the conclusion of his training was engaged on special duties with his Battalion at Luton. He did good work guarding munition works, railways and bridges until after the close of the war, and was discharged in October 1919.

40, Lyndhurst Road, Luton.   4937/A.

STYGALL, V. E., Private, 4th Bedfordshire Regt.

He volunteered in October 1915, and was sent to France in May 1917. Whilst on the Western Front he took part in the engagements at Passchendaele, Ypres and Cambrai. Owing to ill-health he was invalided to England and after receiving hospital treatment served on important home duties until demobilised in February 1919. He holds the General Service and Victory Medals.

40, Lyndhürst Road, Luton.   4937/B.

STYGALL, G. M., Private, East Surrey Regiment.

He joined in February 1917, and three months later proceeded overseas. During his service on the Western Front he was engaged with his regiment in the fighting in various sectors and was unfortunately killed in action in the vicinity of Ypres in October 1917. He was entitled to the General Service and Victory Medals.

40, Lyndhurst Road, Luton.   4937/C.

SUCKLING, J., Private, Bedfordshire Regiment.

Volunteering at the outbreak of war he was sent to France in September 1914. He fought in many engagements on the Western Front, and was wounded at Ypres in 1915. He received treatment at the Base hospital and was later drafted to Egypt. He took part in the advance through Palestine and in the fighting at Gaza. He afterwards proceeded to India where he was stationed until 1919. He was a first-class signaller, and throughout his service was engaged on signalling duties. He returned to England and was demobilised in July of that year, and holds the 1914 Star, and the General Service and Victory Medals.

28, Spring Place, Luton.   4974.

SULLIVAN, J., Air Mechanic, Royal Air Force.

He joined in 1916, and at the conclusion of his training served with his Squadron at Farnborough on important duties, which called for a high degree of technical skill. He did excellent work as a carpenter but was unable to obtain his transfer overseas on account of medical unfitness, and was demobilised in January 1919.

41, Ashby Road, North Watford.   X4969.

SUMMERFIELD, B., Driver, R.A.S.C.

He volunteered in April 1915, and in November of the same year was sent to Egypt. He served at Alexandria on important duties with his unit in connection with transport, and did very good work. He suffered from malaria and was invalided home in 1917, and after spending some time in hospital was eventually discharged unfit for further service in October 1917. He holds the 1914-15 Star, and the General Service and Victory Medals.

Campton Turn, Shefford.   Z4979.

SUMMERFIELD, W., Private, 8th Bedfordshire Regiment.

He volunteered in January 1915, and in February of the following year he was drafted overseas. He was engaged in various sectors of the Western Front and was wounded on the Somme in May 1916. After receiving medical treatment he returned to the firing line and fought at Vimy Ridge, Ypres and Cambrai. He was demobilised in March 1919, and holds the General Service and Victory Medals.

"The Knoll," Maulden, Beds.   4976.

SUMMERFIELD, W. J., Private, 5th Bedfordshire Regiment.

He volunteered in January 1915, and after his training served at many stations on important duties with his Battalion. He did good work but was unable to obtain his transfer overseas owing to medical unfitness, and in consequence was discharged in July 1915.

Ampthill Road, Maulden, Beds.   4977.

SUMMERFIELD, W. J. (D.C.M.), Sergeant-Major, 1st Bedfordshire Regiment.

He was serving at the outbreak of war, and was mobilised and shortly afterwards sent to France. He fought in the Retreat from Mons, and the subsequent Battles of the Marne and La Bassée. In April 1915, he was awarded the Distinguished Conduct Medal for conspicuous bravery and devotion to duty in the Field at Hill 60. He was later killed near Oppy Wood on June 28th, 1917, whilst leading his men into action. He was entitled to the Mons Star, and the General Service and Victory Medals.

Wilshampstead, Beds.   Z4978/A.

SUMMERLIN, A., Sapper, Royal Engineers.

He joined in March 1918, on attaining military age, and after training served with his unit at various stations He was unable to obtain a transfer overseas before the cessation of hostilities, but after the Armistice was sent with the Army of Occupation into Germany, where he remained until his return to England for demobilisation in October 1919.

12, Dunstable Road, Luton.   4972/A.

SUMMERLIN, G., Private, 7th Bedfordshire Regt.

He volunteered in June 1915, and in the same year was drafted overseas. He saw much service on the Western Front and took part in several important engagements and was reported missing on May 3rd, 1917. He was later presumed to have been killed in action on that date, and was entitled to the 1914-15 Star, and the General Service and Victory Medals.

9, Dunstable Place, Luton.   4973.

SUMMERLIN, A., Private, Machine Gun Corps.
He volunteered in 1915, and in the following year was sent to France, where he served for three years. During this period he fought in many important engagements, including the Battles of the Somme, Arras, Ypres and Cambrai, and was wounded. He was demobilised in January 1919, and holds the General Service and Victory Medals.
12, Dunstable Place, Luton. 4972/C.

SUMMERLIN, C., Private, 3/5th Bedfordshire Regiment.
Volunteering in 1915, he embarked for France in the same year and served with his unit in various parts of the British front. He was in action in several important engagements, including those on the Somme, at Ypres, and Cambrai, and was twice wounded. Invalided home he was discharged as medically unfit for further service in December 1918, and holds the 1914-15 Star, and the General Service and Victory Medals.
12, Dunstable Place, Luton. 4972/B.

SURRIDGE, A. J., Private, Essex Regiment.
He was mobilised on the outbreak of war and was almost immediately sent to France. He fought in the Retreat from Mons, and in the Battles of Ypres, Cambrai and the Somme, and was gassed and wounded. Returning to England after the conclusion of hostilities, he was demobilised in October 1919, and holds the Mons Star, and the General Service and Victory Medals.
254, Chester Road, Watford. X4975.

SUSSEX, J., Private, 17th Royal Fusiliers.
He joined in February 1917, and in the following January was despatched to the Western Front. He was in action at the second Battle of the Somme, and during the German Offensive was wounded in the vicinity of Cambrai in 1918. Rejoining his unit on recovery he served overseas until after the close of the war. He was demobilised in February 1920, and holds the General Service and Victory Medals.
88, Edward Street, Dunstable. 4967.

SUTTERBY, W. F., Pte., 1st Hertfordshire Regt.
He volunteered in 1915, and in November of the same year was sent to France. He fought in the Battles of Ypres, the Somme, Béthune and Arras, and was wounded in 1917. Invalided to hospital at Woolwich, he was afterwards engaged on home service duties until demobilised in May 1919. He holds the 1914-15 Star, and the General Service and Victory Medals.
5, Salisbury Square, Hatfield. X4971.

SUTTON, A. G., Private, Labour Corps.
He joined in March 1917, and in the same year proceeded to the Western Front. There he was engaged on trench digging and other duties in the forward areas in connection with operations. He was also employed in guarding German prisoners. He returned to England after the Armistice and was demobilised in September 1919, and holds the General Service and Victory Medals.
69, Elfrida Road, Watford. X4970.

SUTTON, W. S., 1st Class Stoker, Royal Navy.
He volunteered in June 1915, and was posted to H.M.S. "Abdiel," which vessel was engaged on mine-laying and other duties in the North Sea. His ship was in action at the Battle of Jutland and was employed on special duties at Scapa Flow. He holds the 1914-15 Star, and the General Service and Victory Medals, and was demobilised in May 1919.
2, Woodman's Yard, Watford. X4968.

SWAFFER, C. R., Private, 8th Canadian Infantry.
He volunteered in August 1914, and in the same year embarked for France, where he took part in the Battle of Ypres, and in several other important engagements. He was gassed near Arras and sent to hospital in England, and after receiving medical treatment was invalided out of the Army in May 1916. He holds the 1914 Star, and the General Service and Victory Medals.
Weymouth Street, Apsley End. X4992.

SWAIN, A., Sapper, Royal Engineers.
He joined in March 1916, and was later drafted overseas. Serving in various sectors of the Western Front he was engaged on important duties in connection with operations and was present at the Battles of Arras, Cambrai, and other operations until the close of the war. He was demobilised in April 1919, and holds the General Service and Victory Medals.
Breachwood Green, near Welwyn. 4989/B.

SWAIN, A., Private, R.A.S.C.
He volunteered in August 1915, and after completing his training was engaged on important transport duties at various stations. He did excellent work but was unable to obtain a transfer overseas on account of medical unfitness, and was discharged on account of service in 1916. He saw much service in the South African War, and holds medals for that campaign.
44, Clifford Street, Watford. X4988.

SWAIN, A., Private, East Surrey Regiment.
Joining in October 1917, in the following March he proceeded to the Western Front and served there for nearly a year. During this period he fought in several engagements, and was wounded in action on the Somme during the Offensive of 1918, and sent to hospital. He returned to England for demobilisation in March 1919, and holds the General Service and Victory Medals.
17, Hillside Road, Luton. 4982/A.

SWAIN, A. G., 1st Class Boy, Royal Navy.
He volunteered in December 1915, and was posted to H.M.S. "Genista," which vessel was engaged on patrol duties in the North Sea and other waters. He lost his life on October 23rd, 1916, when his ship was torpedoed and sunk by a German submarine in the Irish Channel, and was entitled to the General Service and Victory Medals.
30, Arthur Street, Luton. 4991/A.

SWAIN, C. E., L/Cpl., Loyal North Lancashire Regiment.
He joined in 1916, and in the same year was drafted to France, where he saw much service. He was in action in several important engagements, including the Battles of the Somme, Arras and Cambrai, and was severely wounded. In consequence of his injuries one of his arms had to amputated and on recovery he was invalided out of the Army in 1918. He was entitled to the General Service and Victory Medals.
The Folly, Wheathampstead. 4995.

SWAIN, C. H., 2nd Corporal, Royal Engineers.
He volunteered in October 1914, and in the following year was drafted overseas. Serving on the Western Front he was engaged on important duties in connection with the railways in the forward areas, and was present at the Battles of Arras, Albert, Cambrai and the Somme. He returned home for demobilisation in February 1919, and holds the 1914-15 Star, and the General Service and Victory Medals.
Station Road, Flitwick. 4994.

SWAIN, D. O., Private, R.A.M.C. (T.)
Volunteering in October 1914, he proceeded to the Western Front shortly afterwards and served there for four years. He did excellent work with the Field Ambulance at Ypres, Festubert, Loos, Albert, Arras, Cambrai and the Somme, and was gassed. He holds the 1914-15 Star, and the General Service and Victory Medals, and was demobilised in March 1919.
95, Whinbush Road, Hitchin. 5002.

SWAIN, E., Rifleman, The Cameronians (Scottish Rifles).
He joined in April 1916, and on completing his training was engaged on important duties with his unit. He rendered valuable services but was unable to obtain a transfer to a theatre of war before the cessation of hostilities, and was demobilised in July 1919.
Breachwood Green, near Welwyn. 4989/A.

SWAIN, F., Sapper, 87th Field Company, R.E.
He volunteered in May 1915, and served with his unit at home until sent to France in April 1917. Whilst on the Western Front he was engaged on important duties in forward areas in various sectors and was present at Haveluy and Villers-Bretonneux and other engagements. Demobilised in February 1919, he holds the General Service and Victory Medals.
35, Boyle Street, Luton. 4999.

SWAIN, F., Private, Middlesex Regiment.
Volunteering in March 1915, in the following year he proceeded overseas. He saw much service in France and was engaged on special duties as a sniper and was wounded. Invalided home, he rejoined his Battalion on recovery and took part in heavy fighting in the Albert and Arras sectors and was again wounded. He was demobilised in January 1919, and holds the General Service and Victory Medals.
50, Grove Road, Luton. 4985.

SWAIN, J., Gunner, Royal Field Artillery.
He volunteered in August 1914, and in the following January was drafted to Mesopotamia, where he served for two years. During this period he was in action in several engagements, including the capture of Amara and the Battles of Kut and Kut-el-Amara. In 1917 he was sent to France and fought at Arras, Ypres, Cambrai, and other places, until the termination of hostilities. He was demobilised in March 1919, and holds the 1914-15 Star, and the General Service and Victory Medals.
6, Baker Street, Leighton Buzzard. 4993.

SWAIN, J., L/Corporal, Middlesex Regiment, and Labour Corps

Volunteering in 1915, he was engaged on important duties with his unit until sent to the Western Front in January 1918. He did valuable work in the Battles of Ypres, the Somme, and in other operations during the final stages of the war. Returning to England, he was demobilised in March 1919, and holds the General Service and Victory Medals.

17, Hillside Road, Luton.   4982/C.

SWAIN, J. W., Private, Northamptonshire Regt.

He joined in August 1916, and two months later proceeded to the Western Front where he saw much service. He was wounded in the course of operations and rejoining his Battalion after recovery was taken prisoner on May 27th, 1918, during the German Offensive. Repatriated in January 1919, he died on September 18th of that year from the effects of privation and ill-treatment whilst a prisoner of war in Germany. He was entitled to the General Service and Victory Medals.

17, Hillside Road, Luton.   4982/B.

SWAIN, R. J., Private, 11th Essex Regiment.

Joining in August 1916, in the following December he embarked for France. Whilst in this theatre of war he was engaged in operations in various sectors and saw much heavy fighting. He was killed in action near Cambrai on November 30th 1917, and was entitled to the General Service and Victory Medals.

"The Cricketers' Arms," Caddington, Beds.   4990.

SWAIN, T. J., Private, Grenadier Guards.

Volunteering in August 1914, he was sent to France two months later and was engaged in the fighting at La Bassée and the subsequent engagements of Hill 60, Ypres, Loos and the Somme Offensive, during which he was killed in action on September 10th, 1916. He was entitled to the 1914 Star, and the General Service and Victory Medals.

30, Arthur Street, Luton.   4991/C.

SWAIN, W. J., Private, 1/5th Bedfordshire Regt.

He volunteered in May 1915, and was drafted overseas in the following December. Sent to Egypt, he took part in operations in the Canal zone and in 1917 fought at Gaza, Haifa, Mejdel, Acre, Beyrout, and other places during the British Advance through Palestine. Returning home on the conclusion of hostilities, he was demobilised in July 1919, and holds the 1914-15 Star, and the General Service and Victory Medals.

30, Arthur Street, Luton.   4991/B.

SWAIN, W. R., Private, 1/5th Bedfordshire Regt.

Volunteering in May 1915, he embarked for Egypt in the following January and did good work in the Lewis Gun section of his company. He was in action at Gaza, and several other important engagements during General Allenby's campaign in Palestine and served there until sent home for demobilisation in June 1919. He holds the General Service and Victory Medals.

30, Arthur Street, Luton.   5001.

SWALES, F., Corporal, Royal Army Cyclist Corps, and 8th Bedfordshire Regiment.

Volunteering in August 1914, he embarked for the Dardanelles in April of the following year, and took part in the first landing at Gallipoli, and in the subsequent fighting until the evacuation of the Peninsula. In January 1916, he proceeded to Egypt and served throughout the Advance in Sinai, Palestine and Syria He was demobilised in August 1919, and holds the 1914-15 Star, and the General Service and Victory Medals, also the Long Service and Good Conduct Medal.

229, High Town Road, Luton.   5000.

SWALLOW, A., L/Corporal, R.A.S.C.

Volunteering in August 1914, he served at various stations on completing his training, and was drafted to the Western Front in 1916, and fought in many important engagements, including those at Ypres, the Somme, Cambrai, and throughout the Retreat and Advance of 1918, and was wounded. He was demobilised in January 1919, and holds the General Service and Victory Medals.

8, Batford Road, Batford, Harpenden.   4996.

SWAN, A. C., Corporal, R.A.M.C.

He volunteered in June 1915, and proceeded to France in October of the following year and served in the forward areas during the fighting at Beaumont-Hamel, Vimy Ridge, Messines and Passchendaele, rendering valuable services attending the wounded under fire in the Field. He was demobilised in June 1919, and holds the General Service and Victory Medals.

119, Sandringham Road, Watford.   X4981.

SWAN, A. J., Private, East Surrey Regiment.

He joined in 1918, and was sent to the Western Front in August of the same year and took part in the fighting in the Retreat of 1918, and was in action on the Somme front and was wounded. He returned to England and after hospital treatment served at various stations until demobilised in September 1919, and holds the General Service and Victory Medals.

70, Norfolk Road, Rickmansworth, Herts.   X4986/B.

SWAN, C. W., Private, 2nd Royal Fusiliers.

A serving soldier, he was mobilised at the commencement of hostilities, and sent to the Dardanelles in the following year. Here he was engaged in heavy fighting until the evacuation of the Peninsula and was twice wounded. He returned to England and was subsequently discharged as medically unfit for further service in 1916. He holds the 1914-15 Star, and the General Service and Victory Medals.

80, Harwood Road, Watford.   X4984/A.

SWAN, E. J., Corporal, 1st Hertfordshire Regt.

He volunteered in September 1914, and embarked for the Western Front in the following year. He fought at Ypres, the Somme, Cambrai, Arras and throughout the Retreat and Advance of 1918, and was twice wounded. He returned to England and was demobilised in 1919, and holds the 1914-15 Star, and the General Service and Victory Medals.

80, Harwood Road, Watford.   X4984/B.

SWAN, H., Private, Royal Scots Fusiliers.

Volunteering in November 1914, he was drafted to France later and served in many sectors, fighting at Arras, and in many other important engagements. Transferred to Egypt, he was in action in many battles on the Palestine front, during the advance through the Holy Land. He returned to England and was demobilised in July 1919, and holds the 1914-15 Star, and the General Service and Victory Medals.

Leavesden Green, near Watford.   X3451/B.

SWAN, H., Private, 7th Bedfordshire Regiment.

He joined in 1917, and embarked for the Western Front later in the same year, and saw considerable fighting in various sectors and was engaged in the Battles of the Somme, Arras and Cambrai, and was wounded in the German Offensive of 1918. After receiving hospital treatment he was invalided out of the Service in August 1918, and holds the General Service and Victory Medals.

70, Norfolk Road, Rickmansworth.   X4986/A.

SWAN, L., L/Corporal, Northamptonshire Regt.

Volunteering in August 1914, he was drafted to France in the following month and was in action at La Bassée, Festubert, Ypres, the Somme, and in the Retreat of 1918. He was wounded three times during his service, at Ypres in 1915, on the Somme in 1916, and in April 1918 during the German Offensive. He was demobilised in January 1919, and holds the 1914 Star, and the General Service and Victory Medals.

5, Lammas Walk, Leighton Buzzard.   4998.

SWAN, R., Private, Highland Light Infantry.

Volunteering in September 1915, he proceeded overseas in the following year and was engaged in various sectors of the Western Front and fought in many important engagements. He was reported missing at the Battle of Vimy Ridge on June 9th, 1918, and later was presumed to have been killed in action on that date. He was entitled to the General Service and Victory Medals.

Leavesden Green, near Watford.   X3451/C.

SWANNELL, L., Sapper, Royal Engineers.

He volunteered in 1914, and was sent to Mesopotamia in 1915, and served throughout the campaign in that theatre of war, engaged on important duties connected with operations. He served in the forward areas and was present at many important engagements. Returning to England he was demobilised in 1919, and holds the 1914-15 Star, and the General Service and Victory Medals.

Littleworth, Wing, Leighton Buzzard.   4380/A.

SWEETING, H., Private, 8th Bedfordshire Regt.

He volunteered in September 1914, and was drafted to the Western Front in the following August and saw considerable service in many parts of the line and was in action at Loos. He was gassed and subsequently died from the effects of gas poisoning on May 26th, 1918, and was entitled to the 1914-15 Star, and the General Service and Victory Medals.

2, Liverpool Road, Watford.   X4997/A.

SWEETING, E., Private, 4th Bedfordshire Regt.
Volunteering in October 1914, he embarked for France in the following July and during his service overseas fought in many important engagements. He was killed in action in the Ypres salient on May 5th, 1918, and was entitled to the 1914-15 Star, and the General Service and Victory Medals.
2, Liverpool Road, Watford. X4997/C.

SWEETING, H., Pte., Royal Army Cyclist Corps.
He joined in June 1916, and on completion of his training was stationed at various depôts with his unit, engaged on guard and other important duties. Medically unfit, he was unable to obtain his transfer overseas, and was invalided out of the Service three months after he joined the Colours.
11, Sydney Road, Watford. X4987.

SWEETING, J. G., Pte., 6th Bedfordshire Regt.
He volunteered in August 1914, and embarked for France in July of the following year, and was in action in many important engagements. In the British Offensive on the Somme in August 1916, he was so severely wounded that it was necessary to amputate one of his legs, and after a protracted course of hospital treatment he was invalided out of the Service in September 1917, and holds the 1914-15 Star, and the General Service and Victory Medals.
2, Liverpool Road, Watford. X4997/B.

SWEETMAN, J. A., Sapper, Royal Engineers.
Volunteering in October 1915, he proceeded to the Western Front in the following September and was present at the fighting at Loupart Wood, Festubert and the Somme, engaged on important duties connected with operations. He was wounded and returned to England in December 1917, and on recovery served at various stations until demobilised in February 1919. He holds the General Service and Victory Medals.
21, Cobden Street, Luton. 4983.

SYGROVE, H. H., Shoeing Smith, R.A.V.C.
Volunteering in August 1914, he was sent to Egypt in the following year and served for two years in the Canal zone at various Veterinary hospitals. In 1917, drafted to the Palestine front, he rendered valuable services in attending to sick and wounded horses, and was present at the Battles of Gaza and throughout the advance into Syria. He returned to England and was demobilised in May 1919, and holds the 1914-15 Star, and the General Service and Victory Medals.
Salisbury Road, Harpenden. 2430/B.

SYGROVE, J. H., Gunner, Royal Field Artillery.
Volunteering in March 1915, he was sent to the Western Front in the same year, and fought in various sectors until 1916, when he was transferred to Mesopotamia and served through many engagements in that theatre of war, including those at Kut and Baghdad. Returning to France in 1917, he was in action at Cambrai, the Somme and throughout the Retreat and Advance of 1918, and was wounded and suffered from shell-shock. He was demobilised in March 1919, and holds the 1914-15 Star, and the General Service and Victory Medals.
2, Heath Road, Harpenden. 4963/A.

SYKES, E., Painter 1st Class, Royal Navy.
He joined the Service in May 1916, and was posted to H.M.S. " Superb," which ship was engaged on patrol duties in the North and Irish Seas, and in escorting convoys of troops and supplies to Egypt and Russia. He rendered excellent services throughout, and was demobilised in May 1919, and holds the General Service and Victory Medals.
31, Alama Road, Hemel Hempstead. X5003.

SYMONDS, A. E., Sergeant, Royal Field Artillery.
He enlisted in February 1909, and on the outbreak of hostilities proceeded to France where he was in action during the Retreat from Mons and the Battles of the Aisne, the Marne, Armentières, Ypres, Arras, and the Somme. Transferred to Egypt, he saw considerable service there, and was twice wounded. He was invalided to England and after receiving hospital treatment was invalided out of the Service in March 1919. He holds the Mons Star, and the General Service and Victory Medals.
81, Ash Road, Luton. 5006.

SYMONDS, P., Private, Manchester Regiment.
He volunteered in February 1916, and embarked for France later in the same year, and was engaged in many important battles, including those of Ypres, Arras, the Somme, Cambrai, and was in action throughout the German Offensive and subsequent Allied Advance of 1918, and was wounded. He was demobilised in September 1919, and holds the General Service and Victory Medals.
52, Norman Road, Luton. 5004.

T

TALBOT, R. A., Sapper, 95th Field Coy., R.E.
He volunteered in January 1915, and in the same year proceeded to France. He was engaged on special work in connection with operations and was present at the Battles of Loos and the Somme, and was wounded in 1916. On recovery he was sent to Italy, and amongst other important engagements was in action in the British Offensive on the Piave. He was demobilised in March 1919, and holds the 1914-15 Star, and the General Service and Victory Medals.
25, St. Mary's Road, Watford. X5007.

TANSLEY, E., Pte., Loyal North Lancashire Regt.
Volunteering in January 1916, he was engaged on important duties with his unit until July 1918, when he was sent to France. He served through the concluding operations of the war, and was in action in several important engagements at Courtrai, Ypres and other places. Demobilised in February 1919, he holds the General Service and Victory Medals.
2a, Liverpool Road, Watford. X5008.

TANSLEY, G., Private, 2nd Bedfordshire and Hertfordshire Regiments.
He volunteered in November 1914, and in June of the following year embarked for France. Taking part in various engagements, he was wounded at Loos in September 1915 and invalided to England. On recovery he was drafted to Egypt in January 1916, and fought in the Battles of Gaza, Jaffa and other operations during the Advance through Palestine, and was twice wounded. He returned home in March 1919, and in 1920 was drafted to India and stationed at Secunderabad. He holds the 1914-15 Star, and the General Service and Victory Medals.
51, Leighton Street, Woburn. Z4510/A.

TANSWELL, W. J., Private, R.A.S.C.
Volunteering in October 1915, he was later drafted to the Western Front, and served in various sectors. He was engaged on important duties in connection with the transport of ammunition and supplies to the forward areas and in conveying the wounded from the firing line to casualty clearing stations. He was demobilised in January 1919, and holds the General Service and Victory Medals.
14, Garfield Street, Watford. X5014.

TAPP, H. W., Gunner, Royal Field Artillery.
He volunteered in August 1915, and was sent overseas in the same year. Serving with his Battery on the Western Front, he fought in many important engagements on the Somme, and in the Arras, Ypres and Cambrai sectors, and was gassed. He was sent with the Army of Occupation into Germany and remained there until his return home for demobilisation in January 1919. He holds the 1914-15 Star, and the General Service and Victory Medals.
27, New Kent Road, St. Albans. X5015.

TARBOX, A. F. (M.M.), Sergeant, Duke of Cornwall's Light Infantry.
He joined in March 1917, and in the following September embarked for the Western Front. During his service he took part in the Battles of Cambrai, the Somme and in the Retreat and Advance of 1918, and was awarded the Military Medal for conspicuous bravery and devotion to duty in the Field. He also holds the General Service and Victory Medals, and was demobilised in October 1919.
29, Stoke Road, Linslade, Leighton Buzzard. 5016.

TARGETT, A. N., A.B. (Gunner), Royal Navy.
He volunteered on the outbreak of war, and was posted to H.M.S. " Royal Arthur," which vessel was engaged on important duties in South American waters. His ship was in action in the Battle off the Falkland Islands, and was later on special duty at Scapa Flow. During his service his ship was twice torpedoed. He was demobilised in May 1919, and holds the 1914-15 Star, and the General Service and Victory Medals.
1, Crispin Terrace, Union Road, Hitchin. 5017.

TARRIER, B., A.B., Royal Navy.
Volunteering in August 1914, he was posted to H.M.S. " Thisbe " and employed on patrol and escort duties in the North Sea. His ship took part in the Battles of Heligoland Bight and Jutland and in the raid on Zeebrugge. He holds the 1914-15 Star, and the General Service and Victory Medals, and in 1920 was still serving.
4, Raymond Cottages, Ickleford, Hitchin. 3647.

TARRIER, G. E., Private, 2nd Bedfordshire Regt.
He volunteered in September 1914, and in the following April proceeded to France. In the course of his service he was engaged in operations in various parts of the line, and fought in the Battles of Arras and Ypres, and was twice wounded. He was taken prisoner in July 1917 and held in captivity in Germany until the signing of the Armistice. Demobilised on his return to England in January 1919, he holds the 1914-15 Star, and the General Service and Victory Medals. 2, Raymond Cottages, Ickleford, Hitchin. 5018.

TARRIER, P. C. (M.M.), Corporal, R.E.
Volunteering in May 1915, he was sent overseas in the same year, and saw much service in France. He was engaged on important duties in connection with laying the lines of communication during the Battles of Beaumont-Hamel, the Somme, Arras and Cambrai. He was awarded the Military Medal in September 1918 for conspicuous bravery and devotion to duty in the Field, and also holds the 1914-15 Star, and the General Service and Victory Medals, and was demobilised in January 1919.
Lower Green, Ickleford, Hitchin.　　　　　5019.

TARRIER, S. F., Private, Labour Corps.
He joined in September 1916, and on the completion of his training served with his unit at various stations. He did excellent work in connection with building operations and in looking after horses, but was unable to secure a transfer overseas before the cessation of hostilities, and was demobilised in June 1919.
12, Orchard Road, Walsworth, Hitchin.　　　5020.

TARRIER, W. G., Private, R.A.M.C.
He volunteered in August 1914, and in the following year embarked for France and did valuable work with his unit in the Battles of Ypres, Festubert and Loos. In 1916 he was drafted to Egypt and was engaged with the Field Ambulance during the operations in the Canal zone, and was at Gaza, Beyrout and other places during the British Advance through Palestine. He returned home for demobilisation in May 1919, and holds the 1914-15 Star, and the General Service and Victory Medals.
49, Brunswick Street, Luton.　　　　　　5021.

TARRY, E., Sergeant, 1/5th and 4th Bedfordshire Regiment.
A Territorial, he was mobilised in August 1914, and in the following year proceeded to Gallipoli. He fought in several engagements from the landing at Suvla Bay until the evacuation of the Peninsula, and was invalided home early in 1916. Sent to France in January 1917, he was in action at Vimy Ridge, Passchendaele, Messines, Cambrai and in other operations until the end of the war. He was demobilised in February 1919, and holds the 1914-15 Star, and the General Service and Victory Medals.
7, New Town, Biggleswade.　　　　　Z5022.

TARSEY, W. J., Private, West Yorkshire Regt.
A serving soldier, having enlisted in 1909, he was mobilised on the outbreak of war, and sent to India. He did good work with his unit on guard and other important duties at Poona, Rawal Pindi and other military stations on the North West Frontier. Owing to ill-health he was invalided to hospital, and unfortunately died in November 1919. He was entitled to the General Service and Victory Medals.
29, Lamb Lane, Redbourn.　　　　　5023.

TASKER, A. J., Private, 11th Royal Sussex Regt.
He joined in February 1917, and in the same year was drafted to the Western Front, where he served for nearly two years. During this period he was in action in the Battles of Ypres, Cambrai and the Somme, and during the Retreat and Advance of 1918, and was wounded. He was demobilised in January 1919, and holds the General Service and Victory Medals.
42, Ridge Avenue, Letchworth.　　　　5024/B.

TASKER, J. H. (M.M.), Private, 2nd Bedfordshire Regiment.
He volunteered in September 1914, and in the following year proceeded overseas. He was engaged in heavy fighting in the Battles of Festubert, Loos and other important engagements, and was awarded the Military Medal for conspicuous gallantry and devotion to duty in the Field in 1916. He was killed in action on the Somme on September 22nd, 1917, and was entitled to the 1914-15 Star, and the General Service and Victory Medals.
42, Ridge Avenue, Letchworth.　　　　5024/A.

TATTAM, W. J., Bombardier, R.G.A.
Joining in July 1917, he was sent to France in the following September, and served in various parts of the Western Front. He was in action at Bullecourt, Passchendaele, Cambrai and several other important engagements, and was wounded. He holds the General Service and Victory Medals, and was demobilised in September 1919.
6, Park Gate Road, Callowland, Herts.　　X5025.

TAVENER, T., Private, Bedfordshire Regiment.
He volunteered in November 1914, and served with his unit on Home duties until drafted to France in May 1916. He served with his Battalion on many fronts and was engaged in almost continuous fighting. He was unfortunately killed in action on the Somme on July 13th, 1916. He was entitled to the General Service and Victory Medals.
6, Cumberland Street, Houghton Regis.　　5026.

TAYLOR, A., Private, 1st Bedfordshire Regt.
Volunteering in September 1914, he was sent overseas in May of the following year. He saw much service on the Western Front, and fought in several important engagements, including the Battles of the Somme, Arras, Ypres and Cambrai, and was three times wounded. As the result of his third wound his right arm had to be amputated, and he was invalided out of the Service in April 1918. He holds the 1914-15 Star, and the General Service and Victory Medals.
6, Elizabeth Street, Luton.　　　　　5027.

TAYLOR, A. A., Trooper, Bedfordshire Lancers.
He was mobilised from the Army Reserve in August 1914, and in the following June embarked for France. He was engaged with his unit on important duties in various sectors and fought in the Battles of Loos, St. Eloi and other operations. He was killed in action in the vicinity of Loos on February 12th, 1916, and was entitled to the 1914-15 Star, and the General Service and Victory Medals.
Home Farm, Clifton, Shefford.　　　　Z5028/B.

TAYLOR, A. E., Private, Bedfordshire and Hertfordshire Regiments.
He joined in September 1917, and proceeded to France in the following January. Whilst on the Western Front he took part in various engagements including those during the Retreat and Advance of 1918. He was afterwards sent with the Army of Occupation into Germany, and stationed at Cologne until his return to England for demobilisation in March 1919. He holds the General Service and Victory Medals.
14, Clifton Road, Luton.　　　　　5029.

TAYLOR, A. G., Private, East Surrey Regiment.
He was mobilised on the declaration of war, and almost immediately sent to France. There he was in action in the Retreat from Mons and in the Battles of Ypres, Festubert and Loos and was wounded at the second Battle of Ypres in May 1915. He returned to the firing line on recovery and was again wounded on the Somme in 1916. He was later in action with his unit and fought in the Battles of Albert and Cambrai, and other engagements until the cessation of hostilities. He was discharged in December 1918, and holds the Mons Star, and the General Service and Victory Medals.
Station Road, Ridgmont.　　　　　Z5030/A.

TAYLOR, A. J., Private, 2/6th and 1/5th South Staffordshire Regiment.
He volunteered in October 1914, and after serving with his unit at various depôts proceeded to the Western Front in February 1917. He was wounded near St. Quentin in the following March, and returning to the firing line took part in the Battles of Ypres, Kemmel Hill, Amiens, and was wounded at Bellenglise in October 1918 during the Allied Advance. He was demobilised in February 1919, and holds the General Service and Victory Medals.
2, Heath Terrace, Sandridge Road, St. Albans.　X4242/A.

TAYLOR, A. V., Private, Royal Inniskilling Fusiliers.
Volunteering in September 1914, he was drafted to Gallipoli in the following year, and fought in the landing at Suvla Bay and was wounded on August 15th, 1915. Invalided home owing to his wounds, he received medical treatment, and on recovery was engaged with his unit on important Home duties. He holds the 1914-15 Star, and the General Service and Victory Medals, and in 1920 was still serving.
33, Arthur Road, St. Albans.　　　　X5031/A.

TAYLOR, B., Private, 35th Machine Gun Corps.
He joined in June 1916, and in the following October proceeded to the Western Front. He served in various parts of the Line, and was in action in the Battles of the Somme, Arras, Ypres, Béthune, Cambrai and other important engagements, and was severely wounded in October 1918. Invalided home, he received hospital treatment, and was eventually demobilised in May 1919, and holds the General Service and Victory Medals.
17, Albert Street, Luton.　　　　　5032.

TAYLOR, C., Gunner, Royal Field Artillery.
He volunteered in December 1915, and in the following August embarked for Salonika. Serving with his Battery, he was engaged in the Allied Advance on the Doiran front and in many other important operations in this theatre of war. Returning home for demobilisation in October 1919, he holds the General Service and Victory Medals.
122, Wellington Street, Luton.　　　5033/A.

TAYLOR, C. H., Private, 8th Bedfordshire Regt.
Volunteering in 1914, he proceeded overseas in the following year, and saw much service on the Western Front. He fought in the Battles of Arras, Ypres, Cambrai, St. Quentin and other operations, and was gassed and wounded. He was demobilised in 1919 on returning to England, and holds the 1914-15 Star, and the General Service and Victory Medals.　4, St. Andrew's Street, Hitchin.　5034.

TAYLOR, C. H., Private, 21st Middlesex Regt.
He volunteered in June 1915, and a year later was sent to the
Western Front. Whilst in this theatre of war he was engaged
on important duties with his unit, and fought in the Somme
Offensive and at the Battle of Arras. He was killed in action
near Ypres on December 28th, 1917, and was entitled to
the General Service and Victory Medals.
33, Arthur Road, St. Albans.   X5031/B.

TAYLOR, E., Private, Bedfordshire Regiment.
He volunteered in August 1914, and after completing his
training served with his unit at various stations on the East
coast, and rendered valuable services in connection with
coastal defence measures. He was not sent overseas owing
to medical unfitness for general service, and was demobilised
in 1919.
49, Astley Hill, Hemel Hempstead.   X2877/B.

**TAYLOR, E., Private, Bedfordshire Regiment
and Essex Regiment.**
Volunteering in May 1915, he was drafted to Egypt in May
of the following year. He fought in the British Advance
through Palestine in many important engagements, including those at Jaffa and Haifa. He was killed in action
in the vicinity of Gaza in December 1917, and was entitled
to the General Service and Victory Medals.
14, Sunnyside, Hitchin.   5241/C.

**TAYLOR, E. C., Sergeant, 1/5th Bedfordshire
Regiment, and Royal Garrison Artillery.**
He was mobilised from the Army Reserve in August 1914,
and was engaged on special duties in the cook house of his
unit until transferred to the Royal Garrison Artillery in 1916.
He was drafted to France, and whilst on the Western Front
fought in several engagements, and was gassed and wounded
during the Somme Offensive, and invalided home. On
recovery he served at various depôts, and was demobilised
in January 1919. He holds the General Service and Victory
Medals. Home Farm, Clifton, Shefford.   Z5028/A.

TAYLOR, E. C., Driver, R.A.S.C.
He volunteered in 1915, and in the same year proceeded to
the Western Front, where he saw much service. He was
engaged on important transport duties in the forward areas,
and was present at the Battles of the Somme, Arras, Cambrai
and other engagements, and was gassed. On the conclusion
of hostilities he was sent with the Army of Occupation into
Germany, returning home for demobilisation in June 1919.
He holds the 1914-15 Star, and the General Service and
Victory Medals.
7, Sydney Road, Watford.   5035.

TAYLOR, F., Private, Bedfordshire Regiment.
Joining in June 1916, he proceeded to Egypt in the following
year. Whilst in the Eastern theatre of war he fought in
the Battles of Gaza, Jaffa, Haifa, Aleppo, Damascus and
other engagements during General Allenby's Advance
through Palestine. He was demobilised in November 1919,
on his return to England, and holds the General Service and
Victory Medals.
22, Camp View Road, St. Albans.   5036/B.

TAYLOR, F., Sergeant, R.A.S.C.
He volunteered in August 1914, and on completing his training was engaged on important duties in the Forage department of his unit. He did valuable work, but was not sent
overseas on account of medical unfitness for active service,
and was demobilised in May 1919.
5, Right of Way, New Town, Hatfield.   X4817/B.

TAYLOR, F., Air Mechanic, Royal Air Force.
He joined in March 1917, and after completing his training
was engaged on duties in connection with the construction
of huts and aerodromes at various stations. He did excellent
work, but was unable to obtain a transfer to a theatre of war
before the cessation of hostilities, and was demobilised in
February 1919.
14, Primrose Cottage, Hatfield.   X5037/A.

**TAYLOR, F. A., Private, Royal Army Medical
Corps (52nd Field Ambulance).**
He volunteered in 1915, and in the same year proceeded to
France, where he served on important duties with the Field
Ambulance during the fighting at Hill 60, the Marne and
many other engagements, until the close of the war. He
was demobilised in 1919, and holds the 1914-15 Star, and
the General Service and Victory Medals.
89, Cecil Street, North Watford.   X5038.

TAYLOR, F. G., Private, 1st Hertfordshire Regt.
He volunteered in September 1914, and was shortly afterwards drafted to France, where he served until the close of
the war. During this period he was engaged in heavy
fighting at Ypres, Arras, St. Quentin, Cambrai, St. Julien
and in the Retreat and Advance of 1918, and was gassed and
wounded. He was demobilised in March 1919, and holds
the 1914 Star, and the General Service and Victory Medals.
Old Vicarage Cottages, Offley.   5039.

TAYLOR, G. H., Gunner, Royal Field Artillery.
He volunteered in September 1915, and three months later
embarked for France, where he served with his Battery, and
was in action in many engagements, including those on the
Somme, at Cambrai and Poperinghe. During his service
overseas he was wounded twice, and returned to England in
March 1918. He holds the 1914-15 Star, and the General
Service and Victory Medals, and was demobilised in February
1919.
122, Wellington Street, Luton.   5033/B.

TAYLOR, H., Private, 2nd Bedfordshire Regt.
He was mobilised at the outbreak of war and drafted to
France with the first Expeditionary Force. He was engaged
in the fighting in the Retreat from Mons and the subsequent
Battles of the Marne, Ypres, Festubert, Loos, Arras,
Arras, and many others until hostilities ceased. He was
demobilised in March 1919, and holds the Mons Star, and the
General Service and Victory Medals.
14, Sunnyside, Hitchin.   5241/A.

TAYLOR, H., Private, 6th Bedfordshire Regt.
He joined in October 1916, and in the following January
was sent to France, where he took part in many engagements,
including the Battle of Arras. He was reported missing
on April 25th, 1917, but was later presumed to have been
unfortunately killed in action on that date. He was entitled
to the General Service and Victory Medals.
16, Russell Rise, Luton.   5040.

**TAYLOR, I. J., Private, Royal Marine Labour
Corps.**
He volunteered in September 1914, and after a period of
training at various stations, was engaged on important duties
aboard transport boats carrying troops to and from France.
Owing to ill-health he was invalided to hospital, and after
receiving medical treatment was discharged unfit for further
service in June 1917. He subsequently died on October 23rd
of the same year, and was entitled to the General Service
and Victory Medals.
The Green, Ickwell, near Biggleswade.   Z1891/B.

TAYLOR, J., Private, Machine Gun Corps.
He joined in July 1917, and was shortly afterwards sent to
India, where he served with his unit, and took part in the
operations on the North West Frontier against the Afghans.
He remained in this theatre of war until January 1920, when
he returned home and was demobilised. He holds the
General Service and Victory Medals, and the India General
Service Medal (with Clasp, Afghanistan, North West Frontier,
1919).
Mill Lane, Greenfield, Ampthill.   5041.

TAYLOR, J., Pte., 1st King's (Liverpool Regt.)
A serving soldier, he was drafted to France at the outbreak
of war. Whilst on the Western Front he fought in the
Retreat from Mons and also in the subsequent Battles of the
Marne, Ypres, the Somme, Arras, Loos and Cambrai. After
so long and honourable a period of service he was wounded
and reported missing on August 4th, 1918. He was later
presumed to have been killed on that date. He was entitled
to the Mons Star, and the General Service and Victory Medals.
13, Sunnyside, Hitchin.   5241/D.

**TAYLOR, J., Private, Queen's Own (Royal West
Kent Regiment).**
He joined in February 1918, on attaining military age, and
three months later was sent to France. In this theatre of
war he was engaged in the Cambrai sector, and took part in
the Retreat and subsequent Allied Advance of 1918. He was
demobilised in August 1919, and holds the General Service
and Victory Medals.
36, Plantation Road, Leighton Buzzard.   5042.

TAYLOR, J. A., Private, 7th Bedfordshire Regt.
He volunteered in May 1915, and in the following month was
sent overseas. He served on the Western Front, and
fought in many battles, including those of Arras, the Somme,
Ypres and Albert. During his long term of service he was
wounded three times. He was discharged as medically
unfit in March 1918, and holds the 1914-15 Star, and the
General Service and Victory Medals.
30, Hitchin Hill, Herts.   2223/A.

**TAYLOR, J. E. (M.M.), Corporal, 1st Hertford-
shire Regiment.**
He volunteered in September 1914, and in November of that
year was drafted to France. Whilst in that theatre of war
he took part in the Battles of Ypres, the Somme, Loos and
Festubert. He was unhappily killed in action in the course
of the fierce conflict at St. Julien on July 31st, 1917. During
his service on the Western Front he was awarded the Military
Medal for gallantry and devotion to duty in the Field. He
was also entitled to the 1914 Star, and the General Service
and Victory Medals.
33, Arthur Road, St. Albans.   X5031/C.

TAYLOR, J. E. S., Pte., Royal Army Medical Corps.
Volunteering in April 1915, he was drafted to France in the
following June. During his service on the Western Front
he was engaged with his unit in the Somme, Ypres and
Cambrai sectors as a stretcher-bearer and in attending to the
wounded. On one occasion he was gassed, and he also
suffered from shell-shock. He was demobilised in February
1919, and holds the 1914-15 Star, and the General Service
and Victory Medals.
22, Camp View Road, St. Albans.   5036/A.

TAYLOR, J. W., Staff-Sergeant, Royal Field
Artillery.
He was mobilised at the outbreak of war, and in 1915 was
sent to Egypt. He served in the British Advance through
Palestine, and was engaged in the fighting at Gaza, Jaffa
and Aleppo, and was also present at the occupation of Jerusalem. He was demobilised in April 1919, and holds the
1914-15 Star, and the General Service and Victory Medals.
38, Elfrida Road, Watford.   X5043.

TAYLOR, J. W., Private, Royal Fusiliers.
He was serving at the outbreak of war, when he was immediately drafted to France. Whilst on the Western Front
he took part in the Retreat from Mons and in the Battles of
Ypres, Arras and Passchendaele. During this long term of
service he was wounded six times. He was demobilised in
April 1919, and holds the Mons Star, and the General Service
and Victory Medals. Prior to the war he served in the South
African War, and also holds the Medals for that campaign.
10, Shaftesbury Road, Watford.   X5044.

TAYLOR, N., Private, Essex Regiment.
He volunteered in May 1915, and at the conclusion of his
training was sent 12 months later to Egypt. Whilst in this
Eastern theatre of war he took part in the operations in
Palestine, and was present in the Battles of Haifa and Jaffa.
He was unfortunately killed in action on March 27th, 1917,
at the third Battle of Gaza. He was entitled to the General
Service and Victory Medals.
14, Sunnyside, Hitchin.   5241/B.

TAYLOR, R., Private, 1st Bedfordshire Regt.
He was serving at the outbreak of war, and was almost
immediately drafted to France. He fought in the Retreat
from Mons and the subsequent Battles of Le Cateau and La
Bassée, and was wounded. He returned to the firing line on
recovery, and was later wounded near Hill 60 in April 1916.
He was invalided to England and was eventually discharged
as medically unfit for further service in February 1917. He
holds the Mons Star, and the General Service and Victory
Medals.
Cotton End, Bedford.   Z5045.

TAYLOR, R. H., 2nd Lieutenant, 5th Sherwood
Foresters.
Volunteering in September 1914, he was sent to France in
June of the following year. During his service on the
Western Front he was engaged in much fighting, taking part
in the Battles of the Somme, at Arras and Ypres. He returned
to England in August 1917, and served at home until his
demobilisation in February 1919. He holds the 1914-15
Star, and the General Service and Victory Medals.
14, Lyndhurst Road, Luton.   5046.

TAYLOR, R. S., Rifleman, Rifle Brigade.
He joined in 1916, and at the conclusion of his training was
engaged with his unit at many stations on important duties.
He rendered valuable service, but owing to medical unfitness
was unable to obtain his transfer overseas, and was demobilised in November 1919.
Mill Road, Greenfields, Ampthill.   5047.

TAYLOR, T., Sergeant, Bedfordshire Regiment.
He volunteered in June 1915, and after his training was
employed on special clerical duties at various depots with
his Battalion. He did excellent work, but was unsuccessful
in obtaining his transfer overseas before hostilities ceased,
and was demobilised in December 1918.
Marlborough House, 1, Norman Road, Luton.   5048.

TAYLOR, T., Sergeant, R.A.S.C. (M.T.)
He volunteered in September 1914, and was later sent overseas. During his service on the Western Front he was engaged
with his unit on special work in the Albert, Arras, Bapaume
and Somme sectors, and was constantly under shell-fire. He
returned to England after the signing of the Armistice and
was demobilised in April 1919, and holds the General Service
and Victory Medals.
75, Oak Road, Luton.   5103.

TAYLOR, T. E. (M.M.), Sergeant, 23rd London
Regiment.
Volunteering at the outbreak of war, he was shortly afterwards sent to France. Whilst on the Western Front he was
engaged in the fighting at Ypres and Neuve Chapelle. and
was wounded and gassed. During his service he was awarded
the Military Medal for conspicuous gallantry and devotion
to duty in the Field. He was invalided to England and
eventually discharged unfit for further service in 1916. He
also holds the 1914 Star, and the General Service and Victory
Medals. 4, Edmunds Place, Hemel Hempstead.   X5049.

TAYLOR, W., Driver, R.A.S.C.
He volunteered in November 1915, and in the same year
was sent to France. In this theatre of war he was employed
with his unit on special transport work, taking ammunition
to the front line trenches, and was frequently under shell-
fire. He was demobilised in March 1919, and holds the 1914-
15 Star, and the General Service and Victory Medals.
29, Clifford Street, Watford.   X5050.

TAYLOR, W., Driver, Royal Field Artillery.
He joined in April 1916, and in December of that year was
sent overseas. He served on the Western Front, and fought
in the engagements of Ypres, Arras, Vimy Ridge and Cambrai.
He was gassed and wounded in March 1918, and invalided to
England. After recovery he was employed on Home duties
until demobilised in January 1919. He holds the General
Service and Victory Medals.
21, Althorpe Road, Luton.   5051.

TAYLOR, W., Private, R.A.S.C.
He joined in October 1916, and in the following April
proceeded overseas. He served at Dieppe on special boot-
repairing duties with his unit, and remained in France until
October 1919. He then returned to England and was demobilised, and holds the General Service and Victory Medals.
66, Cobden Street, Luton.   5052.

TAYLOR, W. E., Private, Bedfordshire Regt.
He volunteered in January 1915, and shortly afterwards
proceeded to France. Whilst on the Western Front he fought
in many engagements, including those at Ypres, Hill 60, the
Somme, Vimy Ridge, Arras, Cambrai and St. Quentin, and
was wounded. He was sent to hospital in England and later
invalided out of the Service in May 1918. He holds the
1914-15 Star, and the General Service and Victory Medals.
92, Bury Road, Hemel Hempstead.   X5053.

TAYLOR, W. R., Q.M.S., 1st Hertfordshire Regt.
He volunteered in September 1914, and at the conclusion
of his training was employed on important work with his
Battalion, but was unable to obtain his transfer overseas
before the signing of the Armistice. He was then drafted to
Germany with the Army of Occupation, and stationed at
Cologne until early in 1920, when he returned home and
was demobilised in February of that year.
22, Camp View Road, St. Albans.   5036/C.

TEARLE, E., Private, 7th Bedfordshire Regt.
He volunteered in September 1914, and in the following
January proceeded overseas. He served on the Western
Front and fought at Loos and the Somme, where he was
wounded. On recovery he rejoined his Battalion, and
was engaged in the fighting at Passchendaele, Cambrai and
in the Retreat and Advance of 1918. He was demobilised
in March 1919, and holds the 1914-15 Star, and the General
Service and Victory Medals.
Tilsworth Road, Stanbridge.   5055/A.

TEARLE, E. G., Private, Labour Corps.
He joined in June 1918, and was shortly afterwards sent to
France. Whilst in this theatre of war he was employed on
important duties with his Battalion, and was frequently in
the forward areas whilst operations were in progress. He was
demobilised in October 1919, and holds the General Service
and Victory Medals.
119, St. James' Road, Watford.   X5056/B.

TEARLE, E. J., Sapper, Royal Engineers.
He volunteered in June 1915, and shortly afterwards sent
to the Dardanelles. He was engaged with his unit at the
landing at Suvla Bay and was wounded. On recovery he
was drafted to Egypt, and served for a time at Ismailia in the
Canal zone until May 1916. He was then sent to the
Western Front. and was frequently in the forward areas
whilst operations were in progress in the Somme and other
sectors. He was demobilised in May 1919, and holds the
1914-15 Star, and the General Service and Victory Medals.
119, St. James' Road, Watford.   X5056/A.

TEARLE, E. J., Private, 1st Bedfordshire Regt.
He joined in November 1916, and in the following January
proceeded overseas. Whilst on the Western Front he fought
in many engagements, including those at Arras, Passchendaele, Ypres, the Somme, and was gassed near Cambrai in
1918. He was demobilised in November 1919, and holds
the General Service and Victory Medals.
22, Chapel Path, Leighton Buzzard.   5057/A.

TEARLE, F., Private, R.A.S.C.
Joining in November 1916, he was drafted shortly afterwards to Ireland. He served at Dublin and various other places on special transport duties with his unit and did very good work, but was unsuccessful in obtaining his transfer to a theatre of war before the cessation of hostilities, and was demobilised in September 1919.
1, Alfred Street, Dunstable. 5058/A.

TEARLE, F. J., Private, 8th Bedfordshire Regt.
He volunteered in March 1915, and in the same year was sent to France. During his service on the Western Front he was engaged in the fighting on the Somme, at Arras, Bullecourt and Cambrai, and was wounded on the Somme during the Retreat of 1918. He was demobilised in November 1919, and holds the 1914-15 Star, and the General Service and Victory Medals.
Tilsworth Road, Stanbridge. 5055/B.

TEARLE, H., Driver, Royal Field Artillery.
Volunteering in June 1915, he was sent to France in the following November. Whilst on the Western Front he was in action at Ypres, La Bassée, the Somme and Arras, and was twice wounded. He was demobilised in October 1919, and holds the 1914-15 Star, and the General Service and Victory Medals.
60, Queen Street, Hemel Hempstead. X5059.

TEARLE, H., Stoker, Royal Navy.
He joined in 1918, and was posted to H.M.S. " Emperor of India." During the war his ship was engaged on special work patrolling the North Sea and other waters, and after the Armistice was employed on important duties off Constantinople. He holds the General Service and Victory Medals, and was still serving in 1920.
22, Chapel Path, Leighton Buzzard. 5057/B.

TEARLE, H. C., Private, Royal Fusiliers.
He joined in April 1917, and at the conclusion of his training served at various stations on the East Coast on important duties with the 327th Works Company. He did excellent work, but was unable to secure his transfer to a theatre of war before hostilities ceased, and was demobilised in January 1919. 58, Queen Street, Hemel Hempstead. X5060.

TEARLE, J., Corporal, 1st Bedfordshire Regt.
He volunteered in August 1914, and was shortly afterwards drafted to France. During his service in this theatre of war he took part in much fierce fighting, and was killed in action at the Battle of La Bassée on October 10th, 1914. He was entitled to the 1914 Star, and the General Service and Victory Medals. 1, Alfred Street, Dunstable. 5058/B.

TEARLE, J., L/Corporal, 6th Bedfordshire Regt.
Volunteering in September 1914, he was sent to France in July 1915. Whilst on the Western Front he fought at the Battle of the Somme and was wounded on July 1st 1916. He later returned to the front line trenches and was again wounded at Arras in April 1917. On recovery he rejoined his Battalion, and was wounded a third time in October 1917 near Ypres. He returned to England in January of the following year and was engaged on Home duties until demobilised in February 1919. He holds the 1914-15 Star, and the General Service and Victory Medals.
" South View," Princess Street, Toddington. 5061.

TEARLE, W., Private, Machine Gun Corps.
He volunteered in January 1915, and in May 1917 was drafted to Egypt. He served in Palestine, was engaged in the fighting at Gaza, and was present at the Occupation of Jerusalem. He was transferred to the Western Front in June 1918, and fought at Arras, Ypres and Vimy Ridge. He was demobilised in February 1919, and holds the General Service and Victory Medals.
" South View," Princess Street, Toddington. 5062.

TEARLE, W. M., Private, 2nd Bedfordshire and Hertfordshire Regiments.
He joined in April 1916, and 12 months later was sent to France. During his service in this theatre of war he fought at Ypres, Passchendaele, the Somme, Cambrai and in the Retreat and Advance of 1918. He holds the General Service and Victory Medals, and in 1920 was serving in India on garrison duties.
The Square, Toddington. 5063.

TEBBEY, W. G., Corporal, 1/5th Bedfordshire Regiment.
A Territorial, he was mobilised at the outbreak of war, and in August 1915 was sent to the Dardanelles. He fought at the landing at Suvla Bay, and in the following December was sent to Egypt. He took part in the Advance through Palestine and the operations at Gaza and Mejdil Yaba, and was mentioned in Despatches for devotion to duty in the Field. He was demobilised in July 1919, and holds the 1914-15 Star, and the General Service and Victory Medals.
8, Wenlock Street, Luton. 5064.

TEBBOTH, H. W., Private, 9th (Queen's Royal) Lancers.
He volunteered in August 1914, and proceeded to the Western Front and fought in the Retreat from Mons, was wounded and taken prisoner. He remained in captivity until hostilities ceased, when he was repatriated. He was still serving in 1920, and holds the Mons Star, and the General Service and Victory Medals.
22, Clifton Street, St. Albans. X5065.

TERRY, C. A., Private, 2nd London Regiment (Royal Fusiliers).
Joining in January 1917, he was drafted to France later in the same year, and was in action at Arras, Vimy Ridge and Passchendaele and many other engagements of note. He was unfortunately killed in action on the Menin Road on October 1st, 1917, and was entitled to the General Service and Victory Medals.
68, Souldern Street, Watford. X5067.

TERRY, D., Private, Wiltshire, Dorsetshire, and Devonshire Regiments.
Volunteering in November 1915, he embarked for the Western Front in the following year, and saw much service in various parts of the line, and fought on the Somme and in other engagements. He returned to England in 1917 and served at various stations until after the Armistice, when he was sent into Germany with the Army of Occupation, and remained there until his return to England for demobilisation in April 1919. He holds the General Service and Victory Medals.
112, Judge Street, North Watford. X5068.

TERRY, E. G., Gunner, Royal Field Artillery.
He volunteered in April 1915, and later proceeded to the Western Front. He was in action in the Battles of Ypres, Arras, Passchendaele, and in many other important engagements. He also served in the German offensive and subsequent Allied Advance in 1918, and was twice gassed. He was demobilised in May 1919, and holds the General Service and Victory Medals.
Ganders Ash, Leavesden Green, Watford. X2610/A—X2611/A.

TERRY, G. E., Bombardier, R.G.A.
He joined in June 1916, and later was drafted to France, where he served with both Siege and Field Batteries, fighting in many important engagements, including those at the Somme, Arras, Ypres and in the Retreat and Advance of 1918, during which operations he was wounded on August 23rd. He was demobilised in December 1918, and holds the General Service and Victory Medals.
44, Ridge Avenue, Letchworth. 5069.

TERRY, H., Sapper, Royal Engineers.
He joined in 1916, and embarked for the Western Front later in the same year and was engaged on important duties in connection with operations in the forward areas during the Battles at Pozières, Loos, the Somme, Arras and in the Retreat and Advance of 1918. He was demobilised in 1919, and holds the General Service and Victory Medals.
49, Breakspeare Road, Abbots Langley. X5070.

TERRY, H. J., Private, Bedfordshire Regiment.
He joined in November 1916, and was drafted to France. In this theatre of war he was in action at Arras, Ypres, Cambrai and in many other important engagements. Later transferred to Italy, he saw much fighting in various sectors of the Piave front, and was wounded during his service overseas. He was demobilised in February 1919, and holds the General Service and Victory Medals.
Ganders Ash, Leavesden Green, Watford. X2610/B—X2611/B.

TEW, C. E., Corporal, 2nd Bedfordshire Regt.
He joined in June 1917, and completing his training served at various stations with his unit until drafted to India in October 1919. Here he was stationed at many garrison towns, engaged upon guard and other important duties. He was still serving in that country in 1920.
5, Dordons Road, Leagrave. 5071/A.

TEW, D., Sergeant, Royal Fusiliers.
Volunteering in September 1914, he proceeded to France in the following year and saw considerable service in many parts of the line. He fought at Ypres, Arras, Cambrai and in many other important engagements, and was severely wounded on the Somme in 1917. He returned to England, and after receiving hospital treatment was invalided out of the Service in June 1917 with a paralysed arm, the result of wounds received in action. He holds the 1914-15 Star, and the General Service and Victory Medals.
Russell Street, Woburn Sands, Beds. Z5072.

TEW, L., Sapper, Royal Engineers.
On attaining military age he joined H.M. Forces in January 1920, and completing his training was stationed at various depôts, engaged on guard and other important duties. He rendered excellent services and was still serving later in that year.
5, Dordons Road, Leagrave. 5071/B.

TEW, P. (M.S.M.), Sergeant, 7th Bedfordshire Regiment.
Mobilised at the outbreak of hostilities, he was sent overseas in July 1915. During his service on the Western Front he fought in many important battles, including those of Arras, Cambrai and Ypres, and throughout the Retreat and Advance of 1918. He was awarded the Meritorious Service Medal for consistently good work in the Field, and was demobilised in March 1919. He also holds the 1914-15 Star, and the General Service and Victory Medals.
5, Dordons Road, Leagrave. 5071/C.

THATCHER, C. B., Driver, R.F.A.
Volunteering in May 1915, he was sent to the Western Front in November of the following year, and was in action at many important engagements, including those of Ypres and Arras. In 1917, transferred to Egypt, he fought at Gaza and in many other actions during the Advance through Palestine. He returned to England and was demobilised in March 1919, and holds the General Service and Victory Medals.
8, Adrian Road, Abbots Langley. X5073/A.

THATCHER, E. J., Driver, R.F.A.
He joined in August 1916, and was sent to the Western Front in October 1917, and fought in various sectors until drafted to Italy two months later. Here he saw much service and fought in many engagements, and in March 1918 proceeded to Egypt. He served throughout the Advance in Palestine and Syria, and was wounded in the Riots in Cairo in 1919. He returned to England and was demobilised in October 1919, and holds the General Service and Victory Medals.
8, Adrian Road, Abbots Langley. X5073/B.

THATCHER, G. J., Private, 1st Bedfordshire Regiment.
He volunteered in May 1915, and proceeded to the Western Front in the following September and fought in the Battles of Ypres and the Somme, and was invalided to England in March 1916 owing to ill-health. On recovery he was sent to Italy in October of that year and saw heavy fighting on the Piave front, and returning to France in March 1918 was in action in the Retreat and Advance. He was taken ill with pneumonia, and subsequently died in hospital in France on November 2nd, 1918. He was entitled to the 1914-15 Star, and the General Service and Victory Medals.
9, Ladysmith Road, St. Albans. X2523/B.

THEOBALD, A. R., Private, M.G.C.
He joined in October 1917, and was drafted to France three months later and served throughout the heavy fighting in the German offensive and subsequent Allied Advance. After the Armistice he was sent to Palestine and was engaged on guard and other important duties. Returning to England he was demobilised in April 1920, and holds the General Service and Victory Medals.
38, Garfield Street, Watford. X5074.

THODY, H., Private, Royal Army Service Corps.
He volunteered in September 1914, and in the following year was drafted to France, where he served on the Somme, at Arras, Passchendaele, Lens and Cambrai, engaged in transporting supplies to the front lines, and was wounded. He also served throughout the Retreat and Advance of 1918, and was demobilised in February 1919. He holds the 1914-15 Star, and the General Service and Victory Medals.
Studham, near Dunstable. 693/A.

THOMAS, W. D. T., Pte., Royal Welch Fusiliers.
He joined in April 1917, and on the completion of his training served at various stations on important duties with his unit. He did good work, but was unsuccessful in obtaining his transfer overseas on account of medical unfitness, and was demobilised in February 1919.
1, Park Street, Hatfield, Herts. X531/A—X532/A.

THOMKINS, W., Sapper, Royal Engineers; and Private, 11th Cheshire Regiment.
He volunteered in April 1915, and proceeded to the Western Front in December of the following year and fought in many engagements, including those at the Somme and Arras. He was unfortunately killed in action at Ypres in July 1917, and was entitled to the General Service and Victory Medals.
42, Maple Road, Luton. 5076.

THOMPKINS, C., Private, Labour Corps.
Volunteering in February 1916, he was stationed at various depôts on important duties on completing his training, and was transferred to the Labour Corps in the following year. Embarking for France, he rendered valuable services in the forward areas during the progress of the Battles of Ypres, Poperinghe, Cambrai and the Somme, and after the Armistice served with the Army of Occupation on the Rhine. He was demobilised in November 1919, and holds the General Service and Victory Medals.
36, Essex Street, Luton. 5075.

THOMPSON, A., Private, R.A.S.C. (M.T.)
He joined in December 1916, and later proceeded to the Western Front, where he was engaged on important duties connected with the transport of supplies. He served in the forward areas during heavy fighting, and after hostilities had ceased was sent into Germany with the Army of Occupation. He was demobilised in September 1919, and holds the General Service and Victory Medals.
3, Marquis Lane, Harpenden. 5077.

THOMPSON, A. E., Private, Royal Dublin Fusiliers.
Volunteering in November 1914, he was drafted to the Western Front in June of the following year, and was in action at Hill 60, Ypres, Vimy Ridge, the Somme and in the German Offensive of 1918, and was wounded twice. Invalided to England he received treatment and was discharged in July 1918 unfit for further service. He holds the 1914-15 Star, and the General Service and Victory Medals.
14, St. Saviour's Crescent, Luton. 5078.

THOMPSON, C., Private, Bedfordshire Regiment.
He joined in February 1919, and on completion of his training served at various stations on guard and other important duties with his regiment. He did very good work, and was still serving in 1920.
8, Midland Terrace, St. Albans. X5079/A.

THOMPSON, C., Private, Middlesex Regiment.
He joined in July 1917, and was sent to the Western Front later in the same year, and was engaged in the Battles of Cambrai, Bullecourt, Messines and throughout the fighting in the German Offensive and subsequent Allied Advance of 1918, and was gassed. He was demobilised in February 1919, and holds the General Service and Victory Medals.
8, Midland Terrace, St. Albans. X5079/B.

THOMPSON, E., Driver, Royal Field Artillery.
Volunteering in December 1915, he was drafted to the Western Front in March of the following year, and saw much service in various parts of the line, and was engaged in the Battles of Passchendaele, Messines, Ypres, Arras, the Somme and in the Retreat and Advance of 1918. He was demobilised in May 1919, and holds the General Service and Victory Medals.
68, Hartley Road, Luton. 5080.

THOMPSON, E. F., Air Mechanic, Royal Air Force (late Royal Flying Corps).
He volunteered in August 1914, and in the following July was drafted to German South West Africa, where he served with his Squadron on important duties which called for a high degree of technical skill. He did good work as an aero-engine fitter and tester, and returning to England was subsequently demobilised in October 1919. He holds the 1914-15 Star, and the General Service and Victory Medals.
4, Garden Road, Dunstable. 5142.

THOMPSON, E. G., Gunner, Royal Field Artillery.
He volunteered in August 1915, and embarked for France three months later, and was in action in many important battles, including those of Ypres, the Somme, Cambrai and in the German Offensive and Allied Advance in 1918. He was demobilised in July 1919, and holds the 1914-15 Star, and the General Service and Victory Medals.
1, Stanmore Road, Watford. X5082/B.

THOMPSON, E. J., Rifleman, 15th London Regiment (Civil Service Rifles).
Volunteering in July 1915, he proceeded overseas in the following year. Whilst on the Western Front he fought in many important engagements, and, transferred to Palestine in 1917, served in the Advance through the Holy Land into Syria and took part in much heavy fighting. He also saw service in Salonika. Returning to England he was demobilised in January 1919, and holds the General Service and Victory Medals.
11, Grange Street, St. Albans. X5081.

THOMPSON, F. J., Private, 1st Hertfordshire Regiment.
A Territorial, he was mobilised at the commencement of hostilities and embarked in July 1915 for the Western Front. During his service in this theatre of war he fought at Givenchy, Ypres, Loos and the Somme. He made the supreme sacrifice, being killed in action at Festubert on August 3rd, 1916, and was entitled to the 1914-15 Star, and the General Service and Victory Medals.
3, Barker's Cottages, Hitchin Hill, Hitchin. 5083.

THOMPSON, G., L/Corporal, 4th Bedfordshire Regiment.

Volunteering in November 1914, he completed his training and served at various stations on important duties until drafted to France in July 1916. He was in action at Ypres, the Somme, Arras and other important engagements. He was gassed and taken prisoner on March 24th, 1918, in the German Offensive, and subsequently died in captivity from the effects of gas-poisoning on July 13th of the same year. He was entitled to the General Service and Victory Medals.
3, Oliver Street, Ampthill. 5084.

THOMPSON, R. E., Private, 7th Queen's (Royal West Surrey Regiment).

He joined in October 1917, and was sent to France in the following December and fought in many important engagements. He was severely wounded during the German Offensive of 1918, and subsequently died from the effects of his injuries at Étaples Hospital on April 30th, 1918. He was entitled to the General Service and Victory Medals.
1, Stanmore Road, Watford. X5082/A.

THOMPSON, S., Driver, Royal Field Artillery.

He joined in June 1916, and in the succeeding year proceeded to Russia, where he served in various sectors and fought in many important engagements. He rendered excellent services throughout, and returning to England was demobilised in July 1919. He holds the General Service and Victory Medals.
8, Midland Terrace, St. Albans. X5079/C.

THOMPSON, W., Private, 6th Bedfordshire Regt.

Volunteering in January 1916, he embarked for France in June of the same year and saw active service in many sectors of the Western Front. He fought at the Battles of the Somme and Ypres, where he was killed in action on April 10th, 1917, and was entitled to the General Service and Victory Medals.
1, Stanmore Road, Watford. X5082/C.

THOMPSON, W., Private, Bedfordshire Regt.

He volunteered in August 1915, and was drafted overseas later in the same year and was engaged on important pioneer duties in the forward areas, and was continuously under heavy shell-fire. He rendered valuable services throughout, and on his return to England, after the cessation of hostilities, was demobilised in February 1919, and holds the 1914–15 Star, and the General Service and Victory Medals.
37, Fishpool Street, St. Albans. X5085.

THORN, A. W., Sapper, Royal Engineers.

He joined in 1916, and after training was drafted to the Western Front, where he saw much service. He took part in many important engagements, including those on the Somme, at Ypres and Cambrai. After the signing of the Armistice he proceeded into Germany with the Army of Occupation, and was stationed at Cologne. He returned home in 1919, and was demobilised in that year, and holds the General Service and Victory Medals.
32a, Hagden Lane, Watford. X347/B.

THORN, E. W., Gunner, Royal Field Artillery.

He volunteered in January 1915, and sailed for Mesopotamia in the succeeding year. In this theatre of war he served on the Tigris, and was in action at Kut-el-Amara in 1916 and again in 1917, and was present at the capture of Baghdad and the occupation of Mosul. Returning to England he was demobilised in April 1919, and holds the General Service and Victory Medals.
97, Old London Road, St. Albans. X5088.

THORN, F., Private, 6th Northamptonshire Regt.

He joined in January 1917, and proceeded to the Western Front in the following April. He was engaged in the Battles of Arras, Messines, Passchendaele, Albert and Cambrai, and was reported missing at St. Quentin on April 6th, 1918, during the German Offensive, and later was presumed to have been killed in action on that date. He was entitled to the General Service and Victory Medals.
123, Sun Street, Biggleswade. Z5089/A.

THORN, F. A., L/Corporal, 3rd Northamptonshire Regiment.

Joining in April 1916, he was drafted to Egypt later in the same year and saw considerable service on the Palestine front, and was in action in the Jordan valley and in many other engagements during the Advance into Syria. Returning to England he was demobilised in November 1919, and holds the General Service and Victory Medals.
22, Hagden Lane, Watford. X5090.

THORN, H. A., Driver, Royal Field Artillery.

Volunteering in August 1914, he was sent to France almost immediately and fought in the Retreat from Mons and in the Battles of Arras, Ypres, Passchendaele and throughout the German Offensive and Allied Advance of 1918, and was gassed. He was demobilised in September 1919, and holds the Mons Star, and the General Service and Victory Medals.
14, Cross Street, Watford. X5091/A.

THORN, J., Private, 24th Royal Fusiliers.

He joined in February 1917, and proceeded overseas in the following November and was engaged at the Battles of Albert, St. Quentin, Amiens, Cambrai and throughout the Retreat and Advance of 1918. Proceeding into Germany with the Army of Occupation, he was stationed at Cologne until he returned to England for demobilisation in January 1920. He holds the General Service and Victory Medals.
123, Sun Street, Biggleswade. Z5089/B.

THORN, W. T., Gunner, Royal Field Artillery.

He volunteered in August 1914, and landed in France in time to participate in the Retreat from Mons, during which he was severely wounded. Returning to England he received hospital treatment, and in consequence of his injuries was invalided out of the Service in December 1914. He holds the Mons Star, and the General Service and Victory Medals.
14, Cross Street, Watford. X5091/B.

THORNE, A., Private, R.A.V.C.

He joined in July 1916, and in the following January proceeded to Salonika. In this theatre of war he served with his unit on the Vardar and Struma fronts on important duties in attending to sick and wounded horses. He returned to England after the close of the war, and was demobilised in February 1919. He holds the General Service and Victory Medals.
11, Albion Street, Dunstable. 5092.

THORNE, C. J., Air Mechanic, Royal Air Force (late Royal Flying Corps).

He joined in January 1918, and at the conclusion of his training served at various aerodromes on important duties with his Squadron. He did good work as an aero-engine fitter, but was not successful in obtaining his transfer overseas before the close of the war. He was demobilised in August 1919.
6, Hedley Road, Fleetville, St. Albans. X5093/A.

THORNE, G., Sapper, Royal Engineers.

He joined in 1916, and in the same year was sent overseas. During his service on the Western Front he was employed on special duties in the front lines, and was in action at the Battles of St. Quentin, the Somme, Arras, Cambrai and Givenchy, and was wounded. He returned to England after hostilities ceased, and was demobilised in February 1919. He holds the General Service and Victory Medals.
Slate Corner, Flamstead, Beds. X5094.

THORNE, J. E., Driver, Royal Engineers.

He volunteered in February 1916, and on completion of his training was stationed in Ireland and engaged on special duties with his unit. He did good work as a transport motor driver, but was not successful in obtaining his transfer to a theatre of war before the cessation of hostilities. He was demobilised in March 1919.
50, Hockliffe Street, Leighton Buzzard. 5095.

THORNE, J. W., Sapper, Royal Engineers.

He joined in February 1917, and served at various stations with the Royal Engineers engaged on work in connection with the construction of pontoon bridges. He rendered valuable services in this capacity, but owing to medical unfitness was not sent overseas. He was invalided out of the Service in November 1918.
8, Cecil Street, North Watford. X5096.

THORNE, R. J., Sapper, Royal Engineers, 338th Field Company.

He volunteered in August 1915, and after completing his training served with his unit at home until September 1917, when he proceeded to France. He was stationed at Dunkirk and other places on the Western Front, and employed on special duties in connection with the Inland Water Transport. In December 1917 he returned to England, and was subsequently discharged on account of service in October 1918. He holds the General Service and Victory Medals.
6, Hedley Road, Fleetville, St. Albans. X5093/B.

THORNTON, H., Driver, Royal Field Artillery.

He enlisted in 1901, and was mobilised at the outbreak of hostilities and drafted to France in November 1914. In this theatre of war he was engaged in the fighting at the Battles of Ypres, the Somme, Arras, Cambrai and many others until the signing of the Armistice. He was discharged in May 1919, and holds the 1914 Star, and the General Service and Victory Medals.
58, Upper Paddock Road, Oxhey, Herts. X5097.

THOROGOOD, H. A., Private, R.A.V.C.

He joined in May 1916, and in the same year was sent to
Salonika, where he served on the Struma and Doiran fronts
on special duties in connection with the care of sick and
wounded horses. He was invalided to hospital suffering
from malaria, and returning to England was discharged in
consequence in September 1919. He holds the General
Service and Victory Medals.

24, King's Road, Hitchin.   5086.

THOROGOOD, T. G., Private, Australian Imperial Forces.

He volunteered in 1914, and in the following year was drafted
to France, where he served with his unit in many engagements
and fought at the Battles of the Somme, Arras, Lens and many
others. He made the supreme sacrifice, and was killed in
action at Loos on August 6th, 1916. He was entitled to the
1914-15 Star, and the General Service and Victory Medals.

26, Ickleford Road, Hitchin.   5087.

THRALE, E. (Mrs.), Special War Worker.

This lady volunteered her services for work of National importance during the war, and from January 1916 until
February 1919 was engaged at Messrs. George Kent's
Munition Factory on important duties connected with the
making of fuses. She rendered valuable services throughout.

61, Grange Road, Luton.   5098.

THRALE, J., Sapper, Royal Engineers.

He joined in 1916, and in the following year proceeded to
France, and served with his unit until after the close of the
war. During this period he was employed on special duties
in the forward areas, and was in action at the Battles of
Ypres, Arras, Cambrai and in the Retreat and Advance of
1918, and was gassed. He was demobilised in November
1919, and holds the General Service and Victory Medals.

New Marford, Wheathampstead.   5099 /A.

THRALE, W. T., Private, Machine Gun Corps.

He joined in 1916, and was later drafted overseas. He
served on the Western Front, and fought in many engagements, including those at Arras and Ypres. He was taken
prisoner on the Somme in March 1917, and held captive in
Germany until after the Armistice. He was then repatriated and demobilised in 1919, and holds the General
Service and Victory Medals.

New Marford, Wheathampstead.   5099 /B.

THROSELL, W., Gunner, Royal Field Artillery.

He volunteered in August 1914, and after completing his
training served at home for a time. He was then drafted
to France and served with his Battery on various fronts,
and fought in the Battles of the Somme, Arras, Messines
Ridge, Cambrai and many other engagements, and was
wounded. He was demobilised in 1919, and holds the
General Service and Victory Medals.

12, Dolphin Yard, St. Albans.   X5100.

THRUSSELL, C., Private, East Surrey Regt.

He volunteered in January 1916, and five months later
proceeded to France, where he served with his Battalion,
and was engaged in heavy fighting in the Somme, Arras and
Ypres sectors and was wounded. On recovery he returned
to the firing line and was subsequently killed in action in the
vicinity of Ypres in August 1917. He was entitled to the
General Service and Victory Medals.

Ley Green, King's Walden.   201 /A.

THURGOOD, L., Sergeant, 7th Bedfordshire Regt.

Volunteering in August 1914, he embarked for the Western
Front later in the same year, and was in action in many important engagements, including those of Arras, Ypres and the
Somme, and was wounded three times, the last wound
necessitating his return to England. He received hospital
treatment, and was invalided out of the Service in June 1917,
and holds the 1914 Star, and the General Service and Victory
Medals.

109, Althorpe Road, Luton.   5101.

THURLOW, A. R., Sapper, Royal Engineers.

He volunteered in September 1914, and after his training
was stationed at various depôts, engaged on important duties
in connection with the maintenance of the lines of communication on the East coast. Owing to medical unfitness he
was not transferred overseas, and was discharged unfit for
further service in September 1916.

216, Wellington Street, Luton.   5102 /A.

THURLOW, F. W., Private, 1/5th Bedfordshire Regiment.

A Reservist, he was mobilised at the outbreak of hostilities,
and sent overseas to Gallipoli in the following July. He took
part in the landing at Suvla Bay, and was severely wounded.
He subsequently succumbed to his injuries on August
17th, 1915, and was entitled to the 1914-15 Star, and the
General Service and Victory Medals.

216, Wellington Road, Luton.   5102 /B.

THURLOW, P., Private, 1/5th Bedfordshire Regiment.

Mobilised at the commencement of the war, he served at
various stations until drafted to Egypt in February 1916,
and fought throughout the British Advance in Sinai, and was
unfortunately killed in action in the operations at Gaza on
July 20th, 1917. He was entitled to the General Service
and Victory Medals.

216, Wellington Road, Luton.   5102 /C.

THURSH, H., Captain, Lancashire Fusiliers.

Volunteering in 1914, he proceeded to Egypt in the following
year, and saw considerable service there until 1916. He
was granted a commission for consistently good work in the
Field. Transferred to France he fought in many sectors
of the line and was taken prisoner in March 1918 during
the German Offensive. Repatriated, he was demobilised
in November 1918, and holds the 1914-15 Star, and the
General Service and Victory Medals.

121, Pinner Road, Oxhey.   X2863 /C.

TIBBLES, A. C., Private, Labour Corps.

Joining in 1916, he was sent to the Western Front later in the
same year, and served in the forward areas on important
duties with his unit during the Battles of Arras, Cambrai,
the Somme and in the German Offensive and the subsequent
Allied Advance in 1918. He was demobilised in February
1919, and holds the General Service and Victory Medals.

13, Holywell Road, Watford.   X5104.

TIBBLES, H. H., Private, Bedfordshire Regt.

He joined in 1916, and proceeded to France in the same year.
During his service on the Western Front he was in action at
the Battles of Cambrai, Ypres, Arras, and was killed in action
on the Somme on March 16th, 1917. He was entitled to the
General Service and Victory Medals.

89, Norfolk Road, Rickmansworth, Herts.   572 /A.

TIBBLES, W., Private, Royal Sussex Regiment.

Volunteering in August 1914, he completed his training, and,
engaged on guard and other important duties, served at
various stations with his unit. He was unable to obtain his
transfer to a theatre of war owing to medical unfitness, and
was discharged in March 1919.

10, Mill Road, Leighton Buzzard.   5105.

TIBBLES, W., Gunner, Royal Garrison Artillery.

He volunteered on the outbreak of hostilities, and was drafted
to France, where he fought in the Retreat from Mons, and
in the Battles of Ypres, the Somme, Arras and many other
important engagements. He made the supreme sacrifice,
being killed in action on August 27th, 1917, and was entitled
to the Mons Star, and the General Service and Victory
Medals.

69, Church Street, Rickmansworth.   X5106.

TIFT, H. R., Private, Royal Fusiliers.

He joined in August 1918, on attaining military age, and on
completion of his training was stationed at various depôts
on important duties with his Battalion. He was not sent
overseas before hostilities ceased, but after the signing of the
Armistice was drafted to Germany to the Army of Occupation
and was stationed at Cologne. He was still serving in 1920.

27, Springfields, Linslade, Bucks.   5107 /A.

TIFT, T., Shoeing-smith, R.A.S.C.

Volunteering in February 1915, he sailed for the Dardanelles
in the following month, and was present at the first landing
at Gallipoli and the subsequent fighting until the Evacuation
of the Peninsula. Transferred to Egypt he served on the
Palestine front and saw considerable service throughout
the Advance into Syria. Returning to England he was
demobilised in March 1919, and holds the 1914-15 Star,
and the General Service and Victory Medals.

27, Springfield Road, Linslade.   5107 /B.

TILBROOK, A. J., Rifleman, 4th King's Royal Rifle Corps.

He joined in May 1916, and was sent to Salonika four months
later, and saw much service on the Vardar front and in
various other sectors until drafted to France in July 1918.
Here he fought in the Retreat and Advance of 1918, and was
severely wounded near Cambrai. He subsequently died
from the effects of his injuries on November 5th, 1918, and
was entitled to the General Service and Victory Medals.

25, Dudley Street, Leighton Buzzard.   5108.

TILBROOK, G., Sapper, Royal Engineers.

Joining in July 1918, he was sent to Egypt later in the year
and saw much service on the Palestine front, during the
Advance through the Holy Land. He was present at many
engagements and at the occupation of Beyrout. He returned
to England, and was demobilised in February 1920, and holds
the General Service and Victory Medals.

24, Longmire Road, St. Albans.   X5109 /A.

TILLBROOK, T., Staff-Sergeant, R.A.S.C.
Volunteering in August 1914, he embarked for the Dardanelles in August of the following year and took part in the landing at Suvla Bay and the subsequent operations until the Peninsula was evacuated. Proceeding to Egypt he served in the Advance through Sinai, Palestine and Syria, and was present at the Battles of Romani and Gaza. On his return to England he was demobilised in June 1919, and holds the 1914-15 Star, and the General Service and Victory Medals.
Una Villa, Seaton Road, London Colney. X5110.

TILBURY, E. J., Shoeing-Smith, R.A.V.C.
He volunteered in 1914, and was sent to the Western Front in the following year and served in the forward areas on important duties in connection with the shoeing of horses, and in this capacity rendered valuable services until demobilised in 1919. He holds the 1914-15 Star, and the General Service and Victory Medals.
31, Park Street, St. Albans. X5111.

TILBURY, H. R., 1st Air Mechanic, R.A.F.
He volunteered, in January 1915, and served at Norwich Aerodrome on important duties as a rigger, work which demanded a high degree of technical knowledge. He was drafted to France in 1917, and was stationed at Dunkirk, Calais and Ypres, and rendered excellent services until demobilised in 1919. He holds the General Service and Victory Medals.
102, Norfolk Road, Rickmansworth. X5112.

TILCOCK, T. J., Sergeant, 1st Bedfordshire Regt.
Mobilised in August 1914, he proceeded to the Western Front and fought in the Retreat from Mons and was wounded. On recovery he rejoined his unit and was in action in many other engagements and was again wounded and returned to England in October 1914. After a protracted course of hospital treatment he was discharged unfit for further service in April 1915, and holds the Mons Star, and the General Service and Victory Medals.
1, England Lane, Dunstable. 5113.

TILLER, F. C., Staff-Sergeant, R.A.S.C. (M.T.)
He volunteered in November 1915, and was drafted to Salonika in the following September, and saw much service on the Vardar and Struma fronts and was present in the final Allied Advance in 1918. In January 1919 he was sent to Constantinople and served there with the Army of Occupation for one month, and was then transferred to Russia, where he rendered valuable services until demobilised in November 1919, after returning to England. He holds the General Service and Victory Medals.
10, West Street, St. Albans Road, Watford. X5114.

TILLING, H. E., Private, Bedfordshire Regt.
Joining in 1918, he was drafted to France on completion of his training and saw heavy fighting during the German offensive and subsequent Allied Advance, taking part in many engagements. He returned to England and was demobilised in March 1919, and holds the General Service and Victory Medals.
49, Jubilee Road, North Watford. X5115/A.

TILLING, V. A., Private, Sherwood Foresters.
He volunteered in 1914, and embarked for the Western Front in the following year. During his service in this theatre of war he was in action in many important engagements and was wounded. He returned to the front lines on recovery and saw more fighting, and was captured in the German Offensive in 1918. Repatriated, he was demobilised in December 1919, and holds the 1914-15 Star, and the General Service and Victory Medals.
49, Jubilee Road, North Watford. X5115/B.

TIMBERLAKE, F. W., Private, 9th Royal Fusiliers.
Joining in June 1916, he proceeded overseas five months later, and whilst on the Western Front fought in many important engagements, including those of the Somme, Arras and Ypres, where he was wounded. On recovery he returned to the front, and was in action almost continuously until severely wounded in Flanders on November 14th, 1917. His injuries were such that it was necessary to amputate his right leg, and after hospital treatment he was invalided out of the Service in June 1918, and holds the General Service and Victory Medals.
Church Lane, King's Langley, Herts. X5116.

TIMBERLAKE, R. G., Private, South Staffordshire Regiment.
He volunteered in April 1915, and was drafted to the Western Front in the following January and saw much service in various parts of the line, fighting at the Battles of the Somme, Arras, Cambrai and throughout the German Offensive and Allied Advance in 1918. He was demobilised in February 1919, and holds the General Service and Victory Medals.
32, George Street, Markyate. 5117.

TIMMS, F. J., Signalman, Royal Navy.
He volunteered on the outbreak of war, and was posted to H.M.S. " Princess Irene." Aboard this vessel he was engaged on patrol and other important duties in the North and Baltic Seas and other waters until killed when his ship was blown up at Sheerness on May 27th, 1915. He was buried at Chatham, and was entitled to the 1914-15 Star, and the General Service and Victory Medals.
53, Breakspeare Road, Abbots Langley. X389/B.

TIMMS, H., L/Corporal, Royal Engineers.
He joined in March 1916, and was drafted to the Macedonian theatre of war later in the same year, and served on the Vardar and Monastir fronts in the forward areas engaged on important duties in connection with the operations, and was present at many battles. He returned to England and was demobilised in March 1919, and holds the General Service and Victory Medals.
Tilsworth, Leighton Buzzard. 5118/A.

TIMMS, R. J., A.B., Royal Naval Division.
He joined in January 1917, and proceeded to the Western Front in the following March. Here he saw much service in many sectors, fighting at Bullecourt, Ypres, Cambrai, the Somme, and throughout the Retreat and Advance of 1918. Returning to England in October 1918 with trench feet, it was found necessary to amputate one of his feet, and after treatment he was invalided out of the Service in December 1918. He holds the General Service and Victory Medals.
3, Hicks Road, Markyate. 5119.

TIMMS, T. C., Sapper, Royal Engineers.
Volunteering in July 1915, he embarked for France in the following November and served in the forward areas whilst the Battles of Cambrai and the Somme were in progress engaged on important duties connected with the maintenance of communications. He was also present at the fighting in the Retreat and Advance of 1918, and was demobilised in March 1919, and holds the 1914-15 Star, and the General Service and Victory Medals.
Tilsworth, Leighton Buzzard. 5118/B.

TIMSON, B., Private, East Surrey Regiment.
He volunteered in August 1914, and in the following year was sent to France. Whilst in this theatre of war he took part in many operations and fought in the Battles of Ypres and other important engagements. He was killed in action on October 12th, 1917, and was entitled to the 1914-15 Star, and the General Service and Victory Medals.
75, Grover Road, Oxhey. X5120/A.

TIMSON, F., Rifleman, Rifle Brigade.
Volunteering in June 1915, he was drafted overseas in the same year and was engaged on important duties in Egypt and fought in several engagements during the British Advance through Palestine. In 1918 he was sent to France and was in action in many of the concluding operations of the war, and was wounded. He also saw service in India, and, returning to England, was demobilised in August 1919. He holds the 1914-15 Star, and the General Service and Victory Medals.
75, Grover Road, Oxhey. X5120/B.

TINDALL, F. J., Private, Royal Berkshire Regt.
A serving soldier, he was mobilised on the outbreak of war and was engaged on postal duties at various stations with his unit. He did excellent work, but was not drafted to a theatre of war owing to his being over age for service overseas. He was discharged on account of service in August 1919.
Janus Cottage, New Road, Ascot. 5012-3/A.

TINDALL, G. F., Signalman, Royal Navy.
He was serving in the Royal Navy when war broke out, and was posted to H.M.S. " Tralee," which vessel was engaged on patrol and other duties with the Grand Fleet in the North Sea and other waters, and was in action at the Battle of Jutland. His ship was also employed on mine-sweeping duties. He holds the 1914-15 Star, and the General Service and Victory Medals, and in 1920 was still serving.
Forbes Buildings, Stevenson Street, Oban. 5012-3/B.

TINDALL, G. F., Private, Duke of Wellington's (West Riding Regiment).
He was mobilised on the declaration of war, and almost immediately sent to France. He was engaged in heavy fighting during the Retreat from Mons and was wounded and taken prisoner. Held in captivity in various detention camps in Germany, he was repatriated in December 1918 and demobilised in the following January. He holds the Mons Star, and the General Service and Victory Medals.
9, Lyles Row, Hitchin. 5121.

TINDALL, H. B., Private, 1st Bedfordshire Regt. and Hertfordshire Regiment.
He joined in January 1919, and on the completion of his training was engaged on important postal duties with his unit at various Home stations. He did excellent work, and in 1920 was still serving.
2, Dumfries Street, Luton.   5012–3/C.

TINGEY, H. S., Sergeant, 1/4th Somerset Light Infantry.
He volunteered in 1915, and was employed as Sergeant-cook with his Battalion until 1917. He was then sent to Egypt, where he served for a time, later being drafted to Mesopotamia. Here he was engaged in many operations, including the capture of Baghdad, and returning to England on the cessation of hostilities, was demobilised in March 1919, and holds the General Service and Victory Medals.
Fern Cottage, Ampthill Road, Shefford   Z5122.

TINGEY, J. E., Trooper, Bedfordshire Lancers.
He volunteered in September 1914, and in the following June embarked for France. In the course of his service on the Western Front he was in action in the Battles of Festubert, the Somme, Arras, Ypres, Vimy Ridge and other operations. He returned to England for demobilisation in February 1919, and holds the 1914–15 Star, and the General Service and Victory Medals.
49, Ratcliffe Road, Hitchin.   2879/B.

TITMUS, A., Sergeant, South Wales Borderers.
He volunteered in November 1914, and was sent to the Western Front in January 1916, and was in action in various parts of the Line and fought in the Battles of the Somme and Cambrai, and in the German Offensive and subsequent Allied Advance until wounded in September 1918. He returned to England, and after receiving hospital treatment was discharged unfit for further service in February 1919, and holds the General Service and Victory Medals.
83, Hastings Street, Luton.   5123.

TITMUS, C. W., Trooper, Hertfordshire Dragoons.
He joined in September 1916, and three months later proceeded to the Western Front, where he saw much service. He took part in the Battles of the Somme, Arras, Passchendaele, Vimy Ridge and Cambrai, and in the Retreat and Advance of 1918. Demobilised in March 1919, he holds the General Service and Victory Medals.
Upper Sundon, near Dunstable.   5124/A.

TITMUS, H., Private, Bedfordshire Regiment.
He volunteered in January 1915, and in June of the same year was sent overseas. Serving on the Western Front he was engaged in operations on the Somme, at Arras, Ypres and Passchendaele. He was unfortunately killed in action near Ypres in December 1917, and was entitled to the 1914–15 Star, and the General Service and Victory Medals.
Upper Sundon, Dunstable.   5124/B.

TITMUS, W. (M.M.), Private, Sherwood Foresters.
A serving soldier, he was mobilised when war broke out and was shortly afterwards sent to France. Whilst in this theatre of operations he fought in the Battles of Arras, Cambrai, St. Quentin and other engagements, and was wounded three times. He was awarded the Military Medal for conspicuous bravery and devotion to duty in the Field, and also holds the 1914–15 Star, and the General Service and Victory Medals. He was discharged on account of service in July 1919.   near School, Walsworth.   5125.

TITMUSS, A. E., Corporal, 1/5th Bedfordshire Regiment.
He volunteered in September 1914, and in the following year was sent to Gallipoli. He was in almost continuous fighting from the landing at Suvla Bay until severely wounded at "Chocolate Hill" on August 22nd, 1915. Invalided home to hospital, he was subsequently discharged as medically unfit for further service in July 1916, and holds the 1914–15 Star, and the General Service and Victory Medals.
105, North Street, Luton.   5126.

TITMUSS, F., Corporal, Royal Air Force.
Joining in March 1917, he proceeded to France two months later and served there for nearly two years. During this period he was engaged on important duties as an aero-engine fitter at Ypres, Rouen, Dunkirk and other aerodromes, and did very valuable work. He was demobilised in March 1919, and holds the General Service and Victory Medals.
Limbury Road, Leagrave.   5127.

TITMUSS, H., Private, 3rd Essex Regiment.
He joined in August 1918, and after completing his training served with his unit at various stations on the East Coast, and did good work in connection with coastal defence measures. Owing to medical unfitness for general service he was not drafted overseas, and was demobilised in February 1919.
15, High Street, Lilley, near Luton.   5128/B.

TITMUSS, J., Sergeant, R.A.V.C.
He volunteered in June 1915, and in February of the following year embarked for Egypt. He rendered valuable services attending to sick and wounded horses and mules during the British Advance through Palestine, and was present at the Battle of Gaza and other operations, and was twice wounded. Returning home, he was demobilised in September 1919, and holds the General Service and Victory Medals.
Lilley, near Luton.   5129.

TITMUSS, L., Private, Essex Regiment.
He joined in February 1917, and was shortly afterwards drafted to France. There he served with his unit in various parts of the line, and fought in several engagements. He was killed in action at Arras on September 20th, 1917, and was entitled to the General Service and Victory Medals.
13, Dacre Road, Hitchin.   5130.

TITMUSS, W., Private, Machine Gun Corps.
He volunteered in October 1915, and in the following August was sent overseas. After serving in France for a time he was drafted to Salonika in December 1916, and took part in various operations until March 1917. Owing to fever he was invalided to hospital, and after receiving medical treatment at Malta and later in England, was demobilised in February 1919. He holds the General Service and Victory Medals.
15, High Street, Lilley, near Luton.   5128/A.

TITMUSS, W. J., Private, Suffolk Regiment.
He volunteered in 1916, and in the same year proceeded to the Western Front, where he served for three years. During this period he was in action in the Battles of the Somme, Arras, Ypres, Passchendaele, Albert, Le Cateau and Cambrai, and other engagements. He holds the General Service and Victory Medals, and was demobilised in September 1919.
Catherine Cottages, Upper Green, Ickleford, Hitchin.   5131.

TODD, W., Corporal, 1st Bedfordshire Regt.
He was mobilised on the outbreak of war and drafted to France in September 1914. In this theatre of operations he took part in heavy fighting in the early engagements of the war. He was killed in action on March 18th, 1915, at the Battle of Neuve Chapelle, and was entitled to the 1914 Star, and the General Service and Victory Medals.
35, Cannon Road, Watford.   X3539.

TOFIELD, H. W., Stoker, Royal Navy.
He joined in February 1918, and was posted to H.M.S. "Yarmouth," which vessel was engaged on important patrol duties in the North Sea until after the cessation of hostilities. His ship was also present at Scapa Flow when the German Fleet was surrendered. He holds the General Service and Victory Medals, and was demobilised in October 1919.
31, Kingston Road, Luton.   5132.

TOLLEY, A. W., Private, Machine Gun Corps.
Volunteering in October 1915, he was sent to Mesopotamia in August of the following year. He took part in the capture of Baghdad and other operations, and was wounded at Kut in January 1917, and again at Mosul in the following May. Sent to Persia in May 1919, he served there until the following December. He returned to England and was demobilised in January 1920, and holds the General Service and Victory Medals.
130, Liverpool Road, Watford.   X5133.

TOLLEY, H. A., A.B. (Gunner), Royal Navy.
He joined in February 1917, and was posted to H.M.S. "Shannon," which vessel was engaged in the North Sea and other waters on important patrol and other duties. His ship was in action at Heligoland Bight, and during his service he was twice wounded. He was demobilised in March 1919, and holds the General Service and Victory Medals.
130, Liverpool Road, Watford.   X5134.

TOMKINS, A. N., Driver, Royal Field Artillery.
He volunteered in November 1914, and in the following March was sent overseas. Serving with his Battery on the Western Front, he fought in the Offensive on the Somme and in other important engagements, including the Battles of Ypres and Cambrai. He was demobilised in June 1919, and holds the 1914–15 Star, and the General Service and Victory Medals.
66, Talbot Road, Luton.   5135/A.

TOMKINS, P. G., Telegraphist, Royal Navy.
He joined in 1916, and was posted to H.M.S. "William Cogswell." His ship was engaged on important submarine patrol work in the North, Baltic and Mediterranean Seas during the whole period of the war. After the Armistice his ship was stationed in Turkish waters for a time. He was demobilised in June 1919, and holds the General Service and Victory Medals.
66, Talbot Road, Luton.   5135/B.

TOMLIN, A., Private, R.A.S.C.

Joining in March 1917, he was shortly afterwards drafted to France, and stationed at Calais, where he did valuable work as a baker. On the conclusion of hostilities he returned home, and was demobilised in January 1919. He holds the General Service and Victory Medals.
38, Peach Street, Luton. 5137.

TOMLIN, C., Private, 1st Bedfordshire Regiment.

He volunteered in September 1914, and in the following November proceeded to the Western Front. He was engaged in heavy fighting in various parts of the line, and fought in the Battle of Ypres and other important operations. He was killed in action near Ypres on February 20th, 1915, and was entitled to the 1914 Star, and the General Service and Victory Medals.
54, Sunnyside, Hitchin. 1813/B.

TOMLIN, G., Private, 1st Hertfordshire Regt.

He joined in 1916, and in the same year embarked for France. He saw much service in this theatre of war, and fought in the Battles of the Somme, Arras, Ypres, Cambrai and other important engagements. He was wounded and taken prisoner on July 31st, 1918, and sent to Germany. Released from captivity after the Armistice, he returned to England for demobilisation in December 1919, and holds the General Service and Victory Medals.
66, Norfolk Road, Rickmansworth. X5138.

TOMLIN, H., Driver, R.A.S.C. (M.T.)

He volunteered in August 1915, and in the following January was sent to France. He was engaged on important duties in connection with the transport of ammunition and supplies to the front lines during the Battles of the Somme, Arras, Ypres, Cambrai and Le Cateau (II.). He was demobilised in March 1919, and holds the General Service and Victory Medals.
54, Sunnyside, Hitchin. 1813/C.

TOMLIN, J., Private, Gloucestershire Regiment.

He joined in March 1916, and was drafted overseas six months later. During his service on the Western Front he saw much service, fighting at the Battle of the Somme and in other important engagements. Transferred to Italy in November 1916, he met with an accident shortly after his arrival, breaking a leg and ankle. He was invalided to England, and after protracted hospital treatment was discharged unfit for further service in September 1918. He holds the General Service and Victory Medals.
7, Black Horse Lane, Sunnyside, Hitchin. 5139.

TOMPKINS, A. J., Private, R.A.S.C. (M.T.)

He joined in April 1916, and in May of the following year was drafted overseas. He served on the Western Front for six months and was then sent to Italy, where he was engaged on important transport duties in operations on the Piave. He returned to England for demobilisation in February 1919, and holds the General Service and Victory Medals.
11, Cumberland Street, Houghton Regis. 5140.

TOMPKINS, E. D., A.B., Royal Navy.

He volunteered in August 1914, and after completing his training was engaged as Gunnery Instructor at Portsmouth. He did very good work in this capacity, but owing to ill-health he was not sent to sea, and was subsequently invalided out of the Service in June 1918.
14, Billington Road, Leighton Buzzard. 5141/A.

TOMPKINS, E. G., Private, Sherwood Foresters.

He joined in June 1917, and was sent to France in the following October. He served in various sectors of the Western Front and fought in the Battle of the Somme and in several engagements during the Retreat and Advance of 1918, and was wounded near Cambrai. He holds the General Service and Victory Medals, and was demobilised in February 1919.
14, Billington Road, Leighton Buzzard. 5141/B.

TOMPKINS, F., Private, Tank Corps.

He joined in December 1916, and after completing his training served with his unit on important duties until June 1918, when he was drafted to France. He served at Ypres, Arras and Cambrai during the Allied Advance, and in September was invalided to Sheffield Hospital with poisoned hands, caused by shrapnel. He was demobilised in December 1918, and holds the General Service and Victory Medals.
59, High Street, Houghton Regis. 5143.

TOMPKINS, G., Shoeing Smith, R.A.V.C.

He volunteered in December 1915, and three months later embarked for France, where he served in various parts of the line with his unit on important duties as a shoeing-smith until after the signing of the Armistice. He returned to England and was demobilised in April 1919, and holds the General Service and Victory Medals.
12, Roberts Road, Watford. X5144/A.

TOMPKINS, J. R., Private, 7th Durham Light Infantry.

Volunteering in September 1915, he served at home on special duties until drafted to France in January 1918. He fought with his Battalion in various sectors of the Western Front and was seriously wounded in action at Merville in April 1918. He was sent to hospital in England, and in consequence of his wounds his left arm was paralysed. He was invalided out of the Service in March 1919, and holds the General Service and Victory Medals.
2, Alfred Street, Dunstable. 5145.

TOMPKINS, J. W., Rifleman, K.R.R.C.

Joining in August 1918 on attaining military age, he completed his training and was engaged on important duties with his unit. He was unable to obtain his transfer to a theatre of war before hostilities ceased, but was sent with the Army of Occupation into Germany in December 1918. He returned to England for demobilisation in February 1920.
44, Stanbridge Road, Leighton Buzzard. 1684/A.

TOMPKINS, L., Air Mechanic, Royal Air Force.

He joined in February 1917, and on completion of his training was engaged on important duties at various aerodromes. He did valuable work as a fitter and tester of aero engines, but owing to medical unfitness was unable to obtain his transfer overseas before the cessation of hostilities, and was demobilised in April 1919.
100, Victoria Street, Dunstable. 3957/B.

TOMPKINS, L. A., Sapper, Royal Engineers (T.T. Cable Section).

He volunteered in October 1914, and in the following July was drafted overseas. During his service on the Western Front he was employed on special duties in the front lines, and served in the Battles of Arras, Ypres and the Somme. He returned to England after the Armistice, and was demobilised in May 1919, and holds the 1914-15 Star, and the General Service and Victory Medals.
31, Lyndhurst Road, Luton. 5146/A.

TOMPKINS, O., Gunner, Royal Field Artillery.

He volunteered in July 1915, and in the following March proceeded overseas. Whilst on the Western Front he was engaged in the fighting on the Somme, at Loos, Armentières, Passchendaele where he was gassed on December 24th, 1917), Ypres, Kemmel Hill and in the Retreat and Advance of 1918, and was again gassed. He was demobilised in September 1919, and holds the General Service and Victory Medals.
2, Bolton Road, Luton. 5147.

TOMPKINS, R. A., Private, 13th London Regiment (Kensingtons).

He joined in March 1917, and in the following February was drafted to France, where he served with his Battalion, and during the fighting at St. Quentin was taken prisoner on March 21st, 1918. He was held in captivity until after the Armistice, when he was repatriated. In June 1919 he proceeded to Egypt and remained there until 1920, he then returned to England and was demobilised in February of that year. He holds the General Service and Victory Medals.
31, Frederic Street, Luton. 5148.

TOMPKINS, S., Corporal, Army Intelligence Corps (attached Royal Air Force.)

Volunteering in October 1915, he was drafted to France in the following March and engaged on special duties with his unit in various parts of the line. He was present at many battles, including those of the Somme, Ypres and Arras, and invalided home in March 1918, returned to the Western Front two months later, and served until after hostilities ceased. He was demobilised in March 1919, and holds the General Service and Victory Medals.
31, Lyndhurst Road, Luton. 5146/B.

TOMPKINS, S. W. A., Private, Bedfordshire and Hertfordshire Regiment.

Joining in August 1918, he underwent a course of training and was engaged on special duties at various stations with his Regiment. He was not sent overseas before hostilities ceased, but was drafted to Germany in March 1919 to the Army of Occupation, and served there until the following August. He then returned home and was demobilised in April 1920.
12, Roberts Road, Watford X5144/B.

TOMPKINS, W. H. (M.S.M.), Sergeant, 1st Bedfordshire Lancers.

A Territorial, he was mobilised on the declaration of war and drafted to France in June 1915. During his service on the Western Front he took part in many engagements, including those on the Somme, at Ypres, Arras and Cambrai. He was awarded the Meritorious Service Medal for consistent good work in the Field. He also holds the 1914-15 Star, and the General Service and Victory Medals, and was discharged on account of service in February 1917.
139, High Street, Houghton Regis. 5149.

TOMPKINS, W. M., Sapper, Royal Engineers.
He joined in July 1916, and four months later was sent to the Western Front, where he served for nearly three years. During this period he was engaged in making trenches and roads in the forward areas, and was present at several battles. He was demobilised in March 1919, and holds the General Service and Victory Medals.
Tilsworth, near Leighton Buzzard   5136.

TOMS, E., Driver, Royal Field Artillery.
He volunteered in October 1914, and in November of the following year was drafted overseas. He saw much service on the Western Front and fought in the Battle of Ypres and other engagements, and in 1916 was sent to Egypt. There he took part in various operations during the British Advance through Palestine and, amongst others, fought in the Battle of Gaza. Returning home for demobilisation in June 1919, he holds the 1914–15 Star, and the General Service and Victory Medals.
30, Cavendish Road, St. Albans.   X5173.

TOMS, F. W., Bugler, 4th Oxfordshire and Buckinghamshire Light Infantry.
He joined in April 1918, and on the conclusion of his training served with his unit at Home. Engaged on guard and other duties, he did good work, but was unable to obtain a transfer overseas before the end of the war, and was demobilised in December 1918.
61, Park Street, St. Albans.   X5150.

TOMS, G., Private, Suffolk Regiment.
Volunteering in September 1914, he proceeded to the Western Front in the following year. In the course of his service overseas he fought in the Battles of Festubert, Loos, Ypres, Arras, the Somme, Albert, Cambrai and in several other important engagements. He was severely wounded in action, and subsequently died from the effects of his injuries on October 20th, 1918, and was entitled to the 1914–15 Star, and the General Service and Victory Medals.
97, Park Street, St. Albans.   X5151.

TOMS, H., Sergeant, Bedfordshire Regiment and Machine Gun Corps.
He volunteered in August 1914, and was engaged as a Drill Instructor and in conducting troops to and from France. He also served in various parts of the Western Front and was in action in several operations. Severely wounded, he lost the sight of an eye, and was invalided out of the Army in October 1918. He holds the General Service and Victory Medals.
34, Sotheron Road, Watford.   X5152.

TOMS, J., Corporal, Middlesex Regiment.
Volunteering in August 1915, on completing his training he was engaged as an Instructor and in training recruits for the New Armies. He also did good work in the orderly room of his unit. Owing to medical unfitness for general service he was not sent overseas, and was demobilised in February 1919.
5, Heath Road, Leighton Buzzard.   5153.

TOMS, J. C., Private, Hertfordshire Regiment.
He volunteered in August 1914, and was later drafted to France. Whilst on the Western Front he fought in the Somme offensive and in the Battles of Arras and Ypres, and was gassed and wounded. He was taken prisoner on the Somme in 1917 and held in captivity in Germany until the signing of the Armistice. He then returned to England and was demobilised in December 1918, and holds the 1914–15 Star, and the General Service and Victory Medals.
55, Sopwell Lane, St. Albans.   X5154.

TOMS, W., Private, 9th Middlesex Regiment; and Rifleman, 17th London Regiment (Rifles).
Volunteering in 1915, in the same year he embarked for the Western Front. During his service overseas he was in action at Hill 60, Ypres, Givenchy, Arras, St. Quentin and on the Somme, and was twice wounded. On the conclusion of hostilities he returned to England for demobilisation in February 1919, and holds the 1914–15 Star, and the General Service and Victory Medals.
6, College Place, St. Albans.   5155.

TOOKE, W. H., Sapper, Royal Engineers.
He volunteered in August 1915, and was drafted to France in the same year. He was engaged on important duties in connection with operations, and was present at the Battles of the Somme, Arras, Ypres, Cambrai, the Marne and the Aisne. He was gassed and wounded in the course of his overseas service and returned to England on the termination of hostilities Demobilised in February 1919, he holds the 1914–15 Star, and the General Service and Victory Medals.
3, Alexandra Road, St. Albans.   X5157.

TOOTH, J. G., Sergeant R.G.A.
Having enlisted in 1905, when 14 years of age, he was mobilised on the declaration of war and shortly afterwards proceeded to France. He saw much service on the Western Front and contracted shell-shock and was severely wounded in November 1917. Invalided to hospital in England, he died from the effects of his wounds in January 1918. He had been recommended for a commission, and was entitled to the 1914 Star, and the General Service and Victory Medals.
92a, Crawley Road, Luton.   5158.

TOPHAM, A. W., Gunner, R.G.A.
He volunteered in August 1914, and in the following year embarked for France. Whilst in this theatre of war he fought at Hill 60 and Ypres, and was also in action in the Somme offensive, and the Battles of Arras and Cambrai, and was gassed and suffered from shell-shock. He was demobilised in January 1920, and holds the 1914–15 Star, and the General Service and Victory Medals.
23, Ridge Avenue, Letchworth.   5156.

TOWLE, F., Special War Worker.
During the war he volunteered his services for work of National importance and was engaged as a foreman furnaceman at Messrs. MacLennan's Factory in Scotland and afterwards at the works of Messrs. Geo Kent, Ltd., Luton. He rendered valuable services from January 1915 until the cessation of hostilities, and in 1920 was still employed by Messrs. Geo. Kent, Ltd.
70, Selbourne Road, Luton.   5159.

TOWNROW, F., Sapper, Royal Engineers.
He volunteered in September 1914, and in the following July proceeded to Gallipoli. There he served at the landing at Suvla Bay and in many other engagements until the Evacuation of the Peninsula. He was then sent to Egypt, and was engaged on important duties in connection with the British Advance through Palestine, and was present at the fall of Jerusalem. Returning to England, he was demobilised in June 1919, and holds the 1914–15 Star, and the General Service and Victory Medals.
88, Oak Road, Luton.   5160.

TOYER, C., Private, R.A.S.C.
Volunteering in March 1915, he was sent to Salonika in the same year. He did valuable work with his corps during operations in the Balkans, and after two years' service there proceeded to Egypt. Taking part in the Advance through Palestine, he was engaged on important transport duties in the Battles of Gaza, Jaffa and Ludd, and was invalided home owing to illness in 1918. He was discharged in consequence in August of that year, and holds the 1914–15 Star, and the General Service and Victory Medals.
60, Alexandra Road, St. Albans.   X4529/A.

TOYER, C., Private, 5th Royal Inniskilling Fusiliers.
He joined in July 1916, and in the following December was sent to Salonika, where he took part in the Advance on the Doiran Front and in other engagements in the Balkans. Drafted to Egypt in 1917, he was in action at Gaza and other places during the British Advance through Palestine, and was sent to France in 1918. He fought in the final operations of the war, and returned to England for demobilisation in November 1919, and holds the General Service and Victory Medals.   37, Cobden Street, Luton.   5162.

TOYER, F., L/Corporal, Royal Engineers.
He volunteered in March 1915, and in the following October proceeded to the Western Front. He was engaged on important duties during the Battles of Loos, Vimy Ridge and the Somme, and was invalided home in 1917 owing to illness. On recovery he served with his unit on Home service duties until demobilised in January 1919, and holds the 1914–15 Star, and the General Service and Victory Medals. 90, Ashton Road, Luton.   5163.

TOYER, G. A., Private, 9th Norfolk Regiment.
He joined in December 1917, and embarked for the Western Front in the following year. During his service overseas he fought in the Battles of Ypres, the Somme, Cambrai and St. Quentin, and was gassed in September 1918. He was afterwards sent with the Army of Occupation into Germany and stationed at Cologne. He holds the General Service and Victory Medals, and was demobilised in March 1920.
15, Tavistock Street, Luton.   5164/A.

TOYER, H., Private, 1/5th Bedfordshire Regt.
He volunteered in September 1914, and was drafted to Gallipoli in the following year. He fought at the landing at Suvla Bay and in several other operations, and was wounded at Chocolate Hill on August 15th, 1915. On the Evacuation of the Peninsula he was sent to Egypt in December 1915 and served in the Canal zone, and later took part in the British Advance through Palestine and was in action at Gaza, Haifa, Acre, Damascus and Beyrout. He returned to England for demobilisation in April 1919, and holds the 1914–15 Star, and the General Service and Victory Medals.
22, Duke Street, Luton.   5165.

TOYER, H. A., Private, 45th Welch Fusiliers.
He joined in January 1918, and served with his unit at various stations on the East Coast and in Ireland, and did good work on guard and other duties. He was unsuccessful in his efforts to secure a transfer overseas before the cessation of hostilities, but was sent to Archangel in June 1919, and served in Northern Russia for several months. He returned to England, for demobilisation in October 1919.
24, Tavistock Street, Luton.   5166/A.

TOYER, H. C., Gunner (Signaller), R.H.A.
He joined in July 1916, and in the following May was drafted to France. He saw service in several sectors of the Western Front, and was in action at Ypres, Albert, Cambrai and in many other important engagements, and was gassed. On the conclusion of hostilities he was sent into Germany with the Army of Occupation and was stationed at Cologne, He was demobilised in October 1919, and holds the General Service and Victory Medals.
7, Burr Street, Luton.   1893—1892.

TOYER, J., Driver, Royal Engineers.
He joined in September 1916, and was shortly afterwards sent to Egypt. He was in action in the Battles of Gaza and other operations during the British Advance through Palestine and was present at the fall of Jerusalem. Returning to England, he was demobilised in January 1919, and holds the General Service and Victory Medals.
Front Street, Slip End.   -   5167/B.

TOYER, J. H., Private, R.A.S.C.
Joining in January 1917, he proceeded to France in the following October, and served at the Battles of Ypres and Cambrai. He was drafted to Italy in November 1917, and was engaged on transport duties during the Advance on the Piave and in other operations until the end of the war. Sent to Austria in December 1918, he was employed there for a time on special duties. In March 1919 he was sent to Egypt, and was stationed at Alexandria and later at Kantara. He returned to England for demobilisation in January 1920, and holds the General Service and Victory Medals.
24, Tavistock Street, Luton.   5166/B.

TOYER, P. W., Rifleman, 20th King's Royal Rifle Corps.
He volunteered in December 1915, and in the following March embarked for France. He was in action at Arras, Ypres, Lens, Cambrai and on the Marne, and was gassed at Arras. He served until the conclusion of hostilities and was sent with the Army of Occupation into Germany, being stationed at Cologne. He holds the General Service and Victory Medals, and was discharged on account of service in March 1919.
15, Tavistock Street, Luton.   5164/C.

TOYER, S. W., Sergeant, 25th Middlesex Regt.
Volunteering in December 1914, he was shortly afterwards sent to France and took part in several important engagements, including those at Ypres, Hill 60, and the Somme, and was wounded in 1916. On recovery he was drafted to Siberia, and whilst on the voyage his ship struck a mine on February 6th, 1917, but he was fortunately saved. He returned to England for demobilisation in October 1919, and holds the 1914–15 Star, and the General Service and Victory Medals.
15, Tavistock Street, Luton.   5164/B.

TOYER, W., Private, 1st Hertfordshire Regt.
He volunteered in February 1915, and was sent overseas in the same year. Serving on the Western Front he was in action in several engagements, including those during the Somme offensive. Owing to illness he was sent to hospital at Calais, where he died on July 22nd, 1917. He was entitled to the 1914–15 Star, and the General Service and Victory Medals.
60, Alexandra Road, St. Albans.   X1529/B.

TRAFFORD, C. S., Driver, R.A.S.C.
He volunteered in 1915, and proceeded to the Western Front in September of the same year. Serving on important transport duties he did valuable work throughout the war, and was present at the Battles of the Somme, Arras and Cambrai. He was sent with the Army of Occupation into Germany in December 1918, and was stationed at Cologne for several months. He holds the 1914–15 Star, and the General Service and Victory Medals, and was demobilised in April 1919.
20, Grover Road, Oxhey.   X5168.

TREACHER, J. E., 1st Air Mechanic, Royal Air Force (late Royal Naval Air Service).
He joined in May 1916, and on completion of his training was engaged on important duties at a large air-ship station in the Eastern Counties. He did excellent work in connection with the construction of airships, but was unsuccessful in securing a transfer overseas before the end of the war, and was demobilised in August 1919.
68, Villiers Road, Oxhey, Watford.   X5169/A.

TREACHER, R. W., Trooper, Hertfordshire Dragoons.
He volunteered in March 1915, and in the same year was sent to Egypt. Attached to the Machine Gun Section of his unit, he fought at Gaza, Haifa, Acre and Jerusalem during the British Advance through Palestine, and was present at the occupation of Damascus. He returned to England for demobilisation in 1918, and holds the 1914–15 Star, and the General Service and Victory Medals.
68, Villiers Road, Oxhey.   X5169/B.

TREASURE, E., Sapper, Royal Engineers.
Volunteering in January 1915, he was engaged on important duties with his unit until drafted to France in June 1918. He served on the Western Front and did good work on the lines of communication, during the Battle of Ypres and other important engagements. He was demobilised in June 1919, and holds the General Service and Victory Medals.
339, High Town Road, Luton.   5172/B.

TREGIDGO, W. H., Driver, R.F.A.
He volunteered in September 1915, and in the following year was sent to the Western Front. There he was engaged on important duties at Divisional Headquarters, and later fought at Ypres and on the Somme, and was severely wounded in 1918. He was demobilised in December 1919, and holds the General Service and Victory Medals, and in 1920 was still under medical treatment.
Railway Crossing, Potton.   Z5170.

TRENCHARD, C. J., Private, Middlesex Regt.
Volunteering in August 1915, he embarked for Egypt in the following December and fought at Gaza, Jerusalem and other places during the Advance through Palestine. After the conclusion of hostilities he was sent to Salonika in January 1919, and served there for a time. He was demobilised in May 1919 on returning home, and holds the 1914–15 Star, and the General Service and Victory Medals.
8, Cross Street, Watford.   X5171/A.

TRENCHARD, H., Air Mechanic, Royal Air Force.
He joined in May 1919, and after completing his training was engaged on important duties with his Squadron at various aerodromes. Sent to Ireland, he did good work, and in 1920 was still serving.
8, Cross Street, Watford.   X5171/B.

TROTT, S., Private, 3rd (King's Own) Hussars.
A serving soldier, he was mobilised and proceeded to France at the commencement of hostilities, and was in action in the Retreat from Mons and the Battles of Ypres, Arras, Cambrai, and in the German Offensive and Allied Advance of 1918, and was wounded. He was demobilised in January 1919, and holds the Mons Star, and the General Service and Victory Medals.
13, Edward Street, Luton.   5174.

TRUMAN, H. W., Shoeing-smith, R.F.A.
He joined in 1916, and on completing his training served at various stations engaged on guard and other important duties with his Battery. He did good work, but was unsuccessful in obtaining his transfer overseas before the signing of the Armistice. He was demobilised in 1919.
90, Harwood Road, Watford.   X5175.

TRUMPER, F. L., Sergeant, Rifle Brigade.
Volunteering in November 1914, he completed his training and served with his Regiment on Home duties for a time. He embarked for India in January 1916, and was engaged at various garrison towns on guard and other important duties. He returned to England in 1919 and was demobilised in November of that year, and holds the General Service and Victory Medals.
64, Regent Street, North Watford.   X5176.

TRUNDLER, G. D., Private, 7th Suffolk Regt.
He joined in March 1916, and was sent to the Western Front four months later, and saw much service in various sectors, fighting in the Battle at Vimy Ridge and many others. He was killed in action on the Somme on August 11th, 1916, and was entitled to the General Service and Victory Medals.
High Street, Over, Cambs.   240/A.

TRUSS, J. J., Sergeant, 1/6th Essex Regiment.
Volunteering in August 1914, he proceeded to Egypt in the following year, and served on the Palestine front and fought at the Battles of Gaza, in the operations resulting in the capture of Jerusalem, and throughout the Advance into Syria. He returned to England and was demobilised in March 1919, and holds the 1914–15 Star, and the General Service and Victory Medals.
3, Mullingar Terrace, London Colney.   X5177.

TRUSSELL, C. W., Private, Suffolk Regiment.
Joining in September 1917, he was sent to Salonika later in the same year and saw much service in this theatre of war, fighting in many important engagements. After the cessation of hostilities he proceeded to Constantinople with the Army of Occupation and served there until returning to England for demobilisation in April 1919. He holds the General Service and Victory Medals.
40, Old Park Road, Hitchin.   5178.

TUCK, F., Driver, Royal Field Artillery.
Joining in April 1917, he embarked for the Western Front two months later, and was in action in the engagements at Ypres, Cambrai, and Loos, and in the German Offensive and subsequent Allied Advance in 1918. He was demobilised in July 1919, and holds the General Service and Victory Medals.
Homeleigh, Waller Avenue, Leagrave, Luton.   5179.

TUCKER, A. T. G., Rifleman, 12th London Regiment (Rangers).
Volunteering in 1915, he proceeded to France later in the same year and was engaged in the fighting at the Battles of Ypres, Arras and Cambrai, and was wounded on the Somme in 1917. Returning to England, he received hospital treatment, and was subsequently discharged unfit for further service in August of that year. He holds the 1914-15 Star, and the General Service and Victory Medals.
27, Fearnley Street, Watford.   X5180.

TUCKER, W. J., Private, 6th Bedfordshire Regt.
He joined in June 1916, and embarked for the Western Front in the following December. During his service overseas he fought in many important engagements, and was wounded at Arras in April 1917. He returned to England, and after receiving hospital treatment was invalided out of the Service in November 1917, and holds the General Service and Victory Medals.
Hockliffe Hill, Leighton Buzzard.   5181.

TUFFIELD, A. A., Private, 2nd Norfolk Regt.
A serving soldier, he was stationed in India at the outbreak of war and was drafted to France in October 1914, and fought at Ypres, Hill 60, Givenchy and the Somme, and was twice wounded and gassed in 1915. He was invalided to England, and on recovery was sent to Mesopotamia in 1916 and saw much service there, until, contracting malaria, he was sent to hospital in Malta. In 1917 he proceeded to Salonika, and was in action on the Vardar, Doiran and Struma fronts until hostilities ceased. He was still serving in 1920, and holds the 1914 Star, and the General Service and Victory Medals.
74, Queen's Street, Hitchin.   1855/B.

TUFFIN, H., Sapper, Royal Engineers
Joining in March 1917, he embarked for France later in the same year. During his service in this theatre of war he was employed on important duties in connection with operations and was in action at Arras, the Somme, Ypres, Amiens and during the German Offensive and subsequent Allied Advance of 1918. He was demobilised in March 1919, and holds the General Service and Victory Medals.
3, Queen's Road, Harpenden.   5182/A.

TUFFNELL, B. W., Bombardier, R.F.A.
He volunteered in September 1915, and embarked for Egypt six months later. During his service in this theatre of war he was in action at the Battles of Gaza and in operations preceding the capture of Jerusalem. He fought throughout the Advance into Syria in September and October 1918, and returning to England was demobilised in June 1919, and holds the General Service and Victory Medals.
36, Curzon Road, Luton.   5183.

TUFFNELL, W., Private, 1st Bedfordshire Regt.
He volunteered in September 1914, and proceeded to the Western Front two months later, and fought in many important engagements, including those of Ypres and Neuve Chapelle. He was unfortunately killed in action at the Battle of Hill 60 on April 18th, 1915, and was entitled to the 1914-15 Star, and the General Service and Victory Medals.
Wilshamstead, Beds.   Z4978/B.

TULEY, T. A., L/Corporal, Military Foot Police.
Volunteering in December 1914, he completed his training and was stationed at various depôts engaged on important duties with his unit. He was unable to obtain his transfer overseas owing to ill health, but rendered valuable services until after the cessation of hostilities. He was then drafted to Gibraltar, where in 1920 he was still serving.
42, Old Park Road, Hitchin.   5184.

TUNNELL, S., Sapper, Royal Engineers.
Volunteering in May 1915, he was sent to France later in the same year and saw much service in various sectors, being present at the Battles of Ypres and Arras. In 1917 he was transferred to Egypt, and rendered valuable services on the Palestine front engaged on important duties in connection with the operations during the Advance into Syria. He returned to England and was demobilised in March 1919, and holds the 1914-15 Star, and the General Service and Victory Medals.
20, Brightwell Road, Watford.   X5185.

TURLAND, W. J., Private, R.A.S.C.
Joining in November 1917, he completed his training and served at various stations with his unit engaged on transport and other duties. Unable to obtain his transfer overseas prior to the cessation of hostilities, owing to ill-health, he rendered valuable services until discharged in November 1918.
10, Cecil Street, North Watford.   X5186.

TURNER, C., Rifleman, 18th London Regiment (London Irish Rifles).
He volunteered in 1915, and was sent to the Western Front in the same year, and fought on the Somme, at Arras, Messines, Loos, Albert, and was wounded at Cambrai. He was also in action during the Retreat and Advance of 1918, and returned to England and was demobilised in February 1919. He holds the 1914-15 Star, and the General Service and Victory Medals.
Brampton Park Road, Hitchin.   5187.

TURNER, C. H., Private, Royal Fusiliers (attached Royal Army Service Corps).
He joined in July 1916, and on conclusion of his training served at various depôts in England and Ireland on important transport duties with his unit. Medically unfit for service overseas, he was unable to obtain his transfer to a theatre of war, but rendered excellent services until demobilised in 1920.
15, Havelock Road, Biggleswade.   Z5188/A.

TURNER, E. A. (M.M.), Company Sergeant-Major, 5th Middlesex Regiment.
Volunteering in March 1915, he was engaged in training recruits for the New Armies at various depôts until drafted to the Western Front in June 1918. He fought in many engagements during the Retreat and Advance of 1918, and was wounded. He was awarded the Military Medal for conspicuous gallantry in the Field in saving the life of an officer. He was still serving in 1920, and also holds the General Service and Victory Medals.
102, Estcourt Road, Watford.   X5189/A.

TURNER, F., Private, 13th Australian Imperial Forces.
Volunteering in January 1915, he embarked for the Dardanelles in the following August, and was in action at the landing at Suvla Bay. He was killed in action at Lone Tree Hill on August 23rd of the same year, and was entitled to the 1914-15 Star, and the General Service and Victory Medals.
8, Ash Road, Luton.   5242/A.

TURNER, G. A., Private, Middlesex Regiment.
He joined in 1916, and later was drafted to the Western Front, where he saw much service in various parts of the line, fighting at the Somme, Neuve Chapelle, Arras, Ypres, Cambrai, and throughout the Retreat and Advance of 1918, and was twice wounded. After the Armistice he went into Germany with the Army of Occupation, and served at various stations on the Rhine until he returned to England and was demobilised in 1919. He holds the General Service and Victory Medals.
15, Havelock Road, Biggleswade.   Z5188/B.

TURNER, G. E., Corporal, Bedfordshire Regt.
Joining in 1916, he proceeded overseas later in the same year. During his service on the Western Front he was engaged in many important battles, including those of Arras, Ypres, and the Somme, and fought throughout the German Offensive and subsequent Allied Advance in 1918, and was wounded. He was demobilised in 1919, and holds the General Service and Victory Medals.
5, Grange Street, St. Albans.   X5190.

TURNER, H. F., Sergeant, R.A.S.C.
He volunteered in June 1915, and embarked for the Western Front in the following March, and was engaged on important supply duties until December 1916, when he was transferred to Mesopotamia. In this theatre of war he served in the forward areas in various parts of the front and did very good work. He returned to England in December 1918 and was demobilised in March 1919, holding the General Service and Victory Medals.
102, Estcourt Road, Watford.   X5189/B.

TURNER, H. J., Private, Royal Scots.
Joining in 1917, he was sent to France later in the same year, and was in action in many engagements of note, including those of Arras, Ypres, the Somme, Cambrai and in the Retreat and Advance of 1918. After the Armistice he proceeded into Germany with the Army of Occupation and served on the Rhine until he returned to England for demobilisation in 1919. He holds the General Service and Victory Medals.
15, Havelock Road, Biggleswade.   Z5188/C.

TURNER, J., Driver, Royal Engineers.
Mobilised in August 1914, he embarked for France at a later date and served in the advanced areas on important duties in the Battles of Hill 60, Loos, Vimy Ridge, Passchendaele, and in the German Offensive and Allied Advance of 1918. After hostilities ceased he went to Germany with the Army of Occupation and was stationed at Cologne. He was demobilised in March 1919, and holds the 1914–15 Star, and the General Service and Victory Medals.
8, Ash Road, Luton.   5242/B.

TURNER, J. A., Private, Hertfordshire Regt.
He volunteered in February 1916, and was drafted to the Western Front in the following year. During his service in this theatre of war he fought on the Somme, at Ypres and in the German Offensive and subsequent Allied Advance in 1918, and was wounded. Returning to England, he was demobilised in September 1919, and holds the General Service and Victory Medals.
52, King's Road, Hitchin.   5191/A.

TURNER, J. H., Private, R.A.S.C. (M.T.)
He joined in June 1916, and on completing his training served at various stations on important duties in connection with anti-aircraft work until drafted to France in November 1918. Here he was engaged with his unit on special work, and in the following year returned to England and was demobilised in February 1919, and holds the General Service and Victory Medals.
22, Langley Road, Luton.   5192.

TURNER, R. H., Private, 8th East Surrey Regt.
He joined in August 1917, and proceeded overseas in the following January, and was in action in many important engagements during his service on the Western Front. He was taken prisoner in April 1918 at Villers-Bretonneux in the German Offensive of that year. Repatriated after the Armistice he was demobilised in September 1919, and holds the General Service and Victory Medals.
12, Black Horse Lane, Hitchin.   5193.

TURNER, S., Private, 1/5th Bedfordshire Regt.
Volunteering in September 1914, he embarked for the Dardanelles in the following year and fought in the landing at Suvla Bay and the subsequent engagement at Anzac, and was wounded in August 1915. Drafted to Egypt after recovery he served on the Palestine front fighting at Gaza, Mejdil, Yarba and throughout the Advance into Syria. He returned to England and was demobilised in February 1919, and holds the 1914–15 Star, and the General Service and Victory Medals.
8, Ash Road, Luton.   5242/D.

TURNER, S. F., Corporal, 2nd and 11th Middlesex Regiment.
Volunteering in August 1914, he was sent to France in the following May, and was engaged in many important battles, including those of Ypres, the Somme, Armentières, and Arras, and was wounded in July 1916. On recovery he returned to the front lines, and again saw heavy fighting, being wounded twice more and taken prisoner on May 27th, 1918, during the German Offensive. He was repatriated and demobilised in April 1919, and holds the 1914–15 Star, and the General Service and Victory Medals.
102, Estcourt Road, Watford.   X5189/C.

TURNER, W., Driver, R.A.S.C.
Volunteering in September 1914, he was sent to the Western Front six months later, and served in the advanced areas on important transport duties during many important engagements, including those of Arras, Ypres, the Somme and in the Retreat and Advance of 1918. He was demobilised in April 1919, and holds the 1914–15 Star, and the General Service and Victory Medals.
11, Park Street, St. Albans.   X5194.

TURNER, W., Private, Bedfordshire Regiment and Labour Corps.
Joining in April 1917, he proceeded to the Western Front later in the same year and served in many sectors, and was present at the Battles of Ypres, Arras, Messines, the Somme, and Cambrai. He rendered excellent services, and returning to England was demobilised in March 1919, and holds the General Service and Victory Medals.
8, Ash Road, Luton.   5242/C.

TURNER, W. L., Private, Duke of Wellington's (West Riding Regiment).
He joined in December 1917, and proceeded overseas in the following March, and was in action almost continuously during the German Offensive, and subsequent Allied Advance until wounded in October 1918. He returned to England, and after receiving hospital treatment served at various stations until demobilised in December 1919. He holds the General Service and Victory Medals.
52, King's Road, Hitchin.   5191/B.

TURNEY, C., Private, Bedfordshire Regiment.
He volunteered in August 1914, and in the following month was sent to France. During his long term of service he fought in many battles, including those of La Bassée, Ypres, Loos, Arras, the Somme and Cambrai. He also took part in the Retreat and Advance of 1918. On one occasion he was gassed. He was demobilised in April 1919, and holds the 1914 Star, and the General Service and Victory Medals.
36, Mill Road, Leighton Buzzard.   5195/A.

TURNEY, C. T., Private, Bedfordshire Regiment.
He joined in May 1916, and after his preliminary training was sent in the same year to the Western Front, where he took part in the Battles of the Somme, Arras, Ypres and Cambrai. At the conclusion of hostilities he was sent to Germany with the Army of Occupation, and was stationed at Cologne. He was demobilised in November 1919, and holds the General Service and Victory Medals.
47, Leighton Street, Woburn.   Z632/A.

TURNEY, E., Rifleman, King's Royal Rifle Corps.
He joined in June 1917, and in the same year was sent to France. Serving in several sectors of the Western Front, he fought in the Battles of Bullecourt, Ypres (III.) and the Somme (II.). He also took part in the Retreat and Advance of 1918. He was demobilised in March 1919, and holds the General Service and Victory Medals.
36, Mill Road, Leighton Buzzard.   5195/B.

TURNEY, T., Private, Essex Regiment.
Volunteering in August 1914, he was sent in the following March to Egypt, where he served in the Canal zone. He was subsequently engaged in the fighting at Gaza, and was present at the occupation of Jerusalem. He returned to England after the cessation of hostilities, and was demobilised in March 1919, and holds the 1914–15 Star, and the General Service and Victory Medals.
3, Heath Road, Leighton Buzzard.   5196/A.

TURNEY, W., Private, Royal Inniskilling Fusiliers.
He joined in May 1916, and on the completion of his training was sent overseas in the following November. Whilst on the Western Front he fought in many engagements, including those on the Somme, at Arras, Passchendaele and Cambrai. He also took part in the Retreat and subsequent Advance of 1918. He was demobilised in March 1919, and holds the General Service and Victory Medals.
3, Heath Road, Leighton Buzzard.   5196/B.

TURNEY, W., Private, Labour Corps.
He joined in February 1917, and in the following March was drafted to France. He served in many sectors of the Western Front, including those of Arras, the Somme, and Cambrai, and was engaged in road-making, carrying rations and ammunition, and in trench-digging. He also took part in the Retreat of March 1918, and was discharged in the following June. He holds the General Service and Victory Medals.
14, Dudley Street, Leighton Buzzard.   5197.

TURNEY, W. E., Private, 1st Wiltshire Regt.
Joining in August 1916, the proceeded overseas in the following January. He took part in much fighting on the Western Front, at Arras and at Ypres, where he was wounded in March 1917. He was invalided to England and after many months' hospital treatment at Newcastle, Staffordshire, was engaged on Home duties until he was demobilised in December 1918. He holds the General Service and Victory Medals.
7, Waterloo Road, Linslade, Bucks.   5198/A.

TURNEY, W. H., Private, 36th Training Reserve Battalion.
He joined in July 1918 on attaining military age, and was engaged on special duties with his Battalion at Portsmouth, where his Regiment was stationed. He did good work, but owing to medical unfitness was not sent overseas, and was demobilised in February 1919.
7, Waterloo Road, Linslade, Bucks.   5198/B.

TURPIN, J. H., Private, Queen's (Royal West Surrey Regiment).
Joining in February 1917, he was drafted to France in the succeeding month. Whilst on the Western Front he was engaged in the Battles of Ypres, the Somme and Cambrai. He also took part in the German Offensive and subsequent Allied Advance of 1918. He was demobilised in November 1919, and holds the General Service and Victory Medals.
12, Merton Road, Watford.   X5199.

TURTLEBURY, J., Staff-Sergeant, 5th (Princess Charlotte of Wales') Dragoon Guards.
Having enlisted in 1898, he served for two years after the outbreak of war as Farrier Staff-Sergeant at Aldershot. He was then drafted to France, where he was engaged on important duties at Abbeville, Arras, Ypres, the Somme and Cambrai. He was demobilised in May 1919, and holds the General Service and Victory Medals.
24, St. John Street, Biggleswade.   Z5200.

TURVEY, A., Private, 7th Bedfordshire Regt.
He volunteered in September 1914, and during his training was stationed at Aldershot. In July 1915 he proceeded to France, where he fought at Ypres, Festubert and Loos. He was unfortunately killed in action in the Battle of the Somme on November 16th, 1916. He was entitled to the 1914-15 Star, and the General Service and Victory Medals. His memory is cherished with pride.
High Street, Houghton Conquest, near Ampthill. Z5243/B.

TURVEY, G., Private, Bedfordshire Regiment and Cheshire Regiment.
Joining in 1916, he was drafted to France in the following year. He fought on the Somme front, and was severely wounded and taken prisoner in March 1917. He unfortunately died from the effects of his wounds, whilst still a prisoner, on May 6th, 1918, and was buried at Tourcoing. He was entitled to the General Service and Victory Medals.
High Street, Houghton Conquest, near Ampthill. Z5243/C.

TURVEY, H., Private, Royal Army Service Corps.
He joined in October 1916, and in the following January proceeded overseas. During his service on the Western Front he was engaged in the transport of rations and ammunition in the Arras and Cambrai sectors. He was demobilised in September 1919, and holds the General Service and Victory Medals.
7, Alfred Street, Dunstable.   5201.

TURVEY, S. C., Corporal, Dorsetshire Regiment and Labour Corps.
He joined in March 1917, and in January of the following year was sent to France. He was engaged in guarding German prisoners since he was medically unfit for service in the Field. He did excellent work, and returned to England for demobilisation in October 1919. He holds the General Service and Victory Medals.
41, Great Northern Road, Dunstable.   5202/B.

TURVEY, S. J. (M.M.), Corporal, R.E.
Volunteering at the outbreak of war, he was sent to France in 1915. During a long period of service he was engaged on important work with a cable section. He was awarded the Military Medal for conspicuous bravery and devotion to duty in the Field. He was demobilised in March 1919, and holds the 1914-15 Star, and the General Service and Victory Medals.
41, Great Northern Road, Dunstable.   5202/A.

TURVEY, T., Rifleman, Rifle Brigade.
Joining in March 1918, he served at the conclusion of his training with his unit at Nottingham. Although he was unsuccessful in securing his transfer overseas before the cessation of hostilities, he was drafted to Germany with the Army of Occupation, and was stationed at Cologne. He was demobilised in 1919.
High Street, Houghton Conquest, near Ampthill. Z5243/D.

TURVEY, W., Private, 11th Suffolk Regiment.
He joined in July 1918 on attaining military age, and was drafted to France in the following October. Whilst on the Western Front he was engaged in the fighting in the Cambrai sector, where he remained until he was demobilised in February 1919. He holds the General Service and Victory Medals. 13, Park Street, Dunstable.   5203.

TURVEY, W. (M.M.), Sergeant, 5th M.G.C.
He volunteered in September 1914, and in December of the same year was sent to France. He fought at Hill 60, Vimy Ridge, Arras, the Somme and at Passchendaele, and was awarded the Medaille Militaire for conspicuous gallantry in the Field. He was later transferred to the Italian front and served in the fighting on the Piave. He was demobilised in February 1919, and also holds the 1914-15 Star, and the General Service and Victory Medals.
81, King Street, Houghton Regis.   5204.

TURVEY, W., Private, 7th Bedfordshire Regt.
He volunteered in September 1914, and in the following July was sent overseas. During his long and varied service on the Western Front he was engaged in the fighting on the Somme, at Ypres, Vimy Ridge, Lens and Cambrai. He was demobilised in March 1919, and holds the 1914-15 Star, and the General Service and Victory Medals.
High Street, Houghton Conquest, near Ampthill. Z5243/A.

TUTTEY, C. E., Private, 7th Lincolnshire Regt.
He volunteered in November 1914, and was drafted to France in 1916. During his service on the Western Front he was in action in the Battles of the Somme, Arras and Ypres, and was wounded in October 1918. He was invalided home, and after receiving hospital treatment was discharged in March 1919. He holds the General Service and Victory Medals.
12, Keyfield West, St. Albans.   X5205.

TWIGG, J., Corporal, North Staffordshire Regt.
Volunteering at the outbreak of war, he was drafted to France in January 1915. He fought in many battles, including those of Loos and Ypres, and was seriously wounded at the first Battle of the Somme in July 1916. He was sent to hospital in England and was eventually invalided out of the Service in September 1916. He holds the 1914-15 Star, and the General Service and Victory Medals.
13, Blacksmith Lane, St. Albans.   12/B.

TYLER, C. S., Special War Worker.
He offered his services for work of National importance during the war, and held a responsible post at the Vauxhall Motor Works, Luton, engaged on important work connected with the production of munitions. He rendered valuable services and discharged his duties in an efficient and satisfactory manner.
156, New Town Street, Luton.   5206/A.

TYLER, H. W., Leading Seaman, Royal Navy.
He was serving at the outbreak of war, and was drafted to the Dardanelles aboard H.M.S. "Ocean." His ship took part in the attempt to force the Narrows and was blown up by a mine, but he fortunately was saved. He also served in the Persian Gulf, and was discharged on account of the expiration of his term of service in March 1917. He holds the 1914-15 Star, and the General Service and Victory Medals.
43, Prospect Road, St. Albans.   X5207.

TYLER, R., Private, 1/5th Bedfordshire Regt.
He was mobilised as a Territorial at the outbreak of war, and in July 1915 was drafted to Gallipoli, where he fought at the landing at Suvla Bay. He was subsequently transferred to Egypt, whence he was drafted to Palestine. There he took part in the Battle of Gaza. After his long and varied service he returned to England and was demobilised in June 1919. He holds the 1914-15 Star, and the General Service and Victory Medals.
156, New Town Street, Luton.   5206/B.

TYRRELL, A., Private, 4th East Surrey Regt.
He volunteered in September 1914, and in 1916 was sent to France. Whilst in this theatre of war he fought on the Somme, at Ypres and Cambrai, and was afterwards drafted to Italy, where he was engaged in the fighting on the Piave. Returning in April 1918 to the Western Front, he took part in the final operations of the war. He was demobilised in January 1919, and holds the General Service and Victory Medals.
59, Liverpool Road, Watford.   X5240/D.

TYRRELL, F., Private, R.A.V.C.
He joined in November 1916, and in the following April was sent to Salonika. Whilst in this theatre of war he was engaged upon responsible duties with his unit, attending to sick and wounded horses. He returned to England after the cessation of hostilities, and was demobilised in February 1919. He holds the General Service and Victory Medals.
59, Liverpool Road, Watford.   X5240/A.

TYRRELL, P., Sergeant, R.E. (Signal Section).
He was mobilised at the outbreak of war, and was drafted to the Dardanelles in July 1915. He was engaged on special duties at the landing at Suvla Bay and in many subsequent engagements until transferred to Egypt. Joining in the Palestine campaign, he was engaged upon responsible work at Gaza and Jerusalem, but was unfortunately wounded in July 1917. He was discharged in January 1919, and holds the 1914-15 Star, and the General Service and Victory Medals.
59, Liverpool Road, Watford.   X5240/C.

TYRRELL, S., Sergeant, King's African Rifles.
Volunteering in September 1914, he was almost immediately sent to France, where he fought at Ypres and Festubert. In 1917 he proceeded to German East Africa, where he remained until early in 1919. He then returned to England and was demobilised in February of that year. He holds the Mons Star, and the General Service and Victory Medals.
59, Liverpool Road, Watford.   X5240/B.

TYSOM, C. J., Rifleman, King's Royal Rifle Corps.
He joined in 1917, and in the same year was sent to France. He served on the Western Front and at one time fought with the Guards. He was also engaged on special duties with his unit at Le Havre. He was wounded on two occasions. He returned to England after the signing of the Armistice, and was demobilised in December 1919, holding the General Service and Victory Medals.
31, Hastings Street, Luton. 5209.

TYSOM, H. (M.M.), Corporal 1/20th London Regt.
He volunteered in May 1915, and in March of the following year was sent overseas. He was engaged in the fighting at Messines Ridge, Vimy Ridge, Ypres and Cambrai, and was wounded in the Battle of the Somme on October 1st, 1916. He was awarded the Military Medal for bravery and devotion to duty in the Field on September 1st, 1918. He was discharged on account of service in November 1918, and holds the General Service and Victory Medals.
33, Grove Road, Luton. 2806/B—2807/B.

TYSOM, H., Private, Royal Army Service Corps.
He joined in March 1916, and in the following November was drafted to Salonika. Whilst in this theatre of war he was employed on special work with his unit. He took part in the final Advance into Bulgaria. Returning to England, he was demobilised in September 1919, and holds the General Service and Victory Medals.
178, Wellington Street, Luton. 5210/A.

TYSOM, J. F., Private, R.A.S.C.
He joined in February 1918, and was almost immediately sent to Italy. He was engaged with his unit on important duties during the fighting on the Piave, and for a time was stationed at Taranto. He returned to England after the signing of the Armistice, and was demobilised in 1919. He holds the General Service and Victory Medals.
178, Wellington Street, Luton. 5210/B.

TYSOM, W. B., Sapper, Royal Engineers.
He volunteered in March 1915, and embarked for Egypt in December 1917 aboard S.S. "Arrogant." This vessel, however, was shipwrecked in the Mediterranean, but he survived and reached Egypt. He subsequently served in Palestine and was engaged in the fighting at Mejdel, Haifa and Beyrout. He returned to England and was demobilised in July 1919, and holds the General Service and Victory Medals.
178, Wellington Street, Luton. 5210/C.

TYSOME, F., Private, 2nd Bedfordshire Regt.
A serving soldier, he was drafted to France in October 1914. He fought in many engagements, including those of Ypres, Festubert, Loos, Givenchy and the Somme. He was badly gassed and sent to England in March 1917, and was invalided out of the Service two months later. He holds the 1914 Star, and the General Service and Victory Medals.
Little Lane, Clophill, Ampthill. 5208.

U

UNDERWOOD, A., Sergeant, Tank Corps.
He joined in November 1916, and on completion of his training served at home until December 1917, when he was drafted to France. During his service on the Western Front he fought in the Battles of Cambrai and Albert and in the Retreat and Advance of 1918. He returned to England in November of that year and later proceeded to Ireland, and in 1920 was still serving. He holds the General Service and Victory Medals. 5, George Street, Leighton Buzzard. 5211.

UNDERWOOD, A., Sapper, Royal Engineers.
He joined in July 1916, and at the conclusion of his training served with his unit on important duties at a large port in the West of England. He did very good work in the dockyards, but was unsuccessful in securing his transfer overseas before hostilities ceased. He was demobilised in November 1918.
67, Beech Road, Luton. 5212.

UNDERWOOD, E., Sapper, Royal Engineers.
He joined in March 1918 on attaining military age, and on completion of his training was engaged on special work with his unit. He rendered valuable services, but was not able to obtain his transfer to a theatre of war before the close of hostilities. In December 1918 he was drafted to Germany to the Army of Occupation, and was stationed at Cologne, where he served until 1920. Returning to England he was demobilised in March of that year.
118, Vandyke Street, Leighton Buzzard. 5213/A.

UNDERWOOD, E., Q.M.S. (Farrier), R.F.A.
He was mobilised at the outbreak of war and drafted to France, where he was engaged in the fighting in the Retreat from Mons and the subsequent Battles of the Somme, Arras, Cambrai and many others until the Armistice. He then went into Germany with the Army of Occupation and served there for a time. In 1920 he was still serving, and holds the Mons Star, and the General Service and Victory Medals, also the Long Service and Good Conduct Medal.
58, Church Street, Leighton Buzzard. 5214.

UNDERWOOD, F. T., Private, 8th Bedfordshire Regiment.
He volunteered in August 1914, and shortly afterwards proceeded overseas to France. In this theatre of war he served with his Battalion and was engaged in much heavy fighting. He made the supreme sacrifice, being killed in action at the second Battle of Ypres on May 17th, 1915. He was entitled to the Mons Star, and the General Service and Victory Medals.
Bygrave Cottages, Ickleford, Hitchin. 5215/B.

UNDERWOOD, G. A., Private, Manchester Regt.
Volunteering in 1915, he was drafted to France in the same year. During his service on the Western Front he took part in many important engagements, including those of Ypres and Loos. He was taken prisoner at the Battle of Arras, and held captive in Germany until after the Armistice, when he was repatriated and subsequently demobilised in September 1919. He holds the 1914-15 Star, and the General Service and Victory Medals.
Bygrave Cottages, Ickleford, Hitchin. 5215/A.

UNDERWOOD, H., Sergeant, M.G.C.
A serving soldier, he was mobilised at the outbreak of war, and drafted to France in September 1914. In this theatre of operations he was engaged in heavy fighting in the Battles of the Somme and Arras, and was wounded at Neuve Chapelle in May 1917. On recovery he returned to the firing line and fought at Cambrai, and during the German Offensive was again wounded at Gommecourt in May 1918. He was invalided to England and eventually discharged in May 1919. He holds the 1914 Star, and the General Service and Victory Medals. 118, Vandyke Road, Leighton Buzzard. 5216/B.

UNDERWOOD, J. J., Corporal, Royal Fusiliers.
Volunteering in August 1914, he served at home for a time, and was drafted to France in 1916. He was in action in many engagements on the Somme, and was wounded. On recovery he was sent to Italy in 1917, and fought on the Piave and Trentino fronts until 1918, when he returned to the Western Front, and was actively engaged in the fighting at Arras and Cambrai, and was again wounded. He holds the General Service and Victory Medals, and was demobilised in April 1919.
118, Vandyke Road, Leighton Buzzard. 5216/A.

UNDERWOOD, P. S., Private, Northamptonshire Regiment.
He joined in October 1916, and two months later proceeded to France. He served in many engagements and was in action on the Somme, at Arras, Vimy Ridge and Ypres. Owing to ill-health he was invalided home, and after receiving hospital treatment was discharged as medically unfit for further military service in August 1918. He holds the General Service and Victory Medals.
3, Shirley Road, Luton. 3842/A.

UNDERWOOD, T., Pte., 2nd Bedfordshire Regt.
He volunteered in August 1914, and three months later was sent to France. In this theatre of war he served with his Battalion and took part in the Battles of Ypres and Neuve Chapelle. He made the supreme sacrifice and was killed in action during the Battle of Hill 60 on April 21st, 1915. He was entitled to the 1914 Star, and the General Service and Victory Medals.
11, Cardiff Road, Watford. 5213/B.

UNDERWOOD, W. C., Private, R.A.O.C.
He joined in August 1916, and in the following December was sent to France, where he remained until after the close of the war. During this period he was engaged on special clerical duties at Headquarters of his unit, and did very good work. He was demobilised in September 1919, and holds the General Service and Victory Medals.
11, Cardiff Road, Watford. X5217.

UPCHURCH, C., Rifleman, 12th K.R.R.C.
He joined in October 1917, and in the following April proceeded to France, where he was in action in the Battles of Amiens and Le Cateau, and during the Retreat and Advance of 1918. After the Armistice he was sent into Germany with the Army of Occupation and was engaged on guard and other duties on the Rhine. He returned home in May 1919, and holds the General Service and Victory Medals, and in 1920 was still serving.
17, St. Michael's Mount, Hitchin. 5218/A.

UPCHURCH, F. G., Corporal, 5th Sherwood Foresters.
He joined in March 1916, and four months later embarked for the Western Front. Whilst overseas he fought in the Battles of Arras, Armentières, Vimy Ridge, and was wounded on the Somme in September 1917. Returning to the Field, he took part in the Battle of Cambrai and other engagements during the concluding stages of the war. He was demobilised in September 1919, and holds the General Service and Victory Medals.
17, St. Michael's Mount, Hitchin 5218/B.

UPCHURCH, W., A.B., Royal Navy.

He volunteered in December 1915, and, posted to H.M.S. "Tancred," served aboard that vessel throughout the war. Attached to the Grand Fleet, his ship was engaged on important submarine patrol duties in the North Sea, and was later employed on escort duties in American waters. He holds the 1914–15 Star, and the General Service and Victory Medals, and in 1920 was still serving.
11, Midland Cottages, Nightingale Road, Hitchin.   5219.

UPCHURCH, W., Private, Royal Warwickshire Regiment.

Volunteering in January 1915, he was shortly afterwards sent to France and fought in the Battles of Festubert and Loos. He was drafted to Italy in 1916, and took part in heavy fighting on the Piave, Asiago and Trentino fronts, and was invalided home owing to illness in 1918. After treatment he was discharged as medically unfit for further service in November 1919, and holds the 1914–15 Star, and the General Service and Victory Medals.
35, Orchard Road, Walsworth, Hitchin.   5220.

UPPERTON, T. W., L/Corporal, Royal Engineers.

Joining in July 1917, he proceeded to Italy shortly afterwards and served there on the Piave until sent to France in the following year. Whilst on the Western Front he was engaged on important duties during the Battles of the Somme and Cambrai, and returned home for demobilisation in November 1919. He holds the General Service and Victory Medals.
83, Regent Street, North Watford.   X5221.

UPSON, W. A., Sapper, Royal Engineers; and Private, Durham Light Infantry.

He joined in February 1917, and in the same year embarked for France. Whilst in this theatre of war he was in action in several important engagements, including the Battles of Ypres, Cambrai and the Somme, and was wounded. On recovery he returned to the front lines, and was subsequently taken prisoner in May 1918. He was held in captivity in Germany until the Armistice, when he was repatriated, and demobilised in February 1919. He holds the General Service and Victory Medals.
116, Rushbymead, Letchworth.   5222–3.

UPTON, C. R., Private, 1st Bedfordshire Regt.

Joining in April 1918, he completed his training and was engaged on guard, cookhouse and other duties with his unit, and rendered valuable services. He was unsuccessful in obtaining a transfer to a theatre of war before the cessation of hostilities, and was demobilised in November 1919.
37, Spencer Street, St. Albans.   X5224.

UPTON, H., Private, Sherwood Foresters.

He joined in February 1917, and later in that year proceeded to the Western Front, in several sectors of which he saw much service. He took part in the Battles of Ypres and Cambrai and, severely wounded near Ypres, was sent to a Base hospital. Rejoining his unit after recovery he served until hostilities ceased. He returned home for demobilisation in October 1919, and holds the General Service and Victory Medals.
43, Silsoe, near Ampthill.   5225.

UPTON, H. W., A/Corporal, Bedfordshire Regt.

He volunteered in 1915, and in the same year was sent overseas. Serving on the Western Front he took part in several engagements, including the Battle of Ypres, and was gassed and wounded at Hill 60. Rejoining his Battalion, he fought at Arras and in other operations until hostilities ceased. He was then sent with the Army of Occupation into Germany, and returning to England was demobilised in 1919, and holds the 1914–15 Star, and the General Service and Victory Medals.
37, Spencer Street, St. Albans.   X5226.

USHER, P., Private, 1/5th Bedfordshire Regt.

Volunteering in August 1914, he was drafted overseas a year later, and saw much service in Egypt. He was in action near Jerusalem and in several other engagements during the British Advance through Palestine. He returned to England for demobilisation in July 1919, and holds the 1914–15 Star, and the General Service and Victory Medals.
46, King's Road, Luton.   5227.

V

VANDYKE, A. J., Pioneer, Royal Engineers.

He volunteered in August 1915, and in the following year proceeded to the Western Front. He was engaged on special duties in connection with operations in the forward areas, and was present at the Battles of the Somme, Arras, Ypres and Cambrai. He holds the General Service and Victory Medals, and was demobilised in January 1919.
5, Common View Square, Letchworth.   5228.

VANSCHAGEN, G., L/Corporal, Prince of Wales' Leinster Regiment.

Joining in June 1916, he was sent to Salonika in the following December and fought in engagements on the Doiran front and in other operations in the Balkans. He was afterwards drafted to Egypt and was in action at Gaza and other places during the Palestine campaign. He returned to England for demobilisation in February 1919, and holds the General Service and Victory Medals.
102, Cobden Street, Luton.   1631/A.

VARNEY, H., Sapper, Royal Engineers.

He volunteered in January 1916, and was drafted overseas six months later. Whilst on the Western Front he served on the lines of communication and in wiring and digging trenches during operations on the Somme, at Arras, Cambrai and other places until the end of hostilities. He holds the General Service and Victory Medals, and was demobilised in October 1919.
Lily Crescent, Leighton Road, Wing, Bucks.   2612/A.

VARNEY, W., Private, Bedfordshire Regiment.

He joined in November 1916, and in the following year embarked for the Western Front. During his service overseas he took part in several important engagements, including those at Ypres and on the Somme, and was wounded, gassed and suffered from shell-shock. He was demobilised in February 1919, and holds the General Service and Victory Medals.
35, Chapel Street, Hemel Hempstead.   X5229.

VARNEY, W. J., Private, Coldstream Guards.

He volunteered in January 1915, and in the following July proceeded to France, where he fought during the Somme Offensive and in several other engagements. Wounded in action near Arras in 1917, he was sent to hospital in England and invalided out of the Service in November 1917. He holds the 1914–15 Star, and the General Service and Victory Medals.
High Street, Wing, Bucks.   5230.

VASS, W., Sapper, Royal Engineers.

He volunteered in June 1915, and in the same year proceeded to the Western Front, where he served for nearly four years. During this period he was engaged on important duties in connection with operations at Festubert, Arras, Cambrai and on the Somme. He holds the 1914–15 Star, and the General Service and Victory Medals, and was demobilised in March 1919.
86, Sopwell Lane, St. Albans.   X5231.

VENESS, J., Private, 2nd Royal Sussex Regiment.

Mobilised on the outbreak of war, he was almost immediately sent to France and fought in the Retreat from Mons, the Battle of Ypres, and was wounded near La Bassée on May 9th, 1915. On recovery he was drafted to India in February 1916, and served there on guard and other important duties for over three years. He was demobilised in November 1919 on his return to England, and holds the Mons Star, and the General Service and Victory Medals.
33, Brighton Road, Watford.   X5232.

VESEY, W. L. J., Private, Royal Irish Fusiliers.

Volunteering in August 1915, he proceeded to the Balkan theatre of war in November of the following year and fought in many engagements on the Vardar front. Transferred to France in August 1916, he was in action at the Somme and Cambrai and throughout the German Offensive and Allied Advance of 1918. He was demobilised in December 1918, and holds the 1914–15 Star, and the General Service and Victory Medals.
Ley Green, King's Walden.   5233.

VIALS, E., Private, 4th Northamptonshire Regt.

He volunteered in September 1914, and was drafted to Gallipoli in the following July and took part in the landing at Suvla Bay and in other operations until the evacuation of the Peninsula. In August 1916 he was sent to France and fought in several engagements, including that at Vimy Ridge, and was wounded at Merlancourt on September 10th, 1918, during the Allied Advance. He was demobilised in March 1919, and holds the 1914–15 Star, and the General Service and Victory Medals.
44, King's Road, St. Albans.   5234.

VICKERS, A., Air Mechanic, Royal Air Force.

He joined in January 1917, and after training was engaged on important duties at aerodromes on the South and East coasts. He did valuable work as a fitter, but was unable to secure a transfer overseas before the cessation of hostilities, and was demobilised in March 1919.
24, Springfield Road, Linslade.   5235.

VICKERS, F. G., Driver, Royal Field Artillery.

He volunteered in August 1914, and proceeded overseas
shortly afterwards. He served in various parts of India and
was stationed at Rawal Pindi, where he was engaged on guard
and other important duties. He returned to England for
demobilisation in April 1919, and holds the General Service
and Victory Medals.
41, Fishpool Street, St. Albans.   X5236/B.

VICKERS, F. W., Pioneer, Royal Engineers.

He volunteered in August 1915, and was sent to the Western
Front in the following year. During his service overseas he
was engaged on important duties in connection with operations on the Somme and in the Arras, Ypres and Festubert
sectors. He holds the General Service and Victory Medals,
and was demobilised in March 1919.
41, Fishpool Street, St. Albans.   X5236/A.

VICKERS, P. W., Private, Machine Gun Corps.

Joining in April 1917, he was sent to Italy in the same year
and served with the Lewis guns in various operations on the
Piave and Asiago fronts until the termination of hostilities.
He was demobilised in March 1920 on his return to England,
and holds the General Service and Victory Medals.
41, Fishpool Street, St. Albans.   X5236/C.

VICKERS, W., Private, Machine Gun Corps.

He volunteered in September 1914, and in the following
August proceeded to France, where he was in action in the
Battles of the Somme, Ypres, Arras and Passchendaele. In
November 1917 he was sent to Italy and fought in many
engagements in the Trentino and Piave sectors. He returned
to England for demobilisation in January 1919, and holds the
1914-15 Star, and the General Service and Victory Medals.
24, Springfield Road, Linslade, Leighton Buzzard.   5237.

VICKERY, C. H., Private, Royal Fusiliers.

Joining in February 1917, he embarked for France four
months later and took part in heavy fighting on the Somme
and at Passchendaele. He was reported missing on August
10th, 1917, after an engagement near Arras, and was later
presumed to have been killed in action on that date. He
was entitled to the General Service and Victory Medals.
35, Camp Road, St. Albans.   X4244/A.

VINCENT, A. W., Tpr., Hertfordshire Dragoons.

Volunteering in May 1915, in the following January he was
sent overseas. He served in Egypt for over three years,
and fought in several engagements during the British Advance
through Palestine. On returning to England he was demobilised in August 1919, and holds the General Service and
Victory Medals.
114, St. James' Road, Watford.   X5238/A.

VINCENT, E. C., Corporal, Bedfordshire Lancers and 15th (The King's) Hussars.

Mobilised on the outbreak of war, he was soon afterwards
sent to France and fought in the Retreat from Mons, the
Battles of Ypres and Loos, and was wounded on the Somme
in 1916 and near Ypres in the following year. He was also
in action at Arras and Cambrai and during the Retreat of
1918. He holds the Mons Star, and the General Service and
Victory Medals, and was demobilised in January 1919.
3, South Street, Leighton Buzzard.   5239.

VINCENT, E. H. T., Stoker, Royal Navy.

Joining in January 1917, he was posted to H.M.S.
"Forward," which vessel was engaged on important duties
in the North, Black and Ægean Seas and on the Danube
until the end of the war. He was discharged on account of
service in April 1919, and holds the General Service and
Victory Medals.
114, St. James' Road, Watford.   X5238/B.

VINCENT, T. W., Private, Labour Corps.

He joined in June 1916, and in the same year was drafted to
France. During his service overseas he was engaged on
important duties in the forward areas and was present at the
Battles of the Somme, Passchendaele and St. Quentin. He
was demobilised in February 1919, and holds the General
Service and Victory Medals.
114, St. James' Road, Watford.   X5238/C.

VINTNER, C., Corporal, Grenadier Guards.

He volunteered in August 1914, and a month later proceeded
to France and was in action on the Marne and at La Bassée
and Ypres. He was unfortunately killed in action at Neuve
Chapelle on March 12th, 1915, and was entitled to the 1914
Star, and the General Service and Victory Medals.
7, North Bridge Street, Shefford.   Z3702/B.

VIRGIN, G., Corporal, Queen's (Royal West Surrey Regiment).

Volunteering in August 1914, he was sent to France in the
same year and took part in heavy fighting on the Marne and
in the Ypres sector. He was reported wounded and missing
in September 1915, during the Battle of Loos, but was later
believed to have been killed in action. He was entitled to
the 1914 Star, and the General Service and Victory Medals.
41, Vale Road, Bushey.   X4010/A.

VIRGIN, H., Trooper, Essex Dragoons.

He joined in 1918 on attaining military age, and on the completion of his training served with his unit in Ireland. He
rendered valuable services, but was unable to obtain a
transfer to a theatre of war before the cessation of hostilities,
and was demobilised in November 1919.
41, Vale Road, Bushey.   X4010/C.

W

WADE, G. H., Gunner, Royal Marine Artillery.

Joining in December 1917, he completed his training and
was sent to Russia in the following May and saw much service
on the Murmansk coast and took part in many engagements.
Returning to England, he was demobilised in July 1919, and
holds the General Service and Victory Medals.
4, Church Street, Biggleswade.   Z5244.

WADE, J., Private, Essex Regiment.

Volunteering in January 1916, he was drafted overseas later
in the same year. During his service on the Western Front
he fought at the Battles of Loos, Albert, Vimy Ridge and
many other engagements, and was wounded in 1916. On
recovery he rejoined his regiment and was in action in various
parts of the line, and was again wounded. Invalided to
England he received hospital treatment, and on recovery
was sent to Ireland, and served there until demobilised in
September 1919. He holds the General Service and Victory
Medals. 39, Sun Street, Biggleswade.   Z5245.

WADE, T., L/Corporal, Welch Regiment.

He joined in November 1916, and was sent to France in the
following year and fought in many important engagements,
including those at Loos, the Somme, Arras, and in the
Retreat and Advance of 1918. He was demobilised in 1919,
and holds the General Service and Victory Medals.
Weathercock Lane, Woburn Sands.   Z5246

WAKE, F., Sapper, Royal Engineers.

Joining in June 1916, he proceeded to the Western Front in
the following December and served in the forward areas,
engaged on important duties in connection with operations
whilst the Battles of Ypres, the Somme, Arras and Albert
were in progress, and was gassed. On recovery he rejoined
his unit and was under fire during the Retreat and Advance
of 1918. He was demobilised in June 1919, and holds the
General Service and Victory Medals.
8, Roberts Road, Watford.   X5247.

WAKELEY, C. G., Gunner, R.G.A.

He joined in September 1916, and proceeded to France in
the following June and saw much service in various parts of
the line, and was in action at Arras, Ypres and throughout
the German Offensive and subsequent Allied Advance in
1918. He was demobilised in February 1919, and holds
the General Service and Victory Medals.
Saunder's Piece, Ampthill.   5248.

WAKELIN, F. G., Gunner, R.G.A.

Volunteering in September 1915, he served at various depôts
with his unit until sent to the Western Front in March 1917.
He was in action at Ypres, the Somme, Arras and in many
other engagements until August 1917, when he returned to
England and after a period of Home service was invalided out
of the Army in January 1918, and holds the General Service
and Victory Medals. 4, Cardiff Road, Watford.   X5250.

WAKELIN, G., Gunner, Royal Garrison Artillery.

He volunteered in September 1915, and was drafted to
France in the following January and saw much service in
various sectors. He fought in many important engagements, including those of Ypres and the Somme, and was
wounded during the German Offensive in March 1918, and
returned to England. After treatment he served at various
stations until demobilised in March 1919, and holds the
General Service and Victory Medals.
39, Cannon Road, Watford.   X5249.

WAKELIN, H., Gunner, Royal Garrison Artillery (9th Siege Battery).

He volunteered in September 1915, and was drafted overseas
in January of the following year. During his service in
France he was in action in many important engagements,
including those at Bapaume, Albert, Cambrai, the Somme
and throughout the German Offensive and subsequent Allied
Advance of 1918. He was demobilised in July 1919, and
holds the General Service and Victory Medals.
9, Rookery Cottages, Watford.   X5251.

WAKEMAN, E., Private, 1st Oxfordshire and Buckinghamshire Light Infantry.
Joining in June 1916, he was sent to Mesopotamia in the following May and fought in many important engagements, including those of Khan-Baghdadie and Hit, and was engaged during the final operations of the campaign in that theatre of war. He returned to England and was demobilised in January 1920, and holds the General Service and Victory Medals. 167, Sandringham Road, Watford.   X5252.

WAKES, F., Private, 8th Lincolnshire Regiment.
He volunteered in August 1914, and embarked for France later in the same year. During his service in this theatre of war he was engaged in the heavy fighting at Ypres, Lille and Arras, and in many other important engagements. He was also in action during the Retreat and Advance of 1918, and was gassed. He was demobilised in February 1919, and holds the 1914 Star, and the General Service and Victory Medals. 1, Stanbridge Road, Leighton Buzzard.   5253/A.

WALBY, C., Private, Bedfordshire and Essex Regiments and Labour Corps.
Volunteering in October 1915, he proceeded to the Western Front in the following February. While at the Base he was taken ill and invalided to England in August 1916. On recovery he served at various stations on Home duties until transferred to the Labour Corps, with which unit he was engaged on important work connected with food production. He was demobilised in April 1919, and holds the General Service and Victory Medals. 78, Shortmead Street, Biggleswade.   Z5254.

WALBY, H., Private, Labour Corps.
He joined in 1916, and was sent to France in the following year and served in the forward areas on important duties connected with operations whilst the Battles of Ypres, Arras, Cambrai and Albert were in progress. He was also present at the fighting during the Retreat and Advance of 1918, and was demobilised in November 1919. He holds the General Service and Victory Medals. 81, Sun Street, Biggleswade.   Z5255.

WALDOCK, A. T., Private, Leicestershire Regt.
Joining in 1917, he completed his training and served at various stations in England and Ireland on important duties with his unit. He was unsuccessful in obtaining his transfer overseas prior to the cessation of hostilities, but rendered valuable service until demobilised in 1919. Leighton Street, Woburn, Beds.   Z5256.

WALDOCK, E. F. G., Rifleman, 16th K.R.R.C.
He volunteered in 1914, and proceeded to the Western Front in November of the following year. In this theatre of war he fought in many important engagements, including those of Ypres and Arras. He was unfortunately killed in action on the Somme on July 20th, 1916, and was entitled to the 1914-15 Star, and the General Service and Victory Medals. 1, Thorpe Road, St. Albans.   X5257.

WALDOCK, T. E., Company Sergeant-Major, London Regiment (Royal Fusiliers).
A Reservist, he was mobilised on the outbreak of hostilities and was sent to France in November 1914. He was in action at the Battles of La Bassée, Festubert, Givenchy, Ypres and Arras, where he was wounded on April 9th, 1917. He also fought in the Retreat and Advance of 1918, and was demobilised in March 1919, and holds the 1914 Star, and the General Service and Victory Medals. 14, Verulam Road, Hitchin.   5258.

WALKER, A., Corporal, R.A.M.C.
He joined in October 1916, and on completion of his training was stationed at various depôts, engaged on important clerical duties. He was unable to procure his transfer to a theatre of war, but rendered excellent services until the cessation of hostilities. He was still serving in 1920. 124, Wellington Street, Luton.   5259.

WALKER, A., Gunner, Royal Garrison Artillery.
Volunteering in August 1914, he was drafted to France four months later and saw much service in various parts of the line. He fought at Ypres, Arras and the second Battle of the Marne during the German Offensive of 1918, and was wounded and gassed. He was sent to India in November 1919, and was still serving in 1920. He holds the 1914-15 Star, and the General Service and Victory Medals. 31, Fishpool Street, St. Albans.   X5260.

WALKER, A., Private, Queen's (Royal West Surrey Regiment).
He joined in June 1916, and proceeded to France later in the same year and was engaged at the Battles of the Somme, Loos, Ypres, and saw heavy fighting on the Menin Road and at Delville Wood. He also fought in the Retreat and Advance of 1918, and was demobilised in March 1919, and holds the General Service and Victory Medals. Broad Street, Clifton, Shefford.   Z5261.

WALKER, A., Private, Oxfordshire and Buckinghamshire Light Infantry, and York and Lancaster Regiment.
Volunteering in September 1914, in the following June he was sent to the Western Front, and on arrival there was transferred to the York and Lancaster Regiment, and fought in many important engagements, including those of the Somme, Ypres, Cambrai and throughout the Retreat and Advance of 1918, and was twice wounded. He was demobilised in March 1919, and holds the 1914-15 Star, and the General Service and Victory Medals. 38, New Road, Linslade, Bucks.   5262/A.

WALKER, A. (M.M.), Air Mechanic, R.A.F.
He volunteered in December 1915, and proceeded to France in the following March and was stationed at various aerodromes engaged on important duties as a fitter. He was awarded the Military Medal for consistently good work and devotion to duty. Returning to England, he was demobilised in April 1919, and holds the General Service and Victory Medals. 3, Chapel Path, Leighton Buzzard.   5263.

WALKER, A. J., A.B., Royal Navy.
He joined the Service prior to the outbreak of war, and was posted to H.M.S. "Commonwealth," in which ship he served at the Dardanelles in 1915 and with the Grand Fleet in the North Sea. He was serving on H.M.S. "Russell" when she was blown up by a mine on April 17th, 1916, but he was fortunately saved. He was still serving in 1920, and holds the 1914-15 Star, and the General Service and Victory Medals. Caddington, Luton.   5264.

WALKER, B., Private, R.A.M.C.
Volunteering in August 1914, he concluded his training and was stationed at various depôts with his unit engaged on important duties. He rendered valuable services throughout, but was not able to obtain his transfer overseas before the close of the war. He was demobilised in 1919. High Street, Lidlington, Beds.   Z5265/C.

WALKER, C., Battery Sergeant-Major, R.F.A.
He volunteered in May 1915, and later in the same year embarked for Salonika and saw much service on the Doiran and Struma fronts, and was in action during the operations in the final Allied Advance. After the cessation of hostilities he was sent to Russia and served in many engagements. He was demobilised in 1919, and holds the 1914-15 Star, and the General Service and Victory Medals. High Street, Lidlington.   Z5265/B.

WALKER, E., Private, 2nd Bedfordshire Regt.
He volunteered in August 1914, and was drafted to the Western Front later in the same year. Here he was in action in various parts of the line, and fought at Ypres and many other important engagements. He was unfortunately killed in action in December 1914, and was entitled to the 1914 Star, and the General Service and Victory Medals. 58, Holywell Road, Watford.   X1476/C.

WALKER, F., Private, 1/5th Bedfordshire Regt. and Royal Army Service Corps.
He volunteered in September 1914, and was sent to the Western Front in the following July and fought in many important engagements, including those of Ypres and Loos. In 1916 he returned to England owing to ill-health, and after receiving hospital treatment was discharged unfit for further service in the same year. He holds the 1914-15 Star, and the General Service and Victory Medals. 32, Cowfair Lands, Biggleswade.   Z5266.

WALKER, F. A., Private, King's Own Yorkshire Light Infantry.
He volunteered in September 1914, and later embarked for France, where he was in action in various sectors, and fought at the Battles of the Somme and Arras and during the German Offensive and subsequent Allied Advance in 1918. He was demobilised in March 1919, and holds the 1914-15 Star, and the General Service and Victory Medals. 3, Southwell Road, Callowland, Watford.   X5267.

WALKER, F. C., Private, Bedfordshire Regt.
Joining in March 1918, he completed his training and served at various stations on important duties until after the cessation of hostilities, when he was sent into Germany with the Army of Occupation. Here he was stationed at various towns on important garrison duties for eight months. He then returned to England and was demobilised in November 1919. Caddington, near Luton.   5268.

WALKER, F. G., Private, 1st Hertfordshire Regt.
Joining in September 1916, he embarked for France in the following January and was engaged in the Battles of St. Quentin, Gozeaucourt, the Somme, Arras and Cambrai, and was in action during the Retreat and Advance of 1918. During his service overseas he was twice wounded, and returning to England was demobilised in February 1919, and holds the General Service and Victory Medals.
Clifton Road, Shefford. Z5269.

WALKER, F. G., Sergeant, Royal Field Artillery.
Volunteering in July 1915, he was drafted to the Western Front in April of the following year and fought in the Battles of Ypres, the Somme, Arras, Cambrai and in the Retreat and Advance of 1918. Returning to England he was demobilised in February 1919, and holds the General Service and Victory Medals.
26, George Street, Markyate. 5270.

WALKER, G., Corporal, Royal Air Force.
He joined in May 1916, and on completion of his training served at various aerodromes on important observation and other duties during hostile air-raids. He did not obtain his transfer to a theatre of war, but rendered excellent services until demobilised in December 1919.
51, Loates Lane, Watford. X5271.

WALKER, H., Private (Gunner), M.G.C.
Joining in 1916, he proceeded overseas in the following year and saw much service in various sectors of the Western Front. He fought in many engagements of note, including those of Ypres, the Somme, Arras, Cambrai and during the German Offensive of 1918. In August of that year he returned to England and was engaged on special agricultural duties until demobilised in February 1919. He holds the General Service and Victory Medals.
106, Shortmead Street, Biggleswade. Z5272.

WALKER, H., Private, Essex Regiment.
He joined in 1916, and was sent to the Western Front in the following year and was in action in various parts of the line, fighting at Arras and the Somme, and was wounded at Passchendaele. On recovery he rejoined his Regiment and was engaged in heavy fighting in the German Offensive and subsequent Allied Advance of 1918, and was again wounded twice. He was demobilised in February 1919, and holds the General Service and Victory Medals.
2, Alma Road, Hemel Hempstead. X5273.

WALKER, H. S., Private, Bedfordshire Regt.
He volunteered in September 1914, and after training served at various stations on important duties with his unit until he embarked for France in 1917. In this theatre of war he saw much service, and fought in the Battles of Cambrai, Arras, Passchendaele, Lens, Loos and in the Retreat and Advance of 1918. He was demobilised in January 1919, and holds the General Service and Victory Medals.
New Street, Shefford. Z5274.

WALKER, J., Private, Bedfordshire Regiment.
He volunteered in November 1915, and concluding his training was stationed at various depôts engaged on guard and other important duties with his unit. He was not successful in obtaining his transfer overseas, but did very good work, and contracting consumption whilst on service, died on April 1st, 1916.
High Street, Lidlington. Z5265/A.

WALKER, J., Private, 2nd Bedfordshire Regt.
A serving soldier, he was sent to France at the commencement of hostilities and fought in the Retreat from Mons, in the Battle of the Marne, and many other important engagements. He was reported missing in December 1914 during operations in the Ypres salient, and later was presumed to have been killed in action. He was entitled to the Mons Star, and the General Service and Victory Medals.
38, New Road, Winslade, Bucks. 5262/B.

WALKER, L., Private, 1st Hertfordshire Regt.
A serving soldier, he was mobilised at the outbreak of war and landed in France in time to participate in the Retreat from Mons. He also fought in the Battles of the Marne, Festubert, Hill 60, St. Quentin and in many other important engagements during the Retreat and Advance of 1918. He was demobilised in January 1919, and holds the Mons Star, and the General Service and Victory Medals.
Anchor Cottage, Walsworth. 1846/C.

WALKER, N. T. A., Corporal, Royal Air Force.
Volunteering in August 1915, he was drafted to Italy in the following year and was engaged on important clerical duties at Headquarters throughout his service overseas. He returned to England and was demobilised in October 1919, and holds the General Service and Victory Medals.
The Bridge, King's Langley, Herts. X5275.

WALKER, O. D., A.B., Royal Navy.
He joined in October 1917, and was posted to H.M.S. "Silkh," which ship was engaged on important patrol and escort duties in the North, Baltic and Mediterranean Seas, and frequently passed through mine-infested areas in the discharge of her duties. He was still serving in 1920, and holds the General Service and Victory Medals.
Anchor Cottage, Walsworth. 1846/B.

WALKER, P., L/Corporal, 2nd Bedfordshire Regiment.
He enlisted in January 1914, and proceeded to France at the outbreak of war. He fought in the Retreat from Mons and in the Battles of Ypres, the Somme, and in many other important engagements. Later he was drafted to India, and was still serving in that country in 1920 on garrison duties. He holds the Mons Star, and the General Service and Victory Medals.
217, Chester Road, Watford. 5276/A.

WALKER, P. J., Gunner, R.G.A.
Volunteering in August 1914, he proceeded to the Western Front almost immediately and fought in the Retreat from Mons, the Battle of Ypres and in many other important engagements. He was wounded three times, on the third occasion so severely that after receiving hospital treatment he was discharged unfit for further service in January 1918. He holds the Mons Star, and the General Service and Victory Medals. 217, Chester Road, Watford. 5276/B.

WALKER, S., Rifleman, 2nd Rifle Brigade.
He volunteered in October 1914, and proceeded to France in the following May. During his service overseas he fought in many important engagements, and was unfortunately killed in action at Armentières on August 1st, 1915. He was entitled to the 1914-15 Star, and the General Service and Victory Medals.
5, Sotheron Road, Watford. X548/B.

WALKER, S., Private, Machine Gun Corps.
He volunteered in 1915, and later in the same year proceeded to Egypt, where he served in the Canal zone until 1917. Then, proceeding to the Palestine Front, he fought at Gaza and in many other engagements during the Advance into Syria, and was present at the capture of Haifa and Aleppo. He returned to England and was demobilised in 1919, and holds the General Service and Victory Medals.
27, Spencer Street, St. Albans. X5277.

WALKER, T., Corporal, R.A.S.C. (M.T.)
He volunteered in August 1914, and was drafted overseas almost immediately and served in the Retreat from Mons and the Battles of Arras, the Somme and in many other important engagements. In 1917 he returned to England and until his demobilisation in April 1920 served at various stations on important duties. He holds the Mons Star, and the General Service and Victory Medals.
65, Church Street, St. Albans. X5278.

WALLACE, H. J., Private, R.A.M.C.
He joined in January 1920, and at the conclusion of his training served with his unit at various stations on important hospital duties. He did good work, and later in 1920 was still serving at Chatham with the Royal Army Medical Corps.
109, Oak Road, Luton. 5279/B.

WALLACE, J. A. P., Private, 3/5th Bedfordshire Regiment
Volunteering in October 1914, he underwent a period of training and afterwards was engaged on special duties with his Battalion at various stations. He did excellent work, but owing to medical unfitness was unable to obtain his transfer overseas, and in consequence was discharged from the Service in April 1915.
109, Oak Road, Luton. 5279/A.

WALLEDGE, A., Private, Middlesex Regiment.
He volunteered in June 1915, and in the following year was sent to France. He fought at Albert and the Somme, and in February 1917 was wounded at Arras. He was invalided home, and on recovery was drafted to Ireland, where he served for a time, and proceeded to France in February 1918. He was engaged in operations on the Somme and at Cambrai, and after the signing of the Armistice returned to England. He was subsequently discharged unfit for further service in March 1919, and holds the General Service and Victory Medals. 126, Shortmead Street, Biggleswade. Z5280.

WALLER, A., Private, 1st Hertfordshire Regt.
He volunteered in August 1914, and in the following year was drafted overseas. Whilst on the Western Front he fought in many engagements, including those on the Somme, at Arras, Ypres, Festubert, Loos, Messines Ridge, Vimy Ridge, Cambrai and the German Offensive and subsequent Allied Advance of 1918. He was demobilised in 1919, and holds the 1914-15 Star, and the General Service and Victory Medals.
4, Whinbush Road, Hitchin 5281.

WALLER, A. E., Sapper, Royal Engineers, Private, Northumberland Fusiliers.
He volunteered in 1914, and in the succeeding year was sent to France. Whilst in this theatre of war he served in many battles, including those at Ypres, Arras, Passchendaele, the Somme and Cambrai. He returned to England in December 1917, and was engaged on important Home duties until his demobilisation in February 1919. He holds the 1914-15 Star, and the General Service and Victory Medals.
25, Langley Street, Luton.   5282/A.

WALLER, A. F., Driver, R.F.A.
Volunteering in December 1915, he served in Ireland for a time and embarked for France in the following September, and was in action on the Somme, at Ypres and Cambrai. He was invalided home in 1917 owing to ill-health, and on recovery returned to France, where he was engaged in heavy fighting and was wounded and gassed in March during the German Offensive of 1918. Returning to England, he received hospital treatment and rejoined his unit on the Western Front, where he served until demobilised in February 1919. He holds the General Service and Victory Medals.
31, Hampton Road, Luton.   5283.

WALLER, B , Sapper, Royal Engineers.
He volunteered in 1915, and in the following year was sent to France. During his service on the Western Front he was engaged on special duties with his unit in many sectors, including those of the Somme and Arras. He was constantly under shell-fire, and was gassed in March 1918. He returned to England after the cessation of hostilities, and was demobilised in 1919, and holds the General Service and Victory Medals.
13, Queen Street, Hitchin.   4020/A.

WALLER, E., Private, Middlesex Regiment.
He volunteered in 1914, and in the following year proceeded overseas. Whilst on the Western Front he was engaged in the fighting at Ypres, St. Julien, Messines, the Somme, Cambrai, and was wounded at Arras in December 1917. He returned to England, and on recovery served on Home duties until demobilised in 1919. He holds the 1914-15 Star, and the General Service and Victory Medals.
25, Langley Street, Luton.   5282/B.

WALLER, E. F., Private, Essex Regiment.
He volunteered in February 1915, and, completing his training, was stationed at various depôts, engaged on guard and other important duties with his unit. He did not obtain his transfer overseas owing to medical unfitness, but rendered excellent services until demobilised in April 1919.
20, Bury Park Road, Luton.   5284/A.

WALLER, F. J., Private, R.A.S.C.
He joined in October 1916, and embarked for France later in the same month, and served at Rouen and other bases on important duties with the Expeditionary Force Canteens. He did excellent work and continued serving in France for some time after the cessation of hostilities. Returning to England he was demobilised in November 1919, and holds the General Service and Victory Medals.
20, Bury Park Road, Luton.   5284/B.

WALLER, G., Sapper, Royal Engineers.
He joined in 1916, and in the same year was sent to France. Whilst in this theatre of war he was engaged on important duties in various sectors with his unit. He was killed in action on the Somme on March 9th, 1918, and was entitled to the General Service and Victory Medals.
13, Queen Street, Hitchin.   4020/C.

WALLER, P., Corporal, R.A.S.C.
He volunteered in May 1915, and at the conclusion of his training was engaged with his unit on special duties at various stations. He did excellent work in connection with the training of horses, but was unsuccessful in obtaining his transfer overseas, and was demobilised in October 1919.
21, North Common, Redbourn.   5285.

WALLER, R. J., Private, Machine Gun Corps.
He volunteered in December 1915, and after his training was employed on special duties at various depôts with his unit. He did very good work, but owing to medical unfitness was not sent overseas, and was demobilised in March 1919.
12, Sutton Road, Watford.   X5286.

WALLER, W. G. H., Ordinary Seaman, Royal Navy.
He joined in August 1917, and was posted to H.M.S. "Skirmisher." His ship was engaged on special blockade duties in the Baltic Sea, and after the signing of the Armistice proceeded to Constantinople and served in the Bosphorus on important patrol work. He was demobilised in May 1919, and holds the General Service and Victory Medals.
39, Portland Street, St. Albans.   5287.

WALLEY, W. J., Company Sergeant-Major, Royal Marine Light Infantry.
He was mobilised at the outbreak of war, and served aboard S.S. "Woodnut." His ship was engaged on special duties in the North Sea at Scapa Flow and off the coast of Spain. He was wounded, and was demobilised in March 1919, and holds the China Medal (1900), the 1914-15 Star, the General Service and Victory Medals, and also the Long Service and Good Conduct Medal.
48, Midland Road, Luton.   5288.

WALLINGTON, G., Corporal, R.A.S.C.
He volunteered in November 1915, and twelve months later was sent to France. Whilst on the Western Front he was engaged on important duties with his unit in the Ypres, Somme, Messines and Arras sectors. He was sent to Italy in November 1917, and served on the Asiago Plateau until 1919, when he returned home and was demobilised in March of that year. He holds the General Service and Victory Medals.
4, Wharf Lane, Rickmansworth.   X5289.

WALPOLE, H. F., L/Corporal, 1st Lincolnshire Regiment.
He joined in June 1917, and in the following April proceeded overseas. During his service on the Western Front he was engaged in heavy fighting, and was wounded and reported missing at the Marne on May 28th, 1918. He was later presumed to have been killed in action on that date, and was entitled to the General Service and Victory Medals.
"The Dog and Badger," Maulden, Ampthill.   5290.

WALTERS, A. W., Royal Naval Volunteer Reserve.
He joined in May 1918, and was shortly afterwards sent to France. He was stationed for a time at Cherbourg, where he served on special duties, and was later sent to Malta. He was afterwards drafted to Italy and engaged at Taranto in preparing the camp for troops returning to England. He returned home in 1919, and was demobilised in May of that year, and holds the General Service and Victory Medals.
63, Souldern Street, Watford.   X5291.

WALTERS, C., Private, Royal Defence Corps.
Being ineligible for service with the Colours, he joined the Royal Defence Corps at the outbreak of war, and after completing his training was engaged on important guard duties for a period of more than four years. He did excellent work, and was demobilised in February 1919.
31, Union Street, Luton.   4263/A.

WALTON, C., Private, Northumberland Fusiliers.
He joined in March 1917, and in November of the following year was sent to France. In this theatre of war he was employed on special duties in guarding and escorting prisoners of war. He returned to England in 1919, and was demobilised in October of that year. He holds the General Service and Victory Medals.
7, Gardenia Avenue, Leagrave.   5292/A.

WALTON, G. H., Private, 3rd Norfolk Regiment.
He joined in February 1917, and after his training was engaged with his Battalion on special duties at Crowborough Camp. He did excellent work, but owing to medical unfitness was not sent overseas, and was invalided out of the Service in May 1917.
Saunder's Piece, Ampthill.   5293.

WALTON, J., Private, 8th Bedfordshire Regiment and Royal Defence Corps.
He volunteered in May 1915, and twelve months later was sent to France. Whilst on the Western Front he was engaged in the fighting in many sectors, and was wounded in March 1917. He returned home and later rejoined his Battalion in the front-line trenches and fought at Ypres, Arras and the Somme. Owing to ill-health he was again sent to England, and after receiving hospital treatment was discharged, unfit for further service, in August 1918. He holds the General Service and Victory Medals.
Oliver Street, Ampthill.   5295.

WALTON, J. W., Private, Labour Corps.
He joined in June 1917, and at the conclusion of his training served with his unit at various camps on special duties. He did good work, but was not successful in obtaining his transfer to a theatre of war before hostilities ceased owing to medical unfitness. In June 1919, however, he was sent to France and was employed on salvage work on the Somme. In 1920 he was still serving.
7, Gardenia Avenue, Leagrave.   5292/B.

WALTON, J. W., Sergeant, Royal Engineers.

He joined in October 1916, and was shortly afterwards drafted to the Western Front. In this theatre of war he was engaged in making railroads and pontoon bridges at Loos, Vermelles and Vimy Ridge, and was constantly under heavy shell-fire. He was demobilised in August 1919, and holds the General Service and Victory Medals.
High Street, Westoning, near Ampthill. 5294/B.

WALTON, R. W., Private, Royal Sussex Regt.

He joined in May 1917, and in the following year was sent to France. He was engaged in the fighting in the Retreat and Advance of 1918, and after the signing of the Armistice proceeded to Germany with the Army of Occupation and was stationed at Cologne. He was demobilised in March 1920, and holds the General Service and Victory Medals.
High Street, Westoning, Ampthill. 5294/A.

WANDSWORTH, G. T., Sapper, Royal Engineers (Signal Section).

He was mobilised at the outbreak of war, and in March 1915 was drafted to the Dardanelles, where he served at the first landing at Gallipoli and the Battle of Cape Helles. He was sent to the Western Front in June 1916, and was gassed on the Somme in November 1916, and wounded at Ypres in July 1917. On recovery he rejoined his unit in the Field, and was again gassed in July 1918. He returned to England in September of the same year, and was demobilised in February 1919, and holds the 1914-15 Star, and the General Service and Victory Medals.
19, Alfred Street, Dunstable. 5296.

WARBY, A., Private, Middlesex Regiment.

He volunteered in December 1915, and later proceeded to the Western Front. During his service in this theatre of war he was engaged in the fighting at Ypres, Arras, Cambrai, Passchendaele, Vimy Ridge and Messines, and was twice wounded. He was demobilised in September 1919, and holds the General Service and Victory Medals.
2, Union Lane, New Town, Hatfield. X5297/A.

WARBY, A., Private R.A.S.C. (M.T.)

He volunteered in April 1915, and in the same year was sent to France, where he was engaged with his unit in transporting troops, supplies and ammunition to the front-line trenches and was frequently under shell-fire. He was demobilised in March 1919, and holds the 1914-15 Star, and the General Service and Victory Medals.
40, Shaftesbury Road, Watford. X5298/C.

WARBY, E. R., Gunner, Royal Garrison Artillery.

He joined in June 1916, and in the following September was sent to France. Whilst on the Western Front he fought in many engagements, including those at Arras, Albert, Cambrai and Béthune, and after the cessation of hostilities proceeded to Germany with the Army of Occupation and was stationed at Cologne. He returned home and was demobilised in September 1919, and holds the General Service and Victory Medals.
51, Shaftesbury Road, Watford. X5298/A.

WARBY, F., Gunner, Royal Garrison Artillery.

He joined in April 1916, and in the same year was drafted to France. In this theatre of war he was in action in many engagements, including those at Cambrai and on the Somme, and after the signing of the Armistice was sent to Germany with the Army of Occupation and was stationed at Cologne. He was demobilised in October 1919, and holds the General Service and Victory Medals.
12, Shaftesbury Road, Watford. X5299/A.

WARBY, H., Private, 17th Lancashire Fusiliers.

He joined in August 1916, and was shortly afterwards drafted to France. He served in many battles on the Western Front, and was engaged in the fighting on the Somme and at Cambrai, and was wounded. He was demobilised in October 1919, and holds the General Service and Victory Medals.
34, Shaftesbury Road, Watford. X5299/B.

WARBY, J., Private, Bedfordshire Regiment.

Volunteering in January 1915, he was sent to France in the same year. In this theatre of war he took part in the fighting at Passchendaele, Ypres and Cambrai, and was wounded. He returned to England, and after receiving hospital treatment was discharged as medically unfit for further military service in 1918. He holds the General Service and Victory Medals.
40, Shaftesbury Road, Watford. X5298/B.

WARBY, R. G., Sapper, Royal Engineers.

He volunteered in January 1915, and after his training was drafted to Ireland. He served with his unit at various stations on important duties. He did excellent work as a carpenter, but was unable to secure his transfer to a theatre of war, and was demobilised in September 1919.
5, Bromfield Cottages, New Town, Hatfield. X5297/B.

WARBY, W., Private, R.A.S.C. (M.T.)

He joined in May 1917, and in the same year was sent to France. Whilst on the Western Front he was engaged with his unit on important transport duties with an ammunition column, and was frequently in the forward areas whilst operations were in progress. After the Armistice he proceeded to Germany with the Army of Occupation and was stationed at Cologne. He was demobilised in October 1919, and holds the General Service and Victory Medals.
44, Shaftesbury Road, Watford. X5299/C.

WARD, A. (Miss), Special War Worker.

During the war this lady volunteered her services for work of National importance, and was employed from 1916 until 1918 by Messrs. George Kent, Ltd., Luton. She was engaged on the inspecting staff in the fuse department, and carried out the duties of her responsible position in a thoroughly capable and efficient manner.
102, Ridgway Road, Luton. 5301.

WARD, A., Telegraphist, Royal Navy

He joined in April 1918, and after completing his training was posted to a Mine-sweeper. He did useful work aboard his ship whilst she was engaged on her hazardous duties in the North Sea and other waters. He was demobilised in January 1919, and holds the General Service and Victory Medals.
33, Estcourt Road, Watford. X5301/A.

WARD, A. G., Private, Machine Gun Corps.

Joining in November 1916, he was sent to France in the following January and served in various parts of the line, taking part in many important engagements. He was killed in action on October 4th, 1918, and was entitled to the General Service and Victory Medals.
139, Verulam Road, St. Albans. X5302.

WARD, B. J., Telegraphist, Royal Navy.

Volunteering in April 1915, he was shortly afterwards drafted to Lemnos, and served there for several months as a wireless operator during operations in the Dardanelles. He was afterwards posted to a ship which was engaged on important duties in various waters during the course of hostilities. He was demobilised in March 1919, and holds the 1914-15 Star, and the General Service and Victory Medals.
33, Estcourt Road, Watford. X5301/B.

WARD, C. S., Rifleman, 15th London Regiment (Civil Service Rifles).

He volunteered in January 1915, and after completing his training proceeded to France in July of the following year. He was later sent to Salonika, and fought in many operations in the Balkans, and was later sent to Egypt. Taking part in the British Advance through Palestine, he was in action in several engagements. He returned to England for demobilisation in February 1919, and holds the General Service and Victory Medals.
33, Estcourt Road, Watford. X5301/C.

WARD, F., Private, Middlesex Regiment and 13th Royal Fusiliers.

He joined in May 1916, and embarked for the Western Front in the following November. He was engaged in heavy fighting in the Somme and Arras sectors, and was reported missing after an engagement near Arras on April 23rd, 1917. He was later presumed to have been killed in action on that date, and was entitled to the General Service and Victory Medals.
7, Church Terrace, Hendon, N.W.4 X5303.

WARD, F. C., Sergeant-Major, 1st Bedfordshire Regiment.

Mobilised on the outbreak of war, he was sent to France in September 1914 and took a prominent part in the Battles of Ypres, Givenchy, Arras, Cambrai, and many other important engagements until hostilities ceased. He returned to England and was demobilised in March 1919, and holds the 1914 Star, and the General Service and Victory Medals.
Fortune Cottage, Lovers' Walk, Dunstable. 5304.

WARD, G. F., Corporal, Royal Field Artillery.

Mobilised at the outbreak of hostilities he completed his training and served at various stations with his unit until sent to France in March 1917. He was in action at Arras and Cambrai, and in many other engagements, and was gassed in the Cambrai sector in March 1918, and returned to England. He received hospital treatment, and on recovery was stationed at various depôts until demobilised in January 1919. He holds the General Service and Victory Medals.
33, Camp Road, St. Albans. X5307.

WARD, F. O., Private, Buffs (East Kent Regt.)
Joining in April 1917, he was drafted to Egypt three months later¶and was engaged in the British Advance through Palestine, and was wounded at Gaza on December 23rd, 1917. He was sent to the Western Front on recovery in March 1918, and fought at Ypres and on the Somme during the Retreat and Advance of that year. Demobilised in January 1919, he holds the General Service and Victory Medals.
40, Waterlow Road, Dunstable. 5305.

WARD, G., Private, Queen's Own (Royal West Kent Regiment).
He joined in June 1916, and in the same year proceeded to Italy, where he served for a time. He was then sent to France, and whilst on the Western Front fought in the Battles of the Somme, Arras, Ypres and Cambrai, and was wounded. He was sent into Germany with the Army of Occupation, and returning to England was demobilised in March 1919. He holds the General Service and Victory Medals.
5, Spring Place, Luton. 5306.

WARD, H., 1st Air Mechanic, Royal Air Force (late Royal Naval Air Service).
He volunteered in December 1915, and a year later was sent to France. He was engaged with his Squadron at various aerodromes and did excellent work in connection with the repairing of aero-engines. He was demobilised in February 1918, and holds the General Service and Victory Medals.
1, Mansfield Road, Luton. 5308/B.

WARD, J., Private 1/5th Bedfordshire Regt.
Volunteering in August 1914, he was sent to Gallipoli in the following year and took part in the landing at Suvla Bay and various other operations, and was wounded at Chocolate Hill on August 21st, 1915. In December 1915 he proceeded to Egypt and served in the Canal zone and at El Arish, Gaza, Mejdil and Haifa during the Palestine campaign. He returned to England for demobilisation in February 1919, and holds the 1914-15 Star, and the General Service and Victory Medals.
Mill View, Letchworth Road, Leagrave. 5309.

WARD, M., Pioneer, Royal Engineers.
He joined in August 1917, and in the same year embarked for¶France. Whilst in this theatre of war he was engaged on important transport duties on the canals, and was present at engagements in the Marne and Arras sectors. He was demobilised in May 1919, and holds the General Service and Victory Medals.
111, Church Street, Rickmansworth. X5310.

WARD, P. G., Private, 11th Queen's Own (Royal West Surrey Regiment).
Joining in June 1918, he completed his training and served with his unit at various depôts. He was unable to obtain a transfer overseas before the cessation of hostilities, but was sent into Germany with the Army of Occupation after the Armistice, and was stationed at Cologne for over a year. He returned home for demobilisation in April 1920.
8, School Walk, Letchworth. 5311.

WARD, S., Private, R.A.M.C.
He volunteered in January 1915, and was later drafted to the Western Front. Serving with the Field Ambulance, he did good work at the Battles of Hill 60, Givenchy, Vimy Ridge, Cambrai, the Somme, and many other engagements until the termination of hostilities. He was demobilised in January 1919, and holds the General Service and Victory Medals.
46, Pondswick Road, Luton. 5312.

WARD, S. W., Private, R.A.M.C.
He volunteered in September 1914, and after completing his training served with his unit at various stations on special work. He rendered excellent services, but was unable to obtain a transfer to a theatre of war owing to medical unfitness for general service, and was discharged in consequence in February 1916.
1, Mansfield Road, Luton. 5308/A.

WARD, W., Private, Canadian Forestry Corps.
He volunteered in March 1916, and was shortly afterwards drafted overseas. Serving on the Western Front, he was engaged in felling timber for use in the Field, and was also employed on duties in connection with the food supplies of the Army. He was demobilised in March 1919, and holds the General Service and Victory Medals.
Waterside, London Colney. X5314.

WARD, W. G., Telegraphist, R.N.V.R.
He joined in July 1918, and after completing his training was engaged on important duties at home. He did good work as a wireless operator, but was not successful in being sent to sea before the termination of the war, and was demobilised in January 1919.
62, Union Street, Dunstable. 5315.

WARD, W. H., Trooper, Hertfordshire Dragoons.
Volunteering in September 1914, he proceeded to France in the following year and was in action at Festubert, Loos, Arras, Ypres, Messines, Lens, Cambrai and on the Somme. On the conclusion of hostilities he went into Germany with the Army of Occupation and served at Cologne for a year. Demobilised in April 1920, he holds the 1914-15 Star, and the General Service and Victory Medals.
76, Rushby Walk, Letchworth. 5316.

WARD, W. N., Private, R.A.O.C.
He joined in August 1918, and on the conclusion of his training served with his unit at various stations and did valuable work. He was ineligible for service overseas owing to his age, and was demobilised in February 1919.
23, Chatsworth Road, Luton. 5317.

WARMAN, W., Private, Bedfordshire Regiment.
Volunteering in September 1914, he was sent overseas three months later. He saw much service in Egypt and Palestine, and fought in the Battles of Gaza and Haifa and was present at the occupation of Jerusalem. He returned home for demobilisation in March 1919, and holds the 1914-15 Star, and the General Service and Victory Medals.
42, Bancroft, Hitchin. 1810/C.

WARNER, A. J., Sapper, Royal Engineers.
He volunteered in November 1914, and proceeding to the Western Front in the following year was engaged on important duties during the Battles of Ypres, Passchendaele and the Somme. On the conclusion of hostilities in 1918 he was sent with the Army of Occupation into Germany and served on the Rhine. He was demobilised in 1919, on his return to England, and holds the 1914-15 Star, and the General Service and Victory Medals.
6, Lea Mead, Letchworth. 4719/B.

WARNER, A. W., L/Corporal, 12th Suffolk Regt.
Volunteering in September 1915, he was sent to France in the following June and took part in several important engagements at Ypres and on the Somme, and was wounded in December 1917. He was sent home for treatment, and on recovery returned to France in November 1918 and served there until after the Armistice. He was demobilised in January 1919, and holds the General Service and Victory Medals. 4, Ashton Road, Luton. 5318.

WARNER, C., Private, Bedfordshire Regiment.
He volunteered in February 1915, and embarking for France in the same year was in action in several engagements, including those at Ypres, Arras and Cambrai, and was wounded on the Somme. He was demobilised in 1919, and holds the 1914-15 Star, and the General Service and Victory Medals.
The Hill, Wheathampstead. 2711/A.

WARNER, C., Rifleman, Royal Irish Rifles.
Volunteering in 1915, he proceeded to the Western Front in the following year and saw service in various sectors. He fought in the Battles of Arras, Messines, Cambrai and the Somme, and was twice wounded, and in consequence had two of his fingers amputated. He was demobilised in 1919, and holds the General Service and Victory Medals.
5, Bedford Road, Aspley Guise. Z5319.

WARNER, C., Private, 7th Essex Regiment.
He joined in June 1918, and on the conclusion of his training was engaged on important duties in the Eastern Counties. He rendered valuable services, but was not successful in securing a transfer overseas before hostilities ceased, and was demobilised in January 1919.
4, Ashton Road, Luton. 5320.

WARNER, E., Gunner, Royal Field Artillery.
Volunteering in 1915, he was drafted to the Western Front in the following year and served until the end of the war. During this period he fought in the Battles of the Somme, Arras, Messines and Cambrai, and was also in action during the Retreat and Advance of 1918. He was demobilised in 1919, and holds the General Service and Victory Medals.
Barber's Yard, Wheathampstead. 551/B.

WARNER, E. A., Driver, Royal Engineers.
He volunteered in January 1916, and proceeded to France in the following May. During his service on the Western Front he was engaged on important duties in the Battles of Ypres, Arras, Messines, Cambrai and the Somme, and did good work during the Retreat and Advance of 1918. He was demobilised in December 1919, and holds the General Service and Victory Medals.
5, Wootton Terrace, Walsworth. 5321.

WARNER, F., Private, 7th Bedfordshire Regt.
Volunteering in September 1914, he was drafted to the Western Front in the following July and served there for upwards of four years. During this period he was engaged in heavy fighting on the Somme, at Arras, Ypres, Havrincourt and Cambrai. He was demobilised in January 1919, and holds the 1914-15 Star, and the General Service and Victory Medals. 5, Surrey Street, Luton. 5322/A.

WARNER, H. J., Private, 2nd Bedfordshire Regt.
Mobilised in August 1914, he embarked for France in the following year and was in action at Hill 60, Festubert, Vimy Ridge and several other engagements. He was wounded and taken prisoner on March 21st, 1918, at the second Battle of the Somme, and held in captivity in Germany until after the Armistice. He then returned to England and was demobilised in December 1919, and holds the 1914-15 Star, and the General Service and Victory Medals.
14, Primrose Cottage, Hatfield. X5037/B.

WARNER, J., Gunner, Royal Field Artillery.
He joined in July 1916, and in the following April was sent to Salonika and served in the Balkans for three years. Whilst in this theatre of war he was in action on the Vardar and at Monastir, and was with the first British Division to enter Bulgaria. He returned to England in April 1919, and was demobilised in the following November, and holds the General Service and Victory Medals.
26, Warwick Road, Luton. 5323.

WARNER, R., A.B., Royal Navy.
He was serving in the Royal Navy when war broke out, and his ship was engaged on important patrol duties in the North, Baltic and Mediterranean Seas. She was in action in the Battle of Jutland and had several other encounters with the German Fleet. He holds the 1914-15 Star, and the General Service and Victory Medals, and in 1920 was serving at Gibraltar.
1, Park Street, Hatfield. X5324.

WARREN, A., Gunner, Royal Garrison Artillery.
He joined in April 1916, and four months later proceeded to Salonika, where he served with his Battery in many engagements on the Doiran and Monastir fronts. In 1917 he was sent to Egypt and fought in the Battle of Gaza during the Advance through Palestine. He returned to England in 1919, and was demobilised in October of that year, and holds the General Service and Victory Medals.
12, New Dalton Street, St. Albans. X5325.

WARREN, A., Private, Argyll and Sutherland Highlanders.
He volunteered in February 1915, and in the following August was sent to France, where he was engaged in the fighting at Loos, Vimy Ridge, Beaucourt, Arras and Messines. He was unfortunately killed in action at Grévillers in December 1917, and was entitled to the 1914-15 Star, and the General Service and Victory Medals.
89, Jallon, near Stirling. 5326/A.

WARREN, A. R. (Miss), Special War Worker.
This lady offered her services for work of National importance during the war, and from October 1915 until July 1918 was employed in Messrs. George Kent, Ltd., Munition Factory, on duties in connection with the output of munitions. In August 1918 she joined the Land Army and served in the Forestry Section of this unit until April 1919. She rendered valuable services throughout.
Cromwell House, Rothesay Road, Luton. 5327.

WARREN, B., Private, 1/5th Bedfordshire Regt.
Volunteering in September 1914, he was drafted to the Dardanelles in the following March, and took part in the first landing on the Peninsula, and was wounded on April 25th, 1915. On recovery he was again in action in this theatre of war, and was wounded at the landing at Suvla Bay on August 6th, 1915. He returned to England and was discharged on account of service in May 1917, and holds the 1914-15 Star, and the General Service and Victory Medals.
17, Albert Street, Markyate. 5328.

WARREN, C., Private, King's Own Scottish Borderers.
He joined in May 1916, and in the following January was sent overseas. During his service on the Western Front he took part in engagements at Ypres, Vimy Ridge and Passchendaele, and in August 1917 was drafted to Italy. In that theatre of war he fought in operations on the Piave front until January 1918, when he returned to France and served in the concluding operations of the war, and was gassed at Ypres and Merville. He was demobilised in March 1919, and holds the General Service and Victory Medals.
44, Hitchin Hill, Hitchin. 5329.

WARREN, C. V. (Mrs.), A/Section Leader, Women's Royal Air Force.
She joined in June 1917, and on completion of training was engaged at Henlow Aerodrome on clerical duties with her Squadron. She did excellent work, but was not successful in securing her transfer overseas before hostilities ceased. She was discharged in June 1919.
81, Balmoral Road, Hitchin. 4839/B.

WARREN, E. G., Driver, Royal Engineers.
He volunteered in April 1915, and later in the same year proceeded to France. Whilst in this theatre of war he was engaged on special work with his unit whilst operations were in progress at the Battles of Ypres, Arras, the Somme, Cambrai and St. Quentin, and was wounded. He holds the 1914-15 Star and the General Service and Victory Medals, and was demobilised in July 1919.
2, School Lane, Leagrave. 5330/A.

WARREN, F., Air Mechanic, Royal Air Force.
He joined in January 1918, and after completing his training was drafted overseas. He served with his Squadron on the Western Front at various aerodromes, and was wounded and gassed during a hostile air raid near Cambrai. He returned to England and was demobilised in November 1919, and holds the General Service and Victory Medals.
154, Dallow Road, Luton. 5331.

WARREN, F., Air Mechanic, Royal Air Force.
He joined in February 1917, and at the conclusion of his training proceeded to France, where he was engaged with his Squadron on special work which called for a high degree of technical skill. He served in the Somme and Cambrai sectors, and during his service overseas was wounded. He holds the General Service and Victory Medals, and in 1920 was still serving.
23, Alfred Street, Luton. 5326/B.

WARREN, F., Private, 7th Royal Sussex Regt.
He joined in May 1917, and later in the same year proceeded to France, where he served with his Battalion in many engagements and fought in the Battles of Ypres and Arras, and was wounded in action at Cambrai in 1918. He returned to England and on recovery was subsequently demobilised in December of that year. He holds the General Service and Victory Medals.
86, Boyle Street, Luton. 5332/B.

WARREN, F. F., Rifleman, 15th London Regt. (Civil Service Rifles).
Volunteering in January 1916, he was drafted to France five months later and served with his Battalion in various sectors. He was engaged in heavy fighting during the Somme Offensive and was unfortunately killed in action on September 15th, 1916. He was entitled to the General Service and Victory Medals.
1a, Garfield Street, Watford. X5333.

WARREN, F. F., 1st Air Mechanic, Royal Air Force (late Royal Naval Air Service).
He volunteered in January 1915, and after completing his training served with his Squadron at various aerodromes on special duties which demanded a high degree of technical knowledge and skill. In 1917 he was drafted to France and was stationed at Dunkirk, where he was employed in the repairing of damaged aeroplanes. He was demobilised in December 1918, and holds the General Service and Victory Medals.
81, Balmoral Road, Hitchin. 4839/A.

WARREN, G., Private, Royal Marine Light Infantry.
He volunteered in January 1915, and proceeded to Salonika, from which place his ship was engaged on patrol duties in the Ægean Sea until 1917. In April 1918 he took part in the raid on Zeebrugge, and in the following October was present at the occupation of Ostend. He was still serving in 1920, and holds the 1914-15 Star, and the General Service and Victory Medals.
35, Old London Road, St Albans. X4681/B.

WARREN, G. J., Private, 1st Bedfordshire Regt.
A serving soldier, he was mobilised at the outbreak of war, and sent to France in September 1914 and fought in the Ypres salient, and was wounded at Hill 60, and was in action in various sectors of the Western Front until drafted to Egypt in June 1915. On the Palestine Front he was engaged in the fighting at Gaza, and was present at the occupation of Jerusalem and served during the Advance into Syria. Returning to England he was demobilised in September 1919, and holds the 1914 Star, and the General Service and Victory Medals.
20, Cross Street, Watford. X5334.

WARREN, H., L/Corporal, Military Foot Police.
He joined in June 1916, and was sent to France three months later, and was engaged on important duties during the Battles of the Somme and Cambrai, and in many other important engagements. He also served in the German Offensive and subsequent Allied Advance in 1918, and was wounded. He was demobilised in January 1920, and holds the General Service and Victory Medals.
Victoria Road, Leagrave. 5335.

WARREN, H., L/Corporal, R.A.M.C.
Volunteering in January 1915, he was drafted to the Western Front on the termination of his training, and served in the advanced areas of the Ypres salient in the Cambrai and Arras sectors. He was engaged on important duties in connection with the care of sick and wounded troops, and rendered excellent services. He was demobilised in February 1919, and holds the General Service and Victory Medals.
36, Kimpton Road, Luton.   5336.

WARREN, H. S., Private, R.A.V.C.
He volunteered in October 1914, and was sent to France in June 1916, and served on the Somme and Arras fronts until transferred to Salonika in November 1916. Here he served on the Doiran, Struma, and Vardar fronts, engaged on duties connected with the care of sick and wounded horses, until the cessation of hostilities. In January 1919 he was sent into Turkey with the Army of Occupation, and was stationed at Constantinople. He returned to England and was demobilised in April 1919, and holds the General Service and Victory Medals.
35, Old London Road, St. Albans.   X4681/C.

WARREN, J., Private, 1/5th Cheshire Regt.
He joined in October 1916, and proceeded to the Western Front five months later, and served in various parts of the line in many important battles. He was transferred to Italy in January 1918, and fought in several engagements until returning to France in the following March. He was in action throughout the German Offensive and subsequent Allied Advance, and was demobilised in November 1919. He holds the General Service and Victory Medals.
86, Boyle Street, Luton.   5332/A.

WARREN, J. J., Private, 2nd Bedfordshire Regt.
A serving soldier, he proceeded to France at the outbreak of hostilities and fought in the Retreat from Mons and at the Battle of Ypres. Transferred to Egypt in 1915, he saw much service on the Palestine front, engaged on important guard duties at Jerusalem and Jaffa, and was wounded. He returned to England and was discharged in December 1918, and holds the Mons Star, and the General Service and Victory Medals.
49, Park Road, Bushey.   X5337/A.

WARREN, P. (Miss), Special War Worker.
This lady volunteered her services for work of National importance, and from October 1915 until March 1919 was employed at Messrs. Kent's Munition Factory, Luton, and rendered very valuable services throughout.
16, Rothesay Road, Luton.   5338.

WARREN, R. J., Private, 5th Northamptonshire Regiment.
He joined in December 1917, and proceeded overseas in the following May. During his service on the Western Front he fought in the Battles of Arras, Cambrai, St. Quentin and many other engagements in the German Offensive and Allied Advance. He was demobilised in November 1919, and holds the General Service and Victory Medals.
2, School Lane, Leagrave.   5330/B.

WARREN, S., Private, Middlesex and Suffolk Regiments.
Joining in June 1916, he was sent to France later in the same year and saw much service with his Battalion, and fought at Ypres, Arras and in many other important engagements until admitted into hospital suffering from fever. On recovery he served at the Base on important duties until demobilised in May 1919. He holds the General Service and Victory Medals.
9, Fearnley Street, Watford.   X5339.

WARREN, S., Trooper, Hertfordshire Dragoons.
Volunteering in August 1914, after training he was stationed at various depôts engaged on important duties until drafted to Egypt in 1916. On the Palestine front he was in action in many important engagements, including the Battles of Gaza, during the Advance through the Holy Land into Syria. He returned to England and was demobilised in March 1919, and holds the General Service and Victory Medals.
49, Park Road, Bushey.   X5337/B.

WARREN, W. C., Sapper, Royal Engineers.
He joined in August 1917, and proceeded to the Western Front later in the same year and served in the forward areas on important duties in connection with the laying of railways, and was present at the Battles of Ypres, Arras, Cambrai, St. Quentin, and rendered valuable service in the Retreat and Advance of 1918. He was demobilised in December 1919, and holds the General Service and Victory Medals.
New Marford, Wheathampstead.   5340.

WARREN, W. J., Private, 12th West Yorkshire Regiment and Labour Corps.
Volunteering in September 1914, he was sent to France in September of the following year, and was in action in many important engagements, including those of Festubert and Loos. He was wounded on the Somme in July 1916, and returned to England. After receiving hospital treatment he was transferred to the Labour Corps and served at various stations until demobilised in April 1919. He holds the 1914–15 Star, and the General Service and Victory Medals.
61, Crow Lane, Husbourne Crawley, Beds.   Z4647/A.

WARRICK, G. C., Private, 29th Middlesex Regt. and Labour Corps.
He joined in November 1916, and on completion of his training served at various stations with his unit. He did not obtain his transfer overseas owing to medical unfitness, but rendered very valuable services engaged on agricultural duties until demobilised in November 1919.
50, Yarmouth Road, Callowland, Herts.   X5341.

WARWICK, W., Air Mechanic, Royal Air Force.
He joined in August 1918, and after training served at various aerodromes engaged on important duties as a fitter. He was over military age and consequently was not successful in obtaining his transfer overseas prior to the cessation of hostilities, and was demobilised in March 1919.
Station Road, Ridgmont, Beds.   Z5342.

WASH, A. V., Bugler, Bedfordshire V.T.C.
Ineligible for service with the Colours, he joined the Volunteer Training Corps in August 1917, and served at various stations on the East Coast with his unit, engaged on guard and other important duties. He rendered excellent services until demobilised in June 1919.
27, Ivy Road, Luton.   5343/B.

WASH, S., Private, 12th Bedfordshire Regt.
Joining in January 1917, he was stationed at various depôts on completing his training and was engaged on guard and other important duties. He was unsuccessful in obtaining his transfer to a theatre of war, but did excellent work until demobilised in February 1919.
27, Ivy Road, Luton.   5343/A.

WASHINGTON, A., Gunner, R.F.A.
Volunteering in February 1915, he proceeded to France in November of the following year and fought in many important engagements, including those of Arras and Cambrai, and during the Retreat and Advance of 1918. Returning to England, he was demobilised in February 1919, and holds the General Service and Victory Medals.
Eggington, Leighton Buzzard.   5344.

WASSELL, C. D., Corporal, R.G.A.
A serving soldier, he proceeded to France at the commencement of hostilities and fought in the Retreat from Mons and in the Battles of Neuve Chapelle, Arras, Cambrai and in the German Offensive and subsequent Allied Advance of 1918, and was wounded. He was demobilised in April 1920, and holds the Mons Star, and the General Service and Victory Medals.
2, Batford Road, Harpenden.   5345/A.

WASSELL, S. A., Corporal, 1st Hertfordshire Regiment.
He was mobilised at the outbreak of war, and embarked for the Western Front in June of the following year. He fought in many engagements, including those at Ypres, the Somme and Hill 60 and was engaged in the heavy fighting during the Retreat and Advance of 1918. He was demobilised in October 1919, and holds the 1914–15 Star, and the General Service and Victory Medals.
1, Newcombe Street, Harpenden.   5345/B.

WATERS, A. G., Gunner, Royal Horse Artillery.
Mobilised in August 1914, he was sent to France almost immediately and fought in the Retreat from Mons and in many other important engagements. He was unfortunately killed in action on May 25th, 1915, and was entitled to the Mons Star, and the General Service and Victory Medals.
75, Norman Road, Luton.   5346/A.

WATERS, F., Pioneer, Royal Engineers.
He joined in June 1918, on attaining military age, and after training was stationed at various depôts engaged on important duties with his unit. He failed to procure his transfer overseas prior to the cessation of hostilities, but rendered excellent services until demobilised in January 1920.
24, George Street, Markyate.   5347.

WATERS, F., Private, 3rd Bedfordshire Regt. (attached 9th Essex Regiment).
He volunteered in January 1916, and was sent to France four months later and served in many parts of the line, and fought on the Somme, where he was wounded in July 1916. He returned to England, and after a protracted course of hospital treatment was discharged unfit for further service in June 1918, and holds the General Service and Victory Medals.
7, Cleveland Road, Markyate. 4245/B.

WATERS, F. W. (M.M.), Corporal, 1st Hertfordshire Regiment.
Mobilised at the commencement of hostilities, he landed in France in time to participate in the Retreat from Mons, and fought in the Battle of Ypres and in various other important engagements, and was wounded. He was awarded the Military Medal for conspicuous bravery and devotion to duty in the Field. He was killed in action at Passchendaele on July 31st, 1917, and was entitled to the Mons Star, and the General Service and Victory Medals.
21, Westbourne Terrace, St. Albans. X5348/B.

WATERS, J. C., Gunner, Royal Field Artillery.
Volunteering in August 1914, he proceeded to Egypt later in the same year, and until 1916 served at various stations in the Canal zone. He was unfortunately killed in action at Romani on August 12th, 1916, and was entitled to the 1914-15 Star, and the General Service and Victory Medals.
21, Westbourne Terrace, St. Albans. X5348/A.

WATERS, J. F. Private, 1st Devonshire Regt.
He volunteered in August 1914, and embarked for France in the following year, and was in action at La Bassée, Ypres, Arras, and in many sectors of the Western Front. In 1917, transferred to Italy, he saw active service on the Piave and fought in many engagements. During his service overseas he was wounded three times, and after the Armistice was sent into Austria with the Army of Occupation. He returned to England and was still serving in 1920, and holds the 1914-15 Star, and the General Service and Victory Medals.
21, Westbourne Terrace, St. Albans. X5348/C.

WATERS, S., Q.M.S., Tank Corps.
He joined in April 1916, and was drafted to France later in the same year. Here he saw much service in various parts of the line, fighting in the Battles of Arras, Cambrai, Albert, Ypres, Bullecourt and Passchendaele, and was wounded and gassed. After the Armistice he proceeded into Germany with the Army of Occupation and was stationed at Cologne. He returned to England in 1919, and was demobilised in September of that year, and holds the General Service and Victory Medals.
56, Bearton Road, Hitchin. 5349.

WATERS, W. J., Corporal, 1st Hertfordshire Regiment.
Volunteering in September 1914, he embarked for France later in that year, and fought in many important battles, including those of the Somme, Ypres, Arras and also throughout the German Offensive and subsequent Allied Advance of 1918, and was wounded three times. He was demobilised in March 1919, and holds the 1914 Star, and the General Service and Victory Medals.
75, Norman Road, Luton. 5346/B.

WATKINS, J. W., Private, 2nd Dorsetshire Regt.
He joined in 1916, and was drafted to India, where he served on garrison duties until 1917. He was then sent to Palestine and fought in the engagements at Gaza, Haifa, Jaffa, Damascus and Aleppo. After the cessation of hostilities he was stationed at Cairo until 1919. He then returned to England and was demobilised in April of that year. He holds the General Service and Victory Medals.
101, Norfolk Road, Rickmansworth. X4744/B.

WATSON, A., Gunner, Royal Field Artillery.
He volunteered in August 1914, and after completing his training was drafted to France. In this theatre of war he served for two years, and took part in many engagements, including those of Ypres and Messines, and was gassed. He was later sent to Salonika and fought in many battles on the Macedonian front until hostilities ceased. He returned to England and was demobilised in March 1919, and holds the 1914-15 Star, and the General Service and Victory Medals.
41, Albert Road, Luton. 1064/B.

WATSON, A., Private, Royal Naval Division (Nelson Battalion).
He volunteered in April 1915, and in the following July was drafted to the Dardanelles, and fought at the landing at Suvla Bay and other engagements. He was sent to the Western Front in October 1915, but under age for service with the Colours he was sent back to England and discharged from the Service in August 1917. He holds the 1914-15 Star, and the General Service and Victory Medals.
54, Grange Road, Luton. 5350/B.

WATSON, C., Private (Bandsman), 26th Royal Fusiliers.
Volunteering at the outbreak of war, he was sent to France in 1916. Whilst in this theatre of war he was engaged on special duties with the Band of his Battalion in various sectors of the Western Front, and was constantly under shell-fire. He later served for a time in Italy, and returned home for demobilisation in May 1919. He holds the General Service and Victory Medals. 38, Butlin Road, Luton. 5351.

WATSON, C., Corporal, Royal Defence Corps.
Being ineligible for service with the Colours, he volunteered in 1914 in the Royal Defence Corps. After a course of training he was engaged with his unit at various stations on important guard duties, and did very good work. He was demobilised in March 1919. Brickyard Cottages, Woburn Sands. Z5352.

WATSON, E. C., Private, R.A.S.C.
He volunteered in 1915, and in the same year was drafted overseas. Whilst on the Western Front he was employed on special transport duties with his unit, and was frequently in the forward areas whilst operations were in progress at Loos, Ypres, Arras and on the Somme, and was twice wounded. He was demobilised in 1919, and holds the 1914-15 Star, and the General Service and Victory Medals.
Lower Green, Ickleford, Hitchin. 4841/B.

WATSON, F., Gunner, Royal Field Artillery.
He volunteered in May 1915, and in August of the same year was sent to France. He served in many sectors of the Western Front, including those of Festubert, Loos, Arras, the Somme and Cambrai, and after hostilities ceased proceeded with the Army of Occupation to Germany, and was stationed at Cologne. He was demobilised in June 1919, and holds the 1914-15 Star, and the General Service and Victory Medals.
3, Common View Square, Letchworth. 2826/A.

WATSON, H. (M.M.), Private, 2nd Life Guards.
He volunteered in November 1914, and in 1916 was sent to France. During his service in this theatre of war he fought at the Battles of Ypres, Arras, the Somme, the Aisne, Vimy Ridge and Cambrai, and was awarded the Military Medal for conspicuous bravery and devotion to duty in the Field. He also holds the General Service and Victory Medals, and was demobilised in December 1918.
84, Brightwell Road, Watford. X5353.

WATSON, H. F., Private, Labour Corps.
He volunteered in 1914, but was rejected owing to medical unfitness. However, in October 1915, he volunteered again, and in the following year was sent to France, where he served on special duties as a plumber in the Arras, Ypres and Cambrai sectors. He did very good work, and was demobilised in October 1919, and holds the General Service and Victory Medals
8, San Remo Road, Aspley Guise. Z5354.

WATSON, H. J., Corporal, Middlesex Regiment.
A serving soldier, he was drafted to France in August 1914, and fought in the Retreat from Mons and the subsequent engagements on the Marne, the Somme, the Aisne, Ypres and Cambrai, and was twice wounded. He was sent to England in 1917, and invalided out of the Service in January of that year. He holds the Mons Star, and the General Service and Victory Medals.
208, Harwood Road, Watford. X5355/B.

WATSON, L., Corporal (Shoeing Smith), R.E.
He volunteered at the outbreak of war, and in August 1916 was sent to France, where he served with his unit until the following October, when, owing to ill-health, he was invalided home. On recovery he was drafted to Mesopotamia in June 1917, and was in action at Kut, Baghdad and Basra. He proceeded to India in April 1919, and returned to England in 1920, and was demobilised in June of that year. He holds the General Service and Victory Medals.
8, New Town, Potton. Z5356.

WATSON, R. (jun.), Sergeant, 2/5th Bedfordshire Regiment and Northumberland Fusiliers.
He volunteered in September 1914, and a year later proceeded to France. Whilst in this theatre of war he was in action in the Battles of Loos, Ypres and the Somme, and was gassed. He was taken prisoner near Rheims in May 1916, and held in captivity until repatriated in February 1919. He was discharged on account of service in the same month, and holds the 1914-15 Star, and the General Service and Victory Medals.
54, Grange Road, Luton. 5350/C.

WATSON, R., Company Sergeant-Major, 2/5th Bedfordshire Regt. and Sherwood Foresters.
Volunteering in September 1914, he served with his unit on special duties until drafted overseas two year later. He saw much service on the Western Front and fought on the Somme at Bullecourt, Arras, Cambrai, and during the Retreat and Advance of 1918. He was demobilised in March 1919, and holds the General Service and Victory Medals.
54, Grange Road, Luton. 5350/A.

WATSON, S. H., L/Corporal, South Stafford-shire Regiment.
Joining in January 1917, he embarked for France in the same year and was in action at Arras, Bullecourt and Ypres. He was sent to Italy in 1918, and took part in the Advance on the Piave and in several other engagements. He returned to England for demobilisation in February 1919, and holds the General Service and Victory Medals.
33, Brunswick Street, Luton.   1719/B.

WATSON, W. C., R.Q.M.S., King's Own (York-shire Light Infantry).
He volunteered in September 1914, and a year later was sent to France. Engaged on important clerical and other duties at Rouen, he did excellent work until sent home in March 1917, owing to severe illness, and died on August 5th, 1919. He was entitled to the 1914-15 Star, and the General Service and Victory Medals.
Mount Pleasant, Aspley Guise.   Z5357.

WATSON, W. G., Private, 3rd Grenadier Guards.
Volunteering in February 1916, he was drafted to the Western Front in the following November, and was in action on the Somme, at Givenchy and Saillisel, and owing to ill-health was invalided home in March 1917. He returned to France on recovery in April of the following year and took part in several engagements during the Retreat and Advance of 1918. He was demobilised in June 1919, and holds the General Service and Victory Medals.
28, Church Yard, Hitchin.   5358.

WATSON, W. H., Sergeant, 11th (Prince Albert's Own) Hussars.
A serving soldier, he was mobilised on the outbreak of war, and was engaged with his unit on important duties until sent to France in October 1916. Whilst overseas he was in action on the Somme, at Ypres, Cambrai and St. Quentin, and suffered from shell-shock. On the termination of hostilities he accompanied the Army of Occupation into Germany, returning home in 1919. He holds the General Service and Victory Medals, and in 1920 was still serving.
32, Merton Road, Watford.   X5359.

WATSON, W. T., Private, Royal Fusiliers and Labour Corps.
He was mobilised when war broke out, and almost immediately proceeding to France, fought in the Retreat from Mons and the Battles of Ypres, Armentières, the Marne and the Aisne. Sent to Mesopotamia in April 1916, he took part in many operations, including the relief of Kut and the capture of Baghdad. He was demobilised in April 1919 on his return to England, and holds the Mons Star, and the General Service and Victory Medals.
208, Harwood Road, Watford.   X5355/A.

WATTS, A., Rifleman, 2nd K.R.R.C.
Mobilised on the declaration of war, he was shortly afterwards drafted to France, and was engaged in heavy fighting during the Retreat from Mons and in the Battles of the Marne and the Aisne. He was unfortunately killed in action at La Bassée in October 1914, and was entitled to the Mons Star, and the General Service and Victory Medals.
9, Bensons Row, Biggleswade.   Z4820/C.

WATTS, A. E., Private, 2nd Bedfordshire Regt.; and Gunner, Royal Field Artillery.
He volunteered in November 1914, and in the same year embarked for the Western Front. During his service in this theatre of war he fought in the Battles of Neuve Chapelle, Hill 60, Ypres, the Somme and Cambrai. He was demobilised in February 1919, and holds the 1914-15 Star, and the General Service and Victory Medals.
15, Buckingham Road, Callowland.   X5360/C.

WATTS, A. J., Private, R.A.S.C.
Volunteering in June 1915, he was afterwards sent to France, and served on important duties with his unit. Whilst overseas he was present at several important engagements, including those at Arras and on the Somme, and was wounded four times. He was discharged on account of service in 1917, and holds the General Service and Victory Medals.
15, Buckingham Road, Callowland.   X5361/A.

WATTS, C. W., Private, 8th Bedfordshire Regt.
He volunteered in April 1915, and in the following January proceeded to the Western Front, where he was in action in several engagements. He was wounded and taken prisoner on April 19th, 1916, and held in captivity in Germany until after the Armistice. He then returned to England, and was demobilised in March 1919, and holds the General Service and Victory Medals.
Moggerhanger, Sandy.   Z5363.

WATTS, E. A., Private, Coldstream Guards.
He joined in October 1916, and after serving with his unit on Home Service duties embarked for France in March 1918, and was engaged in severe fighting during the German Offensive of that year. He made the supreme sacrifice, and was killed in action at Ypres on April 27th, 1918, and was entitled to the General Service and Victory Medals.
9, Benson's Row, Biggleswade.   Z4820/B.

WATTS, G., Private, R.A.S.C. (N.A.C.B.)
Volunteering in April 1915, he was later sent to Egypt and then to Russia, and afterwards to Salonika. During his service in these theatres of war he was engaged on important duties in connection with the transport of stores and supplies for the troops in the Field, and was wounded. On returning to England he was demobilised in February 1919, and holds the General Service and Victory Medals.
14, Catherine Street, St. Albans.   X464/C.

WATTS, G. W., Private, 7th Bedfordshire Regt.
Volunteering in September 1914, he proceeded to the Western Front in the following September and fought in the Battles of the Somme, Ypres, Cambrai, and was twice wounded. He was invalided home on account of his wounds and discharged as medically unfit for further service in April 1917, and holds the 1914-15 Star, and the General Service and Victory Medals.
66, Church Street, Leighton Buzzard.   4887/A.

WATTS, J., Private, 1st Bedfordshire Regiment.
He volunteered in February 1916, and in the same year was drafted to France, where he took part in several engagements, including the Battles of Messines and Ypres. He was reported missing on October 22nd, 1917, and was later presumed to have been killed in action near Ypres on that date. He was entitled to the General Service and Victory Medals.
10, Chapel Fields, Biggleswade.   Z5362.

WATTS, J. E., Private, Machine Gun Corps.
He joined in November 1919, and on the conclusion of his training was engaged on important duties with his unit. He did much good work, and was later drafted to India, where he was still serving in 1920.
15, Buckingham Road, Callowland.   X5361/B.

WATTS, L., Private, 1st Hertfordshire Regiment.
Volunteering in February 1916, he embarked for the Western Front in the same year, and saw service in various sectors. He was in action in the Battles of the Somme, Beaumont-Hamel and Cambrai, and was gassed and wounded. He holds the General Service and Victory Medals, and was demobilised in March 1919.
15, Buckingham Road, Callowland.   X5360/A.

WATTS, W. C., Private, Lancashire Fusiliers.
He joined in 1916, and in the following year was sent overseas. Serving in France, he was engaged in heavy fighting on the Somme, at Ypres, Arras, La Bassée, and was gassed. Later, owing to ill-health, he was invalided home in September 1918, and after receiving hospital treatment was demobilised in August 1919. He holds the General Service and Victory Medals.   17, Chapel Fields, Biggleswade.   Z5364.

WATTS, W. J., Private, Middlesex Regiment.
He joined in September 1918, and after completing his training was engaged with his unit on guard and other duties. He rendered valuable services, but was not sent to a theatre of war owing to medical unfitness for active service, and was demobilised in 1919.
15, Buckingham Road, Callowland.   X5360/B.

WATTS, W. W., Private, Bedfordshire Regt.
Volunteering in December 1915, he was drafted to the Western Front in the following July, and was in action on the Somme and at Armentières, Arras and Cambrai. He returned home for demobilisation in January 1919, and holds the General Service and Victory Medals.
125, High Street South, Dunstable.   5365.

WAYMAN, C., L/Corporal, Royal Engineers.
He volunteered in 1914, and proceeding to the Western Front in the same year was engaged on important duties in the forward areas, and was wounded at Hill 60 in 1915, and invalided home. Rejoining his unit on recovery, he served during engagements at Ypres, Arras, Cambrai and on the Somme, and was again wounded and sent to hospital in England. He was demobilised in March 1919, and holds the 1914 Star, and the General Service and Victory Medals.
Austin's Lane, Ampthill.   3871/A.

WEATHERLY, J., Private, Middlesex Regiment.
He volunteered in 1915, and in the same year was sent to Mesopotamia, where he took part in several engagements, including the capture of Baghdad. He was later drafted to India and stationed at Bangalore, and served until his return to England for demobilisation in 1919. He holds the 1914-15 Star, and the General Service and Victory Medals.
34a, Pinner Road, Oxhey.   X5367

WEAVER, W. H., Private, 2nd Bedfordshire Regt.
Volunteering in August 1914, he was drafted to France in the following year, and was in action in many engagements, including those at Festubert and the Somme, and was wounded three times. He was taken prisoner at Ypres in May 1917, and held in captivity in Germany until repatriated after the Armistice. He was discharged on account of service in January 1919, and holds the 1914-15 Star, and the General Service and Victory Medals.
19, Market Street, Watford. X5368.

WEBB, A., Private, Royal Sussex Regiment.
Volunteering in December 1915, he was sent to France in the following July and took part in almost continuous fighting in the Somme sector. He was unfortunately killed in action on October 27th, 1916, during the first Battle of the Somme, and was entitled to the General Service and Victory Medals.
68, Lilley, near Luton. 5369/B.

WEBB, A. W. J., Private, R.A.S.C.
Joining in October 1916, he was drafted to the Western Front three months later and served in various sectors. He was engaged on important duties in connection with the transport of ammunition and supplies to the front lines during the Battles of Arras, Ypres, Cambrai and the Somme. He was demobilised in December 1919, and holds the General Service and Victory Medals.
Luton Road, Stopsley. 5370/A.

WEBB, B. J., Driver, R.A.S.C. (M.T.)
He volunteered in June 1915, and in the following month proceeded overseas. Whilst on the Western Front he was engaged on important transport duties in the Loos, Arras, Cambrai and Somme sectors, and did excellent work until the cessation of hostilities. He holds the 1914-15 Star, and the General Service and Victory Medals, and was demobilised in June 1919.
The Nook, Clophill, Ampthill. 5371.

WEBB, E., Private, 5th Bedfordshire Regiment and 4th Royal Welch Fusiliers.
Volunteering in January 1915, he proceeded to France in the same year, and fought at Loos and Givenchy, and was wounded on the Somme in September 1916. He was later in action at Arras and Vimy Ridge, and was wounded in 1917 at Ypres. On recovery he rejoined his Battalion and fought at Albert and Cambrai during the final operations of the war. He holds the 1914-15 Star, and the General Service and Victory Medals, and was demobilised in July 1919.
Long Row, Ampthill. 5372.

WEBB, E. G., Private, 3rd Queen's Own (Royal West Kent Regiment).
He joined in June 1918, and was shortly afterwards sent to the Western Front, where he took part in the Battles of Arras, Ypres and Cambrai. On the cessation of hostilities he proceeded into Germany with the Army of Occupation, returning home for demobilisation in October 1919. He holds the General Service and Victory Medals.
"Oruba," Gardenia Avenue, Leagrave. 5373.

WEBB, F., Private, Middlesex Regiment.
He volunteered in November 1914, and on the conclusion of his training was engaged on important guard and other duties with his unit. He rendered valuable services, but was unable to obtain a transfer to a theatre of war before the cessation of hostilities owing to medical unfitness, and was demobilised in February 1919.
69, Judge Street, North Watford X2038/B.

WEBB, F., Sapper, Royal Engineers.
Mobilised on the declaration of war, he served with his unit at home until drafted to France in 1917. Whilst on the Western Front he was engaged on important duties in connection with operations on the Somme and at Cambrai, and was gassed on July 21st, 1918. He was sent home for treatment in the following month, and was demobilised in March 1919, and holds the General Service and Victory Medals.
39, King's Road, Luton. 5374.

WEBB, F. J., Private, Bedfordshire Regiment.
He volunteered in September 1914, and embarked for France in the following January. In this theatre of war he was in action in the Battles of Ypres, Arras, Vimy Ridge and the Somme, and was badly wounded near Ypres and sent to hospital in England. After receiving medical treatment he was invalided out of the Service in July 1917, and holds the 1914-15 Star, and the General Service and Victory Medals.
Luton Road, Stopsley. 5370/B.

WEBB, F. M., Air Mechanic, Royal Air Force.
He joined in October 1917, and after completing his training was engaged with his Squadron at various aerodromes on important duties, which called for a high degree of technical skill. He did excellent work in assembling and repairing aeroplanes, but was unable to secure a transfer overseas before the cessation of hostilities, and was demobilised in February 1919.
Dairy Farm, Redbourn. 5375.

WEBB, F. W., Private, Royal Defence Corps.
He volunteered in the Bedfordshire Regiment in August 1914, and being medically unfit for general service was transferred to the Royal Defence Corps. After his training was completed he was engaged at various detention camps guarding German prisoners. He did good work, and was discharged in March 1919.
15, Dordans Road, Leagrave. 5376/A.

WEBB, F. W. (jun.), Trooper, Bedfordshire Lancers; and Private, Royal Army Cyclist Corps.
He joined in March 1916, and later proceeded to the Western Front, where he did excellent work as a Despatch Rider in several sectors, and was wounded in the course of his duties. After the Armistice he was sent with the Army of Occupation into Germany and was stationed on the Rhine. He returned to England for demobilisation in September 1919, and holds the General Service and Victory Medals.
15, Dordans Road, Leagrave. 5376/B.

WEBB, G. W., L/Corporal, Royal Engineers.
He volunteered in January 1915, and three months later was drafted to the Western Front, in which theatre of war he served in several engagements. He was severely wounded on the Somme in September 1916, and lost the sight of an eye and was sent to hospital at Boulogne, and in the following October was transferred to England for medical treatment. He was discharged as medically unfit for further service in October 1917, and holds the 1914-15 Star, and the General Service and Victory Medals.
Rose Cottage, Ramridge End, Stopsley. 3207/A.

WEBB, H., Sapper, Royal Engineers.
Joining in March 1917, he was drafted to Salonika in the same year, and was engaged on important duties during the Advance across the Vardar and in several other operations in the Balkans until the close of the war. He returned home for demobilisation in October 1919, and holds the General Service and Victory Medals.
The Ridgway, Flitwick. 5377/B.

WEBB, H., Private, Cambridge Regiment and 22nd Royal Fusiliers.
He joined in April 1917, and in the following October proceeded to the Western Front. During his service overseas he took part in many important engagements, and was wounded near Cambrai. Rejoining his unit, he served through the concluding operations of the war, and was demobilised on his return home in August 1919. He holds the General Service and Victory Medals.
3, Brache Street, Luton. 5378.

WEBB, J., Private, Suffolk Regiment.
He was mobilised in August 1914, and on the conclusion of his training served with his unit on the East Coast. Owing to medical unfitness for general service he was not sent overseas, and he died on July 26th, 1917, from an illness contracted whilst on military duties.
23, Back Street, Luton. 1962/B.

WEBB, J., Private, York and Lancaster Regt.
He volunteered in May 1915, and in August of the following year was drafted overseas. Serving on the Western Front he was in action at Vimy Ridge, Beaumont-Hamel, Arras, Ypres and in other engagements. He was discharged on account of service in March 1917, and holds the General Service and Victory Medals.
28, Frogmore, near St. Albans. X5379.

WEBB, J., Sergeant-Major, R.F.A.
He volunteered in August 1914, and embarked for France in the following year. Whilst on the Western Front he fought in the Battles of Neuve Chapelle, Arras, Ypres and Cambrai, and was wounded three times. He returned to England and was invalided out of the Army in consequence of his wounds in October 1918. He holds the 1914-15 Star, and the General Service and Victory Medals.
The Ridgway, Flitwick. 5377/A.

WEBB, J. M., Ordinary Seaman, Royal Navy.
He joined in September 1917, and posted to H.M.S. "Royal Oak," served aboard that vessel until the cessation of hostilities. His ship was engaged on important patrol duties in the North Sea, and was also sent on special duty to Scapa Flow. He was demobilised in July 1919, and holds the General Service and Victory Medals.
"Old Farm Cottage," Park Street, St. Albans. X3336/A.

WEBB, J. T., Private, 3rd Bedfordshire Regt.
Volunteering in October 1915, he proceeded to Egypt in the following April and served in this theatre of war for over three years. During this period he was engaged in the fighting during the British Advance through Palestine, and fought at Gaza and in the vicinity of Jerusalem. He was demobilised in July 1919, on his return to England, and holds the General Service and Victory Medals.
30, Jubilee Street, Luton. 5380/A—5381/A—5382/A.

WEBB, J. T., Sergeant, Machine Gun Corps.
He volunteered in September 1914, and was sent to France in the following year. During his service on the Western Front he was engaged in heavy fighting at Arras, Ypres, Cambrai and on the Somme, and was twice wounded. He was demobilised in May 1919, and holds the 1914-15 Star, and the General Service and Victory Medals.
" Batford House," Salisbury Road, Harpenden.   5383.

WEBB, J. W., Private, Royal Fusiliers.
Volunteering in June 1915, he was drafted to France in the following December, and fought in many important engagements, including those on the Somme, at Arras and Ypres, and was wounded. He returned to the Field, and was again wounded on June 7th 1918, near Cambrai, and was invalided home. After receiving medical treatment he was demobilised in February 1919, and holds the 1914-15 Star, and the General Service and Victory Medals.
17, Portland Street, St. Albans.   5384.

WEBB, L. W., Pioneer, Royal Engineers.
Volunteering in February 1915, he proceeded to Salonika in December of the following year, and was engaged in laying light railroads for transport purposes until sent to hospital suffering from malaria in August 1917. He was invalided home in May 1918, and on recovery was drafted to France in the following September and served on the Cambrai front during the final operations of the war. He holds the General Service and Victory Medals, and was demobilised in May 1919.
59, Lilley, near Luton.   5385.

WEBB, R., Air Mechanic, Royal Air Force.
He joined in August 1918, and in the same year embarked for France and did good work with his Squadron at various aerodromes until the end of hostilities. In 1919 he was sent with the Army of Occupation into Mesopotamia, and was stationed at Mosul. He returned to England for demobilisation in March 1920, and holds the General Service and Victory Medals.
69, Cotterells Road, Hemel Hempstead.   X2876/B.

WEBB, R. F., Private, Lancashire Fusiliers.
Joining in 1916, he proceeded overseas in the same year, and saw much service on the Western Front. Whilst in this theatre of war he was in action on the Somme, at Arras and Cambrai, and was gassed. He was demobilised in 1919, and holds the General Service and Victory Medals.
64, Cecil Street, North Watford.   X5386.

WEBB, S., Gunner, Royal Field Artillery.
He volunteered in September 1914, and was shortly afterwards drafted to the Western Front. During his service overseas he fought in the Battles of Loos, the Somme, Arras, Ypres and Cambrai, and was wounded. Returning home, he was demobilised in June 1919, and holds the 1914-15 Star, and the General Service and Victory Medals.
Fern Cottage, Shenley Lane, London Colney.   X5387.

WEBB, S. J., Private, 3rd Bedfordshire Regt.
He joined in June 1916, and in the following January embarked for France. He saw much service in this theatre of war and was in action in several engagements, including the Battles of Arras, Ypres and the Somme. He was wounded on September 2nd, 1918, during the Allied Advance, and sent home to hospital. He was demobilised in August 1919, and holds the General Service and Victory Medals.
30, Jubilee Street, Luton.   5380/B—1/B—2/B.

WEBB, W., Sapper, R.E. (Signal Section).
Volunteering in April 1915, he was drafted to Egypt in the following March and served on the lines of communication on signalling duties at Gaza and other places during the British Advance through Palestine. Sent to France in March 1918, he was engaged on the Somme and in many other operations of the concluding stages of the war. He was demobilised in August 1919, and holds the General Service and Victory Medals.
30, Jubilee Street, Luton.   5380/C—1/C—2/C.

WEBB, W. A., A.B., Royal Navy.
He joined in 1919, and on completing his training was posted to H.M.S. " Powerful," in which ship he was engaged on important duties. He was transferred to H.M.S " Curlew," and in 1920 was serving in China.
69, Cotterells Road, Hemel Hempstead.   X2876/A.

WEBB, W. G., Sergeant, 9th Royal Scots.
A serving soldier, he was mobilised on the outbreak of war and almost immediately drafted to France, where he fought in the Retreat from Mons, and was wounded at Ypres on November 6th, 1914. On recovery, he was in action in the Battles of Hill 60, the Somme, Arras, Passchendaele and Cambrai, and was again wounded. He was demobilised in July 1919, and holds the Mons Star, and the General Service and Victory Medals.
68, Lilley, near Luton.   5369/A.

WEBB, W. H., L/Corporal, K.R.R.C.
He joined in 1916, and in the following October proceeded to the Western Front, where he served for upwards of three years. During this period he was engaged in heavy fighting on the Somme, at Arras, Ypres and Cambrai and in several other important operations until the termination of hostilities. He holds the General Service and Victory Medals, and was demobilised in February 1919.
3, St. Faith's Terrace, Orchard Road, Walsworth.   5388.

WEBSTER, J. C., Private, Bedfordshire Regt.
He joined in February 1916, and in the following year was drafted to the Western Front. During his service in France he fought at Arras, Ypres and Cambrai, and after the Armistice proceeded into Germany with the Army of Occupation. He was stationed on the Rhine until October 1919, when he returned home and was demobilised. He holds the General Service and Victory Medals.
37, Alexandra Terrace, Biggleswade.   Z5389.

WEBSTER, W., Sergeant, Royal Field Artillery.
He was mobilised at the outbreak of hostilities, and being medically unfit for foreign service was stationed at various depôts on special duties and did valuable work. He was demobilised in January 1919, after 4½ years with the Colours.
3, Russell Rise, Luton.   5390.

WEDGERFIELD, A. E., Private, Royal Army Service Corps (M.T.)
He volunteered in May 1915, and in the same year was drafted to France, where he was engaged on important transport duties in various sectors. He was present at the engagements at Ypres, Albert, Béthune, Arras and the Somme, and being twice wounded was invalided home to hospital. He was subsequently discharged in June 1918, and holds the 1914-15 Star, and the General Service and Victory Medals.
The Gables, Loat's Lane, Watford.   X2065/B.

WEDGERFIELD, E. (Mrs.), Special War Worker.
For two years during the war this lady held a responsible position in the engine section of the Aeronautical Inspection Department, where she was engaged as a first-grade viewer. She served at Messrs. North's Factory, Watford; Messrs. Robertson's, Putney; and Messrs. Fellowe's, Harlesden, and rendered valuable services at each place. She gave up her duties in February 1919 after performing highly efficient work.
85, Cardiff Road, Watford.   X2065/C.

WEEDEN, S. F., Private, Bedfordshire Regt.
Volunteering at the outbreak of war, he was drafted to France on the completion of his training. He fought in the Arras and Cambrai sectors, and was killed in action on April 19th, 1916. He was entitled to the General Service and Victory Medals.
Holly Cottage, King's Walden.   2762/A.

WEEDON, F., Private, Durham Light Infantry.
He joined in November 1917, and after his training served at various stations on important duties with his unit. He did good work, but was not able to secure his transfer overseas owing to persistent ill-health, and was invalided out of the Service in November 1918.
3, Salisbury Road, Leagrave.   5391.

WEEDON, F., Corporal, Bedfordshire Regiment.
He volunteered in August 1914, and in the following year was sent to France, where he served for 2½ years. During this period he fought at Ypres and Cambrai, and was mortally wounded in an engagement in January 1918. He died of his injuries on January 11th, and was entitled to the 1914-15 Star, and the General Service and Victory Medals.
8, Chater's Yard, High Street, Watford.   X4484/A.

WEEKES, G. F., Q.M.S.I., Royal Engineers (Signal Section).
He was serving at the outbreak of war and was soon drafted to France, where he was engaged on important duties in connection with the operations and was frequently in the forward areas. In July 1915 he met with a serious accident, and was in hospital in England for four months. After his discharge from hospital he was engaged at various Home stations as an Instructor in Signalling. In 1920 he was still serving, and holds the 1914 Star, and the General Service and Victory Medals.
71, High Street, Houghton Regis, near Dunstable.   5392.

WEEKS, R. C., L/Sergeant, 2nd Bedfordshire Regiment.
He volunteered early in November 1915, and in the following February was drafted to France. During his service on the Western Front he fought at the Somme, Vimy Ridge, Passchendaele, Cambrai and Bapaume, and was killed in action in an engagement on the Cambrai front on August 17, 1918. He was entitled to the General Service and Victory Medals.
Upper Sundon, Dunstable.   5393.

WELCH, A., Gunner, Royal Garrison Artillery.
He joined in January 1916, and in the following June, on the completion of his training, was drafted to France. During his service on the Western Front he fought at Arras, Ypres, Cambrai and the Somme, and was wounded. After his recovery he took part in several of the final operations, and was demobilised in March 1919. He holds the General Service and Victory Medals.
18, Camp View Road, St. Albans. X4438/A.

WELCH, A. W., Gunner, R.F.A.
He volunteered in 1915, and after his training was completed was sent to Egypt. He afterwards served with the British Forces under General Allenby in their advance through Palestine and did good work as a gunner in various important engagements, being present at the fall of Jerusalem. He was wounded during his service in July 1919. He was demobilised after his return to England, and holds the General Service and Victory Medals.
46, Oxford Street, Watford. X5395.

WELCH, A. W., Private, Middlesex Regiment.
Volunteering in December 1915, he was drafted to Egypt in the following year, and fought in many engagements on the Palestine front, including those at Gaza and in the operations resulting in the capture of Jerusalem, and was wounded. He also served throughout the Advance through the Holy Land into Syria in 1918. Returning to England he was discharged in February 1918 unfit for further service, and holds the General Service and Victory Medals.
near The Bell Inn, Flamstead. X5394.

WELCH, G., Corporal, 3rd Hampshire Regiment.
He volunteered in January 1915, and was first sent to the Dardanelles, where he took part in various engagements until the Evacuation of the Peninsula. Later he served in the Balkan campaign and was in action in Serbia in various operations until the cessation of hostilities. He was demobilised after his return home in February 1919, and holds the 1914-15 Star, and the General Service and Victory Medals.
45, Upper Culver Road, St. Albans. X5396.

WELCH, H., Private, Bedfordshire Regiment.
Volunteering in 1914, he was engaged after the completion of his training at various stations on important duties with his unit. He was not able to secure his transfer overseas owing to persistent ill-health, and was discharged as medically unfit for further duty in 1915.
88, Apsley End. X5397/A.

WELCH, H., Corporal, 1st Hertfordshire Regt.
He volunteered in August 1914, and after the completion of his training in the following January was drafted overseas. During his service in France he fought in numerous important battles, including those of Loos, the Somme, Beaumont-Hamel, Arras, Vimy Ridge, Ypres, Passchendaele Ridge and St. Quentin and in subsequent operations until the cessation of hostilities. He was demobilised in January 1919, and holds the 1914-15 Star, and the General Service and Victory Medals.
5, Barker's Cottage, Hitchin Hill, Hitchin. 5398/A.

WELCH, J., Corporal, 1st Buffs (East Kent Regiment).
He joined in April 1916, and in March of the following year was drafted to France. During his service on the Western Front he fought at Albert, Arras, Messines, Ypres, Cambrai and in many subsequent engagements until the conclusion of hostilities. He returned to England in 1919, and in the following year was still serving. He holds the General Service and Victory Medals.
5, Barker's Cottages, Hitchin Hill, Hitchin. 5398/B.

WELCH, L., Sapper, Royal Engineers.
He volunteered at the outbreak of war, and in the following year was drafted to France, where he was frequently engaged until the end of the war in the forward areas whilst operations were in progress, especially in the Somme, Ypres and Cambrai sectors. He was demobilised in February 1919, and holds the 1914-15 Star, and the General Servce and Victory Medals.
88, Apsley End. X5397/B.

WELCH, W., Private, Royal Warwickshire Regt.
He volunteered in November 1915, and in the following February was drafted to Egypt. He afterwards took part in the Advance through Palestine, and was in action at Beersheba and the Jordan Valley. He was also present at the entry into Jerusalem and Damascus. In April 1919 he returned to England and was demobilised, holding the General Service and Victory Medals.
42, Queen Street, Luton. 5400.

WELCH, W., Private, 2nd Bedfordshire Regt.
He was mobilised at the outbreak of hostilities, and was almost immediately drafted to France, where he fought in the Retreat from Mons and in the Battles of La Bassée and Ypres. He was killed in action in the fierce fighting at Loos on September 25th, 1915, and was entitled to the Mons Star, and the General Service and Victory Medals.
2, Cape Road, St. Albans X5416.

WELLING, A. T., Private, R.A.S.C.
He volunteered in 1915, and at the conclusion of his training was drafted to the Western Front, where he served for over three years. During this time he did valuable work in connection with the transport of supplies, and was present at the Battles of Ypres, the Somme, Arras and Cambrai. He was also gassed. He holds the 1914-15 Star, and the General Service and Victory Medals, and was demobilised after his return to England in 1919.
8, Willow Lane, Watford. X5402.

WELLING, B. A., Gunner, R.F.A.
Volunteering in December 1914, he embarked for the Dardanelles in the following July, and was in action at the landing at Suvla Bay and in the subsequent engagements until the Evacuation of the Peninsula. Drafted to Salonika, he fought in various sectors on the Vardar and Doiran fronts and in the final Advance in 1918. He was demobilised in December 1918, and holds the 1914-15 Star, and the General Service and Victory Medals.
48, Upper Paddock Road, Oxhey. X5403/A.

WELLING, F. A., A.B. Gunner, Royal Navy.
He joined the Service in August 1914, and was posted to H.M.S. "Royal Oak," which ship was engaged on patrol and other important duties in the North and Baltic Seas and was in action at the Battle of Jutland. He was wounded at Chatham during an air-raid, and on recovery rendered valuable services until the cessation of hostilities. He was still serving in 1920, and holds the 1914-15 Star, and the General Service and Victory Medals.
48, Upper Paddock Road, Oxhey. X5403/B.

WELLS, A., Private, Queen's (Royal West Surrey Regiment).
He joined in March 1916, and after his training was sent to the Western Front, where he took part in several important engagements, including those at Ypres and Cambrai, and was wounded four times. He was demobilised after his return to England in February 1919, and holds the General Service and Victory Medals.
35, Red Lion Yard, Watford X5404.

WELLS, A., L/Corporal, 1st Essex Regiment.
He volunteered in January 1916, and nine months later was sent to the Western Front. Whilst in this theatre of war he was engaged in the fighting at Arras, Ypres, Langemarck, and Cambrai, and in April 1918 was severely wounded in action on the Somme. Returning to England, he was under treatment for some time before being demobilised in November 1918. He holds the General Service and Victory Medals.
Mimram Road, Welwyn. 5405.

WELLS, A. H., Private, Royal Fusiliers.
He joined in July 1917, and after his training was engaged on duties of an important nature with his unit. He was not successful in obtaining his transfer overseas before the termination of hostilities, but nevertheless rendered valuable services before he was demobilised in 1919.
91, Regent Street, North Watford. X5406.

WELLS, B., Private, 1/5th Bedfordshire Regt.
Volunteering in June 1915, he was sent to Egypt five months later, and took part in several minor engagements on that front. Later he served in the Palestine campaign, during which he fought at Gaza and on the Jordan, and was present at the capture of Jerusalem. He returned to England in March 1919, and was demobilised the following month, and holds the 1914-15 Star, and the General Service and Victory Medals.
85, Sun Street, Biggleswade. Z2660/C.

WELLS, C., Corporal, 5th Northamptonshire Regt.
He joined in April 1918, and in the following July was sent to the Western Front, where, during the final Advance, he fought in several engagements, including those at Arras, Bapaume, the Somme, Cambrai and Amiens, and the second Battle of the Marne. He holds the General Service and Victory Medals, and was demobilised after his return to England in January 1920.
4, Crawley Road, Luton 5407/A.

WELLS, C. A., Signalman, Royal Navy.

He volunteered in 1914, and during the period of hostilities served on important duties with his ship in the North Sea, the Baltic, and various other waters. He rendered valuable services until he was demobilised in August 1919, and holds the 1914–15 Star, and the General Service and Victory Medals.

8, Jubilee Road, Watford.   X3104/B.

WELLS, E., Private, Labour Corps.

He joined in October 1916, and after his training was engaged on important agricultural duties at various stations. He was unable to secure his transfer overseas before the termination of hostilities, but nevertheless did valuable work until he was demobilised in March 1919.

180, Wellington Street, Luton.   5408.

WELLS, F., Private, 8th Suffolk Regiment.

Joining early in 1916, he was sent to France in August of that year, but was killed in the Somme sector on September 29th, 1916, in his first engagement. He was entitled to the General Service and Victory Medals.

85, Sun Street, Biggleswade.   Z2660/B.

WELLS, G., Private, 1st Black Watch.

Joining in May 1916, he was sent overseas in the following year. Whilst on the Western Front he fought at Ypres, Cambrai and the Somme, where he was severely wounded. Returning to England, he was invalided out of the Service in January 1918, and holds the General Service and Victory Medals.

37, Ivy Road, Luton.   5409.

WELLS, G. A., Private, Royal Fusiliers.

He joined in March 1917, and during his service on the Western Front was engaged on important canteen duties, and was stationed principally at Étaples. He holds the General Service and Victory Medals, and was demobilised in April 1919.

87, Copsewood Road, Watford.   X5410.

WELLS, H. F., Private, 2nd Bedfordshire Regt.

He joined in June 1918, and after his training was drafted to India, where he was engaged on important garrison duties at Poona, Rawal Pindi and Calcutta, and in 1920 was still serving. He holds the General Service and Victory Medals.

130, Victoria Street, St. Albans.   X5411/B.

WELLS, H. J., Sergeant, R.A.M.C.

Volunteering in November 1915, he was sent to the Western Front in the following June. During his overseas service he was attached to the 137th Field Ambulance, in which he did valuable work in many important sectors, notably the Somme, the Ancre, Messines, Ypres, Havrincourt Wood and Cambrai, where he was wounded. He was demobilised on his return to England in August 1919, and holds the General Service and Victory Medals.

4, Crawley Road, Luton.   5407/C.

WELLS, P., Sergeant, Royal Horse Artillery.

He enlisted in 1910, and when war broke out was serving in Africa, where he remained with his unit during the period of hostilities, and was mentioned in Despatches for his splendid work. Later he contracted fever, of which he subsequently died at Dar-es-Salaam on August 19th, 1918. He was entitled to the 1914–15 Star, and the General Service and Victory Medals.

4, Crawley Road, Luton.   5407/B.

WELLS, P. H., Private, R.A.V.C.

He volunteered in October 1914, and after his training was sent to Egypt, where he took part in several minor engagements. Later he served in the Palestine campaign, during which he fought at Gaza, Haifa and Beyrout, and was wounded. He was demobilised on his return to England in February 1919, and holds the 1914–15 Star, and the General Service and Victory Medals.

16, Spencer Street, St. Albans.   X5412.

WELLS, R. R., Private, Royal Defence Corps.

Being ineligible for service overseas owing to his age, he joined the Royal Defence Corps in July 1915, and for the remaining period of hostilities was engaged on important duties with his unit at various stations. He rendered services of a very valuable nature until March 1919, when he was demobilised.

Woburn Road, Aspley Guise.   Z5413.

WELLS, W. C., Rifleman, K.R.R.C.

He joined in August 1917, and during his service on the Western Front, acted as Divisional Runner. In this capacity he did valuable work in many important sectors, and after being wounded three times, was taken prisoner near Arras in August 1918. After his release at the cessation of hostilities he rejoined his unit, and in April 1919 was invalided out of the Service. He holds the General Service and Victory Medals.

130, Victoria Street, St. Albans.   X5411/A.

WELLS, W. C., Air Mechanic, Royal Air Force (late Royal Flying Corps).

He joined in February 1916, and at the conclusion of his training was drafted to Mesopotamia, where he was present at the capture of Baghdad and the occupation of Mosul, and was wounded. He was demobilised on his return to England in May 1919, and holds the General Service and Victory Medals.   12, New Street, Shefford.   Z5414.

WELLS, W. G., Private, Queen's (Royal West Surrey Regiment).

He volunteered in December 1914, and after the completion of his training proceeded to France in January 1916. During his service overseas he took part in numerous engagements of great importance, including those at the Somme in 1916, Ypres in 1917, and Albert and Amiens in the Offensive of 1918. He was unfortunately killed in action at Amiens on September 2nd, 1918, and was entitled to the General Service and Victory Medals.

3, Chapel Fields, Biggleswade.   Z5401.

WELSH, A. E., Sergeant-Major, R.A.O.C.

He volunteered in March 1915, and served in France and Salonika. He was engaged as an armourer in the repair of guns. His duties, which demanded a high degree of technical skill, were carried out with great care and accuracy and he rendered valuable services. He was demobilised in July 1919, and holds the General Service and Victory Medals.

4, Lowestoft Road, Watford.   X2946/A.

WELSH, E. W., L/Corporal, 4th (Reserve) Yorkshire Regiment.

He joined in July 1916, and after his training served at various stations on important duties with his unit. He rendered valuable services, but was not successful in obtaining his transfer overseas before the cessation of hostilities. He was demobilised in February 1919.

11, Brighton Road, Watford.   X5415.

WENDEL, E. T., Cook, R.N., H.M.S. "Carysfort."

He joined in June 1916, and served with the Grand Fleet in the North Sea on patrol duties off the coasts of Denmark and Germany. He was engaged on duties of a responsible nature and rendered valuable services. He was demobilised in December 1919, and holds the General Service and Victory Medals. 151, Leavesden Road, Watford.   X5417/A.

WENDEL, L. H., Private, K.O.S.B.

He volunteered in April 1915, and after his training was drafted to the Western Front, where he took part in numerous engagements, including that at Ypres, and was gassed. He was invalided home, and in August 1917 was discharged as medically unfit for further service, holding the 1914–15 Star, and the General Service and Victory Medals.

151, Leavesden Road, Watford.   X5417/B.

WESLEY, G. H., Private, Royal Welch Fusiliers.

Volunteering in December 1915, he was later drafted to France, where he took part in severe fighting at Albert, the Somme and Ypres, and was wounded and suffered from shell-shock. He was invalided home and discharged as medically unfit in October 1917, and holds the General Service and Victory Medals.

15, Park Road West, Luton.   5419.

WESLEY, H., Private, Labour Corps.

He joined in February 1916, and was drafted to France in the same year. He served in various important engagements, including those on the Somme and at Arras, Cambrai and St. Quentin, and was wounded. He was demobilised in April 1919, and holds the General Service and Victory Medals.

3, Queen's Street, Hitchin.   5418.

WESLEY, W., Private, R.A.M.C.

Joining in June 1916, he was drafted to France in December of the same year. He took part in numerous engagements, including those at Arras, Ypres and Passchendaele, and was wounded. He was demobilised in September 1919, and holds the General Service and Victory Medals.

15, Brixton Road, Watford.   X5420.

WESSON, A., Private, R.A.S.C. (M.T.)

He volunteered in June 1915, and in January of the following year was drafted to the Western Front. He was engaged in many sectors, including the Somme, Arras and Ypres, in the transport of ammunition and supplies and rendered valuable services. He was demobilised in March 1919, and holds the General Service and Victory Medals.

19, Ebury Road, Watford.   X939/B.

WEST, A., Private, 10th Queen's (Royal West Surrey Regiment).

He volunteered in August 1914, and in the following year was drafted to the Western Front, where he took part in severe fighting at Ypres, Loos and Arras, and was twice wounded and gassed. He was demobilised in May 1919, and holds the 1914–15 Star, and the General Service and Victory Medals.

39, Temperance Street, St. Albans.   3422/B.

WEST, F. J., Private, 4th Bedfordshire Regiment.
He volunteered in August 1914, and was sent to France in
the same year and took part in numerous engagements,
including that at Ypres. He was reported missing and is
presumed to have been killed in action at Passchendaele on
October 30th, 1917. He was entitled to the 1914-15 Star,
and the General Service and Victory Medals.
1, Stanbridge Road, Leighton Buzzard.   5253/B.

WEST, F. R., Private, 2nd Middlesex Regiment.
He joined in June 1916, and was drafted to France in October
of the same year. He took part in severe fighting on the
Somme and at Ypres, Passchendaele and Cambrai, where he
was severely wounded and taken prisoner. He was held in
captivity until after the Armistice, when he was released, and
returning to England was demobilised in March 1919, holding
the General Service and Victory Medals.
Sharpenhoe Road, Barton.   5421.

WEST, G. D., Sapper, Royal Engineers.
He joined in 1916, and after his training served at various
stations on important duties with his unit. He rendered
valuable services, but was not successful in obtaining his
transfer overseas before the cessation of hostilities owing to
his medical unfitness for active service. He was demobilised
in 1919.
1, San Remo Road, Aspley Guise.   • Z5422.

WEST, H. J., Private, R.A.S.C.
He volunteered in 1915, and in the following year was drafted
to Egypt and thence to Palestine, where he served in
various engagements, including those at Gaza, Jaffa, Haifa,
Aleppo, Damascus and Beyrout. He returned home and was
demobilised in May 1919, and holds the General Service and
Victory Medals.
55, Breakspeare Road, Abbots Langley.   X5423.

WEST, H. W., Sapper, Royal Engineers.
He volunteered in June 1915, and in August of the same
year was drafted to the Western Front, where he was present
at numerous engagements, including those on the Somme and
at Arras and Ypres, being employed as an engine-driver. He
was demobilised in April 1919, and holds the 1914-15 Star,
and the General Service and Victory Medals.
6, Black Horse Lane, Sunnyside, Hitchin.   5424.

WEST, J. C., Lieutenant, R.A.S.C. (M.T.)
He volunteered in August 1914, and in the following year
proceeded to Gallipoli, where he was in charge of the transport
of supplies. His duties, which were of a most responsible
nature, were carried out with great care and efficiency, and
he rendered valuable services. He was later transferred to
Egypt and was engaged on similar work. He was demobilised in February 1919, and holds the 1914-15 Star, and the
General Service and Victory Medals.
32, Dale Road, Luton.   5425.

WEST, W., Private, 11th Essex Regiment.
Volunteering in October 1915, he was drafted to France in the
following year and took part in severe fighting at Vimy Ridge,
the Somme and many other important engagements. He
was killed in action in the Ancre sector on March 21st, 1917,
and was entitled to the General Service and Victory Medals.
Green End, Shillington.   5426

WEST, W., Gunner, Royal Field Artillery.
He volunteered in 1915, and in the following year was drafted
to the Western Front, where he took part in heavy fighting
on the Somme and at Arras, Ypres, Passchendaele Ridge and
Armentières. He was discharged in September 1918 in
consequence of his service, and holds the General Service and
Victory Medals.
22, Portland Street, St. Albans.   5427.

WEST, W. J., Private, 20th Middlesex Regiment.
He joined in February 1917, and was sent to France in January
of the following year. He took part in various engagements
in the Armentières sector, and was gassed and taken prisoner
at Fleurbaix in April 1918. On his release he returned home
and was demobilised in September 1919, and holds the
General Service and Victory Medals.
18, King's Road, St. Albans.   X5750.

WEST, W. S., Private, Bedfordshire Regiment.
He volunteered in August 1914, and in the following year
was drafted to the Western Front, where he took part in severe
fighting at Hill 60, Ypres, Loos, Vimy Ridge, the Somme
and Cambrai. He was demobilised in January 1919, and
holds the 1914-15 Star, and the General Service and Victory
Medals.
5, Surrey Street, Luton.   5322/B.

WEST, W. W., Driver, Royal Horse Artillery.
Volunteering in April 1915, he was drafted to France in July
of the same year. He took part in various engagements,
including those at Albert, Ypres and Armentières. Later
in the same year he proceeded to Mesopotamia, where he
contracted malaria. He returned home and was demobilised
in February 1919, and holds the 1914-15 Star, and the
General Service and Victory Medals.
14, Lattimore Road, St. Albans.   X5428.

WESTCOTT, E., Driver, Royal Field Artillery.
He joined in May 1916, and after proceeding to France
did valuable work with his unit during operations at Arras,
Albert and in the second Battle of the Aisne. After the
cessation of hostilities he was drafted to Germany with the
Army of Occupation, and was demobilised on his return to
England in September 1919. He holds the General Service
and Victory Medals.
6, Pretoria Road, Watford.   X5429.

WESTCOTT, F., Private, 10th South Wales Borderers.
Joining in November 1916, he was drafted to France two
months later. During his service overseas he was engaged
in the fighting at Ypres, the Somme, Armentières and
Cambrai, but in consequence of being wounded three times
returned to England in September 1918. After protracted
hospital treatment, he was demobilised in December 1919,
and holds the General Service and Victory Medals.
70, Sotheron Road, Watford.   X5430.

WESTCOTT, J., Private, 2nd Suffolk Regiment.
He volunteered in July 1915, and after his training was sent
to the Western Front. Here he fought in many important
engagements, including those at the Somme and Beaumont-
Hamel, and on three occasions was severely wounded.
Returning to England in May 1917, he was invalided out of
the Service a year later, and holds the General Service and
Victory Medals.
70, Sotheron Road, Watford.   X5431.

WESTNUTT, J., Sapper, Royal Engineers.
He joined in July 1916, and at the conclusion of his training
was engaged on important duties in connection with the
searchlight section. In this capacity he did excellent work,
and, although owing to physical disability he was unable to
secure his transfer overseas, rendered valuable services until
demobilised in February 1919.
21, Alfred Street, Dunstable.   5432.

WESTON, A., Corporal, K.R.R.C.
Joining in March 1916, he was sent to the Western Front
in the same year at the conclusion of his training. He
fought in the Battles of the Somme, Arras, Ypres and Cambrai, and in the Retreat and Advance of 1918, after which
he served for a time with the Army of Occupation at Cologne.
He was demobilised in August 1919, and holds the General
Service and Victory Medals.
Mill Lane, Greenfield, near Ampthill.   5433.

WESTON, C., Sergeant, Royal Air Force.
A serving soldier in the 2nd Oxfordshire and Buckinghamshire Light Infantry, he was sent to the Western Front at
the outbreak of war, and fought in the Retreat from Mons.
He also took part in many subsequent engagements, notably
those at the Aisne, Ypres, the Somme and Cambrai, and did
valuable work with his unit. During his service he was
transferred to the Royal Air Force, in which in 1920 he was
still engaged. He holds the Mons Star, and the General
Service and Victory Medals.
1, Field Terrace, Smith Street, Watford.   5434.

WESTON, D. G., Private, Machine Gun Corps.
Volunteering in 1915, he was drafted to France at the conclusion of his training in August 1916. After taking part
in several important engagements he was killed in action on
September 9th, 1916, and buried near Delville Wood. He
was entitled to the General Service and Victory Medals.
21, Pinner Road, Oxhey.   X5435.

WESTON, F. C., Driver, R.A.S.C.
He volunteered in January 1915, and after his training was
drafted to Salonika, where he served principally at the base
engaged on important duties in connection with the supply
of rations to our troops in the lines. In this capacity he
did valuable work until after the cessation of hostilities,
and on his return to England in February 1919, was demobilised. He holds the 1914-15 Star, and the General Service
and Victory Medals.
54, Sopwell Lane, St. Albans.   X5436

**WESTON, H. G., Corporal, Loyal North Lan-
cashire Regiment.**
Volunteering in February 1915, he was sent to the Western
Front at the conclusion of his training. After taking part in
the operations at Neuve Chapelle and Ypres he is believed
to have been killed in action at Festubert. He was entitled
to the 1914-15 Star and the General Service and Victory
Medals. East End, Flitwick.   2327/B.

WESTON, S., Private, 2nd Bedfordshire Volunteer Battalion.
Being ineligible for service with the Colours, he joined the Volunteers in June 1916, and was subsequently engaged on important guard duties at various stations. He rendered valuable services until he was discharged in September 1919.
108, Clarendon Road, Luton. 5438.

WESTON, S. C., L/Corporal, 6th Royal Warwickshire Regiment.
He joined in January 1917, and after his training was drafted to the Italian Front, where he served for 18 months. During this period he did valuable work with his unit on the Piave, and was also for a time at Taranto. He was demobilised in May 1919, and holds the General Service and Victory Medals.
47, Whitby Road, Luton. 5437.

WESTWOOD, J. C., Gunner (Fitter), R.G.A.
He joined the Territorials in April 1914, and was mobilised at the outbreak of war. In December 1915 he was sent to France, where he was subsequently engaged in the fighting at Ypres, Vimy Ridge, the Somme and the Ancre. He was invalided home owing to a severe wound in May 1917, but on his recovery returned to the Western Front, and after taking part in the concluding operations of the war, proceeded to Germany with the Army of Occupation. He was demobilised in May 1919, and holds the 1914–15 Star, and the General Service and Victory Medals.
10, Beech Road, Luton. 5439.

WESTWOOD, T., L/Corporal, 1st Cambridgeshire Regiment.
He volunteered in 1915, and after his training served in France for over three years. During this period he fought in many important battles, notably those of the Somme, Arras and Ypres, and did valuable work with his unit throughout. He holds the 1914–15 Star, and the General Service and Victory Medals, and was demobilised in February 1919.
56, Yarmouth Road, Callowland. X5440.

WESTWOOD, W., Private, Machine Gun Corps.
Volunteering in May 1915, he was drafted to Egypt at the conclusion of his training, and later served in Palestine. In this theatre of war he did important work with his unit during operations at Gaza, Haifa, Jerusalem and Jaffa. He was demobilised on his return to England in April 1919, and holds the General Service and Victory Medals.
18, Sunnyside, Hitchin. 5441.

WHEATLEY, A., Air Mechanic, R.A.F.
He joined in December 1916, and in the following year, after completing his training, was drafted to France. During his service in this theatre of war he was engaged in various sectors of our line on important duties which demanded a high degree of technical skill. He was demobilised in January 1919, and holds the General Service and Victory Medals.
23, Pretoria Road, Watford. 1658/C.

WHEATLEY, A. J., Sapper, Royal Engineers.
He joined in May 1917, and in the following September was sent to Egypt and served in the Offensive on Palestine under General Allenby. He was engaged on important railway duties in connection with the military operations and was in the fighting areas at Gaza and Jaffa, and present at the fall of Jerusalem. He was demobilised in March 1919, after his return to England, and holds the General Service and Victory Medals.
31, Cemetery Street, Biggleswade. Z5442.

WHEATLEY, C. E., Sapper, Royal Engineers.
He joined in April 1916, and in the following June was drafted to France, where he served on important duties in connection with the operations, and was frequently in the forward areas. He was demobilised in May 1919, after nearly three years' service overseas, and holds the General Service and Victory Medals.
Magpie Row, George Street, Maulden, near Ampthill. 5443.

WHEATLEY, H., Rifleman, Rifle Brigade.
He volunteered in August 1914, and after his training was completed was sent to India, where he was engaged on important duties at Calcutta for over five years. In January 1920 he returned to England and was demobilised, holding the General Service and Victory Medals.
109, Chester Road, Watford. X5366/A.

WHEATLEY, J., Sergeant, Suffolk Regiment.
Volunteering in August 1914, he served at first on important duties as a Drill Instructor until he was drafted to France. Here he fought in numerous engagements, including the Battles of Arras and Cambrai, and was gassed. After the cessation of hostilities he returned to England, and in February 1919 was demobilised, holding the General Service and Victory Medals.
64, Brighton Road, Watford. X5444.

WHEATLEY, J. C., Private, Bedfordshire Regt.
Volunteering in January 1915, he was drafted to France in the following March and served in various sectors of the Western Front. He was in action on the Somme, and at Albert, Arras, Ypres and Cambrai, and was wounded during this period. He was demobilised in March 1919, after exactly three years' overseas service, and holds the General Service and Victory Medals.
6, Ivel Terrace, Biggleswade. Z5445.

WHEELER, A. H., L/Corporal, Queen's Own (Royal West Kent Regiment).
He joined in 1918, and after his training was engaged in conducting the released German prisoners to Holland until October 1919, when he was sent to India. Here he was engaged on important garrison duties, and in 1920 was still serving at Agra.
5, Wharf Lane, Rickmansworth. X5446/A.

WHEELER, B. R., R.S.M., R.A.S.C.
He volunteered in September 1914, and in the following year was drafted to the Dardanelles, and served at the landing at Suvla Bay and in the engagement at Cape Helles. In 1917 he was sent to Egypt and from thence to Palestine, where he was present in numerous battles, including those at Gaza, Jaffa, Haifa and Aleppo. He was mentioned in Despatches in June 1918 for consistently good service, and holds the 1914–15 Star, and the General Service and Victory Medals. After the cessation of hostilities he returned to England and was demobilised in June 1919.
161, Whippendell Road, Watford. X5447.

WHEELER, F. G., Corporal, Royal Fusiliers.
He volunteered in 1914, and in the following year was drafted to France. During his service on the Western Front he fought at Ypres, Loos, the Somme, Cambrai and St. Quentin, and in various subsequent engagements until the cessation of hostilities. He was demobilised in 1919, and holds the 1914–15 Star, and the General Service and Victory Medals.
Raymond Villa, Ickleford, Hitchin. 5448.

WHEELER, W. (M.M.), Private, Bedfordshire Regiment.
He volunteered in October 1914, and in the same year was drafted to France, where he saw much service. He fought with distinction at Hill 60, Ypres, the Somme and Cambrai, and was four times wounded and gassed. Whilst serving at Cambrai he was awarded the Military Medal for conspicuous gallantry and devotion to duty on the Field. He holds in addition the 1914 Star, and the General Service and Victory Medals, and was demobilised in March 1919.
River Hill, Flamstead, Dunstable. X5449.

WHEELER, W. A., Private, East Surrey Regt. and Royal Air Force.
He volunteered in September 1914, and early in the following year was drafted overseas. During his service in France he was severely wounded at Hill 60, where he was blown up by the explosion of a shell. After his recovery he was in action in various sectors until the conclusion of hostilities. He was demobilised in March 1919, and holds the 1914–15 Star, and the General Service and Victory Medals.
455, Whippendell Road, Watford. X5450.

WHEELER, W. D., Private, 1st East Surrey Regiment.
He joined in May 1917, and in the following August was drafted to France, and served in various important engagements, including that of St. Quentin. He was wounded near Cambrai in 1918, and after his recovery was in action in the final operations until the cessation of hostilities. He holds the General Service and Victory Medals, and in 1920 was still serving.
5, Chaters Yard, High Street, Watford. X5451.

WHEEWALL, S. H., Private, M.G.C.
He was called up from the Reserve at the outbreak of war, and until February 1915, when he was sent to France, was engaged upon duties of an important nature. Whilst overseas he fought in many battles, notably those of the Somme, Ypres and Arras, where he was wounded, and when hostilities ceased was at Courtrai. He holds the 1914–15 Star, and the General Service and Victory Medals, and was demobilised in February 1919.
73, Cowper Street, Luton. 5452.

WHIFFIN, S., Driver, Royal Engineers.
He volunteered in January 1915, and after his training was drafted to Egypt and Palestine. Whilst in this theatre of war he did valuable work with his unit during operations at Gaza and Jerusalem, and before returning to England was stationed for a time at Cairo. He was demobilised in August 1919, and holds the General Service and Victory Medals.
75, West End, Silsoe. 5453.

WHITBREAD, A. J., Private, Bedfordshire Regiment.
He volunteered in 1915, and after his training served on important duties with his unit at various stations. He was not successful in obtaining his transfer overseas before the termination of hostilities, but nevertheless did valuable work until he was demobilised in December 1919.
7, New Street, Luton. 5454/B.

WHITBREAD, E. J., Private, Middlesex Regt.
He volunteered in August 1914, and at the conclusion of his training was drafted to France, where he fought in many important engagements, including those at Cambrai, Ypres and Arras. During his service he suffered from shell-shock. He was demobilised on his return to England in February 1919, and holds the General Service and Victory Medals.
7, New Street, Luton. 5454/A.

WHITBREAD, F., Private, Royal Fusiliers.
He volunteered in May 1915, and two months later was drafted to the Western Front. Subsequently he was engaged in the fighting at Loos, the Somme, Arras and Ypres, and was wounded and taken prisoner in September 1917, whilst in action near Passchendaele. During his captivity he suffered much ill-treatment at the hands of the enemy' and died on December 4th of the same year. He was entitled to the 1914–15 Star, and the General Service and Victory Medals.
Gas Street, Toddington. 5487/B.

WHITBREAD, J., Private, Bedfordshire Regt.
Volunteering in August 1914, he was drafted to the Western Front at the conclusion of his training, and during his service in France fought at Ypres, Loos, Arras and Cambrai, and was wounded. He holds the 1914 Star, and the General Service and Victory Medals, and was demobilised in 1919.
High Street, Barton, Ampthill. 5455.

WHITBREAD, R., Private, 3rd Essex Regiment.
He joined in July 1916, and in November of the same year was drafted to the Western Front. During his service in France he was in action in the Battles of the Somme, Arras, Ypres and Passchendaele, and was severely wounded on September 21st, 1917. He was invalided home to hospital, where he was for five months under treatment, and later was discharged as medically unfit for further duty in May 1918. He holds the General Service and Victory Medals.
Gas Street, Toddington. 5487/A.

WHITE, A., Private, Bedfordshire Regiment and South Wales Borderers.
He joined in 1916, and on the completion of his training was in the following year drafted to Mesopotamia, where he took part in the campaign against the Turks. He was in action at Kut-el-Amara, Baghdad and Basra, and after the termination of hostilities returned to England and was demobilised, holding the General Service and Victory Medals.
Station Road, Ridgmont. Z5459.

WHITE, A., L/Sergeant, Bedfordshire and Leicestershire Regiments.
He volunteered in August 1914, and in the following July was drafted to the Western Front, where he took part in numerous engagements, including those at Arras, Ypres, Passchendaele and Cambrai, and was wounded. He also served in the Retreat and Advance of 1918, and holding the 1914–15 Star, and the General Service and Victory Medals, was still serving in 1920.
Woodland Villas, Dunstable Street, Ampthill. 5458.

WHITE, A., Driver, R.A.S.C.
Volunteering in August 1914, he was immediately drafted to the Western Front, where he served on important duties and was present during the Retreat from Mons and the Battles of Ypres, Loos, Arras and Cambrai. He holds the Mons Star, and the General Service and Victory Medals, and was demobilised in June 1920.
41, Holywell Road, Watford. X5457.

WHITE, A., Private, Royal Army Pay Corps.
Volunteering in March 1915. he proceeded to the Western Front in the following September, and served at Calais, Rouen and Boulogne, engaged on important clerical duties in the Pay Office. He rendered valuable services throughout, and was demobilised in July 1919, and holds the 1914–15 Star, and the General Service and Victory Medals.
near Chapel, Flamstead, Beds. X5456/A.

WHITE, A. E., Aircraftsman, R.A.F.
He joined in November 1917, and after his training served at various stations on important duties with his unit. His work. which demanded a high degree of skill, was carried out with great efficiency, and he rendered valuable services, but was not successful in obtaining his transfer overseas before the cessation of hostilities. He was demobilised in November 1919.
134, Victoria Street, St. Albans. X5460.

WHITE, A. J. (M.S.M.), Sergt., Royal Engineers.
He volunteered in December 1914, and in February of the following year was drafted to the Western Front, where he took part in numerous engagements, including those of Hill 60, Ypres, the Somme, Arras, Passchendaele and Cambrai. He was awarded the Meritorious Service Medal for devotion to duty, and also holds the 1914–15 Star, and the General Service and Victory Medals. He was demobilised in March 1919.
4, Periwinkle Lane, Hitchin. 5461.

WHITE, C., Private, Bedfordshire Regiment.
He volunteered in 1915, and after his training served at various stations on important duties with his unit. He rendered valuable services, but was not successful in obtaining his transfer overseas before the cessation of hostilities. He was demobilised in May 1919.
124, Cotterells Road, Hemel Hempstead. X5462.

WHITE, C. H., Sergeant, 2nd Bedfordshire Regt. and Hertfordshire Regiment.
He volunteered in September 1914, and in the following year was drafted to the Dardanelles and took part in the landing at Suvla Bay. In 1917 he was transferred to France and was in action at Arras and Ypres, and was wounded. He was afterwards sent to India, where he was still serving in 1920, and holds the 1914–15 Star, and the General Service and Victory Medals.
66, Frederic Street, Luton. 5463.

WHITE, C. W., Private, Labour Corps.
He joined in October 1916, and in March of the following year was sent to France. He was engaged on road-making and other important duties with his unit, and rendered valuable services. He was demobilised in March 1919, and holds the General Service and Victory Medals.
33, Cobden Street, Luton. 5466.

WHITE, E. W., Private, 5th South Staffordshire Regiment.
He joined in April 1916, and proceeded overseas in the following August. During his service in France he fought in many important engagements, and was unfortunately killed in action on the Somme on October 4th, 1916. He was entitled to the General Service and Victory Medals.
142, New Town Street, Luton. 796/A.

WHITE, F., Private, Bedfordshire Regiment.
He joined in 1916, and after his training was drafted to the Western Front. He was engaged in various sectors on important duties with his unit and rendered valuable services. He returned home and was demobilised in December 1919, and holds the General Service and Victory Medals.
114, Talbot Road, Luton. 5467.

WHITE, F., Private, 5th Bedfordshire Regiment.
Volunteering in August 1915, he was sent to France in March of the following year. He took part in severe fighting on the Somme and was wounded. He was invalided home and discharged in August 1918, and holds the General Service and Victory Medals.
21, Winfield Street, Dunstable. 5468.

WHITE, H., Driver, R.A.S.C.
He joined in 1916, and after his training served at various stations on important duties with his unit. He rendered valuable services, but was not successful in obtaining his transfer overseas before the cessation of hostilities. He was demobilised in November 1919.
Salford Road, Aspley Guise. Z5469.

WHITE, H. C., Private, 13th Royal Sussex Regt.
He volunteered in November 1914, and served on important duties with his unit until July 1916, when he was drafted to France. He took part in severe fighting on the Somme, where he was killed in action on October 21st, 1916, and was entitled to the General Service and Victory Medals.
Mill Lane, Clophill, near Ampthill. 5470.

WHITE, H. S., L/Corporal, Military Foot Police.
He volunteered in June 1915, and was drafted to France in the same year. He was engaged on various important duties with his unit until, contracting dysentery, he was invalided home. Later he was discharged as medically unfit for further service in April 1917. Afterwards he died on July 25th, 1918, and was entitled to the 1914–15 Star, and the General Service and Victory Medals.
15, Ickleford Road, Hitchin. 5471.

WHITE, J., Private, 4th Bedfordshire Regiment.
He volunteered in August 1914, and was sent to France in the same month. He took part in severe fighting at Mons, Ypres, Arras and Albert, and was killed in action near the last-named place on June 2nd, 1918. He was entitled to the Mons Star, and the General Service and Victory Medals.
4, Wright's Cottages, St. Albans Road, Watford X5472.

WHITE, L. A., Gunner, R.F.A.

Joining in April 1917, he was sent to the Western Front six months later, and saw much service in many parts of the line, fighting at Cambrai and throughout the German Offensive and subsequent Allied Advance in 1918. He returned to England and was demobilised in February 1919, and holds the General Service and Victory Medals.

near Chapel, Flamstead, Beds. X5456/B.

WHITE, M. R. (Miss), Special War Worker.

This lady was engaged at Messrs. Kent's Munition Factory, Luton, on the inspection of fuses for naval shells, and later in making and drilling the same at the Vauxhall Works, Luton. Her duties, which were of a highly responsible nature, were carried out with great care and efficiency, and she rendered valuable services during the war.

8, Boyle Street, Luton. 5473.

WHITE, P. H., L/Corporal, 6th Bedfordshire Regiment.

He volunteered in September 1914, and was drafted to France in July of the following year. He took part in severe fighting at Loos, Ypres and Passchendaele, and was twice wounded. He was demobilised in February 1919, and holds the 1914-15 Star, and the General Service and Victory Medals.

North End, Lemsford, Hatfield. 5474.

WHITE, S. C., Private, 7th Bedfordshire Regt.

He volunteered in August 1914, and in the following year was drafted to the Western Front. He took part in various engagements, including those on the Somme, and was severely wounded on July 1st, 1916, and two days later died of his injuries. He was entitled to the 1914-15 Star, and the General Service and Victory Medals.

Station Grove, Woburn Sands. Z5475.

WHITE, T., Private, 2nd Bedfordshire Regiment.

He volunteered in November 1914, and in the following year was sent to France. He took part in severe fighting at Festubert, the Somme and in other engagements, and was wounded. He was invalided home and afterwards transferred to the Labour Corps. He was demobilised in February 1919, and holds the 1914-15 Star, and the General Service and Victory Medals. Station Road, Ridgmont. Z5476.

WHITE, W., Private, 2nd Bedfordshire Regiment.

He volunteered in October 1914, and was drafted to the Western Front in the following year. He took part in numerous engagements, including those at Hill 60, Vimy Ridge, the Somme, Arras, Cambrai and Albert. He was killed in action at the latter place on May 8th, 1918, and was entitled to the 1914-15 Star, and the General Service and Victory Medals. Duke Street, Aspley Guise. Z5477.

WHITE, W. G., Private, 16th Cheshire Regiment.

He volunteered in November 1914, and served on important duties with his unit until 1916, when he was sent to France, where he took part in various engagements and served in many sectors. He was demobilised in March 1919, and holds the General Service and Victory Medals.

79, Southam, North Kensington, W.10 X5478.

WHITE, W. G., Private, 11th Royal Fusiliers.

He volunteered in April 1915, and was sent to France in October of the same year. He took part in severe fighting on the Somme and at Ypres, and was wounded. He was killed in action in August 1918, and was entitled to the 1914-15 Star, and the General Service and Victory Medals.

86, Cromwell Road, Luton. 5479.

WHITE, W. G., Private, R.A.S.C. (M.T.)

He joined in February 1917, and after his training served at various stations on important duties with his unit. He rendered valuable services, but was not successful in obtaining his transfer overseas before the cessation of hostilities. He was demobilised in November 1919.

41, High Street, Silsoe. 5480.

WHITE, W. H., Private, Northamptonshire Regt.

He volunteered in December 1915, and was sent to France in July of the following year. He took part in various engagements, including those on the Somme, where he was severely wounded and suffered the amputation of his right leg. He was invalided home and discharged in January 1918, and holds the General Service and Victory Medals.

33, High Street, Ridgmont. Z5481.

WHITE, W. J., Private, 1st Prince of Wales' Leinster Regiment.

Volunteering in August 1916, he was sent to Salonika in the following year. He took part in the Balkan campaign, and was afterwards transferred to Egypt and thence to Palestine, where he served in various engagements, including that at Gaza. He was demobilised in June 1919, and holds the 1914-15 Star, and the General Service and Victory Medals.

268, High Street North, Dunstable. 5482.

WHITEHEAD, T. H., Private, R.A.S.C. (M.T.)

He joined in June 1916, and after his training served at various stations on important duties with his unit until March 1918, when he was drafted to the Western Front. He was engaged in the transport of guns and ammunition to the front line and was wounded. He was demobilised in February 1919, and holds the General Service and Victory Medals. 60, Newcombe Road, Luton. 5483.

WHITEHOUSE, T., Gunner, R.G.A.

He volunteered in 1915, and after his training was drafted to the Western Front, where he took part in severe fighting on the Somme and in other engagements, and was wounded. He was invalided home and discharged in February 1918, and holds the General Service and Victory Medals.

44, Puller Road, Boxmoor. X5484.

WHITELL, E., Shoeing-smith, 3rd (Prince of Wales's) Dragoon Guards.

He was serving at the outbreak of hostilities, and in September 1914 was drafted to the Western Front. He took an active part in the Battles of Mons, La Bassée, Ypres, Hill 60 and in other important engagements up to the cessation of hostilities. He also did much valuable service as a shoeing-smith behind the lines. He returned home and was demobilised in February 1919, and holds the Mons Star, and the General Service and Victory Medals.

63, Ridge Avenue, Letchworth. 5485.

WHITFIELD, W., Private, Bedfordshire Regt.

He volunteered in August 1914, and was sent to France immediately afterwards. He took part in severe fighting during the Retreat from Mons, and was wounded and invalided home. Later he was discharged as medically unfit in August 1915, and holds the Mons Star and the General Service and Victory Medals.

39, Sutton Road, Watford. X5486.

WHITING, R. H., Trooper, Herts. Dragoons; and Private, Hertfordshire Regiment.

He volunteered in May 1915, and served on important duties with his unit until December 1916, when he was sent to France, where he took part in severe fighting at Ypres, the Somme and Albert, and was twice wounded. He was demobilised in April 1919, and holds the General Service and Victory Medals. 63, Diamond Road, Watford. X5488.

WHITNEY, A., Private, 1/5th Bedfordshire Regiment.

He volunteered in August 1914, and was sent to Egypt in the following March. In this theatre of war he served in the Advance through Sinai, Palestine and Syria, and fought at the Battles of Gaza and in the operations prior to the capture of Jerusalem, and was wounded. He returned to England and was demobilised in March 1919, and holds the 1914-15 Star, and the General Service and Victory Medals.

27, Ship Road, Linslade. 3874/A.

WHITNEY, W., Corporal, R.A.M.C.

Volunteering in August 1914, he embarked for Salonika in the following year and served in the advanced areas on the Vardar and Struma fronts, engaged on important ambulance duties whilst heavy fighting was in progress, and was wounded. He also served throughout the final Allied Advance in the Balkans, and returning to England was demobilised in March 1919, and holds the 1914-15 Star, and the General Service and Victory Medals.

32, Church Street, Leighton Buzzard. 5489.

WHITTEMORE, C., Private, 7th Bedfordshire Regiment.

Volunteering in September 1914, he was drafted to the Western Front in July of the following year, and fought at Loos, Arras, Ypres, Cambrai and the Somme. He was unfortunately killed in action on August 27th, 1918, in the vicinity of Bapaume, whilst acting as a stretcher-bearer. He was entitled to the 1914-15 Star, and the General Service and Victory Medals.

Campton, Shefford. Z5464/C.

WHITTEMORE, E. G., Private, Royal Fusiliers.

He joined in September 1918, and on concluding his training was stationed at various depôts on important duties with his unit. He was not successful in obtaining his transfer to a theatre of war before the cessation of hostilities, but rendered valuable services until demobilised in January 1919.

Campton, Shefford. Z5464/B.

WHITTEMORE, F. A. (M.M.), Private, Royal Sussex Regiment.

He volunteered in September 1914, and was sent to France in August 1916, and was in action at many important engagements, including those at Wiencourt and Wytschaete. He was awarded the Military Medal in March 1918 for conspicuous bravery and devotion to duty in the field. He was killed in action on August 26th, 1918, and was entitled to the General Service and Victory Medals.

Campton, Shefford. Z5464/D.

WHITTEMORE, H., Gunner, R.M.A.
A serving soldier, he was serving aboard ship in Russian waters at the outbreak of war. He was sent with his ship to the North Sea, where she was in action at the Naval engagements at Heligoland Bight, Jutland and the Dogger Bank, and was also engaged on patrol and other important duties. He was serving at Constantinople in 1920, and holds the 1914-15 Star, and the General Service and Victory Medals. Campton, Shefford. Z5464/A.

WHITTERN, T., Private, Middlesex Regiment.
He volunteered in August 1914, and on completing his training served at various depôts with his unit engaged on guard and other important duties. He was unsuccessful in obtaining his transfer to a theatre of war, but rendered excellent services until demobilised in September 1919.
128, St. James' Road, Watford. X5490.

WHITTINGHAM, H., Private, 2/4th London Regiment (Royal Fusiliers).
Volunteering in January 1915, he was drafted overseas seven months later. During his service on the Western Front he fought in many important engagements. He made the supreme sacrifice at Ypres on September 21st, 1917, and was entitled to the 1914-15 Star, and the General Service and Victory Medals.
29, Copsewood Road, Watford. X5491.

WHITTINGTON, C. J., L/Corporal, 6th Northamptonshire Regiment.
Volunteering in January 1916, he embarked for the Western Front in the following December and saw active service in many parts of the line, and was in action at the battles of Beaumont-Hamel, Arras and St. Quentin, where he was wounded and taken prisoner on April 24th, 1917. He later died in captivity at Cologne on May 24th of the following year, and was entitled to the General Service and Victory Medals.
85, Ash Road, Luton. 5492.

WHITTINGTON, S. G., Corporal, 7th Bedfordshire Regiment.
He volunteered in September 1914, and was sent to France in the following year. In this theatre of war he was in action in many engagements, including those at Hill 60, Vimy Ridge, Bullecourt and Messines. He was unfortunately killed in action at Ypres on July 31st, 1917, and was entitled to the 1941-15 Star, and the General Service and Victory Medals.
79, Hastings Street, Luton. 5493.

WHITTRED, F. E., Private, 1/5th Yorkshire Regiment.
He joined in 1916, and on conclusion of his training served at various stations until proceeding to France in the following January. Here he fought in many engagements and was taken prisoner during the German Offensive of 1918. He died in captivity on July 28th, 1918, from the effects of exposure and privation, and was entitled to the General Service and Victory Medals.
5, White Hill, Hitchin. 5494.

WHY, A., Sergeant, Royal Engineers.
He was mobilised in August 1914, and was stationed at various depôts with his unit. He was medically unfit and consequently was not able to obtain his transfer overseas, but rendered excellent services engaged on the construction of defences on the East Coast. He was still serving in 1920.
10, Park Street, Dunstable. 5495/A.

WHY, F., Private, 4th Essex Regiment.
He joined in June 1916 and was drafted to the Egyptian Expeditionary Force in the following January. He saw much service on the Palestine front, serving as despatch-rider, and was unfortunately killed in action in the Gaza sector on November 25th, 1917. He was entitled to the General Service and Victory Medals.
10, Park Street, Dunstable. 5495/B.

WICKENS, E. T., Private, Canadian Forestry Corps.
He volunteered in December 1915, and after his training served at various stations engaged on important duties. He was unfit for service overseas, and consequently did not obtain his transfer to a theatre of war, but rendered valuable services until demobilised in April 1919.
61, Crow Lane, Husborne Crawley, Beds. Z5496.

WICKERSHAM, A. J., Private, Loyal North Lancashire Regiment.
A serving soldier, he was stationed in India at the outbreak of hostilities and was drafted to German East Africa, and fought in many important engagements. Severely wounded in 1915, he was invalided to England and after protracted hospital treatment was discharged unfit for further service in January 1916. He holds the 1914-15 Star, and the General Service and Victory Medals.
50, Brightwell Road, Watford. X5497.

WICKS, E., Trooper, Bedfordshire Lancers.
He joined in March 1916, and on the conclusion of his training was stationed at various depôts engaged on important duties with his unit. Medically unfit, he was unable to obtain his transfer overseas, but did excellent work until invalided out of the Service in September 1916.
Upper Sundon, Dunstable. 443/A.

WICKS, H. C., Private, 1st Hertfordshire Regt.
Mobilised at the outbreak of hostilities, he was sent to France later in 1914, and fought in many important engagements, including those at Ypres and Arras. He was killed in action at St. Julien on July 31st, 1917, and was entitled to the 1914 Star, and the General Service and Victory Medals.
13, Wells Yard, Watford. X5498.

WICKSON, A. J., Pte., 1/5th Bedfordshire Regt.
Volunteering in August 1914, he was drafted to Egypt in the following year and saw much service there. He fought at the Battles of Gaza and served throughout the Advance through Palestine into Syria, and was wounded twice. He returned to England and was demobilised in February 1919, and holds the 1914-15 Star, and the General Service and Victory Medals. 71, Dordans Road, Leagrave. 5499.

WIDDOWSON, W., Corporal, 2/8th Sherwood Foresters.
He volunteered in November 1914, and was stationed in Ireland, where he served in the riots of April 1916. Proceeding to France in the following year, he fought in the Battles of the Somme, Cambrai, Ypres and in the German Offensive and subsequent Allied Advance of 1918. He was demobilised in March 1919, and holds the General Service and Victory Medals.
50, Ebury Road, Watford. X363/B—X364/B.

WIDDUP, G., Corporal, Royal Engineers.
Volunteering in September 1914, he was engaged on Home service duties at various stations until March 1916, when he was sent to Egypt. He served throughout the Advance in Sinai and Palestine into Syria, and was present at the Battles of Gaza, the capture of Damascus and many other important engagements. He returned to England and was demobilised in June 1919, and holds the General Service and Victory Medals. Bedford Road, Shefford. Z5500.

WIGGEN, R. H. (M.C.), 2nd Lieutenant, Foreign Legion; 15th and 23rd Royal Fusiliers.
He volunteered in August 1914, and was drafted to France in the same year and took a prominent part in the heavy fighting at the Retreat from Mons and in several other engagements, and was wounded. On recovery he was again in action, and was mentioned in Despatches and awarded the Military Cross for conspicuous gallantry and devotion to duty in the Field. He was unfortunately killed in action on February 17th, 1917, and was entitled to the Mons Star, and the General Service and Victory Medals.
Tregantle, Luton Road, Harpenden. 5501/A.

WIGGEN, Y. F., Trooper, City of London Lancers (Rough Riders).
Volunteering in September 1915, he was sent to Egypt and later to Gallipoli, where he took part in the landing at Suvla Bay and many other operations until the evacuation of the Peninsula. Contracting fever whilst on service, he was removed to hospital in Mudros, and died there on December 1st, 1916. He was entitled to the 1914-15 Star, and the General Service and Victory Medals.
Maple Dene, Shinfield, near Reading 5501/B.

WIGGS, W., L/Corporal, R.A.S.C.
He was mobilised on the outbreak of hostilities, and almost immediately embarked for France, where he served during the Retreat from Mons and in the Battles of Ypres, Arras and Cambrai. In 1916 he was sent to Italy, and did good work in that theatre of operations with the Forage department. He returned home for demobilisation in March 1919, and holds the Mons Star, and the General Service and Victory Medals. 8, Blacksmith Lane, St. Albans. 5502.

WIGGS, W. H., L/Corporal, Royal Engineers.
Joining in July 1916, he was sent to France in the same month and was employed on important duties in connection with operations during the Battle of the Somme and other engagements. In November 1917 he proceeded to Italy, and served on the Piave and other sectors for some time. He returned to England and was demobilised in March 1919, and holds the General Service and Victory Medals.
2, Muriel Avenue, Watford. X5503/B.

WIGGS, W. H., 1st Class Stoker, Royal Navy.
He was serving in the Royal Navy when war broke out, and aboard H.M.S. "Sandpiper" served in the North Sea and other waters. His ship was torpedoed in the Battle of Jutland, but he was fortunately rescued. In 1920 he was serving in Chinese waters, and holds the 1914-15 Star, and the General Service and Victory Medals.
2, Muriel Avenue, Watford. X5503/C.

WIGGS, W. J., Private, 1st Hertfordshire Regt.
Mobilised on the declaration of war, he was shortly afterwards drafted to the Western Front and took part in the Retreat from Mons and in several other important engagements. He was killed by a sniper whilst acting as a runner on May 1st, 1917, and was entitled to the Mons Star, and the General Service and Victory Medals.
2, Muriel Avenue, Watford. X5503/A.

WIGMORE, J., Private, Royal Scots.
He was mobilised in August 1914, and proceeded to France in the following year. Whilst overseas he fought in several important engagements, including the Battles of Hill 60 and Ypres, and was wounded. He was later killed in action on September 20th, 1917, and was entitled to the 1914-15 Star, and the General Service and Victory Medals.
Ayot Green, near Welwyn. 3118/F.

WILD, E. C., Signalman, Royal Navy.
He joined in October 1917, and was posted to H.M.S. "Phaeton," and served in that vessel during the course of hostilities. His ship was engaged on important submarine patrol duties in the North Sea, and was also on duty in Russian and Scandinavian waters. He holds the General Service and Victory Medals, and in 1920 was still serving.
46, Inkerman Road, St. Albans. X5504.

WILD, E. W., Sapper, Royal Engineers.
He volunteered in November 1915, and in the following January was sent to the Western Front. During his service overseas he was engaged on important duties in connection with fixing machine-guns in gun-pits, and was present at many battles, including those of Neuve Chapelle and Nieuport. He was demobilised in April 1919, and holds the General Service and Victory Medals.
46, Inkerman Road, St. Albans. X5504/A.

WILDERS, A. H., Gunner, R.F.A.
Volunteering in October 1915, he served with his Battery on special duties until drafted to Mesopotamia in June 1917. Whilst overseas he fought at Kut and Baghdad, and was present at the occupation of Mosul. Contracting illness, he was sent home and discharged on account of service in March 1918, and holds the General Service and Victory Medals.
28, Castle Road, St. Albans. X5505/A.

WILDERS, B., Private, R.M.L.I.
He joined in May 1917, and after completing his training was engaged with his unit on important duties in connection with the coastal defences. Owing to medical unfitness he was not sent overseas, and was discharged in consequence in August 1918.
28, Castle Road, St. Albans. X5506.

WILDERS, G., A.B., Royal Navy.
Volunteering in March 1915, he was posted to H.M.S. "Hyacinth," and served aboard that vessel for five years. During this period his ship took part in the sinking of the "Konigsberg" and the shelling of the ports of German East Africa. She was later on duty in the North Sea and Russian waters, and was in action during the raid on Kronstadt. He was demobilised in March 1920, and holds the 1914-15 Star, and the General Service and Victory Medals.
28, Castle Road, St. Albans. X5505/B.

WILDMAN, A., Private, 9th Suffolk Regiment.
Joining in January 1917, he proceeded to the Western Front in the following June and was engaged in heavy fighting at Ypres and Passchendaele. He was unfortunately killed in action at the Battle of Cambrai on November 20th, 1917, and was entitled to the General Service and Victory Medals.
High Street, Eaton Bray, Dunstable. 5507.

WILDMAN, J. T., Sapper, Royal Engineers.
He joined in October 1916, and, drafted overseas in the following May, saw service in various sectors of the Western Front. He was in action in several important engagements, and was severely gassed in May 1918. Invalided to hospital, he died from the effects of gas-poisoning on July 6th of that year, and was entitled to the General Service and Victory Medals.
Arthur Street, Ampthill. 3090/B.

WILDMAN, P. E., L/Corporal, 1/5th Bedfordshire Regiment.
A Territorial, he was mobilised on the outbreak of war and sent to Gallipoli in the following year. He fought at the landing of Suvla Bay and in several other engagements until the evacuation of the Peninsula. He was then drafted to Egypt and was in action at Gaza, Mejdil and other places during the British Advance through Palestine. Returning to England for demobilisation in June 1919, he holds the 1914-15 Star, and the General Service and Victory Medals.
66, Oak Road, Luton. 5508.

WILDSMITH, H. G., A.B., Royal Navy.
He volunteered in February 1915, and, posted to H.M.S. "Neptune," served aboard that vessel during the bombardment of the Dardanelles forts. His ship was also in action at the Battle of Jutland and took part in the raid on Zeebrugge. He was wounded in the course of his service afloat, and, demobilised in March 1919, holds the 1914-15 Star, and the General Service and Victory Medals.
22, Collingdon Street, Luton. 336/B.

WILES, F. E., Private, Royal Fusiliers.
He joined in October 1916, and embarked for France shortly afterwards. During his service on the Western Front he fought in many engagements, including the Battles of the Somme, Bapaume and Cambrai. He made the supreme sacrifice on November 22nd, 1917, and was entitled to the General Service and Victory Medals.
49, Oak Road, Luton. 5509.

WILKIN, E. (Miss), Special War Worker.
This lady volunteered for work of National importance, and from January 1915 until December 1918 was employed in the Fuse Department of the Chaul End Munition Factory, Luton. Throughout her service she discharged her duties in a thoroughly capable and efficient manner, and to the entire satisfaction of her employers.
7, Dordans Road, Leagrave. 3433/C.

WILKINS, F., Sapper, Royal Engineers.
Joining in April 1917, on the conclusion of his training he was engaged on important duties with his unit at various depôts. He rendered valuable services, but was unable to obtain a transfer to a theatre of war before hostilities ceased, and was demobilised in December 1919.
74, Bury Road, Hemel Hempstead. X5510.

WILKINS, N. (Mrs.), Nurse, St. John Ambulance Brigade.
She volunteered her services in 1915, and after serving with the Watford Branch was engaged on important duties at the Charing Cross and Whitechapel Hospitals. She gained two certificates for nursing in 1916, and rendered most valuable services throughout the war. She was still serving in 1920.
84, Harwood Road, Watford. X5511/B.

WILKINS, S., Telegraphist, R.N.V.R.
He joined in May 1918, and after completing his training was engaged on important duties with his unit. He did excellent work as a wireless operator, but was not successful in being sent to sea before the conclusion of hostilities, and was demobilised in January 1919.
3, New Kent Road, St. Albans. X5512.

WILKINS, W. (M.S.M.), Private, R.A.O.C.
He volunteered in August 1914, and proceeding to France in the following year, was in action in several important engagements, including those at Cambrai and Kemmel Hill. He was awarded the Meritorious Service Medal on May 1st, 1917, for consistent good work in the Field, and also holds the 1914-15 Star, and the General Service and Victory Medals. He was demobilised in February 1919.
84, Harwood Road, Watford. X5511/A.

WILKINSON, H. S. P., Trooper, East Riding of Yorkshire Lancers.
Joining in January 1918, on the completion of his training he served with his unit until sent to Ireland in the following April. Stationed at Dublin, Fermoy and Cork, he did good work in maintaining order, and returned home for demobilisation in November 1919.
51, Dale Road, Luton. 5513.

WILKINSON, J. E., Private, R.A.S.C. (M.T.)
He volunteered in 1915, and in the same year was drafted to France. Whilst in this theatre of war he was engaged on important transport duties in the forward areas, and was present at the Battles of the Somme, Arras and Ypres. He was demobilised in 1919, and holds the 1914-15 Star, and the General Service and Victory Medals.
14, Yarmouth Road, Callowland. X5514.

WILKINSON, W. H., Private, R.A.S.C.
Volunteering in 1915, he was sent to the Western Front in the same year and served in various sectors. He was engaged on important duties in connection with the transport of supplies during the Battles of the Somme, the Aisne, Arras, Ypres, Passchendaele and many others. He holds the 1914-15 Star, and the General Service and Victory Medals, and was demobilised in March 1919.
72, Norfolk Road, Rickmansworth. X5515.

WILLES, A. H., 1st Prize Gunner, R.M.A.
Joining in 1917, he was posted to H.M.S. "Iron Duke" and served in that vessel in the North and Baltic Seas and other waters. His ship was also sent to Turkish waters after the Armistice, and was on special duty at Constantinople. He holds the General Service and Victory Medals, and in 1920 was still serving. 21, College Place, St. Albans. 5516.

WILLETT, C. F. G., Trooper, Hertfordshire Dragoons.

He volunteered in August 1915, and in the same year was drafted to France, where he took part in several engagements, and in July 1916 proceeded to Egypt. During his service in this theatre of war he fought in many operations in the course of the British Advance through Palestine. He was demobilised in April 1919 on his return to England, and holds the 1914-15 Star, and the General Service and Victory Medals.
90, Brightwell Road, Watford.   X5517/C.

WILLETT, J. A., Private, Machine Gun Corps.

Joining in March 1916, he embarked for the Western Front in the same year and was engaged in heavy fighting at Ypres and other places. He was unfortunately killed in action near Ypres during the German Offensive on April 25th, 1918, and was entitled to the General Service and Victory Medals.
90, Brightwell Road, Watford.   X5517/A.

WILLETT, J. R. F., Private, Machine Gun Corps.

Volunteering at the outbreak of war, he was sent to France shortly afterwards. During his service on the Western Front he was engaged in much heavy fighting and took part in many important engagements. He was killed in action on November 7th, 1916, and was entitled to the 1914 Star, and the General Service and Victory Medals.
90, Brightwell Road, Watford.   X5517/B.

WILLEY, C. A., Rifleman, Rifle Brigade.

He joined in April 1918 on attaining military age, and at the conclusion of his training served on important duties at various stations with his unit. He did very good work, but was not able to secure his transfer overseas before the end of the war, and was demobilised in December 1919.
Park View, St. John's Path, Hitchin.   5518/A.

WILLEY, E., Sapper, Royal Engineers.

He volunteered in April 1915, and in the following September was drafted to Egypt. He served in Palestine and was engaged in wiring, trench-digging and pontooning, and also served on the lines of communication in the forward areas whilst operations were in progress, and was present at the Battles of Gaza. He contracted malaria and was invalided to hospital in Alexandria, where he subsequently died on October 15th, 1918. He was entitled to the 1914-15 Star, and the General Service and Victory Medals.
Pretoria Cottages, Harlington.   5519.

WILLEY, H., Cpl., Royal Army Service Corps.

He joined in December 1916, and in the following July was sent to Salonika. In this theatre of war he served on special transport duties with his unit on the Vardar, Doiran and Struma fronts, and was constantly under shell-fire. He returned to England in 1919, and was demobilised in March of that year, and holds the General Service and Victory Medals.
Park View, St. John's Path, Hitchin.   5518/B.

WILLIAMS, A. H., Sergeant, R.A.S.C.

He joined in August 1916, and completing his training served at various stations with his unit engaged on important supply and transport duties. Medically unfit, he was unable to obtain his transfer overseas, but rendered valuable services until demobilised in November 1919.
68, Regent Street, North Watford.   X5521.

WILLIAMS, C. P., Driver, R.F.A.

He volunteered in April 1915, and on the conclusion of his training served at various stations until proceeding overseas in 1917. During his service on the Western Front he fought at Ypres, Arras, Cambrai and in the German Offensive and Allied Advance of 1918, and was wounded. He was demobilised in May 1919, and holds the General Service and Victory Medals.
New Marford, Wheathampstead.   4078/A.

WILLIAMS, E. F., Gunner (Signaller), R.F.A.

He volunteered in April 1915, and was sent to France in the following November and was in action at Armentières, Loos and many other important engagements. Transferred to Egypt in February 1916, he fought at Gaza and in other battles during the Advance into Syria. He returned to England and was demobilised in April 1919, and holds the General Service and Victory Medals.
46, Castle Road, Fleetville, St. Albans.   X5524.

WILLIAMS, F., Gunner, Royal Field Artillery.

He joined in July 1916, and proceeded to the Western Front in the following May, and serving in many parts of the line, fought at Ypres, Arras, Albert, Cambrai and throughout the Retreat and Advance of 1918. He returned to England and was demobilised in May 1919, and holds the General Service and Victory Medals.
32, Watford Fields, Watford.   X5523.

WILLIAMS, G., Private, Royal Sussex Regiment.

Volunteering in November 1915, he embarked for German East Africa two years later and saw much service during the campaign in this theatre of war, and fought in many important engagements. In 1918 he was transferred to India, and stationed at various garrison towns, assisted to restore order in the riots in 1918. Returning to England he was demobilised in December 1919, and holds the General Service and Victory Medals.
15, Bedford Road, St. Albans.   X5525.

WILLIAMS, J. H., Private, 6th Bedfordshire Regiment.

Volunteering in January 1916, he was sent to the Western Front five months later. Here he saw much service and fought in many important engagements. He was reported wounded and missing during the fighting at Mailly-Maillet on November 16th, 1916, and later was presumed to have been killed in action on that date. He was entitled to the General Service and Victory Medals.
58, Shaftesbury Road, Watford.   4723/B.

WILLIAMS, J. H., Private, 7th Bedfordshire Regiment.

He volunteered in March 1915, and was drafted to France later in the same year and was engaged in the Battles of Ypres, the Somme, Arras and in many other important engagements. He was unfortunately killed in action on September 27th, 1916, during the British Offensive on the Somme, and was entitled to the 1914-15 Star, and the General Service and Victory Medals.
Oliver Street, Ampthill.   5528.

WILLIAMS, J. H., Pte., 1st Essex Regiment.

After volunteering in April 1915 and going through his course of training, he crossed to France early in 1916. He took an active part in many engagements up to the close of the fighting, including those at the Somme, Arras, Ypres and Cambrai, and was wounded near Lille in October 1918. After the Armistice he proceeded with the Army of Occupation into Germany, and did valuable service at Cologne until his return to England. He was demobilised in February 1919, and holds the General Service and Victory Medals.
10, Husborne Crawley, Aspley Guise.   Z5527.

WILLIAMS, R. H., Private, Royal Welch Fusiliers.

A Reservist, he was mobilised at the outbreak of hostilities, and embarked for the Western Front in September 1914 and fought in the latter part of the Retreat from Mons, the Battle of La Bassée and in many other engagements. Wounded in November 1916, on the Somme, he returned to England and received hospital treatment. On recovery he was sent again to France in August 1917, and fought throughout the Retreat and Advance of 1918. He was demobilised in June 1919, and holds the 1914 Star, and the General Service and Victory Medals.
Northill, near Biggleswade.   Z5520.

WILLIAMS, W., Private, 1st Hertfordshire Regiment and Royal Defence Corps.

He volunteered in November 1914, and on the conclusion of his training was stationed at various depôts engaged on guard and other important duties. Medically unfit, he was unable to obtain his transfer overseas, but rendered excellent services until invalided out of the Army in April 1918.
23, Park Road, Bushey.   X5529.

WILLIAMSON, B., Q.M.S., 2nd Bedfordshire and Hertfordshire Regiments.

Mobilised at the declaration of war, he embarked for the Dardanelles in the following July and fought at the landing at Suvla Bay and in the subsequent engagements until the evacuation of the Peninsula. He was then drafted to Egypt, and in 1916 was invalided to England owing to ill-health. On recovery he returned to Egypt and served on the Palestine front, and was in action in the operations in the Jordan Valley and in many other engagements during the Advance through the Holy Land. He was still serving in 1920, and holds the 1914-15 Star, and the General Service and Victory Medals.
Station Road, Ridgmont.   Z5030/B.

WILLIAMSON, C. C., Private, R.A.M.C.

Joining in July 1917, he was drafted to the Western Front in the following September. During his service overseas he saw much fighting and was engaged on important ambulance duties during the Battles at Abbéville and the Somme and in the German Offensive and Allied Advance in 1918. After the Armistice he was sent into Germany with the Army of Occupation and served there until March 1919. He returned to England and was demobilised in February 1920, and holds the General Service and Victory Medals.
57, Russell Street, Luton.   5522.

WILLIAMSON, F., Air Mechanic, R.A.F.
He joined in May 1917, and on completion of his training embarked for Egypt in the following January. Here he served at the aerodromes at Alexandria and Cairo engaged on important aircraft repair work until after the close of the war. He returned to England and was demobilised in October 1919, and holds the General Service and Victory Medals.
Station Road, Ridgmont.   Z5530/A.

WILLIAMSON, J., Private, 2nd London Regt. (Royal Fusiliers).
He joined in May 1917, and proceeded overseas in the following September and saw much service in various sectors of the Western Front. He fought in many important engagements and was killed in action at Combles on October 2nd, 1917. He was entitled to the General Service and Victory Medals.
Station Road, Ridgmont.   Z5030/C.

WILLIAMSON, J., Air Mechanic, R.A.F.
He joined in May 1917, and completing his training served at various aerodromes on important aeroplane repair work. He was unsuccessful in obtaining his transfer overseas prior to the cessation of hostilities, but rendered excellent services until demobilised in March 1919.
Station Road, Ridgmont.   Z5530/B.

WILLIAMSON, R., Corporal, Bedfordshire and Essex Regiments.
He volunteered in August 1914, and was drafted to the Western Front in the following July and was in action in many important engagements, including those at the Somme, Arras, Ypres and Cambrai. He fought throughout the German Offensive and subsequent Allied Advance in 1918, and was twice wounded during his service overseas. Invalided to England as a result of his second wound, he was discharged in December 1919 after protracted hospital treatment, and holds the 1914-15 Star, and the General Service and Victory Medals.
58, Crawley Road, Ridgmont.   Z5531.

WILLINGHAM, A. L., L/Corporal, 4th Bedfordshire Regiment.
Volunteering in 1915, he proceeded to the Western Front later in the same year and was in action on the Somme, Arras and Ypres sectors, and fought in many important engagements. He made the supreme sacrifice, being killed in action on October 30th, 1917, and was entitled to the 1914-15 Star, and the General Service and Victory Medals.
Brook Lane, Flitton.   5532.

WILLIS, A., Gunner, Royal Garrison Artillery.
Volunteering at the commencement of hostilities, he was drafted to France almost immediately and fought in the Retreat from Mons and many other important engagements, including the Battles of the Somme, Ypres and Arras. He was also in action throughout the Retreat and Advance of 1918, and was wounded. He was demobilised in 1919, and holds the Mons Star, and the General Service and Victory Medals. 24, Longmire Road, St. Albans.   X5109/B.

WILLIS, A. G., Corporal, R.A.M.C.
He joined in March 1916, and on completion of his training served at various military hospitals on important duties. Unable to obtain his transfer overseas owing to medical unfitness, he rendered valuable services attending the sick and wounded troops until demobilised in January 1919.
George Street, Wing, Bucks.   5533/A.

WILLIS, F. J., Private, 13th Bedfordshire Regt.
Volunteering in January 1916, he concluded his training and was stationed at various depôts engaged on important duties with his unit. Medically unfit, he was unable to obtain his transfer to a theatre of war before the Armistice, but did excellent work until demobilised in January 1919.
16, Estcourt Road, Watford.   X5534.

WILLIS, G. R., Corporal, Royal Engineers.
Volunteering in May 1915, he embarked for Egypt later in the same year. On the Palestine Front he saw much service and was present at many important engagements, employed on important duties connected with operations, and served throughout the Advance into Syria. He was mentioned in Despatches for devotion to duty in the Field. He died from an illness contracted on service in February 1919, and was entitled to the 1914-15 Star, and the General Service and Victory Medals.
24, Laurel Street, Luke's Road, Maidenhead.   5535/A.

WILLIS, H. H., Private, R.A.S.C. (N.A.C.B.)
He volunteered in 1915, and embarked for the Western Front later in the same year. Here he was stationed at Etaples, engaged on important duties connected with the canteens, and rendered valuable services. Returning to England he was demobilised in April 1919, and holds the 1914-15 Star, and the General Service and Victory Medals.
7, Pinner Road, Oxhey.   X3457/B.

WILLIS, H. S., Bombardier, R.F.A.
Volunteering in August 1915, he was sent to France five months later and was in action in many important engagements, including those at Ypres, the Somme, Cambrai and Arras. He also fought in the Retreat and Advance of 1918, and was demobilised in July of the following year. He holds the General Service and Victory Medals.
24, Sotheron Road, Watford.   X5536.

WILLIS, J. R., Private, King's Own (Royal Lancaster Regiment).
Volunteering in February 1915, he completed his training and served at various stations until drafted to Salonika in November 1916. He fought in many engagements on the Vardar and Doiran fronts, and was in action in the final Allied Advance. He returned to England and was demobilised in January 1919, and holds the General Service and Victory Medals.
37, Adrian Road, Abbots Langley.   X5537.

WILLIS, L., Air Mechanic, Royal Air Force.
He volunteered in May 1915, and was drafted to France in the following July and rendered excellent services as despatch-rider during the Battles of Ypres, Vimy Ridge, the Somme and throughout the German Offensive and Allied Advance of 1918. He was demobilised in February 1919, and holds the 1914-15 Star, and the General Service and Victory Medals.
Elspeth, Cowper Road, Harpenden.   5535/B.

WILLIS, L. C., Boy Corporal, R.A.F.
He joined in December 1917, on attaining military age, and after training was stationed at various aerodromes engaged on important duties. He was unsuccessful in obtaining his transfer overseas on account of his age, but rendered excellent services until demobilised in June 1920.
1, Wright's Cottages, St. Albans Road, Watford.   X5538.

WILLIS, R., Sapper, Royal Engineers.
Volunteering in July 1915, he was drafted to the Egyptian Expeditionary Force in the following year. On the Palestine Front he saw much service, and was present at the Battles of Gaza and many other important engagements during the Advance through the Holy Land and Syria. He returned to England and was demobilised in July 1919, and holds the General Service and Victory Medals.
32, Ashwell Street, Leighton Buzzard.   5539.

WILLIS, T., Sapper, Royal Engineers.
He joined in 1916, and was sent to the Western Front later in the same year. He served in the forward areas whilst the Battles of Ypres, Arras and the Somme were in progress, and rendered valuable services engaged on duties connected with the operations during the Retreat and Advance of 1918, and returning to England was demobilised in December 1919. He holds the General Service and Victory Medals.
76, Regent Street, North Watford.   X5540.

WILLIS, W. J., Bombardier, R.G.A.
He joined in May 1916, and embarked for the Western Front five months later, and was in action at the Battles of Ypres, the Somme, Cambrai, Arras and throughout the German Offensive and subsequent Allied Advance of 1918. He returned to England and was demobilised in October 1919, and holds the General Service and Victory Medals.
George Street, Wing, Bucks.   5533/B.

WILLISON, F., Private, 4th Bedfordshire Regt.
Volunteering in November 1915, he was drafted to the Western Front in the following July. Here he saw much service, fighting in the engagements at Ypres, the Somme, Beaumont-Hamel and in the Retreat and Advance of 1918, and was three times wounded. He was demobilised in March 1919, and holds the General Service and Victory Medals.
Jacques Lane, Clophill.   5541.

WILLISON, F. W. T., Private, Middlesex Regt.
He joined in July 1916, and on conclusion of his training served at various stations with his unit engaged on guard and other important duties. Medically unfit, he was unable to obtain his transfer to a theatre of war, but did excellent work until demobilised in December 1919.
Tilsworth, near Leighton Buzzard.   5542.

WILLMORE, C. H., Private, Hertfordshire and Bedfordshire Regiments.
He was mobilised with the Territorials at the outbreak of war and was almost immediately drafted to France, and took part in the Retreat from Mons. He also served in numerous later engagements, including those at Arras and Ypres, and in various final operations until the cessation of hostilities. He was demobilised in February 1919, after 4½ years with the Colours, and holds the Mons Star, and the General Service and Victory Medals.   X5543/B.
41, Loates Lane, Watford.

WILLMORE, W. H., C.S.M., 1st Hertfordshire and Bedfordshire Regiments.

He was mobilised with the Territorials at the commencement of hostilities, and was almost immediately drafted to France, and took part in the Retreat from Mons. Later he was mainly engaged as Instructor in musketry and signalling duties until the cessation of hostilities. He was demobilised in February 1919, after 4½ years' service, and holds the Mons Star, and the General Service and Victory Medals.
41, Loates Lane, Watford. X5543/A.

WILLN, R., Driver, Royal Field Artillery.

He joined in March 1916, and in the following December was drafted to the Western Front. During his service in France he did excellent work as a Driver for the Royal Field Artillery at Arras, Messines, Ypres and in subsequent engagements until the conclusion of hostilities. He returned to England in September 1919, and was demobilised in the following November, holding the General Service and Victory Medals.
156, Hitchin Road, Luton. 5544

WILLS, J., Corporal, Labour Corps.

He volunteered in December 1915, and was almost immediately drafted to France, where he was engaged on important duties in the loading and unloading of ammunition. He served at Festubert, Loos, the Somme, Ypres, Cambrai and in the engagements which followed until the cessation of hostilities. He was demobilised in February 1919, and holds the 1914–15 Star, and the General Service and Victory Medals.
25, Common View, Letchworth. 4565/A.

WILLS, J., Driver, Royal Army Service Corps.

Volunteering in September 1914, he was sent to France in the following year and served on important transport duties connected with the distribution of rations for the troops for about four years. He was demobilised in March 1919, and holds the 1914–15 Star, and the General Service and Victory Medals.
31, Loates Lane, Watford. X5545.

WILLSON, E. R., Private, Labour Corps.

He joined in 1916, and after his training was concluded was drafted to France, where he was engaged on important duties with his Corps and served at Ypres, Cambrai and the Somme. He was severely gassed during this period, and was invalided home and discharged as medically unfit for further duty in March 1918. He holds the General Service and Victory Medals.
42, Oxford Street, Watford. X5546.

WILMOT, A. E., Private, 1/5th East Surrey Regt.

He volunteered in October 1914, and was drafted to France in June of the following year, and saw much service in various parts of the line, fighting in many important engagements, including that of the Somme, where he was wounded in July 1916. He was invalided to England, and on recovery proceeded to Mesopotamia, where he fought in the Battle of Kut and in the operations preceding the fall of Baghdad. He returned to England and was demobilised in October 1919, and holds the 1914–15 Star, and the General Service and Victory Medals.
103, Old London Road, St. Albans. X5547.

WILMOT, C. J., Driver, R.A.S.C. (M.T.)

He volunteered in November 1914, and in the following January was drafted to France. Here he was engaged on motor transport duties, driving to and from the front lines, and served at Hill 60, Ypres, Loos and the Somme, and later at Cambrai and Amiens. He was demobilised in April 1919, after nearly 4½ years' service, and holds the 1914–15 Star, and the General Service and Victory Medals.
9, Stuart Street, Luton. 120/A.

WILSHER, A., Private, R.A.S.C.

He joined in June 1918, and after his training served at various stations on important duties with his unit. He did good work, but owing to the termination of the war was not able to secure his transfer overseas, and was demobilised in December 1919.
Husborne Crawley, Aspley Guise, Beds. Z5548.

WILSHER, J., Sapper, R.E. ; and Pte., R.A.S.C.

He volunteered in May 1915, and in the following year was drafted to Salonika, where he served on important transport duties and was present at engagements on the Vardar front, the Offensive on the Doiran and the Advance across the Struma. He was subsequently demobilised in February 1919, and holds the General Service and Victory Medals.
Bygreave's Cottages, Ickleford, Hitchin. 5549.

WILSHERE, S. A., Private, Loyal North Lancashire Regiment.

He volunteered in January 1916, and in the following April was drafted to France. After taking part in several minor engagements he was killed in the heavy fighting on the Somme on September 3rd, 1916. He was entitled to the General Service and Victory Medals.
9, St. Michael's Mount, Hitchin. 5550.

WILSON, A., Private, R.A.M.C.

He volunteered in September 1914, and after his training served at various stations on important duties with his unit until November 1916, when he was drafted to France. During his service on the Western Front he was present at engagements on the Ancre, at Arras, Vimy Ridge, Passchendaele, the Somme and Cambrai, and suffered from shell-shock. He was demobilised in May 1919, and holds the General Service and Victory Medals.
38, May Street, Luton. 5551.

WILSON, A., Private, Bedfordshire Regiment.

He joined in March 1916, and in the following April was sent to France. Whilst in this theatre of war he was severely wounded at Vimy Ridge and was invalided to hospital. In November of the same year he was drafted to India, and served on important garrison duties at Rawal Pindi, Rangoon and Lucknow until December 1919, when he returned to England. He was demobilised in the following month, and holds the General Service and Victory Medals.
3a, Right of Way, New Town, Hatfield. 13/A.

WILSON, A., Private, 7th Bedfordshire Regt.

Volunteering in September 1914, he was sent to the Western Front in the following year, and during his service in France fought at Hill 60, Ypres, the Somme, Arras and the second Battle of the Marne, and was wounded. Returning to England, he was demobilised in March 1919, after 4½ years' service with the Colours. He holds the 1914–15 Star, and the General Service and Victory Medals.
53, Grover Road, Oxhey, Watford. X5552.

WILSON, A. W., Private (Signaller), 3rd Queen's (Royal West Surrey Regiment).

He joined in April 1918, and after his training served at various stations on important signalling duties. He rendered valuable services, but owing to the conclusion of hostilities was unable to obtain his transfer overseas, and was demobilised in February 1919.
58, Dane Road, Luton. 5553/A.

WILSON, A. W. (D.S.M.), A.B. (Gunner), R.N., H.M.S. " Inflexible."

He joined in 1912, and was sent to the North Sea in H.M.S. " Inflexible " at the outbreak of war, and was later drafted to the Dardanelles. Whilst his ship was in action in these waters he was awarded the Distinguished Service Medal for his conspicuous gallantry in bringing back a picket-boat single-handed. During his service he was three times wounded, and after the evacuation of Gallipoli he returned with his ship to the North Sea, where he continued to serve until July 1919, when he was demobilised. He holds in addition to the Distinguished Service Medal the 1914–15 Star, and the General Service and Victory Medals.
Jacques Lane, Clophill, Ampthill. 5554.

WILSON, B., Rifleman, K.R.R.C.

A serving soldier, he was sent to the Western Front immediately upon the outbreak of hostilities and took part in the Retreat from Mons, in which he was severely wounded. He returned to England in 1915, and was then released for important munition work, in which he was highly skilled. In this capacity he was stationed at Woolwich and Luton, and did valuable work until he was demobilised in February 1919. He holds the Mons Star, and the General Service and Victory Medals.
2, Kingcroft Road, Harpenden. 5182

WILSON, C. F., Private, Bedfordshire Regiment.

He was already in the Army, and when war broke out was immediately sent to France, where he fought in the Retreat from Mons. He also took part in many of the engagements which followed, notably those at Ypres, Kemmel Hill, the Somme and Arras, and was wounded five times and gassed. During his service he was awarded the Croix de Guerre for an act of distinguished gallantry, and in addition holds the Mons Star, and the General Service and Victory Medals. He was demobilised on his return to England in February 1919.
114, Norfolk Road, Rickmansworth. X5465/D.

WILSON, C. H., Private, Queen's Own (Royal West Kent Regiment).

Joining in June 1916, he was drafted to Mesopotamia four months later. His service in this theatre of war lasted for three years, during which time he fought in many important engagements and did valuable work with his unit throughout. He was demobilised on his return to England in December 1919, and holds the General Service and Victory Medals. 29, King's Road, Luton. 5555.

WILSON, D., Private, Bedfordshire Regiment.

Called up from the Reserve at the outbreak of hostilities, he was immediately sent to France and fought in the Retreat from Mons and the engagements at Ypres, Arras and Albert. He was discharged in March 1916 through causes due to his service, and holds the Mons Star, and the General Service and Victory Medals.
Leavesden Green, Herts. X5556/A.

WILSON, E., Sapper, Royal Engineers.
Volunteering in September 1914, he was drafted to the Dardanelles in the following April and did valuable work with his unit during the landing at Gallipoli and the ensuing operations on the Peninsula   After the evacuation he was sent to Egypt and later served on important duties in the forward areas of the Palestine front, where he was present at engagements at Gaza and Mejdel and at the capture of Jerusalem.   He was demobilised in June 1919, and holds the 1914–15 Star, and the General Service and Victory Medals.
20, Ash Road, Luton.   5557.

WILSON, E. J., Private, Middlesex Regiment.
Joining in October 1917, he was drafted to France in the following March, and a month later was taken prisoner near Cambrai.   After his release in December 1918 he rejoined his unit, and later was sent to India, where in 1920 he was still serving.   He holds the General Service and Victory Medals.
73, Liverpool Road, Watford.   X5558/B.

WILSON, E. R., Private, 1st Hertfordshire Regt.
A serving soldier, he was engaged on important duties until he was sent to France early in 1915.   During his service overseas he did valuable work as a first-class bomber, and in this capacity took part in many of the principal engagements until he was killed in action on the Somme on July 31st, 1917.   He was entitled to the 1914–15 Star, and the General Service and Victory Medals.
73, Liverpool Road, Watford.   X5558/A.

WILSON, E. T., 2nd Corporal, Royal Engineers.
He volunteered in January 1915, and at the conclusion of his training in the following July was drafted to Egypt. Later he was sent to Palestine, where he was engaged on duties of an important nature in the forward areas, and was wounded.   Later he was killed in action on April 21st, 1917, and was entitled to the 1914–15 Star, and the General Service and Victory Medals
14, Maple Road, Luton.   5559.

WILSON, E. T., Sapper, Royal Engineers.
He joined in June 1916, and at the conclusion of his training served at various stations on important duties with his unit. He was not successful in obtaining his transfer overseas before the termination of hostilities, but nevertheless did valuable work until he was demobilised in April 1919.
13, Arthur Road, St. Albans.   5560.

WILSON, F., Sapper, Royal Engineers (R.O.D.)
He joined in January 1916, and during his service on the Western Front was engaged on important duties in connection with laying light railways.   In this capacity he served in many important sectors, and was present during the fighting at Ypres and Amiens.   He was demobilised in November 1919, and holds the General Service and Victory Medals.
40, Cannon Street, St. Albans.   2926/A.

WILSON, F., Private, Northamptonshire Regt.
He joined in May 1917, and two months later was sent to Mesopotamia, where he subsequently fought in many important engagements, including that at Baghdad.   He was demobilised on his return to England in December 1918, and holds the General Service and Victory Medals.
114, Norfolk Road, Rickmansworth.   X5465/A.

WILSON, G., Private, 1st Northamptonshire Regt.
Volunteering in September 1914, he was sent to the Western Front three months later, and on December 28th of the same year was killed by a sniper.   He was entitled to the 1914 Star, and the General Service and Victory Medals.
114, Norfolk Road, Rickmansworth.   X5465/C.

WILSON, G. E., Private, R.A.S.C. (M.T.)
He volunteered in September 1914, and in the following March was drafted to the Western Front.   During his service in this theatre of war he was engaged on important duties in connection with the transport of supplies, and was present at engagements on the Somme and at Arras and Cambrai.   He was demobilised on his return to England in March 1919, and holds the 1914–15 Star, and the General Service and Victory Medals.
5, Queen Street, St. Albans.   5561.

WILSON, H., Private, Northamptonshire Regt.
He joined in July 1916, and during his two years' service on the Western Front took part in many battles, including those of the Somme and Cambrai, and was wounded.   He was demobilised on his return to England in February 1919, and holds the General Service and Victory Medals.
44, York Road, Watford.   X5562.

WILSON, H., Gunner, Royal Garrison Artillery.
He joined in December 1916, and after his training was drafted to the Western Front, where he fought in many important battles, notably those of Arras and Cambrai.   He holds the General Service and Victory Medals, and was demobilised on returning to England in February 1919.
24, Pretoria Road, Watford.   X5563/A.

WILSON, H. J., Gunner, Royal Field Artillery.
He volunteered in May 1915, and in the same year was sent to Egypt, where he took part in several minor engagements, and was later drafted to Palestine.   In this theatre of war he again fought in many battles, notably that of Gaza, and did excellent work with his Battery throughout the campaign on that front.   He holds the 1914–15 Star, and the General Service and Victory Medals, and was demobilised in February 1919.
24, Pretoria Road, Watford.   X5563/B.

WILSON, J. D., Private, 7th Sussex Regiment.
He joined in May 1916, and after a brief training was drafted to France.   Whilst there he fought in the Battles of Ypres and Arras, and in August of the same year was killed in action.   He was entitled to the General Service and Victory Medals.
144, Norfolk Road, Rickmansworth.   X5465/B.

WILSON, L. W., Private, 8th Suffolk Regiment.
He joined in July 1916, and in October of the same year was drafted to France.   In this theatre of war he took part in numerous battles, including those of Vimy Ridge, the Somme, Arras and Ypres, and was wounded.   After being in hospital some considerable time he was discharged in August 1917, and holds the General Service and Victory Medals.
37, Cannon Road, Watford.   X5564.

WILSON, M., Sapper, Royal Engineers.
Volunteering in 1915, he was drafted after a period of training to Mesopotamia, where he took part in many important engagements.   In 1917 he proceeded to France and fought in the Battles of Arras and Cambrai, during which time he was wounded.   He holds the General Service and Victory Medals, and was demobilised in 1919.
52, Brightwell Road, Watford.   X5565.

WILSON, O., Private, 2nd Worcestershire Regt.
Volunteering in August 1914, he was drafted on completion of his training to the Western Front.   There he took part in many important engagements, including those of Arras, Ypres, Cambrai and Passchendaele, remaining in the fighting area until the cessation of hostilities.   In December 1919 he was demobilised, and holds the General Service and Victory Medals.
Leavesden Green, Watford.   X5556/B.

WILSON, O. E. (Miss), Special War Worker.
From August 1916 until January 1919 this lady held an important position at Messrs. George Kent's Munition Works, Luton.   She was principally engaged in inspecting fuses, and carried out her duties with great care and efficiency.
58, Dane Road, Luton.   5553/B.

WILSON, R. J., Private, Bedfordshire Regiment.
He joined in February 1916, and in July of the same year proceeded to the Western Front.   There he was in action on the Somme, at Arras and Cambrai, and in many other engagements until the cessation of hostilities.   In February 1919 he was demobilised, and holds the General Service and Victory Medals.
10, South Road, Luton.   5566/A.

WILSON, T., Private, Machine Gun Corps.
He joined in February 1916, and early in the following year proceeded to France.   Whilst in this theatre of war he took part in much of the severe fighting on the Somme and at Cambrai, where he was wounded and taken prisoner in August 1918.   He was released and demobilised in December 1919, and holds the General Service and Victory Medals.
5, Crown Terrace, Watford.   X5567.

WILSON, T. G., Sapper, Royal Engineers.
Volunteering in October 1914, he was drafted on completion of his training to the Western Front.   There he took part in the severe fighting on the Somme and at Arras, Cambrai and in various other battles until the signing of the Armistice.   He returned to England and was demobilised in April 1919, and holds the General Service and Victory Medals.
20, Jubilee Road, North Watford.   X5568.

WILSON, W., A.B., Royal Navy.
Joining the Service at the outbreak of hostilities, he was posted to H.M.S. "Shannon," which vessel was engaged in the Battle of Jutland in May 1916, and also rendered valuable services engaged on important patrol and escort duties.   He was discharged in March 1920, and holds the 1914–15 Star, and the General Service and Victory Medals.
76, Cecil Street, North Watford.   X5570.

WILSON, W., Corporal, 7th Bedfordshire Regt.
He was in the Army at the outbreak of hostilities, and immediately proceeded to France, where he fought in the memorable Retreat from Mons.   He also took part in the Battles of Hill 60, Ypres, Arras, Guillemont, Cambrai, and was gassed, In February 1919 he was demobilised, holding the Mons Star, and the General Service and Victory Medals.
184, North Street, Luton.   5569.

WILSON, W., Sapper, Royal Engineers.
Volunteering in August 1914, he was drafted in September of the same year to the Western Front. There he took part in the Battles of the Marne, La Bassée, Ypres and the Somme, and was wounded twice. Later he proceeded to German East Africa, and during his service in this theatre of war suffered from malaria. He returned home and was demobilised in January 1919, and holds the 1914–15 Star, and the General Service and Victory Medals.
119, Whinbush Road, Hitchin. 3481/B.

WILSON, W. A., Sapper, Royal Engineers.
He joined in April 1918, and in July of the same year was drafted to France. He was engaged on important duties at Rouen, Boulogne and Calais, being under age for service in the trenches. He returned to England for demobilisation in September 1919, and holds the General Service and Victory Medals.
47, King Street, Dunstable. 5571.

WILSON, W. C., Private, 1st Hertfordshire Regt.
He volunteered in August 1914, and in the same year was drafted to the Western Front. He fought in many battles, including those of Loos, Arras, Lens and Cambrai, and on April 25th, 1918, was killed in action on the Somme. He was entitled to the 1914 Star, and the General Service and Victory Medals.
2, Taylor Cottages, Old Park Road, Hitchin. 3686/B.

WILSON, W. E., Leading Mechanic, Royal Air Force (late Royal Naval Air Service).
He joined in May 1916, and was speedily drafted to France. He served with his Squadron at various aerodromes as a rigger on duties which required a high degree of technical skill. In March 1919 he returned to England, and was demobilised, holding the General Service and Victory Medals. 11, Oxford Street, Watford. X5572.

WILSON, W. H., Private, 1st Gloucestershire Regiment.
Having previously served in the South African War, he re-enlisted in September 1914, and was drafted in the following year to France. Whilst there he took part in much of the heavy fighting in the Ypres sector and in other engagements until January 1916, when he returned to England and was discharged in consequence of his service. He holds the 1914–15 Star, and the General Service and Victory Medals.
30, Lammas Road, Watford. X3276/B.

WILSON, W. H., Private, R.A.M.C.
Volunteering in September 1914, he proceeded in the following year to France. There he did splendid work in tending the wounded until August 9th, 1918, when he was killed by the explosion of a bomb. He was entitled to the 1914–15 Star, and the General Service and Victory Medals.
10, South Road, Luton. 5566/B.

WINCH, A. G., Private, Bedfordshire Regiment and Tank Corps.
Volunteering in September 1914, he was drafted to France in the following March. In this theatre of war he served with his unit in various sectors and fought in many important engagements, including those of Ypres, the Somme, Messines, Arras and during the Retreat and Advance of 1918, and was wounded twice. He holds the 1914–15 Star, and the General Service and Victory Medals, and was demobilised in February 1919.
61, Diamond Road, Watford. X5573.

WINCH, F. C., Corporal, Machine Gun Corps.
He joined in December 1916, and in the following September proceeded overseas. During his service on the Western Front he was engaged in much fighting and, taken prisoner at Ploegsteert on April 10th, 1918, was held captive in Germany until after the cessation of hostilities. He was then released and returned to England, and in 1920 was still serving. He holds the General Service and Victory Medals. 104, Ashton Road, Luton. 5574.

WINCH, G., Sapper, Royal Engineers.
He was mobilised at the outbreak of war, and was later drafted to France. Whilst on the Western Front he served in the Arras, Ypres and Cambrai sectors, and was engaged with his unit on special trenching and telephone duties. He was demobilised in February 1919, and holds the General Service and Victory Medals.
Leavesden Green, near Watford. X5575.

WINCH, R. L., L/Corporal, Royal Engineers.
He volunteered in April 1915, and in the following October was sent to France. In this theatre of war he served on important work in the Ypres, Somme and Arras sectors, and during the Retreat of 1918, and, acting as a Despatch-rider, did excellent work. He returned to England after the signing of the Armistice, and was demobilised in March 1919, and holds the 1914–15 Star, and the General Service and Victory Medals.
61, Diamond Street, Watford. X5576.

WINDMILL, B. C. T., Pioneer, Royal Engineers.
He joined in June 1916, and five months later was sent to France. In this theatre of war he was employed in making and wiring trenches and constructing roads to the forward areas, and was constantly under heavy shell-fire in the Somme, Arras and Cambrai sectors. He was demobilised in February 1919, and holds the General Service and Victory Medals. 36, New Road, Linslade, Bucks. 5577.

WINDMILL, G., Sapper, Royal Engineers.
Joining in November 1916, in the following year he was drafted overseas. He served on the Western Front on special work during the heavy fighting on the Somme, at Ypres and Passchendaele, and was wounded and suffered from shellshock. He returned to England after the signing of the Armistice, and was demobilised in January 1919, and holds the General Service and Victory Medals.
65, Breakspeare Road, Abbots Langley. X5578.

WINDMILL, J. A., Pte., Sherwood Foresters.
Volunteering in February 1915, he was sent to the Western Front five months later and was in action in many battles, including those of the Somme, Arras and Cambrai and in the German Offensive of 1918, and was gassed. Returning to England he received hospital treatment and was invalided out of the Service and subsequently died in September 1920. He was entitled to the 1914–15 Star, and the General Service and Victory Medals.
71, Breakspeare Road, Abbots Langley. X5580.

WINDMILL, W. T., Sapper, Royal Engineers.
Joining in June 1917, he was drafted overseas in the same year. Whilst on the Western Front he was engaged on important road and rail construction work in the Arras, Ypres and Somme sectors. He was wounded near Cambrai in 1918, and after recovery returned to his unit and served in the final operations of the war. He was demobilised in October 1919, and holds the General Service and Victory Medals.
69, Hockliffe Road, Leighton Buzzard. 1288/B—1289/B.

WINDWOOD, J., Sapper, Royal Engineers; and Private, Labour Corps.
He volunteered in March 1915, and at the conclusion of his training was engaged on important duties with his unit at various depôts. He did very good work, but owing to injuries received in an accident was unable to obtain his transfer overseas, and was demobilised in May 1919.
4, Cannon's Cottages, Hitchin. 5579.

WINFIELD, A., Private, 1/5th Buffs (East Kent Regiment).
He volunteered in September 1915, and later proceeded to Mesopotamia. Whilst in this theatre of war he took part in many engagements and fought at Kut and other places. He returned to England after the cessation of hostilities, and was demobilised in February 1919, and holds the General Service and Victory Medals.
10, Clifford Street, Watford X3311/B.

WINFIELD, F. A., Private, East Surrey Regt.
Volunteering in 1914, he was drafted to France in the following year. During his service on the Western Front he fought in many battles, including those of the Somme, Ypres and Festubert. He was seriously wounded on August 22nd, 1916, and died a few hours later, and was entitled to the 1914–15 Star, and the General Service and Victory Medals.
77, Grover Road, Oxhey. X5581.

WINFIELD, G., Corporal, 7th Bedfordshire Regt.
Volunteering at the outbreak of war, he was sent to France in the following year In this theatre of war he took part in much heavy fighting and was killed in action at the Battle of Thiepval on September 27th, 1916. He was entitled to the 1914–15 Star, and the General Service and Victory Medals.
10, Clifford Street, Watford. X3311/A.

WINFIELD, H. C., Rifleman, 7th Rifle Brigade.
He volunteered in November 1914, and in August of the following year was drafted overseas. During his service on the Western Front he fought at Ypres and Arras, and was seriously wounded at the Battle of the Somme on September 15th, 1916. He was sent to hospital in England and in consequence of his injuries his left arm had to be amputated, and he was invalided out of the Service in June 1917. He holds the 1914–15 Star, and the General Service and Victory Medals. 9, Ashdown Road, Bushey. X5582.

WINFIELD, H. J., Private, Labour Corps.
He joined in February 1917, and in the same year proceeded overseas. Whilst on the Western Front he served on important duties as stretcher-bearer during the fighting on the Somme, at Cambrai and other places, and did very good work. He was demobilised in January 1919, and holds the General Service and Victory Medals.
3, Sherbourne Cottages, Watford Fields, Watford. X5583.

WINFIELD, J. J., Private, King's (Liverpool Regiment).
He joined in July 1917, and in the same year was drafted to France. In this theatre of war he fought in many engagements, including those at Ypres, the Somme and Cambrai, and was present at the entry into Mons at dawn on November 11th, 1918, and was twice wounded. He was demobilised in 1919, and holds the General Service and Victory Medals.
121, Judge Street, Callowland. X5584.

WING, G. C., Sapper, Royal Engineers.
He volunteered in September 1914, and in the following year was drafted to the Dardanelles. He served in the landing at Suvla Bay and many subsequent engagements until the evacuation of Gallipoli. He was then sent to Egypt and was engaged for a time in the Canal zone. He later took part in the operations in Palestine, and was present at the Battles of Gaza, Haifa, Acre and Beyrout. He returned to England and was demobilised in July 1919, and holds the 1914–15 Star, and the General Service and Victory Medals.
35, Beech Road, Luton. 5585.

WINGER, J., Corporal, Royal Army Service Corps.
Volunteering at the outbreak of war, he was sent to France in 1915. Whilst on the Western Front he was engaged with his unit on special duties as Ambulance Driver, taking the wounded from the Field Dressing Stations to the Casualty Clearing Stations. He did excellent work, and was frequently under shell-fire in the Arras, Aisne and Ypres sectors. He was demobilised in February 1919, and holds the 1914–15 Star, and the General Service and Victory Medals.
109, Chester Road, Watford. X5366/B.

WINGFIELD, R., Sergeant, R.F.A.
Volunteering at the outbreak of hostilities, he served on special duties with his Battery at various depôts. He was employed as an Instructor and did very good work, but was unable to secure his transfer to a theatre of war before the signing of the Armistice, and was demobilised in January 1919
53, Loates Lane, Watford. X5586.

WINGRAVE, F. C., Air Mechanic, Royal Air Force.
He joined in June 1917, and on completion of his training was stationed at various aerodromes, engaged on important observation and other duties. He was unsuccessful in obtaining his transfer overseas, but rendered valuable services as an Instructor in wireless telegraphy to the cadets of the Royal Air Force. He was demobilised in February 1919, and holds the General Service Medal.
73, Frederic Street, Luton. 5587.

WINGRAVE, J. F., Air Mechanic, Royal Air Force.
He volunteered in August 1915, and at the conclusion of his training was engaged at various aerodromes in Scotland with his Squadron on important duties, which called for a high degree of technical skill. He did excellent work as a carpenter, but was not successful in obtaining his transfer to a theatre of war before hostilities ceased. He was demobilised in February 1919.
30, Ridgway Road, Luton. 5588.

WINTER, G. F., Private, R.M.L.I.
He was serving at the outbreak of hostilities, and in the following March was drafted to the Dardanelles. In this theatre of war he fought at the first landing at Gallipoli and many subsequent engagements in that theatre of war. He later served in the Battle of Jutland and during the bombardment of Zeebrugge. He was demobilised in December 1919, and holds the 1914–15 Star, and the General Service and Victory Medals.
69, Hockliffe Road, Leighton Buzzard. 1288/C—1289/C.

WINTERS, F. W., Seaman, Royal Navy.
He joined in February 1918, and was posted to H.M.S. "Calliope," which vessel was engaged with the Grand Fleet in the North Sea on important patrol duties until after the Armistice. He was demobilised in March 1919, and holds the General Service and Victory Medals.
11, Nightingale Road, Hitchin. 5589.

WINUP, R. H., Signalman, Royal Navy.
He joined in August 1917, and was posted to H.M.S. "Opossum." His ship was engaged in the North Sea and the English Channel on important patrol duties, and served with the Home Seas Fleet. He was demobilised in January 1919, and holds the General Service and Victory Medals.
99, High Town Road, Luton. 5590.

WINWILL, C. S. H., Lieutenant, 2nd Canadian Infantry.
Volunteering at the outbreak of war, he was drafted to France in January 1915. He fought at Ypres and the Somme, and was granted a commission in the Field for consistently good work. He was twice mentioned in Despatches for bomb-throwing and devotion to duty during operations, and was wounded three times and gassed. He was subsequently invalided out of the Service in 1918 in consequence of his wounds, and holds the 1914–15 Star, and the General Service and Victory Medals.
68, Church Street, Leighton Buzzard. 4175/B—4176/B.

WISE, F. J., A/Corporal, Royal Air Force.
He joined in August 1916, and in the following December was sent to Mudros, where he was engaged on important duties in connection with aerial photography, and did very good work. He returned to England and was demobilised in January 1919, and holds the General Service and Victory Medals. 34, Neal Street, Watford. X5591.

WISE, G. H., Pte., 17th South Lancashire Regt.
He joined in January 1917, and at the conclusion of his training served at various stations on important duties with his Battalion. He rendered valuable services, but was unable to obtain his transfer overseas before the close of the war, and was demobilised in March 1919.
Bolnhurst, Limbury Road, Leagrave. 5592.

WISE, H., 1st Class Petty Officer, Royal Navy.
He volunteered in August 1914, and was posted to H.M.S. "Dalhousie," which vessel took part in many engagements and was present at the sinking of the "Königsberg," and later proceeded to Mesopotamia, where he served under General Townshend and was besieged in Kut and was twice wounded. He was demobilised in April 1919, and holds the 1914–15 Star, and the General Service and Victory Medals.
60, Acme Road, North Watford. X5593.

WITHEY, F. J., Private, 23rd Royal Fusiliers.
He volunteered in June 1915, and in the following year was drafted to France. Whilst in this theatre of war he was in action at the Battles of Ypres, the Somme, Cambrai and many other engagements, and was wounded. He returned to England after the cessation of hostilities, and was demobilised in March 1919. He holds the General Service and Victory Medals. 112, Harwood Road, Watford. X5594.

WITT, J. E., Private, 21st Middlesex Regiment.
He volunteered in June 1915, and four months later proceeded to France, where he fought in many battles, including that of Loos, during which he was severely wounded. He was invalided to hospital in England, and in consequence of his injuries his right leg had to be amputated. After protracted medical treatment he was discharged as physically unfit for further military service in May 1917. He holds the 1914–15 Star, and the General Service and Victory Medals. 7, Union Street, Dunstable. 5595.

WOOD, B., Private, Leicestershire Regiment.
He volunteered in August 1914, and in the following January was drafted to the Western Front. During his service in this theatre of war he was engaged in heavy fighting in the Battles of Ypres, Arras and the Somme. He was taken prisoner in the Cambrai sector in March 1918, and in consequence of hardships and ill-treatment received during his captivity died as a prisoner of war in Germany on October 18th, 1918. He was entitled to the 1914–15 Star, and the General Service and Victory Medals.
The Limes, Summer Street, Slip End. 5597/A.

WOOD, C., Private, 1/5th Bedfordshire Regiment.
Joining in March 1916, he was drafted to France three months later, and served with his Battalion in various parts of the line and fought in many engagements, including the Battle of the Somme, where he made the supreme sacrifice, being killed in action on September 5th, 1916. He was entitled to the General Service and Victory Medals.
74, Hitchin Road, Luton. 5598.

WOOD, C. R., Corporal, Royal Air Force.
He joined in August 1916, and on the completion of his training served with his Squadron at various aerodromes on important duties which called for a high degree of technical skill. He did very good work, but owing to medical unfitness was not successful in securing his transfer overseas before hostilities ceased. He was demobilised in 1919.
105, High Street, Markyate. 5603.

WOOD, D. M. (Miss), Special War Worker.
During the war this lady offered her services for work of National importance and was engaged at Messrs. Kent's Factory, Luton, on an engraving machine. Her duties were in connection with the manufacture of aeroplane parts, and, throughout, her work was carried out with every satisfaction.
29, St. Saviour's Crescent, Luton. 5599.

WOOD, E. A., Private, 7th Bedfordshire Regt.
He joined in June 1916, and in the following November embarked for France. Whilst on the Western Front he was engaged in heavy fighting in many parts of the line, and was seriously wounded in action on March 13th, 1917. He was invalided to hospital, where he unfortunately died from the effects of his injuries 13 days later. He was entitled to the General Service and Victory Medals.
Belmont, Princess Street, Dunstable. 5600

WOOD, E. J., 1st Air Mechanic, Royal Air Force.
He joined in March 1918, and after completing his training was sent to France in the following October. Here he served with his Squadron in the Somme and Cambrai sectors, and after the Armistice went with the Army of Occupation into Germany, where he remained until August 1919. He is one of the crew of the airship " R.33," and in 1920 was serving at Howden. He holds the General Service and Victory Medals.
24, Beech Road, Luton. 5601.

WOOD, F. J., Private, Royal Army Service Corps.
He joined in February 1918, and on completion of his training was stationed at various places, engaged on important duties driving a caterpillar tractor. He was not able to obtain his transfer overseas before the cessation of hostilities, and was demobilised in February 1919.
68, Holywell Road, Watford, Herts. 30/A.

WOOD, G., Private, 2nd Bedfordshire Regiment.
He joined in April 1916, and six months later was drafted to the Western Front. During his service in this theatre of war he took part in the fighting in many engagements, including the Battles of the Somme, Ypres and Arras. He was wounded in action in April 1917 in the vicinity of Arras, and invalided to hospital in France. Later in 1917 he returned to England and served on Home Defence duties until his demobilisation in January 1920. He holds the General Service and Victory Medals.
Green Hill Farm, Tilsworth, Beds. 5602/B.

WOOD, G. T., Corporal, Royal Engineers.
He enlisted in July 1906, and was mobilised at the outbreak of war, and shortly afterwards proceeded to France, where he was engaged on special duties in connection with operations during the Retreat from Mons and the subsequent Battles of the Marne, Festubert, Loos, Arras, Cambrai, the Somme, Ypres and many others. He returned to England in May 1919, and was discharged in the following month, and holds the Mons Star, and the General Service and Victory Medals.
5, St. Michael's Mount, Hitchin. 5604.

WOOD, H. C., Private, R.A.O.C.
Volunteering in August 1915, he proceeded to France in the following March and served with his unit in the Arras, Ypres, Somme and Cambrai sectors on important duties. He was frequently under shell-fire, and in June 1917 was wounded. He returned to England after the close of the war, and was demobilised in November 1919, and holds the General Service and Victory Medals.
12, King's Road, St. Albans. 5605.

WOOD, H. L., Marconi Operator, Merchant Service.
He joined in March 1918, and after completing his training was posted to the " Epsom," which vessel was engaged in conveying troops from England to France, Egypt and various other theatres of war. He did very good work, and was demobilised in October 1919. He holds the General Service and Mercantile Marine War Medals.
88, Leagrave Road, Luton. 5606.

WOOD, J., L/Corporal, East Surrey Regiment.
He joined in February 1917, and three months later was drafted to France. In this theatre of war he served with his Regiment in various sectors and fought in many engagements, including the Battle of Ypres. He was unfortunately killed in action during the Allied Advance on September 30th, 1918, and was entitled to the General Service and Victory Medals.
6, Athol Cottages, Colney Street, St. Albans. X5607.

WOOD, J., Private, Northamptonshire Regiment.
He joined in June 1916, and was later drafted to France, where he served with his Battalion and was engaged in the fighting in many important battles, including those of Ypres and the Somme. He returned to England after the signing of the Armistice, and was demobilised in April 1919, and holds the General Service and Victory Medals.
13, St. Michael's Street, St. Albans. 5608.

WOOD, J., Private, Bedfordshire Regiment.
He volunteered in August 1914, and after completing his training served at various stations in England and Ireland on guard and other important duties with his unit. He did very good work, but owing to medical unfitness was not able to secure his transfer overseas. He was still serving in 1920.
The Limes, Summer Street, Slip End. 5597/B.

WOOD, J., Private, 2nd Bedfordshire Regiment.
He joined in April 1916, and in the following October was sent to the Western Front, where he took part in heavy fighting in the Somme and Arras sectors. Severely wounded in the vicinity of Arras in 1917, he was invalided to hospital in England, and in 1920 was still receiving medical treatment. He holds the General Service and Victory Medals.
The Green Hill Farm, Tilsworth. 5602/A.

WOOD, J., Private, 4th Bedfordshire Regiment and Hertfordshire Regiment.
Joining in June 1916, he proceeded overseas in the following year and saw much service in France. Whilst in this theatre of war he was engaged in the Battles of Ypres, Passchendaele, Messines and Cambrai. He was unfortunately killed in action on the Somme on March 27th, 1918, and was entitled to the General Service and Victory Medals.
15, York Street, Luton. 5609.

WOOD, J. E., Sergeant, 2nd Durham L.I.
Mobilised on the outbreak of war, he was drafted to the Western Front in September 1914, and was in action at Hooge, Ypres and Armentières. He returned to England in May 1916, and was engaged with his unit on important duties until demobilised in February 1919. He holds the 1914 Star, and the General Service and Victory Medals.
144, Sandringham Road, Watford. X5610.

WOOD, J. J., Sapper, Royal Engineers.
Volunteering in November 1915, in the following April he embarked for the Western Front and was engaged on important duties in the forward areas. He was present during operations on the Somme, at Albert, Givenchy, Combles and Oppy, and was gassed at Arras in 1917. Returning to England in January 1919, he was demobilised in the following March, and holds the General Service and Victory Medals.
8, Lammas Road, Watford. X856/A.

WOOD, J. P., Driver, Royal Field Artillery.
He volunteered in May 1915, and was later sent to France. Serving with his Battery he did good work throughout the course of hostilities, and was in action in many engagements. He was principally employed in moving guns in the forward areas. He was demobilised in January 1919, and holds the General Service and Victory Medals.
11, Summer Street, Slip End. 5611.

WOOD, P. A., Private, 2nd Northamptonshire Regiment and Labour Corps.
He joined in April 1917, and three months later was drafted overseas. He served in Egypt and was engaged on important duties during the British Advance through Palestine. Returning to England after hostilities ceased, he was demobilised in February 1920, and holds the General Service and Victory Medals.
3, Neal Street, Watford. X5612.

WOOD, R., Private, 7th Bedfordshire Regiment.
Volunteering in August 1914, in the following June he proceeded to the Western Front and served there for upwards of three years. During this period he was in action in the Battles of Arras, Ypres, Cambrai and the Somme, and was gassed and invalided home. He was discharged on account of service in June 1918, and holds the 1914–15 Star, and the General Service and Victory Medals.
11, Bailey Street, Luton. 5613.

WOOD, V., Air Mechanic, Royal Air Force.
He volunteered in February 1915, and after completing his training served with his Squadron at various stations, where he was engaged on aeroplane repairs, work calling for a high degree of technical knowledge and skill. He rendered valuable services, but was not successful in obtaining his transfer to a theatre of war before hostilities ceased. After the Armistice, however, he proceeded to Germany with the Army of Occupation, and returned home for demobilisation in June 1919.
13, Parker Street, Watford. X685/C—X686/C.

WOOD, W., L/Corporal, Royal Engineers.
Volunteering in 1914, he embarked for France in the same year and was engaged on special duties in the cookhouse of his unit. Owing to ill-health he was invalided to England, and after receiving medical treatment served at home on special duties until demobilised in March 1919. He holds the 1914 Star, and the General Service and Victory Medals.
Bolnhurst, Limbury Road, Leagrave. 5614.

WOODALL, W. H., Sapper, Royal Engineers.
He volunteered in November 1914, and embarking for Gallipoli in the following June served in the landing at Suvla Bay and was wounded on August 20th, 1915. On recovery he was sent to East Africa in August 1916, and was engaged there on important duties during operations in German East Africa. He returned home in March 1919, and was demobilised in the following month, and holds the 1914–15 Star, and the General Service and Victory Medals.
52, King's Road, Hitchin. 5191/C.

WOODBRIDGE, J., Air Mechanic, R.A.F.
He joined in June 1918, and two months later proceeded to the Western Front, where he served with his Squadron at Dunkirk and Boulogne aerodromes. Whilst overseas he was engaged on aeroplane repair work and rendered valuable services. He was demobilised in February 1919, and holds the General Service and Victory Medals.
4, Talbot Road, Luton. 5616.

WOODBRIDGE, W. J., L/Corporal, R.A.S.C.
Volunteering in February 1915, he completed his training and was engaged on important transport duties with his unit. He rendered valuable services, but was not sent overseas owing to medical unfitness for General Service, and was demobilised in 1919.
Dunstable Street, Ampthill. 5615.

WOODCROFT, A., Drummer, Bedfordshire Volunteer Training Corps.
Being ineligible for service with the Colours, he enlisted in the Bedfordshire Volunteer Training Corps in August 1914, and on completing his training was engaged on guard and other important duties. He did excellent work with his unit, and was demobilised in June 1919.
73, Ivy Road, Luton. 5617/A.

WOODCROFT, E., Sergeant, 3rd Bedfordshire Regiment.
He volunteered in November 1914, and served on special duties with his Regiment until drafted to France early in November 1918. Whilst overseas he was engaged in guarding German prisoners of war at detention camps at Etaples, Amiens and other places. He returned to England for demobilisation in February 1919, and holds the General Service and Victory Medals.
73, Ivy Road, Luton. 5617/C.

WOODCROFT, F. E., Sapper, Royal Engineers.
Volunteering in November 1915, he embarked for France in the following June and was engaged on important duties in connection with operations at the Battles of the Somme, Beaumont-Hamel, Arras, Cambrai and other engagements. He was demobilised in July 1919, and holds the General Service and Victory Medals.
Rectory Lane, Houghton Conquest, near Ampthill. 4742/A.

WOODCROFT, N. (Mrs.), Special War Worker.
During the war this lady volunteered her services for work of National importance, and from January 1915 until December 1918 was engaged on munitions with a large engineering firm. Employed on a drilling machine she carried out her important duties in a careful and efficient manner.
73, Ivy Road, Luton. 2077/C.

WOODCROFT, P. E., L/Corporal, 2nd Bedfordshire Regiment.
A serving soldier, he was mobilised on the outbreak of war and drafted to France in October 1914, served in many parts of the line and was engaged in severe fighting. He was unfortunately killed in action at Ypres on November 7th, 1914, and was entitled to the 1914 Star, and the General Service and Victory Medals.
73, Ivy Road, Luton. 5617/B.

WOODCROFT, S., Driver, R.A.S.C.
Attesting in 1915, he was called up in March 1918 on attaining military age, and sent to the Western Front in the following July. During his service overseas he was employed on important transport duties in engagements on the Somme and at Cambrai during the Allied Advance, and, returning to England in July 1919 was demobilised in the following month. He holds the General Service and Victory Medals.
7, New Street, Shefford. Z5618.

WOODCROFT, W. J., Private, Royal Fusiliers.
Joining in 1916, he was drafted to France in the following year and engaged in the Battles of Arras, Ypres and Messines, and was gassed in 1918. Invalided home to hospital for treatment, on recovery he was engaged on farm work until demobilised in 1919. He holds the General Service and Victory Medals.
The Kennels, Haynes Park, near Bedford. 390/C.

WOODCROFT, W. T., Sergeant, 1/5th Bedfordshire Regiment.
Mobilised in August 1914, he proceeded to Gallipoli in the following year and fought in the landing at Suvla Bay and other engagements, including those at Anzac and Chocolate Hill. After the Evacuation of the Peninsula he was sent to Egypt in December 1915, and served in that theatre of war for several months. He returned to England and was discharged on account of his age in August 1916, and holds the 1914-15 Star, and the General Service and Victory Medals.
70, Park Road West, Luton. 287/A.

WOODCROFT, W. W., L/Corporal, R.E.
He volunteered in January 1915, and was later drafted to Gallipoli, where he saw much service until invalided home owing to illness. On recovery he was engaged on important constructional work at various depôts at home until demobilised in January 1919. He holds the 1914-15 Star, and the General Service and Victory Medals.
Southill, Beds. Z5619.

WOODFORD, A., Officers' Steward, R.N.
Serving in the Royal Navy on the outbreak of hostilities aboard H.M.S. "Amazon," his ship was engaged during the war on important submarine patrol duties in the North Sea, and was in action in the Battle of Jutland and in the Naval raid on Zeebrugge. He holds the 1914-15 Star, and the General Service and Victory Medals, and in 1920 was still serving.
Aley Green, near Luton. 5620/C.

WOODFORD, O., A.B., Royal Navy.
He volunteered in April 1915, and posted to H.M.S. "Castor" served in that vessel throughout the war. His ship was engaged with the Grand Fleet on submarine patrol and other duties in the North Sea and took part in the Battle of Jutland and in the raid ou Zeebrugge. He was still serving in 1920, and holds the General Service and Victory Medals.
Aley Green, near Luton. 5620/A.

WOODFORD, W., Staff-Sergeant, 1st Hertfordshire Regiment.
He volunteered in January 1915, and on the conclusion of his training was engaged on important guard and escort duties at various prisoners of war detention camps. He rendered valuable services, but was not sent overseas owing to medical unfitness, and was demobilised in February 1919.
Aley Green, near Luton. 5620/B.

WOODFORTH, J., Private, 5th Lincolnshire Regiment.
He volunteered in November 1914, and after serving at various stations was sent to the Western Front in 1916, and saw much service fighting at Cambrai, Arras and through the German Offensive and Allied Advance of 1918, and was twice wounded. He was demobilised in February 1919, and holds the General Service and Victory Medals.
New Marford, Wheathampstead. 5621.

WOODING, A. G., Private, 1st Bedfordshire Regiment.
Volunteering in September 1915, he embarked for the Western Front in the following August. Serving in many parts of the line, he fought at the Battles of the Somme and Messines and was unfortunately killed in action at Vimy Ridge on April 23rd, 1917. He was entitled to the General Service and Victory Medals.
36, High Street, Ridgmont. Z5622.

WOODING, C., Private, R.A.M.C.
Volunteering in September 1914, he was drafted to France in the following July and served in the advanced areas on important ambulance duties in the Battles of Arras, Ypres, Cambrai and Neuve Chapelle, and in the German Offensive and subsequent Allied Advance of 1918. He was demobilised in February 1919, and holds the 1914-15 Star, and the General Service and Victory Medals.
3, High Street, Ridgmont. Z5623.

WOODING, J. C., Private, 1/5th Bedfordshire Regiment.
He volunteered in September 1914, and in the following year embarked for the Dardanelles and fought at the landing at Suvla Bay and in the subsequent operations until the evacuation of the Peninsula. Proceeding to Egypt, he saw much service during the Advance through Sinai and Palestine into Syria, and fought in many engagements, and was twice wounded. He served with the Royal Army Medical Corps towards the end of the war, and was demobilised in July 1919 on his return to England, and holds the 1914-15 Star, and the General Service and Victory Medals.
How End, Houghton Conquest, Beds. Z5624.

WOODLAND, E. J., L/Corporal, 1/5th Bedfordshire Regiment.
Volunteering in August 1914, he proceeded to the Dardanelles in the following July and was in action at the landing at Suvla Bay and many battles which followed. Owing to ill-health he was invalided to England, and after receiving medical treatment was sent to France in 1917, and fought at Arras, Ypres, Cambrai, and was again wounded in the Allied Advance in 1918. He returned home and on recovery was discharged as medically unfit for further service in January 1919, and holds the 1914-15 Star, and the General Service and Victory Medals.
Dunstable Street, Ampthill. 5625.

WOODMAN, A., Private, Labour Corps.
He joined in March 1917, and on completion of his training was stationed at various depôts engaged on guard and other important duties. He was unsuccessful in obtaining his transfer overseas owing to medical unfitness, but rendered excellent services until demobilised in January 1919.
2, Edward Street, Luton. 5626.

WOODROW, F., L/Corporal, 2nd Queen's (Royal West Surrey Regiment).
He joined in 1916, and was drafted to France later in the same year, and fought in many important engagements, including those at Ypres, Passchendaele and Arras. He was invalided to England in 1918 owing to ill-health, and was eventually discharged unfit for further service in October 1918. He holds the General Service and Victory Medals.
Holly Cottage, Preston, Herts. 5627.

WOODRUFF, W. G., Private, 1st Wiltshire Regt.
Volunteering in September 1914, he embarked for the Western Front in the following September and fought at the Battles of the Somme, Arras, Ypres and in various other engagements. He was wounded on July 8th, 1916, during the heavy fighting, and succumbed to his injuries ten days later. He was entitled to the 1914-15 Star, and the General Service and Victory Medals.
3, Brickfield Cottages, Hitchin Hill. 5628.

WOODS, A. (M.M.), Lieut., Royal Irish Regiment.
He enlisted in September 1908, and proceeded to the Western Front shortly after the outbreak of hostilities and fought in the Battles of the Somme, Ypres, Arras, Cambrai and Loos, and throughout the German Offensive and subsequent Allied Advance of 1918, and was wounded twice. He was awarded the Military Medal and was twice mentioned in Despatches for conspicuous gallantry and devotion to duty in the Field. He was still serving in 1920, and holds the 1914 Star, and the General Service and Victory Medals.
101, Biscot Road, Luton. 5596.

WOODS, A., Private, 1st Northamptonshire Regt.
He joined in April 1916, and was drafted to the Western Front three months later, and was in action in various parts of the line, fighting in many important engagements. He was wounded during the first British Offensive on the Somme, and subsequently died from his injuries on August 18th, 1916. He was entitled to the General Service and Victory Medals.
Lower Caldecote, Biggleswade. Z5629/C.

WOODS, E., Private, 11th Royal Sussex Regt.
He joined in March 1916, and embarked for France in the following August, and was in action in many important engagements. He was wounded in the Ypres salient in October 1917, and returned to England. After receiving medical treatment he was invalided out of the Service in May 1918, and holds the General Service and Victory Medals.
Lower Caldecote, Biggleswade. Z5629/B.

WOODS, F., Private, 2nd Essex Regiment.
Volunteering in January 1915, he embarked for the Western Front in the following March, and serving in various sectors fought at Festubert, Loos, Givenchy, Vimy Ridge and on the Somme. He was unfortunately killed in action at Passchendaele on October 10th, 1917, and was entitled to the 1914-15 Star, and the General Service and Victory Medals.
18, Fox and Crown Cottages, Potton. Z5630.

WOODS, F., Private, East Surrey Regiment.
He volunteered in September 1914, and was sent to France in the following year and was engaged in heavy fighting in the Battles of Loos, Neuve Chapelle, Arras, Ypres, Cambrai and in many other engagements. Later, transferred to Italy, he saw much service in that theatre of war until the cessation of hostilities. He was then sent with the Army of Occupation into Germany and was stationed on the Rhine. He returned to England for demobilisation in March 1919, and holds the 1914-15 Star, and the General Service and Victory Medals.
33, Husborne Crawley, Beds. Z5631/A.

WOODS, G. W., 2nd Lieutenant, Tank Corps.
He joined in February 1917, and was later sent to the Western Front, where he rendered valuable services as an Instructor in Tank warfare. He served in many parts of the line, and returned to England for demobilisation in January 1919. He holds the General Service and Victory Medals.
5, Claremont Road, Luton. 5632.

WOODS, H., Private, 3rd Northamptonshire Regt.
He joined in August 1918, and was sent to France two months later and fought in the Allied Advance. He was in action in many important engagements and was wounded at Arras. He returned to England, and after hospital treatment was stationed in Ireland until demobilised in August 1919. He holds the General Service and Victory Medals.
Lower Caldecote, Biggleswade. Z5629/A.

WOODS, H., Private, East Surrey Regiment.
Volunteering in September 1914, he proceeded to France in the following year and saw much service there, fighting at Arras, Ypres, Cambrai and the Somme, and was later transferred to Italy. Here he fought in various sectors, and was in action in many important engagements. After the Armistice he was sent into Germany with the Army of Occupation and was stationed on the Rhine, returning to England for demobilisation in March 1919. He holds the 1914-15 Star, and the General Service and Victory Medals.
33, Husborne Crawley, Beds. Z5361/B.

WOODS, J. B., Leading Aircraftsman, R.A.F.
He volunteered in October 1915, and was sent to the Western Front in the following year. He served at various aerodromes in the advanced areas, engaged on duties demanding a high degree of technical knowledge and skill. He was wounded near Ypres in May 1917, and on recovery was drafted to Italy, where he saw much service on the Asiago Plateau and was again wounded in September 1918. He returned to England and was demobilised in February 1919, and holds the General Service and Victory Medals.
47, Lower Paddock Road, Oxhey. X5633.

WOODS, J. G., Rifleman, 7th Rifle Brigade.
He joined in April 1916, and embarked for the Western Front three months later. He fought in many important engagements, including those at the Somme, Arras, Ypres and the Menin Road. He was taken prisoner at St. Quentin on March 21st, 1918, during the German Offensive. Repatriated on the cessation of hostilities, he was demobilised in February 1919, and holds the General Service and Victory Medals.
Fern View, Springfield, Linslade. 5634.

WOODS, S., Private, Bedfordshire Regiment.
Volunteering in August 1914, he proceeded overseas shortly afterwards. During his service in France, he was in action at Arras, Cambrai, Beaumont-Hamel, and in various other important engagements. Owing to ill-health he was invalided to England, and after receiving hospital treatment was discharged unfit for further service in June 1917. He holds the General Service and Victory Medals.
Ramridge End, Stopsley. 5635.

WOODSTOCK, C. E., Private, 13th London Regiment (Kensingtons).
He joined in 1916, and shortly afterwards was sent to France. During his service on the Western Front he was engaged in the fighting at the Battles of Ypres, Arras, the Somme, the Aisne, and many other engagements until the close of the war. He returned to England after the signing of the Armistice and was demobilised in 1919, and holds the General Service and Victory Medals.
9, Lower Paddock Road, Oxhey. X5636/B.

WOODSTOCK, H. C., L/Corporal, 11th Middlesex Regiment.
Volunteering in 1914, he completed his training and was later drafted to France. In this theatre of war he fought in many engagements, including those on the Somme, the Aisne, at Ypres and Givenchy, and was gassed. He was demobilised in January 1920, and holds the General Service and Victory Medals.
9, Lower Paddock Road, Oxhey. X5636/C.

WOODSTOCK, T., Driver, R.A.S.C.
He volunteered in February 1916, and was later sent to France, where he served for a time and afterwards proceeded to Egypt. Whilst in this theatre of war he was present at the Advance through Palestine and was engaged on important duties during operations at Gaza, Jaffa, Haifa and Jerusalem. He returned to England after the cessation of hostilities, and was demobilised in September 1919, and holds the General Service and Victory Medals.
9, Lower Paddock Road, Oxhey. X5636/A.

WOODSTOCK, W. H., Sergeant, R.A.S.C.
He volunteered in 1915, and was later sent overseas. He served in France for a time, and was afterwards sent to Salonika, where he was engaged on special duties with his unit. He did very good work as a baker during the course of his service overseas, and returned to England after the cessation of hostilities. He was demobilised in July 1919, and holds the General Service and Victory Medals.
16, Denmark Street, Watford. X5637.

WOODWARD, A. C., Private, 7th Bedfordshire Regiment.
He joined in February 1917, and in the following December was drafted to France. During his service on the Western Front he was engaged in heavy fighting in many important engagements. On March 22nd, 1918, he was reported missing, and was later presumed to have been killed in action on that date near St. Quentin. He was entitled to the General Service and Victory Medals.
132, Dallow Road, Luton.   5638.

WOODWARD, E., Corporal, R.A.S.C.
He volunteered in August 1915, and in the same year was drafted overseas. He served on the Western Front, and was engaged on special duties as a baker with his unit at Boulogne, Calais and Le Havre, and did very good work. He was demobilised in June 1919, and holds the 1914–15 Star, and the General Service and Victory Medals.
34, Lammas Road, Watford.   X263/B.

WOODWARD, E. J., Private, 13th Middlesex Regiment.
He joined in January 1917, and shortly afterwards was drafted to France. In this theatre of war he was engaged in much fierce fighting at the Battles of Vimy Ridge, and Ypres. He was unfortunately killed in action on June 20th, 1917, at Ypres, and was entitled to the General Service and Victory Medals.
12, New Town, Biggleswade.   Z5639.

WOODWARD, F., Private, Bedfordshire Regt. and Royal Warwickshire Regiment.
He joined in January 1917, and in the same year was sent to France. Whilst in this theatre of war, he fought in many battles, including those of the Somme, the Marne and Cambrai. He returned to England after the cessation of hostilities and was demobilised in 1919. He holds the General Service and Victory Medals.
19, Longmire Road, St. Albans.   X5640.

WOODWARD, F. A., A/Sergeant, R.M.L.I.
He was serving at the outbreak of hostilities, and during the war served in H.M.S. "Cressy," which vessel was employed on special duties in the North Sea and other waters until after the signing of the Armistice. He was demobilised in March 1919, having completed 21 years' service with the Colours, and holds the General Service and Victory Medals.
93, St. James' Road, Watford.   X5641.

WOODWARD, F. C., Corporal, Bedfordshire Regt.
Volunteering at the outbreak of war, he was sent to France in January 1915. Whilst on the Western Front he fought at the Battles of Hill 60, Festubert, Loos and the Somme, and in March 1917, was drafted to Egypt, where he was in action during the Advance through the Holy Land and took part in the Battles of Gaza, being present at the occupation of Jerusalem. He returned to England and was subsequently discharged in December 1918, and holds the 1914–15 Star, and the General Service and Victory Medals.
Upper Sundon, near Dunstable.   5642.

WOODWARD, F. W., Private, 1/5th Bedfordshire Regiment .
He volunteered in September 1914, and in the following year was drafted to Gallipoli, where he fought at the landing at Suvla Bay and in many other battles on the Peninsula. In February 1916 he was sent to Egypt, and was engaged in the fighting in the British Advance through Palestine, and was in action at Gaza, Haifa, Rafa, Jaffa and Jerusalem. He returned to England after the signing of the Armistice and was demobilised in March 1919, and holds the 1914–15 Star, and the General Service and Victory Medals.
Clifton Road, Shefford.   Z5643.

WOODWARD, G., Corporal, 11th (Prince Albert's Own) Hussars.
He volunteered in August 1914, and was later sent to France. In this theatre of war he was engaged in much fighting, and fought at the Battles of Ypres, Arras, the Somme and Cambrai, and after the signing of the Armistice proceeded to Germany with the Army of Occupation. He was demobilised in April 1919, and holds the General Service and Victory Medals.
Littleworth, Wing, Bucks.   5644.

WOODWARD, G. H., Private, Queen's Own (Royal West Kent Regiment).
He joined in July 1916, and three months later was sent to France. He fought in many battles, and was wounded at Oppy Wood. He was invalided to England, and on recovery returned to the Western Front, and was again wounded during the fighting at Bapaume in August 1918. He also saw service in Italy, and was in action on the Piave and Asiago fronts. He returned to England and was demobilised in September 1919, and holds the General Service and Victory Medals.
26, New Town, Biggleswade.   Z5645.

WOODWARD, J., Sapper, Royal Engineers.
He joined in June 1916, and in July of the following year was sent to Salonika, where he served on special duties with his unit during the operations on the Vardar front and the Advance into Bulgaria. After the signing of the Armistice he proceeded with the Army of Occupation to Turkey, and was stationed at Constantinople. He returned to England and was demobilised in August 1919, and holds the General Service and Victory Medals.
116, Liverpool Road, Watford.   X5646.

WOODWARD, R., Private, R.M.L.I.
Volunteering at the outbreak of war, he served aboard ship in the North Sea and other waters on patrol and other important duties. His ship was also in action at the Battles of Heligoland Bight and Jutland and had other encounters with the German Fleet. He was demobilised in March 1919, and holds the 1914–15 Star, and the General Service and Victory Medals.
c/o Mr. Abbott, Heath Road, Harpenden.   5647.

WOODWARD, W., Private, 24th Royal Fusiliers.
He joined in February 1917, and was sent to Ireland, where he was employed on important guard duties until drafted to France in the following April. He was engaged in the fighting near Ypres, and was wounded. He later fought at Passchendaele Ridge, Albert and Cambrai, and after the cessation of hostilities, proceeded to Germany with the Army of Occupation and was stationed at Cologne. He was demobilised in March 1919, and holds the General Service and Victory Medals.
20, Rose Terrace, Biggleswade.   Z5648.

WOOLEY, H. J., Driver, R.A.S.C.
Joining in 1916, he was drafted to France in the same year. During his service on the Western Front he was engaged with his unit on important duties in the Cambrai, Arras and the Somme sectors, and was frequently under shell-fire. He was demobilised in March 1919, and holds the General Service and Victory Medals.
4, Caroline Cottages, Capel Road, Oxhey.   X307/B.

WOOLF, J. (M.M.), Private, 11th Essex Regt.
He joined in May 1916, and in the following October proceeded overseas. Whilst on the Western Front he fought in many engagements, including those at Arras, Loos, Bullecourt, Cambrai, St. Quentin and during the Retreat and Advance of 1918. He was awarded the Military Medal for conspicuous bravery and devotion to duty in the Field, and also holds the General Service and Victory Medals. He was demobilised in August 1919.
Saunder's Piece, Ampthill.   5649.

WOOLFORD, A., Rifleman, 16th London Regt. (Queen's Westminster Rifles).
Volunteering in August 1914, he was sent to France in October of the same year. In this theatre of war he fought at the Battles of Armentières, Ypres, Arras, the Somme, Cambrai, Combles, Bullecourt and many other engagements, and was wounded. He was demobilised in February 1919, and holds the 1914 Star, and the General Service and Victory Medals.
7, Hartwell Grove, Leighton Buzzard.   5650.

WOOLHEAD, A., A.B., Royal Navy.
Joining the Royal Navy in 1910, he was mobilised on the outbreak of hostilities, and aboard H.M.S. "Egremont" was engaged on important patrol duties in the North and Baltic Seas. His ship was in action in the Battle of Jutland and in several encounters with enemy vessels whilst escorting transports to France and other theatres of war. He was demobilised in February 1920, and holds the 1914–15 Star, and the General Service and Victory Medals.
Church Street, Wing.   5651.

WOOLHEAD, C., Private, 2/1st Oxfordshire and Buckinghamshire Light Infantry.
Joining in June 1916, he embarked for the Western Front in the same year, and fought in the Battles of the Somme and Cambrai. During the Retreat of 1918 he was unfortunately killed in action on March 24th, 1918. He was entitled to the General Service and Victory Medals.
Vine Cottage, Leighton Road, Wing.   5653.

WOOLHEAD, E., L/Corporal, Essex Regiment.
He volunteered in June 1915, and in the following March proceeded to France, and was in action on the Somme. Sent to Salonika in May 1916, he took part in several engagements, including the Advance on the Vardar, and proceeded to Egypt in the following April. He fought in the Battle of Gaza and other operations during the Palestine campaign, and returned to England for demobilisation in July 1919. He holds the General Service and Victory Medals.
48, Old Road, Linslade, near Leighton Buzzard.   5719/C.

WOOLHEAD, E., L/Corporal, Bedfordshire Regt.
Volunteering in August 1914, he was quickly sent to the Western Front, where he fought in the majority of the great battles during the next four years. He was wounded near Cambrai in May 1918, and invalided home for treatment. He rejoined his unit in the Field four months later, and was in action in several of the concluding engagements of the war. He was demobilised in July 1919, and holds the 1914 Star, and the General Service and Victory Medals.
48, Old Road, Linslade, near Leighton Buzzard.   5719/B.

WOOLHEAD, E. F., Private, 8th Bedfordshire Regiment,
He volunteered in April 1915, and in the following October was drafted to the Western Front. Whilst in this theatre of war he fought in several engagements, including the Battle of Loos. Taken prisoner near Albert on April 19th, 1916, he suffered considerable hardships and was exposed to heavy shell-fire in the enemy trenches. Returning to England after the Armistice, he was demobilised in March 1919, and holds the 1914-15 Star, and the General Service and Victory Medals.   122, Heath Road, Leighton Buzzard.   5652.

WOOLHEAD, F., Private, R.A.S.C.
He joined in March 1918, on attaining military age, and on completing his training was engaged on important transport duties with his unit. He rendered valuable services, but was unable to obtain a transfer overseas before the end of hostilities, and was demobilised in January 1920.
Littleworth, Wing.   4097/A.

WOOLHEAD, G., Private, Oxfordshire and Buckinghamshire Light Infantry.
Volunteering in 1915, he was drafted overseas in January of the following year. He saw much service on the Western Front and was engaged in heavy fighting in many important battles. He was unfortunately killed in action on the Somme in March 1918 during the Retreat. He was entitled to the General Service and Victory Medals.
Vine Cottage, Leighton Road, Wing   5654.

WOOLHEAD, L., Private, Oxfordshire and Buckinghamshire Light Infantry.
He was mobilised in August 1914, and proceeding to France in the following month, fought in many of the important battles, including those at La Bassée, Loos, the Somme, Ypres and Cambrai. After being invalided home he was discharged in September 1918, as being medically unfit for further service. He holds the 1914 Star, and the General Service and Victory Medals.
48, Old Street, Linslade.   5719/A.

WOOLHEAD, S., Private, Oxfordshire and Buckinghamshire Light Infantry.
Volunteering in July 1915, he proceeded overseas in the following January and served on the Western Front as a signaller. He took part in many engagements, including those on the Somme, at Arras and during the Retreat of 1918, and was wounded three times. Returning to England on the termination of hostilities, he holds the General Service and Victory Medals, and in 1920 was still serving.
School Lane, Wing.   5655.

WOOLHEAD, W., A.B., Royal Navy.
Joining the Royal Navy in 1907, he was mobilised on the outbreak of war, and aboard H.M.S. " Scotsman " was engaged on important patrol duties in the North Sea and the Baltic. His vessel was also engaged in chasing submarines and in escorting transports to France and other theatres of war. She was in action in the Battle of Jutland. He holds the 1914-15 Star, and the General Service and Victory Medals, and in 1920 was still serving.
48, Old Street, Linslade, near Leighton Buzzard.   5719/D.

WOOLLAMS, A. G., Sergeant, 11th (Prince Albert's Own) Hussars.
He volunteered in August 1914, and embarking for France shortly afterwards, served there for upwards of five years. During this period he was in action in the Battle of Ypres, and in many other important engagements, being wounded on one occasion. On the termination of hostilities he was sent to Germany with the Army of Occupation and stationed on the Rhine. He was demobilised in April 1919, on his return home, and holds the 1914 Star, and the General Service and Victory Medals
55, Fearnley Street, Watford.   X5656/A.

WOOLLAMS, J., Private, 32nd Middlesex Regt.
Volunteering in 1915, on completing his training he was engaged on the East Coast on important coastal defence duties and rendered valuable services. He was unable to obtain a transfer to a theatre of war before the cessation of hostilities owing to his age. He was demobilised in 1919.
55, Fearnley Street, Watford.   X5656/B.

WOOLLAMS, J. F., Private, 7th Leicestershire Regiment.
He joined in January 1917, and after completion of his training served with his unit until drafted to the Western Front in the following year. He was unfortunately killed on his first day in action near Ypres on April 19th, 1918, and was buried at Dickebusch. He was entitled to the General Service and Victory Medals. His memory is cherished with pride.
74, Norfolk Road, Rickmansworth.   X5657.

WOOLLARD, J. H., Private, 6th Bedfordshire Regiment.
Volunteering in September 1914, in the following August he proceeded to the Western Front. Whilst overseas he was engaged in heavy fighting in the Battle of Loos and other operations. He was unfortunately killed on June 26th, 1916, in a raid which was preparatory to the Battle of the Somme. He was entitled to the 1914-15 Star, and the General Service and Victory Medals.
57, Lyndhurst Road, Luton.   5658/B.

WOOLLARD, J. K., Bombardier, R.F.A.
He volunteered in August 1915, and in the following June was sent to Mesopotamia, where he fought in the Battles of Kut and Baghdad. Sent to Egypt in 1917, he was in action in the third Battle of Gaza, and at Jerusalem, Aleppo and other places during the British Advance through Palestine. He returned to England for demobilisation in March 1919, and holds the General Service and Victory Medals.
57, Lyndhurst Road, Luton.   5658/A

WOOLLEY, H., Sapper, R.E.
He volunteered in January 1915, and on the conclusion of his training served with his unit in the Eastern Counties and in other parts of England. He did excellent work as a despatch-rider and was also employed on important duties in several workshops. He was unable to obtain a transfer overseas before the termination of hostilities, and was demobilised in January 1919.
16, Florence Street, Hitchin.   5659.

WOOLLISON, G., Sergt., Sherwood Foresters.
Mobilised on the outbreak of war and almost immediately drafted to France, he fought in the Retreat from Mons and was wounded. He was later in action in the Battles of Ypres, La Bassée, Loos, the Somme, Arras, Cambrai and during the Retreat of 1918. During his service he took charge of parties in many trench-bombing raids. He holds the Mons Star, and the General Service and Victory Medals, and was demobilised in March 1919.
70, Church Street, Dunstable.   5660.

WOOLNOUGH, J. A., Corpl., Military Mounted Police.
He volunteered in May 1915, and proceeded to the Western Front in the following month, where he was engaged on important police duties in the forward areas. In the course of his service he was constantly exposed to heavy shell-fire during the Battles of Loos, Arras, Ypres, Cambrai and Bapaume. Returning to England for demobilisation in February 1919, he holds the 1914-15 Star, and the General Service and Victory Medals.
35, York Road, Watford.   X5661.

WOOLSTON, C. W. T., Sapper, Royal Engineers.
He joined in December 1917, and on the completion of his training was engaged on important duties on the South-East Coast at the mystery port Richborough. He rendered valuable services, but was unsuccessful in obtaining a transfer overseas before the cessation of hostilities, and was demobilised in 1919.
85, Cecil Street, North Watford.   X5662.

WOOTTEN, E., Private, 9th Queen's (Royal West Surrey Regiment).
Volunteering in August 1914, he completed his training and served with his unit until he was sent to India. There he was engaged on important guard and garrison duties, and took part in various operations on the North Western Frontier. He unfortunately died in India on October 18th, 1918. He was entitled to the General Service and Victory Medals, in addition to the Indian General Service Medal, 1908 (with Clasp, Afghanistan, North West Frontier, 1919).
5, Paynes Park, Hitchin.   5663/A

WOOTTON, B., L/Corporal, R.A.S.C. (M.T.)
He was mobilised on the declaration of war, and proceeding to France shortly afterwards, served on important transport duties during the Retreat from Mons, and in the Battles of Arras, Ypres, Cambrai and the Somme. He did valuable work throughout the course of hostilities, returning to England in February 1919, when he was demobilised. He holds the Mons Star, and the General Service and Victory Medals.
7, Brighton Road, Watford.   X5664.

WOOTON, L., Sapper, R.E. (R.O.D.)
He joined in January 1917, and in the following month was drafted overseas. He saw much service on the Western Front where he was engaged on the lines of communication during the Battles of Arras, Bapaume Cambrai and the Somme. Returning home for demobilisation in October 1919, he holds the General Service and Victory Medals.
8, Liverpool Road, Watford. X5666.

WORBEY, H., Saddler, R.A.S.C.
He volunteered at the outbreak of war, and was drafted to France in 1915. He was engaged on important duties with his unit whilst operations were in progress at Hill 60, Ypres and in other sectors, and was frequently under shell-fire. Owing to ill-health he was invalided to England, and after receiving hospital treatment was subsequently discharged unfit for further service in December 1915. He holds the 1914–15 Star, and the General Service and Victory Medals.
Nelson House, Brampton Park Road, Hitchin. 5669.

WORBEY, J., Pte., South Staffordshire Regt.
He joined in June 1916, and after the completion of his training was engaged on important duties with his unit at various stations. Owing to medical unfitness he was not successful in obtaining his transfer to a fighting front while hostilities continued, but he rendered valuable services until his demobilisation in March 1919.
3, St. Andrew's Street, Hitchin. 5670/A.

WORBEY, W., Corporal, Bedfordshire Regiment.
He volunteered in September 1914, and in the following April, after the completion of his course of training, was drafted to the Western Front. While overseas he took part in many important engagements, including those at Ypres, Festubert, the Somme, Arras and Cambrai, and was wounded on three occasions. After his return to England he was demobilised in March 1919, and holds the 1914–15 Star, and the General Service and Victory Medals.
3, St. Andrew's Street, Hitchin. 5670/B.

WORBEY, W., 1st Air Mechanic, Royal Air Force.
He joined in March 1917, and shortly afterwards was sent to France. He was engaged on special duties with his Squadron at Dunkirk aerodrome. He did very good work as a fitter and repairer of aero-engines, and remained in this theatre of war until 1919, when he returned to England and was demobilised. He holds the General Service and Victory Medals.
20, Ratcliffe Road, Hitchin. 5300.

WORBOYS, A. E., Private, 3rd Bedfordshire Regt.
He volunteered in February 1915, and at the conclusion of his training was engaged with his Battalion at various stations on guard and other duties. He did very good work, but owing to medical unfitness was unable to secure his transfer overseas, and was subsequently invalided out of the Service in December 1915.
177, Park Street. Luton. 5720/C.

WORBOYS, A. R., Gunner, R.F.A.
He joined in September 1916, and after completing his training rendered valuable services with his Battery until drafted to India in September 1918. He served at various stations on special duties and returned to England after the cessation of hostilities. He was demobilised in May 1919, and holds the General Service and Victory Medals.
177, Park Street, Luton. 5720/A.

WORBOYS, C. (M.M.), Sergeant, 3rd Bedfordshire Regiment.
He volunteered in August 1914, and in the following year was sent to France. In this theatre of war he fought at Hill 60, and was mentioned in Despatches and awarded the Military Medal for conspicuous bravery and devotion to duty in the Field at Ypres on April 22nd, 1915. He was wounded during the fighting at Ypres and also on two other occasions on the Somme, and later fought in the Retreat and Advance of 1918. He was demobilised in September 1919, and holds the 1914–15 Star, and the General Service and Victory Medals.
177, Park Street, Luton. 5720/B.

WORBOYS, C. W., Private, 10th (Prince of Wales' Own Royal) Hussars.
A serving soldier, he was mobilised and drafted to France at the outbreak of war. He was actively engaged in the Retreat from Mons and during the fierce fighting in subsequent engagements. He was killed in action on October 17th, 1914, and was entitled to the Mons Star, and the General Service and Victory Medals.
12, Alfred Street, Luton. 5671/B.

WORBOYS, F. A., Sapper, Royal Engineers.
He volunteered in October 1914, and was later drafted to France. Whilst on the Western Front he was engaged on important duties with his unit during operations in the Bapaume, Arras and Ypres sectors. He returned to England after the cessation of hostilities, and was demobilised in June 1919, and holds the General Service and Victory Medals.
12, Alfred Street, Luton. 5671/A.

WORBOYS, F. G., Sergeant, R.A.M.C. and King's Royal Rifle Corps.
He volunteered in August 1914, and in the following year was drafted to the Dardanelles, where he was engaged at the landing at Suvla Bay and many other engagements until the evacuation of Gallipoli in December of that year. He was drafted to France in 1916, and fought at the Battles of Ypres, Arras, the Somme, Cambrai and St. Quentin. He was demobilised in November 1918, and holds the 1914–15 Star, and the General Service and Victory Medals.
177, Park Street, Luton. 5720/D.

WORBOYS, W. G., Private, Suffolk Regiment.
He joined in 1916, and in the same year was sent to Egypt. Whilst in this theatre of war he served at Ismailia and was engaged in the British Advance through Palestine and took part in the engagements at El Arish, Gaza, Haifa, Acre and Beyrout. He also saw service in France and returned to England after the Armistice, and was demobilised in September 1919. He holds the General Service and Victory Medals.
57, Brunswick Street, Luton. 5672.

WORKER, C., Rifleman, 12th Rifle Brigade.
He joined in January 1917, and after his training was drafted to France in January 1918. Whilst on the Western Front he took part in much heavy fighting and was seriously wounded on the Somme in March. He was removed to hospital in England, and in consequence of his injuries one of his legs had to be amputated. He was invalided out of the Service later in 1918, and holds the General Service and Victory Medals.
Silsoe Road, Barton 5667/C

WORKER, S., Bandsman, Leicestershire Regt.
He joined in March 1916, and in the following December was sent to France. In this theatre of war he served with his Battalion and was in action during the fighting on the Somme, and was constantly under shell-fire. He was killed in action in March 1918 on the Cambrai front, and was entitled to the General Service and Victory Medals.
Silsoe Road, Barton, Beds. 5667/B.

WORKER, S. G., Private, R.A.S.C. and Royal Welch Fusiliers.
He joined in November 1916, and at the conclusion of his training served with his unit at various stations on important transport duties, and was later employed on agricultural work. He rendered valuable services, but owing to medical unfitness was unable to secure his transfer overseas, and was demobilised in January 1919.
Sharpenhoe Road, Barton, Beds. 5668.

WORKER, T., Sergeant, 4th Bedfordshire Regt.
He volunteered in October 1915, and in the following July was sent to France. During his service on the Western Front he fought at the Battles of Ypres, the Somme, and was unfortunately killed in action at Arras on April 23rd, 1917. He was entitled to the General Service and Victory Medals.
Silsoe Road, Barton, Beds. 5667/A.

WORLAND, W. C., Private, R.A.S.C. (Rough Rider).
He volunteered in September 1914, and in the following month was drafted to France. In this theatre of war he was engaged on important duties at the Battles of the Marne, the Aisne, Ypres and the Somme. He was severely gassed and sent to England, and after receiving hospital treatment was discharged unfit for further service in June 1916. He holds the 1914 Star, and the General Service and Victory Medals.
62, Shott Lane, Letchworth. 5673

WORRALL, H. T., Private, 1st Bedfordshire Regiment.
He volunteered in September 1914, and was later sent to France. Whilst on the Western Front he served with his Battalion in many parts of the line and fought in several battles. He was unfortunately killed in action on April 28th, 1918, and was entitled to the 1914–15 Star, and the General Service and Victory Medals.
Lower Luton Road, Harpenden. 5674.

WORRELL, H., Private, 7th Essex Regiment; and Air Mechanic, Royal Air Force.
He volunteered in December 1915, and at the conclusion of his training was engaged with his unit on important duties, which called for a high degree of technical skill. He did excellent work at various aerodromes, but owing to medical unfitness was not sent overseas, and was demobilised in July 1919.
2, The Rookery, Watford. X5675.

WORSLEY, A. F. (Miss), Special War Worker.
During the war, for a period of four years, this lady was engaged on work of National importance at the Admiralty Inspection Buildings, Luton. Her duties, which were in connection with the output of munitions, were carried out in a highly satisfactory manner.
113, Oak Road, Luton. 5676/C.

WORSLEY, E. M. (Miss), Special War Worker.
This lady offered her services and was engaged for four years during the war on important work at the Admiralty Inspection Buildings, Bute Street, Luton. She did very good work in the making of munitions and carried out her duties in a very efficient manner.
113, Oak Road, Luton. 5676/C.

WORSLEY, L. A., Gunner, R.F.A.
He volunteered at the outbreak of hostilities, and in July 1915 was drafted to France, where he was engaged in the fighting at the Battles of the Somme, Vimy Ridge, Messines Ridge, Ypres, and was wounded on July 22nd, 1917. On recovery he rejoined his Battery and served at St. Quentin, Villers-Bretonneux and Le Cateau during the closing stages of the war. He was demobilised in March 1919, and holds the 1914–15 Star, and the General Service and Victory Medals.
113, Oak Road, Luton. 5676/A.

WORSOP, F., Private, R.A.S.C. (M.T.)
He joined in April 1916, and at the conclusion of his training was engaged on special duties with his unit at various stations. He did excellent work as a motor engine fitter, but owing to medical unfitness was unsuccessful in obtaining his transfer overseas before hostilities ceased, and was still serving in 1920.
5, Payne's Park, Hitchin. 5663/B.

WRAIGHT, G. R., Private, R.A.O.C.
Volunteering in October 1915, he embarked for the Western Front in the following January. Here he saw much service in the forward areas during the Battles of Ypres, Arras, Cambrai, the Somme, St. Quentin and in the German Offensive and subsequent Allied Advance of 1918. He was demobilised in September 1919, and holds the General Service and Victory Medals.
128, Estcourt Road, Watford. X5677.

WRAY, F., Private, Bedfordshire Regiment.
He joined in 1917, and proceeded overseas later in the same year. During his service on the Western Front he fought in the Battles of Ypres, Cambrai, the Somme, Neuve Chapelle, and in the Retreat and Advance of 1918, and was wounded. After the Armistice he was sent into Germany with the Army of Occupation and served on the Rhine. He returned to England in 1920, and was demobilised in April of that year, and holds the General Service and Victory Medals.
Preston, Herts. 5678/B.

WRAY, R., Private, Bedfordshire Regiment.
Volunteering in August 1914, he proceeded to France in the following year, and was in action in many important battles, including those of Festubert, Arras, Albert, Vimy Ridge, and fought throughout the Retreat and Advance of 1918. During his service overseas he was wounded three times, and returning to England, was demobilised in December 1919. He holds the 1914–15 Star, and the General Service and Victory Medals.
Preston, Herts. 5678/A.

WRIGHT, A., Air Mechnaic, Royal Air Force.
He joined in June 1918, and was sent to France later in the same year and served at various aerodromes with the Independent Air Force, employed on testing aero-engines, work which demanded a high degree of technical knowledge. He rendered valuable services throughout, and was demobilised in January 1919, and holds the General Service and Victory Medals.
18, Newcombe Road, Luton. 5679.

WRIGHT, A., Driver, R.A.S.C.
Volunteering in December 1914, he was drafted to France in the following month and was present at the Battles of Loos and Vimy Ridge and various other engagements. He was invalided to England in 1916 with an injured foot, and on recovery was transferred to the North Staffordshire Regiment. He returned to France and fought at the Somme, Ypres, Cambrai, and was wounded at Bullecourt. He later rejoined his unit and was taken prisoner on March 21st, 1918, during the German Offensive. Repatriated, he was demobilised in August 1919, and holds the 1914–15 Star, and the General Service and Victory Medals.
The Hill, Wheathampstead. 5680.

WRIGHT, A., Sergeant, 2nd Suffolk Regiment.
A serving soldier, he was mobilised and sent to the Western Front at the outbreak of hostilities, and fought in the Retreat from Mons and at the Battles of Arras, Ypres, the Somme and in many other important engagements during the Retreat and Advance of 1918, and was wounded four times. He was still serving in 1920, and holds the Mons Star, and the General Service and Victory Medals.
The Barracks, Bury St. Edmund's. 5681.

WRIGHT, A., Air Mechanic, Royal Air Force.
He joined in July 1916, and was sent to France in the following month and served at various aerodromes on the Somme, Cambrai and Ypres fronts, engaged on important duties, fitting and testing aero-engines. He returned to England in January 1918, and served at many home stations until demobilised in March 1919, and holds the General Service and Victory Medals.
4, George Street, Markyate. 5682.

WRIGHT, A. C., Private, 3rd, 5th and 8th Bedfordshire Regiment.
Joining in June 1916, he was sent to France in the same year and saw much service in various parts of the line. He fought in many important engagements, including those at Cambrai, the Somme, and was gassed and wounded in action at Loos. He also fought in the Retreat and Advance of 1918, and was demobilised in February 1919, and holds the General Service and Victory Medals.
86, High Street, Markyate. 5684.

WRIGHT, A. C., Sapper, Royal Engineers.
He volunteered in August 1914, and was sent to the Dardanelles in the following April, and served at the first landing and in many engagements until the Evacuation of the Peninsula. He was drafted to France in 1917, and rendered valuable services wiring, trench-digging and maintaining the lines of communication on the Arras and Ypres fronts and throughout the Retreat and Advance of 1918. He was demobilised in May 1919, and holds the 1914–15 Star, and the General Service and Victory Medals.
36, St. Mary's Street, Dunstable. 5685.

WRIGHT, A. C., Sapper, Royal Engineers.
Volunteering in July 1915, he served in Ireland for a time, and later proceeded to France, where he served in the forward areas on important duties, whilst the Battles of Ypres, Cambrai and the Somme were in progress. He did valuable work during the German Offensive and Allied Advance in 1918, and was gassed. He was demobilised in January 1919, and holds the General Service and Victory Medals.
52, Salisbury Road, Luton. 5686.

WRIGHT, A. E., Rifleman, K.R.R.C.
He volunteered in August 1915, and was drafted to the Western Front later in the same year. In this theatre of war he fought at the Battles of Arras, Ypres, Cambrai, the Somme, Passchendaele and in the Retreat and Advance of 1918. He was demobilised in February 1919, and holds the 1914–15 Star, and the General Service and Victory Medals.
54, Brighton Road, Watford. X5687.

WRIGHT, A. E., Private, King's Own Scottish Borderers.
Volunteering in 1914, he completed his training, and after serving at various stations proceeded to France in 1916. He fought in many important engagements, including those at Ypres, Arras, the Somme and in the German Offensive and Allied Advance of 1918. He was demobilised in February 1919, and holds the General Service and Victory Medals. 110, Fishpool Street, St. Albans. X5688.

WRIGHT, A. F., 1st Air Mechanic, Royal Air Force (late Royal Naval Air Service).
Joining in March 1917, he completed his training and served at various aerodromes on the South Coast engaged on important duties, which called for a high degree of technical knowledge and skill. He was unsuccessful in obtaining his transfer overseas prior to the cessation of hostilities, but rendered valuable services until demobilised in March 1919.
11, Luton Road, Markyate. 5689/A.

WRIGHT, A. J., Telegraphist, Royal Navy.
He joined the Service in 1917, and was posted to H.M.S. "Valiant," which vessel was engaged on important patrol duties in the North and Baltic Seas until the cessation of hostilities. His ship frequently passed through mine-infested areas in the discharge of her duties, and did good work throughout. He was discharged in December 1919, and holds the General Service and Victory Medals.
18, Cross Street, Watford X5691/C.

WRIGHT, A. J., Private, 8th Bedfordshire Regt.
He joined in May 1916, and proceeded overseas in the following January. During his service on the Western Front he served with his Battalion in various sectors and fought in many important engagements. He made the supreme sacrifice, being killed in action on April 15th, 1917, and was entitled to the General Service and Victory Medals.
6, Clarendon Road, Luton. 5690.

WRIGHT, B., Bugler, King's Own Scottish Borderers.

Volunteering in November 1915, he completed his training and served at various depôts engaged on guard and other important duties. He was unsuccessful in obtaining his transfer overseas before hostilities ceased, but did excellent work until demobilised in January 1919.
9, Pondwick's Road, Luton. 5692/A.

WRIGHT, B. (M.M.), Q.M.S., Grenadier Guards.

A serving soldier, he was sent to France at the commencement of hostilities and fought in the Retreat from Mons and in many other important engagements, including those at Ypres, Cambrai and in the Retreat and Advance of 1918. He was awarded the Military Medal for conspicuous gallantry and devotion to duty in the Field, and was twice wounded. He was demobilised in March 1919, and holds the Mons Star, and the General Service and Victory Medals.
46, Arthur Road, Fleetville, St. Albans. X5693.

WRIGHT, C., Trooper, Royal Buckinghamshire Hussars.

Mobilised in August 1914, he was drafted to the Egyptian Expeditionary Force in the following March and served throughout the Advance through Sinai and Palestine into Syria, fighting in many important engagements, including those at Gaza, and was wounded. He returned to England and was demobilised in July 1919, and holds the 1914-15 Star and the General Service and Victory Medals.
76, Old Road, Linslade. 5694/A.

WRIGHT, E. E., Trooper, Warwickshire Hussars.

He volunteered in 1915, and was sent to the Western Front in the following year. In this theatre of war he saw much service in various parts of the line, and fought at the Battles of Ypres and Arras and in the German Offensive and subsequent Allied Advance of 1918, and was wounded. He was demobilised in 1919, and holds the General Service and Victory Medals.
40, Puller Road, Boxmoor. X5695.

WRIGHT, E. J., Sergeant, Royal Field Artillery.

He joined in February 1916, and was sent to Mesopotamia in the following January, and fought in many engagements and was wounded in December 1917. Later he proceeded to India and served at various garrison towns engaged on guard and other important duties. He returned to England and was demobilised in April 1920, and holds the General Service and Victory Medals.
31, Sutton Road, Watford. X5696.

WRIGHT, F., Private, Royal Sussex Regiment.

He joined in 1917, and on completion of his training was drafted to India later in the same year, and served with his Regiment at various stations engaged on guard and other important duties. He did very good work and was still serving there in 1920.
14, Birds Hill, Letchworth. 5697.

WRIGHT, F., Pte., Loyal North Lancashire Regt.

He joined in April 1916, and proceeded overseas in the following year. During his service in France he was engaged in heavy fighting in the Battles of Givenchy and Arras, and in the German Offensive and Allied Advance of 1918. After the cessation of hostilities he was sent into Germany with the Army of Occupation and served on the Rhine until he returned to England and was demobilised in September 1919. He holds the General Service and Victory Medals.
112, Wenlock Street, Luton. 1723/A.

WRIGHT, F., Private, 1st Bedfordshire Regt.

He volunteered in March 1915, and embarked for the Western Front later in the same year. Here he was in action in many parts of the line and fought at the Battles of Arras, Ypres, the Somme, and throughout the Retreat and Advance of 1918, and was wounded three times. He was demobilised in 1919, and holds the 1914-15 Star, and the General Service and Victory Medals.
314, High Street North, Dunstable. 5698.

WRIGHT, F. A., Driver, Royal Horse Artillery.

He volunteered in August 1914, and in September of the same year was drafted to the Western Front, where he served in various sectors and fought at the Battles of Ypres, the Somme, Arras and Cambrai and in the Retreat and Advance of 1918. He was demobilised in March 1919, and holds the 1914 Star, and the General Service and Victory Medals.
26, Regent Street, Leighton Buzzard. 1590/A.

WRIGHT, G., Corporal, Royal Field Artillery.

He enlisted in August 1900, and was mobilised and drafted to France on the outbreak of war. He fought in the Retreat from Mons and in the Battles of the Aisne, the Marne, Ypres, the Somme and throughout the German Offensive and subsequent Allied Advance of 1918. He was discharged in April 1919, and holds the Mons Star, and the General Service and Victory Medals.
38a, Guildford Street, Luton. 5699.

WRIGHT, G., Gunner, Royal Garrison Artillery.

He joined in 1916, and was sent to the Western Front later in the same year. Here he saw much service and fought in many important engagements, including those of Cambrai, Arras and the Somme, and was in action in the Retreat and Advance of 1918. After the Armistice he proceeded into Germany with the Army of Occupation and served there for a time. He returned to England in 1919, and was demobilised in December of that year, and holds the General Service and Victory Medals.
New Marford, Wheathampstead. 5700

WRIGHT, H., Private, Bedfordshire Regiment.

Volunteering in August 1914, he proceeded overseas in the following June. During his service on the Western Front he was engaged in heavy fighting in the Battles of Loos, the Somme, Vimy Ridge, Arras, Cambrai, Ypres and during the Retreat and Advance of 1918. He was demobilised in March 1919, and holds the 1914-15 Star, and the General Service and Victory Medals.
21, Albert Street, Markyate. 5701.

WRIGHT, H. W., Private, 1st Bedfordshire Regt.

He volunteered in August 1914, and on completion of his training served with the Army in France in 1916. Here he fought at Loos, St. Eloi and the Somme, and was wounded in 1917 and returned to England. On recovery he was transferred to the Labour Corps, and with this unit rendered excellent services on agricultural work until demobilised in February 1919. He holds the General Service and Victory Medals. High Street, Lidlington, Beds. Z5703.

WRIGHT, I. J., Private, 1st Norfolk Regiment.

Volunteering in August 1914, he was later drafted to the Western Front, where he saw much service. He fought in many important battles, including those of Ypres, Arras and Passchendaele, and was killed in action at Roclincourt on June 6th, 1916. He was entitled to the 1914-15 Star, and the General Service and Victory Medals.
18, Cherry Bounce, Hemel Hempstead. X3077/B.

WRIGHT, J., Private, Bedfordshire Regiment.

He volunteered in January 1915, and proceeded overseas in the following August. Serving in Egypt he fought in the Battle of Gaza and other important engagements during the British Advance through Palestine, and was invalided home, owing to illness, in August 1917. He received medical treatment, and after recovery served at home until demobilised in November 1919. He holds the General Service and Victory Medals.
76, Old Road, Linslade, Bucks. 5694/B.

WRIGHT, J., Private, R.A.S.C. (M.T.)

Volunteering in February 1915, he embarked for the Western Front in the same year, and was engaged on important duties in various sectors. He did excellent work in connection with the transport of ammunition and supplies to the forward areas, whilst heavy fighting was in progress. Owing to ill-health he was invalided to hospital and subsequently died in December 1918, and was entitled to the 1914-15 Star, and the General Service and Victory Medals.
18, Cross Street, Watford. X5691/A.

WRIGHT, J. G., Private, 1st Bedfordshire Regt.

Volunteering in February 1915, he was later drafted to the Western Front. Whilst in this theatre of war he was in action at Delville Wood, Arras and Cambrai and was wounded on the Somme on July 27th, 1916. He was sent home to hospital, and after receiving medical treatment was invalided out of the Service in September 1917, and holds the General Service and Victory Medals.
48, Bunyan Road, Hitchin. 5704.

WRIGHT, J. H., Private, 11th and 12th Middlesex Regiment.

He volunteered in March 1915, and drafted to France in the same year was engaged in heavy fighting in the Somme and Bapaume sectors. He was unfortunately killed in action on November 4th, 1917, and was entitled to the 1914-15 Star, and the General Service and Victory Medals.
11, Luton Road, Markyate. 5689/B.

WRIGHT, J. H., Driver, R.E. (486th Field Coy.)

He volunteered in September 1914, and was engaged on important duties with his unit until sent overseas in February 1916. Serving in Egypt, he took part in the Advance through Palestine, and was present at the Battles of Gaza and Jericho and the occupation of Jaffa and Jerusalem. He returned to England for demobilisation in July 1919, and holds the General Service and Victory Medals.
46, Vernon Road, Luton. 5705.

WRIGHT, L., Corporal, Bedfordshire Regiment.
He was mobilised when war broke out and drafted to France
shortly afterwards. Whilst on the Western Front he was
in action during the Retreat from Mons, and in the Battles of
the Somme, Arras, Ypres, Cambrai and Armentiéres, and was
wounded and gassed. He was demobilised in March 1919,
and holds the Mons Star, and the General Service and Victory
Medals.
The Hill, Wheathampstead. 5706.

**WRIGHT, P. P., Private, Hertfordshire Regt.;
and Air Mechanic, Royal Air Force.**
He joined the Hertfordshire Regiment in July 1916, and in
the following November embarked for France. During his
service overseas he fought in the Battles of the Somme,
the Marne, Arras, Amiens and Cambrai, and was wounded.
Transferred to the Royal Air Force, he did good work with his
Squadron until the end of hostilities. He was demobilised
in January 1919, and holds the General Service and Victory
Medals.
71, Highbury Road, Luton. 5707.

WRIGHT, P. R., Chief Petty Officer, Royal Navy.
He was serving in the Royal Navy when war was declared,
and aboard H.M.S. "Scorpion" took part in the naval
operations at the Dardanelles and assisted in the landing of
troops on the Peninsula. Taken ill whilst on service he
died in November 1915, and was entitled to the 1914-15
Star, and the General Service and Victory Medals.
18, Cross Street, Watford. X5691/B.

WRIGHT, R. C., Private, East Surrey Regiment.
He volunteered in August 1914, and in the following year
embarked for the Western Front. Whilst overseas he fought
in several important engagements, including those at Arras
and Ypres, and was wounded. Rejoining his unit on recovery,
he was killed in action at Loos on September 25th, 1915,
and was entitled to the 1914-15 Star, and the General Service
and Victory Medals.
18, Cherry Bounce, Hemel Hempstead. X3677/C.

WRIGHT, S., Private, R.A.S.C. (M.T.)
He joined in April 1916, and two months later was drafted
overseas. Serving in Mesopotamia he was engaged on
important duties in connection with the transport of ammunition and supplies to the forward areas. Owing to illness
he was removed to hospital at Amara, where he died on
November 7th, 1918, and was entitled to the General Service
and Victory Medals.
26, Curzon Road, Luton. 5708.

WRIGHT, T. D., Bombardier, R.F.A.
He volunteered in April 1915, and after completing his training
served with his unit at various depôts on special duties. He
did valuable work, breaking in and training horses for active
service, but was unable to obtain a transfer overseas before
hostilities ceased. He was demobilised in January 1919.
73, Beech Road, Luton. 5709.

WRIGHT, W., Private, R.A.S.C.
Volunteering in October 1914, he was sent to France in the
following July and served there for four years. During this
period he was engaged on important duties in connection
with the transport of ammunition and supplies to the front
line during the Battles of Arras, Ypres, Cambrai and the
Somme. He holds the 1914-15 Star, and the General Service
and Victory Medals, and was discharged on account of service
in July 1919.
33, Cannon Road, Watford. X5710.

WRIGHT, W., Private (Gunner), Tank Corps.
Volunteering in January 1915, he completed his training and
was engaged on special work at home until sent to the
Western Front in December 1917. He served in various
sectors in this theatre of war, and was in action at Arras,
Ypres, Messines and other important engagements. He
returned home for demobilisation in January 1919, and
holds the General Service and Victory Medals.
13, Marsh Road, Leagrave. 5711.

WRIGHT, W., Sapper, Royal Engineers.
He volunteered in May 1915, and in the same year proceeded
to the Western Front. Whilst in this theatre of war he
was engaged on important duties in connection with operations at Hill 60, Givenchy, Ypres, Cambrai and on the
Somme. He was demobilised in May 1919, and holds the
1914-15 Star, and the General Service and Victory Medals.
9, Pondwick's Road, Luton. 5692/B.

**WRIGHT, W. H., Private, Queen's (Royal West
Surrey Regiment) and Machine Gun Corps.**
He joined in March 1917, and shortly afterwards embarked
for the Western Front. During his service overseas he was
in action at the Somme and in the Battles of Arras and Ypres,
and was gassed. He holds the General Service and Victory
Medals, and was demobilised in June 1919.
6, Cross Street North, St. Albans. X5712.

WRIGHT, W. T., Private, 1st Middlesex Regiment
Joining in March 1916, he was sent to France four months
later, and was engaged with his Battalion in heavy fighting
on the Somme. He was unfortunately killed in action on
August 28th, 1916, and was entitled to the General Service
and Victory Medals.
99, Sutton Road, Watford. X5714

**WRIGHTSON, F. V., Private, Queen's (Royal
West Surrey Regiment).**
He joined in May 1917, and in the same year embarked for
the Western Front. In the course of his service overseas
he fought in several important engagements, including the
Battles of the Somme and Arras. He was killed in action
in October 1918, and was entitled to the General Service and
Victory Medals.
Waller Avenue, Leagrave. 5715.

WYATT, A. L., L/Corporal, Royal Engineers.
A serving soldier, having enlisted in October 1911, he was
mobilised on the outbreak of war, and almost immediately
drafted to France. He served during the Retreat from
Mons and in the Battles of Arras, Ypres, Neuve Chapelle,
Cambrai and Armentières, and was wounded at Loos on
September 26th, 1915, and was gassed in April 1918. Returning home in July 1918 he served at various stations until
demobilised in February 1919, and holds the Mons Star,
and the General Service and Victory Medals.
20, St. Andrew's Street, Leighton Buzzard. 5716.

WYATT, C. H., Driver, Royal Field Artillery.
He volunteered in February 1915, and in the following April
proceeded to France. During his service on the Western
Front he was engaged in heavy fighting at St. Eloi and Vimy
Ridge. As he was under age for service overseas he was sent
home in August 1916, and served with his unit in England
and Ireland until demobilised in March 1919. He holds
the General Service and Victory Medals.
36, Bailey Street, Luton. 5717.

WYATT, F. G., Corporal, R.A.S.C. (M.T.)
A serving solider, he was mobilised on the outbreak of hostilities and was soon afterwards drafted to the Western Front.
He was engaged on important transport duties during the
early fighting in France, and, attached to the 8th Siege Battery,
Royal Garrison Artillery, rendered valuable services in
numerous engagements until the end of the war. He holds
the Mons Star, and the General Service and Victory Medals,
and was demobilised in April 1919.
10, Neal Street, Watford. X5718.

Y

YARROW, C. J., Sapper (Signaller), R.E.
He volunteered in October 1915, and, drafted to France in
the following year, was engaged on the lines of communication
in the forward areas. He was present at several engagements,
including those on the Ancre and at Cambrai, and suffered
from shell-shock. He was mentioned in Despatches for
consistent good work in the Field in 1918, and holds the
General Service and Victory Medals. He was demobilised
in April 1919.
52, Westbourne Road, Luton. 5721.

YATES, E., Gunner, Royal Field Artillery.
A serving soldier, he was mobilised on the declaration of
war, and almost immediately sent to the Western Front.
He was engaged in severe fighting during the Retreat from
Mons and at the Battle of Ypres, and was wounded at Loos on
September 17th, 1915. Returning to the Field on recovery,
he fought in the Battles of the Somme, Vimy Ridge, Passchendaele, Cambrai and Messines. He was demobilised in May
1919, and holds the Mons Star, and the General Service and
Victory Medals.
13, Houghton Road, Dunstable. 5722.

YATES, E. H., Gunner, Royal Field Artillery.
Volunteering in March 1915, he proceeded overseas in the
following July and served on the Western Front for upwards
of four years. During this period he was in action at Loos,
Vimy Ridge, Cambrai, Arras, Ypres, the Somme and during
the Retreat of 1918. Demobilised in March 1919, he holds
the 1914-15 Star, and the General Service and Victory
Medals.
13, Houghton Road, Dunstable. 5723/A.

**YATES, F. A., L/Corporal, 1st Bedfordshire
Regiment.**
He joined in May 1916, and in the same year embarked for
France. Whilst in this theatre of war he fought in several
important engagements, including those at Arras, Ypres,
Cambrai and on the Somme, and was wounded. He was
sent to hospital at Rouen, and after receiving medical treat-
ment served on the Italian front until the end of hostilities.
He was demobilised in January 1919, and holds the General
Service and Victory Medals.
11, Husborne Crawley, Aspley Guise. Z5724

YATES, W. T., Private, Labour Corps.
He volunteered in March 1915, and in the following August was sent to the Western Front, where he was engaged on important duties in the forward areas. He was present at several engagements, including those on the Somme, at Ypres and Cambrai, and returned to England on the conclusion of hostilities. In 1920 he was still serving, and holds the 1914-15 Star, and the General Service and Victory Medals.
13, Houghton Road, Dunstable.   5723/B.

YELLOP, C., A.B., Royal Navy.
Volunteering in August 1914, he was posted to H.M.S. "Hawkins," and served aboard that vessel throughout the war. His ship was engaged on important duties in the North Sea with the Grand Fleet and off the coasts of France, and was in action in the Battle of Jutland and in the raid on Zeebrugge. He holds the 1914-15 Star, and the General Service and Victory Medals, and in 1920 was serving in China.
38, Longmire Road, St. Albans.   1465/A.

YELLOP, J., Gunner, Royal Field Artillery.
He volunteered in August 1914, and later embarked for the Western Front. During his service in this theatre of war, where he fought in several engagements, including the Battles of Arras, Ypres, and Cambrai, he was wounded. He was demobilised in February 1919, and holds the General Service and Victory Medals.
38, Longmire Road, St. Albans.   1465/C.

YELLOP, J. C, Private, Queen's (Royal West Surrey Regiment).
Volunteering in August 1914, he proceeded overseas in the following year and served on the Western Front throughout the war. He took part in many important engagements and suffered from shell-shock. In May 1919 he was sent to Russia, and was engaged on important duties until his return home for demobilisation later in 1919. He holds the 1914-15 Star, and the General Service and Victory Medals.
36, Spencer Street, St. Albans.   X5725.

YERRILL, J., Private, 1st Bedfordshire Regt.
Joining in May 1916, in the following month he embarked for France and was wounded in action on the Somme in September 1916. He was invalided home and on recovery returned to the Western Front in July 1917, and was gassed at Passchendaele in November of that year, he afterwards fought at Albert, Cambrai and in other concluding engagements of the war. He holds the General Service and Victory Medals, and was demobilised in March 1919.
50, Sun Street, Biggleswade.   Z5727.

YERRILL, J., Private, Suffolk Regiment.
He joined in July 1916, and in the same year was drafted to the Western Front, in several sectors of which he was engaged in much heavy fighting. He was unfortunately killed in action on April 29th, 1917, and was entitled to the General Service and Victory Medals.
36, Langley Road, Watford.   X5726.

YERRILL, W. T., Private, Hertfordshire and Lincolnshire Regiments.
Volunteering in December 1914, he was sent to France in the following year. Whilst on the Western Front he fought in many important engagements, including the Battles of Ypres and the Somme, and was wounded and gassed. He was invalided home and ultimately discharged as medically unfit for further service in December 1917. He holds the 1914-15 Star, and the General Service and Victory Medals.
24, Stanmore Road, Watford.   5728.

YIRRELL, B., Private, Oxfordshire and Buckinghamshire Light Infantry.
He volunteered in February 1916, and in the same year proceeded to the Western Front. He fought in several important operations and, wounded on the Somme, was sent to hospital in England. On recovery he was drafted to Egypt and took part in the Battle of Gaza and the capture of Jerusalem during the British Advance through Palestine. Returning home for demobilisation in March 1919, he holds the General Service and Victory Medals.
"Brooklyns," Rothschild Road, Wing, Leighton Buzzard. 5729.

YIRRELL, E., Private, 9th King's Own (Yorkshire Light Infantry).
He joined in September 1916, and in the following January was drafted overseas. Serving on the Western Front he fought in the Battles of Ypres, Passchendaele, Maubeuge and the Somme, and was wounded at Epéhy on March 21st, 1918, and near Cambrai in the following October. He was demobilised in February 1919, and holds the General Service and Victory Medals.
35, Soulbury Road, Linslade, Bucks.   5730.

YIRRELL, R., Gunner, Royal Field Artillery.
He volunteered in August 1914, and was engaged on important duties with his Battery until sent to France in 1916. Whilst overseas he was in action on the Somme, at Albert and Passchendaele, and was wounded and buried by a shell explosion during the Battle of the Somme. He holds the General Service and Victory Medals, and was demobilised in 1919.
12, Lower Paxton Road, St. Albans.   X5732.

YORK, A. J., Private, Bedfordshire Regiment.
Volunteering in September 1914, he embarked for the Western Front in the following year. He served with his Battalion in various sectors and was engaged in severe fighting at the Battles of the Somme, Arras, Ypres and Cambrai, and was wounded and gassed. Rejoining his unit on recovery he fought in other operations until the end of hostilities. He was demobilised in March 1919, and holds the 1914-15 Star, and the General Service and Victory Medals
63, St. John's Street, Biggleswade.   Z5733/A.

YORK, C. H., Private, 2nd Lancashire Fusiliers.
A serving soldier, he was mobilised on the outbreak of war, and shortly afterwards sent to France. There he fought during the Retreat from Mons, and in the Battles of the Marne and the Aisne, and was severely wounded at Ypres on September 23rd, 1915. Sent home in consequence of his wounds he received hospital treatment, and was invalided out of the Service in February 1916, and holds the Mons Star, and the General Service and Victory Medals.
2, Dumfries Street, Luton.   5012/E—5013/E.

YORK, H. N. (Mrs.), Special War Worker.
Volunteering for work of National importance during the war, this lady was engaged in a T.N.T. Filling Factory for two years. Her work, which was in connection with pellet making and bomb filling, was of a highly dangerous character, and was carried out in a thoroughly capable and efficient manner. 2, Dumfries Street, Luton.   5012/D—5013/D.

YORK, W., Corporal, 5th Royal Scots Fusiliers.
Joining in August 1916, after completing his training he was engaged on important guard duties with his unit. He rendered valuable services, but was not sent overseas owing to medical unfitness for general service, and was demobilised in March 1919.
Caddington, near Luton.   5734/B.

YORK, W H., C.S.M., Canadian Engineers.
He joined in 1916, and on the completion of his training proceeded to Siberia, where he was engaged on important duties with his unit. He also acted as an Instructor and rendered valuable services in that capacity until his return to England for demobilisation in June 1919. He holds the General Service and Victory Medals.
63, St. John's Street, Biggleswade.   Z5733/B.

YOUNG, A., Corporal, Suffolk Regiment
He joined in 1917, and in the same year proceeded overseas. He served in various sectors of the Western Front, and was in action on the Somme and in the Battle of Cambrai. After the Armistice he was sent with the Army of Occupation into Germany and was stationed at Cologne. Returning to England he was demobilised in September 1919, and holds the General Service and Victory Medals.
103, Windmill Road, Luton.   5735/A.

YOUNG, A., Private, 1/5th Bedfordshire Regt.
Volunteering in August 1914, he served at various stations, and was later transferred to the Tank Corps, with which unit he was drafted to France in 1916, with the first Battalion of Tanks to proceed overseas. Here he fought in many important engagements, including those at Ypres, Arras, Passchendaele, the Somme and in the Retreat and Advance of 1918, and was wounded. He was demobilised in March 1919, and holds the 1914-15 Star, and the General Service and Victory Medals.
103, Windmill Road, Luton.   5735/B.

YOUNG, A., L/Corporal, Royal Engineers.
He volunteered in September 1914, and in the following January was sent to France. Whilst on the Western Front he was engaged on important duties with his unit in the Ypres and Somme sectors, and was severely gassed at Hill 60 in August 1917. He was invalided home and subsequently discharged unfit for further service in March 1918. He holds the 1914-15 Star, and the General Service and Victory Medals.
5, Sutton Road, Watford.   X5736.

YOUNG, D., Private, 19th London Regiment.
A serving soldier, he was mobilised and drafted to France at the outbreak of war. Whilst on the Western Front he fought in the Retreat from Mons and the subsequent engagements at Arras, Ypres, Hill 60, and Cambrai, and was twice wounded. He was demobilised in February 1919, and holds the Mons Star, and the General Service and Victory Medals.
64, Clifford Street, Watford.   X5737.

YOUNG, F., Driver, Royal Engineers (E.A.)

He volunteered in January 1915, and in December of that year was sent to Egypt. He served for a time at Ismailia in the Canal zone, and was afterwards engaged on important duties, whilst operations were in progress at Gaza, Mejdel, Haifa, Acre and Beyrout. Owing to ill-health he was sent to England, and after receiving hospital treatment was invalided out of the Service in October 1918. He holds the 1914-15 Star, and the General Service and Victory Medals.
34, Spring Place, Luton. 5738.

YOUNG, F. J. (M.M.), Private, Bedfordshire Regiment, 5th Royal Irish Regiment and Royal Irish Fusiliers.

He volunteered in September 1914, and in February of the following year was sent to France. He fought at Hill 60, and was wounded in April 1915. In the following November he was drafted to Salonika, where he was in action until August 1917, and was then drafted to Egypt. He took part in the Advance through Palestine and fought at Gaza, Mejdel, Haifa and Jerusalem, and was awarded the Military Medal for devotion to duty in the Field in January 1918. He was severely wounded and subsequently succumbed to his injuries on August 30th, 1918. He was entitled to the 1914-15 Star, and the General Service and Victory Medals.
The Hill, Welwyn. 5739.

YOUNG, F. J., Private, R.A.O.C.

He volunteered in August 1914, and in the following January was drafted to France. During his service on the Western Front he was engaged on special duties in the stores department of his unit, and did very good work. He was demobilised in May 1919, and holds the 1914-15 Star, and the General Service and Victory Medals.
10, Park Gate Road, Callowland, Watford. X5740.

YOUNG, F. R., Trooper, Bedfordshire Lancers.

He volunteered in February 1916, and in the following October was sent overseas. Whilst on the Western Front he fought at Arras, Vimy Ridge, Oppy Wood, Cambrai, Amiens and in the Retreat and Advance of 1918. He was demobilised in January 1919, and holds the General Service and Victory Medals.
Hall End, Maulden, Ampthill. 5741.

YOUNG, G., Corporal, Queen's (Royal West Surrey Regiment).

He joined in May 1916, and in the same year was drafted to France. He served on the Western Front, and was engaged in the fighting on the Somme, at Arras and Cambrai, and was wounded at Bullecourt. He was demobilised in November 1918, and holds the General Service and Victory Medals.
50, Highbury Road, Luton. 5742.

YOUNG, G. F., Private, R.A.V.C.

He joined in September 1916, and was shortly afterwards sent to France. He was employed with his unit on special duties in the Loos, Lille and Cambrai sectors, and was frequently under shell-fire. He was demobilised in May 1919, and holds the General Service and Victory Medals.
72, Boyle Street, Luton. 5743.

YOUNG, G. F., Private, R.A.V.C.

He volunteered in January 1916, and in May of the following year proceeded to France. During his service on the Western Front he served on important duties in attending to sick and wounded horses, and did good work. Owing to ill-health he was invalided home in May 1918, and was demobilised in May 1919. He holds the General Service and Victory Medals.
72, Boyle Street, Luton. 5744.

YOUNG, G. T., A/Sergeant, Machine Gun Corps and Royal Warwickshire Regiment.

He joined in May 1917, and 12 months later was sent to France. He fought at the Battles of the Marne and Cambrai, and was gassed at Beaumont-Hamel in June 1918. On recovery he rejoined his Battalion, and after the cessation of hostilities served with the Army of Occupation on the Rhine. He was demobilised in December 1919, and holds the General Service and Victory Medals.
Moat Cottage, Waterside, King's Langley. X5745.

YOUNG, H., Private, 1/5th Bedfordshire Regt.

He volunteered at the outbreak of war, and in August 1915 was sent to the Dardanelles. He fought at the landing at Suvla Bay and many subsequent engagements until the evacuation of Gallipoli. He afterwards served in the Canal zone and later proceeded to Egypt, where he took part in the fighting at Gaza, Mejdel, Haifa and Beyrout, and was invalided to hospital suffering from malaria. He was demobilised in October 1919, and holds the 1914-15 Star, and the General Service and Victory Medals.
103, Windmill Road, Luton. 5735/C.

YOUNG, H., 1st Class Stoker, Royal Navy.

He was mobilised at the outbreak of hostilities, and aboard H.M.S. "Cæsar" served on important transport duties conveying troops and supplies to the Western Front and other theatres of war. He also served in the "Aquitania" bringing American troops from U.S.A. to France. He was demobilised in January 1919, and holds the 1914-15 Star, and the General Service and Victory Medals
24, Husbourne Crawley, Beds. Z1107/B.

YOUNG, H. D., Sapper, Royal Engineers.

He joined in May 1916, and in the following January was drafted to France. Whilst on the Western Front he was engaged on important duties with his unit in the Ypres and Arras sectors, and was constantly under shell-fire. He was invalided home in June 1917, and on recovery served on home duties until demobilised in October 1919. He holds the General Service and Victory Medals.
21, Sotheron Road, Watford. X4481/B.

YOUNG, H. V., Private, Norfolk Regiment.

He joined in May 1918, and at the conclusion of his training was drafted to France. During his service on the Western Front he fought in many battles, including those of Ypres and Cambrai, and in the Retreat and Advance of 1918. He was demobilised in September 1919, and holds the General Service and Victory Medals.
138, Baker Street, Luton. 5746/B.

YOUNG, M. (Mrs.), Worker, Q.M.A.A.C.

She joined in May 1917, and proceeded overseas in the following month. During her service in France she rendered valuable services engaged on special clerical duties attached to the Royal Army Pay Corps. She returned to England and was demobilised in April 1919, and holds the General Service and Victory Medals.
35, Turners Road, Luton. 5747/A.

YOUNG, P. C., Private, R.A.M.C.

He joined in July 1918, and at the conclusion of his training served on important duties with his unit. He did much good work, but was unable to secure his transfer overseas until after the signing of the Armistice. He was then sent to Germany with the Army of Occupation, and was stationed at Cologne. He was still serving in 1920.
138, Baker Street, Luton. 5746/A.

YOUNG, R. W., Private, Labour Corps.

He joined in November 1917, and after training was drafted to France in the following March. He served in the forward areas on important duties in engagements at the Somme, the Marne, Ypres, Arras and Cambrai, during the German Offensive and Allied Advance of 1918, and rendered excellent services throughout. He was demobilised in March 1919, and holds the General Service and Victory Medals.
138, Baker Street, Luton. 5746/C.

YOUNG, R. W., Private, 8th Lincolnshire Regt.

He volunteered in January 1915, and was drafted to the Western Front in the following year. Here he fought in many important engagements, including the Battle of Passchendaele, and was in action throughout the German Offensive and subsequent Allied Advance of 1918, and was wounded. He was demobilised in March 1919, and holds the General Service and Victory Medals
45, Chapel Street, Hemel Hempstead. X5748.

YOUNG, W., A.B., Royal Navy.

On attaining military age, he joined the Service in 1918, and was posted to H.M.S. "Weymouth." His ship was engaged on patrol and other important duties in the Mediterranean, North and Baltic Seas, he frequently passed through mine-infested areas in the discharge of his duties. He was still serving in 1920, and holds the General Service and Victory Medals.
34, Mill Road, Leighton Buzzard. 4337/B.

YOUNG, W. R., C.S.M., 4th Bedfordshire Regt. and 4th South Wales Borderers.

Volunteering in September 1914, he served at various stations until drafted to Mesopotamia in May 1917. Here he fought in many important engagements, until transferred to Salonika in October 1918. In this theatre of war he was in action during the final Advance, and returned to England for demobilisation in March 1919, and holds the General Service and Victory Medals.
35, Turners Road, Luton. 5747/C.

Printed in the United Kingdom
by Lightning Source UK Ltd.
127374UK00002B/103-200/A